THE HANDBOOK OF POLITICAL SOCIOLOGY

Written by a distinguished group of leading scholars, *The Handbook of Political Sociology* provides the first complete survey of the vibrant field of political sociology. Part I begins by exploring the theories of political sociology. Part II focuses on the formation, transitions, and regime structure of the state. Part III takes up various aspects of the state that respond to pressures from civil society, including welfare, gender, and military policies. Part IV examines globalization. The handbook is dedicated to the memory of coeditor Robert Alford.

Thomas Janoski is Associate Professor of Sociology at the University of Kentucky. He has taught at the University of California, Berkeley, and at Duke University. He is the author of *Citizenship and Civil Society* and *The Political Economy of Unemployment*, which in 1992 won the political sociology section of ASA's Distinguished Contribution to Scholarship Award. Professor Janoski has published articles in journals such as *Social Forces* and *Comparative Social Research* as well as in edited books. He is currently completing a book called *The Ironies of Citizenship*.

Robert R. Alford, Distinguished Professor of Sociology, City University of New York - Graduate Center, was a respected scholar of political sociology and a dedicated teacher. At the time of his death he was working with a former student on the development of a new theory of misinformation. This book is dedicated to his memory; the preface details his remarkable life.

Alexander M. Hicks is Professor of Sociology at Emory University. His articles have appeared in leading sociology and political science journals, including *American Sociological Review*, *American Journal of Sociology*, and *American Political Science Review*. Since 2001 he has served on the editorial board for the *American Sociological Review* and as inaugural coeditor of the *Socioeconomic Review*. Professor Hicks's publications include *The Political Economy of the Welfare State* (coauthored with Thomas Janoski) and *Social Democracy and Welfare Capitalism*, for which he won the Luebbert Award in the Comparative Politics section of the American Political Science Association for best book on comparative politics in 1998–1999.

Mildred A. Schwartz is Professor Emeritus at the University of Illinois at Chicago and Visiting Scholar in the Department of Sociology at New York University. In 2004 she received a citation for Distinguished Scholarship in Canadian Studies from the Association for Canadian Studies in the United States. Professor Schwartz is the author or coauthor of eight previous books, including *The Party Network* and *Politics and Territory*, which, twenty-five years after publication, became the theme of a conference and a later Festschrift, *Regionalism and Political Parties*, edited by Lisa Young and Keith Archer. She has published articles on the subject of political science and public policy, many as chapters in edited volumes.

The Handbook of Political Sociology

STATES, CIVIL SOCIETIES, AND GLOBALIZATION

Edited by
THOMAS JANOSKI
University of Kentucky

ROBERT R. ALFORD

ALEXANDER M. HICKS
Emory University

MILDRED A. SCHWARTZ
University of Illinois, Chicago

CAMBRIDGE
UNIVERSITY PRESS

CAMBRIDGE UNIVERSITY PRESS
Cambridge, New York, Melbourne, Madrid, Cape Town, Singapore, São Paulo

Cambridge University Press
40 West 20th Street, New York, NY 10011-4211, USA

www.cambridge.org
Information on this title: www.cambridge.org/9780521819909

First published 2005

Printed in the United States of America

A catalog record for this publication is available from the British Library.

Library of Congress Cataloging in Publication Data

The handbook of political sociology : states, civil societies, and globalization / edited by Thomas Janoski . . . [et al.].

p. cm.

Includes bibliographical references and index.

ISBN 0-521-81990-3 – ISBN 0-521-52620-5 (pbk.)

1. Political sociology. 2. Civil society. 3. State, The. 4. Globalization. I. Janoski, Thomas.

JA76.H383 2005
306.2–dc22 2004052604

ISBN-13 978-0-521-81990-9 hardback
ISBN-10 0-521-81990-3 hardback

ISBN-13 978-0-521-52620-3 paperback
ISBN-10 0-521-52620-5 paperback

in memory of
Robert Alford

—

A political sociologist
of world renown
and friend

Contents

PART II: CIVIL SOCIETY: THE ROOTS AND PROCESSES OF POLITICAL ACTION

PART III: THE STATE AND ITS MANIFESTATIONS

PART IV: STATE POLICY AND INNOVATIONS

Preface

Quite unexpectedly and tragically, our coeditor, Robert Alford, died of pancreatic cancer on February 14, 2003, at the age of 74. We would like to tell you a little bit about him. Bob grew up near the Sierras in California where his parents had a ranch in Avery near Angels Camp, of jumping-frog-contest fame. Bob was well over six feet tall and he loved to walk in the forest, orchards, and mountains. He graduated from Bret Harte High School in the gold country of Northern California and attended the University of California at Berkeley in 1946. He was president of Stiles' Hall and active in the campus YMCA and the Labor Youth League. He regularly played classical piano in the Berkeley Chamber Music Group and loved folk music. Bob began work on an MA in sociology at California during the days of the controversial Loyalty Oath and left the university in 1951 rather than sign.

In 1952, Bob started working at the International Harvester truck plant in Emeryville, California. Bob Blauner, who was a coworker, describes their first meeting. "He was wearing goggles to protect his eyes and a gray apron or smock over his work clothes to collect the metallic dust coming from the machine he was operating" that made fenders for diesel trucks. Bob served as a shop steward and, with Blauner and others, pushed the UAW further to the left than it might otherwise have gone. Roger Friedland and Bob Blauner report that after Khrushchev's "secret" speech that detailed Stalin's crimes, including executions of supposed enemies who were actually loyal communists, Bob refocused politically and entered the sociology department at the University of California at Berkeley. Friedland comments that, for Bob, the "state's promulgation of information that was, in fact, disinformation, or outright lies, would later become a theme in his work."

A graduate student of Seymour Martin Lipset, Blauner reports that Bob Alford was Lipset's research assistant for – and even did some of the writing on – the classic *Political Man*. Alford finished his doctoral dissertation in 1961 on class voting in Anglo-American democracies, and it was published as *Party and Politics*. He left Berkeley to take his first academic job at the University of Wisconsin, where he helped lead the Social Organization Program for just over ten years. Bob took his students through a critical engagement with the classic debates with Marxism. In seminars, Bob demonstrated both personal care and political critique as he molded a generation of sociologists. Freidland says that "Teaching for him was a kind of wrestling, a loving combat." And a lifetime of teaching accomplishments was recognized in 1997 with the American Sociological Association's Distinguished Contribution to Teaching Award. Some of the knowledge built over the years of teaching was laid out in his 1998 book, *The Craft of Inquiry: Theories, Methods, Evidence*, and covers historical, quantitative, and interpretative methods and how to develop sociological problems in proposals and prospectuses. In large part, the book teaches the reader how to think about formulating sociological issues.

In 1974, Bob left Wisconsin for the University of California at Santa Cruz, which was closer to his beloved Sierra Mountains. In 1975, he published *Health Care Politics: Ideological and Interest Group Barriers to Reform*. This work showed how rationality developed as a form of symbolic politics, shaping how interest groups, organizations, and politicians could block reform in medical care. It won the C. Wright Mills Award given by the Society for the Study of Social Problems. In 1986 he and Roger Friedland published *The Powers of Theory*. This magisterial study of political sociology is a classic in the field and, in many ways, is the starting point for much of the work in this volume.

Bob never lost his love for music. A gifted pianist in his earlier life, he continued to play the piano. Tragically, in his later years he progressively lost his hearing, leaving him bereft of the joy of even listening to music. It was a supreme loss to him as a musician, yet he, as the consummate sociologist he was, found a way to live with that loss. He turned to writing about music with Andras Szanto in *Theory and Society* in an article titled "Orpheus Wounded: The Experience of Pain in the Professional Worlds of the Piano," published in 1996.

In 1988, Bob took a position as Distinguished Professor of Sociology at the City University of New York, Graduate Center. Friedland reports that "Bob had fallen in love with New York City as a result of doing research there for his health care politics book." In 1999, we four editors began working together on *The Handbook of Political Sociology*. Bob insisted on editing every chapter of the handbook, initially planned to be thirty-five chapters. He would type out his comments and send them by mail from New York, Avery, or wherever he might be. Bob pursued this work with so much gusto up to the end that we had no inkling of our impending loss. He was a man of tremendous principle, goodness, loyalty, and modesty as Friedland and Blauner describe and as we ourselves know. Bob neither complained nor ever said a word to us about being ill. He was to write the final chapter of this volume, to summarize and comment on the preceding thirty-two contributions. We leave this final and carefully probed and deliberated task undone, as a symbol of his unfinished concerto.

The genesis of the handbook project began with a number of articles by Thomas Janoski in the political sociology newsletter *Political Sociology: States, Power, and Society* (see the 1997–1998 issues) and was followed by a session he organized at the 1998 ASA Convention called "Visions of Political Sociology: Directions,

Emphases and Roads Not Taken." Anthony Orum of the University of Illinois–Chicago, Richard Weil of Louisiana State University, Margaret Somers of the University of Michigan, and Robert Alford of the City University of New York–Graduate Center made presentations and answered questions on the "visions of political sociology" in a lively and well-attended session. Afterward, Robert Alford, Alexander Hicks, and Mildred Schwartz agreed to be coeditors along with Thomas Janoski. The project began with the circulation of a position paper that was, in many ways, a reaction to Baruch Kimmerling's *Political Sociology at the Crossroads*. That book assessed the state of political sociology in the United States, United Kingdom, Scandinavia, Russia, India, Poland, Germany, and a number of other countries. Anthony Orum's article (1996) in *Crossroads* about political sociology in the United States was also influential.

Funding was provided by the American Sociological Association and National Science Foundation Fund for the Advancement of the Profession for a conference on "Challenges to Theories of Political Sociology," held on May 25th and 26th, 2001, in New York City. The departments of sociology at the Graduate Center and New York University generously augmented those funds. Beginning versions of most of the theory chapters in the handbook were presented at this conference. The following presentations were made: Thomas Janoski and Axel van den Berg on "Political Economy, Neo-Marxist, Power-Resources Theory," Frances Fox Piven discussant; Edwin Amenta on "State-Centric and Institutional Theories," Robert Alford discussant; James Jasper on "Cultural and Post-Modern Theories," Francesca Polletta discussant; Thomas Janoski on "Neo-Pluralist Theories and Political Sociology," Jeff Goodwin discussant; and Edgar Kiser on "Rational Choice Theories," Edward Lehman discussant.

Planning continued in meetings by the four coeditors in New York and Chicago. After Bob's death, the three of us met in New York in 2003 to reassign responsibilities, select new authors, and iron out other details.

More than fifty authors and coauthors were recruited over a two-year period for the various theoretical and substantive chapters. Each author was asked to provide a review of the literature that had an angle or edge that might reflect his or her new position on each topic. Given the highly charged nature of the field, personal views and ideological orientations at times intruded on analysis in ways that may add a controversial tenor to the result. But we did not ask authors to avoid controversy, and many of them made their statements as strong as our field's standards of discourse might allow.

As each chapter went through a three-stage review process, some authors complained of an *American Sociological Review*-like process. We lost a few who did not want to change their focus but the vast majority revised their chapters, and some even wrote totally new chapters. At a late date, we had to seek new authors for four chapters. They did truly outstanding work, and we thank them for writing and editing with grace under short deadlines and imposing time pressures.

The handbook project took longer than expected, and we worked with a number of editors at Cambridge University Press. We especially thank Mary Child for helping us to initially conceptualize the handbook, attending our meetings in

New York, and allowing us the leeway to produce an exceptionally long work. And we thank Ed Parsons and Cathy Felgar of Cambridge University Press, and especially Michie Shaw of TechBooks for shepherding the work through its production and final stages.

We are also indebted to friends and colleagues in New York and Lexington. At the City University of New York – Graduate Center, we thank the Department of Sociology and Julia Wrigley for generous support. A number of Bob's graduate students helped during the conference and we particularly want to thank Lorna Mason. We also thank Noll Anne Richardson for her hospitality during the conference and keeping us informed on critical issues. At New York University we are indebted to Edwin Amenta and Kathleen Gerson for support from the sociology department and to Tom Lynch for arranging accommodations for the conference. We also thank former chairs Jim Hougland and William Skinner at the Sociology Department of the University of Kentucky for their support and Donna Wheeler, Agnes Palmgreen, Brian Foudray, Leigh Ann Nally, and Fengjuan Wang for production assistance. And last but not least we would like to thank Natalia Ruiz Junco and Kathleen Powers for assisting Thomas Janoski in constructing the index in the XML system.

Lexington, Atlanta, and New York, 2004

Contributors

EDWIN AMENTA (Sociology Department, University of California, Irvine) is the author of *Bold Relief: Institutional Politics and the Origins of Modern American Social Policy* (1998). His articles on political sociology, social movements, and social policy have appeared in the *American Sociological Review*, the *American Journal of Sociology*, *Social Forces*, and the *Annual Review of Sociology*. He is presently competing a book, forthcoming from Princeton University Press, titled *When Movements Matter: The Townsend Plan, the Old Age Pension Movement, and Social Security*.

SHAWN BAULDRY (University of Washington in Seattle) is currently a Research Associate at Public/Private Ventures. His research has centered on program evaluation, particularly programs operated by faith-based organizations working with high-risk youth or ex-offenders. He has recently co-authored *The Promise and Challenge of Mentoring High-Risk Youth: Findings from the National Faith-based Initiative* and a report on the implementation of a national faith-based re-entry program.

DEBORAH M. BEY (Sociology Department, University of Michigan) is pursuing a doctorate degree in the Sociology Department of the University of Michigan. She has been granted The National Institute on Aging Fellowship and is also an instructor with the university.

VIVIANE BRACHET-MÁRQUEZ (Centrode Estudios Sociology, El Colegio de México) has published *The Dynamics of Domination* (1994) and *Entre Polis y mercado* (2001). She has worked on democracy and the politics of health and social security reform in Latin America. Her current project is a comparative study of state formation and democracy in Latin America since independence from Spain.

CLEM BROOKS (Sociology Department, Indiana University) has interests in electoral politics, public opinion, and welfare states in developed democracies. He is working with Jeff Manza on a book entitled *Why Welfare States Persist* developing a new theoretical approach to understanding sources of cross-national variation in social policy. Other projects include a study that evaluates economic versus sociological approaches to understanding mechanisms behind mass policy preferences.

The Late RICHARD CLOWARD (School of Social Work, Columbia University, New York) published *Delinquency and Opportunity* (1960) with Lloyd Ohlin and authored *The Politics of Turmoil* (1974) and *Illegitimate Means, Anomie and Deviant Behavior* (1993). With Frances Fox Piven, he co-authored *Poor People's Movements: Why They Succeed, How they Fail* (1977), *Why Americans Don't Vote and Why Politicians Want it That Way* (1988), *The Breaking of the American Social Compact* (1997), *Regulating the Poor: The Functions of Public Welfare* (1971, and 1993, updated edition). The last named book was listed among the "Forty Most Notable Books" by the American Library Association, and the

2nd Edition won the 1993 Political Sociology Section Distinguished Contribution to Scholarship Career Award. His many other books and articles are too numerous to mention. As an activist, he was a force for change in many protest movements having co-founded the National Welfare Rights Organization, which aimed to federalize Aid to Families with Dependent Children. He co-founded Service Employees Registration and Voter Education and advocated for the Motor Voter Act of 1992. At Columbia University from 1954 to 2001, he was an academic and an activist who saw a number of his proposals become the law of the land.

JONATHAN EASTWOOD (Committee on Degrees in Social Studies, Harvard University, Lecturer) is currently completing a study of nationalism in Spain and Latin America, as well as working on a number of related questions in sociological theory and the sociology of culture. His most recent publication, an article titled "Positivism and Nationalism in 19th Century France and Mexico" appeared in the December 2004 issue of the *Journal of Historical Sociology.*

THOMAS ERTMAN (Department of Sociology at New York University) teaches and researches in comparative/historical sociology, political sociology, social theory, and sociology of the arts. His book, *Birth of the Leviathan: Building States and Regimes in Medieval and Early Modern Europe*, was awarded the Barrington Moore Prize of the ASA in 1998. Currently he is writing *Taming the Leviathan: Building Democratic Nation-States in 19th and 20th Century Western Europe.*

GØSTA ESPING-ANDERSEN (Sociology at the Departamende Ciencies Politques i Sociales, University Pompeau Fabra in Barcelona, Spain) has recently published *Social Foundations of Postindustrial Economies* (1999), *Why De-regulate Labour Markets?* (2001) and *Why We Need a New Welfare State* (2003).

PETER EVANS (Sociology Department at the University of California, Berkeley) holds the Marjorie Meyer Eliaser Chair of International Studies. His past research has been on the role of the state in industrial development, an interest reflected in his book *Embedded Autonomy: States and Industrial Transformation* (1995). He has also worked on urban environmental issues, producing an edited volume, *Livable Cities: Urban Struggles for Livelihood and Sustainability* (2002) and is currently working on labor as a global social movement.

WILLIAM FORM (Sociology Department, Professor emeritus, The Ohio State University) has published widely in economic sociology, social stratification, and industrial organization in Italy, Argentina, India, Korea and the United States. Currently, he is studying the response of downtown churches to the daytime downtown population as well as the economic stratification of churches in the metropolis.

JEFFREY GOODWIN (Sociology Department, New York University) is author of *No Other Way Out: States and Revolutionary Movements, 1945–1991* (2001) and co-editor of *Passionate Politics: Emotions and Social Movements* (2001), *Rethinking Social Movements* (2003) and *The Social Movements Reader* (2003).

FRANCISCO J. GRANADOS (Sociology Department, Southern Methodist University) wrote "Interorganizational Alliance Diversity, Firm Status Change, and Performance in the Global Information Sector, 1989–2000" (with David Knoke). He was awarded the 2004 NSF Dissertation Improvement Grant (with David Knoke), as well as the 2003 American Sociological Association Economic Sociology Section Graduate Student Paper Award when he attended the University of Minnesota.

LIAH GREENFELD (Political Science Department, Boston University) has published widely on questions of art, economics, history, language and literature, philosophy, politics, religion and science. She is a preeminent authority on nationalism, a stature reinforced by the publication of *The Spirit of Capitalism: Nationalism and Economic Growth* (2001). In 2002, she received the Kagan Prize of the

Historical Society for the best book in European History for *The Spirit of Capitalism* and in 2004 delivered the Gellner lecture at the London School of Economics.

ALEXANDER HICKS (Department of Sociology, Emory University) authored *Social Democracy and Welfare Capitalism* (winner of the 1999 Luebbert Award). He has first-authored papers in the *American Journal of Sociology, the American Political Science Review,* the *American Sociological Review,* and other leading journals of sociology and political science on the political economy of social and economic policy, on which he continues to write. In 2001 he began service as founding co-editor (with David Marsden) of the *Socioeconomic Review.*

BARBARA HOBSON (Sociology Department, Stockholm University) has published numerous articles on gender and citizenship concerning welfare regimes and social movements, and most recently transnational institutions and diversity. Her most recent books are *Recognition Struggles and Social Movements* (2003); *Making Men Into Fathers: Men, Masculinities and the Social Politics of Fatherhood* (2002), *Contested Concepts in Gender and Social Policy* (with Lewis and Siim, 2002 Edward Elgar). She is founder and an editor of the journal, *Social Politics.*

GREGORY HOOKS (Departments of Sociology and Rural Sociology, Washington State University) has contributed to several sub-areas within sociology, including political sociology, urban and regional sociology, and organizations. He is currently involved in research into the rhetoric and the impact of prisons on local economic. Among his publications is "Guns and Butter, North and South: The Federal Contribution to Manufacturing Growth, 1940–1990," in Scranton (ed.), *The Second Wave: Southern Industrialization, 1940–1970* (2000).

EVELYN HUBER (Political Science Department, University of North Carolina, Chapel Hill) is the Morehead Alumni Distinguished Professor of Political Science and Director of the Institute of Latin American Studies. She was awarded 2001 Best Book on Political Economy from the Political Economy Section of the American Political Science Association. Among her publications are *Development and Crisis of the Welfare State: Parties and Policies in Global Markets* (with John D. Stephens, 2001) and *Models of Capitalism: Lessons for Latin America* (2002).

DAVID JAMES (Sociology Department, Indiana University) focuses his research on the politics of race and class stratification in the United States. His published works include articles on racial differences in education in the South, determinants of voter registration rates during the 1960s, and residential segregation in urban areas of the United States. At present, he is engaged in collaborative research (with Kent Redding) on the determinants of racial differences in voter turnout in the American South during the late 19th and early 20th centuries.

THOMAS JANOSKI (Sociology Department, University of Kentucky) has published *The Political Economy of Unemployment* (1990), which won the Distinguished Contribution to Scholarship Award in political sociology, and *Citizenship and Civil Society* (1998). His work has appeared in *Social Forces, Comparative Sociological Research*, a co-edited volume with Alexander Hicks called *The Comparative Political Economy of the Welfare State* (1994), and other books and journals. He is currently writing a book called *The Ironies of Citizenship.*

JAMES JASPER (Independent scholar in New York City) is editor of *Contexts* published by the American Sociological Association. He wrote *Restless Nation: Starting Over in America* (2002), *The Art of Moral Protest* (1999), *Nuclear Politics* (1990) and co-authored *Rethinking Social Movements* (2003) and *Animal Rights Crusade* (1991). He co-edited *Passionate Politics* (2003), and *Social Movements Reader* (2003).

CRAIG JENKINS (Sociology Department and Faculty Associate, Mershon Center for International Security, Ohio State University) has published *The Politics of Insurgency* (1985) and co-edited *The*

Politics of Social Protest (1995) with Bert Klandermans. His articles have appeared in the *American Sociological Review*, the *American Journal of Sociology, Social Forces* and numerous other journals and collections. He is currently working with Charles Taylor on *The World Handbook of Political Indicators IV*, a study on high technology policy, and the development of the environmental movement in the United States.

LANE KENWORTHY (Department of Sociology at the University of Arizona) studies the impact of institutions and government policies on economic performance in affluent countries. His publications include *Egalitarian Capitalism* (2004), *In Search of National Economic Success: Balancing Competition and Cooperation* (1995), and articles in the *American Journal of Sociology, American Sociological Review, Comparative Political Studies, European Journal of Political Research, Social Forces* and *World Politics.*

LESLIE KING (Department of Sociology and Environmental Science & Policy, Smith College) focuses her research on population policies, mainly in countries with relatively low fertility. She is especially interested in how ideologies of nationalism, gender, race/ethnicity and class are implicated in the construction and implementation of population policies. Leslie's articles on population-related issues have appeared in *Ethnic and Racial Studies, European Journal of Population, The Sociological Quarterly*, and *Gender & Society*. She is currently beginning a project that will examine debates within the Sierra Club over immigration to the United States.

EDGAR KISER (Sociology Department, University of Washington in Seattle) has published articles in sociology, political science, and economics journals on topics including the determinants of war and revolt, the development and decline of voting institutions, the centralization and bureaucratization of state administration, and the methodology of historical sociology.

JOSHUA KLUGMAN (Sociology Department, Indiana University) is a doctoral student. His dissertation is about resource inequalities among U.S. public schools and the consequences for their students. He also teaches undergraduate courses for the university.

DAVID KNOKE (Sociology Department, University of Minnesota) is author of *Changing Organizations: Business Networks in the New Political Economy* (2001) and co-author of *Comparing Policy Networks* (1996). His current project analyzes the changing strategic alliance network of the Global Information Sector.

KAY LAWSON (Political Science Department, Professor emerita, San Francisco State University) is co editor of *International Political Science Review*, and her most recent publications are the fifth edition of *The Human Polity: A Comparative Introduction to Political Science* (2003), and *How Political Parties Respond: Interest Aggregation Revisited* (Co-edited with Thomas Poguntke, Routledge, 2004).

FRANK LECHNER (Sociology Department, Emory University) has edited *The Globalization Reader* (2000, 2004) and written *World Culture: Origins and Consequences* (2005), both with John Boli, in addition to publishing numerous papers on religion, globalization, and sociological theory. His current work focuses on globalization and national identity, using the Netherlands as an illustrative case.

JEFFREY MANZA (Sociology Department and Institute for Policy Research at Northwestern University) has co-authored *Social Cleavages and Political Change: Voter Alignments and U.S. Party Coalitions* (1999) and *Locked Out: Felon Disenfranchisement and American Democracy* (forthcoming). He is also the co editor of *Navigating Public Opinion: Polls, Policy and the Future of Democracy*. He is currently writing a book with Clem Brooks on the impact of public opinion on welfare state effort in comparative perspective.

JOHN MARKOFF (Department of Sociology, University of Pittsburgh) Professor of Sociology, History and Political Science, has published *Waves of Democracy: Social Movements and Political Change* (1996), *The Abolition of Feudalism: Peasants, Lords and Legislators in the French Revolution* (1996), and (with Gilbert Shapiro) *Revolutionary Demands: A Content Analysis of the Cahiers of Doléances of 1789* (1998). He is working on the history of democracy.

PHILIP MCMICHAEL (Development Sociology, Cornell University) has authored *Settlers and the Agrarian Question* (1984), *Development and Social Change: A Global Perspective* (2004, 3rd edition), edited *The Global Restructuring of Agro-Food Systems* (1994), *Food and Agrarian Orders in the World Economy* (1995), and co-edited *Looking Backward and Looking Forward: Perspectives on Social Science History* (2005). He has published in *The American Sociological Review, Theory and Society, International Social Science Journal,* and *Review of International Political Economy.* His research concerns food regimes and counter-movements.

JOYA MISRA (Sociology Department and Center for Public Policy and Administration, University of Massachusetts, Amherst) has published articles in a variety of journals, including *Social Problems, Social Politics, Gender & Society,* the *American Journal of Sociology,* and the *American Sociological Review.* She is currently finishing a project focused on neoliberal economic restructuring, immigration, and carework, and beginning another cross-national project that examines the effect of family policies on employment, wages, poverty by gender, marital status and parenthood status.

MARK MIZRUCHI (Department of Sociology and Business Administration at the University of Michigan) is the author of *The Structure of Corporate Political Action, The American Corporate Network, 1904–1974* and more than 80 articles and reviews. His recent publications have appeared in the *American Sociological Review, Theory and Society,* and *The Journal of Corporate Finance.* His current work includes a study of the changing nature of the American Corporate Elite over the past three decades.

OSCAR OSZLAK (Director of the Masters Program in Public Administration, University of Buenos Aires in Argentina) has published *La Formacion del Estado Argentino* (1982, 2nd Edition 1997), *Merecer la Ciudad* (1983), *Estado y Sociedad: nuevas reglas de juego*, and *Civil Service Systems in Latin America and the Caribbean* (2002). His work has appeared in the *Latin American Research Review, International Social Science Journal,* and *Asian Review of Public Administration.* He is currently writing the second part of *The Formation of the Argentine State, 1880–1945*.

FRANCES FOX PIVEN (Department of Sociology at the City University of New York, Graduate Center) is Distinguished Professor of Political Science and Sociology. She was the first recipient of the Lifetime Achievement Award of the Political Sociology Section of the American Sociological Association. More recently, in 2000, she received the American Sociological Association's Distinguished Career Award for the Practice of Sociology. Among her publications is *Regulating the Poor* (with Richard Cloward, 1972/1993), a landmark analysis of the role of welfare policy in the economic and political control of the poor and working class.

KENT REDDING (Sociology Department, the University of Wisconsin in Milwaukee) has published *Making Race, Making Power: North Carolina's Road to Disfranchisement* (2003). His work has also appeared in the *American Sociological Review, Historical Methods, Social Forces, Sociological Forum*, and other journals. Current projects include an examination of the comparative success of extreme right political parties in the past two decades and comparative analysis of the incorporations of labor, women, and racial and ethnic minorities into western democracies over the past 150 years.

JAMES RICE (Departments of Sociology and Rural Sociology, Washington State University) is pursuing a doctorate degree in Sociology from Washington State University. He is also a teaching assistant for the university.

MICHAEL EDWARD SAUDER (Department of Sociology, Northwestern University) is pursuing a doctorate in Sociology at Northwestern University. He was awarded the 2004 American Sociological Association's Graduate Student Paper prize (with Ryon Lancaster) for "Law School Rankings and Admissions: The Effects of the Redefinition of a Status Hierarchy."

MICHAEL SCHUDSON (Communication Department, University of California, San Diego) is the author of *Discovering the News* (1978), *Advertising, the Uneasy Persuasion* (1984), *Watergate in American Memory* (1992), The Power of News (1995), *The Good Citizen: A History of American Civic Life* (1998) and *The Sociology of News* (2003). He is presently working on changing norms and practices of public expression in the United States since 1960.

MILDRED A. SCHWARTZ (University of Illinois-Chicago, professor emerita, and New York University) includes among her books *Persisting Political Challengers* (2005), *The Party Network* (1990), and *A Sociological Perspective on Politics* (1990). She has also published widely in sociology and political science journals and in edited volumes. She is now beginning work on the deterrents to corruption. In 1999, she held the Thomas O. Enders Chair in Canada – U.S. Relations at the University of Calgary.

JOHN D. STEPHENS (Political Science Department, University of North Carolina, Chapel Hill) is the Gerhard E. Lenski, Jr. Professor whose main interests are comparative social policy and political economy, with area foci on Europe, the Antipodes, Latin America, and the Caribbean. He is author or co-author of four books including *Transitions to Socialism* (1978) and *Capitalist Development and Democracy* (1992) and *Development and Crisis of the Welfare State*, (2001). He also has authored numerous journal articles.

WOLFGANG STREECK (Department of Sociology and Director of the Max Planck Institute for the Study of Societies in Cologne, Germany). From 1988 to 1995, he was Professor of Sociology and Industrial Relations at the University of Wisconsin, Madison. He has written on industrial relations and comparative political economy. His recent books include *Beyond Continuity: Institutional Change in Advanced Political Economies* (with Kathleen Thelen, 2005) and *Germany: Beyond the Stable State* (with Herbert Kitschelt, 2003).

CHARLES TILLY (Social Science, Columbia University in New York) is The Joseph L. Buttenweiser Professor of Social Science and has recent books that include *Stories, Identities, and Political Change* (2002), *The Politics of Collective Violence* (2003), *Contention and Democracy in Europe, 1650-2000* (2004), *Social Movements, 1768-2004* (2004), *Trust and Rule* (2005), and *Identities, Boundaries, and Social Ties* (2005).

JACOB TORFING (Politics and Institutions, Department of Social Sciences, Roskilde University, Denmark) has published *Politics, Regulation and the Welfare State* (1995) *New Theories of Discourse* (1999) and *Discourse Theory in European Politics* (2005). He is co-founder of the Danish Center for Discourse Theory and Director of the Centre for Democratic Network Governance. He is currently writing about the role of discourse in new forms of democratic network governance.

AXEL VAN DEN BERG (Sociology, McGill University) has published books and articles on Marxist state theory and other kinds of "critical" and sociological theory, rational choice theory, comparative labor market regimes, and cross-cultural differences in aesthetic preferences. He is currently European Commission Incoming International Marie Curie Fellow charged with the formulation of a multi-country collaborative research plan on "transitional labor markets" and the evolution of current social protection regimes.

SILVIO WAISBORD (Department of Journalism and Mass Media, The State University of Rutgers) is the author of *Watchdog Journalism in South America: News, Accountability and Democracy* (2000), *El Gran Desfile: Campañas Electorales y Medios de Comunicación en la Argentina* (1995) and co-edited *Media and Globalization: Why the State Matters* (2001) and *Local Politics, Global Media: Latin American Broadcasting and Policy* (2002). He was a fellow at the Kellogg Institute for International Studies at the University of Notre Dame, the Annenberg School for Communication, the Media Studies Center at the Freedom Forum, and the Center for Critical Analysis of Contemporary Cultures. His research interests are media and politics, audiovisual industries, nation and cultures, globalization, and Latin America.

FENGJUAN WANG (Department of Sociology, University of Kentucky) wrote her thesis, *A Comparative Analysis of Ethnic Niche Effects on Immigrants' Earning Returns*, comparing the income gains of four Asian and two Hispanic immigrant groups in the United States. She is currently finishing a master's degree in statistics.

DAVID WEAKLIEM (Department of Sociology, University of Connecticut) is interim director of the Roper Center for Public Opinion Research. His current projects include a historical study of class politics (with Julia Adams) and an examination of ideological change in the United States since the 1970s. His articles have appeared in the *American Journal of Sociology, British Journal of Political Science, American Sociological Review,* and other journals.

INTRODUCTION

Political Sociology in the New Millennium

Alexander M. Hicks, Thomas Janoski, and Mildred A. Schwartz

Although modern political sociology has existed for more than a century, it came into its own during the decades bridging the victory at the end of World War II and the anti-Vietnam War movement. Especially important in setting the direction for political research with a distinctive focus on "the social bases of politics" was Seymour Martin Lipset's *Political Man* (1960), published in twenty countries and deemed a "citation classic" by the *Social Science Citation Index*. The transformative potentials of the social bases of politics were redirected away from the pluralist theoretical tradition by William G. Domhoff's *Who Rules America?* (1967), which stimulated interest in capitalist power; William Gamson's *The Strategy of Social Protest* (1975), which expanded attention to the popular bases of power beyond interest groups to social movements; and James Petras and Maurice Zeitlin's *Latin America: Reform or Revolution* (1967), which excited new interest in the politics of labor movements. The 1980s' ascent of state-centric institutionalism registered a major impact on political sociology with its *Bringing the State Back In*, edited by Peter Evans, Dietrich Rueschemeyer, and Theda Skocpol (1985). The works of these times had a common focus on the societal determination of political processes and outcomes and on how state structures cause varied outcomes in different countries.

Since the early 1980s, political sociology has moved to include the unique and powerful perspectives of Michel Foucault (1979, 1980, 1984, 1990, 1991), Pierre Bourdieu (1994, 1998a, 1998b), and other poststructuralist or culturally oriented theorists; of feminism (Butler, 1990; Hobson, 1990; Hobson and Lindholm, 1997; Young, 1990); of racialization theory (Goldberg, 2002; Omi and Winant, 1994; Winant, 2001); and of rational choice theories (Coleman, 1966; Hechter, 1987; Lange and Garrett, 1985, 1987; North, 1990; Tsebellis, 1990, 1999; Wallerstein, 1999). Along with other perspectives, these have all shaken the theoretical dominance of pluralist, political/economic, and state-centric theories.

Today, political sociology stands out as one of the major areas in sociology. Its share of articles and books published is impressive. For example, in 1999, 17 to 20 percent of the articles in the *American Journal of Sociology* and the *American Sociological Review* and about 20 percent of the books reviewed by *Contemporary Sociology*, the major reviewing journal in American sociology, dealt with political sociology. A number of political sociologists, including Seymour Martin Lipset, William Gamson, and Jill Quadagno, have served as president of the American Sociological Association (ASA). The political sociology section of the ASA continues to attract an above-average membership.[1] Yet, along with all this vitality, the field remains fluid, stimulated by the following processes and theoretical transformations.

[1] In 2003, membership stood at 560 compared to the average of 463 for all sections. Dobratz et al. (2002b) also report that a high percentage of articles in the *Annual Review of Sociology* are on the topic of political sociology.

First, although state-centered, and later policy-centered, theory associated with Theda Skocpol and others (e.g., Evans, Rueschmeyer, and Skocpol, 1985; Skocpol, 1979, 1992) has garnered a great deal of attention in political sociology; new developments in pluralist, political/economic, and elitist theoretical traditions have largely flown beneath the radar these past two decades. With similar stealth, new approaches to policy domains (Burstein, 1991; Knoke et al., 1994) and civil society (Hall, 1995; Jacobs, 2002; Janoski, 1998; Keane, 1988) have emerged without widespread recognition from political sociologists. These developments indicate that the time is ripe to move from differentiation of theoretical work to more synthetic theory building by bringing civil society, policy domains, voluntary associations, social movements, interest groups, and the state into more meaningful theoretical relations.

Second, although the print and electronic media have been studied in detail, these institutions have not been adequately integrated into political sociology. Even though political sociology may often refer to the media, within its own theory it has failed to integrate the media as an oblique force that has strong but not always clear impacts on political candidates, elections, ideologies, and legislation, and on the implementation and evaluation of policy. Except where political parties or candidates control the media, such as in Italy with Prime Minister Silvio Berlusconi, the impact of mass media is often indirect and not obviously, or at least continuously, in favor of any party. But the media are political actors, not just fuzzy filters of news and views. The integration of the media into empirical research, especially comparative work, is particularly important for the comprehension of the role of mass media in the public sphere (Keane, 1991; Kellner, 1990; Schudson and Waisbord, Chapter 17, this volume; Wheeler, 1997; Zaller, forthcoming).

Third, some process-oriented subtheories in political sociology have been underemphasized. Public opinion needs to be pushed in the direction of social network and media contexts rather than seen as something that is just out there (Burstein, 2003; Gamson, 1992; Huckfeldt and Sprague, 1995). Theories of political deliberation certainly should play a stronger role, especially in considering the impact of small group democracy, deliberative polling, and electronic town meetings (Bohman, 1996; Fishkin, 1991; Fishkin and Laslett, 2003; Habermas, 1984, 1987, 1996). Process theories of democracy are important as well in regard to the transformation of political parties and trade unions, multiple and changing political identities, and participation in voluntary groups that cause cross-cutting cleavages (Manza, Brooks, and Sauder, Chapter 10, and Schwartz and Lawson, Chapter 13, this volume). Structural and process explanations involving political mechanisms need to be brought more into play, and the growing area of cultural explanation needs to be integrated into this mix (Diamond, 1999; Fung and Wright, 2003; McAdam, Tarrow, and Tilly, 2001; Mutz and Martin, 2001; Tilly, 2003).

Fourth, the conceptual gulf between the two vastly different locations in space – "all politics are local" and "all politics are global" – needs to be bridged, as is being done in the literature on antiglobalization movements and perhaps with the political slogan to "Think Globally, Act Locally" (e.g., Khagram et al., 2002; see the McMichael and Evans chapters [Chapters 30 and 32] in this volume). More attention needs to be paid to the urban and local studies of the political and neighborhood politics of William Gamson in *Talking Politics* (1992) (see also Berry et al., 1993). Means need to be found that integrate theories as diverse as the world systems theory of Immanuel Wallerstein in *The Modern World System* (1989) and Michael Hardt and Antonio Negri's *Empire* (2000). Finally, efforts that directly link the local and the global (e.g., Fourcade-Gourinchas and Babb, 2002; Hay, 2001; Ranney, 2003) need to be encouraged.

Fifth, although it is sometimes denied, the study of politics is affected by cycles of political power. On the one hand, politics and policies themselves change, depending on whether the right or left is in power. On the other hand, social and political hegemony can shift from democratic processes in the community and the welfare state to privatization and market processes. This creates oscillations in political research, such as the leftward and rightward tilts, respectively, in the political scholarship of the 1960s and then the 1980s and early 1990s (e.g., see Hunter, 1991, on "culture wars" and Linz and Stepan, 1978a, 1978b, and Diamond et al., 1988, on "cycles of democratization"). Yet the eagerness to explain the expanding welfare state is hardly matched by the comparative lack of enthusiasm to theorize and explain its decline (Korpi and Palme, 2003; Pierson, 2001). Moreover, social movement research seems much more enthusiastic about the civil rights movement than the New Right/fundamentalist and neoliberalism movements. Still, the mobilization of the religious right has attracted significant attention from sociologists (e.g., Diamond, 1995; Liebman and Wuthnow, 1983; Luker, 1984; Marshall, 1994). Indeed, the sociological study of the neoliberal movement looks like a burgeoning academic cottage industry (e.g., Campbell and Pederson, 2001; Fourcade-Gourinchas and Babb, 2002; Simmons, Garrett, and Dobbin, 2003; Swank, 2003).

Sixth, the influence of poststructuralist and postmodern theories, and the feminist expansion of the "political," have broadened the concept of power from formal political institutions to the informal political processes often involved with the market or private spheres (Dyrberg, 1997; Foucault, 1979, 1980, 1984, 1991; Torfing, 1999). Poststructuralist and postmodern authors have also questioned the objectivity and narrowed the empirical scope of sociology (at least insofar as any theoretical/empirical correspondence is concerned), sometimes to the extent of denying the possibility of theoretical realism and trading away the theoretical domain to be explained for the specific case to be interpreted. These authors have equated political sociology with nearly "all of sociology," revealing previously neglected aspects of politics. However, when everything is political, political sociology itself becomes diffuse and unfocused. Although researchers, especially those who look for the wide-ranging "social bases of politics," naturally abhor the imposition of boundaries on the political, some redelineation of what constitutes political sociology is necessary. The denial of theoretical realism conflates sociology and literary fiction, whereas the diminution of theoretical domains (at times to a vanishing point) blurs the distinctiveness of sociology from biography, journalism, and descriptive historiography.

Seventh, although institutions have always been the mainstay of sociological explanations, new challenges have emerged from alternative perspectives. In recent years, economists and political scientists have been applying rational choice theory to the formation of institutions and to action in an institutional context (Booth, James, and Meadwell, 1993; Hardin, 1995; Kiser and Bauldry, Chapter 8, this volume; Knight and Sened, 1995; Lewin, 1988, 1991; North, 1990; and Tsebelis, 1990). The *Journal of Institutional and Theoretical Economics* has been at the forefront of these efforts, reinforced by the Nobel Prize awarded to its preeminent spokesman, Douglas North (1990). Political sociologists have been stimulated to move beyond verifying and describing the existence of institutions to explaining their creation and transformation (Brinton and Nee, 1998; Steinmo, Thelen, and Longstreth, 1992), as well as examining how emotions affect political outcomes (Goodwin, Jasper, and Polletta, 2001; Hochschild, 1983). Yet we still see the need for much more theoretical and cumulative work on institutions (Boudon, 2003).

Amidst this swirl of change, there is a need for intellectual tools that can survey and integrate the family of disparate subfields called political sociology (Turner and Power, 1981). Such a survey needs to do the following four things: (1) bring the diverse contributions to the field of political sociology together and place them within a clear and encompassing conceptual framework; (2) synthesize, or at least counterpose, new developments in theories of political sociology in ways that still recognize some residual fragmentation; (3) consolidate sociological explanations of politics through the "social bases of politics" and state institutionalism while advancing the recognition of "civil society" as a key aspect of the state's social foundations and achievements; and (4) incorporate the expanding theories of globalization and empire. We present the *Handbook of Political Sociology*, partly based on a "Visions of Political Sociology" session at the 1998 American Sociological Association convention and a 2001 conference on "Theories of Political Sociology," as a means to reorient sociological explanation of politics. We believe that it can advance political explanation not only by providing new directions but also by energizing students of politics with creative insights from previously unassimilated literatures.

THE PLACE OF A HANDBOOK IN POLITICAL SOCIOLOGY

The purpose of this handbook is to sharpen our focus on what has been somewhat blurred by the seven entropic developments just discussed. Although political sociology has had considerable success with its focus on "the social bases of politics" and its new institutional approaches, it needs to be more inclusive of recent developments while retaining a critical sensibility. Reintegration of the field and a possible synthesis of new developments into existing theories, where practicable, are important ways to extend and refocus the goals of political sociology.

The second, most obvious, reason that a *Handbook of Political Sociology* is needed to clarify political sociology is that one has never been assembled before. This handbook is the first of its kind to bring together original articles covering a coherent range of topics. The gap it fills was dealt with in the past by a number of edited volumes that included both classical and current readings, including Lewis Coser (1966), Frank Lindenfeld (1968), S. N. Eisenstadt (1971), and Kate Nash (2000a). One two-volume collection by William Outhwaite and Luke Martell (1998) contains classical statements by Marx, Weber, and Gramsci along with a large number of reprints of more current articles. These compendia relied on previously published sources to construct an overview of the field. Instructive surveys of the field were also written, such as those by Barrington Moore (1962), Morris Janowitz (1970), Edward H. Lehman (1977), Tom Bottomore (1979), Mildred A. Schwartz (1990), Keith Faulks (2000), Anthony Orum (1977), Philo C. Washburn (1982), Robert Dowse and John Hughes (1972), Arnold K. Sherman and Aliza Kolker (1987), George Kourvetaris (1997), Kate Nash (2000b), and Baruch Kimmerling's edited volume (1996).[2] One may also read Richard Braungart (1981), Jonathan Turner and C. Power (1981), and Anthony Orum (1988) for summary essays on the field. Robert Alford and Roger Friedland did an impressive review of pluralist, managerial, and class theories of political sociology (1985), which we examine in more detail shortly, and Martin Marger followed with a somewhat similar classification (1987).

More recently, edited volumes have emphasized particular theories or approaches. An emphasis on "state-centered" theories is presented in the Evans, Rueschemeyer, and Skocpol book (1985). George Steinmetz (1999) and Julia Adams, Elisabeth Clemens, and Ann Shola Orloff (2004) emphasize the fusing of the "cultural turn" and rational choice in political sociology. This handbook differs in not arguing for a single perspective. We shall err toward presenting as many points of view as possible, and we indicate where theoretical explorations, syntheses, or other responses are needed.

Other edited volumes address methodological approaches. Theda Skocpol (1984) examines historical methodologies. Thomas Janoski and Alexander Hicks (1994) cover a range of quantitative methods and formal qualitative approaches like those presented in Charles Ragin (1987, 2002). In addition, a recent survey of historical/comparative sociology by James Mahoney and Dietrich Rueschemeyer (2003) focuses largely on political sociology. As with theory, we believe allowing a thousand flowers

[2] Two widely used textbooks using elite theory, one in sociology and the other in political science, make little attempt to cover a broad range of theories but, nonetheless, connect to parties, interest groups, legislatures, and government: G. William Domhoff (1967, 1983, 1998, 2002) and Thomas Dye and Harmon Zeigler (2000). Kate Nash (2000a, 2000b) captures the cultural turn in political sociology but rarely mentions political parties, interest groups, legislatures, or government. She focuses on cultural theory with most of her attention on social movements, citizenship and rights, identity politics, international organizations and movements, and the displacement of the nation-state.

to bloom is preferable to confining investigative methods to a few strains.

Betty Dobratz, Lisa Waldner, and Timothy Buzzell have recently edited three special issues of *Research in Political Sociology* with the intent of "assessing the state of the field of political sociology at the start of the twenty-first century" (2003:1). The first, more specialized, volume looks at social movements and the state along with a symposium on the 2000 presidential election in the United States (2002a). The editors describe the second volume on theory (2002b) as "not a comprehensive overview" but a volume that gives "examples of several new promising trends" and "a critique of current approaches" in the areas of pluralist, class, elite, world systems, and postmodern debates (Waldner et al., 2002:xiii–xiv). The third volume (2003) is a more general survey of public opinion, civil society, electoral politics, social movements, and a historical/comparative analysis of the state. It also contains a few more specialized chapters such as Paul Luebke's reflections on being a progressive legislator in a very conservative state and Eduardo Bonilla-Silva et al.'s article on the new racism in present-day American society. The result is an important contribution, but one, as the editors make clear, without the intention of providing the kind of comprehensive overview that is our objective.[3]

This handbook intends to provide readers with an integrated overview of major theories and findings, lead them conveniently to topics of interest, and assist them in the common challenge of synthesizing a disparate field. For many researchers in specialized areas, this integrative view should bring cutting edge research in adjacent fields and also offer as definitive a panorama of political sociology as space permits. In addition to the intellectual need for integrating theory, delineating the scope of the field, and developing multiple perspectives on society and politics, a *Handbook of Political Sociology* of this scope has never been done. We, and the authors of subsequent chapters, offer this work as an attempt to provide what has until now been missing.

TWO NEW CHALLENGES

In the mid-1980s, the field of political sociological theory was effectively summarized and partially synthesized in Robert Alford and Roger Friedland's *The Powers of Theory*. In their masterful book, action and structure are analyzed at three levels (individual, organizational, and societal) each with its characteristic mode of power (situational, bureaucratic, or systemic). Three major theoretical perspectives, each closely tied to a level and to a mode of power, anchor their conceptions of theory. One is the pluralist perspective: individualistic, situational, and tied to a characteristic problematic of governance, in particular democratic governance. A second is the managerial perspective: organizational, bureaucratic, and focused on problems of state capacity that is comparative. A third is the class perspective: societal, systemic, and focused on the conundrums of resistance to economic inequality and societal "crisis." To these theoretical perspectives and elements are added an additional emphasis on either politics (political structure and process) or function (the consequences of politics). As with many holistic articulations of social science phenomena, this scheme evokes the metalanguage of systems theory. Individual and group actions link the societal environment and the organization(s) of the state. Insofar as modes of power are concerned, situationally embedded actions have their impact as inputs and throughputs on and through the bureaucratic structure of the state, feeding

[3] There are also a number of handbooks in political science, such as those by Fred Greenstein and Nelson Polsby (1975), Robert Goodin and Hans-Dieter Klingemann (1997), and, in its overall effect, Ira Katznelson and Helen Milner (2002). However, political science does not emphasize the "social bases of politics" to the extent that sociology does, and much of its approach to political behavior in international, comparative, and national politics involves more psychological and rational choice approaches. Although much closer to us in subject matter, a recent handbook in political psychology refracts the political through the lens of psychology (Sears, Huddy, and Jervis, 2003). The present handbook responds to our perceptions of what is missing in sociology itself, where we also learn from political science and allied fields and borrow freely from their accomplishments.

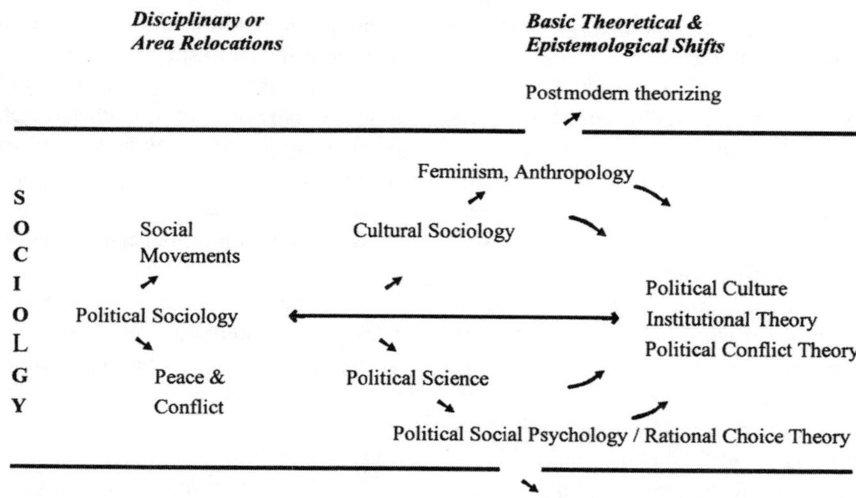

Figure 1.1. The Directions and Redirections of Political Sociology.

back, in systemslike fashion, on actors and their social situations (organization and society). In short, although beginning from some distinctive roots and moving toward a number of original objectives, Alford and Friedland echo long-held views in sociology and political science about how to conceptualize the social and political world (e.g., Easton, 1965; Parsons, 1969; Wallerstein, 1989).

But much has changed in the nearly twenty years since they presented their work. From one direction, the epistemology of science has been challenged by more contextualized and cultural conceptions of politics and by less positivist (e.g., more realist and interpretivist) views of causal origins. Although frequently stopping short of an antiscientific "postmodernity," a postmodern influence can be seen in the emphasis on subjectivity and "capillarity" (a Foucaultian term for diffused and extensively networked power), a turn to structural and discursive conceptions of *objective* culture, and a major rejection of materialist and other determinisms. From the direction of economics and political science, rational choice and game theorists have influenced political sociologists with an innovative stress on rational motivation that brackets most forms of "subjectivity" – everything beyond preferences, information and rational calculation – and increasingly assesses politics in complex, even nested, situations.

To some degree, these postmodern and rational choice positions lead in orthogonal or even opposite directions as follows: (1) with a diffusion and *de*construction of power (and domains for its explanation) associated with postmodernism and the cultural turn and, at times, emphasized in feminist orientations toward the private sphere, and (2) with the integration of all social science around modes of rational action (that arguably are more psychological and economic than sociological) associated with the rational choice approach. These diverse and contradictory pressures are illustrated in Figure 1.1.

The cultural and feminist paths lie within sociology but may lead to postmodern theory in anthropology and the humanities, both of which strongly emphasize culture. The rational choice approach has seeds in much of power resources and political economy theory but leads outward toward political science and economics. In many ways, both theories lay claim to institutional theory. A coherent approach to political sociology would strive toward the sort of *rapprochement* between, or even integration of, two of the theoretical orientations that Campbell and Pedersen (2001) sketch out for conflicting schools of institutional theory: "rational choice" and "discursive" institutionalism. These orientations differ greatly in their views of how universal or historically specific (or "local") theories should be, with rational choice theory at one, universalistic, pole and historical and discursive theories at the other, highly particular, pole. These are at opposite ends as well in their views of how positivistic or interpretivist theories should be. Yet although new theories from across the aisle from one's own preferred side of the universalistic/local and the positivist/interpretivist divides often are dreaded, Campbell and Pedersen show how institutionalists of every stripe are "finding ways to connect their turf to others" (2001:273). We return to these distinctions when we discuss the challenges presented to political sociology by the "cultural turn" and the rise of rational choice theory.

The First Challenge: Culture (and Postmodernity)

From the perspective of the new cultural sociology, the theory that had dominated sociology following World War II was modern in epistemology (objectivist and scientific) and modern in politics (a creature of industrial society).[4] Epistemologically, it was marked by an antitraditionalist and antireductionist skepticism that preceded the postmodern skepticism toward scientific objectivity certainty yet remained objectivist (or "realist") and scientific. Politically, it was founded on the assumption that social cleavages and interest groups shape the election, legislation, and social and foreign policy outcomes of states. The theory's conceptualizations, much like those stressed by Alford and Friedland (1985), are tersely characterized by Adams, Clemens, and Orloff (2004) as involving a "double reduction" of phenomena to social (and state) structure and to utilitarian action (the last constrained, if not prefigured, by structure). In case the quoted use of "reduction" appears pejorative, we note that "reduction" was a respectable theoretical goal for the modernists in question and remains so to the many modernists (or perhaps "neomodernists") who continue in political sociology today, two decades after Alford and Friedland's (to use a literary trope) "high modernist" work.

Adams, Clemens, and Orloff's critique is not entirely new, having been anticipated by microinteractionist theories ranging from symbolic interactionism and ethnomethodology in the United States (e.g., Herbert Blumer, Howard Garfinkel, Anselm Strauss, and Erving Goffman) to hermeneutics, phenomenology, and historicism in Europe (e.g., Edmund Husserl, Alfred Schutz, Paul Ricouer, and Hans-Georg Gadamer). As described by Stephen Pepper (1972), the epistemological basis for this new contextualism lies in the meaning created in small contexts, with its strands dissipating as it moves beyond the originating context to other situations. Such contextualism is commonplace within the more encompassing orientation toward social reality sometimes termed interpretivist (Steinmetz, 1999). By and large, the postmodernists, feminists, and race/ethnic social constructionists may be termed interpretivists. However, as we shall see, we believe that interpretivism leaves social scientists in need of an epistemological midpoint between such antimonies as explanatory theory and orienting framework; and between covering law explanation and contextually specific interpretation.

The path to the assimilation of culture into *political* sociology has been a lengthy one. In the 1950s and 1960s, political sociology focused on power structure research and pluralism and on

[4] The "modernist political sociology" presented by Alford and Friedland articulates not merely a scientifically ambitious concatenation of accounts of theories of the state – that is, of state, state and society, state and economy, state in capitalist society, and the like – it conveys an ontology appropriate to the scientific sociological study of states. *The Powers of Theory* world is one of action and structure, structure and function, and function and process, where structures are presumed to be like the social relational structure articulated by Peter Blau (1964) or Erik Olin Wright (2002, 1997) but not like the symbolic structures described by Mary Douglas and Baron Isherwoood (1979) or William Sewell, Jr. (1980, 1985, 1992, 1994). And it is from this latter direction that the first major challenge to political sociology has come.

value consensus and functionalist equilibrium. Political culture was often viewed in what has come to be known as "essentialist" nationalist terms, which left most cultural variability as a distinction between nations. Gabriel Almond and Sydney Verba set the tone of early cultural studies with *The Civic Culture* (1963), in which they examined the cultural constants affecting political participation in five nations. Laboring long in the gardens of political culture, Ronald Inglehart presaged some aspects of postmodernity through his studies of postmaterialist values (1990, 1997). Murray J. Edelman (1964) took an early look at symbolic culture from an interpretivist perspective unusual for American social scientists during the first post–World War II decades.

Under the aegis of neo-Marxist concerns with capitalism and the rise of the working class, various scholars did cultural research in political sociology. Edward P. Thompson probed the meaning of religion and craft in *The Making of the English Working Class* (1966) and helped create a "social history" movement that explored the meaning of everyday life under the shadow of capitalism. Basil Bernstein (1975), Raymond Williams (1973, 1977), and Garth Stedman-Jones (1983) examined how language and symbols in a social context affected socialization, learning, and action. Later in the 1970s and 1980s, much of the upsurge in critical theory was oriented toward advertising, gender, the media, and culture in general.

An important precursor to all of this was Weber's (1922, 1930) cultural work on religion. Weber argued that capitalism was created through the religious insecurities of a band of religious heretics "irrationally" believing in predestination.[5] Weber, working largely within the German tradition of the "cultural" or "human sciences" (e.g., Dilthey, 1989) and influenced by Friedrich Nietzche (Turner, 1992: chapter 10), can be interpreted as equally as antipositivist as the previously mentioned neo-Marxist practitioners of cultural political analysis.

Despite Weber's dynamic account of capitalism and Thompson's nuanced view of the working class, prevailing approaches to political culture were severely criticized for their static nature and for their stereotyping of entire peoples (e.g., Almond and Verba, 1963). Culture itself became infused with a fixity that clearly overgeneralized. Although Weber and Thompson had shown one way out of this bind, cultural studies did not really emerge as a force until it embraced a vibrant intellectual community relatively isolated from the kind of social science practiced in the Anglo-American world, namely the French poststructuralist community of Michel Foucault, Frederik Barth, Roland Barthes, and (in some ways) Raymond Boudon and Pierre Bourdieu, plus such postmodernists as Jean Baudrillard, Jacques Derrida, Jacques Lacan, and Jean-Francois Lyotard.

Foucault removed the critical aspect of determinism from his theories by talking about "what was possible" in various social contexts between groups and people with varying levels of power/knowledge. This changed the analyst's viewpoint toward culture as something of an epiphenomenon of industrialization to one that perceived cultural processes to cause material outcomes or even to supplant the "social as material" with the "social as text." This approach allowed the static theories of culture to become dynamic and the secondary nature of culture under capitalism to become primary. It also declared as essentialist both the predictions about revolution and the leadership role of the working class in Marxist theory and the social scientific laws and generalizations about the inevitability of progress or economic development.

For many advocates of the cultural turn, claims for culture's broad relevance to the constitution and explanation of social reality come laden with epistemological and methodological implications. For them, social reality is evanescent – frequently changing and subject to unpredictable change – as well as geographically heterogeneous. If culture as a pervasive source and constituent of social institutions

[5] The Weberian framework of social action utilizes four types of rationality – instrumental, practical, subjective, and theoretical – but it also recognizes traditional and emotional action as equal components (Janoski, 1998; Kalberg, 1980).

is thus impermanent and heterogeneous, then such cultural volatility undermines the degree of social stability needed for the sort of stable and homogenous domains required for valid "universal" theorizing (Adams, Clemens, and Orloff, 2004; Steinmetz, 1998, 1999).

Culturally induced social-theoretical instability raises some disturbing questions. What if cogent causal regularities, and thus robust theoretical domains, are not only institutionally conditioned, as is typically assumed for middle-range theories? What if institutions themselves have an irreducibly cultural aspect, as in William Sewell's (1992) Janus-faced view of institution and social structure?[6] Then class groupings and actions would be contingent on workers' own historically contingent conceptions of themselves and their labor.

What if the political movements of even class-conscious workers are dependent on workers' conceptions of the movements in which they participate? Here one outcome is described by Nader Sohrabi (1995, 2002), for whom revolutionaries in the early twentieth century (e.g., the Russian of 1905, the Iranian "Constitutionalist" insurrectionaries of 1906, and the Young Turks of 1908) enacted a constitutionalist/parliamentary paradigm of political revolution while themselves members of the paradigm's ecumenical, and by no means simply class, variety of revolutionary coalition. If workers did not enact socialist revolutions as members of *class*, or even cross-class, projects, then the universalizing aspirations of class theories to theorize politics for the entire industrial age contracts into a relatively small, culturally restricted space, confined mainly to the Soviet era. Not only does much of the pre-Soviet era lack "worker" as its revolutionary actor or "socialist revolution" as its dominant revolutionary project, the Soviet era of class revolutions ends with the collapse of the Soviet bloc, which vitiates the socialist revolutionary vision. In other words, theoretical domains can be hemmed in by history and its cultural infrastructure (Goodwin and Jasper, 1999), leaving them at risk of sudden and unpredictable terminations beyond which new theory is needed.[7]

If in natural science the history of concepts and theories tends to play catch-up with reality, in social science the histories of scientific sign and social referent rush forward on separate tracks running in rough tandem. In this latter case they do so as new social phenomena enter the world, requiring new concepts and opening the door to new theoretical domains (Somers, 1995). True, the challenge of such volatility may be manageable. Historical and institutional specificity may, at times, only call for carefully constructed middle-range theoretical domains (Paige, 1999), a move anticipated by Merton (1968:39–72). It may merely require the kind of attention to statistical interactions that now permeates institutionally sensitive macro studies of politics (e.g., Esping-Andersen, 1993; Garrett, 1998; Goodwin, 2001; Pampel and Williamson, 1989; Steinmetz, 1993; Swank, 2002). Yet, as Janoski and Hicks (1994:10–12) indicate, there are times when an explanatory domain may be quite specific, even to a particular nation in a particular era. The degree to which a theoretical domain is temporally and spatially localized must be evaluated through the lens of history (Goodwin, 2001:293–306).

The cultural turn and the uses of culture in political sociology come in close association with other new directions in sociology, for

[6] Moreover, the resulting variance in social regularities across time and place appears more perturbed by cultural volatility if one is a realist who sees social phenomena as "over determined" (e.g., Steinmetz, 1998). The same hypervariability reigns for an interpretivist, who will tend to see any given account of social (or regularity) as an artifact of the interpretive scheme in use and who will tend to see the scheme as bracketting the favored foci of other schema (e.g., Steinmetz, 2003). As advocates of the cultural turn have long been and increasingly are realist, interpretivist, or both (Adams, Orloff, and Clemens, 2004), skepticism toward theoretical universalism in the sense of causal regularities invariant across wide swaths of time and space is especially rife.

[7] This is not simply a state of affairs unique to a few theoretical entities. For example, what appears to be a quite general "interest group" in one theory may turn out to be a local creation of Progressive Era politics (Clemens, 1997), and the truths about *Finanzkapital* (Hilferding, 1981[1910]; Lenin, 1933[1916]) may turn out to be local and transient German truths (Hicks, 1988; Zysman, 1984).

example the feminist one (e.g., Adams, 1999; Orloff, 1993). Feminist thought may not only add new variables, unsettling old theories and investigations (e.g., Orloff, 1993), it may also introduce new cultural dimensions to the analysis of power with all their potential complications (Adams, 2003; Misra, 2003).

In short, many participants in the cultural turn – for example, postmodernists, feminists, and race/ethic social constructionists – may be regarded as interpretivists, who view theoretical domains as local and evanescent because of the operation of culture (Goodwin and Jasper, 1999). This elaborates our earlier claim that participants in the cultural turn need, if their advance is to strike a healthy balance, to find an epistemological midpoint between positivist universalism and interpretivist historical and institutional specificity. The cultural turn directs political sociologists down a slippery slope from positivistic universalism, through increasing degrees of institutional and historical specification of theoretical domains, into a realm where theory serves not so much to capture social regularities as to regulate the interpretation of unique events. In our view, middle-range theory provides the missing midpoint. Of course, the objects of some quests for theoretical understanding may prove elusive, receding from the general to the particular. However, we think sociologists should strive to resist the pull of cultural theorizing into particularism. Our methodological injunction should be, with due institutional and historical alertness, to find the interaction that clarifies the order that lies beneath what at first appears to be confusingly heterogeneous processes, never to lightly abdicate the search for explanatory empirical patterns (Paige, 1999).

As one of three different approaches to the new cultural sociology, Robert Wuthnow's *Communities of Discourse* (1989) provides an explanation for major political changes. He examines environmental conditions, institutional contexts, and action sequences to demonstrate how ideologies of change are produced and how subsets of these are then selected for institutionalization into roles of world-historic importance. The "performativity" of such cultural articulations establish the mechanisms by which entirely new cultural formations are created: the selection of new ideas by actors (Protestant ministers, *philosophes*, or labor organizers) who use specific behavioral scripts to create figural actors (i.e., narrative heroes or heroines of the pilgrim, freethinker, or worker) of new ideologies and the different institutional carriers of these ideas (1989:5–18). Wuthnow goes on to explain these three ideologies appearing on the Western stage: the Reformation (joining the pious in church, as guided from the pulpit, in direct communion with God), the Enlightenment (rational, secular intellectuals based in royal courts and later in bourgeois salons), and Socialism (as a party and labor union project mobilizing employees for revolution and the future leadership of society). Wuthnow's focus is on ideologies as ideas that promote momentous change, much as we see in Weber's (1930) consideration of the Protestant ethic in promotion of capitalism, Philip Gorski's (1999, 2003) examination of religious pietism in the formation of the bureaucratic disciplinary state in Prussia, and Steinmetz's (2003) account of "pre-colonial ethnographic discourse" in the construction of Wilhemine colonial governance.

For a second approach, fusing postmodern and Marxist theory, Ernesto Laclau and Chantal Mouffe (1985) present a skeptical two-stage theory that avoids essentialism by proposing a pluralist governing scenario and a leftist strategy within it. Their politics embody a radical plural democracy that accepts liberal democracy to the extent that the left extends and deepens the principles inherent in it (Mouffe, 1992). Liberal democracy is seen as a contradiction between libertarian norms of unrestricted rights and communitarian norms of cooperation (Mouffe, 1993; Torfing, 1999:249–52). From this tension emerges an "agonistic democracy" that gives political space for varied and even contradictory political strategies that allow for a wide diversity of viewpoints without striving for an ultimate utopia (Mouffe, 1993:4, 1996; Torfing, 1999:255).

A third approach is supplied by feminist analysts of politics who have challenged much that had been conventional wisdom in political sociology. For example, feminist scholars of the welfare state, like Orloff (1993) and O'Connor, Orloff, and Shaver (1999), expose the distortions in current views of social needs and care, both public and private, that do not take account of the care provided by unpaid female workers. Joya Misra (2003) shows how women were key actors in developing family allowances in the welfare state. In areas other than the welfare state, Adams (1994) reveals how Dutch, English, and French representatives of family lineages mobilized signifiers of paternal identity in constituting patrimonial political structures; and, in so doing, she uncovers the gendered contents of long-standing sociological concepts and institutions. And Kathleen Blee shows how the interaction of race and gender operated within the culture of the Klu Klux Klan (1991).

For political sociologists interested in generalizations about political phenomena – whether historically, institutionally, or culturally nested, whether culturally wide-ranging or contextually hemmed in, whether meant to capture the one best map for a theoretically comprehensible reality or to merely provide theoretical flashlights able to help orient us to a stubbornly obscure reality – this cultural turn calls attention to new investigative possibilities. The turn may then direct political investigators to historically specific and historically unfolding cultural aspects of social reality. This leads toward a greater historicization of political sociological theory and method. At the same time, such awareness does not eclipse earlier concentrations on social structure and utilitarian action. Nor does it eliminate the need for generalizing theory and explanation.

The Second Challenge – Rational Choice Theory

The commitment to rational choice theory, currently evident in as much as, say, 40 percent of political science writing, presents a strong challenge to political sociology. Rational choice approaches politics in much more rationalistic, theoretically mathematical, and individualistic ways than have been the tendency in political sociology. True, a number of political sociologists have been influenced by the theory and practice of rational choice (e.g., Adams, 1996; Brustein, 1996; Coleman, 1990; Ermakoff, 1997; Gould, 2004; Hardin, 1995; Hechter, 1987, 1999; Hopcroft, 1999; Kiser, 1999; Kiser and Kane, 2001a, 2001b; Oberschall, 1993). It would require a longer story than we can accommodate here to indicate how neoclassical economic thought came to play such a strong role in the discipline of political science, but suffice it to say that the prestige of Nobel prizes, the increasing market orientation of society, and the rise of neoconservative and antigovernment sentiments have helped advance this ascent. Even sociologists have adopted economic terms such as human, social, and cultural *capital*. The influence of human capital, associated with Gary Becker, a Nobel prize-winning economist, was given additional legitimacy in sociology with his joint appointment to the department of sociology at the University of Chicago. The rational choice orientation, which is almost diametrically opposed to the cultural turn, constitutes a second challenge, this one from economics via political science.

In parallel to rational choice theory in political science, sociology has its own micro-based exchange theory. Its precursor, Georg Simmel (1950, 1955), focused on the dyad and triad, and in so doing laid the basis for social exchange theory. George Homans (1964) and Peter Blau (1964) developed a theory of exchange and power based on expected rewards from exchange (e.g., money, approval, esteem, and compliance), norms of reciprocity and fair exchange, and the belief that balanced exchanges in one sphere tend to produce imbalanced exchanges in others. From this, Richard Emerson (1972, 1976) and others developed a microtheory of power based on how much one actor depends on the other. Group exchange theorists, such as Samuel Bacharach and Edward Lawler (1980, 1981), extend this power-dependence analysis to unions/management, political parties, and other groups. However, social exchange theory has not, by and large, penetrated nearly as far into political sociology as rational choice theory has into political science. Paradoxically, it may be that rational choice theory, though less ostensibly sociological than exchange theory, might have better prospects within political sociology than exchange theory ever did. However, the reasons for rational choice theory's potential appeal to sociologists are, as we shall see, closely tied to its arguable limitations.

Rational choice theory is a generalization of the basic theoretical method of economics devised to move onto terrain beyond the market (Becker, 1991, 1995; Suzumura, 1989). First of these new substantive domains was the polity, focus of the new economic subfield of "public choice." Public choice theory extends economic models into such topics as optimal location theory, rent-seeking theory, and political supply theory. Optimal location theory addresses the question, "How does the institutional structure of the state determine the number of political parties and party platforms?" (Downs, 1957; Riker, 1962). Rent-seeking theory addresses the question, "What are the consequences of actors lobbying the state to intervene in the market?" (Wicksell, 1954.) Principal agent and policy supply theories are theories that ask, "Are elected politicians and state officials able to adequately control appointed bureaucrats and the political economic consequences of their actions?" (Niskanen, 1971). As these theories developed outside the market arena and the specific theoretical formulations that had sought to capture market logic, a more general theoretical logic was formalized (Becker, 1991, 1995). This logic clarifies, or rearticulates, economic theory as rational choice theory: as a theory of the optimizing decision-making decisions (and behaviors) of rational egoists (Suzumura, 1989).

Undiluted rational choice theory comes inextricably linked with a family of formal, mathematical methods of theoretical articulation, development, and analysis that conform closely to the logicodeductive conception of theory as a logical structure of statements derived through formal logic or mathematics from explicit premises. This conception of theory is, in turn, linked to a "positive" method of empirical investigation (Friedman, 1953; Keat and Urry, 1983:chapter 2).

Major developments in rational choice decision-making theory include articulating a theory of constrained optimization and the incorporation of game theory. The first includes social (and cognitive) structural contexts in the elaboration of optimizing behaviors (Alt and Crystal, 1983; Becker and Murphy, 2003; Tinbergen, 1952). The second makes an even more direct appeal to the sociological imagination by addressing the problem of strategic choice in the context of interaction between two or more actors, each of whom takes account of the anticipated actions of the other (Schotter, 1981). We almost hear the voice of Weber (1978:4) on action as "social" insofar as it "takes account of the behavior of others" as it is "oriented in its course."

An axiomatic theoretical structure that can embolden its practitioners to theorize in diverse domains not only encourages cumulative theory building but also establishes an abstract domain hospitable to universal theoretical claims, namely the logical structure of the theory itself, a kind of laboratory of the mind aloof from the noisy empirical fray. Just as cases can be made for the "realism of the abstract structures of logic and mathematics" (e.g., Putnam, 1983), ones can be made for the realism of the abstract generalizations of economic theory as the structure – or a modal structure – of rational action (Riker and Ordeshook, 1973). More substantively, rational choice theory's treatment of strategic rationality in the theory's "game-theoretic" mode also seems likely to appeal to those focused on social exchange. Similarly, rational choice theory's efforts to situate action in social context can only improve the theory's favor in the eyes of sociologists even though, as we shall see, such favor comes sparingly.

In resonating with sociologists of exchange, the work of Lief Lewin (1991) shows how, in the context of the welfare state, weaker groups gain power to manipulate stronger groups or coalitions. Addressing eight crisis periods in Swedish politics – the tariff, suffrage and mass franchise, parliamentarism, the Saltsjöbaden agreement, economic planning, supplementary pensions, nuclear power, and the employee investment funds crisis – Lewin shows how distinct bargaining strategies enacted in each policy arena explain resolutions of the crises (see other political examples in Edling and Stern, 2003; Przeworski, 1985; and Wallerstein, 1999).[8]

Heckscher (1996) and Fischer and Ury (1981), along similar lines, extend rational choice analysis to a multilateral bargaining model that includes multiple participants with diverse social bases (i.e., class, race, ethnicity, gender, region, religion, and so on). This model avoids positional bargaining (i.e., stating concrete bargaining demands in two-party bargaining) and embraces cooperative bargaining that focuses on problem solving from many different perspectives.[9] In a similar way, Bacharach and Lawler (1980, 1981) build a sociological theory of bargaining based on group power.

Rational choice theory has the ability to offer new explanations for socially embedded behaviors that would once have been treated by sociologists as based solely on emotional orientation (e.g., attitude) or political tradition. So Brustein (1991) finds the roots of Mussolini's support in his fascist appeals to the material interests of various constituencies, in particular agricultural small holders. He does much the same in examining support for the Nazi movement (Brustein, 1996). Finally, in *Roots of Hate* (2003), he extends the rational choice explanation for the roots of anti-Semitic politics to all of interwar Europe. Critical to much of his analysis is the Nazis' ability to mobilize rural small holders in reaction to left parties that opted for agricultural collectivization policies.[10]

One criticism of rational choice theory commonly made by sociologists is that it relies on an implausibly rational, even hyperrational, theory of human behavior. However, rational choice theory has made advances that dull this criticism – for example, by providing insights about interests as they stray from strict individualistic rationality (Gould, 2004). George Tsebellis (1990, 1999) puts decisions and coalitions into a more realistic societal situation based on games nested within other games, which are themselves nested within institutions. This becomes a basis for a new and more complex institutional theory. Decisions are made in a rational fashion but with considerable room for context as nesting alters payoffs and hence decisions (see Cook, 2002, on alliances and nesting).

[8] For example, in the suffrage crisis of the 1900s, the Social Democrats wanted universal suffrage to be declared the law of the land. They were growing in numbers through incremental changes in the franchise rule, and they were bound to be the majority party when an eventual franchise bill was passed. The conservatives, seeing the writing on the wall and acting early, pursued a strategy of making additions to the agenda. They backed universal suffrage, despite internal conservative protests, but attached the principle of proportional rule. This meant that the conservative party would survive the postuniversal suffrage change and not die with a "winner-take-all" election. The Social Democrats were divided partly because they were not prepared for the agenda amendment. As a result, the weaker party had the basis to survive into the future and, indeed, survives to this day. In general, the weaker party (e.g., the conservatives facing possible oblivion with the mass franchise) often wins because it can more clearly pursue its goals with specific strategies, whereas larger or more powerful groups have more difficulty maneuvering because of internal factions.

[9] In international relations, similar forms of multilateral bargaining are starting to emerge, especially bargaining in NAFTA, the European Union, and various international gatherings (Cameron and Tomlin, 2000; Keohane, 1989; Putnam, 1993). However, as its descriptive scope is expanded, the predictive value of rational choice theory in studying political conflict is reduced because the constrained situation is lost.

[10] Social Democratic agricultural platforms offering subsidies and supports for cooperative arrangements often appealed to agricultural small holders. Communist platforms aimed at public agricultural collectivization often made sense to agricultural laborers. However, in countries where they were strong, Communist plans for collectivization were so anathema to small holders that they tended to drive small holders and, with them, much of the rural population straight into the arms of National Socialist and Fascist parties brandishing appeals to the property rights and economic security of farm proprietors. In short, communist agricultural planks were so inconsistent with the cost–benefit ratios of agricultural proprietors that they tipped the balance of farmer preferences for a mixed economy, and, where Communist parties were electorally strong, they split the left and tended to push the economically rational political choices of economically insecure but ultimately proproprietorial farmers to the far Right (Brustein, 2003).

Dennis Chong integrates sociological and economic mechanisms into bargaining and aims to account for the conflict between groups over norms and values. He proposes a status politics that is "based on subjective calculations of self-interests" that are "motivated by both material and social goals" (Chong, 2000:1, 220). Interests are consequently based on "the history of one's choices, including the values, identifications, and knowledge that one has acquired through socialization" (Chong, 2000:6–7). Frank Knight (1992) puts inequality directly into a bargaining theory of institutions by incorporating distributional inequalities into a mixed game of choice. This systemic inequality inevitably leads to differential bargaining power, which, in the construction of political institutions, provides for unequal benefits. He couches this formulation in an evolutionary framework (e.g., variation, selection, and inheritance) whereby citizens will make decisions depending on whether the costs are sufficient to change or accept these institutions. Edgar Kiser and collaborators explore many other aspects of state formation and development employing the principal agent theory (e.g., Kiser and Bauldry, Chapter 8, this volume; Kiser and Kane, 2001; Kiser and Linton, 2002).

However, for all its appeals to, and inroads into, sociology, rational choice has been greeted with much more resistance by sociologists than by political scientists. Its degree of logicodeductive theoretical method and universalism, its rational empiricism (or positivism), the stylized character of its models of strategic action, and its *ad hoc* (when not negligible) treatment of social context have all been copiously criticized (Gould, 2004; Green and Shapiro, 1995). Moreover, the simplicity of its assumptions about human rationality and egoism and of its claims for the "exogeneity" of preferences have been viewed with widespread skepticism by social scientists, especially sociologists (Elster, 1989; Gould, 2004; Hastie, 2001; Rabin, 1998). Although such criticisms have been extensive among political scientists as well as sociologists, sociology has clearly offered much resistance to the spread of rational choice theory. Some reasons for this differential will appear when we examine the implications of rational choice, along with cultural theory, for the future of political sociology.

The Challengers and the Challenged

One major advantage held by the challengers is that they have momentum, support, and emotion on their side. Their theories enthrall highly motivated and malleable graduate students and dismay aging faculty with sunk-costs in other theories. Although one might be tempted to describe every challenge in Kuhnian terms, as revolutionary science overthrowing normal science, we should remember that many challenges to this or that theory or metatheoretical thrust come and go. There have been many more fads with little lasting impact on the field than there have been tectonic shifts in political sociology's underlying conceptual strata.

Although theorists of the new approaches often show disdain for previous theories, especially when they demand mastery of new jargons, challenges ebb. New directions sometimes double back onto old terrain as when Foucaultian scholars rediscover the long sociological tradition on social control and total institutions (Goffman, 1961). Just how different is capillarity (Foucault) from power in social exchange networks, Korpian power resources from earlier pluralist ones (Rogers, 1974), *bricoulage* from pluralism? The key point is not that these concepts are exactly the same but rather to question whether there has been any attempt at cumulation in sociological work (see Boudon, 2003). As stated, cultural and postmodern theories needed the isolation of French intellectual circles to escape the determinism of Anglo-American, German, Marxist, and other more neutral or scientistic theories. But in the end, theorists must make sense of the cacophony of terminology and ask, "What is really new here?" Sociology, inherently a composite of structure and culture, with individual and group social action that is rational and emotional, will operate to create, oppose, or ignore constraints from challengers with varying degrees of success. We may ask what these challengers' ideas might look like if they are absorbed or ignored, perhaps to live a life of their own in a parallel but separate realm of ideas.

In answer to the cultural challenge, we find the amount of determinism or essentialism attributed to political sociological theory to be overstated by practitioners of the turn. It would be false to characterize those political sociological theorists not committed to the cultural turn as pursuing "covering law" explanations, insensitive to cultural, historical, and institutional specificity. For example, the once-strong deterministic vein within Marxist political sociology continues to recede as cultural critiques of determinism by Thompson (1966) and Garth Stedman-Jones (1983) are reinforced by a new post-Soviet wave of cultural critiques (Gibson-Graham, 2002; Harvey, 2000; and the journal *Rethinking Marxism*).

Although a case for a deterministic Weber was recently constructed in an attempt to locate the progressive triumph of rationalism as the central theme in Weber's *ouevre* (Hennis, 1987; Schluchter, 1981), others have accentuated an antideterministic Weber that appears truer to his era and his main thrust. In particular, Bryan Turner, using Stephen Kalberg (1985) to address "religion and state-formation," has described Weber as follows:

> Weber approached society as a diversified, fragmented and competitive collection of semi-independent institutions, sectors and social groups which fought with each other for the monopolization of social resources. (Turner, 1992:111)

The nondeterministic Weber has long been reflected in the sensitive use of "themes" rather than "theory" in the work of Reinhard Bendix (1964, 1970, 1984), echoed in Skocpol and Somers (1980) on Bendix. It recurs again in the turn from covering laws to "social mechanisms" in the work of Charles Tilly (2003 and in this volume). Further, Richard Swedberg (2003) points to a new interpretation of Weber based on interests and emotions in institutions that combines both rational choice and interests embedded in culture. Still, although consideration of Weber and Bendix undercuts claims for the novelty of the new cultural turn, consideration of Tilly (2003) and Swedberg (2003) catches us up in the new turn and reveals the tension between much of culturally oriented political sociology and the prevailing empiricist bent of contemporary political sociology.

One challenge issuing from participants in the cultural turn involves a generalization of the political. For example, Agger and Luke (2003:189) in citing Baudrillard, claim that:

> The political in this context is found not in parliaments, but rather in professional-technical conflicts or the competition of capital: the non-political becomes political as power rushes into sub-political realms of action. The allegedly political dimension, in turn, of elections, parliaments or parties decays into a non-politics of spectacle, quietism or plain ignorance . . . .

A new substructure has been found for the overtly but derivatively political in cultural discourse over identity, family, professions, and other aspects of the private and market spheres. The state, as it was in early Marxism, is again an epiphenomenon; and political science should either demote itself as a discipline or plunge into the all-consuming investigation of culture.

The claim that political sociology will or should devolve into a power perspective on "society in general" simply does not hold. The politics of elections, legislation, and state policy actions are not epiphenomena totally ruled by cultural forces. This does not mean that there are no new social forces in identity, the private sphere, and so on. Few political sociologists, however, are disposed to accept such a diffusion of the political out into the whole metatheoretical domain of sociology. Indeed, by no means can most political sociological participants in the cultural turn be said to take this extreme postmodern position. What we can affirm is that state- or polity-centered theory is not ready for the dustbin of history.

Our preference for theories that claim to articulate an "objective" reality over theories that principally claim to orient interpretations of a subjective (or explosively intersubjective) reality goes along with our guarded respect for the many methodological and epistemological challenges posed by the cultural turn and its counsel of alertness to the particularity of history, institutions, and culture (and an underlying cultural volatility). We suggest that the tensions generated by the encounter between heavily cultural and social-relational (and psychological) views of social phenomena may find satisfactory resolution for many realists and positivists in the use of three regulative ideals: middle range theory, statistical interactions (Paige, 1999; Swank, 2002), and "multiple conjunctural causation" (Ragin, 1987). Furthermore, realists who doubt the accessibility of open concrete systems to robust regularities in phenomena may still find assurance in experimental and quasi-experimental modes of theory testing (Cook and Campbell, 1979). Certainly, the relevance of theory stressing "orienting" concepts (cf. Skocpol and Somers, 1980) remains robust far down such risky "slippery slopes" as we have cautioned against here. Indeed space may be found for quite universalistic theorizing in that realm of rational choice theory that devotes itself to elaborating the rational calculi of the stylized *homo economicus*, to whom we soon turn.

The cultural turn may have emerged at a propitious moment, a time when ideological performance moves from the authors and readers of pamphlets and books to the creators and viewers of television, computer monitors, and the Web. Increasing scrutiny of the media's impact on voter preferences and participation, candidate and official behavior, and political competition in general are most welcomed at this point and may be among the major strengths of the cultural approach (Hayles, 1990; Johnston, 1998; Schudson, 2003). Still, many would argue that a cultural emphasis needs to be counterbalanced by a continued interest in the political economy, lest the focus on ideas distract from the importance of resources and interests. Attention to both the culture and political economy need not be strained. For example, in focusing on ideology one might see the role of "public interest" organizations as conduits running from political interests to media representations of politics by spokespersons and talking heads (Gamson, 1992). Indeed political economists have long packed some culture into actors' goals (Moore, 1967).

The second major challenge, rational choice theory, presents a view of politics that is nearly the opposite of the culturally centered one. Despite some allowance for culture in the articulation of options and interest, which is a view virtually dominated by the decision making of instrumentally (and sometimes strategically) oriented egoists. The more economic variety of rational choice emphasizes preferences and, in game-playing situations, strategies that mainly concern material outcomes, whereas the political science versions tend to direct more attention to institutions and consider more diverse goals (such as status or secure incumbency in office). For political sociology, even more weight needs to be given to acknowledging that a person's goals are diverse and complex if the rational choice approach is to seem credible. Although people may want to negotiate the best deal, it may not be entirely clear what their best deal is. Because, until recently, emotion (as well as most subjectivity) has been left off the rational choice table, a hole has marred the domain of such analysis, which is a problem from the cultural perspective (Adams, 1998; Hochschild, 1983; Somers, 1998). As troublesome Weberians point out to rational choice theorists committed to a highly stylized version of instrumental rationality, reason itself has more than a single form (Janoski, 1998:85–7; Kalberg, 1980).

The logicodeductive theoretical apparatus of rational choice theorists is viewed skeptically, if not with hostility, by sociologists who think that it builds on a foundation of simplistic assumptions about human actors (i.e., too selfish or *hyper*rational, too unemotional, too given to fixed "exogenous" preferences) while ignoring the windfalls of inductive discovery (Hirsch, Michaels, and Friedman, 1987). Indeed, the impression that rational choice theory builds on an utterly unrealistic model of the person is strongly held by many social scientists (Elster, 1989; Gould, 2004; Green and Shapiro, 1995; Hastie, 2001; Rabin, 1998). Also, few sociologists are comfortable with Milton Friedman's (1953) argument that rational choice theory is so predictively powerful that it has license to proceed from its assumptions on an "as if" basis (Green and Shapiro, 1995).

Rational choice theory's tendency toward universalistic presumption for its propositions antagonizes those who place high value on the "realists" specification of causal mechanisms grounded in a concrete knowledge of the "thing" or "object of study" at issue (e.g., the unit of analysis in historical and institutional context) (Quadagno and Knapp, 1992). Complementarily, some sociologists view attempts by rational choice authors to work within the constraints of social contexts viewed under considerable historical and institutional specificity (e.g., Kiser and Hechter, 1991) as insufficiently attentive to historical and institution detail and inductive reasoning (Quadagno and Knapp, 1992).

Rational choice theories may be at their best in tightly constrained situations where the range of outcomes are clear and manageable, when social structural (and cognitive and cultural) constraints are well-defined, and where there are either (a) an indefinitely large set of actors, each of which must adjust behavior to all the others as an aggregate, as price takers do in competitive pricing situations, or (b) a limited number of parties, as in such game-theoretic situations as collective bargaining between one representative of management and one of labor (Bacharach and Lawler, 1980, 1981; DeMenil, 1971; Raiffa, 2003). In other words, the participants know whether strategic action is an option and whether the option is manageable.[11]

We suspect that, overall, despite rational choice theory's deductivism and positivism, its increased alertness to social interaction and context, and its accommodations to sociological insight (e.g., Tsebellis, 1992, on nesting and Chong, 2002, on irrationality in action), there still will be effective brakes on the theory's progress within sociology. The long legacy of sociological opposition to highly individualist modes of theorizing, from Marx's (1904, 1909) critiques of classical political economy and Durkheim's (1984) critique of Spencer, will keep rational choice theory from ever exerting the extent of influence already attained by the cultural turn. Just as sociology has pitted the social against the individual and the socialistic against the rationally egotistical, it has favored the cultural, from Durkheim (1915) and Weber (1922, 1930) on religion, to Fine (1987, 1998) on little leaguers and mushroom hunters, and Bourdieu and Passeron (1990) on social orders large and small.

The recent advance of cultural approaches to political sociology also has its limits. Not only does continued regard for political economic issues caution against too strong a cultural stress, the modernist strain of sociological objectivism (realism and science) ascendant in U.S. political sociology throughout most of the postwar period seems likely to contain the culturalist advance. On the one hand, political economy had best accommodate cultural analysis if it is to master such matters as political economic reproduction and diffusion (e.g., Bourdieu and Passeron, 1990; Campbell and Pedersen, 2001). On the other hand, cultural sociology will surely have to accommodate the material and the social relational as well.

We hazard a guess that perhaps one-fifth of political sociologists are substantially within the "culture" camp, whereas another 5 to 10 percent practice a variant of rational choice theory. Unless these guesstimates are short, or shortsighted, a political sociology that is centered on social structure and social action (albeit substantially utilitarian action) can be expected to continue into the foreseeable future. At the same time, we believe that advocates of both postmodernity and rational choice will pull away from their cognate disciplines in the humanities, literature, and neoclassical economics to return and re-create political sociology in conjunction with, rather than as a replacement for, the neopluralist, conflict, and state-centric standard bearers. To refer back to Figure 1.1, these

[11] Most rational choice theorists recognize this, but other rational-action enthusiasts attempt to extend the range to all behavior. Exchange theory in sociology does this most clearly by arguing that, because power emerges from dependency, wherever dependency exists, there are power differences. Oddly enough, this view resembles Foucault's position, at least insofar as power is everywhere.

two movements, represented by outward flowing arrows, will return or curve back to a focus on institutions and other core areas of sociology and enrich the latter with their insights as they engage in a diversified and more complex process of theory building.

THE PURPOSES AND APPROACH OF THE *HANDBOOK OF POLITICAL SOCIOLOGY*

From the future of theory to the task at hand, this handbook pursues an integrated survey of the field of political sociology. We address four sets of questions: How have major theoretical traditions in political sociological theories adapted to changing times over the last several decades? How are the social bases of politics manifested in political sociology? What forms have been taken by the state and why? How are political outcomes reflected in policies, regimes, and international systems? These questions form the basis for dividing the handbook's chapters into five parts. The first, a section on "theories of political sociology," focuses on pluralist, conflict, state-centric, institutional, rational choice, cultural, and postmodern theories. The second, a section on the social bases of politics, focuses on political processes (social cleavages, voting, campaign contributions, public opinion, political attitudes, ideology, and political deliberation) and political organizations (political parties, interest groups, policy organizations, corporations, social movements, and the media). The third, a section on the state and its processes, concentrates on the structural and cultural formation of nation-states, civil and military bureaucracies, and authoritarian political systems. A fourth section focuses on the outcomes of politics in terms of social change, justice, redistribution, and repression. It does so by examining the following two levels: (1) policy changes (welfare state, policies toward minorities, intervention in the economy) and (2) regime transformations (wars, revolutions, and transitions from communism to market-based politics). In the fifth and final section, we examine international systems (imperialism, neocolonialism, trade, transnational corporations, global capitalism, migration/naturalization,genocide/asylum, and national devolutions). In short, our model of national politics stresses the more distal social bases of political action as relatively exogenous variables; the intervening, but also partially autonomous, role of the institutions of the state and its policies and the repercussions of regime change; and the ultimate exogenous force of transnational systems.

Theoretical Approaches to Political Sociology

The core debates among theories of political sociology appear in the first section, which opens with Frances Fox Piven and the late Richard Cloward's argument that, if rule making is a strategy of domination, rule breaking is the essence of opposing, disabling, and even replacing such domination. The question about power in political sociology then becomes "How does the 'human capacity for innovation' bring about these challenges to rule and domination?" Power is based on dependence, but the recognition of dependence requires interpretation on both sides and is often clouded by complexity and/or ideology. How do we and others "see" rules? In other words, the power of rule breakers depends on their recognizing power potential in votes, organization, and mobilization. And much of this requires "staying power," "controlling alternatives," "limiting constraints," and "facing or deflecting crushing force." Thus rule making consists of strategies to control people through the state, whereas challenges to these rules involve defying them and working hard to change them.

The theory section then flows into three chapters that update debates among the new pluralist and neofunctionalist, conflict and political economy, and state-centered or polity-centered perspectives. Alexander Hicks and Frank Lechner's chapter on neopluralism and neofunctionalism in political sociology reviews the rise of new forms of pluralist theories that have penetrated political sociology, whether with theoretical banners flying high or more covertly. The authors show how neopluralism has extended the range of agency to class- and state-based actors within structural contexts. One wave of pluralism comes from recognizing the impact of class, race, ethnicity, gender, and other social forces; another comes from the increasing variety and quantity of interest groups in the policy process; and a third comes from increasing levels of democratization, the media, and openness in the political process. Neofunctionalism's impact has not been as great as pluralism's, but its influence is felt especially through its cognate affinities to cultural sociology and because of the broader theoretical foundation that it provides to the pluralist point of view. Pluralist ideas permeate political sociology, emerging from different directions through a loosely coupled group of scholars.

From an opposing direction, Axel van den Berg and Thomas Janoski's chapter on conflict theories in political sociology argues that functionalism has nearly vanished and that all current theories – pluralism, state-centric, cultural, feminist, and racialization – have adopted the dominant, meta-perspective of conflict. They trace two conflict traditions through Marxist and Weberian lenses. Although traditional Marxist theory has imploded with the pluralization of conflict (e.g., from social bases in gender, race, ethnicity, and religion) and new and more contingent theories have developed with, for example, the "power constellations" theory of Huber and Stephens (2001) – and the "accommodationist" theory of Prechel (2000) – there is a tendency to place too exclusive an emphasis on corporate and elite power. Yet, some of the best work today by Marxists and some others working in this area is less theoretical, more empirical, and indeed exactly in this area of corporate power. For example, it describes exactly how campaign finance and insider influence involving large corporations actually work (Clawson, Neustadtl, and Weller, 1998; Prechel, 2000). The authors side more with the Weberian approach that gives equal weight to class, status, and power in both the political economy and cultural explanations.

In discussing state-centered and political institutional theory, Edwin Amenta shows how state-centered theory grew out of the work of Max Weber and Otto Hintze against the 1950s and 1960s backdrop of pluralist and conflict theories. The struggles that the Marxists were having with the autonomy of the state stimulated Theda Skocpol and others to reexamine Weberian theory and consider how the structure and processes of the state were a causal factor, with considerable force in and of themselves. Processes involving state formation, state interests, state strength, and state autonomy could influence, and even create, interest groups and establish rules of the game favoring some of them. Concern with these issues has led to a political-institutional theory (in Skocpol's latest terms, a polity-centered argument). Amenta shows how this new historical institutionalism emphasizes political contexts rather than the state alone. The key to more elaborate arguments within this tradition is to rely on creative or genealogical aspects of the state in forming politics and shaping interest group desires.

The next five chapters present the main theoretical challenges introduced earlier in this chapter. The cultural challenge comes mainly from within sociology and is discussed in four chapters. The rational choice challenge, although coming partly from within sociology, is largely a phenomenon arising from economics and influencing the discipline of political science. Although important to sociology as well, its outlines are captured in a single chapter.

In James Jasper's survey of the cultural approach, he proclaims that culture has become an increasingly central analytical tool since the early 1970s. He asks why, if capillary power is everywhere in the Foucaultian universe, are political sociologists not happier. Although he does not answer this question, he gives a wide-ranging survey of the cultural approach and extends even wider permission for the cultural study of intrinsically political issues, ranging from those associated with government to personal relations in the bedroom, on the playground, or on the street corner. In his grand tour of the wide world of culture, Jasper examines culture from its presence as civic culture, crowd psychology, structuralism, critical theory, hegemony, postmodernity, and globalization to its forms as ideology, collective identity, text, narrative, ritual, practice, discourse, and rhetoric. He considers how citizens are mobilized outside and inside the state and concludes with suggestions for attending to many of these undeveloped themes.

Jacob Torfing views some of the same material from the perspective of discourse analysis in political sociology, moving beyond Michel Foucault to the subjectivism of Jacques Derrida and Slavjo Žižek. From the subjectivist angle he derives a set of terms and concepts, radically new for most social scientists, such as articulation, constitutiveness, dislocation, sedimentation, sutures, and *bricoulage*. Torfing guides the reader through them with sensitivity and a dissection of the differences in four different theories (and methodologies) of discourse. This is the cultural turn with the sharpest angles, ending with LaClau and Mouffe's "agonistic democracy" and Žižek's contradiction that "we can only save democracy only by taking into account its own radical impossibility" (1989:6).

Barbara Hobson's chapter on feminism takes us away from "monolithic conceptions of state as patriarchy" to a recognition of the complex processes and structures of today's multiple feminisms. For example, she confronts the dilemmas of citizenship posed by maternalist and humanist feminism (i.e., the pull between difference and equality, private and public, needs and rights, and care and justice), and presents contextuality as one way to solve them (i.e., when difference makes a difference). Conceptions of rights in neoliberal, civic republicanism, and Marshallian thinking are all demonstrated to have implications for the different ethic of care that emerges from different political regimes. Hobson shows how the impact of postmodernity and multiculturalism can have surprising counterintuitive effects on universalism in the treatment of women of different racial origins. She concludes by assessing the primary dilemmas for feminist theorizing in political sociology.

David R. James and Kent Redding put race theory in the forefront of an expanded conception of how political sociology needs to address theories of the state. They do this by examining theories about how race and ethnicity are politically constructed. Although there is broad recognition about the ways in which states affect racial policies, the authors direct us to examine the processes by which states create and maintain racial identities and conclude with an analytically sensitive definition of the racial state. Their approach challenges prior theories of racialization in a number of effective ways.

In the final chapter of this section, Edgar Kiser and Shawn Baudry present rational choice theory as having considerable relevance to political sociology. It applies broadly to the new institutionalism, exemplified by studies of aristocrats, tax farmers that control the state, and the pooling of resources through institutions as a way to resolve the tragedy of the commons. Rational choice theory also has applications to culture, for example, as in "focal points," where rituals, holidays and statues that serve legitimation functions can also serve as "focal points" to coordinate collective protests. Yet in explaining collective action, rational choice seems to be at a disadvantage because people can be free riders. Kiser and Baudry respond by tying collective action to repeated games, especially involving "unconditional cooperators." In seemingly spontaneous situations, they use "preference falsification" to explain sudden reversals in political action. They argue as well for a relationship between rational choice and history and make a contribution to institutional theory with their critique of path dependence.

Chapters ranging from conflict to culture to rational choice suggest that the era of grand theorizing is over. As our theoretical scope narrows, it focuses more on mechanisms, constraints, and contexts. Although we began this chapter in anticipation of a move to synthesis, it is apparent, at the present time, that that possibility is still limited. We experienced this personally as our plans for the theory section expanded from four to nine chapters. It appears that the answer is still "yes" to the conflict chapter's question: must we have a separate theory for class, race, gender, and the state? Adams, Clemens, and Orloff (2004) also predict a tripartite dialectic of culture, rational choice, and structure in the next few decades of the twenty-first century. If so, this may lead to a more complex synthesis of theory, but it is difficult at this time to predict what it might be, if it indeed happens at all.

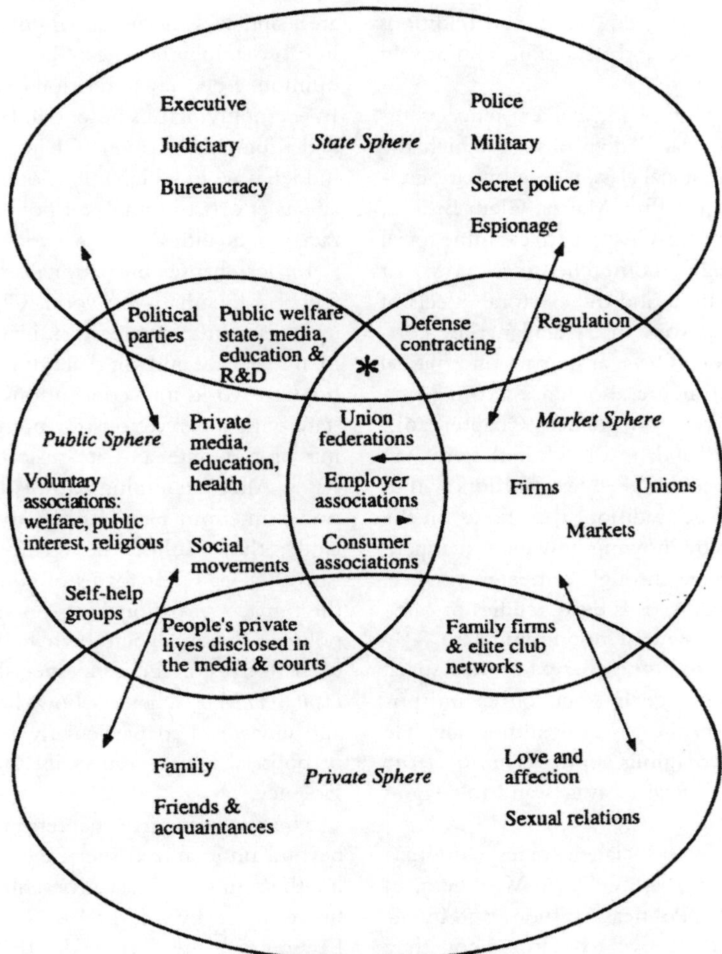

Figure 1.2. The Structure of Civil Society and the State (Janoski, 1998).

The Social Bases or Roots of Politics in Civil Society

The very nature of the field that makes political sociology sociological comes from civil society in the broadest sense – everything about society that is either not the state or where the state has overlapped into other arenas. In Figure 1.2, this would be the three overlapping circles below the circle representing the state, that is, the public, market, and private spheres. The social bases of politics are located not at "Number 10 Downing Street," "the hallowed halls of Congress," "the White House," or "the new Bundestag building in Berlin." Rather they reside with citizens situated in groups like labor unions, women's groups, corporations, voluntary associations, and churches or other religious organizations. They are rudiments of sociology, discussed in Chapters 2, 3, and 27 on theory (this volume). Less directly, social bases are comprised of every citizen and sometimes even noncitizen residents. Collectively, we call all these nonstate entities civil society. They constitute the diverse interests, rationalities, emotions, and traditions that shape the state and its actions and are, in turn, shaped by it.

The complexity of societal existence is reflected in deep-seated divisions, of which the most notable are social class, race, ethnicity, gender, and religion. Jeffrey Manza, Clem Brooks, and Michael Sauder (Chapter 10) examine social cleavages through a comprehensive survey that focuses on elections and the electoral effects of inequalities in power. In particular, they consider how cleavages have an impact on political participation (a theme also addressed in Misra and King's chapter on gender [Chapter 26]), voting behavior, and, in the United States, on campaign finance. Unlike many authors within the social cleavage tradition, they focus on the flip side of class by showing how elites maintain political advantage through campaign finance. To those who say class is dead, studies of campaign finance provide a resounding "no." By placing their topic in the context of how social cleavages were treated by sociologists and political scientists in the past, the authors are able to emphasize remaining controversies over the political role of social cleavages and to suggest avenues for future research.

Still working with social cleavages as unorganized divisions in society, David Weakliem, in "Public Opinion, Political Attitudes, and Ideology" (Chapter 11), moves to examine how they are expressed in opinions and ideas. He looks at both sides of the equation: what social forces affect the formation of public opinion and what impact public opinion has on political processes. As Manza, Brooks, and Sauder do in Chapter 10, treating the implications growing out of the way cleavages have been studied, Weakliem begins by noting the hiatus between mid-twentieth-century studies of public opinion and the relative loss of interest in the topic until recently. Although Weakliem is appreciative of the early work, particularly in its emphasis on social cleavages, he also sees its deficiencies. One was a lack of attention to processes of thinking, as though opinions were transmitted mainly through contacts. Another was a conception of change that had no place for sudden or discontinuous shifts in opinions. Weakliem evaluates recent work that looks precisely at these formerly neglected areas and sees the potential enrichment of political sociology in renewed scrutinies of public opinion, especially in relation to public policies. In exemplifying this potential, James, Redding, and Klugman's chapter (Chapter 27) traces the hidden ways in which public opinion about race affects efforts to undo past policies that created racial inequalities.

In her chapter on nationalism, Liah Greenfeld and Jonathan Eastwood (Chapter 12) pick up on a solidarity rooted in primordial attachments to place and kin that is transformed in the modern world into conceptions of the nation-state with repercussions for both the functioning of the state and its relations with other states. After examining various theories of nationalism, from Hans Kohn's to Roger Friedland's, they outline the relation of nationalism vis-à-vis other forms of consciousness and the impacts of nationalisms on various types of political action. Their own cultural approach to nationalism, focused especially on *ressentiment* (*à la* Max Scheler), shows how deprivation and envy lead to particularly irrational forms of political action, especially those involving violence.

The remaining five chapters in this section go beyond unorganized social cleavages to examine them in their various organized forms. The first of these, by Mildred A. Schwartz and Kay Lawson (Chapter 13) tackles the quintessential form of political action in the social bases, organization, and environments of political parties. Discussion of the social bases of parties necessarily overlaps with previous chapters on social cleavages but also takes into account the ties between parties and organized interests and the links between government and citizens. The extent to which cleavages are mobilized by parties remains a troubling question in many societies and touches on the difficulty of separating normative concerns from empirical ones. In considering the structure and culture of parties, similar problems arise in evaluating predictions of party decline. Because parties carry out governing functions, there is controversy over whether political parties should be treated as inside or outside civil society, one of the issues raised by considering the environmental context of parties.

Social cleavages can be most directly organized into interest groups – organizations with the goal of influencing public policy – which is the subject of Francisco Granados and David Knoke's chapter (Chapter 14). As political actors, interest groups overlap to some degree with political parties but also with social movements. Interest groups vary according to how they are organized, the extent of resource mobilization, their governance, and the range of interests they represent. Their internal character then has a bearing on how they influence policy. Granados and Knoke capture the range of interests that can be mobilized by examining the extent to which they form policy networks. They also draw attention to the significance of policy institutes as sources of interest group influence (e.g., the American Enterprise Institute and the Brookings Institution). The authors conclude by emphasizing the complexity of issues involved in understanding the role of interest groups and the potential they have in settings outside North America and Europe.

A key tenet of most conflict theories is that some groups are more powerful than others. In current societies, these sites of power are corporations, which Mark Mizruchi and Deborah Bey examine in their chapter (Chapter 15) on corporate power and control, including interfirm relations and networks. Although acknowledging the power of corporations in capitalist societies, the authors also point to the uncertainty in evaluating the role of business just as it is becoming more global. They caution against making too-easy generalizations about the past while mapping a blueprint for future research.

Craig Jenkins and William Form (Chapter 16) move away from those organized groups recognized to have some power to the more informally organized category of social movements. Because social movements are, by definition, committed to bringing about change, the central question for Jenkins and Form is when and how such change takes place. In looking for the causal connections that underlie the possibility that movements will produce change, they draw a portrait of movements embedded in their institutional milieus, dependent for results on their interaction with the mass media, allies and opponents, and political authorities.

In their chapter on the media, Michael Schudson and Silvio Waisbord (Chapter 17) point to the diverse ways that the mass media relate to social cleavages. The roles played by the media are often ambiguous if not contradictory. In societies where they are separate from organs of the state, they make up part of civil society. Their interaction with the state involves efforts at their regulation, on one side, and their attempts to influence the state, on the other. They represent part of the corporate power system while publicizing its abuses. They present themselves as purveyors of news to the general public, regardless of divisions in that public, and at the same time their drive for profit makes for their emphasis on entertainment as a factor in how news are disseminated. In the United States, although close ties between homogeneous news media and a single political party have waned, some highly salient connections obtain, and the media are often unpredictable in the ways in which they treat parties and candidates. At the same time, journalism is an institution that can be examined as a political system in itself, a theme that Schudson and Waisbord find especially compelling.

The roots of politics in civil society are both far-reaching and changing. There is potential for any major social division in a society to become mobilized into political salience. Societal divisions can be expressed in a variety of organized outlets while those organizations can represent anything from portions of a single cleavage to cross-cutting cleavages and interests. Structural divisions coexist with cultural ones, sometimes reinforcing each other, leading to disintegration, or retreating from salience. What these chapters all make clear is how the relation between the social/cultural and the political varies over time and from society to society. Their message is that what we have learned in the past, although remaining relevant, cannot replace a continuing search for how the political is transformed.

Explaining the State and Its Policies in Political Sociology

Influencing the state itself is the ultimate aim of most social movements, interest groups, and parties. This section is concerned with how the state is created, various forms of states, transitions between states, and how the state creates, implements, and evaluates its policies. In Chapter 18, Thomas Ertman discusses the formation and building of nation-states in Europe. He contrasts the founding work of Weber and Hintze and the renaissance of state and war theory of the 1960s to that of the 1980s by Anderson and Tilly.

Currently, the strongest factors influencing the formation of the state are warfare, rational choice, and culture. For Ertman and Downing's (1992) bellicist (warfare) approach, combined with the variable strength of medieval constitutionalism (legislatures), provides a useful cross-national explanation of state formation. In single-country studies, the rational choice approach of North highlights how relative power affects the extent to which rulers may enter into durable bargains with representative institutions to constrain predatory behavior and create an efficient property rights system. Using cultural case studies, Adams (1994) develops patrimonial theory of how families gain state power and resist bureaucracy in the Dutch Republic, and Gorski (2003) explains how the Calvinist rather than Lutheran religion shaped the disciplinary aspects of the Prussian state. Ertman finds the key to these three (bellicist, rational choice and cultural) approaches in a fundamental question: how do participatory local governments gain enough strength to avoid both the rent seeking associated with patrimonial corruption and the authoritarian solutions to state formation processes?

In Chapter 19, John Markoff follows with a survey of the transitions to democracy whose variable beginnings have helped to mold their diverse end points. Given such constraints, "transitologists" have increasingly studied the deals and strategies pursued, especially those among radicals, moderates, and hardliners. This necessarily includes elites but not to the exclusion of social movements of workers, farmers, and the like. Interim regimes and consolidation are the next step in process theories of transition. Moving from case studies to macrotransitions and waves of democratization in many countries, he finds that challenges to scholarship include the historically and culturally shifting definitions or domains of democracy, the theoretical combining of levels of organization and results, and the methodological issues involved in the measurement of democratic rights.

In his chapter on revolutions and revolutionary movements (Chapter 20), Jeff Goodwin reviews several general theoretical approaches to these phenomena, including modernization and Marxist theory. He suggests that state-centered approaches may shed the brightest light on the key questions of where and when revolutionary movements become powerful forces and sometimes seize state power. (Not all revolutionary movements, even powerful ones, actually seize power.) Revolutionary movements are likely to become especially strong where infrastructurally weak authoritarian states radicalize their political opponents by, among other things, politically excluding and indiscriminately repressing them. Weak authoritarian states that are also corrupt and clientelistic, thereby alienating or dividing potentially counterrevolutionary elites (economic, political, and military), are especially prone to being overthrown by the revolutionary movements that they unintentionally help to foster. Goodwin suggests that democratic political regimes, by contrast, rarely radicalize social movements because they generally provide the "political space" in which movements may demand reforms from the state, sometimes successfully.

Denying that a general, lawlike theory of regime change is possible, Charles Tilly (Chapter 21) examines the increasing focus on robust mechanisms for change rooted in contentious politics. Tilly formulates a taxonomy of state regimes based on five dimensions: state capacity to shape resources and action within its social realm, the breadth of representation in the polity, the equality of representation throughout the polity, the strength of consultation among polity members, and the protection of members of the political system. He discusses the most likely of the thirty-two combinations of binary categorizations of these five variables, and within each one there are "contentious repertoires" that provide collective claim-making routines that characterize the conflicting actors within each regime type. Tilly leaves us with three important questions: How does the basic character of a regime affect the form and dynamics of contentious politics? How do changes in a regime's character affect changes in the forms and dynamics of contention? And how do changes in repertoires of contention, paths of claim making, and claim-making parties affect the trajectories of regimes?

In their chapter on neocorporatism (Chapter 22), Wolfgang Streeck and Lane Kenworthy describe the evolution of corporatism's conceptualization in political thought and of its role as a key institution in the political economies of affluent nations. They examine the distinctions between corporatism and pluralism and among corporatist organizational structure, concertation, and private-interest government. They survey theory and research on the impact of corporatism on economic performance. And they consider the extent to which current processes – such as heightened capital mobility, union fragmentation, labor market deregulation, and European integration – threaten to undermine democratic corporatism.

Despite waves of seemingly political freedom, all is not well with either democratic or undemocratic states. Viviane Brachet-Marquez (Chapter 23) focuses on the nature of undemocratic states that employ repression and deal in death. She develops a three-part typology of regimes: totalitarianism with a strong guiding ideology, authoritarianism without such an ideology, and sultanistic states that have extreme patrimonialism. Given that totalitarianism seems to be a thing of the communist and fascist past, she looks at leftist movements against authoritarian and sultanistic regimes in Latin America that, ironically, become quite undemocratic and violent themselves. Shifting focus, she examines a broad range of right-wing parties and movements in more democratic circumstances and casts them into a typology of liberal or populist versus ultraconservative or extreme Right. She concludes that democratic and undemocratic are linked together both within democracies and outside them in the international arena. Thus, undemocracy surfaces in nominally democratic states where there is a lack of enforcement of laws to protect the vulnerable and with vast inequalities of income. It exists at the international level with arms deals, money laundering, aid packages, and covert action to undermine social movements and to promote (often undemocratic) regime stability. This spread of undemocracy takes the political sociologist well beyond the limits of the communist and fascist regimes of the past.

State policies are most often implemented by civil bureaucracies. Oskar Oszlak (Chapter 24) examines these processes of public administration, many of which are often ignored by political and even organizational sociologists. Oszlak sees the formation of the state, nationhood, and capitalism as simultaneously involved in the development of bureaucracy, which then reacts to political and policy developments as they occur over time. These bureaucracies operate in diverse environments with varying degrees of productivity, different behaviors and norms, many structures, and, especially, miniscule to sufficient resources in terms of budgets, employees, and mandates. The policy realm is where each new regime attempts to alter the power relationships within civil society and between it and the bureaucracy itself. Consequently, resources come and go within the constraints of technology, culture, clientele, and, of course, the regime itself. His chapter provides a justification for bureaucracy in public policy and a model of its internal and external dynamics. He concludes that technology and culture may have strong impacts on bureaucratic productivity and performance, but the strongest factor is the state regime, which must be adequately characterized to measure its impact on the bureaucracy.

In their chapter on the comparative study of welfare states (Chapter 25) Alexander M. Hicks and Gøsta Esping-Andersen review the literature on the origins of welfare policies in the narrow sense of social insurance and other income maintenance policies. In addition, true to the spirit of current welfare state theories and investigations, they examine a range of family and labor market policies, examine the egalitarian/redistributive and, more generally, stratification dimension of state policies as a further aspect of welfare states, and stress gendered aspects of all of these policy outputs and outcomes. They view the welfare state as a political nexus between the causally powerful and the politically dependent aspects of social stratification. In reviewing explanations, class-linked power resources (e.g., business and union organization and partisan politics) loom large, and globalization emerges as a less compelling and transformative force than domestic economic and demographic trajectories from factors such as increasingly high and long-term unemployment to societal aging. Although the stratification/welfare nexus is used to highlight the study of the welfare state as central to the contemporary response to the old question "Who gets what from government?," attention to material struggle and allocation is complemented by attention to social rights and citizenship. Hicks and Esping-Andersen open and conclude their "introduction" with historical as well as theoretical background and analysis.

Joya Misra and Leslie King, in looking at state policies toward women (Chapter 26), identify gender as an inherently political concept because it is involved in the distribution of power, generally resulting in a system of inequality. But that does not make gender a passive component, always at the mercy of unilateral state actions. They emphasize that the relation between gender and the state is bidirectional, dependent on such factors as political resources and structures, the strength of interest groups and social movements, women's inclusion in these, prevailing ideologies, and the degree of state autonomy. In selecting three policy areas of special relevance to gender, those concerning the labor market, social welfare, and population, Misra and King point to the need for considering how state policies affect gender, even when they do so implicitly, as in employment-related pensions geared only to full-time workers.

Kent Redding, David R. James, and Joshua Klugman trace the interconnections between race and state actions in their chapter on the politics of racial policy (Chapter 27). They emphasize how existing racial identities and social inequalities affect how states construct racial categories and race-based policies in a continuing process. Although concentrating on the experiences of the United States from the days of slavery to the present, their comparative sweep allows them to point out when race produces policy outcomes unique to national settings. The strength of historical constraints, institutionalized in a range of social patterns and unarticulated public attitudes, leads them to caution against the wholesale adoption of race-neutral policies even after some of the worst race-based abuses have disappeared.

In Chapter 28 Gregory Hooks and James Rice examine the processes and effects of conducting, winning, and losing wars. Despite Morris Janowitz's early work, sociology largely emphasizes the domestic or "homefront" to the neglect of war. But more recently this has changed with works by Skocpol, Moore, Tilly, Giddens, Mann, and many others. War clearly impacts demography, budgets and governmental planning, industrial production, citizenship rights and the welfare state, contentious politics and state breakdown, battles between military and civilian power, and the state itself as it moves toward empire or defeat. Disgust with war may even produce major advances in human rights and some global governance. Hooks and Rice make a strong plea for taking the political sociology of war off the sideline and putting it into a more central place, which they say may come about through the confluence of world systems and neoinstitutionalist work on how war molds society.

The Globalization of the World and Politics

Although some may proclaim the end of politics, the nation-state or multinational state is a strong entity. The loss of sovereignty often proclaimed is based on an exaggerated sovereignty that may have existed for only the most powerful state, and even then, all states encounter resistance and constraint. This section looks at the processes of globalization and how it is affecting politics, mobilization, and the movement of people and capital.

In Chapter 29, Philip McMichael casts a critical eye on the process of globalization, suggesting that it takes different forms across time and space. He specifies contemporary globalization as a discursive project, geared to institutionalizing corporate markets through multilateral and regional economic agreements driven by powerful states. From this perspective of depicting globalization as an exercise in power, he examines political countermovements to globalization. Global justice movements, he argues, are globalization's "historical and relational barometer," and they operate at various, but often interrelated, scales. Working from Karl Polanyi's "double movement" of implementation of and resistance to economic liberalism, McMichael questions the adequacy of Polanyi's formulation for the elaboration of market rule in the twenty-first century. This question concerns the conventional interpretation of "sovereignty" as the centerpiece of nation-state formation, including the development of citizenship. Here, globalization is viewed through the lens of a sovereignty crisis, where corporate market rule compromises the social contract upon which the state/citizen relation is founded. The crisis is expressed differently across the world, as the impact of market rule generates alternative social movement conceptions of sovereignty, especially in the global south where corporate globalization is realized through a drastic intensification of social exclusion.

In Chapter 30, on the politics and economics of global capitalism, Evelyn Huber and John D. Stephens map current political sociological and political economic views of the impact of global capitalism on state policy in the more affluent democracies of the Organization for Economic Cooperation and Development (OECD) nations and Latin America. They find that the results seem thin, equivocal, or highly conditional upon institutional context in the affluent OECD democracies but indicative of real global pressures for neoliberal policy reform in Latin America. Indeed they see little evidence of policy-relevant global pressures other than those of liberalized capital flows upon the freedom to pursue traditional Golden Age fiscal and monetary stabilization policies. In general, they question the importance of global economic pressures – in comparison with neoliberal ideological pressures, societal aging, and increasing long-term unemployment – for the actions of state.

Thomas Janoski and Fengjuan Wang (Chapter 31) examine the politics of both the most often poor and nondemocratic "sending countries" and the predominately rich and democratic "receiving countries." One focuses more on "emigration" and what population movements do to those left behind and what governments do to control immigration; the other looks at "immigration" and what the continuous influx of new people do to society and then how they may be integrated through naturalization and citizenship. Their first point is that theories of immigration need to combine the perspectives of sending and receiving countries in their political sociological analyses. A second point is that the increase in welfare and other payments for refugees seeking and obtaining asylum have politicized immigration debates such that the Left and Right have become much more polarized on this issue. At the same time, transnational immigration processes aided by air travel and the transmission of remittances to support whole towns make this global process much more fluid, whereas the reacceptance of "dual nationality" and the view of immigration as an investment process makes the issue more complex than in the past. All of this will become much more important as the retirement of the baby boomers causes vastly increased immigration to most receiving countries.

Peter Evans, in his chapter on counterhegemonic globalization (Chapter 32), brings the emerging global drama of transnational social movements of labor, gender, and the environment into a sharp, new, and wide-screen focus. Evans argues that analysis of the dynamics of transnational social movements should be central to the core agenda of political sociology, both because we cannot understand the politics of global governance institutions without taking into account the role of oppositional movements and because the idea of a purely "domestic" or "national" social movement is becoming an anachronism. Evans makes a sharp distinction between antiglobalization movements, which aspire to somehow retrieve a world in which power and values might be defined primarily on a local basis, and what he calls counterhegemonic globalization. The transnational labor, women's and environmental movements are not trying to negate globalization so much as they are trying to provide global support for the values and interests of their constituents. In going about their global project these movements not only build their own networks, organizations, and "collective action frames" but also simultaneously leverage ideologies and organizational structures that have been constructed by the neoliberal globalization that they oppose. "Basic human rights" and "democratic governance," for example, are central to the hegemonic ideology of neoliberal globalization, but they are also valuable ideological tools for counterhegemonic globalization. Evans illustrates his perspective with a number of examples of successful transnational campaigns but also admits that his approach only demonstrates the possibility of a counterhegemonic globalization.

CONCLUSION

Political sociology points in a number of theoretical directions for the new millennium. We anticipate that the most influential theories will prominently include those that most successfully allow researchers to answer the questions posed earlier in this introduction. How do we solve the apparent contradiction between conflict theory of elites and the new pluralism within policy domains? In what ways do we make the media a central part of theories of political sociology and not just a theory of how the media works? How do we optimally blend culture into political sociology, previously dominated by social-relational or structural conceptions of social action? How do we incorporate the analytical tools and substantive insights of rational choice without underplaying cultural and nonrational motivations and frames for action? How do we develop middle-range theories and mechanisms for understanding political processes, sensitive to historical and institutional particularity? How do we blend the local and the global in a meaningful way? How do we all balance the field's focus despite the cycling of political power among Left, Center, and Right? How do we develop a view of power that is useful in explaining urgent, concrete political phenomena? How do we revise the study of the politics of stratification, its parties and institutions in the globalizing, aging, environmentally constricting new world? How do we revise the theory of institutions in civil society enlightened by perspectives on rationality and emotion, action and tradition, culture and social structure?

The political theories that are used to answer these questions are likely to develop in four ways: (1) by incorporating both rational agency and culture into our conceptualizations and analyses of institutions; (2) by not privileging any simple status or class category, which creates exclusions, but focusing on many status and class groups in creating a more complex theory of the social bases of politics; (3) by creating studies of political sociology focusing on the development of agency and microsocial mechanisms, process theories of democracy, deliberation, and the media, and how politics filters through protopolitical groups into more directly political actors; and (4) by expanding conceptions of diffused and networked power in societies and incorporating the cultural, martial, economic, and political forces in the globalized world beyond boundaries.

We began our work conscious of how pressing were the foregoing questions, along with their related theoretical challenges but with no illusions that we could, in the space of the handbook, provide definitive answers. We hope that our four objectives – providing an encompassing framework, surveying the possibility of synthesis, consolidating the social bases, and incorporating the global – have been more modest and realistic. We conclude by reviewing those objectives and how we have fulfilled them, mindful that, ultimately, it will be our readers who assess the usefulness of our work.

Our first objective was to gather under the roof of the handbook all the theories and substantive areas that could legitimately be called political sociology. We began with well-established and contending theories – neopluralism, neofunctionalism, conflict and political economy, and institutionalist and state-centric theories. We included as well new challenges from culture, discourse, feminist, racialist, and rational choice theories, which we anticipate to become even more influential. Our substantive reach led us to look at adjacent sociological subfields of social movements, peace and conflict, race and ethnic studies, and sex and gender. We are also alert to developments in adjacent disciplines, particularly political science. As a result, we devote eight chapters to aspects of civil society, ranging from social cleavages to public opinion to organized efforts in mobilizing the public and influencing the state. Another eleven chapters are devoted to the state in all its forms and variations and in policies as they affect social welfare, gender, and military operations. The briefest section, consisting of four chapters, deals with globalization, an area where scholarly attention can be expected to grow as relations among states change and movements of people and capital break out from the confines of state boundaries. Although some topics may not have been treated with as much thoroughness as possible, and some arguably notable topics may not have been included, we think that the coverage largely realizes our first objective.

Our second objective was to draw together relevant theories with an eye to possible consolidation. It required recognizing that underlying every theoretical venture in political sociology there is some conception of power. Although moving away from seeing political power only in terms of actions of the state or its organs, as Piven and Cloward do by directing us to a range of institutions in which power is a primary process – religion, family, work, the media, and other cultural forces – we remain committed to a focus on the state. One whole section of the handbook is given over to the state in all its varieties and activities. That is, although power is diffused throughout society and emerges in networks of relations, we still believe it important to keep a central focus on the state as an institution whose rationale is the consolidation and exercise of power. States can be influenced by all the social forces that make up civil society, but also retain a level of autonomy that makes them social actors in their own right.

Our third objective was to consolidate the widening range of the "social bases of politics." This is because power is also located outside the state, making it equally important to adopt some of the prompts from cultural theory in taking account of diffused power as well as the interest-based organizational forces long studied in political sociology. Just as social characteristics change over time in their relevance to social cleavages, so too do they alter in their ability to become politicized. Here we have valuable contributions from feminist and racialist perspectives in showing how problems become political issues in proto-political groups – families, neighborhoods, corporations, and voluntary associations including churches and charitable groups – which are then passed on and modified in more directly political groups – social movements, interest groups, corporate action committees, the police and judicial system, political parties, and the media.

Finally, our fourth objective was to incorporate globalization and empire within political sociology. Clearly, power is also located outside the state (and state system) in an increasingly globalized economy and this necessitates a focus on political economy. Global power is encountered when states attempt to use economic policy to deal with foreign competition or even simply to regulate their domestic economies and exchange rates. Global influences are complicated by processes of international migration that since the early 1950s have allowed migrants to travel with increasing speed. Cultural factors also shape how these migrants are treated and integrated with powerful influences exerted both by domestic politics and international civil society, including the UN and transnational movements. Meanwhile, countermeasures against globalization and related international forces are being mounted by social movements and other forms of protests. Clearly, the international arena forms an engrossing stage for political economy and cultural explanation.

We still see a divided theoretical arena. Longstanding and established theories in the field coexist in uneasy tension while contentious new theories have entered political sociology, sometimes with as little regard to competing approaches as they feel that they have received from established ones. To us, the field's great diversity of theoretical arguments is a sign of its health, stimulating vigorous debate and self-examination. Our own assessment is that rational choice theory, on the one hand, and the cultural turn, on the other, can together enrich political sociological theory, indeed enrich theories beyond themselves. Some authors have already pointed to areas where bridging may occur and where fruitful borrowing can develop. For example, Kiser and Baudry discuss where rational choice theory can benefit from culture and Hobson notes how feminist theory draws on structuralist approaches to the state. In some fashion, all the handbook chapters, theoretical and substantive, grapple with theoretical tensions and suggest pathways for a vibrant political sociology in the new millenium.

PART I

THEORIES OF POLITICAL SOCIOLOGY

CHAPTER ONE

Rule Making, Rule Breaking, and Power[1]

Frances Fox Piven and Richard A. Cloward

Social life is inevitably organized by rules, whether these rules are rooted in custom or in the laws of an organized state. Rules are usually treated as ubiquitous, the most elementary feature of society. But obedience to rules cannot be taken for granted. People everywhere both conform to the rules that organize social life and violate them. In this chapter we explore the question of why women and men break the rules of their society and why they break particular rules. And we focus on this question because we think it illuminates the dialectic of power – of domination and resistance – in human relations.

The crux of our argument is that just as rule making is a strategy of domination, so is rule breaking a strategy in challenges to domination. We make our case in several steps. First, we discuss concepts of power and focus on the particular understanding of power as embedded in interdependent social relations that undergirds our argument. We contend that rule making and rule breaking can be understood as strategies to inhibit or activate the leverage inherent in contributions to social interdependencies. And finally, we briefly consider the bearing of theories of agency, of the human capacity for innovation, on the emergence of challenges to the rules.

Our interest in the bearing of rules on power arises from our career-long study of the dynamics of social movements, and particularly the unruly collective protests that periodically disrupt the normal workings of the American political system. We think these events play a key role in the process of reform in American politics. But the disorder associated with protest is nevertheless widely criticized; even those who sympathize with the grievances of the protestors often complain that they ought to have chosen more conventional and rule-abiding ways of advancing their cause. Our historical studies of American protest movements lead us to the quite different conclusion that defiance of the rules of normal politics is an essential aspect of the development of such power as the protestors are able to wield. Our earlier work traced the impact of collective defiance on American political institutions. Here we put institutional outcomes aside to consider more specifically and theoretically the bearing of rules and rule breaking on power relations.

In contemporary social science, the study of rule breaking has been dominated by the field of "deviance" and then further divided into specialties according to forms of rule violation or the demographic characteristics of the rule violators. The result is to tear the study of rule breaking away from larger questions about the nature of social order. In the past, however,

[1] We thank the editors of this volume for their editorial suggestions. Our good friend the late Robert Alford took special pains in offering his help. We also thank other colleagues who gave us their careful reading and criticisms, including Peter Bratsis, Jonathan Fox, Chad Goldberg, Margaret Groarke, and Sid Tarrow. We are particularly grateful to Lori Minnite, Leo Panitch, and Susan Woodward, who not only read the manuscript but also argued at length for the critical amendments they suggested.

thinkers who tried to understand why people sometimes broke the rules of their society were preoccupied with the connection between rule breaking and threats to the established order or to constituted authority. Aristotle's (1962:193) catalog of the "origins and causes of the disorders" leading to the dissolution of governments was an effort to identify the conditions that would prevent internal strife. Thomas Hobbes excoriated such iniquitous doctrines as that of individual conscience, not to mention the notion that the sovereign himself ought to be subject to civil law as "Those things That Weaken or Tend to the Dissolution of a Commonwealth." Modern sociological ideas have also been explained by Nisbet (1966:21) as "responses to the problem of order created at the beginning of the nineteenth century by the collapse of the old regime under the blows of industrialism and revolutionary democracy."

Thinkers who turned these political assessments on their head, who abjured constituted authority as a source of oppression, also focused on the corpus of law because it was the handmaiden of authority. "The universal spirit of Laws, in all countries" pronounced Rousseau (1962:200), "is to favor the strong in opposition to the weak, and to assist those who have possessions against those who have none." This conclusion was shared by Adam Smith as follows:

> Laws and governments may be considered in this and indeed in every case as a combination of the rich to oppress the poor, and preserve to themselves the inequality of the goods which would otherwise be soon destroyed by the attacks of the poor, who if not hindered by the government would soon reduce the others to an equality with themselves by open violence. (cited in *Monthly Review* 32(5):13)

Aristotle wrote at a time when the Greek city-states were seething with rebellion, Machiavelli in the midst of the intrigue and turmoil of late medieval Florence, Hobbes in the aftermath of two civil wars in England, and Rousseau and Smith on the eve of what was to be "the age of revolution." The grand theorists of sociology wrote in the midst of the social and political turmoil of the second half of the nineteenth century. All of these thinkers, whatever their political allegiance, saw in the rising disorder that surrounded them a contest for or against domination. They saw, in short, that rule breaking and rule making are at the core of the struggle for power in human society.

DEFINITIONS OF POWER

We think that when people either make rules or break rules they are expressing a fundamental human propensity to try to exert power. To be sure, talk about fundamental human propensities is hazardous, but we believe our focus on rules and power is undergirded by assumptions that are straightforward and uncontroversial.

First, we take for granted the sociological premise that people are inherently social and that the experience of collective life profoundly influences the identities people develop, the purposes to which they are oriented, and the interpretations of their reality that informs the actions they take to pursue those purposes.

Second, we assume a human capacity to reconstruct learned identities, discover different and conflictual purposes from that imposed by the group, and invent new interpretations of social reality in the course of pursuing those purposes. We thus take for granted that human beings are to some extent purposeful and reflective agents.[2] For this reason, and despite the force of group influence, every actor confronts the social constructions imposed by other actors, including collective and institutionalized constructions, as an exterior and constraining force. Social relationships are both a means of cooperation in the pursuit of shared goals and also a means of conflict, of acting on disparate individual and group goals.[3]

[2] We use the term "purposeful" with some hesitation. We agree with Giddens (1984:6) that much day-to-day action is routine and as such is subject only to "reflexive monitoring and rationalization." By contrast, "motives tend to have a direct purchase on action only in relatively unusual circumstances."

[3] The oft-cited argument about sociology's "oversocialized conception of man" is by Dennis Wrong. Both the original essay and Wrong's contemporary comments on the problem can be found in Wrong (1999).

Third, we think the complex patterns of cooperation that constitute group life shape and constrain peoples' capacities for agency. But group life is also the context in which agency is realized, in which people discover divergent identities, invent new interpretations, and find the power to act on their divergent purposes.[4]

These minimal assumptions allow us to claim that action to make or break rules can be understood as an expression of the perennial efforts of women and men to use their relations with others in the pursuit of outcomes they desire, to exercise power. We recognize, of course, that everything depends on the concrete character of ongoing social relations, on the specific goals of different parties to those relations, and on the vast accumulated repertoire of institutionalized practices and beliefs within which these concrete relations exist and goals are pursued.

Having asserted that rule making and rule breaking reflect efforts to exercise power, we need to discuss that much belabored term.[5] Our usage so far is familiar enough, similar to the understanding of power running through the arguments of theorists from Thomas Hobbes to Steven Lukes. The most widely cited formulation is Max Weber's (1968:926–40): power is understood as "the chance of a man or a number of men to realize their own will in a social action even against the resistance of others who are participating in the action." R. H. Tawney (1931:229) proposes a similar though more explicitly reciprocal definition: "Power may be defined as the capacity of an individual, or group of individuals, to modify the conduct of other individuals or groups in the manner which he desires, and to prevent his own conduct being modified in the manner in which he does not."

This understanding of power as inherently conflictual is sometimes referred to as the *zero-sum* conception. What an actor on one side of a power relationship achieves is at the expense of another actor. It contrasts with an understanding of power as simply the capacity to realize ends, as when Bertrand Russell (1938:2) defined power as "the production of intended effects." It also contrasts with the Parsonian (1967:297; 1969:352–429) view of power as the communal capacity to secure or enforce compliance for collective purposes, or power conceived as a

> generalized capacity to secure the performance of binding obligations, when the obligations are legitimized with reference to their bearing on collective goals and where, in the case of recalcitrance, there is a presumption of enforcement by negative sanctions. (1967:297)[6]

Anthony Giddens (1976:11–112) also notes the difference between the use of power in the sense of the capacity of an actor to alter the course of events and what he calls the narrower, relational sense, as a "property of interaction" which may be defined as "the capability to secure outcomes where the realization of these outcomes depends on the agency of others . . . is power as *domination*" (emphasis in the original). To Giddens, the relationship between power and conflict is contingent, because power presupposes conflict only when resistance has to be overcome. But resistance often does have to be overcome. Hobbes (1958:160) was not the only one to note the following:

> And therefore if any two men desire the same thing, which nevertheless they cannot both enjoy, they

[4] The dualism of social action and social structure is an argument that runs through Giddens work, beginning with Giddens (1976). See also Norbert Elias (1978:94–6) for a parallel argument about "figuration" and the psychological capabilities of actors, and see Zygmunt Bauman (1989) for a critical commentary.

[5] In the discussion that follows we do not attempt to consider the entire voluminous literature on power but rather focus on the work that applies to our argument. Recent publications not covered include Dowding (1996), Haugaard (1997, 2002), Flyvbjerg (1998), Klein (1998), Morriss (1987), Poggi (2001), Scott (1996), Stewart, (2001), and Wartenberg (1992).

[6] We note in passing that although there are differences between the Parsonian view of power and the conception developed by Michel Foucault (2000), there are also strong and striking similarities. For Parsons, power is total, a generalized feature of a social system, rooted in a normative consensus, which includes a consensus on the use of sanctions against those who deviate. For Foucault, power is embedded in a system of knowledge and classification which penetrates institutional life and embraces and controls everything and everyone. See also Dyrberg (1997).

become enemies; and in the way to their end, which is principally their own conservation, and sometimes their delectation only, endeavor to destroy or subdue one another.

Power is thus inextricably linked with conflict in actual social life, simply because social life implies zero-sum contests, whether, as in the Hobbesian example, because men and women compete over the same things or because they contest the terms and ends of cooperative efforts. Moreover, the fact of group life means that people try to use each other to reach their goals, a point that Parsons (1949:93) makes in his discussion – but ultimate dismissal – of the Hobbesian perspective. Thus pervasive conflict is "inherent in the very existence of social relations themselves. For it is inherent in the latter that the actions of men should be potential means to each other's ends."[7]

Although the disputes generated by these different conceptions have received enormous attention,[8] we do not need to do more than note them here.[9] It is sufficient to say that we are using the term *power* in the Weberian zero-sum sense that postulates conflict as endemic to social life.

Power Resources: The Distributional Perspective

A zero-sum view of power leaves much unsettled, including such perennial disputes as whether power is a latent capacity or whether it must be actualized to be called power. Also, are the unintended consequences of action evidence of power? These disputes have given rise to a good many refined redefinitions that are also not important for our discussion. One familiar and nagging issue does bear on our argument, however, and it is perhaps the most important dispute in the discussion of power. What are to be regarded as power resources? Weber's (1968:53) definition may be widely accepted precisely because of what it does *not* specify, "the basis on which this probability [of exerting power] rests." Weber himself thought the bases for power could not be explicated: "The concept of power is sociologically amorphous. All conceivable qualities of a person and all conceivable combinations of circumstances may put him in a position to impose his will in a given situation" (cited in Wrong, 1979:23). That position forecloses the possibility of analyzing the patterned distribution of power in any society, which a good many analysts have not been satisfied to accept. Instead, there are major and recurrent disputes about the bases (i.e. the resources) for domination in social interaction. Our own position on power resources is central to our argument about the relations among rule making, rule breaking, and power.

The usual understanding about resources for power in social science is that power rests on attributes or things, such as personal skills, technical expertise, money the control of opportunities to make money, prestige or access to prestige, numbers of people, or the capacity to mobilize numbers of people. Randall Collins (1975:60–1) summarizes the prevailing wisdom as follows:

> Look for the material things that affect interaction: the physical places, the modes of communication, the supply of weapons, devices for staging one's public impression, tools, and goods. Assess the relative resources available to each individual: their potential for physical coercion, their access to other persons with whom to negotiate, their sexual attractiveness, their store of cultural devices for invoking emotional solidarity, as well as the physical arrangements just mentioned . . . . The resources for conflict are complex.

Collins's catalog is familiar and not notably different from Dahl's (1961:226) "common sense" list of "anything that can be used to sway the specific choices or the strategies of another individual" or Oberschall's (1973:28) discussion of

[7] We should note here the work of Adam Przeworski and Michael Wallerstein (1982, 1985), who develop the argument that under specified conditions class conflict in capitalist and democratic societies can produce a mutually beneficial class compromise institutionalized and coordinated by the state.

[8] See, for example, Parsons's (1960:220) well-known attack on C. Wright Mills (1956). Alvin Gouldner (1970) is virtually a book-length polemic against Parsons, but see especially Chapter 8.

[9] See also Dennis Wrong (1979:237–47), for a good discussion of this dispute. And see Anthony Giddens (1977).

"anything from material resources – jobs, income, savings, and the right to material goods and services – to nonmaterial resources – authority, moral commitment, trust, friendship, skills, habits of industry, and so on." Others have tried to classify resources according to some discriminating principle, as when Giddens (1985:7) distinguishes between "allocative resources," meaning control over material goods and the natural forces that can be harnessed in their production, and "authoritative resources," meaning control over the activities of human beings. Etzioni (1968:357–59) distinguishes between utilitarian resources or material inducements, coercive resources that can be used to do violence to bodies or psyches and normative or symbolic rewards or threats.[10] Tilly (1978:69) takes a more strictly economistic tack, emphasizing "the economist's factors of production: land, labor, capital, perhaps technical expertise as well." Mills (1956:9,23) makes the important additional point that the "truly powerful" are those "who occupy the command posts" of major institutions," because such institutions are the bases for great concentrations of resources.[11] And everyone appears to agree that one kind of resource can be used to gain another, as resources are "transferred, assembled, reallocated, exchanged" and invested.[12] In sum, from this perspective, power resources are the attributes or things that one actor can use to coerce or induce another actor.[13]

The sheer proliferation of lists of resources that can result from this perspective, from money to popularity to numbers to spare time, has sometimes been the basis for arguing for a considerable indeterminacy in the patterning of power.[14] By extension, if all sorts of things matter as resources, almost everyone has something that can be used to influence somebody, a perspective embodied in pluralist studies of community power structure.[15] Even those who would seem to have virtually nothing that anyone might desire or fear have at least their numbers, an argument often regarded as self-evident. We consider these claims to be both empirically contestable and theoretically opaque.

Typically, however, the kinds of goods and traits singled out by analysts as key resources are not widely distributed but are concentrated at the top of the social hierarchy. This is what Giddens intends to convey by identifying "allocative" and "authoritative" resources as the bases for power and what Etzioni implies with his classification of resources as utilitarian, coercive, and normative. It is also the implication of schemes such as Tilly's land, labor, capital, and technical expertise and is the obvious meaning of Mill's definition. It follows that power is also concentrated at the top. The reasoning is straightforward. Some attributes and things matter more to people than others. Wealth, prestige, and the instruments of physical coercion are all reliable bases for dominating others. Because these traits and goods are, everyone agrees, distributed by social rank, it appears to follow as night after day that people with higher social rank have more power and people with lower social rank have less.

This distributional view of power is certainly not altogether wrong. Indeed, it matches much ordinary human experience. Most of the time, those who have riches, or prestige, technical skill, or guns do dominate those who have none of these things. Moreover, riches and prestige and skill tend to flow together, creating a class hierarchy. But if this pattern of power were entirely and inevitably so, all efforts by people at lower positions in the social hierarchy to exert power, including by actions that break the rules,

[10] William Gamson's (1968:100–4) classification of resources according to whether they are used for inducement, constraint, or persuasion is similar to Etzioni's.

[11] This point about the organizational bases of power was later developed by Robert Presthus (1964).

[12] The language here is taken from Oberschall (1973: 28); for the identical point in different language, see Dahl (1961:227). The obvious point that wealth, status, and power are each all potential means to the other was originally made by Weber and is discussed in Wrong (1979:229).

[13] Other and more elaborate lists of resources can be found in Lasswell and Kaplan (1950:83–92).

[14] Dahl (1961:226), for example, begins his own list with "control over an individual's time." By this sort of reasoning, the unemployed should be expected to exert substantial influence.

[15] The classic study is Dahl (1961). See also Polsby (1963).

would be in vain. Perhaps such efforts could be understood as an expression of an enduring human proclivity to try to influence others, but the proclivity is inevitably without consequence if resources for power are fixed in advance by patterned inequalities in the distribution of things and traits.

Thus, if the distribution of power simply reflected other structured inequalities, then political challenges from below would always be without effect. The realm of power and politics would inevitably reiterate other inequalities. And social thinkers observing very unequal societies would not worry about defiance and disorder as potential challenges to established authority.

INTERDEPENDENT RELATIONS AND RESOURCES FOR POWER

We believe that a different way of thinking about resources for power is more useful in interpreting rule breaking and rule making. Examples that focus on specific institutional settings point us in the right direction. The effective exercise of power in electoral representative institutions, for example, or in industry or in mating relationships, does not result simply from a general currency of things or traits and the pattern of their distribution but rather depends on the specific relationships that make particular things or traits useful and important. Thus, political analyses that focus on formal electoral arrangements identify votes as a key resource. Although disembodied votes mean nothing, in formal democratic theory votes matter greatly because state leaders are dependent on voting majorities to retain office. Analyses that assume relations of production to be preeminent identify control of capital or labor as key resources for the exercise of power by contending classes. A focus on religious institutions might highlight the priesthood's control over religious revelation and salvation, on the one side, and the laity's control of acknowledged faith, on the other. These perspectives may not be right, but if they are not right it is because they have misspecified the key relationships within which power is to be exercised or assumed that power in electoral relations, labor-capital relations, marriages, or churches can be explained in isolation from each other (which leads us to another version of the pluralist concept of power). The formally democratic state may be only formally democratic and the key relations may not be between citizen-voters and state leaders but perhaps between the owners of property and state leaders. But even when they are wrong, such perspectives have the virtue of a certain coherence, in the sense that ideas about the power resources that enable one group or individual to dominate another are firmly rooted in ideas about the patterned relationships that bind them together. We know why a thing or trait can be employed by one actor to sway another because we know something about how they depend on each other. This patterned interdependence is what Michael Schwartz (1976:172–3) has in mind when he writes about "structural power" as follows:

> Since a structure cannot function without the routinized exercise of structural power, any threat to structural power becomes a threat to that system itself. Thus if employees suddenly began refusing to obey orders, the company in question could not function. Or if tenants simply disobeyed the merchant's order to grow cotton, the tenancy system would collapse.... Thus, we see a subtle, but very important, relationship between structural power and those who are subject to it. On the one hand, these power relations define the functioning of any ongoing system; on the other hand, the ability to disrupt these relationships is exactly the sort of leverage which can be used to alter the functioning of the system.... Any system contains within itself the possibility of power strong enough to alter it.

These observations suggest a general perspective on resources for power that is less static than the distributional perspective and that is capable of explaining not only why those who have riches or status usually prevail but also why those without riches or status nevertheless try to prevail and sometimes even succeed. It also helps to explain, as a distributional perspective cannot, why the making and breaking of rules is central to the pervasive contests of social life.

Resources for power are not only or primarily the disembodied attributes or things that can be used to induce or coerce others but in addition are derived from the patterns of interdependence that characterize all social life.[16] Of course, systems of economic or political or religious or military or ideological or kinship interdependence vary from one society to another and from one location in a given society to another. Such variations matter greatly in deciphering the actual distribution of power and the potential for the exercise of power. Our point for now, however, is that *whatever* the specific pattern of social relations, the social fact of relationship and interdependence generates the resources, as well as the occasions, for the exercise of power.

In other words, power resources are embedded in the patterns of expectation and cooperation that bind people together, even when all that is expected or required of particular people is their quiescence. Cooperation implies patterns of mutual dependence, and mutual dependence implies the possibility of using others for desired ends – to exert power. *People have potential power, the ability to make others do what they want, when those others depend on them for the contributions they make to the interdependent relations that are social life.* Just as the effort to exert power is a feature of all social interaction, so is the capacity to exert power at least potentially inherent in all social interaction. And because cooperative and interdependent social relations are by definition reciprocal, so is the potential for the exercise of power.[17]

Moreover, many of the things and attributes emphasized by other writers as resources for power are effective inducements or sanctions only because of the social relations in which the actors are enmeshed.[18] Control over capital is an effective resource for exercising power over others because those others are already entangled in a system of economic relations that makes them dependent on entrepreneurs for the means of production and subsistence, or they are enmeshed in a political system that makes government dependent on tax revenues generated by private wealth. Numbers are considered a political resource because the parties to a conflict contend within a set of political relationships that gives voting majorities, and hence numbers, significance in determining who will hold constituted state authority. Or a thing called money carries great weight because it is a script that governs the distribution of material goods in a specific system of economic relationships.

The large and important exception to this understanding of power resources as rooted in social interdependence are the things and traits that allow one actor to dominate another by using or threatening to use physical force. Force cannot reasonably be said to depend on any social relationship. Indeed, modern military technology has made even the minimal relationship implied by physical proximity unnecessary for the exercise of power through force. This is a large exception, not only because force is employed or threatened more widely than is usually acknowledged but also because the threat of force lurks in the background even in the manifold interdependent relationships in which it plays no direct role, as is obvious in the pervasive influence of state coercion in regulating social life.

Even putting aside this important exception, we quickly admit that at first glance our perspective on power resources as embedded in social interdependencies makes rather less sense of our common experiences than does the distributional perspective. The focus on interdependence suggests a strain toward equality, whereas social life as we know it is everywhere unequal. A great deal remains therefore to be explained. Still, it is worth recalling that Thomas Hobbes,

[16] The foundational statement is Hegel's discussion of independence and dependence in the relationship of master and servant. See Carl J. Friedrich (ed.) *The Philosophy of Hegel*, Modern Library Edition, New York: Random House, 1953:399–411. Michael Mann's argument that we "conceive of societies as federated, overlapping, intersecting networks rather than as simple totalities" complements this discussion of power. See Michael Mann, *The Sources of Social Power: A History of Power from the Beginning to A.D. 1760*, Cambridge, UK: Cambridge University Press, 1986:17.

[17] A quite different argument roots power relations in social cooperation by arguing that cooperation toward a common purpose makes necessary some hierarchy of command in order to coordinate activities. See Collingwood (1942:153–4).

[18] Giddens (1984:33) says something like this when he claims that what he calls "allocative resources" become resources "only when incorporated within processes of structuration."

an astute theorist of power, took the essential equality among people as his starting point. The Hobbesian understanding stressed endemic and rapacious conflict precisely because all people have the resources for conflict. It is not inequality of resources for power, and the resulting entrenched patterns of domination, that are natural as in the distributional perspective, but a rough equality of resources, and the ensuing endemic and pervasive conflict, that is natural.

At least some part of our experience confirms this seemingly paradoxical view as well. To be sure, rural overlords have wealth, social standing, and force of arms, and peasants have none of these things. Most of the time, the overlords are the powerful, the peasants are the powerless, and the distributional conception of power seems confirmed. But sometimes peasants rise up against their overlords. They refuse to labor in the lord's fields or withhold their rents or taxes or take to arms or to the hills. When they do, the outcome often goes against them. But it does not inevitably go against them. Sometimes, in some places, peasants prevail. Or at least, they win something, perhaps some moderation of the terms of their subjugation. And sometimes, whether in the end for better or worse, their actions become part of the chain of events that transforms their society. Workers may refuse to labor or take to the streets or to the barricades. When they do, the outcome is not necessarily foretold. Insurgent workers sometimes win something. Sometimes, they win shorter hours or higher wages. More rarely still, they help set in motion the forces that topple governments. Even the marginal poor, those on the fringes of social life, the people who seem to have no role in ongoing patterns of economic, social, or political activity, can become the urban mobs of the American or French Revolutions or the urban rioters of contemporary Latin America. And even rioters sometimes win something.[19]

If people without wealth or status or technical skill sometimes prevail, then they must have some kind of power. Their power, the power of people we ordinarily consider powerless, derives from the patterns of interdependence that constitute social life and from the leverage embedded in interdependent relations. In a feudal system of production, not only do peasants need overlords, but overlords need peasants. There is no production and no surplus for the overlord without peasant labor. Similarly, not only does labor need capital in an industrial system of production. Just as land is not a means of production without those who work it, so is capital not capital without labor. And it is not only the poor who need contributions from the rich; in a society of densely interdependent relations, the rich also need contributions from the poor. If nothing else, they need them to be quiescent.

The systems of interdependence that constitute societies determine the main lines of strategic action available to contending actors or, in another language, shape the repertoires of political action.[20] Thus contention in economic relations takes broadly predictable forms as different groups try to exert leverage by withholding or threatening to withhold their contributions to production: owners or managers engage in lockouts or blacklists or capital flight on the one side; workers engage in labor strikes or slowdowns or sabotage on the other. In religious institutions, the priesthood can threaten to withhold the promise of salvation whereas adherents and acolytes can threaten a withdrawal of faith. In political institutions, the complex interdependencies between state actors and private property owners are activated by curbs on property rights on the one side, by capital flight or tax rebellions on the other.

These examples are certainly too broad; they are virtual caricatures of the actually diverse and specific interdependent relations that characterize real societies, especially complex modern societies. For one thing, few relationships are simple dyadic relations as in our examples so far.

[19] The literature on the reverberations of challenges from below is, of course, enormous. "Social movements based on power resources," Janoski (1998) asserts boldly, "provide the *pressure for change* in citizenship rights." For a series of studies on contemporary protest movements and their outcomes in Latin America, see Eckstein and Wickham-Crowley (2002).

[20] The term *repertoire* is used by Charles Tilly (1982: 21–51, 1984:308, 1986:253–80) to describe the characteristic forms of collective action employed by a group.

A web of complex networks of political, economic, and cultural interdependencies has to be analyzed if the actual potential for power by different participants in these networks is to be deciphered. Moreover, the myriad relations of everyday life in which people try to exert power may not be the classical hierarchical relations between overlords and peasants, or even capital and labor. Contemporary power relations are also between foremen and workers, guards and prisoners, merchants and customers, landlords and tenants, husbands and wives, bureaucrats and clients, doctors and patients, teachers and students. Lateral relations are also grids of interdependency, as in the relations among workers or prisoners or students. For some purposes these multiple concrete relations may not be very important. When doctors and patients, or wives and husbands, try to use the leverage inherent in these interdependent relationships to exercise power, each on the other, the reverberations of their actions are usually limited. They are not likely to transform institutions or societies. Nevertheless, the concrete relations of everyday life may loom very large in patterning the real efforts of people to exercise power and to exercise power by breaking rules. Most of the time, people only try to make their everyday lives. They do not try to make history.[21]

Our perspective shares a premise with the conception of power developed by "exchange theorists" in sociology. The initiating insight of exchange theory was contained in an article by Richard M. Emerson (1962),[22] who proposed that power was an attribute not of social actors but of relationships. Power resides in the dependence that one actor has on another in social relationships. In this and later work, Emerson puzzled over the processes through which power inequalities were reduced by what he called "balancing operations" – intrapsychic or intrapersonal strategies by which actors reduced their power disadvantages by reducing their own motivational investment in the power-dependence relationship or by increasing the investment of their antagonist. These ideas were tested in a series of experiments in small group settings. This narrow and ahistorical tack, however, probably goes far to account for the limited influence of Emerson's perspective.

Peter Blau's (1964) subsequent development of Emerson's work has received more attention, prompting Coser (1976:157) to call it "one of the most significant advances" in the study of power. But although Blau rightly faulted Emerson for a focus on "balancing operations" that diverted attention from the actuality of power imbalances, Blau himself made changes in Emerson's initial premise that had the effect of naturalizing – and legitimating – existing power relations. Where Emerson (1962:32) had begun from the premise that social relations "commonly entail ties of mutual dependence between the parties," Blau (1964:118) emphasized a one-sided and unilateral dependence and proposed that such dependence could be explained by the unequal contributions that different parties made to a relationship:

> By supplying services in demand to others, a person establishes power over them. If he regularly renders needed services they cannot readily obtain elsewhere, others become dependent on and obligated to him for these services, ... unless they can furnish other benefits to him that produce interdependence ....

Blau thus treats power imbalances as a reflection of imbalances in the contributions different people make to collective life. Concentrations of power merely register dependence on services and benefits. The power that employers have over their employees, or husbands over wives, is the result of the benefits they provide that employees and wives need and cannot get elsewhere. By resting the case there, Blau in effect eliminates the moral problematic and empirical tension in power relations. Those who are dominant are those who contribute more; those who are subordinate contribute less. Even casual attention to real historical patterns of domination and subordination – of tenant

[21] A point forcefully made by Flacks (1988).

[22] Emerson's perspective in turn had antecedents in the work of Waller (1951) and (1949) who both argued that in sexual relations the partner who is less involved and therefore less dependent on the other has greater power. And see Bacharach and Lawler (1980) for a discussion of mutual dependence in organizational and labor-management bargaining situations.

farmers by plantation owners, for example, or of wives by husbands, or servants by masters – and the key assumption of the exchange theory of power, that domination reflects greater contributions to social relationships, collapses. Landowners and railroad magnates did not, after all, become dominant because their contributions in the form of what Blau (1964:118) calls "needed services" were inherently greater than the contributions of those who tilled the prairies or laid the tracks or succored the children.

Although we share Emerson's premise that the sources of power are to be found in interdependent social relations, we do not think that power inequalities reflect unequal contributions to these relations. On the contrary, notions about unequal contributions to systems of social cooperation are usually intensely ideological. The view that landlords or capitalists or breadwinners make greater contributions to interdependent relations than those who are subordinate to them is just that sort of notion. The belief that a landowner "owns" land, and can therefore supply it to those who don't, or that investors "own" capital, is itself variable and contingent, a reflection of the system of rules and interpretations within which social interdependencies develop. Contributions to interdependent relations can be real, in the sense that they involve action on and in the material world. And they are real in the sense that they generate real responses from actual others. They are also, however, socially and ideologically constructed, and they are socially constructed differently by different people.[23] Moreover, socially constructed ideas about contributions can and do change, a point we discuss in the next section.[24]

Virtually by definition, reciprocal interdependencies argue a rough equality of contributions, in the sense that the contributions of different parties are equally necessary to the ongoing relationship. Why, then, is nothing else equally distributed? Or more specifically, why don't people use the potential power embedded in social interdependence to secure a more equal distribution of the things that they value?

The Problem of Actionability

A large part of the answer is that some contributions to interdependencies can more readily be used to exert leverage than others. The lines of power, of domination and exploitation, tend to reflect not the actual value of the contribution of services or benefits to others, as Blau argues, but rather differences in the "actionability" of contributions. Interdependencies generate potential resources for power. Whether they can be acted on or not is, however, a highly contingent matter.

The basic power tactic that arises out of interdependency is to withhold or threaten to withhold what others need. But that is usually easier for some participants than for others, and easier under some conditions than under others, and for several reasons.

First, contributions to interdependent relations must be recognized before they can become actionable. Interdependencies are real in the sense that they have real ramifications in the material bases of social life. But they are also cultural constructions. At first glance it might seem that the very fact of participation in cooperative activities would lead people to recognize their own contributions. Perhaps so, or at least to some extent and under some conditions, as explained in the next section. But this recognition must overcome inherited interpretations that privilege the contributions of dominant groups, as well as the continuing ability of dominant groups to project new and obscuring interpretations. Simply put, people must *recognize their potential power* before they can act on it.

Second, to effectively threaten to disrupt ongoing interdependencies requires, where contributions are collective, that the power seekers themselves coordinate their actions, something that is easier for an organized church, state, or firm, for example, than for numerous dispersed believers or citizens or workers. Note that our

[23] That this is so, and may nevertheless not be readily observable, is perhaps James C. Scott's (1985, 1990) main point about peasant resistance.

[24] The shift in public opinion effected by the campaign in the United States to "reform" welfare is an example. Where prior to the campaign, the mothering activities of poor women had been accorded some legitimacy, the campaign persuaded the public that only wage work was a legitimate social contribution.

meaning here is not simply the usual organizing idea that individuals and their resources must be aggregated but rather that it is the contributions necessary for the functioning of an ongoing social relationship that must be aggregated. We call this the problem of *coordination*.

Third, power seekers must be able themselves to tolerate the costs imposed by a halt in cooperative activities, which is usually (but not inevitably) easier for capitalists than for workers, for example, or for landlords than tenants. This is the problem of endurance or *staying power*.

The fourth condition for effective action on contributions is that the power seekers be able to prevent those with whom they are contending from finding substitute contributions. For example, striking workers try to prevent their employers from hiring other workers or wives try to limit their husbands' access to other women. This is the problem of *controlling the supply of alternatives*.

A fifth condition for the exercise of power in interdependent relations is that contenders do not respond to challenges by simply exiting from the relationship, or threatening to exit, as when peasants evade the exactions of an overbearing prince simply by moving elsewhere or employers facing strike actions threaten to close down. This is the well-known problem of *exit*.

Sixth, the effective use of the leverage inherent in interdependencies requires that the power seekers be free from constraints that might be imposed by their interdependent relationships with other parties, as when would-be peasant insurgents are constrained by the threat of religious excommunication or when labor insurgents are constrained by the threat of intervention by the courts. Indeed, it is widely agreed that recurrent defeats of American labor struggles were the result of just such "third party" state interventions.[25] This is the problem of *multiple and constraining bonds*.

Seventh and last, the realization of the power potential inherent in interdependent social relations depends on whether the challengers confront the threat of physical coercion. Again, the history of the use of force to crush American labor insurgencies provides a vivid illustration.[26] This is the problem of *force*.

Or, to put the problem of actionability another way, some contributions to interdependent relations are more liquid, more readily converted into power resources, than others.[27] Further, some contributors who try to activate interdependencies risk more than others, which matters greatly for the possiblity of transforming interdependencies into power. Even so, however, this is not the whole of it. The actionability of different contributions is variable and contingent: people who are dispersed and divided do sometimes manage to forge unified action; those who are hard-pressed sometimes accomplish stunning feats of endurance; under some conditions, contributions from below cannot easily be replaced; exit may mean forfeiting whatever was desirable in the relationship; and the threat of force has both limits and costs. Much of the social movement literature about the conditions that give rise to new collective claims from below can be recast as being about the conditions that make it possible for lower status people to act on interdependent power.

But there is another large part of the answer to why reciprocity in contributions to social life does not lead to greater equality in power relations, and this part of the answer is ordinarily ignored. Social rules inhibit the activation of interdependencies and hence restrict the wide exercise of power.

RULES AS INSTRUMENTS OF POWER

Rules are often treated as simply the basic postulates of collective life, so elementary a feature that they do not themselves have to be

[25] The role of government in crushing labor insurgency is one of our main points in *Poor People's Movements* (1977, Chapter 3), and it explains the continuing emphasis of American unions on building its electoral leverage. See for illustrations of these contemporary efforts Lazarovici (2002:14–17).

[26] For a recent discussion, see Goldstein (2001).

[27] William Gamson (1968:94–5), who relies on a distributional concept of power, uses the term *liquidity* to differentiate between power resources and potential resources that must be deployed or mobilized before they can be used to influence others. Immediately available power resources are more "liquid."

explained.[28] But rules are also the achievement of social life: created by people, enforced by people, and violated by people. Rule making is, whatever else it may be, a power strategy with which some people try to make others do what they want. Rules do this by specifying the behaviors that are permissible by different parties in interdependent relations. And because the rules are fashioned to reflect prevailing patterns of domination, they prohibit some people but not other people from using the leverage yielded by social interdependence.

Although the view that rules are an instrument of power will surely not be unfamiliar, and has in fact been advanced from time to time and perhaps most boldly by sociologists in the field of criminology,[29] it nevertheless seems too brash and too simple. And it surely is too simple, which is part of the reason this argument has not seemed credible when it has been advanced in the past. It is too simple insofar that the quest for power certainly does not exhaust the social meaning of rules and rule making. Rules order human activities in ways that have little direct bearing on power. Thus the rules that guide people in their everyday behavior, that tell them how to till the fields or work their machines or mate or die, do much more than establish and maintain patterns of hierarchy. They make available to people the wisdom of accumulated experience, and they secure people against the totally unexpected in social encounters. They also make possible the tacit cooperation that underpins social life. In the classical line of sociological thinking from Durkheim to Parsons, rules originate and persist in the effort to solve these problems of collective life.

Thus the age-old rules the peasant follows when he tills the fields, even when these rules are endowed with sacred meanings that reinforce a pattern of worldly hierarchy, nevertheless do not usually mainly reflect domination but rather distill a centuries-old reservoir of communal knowledge. James C. Scott (1976) describes the rules to ensure against subsistence crises among Southeast Asian peasants, including rules commanding redistribution when dearth is threatened. Carol Stack's (1974) account of rules governing the exchange of gifts and services in an urban ghetto are similarly strategies honed by experience to ensure community survival in the face of scarcity and uncertainty. The laws of contract that made possible the growth of merchant capitalism in Europe were not – although they would later be put to that purpose in relations with labor – primarily instruments of domination but rather facilitated exchange by making the terms of contract more secure. Perhaps most of the myriad rules that govern the daily actions of people – driving to work, crossing the street, responding to a fire alarm – are merely the regulating framework that makes group life possible.

However, this functional perspective on rules does not help to make sense of those important rules that are the lynchpins of the patterns of domination of a given society. Rules are basic to group life, but so is the play of power, the effort to use others to achieve ends even against opposition. Perhaps the most important way that people try to use social relationships to achieve their ends over time is by rule making. The ability of social actors to use the leverage generated by interdependent social relations is contingent and subject to change, for all of the reasons we have already given. But power can be made more secure by fashioning rules that define or redefine the contributions made by different contenders in interdependent relations, thus making the contributions of some recognizable and obscuring the contributions of others. In so doing, rules also legitimate the actions available to some contenders while delegitimating the actions available to others.

The first aspect of these power rules might be called the social construction of contributions. Recall Blau's mistake in assuming that power

[28] "Humans are rule makers," says Guillermina Jasso (2001:48). "Every day, and in every area of life, they make rules – rules for themselves, rules for other individuals, and rules for groups and societies." We should add that recently rational choice analysts have in fact given a good deal of attention to the effort to explain the evolution of rules. See, for example, Jonathan Bendor and Piotr Swistak (2001:1493–545). See also Hechter and Opp (2001).

[29] See, for example, Vold (1958), Turk (1966), Sutherland (1943:99–111), Quinney (1973), Chambliss (1975:149–70).

inequalities flowed from inequalities of contributions. A vivid example is the legal construction of private property. Once a legal right is established that confers total possession of land or goods on certain actors, that possession in turn is understood as their contribution to interdependent relations. When commercializing landowners across Europe and Asia apppropriated common lands and wastelands, they turned to the state to make and enforce laws that upheld their right to do so in the face of local resistance and to sanction those who resisted. Once "ownership" of the disputed lands was established, it became the basis for new relations between owners and the working peasantry. Similarly, the French colonial regime in Algeria replaced a complex system of communal rights to use the land with a new law of private property. At one stroke the law "threw all land held by Muslims upon the open market, and made it available for purchase or seizure by French colonists" on whom the Algerian peasantry then depended for access to land (Wolf, 1969:213).

The property laws that now regulate social and economic relations also construct contributions in ways that legitimate power. As economic activity in evolving capitalist societies came to depend less on the control of land and more on the control of capital and goods, so were laws developed and elaborated that secured the access of some groups to these new or newly important forms of property and ensured their exclusive rights to dispose of property, while limiting the access and rights of other groups.

Ongoing patterns of interdependence thus continually stimulate efforts by some parties to make rules that simultaneously legitimate their domination in interdependent relations and limit what others can do in these relations. In the course of these contests, what some contenders expropriate comes to be defined as private property, what others expropriate is defined as stolen goods.[30] In other words, rule making curbs the use of power resources inherent in the fact of social interdependency, and it curbs the use of power by some people and not by others. The play of power is never free play.

Rule making is thus the exercise of the power of some to neutralize the power of others in interdependent relations. This exercise of power stabilizes power by institutionalizing it. The force of tradition, the authority of the group and the state, and the force of group and state sanctions against the rule violator are added to the exercise of power. Simmel (1950:263) grasped some of this when he wrote the following:

> As soon as the ruler gives the law as law, he documents himself, to this extent, as the organ of an ideal necessity. He merely reveals a norm which is plainly valid on the ground of its inner sense and that of the situation, whether or not the ruler actually enunciates it.

Simmel made this comment in the context of arguing that the ruler himself becomes subject to the law he promulgates, a point of some importance, especially in understanding why insurgents often invoke some aspect of the law itself to justify their defiance. But he also said that the law, as an "objective power," enforces subordination by objectifying it. Thus when the worker is under contract, the character of his subordination changes, for then "The worker is no longer subject as a person but only as the servant of an objective, economic procedure," a procedure dictated by "objective requirements" (262–3). In a similar way, contracts imposed by employers on workers, or by welfare staff on recipients, seem to be neutral agreements between freely negotiating and equal parties.[31]

We can now comment on a feature of rule making in modern societies that has been the source of some dispute. "It is inherent in the special character of the law, as a body of rules and procedures," says E. P. Thompson (1975:262–3), "that it shall apply logical criteria with reference to standards of universality and equity .... The essential precondition for the effectiveness

[30] For historical illustrations, see the accounts in Hall (1952:62–79), Douglas Hay (1975a, 1975b), Thompson (1975).

[31] Sanford Schram (2000:chapter 1) makes the argument that the use of "contracts" between welfare departments and welfare recipients is deceptively neutral. For a more general discussion of the criminal law and its implementation as political domination, see Turk (1982).

of law . . . is that it shall display an independence from gross manipulation and shall seem to be just." Even when due account is taken for what may be the distinctly Western and modern focus of Thompson's generalization, we think the universal character of law has to be seen in a different light. Rules cast in the language of universality nevertheless discriminate among different kinds of contributions to interdependent relations and thus restrict the power strategies of different actors differently.

We think this observation clarifies the sometimes belabored and confusing argument by "critical" criminologists, who weave unsteadily between the view that the substance of the law is inherently biased against the lower orders and the alternative argument that the enforcement of the law is uneven, exempting dominant groups.[32] Gouldner (1950:296) contributed to this confusion with his breezy charge that the law is not an objective power at all. On the contrary, "the possession of power itself enables some to default on their moral obligations . . . and . . . this default of morality is itself established as customary."[33] That the powerful evade moral sanctions is surely true, at least much of the time.[34]

However, we believe our point is more telling. Rules shore up power not just because they are biased or enforced unequally. Rather, the rules are only superficially universal, as in Anatole France's jibe about the law that prohibits the rich and the poor alike from sleeping under bridges. Laws shore up power not mainly by unequal enforcement but by singling out for prohibition or restriction the strategies available to some actors and not the strategies available to others. That laws restricting strikes apply to workers and employers alike is not significant. What is significant is that laws governing labor strikes have always been far harsher than laws that restrain capital strikes by investors.

The rules themselves are therefore a major focus of contention. People will do battle about what actions are permissable by whom in interdependent relations, about which parties to a relationship have the legitimate right to withhold or threaten to withhold their contributions or, less directly, which parties have the right to undertake the organizing activities that will make their contributions actionable. The bitter labor struggles in Europe and the United States precisely over the right to strike were struggles over the right to use contributions to interdependent relations as a power resource. Other statutes were devised that forbid the organization of workers employed by the emerging manufacturing class (Orren, 1991; Hattam, 1993; Forbath, 1989:1111–256). Nineteenth-century struggles for freedom of speech, or worship, or assembly were similarly struggles over the right to organize contributions to interdependent relations (Pope 1997:941–1031).[35] The outcome of these struggles may be to reaffirm existing power rules, but it may also lead to their modification. Popular struggles did win freedom of speech and worship; workers did win the right to unionize and the right to strike, albeit on closely defined terms. Also, rules can be modified by the powerful, as when long-standing rights to the use of the commons or the forests are withdrawn, the right to unionize is whittled back, or speech

[32] See, for example, the discussion of crime and law enforcement in Nigeria in Chambliss (1975).

[33] Gouldner goes on to say "The more powerful are . . . both ready and able to institutionalize compliance with the moral code at levels congenial to themselves and more costly to those with less power . . . . The powerful can thus conventionalize their moral defaults (emphasis in the original, 1950:297). Relatedly, Hechter and Borland (2001:186–233) argue that ambiguity in the norm of national self-determination enables more powerful actors to employ the norm strategically.

[34] E. P. Thompson (1975:262) rightly criticizes this overgeneralized view of the law "as a pliant medium to be twisted this way and that by whichever interests already possess effective power."

[35] See Pope (1997) for a discussion of labor's effort to use the 13th amendment to establish "Labor's Constitution of Freedom." Much of the literature treats New Deal labor legislation as if it allowed labor to break free of this tradition of legal constraint. More accurately, whereas New Deal legislation, and the court decisions which followed, created a new legal framework, that framework also limited and channeled labor's efforts to use interdependent power. See Piven and Cloward (1977:155–75). Nelson Lichtenstein (2002) also makes the case that the sorry state of contemporary unions is very much owed to the New Deal legal framework.

rights are curtailed. Such changes in the structure of rules alter the legitimate repertoire of political action by different participants in interdependent relationships. And the inevitable recurrence of such power conflicts means that the structure of rules is never stable for long.

THE STATE AS PROMULGATOR AND ENFORCER OF RULES

In modern societies, the rules that sustain important forms of domination are typically formulated and imposed by the state. "The modern state," Weber (1946:82) says bluntly, "is a compulsory association which organizes domination." The laws that prohibit certain behaviors in interdependent relations, and prescribe the penalties to be imposed on violators, should be understood as the use of power to stabilize power, by means of the state's bureaucratic apparatus for promulgating and elaborating rules and monitoring compliance, and by means of its coercive resources for enforcing compliance. Lawmaking and law enforcement in the modern world is, whatever else it may also be, the use of the formidable arsenal of the state to inhibit challenges to ongoing patterns of domination in interdependent relations. This argues that the most telling kind of power, at least in modern societies, is political power. Effective leverage in political relations results in the promulgation and enforcement of state laws that enhance or constrain the exercise of power in any of the myriad social networks of a society.

The system of law thus constitutes a new constraining social reality, a structure of power built by the accumulation and objectification of the outcome of past power struggles.[36] Once successfully institutionalized, the law shapes ongoing conflicts by constraining or enhancing the ability of contemporary actors to use whatever leverage they have in interdependent social relations.

Because the power relations underlying the introduction of systems of rules tend to emerge more vividly as the events recede in time and space, we turn to some historical examples. The feudal laws that governed the relations between lord and vassal were cemented by an oath of fealty at a time when the breaking of an oath held the palpable terror of everlasting damnation. The vassal was obliged by law to work the lord's domain, to serve in and supply the lord's armed retinue, and to submit to the lord's will in matters of marriage or trade (Tigar and Levy, 1977; Markoff, 1996). Such laws were certainly functional for feudal communities, aside from their role in maintaining a power structure. They made possible a system of armed protectorates that provided a measure of security for lords and vassals alike in an era of violence and pillage. Feudal law, like any system of rules, also established a framework to regulate multiple forms of cooperation and secure people against the unexpected contingencies of social life. Moreover, these rules obligated the lord to provide for his vassals in bad years. Christopher Hill (1952:36) argues that undergirding feudal notions of the responsibility of lord to vassal was the economic imperative of keeping the people who worked the land alive during periods of dearth. This limited reciprocity may have also indicated that the power of the dominant class was not total. In any case, whatever else it did, an important consequence of feudal law was to stabilize the raw power of a ruling class that had initially been based largely on force.

The main recourse of subordinate groups was evasion or flight.[37] It was not easy to counter these stratagems with armies. Then, as later, surveillance was difficult, and the geographical reach of military forces was limited. But the ritual meanings and legitimate sanctions embodied in the feudal code inhibited recourse to the vassal's stratagems of evasion and flight and thus also reduced the leverage they might otherwise have

[36] Our definition of structure here is broadly similar to Giddens's (1984:xxxi) definition of structure as "rules and resources recursively implicated in social reproduction." Giddens goes on to offer an extremely abstract elaboration of what he means by rules and resources.

[37] Michael Mann (1986:49 passim) argues flight was historically the main recourse of subordinate groups confronted by the exactions military rulers who, in turn, strove to reinforce the "caging of social life."

exerted, albeit at the cost of fleeing the lord's protectorate.

In the midfourteenth century, the plague that killed off an estimated half of Europe's population shifted the balance of interdependent power in favor of workers. The poor took to the road in vast numbers to better the terms of their employment, prompting a rush of lawmaking across Europe to prohibit vagrancy and beggary and to enforce work on the terms offered by local landlords. These laws were no doubt in part an effort to secure a modicum of social order in the face of the breakdown of medieval social arrangements. But they were also intended to ensure the domination of landlords over laborers. The English Statute of Laborers of 1349 attempted to eliminate the leverage the poor had gained from labor scarcity (enhanced by the newly available option of service in the King's army), by requiring that all able-bodied men and women under sixty and without income accept employment at wage rates that prevailed before the plague (Lis and Soly, 1979:48) and forbidding those already employed to depart without good cause (Chambliss, 1964:66–7; Piven and Cloward, 1993, Chapter 1). The option of exit was thereby prohibited. The new law limited exit in other ways as well. Many of the poor tried to survive by taking to the road and pleading for alms. Not only did this make the supply of workers and servants insecure, but the sheer numbers of vagrants terrified the landed gentry. They responded by securing laws that prohibited the giving of alms on the one side, and vagrancy and beggary on the other, and enforcing the latter prohibitions by the brand and the lash and, later, the workhouse.

The evolution in tandem of new laws creating and elaborating the terms of ownership of private property, on the one hand, and of criminal theft or property destruction, on the other, also reveals the effort to shore up power. Consider the struggle over access to English forest lands that culminated in the Black Acts in the eighteenth century. An aristocracy intent on the exclusive use of the forests as pleasure parks, in contravention of custom, turned to the state to legalize their dispossession of commoners and to enforce that dispossession in the face of resistance. Draconian punishments were meted out to those who tried to sabotage the new parks or even those who simply took advantage of proximity and uneven surveillance to persist in the exercise of hunting and other customary ancient use rights (Thompson, 1975; Hay, 1975a).

As commerce, manufacturing, and wealth expanded in the eighteenth century, and the forms of property became more complex, opportunities for theft and fraud also expanded. Accordingly, the laws sanctioning theft were also elaborated. The process was not indirect or obscure; it was simple and bald, interest-group politics. Three examples are illustrative. In 1753, Parliament enacted a new statute prescribing hanging as the penalty for stealing shipwrecked goods. The "Merchants, Traders and Insurers of the City of London" thought existing laws insufficiently tough to discourage the scavengers who were reducing their profits. In 1764, Parliament decreed the death penalty for those who broke into buildings to steal or damage linen or the tools to make it, as part of an act incorporating the English Linen Company. In 1769, an act making the destruction of mills by food rioters punishable by death had quickly appended to it measures providing for the punishment by transportation of those who rioted against enclosure and also those who meddled with bridges and steam engines used in the mines, as one group of gentlemen after another named the economic interests they wished to protect (Hay, 1975b:20–1).

Evolving English and American labor law also reveals the uses of lawmaking to shore up power. Ceilings on wages were established. Refusal of work became a crime. Laws against unionization were succeeded by contemporary laws that closely prescribe the terms on which workers can strike. All such rules limit the ability of workers to use their contributions to economic relationships to change the terms of those relationships. Lawmaking in other institutional areas, such as laws against heresy or laws establishing patriarchal prerogatives in family relations, also buttress power. The electoral-representative system itself, precisely because it raises the threat and possibility of equalizing power relations, is shaped and twisted by laws and regulations that give the votes of some people more weight than other people.[38] Once we move beyond the view that social norms mainly reflect a value consensus or support key social functions, it is clear that rule making in the modern world is, whatever else it may also be, an effort by some people to use the state to ensure their domination in relations with other people.

RULE BREAKING

A focus on rules and rule making can be misleading, for it fits too neatly with traditional sociological perspectives that deny agency and conceive of social life as systems of total domination. But domination is never total. People obey rules, but they also defy rules. The classical sociological tradition explains rule breaking as a byproduct of a breakdown or rupture in the larger society. There is surely something to this. But although breakdown or disorganization, conceived of as the weakening of socialization processes, may open the way for defiance, we think rule breaking also has to be understood as the effort of purposeful and reflexive human agents to exercise power. This is virtually a corollary of our perspective on rule making. If rules are strategies of domination evolved by purposeful and reflexive human agents, challenges to these rules by other agents will take the form of defying the rules, along with other more and less legal attempts to change the rules. At the very least, defiance will be a recurrent element in such challenges when they occur. Observers of such events may shudder at the threat to social order inherent in defiance of the rules and hurry to recommend alternative and law-abiding remedies, whether through appeals to God or appeals to the Congress. Such remedies are not remedies. The crucial point is that precisely the actions which the law forbids give paupers or workers or peasants some leverage in interdependent relations.

People do challenge domination. Each instance of lawmaking as an exercise of power is paralleled by instances of efforts of women and men to refuse, evade, or resist the constraints of the law. The poor who were prohibited by law from vagrancy and beggary took to the road nevertheless. Starving rural people flocked to the towns, where they laid siege to the rich with their pleas for alms and theft and where their very presence was perceived as threatening, as indeed it often was, and particularly so because disease epidemics often followed in the wake of hunger. "The permanent confrontation with the migrating possessionless became an obsession for the 'right-minded' European," say Lis and Soly (1979:115), and especially so in the wake of bad harvests or the expropriation of small holders.[39] Moreover, the dispossessed seemed to think they had some rights, a reflection perhaps of feudal ideas of reciprocity (Markoff, 1996:40).[40] Consequently, prohibitions and punishments came to be complemented by provisions for relief of the poor.

The artisans and tradesmen in the small towns of medieval Europe also defied feudal law and took up arms to secure their freedom from feudal obligation. Villagers forbidden access to the forests or the streams nevertheless poached and sometimes pillaged. In the eighteenth century, as enlarging urban markets and growing armies depleted rural grain supplies, outraged crowds simply commandeered the local grain, often selling it at a "just" price (Rudé, 1964; Thompson, 1971; Tilly, 1969).[41] Workers who could not openly combine, did so secretly, and when they could not strike legally

[38] Most such electoral rules come over time to be regarded as functionally necessary for the conduct of elections. See Piven and Cloward (2000:1–36). For an interesting examination of the power implications of the customary rules requiring the secrecy of the ballot, see Barbalet (2002:129–40).

[39] See also Jutte (1994) and Hill (1952).

[40] On this point, see John Markoff (1996:40) and Jutte (1994:27).

[41] See George Rudé (1964), Thompson (1971), Tilly (1969). The tendency in this material is to understate the element of defiance in the food riot by emphasizing that when the rioters commandeered grain and called for a "just price" they were merely acting out the role that the magistrates should have played according to medieval custom and law. But, of course, nothing in medieval tradition allowed the crowd to assume the authority of magistrates.

they sometimes struck illegally. And everywhere at all times, heresy is not stamped out by the laws against it, for the law intended to ensure ideological hegemony is matched by challenges to hegemony.

These examples should not mislead by their drama, for defiance does not have to be bold. Sometimes people do riot and burn and pillage. But the penalties for open defiance can be terrible. More often subordinate and vulnerable people turn to the age-old ruses and evasions of the peasantry, the foot dragging and desertions of the infantry, the soldiering and sabotage of the factory worker, and the pilfering and deceits of the servant. All such actions express the human inclination to use social relationships to realize ends and thus to exercise power. For those on the underside of relationships of domination, that inclination takes the form of resisting, evading, and defying the rules that have secured their domination.

RULE BREAKING AND AGENCY

With these comments on rule breaking, we have taken one side in the debate over whether human agents matter, whether reflective and purposeful people make a difference in the patterns of collective life.[42]

The question of whether reflective human agents play a role in social causation has only recently come to the fore in social explanation. True, some conception of agency was always at least implicit in the various "interpretive" sociologies descended from Husserl,[43] as well as in the American interactionist tradition.[44] But for a long time, these approaches remained marginal, and social science was dominated by a social determinism inherited from Durkheim (or at least a particular reading of Durkheim), who had sought to overturn nineteenth-century theories of the biological and environmental determinism of human behavior by enjoining his readers to believe in the facticity of society, in the actuality of what he called "social facts" as causal forces.[45] This brilliant stroke became an intellectual rallying cry. He commanded us to shift our focus from the natural to the social world to explain human behavior. The simplicity and clarity that made the injunction so compelling also helped to produce a sociology in which the ideas and actions of people were interpreted as solely or primarily the products of social structure. The main theoretical task of social science came to be understood as the identification of structural determinants of human action. The structural determinants favored at different times ranged from Parsonian structural-functionalism[46] to a similarly deterministic Marxism and then to the structural determinism of the purely ideal realm of "knowledge" exemplified by Foucault. With the decline of both the functionalist and Marxist paradigms, the ascendance of postmodernist interpretive schools, and the simultaneous rise of rational choice perspectives with their emphasis on the rational egoist as the prime mover in history, the issue of human agency has moved to the fore.

The idea of human agency, with its connotations of a retreat from scientific explanation of

[42] Or, to use Gidden's (1977:8) words, because this is one of his preoccupations, it is the question of whether social life is shaped in part by "rationalized conduct ordered reflexively by human agents."

[43] For discussion of this point, see Dawe (1978:362–417) and Miller (1979).

[44] See, for example, Cooley (1902); Mead (1936), Blumer (1978), Goffman (1959), Strauss (1958), Dunier (1999), Anderson (1999).

[45] The well-known Durkheimian imperative was to "consider social phenomena in themselves as distinct from the consciously formed representations of them in the mind . . . ." See Durkheim (1938:28).

[46] A number of authors have made the point that Parsons in fact began his formidable theoretical journey preoccupied with the voluntaristic element in human conduct, a preoccupation that some writers say was later submerged by the elaboration of a deterministic functionalism. See, for example, Dawe (1978) and Therborn (1976). Thus the ostensible goal of *The Structure of Social Action* (1949) was to provide a theoretical basis for the voluntaristic and creative element in human action, although John Finley Scott (1963:716–35) argues that as early as the writing of *The Structure of Social Action*, Parson's interest in the voluntaristic element in action had receded and that the better expression of these earlier ideas appeared only in an earlier article by Parsons (1935:282–316).

social phenomena into an unsatisfactory voluntarism, raises difficult and troubling issues. But we need the concept of agency when we try to understand not why people obey the rules, not why they do what they know will be approved and rewarded, but why they break the rules, defy the expectations of their community, and risk sometimes terrible penalties.

Most discussions of agency rest their case on a distinctive human capacity for reflection on action (or "reflexivity") and for innovative interpretation, despite the constraints of social structure. This capacity is said to defeat efforts at formulating deterministic laws about social action in two different ways. One is simply that reflection and interpretation complicate causality by intruding psychological and semantic processes into models of explanation, thus creating a fundamental divide between the natural sciences and social explanation. "The human capacity for the construction of meaning," says Dawe (1978:373) "... constitute[s] the crucial difference between the conceptualizing subject matter of sociology and the nonconceptualizing subject matter of natural science."[47]

The other is that thinking human agents can anticipate and upturn even complex causal generalizations. Giddens (1984:xxxii–xxxiii) calls this the "double hermeneutic" through which social actors anticipate and innovate in the face of efforts by social scientists, or indeed any social observers, to predict behavior. "[R]eflection on social processes (theories and observations about them) continually enter into, become disentangled with [sic] and re-enter the universe of events that they describe."

The possibility for human agency, however, does not rest only on inherent capacities for reflection and innovation. Social structure itself encourages or inhibits self-consciousness and innovation, with consequences that can in turn lead to the power challenges that change structure, including both the rules governing social relations and the body of inherited meanings we call culture.

Most social science has focused on the way social structure constrains thought and behavior. People internalize structural constraints through socialization and then confront structural constraints again as externally imposed sanctions on behavior. So long as structure is conceived of as entirely constraining, the idea of human agency rests on the premise of structural lacunae, on the notion that socialization can somehow be incomplete or that there are gaps or inconsistencies in the structural constraints that confront the actor.

On the contrary, structure can facilitate not only by its gaps or incompleteness or weakness but also by its sheer denseness and complexity.[48] Some features of social structure enable people to be something more than manipulable objects shaped by a social environment. The key question is "How?" Structural constraints, says Giddens (1984:174), "serve to open up certain possibilities of action at the same time as they restrict or deny others" but his discussion remains elusive and abstract. Lukes' (1977:6–7) assertion that "although agents operate within structurally determined limits, they nonetheless have a certain relative autonomy and could have acted differently"(1977:6–7) is also unconvincing. Lukes never tells us what it is about the changing and variable features of structure that permits or nurtures "relative autonomy."

Our argument about interdependent power may provide a conceptual bridge between social structure and the self-conscious and purposeful actor. We think the ability of human agents to invent new interpretations and action strategies in the face of dominant interpretations, including strategies that defy authoritative rules, may be rooted in their experience of social life, and specifically in the experience of their own contributions to the web of interdependencies that constitute social structure.

Peasants till the fields and provide the surplus on which the overlords depend. Irish laborers

[47] See Alan Dawe, 1978, *op. cit.*, 373.

[48] Analysts point to a number of processes through which structure may facilitate agency. See the argument that market economies tend to create autonomous and complex personalities (see Lane, 1978:2–24); Sewell (1992) sees institutionally complex societies as providing alternative rules and resources that can encourage agency. Habermas (1984) sees the potential for critical reason inherent in Western modernization.

on the railroads laid the tracks that made the railroad magnates rich; Blacks in the gold mines of South Africa work the lodes on which the mining companies depend; and so on. Human agents necessarily reflect on these social relations, and on their own contributions to them. Barrington Moore (1966:471) had something like this in mind when he asserted that "Folk conceptions of justice . . . . do have a rational and realistic basis." Moore was looking at the top side of interdependent relations, and he proposed that peasants evaluate the contributions of overlords to the community in relation to the surplus they extract in deciding whether an injustice is being done. We are arguing more generally that the actual experience of making contributions to social relationships is the objective and material basis for the self-conscious reevaluation of social relationships by human agents.

Of course, social structure *is* constraining. Human agents do not construct interpretations out of whole cloth. Rather, they reevaluate their circumstances within an ideological framework that is largely inherited, to which they are largely socialized. To assert a capacity for reflection and innovation is not to deny this but rather to say that people continue to probe and question the dominant interpretations that they inherit and to modify those interpretations in the light of their experience. That experience includes the reflexive observation of their contributions to social life. The fact of interdependence may be the foundation for alternative evaluations of existing social arrangements, and for alternative visions of how social life could be organized, including how socially valued goods and symbols could be distributed.

In this way, social structure provides the objective grounding for agency, for the development of alternative ideas of what is right and what is possible. Of course, even real contributions are often not actionable, for all of the reasons we have explored. But the complex contingencies that determine whether contributions are actionable change. As they do reflective and innovative human agents, drawing on the reservoir of alternative interpretations created by human agents in the past, probe anew the shifting possibilities for exercising power. Underlying this testing of possibility are the realities of social interdependence and the potential for realizing disparate purposes it generates.

Rule making and rule breaking, conformity and deviance, are an expression of the dialectical and conflict-ridden character of social relations. The interdependent and cooperative social relations in which people are lodged are also relations of domination and potential conflict. People try to exercise power by making and breaking the rules governing these relations. Or, to shift to another idiom, people make rules and break rules because because rules and rule breaking are rational means to desired ends in social life. Both those on top and those below try to use the very links that bind them to others to make or remake some aspect of their lives. As Thompson (1978:240) put it,

> . . . [T]he fact is that all histories hinge on power. The power of some men [sic] has repressed the potential nature of other men. These other men have discovered their own nature only in resisting this power. Not only their economic being, but their intellectual being – their ideas, knowledge, values – have been coloured by the possession of or the resistance to power; at this point all "histories" have found a common nexus.

But there is a good deal that remains to be explained. For one thing, to understand the quest for power from the underside of social relations, we have to begin to examine the power implications of systems of law and regulation. Only when the power implications of the rules governing specific systems of social relations are analyzed as structures of power, in all their complexity, can we appreciate what it is that rule makers and rule breakers as trying to accomplish.

Moreover, the quest for power is hardly the whole of an explanation. If it were, then the answer to the question of why people break the rules would be simple and clear-cut, and we would have already answered it: they do so to assert power, to bend the actions of others in the pursuit of their own disparate interests and aspirations. But in most places most of the time, people don't challenge the rules that enforce their domination.[49] In everyday life, people mainly endure and obey. If rule violation is a politics embedded in the power dimension of all social relations, then the question experience forces on us is not only why some people sometimes break the rules that enforce domination, but why do most people most of time obey those rules. Why, in other words, if human beings are political beings, if they try to act on their divergent purposes in group life, don't they try to break the rules they must break to exert power? A perspective on rule making and rule breaking as the play of power requires us to wonder not only why there is disobedience, but why there is obedience. If there is disorder some of the time, why is there social order most of the time?

Further, Thompson's paean to resistance notwithstanding, actual patterns of rule breaking are often not easily seen as power strategies. Sometimes people poach and burn and pillage and riot. Sometimes, they pilfer and smuggle and sabotage and evade. But women and men break a good many rules that cannot reasonably be regarded as instruments of domination. They take their own lives and not the lives of their rulers; they turn on their own bodies in hysteria and hypochondria instead of the bodies of their antagonists; they join together in millenial movements of self-destruction instead of joining in revolutionary movements of self-assertion. Why? Why do women and men defy, evade, and resist rules against narcotics or homicide or child abuse which seem to have no bearing on domination?

Why, in short, if all men and women are endowed with a capacity for politics, do they obey the rules of domination as much as they do? And why do they defy rules that have little to do with power? Why do they rebel so infrequently and go mad so frequently? These are the difficult questions in an inquiry into rule breaking and power.

[49] The problem has not been entirely neglected. It is in fact the distinctive Gramscian problem. See Gramsci (1971), Burawoy (1979), and Scott (1990).

CHAPTER TWO

Neopluralism and Neofunctionalism in Political Sociology

Alexander Hicks and Frank J. Lechner

A broadly pluralist tradition of political sociology flourishes today in its neopluralist reconstructions in political science and, to a lesser extent, sociology. Since the 1970s the pluralist tradition of political analysis, which stressed the causal primacy of a plurality of collective social actors, has passed into a neopluralist phase. This transition entailed an extension of the pluralist repertoire of actors into the once-forbidden territory of Marxian class and antiestablishment social movements, as well as an enhanced recognition of the grounding and embeddedness of politically influential actors in social structures and systemic dynamics beyond those of culture. Neopluralism expands the pluralist stress on multiple bases of social action to encompass a yet fuller range of actors (class ones in particular), an increased sensitivity to structural and systemic modes of power not reducible to social action, and a more complex articulation of agency and structure. Insofar as frameworks and theories of political analysis today reflect *both* this ecumenical approach to the varieties of potentially important actors (for example, union movements as well as business lobbies and interest associations) *and* the approach's openness to the causal powers of both agency and structure (for example, macroeconomic and political institutional constraints upon as well as ground for action) today we are all neo-pluralists.

Neofunctionalism is a notable complement to neopluralism, much as functionalism was an important complement to classical pluralism. Neofunctionalism is hardly the pervasive force that functionalism was during the first two decades following World War II. Nevertheless it remains a significant presence in sociology, especially political sociology, neopluralist political sociology most particularly.

We begin with neopluralism. First, we place neopluralism within its pluralist legacy, especially that of the "classical" pluralism of post–World War II political science. Second, we trace the emergence and articulation of neopluralism as a series of complicating revisions of the pluralist orientation in response to the critics of pluralism who took issue with the scope of its repertoire of social agents and with its relative disembodiment of its key social actors from structural context. We next examine neopluralism in terms of a series of marriages with other theoretical orientations as well as a number of innovations not evidently made in response to pluralism's external critics. We finally turn to a brief summary of what neopluralism is and is not in relation to its pluralist heritage and its many theoretical competitors.

These things done, we continue with neofunctionalism, showing its historical affinity with pluralism, its independent development of a more systemic conception of polities, and its partial convergence with neopluralism in work that links a plurality of actors and conflicts to structural contexts. We end with a summary of what we have written and an eye to the future of neopluralism and neofunctionalism.

NEOPLURALISM, ITS PLURALIST TRADITION, AND ITS COMPETITORS

Who rules, asked Aristotle, "the one, the few or the many?" Theoretical perspectives on politics vary in their answer to his question. Though no currently influential theory posits the theoretical generalization that individual positions or single individuals rule entire polities, some nevertheless may suggest that, in a sense, "the one" does rule.[1] For example, class theories have sometimes tended to view each polity as dominated by one "ruling class" (Domhoff, 1967), whereas elite theories have sometimes granted rule to single, homogeneous elites (Hunter, 1953). Nevertheless, such class and elite theories do typically propose, whether as working hypothesis or fine-grained conclusion, that "the few" rule. Thus, the apparent "one" of a "ruling class" or a single, homogeneous "ruling elite" may in fact be internally differentiated like Domhoff's (2001) class analytical "power elite" or Mills' (1956) more classically elitist "power elite."

The classic pluralist answer to Aristotle's question was "the many" (Polsby, 1960). Pluralists claimed that power is exercised by, or on behalf of, either the whole of a population or at least a wide range of the population's subgroups. Yet pluralism has been transformed. In response to criticism of its basic claim about the nature of rule, pluralism has had to concede that advantage might sometimes go to the few, for example to the organized, plural elites from atop the stratification system described by Schattschneider (1960) and Bachrach and Baratz (1962).[2] Moreover, pluralism had to respond to the criticism that it ignored certain actors or that it ignored the role of structural and systemic contexts for – and explanatory complements to – social action. The reconstructed pluralism of the past quarter-century that has responded to challenges of these sorts is our "neopluralism."

Again, to examine neopluralism, we review the pluralist tradition in its classical incarnation, consider neopluralist reincarnations in response to charges that pluralists truncated the cast of political actors or robbed it of set and stage, describe pluralist elements present in the guise of sundry ostensibly non-pluralist theoretical orientations and attempt a final articulation of what neopluralism is and is not, as well as of the pluralist/neopluralist distinction. Neopluralism considered, we turn to neofunctionalism. Conclusions follow.

Classical Pluralism

Central to pluralist theories of politics are conceptions of a polity marked by Aristotle's "unity in diversity" and the early liberals' competitive and representative democracy. Not coincidentally does De Tocqueville emerge as the first renowned modern pluralist political analyst, for in his *Democracy in America* he wrote in closely observed empirical detail about the liberal democracy of a socially diverse people at a time when such political empiricism was rare. Works that came to be called, or dubbed themselves, pluralist were works about the political process in such socially diverse liberal democracies: for example, Arthur F. Bentley's *The Process of Government* (1908), David Truman's *The Governmental Process* (1951), and Robert A. Dahl's *Who Governs?* (1961). In the terms of Dahl's (1971) *Polyarchy*, pluralist theory developed as a theory of power in liberal democracies. This theory is one of power in polyarchies, which are defined by the conjuncture of (a) effective rule by "representative" officials who are (b) chosen by vaguely inclusive electorates and through free and competitive election, who are (c) safeguarded by individual and associational civil liberties and who also are (d) socially grounded in

[1] Some authors also apply their theories to the study of powerful individuals. We do not claim that contemporary scholars never study monarchs (as Trevelyan studied George III) or powerful individuals (as Dahl studied New Haven's Mayor Lee) but they have not done so often. Nor have they prominently, except in some theories of Sultanates, characterized rule as "monarchical" as opposed to more pluralistic elite (e.g., "league," "clique," "coalitional") metaphors.

[2] As Schattschneider (1960) famously wrote, "The pluralist choirs sing with a decidedly upper class accent."

heterogeneous – pluralistic – social structures.[3] Pluralism, in fact, is an explanatory theory of state action, preponderantly in political democratic societies, that stresses the effective agency (i.e., state power) of a plurality of types of actors.[4]

One core pluralist axiom goes back even before De Tocqueville: *a plurality of interest groups and interest group conflict are keys to understanding power and governance* (e.g., Hume, 1987[1739]). This proposition is picked up by Bentley (1908) during the Progressive-era transformation of interest groups from lobbies and partisan tribes to professionalized voluntary associations (Clemens, 1997), and it is revived again by Key (1942) and Truman (1951), who extend the pluralist axioms to include the proposition that *party and public opinion, along with interest groups, are potential vehicles for power and are all largely capacitated by the electoral and representative medium – or roadway – of political democracy.* (For a recent review of public opinion in theory and research see Burstein, 1998.) This pluralist premise states not that *interest groups and conflict among them* must always prevail a *priori* or have, in fact, dominated the empirical record, but that they are key theoretical categories that should be prominently considered when one frames her exact investigation and specifies her theory (e.g., details it propositions or model).

Dahl (1961) and Polsby (1960) elaborate the "pluralist" perspective in response to the perceived intellectual closure of the "power structure" approaches of preceding decades, in particular in response to the work of Hunter (1953) and his sociological disciples (see Aiken and Mott, 1970).[5] In his exceptionally clear and precise articulation of the pluralist stress on a volatile plurality of potentially consequential resources, Polsby (1960:13) offers a partial list of the "many different kinds of resources" that may ground power, "many more, in fact, than stratification theorists"(Polsby's *elite* theorists) "customarily take into account," and a flexible view of "the conditions for their relevance." The list includes economic resources (e.g., "money and credit," "control over jobs," and "control over the information of others"), status resources (e.g., "social standing" and "popularity, esteem, charisma") and authority resources (e.g., "legality, constitutionality, officiallity and legitimacy"), along with some less cleanly classifiable resources (i.e., "knowledge and expertise," "ethnic solidarity," "the right to vote,"

[3] Here *social* is used in an encompassing societal sense rather than in contrast with *political* or *economic*, and *heterogeneity* is used especially as concerns the economy, particularly when this is not excessively centralized or fused with or dominated by the state (Dahl and Lindblom, 1953; Friedman, 1962; Dahl, 1971, 1982; Lindblom, 1977).

[4] One might unpack this "plurality of actors" into a plurality of social-structural and cultural bases of actor identification and a plurality of social resources for, as well as bases of (and enactors of) power. In addition, the pluralist focus on political democracies is so convenient as to suggest that pluralist seek a tautological advantage for their theory. However, it should be noted that pluralism's, and neopluralism's, theoretical competitors commonly challenge, if not disdain, the "pluralist" explanatory stress on a plurality of theoretically anticipated possible sources of rule. For example, Domhoff (2002), as opposed to Amenta (1998), sees economic elites engineering the Social Security Act of 1935 with few democratic (or related nonelite) complications.

One might also think that pluralism's scope is too limited. However, theoretical universalism of the sort that does not specify clear, institutionally homogeneous, theoretical domains, is not without its critics – from the advocates of local knowledge such as Boas (1940) and Geertz (1995) to proponents of historical realism like Skocpol (1975) on revolution in agrarian empires or Paige (1997, 2000) on revolution in coffee-growing modes of production. Here we assume that a political democratic domain is a valid domain for a political theory insofar as the gain in realism and specificity that the theory gets from focus on the democratic domain is large relative to the lose in theoretical scope. Judgments will differ on what constitutes "large" where a particular theory is concerned. The viability of debate over scope versus realism in chose of theoretical domain noted, specific debates over such choice can hardly be settled here. Suffice it to say that a theory of explanatory powers that were comparable within the democratic domain and superior beyond it would have a serious case to make against pluralism for its democratic focus.

[5] Theory should cast a large net designed to catch as wide a variety (a plurality!) of fish as may characterize the waters trawled, as well as one knit to search out the real stuff of policy decisions as opposed to the fish stories of political reputation.

"time," and "personal (human) energy").[6] The "flexibility" involved concerns the skill and, in turn, the aptness of "timing and targeting" with which the resources are employed, for central to the pluralist perspective is the view that the range of potentially empowering resources and of opportunities for their use is so broad that students of politics must cast a wide net. Not only must they be conceptually open to a wide range of potentially powerful categories of actors; they must be epistemologically open to the point of supplementing theoretical logic with methodological induction: "pluralists want to find out" (Polsby, 1960:12). Polsby also offsets the arguably indeterminate breadth of the pluralist view of who may be powerful with a precise conception of where and how power is to be found: at the point of decision and in the identity of whomever made or influenced the decision.

Each of Polsby's stresses came under nearly immediate criticism, criticism that initiated the movement toward a revised (neo-)pluralism. Schattschneider (1960) was among the first to note how greatly the disparate resources detailed by Polsby were associated with class advantage, whereas Bachrach and Baratz (1962) were quick to note that agenda setting (however "decisional" it might be) lay beyond Polsby's final policy decisions. Still, Schattschneider's argument was less with pluralism as theory than it was with the perhaps Pollyannaish views of some pluralists concerning the extent to which the democratic playing field is "level," for example, undistorted by "social standing" and marked by "noncumulative" inequalities in "resources of influence" (Dahl, 1961:7, 229–30). Pluralists stressed that political resources are, in fact, diverse; and that they may substitute for one another, thereby empowering actors whom a more narrow conception of resources would bar from political opportunity. Nevertheless, such politically "leveling" considerations should not obscure the pluralist's awareness of typically large skewing of the distribution of political resources in favor of a relatively few. In addition, Bachrach and Baratz's argument was not with the breadth of the pluralist inventory of the potentially powerful so much as it was with the shallowness of concentrating attention on a single, final phase of decision making and on conflict over outcomes at that one point. Pluralist (or neopluralist) scholars today often take inquiries up the river of the policy processes from final legislation to bill drafting and from that all the way to the headwaters of agenda setting (e.g., Anderson, 1994; Stone, 1989).[7]

To increasing criticism during the politically and ideologically tumultuous 1960s and 1970s – the era of emergent liberation movements, antiwar and anti-imperialism movements, and the New Left – pluralism responded with self-transformation. Indeed, in responding it metamorphosed into what we term *neopluralism*. Much of the transformation involved arose around criticisms of some limitations in the

[6] These resources, although all are ones that might be attributed to individuals and groups and capacitate their action, also are ones that vary in level of analysis for potential attribution (e.g., of "esteem") from individual (e.g., "charisma") through group ("solidarity") to the macro institutional ("economic" and, most especially, "authority" resources).

[7] Underlying the axiomatic premises that *plurality interest groups and interest group conflict are keys to understanding power and governance* and that *party and public opinion are, along with interest groups, potential vehicles for power and are all largely capacitated by political democracy* are two factors. One is the core power resource view underlying a wide range of theories of social action that conceptualizes effective action as centrally, if not exclusively, a function of *predispositions* to action (whether centered in "preferences, values, interests, goals, or the like") and of capacitating *resources* for action, including in some theories of social action situational or contextual *infra* resources (see Rogers, 1974). The second is the behavioral revolution of the 1950s, which privileged the individual (but see the prebehavioral Bentley, 1908, and the postbehavioral Clemens, 1997). This individualism takes forms from the virtual individualist reductionism of behavioral-era classicists like Dahl (1962) and Polsby (1960) and the individualist microfoundationalism of macrocomparativists like Iversen (1999). However, pluralists and neopluralists, defined in terms of the axioms of *plural actors* and *democratic* conduits are not necessarily individualist (e.g., Hume, 1987[1739]; Bentley, 1908, Lijphart, 1984). Thus, we regard methodological individualism, although prominent for some pluralists, as inessential to pluralism and neopluralism, as well as a source of issues related to pluralism and neopluralism that we no longer address here.

pluralist emphasis on agency. This tended to be exclusive, despite its stress on a plurality of agents, and it tended to be volitional beyond many views of social action and its structural embeddedness. In turning to pluralism's response to critics, we turn *ipso facto* to the rise of neopluralism, for pluralism's response to its critics was self-transforming. In articulating the responses, many of which include concessions and revisions of original pluralist positions, we simultaneously delineate the new neopluralism.

Neopluralist Responses to Critics

(Neo-)pluralist Responses to Critics I: Extending the Range of Agency. More theoretically pointed criticism would come. Perhaps the most basic criticism charged neglect of class- and state-based actors, as in Domhoff (1978) on Dahl's (1961) underestimation of business in the latter's New Haven study or Shefter (1978) and Skowronek's (1982) statist framings of bottom-up pressure groups and parties in U.S. policy formation. Responses to such criticism began a transformation of pluralism into a *neo*pluralism. On the statist revisions of pluralism, attention to state initiatives and state-framed mediations of a world of pluralistic associational forces is now commonplace both in the work of Americanist and comparativist investigators. For example, the pluralism of agency is extended to state-based "interest groups" agents by Garand (1988). It is extended to associational state networks in Laumann and Knoke (1987), which is reviewed in Chapter 14 of this volume. In particular, it has been extended, using graph theory conceptualizations and techniques, to a new interest in and affirmation of the importance of lobbyists in Heinz, Laumann, Nelson, and Salisbury (1993) and to a "new institutionalist" framing of group and party action by Clemens (1997). As shown, agency is also extended to class actors; and the importance of class actors is large relative to what it was in classical pluralism.

In their ambitious survey of lobbyist growth, in *The Hollow Core* (1993) John Heinz, Edward Laumann, Robert Nelson, and Robert Salisbury cite six important principles about the exercise of influence.[8] One principle is that "Influence is situation specific." Another is that "Low visibility may be more advantageous than high visibility." A third states that "The merits may count more than clout." A fourth enjoins that "Newcomers would do well to take the advice of regulars." A fifth states that "Interest groups, even those who share common objectives, may be clumsy and get in each other's way." The sixth counsels that ". . . it is dangerous to assume that conventional notions of influence will accurately predict policy outcomes." A key general idea is that elites are not organized into disciplined or predatory swarms of interests that capture or otherwise control government agencies and dictate policy (1993:377–8). Instead they are rather loosely coupled, despite a great increase in numbers (numbers of lobbyists in particular).

Elisabeth Clemens's (1997) *The People's Lobby* focuses on interest-group politics in the United States from 1890 to 1925. It shows that high levels of political participation by interest groups – at least groups with a degree of formal, politically oriented, organizational structure such as the modern voluntary association – were not always the case. Rather, during the pivotal 1890–1925 period group politics was vitally changed in the five following ways: (1) state capacity was increased and rationalized; (2) traditional elites were alienated from party politics and attracted to progressivism; (3) political parties became increasingly regionalized and regulated; (4) new forms of political participation – such as the initiative, the referendum, the recall, and the direct election of senators – were invented; and (5) interest groups were organized outside of political parties to represent a large number of issues (1997:27–8). Focusing on the creation of labor, women, and farmers's interest groups in Washington, California, and Wisconsin, she is able to show how these groups, by means of novel repertoires of action and new organizational forms, could represent their interests in the public sphere in ways that circumvented

[8] The survey questions members of groups that employ lobbyists, government officials who deal with lobbyists, and the lobbyists themselves.

the well-vested elites of business lobbyists and party leaders. Clemens clearly delineates a "new politics of pluralism," albeit with a state-centric twist and new institutionalist theoretical tools.[9]

Where incorporation of class and other actors, often judged as reification of group forces, has been concerned, Americanist pluralists have been less inclined to widen their purview of relevant actors than have comparativist pluralists. However, a clear extension of the role of class actors emerges among established U.S. pluralists around 1980 (e.g., Lindblom, 1977; Dahl, 1982), as also is documented by the chapter of Granados and Knoke in this volume. Suddenly, key pluralist figures were quite open to the relevance of class and variously class-based actors from unions and business associations to confederations of these. Indeed, class-linked organization of interests become prominent within the broadly pluralist tradition. In particular, Dahl (1982:53–4, 67–8, 79–80) identifies salient pluralist emphases on highly fragmented systems of interests and weak class profiles, with pluralist readings of an *extreme* United States case. More fundamentally, in his *Dilemmas of Pluralist Democracy*, Dahl (1982:chapter 4, especially pp. 48–54, 68–80) elaborates the concept of "organizational pluralism." With this he maps and, in turn, helps explain variation in the structure of interest organizations, the aggregate societal – level organization of interests. Elements of this structure range from the relatively decentralized, exclusive, and fragmented forms of U.S. democracy to the relatively centralized, inclusive, and cohesive pluralism of Scandinavia. At this latter pole of the continuum of interest organization, Dahl admits into the pluralist universe precisely those types of "neocorporatist" political economic configurations that have recently captured the imagination of sociologists in recent decades (see Streeck and Kenworthy [Chapter 22] in this volume). These configurations are marked by high "inclusiveness and centralization" of "interest organizations" and of governmental participation in "negotiation" that culminates, to lift a term from Rokkan (1970), in the Scandinavian system of "corporate pluralism" (Dahl, 1982:67–8; Hicks, 1991).

With Dahl's (1982) *Dilemmas*, pluralist theory emerges, whether by transformation or revelation, as more than a theory that is conceptually alert to a fine-grained range of actors, interests, resources, institutions, and other bases of power. It emerges as one that conceptualizes variations in the organization of interests from the fragmented, hyperpluralist United States of modal Americanist "pluralists" to the "corporate pluralism" of such European pluralists as Rokkan. With the theory of organizational pluralism, Dahl (1982) explicitly seeks to balance the pluralist stress on a diversity of possible power bases with an offsetting emphasis on a diversity of actual configurations of active power bases. He also incorporates a highly inclusive, centralized, and coordinated organization of interests into the vocabulary of pluralism by treating such interest organization as one molecular realization of pluralism's eclectic table of theoretical elements. Moreover, he breaks with the theoretical presumption of a greater democratic representativeness in polities characterized by a more "plural" organization of interests. The "dilemmas" of Dahl's title involves polities across his spectrum of degrees of interest organization.[10]

Consistent with Dahl's clarification of pluralism as a variously realized range of possibilities from the hyperpluralism of the United

[9] As Clemens (1997) is more directly focused on institution than actor, it might be regarded as more an new institutionalist work than a neopluralist work. However, it is easily read as a new institutionalist framing and revision of interest group pluralism, whether as one of a new institutional neopluralism or a neopluralist new institutionalism. Note that, moving from substantially sociological projects like Clemens (1997) and Heinz et al. (1993) onto unquestionably political scientist terrain, we find further notable state-structural framings of pluralities of associational and partisan actors (e.g., Boix, 2001b; Brzinski, Lancaster, and Tuschhoff, 1999; Lijphart, 1984: chapter 8).

[10] For example, Dahl contrasts *corporate* pluralism as an admirably effective representation of a few fixed, salient, and shared interests of a relative inclusive constituency with the greater range and flexibility of interests being voiced in more *hyper*pluralist systems. This is a restatement of pluralism as a *neo*pluralism in the sense of a *reconstituted* pluralism.

States to the more centralized interest organization of Scandinavia, comparativist students of European politics have often worked in a virtually class-centered neopluralist mode. This literature, which might be called corporatist neopluralism, is consistent with the traditional pluralist stress on industrialization, heterogeneous social cleavages, organized interests, and electoral politics. However, it is articulated with novel emphases on the European empirical terrain with its unabashedly class-linked organizations (Pierson, 2001). It identifies a *continuum* of structures of "interest intermediation" (Schmitter, 1981), which vary, like Dahl's (1982) "organizational pluralism," from fragmented arrays of interest groups to formally organized corporatists meta-organizations of interest associations (e.g., confederations of business associations and labor unions). This helps explain comparativists' responsiveness to class-analytical, neocorporate and other institutionalist critiques of an unreconstituted pluralism. Central innovations here are the combination of a pluralistic openness to power sources with stresses on class- and state-grounded actors (e.g., union confederations and class parties, politicians, and public organization like central banks). Common too is a balance between social actor and institutional constraint (agent and structure) in policy determination and an eye for broadly political economic structures, outputs, and outcomes as objects of analysis. Some key authors have combined pluralist and class-analytical elements. Moving from works with relatively decided pluralist tilts to works with relatively decided class emphases, we note David Cameron (1978, 1984), John Ruggie (1982, 1996), Peter Katzenstein (1984, 1985), Douglas Hibbs, Jr. (1986a, 1986b), Hicks and Misra (1993), Iversen (1999, 2001), Lange and Garrett (1985, 1986), Garrett (1998a, 1998b), Przeworski and Wallerstein (1982, 1988), Przeworski (1985), Wallerstein (1987, 2000), and Swank (1992).[11]

Pluralists in sociology and political science adapted to the criticism that they neglected class. In doing so they contributed to the construction of neopluralism.

Neopluralist Responses to Critics II: Agency in Context. Perhaps the most telling criticisms of pluralism were those that came from Poulantzas (1968, 1973, 1978), Lukes (1974), Block (1977, 1981), Alford (1975), and Alford and Friedland (1985), arguing that two or three additional structural or systemic levels of power (with their own crucial *explicantia*) operated from beyond immediate policy-making arenas and their fields of political actors. As articulated by Alford (1975) and Alford and Friedland (1985), these involve structural and systemic levels of power *beyond* the situational level in which pluralist agents engage in relatively visible conflicts over relatively final, policy-producing

[11] All of these literatures are clearly nonelitist in their consideration of varied bases of consequential popular or "mass" power (class, religious, ethnic, peripheral as well as core) that effectively utilize electoral/representative institutions. All are nonclass in their conceptualization of virtually every societal structure and process but class – economic, political, or intermediating – in nonclass analytical terms (indeed in their centering of class mobilization in trade/union bourgeois democratic partisan institutions). Still, Douglas Hibbs, Jr. (1986a, 1986b), Lange and Garrett (1985, 1986), Garrett (1998a, 1998b), Przeworski and Wallerstein (1982, 1988), Przeworski (1985), and Wallerstein (1987, 2000) might all appear to be too focused on opposing pairs of class-linked actors to qualify as neopluralist. However, these authors treat classes as large interest groups, reconceptualize class interests in group terms and class capacities in organizational/associational (e.g., party and union) terms; articulate economic issues in orthodox, if inventive and leftist, economic terms; and embrace a view of interest organization that overlaps with Rokkan (1970) or Dahl's (1982) "corporate pluralism." They might be classified – or coclassified – as "conflict theorists" of political democracies; however, self-conscious "conflict theory" has been absent from the minds of political scientists since the 1980s rejections of functionalism, except in some theories of revolution (e.g., Gurr, 1971). They might also be (co-)classified, Hibbs, Jr. (1986a, 1987) aside, as rational choice theorists. However, they tend to embrace certain practices proscribed by rational choice theorists: that is, they pose questions and conduct research at a macroinstitutional level, theorize about collective actors without explicit individual-level micromechanisms, and incorporate a large number of institutional factors that have not been theoretically reconstituted as emergent properties of "the time-tested verities" of optimizing behavior.

or -defeating decisions. It would seem that for any outcome, as for the proximate battles and decisions that bring it about, a structural level (e.g., one of state structural organizational and policy resources, rules and procedures, missions and legacies, options for action, and so on) is present that at once constrains and empowers, modifies, and transcends agency. Simultaneously, an even more encompassing systemic level exists at which political structures are embedded in economic, cultural, and other structures. Yet these contexts for the pluralist arena had been marginalized, when not suppressed.

In particular, this jointly structural/systemic criticism targets pluralist tendencies to neglect or marginalize *both* (1) social and cultural[12] political structures directly impacting on state outcomes (processes, decisions, actions, policies, impacts, and so on) *and* (2) new, deeper levels of state action and reaction situated beyond these structures (as in the decisions behind formation of structures). Further, structural/systemic critics and their neopluralist accommodators see larger systemic forces of economy and culture – plus interdependencies among these and state structures and actors – exerting themselves. For example, a chain of dependencies running from investment to productivity, from productivity to material and symbolic support for state actors, and from support to actions itself is often invoked by the critic (Alford, 1975; Alford and Friedland, 1986:chapter 18) and her respondent (Hibbs, Jr., 1986a, 1986b; Lindblom, 1977).

On neglect of the structural level, (neo-) pluralists have addressed the power implications of social structures and social system dynamics for particular agents (e.g., Hibbs, 1986a, 1986b; Lijphart, 1984); Lijphart (1984, 1998) and Birchfield and Crepaz (1999) on the redistributive implications of unitary state consensus systems; Pampel and Williamson (1989) on the relevance of democracy for the political voice of the elderly; and Katzenstein (1984) and Boix (1999) on the contested class functions of proportional representation provide just a few examples of the sort of work in question. Indeed, these authors all focus on political agency in the contest of structural factors that condition its occurrence or shape its course or consequences.

On the implications of systemic forces for agent power, we have two types of (neo-)pluralist responses. On the one hand, we have pluralist denials that policy maker accommodation to intractable systemic forces counts as evidence of the power of the force favored. Here, for example, we have Rose's (1967:3) stress on "social forces" versus "powerful men" and on "impersonal forces – such as geography and economic – " not as determinants of the "predominance" of certain actors but as "semi-independent forces of social change" that "set marked limits to the power of any elite group to control the actions of society" (p. 7). On the other hand, we have neopluralist acknowledgments of the consequences of systemic forces for political action. These acknowledgments show that openness to a truly encompassing plurality of power bases that we earlier termed *neopluralist*. Here we have Lindblom on the procapitalist power biases of capitalist systems, Swank (1992) on the policy consequences of investment rates for a range of partisan forces and political economic policy outcomes, Hicks and Misra (1993) on the reshaping of groups power by the new post-OPEC economic troubles, and Pierson (2001) on the impacts of globalization – by policy regime or political structure – for welfare state "retrenchment." Each shows the neopluralist openness to structural and systemic

[12] Cultural structures are not prominent in Alford and Friedland (1985). However, social structure may be said to connote symbolic as well as social-relational structure since at least Sewell, Jr. (1992) Indeed, looking back in light of that landmark article, deep cultural constraint is prominent in Lukes (1974; see also Gaventa, 1980), if not in the other critics noted. Indeed, Friedland and Alford (1991) indicates that Alford and Friedland (1985) would been more prominently cultural had it been compelted a half-dozen years later. Almond and Verba's (1963) *The Civic Culture* is, of course, the classic pluralist work on culture and politics, and Robert Putman's (2000) *Bowling Alone* is perhaps its most innovative critical update. Ronald Inglehart (1997) has prompted much work on the "subjective" political culture of "values." For a thoroughly cultural, hyperpluralist theory in a postmodernist vein opposed to distinctions between agency and discourse, see Laclau and Mouffe (1992, 1996).

explanation, in addition to class (and traditional interest group).[13]

For pluralists like Rose, the options for popular "voice" silenced by particular political institutions or rendered prohibitively costly by particular political economic systems typically were not regarded as evidence for the power of any grouping that the institutions might appear to disproportionately advantage. Rather, they tended to be regarded as those inevitably recalcitrant aspects of social reality – the necessity of certain incentives for investment, of adequate investment for prosperity, of prosperity for revenue sufficiency, of revenue adequacy for state efficacy and legitimacy, and state considerations of efficacy and legitimacy for what they do – that agents must, at least typically, take as a given (Rose, 1976). For neopluralists, structural and systemic forces came to be regarded as grounds for, and even aspects of, group (or class) power. Eleventh-hour pluralists, as part of their reconstitution into neopluralists, reached out to augment their explanatory powers by incorporating theoretical elements that they had previously shunned. In part, such pluralists' coming to terms with the limitations of early agency theories of politics gave rise to neopluralism.

That pluralist treatments of structural and systemic power were thin on theoretical accounts of systemic process á la Baran and Sweezy (1966) and O'Connor (1973) seemed to count against them. However, Block's (1977, 1981) especially influential accounts of systemic or structural power shared the pluralist interest in consequences of systemic and structural context for the poltical actions of a range of actors. In addition, they closely resembled Lindblom's (1977) treatment of "the privileged position of business." Since the late 1970s some of the best articulations of systemic dynamics are patently pluralistic (e.g., Boix, 2001, and Katzenstein, 1984, on electoral agency in the context of development and globalization). Furthermore, although institutionalism within the pluralist tradition of political science is hardly synonymous with a clearly pluralistic view of prominent political actors, it certainly has contributed to the neopluralist articulation of political institutions and of agency in its (structural) context (Brzinski et al., 1999; Iversen, 1998; Lijphart, 1998). Indeed, neopluralists have been able to turn to their tradition for many of their insights into institutionally situated action. Neopluralists did not tend to preclude structural and systemic factors as conditions for state policy so much as they tended to downplay them as criteria for the assessment of group power. Neopluralists have been keenly alert to the power implications of structures and systems.

If there is any neopluralist deemphasis of structural and systemic factors as determinants, it has been the result of a neopluralist tendency to stress the degree of free play that actors retain in the face of such (merely partial) structural determinants. Indeed, in line with such sociologists as Berger and Luckman (1966), Giddens (1973), and Powell and DiMaggio (1991), neopluralists place some stress on the constitution and construction of social structure and system by social actors (e.g., see Boix, 1999, and Katzenstein, 1984, on the social construction of proportional representations systems).

Structural/systemic constraints should be understood as variously dependent on agency: for example, agency may operate as a source of structural constraint as in Katzenstein (1984) or Boix (1999) on the partisan political construction of proportional representations. In addition, agency may also may operate as a microfoundation of structural constraints affecting policy as in Iversen (1999) on corporatism and macroeconomic policy. Neopluralists have advanced understanding of the sources of social structure in political action as well as opened the pluralist tradition to concern for the embeddedness of political action in social structure.

[13] To the images of the mediation of social action by structures of social relations already presented previously, we might add images from two works already discussed in a little detail. One is Heinz et al.'s (1993) network-centered account of the mutual determination and cooperation of actor agency and social structure *qua* network. The other is Clemens's (1997) new-institutionalist relocation of social action in concatenating institutional structures that so overdetermine agency that they virtually reduce agency to their own designs.

Higher-Order Integrations and Distal Influences. Imperialistic syntheses of elements of traditional political/sociological approaches such as pluralism, elitism, class analysis – often syntheses centered on one of the initial perspectives – marked the last decades of the twentieth century. These provided us with neo-Marxist, statist (neoelitist) and polity-centered (neostatist), resource mobilization, "new institutionalist" and multicultural innovations like those of Wright (1985), Skocpol (1985), Skocpol (1992), Hicks and Misra (1993), Clemens (1997), and Mouffe and LaClau (1993, 1996). Most of these works place sufficient stress on a plurality of potentially powerful social actors to qualify as neopluralism (if not necessarily *only* neopluralism). For example, Skocpol's (1992) "polity-centered" framework presents a polity in which the wide range of actors – not merely state as well as societal but gendered as well as classist and partisan as well as interest group – is prominent enough to warrant a neopluralist reading, and Skocpol (1996) provides an almost classically pluralist interest-group account of the failure of Clinton's national health care initiative. In revising "political resource" theory, Hicks and Misra 1993:703) argue for "an authentically open political resource theory that is as alert to 'class' and 'state' as it is to 'interest group' and 'electorate.'" Indeed, they free the use of political resource from the "class" usage assigned it by Korpi (1982) despite such more catholic precedents as Rogers (1974). Skocpol and Campbell's (1994) delineation of an "institutional" "theory of the state and politics" is replete with references to generic "actors" (as opposed to their pluralist "groups," elite-theory "elites" or class-analytical "classes"), and this move from a traditional pluralist concentration on "groups" to the yet more open category of actors (albeit actors in state-institutional contexts) qualifies as just such an opening up of the range of potentially powerful political agents as we see at the core of neopluralism. Moreover, in a recent "institutional" work, Amenta (1998) not only shows an openness to a plurality of consequential actors (unions, populist movements, parties and party factions, machine politicians and Dixiecrat autocrats) but also indicates how variation in the institutions in which actors are embedded can ground the differentiation of actors. Further, Amenta (1998) shows how embedding actors in institutions helps knit the variety of relevant political agents into an overall pattern.[14]

We have argued that although neopluralism retains the traditional pluralist openness to a variety of politically consequential actors, it is also marked by a new openness to class structure and agency and by a new attentiveness to the structural and systemic forces embedding agency. Development of a wide range of works along these lines constitutes a major trend. Still, particular political sociologists and political scientists tend to address questions passed on to them by their disciplinary communities. They tend to most fully address those questions that frequent their hallways, conferences, and publishing venues. In doing this, practitioners with particular disciplinary affiliations tend to be most vocal about issues long relatively salient within their particular professional disciplines – say, issues of group and party preference rather than ones of class interests for the case of scholars ensconced in political science. They likewise tend to articulate common issues with distinct emphases – as when political scientist Dahl (1982:66–8) colors Scandinavian "neocorporatism" with an "inclusiveness and centralization" of "interest organization" and sociologist Hicks (1999:230–6) paints the same institutions in terms of the institutionalized incorporation of labor unions into the structures of political economic policy making. So agency may operate in guises of "employee association" or "political incorporation" but are offered similar pictures in either case. Structural/systemic constraints should be understood as variously dependent on agency. For example, agency, as in Iversen (1999) on corporatism and macroeconomic policy, may operate as a microfoundation of structural constraints affecting policy. In addition, agency, as

[14] In its multidimensional conception of the expansion of rights underlying democratic citizenship and of the factors that have engendered these rights, theories of citizenship and citizenship rights might, insofar as they constitute explanatory as well as normative theory and legal taxonomy, be regarded as substantially neopluralist (Janoski, 1998).

in Katzenstein (1984) or Boix (1999) on the partisan political construction of proportional representations, may operate as a source of structural constraint. In addition, agency also may operate as a microfoundation of structural constraints affecting policy as in Iversen (1999) on corporatism and macroeconomic policy.

Neopluralism in Brief

Pluralism is a theoretical orientation stressing the causal potency of a plurality of interest groups and interest-group conflict, as well as of party, public opinion, and election, as determinants of the institutions and actions of governance, democratic governance in particular. Neopluralism is a reconstitution of pluralism extending its conception of interest group to encompass class groupings and social movement organizations and revising its conception of group political agency to an enhanced appreciation not only of the structural foundations and arenas of agency but also of the shaping and the complementation of social action (and political influence) by structural and systemic determinants.

Thus, in the wake of Hibbs (1976), Lindblom (1977), and Cameron (1978), Lipset's (1950, 1960) early focus on class ceases to appear an eccentric digression from the pluralist tradition. In the wake of Lindblom (1977), Lijphart (1984), and Swank (1992), discussion of structural power does not appear alien to that tradition. By the 1990s sociological works full of heterogeneous causal agents operating alongside (or entwined with) institutional and other structural *explicantia*, stand out only for their excellence (e.g., Amenta, 1998; Clemens, 1997; Skocpol, 1992, 1996; Steinmetz, 1993).

As our language has repeatedly stressed, neopluralism is, like pluralism, a theoretical orientation, a loose family of more focused attempts at tightly argued prepositional theory. As our section on higher-order integrations indicated, it may overlap with other theoretical approaches as well as encompass them. For example, if it encompasses Lijphart (1984) and Swank (1992), it overlaps with the substantially neo-Marxist Przeworski and Wallerstein (1988) or the substantially institutionalist Clemens (1997) and Amenta (1998). Indeed, from the perspective of theoretical approaches other than neopluralism itself, neopluralism appears to be the orientation subsumed rather than that doing the subsuming. The multitude of group actors contained within the pages of Clemens (1997) might appear less a neopluralist ensemble of agents couched in a particularly institutionalist conception of social context than as a series of political agents constructed and animated by Clemens varied institutional structures. What looks like a new institutional variant of neopluralism to one person might appear more like a neopluralism of the new institutionalism to another (e.g., Clemens). Still so long as theoretical orientations need not fall into mutually exclusive categories, some orientations that also fit other categorizations might be regarded as neopluralist. The opening assertion that "we are all neopluralists today" may have been an overstatement. However, today many political sociologists sometimes wear neopluralist hats.

NEOFUNCTIONALISM AND ITS FUNCTIONALIST ROOTS

As many of their counterparts in other traditions within political sociology, neopluralists often invoke a general kind of functional analysis. Their arguments are "functional" in a very basic, and epistemologically disputed, sense insofar as they posit certain "needs" on the part of groups, institutions, or even whole societies that are "satisfied" by means of a particular political process or institutional adaptation. A case in point is Giddens's (1973:217–19) "industrial society" variant of structural/functionalist theory, which served as the base of several influential early theories of societal historical development, in particular those pertaining to welfare state development. In this theory, new needs generate new institutions and common needs tend to generate common institutions (e.g., Kerr, Dunlop, Harbison, and Meyers, 1964), a theme that persists today in the literature on the welfare state (e.g., Wilensky, 2002). For example, new needs for security emerge due to transitions from agriculture to industrialism, rural life to urban life, personal relations to impersonal exchange. Thankfully, they emerge complemented by imperatives and capabilities for the operation and maintenance of the new industrial system. Important among the institutions generated to satisfy these imperatives is an expanded state nurtured by the industrial system's plentiful resources (Kerr et al., 1964). Part of the inexorable emergence of this new state is the appearance of the welfare state (Myles 1989:91–3). Explicitly functionalist are Wilensky and Lebeaux (1964), Wilensky (1976), and Stinchcombe (1985), who stress policy responses that are functional for the needs of burgeoning elderly populations. Residues of functionalist industrialism are evident in Pampel and Williamson (1989), Williamson and Pampel (1992), Collier and Messick (1975), and Usui (1993), in which needs arguments sometimes emerge in ways evocative not just of functional inspiration for causal argumentation but also as functional imperatives. Indeed, Hicks's (1999) finding that economic development is a necessary condition for early consolidations of basic repertoires of welfare state programs circa 1920 does not fully break loose with functionalist rhetoric, even though it stresses the causal primacy of class social action within developed societies. Moreover, Wilensky's (2002) treatment of convergent tendencies (e.g., substantial social insurance systems) in modern welfare states rooted in common developmental tendencies of advanced welfare states updates the functionalist account of convergence-inducing functional imperatives for the modern era. In the latter, sophisticated versions, which do not attribute "needs" to societies and do not assume that "need satisfaction" counts as explanation, such functional accounts partly follows the precedent set by Robert K. Merton (1968).

Going beyond functional analysis, the specific theoretical tradition associated above all with the work of Talcott Parsons (1902–1979) shares an affinity with neopluralism in some of its assumptions about the political process and in its imagery of politics in democratic polities. Broadly speaking, this cognate tradition affirms the intrinsic pluralism of power sources in democratic societies. It moves away from a narrowly voluntarist conception of rule by analyzing politics in systemic terms. It also strives for metatheoretical integration by taking into account the multiple (i.e., plural) influences on the political domain that stem from its complex structural setting. Although this tradition provides a theoretical scaffolding that supports neopluralism, it also diverges in some ways. It centrally and uncompromisingly conceives of the polity as a system within a larger social system and, in post-Aristotelian fashion, it dispenses with the idea of the polity as the center of a society striving to realize the good life. With some exceptions, then, neofunctionalism decenters politics conceived in the prevalently state-centered terms of our era: the specific concerns of neopluralism, including its very focus on the political as such, become secondary to a systemic analysis of society, the political dimension of which is only one subsystemic facet of its overall organization. We illustrate this cognate tradition with a brief discussion of several relevant contributions, starting with that of Parsons himself.

Long an influential figure in twentieth-century sociology and a leading exponent of functional analysis, Parsons held an essentially pluralistic view of modern societies: not only were they differentiated along functional lines, they were also comprised of many collectivities. The polity of a society, effectively equivalent to government as a specialized organ of a nation-state, depended for support on a "societal community" consisting of "a complex network of interpenetrating collectivities and collective loyalties, a system of units characterized by both functional differentiation and segmentation" (Parsons, 1969:42–5). The "democratic association," Parsons argued, was grounded in "the solidarities of various kinds and levels of associational communities," which function to some extent independently of politics proper (Parsons, 1969:3). Criticizing C. Wright Mills for sketching a far too monolithic picture of the American "power elite" in the 1950s, Parsons presented his own work as defending the viability of "pluralistic-democratic society" (Parsons, 1969:159). His antielitist, antinostalgic, and antiutopian assessment of liberal/democratic institutions (Holton and Turner, 1986:chapter

5) fits the spirit of the (neo-)pluralism we have described.

Parsons's key step in analyzing the political domain was to conceptualize it as a functionally specialized subsystem of a larger social system, namely as that institutional structure focused on attaining collective goals by mobilizing collective resources. Its key function was to make binding decisions (Parsons, 1969:33, 45). Along with this functional redescription of politics, Parsons also proposed to treat power not as the ability to affect the behavior of others but rather as the "generalized capacity to secure the performance of binding obligations by units in a system of collective organization" (Parsons, 1969:361). Instead of a zero-sum game, therefore, the pursuit of power concerned the non-zero-sum process of mobilizing the means to make decisions advancing a collective interest. Parsons argued that, by analogy with money, power could be treated as a medium of exchange in interaction. Although this type of analysis retained a voluntarist element, insofar as it assumed that actors acted in pursuit of goals inscribed in systemic norms, it construed political action as embedded within a particular systemic context.

Applying functional analysis to the operation of the polity, Parsons focused on the conditions for sustaining an effective democratic polity. These included not only support from the societal community but also legitimation of the powers of government and control of basic facilities. More generally, Parsons represented these conditions as part of a set of exchanges between the polity or "goal-attainment" subsystem and the integrative, pattern-maintenance, and adaptive subsystems, respectively. By showing how the operation of the polity, as one subsystem among others, depended on these multiple exchanges, Parsons also illustrated a broader theoretical strategy, the purpose of which was to devise a conceptual scheme that would integrate different dimensions of action and thereby avoid reductionist explanations of any single domain.

Although in some respects Parsons displayed a substantive and metatheoretical affinity for the neopluralist vision we outlined previously, most notably in his functionalist view of the plurality of power bases and agents, his work diverged in several ways. In keeping with his general view of institutions, Parsons assumed that shared normative commitments under gird pluralist contention (cf. Sciulli, 1990:369–75). Because he focused more emphatically on the polity as a system and treated political action within the context of a larger theoretical agenda, his work lacked a distinctly political agenda resembling the exclusive focus on things political characteristic of neopluralist work. Yet several of Parsons's students systematically applied his theory to political conflict and change.

In his book on *Social Change in the Industrial Revolution*, Smelser (1959) applies Parsonian functional analysis to the transformation of the British cotton industry and working-class family structure between 1770 and the 1840s. He describes these changes as forms of structural differentiation brought about by a specific sequence of dissatisfaction with older structures leading to symptoms of disturbance, followed by attempts at institutional control and the specification and implementation of new ideas (Smelser, 1959:15–16, 404). Functionalist theory serves at least two purposes in this analysis: it helps to identify components of the relevant institutions that were undergoing change, and it suggests the direction in which potential differentiation might proceed. In applying the theory, Smelser relies on an assumption familiar from Parsons' work, namely that in episodes of differentiation values are relative stable, providing criteria by which both initial dissatisfaction and newly defined roles might be legitimated. Most relevant in this context is Smelser's interpretation of new factory legislation from the 1820s to the 1840s. He shows how this legislation constituted a political response to disturbances brought about by specific systemic problems, how attempts at political control of working-class agitation and "regressive" disturbances gave way to "new ideas," and how apparent working-class victories, such as bills limiting working hours, also contributed to the incipient differentiation of working-class families (Smelser, 1959:chapter XI). In analyzing this contentious period, Smelser thus pays close attention to political conflict and political change, but from a distinctively functionalist standpoint, by treating conflict as reflecting underlying structural strains and by treating change as part of a process of reequilibrating a disturbed system.

In one of the most politically relevant and theoretically sophisticated studies in the structural/functional vein, Gould builds on Smelser as well as Parsons to argue that "[t]he English revolutions of the seventeenth century were an outgrowth of internal, inherent movement of the manufacturing mode of production when controlled, as it was in England, by a set of rationalizing values, in contradiction to a political system legitimized within the context of traditional values" (Gould, 1987:114). The revolutions replaced a patrimonial polity with a stronger rational/legal state legitimated by a new egalitarian individualism, a political system more capable of mobilizing people and resources, projecting power, and supporting the rise of machine capitalism (Gould, 1987:362–3). To account for the coming of the Revolution, Gould relies on a structural description of English social structure and on a functional analysis of the tensions generated within it. He dissects the overall episode into revolutions at the levels of facilities, goals, and norms/values, and analyzes each as the outcome of a "value-added" sequence in which functionally relevant strain, combined with suitable opportunity structures, precipitating factors and legitimating beliefs, leads to an attempted political change. Only the specifically political revolution at the level of goals, he argues, represented the "culmination of the tendential development of prerevolutionary English social structure"; neither normative nor value revolution proved sustainable (1987:291). As this brief summary already indicates, Gould's functionalism has a Marxist twist, because he describes relevant changes as "bourgeois" revolutions that resolved a "contradiction" in the English social system in a manner that advanced (a new stage in) the capitalist mode of production. In combining Parsonian and Marxist systems theory to account for political change, Gould implicitly challenges any clear pairing of (neo-)functionalist theories of society with more eclectic (neo-)pluralist theories of society. By assigning factors and actors in the English Revolution a definite place in a general theoretical scheme, he argues that systematic explanation of political change must also be systemic (i.e., structural and functional).

One strand of recent work in the Parsonian vein, which Jeffrey Alexander has labeled neofunctionalism (Alexander, 1985), has loosened Gould's theoretical strictures and moved closer to the neopluralist mainstream by focusing on an empirical agenda concerned with the impact of group conflict and competition. Such politically oriented *neo*functionalist work is guided by two criticisms of Parsons. As Alexander has argued (1983), Parsons' substantive work suffers from idealist conflation, because he turned a presuppositional commitment to the significance of values in action into an overly integrated and consensual view of actual societies. Skirting the rough-and-tumble of actual conflict and competition also hampers causal explanation of actual social processes. Inspired by the work of S. N. Eisenstadt, several neofunctionalists have turned their attention to particular political processes (see Alexander and Colomy, 1990). For example, Colomy (1990) shows how competition among strategic groups in early America produced uneven differentiation of political institutions. Similarly trying to bring "agency" back in, Rhoades (1990:188–9) argues that differentiation in higher education "is largely the product of political competition and state sponsorship." Smelser's later work on education perhaps marks this direction most clearly. To account for the distinct forms of differentiation of primary education in Britain and America, he refers more explicitly than in his earlier work to the role of "political struggles among social groups" with certain vested interests and to "the political resolutions of those struggles" (Smelser, 1990:165). He adds that the condition of the British working class hampered differentiation in the nineteenth century (Smelser, 1990:166). As these examples show, this neofunctionalist work particularly aims to explain how, and to what extent, new, differentiated institutions can emerge. Although such work addresses political processes as independent rather than dependent variables, the imagery of multifaceted contention within a complex institutional setting partly converges with that prevalent in neopluralism.

Alexander has contributed to this neofunctionalist line of thought with his analysis of Watergate (1988a, 1988b). The specific question he addresses is why the initially muted public response in the United States to the Watergate break-in turned into a major societal crisis after the elections of 1972. In a manner familiar to neopluralists, Alexander first describes the political polarization that developed through the 1960s. Different factions in the American polity legitimated their political behavior in very different terms, and these political subcultures had become more polarized over time. When the main Watergate events became known in 1972, a substantial portion of the American public was inclined to treat them as "normal" politics and to resist the more radical interpretation of the break-in as a profoundly deviant act (1988a:167ff). Alexander then shows that as new information suggested that basic political norms had been violated, and as institutional controls and elite cooperation broke down, the definition of the problem became generalized (1988b:198ff). In dealing with this crisis, however, the relevant actors could draw on a broadly shared consensus about the nature of the polity and its purposes. As ritual affirmations of a sacred common culture, the Senate Watergate hearings and the subsequent impeachment hearings in the House of Representatives constituted key steps toward reintegration (1988a:170, 1988b:203). Although this conveys the capacity of the American political system to overcome the divisive impact of modernizing change and polarizing conflict in a manner that fits the Parsonian view of American politics, Alexander argues that understanding this regenerative pattern requires jettisoning the Parsonian assumption that social systems simply "specify" consistent cultural schemas and attend instead to the contingent dynamics of conflict within social systems (1988a).

Though not focused on political matters narrowly conceived, Alexander's related work on civil society aims to rethink the nature of democratic society along neofunctionalist lines. He has argued for the relative autonomy of civil society, described variations in patterns of inclusion, and studied the problematic reintegration of U.S. civil society after Watergate (Alexander, 1988a, 1988b, 1990, 1998a). He thus conveys by example "the pluralism, complexity, and inevitably conflict-ridden nature of democratic social life" (Alexander, 1998a:12). Alexander's work also illustrates how some neofunctionalists have modified the traditional Parsonian emphasis on the symbolic nature of all action. For example, he argues that civil society is "not merely an institutional realm" but also "a realm of structured, socially established consciousness, a network of understandings that operates beneath and above explicit institutions and the self-conscious interests of elites" (Alexander, 1998b:97). This implies that every study of social or subsystem conflict "must be complemented by reference to this civil symbolic sphere" (Alexander, 1998b:97). Rather than analyze this sphere as the normative specification of consensual values, Alexander shows how certain conflicts are discursively organized around polarized (e.g., "democratic" vs. "counter-democratic") codes (Alexander, 1998b). He thus moves beyond the consensual strain in Parsons' treatment of symbolic action, suggesting that neofunctionalism is able to account for political conflict in substantially cultural terms.

The work of Alexander and like-minded colleagues has remained "Parsonian" in its awareness of the cultural nature of political action, its interest in grand themes like differentiation, and its "multidimensional" form of theorizing. Although creatively extending Parsonian functionalism and linking up fruitfully with neopluralists in several respects, some neofunctionalist work risks retreating to a voluntarism more characteristic of the older pluralism and overcome in Parsons' later work. By pursuing a more empirical agenda, it also veers away from the coherent systemic and theoretical thrust historically associated with functionalism and illustrated by Gould's work discussed above. In working through such trade-offs, neofunctionalism faces dilemmas similar to those confronted by neopluralism.

Whereas the concerns of Parsons' American successors partly converge with those of neopluralism, Niklas Luhmann's systems-theoretical response to Parsons breaks decisively with neopluralist assumptions and problems. Regarding functional differentiation as the defining feature of modern society, Luhmann follows Parsons in treating politics as a differentiated subsystem specialized in "issuing binding decisions and creating social power" (Luhmann, 1982:139). But Luhmann's analysis differs from that of Parsons (Luhmann, 1982:chapter 3). For example, he defines systems not as patterned relationships but in terms of the difference they maintain in relation to a complex environment (Luhmann, 1982:139), through the self-reproduction of their operations (Luhmann, 1995). For social systems, treated as forms of communication rather than institutionalized normative patterns, this means that self-referential communication about communication is essential (Luhmann, 1995). Although Parsons focused on the way a society could balance functional differentiation with integration, and Alexander still maintains that there is "a *society* that can be defined in moral terms" (1998b:97; emphasis in original), Luhmann argues that differentiation is sufficiently pervasive to require a new way of thinking about society that does not view it as a community writ large. Applied to politics, this line of thought has several consequences. First, politics becomes a form of communication set apart from communication in other spheres; the key question here is how, once the political system is differentiated, it can be shielded against complexity, entropy, and risk through self-reference and further internal differentiation (Luhmann, 1982:139). Second, power is redefined as the medium in this form of communication, specifically "the possibility of having one's own decision select alternatives or reduce complexity for others," thus transmitting a "selection based on selection" (Luhmann, 1982:150–1). Third, in Luhmann's radically differentiated image of modern society, the very place of politics changes: it becomes simply one part of a society "without a top or a center" (Luhmann, 1990:100). As a consequence of this recasting of politics, finally, contention among groups or parties loses its central place in the political sphere. Contention matters insofar as it presents options to the system, which can thus avoid paralyzing overcommitment to particular decisions or structures and maintain an openness to "other possibilities" that is especially important in a system focused on reducing complexity by making decisions (Luhmann, 1982:162, 164). Not surprisingly, then, Luhmann notes that although pluralism has touched on issues of systemic significance, "its limitation to groups and interests has not been transcended" (1982:383). From a neopluralist standpoint, in turn, the Luhmannian agenda may seem overly systemic and abstract. Thus, although contemporary American (neo-)functionalism remains connected to neopluralism in certain of its assumptions and in its vision of democratic polities, the Luhmannian approach to politics decisively parts company with both kinds of scholarship.

CONCLUSION

The influence of sociological functionalism has waned since the post–World War II, pre–Vietnam War heyday of both functionalism and pluralism. However, as we have shown, some nesting of political analysis in functionalist social theories persists (e.g., Wilensky, 2002; Williamson and Pampel, 1992) and neofunctionalist political analyses, both pluralist and nonpluralistically tilted (e.g., Alexander, 1988a, 1998a; Gould, 1987, 1999; Stinchcombe, 1985), have not left the scene.

By creatively embedding actors and conflicts in systemic accounts of political processes, some varieties of neofunctionalism, as we have shown, continue to be relevant to the evolution of neopluralism. Though its role in political sociology has diminished, neofunctionalism remains a resource to neopluralists concerned about explanatory entropy within a markedly ecumenical tradition.

The role of the pluralist tradition of political analysis with its stress on attention to a plurality of potentially powerful social forces, on social action over structural determination, and on political democracy as a principal theoretical domain is alive today. Within sociology, the broadly pluralist tradition has rebounded, in part because of neopluralists openness to class forces often previously regarded as alternatives to the pluralist repertoire of notable social actors, in part because of neopluralist assimilations of structural arguments, and in part because of a conscious neopluralist recognition of the institutional specificity of the social contexts (such as polyarchy) in which political pluralism is a plausible theoretical prior. Within political science, the pluralist tradition not only has withstood the sociological critique of pluralism; it also has contributed to the neopluralist revision of the pluralist tradition. It has survived the rise of rational choice theories of politics whose radical methodological individualism and formalism place them at some distance from – or in some arcane corner of – neopluralism (see Kiser and Baldry, in this volume [Chapter 8]).

What we here call neopluralist work is a political analysis of state action and its determinants that is centrally open to a variety of politically consequential power bases and actors, class structure and actors among them, as well as racial, ethnic, sectoral, and disparately cultural identifications and groupings, and that is systematically attentive to the structural and systemic contexts embedding action.

Still, students of politics who are not, or at least not foremostly, neopluralists do remain prominent. For example, among sociologists, those who would sharply focus their explanatory efforts with the selective tools of class analysis or neoinstitutionalism remain very notable (e.g., Frank, 2000; Wright, 1997). Among political scientists, not only do some eschew class actors or circumvent economic constraint (e.g., Boix, 2001; Skowronek, 1999) yet remain prominent; much is dominated by the concepts and tools of rational/public choice theory. Still, neopluralism as we have delineated it is now commonplace within both sociology and political science.

Like all wide-ranging and eclectically inclined theoretical orientations, neopluralism has entropic tendencies that pressure for corrective measures. As neopluralist work is somewhat eclectic by virtue of its very openness, it may gain focus when combined with other theoretical stains. Indeed, neopluralist and non-neopluralist theoretical elements often appears in combination. For example, we may speak of Laumann and Knoke (1987) as organizational neopluralists – or as neopluralist theorists of organizational fields. We may dub Hicks and Misra (1993) class-centered neopluralists but Hicks (1999) a neopluralist class analyst. We may term Clemens (1997) and Amenta (1998) new institutional neopluralists – or neopluralist new institutionalists.

A theoretical orientation that can perhaps best pride itself on its Catholicity invites fundamentalist reformation. To entertain a great range of explanatory tools risks loss of explanatory, prescriptive, and predictive specificity. Indeed, neopluralist work tends toward such cognate forms as those offered previously – organizational neopluralism, neoinstitutional neopluralism, class-centered neopluralism. This is so because neopluralism often gains closure and elegance from combination with particular other theoretical orientations. For example, Clemens (1997) and Amenta (1998) use the woof of neoinstitutional analysis to weave together a wide range of political materials.[15] At times, the explanatory accuracy and realism will pressure us away from a plurality of societal actors, as in class accounts of the origins of neocorporatism (see Katzenstein, 1984; Western, 1991). At other times, they will counsel a plurality of actors, as in delineation of U.S policy domains (e.g., Heinz et al., 1993; Laumann and Knoke, 1987). As neopluralists

[15] If one were inclined to view individualism as a primary characteristic of (neo-)pluralism and the (neo-)pluralist stress on interests as highly similar to the rational choice on preferences and goals, one might be inclined to view the current U.S. ascendance of rational choice theory as fundamentalist revision of (neo-)pluralism. We do not regard individualism as essential to (neo-)pluralism; and we think that the relation of interests to preferences and goals is complicated. Thus, we do not see rational choice as simple evolution out of (neo-)pluralism. Nonetheless, we do think that the long highly individualistic thrust of much American political science that is importantly manifested in neopluralism and the pluralist tradition does energize the large presence of rational choice in contemporary U.S. political science, as well as the smaller presence of rational choice in contemporary sociology.

pragmatically work through such options, in continuing engagement with alternative theoretical approaches, they will bolster the vitality of a central tradition in political sociology.

Just as neopluralism emerged from the crucible of an earlier pluralism under critical attack, so new modes of political analysis may arise from critiques of neopluralism and neopluralist mutations.[16]

[16] The authors of this chapter are indebted to Janoski (2001) for inspiration.

CHAPTER THREE

Conflict Theories in Political Sociology[1]

Axel van den Berg and Thomas Janoski

Once upon a time, Parsons's structural functionalism, depicting society as a community founded on a value consensus, was thought, at least in the United States, to be the dominant theoretical paradigm in the discipline. To be sure, there was always a fair amount of resistance to this view (e.g., C. Wright Mills, Ralf Dahrendorf, Dennis Wrong, and others). But it was not until some time during the 1960s, in part no doubt encouraged by the turmoil resulting from the civil rights, antiwar, and gender protests of the era, that a strong reaction set in against the value consensus approach under the label of *conflict theory*. Although different approaches have come under this label, they have one main feature in common: conflict theories emphasize the importance of social cleavages generating social conflict that in turn account for political outcomes, including momentary political events, more enduring policies, and long-lasting political institutions.

It is useful to distinguish two major strands of conflict theory according to the kinds of social cleavages they emphasize as well as the historical role that conflict plays in them. First, there are the conflict theories more or less directly hailing from the Marxist tradition. These theories focus on the fundamental material interests of different groups as they become intertwined with political forces. These conflicting interests are ultimately based in the mode of production, which creates two main classes, in the case of capitalism, labor and capital. It is the conflict or struggle between these two primary classes, and the organizations representing their interests, that is thought to provide the fundamental key to explaining political outcomes. But although the importance of fundamental economic interests had been recognized by non-Marxists from Adam Smith to Max Weber, another feature is more exclusively Marxist: that the working class is ultimately struggling to overthrow the existing mode of production for a more advanced one, culminating in the establishment of "socialism," a mode of production in which fundamental conflicts of material interest will disappear. In this sense, the struggle of the subordinate class is "progressive" and aims at the ultimate elimination of class conflict.

Arguably the most profound difference between Marxists and other conflict theories is that the latter do not entertain a progressive view of history in this sense.[2] Instead, they treat social

[1] An earlier version of this article was presented at the Theories of Political Sociology Conference at the CUNY-Graduate Center and NYU on May 25–27, 2000. We thank Frances Fox Piven, Jeffrey Goodwin, Mildred Schwartz, Alexander Hicks, and Robert Alford for helpful comments and the ASA/NSF "Fund for the Advancement of the Discipline" for financial support.

[2] Which does not mean that they do not recognize any long-term trends, Weber's secular process of rationalization being an obvious example.

and political conflict as an inevitable and permanent feature of social life. Nor do they recognize the primacy of class conflict. Instead they have either posited political power itself as the fundamental source of social cleavage and conflict or insisted on the multiplicity of sources of social conflict such as race, gender, ethnicity, religion, language, age, and so on, in addition to economic interests, arguing that each of these can produce groups that compete and pursue different political ends, and in so doing, dominate or subordinate their competitors. Some cultural, feminist, and racial theories would fit under this rubric as well but their practitioners often reject the label of conflict theory because of its materialist connotations (see Chapters 4, 5, 6, and 9 of this handbook for these theories).

Today, some three decades after it was first introduced as such, there is no longer much talk about conflict theory as a distinctive approach. This does not mean that it has disappeared. To the contrary, it may well be a sign of its success. In fact, the relatively precipitous decline of structural functionalism as a major approach has rendered the label *conflict theory* as a way to designate a new, alternative way of looking at the social world largely redundant. At the same time, the Marxist branch of conflict theory does seem to have lost much of its original appeal since its brief revival in the 1970s. In view of the apparent decline of much of the traditional, class-based left/right politics of the first half of the twentieth century, even in the old European heartland, and the related rise of various alternative forms of "identity" politics involving race, gender, religion, and ethnicity, Marxists have been under much pressure to rethink and reformulate their most basic assumptions.

In this chapter we first review the theoretical traditions based on class from Marx to the present day and then examine more general conflict theories that include status and other factors from Weber to Bourdieu. Finally, we attempt to draw some conclusions from this survey about the likely future trends and fate of conflict theory in political sociology.

CLASS CONFLICT THEORIES: FROM MARX TO HARDT AND NEGRI

Marxism, Leninism, and "Revisionism"

According to the Marxist canon, the state and politics belong to the social "superstructure" that "reflects" or is "determined by" the economic base, in particular the relations of production, that is, the class structure. Such a "reflection" *might* imply that the degree to which the working class and the bourgeoisie, as well as the intermediate strata, are able to exert effective influence on government varies, depending on the class struggle. Marx does sometimes appear to suggest this in his more "conjunctural" analyses (e.g. Marx, 1963, 1972) as well as in his unfailing support for prolabor legislation. On the whole, however, Marx and Engels clearly took a more categorical view as famously expressed in the *The Communist Manifesto*: "Political power, properly so called, is merely the organizing power of one class for suppressing another" (Marx, 1954:56) and "[t]he executive of the modern State is but a committee for managing the common affairs of the whole bourgeoisie" (1954:18).

Until the rise of liberal democracy and universal suffrage, this general position would seem to have been tenable enough. And in their comments on some of the cases where the suffrage was gradually extended during the second half of the nineteenth century, Marx and Engels made it clear that they did not think democracy and capitalism could coexist for long (van den Berg, 2003:77–95). But as working class parties grew more influential *without* provoking the expected cataclysm or swift transition to socialism, Marxists were forced to make a difficult choice: *either* accept that the reformist "parliamentary road" to socialism was to be considerably slower than anticipated *or* insist that parliamentary democracy was really just a cover for continued bourgeois rule.

The reformist position was first proposed by German labor leader Eduard Bernstein (1909) and only much later accepted by German Social Democratic leader Karl Kautsky (1971) and the other social democratic parties of Europe. But Lenin drew the opposite conclusion, namely that the

> democratic republic is the best possible political shell for capitalism, and . . . once capital has gained control . . . it establishes its power so securely, so firmly that *no* change, either of persons, or institutions, or parties in the bourgeois republic can shake it. (Lenin, 1932:14)[3]

In the end, Lenin's position became the undisputed Marxist orthodoxy, energetically enforced by his Third International. Effectively excommunicated from the community of "real" Marxists, reformism came to be seen as a decidedly non-Marxist view of politics and the state in modern capitalism.

The decisive factor in Lenin's thinking, at least since the 1903 split between the Mensheviks and Bolsheviks, was that "the working class, exclusively by its own effort" would never attain a level of class consciousness beyond reformism (Lenin, 1968:40). A succession of Western Marxist theorists have tried to account for this puzzling fact by reassessing the role of the bourgeois cultural realm as having a far more powerful effect in imposing "false consciousness" (Lukács, Korsch), "hegemony" (Gramsci, 1971) or "instrumental rationality" (Horkheimer, Adorno, the Frankfurt School) on the working class than the original base-superstructure model would have allowed (e.g., Anderson, 1976; Kolakowski, 1978). These more "culturalist" arguments would become particularly influential among neo-Marxist theorists from the 1960s and after, whose work we discuss in the next sections.

Marxist and *Marxisant* Theories of the State

With reformism discredited as un-Marxist, the rise of the welfare state, especially under social democratic auspices, posed a special problem for orthodox Marxists: how could such apparent concessions to the working class be made by a state exclusively serving the interests of the capitalists (cf. Alford and Friedland, 1985)? An immediate answer was simple: welfare state reforms have not only done little to advance the cause of socialism, they have actually been "an essential prophylactic against it" (Miliband, 1977:155), the "relatively low . . . price which the dominant classes knew they would have to pay . . . for the maintenance of the existing social order" (Miliband, 1969:100). But this immediately raises a much thornier question: given the apparently democratic institutions and the active participation of the largest working-class parties *through which* such reform has often been implemented, what is it that keeps reform from crossing the line between merely helping to maintain the system and actually *transforming* it? That is, how is reform kept within the limits of ultimate capitalist class interests? Most of the debate among Marxists about the true nature of the "capitalist state," which raged from the late 1960s to the early 1980s, revolved around alternative answers to this question.

One answer, most clearly formulated by Ralph Miliband (1969), was that the capitalist class in effect controlled government policy. Citing a mass of British empirical data on the social class origins and sociopolitical values of the top officials in all branches of government, the judiciary, as well as the educational system and the mass media and even religion, Miliband concludes that the British capitalist class has a firm grip on all levels of public power, as well as on the institutions of opinion formation and legitimation. As a result, Miliband argues, the capitalist class "exercises a *decisive* degree of power" (1969:45), enabling it to block any reform that seriously undermines its long-term interests. The state, in other words, is an instrument of capitalist power, whence the term *instrumentalism* for this particular Marxist theory of the state.

In a much subtler and detailed manner, G. William Domhoff has tried to demonstrate something similar for the United States, paying particularly close attention to some of the landmark legislation of the New Deal. Like Miliband, but in much more painstaking detail, Domhoff shows how members or

[3] For all quotations in this chapter, the emphasis is in the original.

representatives of America's corporate elite are heavily overrepresented in all major political institutions, lobbying organizations, boards of major universities, mass media, and major foundations. But in addition to this, Domhoff traces in detail the process that led to New Deal legislation, especially the 1933 Wagner Act, to show that at every step of the way the formulation of the problems as well as the solutions were decisively influenced by a network of policy and research organizations that was created and controlled by the most far-sighted as well as the most powerful among America's businessmen. Consequently, Domhoff claims, even the most apparently prolabor legislation in the United States was formulated and often advanced by powerful elements of the corporate class, a class that "is able to impose its policies and ideologies in opposition to the leaders of various strata of the non-propertied, wage-earning class" (Domhoff, 1979:16).

Domhoff's argument is often referred to as the "corporate liberalism" thesis, because it holds that the more moderate, far-sighted segment of the corporate business community usually prevails over its more conservative segments. Domhoff has continued to develop an impressive *oeuvre* to support that basic argument and it has generated an extensive secondary literature criticizing various aspects of his account of the genesis of New Deal policies.[4] Empirically, these critics have generally argued that Domhoff tended systematically to underestimate the role of social forces other than the most advanced wing of corporate business, in particular the influence of unions, politicians, and the state.

But whatever the merits of Domhoff's and his critics' detailed arguments about the determinants of the New Deal, he has helped spawn several research traditions empirically examining the extensive interlocks between major corporations and banks, the sources of effective political mobilization of American business interests and corporate funding of political campaigns, all with the more or less instrumentalist intention of documenting the degree to which well-organized business interests potentially exercise a disproportionate amount of influence on public policy making in the United States.[5] In a similar vein, the somewhat more complex "accommodationist" theory of Glasberg and Skidmore (1997:11–16) and Prechel's "contingency theory" (1990, 2003) examine class-based political mobilization and organization in response to perceived political threats and in interaction with politicians and bureaucrats in a dynamic process that modifies both.[6] Thus, in many ways Domhoff's approach, and several approaches like it, have remained a thriving research enterprise. Yet in the eyes of the more theoretically inclined Marxists of the 1970s and early 1980s, the instrumentalism Domhoff's theory shared with Miliband's rendered both decidedly beyond the Marxist pale.[7]

Using structuralist Marxism, Nicos Poulantzas (1967, 1972, 1973b, 1976) mounted a devastating critique of Miliband's (1972, 1973) instrumentalism. As a result of its "empirical and

[4] For Domhoff's own work see 1967, 1970, 1974, 1978, 1979, 1983, 1990, 1998, and 2001 for a summary. His most important critics include Quadagno (1984, 1985, 1996), Skocpol (1980), Skocpol and Amenta (1985), and Skocpol and Orloff (1986). For an extensive critique of Domhoff on both empirical and theoretical grounds, see van den Berg (2003:196–221).

[5] On corporate interlocks see Mintz and Schwartz (1985), Mizruchi (1989), Mizruchi and Koenig (1986), and Sklair (2001), on business mobilization Burris (1987, 1992, 2001). The campaign finance literature developed somewhat later (Clawson, Neustadtl, and Bearden, 1986; Clawson and Neustadtl, 1989; Clawson, Neustadtl, and Scott, 1992; Neustadtl, 1990; Neustadtl and Clawson, 1988).

[6] For further work in the accomodatonist tradition, see Akard (1992), Allen (1991), Allen and Broyles (1989), Brents (1992), Gilbert and Howe (1991), Glasberg (1989), Glasberg and Skidmore (1997), Hooks (1993), Jenkins and Brents (1989), McCammon (1994), Mizruchi (1989), and Prechel (1990, 1991, 2000, 2003).

[7] Domhoff does not consider himself to be a Marxist and he has vehemently rejected the now derisory label of *instrumentalist* (Domhoff, 1976). But for all practical purposes his theory *does* have quite a lot in common with mainstream Marxism and it *does* posit a (most powerful segment of the) capitalist class capable of decisively influencing government policy and consciously and, even more important, *accurately* doing so in the best long-term interests of the class as a whole. *This* is the essence of the instrumentalist position which subsequent, allegedly more sophisticated Marxist theorists were to treat with such contempt (see also Lo, 2002:200–2).

neo-positivist approach," involving a wholly naïve "voluntarism" and "subjectivism," Miliband's argument was, according to Poulantzas, "unconsciously and surreptitiously contaminated by the very epistemological principles of the adversary" (1972:241–2, 1976:67). As a result, Miliband was unable to demonstrate the structural necessity of the coincidence between capitalist state policy and the long-term interests of the capitalist class, *whoever* happens to favor or oppose that policy. Theoretically, Miliband's approach treats the state as a neutral instrument that, hence, could in principle be captured and wielded by *real* anticapitalist forces to undermine capitalism, which comes perilously close to the "revisionism" of Bernstein, Kautsky, and their social democratic heirs. Empirically, he is unable to account for the many kinds of social reform that, though often promoted as radical by labor governments and sometimes vehemently opposed by all or most major fractions of the bourgeoisie, invariably end up *strengthening* the capitalist mode of production rather than undermining it, including welfare state policies, social security, legal protection for unions, and so on. In fact, his approach assumes a degree of omnipotence, omniscience, and unity of the capitalist class that is far beyond its ability.

Basing himself on Althusser's (1969) "structuralism," Poulantzas formulated a rigorously "scientific" Marxist theory of the capitalist state that conceptualizes it as a "relatively autonomous instance" and in modern capitalism as the "dominant" instance as well. According to this

> . . . scientific Marxist conception of the state superstructure . . . the state has the particular function of constituting the factor of cohesion between the levels of a social formation . . . and . . . the regulating factor of its global equilibrium as a system. (Poulantzas, 1973a:44–5)

Although this function serves the long-term interests of the capitalist class, the state can effectively perform only it if it enjoys a considerable degree of "relative autonomy" from that class that is ordinarily far too divided and fragmented to realize or agree on its own long-term interests by itself (1973a:284–5). Instead of treating the state as the willing instrument of the capitalist class, this means that:

> the capitalist State best serves the interests of the capitalist class only when the members of this class do not participate directly in the State apparatus, that is to say when the *ruling class* is not the *politically governing class* . . . this State can only truly serve the ruling class in so far as it is relatively autonomous from the diverse fractions of this class, precisely in order to be able to organize the hegemony of the whole of this class. (1972:246–7)

Thus, the objective function of the state apparatus to serve the interests of the dominant classes has nothing to do with the class origins of its personnel or external pressures from the members of those classes. It is entirely determined by the state's "relation to the structures" (1973a:115). Paradoxically, the political actions of the dominated classes actually help the state in achieving its objective function, allowing it to enforce decisions that are opposed by the dominant classes, too short-sighted to recognize their own long-term interests (1973a:285–9).

Claus Offe arrived at a very similar Marxist theory of the state by way of a system theoretic analysis of "late capitalism." Treating capitalist society as a configuration of interconnected subsystems with their own internal "organizational principles," Offe argues that the state is a necessary "flanking subsystem" (1976:33–5) whose function consists of counteracting the self-destructive tendencies of the dominant economic subsystem, while violating as little as possible the latter's organizational principle of commodity exchange. Thus, the long-term increase in state interventionism in the economy and the expansion of welfare state provisions and programs are efforts by the state to avoid or resolve crises and conflicts provoked by the process of private capitalist accumulation that might otherwise have threatened the very foundations of the capitalist system (Habermas, 1973:50–60; Offe, 1972a:21–5, 1972b; Offe and Ronge, 1975:141–3; van den Berg, 2003:29–31). They fulfill the legitimation function of retaining mass acquiescence, allowing the state to perform its functions favoring the long-term interests of the capitalist class (Offe, 1972b, 1972c:81). Consequently,

> [t]here is no need to equate the capitalist state, either empirically or theoretically with a political alliance of the personnel of the state apparatus on the one side and the class of owners of capital (or certain segments of this class) on the other side. For the abstract principle of making a subject of permanent market exchange relationships out of every citizen does more to keep state policies in tune with the class interests of the agents of accumulation than any supposed "conspiracy" between "overlapping directorates" of state and industry could possibly achieve. (Offe, 1975:251)

Thus, like Poulantzas, Offe claims that the capitalist state has paradoxically been able to gain the required autonomy from the bourgeoisie in the latter's own long-term interest only by utilizing the "formal structures of bourgeois democracy" (Offe, 1974:54).

But somewhat unlike Poulantzas, Offe emphasizes how state interventionism and social welfare policies can only *displace* the contradictions of capitalism, not resolve them. Although the working class may be pacified indefinitely in this way, other sections of society become increasingly "decommodified" and hence unwilling to continue to endorse the state's continuing support of private accumulation, eventually producing a new "legitimation crisis"(1972c:169–88; Habermas, 1973). Efforts to cut back on "excessive" legitimacy commitments (e.g., through social spending cuts and more reliance on repression) will not work because legitimation programs are not readily reversible: they cannot easily be cut back without the danger of "exploding conflict and anarchy" (Offe, 1984a:153, 288, 1984b:240, 1972a:96–102, 1974:4952, 1976:59).

James O'Connor (1973) proposed a very similar argument with respect to the contradictory accumulation and legitimation functions of the U.S. state. As the state's accumulation function forces it to get ever more deeply involved in supporting private monopoly capital, O'Connor argues, it is increasingly forced to conceal its complicity with capital by ever more generous "legitimation" programs. But ultimately this will lead to a "fiscal crisis" eventually culminating in "economic, social, and political crises" (1973:9), as the monopoly sector corporations and labor unions become increasingly reluctant to finance further increases in state expenditures out of their "rightful" share of the economic surplus (1973:7–10).

In any case, the "structuralist" and systems-theoretic criticisms made by Poulantzas, Offe, and others (Therborn, 1977, 1978:129–61; Laclau, 1975) swiftly relegated instrumentalism to "the prehistory of theoretical formalisation" (Laclau, 1975:96). After putting up minor resistance, even Miliband himself seems to have capitulated to the theoretical sophistication of his critics, now arguing, in a much-quoted passage, that Marx and Engels's formula about the state being "but a committee for managing the *common* affairs of the *whole* bourgeoisie" should be interpreted to mean that "the state acts *on behalf* of the dominant 'ruling' class" but not necessarily "*at the behest* of that class" (Miliband, 1973:85 n.4).

Thus "relative autonomy" was quickly established as the "new orthodoxy" (Krieger and Held, 1978:191) among right-thinking Marxists. Yet its effective reign was to be remarkably short. Questions soon arose as to what causal mechanisms, exactly, kept the capitalist state's autonomy *relative*, that is, in line with the long-term interests of the capitalist class, given that class's own inability to understand its own interests and the state's apparent dependence on working class support. Neither Offe nor Poulantzas ever offered anything but a few murky hints about "functional necessity" as an answer to this question. More serious, from a Marxist perspective, however, was the "implacable determinism" (Anderson, 1976:65) that characterized their functionalist approach, leaving no room whatsoever for conscious human agency and hence no "motive force for political action" at all (Appelbaum, 1979:26; Bridges, 1974; Burris, 1979; Esping-Andersen et al., 1976:188; Smith, 1984).

In his last major work, Poulantzas seems to have taken some of these criticisms to heart, now proclaiming, *ad nauseam* in fact, "the primacy of the class struggle over the apparatuses" (1978:38, 45, 53, 126, 149, 151) and conceding that "popular struggles traverse the State"

(1978:141) and even advocating a "democratic road to socialism" that preserves the institutions of "bourgeois" democracy, which were truly "a conquest of the masses" (1978:256). Offe, too, seems to have shifted toward a less functionalist position in his more recent work, now viewing "the state of democratic politics . . . as both determined by, and a potential determinant of social power" (Offe, 1984a:161).

These vague allusions sound somewhat like the "class struggle" or "class dialectic" approach that some Marxist writers have proposed in an effort to rehabilitate "historically dynamic class conflict as a motor of structural change" (Block, 1977; Bridges, 1974:178–80; Esping-Andersen et al., 1976:188; Whitt, 1979a). This approach views state power and government policy "as a complex, contradictory effect of class (and popular-democratic) struggles, mediated through and conditioned by the institutional system of the state" (Gold, Lo, and Wright, 1975a, 1975b; Jessop, 1977:370). That is to say, depending on the effectiveness of those "popular-democratic struggles," state policies may very well serve the interests of the working class rather than just those of the capitalist class. A number of attempts to assess the empirical validity of this "class struggle" approach have generally tended to confirm it (Devine, 1985; Gough, 1975, 1979; Isaac and Kelly, 1981; Quadagno, 1984; Skocpol, 1980; Whitt, 1979a, 1979b, 1982): the capitalist class is not always united and even when it is, it does not always get its way.

But this comes uncomfortably close to the old "revisionist" and "reformist" heresies, of course.[8] Although the proponents of the "class struggle" approach have been loathe to draw this conclusion, the fact remains that post–War Marxist state theory seems to have come around full circle, from instrumentalism to fierce structuralist rejections of *any* reformism, back to a version of the formerly excommunicated revisionism. A second irony worth noting is that although instrumentalists like Domhoff and Miliband may have ingloriously lost the battle of "high theory," in retrospect they appear to have won the war. Although the arguments of their structuralist critics are at most of antiquarian interest by now, there is a rich and continuing research tradition following Domhoff's lead. Moreover, whatever the specifics of his account of the New Deal, his *general* point, that U.S. business interests have far more clout at virtually all levels of policy making than any other real or potential interests, and certainly a great deal more than they were assumed to have in the more complacent versions of 1950s neopluralism, has become a commonplace in this much more cynical age, among the wider public as much as among the erstwhile advocates of neopluralism themselves (e.g., Dahl, 1989, 1990).

Power Resources Theory

The return toward the once-taboo reformism is quite explicit in so-called power resources theory, a.k.a. social democratic or working class strength theory (Korpi, 1983, 1989:312; Korpi and Shalev, 1980; Shalev, 1983, 1992). Korpi starts from the classical Marxist position that capitalist markets create enormous inequalities in access to resources and power, producing a fundamental conflict of interest between the most and the least favored, and capitalists and workers (e.g. Korpi, 1983:227). But although the members of the capitalist class enjoy a great advantage in terms of economic resources, workers have access to some resources of their own, which can be employed in the democratic political arena. Although " . . . wage earners are generally at a disadvantage with respect to power resources . . . through their capacity for collective action, the extent of their disadvantage can vary over time as well as between countries" (Korpi, 1985a:41). The wage earners' "capacity for collective action" depends on a host of factors, including the degree of homogeneity of their working and living conditions, the degree of mobilization and coordination of labor unions and political parties, the lessons learnt from previous conflicts, the institutional setting, and so on. Such factors will determine

[8] This has not been lost on the authors who seek some support for a reformist position in the recent Marxist literature. Both Korpi (1983:19, 245 fn. 20) and Stephens (1979:215, fn. 5) invoke Esping-Andersen et al. (1976) as evidence for the Marxist pedigree of their own approaches.

the strength of working-class organizations relative to those representing the interests of capital, which will, in turn, help determine government policies, particularly those that affect the distribution of economic resources between the social classes.

Thus, the basic power resources approach starts from a classic two-class model to explain political outcomes. The workers and the bourgeoisie mobilize through trade unions and employer associations that may become the bases for left, right, and even centrist political parties. These parties then channel conflicting class interests through the state, bureaucracy, and courts as a result of elections, legislation, and executive decisions. Hence, patterns of change in social welfare legislation can be explained from the relative strength of the two class groups. As labor gains in class strength by the mobilization of resources through trade unions and supporting social democratic parties, it wins greater say in funding and managing the welfare state. In this way the lower classes can use the welfare state for redistributive purposes to compensate to some extent for the unequal distribution by markets.

With this general theory, Korpi, Esping-Andersen, Shalev, and many others seek to explain how different "models of capitalism" – arrangements for the distribution of economic resources through the labor market and industrial relations (Coates, 2000; Crouch, 1997; Crouch et al., 1999) – have produced different political power alignments between labor and capital, which, in turn, generate different "welfare state regimes" that restructure income distributions and incentives through pensions, health care, education, and other state and sometimes private services. This is how power resource theorists explain the rise of the highly developed and redistributive Scandinavian welfare states and how Esping-Andersen explains the emergence the three regimes of welfare capitalism – liberal, traditional, and social democratic regimes (1990; Esping-Andersen and Korpi, 1987; Korpi, 1983; Stephens, 1979).

But the basic two-class model of power resources theory has been criticized for being too simplistic in several respects. Some critics claim that it has a simplified view of the state as nothing but a "transmission belt" for the class interests of various interest groups (Weir and Skocpol, 1985:117), others fault it for focusing too narrowly on the primary social classes and on material interests (Lister, 2002). Against such criticisms, Korpi in particular has recognized the importance of built-in arrangements in all societal institutions, including the state, that favor some interests at the expense of others and that reflect not only past conflicts and the current balance of societal power (Korpi, 1985a, 1985b) but also strategic interactions among politicians, bureaucrats, and interest-group leaders that make outcomes highly contingent. As a result, state officials may have "considerable freedom of choice" although their autonomy remains "circumscribed" by the broad mandate of their constituents (Korpi, 1989:314). Second, Korpi claims to take norms and ideology quite seriously. Ideology can be a method by which power resources based on coercion or remunerative power can be converted into normative incentives, and it is an important normative resource in mobilizing groups and overcoming the "free rider" problem (1985a:39). Nor does ideology necessarily always serve the interests of the most privileged. In the opposite direction, "contagion from the left" may lead to working-class demands being adopted by other political parties (Korpi, 1989:313, 1985a, 2003; Rogers, 1974). As for the narrow class focus, Korpi argues that "[t]he power resources approach does not . . . imply that social policy development is based on the organizational and political power of the working class and left parties alone," because in the Swedish case as elsewhere it emphasizes the importance of coalitions with "farmers' parties, conservative parties, and Catholic parties," among others (1989:313). In fact, Korpi insists, it offers a "game theoretical perspective on the analysis of interdependent actors" (1989:313). Similarly, Esping-Andersen emphasizes the importance of coalitions in Scandinavian social policy development (1985:36–7; Baldwin, 1990; Hicks, 2000; Van Kersbergen, 1996).

In practice, however, even where they explicitly mention bureaucrats and politicians, power resources theorists tend to subordinate their interests to those of the primary social classes, either capital or labor (e.g., Esping-Andersen, 1985:30, 1990; Korpi, 1985a:106; Stephens, 1979:65–8, 79, 131). But more recently, there have been several serious attempts to incorporate many aspects of state-centric theory – constitutional structures, state centralization, corporatism, and bureaucratic paternalism – into the power resources and related approaches (Hicks and Misra, 1993; Huber, Ragin, and Stephens, 1993). Most often they concentrate on constitutions, welfare state structures, and modes of deregulation (Korpi and Palme, 2003).

A number of scholars referring to themselves as "analytical Marxists" have attempted quite explicitly to provide Marxism with microfoundations based on rational choice theory (Carver and Thomas, 1995; Elster, 1982, 1985; Przeworski, 1985a; Roemer, 1986). Interestingly, with respect to political sociology this brings them very close to power resources theory when explaining the rise of working-class reformism and the welfare state (Lo, 2002:207–8). The starting point for analytical Marxism is the assumption that individual workers as well as their representatives in unions and labor parties will act according to what they perceive to be their best immediate interests, given the existing balance of power and the most likely actions and options of their political opponents. From this they argue that, in the absence of any clear revolutionary alternative, the labor movement has rationally opted for a reformist strategy that has subsequently produced welfare states offering a range of social security benefits and income redistributions, depending on the power of their respective labor movements (e.g., Przeworski, 1985b, 1991; Przeworski and Sprague, 1988; Wallerstein, 1999).

Beginning with Skocpol and Orloff (1986) and followed by Janoski (1990:9–36; 1998:148–65) and Hicks and Misra (1993), a basis was laid for combining a multigroup approach to power resources and state-centric theory. Rueschemeyer et al. (1992) and Huber and Stephens (2001) propose a power constellation theory that also addresses more diverse groups. This approach stays centered on the importance of class groupings in trade unions and political parties, and even reinforces a sort of mode of production argument with their recent emphasis on production regimes. But they add gender and racial groups combining them into so-called constellations of power (Huber and Stephens, 2001:17–20, 23). Huber and Stephens agree with the state-centric critics in seeing state structures as potential veto points defined by constitutions, and in the importance of policy legacies, which can easily be interpreted as the results of previous battles over power resources. But they remain "quite skeptical" (2001:21) of state bureaucrats significantly affecting policy because they appear to have no obvious interests of their own with respect to policy, and more importantly, the power resources of parties and interest groups "profoundly limit the range of policies that bureaucrats are able to suggest" (2001:21). Thus, in this broadened power resources approach, the *pressure* for change may still come from societal groups and particularly labor and capital, but state structures in the legislature via the constitution, and policy legacies in the bureaucracy can *channel* that pressure to varying degrees (Janoski, 1998:143–4). Although this may not satisfy state-centric theorists, it constitutes a significant extension of the original power resources model.

Paul Pierson, in the "new politics" approach, maintains that power resources theory is very useful in explaining the rise of the welfare state but not in accounting for the retrenchment process (1994, 2001). However, Korpi points out that groups other than labor and capital – pensioners, health care consumers, and the disabled – are the "new client groups of benefit recipients generated by welfare states themselves" who play a more prominent role in resisting government cutbacks (2003:591). This is, of course, perfectly compatible with the wider power resources theory just outlined. Korpi and Palme use this to further demonstrate that class factors, state structures, and citizenship variables explain retrenchment in eighteen countries (2003:426–42).

Thus, some power resources theorists have begun at least to acknowledge the importance of other causal factors such as the state, culture, and nonclass group interests. There certainly is nothing in principle to preclude a general power resources theory from being extended in these directions.[9] At the same time, when this is seriously attempted, that is, when current state structures are seen not only as the results of struggles for power in the past but are also treated as effective causal forces in the present, and when status groups such as blacks, women, gays, and ethnic minorities are treated as groups capable of accumulating and wielding power resources on a par with labor and capital, then the theory does tend to take on an uncanny resemblance to the neo-Weberian conflict theories discussed under "Class, Status, and Symbolic Conflict: From Weber to Bourdieu."

Critical and Emancipatory Theory

In the 1920s and 1930s a group of neo-Hegelian Marxists known as the "Frankfurt School" began to formulate a "Critical Theory" to analyze how the working class's "false consciousness" was the result of the triumph of "instrumental reason" over "substantive reason." Max Horkheimer, Theodor Adorno, Herbert Marcuse, and others loosely associated with their original institute in Frankfurt saw as their principal task the search for new social and philosophical sources of true reason with which to counter the manifest unreason of modern capitalism (Jay, 1973).

Jürgen Habermas is the leading exponent of the second generation of critical theorists. Like his erstwhile mentors Habermas has spent an intellectual lifetime searching for an effective philosophical and social antidote to the relentless march of "instrumental rationality" characterizing modern capitalism and its bureaucratized states. Most of Habermas' work has been concerned with establishing the *philosophical* grounds for a critical, emancipatory practice resisting the spread of instrumental rationality. These grounds ultimately rest on the "central intuition" (Dews, 1986:99; Honneth et al., 1981:9) that the "ideal speech situation," a situation that "excludes all force . . . except the force of the better argument" (Habermas, 1984:25) is in some way "the inherent *telos* of human speech" (Habermas, 1984:287).

It is only in *The Theory of Communicative Action* (1984, 1987) that Habermas finally clearly attempts to identify the potential *social* carriers of critical emancipatory, communicative reason who will form the progressive forces in the central social conflicts of the near future. In it, Habermas proposes a "two-level" theory of modern society pitting the Schutzean "lifeworld" of culture, social norms, and personal identities against the anonymous commercial and bureaucratic "systems" of modern capitalist society. The principle of organization of the lifeworld, Habermas maintains, is interpersonal communication that ultimately rests on the ideal of an "ideal speech situation" among free and equal participants. Although this ideal speech situation must always remain an unattained ideal, Habermas claims, there is nevertheless a historical tendency for the lifeworld in modern societies to become *more and more* "rationalized," that is, more closely approaching an "ideal speech situation," relying more and more on "*discursive will-formation*" rather than the automatisms of received tradition (Habermas, 1987:147).

At the same time, large domains of modern society, and in particular the economy and the legal-political system, have become so complex that they can only be effectively steered by mechanisms that do not appeal directly to actors' intentions and orientations. These systems of purposive-rational action are instead increasingly coordinated by the generalized "delinguistified steering media" of money and power (Habermas, 1984:341–2). But although this "uncoupling" of system from lifeworld is a necessary part of the overall process of rationalization, according to Habermas, the process is "contradictory from the start" (Habermas, 1984:342), with the two antithetical principles of coordination clashing as the subsystems of purposive-rational action tend inexorably to

[9] In some ways, the European ties of power resources theorists in countries with strong labor movements seemed to blind them to making these developments. Just as new social movements seem new to countries long dominated by class, other countries with a history of ethnic and/or racial conflicts do not see them as all that new.

expand their reach beyond their original domains. As a result, there is the growing danger of a "colonization of the lifeworld" by the subsystems of purposive-rational action, as manifested in persistent tendencies toward state regulation on the basis of administrative rationality as well as the commercialization of the lifeworld (Habermas, 1987:153–97, 301–31).

Clearly the working class and its organizations are in no position to resist this colonization as they are themselves hopelessly implicated in the ongoing processes of bureaucratization and monetarization. But there are, according to Habermas, a number of significant sociopolitical movements that have recently emerged, including feminism, the Greens, peace movements, human rights activists, ethnic and geographically based movements, and youth and "alternative" movements, which are both products and proponents of the communicatively rational discourse increasingly shaping the lifeworld. These so-called new social movements, Habermas expects, will take up the banner of the embattled "lifeworld" and the struggle against the encroachments of monetary and bureaucratic principles of organization (Habermas, 1981, 1986, 1987:391–6).

Thus, Habermas predicts the outbreak of a new set of central social conflicts in the advanced capitalist countries based on the fundamental tensions, the contradiction in fact, between the expansion of ever more encompassing systems of impersonal organization in politics and economy and the increasingly democratized lifeworld of cultural identity and social action. This accounts for the rise and recent prominence of those much-discussed new social movements that seem to be based more on matters of identity and principle than on their members' immediate interests. It may be a far cry from the erstwhile certainties of classical mode-of-production Marxism, but it does, quite unlike the neo-Weberian conflict theories, predict the predominance of one particular kind of social conflict over others and provide the not inconsiderable comfort of identifying the progressive forces in the battles to come.

A third generation of critical theorists has emerged but most of its work is in the philosophical realm and its sociological implications remain underdeveloped. John Keane has extensively written about the potential for resistance against the dominant ideology in civil society (Keane, 1987a, 1988a, 1988b, 1991, 1998; Arato and Cohen, 1984). Axel Honneth attempts a pluralization of the left beyond economic domination and sees the civil sphere as a location for "practical-critical activity" (Honneth, 1991:19–31) and the development of a "moral logic of social conflicts" using Hegel and Mead (Honneth, 1996:160–79). Seyla Benhabib (2001, 2002) attempts to formulate a communicative ethics with much more of a gender and racial emphasis. But very much in keeping with the earlier Frankfurt School tradition, all of these writers are much concerned with finding the philosophical and moral principles on which to build a critical stance, although some attempts have been made, inspired by Habermas and his followers, to promote deliberation in the public sphere at a much more practical level (Fung, 2003; Fung and Wright, 2003; Sargeant and Janoski, 2001).

In a somewhat similar vein, Ernesto Laclau and Chantal Mouffe (1985) have attempted to combine Marxism and postmodernism into something they call "postmarxism." Taking Gramsci's emphasis on political activity as the basis of hegemony to its logical extreme, they categorically deny that *any* social agent takes a privileged position within the emancipatory struggle: "in certain instances it may very well be that ecological, feminist or gay/lesbian liberation movements constitute the most radical forms of hegemonic struggle against an existing set of power structures" (Daly, 1999:71). The task of the political left, according to Laclau and Mouffe, is to radicalize plural democracy by exploiting the tensions created by the contradiction, inherent in liberal democracy, between the individualist and libertarian aspects of unrestricted rights and the cooperative and norm-building nature of a democratic community (Mouffe, 1992a, 1993a; Rosenau, 1992:14–17; Torfing, 1999:245, 249–52). Such "agonistic pluralism" (Mouffe, 1999) will have a radical democratizing effect, transforming citizens from passive bearers of rights into active constructors of associations creating and exercising further rights. It will lead to entirely new relations between citizens and the state, between the private and the public sphere, and so on. But because no kind of struggle is a priori privileged over, or more fundamental than any other, there also cannot be any future socialism in which the most fundamental conflicts are resolved once and for all. Therefore, the struggle for liberty and equality will continue forever, being taken up by a succession of different social agents forging their hegemonic projects *ad infinitum*. In short, Laclau and Mouffe end up redefining the socialist project as a never-ending "radicalization of democracy; that is, as the articulation of struggles against different forms of subordination – class, gender, race, as well as those others opposed by ecological, anti-nuclear, and anti-institutional movements" (Laclau and Mouffe, 1985:ix).[10]

World Systems and Globalization Theories

The main point of world systems theory is to shift our focus from social cleavages within to those between states and nations. The major cleavage is that between the core country or countries dominating the capitalist world system and the peripheral and semiperipheral countries dominated and exploited by them through an international division of labor characterized by "unequal exchange." Immanuel Wallerstein's work (1974, 1980, 1989) has focused on distinct periods in world history applying the up and down trends of Kondratieff cycles to help explain changes in the world economic and political order. Many others, including Christopher Chase-Dunn (1983) and Terry Boswell and Albert Bergesen (1987), have contributed to this literature. Daniel Chirot (1986) and others have provided a non-Marxist alternative to world systems theory.

Many of the debates in and about world systems theory have focused on whether and to what extent exploitation of the periphery is necessary for core country prosperity and dominance, and on the nature, length, and relations between the various economic and political cycles of the capitalist world system (Hall, 2002). But political power, and its intimate connection with powerful economic interests, plays a central role in the dynamics of world systems. In turn, political outcomes within as well as between countries are explained by world system theorists as the outcome of the struggle for domination and resistance within the world system. Thus, the emergence of strong, formally democratic, somewhat redistributive states depending heavily on popular legitimacy in the core countries, as well as the rise and persistence of weak, corrupt, and often brutally coercive comprador states in the periphery are explained by, but also help explain, the respective countries' position within the overall world system.

As with other approaches with Marxist roots, world systems theory has been criticized for paying insufficient attention to nonclass groups and issues such as gender, race, and ethnicity (Dunaway, 2001; Misra, 2000; Ward, 1993). But here as elsewhere proponents claim to have made amends in this regard in recent years (e.g., Hall, 2003).[11]

[10] Although recognizing that all programs are a partial hegemony, Mouffe specifies that the new leftist project opposes complexity, bureaucracy, and massified life and pursues a form of associational democracy (Hirst, 1988, 1994; Cohen, 1995). This associational socialism would include (1) cooperatively owned and democratically managed economic units, (2) challenges to hierarchies and inequalities, and (3) decentralized, democratic governance. The state would be transformed in a reflexive manner to ensure equity and balance between associations and protect the rights of individuals and associations. Representative democracy would continue but be transformed by deliberative democracy and the socialism pursued by the left would be forever "becoming" in a truly pluralist society (Hirst, 1994).

[11] There are some interesting parallels between world systems theory and some critical versions of globalization theory that stress the combination of powerful multinational corporations, U.S. political and military might, and Western or U.S. culture imposing a new world order benefitting primarily the advanced West while dominating and exploiting the rest of the world (Robertson, 1992, 1995; Roudometof, 1995; Sanderson, 1995). But world systems theorists generally see globalization as merely the latest wave of an age-old dynamic and tend to dismiss overly excited globalization theories as lacking historical perspective (Hall, 2002:103–7).

Perhaps the most discussed attempt to refurbish Marxism by transferring the class struggle to the international arena is *Empire* (2000) by Michael Hardt and Antonio Negri.[12] They seek to go beyond postmodern localism and poststructuralist pessimism to recapture Marxism's original promise of the eventual overthrow of capitalism. Their principal claim is that capitalism has, partly in response to the crises provoked by the various oppositional movements that emerged since the 1960s, transformed itself from an imperialism based on sovereign nation-states and Foucauldian disciplinary power to what they call *empire*, an entirely new stage characterized by deterritorialized global control through the internationalization of the capitalist market, the "informatization" of labor and a seamless web of interconnected economic, political, and cultural control mechanisms completely permeating the minds and bodies of the multitudes it brings under its sway across the globe, amounting to an entirely new form of power: "biopower."

This new system of control does not depend on the old binary categories and exclusions attacked by the postmodernists anymore, nor does it have any trouble accommodating and incorporating those local identities and differences that postmodernists and poststructuralists hold so dear, rendering them entirely harmless and even celebrating them. In this sense, Hardt and Negri argue, empire is actually a progressive force in that it effectively sweeps aside or neutralizes those narrowly parochial nationalisms and localisms in which postmodernists and postcolonialists see the sources of resistance (2000:138). It globalizes capitalism in a way not even imperialism could, creating a new, broader basis for anticapitalist struggle in the multitude, a much-expanded version of the former Marxist proletariat defined as "a broad category that includes all those whose labor is directly or indirectly exploited by and subjected to capitalist norms of production and reproduction" (Hardt and Negri, 2000:52).

[12] The journal *Rethinking Marxism* recently devoted an entire double issue, Fall/Winter 2001, to discussions of the book.

Hardt and Negri's reasons, though not always clear, for expecting the multitude to turn against capitalism are instructive, as they are a throwback of sorts to classical Marxism. The multitude, they argue, constitutes the "real productive force" (Hardt and Negri, 2000:62) in a labor process of unprecedented sociality. But this unprecedented socialization of the now-international labor process also gives the multitude unprecedented powers of resistance against the globalizing capital of empire. For however local the struggles may appear, they are immediately globalized in their effect and impact. Examples include, according to Hardt and Negri, such seemingly local struggles as the Palestinian Intifada, the rebellion in Chiapas, the race riots in Watts, and the student protests in Tiananmien Square. All these are united, they insist, by the fact that they "directly attack the global order of Empire and seek a real alternative" (Hardt and Negri, 2000:56–7). They represent the multitude's struggle for freedom from the control of Empire. Although this identifies a new, albeit rather fragmented and disparate worldwide social conflict with presumably far-reaching consequences, Hardt and Negri do not venture any clear predictions as to what the political outcomes are likely to be.

CLASS, STATUS, AND SYMBOLIC CONFLICT: FROM WEBER TO BOURDIEU

Weber's Multiple Conflict Theory

Of all the classical theorists, Weber was perhaps the one who took politics in all its forms most seriously. For Weber, politics was, first and foremost, an incessant struggle for power, the power to control or influence the collective actions of the community. In relatively organized communities such action takes place through, or is sanctioned by, a state, defined by Weber as "a human community that (successfully) claims the *monopoly of the legitimate use of physical force* within a given territory" (Weber, 1948:78, 1978:56). Weber distinguished three pure types of legitimate rule or domination, each with its own characteristic internal dynamic: rational-legal rule based on the belief in the legality of the process by which policies are enacted and authority is conferred; traditional rule resting on the belief in the "sanctity of immemorial traditions and the legitimacy of those exercising authority under them" (Weber, 1978:215); and charismatic rule, resting on the belief in the exceptional qualities of an individual political leader. Although Weber's emphasis on legitimacy points to the fact that political rule depends for its stability to some extent on its cultural justification, he was far from a consensus theorist. To the contrary, his detailed discussions of the various historical subtypes of legitimate rule all revolve around the perpetual struggles between rulers and ruled, and especially between rulers and their lieutentants and officials, yielding never-ending cycles of concentration and fragmentation, usurpation and legitimation (1978:Part I, chapter III; Bendix, 1960:285–468). In fact, Weber treated the underlying values, and the religious beliefs on which they were based, themselves as outcomes of struggles between a variety of groups with clashing ideal and material interests (1978:Part II, chapter VI; Bendix, 1960:83–281).

That Weber was, first and foremost, a conflict theorist, even when considering culture and politics, is quite clear from his well-known passage on "Class, Status, Party" (Weber, 1978:926–40). This passage was intended as a conceptual introductory statement on "The Distribution of Power Within the Political Community." In other words, Weber was trying to systematize the multiplicity of interests around which citizens can get mobilized to try and affect the distribution and use of political power in their own favor. Of course, the passage was also quite deliberately meant to counter the unidimensional Marxist idea that all major struggles were at bottom class struggles.

Weber certainly does not deny the importance of economic interest as a basis for mobilization and conflict throughout history. But he revises Marxist doctrine on two crucial points. First, he defines class position as determined by similarity of "market situation," that is, similarity in the extent to which one has access to valuable goods and services as determined by one's ability to trade one's assets on labor and commodity markets. This is a broader definition of class than the Marxist definition of (lack of) control over the means of production, which is only one kind of class in Weber's scheme. As Marxists have often pointed out, Weber's definition of class focuses on inequality of consumption opportunities, as opposed to the production side and its relations of "exploitation" (e.g., Wright, 2002).[13]

The second, and more important way in which Weber departs from Marx is that he argues that class, however defined, is neither the only nor even the historically most important basis for "communal action." Classes are not, according to Weber, natural communities. It takes a great deal of effort and favorable conditions for large numbers of people in comparable class situations to actually get mobilized as a class (Weber, 1978:928–32). Conversely, status groups, that is, groups of individuals who share positive or negative social estimation of honor based on some shared characteristic, "are normally groups" (1978:932). The characteristic in question may be "any quality shared by a plurality," including race, ethnicity, gender, religion, language, occupation, and so on (1978:932). Any one of these may be a source of status in a given community and, as such, a source of conflict and struggle for power. Status groups often involve a distinctive lifestyle as well as restrictions on interactions with "outsiders." Given that they are, almost by definition, already self-conscious groups, status groups are relatively easily mobilized and hence *at least* as likely to play an important role in the perennial struggle for power as classes are, according to Weber (1978:932–8). Moreover, status distinctions can cut across and even run counter to class distinctions in a variety of ways. At the

[13] This does not mean, however, that class inequalities are not a result of "domination" for Weber (Scott, 1996:188–92). But a critique of Weber for not having a theory of exploitation (e.g., Wright, 2002) largely misses the point. For Weber *exploitation* was a term of moral disapproval, not a social-scientific concept adding to our explanatory understanding of economic inequality and its correlates.

same time, Weber insisted that class and status (and, presumably, political power) do tend to reinforce one another in the long run. Although "[p]roperty as such is not always recognized as a status qualification . . . in the long run it is, and with extraordinary regularity" (1978:932).

The section on party is rather short, but it is clear that Weber had intended to treat it as a third major source of political organization, struggle, and domination. A party is any association aiming to influence "social action no matter what its content" (Weber, 1978:938). Thus, a party may represent primarily economic class interests or status groups or, more likely, a combination of both. But it may also fight for the realization of ideal interests or it may, for that matter, primarily serve to provide political office and benefits for its members (as in pure patronage parties) although "[u]sually the party aims at all these simultaneously" (1978:938).

Thus, Weber's approach is, if anything, even more unflinchingly a conflict theory than Marx's. For Weber, conflict is endemic in social and especially political life, and it has as many sources as there are types of life chances and social advantages that people can pursue. None of these sources or types of conflict has primacy over any of the other, either in the sense of being causally more fundamental or in the sense of having some special place in determining the grand sweep of history. Unlike either Marx or the neo-Machiavellians, Weber takes culture very seriously, both as a binding force and as a source of division and conflict. Unlike Marx, Weber takes politics very seriously as well and sees it, too, as the source of an inevitable and unending struggle for power in its own right as well as a means to satisfy other ideal and material interests.

Weber had a profound influence on a variety of social thinkers from Talcott Parsons to the Frankfurt School. Schumpeter's argument for democratic elitism and his dark predictions of the impending rise of a bureaucratized socialism, in particular, owed much to Weber's insights (Schumpeter, 1950). After WWII, with the rise of political sociology proper, much of the mainstream more or less naturally adopted a Weberian perspective, examining the difficulties in maintaining organizational democracy (Lipset, Trow, and Coleman, 1956), tracing the interactions between class and status group membership in determining political behavior and outcomes (Lipset, 1981) or working out the complex historical patterns of interaction among class, status group, and forms of political domination to account for the long-term rise of democracy and dictatorship (Moore, 1966).

Political Power Elite Theory

Other early critics of Marxism sought to replace the class struggle with the struggle for political power itself as the "motor force of history." These were the classical power elite theorists, Vilfredo Pareto, Gaetano Mosca, and Robert Michels, sometimes referred to as the neo-Machiavellians for their hard-nosed, even cynical, view of the world. The primary conflict in society was not one between classes struggling for control of the means of production but between elites and would-be elites struggling for control over the means of coercion. For every social endeavor, according to Pareto, there are those naturally endowed to excel and those who will not, and the former are the elite. The most important of these elites, the *governing elite*, is the one that controls government and politics. By virtue of its control of the means of coercion, it effectively dominates the rest of society as well. So the main line of social cleavage in all societies runs between the governing elite trying to hold on to power and aspiring counterelites trying to conquer it. To stay in power, the governing elite must use a judicious mix of physical force, religion, intelligence, and cunning. But this requires the presence of sufficient numbers of elite members with the appropriate talents (lions as well as foxes). Yet elites have a tendency to close themselves off to the talented offspring of nonelite members, which produces, over time, an imbalance between an increasingly decadent elite and a rising number of talented but frustrated subjects. In the absence of a proper circulation of elites ensuring the incorporation of new talent, then, those ruthless and talented enough will eventually stage a revolution to overthrow and replace the existing elite, starting the eternal cycle all over again (Pareto, 1963).

Thus, Pareto proposed a theory of revolution as well as a cyclical theory of political regimes and an argument about the essentially illusory character of all democracies, based on a simple set of assumptions about the random (biologically determined) distributions of various talents within any human population. Mosca's argument (1939) is similar, albeit less directly derived from biology. All societies are, according to Mosca, divided between a minority class that rules by virtue of its political power and a majority that is ruled by it. A successful ruling class will combine the use of force with a "political formula," that is, an ideology capable of uniting society under its leadership. Thus, parliamentary systems are merely a modern way of ensuring the stable command of the current ruling class.

Michels set out to examine the presumably most democratic of modern institutions, political parties, and especially those representing the working classes, to find the mechanisms by which such organizations manage to overcome this tendency toward the concentration of power. What he discovered, instead, was his "Iron Law of Oligarchy." Large-scale organization, no matter how democratic its official ideology, requires a division of labor between expert officials and rank-and-file members. This inexorably leads to oligarchic control by a small insider elite. "Who says organization says oligarchy" (Michels, 1962:365).

Thus, neo-Machiavellian theorists view the conflict between the rulers and the ruled, between those in control of the political system and those whom it controls, as the primary conflict in all societies (see also Lukes, 2001; McCormick, 2001). It tends to view the democratic pretensions of modern democracies with suspicion and treats the cultural realm as an appendage (Pareto's derivatives, Mosca's political formula) in the *real* struggle between rulers and ruled. It also appears to have been of limited use as an *explanatory* conflict approach in political sociology because it fundamentally takes political inequality for granted instead of seeking to explain it.

Early Postwar Conflict Theory – Dahrendorf

By combining elements from Marx and Weber, Ralf Dahrendorf (1959, 1968) formulated a conflict theory, explicitly in opposition to the structural-functionalist consensus theory, based on the inevitable inequality of authority. Complex societies, according to Dahrendorf, are populated by imperatively coordinated associations centered around major societal tasks, which can be political, economic, cultural, and so on. By definition, these associations are characterized by a division between those with authority and those without. This creates an inevitable conflict of interest within each such association between the dominant class, which has an interest in maintaining the status quo, and the subordinate class challenging that status quo. Thus, Dahrendorf claims to generalize Marx's two-class model beyond the sphere of production on the basis of the division of power characteristic of *all* forms of complex organization. But given the variety and multiplicity of imperatively coordinated associations there will also be any number of two-class systems and most invidividuals will occupy different class positions in different associations. The result is a proliferation of classes and class positions, many of them cross-cutting, having the effect of *preventing* any single, societywide class conflict from dominating all others, except under unusual conditions of coinciding multiple cleavages.

Hence, although organizational power-based conflict is ubiquitous and inevitable, according to Dahrendorf, it predicts no single or simple political outcomes. The latter depend on the distribution of resources between dominant and subordinate classes at any one time, which in turn depends on technology, the shape of organizations and institutions, overlapping class divisions, degree of mobilization and much else. But although Dahrendorf accepted the inevitability of conflict over political power as the neo-Machiavellians had done (see also Lenski, 1966), he did not share their jaundiced view of modern democracy and spent much time and energy arguing for various improvements and strengthening of the democratic process (1967, 1974, 1987, 1988, 1994).

General Neo-Weberian Conflict Theories – Collins and Turner

From at least the early 1970s, a number of 'left-Weberians' have attempted to resurrect a Weberian approach centered on group conflict, in explicit opposition to the Parsonian appropriation of Weber as a theorist emphasizing culture and consensus. They have argued that Marxian classes are only one among several sources of power and conflict and by no means necessarily the most important or the determinant ones, not even "in the last instance." Social exclusion and the monopolization of privilege occurs at least as frequently and effectively on the basis of status characteristics and political power.

Perhaps the most prominent, and certainly the most explicit, attempt to advance the conflict tradition is Randall Collins's *Conflict Sociology* (1975). Collins sets out to formulate a general neo-Weberian conflict theory that "may be applied to any empirical areas," based on the simple assumptions that:

> men [and women] live in self-constructed subjective worlds; that others pull many of the strings that control one's subjective experience; and that there are frequent conflicts over control. Life is basically a struggle for status in which no one can afford to be oblivious to the power of others around him [or her] [and] everyone uses what resources are available to have others aid him [or her] in putting on the best possible face under the circumstances. (1975:60)

Armed with this fairly rudimentary set of assumptions, Collins tackles a wide range of traditional sociological issues, from occupational, sex, and gender stratification to complex organizations, the distribution of wealth and social mobility, educational sociology, and even the sociology of knowledge and philosophy (1971, 1975, 1979, 1998). In each case, Collins tries to show how outcomes can be explained as the result of ongoing struggles between groups formed around shared experiences of privilege and exclusion, order giving and order taking, and attempting to improve the relative standing of their members. Such groups are neither necessarily class-based in the Marxian sense, nor exclusively based on organizational power as assumed by the neo-Machiavellians and their latter-day followers. In true neo-Weberian, multidimensional fashion, Collins seeks to explain the formation of specific conflicting groups as the result of shared experience, available resources and technology, networks of communication and cooperation, and so on. The result is a plethora of sometimes primarily culture-based, sometimes occupation or wealth-based, and sometimes organizational power-based groups jockeying for relative advantage.

Several things about Collins's general approach foreshadow more recent developments in conflict theory. First, as the emphasis on subjective experience already suggests, Collins is keenly sensitive to two aspects of the social stratification process that have generally escaped the close attention of the more macro-oriented theorists of stratification. The first is the importance of repeated face-to-face interaction as the ultimate microsociological foundation of the social stratification process (1975:chapter 3, 1988:188–228). The other is the recognition of culture as both the product of shared experiences of repeated unequal encounters and as a major source on the mobilization and realization of group interests (1990, 1998). Finally, Collins strongly emphasizes the importance of the nature and scope of communication and cooperation networks for social outcomes, ranging from the distribution of wealth to that of ideas (1975: chapter 8, 1998).

Although Collins himself has primarily applied his conflict approach to other matters, its implications for political outcomes and structures are nonetheless clear. Much of his analysis of credentialism, for example, is devoted to showing how public policy with respect to school curricula is the outcome of sometimes-fierce battles between groups representing different social strata trying to gain relative advantage for their members' children within the educational system (Collins, 1979). In keeping with the Weberian tradition, Collins treats politics as a form of overt or covert violence and defines the state as "the way in which violence is organized" (1975:351). Thus, the politics of premodern societies are, in Collins's view, primarily determined by the technology of violence and administrative coercion, which in turn depend in large part on economic resources.

At the same time, coercion alone always meets resistance and requires a legitimating ideology, usually in the form of a state religion, at least to keep those doing the coercing solidary and those being coerced passive. The larger the empire, the more universalistic such religions have to be to maintain a semblance of legitimacy and cohesion over and among increasingly diverse populations and administrators. Collins treats the politics of modern bureaucratized states in entirely Weberian terms as well, with an ever-changing array of mobilized representatives of classes, status groups, and parties seeking to enlist the state's coercive powers to serve their constituents' interests. Democracy is, according to Collins, not the rule of the people resulting from inevitable historical progress but a relatively more inclusive form of coercive rule by mobilized interests necessitated by conditions of relatively even distributions of coercive and administrative resources among separate but interdependent mobilized groups. Thus politics are and remain a matter of continuous conflict and struggle between groups more or less mobilized around varied material, coercive and cultural interests that are neither reducible to any one "master cleavage" nor ultimately resolvable (Collins, 1975: chapter 7).[14]

By contrast, Bryan Turner's analyses of the politics of citizenship can be seen as an application of this kind of neo-Weberian conflict theory (1981, 1986a, 1986b, 1990, 1992, 1993a, 1993b; also Janoski, 1990, 1998). Turner describes the battles among a variety of excluding groups pursuing "personhood" – the initial right to be considered a citizen and thus be a member of the society and nation in question. These groups may get mobilized along class lines, through trade unions and employers, left and right parties, and other organizations representing workers and the intelligensia or as status groups, such as ethnic/racial groups, women, religious groups, and so on (Turner, 1988:42–64). Interest groups and organizations representing these emerging citizens may be strengthened or weakened by economic, demographic, ideological, or international developments. Generally, in the battles for citizenship, status groups tend to cut across classes rather than coincide with them (Parkin, 1982:98–9), rendering the politics more fragmented than it would otherwise be. As a result, the criss-crossing of different types of groups and interest representation produces many types of social policy outcomes. This is then embedded within the larger conflict of capitalism and its markets versus citizenship and its rights (Janoski, 1998:147–64).

Mann's Integration of Ideological, Economic, Military, and Political Power

By far the most ambitious, as well as *politically* sociological exponent of the neo-Weberian current is Michael Mann's attempt to recast the entire "history of social power" (Mann, 1986, 1994) in terms of a neo-Weberian conceptual scheme. As his fellow neo-Weberians, Mann is concerned to show that control over economic resources is only one source of social power among several, none of which are always or entirely reducible to or based on the others. But Mann introduces several major conceptual innovations that make his approach distinctive. First, he replaces the traditional Weberian triad of stratification dimensions – class, status, and power – with four mutually irreducible kinds of social power: economic power based on control over material resources, ideological power based on the need for meaning, military power based on physical coercion, and political power based on more or less centralized territorial administration (1986:chapter 1). This yields the so-called IEMP model of social power. In other words, by splitting the traditional Weberian dimension

[14] Collins's approach has much in common with Parkin's (1980) theory of social closure, implying a perpetual and many-sided group struggle for access to, and exclusion from, any number of valued resources and opportunities. Raymond Murphy (1988) has attempted to combine and refine Collins's and Parkin's arguments (see also Janoski, 1998:235–6).

of political power into two, one based on physical coercion and the other on administrative control, Mann explicitly rejects the tight Weberian connection between statehood and the monopoly of the means of physical coercion. To the contrary, Mann argues, administrative and military control historically rarely overlap completely and their conceptual separation allows for the analysis and recognition of a much greater variety of political forms beyond the European state (1986:25–8).

Mann's treatment of ideology as a source of social power similarly elaborates and refines the traditional Weberian approach. Although that approach treats status as an important source of stratification and conflict, and pays some attention to the importance of ideas, especially religion, as a basis for and resource in such conflicts, it does not explicitly conceptualize the important difference between *transcendent* ideologies that are able to appeal across, and somewhat independently *of*, other sources of power and *immanent* ideologies that mainly serve to sustain the morale of existing groups or organizations. For Mann, this distinction enables us much better to understand why certain religious currents, in particular the great world religions, were and are able to appeal widely across class and political boundaries and thus able to provide the basis for quite independent and powerful networks of ideological power, whereas others are primarily effective as symbolic sources of narrower group cohesion and mobilization.

Third, Mann conceives of social power, much like Collins, as a matter of the active organization of social networks of varying reach and sophistication that are built to acquire and harness, to cultivate and monopolize, the various sources of power to the benefit of their members. Such networks can be *extensive*, that is, far-flung but relatively superficial in their effects, or *intensive*, capable of commanding high concentrations of commitment and mobilization. Also, these networks are not neatly bounded entities but more like disorderly bundles of interactions of various reach and strength that are rather frayed at the edges. As a result, Mann argues, it is misleading to think of societies as neatly bounded unitary entities (1986:9). Instead, they are bundles of several intertwined, partially overlapping, power networks that have highly variable connections beyond the society's supposed boundaries, which are themselves continuously shifting and being contested.

With this expanded, but still rather spare, Weberian toolkit, Mann recasts the history of social power from the dawn of time to the present. In this way, he eventually hopes to discover historical patterns and regularities that may yield some empirically grounded higher-level generalizations. His account emphasizes how different power networks are entangled in a continuous and remarkably "promiscuous" process of interaction and intertwining, as they are constantly being mixed and matched in various combinations, never wholly independent of one another, yet never entirely reducible to one another either. Periodically, the process crystallizes into recognizable, durable social structures in which one of the distinct sources of power tends to dominate. But Mann insists again and again that such dominance is historically contingent and that no source of power ever has ultimate determining primacy.

Mann's massive reconsideration of the major turning points in history has produced an array of novel, and thus inevitably controversial, interpretations and generalizations. He argues, for instance, that sociogeographic "caging" of subject populations by a well-organized minority is perhaps the most important factor accounting for the rise of early stratification systems generating the first major civilizations. Similarly, the caging of populations into increasingly tightly administered nation-states in the early modern era, ultimately produced demands for democracy as they were the only option of improvement left open. Another intriguing notion Mann has gleaned from his inductive study of major historical turning points is the "interstitial emergence" of new power networks (1986:15–19, 537–8). Such networks tend to arise in the interstices or pores – the empty spaces left by the incomplete institutionalization and disorderly interaction – of existing power networks. This was the case with the rise of Christianity, as it was, in a quite different setting, with the emergence of modern capitalism.

The second volume of *Sources of Social Power* (1994) uses his framework to address the modern period from 1760 to 1914. Against much conventional wisdom, Mann tends to downplay the role of capitalism and industrialism and to emphasize instead the early modern "revolution" in military organization and technology as the key to the rise of the modern, strong administrative state. He then proceeds to depict both class politics and nationalism as in large part the product of the creation of a national political arena by the revenue-extracting infrastructure-building modern nation-state. The same historical dynamic helps to explain the later mobilization of a plethora of social movements, representing gender, ethnic, sexual, environmental, religious, and many other interests. In a similar vein, Mann insists that the degree to which globalization is a new phenomenon and is likely to weaken the powers and sovereignty of the modern state is much exaggerated (Mann, 1997, 2001).

Although these middle-level generalizations are certainly fascinating, Mann has not, thus far, arrived at the kind of cross-temporal and cross-cultural generalizations that might constitute a coherent, general theory of inequality or social evolution. Instead, he has concentrated on issues specific to the twentieth century that he could not deal with in earlier volumes (Mann, 1999, 2000). This is, perhaps, not entirely surprising. Much of Mann's work is intended, in true Weberian form, to show how much more multicausal and complex the forces that drive history really are than any a priori grand theoretical synthesis, including Marxism (cf. Anderson, 1974), could ever do justice to. But this basic intent, which is virtually built into Mann's conceptual scheme, tends, for this very reason, to militate against sweeping, cross-epochal generalizations. It remains to be seen, then, whether Mann's approach is capable of delivering the empirically grounded theoretical payoff he aspires to or whether it will remain a monumental and Weberian testimonial to the sheer complexity of the social and political world.

Bourdieu's Field Theory

The late Pierre Bourdieu may well be the most influential of the contemporary neo-Weberian conflict theorists. Although often mistaken for a neo-Marxist (e.g., Alexander, 1995; Jenkins, 1992), particularly for his liberal use of concepts such as *capital, class struggle, domination,* and so on, and his obvious delight in exposing the meritocratic pretensions of elites, Bourdieu's approach is clearly much closer to that of Collins, Parkin, and Turner than it is to any version of (neo-)Marxism. Bourdieu himself did not accept either label, maintaining that his approach transcended all simple classifications and dichotomies.

For Bourdieu, the social world can be viewed as a series of partially overlapping but relatively autonomous domains that are in effect battlefields in which individuals and groups compete for social advantage. Each of these social fields has its own type of reward or distinction, its own rules of engagement, and its own dominant class or elite. The nature of the reward as well as the rules governing the process of its acquisition are themselves subject to struggle as well. The struggle is fought through the deployment and conversion of various forms of *capital,* a term Bourdieu uses in a peculiarly broad sense: there is *social capital,* otherwise known as reputation and social connections, *cultural capital* or cultural/educational advantage, *symbolic capital* or legitimation, as well as *economic and political capital.* In short, Bourdieu uses the term *capital* to designate whatever advantage people struggle for in any particular field to emphasize its uses as both a resource in a struggle and the final prize *of* the struggle. Much of Bourdieu's work is a series of applications of this field theory to a variety of social fields, particularly cultural ones such as the educational system (Bourdieu and Passeron, 1971), aesthetics and the arts (Bourdieu, 1984, 1996), and academia and language (Bourdieu, 1988, 1991) but also the upper strata of the French civil service (Bourdieu, 1996).

At the center of Bourdieu's empirical work is the claim that elites are able to reproduce themselves, that is, pass on their privileges to their offspring, even in the apparently most meritocratic social fields, by converting one kind of capital (e.g., social capital) into another (cultural capital, credentials). They reproduce their own because they can manipulate the very criteria for what counts as worthy in a particular field, such as education or high-brow art, in such a way as to favor their own and their children's tastes and predispositions. Except for the terminology of field and capital, this theory of seemingly meritocratic class reproduction is virtually identical to Collins' theory of credentialism.

Given his preoccupation with social domination, it is perhaps surprising that Bourdeu paid relatively little attention to the fields of politics and to political power, as compared to his studies of various cultural domains. But, very much like his predecessors since at least Althusser (1971), Bourdieu has a typically French preoccupation with how power and domination are "reproduced" symbolically. Arguably most of Bourdieu's work is devoted to showing how dominant classes are able to manipulate symbols, values, knowledge, and tastes so as to uphold their own continued domination by making them appear objectively valid, natural, universalistic, and meritocratic. Thus, his major work on France's civil service elite deals primarily with the way this elite reproduces itself through highly selective elite schools and claims of superiority of character and expertise that appear to be entirely universalistic and meritocratic. Similarly, in one of his rare forays into the field of politics and the state, Bourdieu actually focuses mostly on how the state successfully claims the monopoly of "symbolic violence" by imposing the distinctions, categories, and divisions that come to be accepted as natural by the citizenry and that thereby help produce the "doxic submission to the established order" (1994:15) that legitimates and upholds the state.

The one essay in which Bourdieu proposes some "elements for a theory of the political field" (Bourdieu, 1991:chapter 8) deals primarily with the professionalization of politics and the resulting problems of accountable political representation, particularly by politicians and parties of the left claiming to represent those most deprived of economic and cultural capital. The political disenfranchisement of the underprivileged is also a major theme in Bourdieu's analyses of political polling, which provides, according to his accusations, "scientific" legitimation for political powerlessness (Bourdieu, 1984:Chapter 8, 1990b: chapter 12). As elsewhere, Bourdieu seems primarily interested in deflating the pretensions of the various experts, bureaucrats and professional politicians who dominate the political field. He does at one point describe "[t]he state [as] the *culmination of a process of concentration of different species of capital*: capital of physical force or instruments of coercion (army, police), economic capital, cultural or (better) informational capital, and symbolic capital," all of which leads "to the *emergence* of a specific, properly statist capital" (Bourdieu, 1994:4). But he never carries out the analysis of the effects of the struggles over these various other kinds of capital on "statist capital." The only clear instance where he examines the effect of the social and economic realms on the political is where he briefly explains political propensities by the cross-pressures of economic capital (read: class) and cultural capital (read: status/lifestyle), which is, of course, standard Weberian fare (Bourdieu, 1998, 1984:451–3).

Conversely, as a major public figure in France, Bourdieu did devote an increasing amount of his energy in his later years to political interventions on behalf of those he saw as most disadvantaged. The *Weight of the World* (Bourdieu et al., 1999) is primarily a lengthy documentation of the many economic and social miseries suffered by the underprivileged in French society that Bourdieu partly attributes to the state's abdication of its social responsibilities under the sway of neoliberal ideology. Bourdieu's later political tracts mostly denounce neoliberalism and the free market ideology, as well as commercialism and patriarchy, as ideologies meant to further strengthen the domination of the already privileged and to exacerbate the repression and powerlessness of the disadvantaged (Bourdieu, 1998a, 1998b, 2001). There is, it must be said, a bit of an unresolved tension between these idealistic efforts and Bourdieu's rather more cynical view of the political field in his more academic work.

For many of his admirers, the appeal of Bourdieu's approach lies no doubt in its promise to unmask the self-serving pretentions of all elites. Although Bourdieu himself did not extensively analyze politics from this vantage point, a full-fledged Bourdieuian study of the political field, thoroughly deflating the rhetorical and ideological ploys used by the political classes to maintain their dominance in this field, is both plausible and likely to be undertaken sooner or later by one of his disciples. Like all the work inspired by Bourdieu, it will firmly put culture and symbolic power at the center of the analysis. But it is worth noting that this use of culture does remain rather narrower than that of Mann, in that it almost exclusively focuses on culture as *ideology*, that is, as a set of symbols and ideas that objectively serve to uphold the domination of the privileged few. Conversely, treating culture as a force potentially capable of genuinely cutting *across* class lines, that is, as being something more than merely the mystifications serving the interest of the dominant class, might deprive Bourdieu's approach of much that his followers find most attractive about it.

CONCLUSION

At first sight, conflict theory, and particularly the neo-Weberian variants, would seem to have conquered all. At the time the term *conflict theory* was first used to describe this approach, it was meant to set it off against the then supposedly dominant consensualist structural functionalism of Talcott Parsons and his followers. Today, that kind of structural functionalism simply is not around anymore. Latter-day admirers of Parsons have attempted to resurrect some of his ideas, but their neofunctionalism explicitly recognizes social conflict as a primary determinant of social outcomes of all kinds (e.g., Alexander, 1985, 1998; Colomy, 1990). In fact, whatever the topic, the standard explanatory strategy in political sociology today is to look for two or more groups with clearly opposed interests, and the resources to make their influence felt, to explain the phenomenon in question as the outcome of the conflict between them. Whether we try to explain the occurrence of revolutions, elections, policies, or political institutions, this is now the standard explanatory model.

So what is the current state of the two theories highlighted in this chapter? First, the long-term trend toward fundamental revision of the basic doctrines of Marxism, a trend that arguably started a century ago with the split between Leninism and revisionism, continues unabated. The major reassessments appearing in today's *marxisant* journals, especially *Rethinking Marxism*, invariably and most energetically question precisely the most central assumptions of historical materialism: the base-superstructure model of society, the primacy of class and production-based interests and struggles, and the belief in historical progress. Traditional mode-of-production Marxism is castigated by its critics for ignoring nonclass and non-production-based interests and conflicts of all kinds: gender, nationality, the environment, culture, politics, globalization, and so on (Gamble, Marsh, and Tant, 1999; Gibson-Graham, 1996; Sherman, 1995). But whatever the merit of such criticisms, there is no question that any attempts to "reinvent" Marxism by abandoning its materialist core and replacing it with social cleavages of a more superstructural provenance are bound to make it lose much of its distinctiveness as a social theory (cf. Burawoy and Wright, 2002).

As we have seen in the first part of this chapter, Marxist and *marxisant* approaches to politics seem to have gone into two quite different directions. On one side there are those who still take class and class conflict to be a fundamental determinant of political outcomes. Among them we may count Domhoff and those doing research on business influence in politics generally, the self-styled "class struggle" theorists, power resources theory and its offshoots, and analytical Marxism. After having been temporarily eclipsed by their "structuralist" foes during the 1970s and early 1980s, this collection of approaches continues to produce much research documenting and explaining how class interests have shaped political institutions and policies. As they have been strongly criticized for their relative neglect of determinants other than class, many have felt compelled, however reluctantly, to pay some attention to nonclass factors such as gender, the state, "new" social movements, and so on. But in doing so their approaches do become less and less distinct from Weberian conflict theory.

The second direction taken by Marxist theorists follows more in the tradition of Western Marxism (Anderson, 1975). They have given up on the working class as the agent of progressive change but not on the possibility of identifying new progressive forces that will challenge the capitalist system in the near future. Among these we can count the several generations of critical theorists, neo-Gramscians such as Laclau and Mouffe and Hardt and Negri's theory of empire. World systems theory is a little more difficult to classify because it remains in some respects firmly materialist in its emphasis on trade and the international division of labor, but it does replace the Western working class with a rather vaguely conceived periphery as the source of future progressive conflict. What is, in any case, most distinctive about this second strand of Marxist theorizing is its strong drift away from materialism and toward more philosophical, normative, or even moral sources of resistance to power.[15]

The general trend in Marxist theorizing about politics, then, and for that matter, Marxism as a whole, is a drift away from the erstwhile materialist assumptions and toward a progressive acceptance of *independent* effects of superstructural forces such as politics, the state, and culture.

What of the second major set of theories examined? Neo-Weberian conflict theorists have always argued that their approach was superior to the Marxist variety of conflict theory in that it recognizes conflicts between groups based on cultural and political interests as no less important than class conflict in the Marxist sense. But, as we have seen, there is today nary a Marxist left who would openly proclaim the primacy of class struggle over other kinds.

Perhaps, then, we are all (neo-)Weberian conflict theorists now. But the victory of neo-Weberianism does seem to be, if not exactly Phyrric, then at least rather a prosaic one. For it may well be true that essentially single-cause theories such as Marxism and neo-Machiavellian power elite theory cannot possibly accommodate the full complexity of the real social world out there, but what neo-Weberians propose to put in their place, that is, the unflinching acceptance of this inescapable complexity, is not exactly going to satisfy our deeper theoretic yearnings either (cf. Rule, 1997). The merit of Marxism and neo-Machiavellian theory is that they offer a grand theoretical vision: a more or less singular key that will unlock all of history's and society's mysteries. As opposed to such grand theoretic visions, Weber and the neo-Weberians offer only a caution that no single key is likely to do the job alone. Is that really the best we can do?

Perhaps this is not entirely fair to the hard explanatory work that has been done and is being done by the whole range of scholars we have discussed. Having accepted the multiplicity of group interests and resources, and hence causal factors, that are likely to be involved in any satisfactory explanation of whatever we are trying to explain, the next step is surely to try and uncover whatever regularities there may be in the relationships between them. What resources are likely to be decisive in what social settings? Are there any historical trends in the relative importance of various types of resources and the groups who have the greatest access to them? What exactly are the mechanisms by which some groups manage to mobilize such resources, whereas others do not? And so on and so forth. And in their various ways these are exactly the sorts of questions that those we have labeled neo-Weberians, and many others like them, have pursued with much energy, intelligence, and ingenuity. As we have mentioned all along, these efforts certainly have borne fruit in terms of producing a range of fascinating and important middle-level generalizations that are

[15] This is, as van den Berg (2003:420–3; also Anderson, 1975) argues, probably a direct result of the self-imposed puzzle they have set out to solve: why do the Western workers refuse to act in their own clear interest when those interests are so obvious and there is no massive repressive state apparatus keeping them from acting on them? There is an interesting parallel here with Parsons' recourse to socialization, culture, and value consensus to solve the "Hobbesian problem of order" *he* had set for himself.

ready for further testing and modification. Perhaps, as Charles Tilly argues (echoing Robert Merton), the best we can do is search for "causal mechanisms that link contingent sets of circumstances" rather than grand theories that predict "recurrent trends on a large scale" (Hedström and Swedberg, 1998; Tilly, 1993:18, 2003).

Furthermore, from the survey we have just concluded one can draw at least some tentative conclusions about promising paths for future work. The ongoing research on the effects of money and well-organized business interests on politics is important and fruitful both for practical reasons and in advancing our theoretical understanding of modern democracies. And it will undoubtedly have to pay more attention to the role of the media in the future. Also, this work would be usefully complemented by more research on the influence of other organized and not-so-organized interests and their underlying causal mechanisms.

Then there is the role of culture. Conflict theorists still appear to be uncomfortable in their attempts to incorporate the role of culture, as can be seen from Bourdieu's and others' persistence in treating it almost exclusively as ideology, as mystification helping to justify and maintain the privileges of the dominant class. Collins and Mann have begun to add more depth to this picture by recognizing how culture can unite as well as divide, and how it can be a weapon in the hands of all kinds of conflict groups, including the subordinate ones. This line of thinking and inquiry looks exceedingly promising and is worthy of further extension and elaboration.

Facing the seemingly unmanageable complexity of the many kinds and sources of social conflict, there is an understandable temptation to take refuge either in specializing in one particular *kind* of conflict – ethnic conflict theories, state-centric theories, economic conflict theories, cultural conflict theories, feminist theories and so on – or else in a multidimensional conflict theory that can easily turn into little more than an excuse for *ad hoc* eclecticism in explaining whatever needs to be explained. But surely conflict theory can be developed beyond these rather unsatisfactory opposites. The way forward, it seems to us, is to try and think about the social and historical contexts in which one rather than another of the many possible types of social conflicts tends to dominate the political arena and what, if any, the most typical political outcomes are. Thus, many potentially fruitful questions present themselves. Are status groups indeed generally more readily mobilized, as Weber suggested, than economic classes? What are the social conditions necessary for economic inequality to become the primary focus of organized political conflict? Is it the case that social conflicts based on economic inequality tend to be more amenable to compromise and gradual reform than conflicts based on ethnic identities or nationalism? Is the success of such compromise dependent on a growing economy rendering the conflict a positive-sum game? Is the rise of strong ethnic and religious movements in part the result of political rather than social exclusion?

These are just some of the many interesting and important questions that the conflict theoretical approach to politics opens up. Answers to such questions, and a better understanding of the underlying mechanisms explaining them, as well as the range of historical contexts and societies for which they hold, offer, it seems to us, the greatest promise for conflict theory to produce well-founded generalizations about the social determinants of political outcomes, which is, after all, what political sociology is all about.

CHAPTER FOUR

State-Centered and Political Institutional Theory: Retrospect and Prospect[1]

Edwin Amenta

A generation ago few political sociologists placed states and other large-scale political institutions at the center of politics and understood states as sets of organizations. But now we do, transforming the way that political sociologists think about states and political processes. This alternative conceptualization of the field of study has opened up numerous questions and empirical terrains. If states and power are the central subjects of political sociology (Orum, 1988), in our understanding of these key concepts we political sociologists are now all "institutionalists."

The rise of self-consciously state-centered scholarship was motivated in part by perceived inadequacies in Marxist, elitist, and pluralist theories and behaviorist approaches to politics, including their conceptions of states and their research programs. State-centered and political institutional scholars confronted these theoretical programs by contesting both what was worth explaining in political sociology and the dominant explanations for political sociological phenomena. Unlike the others, state-centered analysts tended to view states, in the manner of Weber, as a set of organizations, but with unique functions and missions. Thinking about states in this Weberian way shifted what was important to explain in political life, and this approach to politics opened up new research questions and agendas. This has especially been the case for analyses of revolutions and social movements, welfare states and social policy, and the development of states generally. Some of these new questions and research agendas promoted by state-centered scholars employing Weberian understandings of states have been taken up by proponents of varying theoretical persuasions, including Marxists and pluralists, who have provided explanatory answers different from those of state-centered scholars and political institutionalists.

What is more, few social scientists had placed states and political institutions explicitly on what might be called the independent-variable side of causal arguments until the 1980s. Since then there has been much work that gives states and political institutions the primacy of place in explaining political phenomena. These theoretical moves toward statist and political institutional explanations were in part due to pluralist and Marxist explanations of politics. State-centered scholars tended to see state structures and actors as having central influence over politics and states. On the one hand, structural aspects of states shaped the political identities, interests,

[1] My thanks to the participants of the Theoretical Challenges in Political Sociology Conference, CUNY Graduate Center and NYU Departments of Sociology, May 26–27, 2001, the NYU PPP Workshop, the NYU 2003 Political Sociology class, as well as to Vanessa Barker, Neal Caren, Brian Gifford, Thomas Janoski, Edward W. Lehman, Miriam Ryvicker, Mildred Schwartz, and anonymous readers, for their helpful comments. The chapter is dedicated to Bob Alford, master political sociologist.

and strategies of groups that other perspectives took as given. On the other hand, state actors were deemed important players in politics, who depending on their autonomy and capacities might matter more than class or interest group actors in determining political outcomes. The political institutionalists that followed tended to focus more on the systemic and structural aspects of states and the manner of their organization in constructing causal arguments. These institutionalists also sometimes expanded their focus to political party systems in shaping the political identities, interests, and strategies of politically mobilized groups. Nowadays many more political sociologists employ political institutional arguments, even those whose theoretical allegiances are mainly elsewhere. If political sociologists are not all proponents of political institutional theories, we certainly pay far more attention to the potential causal impact of political institutions than 25 years ago.

In what follows I discuss the rise and the distinctiveness of state-centered and political institutional theories, including early proponents and what later scholars were reacting against. From there I address the evolution from state-centered theory to political institutional theory. Along the way I discuss its promise and address some of its achievements through exemplars of this sort of analysis, for it has made profound contributions to political sociology, as well as some of its shortcomings. This critical appreciation, however, is not intended to be comprehensive. In my illustrations I draw especially on work in the area of social policy, which mainly concerns interactions within states but also the literatures on revolutions, social movements, and state building. I argue that the theoretical project has advanced far, but not as far as it might have, because scholars working with these ideas have had countervailing analytical and research aims, based in comparative and historical analyses. I conclude with some ideas about how to advance the theoretical project, within the framework of the comparative and historical analyses that scholars using political institutional ideas most frequently employ.

THE RISK AND SIGNIFICANCE OF EXPLICITLY STATE-CENTERED THEORY

There has always been political institutional and statist-centered work in political science and sociology. In European social science and history at the turn of the century, the centrality of states to politics and political life was posited especially among German scholars, notably Max Weber and Otto Hintze. In American social science, many political scientists, working from the so-called old institutionalist school, placed states and political institutions at the center of their analyses as a matter of course, though not always referring explicitly to them (see Almond, 1990). In the postwar period, however, this older institutional view was mainly abandoned for other perspectives, with pluralists and elitists dominating in U.S. domestic political analysis and with a political cultural approach that placed "political development" and "modernization" at the center of analyses in comparative politics (see review in Hall, 2003).

In the first 30 years after the end of the Second World War, scholars sometimes placed states near the center of their analyses. Pluralists scholars were interested in legislative decisions made by political actors, especially elected officials. Usually they referred to "governments," saw U.S. government processes as largely similar, and focused frequently on the political influence of groups other than political parties, as in the work of David Truman (1951) and Robert Dahl (1961). By contrast, Marxist scholars, who in the 1960s began to contest pluralist images of political processes as inclusive, began to refer explicitly to "the state." But this was typically done in an undifferentiated way and with states remaining conceptually and especially theoretically peripheral to their analyses. In the late 1960s and early 1970s, Marxist scholars in political science and sociology explicitly discussed "the state," though they usually understood it in a singular way, as "the capitalist state," and tended to see states at best as "relatively autonomous" and their actions mainly influenced by class-based determinants, such as economic elites and the needs of capitalism, as in the famous debate between Ralph Miliband and Nicos Poulantzas. Among scholars of American politics, some scholars in international relations field of political science (e.g., Krasner, 1978) also addressed states as such, but worked largely at the geopolitical level and were not concerned with state and society relationships.

Perhaps more important, other scholars more centrally addressed state actors, structures, and state building in a more macrosociological manner. Comparative sociologists and political scientists, notably Reinhard Bendix, Barrington Moore, Samuel Huntington, Seymour Martin Lipset, Stein Rokkan, Juan Linz, Shmuel Eisenstadt, and Charles Tilly, paid close attention to state processes and provided analyses that might be deemed nowadays as state-centered but often viewed and referred to states through the conceptual tools of dominant perspectives. Working from a highly abstract set of social systems concepts pioneered by Talcott Parsons, Lipset, and Rokkan (1968), for instance, argued that to understand long-standing differences in political party systems one had to focus on "nation builders," the situations and crises they faced, and the choices they made (see also Lipset, 1963). The nation builders in their account could also be viewed as "state builders," because their projects were perhaps more institutional than cultural. Huntington (1968) addressed variations in forms of "political modernization" in a manner that focused on characteristics and development of state institutions. Tilly (1975) made the greatest break with previous understandings, explicitly addressing state building rather than political modernization or nation building. In a volume that stood out from in a series largely devoted to nation building, Tilly asked why "national states" came to predominate in Europe rather than other statelike and protostate political organizations. He also made breakthroughs on the explanatory side, arguing that state-led processes of war making in part led to the expansion of states and victory the form. Theda Skocpol (1979) found accounts relying on societal causes of the major revolutions to be unconvincing and argued that states, understood in the Weberian way, were crucial in explaining revolutions.

A Self-Conscious Conceptual Shift to "States"

In American political sociology, however, self-consciously statist and state-centered analyses were developed mainly in the late 1970s and 1980s, largely in reaction to other conceptual constructions and theoretical arguments. A focal point of this shift in attention was the volume by Peter Evans, Dietrich Rueschemeyer, and Skocpol (1985), *Bringing the State Back In*, which brought together a number of scholars working in political sociology as well as related fields. At around the same time many other scholars gave serious theoretical attention to states (see review in Orum, 1988). Skocpol (1985) wrote an introduction that is worth discussing because it was a kind of self-conscious statist manifesto that drew a great deal of critical attention. Many of these ideas were already current, but she harnessed them to a theoretical and research program and call to academic action that placed states at the center of political analysis. To show the distinctiveness of this perspective, Skocpol criticized pluralists and Marxists. Although there were many scholars from each tradition with relatively subtle understandings of states, she argued that these perspectives treated states chiefly as arenas in which political conflicts took place. Pluralists tended to see this arena as largely neutral, one in which all manner of interest groups and citizens could participate and contend but with some advantages being held by elected officials. Marxists tended to see the arena as one in which classes battled, with a tremendous home-field advantage for capitalists, or, alternatively, Marxists saw the state as serving the function of reproducing and legitimating capitalism. Marxists tended to refer to "the state," especially the "capitalist state," rather than to "states," suggesting little variation among them and little importance of states before extensive capitalism. In short, neither set of scholars saw states as complex organizations that were different from other organizations in their political centrality and missions, nor did these scholars see that the way that states were structured or state actors as highly consequential in political life.

Conceptually speaking Skocpol's call was even for scholars of American politics, where executive bureaucracies were relatively weak and lacking in political power, to embrace a Weberian understanding of states – as sets of political organizations that exerted control over territory and people and engaged in legislative, executive, military, and policing activities. Within these territories states held a monopoly on legitimate violence and sought to maintain order, extracting resources from their populations and often seeking territorial expansion in competition with other states. All states engaged in lines of action that could be understood as state policy. States were sets of organizations in some ways like other organizations but with unique political functions, missions, responsibilities, and roles. In their bids to maintain order and exert legitimate authority they structure relationships between political authority and citizens or subjects and social relations among different groups of citizens or subjects; they also interact and compete with other states. Historically states have been structured in ways other than the today's prominent nation-state, have operated in economic contexts other than industrial capitalist ones, and have been only variably subject to democratic forces.

This conceptual shift in thinking about states highlighted aspects of politics ignored by much of pluralist and Marxist scholarship and opened up a series of research questions. Not surprisingly given its Weberian origins, the statist research program was often comparative and historical but could also be employed in quantitative research. The organizational conceptualization of states criticized the empirical focus of pluralism, which centered on who participated and prevailed in various episodes of decision making in American politics, as well as to elite theorists, such as William Domhoff, who also studied these decisions but with a focus on the influence of elite groups. The statist research program also criticized the empirical approach of Marxists with functionalist conceptualizations of the capitalist state; the latter suggested somewhat ahistorically that all states in capitalist societies acted in similar ways and whose research often sought merely to provide empirical illustrations (e.g., O'Connor, 1973) rather than causal analyses. The organizational turn in conceptualizing states implied wider examinations to explore larger differences in patterns of politics and political outcomes across places and times. Issues such as state building, democratization, and revolutions became more central subjects of political sociology. Issues such as social policy that were already examined by political sociologists could be reconceptualized beyond examination of relative spending on programs. All in all, the change in outlook about what was important to understand and worth explaining suggested that political sociologists turn to their attention to addressing major differences in patterns of politics across places and times. Scholars studying one country or even focusing on postwar American politics were encouraged to situate the subject comparatively and historically.

State-centered scholars, however, went beyond the conceptual shift about the subject matter to political analysis to claim that states were crucial causal forces in politics as well. The widest break with other theoretical perspectives concerned the causal influence of state institutions on political life – what Skocpol (1985) calls a "Tocquevillian" conception of states or what Goodwin (2001) recently calls a "state-constructionist" conception. State institutions might be configured in different ways for any number of reasons, including historical accidents of geography, results of wars, constitutional conventions, or uneven processes of political, economic, bureaucratic, and intellectual development. But whatever the reason for their adoption or genesis, if these political arrangements were for long stretches of time impervious to change they would have fundamental influence on political patterns and processes over new issues that might emerge, particularly those concerning industrial capitalism. Invoking the impact of political institutions had been explicitly addressed in a comparative fashion by Huntington (1968) and in American politics by E. E. Schattschneider (1960) and Theodore Lowi (1972) among others, but the new discussions of causal role of state institutions on politics gave the idea a boost among scholars who were dissatisfied with previously dominant approaches. This line of argumentation was in line with criticisms of standard views of power, which concerned decision making or decisions to keep issues off political agendas (Bacharach and Baratz, 1970). Instead it suggested the possibility that political power was structurally determined, in that the basic construction of states would influence which political battles were likely to take place as well as which groups might win political battles.

Arguments about the causal role of state political institutions also implied more fundamental difference with other theories of politics, in that state political institutions were posited to have key impacts on the political identities, interests, preferences, and strategies of groups. Political identities, organization, and action were not things that could be read off market or other relationships but were influenced by political situations. Even if political identities were largely similar for a category of people across different places, political institutional arrangements might encourage some lines of political action and organization by this group across polities or time and discourage others and thus shape political group formation. In short, the political institutional theory rejected arguments that landowners or workers or experts or ethnic minorities would take similar forms and make similar demands in all capitalist societies; instead their political identities and organization would depend on political institutional situations. A signal contribution along these lines was Ira Katznelson's (1981) *City Trenches*, in which he addressed why American workers were organized around their jobs economically, but politically around their neighborhoods and in political parties along ethnic and religious lines, in comparison with workers in other capitalist democracies who were organized consistently in one manner or another.

Leaving aside the geopolitical level, many macro-level political institutional conditions might shape broad patterns of politics. Overall authority in state political institutions might be centralized or decentralized. Political authority might be centralized or spread among localized political authorities in the manner of the United States. The legislative, executive, judicial, policing, and other governmental functions within given political authorities might be located within set of organizations or spread among different ones, each with their own autonomy and operating procedures. Polities might differ greatly in type, depending on the degree to which state rulers had "despotic power," to use Michael Mann's (1986) distinction. State political institutions were subject to different levels and paces of democratization and political rights among citizens. Once democratized they were subject to all manner of electoral rules governing the selection of political officials. States executive organizations were also subject to different levels and paces of bureaucratization and professionalization. Each of these processes might fundamentally influence political life.

The other main line of argumentation, first in the order treated but second in ultimate importance, was that states mattered as actors, an idea already current in the "bureaucratic politics" literature in political science (e.g., Allison, 1971). State actors were understood organizationally, largely in a resource-dependence way. As organizations, different parts of states might have greater or lesser degrees of autonomy and capacity. The autonomy of states or parts thereof was defined as their ability to define independently lines of action. State capacities were defined as the ability to carry out lines of action, however they were devised. These differences in state autonomy and capacity, mainly understood as those in executive bureaucracies, were argued as being important in explaining in political outcomes across times and places. The roles of these actors were deemed both central and variable – and thus likely important in political outcomes and in need of greater investigation, theoretical and empirical, than provided by other perspectives on politics. The idea of states' capacities was sometimes understood in a wider way, with Mann (1986) referring to states' "infrastructural power." The ideas of state autonomy and capacity brought into the discussion the "power to" do something, as in Parsons's treatment of the subject, without neglecting "power over," on which political scientists and sociologists previously had focused (Lukes, 1974).

Sometimes claims by statist theorists about state autonomy and capacity and the importance of state actors have been understood to mean that state actors were more likely to prevail in any particular political decision (Alford and Friedland, 1985), a kind of specific elitist argument. Instead statist theorists posed state actors as potentially key players in political outcomes, given their functions and mandate to carry out state policy. Their role and effectiveness would depend partly on characteristics that made other political actors effective – strategies of action, resources, knowledge, and so on. They might be captured or staffed by politically organized or social groups as well, but the groups might not necessarily be representing capitalists or workers. In addition, the ability of state actors to devise autonomous lines of action might be influenced in turn by the structure of state institutions and other political institutional arrangements.

The state-centered arguments proposed by Skocpol at first were more theoretical framework and conceptional development than theory, however. They suggested that macrostructural aspects of states and large-scale processes of state building influenced politics directly and indirectly. In channeling political activities in some ways rather than others, state structures would influence the identities and actors at this meso level of organized political actors. The way states were structured would also influence who among these organized actors might win political battles and which ones they might win. Thus state structures would also influence the relationships between the actions of politically mobilized groups and political outcomes. Because macrostructural aspects of states were likely to vary substantially across polities and over time, these conditions might be likely to explain longstanding patterns of politics. A second line of argumentation concerned the impact of state actors on political outcomes. State actors were deemed to be potentially autonomous and thus potentially major players in influencing political outcomes. Even if not autonomous, they might be captured by different groups other than those prominently figuring in Marxist theory, such as political parties or non-class-related interest groups. It would not constitute much of a theory, though, until state-centered scholars specified causal claims employing this framework.

State-Centered Theory: An Example and Model

In a 1984 article, Ann Orloff and Skocpol introduced explicitly state-centered theory and applied it to a central problem in political sociology and politics, the development of social policy. The new approach was signaled by the sort of question they asked. They wanted to know why social insurance programs were adopted much sooner in Britain than in the United States, despite the many similarities between these countries. This comparative question also homed in important historical episodes in policy making for each country. The answers they proposed were different, too. They asserted the two means of state causation suggested by Skocpol and used the framework to construct specific causal claims. Most fundamentally they argued that processes of state formation influence how state and political organizations operate; these organizations in turn would have an impact on policy proposals directly and indirectly, by influencing what politically active groups would propose. Behind the processes of state formation were sequences of democratization and bureaucratization. Notably, if a polity had been democratized before it had been bureaucratized, it would produce a state with low bureaucratic capacities and orient political parties toward patronage rather than programs, as they used state positions as sources of employment for their operatives. Patronage-oriented parties would eschew social programs and the underdeveloped states they led would have fewer capacities to run them (see Shefter, 1978). The way that polities were structured in turn had effects on politically organized groups. Despite similarities in backgrounds and goals and contacts across borders, social reformers in different polities, for instance, would have a different orientation toward social politics. They also argued that state bureaucracies and the officials in them might also be sites of autonomous action, employing their capacities and location in struggles with other groups. State domestic bureaucratic capacities were argued to influence political officials, whose proposals would be shaped by the availability of specific capacities to engage in policy (Finegold and Skocpol, 1995), an argument that was later dismissed by some scholars synthesizing class-struggle arguments from a neo-Marxist perspective and political institutionalism (cf. Huber and Stephens, 2001). These capacities, however, were also likely to be constrained at the political institutional level.

The article suggested both the promise of the outlook provided by a wider understanding of states and the potential for political institutional theorizing, as well as the issues raised by them. They were asking questions that few others were asking, given their limited conceptualization of states and their focus on behavioral concepts, such as who made decisions, who voted for which parties, or how much was being spent for a state function. In addressing important differences in these policies across countries, the question went beyond what would have been addressed by functionalist Marxists, who would have seen the issue as a similar matters of accumulation and legitimation. Their research project moved the discussion away from comparative spending on social policy to its adoption, an issue overlooked given previous conceptualizations of states and techniques of analyzing data. The comparative approach also helped to address the issue of why an issue did not reach the political agenda, without anyone needing to make a decision about keeping it off (Lukes, 1974). At the same time, this issue was going to prove useful to theorize about only so long as other scholars felt it was important, perhaps depending on the degree to which state power was involved. In this case, scholars tended to agree about the importance of the adoption of social policy and attempted to explain it (see review in Amenta, 2003). Also, it was somewhat difficult to appraise the importance of these particular episodes of policy making – which is similar to the problem of addressing what constituted "important decisions" for those studying power in communities (Polsby, 1980).

The theoretical explanation combined aspects of macro-level structural and systemic argumentation with meso- or organizational-level argumentation in a novel way that fundamentally contested both Marxist and pluralist claims about the likely actors in the political process and their importance. Orloff and Skocpol (1984) argued that broad processes of social change, democratization, and bureaucratization configured the U.S. polity and party system against the adoption of modern social spending policy and Britain's in favor of it. The macro-level configuration of polities was deemed to influence processes of politics, including how key political actors identified themselves at lower levels and what these actors wanted. Although worker and capitalist political actors, predominant in Marxist theory, would likely matter in all polities, they might see their interests and identities diverge according to the incentives provided for them by political institutions, including the nature of the political party system. Like the pluralists, they argued that a wide group of actors might matter, though the possibilities of organizing interests would be influenced by the political structure and the broad processes that lay behind it.

Left undertheorized, though, were a number of issues. Among them were the fundamental relationships between the large-scale processes and the structure of other polities subject to these processes. Although state capacities were claimed to be important in influencing political officials and these capacities were argued to be constrained by political institutional patterns, it was not clear under what conditions state capacities might vary and matter. The interaction of politically organized groups was largely left undertheorized, with the presumption, though, that those favored by the structure of a given polity would prevail disproportionately in political decision making. Political actors at the meso level were viewed as rational for the most part, as rational choice theorists would expect, shifting the best they could under the circumstances. But as organizations, these actors also might be constrained by the conditions of their founding, as some "old institutional" organizational theorists would have it (see review in Stinchcombe, 1997), or by understandings of their missions that might result from bounded rationality and constraining scripts, templates, and schemas, as "new institutional" organizational theorists would suggest (see review in Clemens and Cook, 1999).

TOWARD POLITICAL-INSTITUTIONAL THEORY

The initial state-centered theoretical program – treating states as important causal forces in politics – has evolved into a political-institutional one over the last decade or so, altering the program in important ways. Scholars have generally employed the Tocquevillian argument about states in an explanatory way and have added further argumentation concerning the construction of other large-scale political institutions, including political party systems. In the hands of some theorists, the arguments became more structural and systemic, with long-standing political institutions influencing all groups and having major influence over outcomes of interest. In the hands of others, political institutionalism has become more historical and focused on historical processes. Here scholars continue to argue that political institutions fundamentally influence political life but focus theoretical attention on the interaction of actors at a medium-systemic, interorganizational, or meso level. These actors are seen as working within institutional constraints, as well as with constraints on resources and other means of action, and attempting to influence state policy. Changes in state policies in turn set processes in motion that influence the interests and strategies of actors that will determine whether programs will feed back in a way that strengthens the program or undermines it or leaves it open to changes at a later time. The main theoretical framework is that macro-level political institutions shape politics and political actors, who act under constraints that may influence their impact on states and policies, refashioning political institutions in the process, and so on.

Before I discuss this political institutionalist theoretical project, I want to say a few words distinguishing it from other uses of the term *institutionalism* among sociologists and political scientists. It is now conventional to say that there are three groups of institutionalists: "new institutionalists" in the sociology of organizations (Powell and DiMaggio, 1991), "institutionalists" employing rational choice theory in political science (Moe, 1987), and "historical institutionalists," political scientists who are distinctive for their comparative and historical methodology (Thelen, 1999; Thelen and Steinmo, 1992; see review in Hall and Taylor, 1996). The new instititionalism is a species of organizational theory, which sees organizations in a particular way and treats states largely like other organizations. For this group, political sociology involves organizations, and thus new institutional theory is expected to be relevant; mainly, however, this theory provides a broad cultural perspective on politics (e.g., Meyer, 2001). By contrast, the rational choice institutionalists in political science employ a style of theorizing based on micro-level foundations; they emphasize deductive theorizing itself as being central to social scientific progress and are concerned less with sustained empirical appraisals of theoretical arguments. They are roughly aligned with economic institutionalists (e.g., North, 1990).

Finally, historical institutionalism is a way of engaging in the social scientific enterprise that places less emphasis on general theorizing in which scholars pose macropolitical or – sociological empirical puzzles and employ comparative and historical analytical research strategies to address them (cf. Immergut, 1998). Institutional structures of all sorts usually matter in these explanations. There is an elective affinity between the approach of the historical institutionalists, who now form a self-conscious academic grouping, and political institutional theorizing, but the overlap is far from complete. Historical institutionalists tend to see political institutions as being distinctive and influential and more than new institutionalists are concerned with issues of power. Those who call themselves historical institutionalists, including Skocpol, often rely on political institutional theorizing. Indeed, that so much of political institutional theoretical argumentation has been developed and appraised by comparative and historical research has strongly influenced the evolution of the political institutional theoretical project. But there is no necessary connection between the historical institutionalist approach, where causation is often presumed to be multiple, conjunctural, and path-dependent, and any given theory or even style of theorizing. Historical institutionalists may not ascribe central causal roles to political institutions in any given analysis and could instead rely on economic or social institutions in their theoretical argumentation. By contrast political institutional argumentation relies on the structure of state and other major political institutions, including electoral systems and political party systems, and processes of state and party building, in the construction of causal political arguments and explanations for macropolitical phenomena.

Developments in political institutional theorizing since the early 1990s have continued to focus more on the impact of political contexts on politics more so than on the role of bureaucratic state actors. Scholars working in this mode have often followed some of the same structural guidelines of Orloff and Skocpol, but focusing on other political institutions and hypothesizing different empirical implications. One line of argument is that political institutions influence the types of actors in a polity, including the form, identities, and interests of political actors, and from there to important processes and outcomes. The second is that political institutions provide distinctive contexts that influence causal relationships at a meso level of political organization and action. Third, there have been attempts to theoretically model the process over time, in which state institutions influence political actors, who maneuver within constraints to influence states, which are altered in turn and then influence real and potential political actors. The theorizing here focuses not structural political institutions and large-scale processes, but smaller scale processes.

Structural Political Institutionalism

An example of the highly structural political institutionalism is the state-centered theory of Third World revolution posed by Jeff Goodwin (2001). He asked why revolutions were peculiarly modern phenomena, why some Third World countries rather than others were beset by revolutionary mobilizations, and why some regimes rather than others were vulnerable to revolutionary overthrow. The answer was neither poverty nor mere authoritarianism, as there were many examples of each throughout history without significant revolutionary movements. Instead there were no revolutions until there were states. From there he found that closed authoritarian regimes provided motivation and a focus for revolutionary groups, whereas even limited inclusionary regimes tended to siphon off opposition. From there he asked which regimes were vulnerable to overthrow by revolutionary movements, that is, contexts in which revolutionary action and actors were likely to succeed. The answer was that there were two different sorts of regimes that tended to be impervious to reform and unable to respond effectively to revolutionary movements: neopatrimonial dictatorships and colonial regimes based on direct rule.

Structural and systemic, this line of argumentation was more elegant and encompassing than the previous state-centered arguments, which involved a variety of processes and a profusion of actors, and provides an example of a strictly political institutionalist argument. The type of regime influenced strongly the interests and identities of potential political actors. In a patrimonial regime, involving personal control by dictators allowing no stable group prerogatives in the policy, businesspeople, landlords, and professionals were likely to go into opposition, reading their interests off political institutional situations, not economic class positions. The type of regime also shaped state repressive capacities, promoting unprofessional and incompetent military forces and making it difficult for them to resist armed revolutionaries, if they were to appear. The argument is not strictly determined, in that these were powerful tendencies, not necessarily leading to armed struggle by revolutionaries, and not ensuring its success once they had formed. There was room for maneuver by these regimes, and room for agency of revolutionaries as well, but the main line of argument was political institutional and helped to separate which states would be subject to revolutionary movements and likely to succumb from those of poor countries suffering under authoritarian regimes that did not. This left somewhat undertheorized, at least by institutional argumentation, the activities of revolutionary movements and other groups that might tip these situations one way or another and required supplementation especially on the side of the political actors.

Another example of structural political institutionalism at the macrosocial level, but addressing differences in policy in democratized polities, is Sven Steinmo's (1993) *Taxation and Democracy*. Steinmo demonstrates that the taxation systems of America, Britain, and Sweden had varied over the past century greatly and often in unexpected ways. American and British taxation has been more redistributive and progressive, imposing stiffer taxes on the rich than Swedish taxation, which generates more revenue. He also demonstrates that American taxation for most of the postwar period was comparatively complex and inefficient, whereas the Swedish taxation system was stable, efficient, and yields high revenues. The British tax system stood out chiefly for its unstable and erratic character. He asks why these comparative differences in taxation policy – given that they matter for redistribution in themselves as well as for all redistributive programs that might be funded by states.

Steinmo's explanation focuses on the structure of a polity's decision-making institutions. American political authority was born fragmented and was never unified. In Sweden, a constitutional convention at the turn of the century created a Lower Chamber elected by proportional representation and an Upper Chamber less responsive to the will of the people. Britain had no constitutional convention and restrained its upper chamber, the House of Lords. According to Steinmo, each set of democratic institutions engendered a specific form of governing: in America, by congressional committee; in Sweden, corporatism; in Britain, strong party government. These forms of government influenced the views and activities of the main actors involved and in turn account for key taxation outcomes. Committee government in America, with its decentralization of power, brought with it low revenues and high tax expenditures, low efficiency, and high complexity. Providing great power but only limited time to exercise it, party government in Britain produced extreme instability in taxation policy. Corporatism in Sweden, based on the continuing power of the Social Democratic party, created a deep and abiding trust between that party and the permanent bureaucracy and produced a stable taxation system in which corporate actors traded off higher taxes for other benefits. In this model the broad patterns of taxation policy over a century are explained by large political institutional differences in electoral systems that translate into differences in the processes by which politics takes place. Corporatism as a mode of state-led interest intermediation has its own influence on social politics (see also Hicks, 1999) but is explained in turn by prior political institutional arrangements. The argumentation is elegant, with large patterns of politics and major differences in important political outcomes explained with few moving structural and systemic political institutional parts.

As with Goodwin's state-centered theory of revolution, Steinmo's institutional argument by design leaves a fair amount unexplained. The structural line of argumentation does not attempt to explain political change or specific outcomes within a given case, especially those resulting from the mobilization and action of groups at the organizational level. Perhaps more important, though, the question is framed with respect to the three countries and not more generally and the implications of the argumentation are not drawn out for other polities. Also, the broad institutional differences among the polities identified by Steinmo are different from the ones that Orloff and Skocpol suggested as being crucial for social politics. Although both pay causal attention to the role of political institutions, Orloff and Skocpol focus on the long-term processes of democratization and bureaucratization in state formation, whereas Steinmo discusses the impact of electoral and political decision-making institutions based on differing constitutional arrangements. This difference in outlook suggests that there are many possibilities for structural political institutional arguments, even in democratized polities and regarding similar objects of explanation.

Toward More Elaborated Institutional Argumentation

Within state-centered and political institutional scholarship there has been something of a shift from comparative theoretical argumentation to explain differences in large outcomes to historical argumentation explaining processes. This theoretical shift addresses the issue of explaining political changes and tries to fill in some of the explanatory gaps in the initial theoretical program. These theoretical moves take the from of claiming that changes in state policies have the potential to reconfigure political contexts and with them political identities, interests, and activity.

A key example of this movement, to stay with the social policy example, was in Theda Skocpol's *Protecting Soldiers and Mothers* (1992). In it she seeks to specify more fully the impact of macro-level political institutions on political actors and action, but she also allows increasing autonomy among meso-level political actors in battling over issues and adds reciprocal argumentation about the impact of state policies on politics. Skocpol drops the state-centered label and instead employs what she calls a "structured polity model," which she uses to explain specific historically and comparatively situated questions regarding U.S. social policy. These include why the United States created in the late nineteenth century a system of veterans' benefits when other countries did not and why the United States did not replace this system of benefits in the early twentieth century with social insurance for male wage-earners, when many other countries did, and instead creating programs for women. As before, she seeks to explain why U.S. social policy diverged from that of countries elsewhere subject to broadly similar economic processes.

As before, too, Skocpol's theoretical model gives primacy of causal place to the structure and formation of political institutions. The state-formation process leads to political organizations with given capacities and operating needs. Early democratization and late bureaucratic development within the U.S. state meant among other things that political parties tended to pursue patronage policies and avoid programmatic social policy (see also Mayhew, 1986:292–4; Amenta, 1998:chapter 1). Skocpol also argues that political institutions strongly influence social identities in politics. State and party structures and the scope of the electorate contribute to the formation of political identities and group political orientations, along with socioeconomic relations and cultural patterns. In this vein she argues, for instance, that U.S. workers did not have to mobilize along class lines to gain the vote and thus did not act as class-conscious actors. By contrast women in the United States reacted as a group against their exclusion from the polity – a process intensified by the fact that elite women in America were more highly educated than their counterparts in other countries.

Yet the argumentation goes beyond these structural and systemic claims to indicate other institutional reasons behind the making of social policy. For according to the logic of the structural, instititutional argumentation, there would be no impulse toward modern social policy in America. To address this, Skocpol makes linkages between the macrostructural level and the organizational level in making claims about the causes of change in social policy. She suggests that to be effective in any polity political actors, however organized and with whatever identities, have to construct a good "fit" between their capabilities and the given political institutions. In a U.S. polity in which elected members to Congress and state legislatures are not constrained by the party discipline imposed by parliamentary political systems and are chosen by way of geographic representation, she argues that the groups likely to gain the greatest leverage are "widespread federated interests." From here she claims that U.S. reformist professionals were likely to succeed in political struggles only when they were allied with groups with popular constituencies organized across many legislative districts. She points to groups such as the Grand Army of the Republic, the Women's Christian Temperance Union, and the Federal Order of Eagles as being exemplars of such organization and effectiveness in policy. Although the argumentation deals with general aspects of polities, these combinations of characteristics is specific to the U.S. polity, whose early policy developments and lack of development in modern social insurance programs she is attempting to explain.

In her final theoretical claim, Skocpol opens the way to see state building and policy making as a reciprocal and path-dependent process. Following Lowi (1972), she argues similarly that once adopted new policies can transform state capacities and produce changes in social groups and their political goals and capabilities. The new state actors can employ these capacities in further political struggles. Political groups may be strengthened by having states sanction them and reward them through policies. New groups may be encouraged by policies. Both of these influence policy at a later point in time. In short, the initial configuration of social policy influences its future; the structure of social policy has important impacts on the politics of social policy and thus the future of it and other policies. In this way the political institutional theory is made "historical" (Abrams, 1984).

Other scholars have argued similarly that the process of social spending policy is path-dependent in this matter. The main line of argumentation is that the form a program assumes may influence its political future by determining whether groups will mobilize around it in support. It has been argued notably that programs whose recipients are confined to the poor tend to gain little support (Weir et al., 1988), because the coalitions that can potentially form behind them are likely to be small and politically weak; programs with larger beneficiary groups, including middle classes, will have a better chance to grow. Pierson (1994) argues further that mature programs have "lock-in" effects that counter bids to cut them, because people have organized their lives around these programs and in many cases interest groups have already formed explicitly around beneficiary categories created by programs. In short, policy changes can cause positive feedback loops that lead to their reinforcement.

Others have extended the project is by supplementing it with other perspectives (Amenta, 1998; Orloff and Skocpol, 1986; see also Janoski, 1998). Although the political institutional argument points to influence on the formation of political interests and identities, it still leaves a great deal of autonomy at this level. New policies often are claimed inadvertently to create new groups and identities, making the arguments compatible with some pluralist and Marxist arguments at the meso level of politics. Many have combined institutional argumentation with Marxist arguments, especially those regarding class struggle (Hicks, 1999; Huber and Stephens, 2001) or class coalitions (Esping-Andersen, 1990), which are more compatible with political institutional theorizing than others. However, these arguments largely see class factors as the driving force behind state development and political change and thus remain located in that camp. Others have similar employed political institutional theorizing with different forms of cultural analysis (Clemens, 1998; Hattam, 1993), including the new institutionalism in the sociology of organizations.

Some Issues in Political Institutional Theoretical Projects

Despite advances and syntheses, many issues remain to be addressed at the each of the three main levels of theorizing in political institutional arguments. Political institutional argumentation has been most coherent in its structural and systemic form. Even here, though, the implications that scholars have drawn for political processes and outcomes are delimited, both in the degree to which they explain outcomes or processes under study and in terms of the situations to which they might apply. Also, there have been divergent claims about the impact of political institutions on politics and these differences need to be addressed by theorists. The opening of this program by scholars specifying linkages between the macro and meso levels of analysis, indicating macrocontextual factors that influence relationships at the organizational level has addressed some issues, but these theoretical linkages need to be traced further. The theoretical argumentation concerning state building as a path-dependent process has opened the theoretical program further and facilitates theorizing processes and change. Yet with the greater the openness of the project, political institutional theorizing runs the danger of returning to a framework for analysis rather than a set of theoretical claims that can provide explicit empirical expectations in different situations.

On the structural and systemic side, scholars in this camp have specified characteristics at the political systemic level of argumentation and given reasons for their likely influences on political processes. Many scholars studying social policy, for instance, now agree that the centralization of the polity promotes the development of redistributive social policy and fragmentation hinders it, because fragmentation facilitates the ability of opponents of social policy to deflect initiatives (Immergut, 1992; Maioni, 1998). Skocpol (1992) argues similarly that the fragmented U.S. polity limits what is possible in social policy. But the argument is multidimensional. Political authority in the United States has never been horizontally or vertically integrated. At the national level of government, the United States has a presidential and nonparliamentary system that allows intramural conflict. Members of Congress from the same party can defect from the president's legislative program without risking loss of office and can initiate competing programs. There are two legislative bodies, and legislators represent geographical districts, not parties. Any laws that make it through this maze can be declared unconstitutional by the U.S. Supreme Court. Scholars have not, however, theoretically sorted out which of these forms of fragmentation matter most and how with regard to social policy making (Amenta, Caren, and Bonastia, 2001). By contrast, Steinmo makes claims about the role of electoral institutions on political processes and makes plausible claims for his three cases but does not follow through with the implications of general theorizing for other cases. Also, Steinmo and Skocpol are making political institutional arguments at the same level but are claiming that different sorts of political institutions matter. These differences in systemic argumentation need to be acknowledged and their implications addressed.

As for the links between the macrostructural level and the meso-organizational level, the political institutionalist line is that the former influences the latter and from there the fundamental course of politics. In the social policy literature, for instance, scholars have made arguments that sequences of democratization and bureaucratization have influenced whether political parties will appeal by way of patronage or programs. Similarly, scholars have made arguments about the impact of the pace and character of democratization on group formation (Amenta and Young, 1999). But for scholars making institutional arguments about social policy, it is important to make further theoretical connections from macro-level conditions to the political organizational level. Skocpol (1992), for instance, argues that the particular way that democratization took place in the United States had an impact on the political group formation and identities. The argument is set out in a general way but is not conceptualized or extended beyond the case at hand to see how applicable it might be to others.

Policy feedback claims similarly have advanced, but need further specification to be transformed into systematic theoretical arguments. To return to the social policy case again, despite the incentives to organize around new categories and benefits created by state programs, groups sometimes form in support of programs and identify themselves with them and sometimes not. Those groups that supported the adoption of mothers' pensions programs in 1910, for instance, had lost interest in them by 1930. Although need-based programs tend not be supported, they sometimes have been politically popular, as work programs were during the Depression and is Medicaid nowadays (Amenta, 1998; Howard, 1999). The nature of policy feedback arguments been conceptualized in ways that would it possible to construct theoretically coherent path-dependent arguments (see Abbott, 1992; Griffin, 1992; Mahoney, 2000; Pierson, 2000a). Scholars making these claims, however, need to provide more specific expectations linking aspects of policy to the processes that influence their fate. That is to say, they need to identify aspects of social policies that induce the formation of groups around them or that are expected to influence their politics and fates in other ways. It would fit with the political institutional project that the policies that would matter the most in reconfiguring political life would be those that influence systemic aspects of politics.

RESEARCH PRACTICE AND THE NEXT STEPS

Political institutional projects have gone great distances since the early 1980s, but the type of progress made and the lack of progress in some areas has been due chiefly to how political institutionalists typically engage in social scientific inquiry. Although not all historical institutionalists are political institutionalists, most political institutionalists mainly employ comparative and historical methods, which in turn influence the strengths and weaknesses in the political institutional mode of theorizing. The style is bold in some ways (in asking questions) and reticent in others (in extending theoretical claims beyond cases of interest). Together these characteristics have led to many new and promising political institutional hypotheses and theoretical argumentation, buttressed by compelling historical and comparative research, but the theoretical claims have not been carried through as far as they might be.

Boldness and Reticence in Comparative and Historical Analyses

Comparative and historical scholars are not afraid of big questions – empirically at least (for discussions, see Amenta, 2003; Goldstone, 2003; Mahoney and Rueschemeyer, 2003). These analysts often seek to explain differences in major patterns of political development and readily ask why some countries had revolutions, democracies, and welfare states, whereas others did not. These bold comparative questions and research projects have an affinity to structural and systemic explanation. For political institutionalists explaining the differences in large patterns usually involves showing that some structural and systemic political conditions or circumstances hindered a major development in one place and either aided or allowed the development in another. In addition, these scholars use comparisons or trace processes to cast empirical doubt on other possible explanations and to provide further support for their own. This sort of questioning calls attention to large-scale contexts and processes, which are sometimes not noticed in approaches to data analysis that focus on events surrounding specific changes under study and do not look at the big picture.

Usually the impulse is even bolder, however, for comparative and historical scholars are not often content to explain a large part of the variance in their cases, as quantitative investigators are content to do, but often want to explain all of it (see Ragin, 1987). And so after explaining broad patterns, these scholars attempt to trace the processes which helped cases to show change, whether the adoption of a policy or its retrenchment or the development of a revolutionary movement or an issue of state building. This task usually involves some theorizing at the meso level of political organization, often involving with the interaction of politically active groups with state bureaucrats and other actors, or some combination of theorizing at the macro and meso levels. The causal argumentation sometimes gets quite detailed at the organizational level. In the bid to explain all the variance sometimes elements from other theoretical perspectives are added, and sometimes strictly contingent elements are brought into the account.

Bold as they are in their questions and explanatory goals, comparative and historical scholars are often reticent theoretically. They do not frequently bid to theorize beyond the cases and time periods of interest. Often these cases are states, subnational units, and policies or groups within a country or across a few countries, and the studies are limited to a specific period, often lengthy, of time. It is only in rare instances that comparative and historical scholars address populations of theoretically relevant cases in their research. Mainly this gap is due the steep research requirements of doing comparative and historical work, as one needs to gain a deep understanding of the cases involved. Yet there is no reason not to draw out the theoretical implications for other cases that we know less about.

As we have seen, Steinmo (1993) compares across his three countries and is willing to explain major differences in policy-making processes and taxation outcomes over long periods of time but does not follow through with the implications for other democratic states with relatively advanced capitalist economies – the population from which his three cases form a subset. But because his theorizing involves specific countries and their electoral institutions, he leaves it open as to how the process from electoral rules to taxation policy patterns might play out in countries with different electoral laws. Without his specifying the argument further, one might presume that there would be as many different patterns in taxation policies as there were electoral laws and countries to examine. It would also be possible and more theoretically valuable to construct a somewhat more general argument to explain the policy-making processes of other countries, but he stops short of drawing out the implications.

Skocpol (1992) wants to explain developments over a somewhat shorter period than Steinmo and provides more detailed theorizing, as she is hopeful to answer numerous questions about U.S. social policy and explain all the variance she addresses. She makes meso-level arguments about the forms of organization that are likely to work in a polity structured like that of the American one and traces the activities of these organizations over time. She goes on to explain variation in broad patterns of policy – such as why some maternalist programs passed and why ones for male workers did not – as well as the specifics of individual programs. Her theorizing is explicitly situated in the American political context and possibly that context in the decades surrounding 1900. Yet it would be consistent with her argumentation that to make an impact organized groups have to fit political contexts whatever they happen to be – and to specify what that might mean across cases. The form of the argument is that certain combinations of variables or conditions are deemed to have specific effects within a given overarching context, and it seems worth attempting to speculate theoretically about these relationships beyond the her case and time period. This theorizing would mean thinking through the impact of the contexts and whether the combination of variables or conditions would be likely to have implications in many situations or few and what they might be. It would also make it possible for other scholars with deep understandings of other cases to appraise the arguments.

Political institutional scholars do occasionally theorize and examine the relevant cases in a population of interest. In Ertman's (1996) analysis of state formation in early modern Europe, he stands out in placing all cases into four groupings of types of state formation. These are groupings are based on whether the character of the state's infrastructure was patrimonial or bureaucratic and whether the political regime was absolutist or constitutional – more or less along the lines of Mann's (1986) ideas of infrastructural and despotic power. This rephrasing of the question is a major contribution in itself, as he reworks previous concepts of absolutism to show variation in state types where others had seen uniformity and blurred important distinctions. From there he presents a theoretical model that involves initial conditions and processes that combine to order the cases into different patterns. Territorial-based assemblies were more likely than estates-based ones to hold out against the blandishments of would-be absolutist rulers. But early geopolitical conflict, rather than building the state infrastructurally, meant that states could not take advantage of new techniques of administration and finance and the explosion of administrative expertise after 1450. His argument includes path-dependent claims that alter the workings of long-term processes, with states becoming subject to military pressures altering the paths they were set down by initial conditions. As a result he is able to explain all the cases. This sort of theorizing is an exception, however, and is not necessarily due to a difference in attitude about the proper role of theory in comparative and historical research but to one scholar's ability to master many cases. This seems less likely to be possible for most scholars, especially those studying processes over the last centuries, as secondary literatures on individual countries and political issues have exploded, as well as the availability of primary documents.

Findings of comparative and historical analysts are sometimes held suspect because they possibly select on the dependent variable, leading to biased results (King, Keohane, and Verba, 1994; cf. Ragin, 1987, 2000). The theoretical problem resulting from small-N comparative studies is, however, that scholars frequently do not theorize beyond their cases. And so I am calling for scholars to apply some of the same boldness to take on the big questions and explain all relevant variance in research projects to political institutional theorizing. Scholars need to think further about the range of variation across the likely population for which claims can be made and need, too, to take into account the likely result of a lack of diversity in the population (Ragin, 2000). Theoretical programs can advance through a scholarly process in which one person studies three countries and another studies two others and each makes theoretical claims particular to those cases and time periods, but the progress would likely come faster if the comparative and historical analysts would think through the implications of their theoretical arguments and provide some empirical expectations for some relevant cases they do not study.

Extending the Political Institutional Theoretical Project

To advance the theoretical project, the next steps for political institutional scholars are to go beyond preliminary or highly bounded theoretical statements and general orienting concepts to make more extensive theoretical claims. I am not calling for general laws designed to apply everywhere, but middle-range theoretical argumentation in the Mertonian tradition that has implications beyond the cases or times at hand with well-thought-out scope conditions. At the most general level, the theoretical claims could be of the sort that Lipset and Rokkan (1967) did for political parties or Rueschemeyer, Stephens, and Stephens (1996) have done for democratic breakthroughs. Even if scholars develop their theoretical argumentation by way of paired or implicit comparisons as standard in comparative and historical and historical institutional analyses, it is always possible and worthwhile to think through the similarities with other cases and work through the theoretical implications for those cases even if one cannot carry through with the research needed to appraise these arguments.

Let me suggest a few ways to propel this process. One way to develop political institutional theory further would be to modify some of the largely methodological precepts of Przeworski and Teune (1970). They implored comparative scholars to replace proper names of countries as far as possible with variables in their causal analyses. Do not theorize about Sweden or America and Britain or Latin American countries, was their injunction, but instead capitalist democracies, liberal welfare states, or Third World countries. Also, their view of comparative analysis was multilevel, with an emphasis on macro and contextual theoretical argumentation. A comparative argument was one in which differences in theoretical variables at the political systemic level resulted in differences in individual-level causal relationships. Thus the nature of the party system might be argued to influence the relationship between an individual's class position and their political affiliation or voting behavior. In short, they suggested that whenever possible analysts should think more generally and to think about the impact of contexts at one level to influence causal relationships at another.

It would be worth extending these insights, but altering some of the precepts to fit the circumstances faced by political institutional theorists, who usually engage in comparative and historical studies. My call is for them to provide theoretical argumentation with applicability to all capitalist democracies or to all liberal welfare states or to some larger population, perhaps bounded by a time period or process, rather than limiting theoretical discussion to the few cases or time periods being closely studied. Other scholars might try to extend the argumentation to these other cases to see whether they are supported or, if not, whether the initial argumentation would needed to be modified and how. This might help as well to separate what is general from what is specific in the explanation of any given phenomena. The injunction to remove proper names when possible might also be applied to historical contexts, as different periods of time may in themselves stand in for combinations of variables or particular processes that could be conceptualized more generally. The goal would be to theorize about the conditions behind the period in question rather than the specific time itself.

This sort of theoretical development and accumulation can be seen in the literature on revolutions and the retrenchment of the welfare state. Wickham-Crowley (1992) provides a theory of revolution in Latin America, a conjunctural argument with five main conditions that include both political institutional circumstances as well as issues applicable to Latin American countries only. Together the five conditions explain each of the countries that had revolutions in that region. He argues that his explanation applies only to Latin America and does not try to extend it outward. Going further, Goodwin (2001) pitches his argumentation to all Third World countries and sees the different continents as providing different sorts of contextual conditions that can be employed in theoretical argumentation with implications for empirical differences. In his examination of social policy in the United States and Britain in the 1980s Pierson (1994) argues that forces for retrenchment were general across capitalist democracies in the last quarter of the twentieth century (see also Huber and Stephens, 2001; Swank, 2001). By this time most systems of social spending had been completed and expanded – had become "institutionalized" – and bids to cut them back were taken up in force by many political regimes. Later Pierson (2000b) situates some of his arguments in institutional settings. He argues that retrenchment processes are likely to be dependent on the nature of the previous welfare state, whether it is liberal, conservative corporatist, or social democratic, according to Esping-Andersen's (1990) institutional models.

A way to go beyond theorizing about specific historical periods would be for political institutional theorists to make theoretical claims about phases of processes. In the literature on social policy, for instance, scholars have taken seriously the possibility that different phases of development of social policy had different determinants (Flora and Alber, 1981). From this point of view, because they differ as processes, the adoption of social policy may be determined by different causes than its expansion or its retrenchment (see review in Amenta, 2003). This conceptualization can be employed to reflect back on theory and improve it. By breaking social policy into different processes, scholars can theorize that conditions and variables will have a different impact across them. It has been argued with regard to the Marxist- and class-based social democratic explanation of social policy that a period of social democratic rule after the establishment of social policy may have less impact or a different sort of impact than when social policies were being adopted or changed in form (see, e.g., Hicks, 1999). Similarly, it may be useful to consider retrenchment as a recurrent possibility throughout the history of social policy with different determinants when once social policy has been established as compared to when it is at an early stage of institutionalization.

Spelling out as far as possible with concepts the scope conditions of theoretical argumentation in general terms would aid progress in both theory and research. Even if one's theoretical argument provides implications that eventually are not borne out in research – perhaps the largest drawback to theorizing beyond one's cases – the claims will give others something with which to begin their own empirical work and lead to the creation of better theories. This would be true whether one employs the conjunctural sort of theory in which combinations of conditions lead to outcomes (Katznelson, 1997; Ragin, 1987) or the time-order sequence sort in which events or processes must happen in a certain order to produce outcomes (Griffin, 1992). Abbott (1992) notably suggests that scholars making time-order or narrative arguments need to address populations rather than have these arguments always tied to case studies. In short, one should think through that applicability and implications of even path-dependent claims for processes in other settings than the ones at hand.

Another analogy from Przeworski and Teune's methodological precepts would be to extend contextual theorizing concerning the macro level of political institutions on meso-level relationships regarding interactions of political organizations and outcomes of interest. A main line of argumentation of institutional theory is that political institutions not only influence the identities and modes organization of politically active groups; political institutions also constitute contexts that alter relationships at the political organizational level between politically mobilized groups and outcomes of interest. These contexts may alter as well individual-level relationships, such as whether an individual's class position will influence political preferences. The task here would be to address systematically how these contexts influence the relationships at these lower levels between organizations and outcomes or processes.

One way to sort this out is for institutionalists to theorize if they were going to employ Boolean qualitative comparative analysis (Ragin, 1987; see also 2000) to appraise their claims. In a Boolean analysis, an investigator typically examines a set of five or fewer categorical – all or nothing – independent variables and employs them to explain a categorical dependent variable. A set of algorithms indicate the combinations of conditions that are associated with the outcome in question. But the task for institutional scholars would be to theorize in this manner by a stepwise process that first analyzed the connections between macro-level and meso-level developments and then combined the macro- and meso-level elements in an analysis to explain outcomes, using the macro-level elements as contextual factors for the meso-level ones. One would start from theoretical arguments made on a few cases in a specific time period and extend the thinking outward as far as one would think it plausible.

The theorizing process would thus begin by addressing the impact of higher-level institutional conditions or processes on meso-level organizational conditions or processes. In the first step one would theorize about the interaction of macroinstitutional conditions that would be likely to lead to the prevalence of actors at a meso level, including perhaps the existence of certain state bureaus and agencies. The elements of the argument at the either level might include processes and issues of timing, such as whether a polity was democratized before it was bureaucratized. From these one would make claims about the relationship between different meso-level actors and their forms of activity or lines of action within different macrosocial contexts and the outcomes or processes to be explained. In thinking through the different combinations expected to lead to the outcomes in question, one could theorize that multiple combinations might lead to the same outcome. In this way it would be possible to make claims, for instance, about the adoption of major social spending programs across all interwar capitalist democracies or a successful revolutions in post–World War II Third World countries. One would be able to think through which combinations of explanatory circumstances and variables would be impossible or unlikely to appear empirically and tighten theoretical thinking (Stinchcombe, 1968).

In my own work on the development of social policy (Amenta, 1998), I argue along these lines. One claim is that the democratization of the polity, a systemic condition, influences relationships at the meso level between political actors and social policy. For instance, it is generally held among statist scholars that autonomous and resourceful domestic bureaucracies will spur social spending policy. I argue instead that this relationship depends crucially on whether and the degree to which the larger polity is democratized, with autonomous domestic bureaucracies largely uninfluential in underdemocratized polities. I argue as well that the relationship depends in part on the partisan nature of the political regime in power. The larger argument also extends to the influence of other politically mobilized groups on social policy. An underdemocratized polity not only discourages the mobilization of social movements but also attenuates the relationship between their collective action and advances in social policy. Although the theoretical claims are appraised on the development of U.S. social policy, in comparison with that of Britain, the claims are general enough in nature that they could be applied to other cases.

CONCLUSION

The turn toward political institutionalism in political sociology, thinking about states in a Weberian and organizational manner, has opened up a number of questions for research, breaking through the barriers imposed by other perspectives. These questions, such as the development of states, the appearance of revolutions and other social movements, and the development of social policies are of key interest to those who study issues of political power and have helped to transform the subject matter of political sociology.

What is more, scholars have proposed political institutional theories of politics and states to explain these and other social processes and outcomes. These arguments have been mainly structural and systemic but also address relationships at lower levels of organization. Macro-level structures constitute political contexts that influence the politics at the organizational level and the relationship between the forms and lines of action of these organizations and political outcomes of interest. In addition, institutional theories have been opened up to become historical in nature, with the political process modeled as states influencing political action, which influences states at a later point in time.

These advances and evolutions in the theoretical project have also brought with them important theoretical challenges for its proponents. Institutional theories do well in explaining the broad lines on which political contention takes place and the limits on political activity, but less well in explaining changes. Also, the way that political institutional thinking has progressed has depended on groups of researchers mainly making arguments about a few cases in historical periods about which they have detailed knowledge. They have not often extended their theoretical thinking to the relevant populations of cases and processes. This has slowed the development of political institutional theory and the accumulation of research findings in particular areas of study.

To make greater contributions theoretically and to avoid degenerating into a framework or an outlook, political institutionalism needs to be able to make greater portable theoretical claims about the likely consequences of different configurations of political institutions and actors on outcomes and processes of importance. The task here is to develop configurational theoretical claims in which connect political institutions at the systemic level to actors and relationships between them at the meso level to processes and outcomes, such as revolutions or social policy and the like. This theorizing should be done in ways that go beyond the specific cases at hand. Institutional scholars also need to better theorize path-dependent argumentation, in which timing and sequence matter in the explanation of outcomes. This important thing is for this reciprocal process to be modeled and applied more systematically to key comparative and historical questions. These issues, which amount to in essence a call for more middle-range theory with greater historical sophistication built in, are both challenges and opportunities for the next generation of scholars.

CHAPTER FIVE

Culture, Knowledge, Politics

James M. Jasper

In the last thirty years, culture has been taken more seriously as an analytic tool and used more extensively than ever before in the social sciences. A generation of scholars has now demonstrated the cultural dimensions of all political institutions and processes. At the same time, they have shown the political side of all culture, from childrearing to insane asylums, television shows to presidential inaugurations, architecture to the gardens of Versailles, fairy tales to high fashion. Across many disciplines, the study of culture today is about the power of gatekeepers, the rhetorical legitimation of formal organizations, the social determinants of art and ideas, the reproduction of hierarchies, the acquisition of cultural capital, the normalization of the individual self. To show that an idea or institution is socially constructed – one of today's great intellectual pastimes – is normally to reveal the political purposes hidden behind it (Hacking, 1999).

Political sociology should be riding high thanks to the "cultural revolution," as culture and politics have become central, intertwined lenses for viewing all social life. But I suspect the opposite has happened. Rather than defining its domain as the exercise of power, the clash of wills, the construction of favorable ideas and institutions, wherever it happens – in other words, making politics, like culture, a way of seeing the world – political sociology has defined its terrain more narrowly as the institutions of the nation-state: parties and elections, citizenship and boundaries, state agencies and their constituencies. When power is discussed, it is the ability to set urban growth agendas or gain citizenship rights, not to make blockbuster movies or suppress masturbation. What's more, there has been considerable reluctance to recognize the cultural dynamics within the organizations of the state itself. By defining their domain as certain institutions rather than certain processes, most political sociologists – especially in the United States – have chosen a narrow and safe terrain over a broad but treacherous one. Political sociology has yet to fully incorporate meaning in its explanations, and it will be more dynamic and creative when it does.[1]

BRIEF HISTORY

For two hundred years, political analysis has reflected a broader cultural conflict between Enlightenment and Romantic impulses, between "civilization" and "culture" (Elias, 1978/1939). On the one hand is an optimistic, liberal faith

[1] Here is some evidence that cultural sociology has embraced politics more than political sociology has culture. In Smelser's 1988 *Handbook of Sociology*, Anthony Orum's article on political sociology paid virtually no attention to cultural dimensions, despite his enthusiasm for E. P. Thompson, important to Orum for his historical approach not his cultural. Several years later when Diana Crane edited a volume called *The Sociology of Culture* (1994), almost all the chapters in fact concerned power and politics, although the titles were about historical sociology, formal organizations, the integration of national societies, material culture, and art.

in science and rationality, which views people as essentially the same everywhere, differing primarily by how far they have traveled along the same road of progress and development. On the other hand we see a recognition, and sometimes celebration, of abiding cultural differences, thought to be the fount of spiritual values more important than material advancement, a higher source of knowledge than science. The utilitarian tradition that derives from Enlightenment ideals has given us rational choice models of humans as largely material creatures, with mostly universal urges, and a corresponding model of social science as the search for constant laws like those of physics or chemistry. Those suspicious of modernity (whether on esthetic, ecological, or reactionary grounds) have been more likely to analyze culture as a source of resistance and alternative values. For every Bentham there has been a Coleridge, for every Tom Schelling a Clifford Geertz.

Romanticism began to stir at the very height of the Enlightenment. As early as the 1760s, the *Sturm und Drang* movement emphasized the inner self and its emotions over the colder rationality of science. Rousseau published his *Confessions* in 1783, claiming that the truth about individuals lies in their inner workings and sentiments. In 1813, Madame de Staël returned to France from a German sojourn with a new term, "romanticism." Burke (1973/1790) famously described the ancient origins and slow, organic development of British liberties solidly rooted in community – in contrast to the radical social engineering of the French Revolution. Prime Minister Benjamin Disraeli transformed many of Burke's ideas into practice, adding an overlay of medieval nostalgia, while Matthew Arnold and others additionally insisted on the benefits of high culture (also Eliot, 1949). The great turn-of-the-century theorist of hermeneutics, Wilhelm Dilthey (1976), explicitly contrasted his holistic vision of cultural meaning – and the human sciences – with the Enlightenment reductionism and materialism of natural science. Into the twentieth century, theorists like Michael Oakeshott continued Burke's image of government as a natural outgrowth of society, easily disrupted by efforts at sudden transformation. Culture and community were central to this vision.

Political sociology (and perhaps sociology as a whole: Nisbet, 1966; Seidman, 1983) was born out of the tension between Enlightenment and Romanticism. We see this in Marx's search for universal laws of history, placed precariously alongside his faith in the revolutionary action of the proletariat. It is even more striking in Weber's distinction between the value neutrality of social science and the normative commitments of researchers that influence their choice of problems. From this contrast came another: Weber's analysis of the increasing rationalization and rigidity of modern, bureaucratic societies and his desperate hope for charismatic leaders to bring innovation to these systems. Pessimism over Europe's political arrangements in the 1920s fostered a cult of actions and decisions that could set things right.

This brand of Romantic political thought came to a fiery and disreputable end with fascism, its great triumph and debacle. Figures like Carl Schmitt (1976/1932), arguing for a strong state and community, savaged liberalism for its optimism about human nature, indeed for its denial of the need for politics and the state. Inspired by Weber, Schmitt developed an existentialist reverence for powerful leaders who could make decisions and create politics by defining a society's enemies (Wolin, 1992: chapter 4). Mussolini articulated the Romantic spirit of mythical community in proclaiming, "We have created a myth, this myth is a belief, a noble enthusiasm; it does not need to be reality, it is a striving and a hope, belief and courage. Our myth is the nation, the great nation which we want to make into a concrete reality for ourselves" (quoted approvingly in Schmitt, 1985/1923:75–6). In their dread of communism, most conservatives abandoned Burkean principles of organic community to line up behind fascist parties of radical change, thereby discrediting traditional tropes of culture, community, and nation. Romantic political language was made unavailable to the initial postwar generation of political analysts (cf. Alexander, 1995).[2]

Romantic tropes of culture and community could thus be rediscovered in the 1960s, migrating from the Right end of the political spectrum to the Left. The traditional association of the Left with universalist rationality and the Right with cultural singularities was in large part reversed (Gitlin, 1995). Increasingly, political activists and scholars of the Left used cultural analyses to build their followings and criticize their societies, drawing on many antimarket images first developed by conservatives. Collective identities, beginning with Black Power and Third World revolutionaries, became a source of resistance to political and economic structures; community became a rallying cry of the Left more than the Right. Ecology and feminism articulated a critique of the "instrumental reason" of Enlightenment science and self-confidence; new criticism of professions and other experts appeared. Small became beautiful. In a momentous shift, the professional middle classes, once the great supporters of the rationalistic tradition, grew more ambivalent if not critical of the Enlightenment project (Espeland, 1998; Moore, in press). (These concerns find echoes in today's antiglobalization protest.) At the same time, much of the Right embraced promarket utilitarianism with a revolutionary zeal, especially in Britain and the United States.

Political analysis changed as well. Under Enlightenment ideals in the immediate postwar generation, most students of politics believed in two forms of knowledge, that which accurately reflected reality and that which did not. Those with accurate understandings were thought to include scientific scholars, of course, but also citizens who pursued their goals by voting and forming interest groups in good pluralist fashion. Suffering from illusions, on the other hand, were those with ideologies or those who stepped outside normal institutional channels to join social movements led by demagogues (Bell, 1960; Smelser, 1962).

Marxists challenged this vision, but simply reversed the attribution of truth and ideology. The state, in thrall to capital, promulgated false ideology through the schools, the media, and other "apparatuses" (Althusser, 1971; cf. Thompson, 1978), whereas the social position of the working class (and intellectuals aligned with it) allowed it to grasp the truth about capitalist society. If the mainstream blamed fascism on Romantic impulses, the Left frequently attributed it to the Enlightenment (Horkheimer and Adorno, 1979/1944). In postwar political analysis of all stripes, however, people were either right or wrong in their thoughts and actions.

As many activists of the 1960s – such as Todd Gitlin, Richard Flacks, and Stanley Aronowitz – became academics in the 1970s, they frequently turned to culture as a way of criticizing their societies and explaining what went wrong. Social scientists rediscovered the local meanings and practices of culture. They came to appreciate that people do not see and encounter the world around them directly, but through the many lenses of cultural meanings, language, tradition, memory devices, structures of feeling, and cognitive schemas. "False consciousness" was a convenient first effort to explain the failure of revolutions, but it was soon dropped for its arrogant assumption that scholars had the truth while the working class were dupes. Even scientific facts, Thomas Kuhn and others showed, are not entirely free from expectations, theories, and cultural frameworks. All that we know and do as humans occurs through thick webs of meaning. The social sciences took a profound cultural turn, complete with the celebration of diversity that traditionally accompanied a cultural emphasis, but (mostly) without its reactionary associations.

There were broader social sources for the resurgent Romanticism of the 1960s. Most strongly in the United States (where World War II could be viewed as a victory rather than a debacle for the Enlightenment), the 1950s had been an apogee for Enlightenment values. Science was glorified as never before. Modernism

[2] After Nietzsche, Martin Heidegger was the greatest anti-Enlightenment thinker, and it is no accident that he was both a Nazi sympathizer and the trailblazer for environmental ideas, the cultural turn, and the critique of instrumentalism.

in architecture and urban design triumphed through an alliance with developers and planners attracted by its no-frills economy. Architects and developers shared a disregard for local contexts and communities, which stood in the way of broad freeways and International Style blocks (the modernist premise of this architecture was that buildings had their own logics independent of existing contexts). Nuclear reactors and skyscrapers were built regardless of the qualms of local populations. Such hubris was ripe for reaction. In the early 1960s, Jane Jacobs's defense of traditional city life (1961), Rachel Carson's warning of environmental disasters (1962), and SDS's 1963 critique of instrumentalism, the Port Huron Statement, were parallel reactions to an Enlightenment apparently running amok. The movements of the 1960s, populated by those who had not lived under fascism or fought in the war against it, surreptitiously carried Romantic baggage.

Since the 1970s the Left has been torn between Romanticism and Enlightenment, between deconstructing all claims to truth, thereby undermining its own bases for political rhetoric and action, and attacking especially or only the truth claims of the powerful. (Even postmodernists have an ironic, nihilist wing and a political, engaged wing: Rosenau [1992].) In figures like Foucault and Derrida, this tension is never fully resolved; many combine thoroughgoing intellectual critique with political action based on strongly held values – with no necessary connection between the two. Collective movements are similarly torn. Feminists build social movements on the basis of the idea of "woman," for example, but also criticize each other for reifying this concept. Their critique of all metaphysics seems to undermine their own programs. (Anyone who thinks this "postmodern" plight is altogether new should read not only Weber but also Robert Musil's unsurpassed portrait, *The Man Without Qualities*, set in 1914 and written in the 1920s.)

The collapse of the Left at the end of the 1960s also helps explain the shift in scholarly perspectives. When history seems to be on your side and your favored group is doing well, you tend to see the world as rational. When your group acts as you think they should but is blocked anyway, you may tend to turn to structural explanations, as also happened after the 1960s. When your side does not even act as you think they should, in the way the working class has regularly disappointed the intellectuals sympathetic to them, cultural and psychological explanations come naturally to the fore. In the 1970s academic radicals turned to either structure or culture to understand what had gone wrong. Those who entered the humanities could assure themselves they were still "doing politics" while studying Courbet or Shakespeare (e.g., Clark, 1973; Eagleton, 1976; Jameson, 1981).

This momentous flip-flop, in which Right and Left traded tropes of culture and particularism for those of science and universalism, is only part of intellectual history. Alongside the new free-market Right, there persisted a religious Right that continued to appeal to values of community and family. Nor were all scholars of culture and politics leftists inspired by images of popular communities. But more than ever before, progress and social justice came to be associated with criticism of large bureaucracies in the name of the local and the particular. Whatever the motivation, however, the proliferation of cultural concepts since the 1970s has enormously enriched the study of politics.

POSTWAR APPROACHES TO POLITICS AND CULTURE

For twenty years after World War II, efforts to understand politics and culture were dominated by attempts to explain fascism and communism, while at the same time reflecting national differences. Enlightenment approaches triumphed most fully in the United States, perhaps because Americans' experience of World War II was less psychologically devastating than Europeans'. One research program examined the civic culture thought to be necessary for democracy. Another addressed the occasional regression of politics into participation outside normal channels, viewing protestors and insurgents as irrational or immature.

Civic Culture

The main American approach was to examine what was called "political culture," how people thought and behaved in the civic arena (Almond and Verba, 1963). On Enlightenment assumptions, researchers expected Western-style democracy to spread gradually throughout the world. They also sought to promote these systems to counter communism. Civic culture was linked to pluralist ideals of stable institutions within which organized pressure groups could maneuver freely, an amalgam of democratic spirit and deference toward "proper" authorities. Pockets of resistance, such as fascist Germany and many developing nations, could be explained by their backward political cultures (Banfield, 1958). Poor childrearing, as in authoritarian families, was blamed for inadequate veneration of representative elections and institutions (Adorno et al., 1950). The civic culture approach combined a belief in unitary cultures, usually associated with nation-states, faith in attitudinal surveys as the means for getting at cultural meanings, and a Burkean notion that certain national cultures were conducive to democratic institutions.

Research in this vein continues today. One branch has claimed to find increased civic-mindedness in Germany (Baker et al., 1981) and Italy (Inglehart, 1989; Putnam, 1993) and a decline in the United States (Lipset and Schneider, 1983; Putnam, 2000) and Britain (Kavanagh, 1980). Such research shows that civic virtue varies over time, affected by factors like historical events and demographic transformations, rather than being a mysterious emanation from a national population. Another branch has examined diversity within a nation as well as changes over time. Ronald Inglehart (1977, 1989), most prominently, has disclosed the rise of "postmaterial" values among significant minorities in the advanced industrial countries: issues such as environmental protection, the quality of life, and the avoidance of hierarchy, rather than material concerns with a paycheck and what it can buy. Such values are of interest especially for their effects on political trust and participation (Barnes and Kaase, 1979).

Political culture research has come in for its share of criticism (e.g., Elkins and Simeon, 1979; Somers, 1995). It has been accused of inadequately distinguishing between individuals' attitudes and institutional opportunities open to them. It does not fully address differences within populations, especially those who do not fit the "dominant" pattern of values and behaviors; cooperation does not require consensus (Mann, 1970). It does not specify clearly the relationship between political and other domains or the ways in which cultures change over time. Many of these inadequacies have been discussed by Verba himself (1980). Another problem is the conceptualization of culture as individual attitudes measurable through surveys – a view that distinguishes the political culture tradition from the cultural revolution that has appeared alongside it. Today's practitioners, such as Robert Putnam, are at least more sophisticated in the kinds of evidence they deploy.

The Crowd Mentality

Protest movements and other extrainstitutional forms of political action were seen as the opposite of sound civic participation (Almond and Coleman, 1960:5–8). Most postwar academics dismissed them in pejorative fashion, associating them with the mass rallies of fascism and communism. In one view, personality deficiencies led people to join larger entities, to lose themselves in some cause, no matter what it was (Hoffer, 1951); deluded participants were working out internal psychodynamics from their childhoods, with little connection to the world around them (Swanson, 1956, 1957). In another, crowds led members to act irrationally, to do things they would avoid as individuals. Hence social movements were studied in the same "collective behavior" field as fads and panics (Smelser, 1962). More charitably, protestors were immature young people, perhaps working out unresolved Oedipal issues or identity crises, but not hopelessly and permanently pathological (Smelser, 1968; Klapp, 1969). This was a popular academic response to the youth-filled social movements that appeared in the 1960s, and which would eventually evoke a more sympathetic and sophisticated view of protest. Critics of American society at least put the blame on institutional tendencies toward mass society (Kornhauser, 1959), especially after Stanley Milgram (1974) discovered that Americans, and not just Germans, could be bullied into administering electric shocks to research subjects. Psychologizing approaches like these were often crude attempts to grapple with cultural meanings (Jasper, 2004).

Like civic culture, the study of collective behavior continues. Relative deprivation theories have been used as a way of thinking about grievances and discontent in protest (Tyler and Smith, 1998), the importance of which was denied in structural models (e.g., McCarthy and Zald, 1977; Jenkins and Perrow, 1977). David Snow and coauthors (1998) found a breakdown in the routines of daily life to lie behind much collective action. To explain feelings of threat, so important to political mobilization, requires psychology and culture (Jasper, in press, a), one reason that more structural approaches have missed it entirely (cf. Goldstone and Tilly, 2001).

In true Enlightenment style, most American research in the 1950s and early 1960s was deaf to the particularities of culture and community. All nations would follow the same path of progress toward autonomous individuals freed from the cognitive and emotional bonds of local communities. When they did not, psychoanalysis could be used to explain deviations as pathologies. (As always, there were exceptions, such as Lane's [1962] lengthy interviews probing the political beliefs of fifteen men.) After the political conflicts of the 1960s destroyed this Enlightenment complacency, community and cultural embeddedness resurfaced as central categories. Scholars had several traditions, incubated in different national settings, to which they could turn in their efforts to understand the political effects of culture.[3]

Structuralism

From France came a semiotic model (the best history of which is Dosse, 1997). Drawing on Saussure's structural linguistics, anthropologist Claude Lévi-Strauss (1969/1949; 1967/1958) had shown that other cultural phenomena could be treated as though they were tight systems of signs, whose meanings derived from each sign's difference from other signs rather than from the intentions of the user or correspondence to objective reality. Thus we know what "beige" means because we know how it differs from tan, brown, and other colors; it does not reflect any inherent "beigeness." As structuralism's influence grew in France in the 1950s and 1960s, any number of human conventions were analyzed as though they were a tightly organized language. Lacan (1977/1966) reinterpreted Freud's concept of the unconscious as a language. Barthes applied the same ideas to media images (1972/1957), fashion (1983/1967), and Japanese culture (1982/1970). Althusser (1969/1965, 1971) recast Marxism in the same light. A flood of English translations of semiotic works like these appeared in the 1970s.

French structuralism gave central place to culture, but allowed little room for intention or creativity, change in or resistance to the system's meanings. Language strongly constricts its users, whose tiny innovations appear rarely and spread slowly. Indeed, Saussure's linguistics largely dismissed people's spoken speech in favor of the underlying rules of language. Compared to orthodox Marxism, Althusser's concern with ideological state apparatuses was an advance,

[3] Anthropologists such as Victor Turner (1967, 1974), Mary Douglas (1966, 1973), and especially Clifford Geertz (1973, 1983) also provided insights into culture. But these scholars tended to see culture as a search for existential meaning, in contrast to more politically and strategically alert anthropologists like Fredrik Barth (1959, 1969) and F. G. Bailey (1991, 2001). As a result, political sociologists were less influenced by anthropology than other sociologists were.

allowing a "relative autonomy" to noneconomic factors in politics, but economic determinism remained. And structuralists' insistence that they were doing rigorous science through their analysis of signs (for example, Lévi-Strauss hoped to locate binary sources of mythic structures in the human brain) was not the impulse that would draw so many to culture in the 1970s. The great cultural turn was deeply suspicious of science, searching instead for the same "richness" of cultural meaning that had attracted earlier Romantics. The semiotic model was alluring because it highlighted meanings, but it conceptualized them as rigid and relatively unchanging.

Critical Theory

The Frankfurt School provided a more political version of culture, steeped in the horrors of Nazi Germany. Led by philosopher Max Horkheimer, this group began its social analysis in the 1920s, in the same atmosphere of despair as Weber and Schmitt. Drawing on Marxism, they grappled with several historical observations: Modern society seemed increasingly shackled by the iron cages of bureaucracy and industrial production; the working class was not a reliable force for progressive change, accommodating easily to mainstream politics and even to the nationalism of World War I; the world's only socialist nation seemed more and more subject to Stalin's cult of personality and rigid domination by the state; and average citizens were increasingly drawn to the peculiar fascist amalgam of nationalism and populism, anticommunism and communalism. The group's exile to New York in 1934, or more precisely the conditions that forced it, only added to their reasons for pessimism.

Mass culture became the primary culprit used to explain the unfortunate direction the zeitgeist took in the 1930s.[4] The Enlightenment itself, according to Horkheimer and his collaborator Theodor Adorno (1979/1944:xi–xii), led to fascist barbarism, the end result of a process in which "thought inevitably becomes a commodity, and language the means of promoting that commodity." In psychological terms, capitalist crises undermined the power of the father, in struggle against whom boys had traditionally developed their own autonomous egos and superegos. Without these, they were susceptible to mass propaganda from the state. The team – especially Adorno and Marcuse – increasingly turned their attention to art, finding in it a critique of the present and a longing for some future society that would allow freedom and creativity. Yet art was too often an instrument for capitalist docility and alienation, when it suggested that modern societies had already attained social harmony. The culture industry leveled its products to commodities, isolated from any sense of society as a whole or of the possibilities for historical change. Through numbing familiarity, for instance, radio eroded our capacities to listen to music in a sophisticated, critical way (Adorno, 1978/1938).

For former activists hoping to draw lessons from their political failures, critical theory was almost as grim as French structuralism. The culture industry could turn everything, even radical critique, into another fetishized commodity. Jürgen Habermas, primary heir to this tradition, has explicitly looked back to the Enlightenment as a way to rescue the entire Frankfurt project (1987a). Rather than an inherent tendency, barbarism is one possible path down which rationality can take us. Unlike the French, Habermas turns to speech rather than language as the basis for his analysis, finding in it a foundation for action and critique rather than a tight system (1979, 1984, 1987b). Through communicative interaction we can challenge those in power to live up to rules and ideals we all share, asking them to justify their actions. Through his ideal of "undistorted communication," Habermas suggests both an analysis of current distortions and a direction for progressive change. Pitched at such a high level of universalist abstraction, however, his work does not altogether satisfy the curiosity about and fondness for the

[4] The members of the Frankfurt School who studied politics more directly, such as Franz Neumann, Otto Kirchheimer, and Frederick Pollock, receded in prominence over time and were barely read at all when the perspective enjoyed a resurgence in the 1970s.

particularities of culture that motivated many scholars of the 1970s and 1980s. Although he puts meaning at the core of social life, Habermas remains a social theorist, not a cultural analyst.

Hegemony

A third national tradition, hailing from Britain, thoroughly attends to those details of culture and community, the stuff of meaning. Old leftists such as Raymond Williams and E. P. Thompson, heavily involved in working class movements, perceived considerable resistance to the dominant culture. When Williams tried, in *Marxism and Literature*, to give a general description of culture (liberally defined as meanings, values, practices, and relationships), he even smuggled in a model of class conflict. His residual, dominant, and emergent elements of culture all too obviously correspond to the aristocracy, bourgeoisie, and proletariat. Williams escaped Marxism's economic determinism but not its image of history as class struggle. (He gives the game away [1977:123] by the – admittedly "difficult – distinction between emergent elements "which are really elements of some new phase of the dominant culture . . . and those which are substantially alternative or oppositional to it" – a familiar metaphysical distinction between what remains capitalist and what is instead socialist).

No other work on culture and politics matches the influence of E. P. Thompson's *The Making of the English Working Class*, published in 1963. The book's title suggests the central theme of agency, so entirely missing from the semiotic and Frankfurt traditions: The working class was present at and active in its own making. Thompson especially describes the cultural and religious traditions and ideas, with roots deep in the eighteenth century, that were major ingredients. Like Williams, he takes the working class and the class basis of historical change for granted. He assumes it was the same collective actor resisting industrialism on the basis of class interests and consciousness in the 1790s and the 1830s. But much of that resistance, Calhoun (1982) has shown, arose from preindustrial traditions and community solidarities rather than from economic class.

British traditions of seeing class conflict in culture continued. At the University of Birmingham, Stuart Hall, Paul Willis, Dick Hebdige, and others looked to working class subcultures for forms of resistance that fused culture and politics (Hall and Jefferson, 1976). Willis (1977) famously described how youthful rebellion in the schools condemned working class boys to a life of dead-end jobs. Hebdige (1979) found resistance in the safety pins and torn clothes of punk subculture. In a related vein, Stanley Cohen (1972) saw "moral panics" in mainstream institutions' reactions to working class youth, whom they cast as dangerous "folk devils."

The British and eventually others recovered the concept of cultural hegemony from Antonio Gramsci (2000), whose involvement in Italian politics in the 1920s made him sensitive to the real choices to be made in wars of position and wars of maneuver. The term "hegemony" attractively suggested that resistance was possible, even while most power lay with those on top. But elites' hegemony is not automatic; they must constantly work to maintain their position. According to Gramsci, much of that work is cultural, promulgating ideas favorable to their continued power. Like many cultural concepts, hegemony could be read in ways that stress structure and the stability of domination or ways that emphasize struggle and the potential for change.

These basic, if contrasting, models of culture and politics were easily exported to new realms. A good example is R. W. Connell's research. Having written about class relations in the 1970s (Connell, 1977), he turned his attention to gender in the 1980s (1987, 1995). He simply applied his British model, describing hegemonic images of masculinity, subordinate, complicit, and marginalized ones, as well as "protest masculinities." Connell runs into the difficulties characteristic of this tradition, however: Knowing the structure of class or gender in advance, as well as in many cases the direction of historical change, these scholars misrecognize other kinds of political players (Laclau and Mouffe, 1985). They also have trouble linking ideas and concrete actors, or rather they assume a link rather than demonstrating it. Ideas and sensibilities can float more freely than the metaphor of class structure and conflict allows.

Synthesis

Agency, the ingredient missing from French and German cultural studies, had to be imported from Britain. Anthony Giddens (1973, 1979) coined the now-famous term "structuration" to insist that structures must be reproduced by agents even while constraining and channeling their agency. Drawing on interpretive traditions like those of Schutz and Winch, Giddens (1976) insisted that mutual knowledge allows social interaction to be meaningful to agents. In turning away (partially) from structuralism, Pierre Bourdieu's *Outline of a Theory of Practice*, translated into English in 1977, also viewed culture as strategic, seeing it not just in oppressed groups but throughout social life, in marriage ceremonies as well as motorbikes. Whereas Giddens remained at the abstract level of theory, carving out a logical place for meaning in social explanation, Bourdieu reveled in the details of cultural capital (Bourdieu and Passeron, 1979), artistic tastes (1984), academic competition (1988), and artistic production (1996). For both, invoking agency was a way of throwing up their hands at the limits of structural explanations, a kind of residual. (On the incomplete ways in which Giddens and Bourdieu inserted agency into their work, see King [1998, 2000], and for a more cultural approach to structures, Sewell [1992].) By the end of the 1980s, cultural research had transcended the national models that had constrained it in the 1970s.

Postmodernism and Globalization

The influence of the cultural turn was obvious in discussions of postmodernism and globalization in the 1980s and 1990s. Although it has been given many nuances, postmodernism is closely related to the "postindustrial" concept that modern societies are dominated less and less by the extraction of raw materials or their processing into industrial products, and more and more by the production and distribution of symbols, knowledge, and information (Touraine, 1971; Bell, 1973). At the same time, postmodernism in those arts affected by it has resulted from a thoroughgoing cultural constructionism in which the play of human creativity is emphasized over the search for supposedly "deeper" ontological realities (Huyssen, 1986). The increasing efficiency and penetration of communication technologies are said to have created a world of simultaneous, superficial images without any extension in time or space (Meyrowitz, 1985). The result is an increasing "incredulity toward metanarratives," the metaphysical groundings by which we situate ourselves, including both the Science of the Enlightenment and the Soul of the Romantics (Lyotard, 1984). To trace power today one must "read" the polity and economy: The world is a text to be interpreted (Shapiro, 1992). (For more on this tradition, see chapter 6 of this volume.

Culture has also left its mark on debates over globalization (Featherstone, 1990; King, 1997; Tomlinson, 1999). Much of the research conducted under this banner reflects a fusion of the interpretive concern of postmodernism with an older world systems interest in international relationships. The Marxist world systems tradition was resolutely structuralist and antiinterpretive (Wallerstein, 1997), so a generation of scholars interested in the cultural aspects of global trends had to march under a different banner, rediscovering many of the older generation's insights in the process. The speed with which the concept of globalization replaced the more structural idea of the political economy of world systems reflects, I think, the cultural turn. Debates over globalization frequently center around the relative homogenization and resistance of culture – even when disguised as debates over the future of the nation-state.

FORMS OF CULTURE

In this proliferation of work, several trends stand out. Foremost, culture is seen to permeate all knowledge, choices, practices, and institutions, rather than being a restricted part of social life. In this "constructionist" view, all that humans can know and perceive, even the most objective scientific knowledge, is shaped by our frameworks. As a result, there is skepticism about truth claims and efforts to establish foundations in social science, which found its strongest expression in postmodernism. We simply cannot get outside our language and our theories to test the latter with total assurance. The crisp Enlightenment distinction between true and false claims is hard to maintain, as all ideas reflect their social context.

At an implicit level, culture helps constitute our reality; at a more explicit level it is deployed strategically to shape that reality (Laitin, 1988). Culture is therefore viewed as an element of strategy and power, a potential site of contestation rather than automatically a source of social unity (if it does encourage unity, this is because elites have used cultural tools for that purpose). Ann Swidler (1986, 2001) has suggested that we view culture as an open-ended "toolkit" of strategies from which individuals select in pursuing their goals and living their lives, a form of problem solving. Charles Tilly's repertories of action (1978) is a more structural version of the same idea. As a result, the tendency has been to abandon talk of "a culture" (as a coherent entity shared by members of a "society") in favor of discussions of cultural tools, meanings, and rituals. Culture comes in discrete pieces, not as a whole. It is everywhere, but it is not everything.

At the same time, culture has not been collapsed into the subjective beliefs of individuals, which would be a kind of anything-goes relativism. The "social context" of knowledge includes institutional and rhetorical mechanisms – always imperfect – by which we continue to sort better and worse claims. There has been a strong insistence that culture is an objective reality of symbols and rituals that can be interpreted without having to delve inside the minds of individuals (e.g., Wuthnow, 1987:32). Perhaps too strong. Meaning, like language, seems both subjective and objective: We can get at it from the structured, public meanings available to us, but also from interviews with individuals and even introspection (a lost art in sociology). Culture arises from a constant interaction between individual intentions and others' responses. You can use language and culture in new ways, but you will then struggle to be understood. Like the old question of coherence, that of subjectivity turns out to be something of a red herring.

To avoid seeing culture as either a unitary whole or subjective beliefs, we need to recognize that each individual has a unique set of meanings, generated through a lifetime's interaction with the natural and social worlds. The idea that individuals "share" a culture, which they "internalize" so that it means exactly the same to each of them, seems misguided. Turner (2002) grounds this differentiation in the learning structures of the brain, Chodorow (1999) in lifelong psychodynamic interaction.

If culture is everywhere, then we need to distinguish the forms it takes if we are to avoid tautology. Various metaphors and concepts have been used to understand it, which also roughly correspond to different embodiments and uses of culture. Unfortunately, partisans of one or the other of these concepts have regularly inflated them into general theories of culture to the exclusion of other forms and formulations – a strategy good for academic careers but not intellectual progress. Here are some of the most prominent.

Ideology. A relatively coherent and explicit system of ideas, this was the most common way to study culture in politics when observers had more confidence in their ability to distinguish true and false beliefs (the latter being ideology). It lost favor in the cultural turn, but there are signs that the term may be revived to mean simply "a system of meaning that couples assertions and theories about the nature of social life with values and norms relevant to promoting or resisting social change" (Oliver and Johnston, 2000:43). In other words, a rationalized set of images, claims, and values that are a useful tool in political mobilization and argumentation. One limitation is that few parties, movements, or individuals attain such a high degree of coherence in their beliefs.

Frames are cognitive schemas or root metaphors that highlight or encourage certain meanings and feelings rather than others. Even though Snow et al. (1986; also Carruthers and Babb, 1996) insisted on the processes by which leaders and followers came to agree on frames to analyze a problem, in most research frames are analyzed, one at a time, through the static lens of traditional content analysis. Rhetors try on one frame after another until they find one that works with their audiences, but little attention is paid to the development of each frame.

Collective identity is the drawing of group boundaries, us versus them. It is the solidarity often needed for mobilization and is probably more an emotional than a cognitive process (Jasper, 1998). Drawn from the world of structural binary oppositions, collective identity has rarely been seen as an interactive process unfolding over time – although this may be the future direction of research (Polletta and Jasper, 2001). Although analysts emphasize the "social construction" of identities, they are only now turning to the actual work that goes into that construction rather than the structural circumstances that allow it.

Text is the favorite postmodernist metaphor (Shapiro, 1992). Sometimes literal texts are important, as postmodernists, indebted to literary criticism, prefer to read novels, constitutions, and other documents. But they also read everything else *as though* it were a text: cities, wars, geography, political cartoons, the evening news, even fondness for animals. The text metaphor reminds us that our object of study is a human creation, often carefully and consciously fabricated, not a fact of nature, but it can also be used to shift attention from the intentions of the creator to the thing created (Foucault, 1977/1969). Texts lend themselves especially to semiotic and structuralist analysis.

Narrative. Many cultural meanings come packaged in stories with beginnings and ends, told in a variety of social contexts (Hall, 1995; Somers, 1995; Polletta, 1998). Although often treated in static fashion as structural, predictable combinations of characters and events, narratives can be used in a more dynamic fashion – "storytelling" – to get at the interaction between "speakers" (figurative as well as literal) and their audiences (Ricoeur, 1984; Davis, 2002).

Ritual. When meanings are expressed in action, they can get a grip on people without their being aware of it. The most obvious case is ritual, a symbolic expression of shared beliefs at a time and place intended to increase their emotional resonance (Kertzer, 1988). People enjoy rituals for their embodiment of group solidarity, the collective effervescence Durkheim pointed out (Berezin, 1997). Rituals can have external audiences as well as internal, telling outsiders what is important to a group or organization, what kind of entity it is, who its enemies are.

Practice. Bourdieu and Giddens both argued that much of our cultural knowledge is tacit, embodied in practices rather than consciously and explicitly held in the form of something like propositions. The emphasis is on the work that goes into making meanings and knowledge rather than the ideas produced, even though intention is often overlooked. Turner (1994) has raised questions about what exactly is shared in practices – a difficulty avoided by newer formulations which view practices as an engagement with the physical world (Archer, 2000), as in science (Knorr Cetina, 1999). We can learn to accomplish expected tasks without necessarily sharing the same underlying knowledge. This is a radical rethinking of what culture is.

Discourse. Dialogical approaches, inspired by early Soviet scholars such as Bakhtin and Vygotsky, are highly social in their models of the origins of meaning, highlight the open-ended freedom of social life, and include attention to the emotional dimensions of meaning and action (Steinberg, 1999; Barker, 2001). Like texts, however, discourse can be viewed as having a life of its own, independent of the institutional contexts in which it unfolds. (See Chapter 6.)

Rhetoric. Many of these cultural concepts can be rethought as a form of strategic and symbolic interaction by placing them in the context of rhetoric: of speakers and audiences, of emotional and cognitive responses, of the open-ended development of cultural meanings (Billig, 1987). Emotional responses become prominent, and there is room for creativity and innovation as cultural meanings are fabricated in a complex interactive process that can never be predicted in advance. Rhetoric (about which the ancient Greeks and Romans knew so much: Quintilian, 2001) seems a useful way to understand culture in politics, for it focuses on the appeals made – in both words and actions – to a variety of audiences, often simultaneously. And at 2,500 years, it is our oldest tradition of explicit social constructionism.

The first five of these cultural concepts emphasize structured meanings. Ritual and practice put meanings in action, although they usually leave little room for intentionality. The last two focus on social action and interaction as the source of meaning, and they can also be used to show strategic intentions behind cultural work. Each gets at a different form that culture takes.

MOBILIZING CITIZENS

Cultural tools and historical research have enriched each other, especially concerning the rise of the modern state and related practices. The nation-state is notorious in its need to mobilize and discipline large numbers of people, most obviously to fight in and support wars but also to reproduce the population, train it, keep it healthy and productive, acting normally or predictably. The disciplinary techniques of recent centuries are cultural efforts to shape the minds, hearts, and habits of citizens and their families. States are not the only perpetrators: Sometimes rising economic classes craft themselves (and especially the next generation), and economic leaders need to train people for specific kinds of workplaces (as in the abstract notion of time necessary for the coordination of modern factories [Thompson, 1993] or the ability to display certain emotions on demand [Hochschild, 1983]).

As the great student of techniques used to keep people in line, Michel Foucault did more than anyone else to make the cultural turn glamorous. Through the 1960s, Foucault (1965/1961, 1973/1963, 1973/1966) was a fellow traveler of structuralism, showing the extent to which humans are trapped within their languages and languagelike conceptual systems – in what amounted to an assault on the human sciences. In the 1970s, he turned his attention to more institutional settings (1978/1975, 1978/1976), especially the "disciplinary" practices and knowledges that controlled minds and bodies: surveillance in prisons and schools, military drills, psychological tests for "normalcy," statistics on fertility and other demographics that could be helpful to the state. He criticized existing theories of power for focusing so heavily on the state: Power was treated as though it were a thing rather than a relationship, it was seen as too centralized, and it was viewed as primarily negative and constraining. In Foucault's "capillary" model, power also produced actions and knowledge, created new kinds of people and new practices. In the final years of his life, Foucault (1982, 1991) was groping toward a more strategic view of power, based on metaphors of war and conflict rather than the structuralist metaphor of language or economic metaphors of money and exchange.

For politics in a narrower sense than Foucault's, the French Revolution was a great leap forward in techniques of mass mobilization – and its historiography has been a proving ground for new theories. The history of its histories shows the increased appreciation for culture in the 1970s, as studies of the class basis of the revolution (Lefebvre, 1947; Soboul, 1974) were displaced by discussions of the revolution's symbolism, rituals, and language. François Furet (1981/1978) took the lead in attacking traditional accounts that saw the revolution as the triumph of the bourgeoisie, preferring instead to emphasize the struggle over symbols and language (and the right to speak for the nation). Mona Ozouf (1988/1976) analyzed revolutionary festivals as special events in which meanings were constructed, even new images of time and place worked out. Although recognizing that rival festivals were used as part of a conflict between the emerging political parties, she nonetheless found in them a Durkheimian effort to forge a national collective identity. Extending their work, Lynn Hunt (1984:54) showed that politics itself is a cultural creation, an improvisation based on existing values and beliefs but also a crucible for creating new ones: "Political symbols and rituals were not metaphors of power, they were the means and the ends of power itself." This cultural and linguistic reinterpretation of the revolution stressed its creativity and particularity as an "event" (Sewell, 1996) – in contrast to earlier Marxist images of it as an important step forward for universal historical progress. Studying cultural creativity was also a way to break with Lévi-Strauss's semiotic model.[5]

Nationalism was one of the most powerful mobilizing rhetorics used after, and in response to, the universalistic pretensions and imperialist policy of the French Revolution and Napoleonic consolidation. Nationalism consists of the meanings necessary for rousing people to support modern states, usually appealing to some sense of a shared history, even if it had to be fabricated, as well as a common language – itself thought by Romantics to define the essence of a "people." At its heyday from the French Revolution to World War II, nationalism was deployed most often by aristocratic elites who wanted to mobilize the lower orders for war and work but not to help govern. The intellectual history of nationalism is closely tied to that of Romantic political thought (e.g., Fichte, 1968/1807–8), and both of them flourished and then collapsed with fascism. The power of nationalism, long ignored by materialist and universalist interpretations of European history, which expected it (like religion) to whither, began to receive considerable attention in the 1980s (Gellner, 1983; Smith, 1983, 1991; Hobsbawm, 1990) – especially as a form of discourse (Calhoun, 1997).

Benedict Anderson's (1983) suggestion that nations are "imagined communities" opened the way to understanding the elaborate work that goes into constructing national identities, through literature, folk traditions, monuments, buildings, ritual commemorations, museums, and other carriers of collective memory. Almost all commentators have debunked nationalists' own claims to deep-rooted "natural" or essential identities – although Anthony Smith (1986) sees most nationalism as grounded in premodern ethnic identities. Fascist regimes were especially adept at manipulating symbols of national identity. Mabel Berezin (1997) and Simonetta Falasca-Zamponi (1997) have amply shown the aesthetic dimensions of politics, especially the careful staging of rituals designed to bolster Mussolini's regime. (Fascism's foes had to arouse equally strong emotions to defeat it: Dower, 1986.)

Collective identity has been recognized as a crucial building block of political action, even in relatively simple tasks like voting. Most research has focused on legally defined identities involved in citizenship and discrimination, even though all identities (including citizenship: Brubaker, 1992) are a cultural accomplishment that reflect considerable conflict over interpretations and boundaries. Some are more obviously cultural, such as religious or regional identities, which often arise in response to state efforts to suppress them in favor of national identities. In the Islamic world, religious identities today sometimes serve the role that nationalist ones did in Europe a hundred years ago (Jasper, in press, a). We can no longer assume that class will be a primary identity, especially as the most active theorizing over identity in recent years has focused on gender (Scott, 1988; Young,

[5] For Kevin Michael Baker (1990), the revolution resulted from conceptual shifts in the field of discourse that included the word "revolution." Rosenfeld (2001) extended this symbolic approach to other, nonverbal arts in the making of the revolution. Also see Chartier (1991).

1990; Nicholson, 1990) and sexual preference (Gamson, 1995; Bernstein, 1997; Stein, 1997; Lichterman, 1999).

An untheorized tendency persists, in which identities are assumed to form as a kind of cultural icing over a structural cake. For instance, class may be thought the important factor, subject to different ways of living and feeling one's class position. Or sexual preference may be the bedrock, so that theorists can then describe the cultural work it takes to make people aware of the identity that it supports (Taylor and Whittier, 1995). If there are structural positions that are more likely to encourage collective identity, almost no one has successfully theorized about why (cf. Tilly, 1998). And each time a framework privileges one position, another comes along that seems equally important: Gender challenged class in the 1970s, but crashed on the shoals of racial differences, then sexual preferences came along to cut across the others. What is more, we recognize the structural basis only after we encounter the culturally elaborated identity, never before. Some identities form with no conceivable structural supports except what the collectivity creates for itself. We must no longer assume that collective identities exist prior to mobilization efforts – many people identify with a movement, an organization, or in some cases even a political tactic such as nonviolence (Melucci, 1996; Jasper, 1997: 85ff).

It took powerful ideas and feelings – and a lot of blood – to enlist normal people in the projects of state builders and rulers. Rulers regularly maintain their positions by manipulating symbols and rituals. They build edifices that awe their subjects, control flows of information in the media, determine school curricula, and even build gardens to demonstrate the scope of their power (Mukerji, 1997). Words are crucial, but they are not the only carrier of meaning. The power of meanings is every bit as great as that of force, and history has been a fruitful source of evidence in rediscovering the former. The cultural creation of "nations" and "peoples" was necessary for the institutional invention of modern states, the primary focus of political sociology.

OUTSIDE THE STATE

The raw materials of politics – motivations, fantasies, fears, and sensibilities – arise in any sort of practice or institution, but they are especially thought to be formed in the private sphere, whence they shape what happens in the public. The private sphere has proven remarkably amenable to cultural analysis. Studies of national character, for example, stretch back at least to Montesquieu and Tocqueville, if not Herodotus and Thucydides. More recently, to take one example, Lamont (1992) showed how French professionals use intelligence as a central criterion in judging people, whereas Americans rely more on moral probity and material success. Other works are only implicitly comparative. Weiner (1981) found widespread English resistance to industrialism even at its apparent peak in the late nineteenth century, while Perkin (1969) demonstrated the reach of the emerging middle class in the same period, including its increasing dominance of state offices. A number of scholars have addressed the roots of American individualism (Bellah et al., 1984; Merelman, 1984; Gans, 1988), and Macfarlane (1978) traced English individualism deep into medieval history. Such studies (and these are only a tiny sample) trace the social roots of political preferences.

Inspired in part by Habermas's (1989) discussion of the public sphere as the incubator of political goals, understanding, and participation, considerable research has investigated the resources normal citizens use to approach politics. Bellah and his collaborators (1984) found Americans extremely individualistic in their talk, making it hard to see how collective politics could emerge. Gamson (1992), on the other hand, used focus groups to uncover critical ideas and feelings out of which protest might arise. Eliasoph (1998) showed how a pejorative cultural definition of "politics" prevents Americans from taking their "private" opinions into public arenas – in other words, how they work hard to create the apathy so often observed. Citizens' moods, such as cynicism, resignation, or optimism, shape their political participation. Others (Reinarman, 1987; Hochschild, 1995; Block, 1996; Jasper, 2000) have explained Americans' embrace of markets and suspicion of government.

Following the assumptions of the hegemony model, many scholars look to marginalized and oppressed groups for resistance to mainstream institutions, values, and sensibilities. They are seen, for instance, as sources of new tastes and means of expression, as with graffiti and rap (Rose, 1994). Poor African Americans (Duneier, 1999) and working class youth (Charlesworth, 2000) fascinate sociologists not only because of political sympathies but also, one suspects, as Romantic symbols of the "other" (on the blurred line between sociology and moral cheerleading, see Wacquant, 2002). Multiculturalism seems to encompass both sides: a universalist embrace of equal opportunities for cultural expression and a Romantic celebration of particularities. So-called communitarianism insists on membership in a cultural community as a defining property of human beings, even though many of its standard-bearers are rootless academics who move from university to university – and whose "communities" are rather fanciful, nostalgic constructs.

Moral panics are one form of political mobilization that sociologists have investigated, but under the rubric of deviance more often than political sociology. The concept (which as I noted developed in loose connection to the Birmingham School but also echoes crowd theories of the 1950s) describes sudden concern over a group or activity, accompanied by calls for control and suppression. Out of an infinite range of potential perceived threats, one – which may be neither new nor on the rise – suddenly receives considerable attention. The news media, public officials, religious leaders, and private "moral entrepreneurs" focus public attention on the issue, typically by identifying some recognizable group as "folk devils" – usually young people, racial and ethnic minorities, or other relatively powerless groups – responsible for the menace (Cohen, 1972; Rieder, 1985; Beisel, 1997; Springhall, 1998; Glassner, 1999 – not all of whom explicitly use the concept of moral panic). New political or legal policies are sometimes the result, and new symbols and sensibilities (available as the raw materials for future panics) almost always are (Jenkins, 1992, 1998). "Panic" is a pejorative word, but it attracts cultural constructionists by viewing public reactions and rhetoric as a part of cultural struggle rather than linked to any objective measure of threat. Many observers have found the concept useful because it opens a window onto a society's disagreements over basic values, often intuitively felt ones, as well as onto fears and anxieties that are normally submerged.

Social movements and other nongovernmental organizations are today's preferred vehicles for articulating new sentiments and interests. In turn, recent theories of movements have described them as sources of moral, emotional, and cognitive creativity, satisfying to participants less because they pursue group and individual self-interest than because they express emerging knowledge and moral intuitions (Luker, 1984; Melucci, 1989; Eyerman and Jamison, 1991; Jasper, 1997), including new collective identities (Melucci, 1996). Whereas an earlier generation of scholars (summed up in McAdam et al., 1996) concentrated on explicitly political and economic movements, such as labor and civil rights, younger scholars turned their attention to more cultural movements in the 1980s and 1990s (Rose, 1994; Stuempfle, 1995) – sometimes using the misleading label "new social movements" (Calhoun, 1993). A number of cultural dimensions of social movements have been described, including the need to frame arguments in ways that resonate with potential audiences (Snow et al., 1986; Gamson, 1992); the use of discourse (Steinberg, 1999) and narrative (Polletta, 1998; Davis, 2002); the emotions of social movements (Jasper, 1998; Goodwin et al., 2001); and, finally, the use of collective identities for mobilization (Gamson, 1995), strategic outreach (Bernstein, 1997), and the clarification of goals (Polletta and Jasper, 2001).

Revolutions are the most political form that social movements can take, aiming at transformation of the state. Their obvious structural intent (to change state structures themselves, and sometimes economic structures too) seems to have discouraged more cultural views, perhaps combined with the long shadow of Skocpol's (1979) structural reorientation of the field.

Nonetheless, Goldstone (1991) has inserted some role for ideology into his structural model; Foran (1993) and Goodwin (2001) integrated cultural factors more fully with structural ones. (See the chapter in this volume by Goodwin.) Even structural conflicts and transformations are imbued with meaning for participants on both sides.

If cultural meanings channel political aspirations and action, they are also the stuff of politics as a spectator sport. Given the complexity of modern societies, most of us participate in politics indirectly through the media. Dramaturgical metaphors of politics become quite literal. One implication is that we need to distinguish the many audiences for any political choice or action, bringing rhetoric to the fore (Nimmo and Combs, 1980; Jamison, 1988; Popkin, 1991). Politicians carefully "manage their visibility" to achieve the desired impacts on audiences (Thompson, 1995). Robin Wagner-Pacifici (1986), for instance, successfully analyzed the Red Brigades' 1978 kidnaping of Aldo Moro (Italy's prime minister) as a social drama.

For several decades Murray Edelman has shown how politics and policies are aimed at more than one audience at the same time. Apparently drawing on "mass society" models, he distinguished material and symbolic effects of policies, with "organized" interests having sufficient power to grab the "real," namely, material, effects. Although Edelman insisted that elites do not simply use symbols instrumentally as a smokescreen – the opiate of the masses – he did describe symbolic processes pejoratively (1964:40) as "the only means by which groups not in a position to analyze a complex system rationally may adjust themselves to it, through stereotypization, oversimplification, and reassurance." He later expanded the residual contrast between rationality and symbolism into a tougher critique (drawing on French postmodernism) of political language (1977) and images (1988) for the ways in which they hide power in modern societies. When attention is thus refocused on elites rather than on "masses," the critical kernel of the earlier theories – formulated as a critique of complacent pluralism – becomes clear.

The media, as the lens through which most citizens view politics, were important to the emerging cultural perspective in the 1970s and 1980s. A number of scholars examined the characteristic biases of print and television news (Schudson, 1978; Gans, 1979; Bagdikian, 1983; Kellner, 1990). Todd Gitlin (1980) showed not only how media coverage of the New Left distorted its means and ends in the eyes of outsiders, but also how it transformed the movement's sense of its own identity. Fictional programming could also be deconstructed for its political (or apolitical) thrust (e.g., Gitlin, 1983; Jhally and Lewis, 1992). Edward Said (1978) made a large impact by decoding the cultural biases of the West in dealing with the East, showing how the former made the latter appear mysterious, unchanging, and inferior. Critics decried cultural imperialism, implying that the flow of meaning was unidirectional from the center to the periphery (Hamelink, 1983; Schiller, 1992).

This hegemonic view of the media began to give way to a more complex picture in the late 1980s. Under the influence of reader response research in literature, sociologists began to discover the varied interpretations viewers made of the programs they watched (Ang, 1985; Liebes and Katz, 1990) and citizens' ability to mix their own common-sense understandings with media information (Gamson, 1992). By the 1990s, viewers were no longer the passive recipients portrayed by critical theory, but agents actively interpreting the world, using media such as television for a variety of purposes (Tomlinson, 1991; Lembo, 2000). No one can be left in the status of pure victim: not even Islamic women (Saliba et al., 2002; Beaulieu and Roberts, 2002). A vast literature on the political meanings and impacts of other media and arts has followed a similar trajectory toward the recognition of audience agency. (On similar trends in anthropology, see Miller [1995] and Baumann [1996]; in history, Geyer and Bright [1995].) Postcolonial discourse gives a voice to those once framed as others and then as victims (Bhabha, 1994).

Political sociology, alas, has had too little connection to these closely related fields, in which culture and power have been central.

INSIDE THE STATE

The state remains the central focus of political sociology, and here cultural approaches have made the least progress. The biased vision of the 1950s, in which extrainstitutional action was based on ideology and emotion while bureaucrats were driven by interest and instrumentalism, seems to persist. Whether tinged with admiration or indignation, analyses of state actors tend to examine their practical, strategic choices and policies as though they were transparently rational. Admitting that they too operate within culture and emotion, however, would hardly render them irrational – just human.

Scholars have found it easier to examine the cultural dimensions of past states than contemporary ones, and especially practices of state formation. Thus Philip Gorski (1993, 2003) analyzed the "disciplinary revolution," propelled by ascetic Protestantism, which helped create modern state bureaucracies. Eiko Ikegami (1995) described a parallel process in Japan, the "taming of the samurai" as part of modern state building. The works on nationalism and disciplinary power cited above also address state formation in the early modern period (and Steinmetz's *State/Culture*, a central collection addressing the cultural dimensions of the state, has as its content and subtitle, "State-Formation after the Cultural Turn," as though there were no culture in normally functioning states).

State culture has also been probed from the perspective of those oppressed by it. Thus James Scott, with a career devoted primarily to peasant resistance (1985, 1990), could write about what it is like to "see like a state" (1998). Like large-scale capitalism, the modern state controls territory and people by reducing them to simple, homogenized categories and numbers capable of counting and manipulation. Scott decodes the faith in progress and technology that peaked in the twentieth century within subcultures of the state and the experts closely aligned with them.

The "new institutionalism" in sociology emphasizes culture in explanations of organizations and their decisions, including components of the state (Powell and DiMaggio, 1991). But its impact on political sociology has been limited by the backward way the state has been used, primarily to criticize images of firms as autonomous rational actors. The thorough and defining intervention of states in markets has been one of the approach's core ideas (Dobbin, 1994; Fligstein, 2001), but the emphasis has been on the state's effect on corporate policies rather than on state policies themselves. A small current, however, emphasizes normative models of how states should be organized (e.g., democratically, with certain kinds of departments and agencies), and the worldwide spread of a single model of the national state (McNeely, 1995; Meyer et al., 1997; Meyer, 1999).

As part of their broader program to show that organizational development and change are not driven by efficiency, Meyer and Rowan (1977) argued that organizations devote considerable resources to following prevailing conceptions about how organizations should function, in other words increasing their legitimacy more than their efficiency. Strategic efficacy is not the same as technical efficiency. In some ways, the new institutionalists have substituted cognitive components for the norms of structural functionalism as the glue that binds organizations and systems of organizations. At any rate, there is a large opening for cultural analysis of organizations, including state agencies. Fligstein and Mara-Drita (1996), for example, showed how political elites strategically frame arguments to legitimate their policies to one another.

Other scholars have looked inside the state from cultural perspectives. Most common have been accounts of local organizational cultures. For instance, a fatalistic attitude toward accidents and pollution may arise among those who process nuclear materials and wastes daily (Loeb, 1986; Zonabend, 1993). In many cases, organizational cultures reflect the professional training of those who dominate the organizations (Jasper, 1990) – even when these conflict with legal mandates (Bell, 1985). Yet the same profession may contain factions with contrasting assumptions about the world, reflecting in some cases generational differences (Espeland, 1998). Unfortunately, many of these works present the cultural aspects of decision making as though they interfered with rationality, accepting an unrealistic notion of pristine rationality.

Culture becomes a clear explanatory variable when different sets of meanings are compared or traced across different institutional levels. For example, I was able to trace different "policy styles" – based largely but not entirely on professional training – across different organizations involved in nuclear policy making (Jasper, 1990). Disagreements were especially strong between engineers, who relied on developing technologies and transforming the physical world as the solution, and economists, who preferred to let prices reconcile supply and demand, aided by careful cost-benefit analyses. Then, by comparing the organizational distributions of these styles across countries, I could explain policy outcomes. The same policy styles were found inside and outside the state, helping to explain why some preferences affected policies more easily than others. What Haas (1992) calls "epistemic communities" of similarly trained professionals transcend the boundaries of the state and of the nation. The borders of the state are porous, and cultural meanings are one of the things that flow across them.

Finally, a growing body of research has examined the role of ideas in politics and policy making (reviewed in Campbell, 2002). All too much of this literature compares the impacts of ideas and interests, as though the two were competing and mutually exclusive – a starting point encouraged by the boldest rational choice formulations (Jacobsen, 1995; McDonough, 1997). Some research on ideas often pushes into more implicit forms of meaning (such as worldviews: Dobbin, 1994); looks at experts and others who attempt to "own" social problems and policies (Gusfield, 1981); and examines the social networks through which the ideas flow (Keck and Sikkink, 1997). Discussion of ideas rather than less explicit meanings still tends to concede considerable rationality to state officials, however.

Despite this start, the emotions, cognitions, and moral principles and intuitions of elected officials and bureaucrats cry out for closer investigation.

UNDEVELOPED THEMES

Now that they have established that culture matters, researchers seem likely to continue current trends toward distinguishing and refining its many effects. Identities, frames, narratives, and so on operate differently. Once they are distinguished, we can begin to study the relationships among them. In what rhetorical situations are narratives most effective? When do narratives help to construct identities? Do different schemata give rise to different frames or identities? We still need to describe the identities, rhetorics, and so on at work in different countries and groups, now that so much work has been done defining these concepts at an abstract level. We need to know more about the concrete meanings in use; we currently lack even basic typologies for many of them.

Other aspects of culture and politics have been ignored almost entirely.

Emotions, for example, permeate all social life. Long-standing affects such as love and hate (but also trust and respect) are both crucial means and fundamental ends of political life. Other emotions, such as compassion or indignation, are complex cultural constructs that guide much political action. Moods such as depression, hope, or cynicism affect people's ability and willingness to participate in politics. Although some emotions seem hardwired into us, especially reflex emotions like anger and surprise (Griffiths, 1997), most are eminently cultural creations. Political psychologists have examined the effects of emotions on political perceptions and voting (Ottati and Wyer, 1993), and students of social movements have rediscovered the emotional dimensions of protest (Goodwin et al., 2001; Aminzade and McAdam, 2001). Otherwise, even the most culturally oriented analysts of politics have ignored emotions – even though in many cases it may be the associated emotions that give recognized causal mechanisms their real explanatory thrust (Jasper, 1998). It is obvious that emotional workmanship goes into the construction of someone as a victim, for example, but less so how much emotional work must go into constructing someone as rational (Whittier, 2001).

Character. Victims are one example of the character types we commonly construct in political life; the other main ones are heroes and villains. Heroes and villains are both powerful, victims weak. Heroes and victims share moral righteousness, something villains notably lack. Through cartoons, jokes, and direct description, political parties, nations, and other players try to portray themselves as heroes or victims, their opponents as villains. The subject of the epideictic tradition in rhetoric, this kind of praise and blame is a core political activity rarely studied by political sociologists. It is cognitive, moral, and emotional at the same time.

Biography. The self and individuals are another topic inadequately studied – even by postmodernists who dismiss the idea as an illusion. There is little borrowing from the vibrant field of political psychology or mainstream research on personality. We need to understand selves if we are to incorporate individuals into our explanations. Ironically, the more "macro" one's research, the more difference an idiosyncratic individual can make – as historians and readers of biographies understand. Political sociologists are less likely today to try to explain "the state" than they are to explain specific outcomes such as Swedish trade policies in the 1960s, and as soon as we are on concrete historical terrain, key figures loom large in any explanation. A dictator's decision to fight or flee a mob, a prime minister's passion for nuclear energy or ecology, a protest leader's commitment to nonviolence: All these have significant effects, reduced to noise in more structural models (for critique: Jasper, 1990, 1997). Individuals are also widespread symbols (Fine, 2001). Through the intersection of culture and psychology, we should be able to deal with them more effectively. Many of these issues have been covered under the rubric of leadership, a matter central to Weber but so contrary to current trends that it lacks a chapter in this handbook.

Leadership. The subject of leadership has increasingly been left to students of strategy (e.g., Allison and Zelikow, 1999), while political sociologists have looked for "structures." Leaders were a staple of research in the 1950s, aimed at explaining demagogues' ability to manipulate mass followers – a topic that at least focused on rhetorical dynamics (Burke, 1941). The functions of coordinating a team or agency are today collapsed into organizational research. Yet the emotional identifications, rhetorical framings, and other persuasive powers of leaders remain a rich and understudied topic. Cognitive and emotional issues of leader succession, for instance, are crucial for formal organizations, regimes, parties, revolutions, and protest groups (Gouldner, 1954:70–101).

Cognition. The cognitive revolution in psychology has paralleled the cultural one in sociology, but there has been little cross-fertilization. One has universalist pretensions whereas the other does not, but they cover similar topics like memory, basic assumptions, decision making, and so on (Cerulo, 2002). A variety of psychologies may have something to contribute to political sociology. Even psychoanalysis, once popular but now in disfavor, can still tell us something about unconscious motivations, hidden meanings, and personality types (Jasper, 2004). If individual leaders occasionally play pivotal roles in politics, then psychobiographies should have a larger part in our explanations.

Zeitgeist. Analyzed by Mannheim (1952/1928) but forgotten in recent years, every microgeneration comes of age in a slightly different cultural mood, retains different memories. The "structures of feeling" in a society (Williams, 1977) shift rapidly, reframing conflicts and how they are experienced, even shifting the identities of the players involved. Senses of momentum, for instance, shift quickly but influence goals and strategies. Each year's recruits to parties and movements differ somewhat from other years' (Whittier, 1995).

Strategy. Strategic action is a topic that has received both too much and too little attention. Just as rational choice theorists have managed to define rationality in their own narrow way, so the subset of them called game theorists have staked a claim to strategic thinking that has scared away other social scientists. Diverse institutional and cultural contexts disappear in the sparse elegance of game theory. Strategic choice depends heavily on personality traits, know-how, routines, emotions – and a whole range of cultural meanings of every sort. Again, the structural bias of the 1980s has prevented political sociologists from recognizing strategy when they encounter it. They are likely to overestimate the constraints and underestimate the choice involved in any given outcome. A strategic approach might be the key to integrating culture and structure, order and agency (McAdam et al., 2001; Fligstein, 2001; Jasper, in press, b).

Agency. Agency is a concept whose popularity has risen in recent decades alongside that of culture, and the two ideas are often linked. Beginning with Giddens (1979), however, agency is a term most often used by structurally oriented researchers when they reach the limits of their models: a residual category for what is left over, dismissed as unexplainable. Attention to strategy and culture would, I think, help us give a fuller account of agency. People make choices, face dilemmas with no right answers, interact with each other in open-ended ways. In the political realm, this is the source of most freedom, creativity, and contingency (Jasper, 1997; Emirbayer and Mische, 1998).

In addition to these underdeveloped areas, attention to culture could enrich other approaches and dimensions of political life. In recent years scholars have come to appreciate the role of social networks in mobilizing people and influencing policy. Although there remains a frequent tendency to reify the network metaphor in structuralist fashion, the impact of networks is mainly that they allow information to flow, affective loyalties to evolve, and common understandings to grow (Gould, 1995; Emirbayer and Goodwin, 1994) .

Structural approaches more generally might benefit from attention to culture. In their concern to demonstrate the autonomy of state bureaucrats (in a polemic against earlier marxist simplifications), structuralists overlooked one of the main ways that state and nonstate institutions are connected, namely culture (Skocpol, 1979; Block, 1977; Evans et al., 1985). Political sociology has still not entirely recovered from this one-sided paradigm. But as we have seen, the most "structural" institutional settings are permeated by cultural meanings, which account for much of their causal impact.

In addition, many of the criticisms and gaps in rational choice theory can be addressed by supplementing it with culture (Ferejohn, 1991; cf. Adams, 1999). These include the origins of preferences, still often treated as exogenous to rational choice models. Culture may also help us grapple with noncomparable preferences, especially what Taylor (1989) calls moral "hypergoods" that people are reluctant to give up at any cost. A number of the decision-making biases described by cognitive psychologists and behavioral economists are the result of local cultures as well as limitations of the human brain (Kahneman et al., 1982; Thaler, 1992; Camerer, 2003). More broadly still, when actors satisfice rather than maximize, they must follow cultural traditions to tell them what satisfactory levels are, and often bring in culturally determined reference groups in doing so. Culture is the main context within which strategic decisions are made (Jasper, in press, b).

A number of these paths would lead cultural approaches out of their recurrent Romantic celebration of particularism, especially by linking them to abiding strategic concerns. Some scholars have already criticized the emphasis on community and culture for undermining universal standards of justice and equality (Gitlin, 1995; Barry, 2001), others – more dubiously – for abandoning materialism (Palmer, 1990). Habermas views humans as cultural creations yet still seeks universalist agreement through dialogue. In the study of politics it is hard to avoid moral polemics, but cultural approaches have given us a number of taut analytic tools for understanding the politics of social life regardless of our own value judgments. Political sociology will be a more interesting field as it continues to open up dialogues between culturalists and others.

CHAPTER SIX

Feminist Theorizing and Feminisms in Political Sociology

Barbara Hobson

Feminist theorizing in the social sciences covers a vast territory. It emerged from feminist movements and feminisms in politics, and though still in dialogue with them, feminist theory now has its own track in the academy, in academic journals, graduate programs, and has its canon of core feminist texts. Feminist theory has been engaged in debates with mainstream theory, including critiques of theories, concepts, and epistemologies as well as offered alternative explanatory theories of gender differences in power resulting from economic, political, and social structures and processes (Chaftez, 1997). It has a normative side developing models and formulating strategies to achieve gender equality and equity. However, as a result of postmodernism, in feminist theorizing there has been a strong critique of approaches that assume gendered coherent identities and interests. What has remained constant in feminist theorizing is its interdisciplinarity. In the course of this chapter, we will be traveling across disciplinary borders, featuring feminists speaking from traditions of sociology, political science and political philosophy, history and law. My presentation of this kaleidoscopic and fractured theoretical terrain is admittedly selective, based on my own rendering of the core research areas, the key actors, and their exchanges.

The chapter focuses on gender, state, and citizenship using two lenses. The first concentrates on debates among feminist theorists and citizenship around public and private spheres, difference, and universalism; the second turns to feminist theorists in dialogue with mainstream theorizing on citizenship. In gendering the theoretical terrain of citizenship, feminists have challenged the lack of gender perspectives in mainstream approaches as well as introduced new dimensions that have deepened and expanded existing theories, models, and typologies.

In calling this chapter feminist theorizing and feminisms in political sociology, I underscore the plurality in theories and approaches. The plural form, feminisms, mirrors an important shift in the theoretical terrain, from monolithic conceptions of the state and patriarchy toward more complex frameworks that consider processes and social structures of states and state institutions, and embedded notions of citizenship and exclusion within specific histories and political contexts. Finally, feminisms signify the multidimensionality in the category of gender and how this insight informs the framing of gender across class, race/ethnicity, sexual preference, and disability in different political arenas (the local, national, and supranational).

The chapter is divided into four sections. Part one considers the first phase of feminist theorizing of the state, which can be organized into three categories: liberal, socialist, and radical feminisms. The next section addresses mechanisms of exclusion, including the feminist critique of classical theories of citizenship that bifurcated public and private spheres. Part three considers the postmodern turn and its impact on theorizing inclusion and exclusion. This includes both the postmodernist and poststructuralist critique and the challenges made by black feminism, Third World feminism, and feminist scholars from former Soviet regime countries. I also concentrate on the feminist dialogue with two citizenship theoretical traditions, social citizenship and civic republicanism. Here I seek to highlight the ways in which gendering of citizenship reaches the heart of debates on inclusion and exclusion around rights and needs, individual and group rights, and multiculturalism. The concluding section considers current challenges for feminist theorizing and political sociology.

THE STATE, POWER, AND AGENCY

Until the early 1980s, feminist theoretical positions on the state fell into three broad categories: socialist/Marxist, liberal, and radical. Each offered a different account of the state reproducing and perpetuating gender inequalities.

Neo-Marxist and Feminist Dialogues

The state entered feminist theory through socialist feminism and neo-Marxist debates on production and reproduction (Haney, 1996). Within Marxian theory, the state is an agent of elite capitalist power; gender exploitation is viewed as a subset of class exploitation reproducing class relations. Feminist theories sought to modify and extend Marxist theories of production and reproduction (Eisenstein, 1979; Sacks, 1974) to go beyond the analysis of women's unwaged labor in the household as reproducing and maintaining an exploited labor force (Seccombe, 1974; Zaretsky, 1976). Socialist feminists argued in what has been referred to as the domestic labor debate that one had to focus on the underlying social conditions that shaped women's unpaid labor, that gender inequalities in the family were ideologically and practically linked to their responsibility for unwaged work in the family (Barrett, 1980; Hartsock, 1985; Molyneaux, 1979; Vogel, 1983). The state became a focal point in these feminist dialogues through its support of the male breadwinner wage. Mary McIntosh (1978), in "The State and the Oppression of Women," linked the labor process to the institution of the family. The state's support for the male breadwinner reproduced the division of labor in the household and women's dependency, which also made them a source of cheap labor or a latent army of reserve labor (McIntosh, 1978:264). McIntosh emphasized the contradictions in these state interventions in sustaining these relationships. By making women dependent on men's wages, they kept women in a semiproletarianized state – easily exploited.

Another response to the domestic labor debate was the assertion that there was a parallel system of exploitation, patriarchy (gender could not be fit into a Marxist frame), because women's unpaid domestic work not only served the interests of the capitalist economy but also the interests of individual men, as expressed in Heidi Hartmann's classic article, "The Unhappy Marriage of Capitalism and Patriarchy" (Hartmann, 1986). Joan Acker (1988) has provided the most theoretically promising reconciliation of this unhappy marriage of class and gender through her introduction of the concept of distribution, which addresses the role of the state in mediating these relationships. Not two systems but one structure operates, according to Acker. Gender is implicated in the organization of the labor process (deskilling and technology, and the wage structure relation) as well as present in the evolution of the family wage constructed around gender difference. State policies bolster the family wage and women's economic dependency as well as seek to ameliorate the conditions it helped to create (Acker, 1988; Walby, 1990).

Liberal feminist theory views the state as a potentially neutral arbiter lacking any ideology of its own. Recognizing that men dominate the state, liberal feminism maintains that the state and its institutions exist apart from men's domination. Men, like women, are an interest or pressure group. The state is a site in which groups contest and compete with one another, hence a neutral arbiter between them. State processes are legitimate, but men have captured them (Connell, 1987). Given this perspective, liberal feminist approaches embrace strategies for more access and influence (Gelb, 1989; Klein, 1987; Sawer, 1993). Women's agency is a crucial dimension in liberal feminist theorizing on the state and is an explanatory variable for variations across states in terms of women's voice/representation and their influence over gender inequalities.

The Patriarchal State

Radical feminist theory takes as its starting point that the state is a system of structures and institutions created by men in order to sustain and recreate male power and female subordination. Departing from economic analysis of women's exploitation, radical feminist theorist Catherine MacKinnon (1983), in her agenda-setting article, "Feminism, Marxism Method and the State," sought to carve a feminist theory of the state in opposition to Marxist theory. She expressed this in her now classic analogy: Sexuality is to feminism what work is to Marxism. Although both Marxism and feminism were concerned with analyzing power, MacKinnon asserted that they were incompatible. Her theorizing on the state revolves around the sexual subordination of women and how this subordination is embedded in the state apparatus, procedures, and structures (MacKinnon, 1989). Radical feminist theorizing has rejected the essentialism implicit in MacKinnon's stance in which men and women appear as fixed categories of dominant and subordinate. However, her emphasis on sexuality as the core of state patriarchy continues to influence radical feminists' analyses of the state and the governance of gender (Brush, 2003; Elman, 1996). Governance, a central concept in radical feminist framework, derives its inspiration from Foucault and the regulatory function of the state. What they take from Foucault is his formulation of the diffusion of power, that power is fluid, relational, existing in institutions that reflect the gendered power structure. As Lisa Brush (2003) argues in her study of *Gender and Governance*, however, both Foucault's and Weber's definitions of power are gender-blind. Weberian notions of "power over" ignore the sites of resistance and strategies to overcome domination (empowerment) (Brush, 2003; Heckman, 1996). Foucault does not address the gendered dimensions of power as knowledge – that the power to know is gendered. Moreover, in Foucault's analysis, the regulation of sexuality is gender-neutral, ignoring the much greater control of women's bodies (Hartsock, 1985). Still, Foucault reverberates in much of radical feminists' theorizing both because of his emphasis on bodies as sites of power and because of his view of power as permeating everyday life relationships of people, both individually and in institutions.

Radical feminist theorizing assumes the state is a purposive actor reproducing patriarchy, that states are masculinist, designed by men to serve their interest. Although the framework of governance seeks to broaden the analysis to include structures of power, a suspicion and pessimism remain about the potential of state institutions to address feminist politics. There is also skepticism about the usefulness of institutional state theories to accommodate issues of sexual subordination and violence.

In his examination of feminist research on the patriarchal state, Robert Connell (1990), the author of *Gender and Power*, highlighted two important theoretical weaknesses. The state is not monolithic but consists of complex structures and actors, with sites for resistance. In short, the state is not a thing but a process. Connell in his appraisal of feminist theorizing on the patriarchal state argues for more complexity as well as a process-oriented view of the state. The state is constituted within gender relations as the central institutionalization of gendered power. Conversely, gender dynamics are a major force constructing the state, both in the historical creation of state structures and in contemporary politics" (1990:519).

Anna Yeatman (1997) begins from this position – that feminism has been a force in the development of more democratic social relations in public and private domains. She distinguishes state-centric "power over women," or domination – which often includes state interventions to protect women from abusive men, a form of liberal paternalism – from power as capacity. The latter assumes "democratic deployment of legitimate state domination," obtained through feminist demands for a politics of women as rights-bearing subjects and agents (Yeatman, 1997).

Over the past decade, a rich literature on gender and welfare state formation has developed, underscoring the importance of women's agency that implicitly challenges the monolithic view of the patriarchal state (Koven and Michel, 1993; Misra and Atkins, 1998). Skocpol's (1992) distinction between paternalist and maternalist welfare states highlights the importance of women's agency in the development of American welfare states compared to European paternalist ones. Hobson and Lindholm (1997) analyze the power resources of feminist actors in the first years of Swedish social democracy, suggesting a need to pay attention to variations in European welfare state formation.

Feminist actors have been important agents in the making of welfare states and in shaping the different gender logics around paid and unpaid work (Skocpol, 1992; Lewis, 1992b, 1994; Hobson and Lindholm, 1997; O'Connor et al., 1999). Making the argument that political institutions and politics make a difference, feminist research on the Nordic countries has underscored the importance of the government as an actor promoting women's interests (Selle and Karovonen, 1995). In her overview of feminist debates, Bryson (1992) made a similar point about the "women friendly" Scandinavian states: "'the vicious circle' of women's political economic and social disadvantage is being replaced by a 'virtuous circle' through which gains in one area interact with gains in another, to produce a general picture of cumulative progress" (Bryson, 1992:110). Women have been key actors in promoting women's greater participation in political and economic spheres. Although one may disagree with the optimistic prognosis of this assessment, one cannot ignore the variation in women's economic, political, and social position that has been revealed in empirical research on gender and the welfare state.[1]

[1] The ambitious RINGS project on state feminism and movements has sought to demonstrate this: see Mazur (2001); Stetson (2001); and Outsthorn, (2004).

Mechanisms of Exclusion: Public/Private Divide

The initial dialogues in feminist theorizing and the state debated whether the state was positive or negative for women. They asked whether private patriarchy was being replaced by public patriarchy, whether women's dependency on husbands was being shifted to dependency on welfare state bureaucracies (Pascall, 1986; Hernes, 1987). But another strand of feminist theorizing emerged in the late 1980s, which turned the focus toward analyzing the mechanisms of exclusion, particularly the gendered construction of public and private spheres of life.

Rather than presenting a feminist theory of the state, Carole Pateman analyzed the exclusionary mechanism in citizenship theory: the relegation of women's activity to the private sphere. In what has become a classic feminist text, *The Sexual Contract* (1988), she revisited the triad of classical social theorists on citizenship, the state, and the social contract: Rousseau, Hobbes, and Locke. Pateman referred to the social contract as a fiction, a narrative that has provided the theoretical underpinnings for the exclusion of women from an active participation in the polity. Underlying the social contract were constructions of sexual difference. For example, Rousseau conceptualized civic republicanism and political life as male domain; the public sphere of rights of protections did not apply to women, whom he believed lacked the faculties of reason and were unable control their passions, two prerequisites for civic republicanism (Pateman, 1988; Phillips, 1991). The relegation of women to the family, a sphere lacking in rights, meant that women were civilly dead. In the private sphere there was an implicit sexual contract, one in which men had access to women's bodies in marriage through law and women's economic dependency. Hence women were more a kin to slaves than to exploited workers.

Wollestenscraft's Dilemma

In her analysis of "The Patriarchal Welfare State," Pateman (1989) reformulated the classical dilemma in citizenship theory and practice for women, which she called Wollestencraft's dilemma. Referring back to that eighteenth-century feminist philosopher who first recognized the dilemma of difference, Pateman applied it as a theory of modern citizenship: In a patriarchal understanding of citizenship, in which the ideal of citizenship is based on a universalistic gender-neutral social world – in our century connected to paid work – women are lesser men, as norms are built on a male model. In a framework in which women's special talents, needs, and capacities are acknowledged as different from men, whose citizenship is based on rights and duties attached to paid work, then women are lesser citizens as there is an inherent lack of respect for their contribution as mothers and caregivers. These two routes to citizenship lead to a dead-end for women (Pateman, 1989:196). What is obvious in this analysis is that the public/private split has played a dual role, both as an explanation of women's subordinate position and as an ideology constructing that position (Davidoff, 1998). This dichotomy has had the effect of solidifying women's difference and subordination.

Wollenstencraft's dilemma placed the equality and difference debate at the center of the sphere of citizenship. One can trace this theoretical divide back to cleavages in the first wave of feminist politics, both the pre- and post-suffrage movements. Various feminist actors promoted competing agendas: whether strategies for women's emancipation should embrace laws and policies to put women on the same footing as men or whether they should struggle for special protections that recognized women's maternal responsibilities (Koven and Michel, 1993; Harrison, 1988). The debates resurfaced in the second-wave feminism of the 1970s, but the real playing field of the equality/difference divide has been in academia. It covers many different theoretical fields including epistemology, psychology, moral philosophy, and, most relevant to this discussion, citizenship (Bock and James, 1992; Lister, 1998; Phillips, 1992). Within the domain of citizenship and political theory, the equality/difference debate is a fulcrum on which other feminist theoretical issues are hinged – debates around the private/public divide, needs and rights, and an ethic of care versus an ethic of justice.

At the extreme end of the equality/difference debates are theories rooted in essentialist identities that assume an epistemological position that women speak in a different voice (Gilligan, 1982; Offen, 1988). Taking a perspective of differentiated citizenship, maternalist feminists celebrate the private sphere as the realm of women's influence. Rather than seeing women's encapsulation in the private sphere as the means by which they were excluded from the polity and from participatory citizenship (Pateman, 1989; Vogel, 1994; Philips, 1992), maternalist feminists (or social feminists as they are sometimes called) view the private sphere as the uncorrupted domain of women's power and influence (Elshstain, 1992). For Jean Bethke Elshtain, its most uncompromising proponent, mothering and the sphere of the family are the high moral ground where human ties are the most important for articulating values, in contrast to the corrupt world of politics and self-interest. The logic in maternalist thinking is that women's experiences of care and motherhood will create a "politics of compassion," "an ethical policy," that will result in a more just and peaceful world (Elshtain, 1981: Ruddick, 1984).

In proposing an ethic of care, Joan Tronto (1993) has sought to distinguish her position from essentialist/maternalist theories of female identity as well as avoid deepening the rift between public and private. She maintains that her conceptual ground in the ethic of care is gender-neutral. Her purpose is to incorporate gender-sensitive dimensions that stand in opposition to the ethic of justice rooted in Kantian universalistic formulas. Arguing that hers is a "contextual moral position," she is asking us to view care as public concern and consider what social and political institutions should support an ethic of care. Along the same lines as Tronto, Diemut Bubeck (1995) makes the case for care as a resource for political citizenship. She maintains that "private" concerns, values, skills, and understandings can enhance the public practices of citizenship. Nevertheless, although it seeks to go beyond maternalist feminism, the ethic of care tends to fall into similar rhetoric, of "essentialized carers," if not mothers (Leira and Saraceno, 2002). Though rejecting the idea of biologism in maternalist thinking and essentialized identities, many feminist scholars nevertheless are arguing for an alternative vision of collective, interdependent citizens, in opposition to liberal democratic theory rooted in a tradition of the independent rational individual (Hochschild, 1995; Knijn and Kermer, 1997; Sevenhuisjen, 1998).

Feminist scholars have offered different strategies to resolve Wollstencraft's dilemma. One response that seeks to go beyond equality and difference is contextuality: when does difference make a difference. Carole Bacchi has elaborated this position most fully in her book on *Same Difference* (1990). In that study, she locates examples of how feminists have employed different strategies, emphasizing gender distinctiveness and gender neutrality at different moments in time and across societies. The context thesis is also supported by a great deal of historical sociological work, which reveals the importance of institutional variations in shaping the universe of political discourse and political choices (Hobson and Lindholm, 1997; Jenson, 1990; Koven and Michel, 1993).

Legal theorist Martha Minow (1990) has offered the most theoretically powerful analysis of the contextual argument. She claims that by emphasizing difference, we highlight deviance or stigma, but by ignoring it we leave in place all the problems that arise from a false neutrality. Instead of viewing the equality/difference divide as opposites, she suggests that we regard them as practices and sets of relations between people and institutions (Minow, 1990:90).

THE POSTMODERN TURN: GENDERED IDENTITIES AND FEMINISMS

The contests over women's inclusion as full citizens based on their difference or equality have been battles over the category of gender, surrounding collective identities and shared interests. These struggles have intensified as a result of the interventions of postmodernism and poststructuralism and the recognition of differences among women and the diversities in feminisms.

Pateman's two-horned dilemma has become many-sided when confronted with postmodernist/poststructuralist theories. The postmodern turn has imploded the equality and difference debate by destabilizing the very category of woman and the political underpinnings of feminism, which assumed gendered identities and interests based on shared experiences of subordination and exclusion. Postmodernists reject not only the binary oppositions of man/woman, but also those of unity/diversity and universality/distinctiveness. The very idea of making claims based on gendered identities (even those that emerge from political struggles) is viewed as reifying individuals into abstract categories, ignoring their diversity and experience. The idea of gendered collective struggles for justice is rejected on two fronts: the first as a denial of unified experience upon which women can frame claims for rights, and the second as a rejection of universalism as a legitimate base for such claims. The former has been most problematic for feminist critics, who claim that it undermines the potentialities for collective feminist action. There is diversity in postmodernist and poststructuralist theorizing. Indeed, some argue that rather than a theory or theories, postmodernism is more a body of thought bound by conceptual ground in which concepts of language, power, identity, and resistance are central (Bryson, 1992:36). One can find many examples of poststructuralist analyses of discourses of power that view social practices as important in constructing gender identity. From this standpoint, they propose transformative politics (Butler, 1990; Fraser, 1997; Weedon, 1987, 1998).

To the extent that most feminist theory is cautious about generalizing about all women on the basis of what middle class Western women experience – that the experience of gender is context-bound: culturally, structurally, and individually – one can say that a postmodernist/poststructuralist critique has transformed theorizing gender. Moreover, the postmodern emphasis on the importance of discourse and the importance of language as a signifier of power has been integrated into much of feminist theory: in terms of how political subjects are constituted and more generally of how discourse operates in different institutional fields in the construction of social meanings. The inclusion of discourse as a dimension of power is visible in analyses of political opportunity and of the discursive resources of feminist actors (Adams and Padamasee, 2001; Hobson and Lindholm, 1997; Hobson, 2003; Jenson, 1990). It has also been incorporated in social movement theory and recognition politics, of which gender is one key dimension (Gal, 2003; Gamson and Ferree, 2003; Gamson, 1995; Hobson, 2003).

Whereas the critique of gender as an analytical category in postmodernism for the most part has been a deconstructivist enterprise, critical race and gender theory has been a reconstructivist endeavor from which to develop analytical frameworks that take into account the multidimensionality of gender and feminisms. Black feminist scholarship has had a profound impact on feminist theorizing (Crenshaw, 1995). This scholarship has challenged empirically and theoretically feminist analyses of the sources of oppression, the notion of a gendered collectivity formed around common identities and interests. Speaking from different experiences, histories, and political and economic positions, black feminist scholars not only highlighted the exploitation of black and Third World women by white middle class women, but also challenged the basic frameworks of feminist theorizing (Collins, 1991; hooks, 1995).

How gender was incorporated into welfare state formation and citizenship, in addition, has been bound up with constructions of race and ethnicity in different societal contexts. In their genealogy of dependency, Fraser and Gordon (1994) have traced different registers (gender, class, and race) in U.S. history. They reveal the ways in which the construction of welfare became associated with the black single mother, dependent on the state, lacking a male breadwinner, and whose mothering was deemed less worthy than white motherhood.

Moreover, for black feminists, the family, rather than a site of oppression – a central argument in feminist theories of women's subordination – is viewed as a site of resistance against the intrusion of the state and the policing of unmarried mothers (Mink, 1994). Women scholars from the postsocialist transition countries have raised many of the same points in their challenges to Western feminist scholarship. This critique has been captured in a series of dialogues on gender and citizenship (Gal and Kligman, 2000; Special Forum, "East meets West and West meets East," 1995). In the same vein as black feminists, scholars from the former Soviet Regime countries argue that for women under socialism, the private sphere was not viewed as a location of oppression (Szalai, 1991; Havelklova, 2000; Maleck-Lewy, 1995). Rather, it embodied a sphere of protection and refuge against the control of totalitarian regimes – a place to retreat from the surveillance of the state where one could count on the loyalty of family members. It was a place for bartering goods and services, a place to strike out on one's own in the unofficial economy (Gal and Kligman, 2001; Szalai, 1991).

The clash between feminisms is highlighted in Myra Marx Ferree's (2000) analysis of two distinct feminisms in East and West Germany. She has used the terms "private patriarchy" and "public patriarchy" to represent different discourses, identities, and structures of experiences of the East and West German women's movements. Analyzing the sources of oppression from different lenses, East German feminists addressed the structural features of state power (public patriarchy); while Western feminists viewed women's exploitation in terms of the power of individual men over women in families and their acts of violence toward women (private patriarchy). West German feminists characterized their Eastern counterparts as naïve and backward because of their failure to address private patriarchy – women's exploitation in the family. East German feminists in turn charged their West German counterparts with arrogance (Ferree, 2000:165). Paralleling the East–West critique, Third World feminist scholars have also questioned the validity of middle class American and European feminists who have constructed them as powerless victims of patriarchy (Mohanty, 1991) – a South–North critique. Nor do Third World women identify with the public/private dichotomy, claiming that Western feminists' emphasis on the gender division of labor does not resonate in their perception of a struggle for economic survival – a struggle that does not pit men against women (Gordon, 1996).

Critical race and gender theories seek synthetic analyses across race, class, and gender. Evolving from the wellspring of research on gender and the welfare states, Fiona Williams (1995) posits a model of welfare states that views structured social relations across race, class, and gender, all of which are mutually constitutive and shape women's claims for inclusion. Elaborating on Castell and Miller's concept of migration regimes, she extends the theoretical boundaries of citizenship to embrace the intersectionality of race and gender in the processes of nation building, the legacies of racism, and the construction of family and motherhood in welfare states (Williams, 1995:149). Eileen Boris (1994) has coined the terms "racialized gender" and "gendered race" to capture the ways in which gender and race/ethnicity have been interconnected in the constructions of citizenship, policy-making structures, and economic structures. These relationships are also expressed in movements and countermovements around gender and race. She applies these insights to the U.S. case, the paradigm of the gender/racialized state. In *Unequal Freedom*, Evelyn Nakano Glenn (2002) confronts race and gender theory with three case studies: blacks and whites in the Southern United States; Mexicans and Anglos in the Southwest, and Japanese and Haoles in Hawaii. Race and gender are fluid categories in *Unequal Freedom* shaped by one another in locales, constructed by dominant "whites" (which includes whites in the South and Haoles in Hawaii), and contested by subordinate groups. For Glenn, employing Dorothy Smith's notion of the everyday as problematic to the comparative analysis of citizenship, race and gender hierarchies are experienced in the micropolitics of everyday life. Her analysis reflects the focus of feminist theorizing on citizenship as practice rather than status.

There is also a flowering of research seeking to theorize citizenship across gender, race, and class divisions within the context of nation building and colonialism, shifting the focus away from advanced capitalist societies. Postcolonial feminist analyses have succeeded in revealing the ways in which feminists have been complict in colonialist and racist policies (Lake, 2000; Mohanty, 1991, 2003). Research on gender and global restructuring has underscored the exploitation between women, making visible the class/gender positionings across regions (Marchand and Runyan, 2000). Referring to the global care chain, feminist research (Hochschild, 2000; Anderson, 2000; Gavanas and Williams, in 2004) traces the migration of women from the South who travel across continents to do the "dirty work," of middle class white women in the North, leaving behind their own children to be cared for by others. Nevertheless, global restructuring has created a theoretical bridge across North and South, revealing similar processes in the feminization of casualized and irregular labor, that women are employed in temporary irregular employment. The effects of global restructuring are mirrored in the retreat of the state and the effects on the care deficit and the loss of social infrastructure in societies in the North and South (Pearson, 2000; Marchand and Runyan, 2000; Moghadam, 2003). The North–South dialogue in feminist theorizing can be seen in the diverse literature on women and development enriched by transnational networks such as DAWN (Development Alternatives of Women for a New Era) and UN forums in Nairobi, Copenhagen, and Beijing (Stienstra, 1994).

Destabilizing gender as a category of analysis has led to a multidimensional awareness of gender. But it has also produced theoretical dissonance in the response to the challenge of how to develop theories that recognize that people are more than just the sum of their race, class, and gender, but that nevertheless do not surrender to relativism or disregard the patterns of power and inequality. For many feminist scholars, the frame of citizenship has opened up conceptual space for developing theories of women's agency, a theoretical perspective that has been confounded by the postmodernist challenge to the existence of women as collective. The framework of citizenship also has enabled feminist scholars to confront histories of discrimination and exclusion through the lens of social citizenship, which has enhanced the analysis of the role of institutions and welfare state structures in reproducing gender inequalities.

FEMINIST DIALOGUE ACROSS CITIZENSHIP THEORIES

Citizenship became a keyword in feminist theorizing on the state and social politics, part of a much broader development in late-twentieth-century citizenship scholarship, though much of that scholarship continues to be gender-blind. In trying to develop a full vision for gendered citizenship, feminist theorizing has drawn on two traditions: (1) civic republicanism and participatory citizenship, reflected in a range of theories, most recently communitarianism; and (2) citizenship, inclusion, and membership embodied in Marshall's theories of social citizenship.

Civic Republicanism: Participation, Rights, and Obligations

Civic republicanism dates back to ancient Greece and the ideal of civic duty and the political obligations in the polity. As discussed previously, the Enlightenment republican writers such as Rousseau bestowed both the virtues and duties of participatory citizenship to male citizens. However, eighteenth-century feminists used the discourse of civic republicanism to argue for women's inclusion into the ranks of citizens (Bussemaker and Voet, 1998), and the ideals of liberalism to press for equal citizenship with men (Olympe De Gouges Declaration for the Rights of Women, Déclaration des Droits de la Femme et de la Citoyenne, 1791, 1986, is a classic example).

One reason for the renewed interest in civic republicanism in our own day can be traced to the structural reorganizations of global capital, the retrenchment of welfare societies, and what Turner calls the breakup of a reformist consensus (Turner, 1993:33). Hence we have a need for a more active mobilized citizenry. Civic republicanism also offered a theoretical framework for building women's agency into theories of citizenship. It has appealed to feminist theories of agency because it valorizes citizenship from below, that is, politics with a small "p." Because there are no women's political parties and women lack a critical mass of representatives in governments in most countries, citizenship as practice opens up a theoretical framework for the incorporation of women's politics.

Citizenship as practice has engaged feminist scholars (Jones, 1990; Lister, 1997), particularly those who have broken with liberal conceptualizations of citizenship that revolve around the individual's civil and political rights. This approach promotes a more civic-minded service to a community (Jones, 1994:267). Jones defines this dimension of citizenship "as an action practiced by a people of certain identity in a specifiable locale" (1994:261). Citizenship as practice draws on Brian Turner's theory of active citizenship.[2] Concentrating on the moral active subject, Turner (1993) uses the French case as an example of active citizenship, and the challenges from below to the spheres of family, and religion. Although he seeks to overcome the public/private split, Turner does not address at all the gender implications of his analysis (Lister, 1997:125).

Civic republicanism and the notion of citizenship from below has led feminist theorists to revisit Hanna Arendt's theory of participatory democracy. For many second-wave feminists, Arendt appeared as masculinist and at odds with basic principles of feminism, captured in the idiom of the personal is the political. Not only Arendt's strict demarcation of public space as the world of politics, but also her hostility to feminism and unwillingness to recognize particularized identities, such as gender, as a base for politicization, make her an unlikely bedfellow for feminist theorists (Honig, 1995). But feminist theorizing in the 1990s has prompted a reconsideration of her work (Honig, 1995[3]; Landes, 1998a) through the lens of participatory citizenship and civic republicanism. Her work speaks to feminist theorists who are embracing

[2] Turner (1990) viewed his concept of active citizenship in relation to Marshall's evolutionary theory of citizenship (see discussion below).

[3] See the collection of essays published by Bonnie Honig (1995), which seeks to politicize and historicize Arendt's work.

active democratic citizenship that acknowledges pluralism (Mouffe, 1992a).

In contrast to Arendt's strict demarcation of public space as the world of politics, Habermas in his generalized notion of the public sphere (1990) constructs a framework for participatory democracy, which is an intermediary space between the political system and private sectors of lifeworld. According to Nancy Fraser (1989), what is missing in Habermas's analysis is a gendered subtext on the public and private – that there is no meaningful way to reveal the institutional links between the spheres of paid and unpaid work and family and official economy in his distinction of system and lifeworld. But others view his later works (1990, 1998) on the public sphere and his theory of discourse ethics as a corrective to his earlier gender blindness. They note that his theory has much to offer feminist analysis of feminist politics (Cohen, 1995; Benhabib, 1998). Still, feminist theorists query whether his concept of deliberative democracy can truly feminize and democratize the public sphere (Landes, 1998b), in light of his rigid distinctions between needs and interests, and values and norms. To do so would entail a radical restructuring of discursively organized public space to include all social norms, including family norms and the gendered division of labor (Benhabib, 1992).

From another perspective, feminists have challenged Habermas's notion of deliberative democracy in the context of social and economic inequalities in societies. More privileged groups dominate this sphere, men more often than women. Iris Young claims that subordinated groups, minorities, poor people, and women, historically created "subaltern counter publics," often lack the associational life that provides forums for its members to raise issues among themselves (Young, 2000:171–2).

This critique of participatory democracy has been leveled at civic republicanism more generally as it is understood in conventional terms, which assumes that individuals come together and create the common good without partiality or insensitivity to the rights and needs of weaker members of societies. This critique is implicit in the feminist challenge to communitarianism (Phillips, 1991; Bussemaker and Voet, 1998), which shares with civic republicanism a belief that individual needs should be balanced against the common good. A parallel critique can be made against Arendt's concept of public space and Habermas's framework of deliberative democracy in which members of civil society act collectively to democratically resolve the issues that concern them as a political community. Once again, the dominant voices and politically advantaged groups will be the fittest in this competitive setting.

Finally, feminist scholars also have been wary of civic republicanism and communitarianism because of its emphasis on *obligations over rights* (Sevenhuijsen, 1998). Communitarianism, which has been championed by left and right political spokespersons, has laid the basis for a reestablishment of responsibilities of citizens (Etzioni, 1993). This has opened the gates for attacks on welfare mothers as passive dependent citizens, which reflects a failure to understand their caring work is work (Levitas, 1998; Mink, 1999). Within the broader contexts of participatory citizenship, the duty to participate embodied in civicness should be understood in terms of women's lack of resources, including time, money, and social networks (Lister, 1997; Stolle and Lewis, 2002).

The dialogue between feminists and participatory democratic theory has been essentially a feminist interpolation, as much of the theorizing remains gender-blind. Feminist theoretical challenges, feminist movements, and feminist activism in civil society have led to some rethinking of the discursively organized public space and civil society (Cohen, 1995). But the feminist challenge to participatory democratic theory to develop a truly integrative framework for the public and private still remains on the table.

T. H. Marshall: Social Citizenship and Membership

For many feminist theorists, T. H. Marshall provided a framework for confronting histories of exclusion, though class inequality, not gender, underlay Marshall's framework of social citizenship. Marshall defined social citizenship "as a status bestowed on those who are full members of a community. All who possess the status are equal with respect to the rights and duties with which the status is endowed" (1950:28–9). This gender-neutral formula did not explicitly exclude women, but in an era when full membership in community assumed a male breadwinner wage to support a wife and children, social citizenship rights were applied to male citizens.[4] In addition to the critique of the implicit gender blindness in Marshall's concept of citizenship, feminist scholars also made the point that his sequencing of rights, his historical analysis of the evolution of rights – from civil, political, and social – was an androcentric model. Women in many Western societies had access to social rights before they had the right to vote (Fraser and Gordon, 1994; Walby, 1994). Finally, Marshall analysis of the emergence of social citizenship assumed a male subject as it was historically linked to class inequalities and working class mobilization. The working class man armed with the right to vote and mobilized in a trade union emerged as a new category of citizen who required new types of rights (Marshall, 1950:106). This account of the worker-citizen did not embrace the rise of a new woman citizen and the gendered social rights being claimed around widows' pensions, maternal health, and aid to dependent children, as well as protections against dismissal from employment upon marriage and pregnancy (Skocpol, 1992: Hobson and Lindholm, 1997).

There are many reasons why Marshall became a focal point in feminist research. Recognizing that Marshall did not integrate gender in his account of the evolution of citizenship rights, some feminist scholars nevertheless have welcomed Marshall's view of the active state, seeing it as an antidote to the negative state and negative rights in classical liberal theory and neoliberalism. His notion of community flowed from a tradition of social liberalism (Faulks, 1998) and was premised on a vision of the state that would provide a modicum of security for its citizens. When gender was incorporated into this framework, feminist research introduced dimensions of social citizenship that Marshall never could have imagined.

For example, Sheila Shaver (1994) argues that social rights are a precondition for the civil right to abortion; without social rights to abortion, access becomes stratified. Taking this perspective further, one can argue that to deny women the right to choose pregnancy or not is to undermine their right to participate in civil society and the polity (Bryson, 1999; Held, 1989).

Marshall's formulation of inclusion as membership in a community rather than in a nation-state has also provided the basis for a more holistic definition of citizenship that goes beyond formal rights such as voting or the right to carry a passport. The notion of community rather than state leaves room for theorizing around divided communities and differences (Yuval-Davis, 1997) and claims that are linked to EU citizenship (Hobson, 2000). Finally, Marshall's construction of citizenship as full membership has resonated among feminist scholars who advocate it as blueprint, an ideal, or gold standard of citizenship (Lister, 1997; Vogel, 1994), an argument for retaining the universalistic dimension in citizenship rights.

The main thrust of feminist research and social citizenship emerged in a dialogue with welfare state theorists who took Marshall's mantle, particularly the power resource school. Paralleling Marshall analysis of the conflict between class and citizenship, the power resource model in welfare state theorizing recast the conflict in terms of politics and markets, labor parties and employers (Korpi, 1989; Esping-Andersen, 1985). In Gösta Esping-Anderson's well-known book, *The Three Worlds of Welfare Capitalism* (1990), variations in social citizenship across welfare states revolve around two dimensions: stratification and decommodification. The latter, like Marshall's own construction of social

[4] Empirical research on gender and the origins of the welfare state has shown the extent to which the Marshallian model, when applied to the Beveridge welfare state, had negative consequences for dependent wives, excluded from full participation in the community of paid work and the social rights attached to work (see Lewis, 1992; Pedersen, 1993).

citizenship, assumed a male worker model. Decommodification embodies those rights that weakened a worker's dependence on the market. However, this measure of social rights assumed that individuals were already commodified (Hobson, 1994; Knijn and Ostner, 2002; Orloff, 1993). Even in 1990, when *Three Worlds of Welfare Capitalism* was published, the majority of women in the Western welfare states analyzed were not in the labor force or had intermittent employment. More to the point, feminists argued that for many women, commodification could have a beneficial liberating effect by weakening women's dependence on a male breadwinner wage, enhancing women's civil rights by enabling them to exit untenable marriages (Hobson, 1990). Feminist theorizing introduced a gender-sensitive dimension of social citizenship) – the right to form independent households without the risk of poverty (Hobson, 1994; Orloff, 1993). This dimension of gendered social rights challenged mainstream theories that focused on the state/market nexus on two levels. First, feminist challenges affirmed that states not only play a role in the stratification within societies by regulating markets and redistributing resources across families, but also that states stratify and redistribute resources within families. Second, they argued that decommodifying policies are gendered, often those aimed at women workers such as maternity leave and the parent's right to work part-time, and often had the perverse effect of intensifying gender-segregated labor markets, leading to greater gender stratification in the labor market (O'Connor et al., 1999; Mandel and Shalev, 2003).

The paradigm shift in welfare state theorizing toward typologies or clusters of policy regimes also opened up theoretical space for feminists to engage with mainstream theorizing. The mainstream policy regime typology is structured around an institutional triangle of states, markets, and families. This analytical device reflects the ways in which states govern markets (the state/market axis), but also how states redistribute resources and support family forms (Esping-Anderson, 1990; Korpi and Palme, 1998: Korpi, 2000). Feminist research proposed alternative regime typologies that consider women's unpaid work in the family and the social rights for carework. The enterprise of gendering welfare regime typologies implies gendering the gender-neutral subject in welfare state models, who is the average industrial worker. Further, it involves introducing carework as work, incorporating types of services as well as types of benefits in the construction of models of welfare state regimes. Using this framework, feminist typologies of welfare states analyze variations according to the strength or weakness of the male breadwinner logics (Lewis, 1992a). Drawing on theories of welfare regimes, feminist researchers on gender and welfare states have incorporated the concept of social care into the definition of citizenship, which assumes that citizens are both wage workers and unpaid carers and that policy regimes can be clustered along the public and private mix of care, and the role of the state structuring gender choices around paid and unpaid work (Knijn and Kremer, 1997; Daly and Lewis, 2000). Care regimes cluster differently than the policy regime models in Esping-Anderson (1990), and this has become more pronounced as welfare states seek solutions to the care deficit that has resulted from the increasing numbers of women in employment and welfare state retrenchment. Another lens from which to view gendering of welfare state regimes revolves around the degree of individualization in social citizenship rights (Sainsbury, 1996), a perspective that undermines the notion of the family as a unit of shared interests.

In many respects, the feminist dialogues with welfare policy regime theorizing have been a two-way street. Feminists have employed the regime model as a springboard and taken up the challenge of gendering it (Sainsbury, 1994; O'Connor et al., 1999). From the other side, power resource theorists, for example, Gösta Esping-Anderson (1999, 2002) and Walter Korpi (2000), have acknowledged their debt to feminist theorizing. Korpi draws on feminist theorizing most directly in his institutional models of gender inequalities. Andersen, in his subsequent studies and most recently his book on *Why We Need a Welfare State*, confronts the gendered postwar settlement rooted in Marshall's social contract that sought to ensure and uphold the male breadwinner. Esping-Andersen (2002) argues for a changed gender contract that does not assume a male life cycle. However, as feminist research on welfare states has underscored, women's agency is crucial for altering the institutional agenda to allow for a reconciliation of family responsibilities and employment, and for including men as fathers and caretakers in the feminist project (Hobson and Morgan, 2002).

Embedded in the term "women-friendly state," a phrase coined by Scandinavian political scientist Helga Hernes (1987), embraces Marshall's notion of an active state that provides universalistic benefits and services but also enables women to be participants in economic and political spheres. Following a Marshallian framework that links civil, political, and social rights, Hernes and other Scandinavian scholars (Siim, 2000; Dahlerup, 2003) have understood that being a full member of the community is dependent on the possibilities of women's mobilization and representation in discursive arenas and politics. Along similar lines, Walter Korpi (2000), applying Marshall's frame of social citizenship alongside Amartya Sen's concept of capacities, employs the concept of gender agency inequality to reflect women's economic dependency in the family. An active state, with benefits and services, according to Korpi (2000), enhances women's capacities to become independent and active citizens by allowing them to combine employment and family responsibilities. More explicit in her analysis of feminist agency and participatory citizenship, Birte Siim (2000) couples social rights to political rights and vice versa, maintaining that without social rights, women are not in a position to be politically active and engaged in participatory citizenship. According to Siim, it is feminist politics from above and below that leads to extensions in social citizenship.

Thomas Janoski's (1998) concept of participation rights is also relevant to this discussion. Extending Marshall's model of citizenship, he introduces participation rights that embrace workers' councils and organizations that set the course for policy. Gendering this concept of participation rights involves incorporating dimensions of women's inclusion into policy-making bodies. In this context, there is a significant body of research on women's participation in non-governmental agencies as experts influencing policy decision making. The role of femocrats in government can also be analyzed through the lens of participation rights. Though first used in the Australian context (Eisenstein, 1996), the term "femocrats" refers to women with feminist orientations who become part of the welfare state bureaucracy, boring from within and being pushed from without, from feminist movements and non-governmental organizations (NGOs). The concept has been systemically applied to studies of women's policy-making influence across Western industrialized countries (Hernes, 1987; Stetson and Mazur, 2001).

The positioning of women as collective agents cannot ignore the importance of women's social movements in shaping gendered dimensions of citizenship. Even in the welfare state typologies that seek to address gender directly, this dimension is not integrated into welfare state models.[5] Women's agency is operationalized in terms of numbers of women in parliament or ministries, or the strength of confessional parties versus working class parties. To develop a theory of agency that addresses social movements in welfare state development and retrenchment would involve a merging of the two traditions of citizenship. Ruth Lister (1997:36) argues for a dynamic approach that would encompass social citizenship rights and inclusion, embracing women's social, economic and reproductive rights, alongside political participatory rights that recognize collective actors and in which the content of rights is the product of political struggles.

Gendering Citizenship Conflicts

Citizenship defined as membership and inclusion involves struggles over the content of rights

[5] See Huber et al. (1993) and Korpi (2000). For a comment on these analyses of gendered agency: Hobson (2000); Shaver (2002).

(Janoski, 1998; Turner, 1993). Janoski (1998) suggests that conflict enters into citizenship theory on three levels: (1) conflicts between capitalism and citizenship that can be traced back to Marshall's analysis of the inherent tension between class and citizenship; (2) contests between different claim structures, for example, affirmative action can violate equal treatment law; and (3) conflicts entail struggles over the extensions of citizenship of which he includes class and status groups. However, as feminist research reveals, gendered struggles around citizenship concern not only the content of rights, but also the framing of citizenship: as individual and collective rights and needs.

The Discourse on Rights

Throughout the history of feminism, the citizenship discourse on rights has been central to women claims, including such basic rights as education, owning property, custody of children, and suffrage. In current-day feminism, liberalism and its associated rights discourse have been the subject of intense debate and feminist theoretical challenges. One could divide the feminist debate on rights into two strands: those engaged with classical liberal or neoliberal constructions of negative and abstract rights (which are a restatement of classical liberalism); and those in dialogue with the social liberal tradition interpreted by Marshall. The latter has synthesized a collective notion of rights with liberal ideas of individual freedom (often referred to as social liberalism).[6]

Some of the strongest critiques of the democratic liberal tradition of rights have come from American feminist political theorists. Mary Glendon (1991) offers a stern critique of "rights talk" in the United States where the vocabulary of rights is translated into negative rights and the passive state. According to Glendon, this is built on a Lockean fable, which takes as its premise that men possess property in their own person in a state of nature and only give up those parts of this "natural liberty," freedom, that are absolutely necessary. What follows from this narrative of the origins of rights is a highly individualistic view of citizenship rights that assumes rational man should be able to pursue his own interests without undue interference. This framing of negative rights tends to set up a series of dichotomies between public and private, active and passive citizenship, and individual and collective agency (Turner, 1993; Glendon, 1991; Dietz, 1992). Another American political theorist, Mary Dietz, acknowledges these liberal tenets of equal treatment in law have overturned many of the restrictions on women as individuals, but maintains that they do not provide the language or concepts to articulate a feminist vision of citizenship (1992:7). She underscores the limitations in an individualistic notion of rights that override the welfare of society as a whole. Reacting to the lack of collective social responsibility in liberal rights talk, some feminist theorists have found other idioms in needs talk (Kittay, 1999).

Will Kymlicka (1989) maintains that feminist critiques (as well as socialist and communitarian critiques) of liberalism as promoting excessive individualism and atomism do not consider the varied theoretical terrain in liberalism (2–12). Referring to theories of justice, such as Rawls and Dworkin, among others, he claims that interests are socially embedded and emerge from social interactions that are always under revision. Feminist theorists, who have embraced a rights-based framework, have understood that they need to revise theories of justice that have focused on class rather than gender inequalities and ignored rights embedded in the private sphere.

Susan Moller Okin (1989) takes the Rawlsian formula for social justice and applies it to the family. Here she constructs a system of rights employing Rawls's concept of the veil of ignorance or original position, that is, individuals would not have knowledge of their sex. In effect, she asks us to perform a thought experiment: to suppose we did not know our social position before birth, and hence being rational actors we would create more just

[6] This strand of liberalism has been referred to as new liberalism, or social democratic liberalism (O'Connor et al., 1999).

institutions. In her analysis, she provides us with a visual demonstration of her theory in a series of cartoons in which judges are asked to rule on rights for pregnancy leave. In the middle of their deliberations, they grow enormous pregnant bellies.

Others, such as Nancy Fraser (1997), argue for a synthesis of needs and rights, which allows us to "translate justified needs claims into social rights." This approach encourages us to contextualize our discursive strategies, to recognize that the question of whose needs should be met exists in a highly contested arena, continually shifting from the domestic or personal to the political. Thus "needs talk" can act to politicize needs and bring them into the sphere of the public, or needs talk can result in reprivatizing them, defining needs as private concerns.

Struggles around citizenship rights are most visible in the contests around individual versus group rights. These hinge on many other fractures in feminist theorizing around gender identities, agency, and power. How to develop theories that allow for the multidimensionality of gender but avoid the reification of identities? How to address multiple identities and loyalties in citizenship claims while retaining the theoretical framework of women's collective agency? In some respects these questions are simply variations on earlier dilemmas in feminist theorizing surrounding gender as an analytical category, but they have matured in their complexities within the contested theoretical space of multiculturalism and citizenship (Phillips, 1995).

CHALLENGES TO FEMINIST THEORIZING AND CITIZENSHIP

Multiculturalism and Group Difference

In the 1990s, social movements constructed around distinctive identities challenged the universalist framing of rights in theories of citizenship that ignored or denigrated gender, race/ethnicity, sexual preference, disability, or age. An academic discourse on cultural citizenship and cultural claims (Benhabib, 2002; Fraser, 1997, 2003; Hobson, 2003; Kymlicka, 1995; Taylor, 1994) emerged. Purposefully distancing themselves from identity politics, critical political theorists have employed the concept of recognition (Fraser, 1997; Honneth, 1995; Taylor, 1994). Setting the agenda, Charles Taylor (1994) affirmed that to misrecognize someone is more than an individual harm, but a form of oppression; to ignore or make invisible histories of devaluation and exclusionary processes or to denigrate them as persons based on their group difference. Gender disadvantage in this conceptual domain appears as but one of many types of misrecognition; however, it has been salient in both the theoretical and empirical analyses. One reason is that several of the main protagonists in setting the agenda have been engaged with feminist theorizing on citizenship and justice. But perhaps more importantly, feminist challenges to univeralism and theorizing on gender-differentiated citizenship dovetailed with multiculturalist debates. Taylor, for example, acknowledges that struggle for recognition is a "struggle for a changed image," which has been crucial for strands of feminism (Taylor, 1994:65).

Recognition politics brings to the fore the issue of individual rights versus group rights. Individuals can be oppressed by the very same groups that claim to represent them based on their group disadvantage (Kymlicka, 1995; Yuval-Davis, 1997), a concern that has been raised by feminist scholars. In a provocative and controversial article, Susan Moeller Okin (Okin and Cohen, 1999) asks, "Is multiculturalism bad for women?" Her answer is affirmative, arguing that cultural differences and group rights in societies can deny women freedom and basic human rights. Her main examples are genital mutilation, polygamy, and child marriage. Will Kymlicka (1995) incorporates liberal tenets into multiculturalism by asserting that one can make the distinction between group rights that involve the claim of a group against its members and the group's claims against the larger society. He affirms that a liberal theory of multicultural rights does not accept rights that result in gender inequalities (Kymlicka, 1999). Nevertheless, his distinction does not address the power positionings in the group, and empirical studies of group claims suggest women's voices are often silenced or disregarded (Williams, 2003; Yuval-Davis, 1997).

Nira Yuval-Davis (1997; and Yuval-Davis and Werbner, 1999) views multiculturalism less critically than Okin, but also points to its inherent dangers for women. For her, multiculturalism is an "interruptive rhetoric" and antidote against false notions of national homogeneity and unity (1997); however, she nevertheless claims that multiculturalism can reify groups as internally homogenous. In her analysis in *Gender and Nation*, Yuval-Davis argued that fundamentalist religious constructions of family and gender have been overall detrimental to women, an example of how individuals and groups can restrict the autonomy of individuals in the group. They can be oppressed by the very same collectivities that are claiming citizenship rights based on their group's disadvantage. Moreover, she maintains that fundamentalist politics have essentialized identities of ethnic communities. Here she addresses the basic dilemma in the recognition paradigm, that it tends to tends to reify social groups. Feminist theorizing has confronted the issue from different perspectives: in the critique of essentialism or fixed identities and in the formulation of feminisms versus feminism.

Yuval-Davis argues for a multilayering in citizenship that reflects a growing acceptance that citizens are political subjects often involved in more than one political community – the local, ethnic, national, and transnational – often with multidimensional loyalties and interests: gender, nationality, religion and ethnicity, disability, and sexual preference (Yuval-Davis and Werbner, 1999). Her concept of transversal politics seeks to go beyond multiculturalism through coalition building across communities. One such example (Yuval-Davis, 1997) that illustrates a successful transversal politics is *Women Against Fundamentalism*, comprised of women who have crossed borders as migrants, refugees, and dissidents. Because transversal politics understand that individuals are members of various collectivities, they also respond to the dilemma, alluded to above, of multiple loyalties and multiple identities.

Overcoming Reification of Collective Identities

Iris Marion Young's original schema of group-differentiated citizenship began with the assumption that groups "cannot be socially equal unless their specific experience, culture and social contributions are publicly affirmed and recognized" (Young, 1990:174). This is to be done through institutional mechanisms that give oppressed groups a voice in the political arena. A key criticism aimed at Young's position is that it freezes group identities and suppresses differences within groups.

Addressing the dilemma of reification of identities, in her recent study of *Democracy and Inclusion*, Young (2000) suggests one can understand group membership as seriality. This is a concept that she derives from Jean Paul Sartre, who used it to describe unorganized class existence (Young, 1995). Not based on identity or shared attributes, serial collectivities result from "people's historically congealed institutionalized actions and experiences that position and limit individuals in determinate ways that they must deal with" (Young, 2000:119). Applying seriality to gender, Young sidesteps the problem of women as a social unity by claiming that individuals can choose to ignore their serial memberships or join with others and develop group solidarity.

Nancy Fraser (2003) in her recent published work has chosen another route to avoid reification of groups by reconceptualizing recognition in Weberian terms as status inequality. She defines misrecognition as social subordination in the sense of being prevented from participating as a peer in social life, which is grounded in institutionalized patterns of disrespect and devaluation. However, to abandon the conceptual terrain of collective identities is to give up a critical dimension in theorizing women's agency in states and civil society.

For some feminist scholars, process theories of social movements have offered insights and analytical strategies that avoid the reification of women's identities while still embracing the concept of women's collectivities and collective action. This theoretical lens has focused on collective identity formation and the systems of meaning that produce collective action. It provides a way of building-in contingencies, multiple identities, and loyalties into analysis of collectivities in specific locales (Gamson, 1995; Melucci, 1996; Meuller, 1994; Della Porta and Diani, 1999). Frame analysis, representing a cultural turn in social movement theorizing (Snow and Benford, 1992; Hunt et al., 1994), highlighted the importance of cognitive processes that shape collective identity formation. This dynamic model of identity formation allows for analyses of the making of feminist collectivities: How actors (movement activists or feminist spokespersons) construct meanings and frame claims also enables us to understand the boundary-making mechanisms in feminist movements. To reveal these processes is to confront the power dimensions in the making of collectivities and the privileging of certain actors and their claims over others – that is, who and what gets recognized in the public sphere and political arenas (Hobson, 2003).

CONCLUSION

With the recognition of the multitiered layering of citizenship and identities, it is increasingly difficult to fit feminist theorizing into neat categories of socialist, liberal, and radical. From the vantage point of feminist theorizing on citizenship, Wollestencraft's dilemma has grown at least three horns that can be expressed in the *gender-differentiated citizen,* the *gender-neutral citizen*, and the *gender-pluralist citizen* (Hobson and Lister, 2002). However, none of these stances brings us closer to articulating a feminist theory of citizenship that does not either jettison the universalist frame of citizenship as a gold standard of rights or alternatively shade out the particularized experiences of groups with histories of disadvantage and social exclusion. The gender-differentiated citizen falls into the trap of creating sexually segregated norms (Jones, 1990) and freezing identities. The gender-neutral citizen places women in the unequal world of male norms (Phillips, 1991:7), into what Ursala Vogel refers to as illusory, ready-made spaces of traditional conceptions of citizenship. The gender-pluralist citizen, a poststructuralist solution to the classic dilemma, is organized around a democratic conception of citizenship in which the subject is constructed through different discourses and subject positions as opposed to an identity – be it race, class, or gender (Mouffe, 1992b:377). However, this theoretical casing of citizenship tends to undermine collective agency and lead toward a fragmented politics.

The dilemma of universalistic and differentiated citizenship may be unresolvable. Benhabib (1992) in her concept of feminist universalism suggests that we combine universalistic principles with particularistic perspectives, in which we assume a context-specific ambiguity. Also taking a context-bound position, Lister (1998) concludes that universalistic and particularistic rights are always in creative tension, a dilemma reflected in the theory and practice of citizenship.

How to translate the practice of citizenship into theories of agency that are context-specific has been on the agenda of gender research for over a decade. However, the challenge in our century is how to develop theory that addresses the multidimensionality in gender in an era of global actors and supranational institutions and arenas. Citizenship rights and protections are still lodged in national law, but supranational institutions have more and more impact on redefining nationality and membership through laws and their interpretation of international human rights codes (Sassen, 1998). Individuals and groups can leapfrog their own legal systems and seek justice in international and supranational courts. The European Union is a unique example, as EU law supersedes the national law of member states. Though European citizenship has had a limited meaning confined within the framework of the free flow of labor across borders, the Social Charter of Rights, the new directives on parental leave, and informal recommendations on domestic violence and sexual trafficking all suggest the expanding loci of the EU framework of rights (McGlynn, 2001; Carson, 2004).

The idea of the global citizen is metaphor that suggests new legal and political opportunities, which may have significance for marginalized groups. For women's collective agency, the "transnational" has generated new forms of collective action and made available alternative gender frames and discursive resources. Recent feminist research has begun exploring some of the implications of transnational feminism and supranational feminist networks on feminist theorizing (Basu, 2000; Bulbeck, 1998; Alvarez 2000; Tickner, 2001). However, little attention has yet been paid to how global activism and actors reshape institutions and alter the constructions of citizenship. Karen Booth (1998) has made the argument that global actors reject the sovereignty and even the relevance of the nation and the significance of citizen identity (119). Yet this is too simple a formulation, because transnational actors even when they are mobilizing in global forums – the centralizing role played by the UN conferences comes to mind – the transnational networks that they spawned seek to influence and recast rights and claims for full citizenship in respective national settings (Keck and Sikkonk, 1998). In her study of how EU policies are translated into national discourses and legal frameworks, Ulrike Liebert (2003) underscores this point.

The challenge for feminist theorizing is to imagine the practice of citizenship in a multi-dimensional and dynamic context of gendered actors across local, national, and supranational arenas. This is to take into account how global restructuring and new supranational institutions contour the field of claimants and claims.

CHAPTER SEVEN

Poststructuralist Discourse Theory: Foucault, Laclau, Mouffe, and Žižek

Jacob Torfing

Poststructuralist discourse theory is a tool for analyzing the more or less sedimented rules and meanings that condition the political construction of social, political, and cultural identity.[1] It begins with the assertion that what exists only becomes intelligible when it is joined with a specific form which constitutes its identity. The formation of identity is not grounded in some metaphysical instance like God, Nature, Man, Reason, or the Iron Laws of Capitalism. Instead, discourse theory subscribes to an *antiessentialist ontology*, which is opposed to the idea of a self-determining center that structures society and defines identity while itself escaping the process of structuration. Hence it asserts that identity is constructed in and through a multiplicity of overlapping language games. Following Ludwig Wittgenstein (1959), language is conceived neither as a medium for the representation of an extralinguistic reality nor as a medium for the expression of our inner thoughts and emotions. Rather, it constitutes a rulebound system of meaning and action that conditions the ultimately political construction of identity.

The emphasis on the constitutive role of language clearly indicates that discourse theory is a part of the linguistic turn in the social sciences. However, the point of discourse theory is neither to study how we actually speak and write nor to investigate the rules that we draw upon when speaking or writing. Discourse theory aims at a much broader analysis of the construction of discursive forms. The theoretical development from Ferdinand de Saussure's structural linguistics and Louis Hjelmslev's glossematics to Roland Barthes's semiology has purged linguistics of all reference to phonic and semantic substance, thereby transforming it into an analysis of pure forms. Military parades, popular culture, public administration, political demonstrations – everything can be analyzed in terms of the construction of discursive forms. Thus, when Jacques Derrida (1988:148) claims that "there is nothing outside the text," he is not arguing that the state and economy only exist as words or meanings contained in spoken or written messages, but rather that these institutional orders should be analyzed as complex sign systems, which can be analyzed by applying the principles of *linguistic form analysis*.

[1] In the present context "identity" refers not only to peoples' conception of who they are or want to be, but also to the meaning, sense or signification they attach to different objects, experiences, and events. Generally, poststructuralist discourse theory aims to say new things with new words that for outsiders might appear as incomprehensible jargon. The appropriation of the poststructuralist vocabulary is complicated by the fact that many terms are developed and used in particular textual contexts, rather than defined as a part of a systematic conceptual apparatus. Another difficulty lies in the fact that many of the concepts aim to capture the experience of the limits of the modernist quest for a metalanguage that provides a transparent representation of the objectively given social reality. However, as a possible inroad to the conceptual wonderland of poststructuralist discourse theory, I have elsewhere produced a glossary covering most of the key concepts that are found in this chapter (see Torfing, 1999:298–307).

Discourse theory aims to analyze the construction of identity within linguistic systems and it holds a *relationalist and contextualist view* of identity formation. Identity is thus shaped by its relation to other identities within a particular historical context. This means that we can only understand "mother" through the contextualized relationship to "father," "son," and "daughter," we can only see something as "nature" in its historically conditioned opposition to "culture," and we can only account for the historical form of "the state" in relation to historical forms of "economy" and "civil society." These historically specific, relational ensembles of mutually constitutive identities are called discourses.

Identity is always constructed within a particular discourse. However, the formative order of discourse is not a stable self-reproducing structure, but a precarious system that is constantly subjected to political attempts to undermine and restructure the discursive order. There is no deep essence that can guarantee the formation or reproduction of a particular discourse. Rather, the discursive order and the mechanisms ensuring its contingent reproduction are shaped and reshaped through a series of political decisions that are taken in an ultimately undecidable terrain of unresolvable dilemmas and nontotalizable openness. Even though the constitutive decisions might be supported by good reasons and noble motives, the key point is that in an undecidable terrain we never arrive at a situation in which the decision is taken by the structure and then subsequently presented to us as a fait accompli. We are always left with a nonalgorithmic political choice between a series of actual options, which in different ways satisfy the rules prescribed by the discursive context of the decision. This means that the constitutive choice of A necessarily involves the repression of the alternative options B, C, and D. Consequently, the political should be seen as both a constitutive and subversive dimension of the social order. It can neither be reduced to state institutions nor to party politics. Rather, it refers to constitutive and subversive practices that, at least potentially, are found everywhere in society and ultimately prevent it from constituting a closed and unified totality.

Discourse is coexistent with the social, and the discursive order is politically constructed through acts of inclusion and exclusion, or, in other words, by the exercise of power. These stipulations permit us to reject both the liberal and Marxist view of the political as something that is ultimately determined by the social (the pregiven preferences of individuals or the laws of the capitalist economy). Instead discourse theory asserts the *primacy of the political* over the social. Certainly, this assertion does not imply that everything is political, because politically constructed identities and relations over time become sedimented into a recursively validated social realm that is oblivious to its political origin. The political origin of sedimented social identities is not eliminated, but only repressed. Therefore, the possibility of reactivating the political origin of the social through a deconstruction of the discursive hierarchies distinguishing the normal from the deviant, order from disorder, and the sensible from the nonsensical is always present (see Laclau, 1990).

When analyzing the political construction of relational identities within particular discourses, we should, of course, bear in mind the post-positivist insight that no empirical observation can possibly verify the truth of our propositional statements (Popper, 1959). It should also be recognized that even falsification fails to rebut knowledge claims because these are underdetermined by empirical evidence (Quine, 1971) and protected by the armor of the predominant scientific paradigm (Kuhn, 1970). This means that science can no longer be identified with truth as opposed to nontruth. However, it is still possible to insist on the possibility of scientific knowledge by relying on principles of an undogmatic willingness to give up a scientific paradigm or research program when it is confronted with others carrying a larger heuristic value (Lakatos and Musgrave, 1974). The problem with this attempt to rescue science is that it presupposes the existence of a metalanguage which can be applied in evaluating the heuristic value of competing paradigms

(Feyerabend, 1975). The *antifoundationalist stance* of poststructuralist discourse theory renounces this presupposition by asserting that there is no extradiscursive instance in terms of empirical facts, methodological rules, or privileged criteria for scientificity that can safeguard either Truth or Science. Truth is always local and mobile as it is conditioned by a discursive "truth regime" that specifies the criteria for judging an analytical narrative to be convincing (Foucault, 1986a). Science may constitute a particular truth regime that is built around conventional norms about cumulative and intersubjective knowledge, replicability, intellectual honesty, and so forth. However, these criteria are subject to constant renegotiation and there is no way of protecting them from the influence of competing truth regimes. The boundary between science and nonscience is thus blurred and subject to politico-discursive interventions.

The antiessentialist ontology, the linguistic form analysis, the relationalist and contextualist view of identity formation, the assertion of the primacy of politics, and the antifoundationalist epistemology constitute the backbone of the poststructuralist discourse theory advanced by prominent thinkers such as Michel Foucault, Ernesto Laclau, Chantal Mouffe, and Slavoj Žižek. The works of these distinguished theorists have significantly contributed to the development and renewal of political sociology. Their persistent focus on political issues such as power, social movements, populism, democracy, and emancipation, as well as their dedicated attempt to advance new ways of thinking and analyzing these issues, warrant a close study of their thoughts and ideas.

Poststructuralism has had a huge impact on cultural studies, where it has become almost hegemonic. However, in the past decades poststructuralist discourse theory has gained increasing prominence among political theorists and critical political sociologists, attracting special attention from post-Marxists of various kinds. In the mid-1980s discourse theorists were still few and far between, but today there are many places and fields of study where poststructuralist discourse theory constitutes a real challenge to mainstream theory. In others, it has almost become the new mainstream. However, the poststructuralist wave seems to have taken slightly different forms in Europe and the United States. Many European academics were immediately captured by French poststructuralism and developed a strong interest in ontological questions. This was also the case with North American academics like Judith Butler (1990), Craig Calhoun (1994), and Mark Poster (1990). However, in the United States a large group of political sociologists fashioned a discourse theoretical approach that combines new ideas from poststructuralism with basic (methodological) insights from the highly influential currents of symbolic interactionism and ethnomethodology (see Eliasoph, 1998; Gubrium and Holstein, 1997; Reinerman, 1987).

The growing interest in poststructuralist discourse theory stands in sharp contrast to its incomplete character. As yet, there does not exist a coherent theoretical paradigm, only a heterogeneous set of theoretical and analytical contributions that in different ways combine genealogical hermeneutics, deconstructivism, and psychoanalysis with post-Marxism, postanalytical philosophy, and American pragmatism. The number of empirical studies is growing rapidly, but there is a general lack of methodological self-reflection and few discussions about research strategy. On the other hand, the open and tentative character of poststructuralist discourse theory is also its strength, as it makes it possible for people to contribute actively to the elaboration of a strong theoretical and methodological alternative to the dominant approaches of rational choice theory, historical institutionalism, systems theory, and political economy.

A number of historical events have nurtured the emergence and development of poststructuralist discourse theory. The events of May 1968 generated a need for a renewal of social and political theory. The struggle against the dominant forms and contents of higher education and the efforts on the part of progressive intellectuals to ally with oppressed groups of prisoners, immigrants, and so forth prompted a closer study of the relation between power and knowledge.

The transformation of the student revolt into a broad struggle against multiple forms of ideological repression and the proliferation of new social movements fostered a growing interest in the question of how identity was constructed and changed. Finally, the politicization of cultural expressions and private lifestyles generated a need for a broadening of the understanding of politics.

The theoretical crisis and political impotence of Marxism has also played a key role in the development of discourse theory. Many Marxists have lost their faith in economic determinism, the primacy of class struggle vis-à-vis other social and political struggles, and the blessings of centralized state regulation of society. They find in discourse theory a critical theory that explicitly claims to be both *post*-Marxist and post-*Marxist* (Laclau and Mouffe, 1985:4).

The postmodern recognition of the limits of modernity has also exerted a huge influence. The modern conception of a rational, unencumbered individual who liberates himself through the uncovering of an undistorted knowledge is problematized by the postmodern insistence on viewing rationality, identity, and knowledge as contingent products of discursive power strategies. This has stimulated interest in analyzing the historical processes of inclusion and exclusion, which have established and formed the rationalist, individualist, and emancipatory discourse of modernity.

Finally, the emergence of a "new reflexivity," which is characterized by the gradual loss of authoritatively given rules, norms, and values, forces us to engage in the active construction of a provisional foundation for the validation of our actions as reasonable and appropriate. This engagement drives us into a self-reflexive negotiation of rules, norms, and values at the level of discourse. Hence, the death of the grand narratives seems to stimulate our interest in the contingent construction of the many small narratives that can help to structure our identity, actions, and views of the world.

Initially, the growing interest in discourse theory was met with a great deal of skepticism. Very often it was written off as "postmodern nihilism," "antiscientific nonsense," and "anything-goes theory," and students of discourse theory had a tough time trying to justify their position. Many were rescued by the repressive tolerance on the part of mainstream theory, according to which it was acceptable to use discourse theories to analyze "soft" issues such as gender, sexuality, and ethnicity. In this way, the core areas of research were monopolized by the more traditional theories. However, in recent years the hostility toward discourse theory has largely disappeared. Mainstream theorists have gradually become used to the new vocabulary, and poststructuralist discourse theorists have become more open-minded, engaging in a fruitful dialogue with other researchers about the value added from taking a discourse theoretical approach to the study of central problems within political sociology.

In countries like Britain, Denmark, Germany, and Holland and in research areas such as gender and ethnicity studies, Third World studies, and policy analysis, poststructuralist discourse theory has become a highly influential approach. The sudden rise to fame does, however, carry the dangers of trivialization and reabsorption into mainstream theory. It has become increasingly fashionable to talk about discourse, but without buying into the theoretical package of poststructuralist discourse theory. Often people use the term "discourse" merely in order to emphasize the role of ideology, common perceptions, and shared values, and they tend to see discourse as something that is manipulated by rational and willful actors who aim to bend discourse to their own ends. In order to counteract these dangers, we have to insist on the need for a more profound understanding of the key concepts and arguments of poststructuralist discourse theory. The main part of this chapter will be devoted to an exploration of the conceptual and argumentative framework of poststructuralist discourse analysis. This will be followed by a response to some of the standard criticisms of discourse theory. I will then elaborate the consequences of discourse theory for understanding the social basis of politics and conclude with a brief assessment of its future tasks. However, before dealing with the intricacies of discourse theory, I shall provide a brief overview of different kinds of discourse theory in order to show the distinctiveness of the poststructuralist version.

DISCOURSE THEORY AS A STUDY OF MEANING AND POLITICS

Discourse theory developed as a cross-disciplinary attempt to integrate central insights from linguistics and hermeneutics with central insights from social and political science. Such integration is prompted by the widespread recognition of the fact that political and social change is accompanied by linguistic change. However, the latter is not merely a reflection of the former. Linguistic forms and rhetorical operations are constitutive of the social world. Hence, when "workfare" is linked to "opportunity" and "duty" rather than "welfare" and "right," and opposed to "welfare," "greed" and "patronage," the consequence is that social benefits are cut, repressive quid-pro-quo schemes are introduced, and the incentives to take insecure low paid jobs are augmented. This shows that rhetoric cannot be reduced to a quasi-logical art of persuasion that helps politicians to sell their policy by means of providing an eloquent linguistic wrapping. Rhetoric plays a central role in the shaping of our world, and this is exactly what discourse theory explores.

There are many kinds of discourse theory. In linguistics "discourse" refers to a textual unit that is larger than a sentence. A sentence consists of a number of signs, each of which articulates a signifier (an expression or sound–image) and a signified (a content or concept). *Sociolinguistics* (see Downes, 1984) and *content analysis* (see Holsti, 1969) are examples of a linguistic discourse analysis. At the operational level, discourse is defined as spoken language and the aim is to identify patterns in our use of language. Sociolinguistics analyzes the relation between our socioeconomic status and our vocabulary and linguistic code, whereas content analysis analyzes our usage of particular words, word classes, and word combinations. This type of analysis is sometimes extended to include written language. However, there is no attempt to address the crucial issue about the relation between power and the use of language.

Dialogue and conversation analysis (see Sinclair and Coulthard, 1975; Atkinson and Heritage, 1984) also defines discourse as spoken language either in terms of an institutionalized and hierarchical dialogue (e.g., between doctor and patient) or in a more informal dialogue between equals (e.g., a telephone conversation). The focus is not so much on the use of language as on the organization of linguistic interaction. How are conversations initiated and concluded? How are topics chosen and changed during the conversation? What determines turn-taking, and how does one sentence affect the next? However, the ethnomethodological point of departure of this type of analysis precludes a theoretical interest in questions about the exercise of power that, eventually, would lead to more heterogeneous forms of interaction than the ones analyzed by dialogue and conversation analysis.

Discourse psychology (see Labov and Fanshel, 1977; Potter and Wetherell, 1987) is a constructivist branch of social psychology that is also interested in what people actually say to each other. However, the focus has shifted from the organization of linguistic interaction to the strategies of speakers. The speakers want to achieve something in and through the conversation, and they consciously try to produce a shift in the framing of the conversation and in the style in which it is deployed. The social environment of the speakers provides models for what can be said and done in the conversation, but the identity of the speakers is partly determined through their heterogeneous interaction during the conversation. Discourse psychology clearly moves in the direction of a constructivist analysis of discourse, but it fails to relate this analysis to questions of politics, ideology, and power.

The group of so-called *critical linguists* at the University of East Anglia (see Fowler et al., 1979) broadens the notion of discourse to include both spoken and written language. Most importantly, it departs from linguistic discourse analysis by claiming that language cannot be analyzed independent of its social and political function. The critical linguists share with Michel Pêcheux (1982) the interest in how discourse, through its choice and combination of different linguistic expressions, produces a particular representation of reality, and it aims to show that processes of representation often result in an ideological misrepresentation. The interest in the ideological effects of language clearly links the linguistic analysis of discourse to an analysis of power. Hence, it is asserted that ideological discourses contribute to the reproduction of the existing power relations. However, this type of discourse theory is still biased toward linguistic analysis and the notions of ideology and power are undertheorized.

Critical discourse analysis (CDA), as developed most consistently by Norman Fairclough (1992, 1995), aims to balance linguistic analysis with the analysis of power and politics. CDA further expands the notion of discourse to include all linguistically mediated practices. Social practices are discursive practices insofar as they contribute to a semiotic production and interpretation of text in the broad sense of speech, writing, images, and gestures. Discursive practice is ideological insofar as it contains naturalized semiotic elements (i.e., linguistic expressions that are taken for granted). Social classes and ethnic groups use ideological discourse to maintain their hegemonic power or to establish a counterhegemony. Hence, ideological discourse not only contributes to the reproduction of the predominant discursive order, but also to its transformation. CDA clearly demonstrates the power effects of discourse. However, CDA remains unclear about how exactly to understand the relation between discourse and its nondiscursive context, and its explicit reliance on critical realism (see Bhaskar, 1975; Sayer, 1984) tends to reduce discourse to a linguistic mediation of causal mechanisms embedded in the multilayered socioeconomic structure. This significantly reduces the explanatory power of discourse analysis.

Although CDA conceives discourse as something that actors draw upon in their production and interpretation of meaning, there is a tendency to view discourse as an empirical referent, that is, a collection of practices with a semiotic content. As Fairclough (1992:38–9) himself notes, this marks a sharp difference from the French philosopher Michel Foucault's *quasi-transcendental conception of discourse*. Foucault (1985) does not focus on the particular form and contents of linguistic statements and semiotic practices, but on the rules of formation governing the production of such statements and practices. He is concerned neither with the truth nor the meaning of actual statements, but with their conditions of possibility in terms of the discursive rules that regulate what can be said, how it can be said, who can say and from which position, and which discursive strategies can be advanced. Influenced by Marxist theory, which was very strong at the time, Foucault's archaeological approach to discourse analysis insists that the discursive rules of formation are conditioned by nondiscursive relations. However, the criteria for distinguishing the discursive realm from the nondiscursive and the nature of the "conditioning relation" remain unclear.

In his later works, Foucault (1986b, 1986c) seems to be less concerned with the distinction between the discursive and the nondiscursive, and with the development of his genealogical approach he shifts the analytical focus from the rules governing the production of statements to the complex web of power strategies that establish hierarchical relations between global/totalitarian forms of knowledge and local/subjugated forms of knowledge. Foucault's power analytics replaces the classical notion of sovereign power, which basically views power as dominance and repression, with a new notion of discursive power that emphasizes the productive aspects of power (Foucault, 1990). Power is neither a relation of dominance nor a capacity to act, but the way actions affect other actions by means of shaping the identity, capacities, and horizon of meaning of the acting subjectivities (1986d). Hence, power and discourse are mutually constitutive and we cannot have one without the other. This makes Foucault the antidote of the German philosopher Jürgen Habermas (1987, 1990, 1992), who also tends to label his work discourse theory. Whereas Habermas tries to rescue the project of modernity by seeking to eliminate power in order to realize the ideal of a communicative rationality based on free, sincere and truth-seeking dialogue, Foucault tends to view modernity as constituting a particular truth regime that is shaped in and through power struggles. The British-based political theorists Ernesto Laclau and Chantal Mouffe (1985) agree with Foucault's insistence on the internal relation between power and discourse, and they also define discourse in transcendental terms as the historically variable conditions of possibility of what we say, think, imagine, and do. However, they take issue with, and ultimately abandon, the unsustainable distinction between the discursive and the nondiscursive. Hence, they claim that discourse is coextensive with the entire social fabric. Although they still want to pay attention to the discursive rules governing the use of language, they are more concerned with elaborating a set of theoretical concepts and arguments that can help us to account for the construction of such rules in and through power struggles. In this sense, their work can be seen as a continuation of Foucault's later studies, although their theoretical sources of inspiration are different.

POSTSTRUCTURALIST DISCOURSE THEORY IN A NUTSHELL

Whereas Foucault draws on French epistemological studies of the history of ideas, Laclau and Mouffe develop their concept of discourse through a deconstructive reading of structural linguistics. After the publication of their now classic book *Hegemony and Socialist Strategy* (1985), Laclau and Mouffe became heavily influenced by the Slovenian philosopher Slavoj Žižek's poststructuralist psychoanalytic theory. This is particularly evident in Laclau's *New Reflections on the Revolution of Our Time* (1990), which aims to develop a theory of the subject before its subjectivation. Recent debates between Laclau and Žižek published in *Contingency, Hegemony, Universality* (Butler, Laclau, and Žižek, 2000) show that despite the theoretical points of convergence, there is serious disagreement about the political implications of the theoretical arguments (see below).

As noted above, Laclau and Mouffe (1985:4) insist that their discourse theory is both *post*-Marxist and post-*Marxist*. That is to say, whereas they clearly recognize the many pathbreaking insights of Marxism, they insist on the need to transgress the Marxist tradition in order to solve some of the inherent theoretical problems. Both Laclau and Mouffe were part of the Althusserian revolution, which sought to reinterpret Marxism as a structuralist science about the underlying matrix of society in terms of modes of production, social formations, and so forth. They both experienced the shortcomings of the structural Marxism of Louis Althusser, Etienne Balibar, and Nicos Poulantzas in the face of Latin American politics. And although the notions of "hegemony" and "overdetermination" were helpful in understanding populist movements, the class reductionism and economic determinism inherent to structural Marxism constituted a deadweight loss that had to be removed.

Interestingly, Laclau and Mouffe found in the open and undogmatic Marxism of Antonio Gramsci (1971) the theoretical inspiration to deconstruct the Marxist legacy and counteract the paradoxical tendency toward the disappearance of politics within Marxist political theory. In Marxist theory the form and functions of the state, and political class struggles that are fought out at the superstructural level, are seen as determined by the inner movements of the economic infrastructure. When, finally, the productive forces are fully developed, the proletarian revolution will render the Marxist doubling of the political into state and class struggles obsolete. Gramsci attacks the Marxist conception of society and claims that state, economy, and civil society, rather than forming a structured hierarchy of determination, are articulated within a historical bloc, which is shaped and reshaped through political struggles that cannot be reduced to their class content. It was Gramsci's critique of essentialist thinking within Marxism and the radicalization of his key concept of hegemony which inspired Laclau and Mouffe's elaboration of a poststructuralist discourse theory that has recently developed into a new type of postmodern political sociology (see Torfing, 1999).

As such, the intellectual development of Laclau and Mouffe can be divided into three phases. These can be described in terms of the historical situation, the main target of their

Table 7.1. *The Three Phases of Laclau and Mouffe's Intellectual Development*

	A Gramscian Critique of Structural Marxism (the 1970s)	The Elaboration of a Poststructuralist Discourse Theory (the 1980s)	Toward a New Type of Postmodern Theorizing (the 1990s)
Historical situation	Post-1968 era and emerging crisis of the "social democratic" welfare state	The rise of the New Right and the recognition of the political impotency of the Left	The surge of postcommunist identity politics and particular multiculturalist interpretations
Main target of critique and sources of inspiration	Criticize structural Marxism for its class reductionism and its economic determinism and use Gramsci to insist on the independent role of hegemonic politics	Criticize the last remnant of essentialism in Gramsci and use poststructuralist theory to make further theoretical advance	Criticize the structuralist account of subjectivity and use Lacanian psychoanalysis to advance new theory of the subject and the political construction of subjectivity
Theoretical contribution	Notion of popular antagonism (nonclass interpellation) that is still seen as overdetermined by class antagonism	The development of a consistent theory about discourse, hegemony, and criss-crossing social antagonisms that emphasizes the primacy of politics	Distinction between social antagonisms and the dislocations that reveals the undecidability of the social and opens the space for its rearticulation around empty signifiers
Political project advanced	A democratic socialism that can articulate the demands of the new social movements	A radical plural democracy that displaces the struggle for liberty and equality to all spheres of society	An agonistic democracy that reconciles democracy and antagonism

critique, and its sources of inspiration; the most significant theoretical contribution; and the political project advocated. An overview of the three phases of development is provided in Table 7.1.

As already noted, the events of May 1968 stimulated the interest in the struggle against the dominant ideology. In addition, the emerging crisis of the welfare state shattered the belief in crisis-free, rational state planning and intensified popular struggles against the bureaucratization, commodification, and homogenization of social relations. This led to a strengthening of the Left, which in turn stimulated the interest in Marxist theory. Structural Marxism was extremely fashionable among left-wing intellectuals. However, Laclau and Mouffe criticized its essentialist assertions of the necessary class belonging of all ideological elements and the economic determination in the last instance, and sought to develop a theory about ideological interpellations that did not follow the economic and political dividing lines between the social classes (Laclau, 1977; Mouffe, 1979, 1981). The implicit assertion was that such a theory would help to make the struggle for democratic socialism more sensitive to the demands of popular movements.

In the second phase – the 1980s – the rise of the New Right clearly demonstrated the failure of the Left to win the battle of the hearts and minds of the general population. The devastating result was that a large fraction of the British working class voted for the Conservative Thatcher government. Laclau and Mouffe saw the dogmatic assertion of the primacy of class and economy as a major obstacle to the reinvigoration of the Left, and they criticized the last remnant of essentialism in Gramsci, who still asserted that only the fundamental classes were capable of exercising hegemony (Laclau and Mouffe, 1985). The social classes owed their privileged role in the struggle for hegemony to their structural position in the sphere of production, which provided a nonpolitical anchorage point for the political struggles. However, by questioning the idea of a determining center of society and by insisting on the political structuration of the economic field, Laclau and Mouffe not only effectively eliminated the last element of essentialism, but also paved the way for the development of a poststructuralist theory of discourse, hegemony, and social antagonism that asserts the primacy of the political over the social. In addition, the resultant post-Marxist and poststructuralist theory of discourse opposed the privileging of the socialist struggle for the common ownership of the means of production. Indeed, socialism is now seen as but one element in a broader struggle for a radical and plural democracy. Throughout the history of modern society, the egalitarian logic of democracy has proven its ability to mobilize popular antagonistic fronts directed against different kinds of oppression. However, it is important to combine the struggle for democratic equality with the struggle for pluralism in order to avoid totalitarian assertions of the democratic identity between the ruler and the ruled. Hence, democracy should be plural, and the inherent conflict between equality and liberty is exactly what prevents the elimination of the political. Finally, it is argued that a further radicalization of political, rather than economic, liberalism must extend the demand for equality and liberty to all spheres of society and aim to unify the struggles of the new social movements in a progressive hegemonic project (Mouffe, 1988, 1989, 1992).

The 1990s, the third phase of the development of their writings, is marked by the end of the Cold War and the subsequent surge of a multiplicity of nationalist, ethnical, religious, cultural, sexual, and postmaterialist struggles for the construction and assertion of a new set of identities. Some multiculturalist interpretations of the new identity politics abandoned the idea of universal values and celebrated the radical particularism of authentic identities. The new identity politics made it pretty obvious that the structuralist account of subjectivity in terms of its structural locations within a discursive formation was unable to account for the dynamics of identity formation. Inspired by Žižek's interpretation of Lacanian psychoanalysis (Žižek, 1989, 1990), Laclau and Mouffe aimed to develop a theory of the political construction of identity through processes of identification that are prompted by the dislocation of the subject prior to its subjectivation (Laclau, 1990). The articulation of different points of identification is conditioned by the construction of an antagonistic frontier, which in the language of Carl Schmitt divides friends from enemies (Mouffe, 1992). The problem now becomes how to reconcile the ineradicable presence of social antagonism with a plural democracy. This can be achieved through the development of an agonistic democracy, which aims to turn "enemies" into "adversaries" who agree on the basic rules of plural democracy, while disagreeing on their interpretation and their implications for now to organize society (Mouffe, 1993).

The cumulative effect of the continuities and discontinuities in Laclau and Mouffe's intellectual development is the advancement of an increasingly refined theory that is organized around the key concepts of discourse, hegemony, social antagonism, dislocation, and the split subject. Before proceeding to clarify the precise meaning of these concepts, it should be noted that the kind of theory which they put forward is neither a substantive theory covering a particular field or subfield nor an elaborate system of analytical categories and typologies that aims to map the world in an isomorphic way. Instead, it provides a consistent set of concepts and arguments that enables us to answer old and new research questions in a way that takes seriously the assertion of the contingency of all social identities.

Discourse

Discourse is defined as a relational ensemble of signifying sequences that provides the conditions of emergence of any meaningful object. This does not deny the existence of real objects outside discourse, but simply asserts that the construction of such objects as meaningful always take place within discourse.

The notion of *discourse* has its distant roots in classical transcendentalism (Laclau, 1993). Like Kantian transcendentalism, it focuses on the conditions of possibility for our perceptions, utterances, and actions rather than on the factual immediacy or hidden meaning of the world. However, there are two important differences between classical transcendentalism and poststructuralist discourse theory. First, whereas classical transcendentalism conceives the conditions of possibility as ahistorical and invariable, discourse theory insists on their historical variability. That is to say, the transcendental conditions are not purely transcendental, but a provisional horizon of meaning that is continuously changed by empirical events (Laclau, 2000:76). Second, although classical transcendentalism is still in some sense anchored in an idealist conception of the subject as the willful creator of the world, discourse theory conceives the *quasi-transcendental conditions* as a structural feature of discourse. The subject itself is conceived as a part of discourse and analyzed in terms of its different positions within the discursive structure.

The deconstruction of totalizing and deterministic structures leads directly to the notion of discourse. The classical notion of structure is another name for the totalizing closure of a topography, construction, or architecture whose internal order is determined by a privileged center. However, according to Derrida (1978:279), the idea of an ultimate center is contradictorily coherent as it assumes that the center structures the entire structure while itself escaping the very process of structuration. Discourse theory takes the consequence of this and abandons the idea of an ultimate center, which is given in its full presence beyond the reach of the play of meaning. By giving up the idea of a determining center, the process of signification extends almost infinitely. In this situation, everything becomes discourse in the sense of being constituted within relational ensembles of signifying sequences that in the absence of an ultimate center are organized around a multiplicity of mutually substituting centers that fail to invoke a totalizing closure.

A common misunderstanding is that discourse merely designates a linguistic region within a wider social realm. Whereas this might provide an accurate description of the concept of discourse found in the early works of Foucault, it certainly misses the nature of the concept in the works of Laclau and Mouffe (1985). As already mentioned, Laclau and Mouffe reject the distinction between the discursive and the nondiscursive and insist on the interweaving of the semantic aspects of language and the pragmatic aspects of action. Hence, discourse is coextensive with the social and takes the form of a series of overlapping language games.

In the concrete analysis of discourse, we must pay attention to the way that identity is constructed through *relations of difference* and/or *relations of equivalence*. Sometimes it is the differential aspect of the social identities that is emphasized (this is the case in the modern welfare state, which expands a differential logic by constructing everybody as legitimate differences). At other times, it is the equivalential "sameness" of the different identities that is emphasized (this is the case in a revolutionary situation where everyone is constructed either as a part of the people or as a part of the repressive regime). The balance between the differential and equivalential character of social identity is a result of political struggles.

The construction of relations of equivalence is a result of what Sigmund Freud in his *Interpretation of Dreams* (Freud, 1986) called *overdetermination*. Overdetermination occurs at the symbolic level and may take the form of either condensation or displacement. Condensation involves the fusion of a variety of significations and meanings into a single unity. Displacement involves the transferral of the signification or meaning of one particular identity to another identity. In Lacanian psychoanalytic theory, condensation becomes equivalent to *metaphor*, whereas displacement becomes equivalent to *metonymy*. An example here would be the metonymical relation of contiguity between different ethnic groups working together to support each other's social and political demands, but without thereby developing a common cause or identity. The bonds between the different groups might be strengthened in the wake of a right-wing populist attack on refugees and immigrants, which could lead to a metaphorical unification of these groups around a common perception of who they are and for what they are fighting.

A discursive field might be unified by particular *nodal points*, such as "communism," "welfare," "globalization," and so forth. These are signifiers without any precise content that function to construct a knot of meaning which fixes the differential identity of a variety of social identities. For example, "globalization" confers a certain meaning to terms like "regulation," "competitiveness," "the state," and so forth. Hence, we see how in neoliberal discourse the reference to "globalization" tends to redefine "regulation" in terms of "the need for deregulation," "competitiveness" in terms of "structural competitiveness," and "state" in terms of "the enabling state."

It should be noted that the fixation of identity within discourse only results in a *partial fixation* of meaning. There will always be something that escapes the seemingly infinite process of signification within discourse. The partial fixation of identity produces an irreducible surplus of meaning that is not captured by the logic of discourse. The field of irreducible surplus meaning is termed the discursive, or the *field of discursivity*, in order to indicate that what is not fixed within discourse is not extra- or non-discursive, but is discursively constructed within a terrain of unfixity. The field of discursivity provides, at the same time, the condition of possibility and impossibility of discourse. On the one hand, it provides the differential trace structure that every fixation of meaning must necessarily presuppose. On the other hand, it provides an ambiguous realm that overflows and subverts the attempt to fix identity within a stable discourse (Laclau and Mouffe, 1985:111).

Hegemony

Discourse is a result of *articulation*, which is defined as a practice that establishes a relation among elements such that their identities are mutually modified as a result of that practice (Laclau and Mouffe, 1985:105). When, for example, an ethnic identity is articulated with a class identity, both identities are transformed. The class identity can no longer be expressed in purely economic terms, and the ethnic identity has to show its relevance for economic struggles.

Articulations that involve the production of political frontiers are defined as hegemonic articulations. *Hegemony* is an articulatory practice aiming to establish a political as well as moral–intellectual leadership. According to Gramsci (1971), a political force becomes hegemonic insofar as it succeeds to transgress its own interests and present itself as the expression of a collective will with a national and popular character. Lenin saw hegemony merely as the working class's political leadership of a broad class alliance that was made possible by the exceptional situation in Russia, where the bourgeoisie was to weak to carry out its own revolution and capitalism was too scarcely developed to foster a large working class. Trotsky insisted that the "uneven and combined development" in Russia was a general condition in the Western countries and thereby expanded the scope of validity of the contingent logic of hegemony. But it was Gramsci who changed the content of the notion of hegemony by showing that the forging of a political and moral–intellectual leadership involved the articulation of a variety of ideological elements into a common political project that modifies the identity of the political forces behind it. Laclau and Mouffe further radicalized Gramsci's concept of hegemony by removing the ontological assumptions behind the assertion that only the proletariat and the bourgeoisie are capable of exercising hegemony (Gramsci, 1971:161, 182).

Conceiving hegemony as an articulatory practice that unifies a discursive field around a nodal point always involves an element of *ideological totalization* (Laclau, 1996a). However, ideology can no longer be seen as a distorted representation of social reality, as the latter is always-already constructed in and through discourse. Ideology still involves distortion, not of how things really are, but of the undecidability of all social identity. As such, ideology constructs social identity as a part of a totalizing horizon that denies the contingency and precariousness of the constructed identities. Ideology may take the form of a myth or a social imaginary (Laclau, 1990). A myth provides a reading principle that permits the political actors to interpret the cause of societal crisis in a certain way by emphasizing particular empirical events and by suggesting a particular solution to the crisis. Hence, a *myth* constructs a surface for the inscription of particular social demands. A myth is transformed into a *social imaginary* when the symbolic and imaginary content of its story line begins to dominate the empirical events that it inscribes. Hence, in a social imaginary the mythical construction of a crisis-ridden situation is transformed into an unlimited horizon for the inscription of any social demand.

Social Antagonism

The limits and unity of a hegemonic discourse cannot be constituted by reference to an inner essence. Neither can it be constituted in relation to an external element that is different from the moments within the discourse, because in that case the outside is reduced to simply one more difference within the discursive system. Hence, the construction of the limits and unity of a hegemonic discourse involves the positing of a constitutive outside that has no common measure with the discourse in question. Instead, it constitutes a threat to the differential order of the discourse (Laclau, 1996b). The construction of a radical and threatening otherness is a result of the exclusion of a series of discursive elements that are articulated in a chain of equivalence which collapses the differential character of the excluded elements. The chain of equivalence expresses a certain sameness of the excluded elements, but as the number of elements increases, it becomes clear that the only thing they have in common is that they pose a threat to the discourse in question (Laclau and Mouffe, 1985).

This clearly shows why social antagonism has nothing in common with either a "real opposition" in which A clashes with B or with a "logical contradiction" in which A is contradicted by non-A. In both cases A remains a fully constituted identity, whereas in social antagonism the identity of A is problematized by an antagonizing force. In the case of a social antagonism, A cannot be fully A because it is negated by anti-A. However, social antagonism does not simply counterpose a positive, differential pole with a negative, equivalential pole. For when confronted with an antagonizing otherness, the differential moments of the negated discourse tend to become articulated in a chain of equivalence that expresses their sameness vis-à-vis the enemy. We shall return to this problematique later. section 5.

Dislocation

In *Hegemony and Socialist Strategy* (1985), social antagonism is held responsible for the "impossibility of society." The argument is that social antagonism introduces a radical negativity, which prevents society from forming a fully constituted symbolic order. However, according to Žižek, the social identities negated in a social antagonism are always-already negated. In other words, the negation of a social identity in a social antagonism is always the negation of a negation. Žižek (1990) points to the effects of the Lacanian real, which is an unrepresentable kernel of negativity that reveals the ultimate failure of any symbolic order to constitute a completely sutured space.

Žižek's intervention led Laclau (1990) to reformulate his position. A theoretical division of labor is established between *dislocation*, which is responsible for the disruption of the discursive order, and *social antagonism*, which reconstructs the limits and unity of the discursive order while simultaneously preventing its closure. A hegemonic discourse is dislocated when new events cannot be domesticated, integrated, or explained by the discursive system. A discursive order is normally quite flexible and thus capable of inscribing a wide range of new events and developments. However, discourse only leads to a partial fixation of identity. It is therefore bound to come up against events that it cannot inscribe in its symbolic matrix. The failure to domesticate new events will lead to a complete or partial breakdown of the symbolic order. Dislocation shows itself in a structural or organic crisis in which there is a proliferation of floating signifiers. A good example of dislocation is the stagflation crisis that hit many Western economies in the beginning of the 1970s. Keynesianism was stalemated by the joint occurrence of rising unemployment and rising inflation.

Dislocation reveals the undecidability of the social and opens a terrain for totalizing hegemonic attempts to heal the rift in the dislocated structure of society. As such, dislocation is the condition of possibility of political action. Without the disruption of the social order, there can be no hegemonic politics. However, this is not merely replacing an essentialist grounding of society in a fully present positivity with an equally essentialist grounding of society in the abyss of pure negativity. With the assertion of a radical negativity, the concept of "grounding" loses its meaning. That is to say, whereas one can derive a whole series of determinate effects from a positively defined essence, nothing follows from negativity except the contingent political struggle about how to suture the dislocated social space (Laclau, 2000:184).

The Split Subject

The recurrent dislocations of the discursive systems means that the subject cannot be conceived in terms of its structural position within discourse, such as structuralist thinkers have done it. Discourse theory sides with the structuralists in their critique of the notion of a free, atomistic subject. The subject is internal to the structure, but because of the constant dislocations that disrupt the discursive order, the subject always emerges as a *split subject*. The subject has neither a fully achieved structural identity nor a complete lack of identity, but rather a failed structural identity (Laclau, 1990). The subject cannot be what it is because of the dislocating events that function to disrupt the symbolic order of society.

In this situation, the split and traumatized subject will either lapse into paralyzing self-denial or seek to establish an illusionary full identity in and through processes of identification. Identity is not the cause of the actors' political identifications. On the contrary, *identity* is a result of the split subject's *identification* with political discourses that promise to construct a fully achieved subjectivity by eliminating the source of all evil (Laclau, 1990; Butler, Laclau, and Žižek, 2000). Hegemonic struggles aim to articulate the different points of identification into a credible political project, which attempts to solve the problems at hand in accordance with the cherished values of the community and the institutionalized understanding of what is appropriate action.

Taken together, the five key concepts and the related arguments provide the basis for a new type of postmodern theorizing. The concepts may prove to be of great value in empirical analysis of social and political phenomena, but the task of further elaborating and operationalizing the conceptual framework remains. For, as David Howarth (2000) remarks, there is still a gap between some of the abstract ontological concepts and the need for concepts dealing with the ontic level. The task of filling this gap is a challenge that is currently taken up by numerous students of discourse.

DISCOURSE THEORY: ACCUSED AND DEFENDED

Two accusations against poststructuralist discourse theory are repeatedly voiced. The first claims that discourse theory leads to a relativist gloom and the second that discourse theory lapses into idealism. The charge of *relativism* contends that because there are no ultimate foundations and everything is discursive, we end up in a situation where everything is equally true, right, or good (Geras, 1987, 1990; Howard, 1989). This makes it impossible to defend any particular set of claims or values. The premise of the argument is correct because discourse theory insists that there is no extradiscursive truth, moral, or ethics (Rorty, 1989; Mouffe, 1996). However, the conclusion is wrong, as we never arrive at a situation where everything is equally valid. We always find ourselves placed within a particular discourse that provides us with a set of historically contingent criteria for determining what is true, right, and good. Only God is capable of transcending all discursivity; we mortals are stuck within particular discursive frameworks that define our criteria for judging something to be true, right, or good. However, if we were trapped within unified, closed and self-reproducing discourses, the possibility of an agonistic dialogue between different discursive truth claims would be impossible. The different cultures, traditions, and contexts that condition our truth claims are constantly rearticulated through processes of disintegration, mutual influence, and antagonistic conflict. They cannot be protected from contestation and contamination as their boundaries are continuously permeated and redrawn. It is this ongoing destabilization of the multiple contexts of cognitive, normative, and ethical judgment that facilitates a common political dialogue and can prevent a violent clash between pure and self-enclosed particularities.

The charge of *idealism* holds that the idea that everything is discursively constructed leads to an idealist denial of the independent existence of reality (Geras, 1987; Woodiwiss, 1990). However, against this accusation it can be argued that poststructuralist discourse theory is a realist and materialist constructivism of a radical kind (Laclau and Mouffe, 1987; Torfing, 1999). Discourse theory is *realist* in that it asserts that matter exists independently of our language, thoughts, and consciousness. However, matter only becomes intelligible for us when it is joined with a discursively constructed form. A spheric object at the bottom of the sea becomes a "mineral" in the hands of a geologist, a "projectile" in the hands of a desperate soldier, and a "ball" when a child kicks it down the street. A less trivial example would be that the bombing campaign against Serbia becomes a "military aggression" in the discourse of Serbian nationalists and a "humanitarian intervention" within the discourse of UN officials. When social and political identities are initially constructed and classified within discourse, we can judge propositional statements about the world as being true or false, but the world cannot determine the vocabulary by which we render the material entities, events, and feelings intelligible.

Discourse theory is not only realist, but also *materialist* in the sense that it claims that the discursive forms which render the world intelligible cannot be reduced to a reflection of the immanent essence of either the experienced object or the experiencing subject. Discursive forms are determined in and through their relation to other discursive forms within signifying systems that are constantly disrupted by dislocation and hegemonic interventions. The dream of a total fixation of a discursive system of forms that finally describes the world as it really is will never come true as the Lacanian real constitutes a undomesticable kernel which prevents the symbolic order of discourse from fully constituting itself. It is this destabilization of the discursively constructed forms that maintains the irreducible distance between form and matter, which is the defining trait of a materialist position.

Finally, discourse theory can be said to be *radical* in the sense that the material entities, whose forms are constructed in and through discourse, are not simply awaiting their discursive signification which can then be said to provide a more or less correct representation of social reality. According to Žižek (1989), the material entities are retroactively constituted by the discursive forms through which they are signified. Hence, the tendentially empty signifier "welfare state" provides a reference point for the construction of a relative unity of institutions, policies, and social practices that together are signified as "welfare state."

THE RETROACTIVE CONSTRUCTION OF THE SOCIAL BASIS OF POLITICS

If political science studies how politics shapes policy within a certain polity, *political sociology* inquires into the social basis of politics and the state. This raises the important question about the role and impact of class, ethnicity, gender, and so on for the form and function of the state and the political struggles that take place within and outside it.

Recently, the notion of class has lost its capacity to function as the articulating core around which all political identity is constituted (Laclau, 2000:296–301). The working class is in decline both numerically and in terms of its organizational strength. At the same time, class identity is decentered by internal divisions and by the participation of the working classes in a generalized mass culture. Finally, the location of social agents in the productive process seems to lose its centrality in determining their identity. The decentering of class has thus far led to its insertion into an enumerative chain together with other identities that are considered capable of producing a political frontier within a limited social space. In the absence of a political identity capable of unifying the other identities due to its ontologically and epistemologically privileged position, politics becomes a babel of multiple voices that is often referred to as *identity politics*.

The danger implicit to some multiculturalist interpretations of identity politics lies in the conception of the multifarious identities as separate, self-defined, and authentic identities whose particular demands should be reinforced rather than compromised through political struggle. At the theoretical level, the problem is that the contingent and politically constructed character is denied. At the political level, the problem is that the production of broad popular frontiers is prevented, leaving the state with a golden opportunity to deal with the particular demands of each identity in a completely transformist manner. This will make it difficult to advance a progressive politics building on universalizing demands for freedom and equality.

Now, the solution to this problem does not, as Žižek (2000) seems to suggest, lie in the dogmatic reassertion of the privileged role of a universal class, but rather, as Laclau suggests, in analyzing the contingent political recomposition of common political projects. We should not deny the particularity of political identities, but insist on the possibility of articulating broad popular frontiers based on a hegemonic universality.

In his argument, Laclau (1996b, 2000) presupposes the existence of different political groups each aiming to advance their own particular demands through democratic struggles that give rise to conflicts within limited societal sectors. Hence, students demand better financial support, the workers demand higher wages, women demand equal opportunities in the labor market, environmentalist groups demand tough regulation of industrial emissions, and so on. If these particular demands are met by the system, the basis for political conflict will disappear. On the contrary, if they are not met – either because they are rejected by the government for political reasons or because a socioeconomic crisis makes it impossible for them to be met – the particular groups will share with each other a feeling of frustration because of the negation of their demands and will stand up against the negating force, with hopes of overcoming their loss of identity through political action. Despite the different content of the particular demands, they will all be united in their opposition to the system.

What unites the particular groups is the construction of a chain of equivalence that emphasizes a universalizing sameness of the negated demands. As the particular identities might not share any positively defined interest, the sameness constructed by the chain of equivalence can only be expressed by tendentially empty signifiers appealing to universal ideas about Freedom, Progress, Modernization, Revolution, the People, and so on. The more the chain of equivalence is extended, the more empty the signifiers of universality must be, in order to be able to express, metaphorically, all the different negated demands. However, there can be no completely empty signifier, and thus no pure universality, as a signifier always signifies something. There will be an ongoing struggle between different conceptions of universality, and the hegemonic attempt to widen a certain conception of universality to include all other conceptions will always fail to eliminate the reference to particularistic interests. For example, it is often argued that the universal expansion of human rights is an expression of the particular interests of Western capitalism.

It should be noted that the universal dimension of the chain of equivalence does not preexist the particular demands in terms of a common recognition of the normative basis of society or a regulative idea of the future achievement of the good life. Rather, the universal dimension grows out of the negation of particularity and only exists as an attempt to symbolize the chain of equivalence that expresses the common feeling of a lack of identity. The empty universals emerge as an attempt to positivise a radical negativity. The empty universals might provide important reference points for the particular identities, but they do not absorb the particularity of the negated identities into a universal dialectical unity. The particular identities remain split between their own particularity and their universal dimension.

Because the universal dimension of the chain of equivalence does not carry the means of its own representation, a particular political agency must assume the task of expressing the universalizing sameness of the negated identities. This process by which a particular group assumes the function of universal representation is a hegemonic operation as it involves seizing the political and moral–intellectual leadership of an alliance of popular resistance. The hegemonic operation will imply both a universalization of particularity and a particularization of the universal. Hence, on the one hand, the hegemonic agent will have to give up or modify its particular demands in order to be able to speak in the name of the people. The universalization of the particular identity of the hegemonic agent will often lead to its splitting into a group of hardliners, who remain true to the original particularity, and a group of pragmatics who wish to fulfill the role of universal representation.

On the other hand, the hegemonic agent's articulation of a political project that incarnates a certain conception of the universal will eventually provide the empty universality with a particular content that to some degree reflects the hegemonic agent's demands. In order to advance the political struggle, the hegemonic agent will have to operationalize the abstract appeal to empty universal signifiers. The transformation of the empty universals into concrete proposals and legislation will further contribute to their particularization, and this means that more identities will be excluded from the political project. This dilemma indicates the problems involved in making the transition from leading a popular resistance movement to taking over government office.

The argument of Laclau clearly shows that the hegemonization of the empty universals constructs the social basis of politics in a political act of inclusion and exclusion. The universalization of the demands of the hegemonic agent may lead to a recomposition of its social basis as some people might leave the group while others join. Likewise, the particularization of the empty universals may include some particular groups in the hegemonic bloc while excluding others. The conclusion is that although politics clearly has a social basis, this is constructed in and through hegemonic struggles. In other words, politics cannot be read off its social basis, as the latter is retroactively constructed by the politics it engenders.

THE TASKS AHEAD

In order to meet the rising expectations of the rapidly expanding, but still rather new and incomplete, research program of poststructuralist discourse theory, some crucial theoretical, methodological, and empirical tasks must be fulfilled in the future.

Theoretically, there is a need for a further *clarification of the status* of poststructuralist discourse theory (Žižek, 2000). The twin pitfalls consist *either* in insisting on the radical historicism of the historicist approach of discourse theory and delimiting the validity of the different concepts and arguments to the historical, and even textual, context in which they have been developed, *or* in viewing discourse theory as a transcendental truth about radical contingency, which could only be revealed in the present postmodern condition. Whereas the first option risks turning discourse analysis into a strictly local storytelling exercise with no general validity, the second option betrays the discourse theoretical insight into the contingency of all truth claims. Therefore, an important future task of discourse theory is to find ways of recognizing the historicity of its analytical categories without letting that recognition stand in the way of a pragmatic usage of these categories in different social and historical contexts. Hence, it might be that the hegemonic logic of politics only comes to the fore with the development of modern mass society, but, as Laclau notes, we can still use this logic to "interrogate the past, and find there inchoate forms of the same processes that are fully visible today; and, when they did not occur, understand why things were different" (Laclau, 2000:200).

Another theoretical task is to develop further the theoretical resources for understanding the *processes of sedimentation* of politically constructed social identities and relations, the contribution of institutional frameworks to the *stable reproduction* of historical forms of capitalism, and the *path-dependent effects* of institutionalized regimes on the path-shaping hegemonic strategies (see Mouzelis, 1988; Torfing, 1998). The theoretical emphasis on contingency, dislocation and undecidability, which was an important weapon in the struggle against rationalistic, deterministic and functionalistic theories, has discouraged studies of the formation and formative effects of institutionalized discourse. Poststructuralist discourse theory can contribute significantly to the development of the expanding field of (neo)institutional theory. This can be achieved not only by questioning the objectivist assumptions underlying much of the research in this field, but also by directing more attention to the crucial role of sedimented imaginaries, which is not fully captured by the present focus on the regulative, normative, and cognitive dimensions of institutions. However, the realization of this potential requires a serious theoretical engagement with institutional analysis.

The last theoretical task to mentioned in this context is the need to further theorize the *implications of discourse theory for critique, normativity, and ethical questions* (see Critchley, 1998; Žižek, 1999). Critique of political claims and ideologies can no longer take the form of an appeal to universal values or the presence of an undistorted reality. Both values and reality are revealed as malleable discursive constructs and, thus, fail to provide a solid foundation of critique. This does not make critique impossible, but radically changes its form. Hence, a discourse theoretical critique will take the form of a deconstructive attempt to denaturalize social objectivity by revealing the political process of inclusion and exclusion that any totalizing hegemonic operation must necessarily involve (Laclau, 1996a). However, it is not enough to show the contingency of essentialist claims and totalizing ideologies. A constructive political critique should be linked to moral and ethical considerations. There is an urgent need for analyzing the ethical substance of the community (i.e., what Derrida refers to as justice), which is *impossible* because it is incommensurable with any normative order (i.e., what Derrida [1994] refers to as law) and *necessary* because it is constantly invested in particular normative orders. We should pay special attention to the processes through which this ethical substance is constructed through political decisions that are not predetermined by some aprioristic normativity, but, nevertheless, taken within sedimented practices that constitute the normative framework of a certain society (Laclau, 2000:82–5). The distinction between an undecidable justice and an eminently deconstructable law, and the attempt to show how the two are articulated through hegemonic operations, provides a promising starting point for the future elaboration of constructivist account of the relation between politics and ethics.

Many people are struck by the imbalance between the sophisticated and highly elaborated philosophical and theoretical framework of discourse theory and the crude and scarcely developed account of questions about research strategy and methodology. This can be largely explained by the postpositivist and even anti-epistemological stance of discourse theory, which rejects the need for a scientific method enabling us to confront theoretical statements with empirical facts. Unfortunately, the critique of epistemology has thrown the baby out with the bathwater, as poststructuralist discourse theorists have *paid little attention to methodological questions* (see Howarth, 1998; Howarth and Torfing, 2004). Of course, we should not seek to elaborate an authoritative methodological rulebook telling us how to apply discourse theory in empirical studies. Research is not about following rules, but rather about bending and inventing rules as an instance of their usage. However, discourse analysts need to develop some more explicit, systematic, and self-critical reflections about the formative usage of methodological rules. During the research process, discourse analysts are confronted with a series of choices about how to conduct their analyses. There are crucial questions about how to narrow down the theoretical and empirical scope of analysis; how to select the case or cases to be studied; how to select and blend different kinds of qualitative, and even quantitative, data; how to analyze data in a valid and reliable way; how to be sensitive to unexpected and recalcitrant interpretations of events; and how to integrate theoretical and empirical arguments in a fruitful way. All these important questions should be dealt with in a much more explicit way and ought to be subjected to careful arguments about the consequences of the choices made.

Another important methodological task relates to the more fundamental question of *research strategy* (see Howarth, 2000). Different problematiques call for different research strategies. If we want to show the contingency of "Frenchness," as it is constructed within the nationalist discourse of right-wing populism, we need to adopt a deconstructive research strategy, which is quite different from the kind of hegemonic power analytics to be used in the analysis of the outcome of political struggles over environmental regulation. In short, discourse analysts need to be more explicit about what they choose to look for in empirical analysis, why they want to look for it, how they are going to do it, and what kind of research results they are likely to obtain.

At an even more basic level, there is a great need for reflections about the *role of the researcher.* Already Foucault (1986a) gave up the idea of the discourse analyst as a neutral spectator who deciphers discourse from a point outside of it. The discourse analyst is implicated in the power struggles that take place within or around the discourse in question, and brings his or her own discursivity into play in the analysis. The problem of how discourse analysts should handle this implication cannot be reduced to a conflict between the normativity of the discourse analyst and the factual character of the empirical field. Normative and descriptive aspects cannot be entirely separated, but are articulated both in the discourse of the analyst and the discourse to be analyzed (Laclau, 2000:80). Hence, the problem poses itself as a question of the effects of intertextuality, that is, the effects of an interface between different texts. There is no way of preventing the construction of such an interface, but we need to find ways of assessing the effects of this intertextuality. Again, the question is not simply one of the impact of the researcher's pre-interpretations on the interpretative understanding of the discourse, but of the active construction of certain interpretations in the meeting between the researcher and the discourse to be analyzed. It is the form and impact of this meeting that needs further investigation at a general theoretical, as well as practical, level.

Although poststructuralist discourse theory informs an increasing number of empirical studies in a wide range of areas (see Dyrberg, Hansen, and Torfing, 2000; Howarth, Norval, and Stavrakakis, 2000; Norval, 1996; Smith, 1994; Torfing, 1998), there are important empirical tasks to carry out. First of all, we need *systematic in-depth studies* of empirical phenomena that clearly take us beyond the level of illustrative examples of theoretical arguments and theoretically informed redescription of a series of events. However, it is not enough that empirical analysis is rich and detailed. It must also be systematic so as to avoid impressionistic accounts, thus permitting other researchers to follow the various steps in the analysis. Systematicity could be enhanced through a more rigorous application of various techniques of textual analysis. Of course, such methods should not be applied in an instrumental way, and they will never short-circuit the toils of empirical discourse analysis. However, a pragmatic usage of textual analysis methods will help to scrutinize empirical material in a more systematic manner.

An important, and yet unfulfilled, ambition in empirical discourse analysis is carefully to *show the merits* of adopting a discourse theoretical perspective. The comparative advantage of discourse theory in analyzing empirical phenomena and events should be brought out more clearly by highlighting the strengths and weaknesses of discourse theory vis-à-vis other theories. The aim of this exercise should be to show that poststructuralist discourse theory is not merely covering other aspects than the more traditional theories, but opens up new and better ways of dealing with key problems of political sociology.

Last but not least, the current trend toward addressing *core issues of political sociology and political science* should be continued. Not only will it help to prevent the theoretical marginalization of discourse theory while advancing its argumentative and conceptual resources, but it will also further stimulate the dialogue between poststructuralist discourse theorists and more traditional mainstream theories. This will hopefully benefit everybody and help to renew political sociology as a key element in contemporary social science.

CHAPTER EIGHT

Rational Choice Theories in Political Sociology[1]

Edgar Kiser and Shawn Bauldry

Rational choice theory has been dramatically transformed in the past few decades. Many economists are abandoning the sparse mathematical models that dominated neoclassical economics in favor of the more complete and nuanced pictures of institutions, organizations, and action advocated by the "new institutionalism" (North, 1981, 1990; Williamson, 1975) and "behavioral economics" (Thaler, 1991). Rational choice theory in political science and sociology has taken further steps in that direction by developing much broader arguments at both the micro and macro levels. The intellectual diffusion of rational choice is best described as a complex form of assimilation, in which ideas from economics have both shaped and been shaped by their new disciplinary contexts. We believe the new theoretical model that is emerging from this process – which we call a *sociological rational choice theory* (in contrast to the traditional neoclassical approach) – has much to contribute to political sociology.

This chapter has three main goals. First, we outline the core features of sociological rational choice theory. Second, we summarize the contributions of rational choice theory to political sociology in three areas: the analysis of institutions, culture, and history. As rational choice has only recently made significant inroads in political sociology, we include seminal works from political science and economics in our discussions. Third, we discuss the scope of rational choice theory, arguing that it will be useful for many but not all problems of interest to political sociologists.

SOCIOLOGICAL RATIONAL CHOICE THEORY: A BRIEF OUTLINE

This section outlines a sociological version of rational choice theory (Hechter, 1987; Hechter and Kanazawa, 1997; Brinton, 1988; Levi, 1988, 1997; Coleman, 1990; Kiser, 1994, 1999; Adams, 1996; Brustein, 1996; Boudon, 1982, 1996; Lindenberg, 1989; Brinton and Nee, 1998).[2] Rational choice theory consists of separate arguments pertaining to the *motives and goals* of individual actors and to *models* of the conditions within which their action takes place. The

[1] We would like to thank all participants in the conference on "Theoretical Challenges to Political Sociology" (May 2001, New York University) and two reviewers for very helpful comments on an earlier draft.

[2] We believe that this version of rational choice (in contrast to neoclassical economics) has classical roots in the work of Max Weber (Kiser, 1999; Kiser and Baer, in press; Swedberg, 1998; Norkus, 2001). Both perspectives rely on methodological individualism, assumptions about intentional action, and the use of abstract models of organizational and institutional structures. Like earlier readings of Weber (Parsons, 1937; Bendix, 1977; Collins, 1986), our interpretation is shaped by our own theoretical perspective. This rational choice interpretation of Weber is roughly analogous in its intent to the analytical Marxism proposed by Jon Elster (1985) and John Roemer (1986), and thus can be called *Analytical Weberianism*.

focus on motives derives from methodological individualism. This does not imply reductionism (Homans, 1964) – it means simply that all complete explanations must include an analysis of individual motives and actions (Weber, 1968:13; Hechter, 1981; Coleman, 1986). Nor does it imply that corporate actors (classes, firms, states) cannot be used in rational choice models, only that their unity as "actors" must be justified, not just assumed.

Motives consist of orientations to action (either consequentialist or nonconsequentialist) and the goals of action. Instrumental action is consequentialist; nonconsequentialist actions are generally based on either values or emotions. Instrumental action provides the best starting assumption about microfoundations because: (1) it is least ambiguous and therefore most understandable to the analyst; and (2) it yields clear empirical implications.[3] Instrumental microfoundations are used as ideal types, and as such they are also useful in that they clearly reveal anomalies. To resolve these anomalies, modifications of the explanation should be made first in the least central aspects of the theory, with successive movements to more central elements if that tack fails (Lakatos, 1978). More specifically, look first at the way the social structural constraints specified by the model have been operationalized in the particular case. Second, perhaps the wrong model has been used for the case (maybe the case is really a repeated game as opposed to a one-shot game, or maybe it is a chicken game instead of a prisoner's dilemma). The next step is to reassess the microfoundational assumptions. Look first at the specification of the goals of actors – this is no doubt the source of many of the incorrect predictions in rational choice explanations. Finally, perhaps the assumption of instrumental rationality is incorrect and some other form of action should be employed in the explanation.

One of the most difficult things to do in rational choice models is to specify the goals of action. Analysts generally begin by assuming general goals such as wealth, power, and prestige, as these have the advantages of being fungible and having clear behavioral implications. More detailed specifications of preferences are sometimes used. For example, Barry Weingast and Michael Moran (1983) and Terry Moe (1985) were able to construct "ideological indexes" of the Congress as a whole, even for relevant congressional committees and subcommittees. This type of detailed preference specification is very rare in rational choice models – the data availability in this context make it possible.

Rational choice is not just a microlevel theory – it is a multilevel theory that focuses on explaining macrolevel outcomes, and it does so with arguments that always combine macro and micro levels (Coleman, 1986, 1990; Friedman and Hechter, 1988; Hechter and Kanazawa, 1997). In addition to microfoundations, rational choice theory thus also requires abstract macrolevel models of structures and relations. These models sometimes come from within rational choice theory (agency theory, optimal location theory, various types of game theory). However, sociological rational choice has also borrowed models from other parts of sociology that are consistent with the microfoundations of rational choice, such as network theory, Marxist economics, and Weberian ideal types (Coleman, 1990; Przeworski, 1985; Elster, 1985; Roemer, 1986; Adams, 1996; Gould, 2000; Kiser, 1994).

This chapter will show that standard criticisms of rational choice – that it is fatally flawed as a result of its inability to incorporate institutions, culture, and history – are no longer valid.[4] These were reasonable criticisms of rational

[3] Weber (1968:5) argued that "[t]he interpretation of such rationally purposeful action possesses, for the understanding of the choice of means, the highest degree of verifiable certainty."

[4] Anthony Obserschall and Eric Leifer (1986) argued that rational choice theories too often assume that outcomes are efficient and ignore the fact that power differentials often create and sustain inefficient institutions and policies. Mark Granovetter (1985) claimed that many rational choice models ignore the fact that action is always embedded in social contexts and that institutions, networks, and culture often shape choice and action. Margaret Somers (1998) and Philip Gorski (2000) argued that rational choice theory cannot incorporate the important effects of history and culture. Donald Green and Ian Shapiro (1994) listed several problems with rational choice theory, but their primary complaint is that it has very little empirical support.

choice work in neoclassical economics, but sociological rational choice theory is responding to all of them by incorporating institutions, culture, and history into their models (see also Brinton and Nee, 1998). As a result, rational choice theorists are currently producing much more interesting analyses of politics.[5]

RATIONAL CHOICE MODELS OF POLITICAL INSTITUTIONS

Rational choice models in economics are known for their parsimony. One of the ways that neoclassical versions of rational choice have simplified the world (in part to make the mathematics tractable) is to virtually ignore institutions. Gary Becker's (1976) application of the neoclassical model to several sociological topics is a classic example: Everything at the macro level is modeled as a market – there are markets for crime, marriage, and children – as if the market was the only type of institution. This is beginning to change, even within economics, with the rise of the "new institutionalism" (North, 1981, 1990; Williamson, 1975) and the "new growth theory" (Barro, 2002). Contemporary economists have begun to realize something Adam Smith ([1776]1976) knew all along[6] – that all economies are embedded in institutional contexts and that the nature of these institutions has important effects on economic development and growth (for summaries, see Eggertson [1990] and Weingast [1996]). This elaboration of the theory allows rational choice to respond to Mark Granovetter's (1985) criticism that they ignore the embeddedness of action.

Institutions are defined broadly in rational choice theory as equilibria of extensive form games (Shotter, 1981; Calvert, 1995:57–93; Bates et al., 1998:5).[7] They are viewed as solutions to cooperation problems that are self-enforcing (meaning that no actor in a position to change the institution has an incentive to do so) and as mechanisms to resolve coordination problems through providing focal points (Kreps, 1990; Alt and Alesina, 1996; Weingast, 1996).[8] This approach facilitates the use of game theory to explain the origin of institutions and institutional change.

Game theoretic models, however, often produce multiple equilibria. In these cases, they fail to generate clear predictions and thus are often not helpful in testing models. Rational choice theorists have developed the concept of "structure induced equilibrium" to deal with multiple equilibria problems (Shepsle and Weingast, 1987). The key to this argument is that particular features of institutional structure push toward one stable equilibrium point by limiting either the choices available to actors or the range of enforceable outcomes. If these institutional features can be identified, the choice of one equilibrium among the many possible can be explained. For example, Moe's (1989) study of the Environmental Protection Agency (EPA)

[5] We do not attempt to discuss all aspects of rational choice theory that have addressed politics. Three things might be especially conspicuous by their absence: spatial models of politics derived from Anthony Downs (1957), theories of war and international relations, and theories of voting behavior. Downsian models of the "optimal location" of political parties have had little impact on sociology, and we believe they are unlikely to due to their highly mathematical nature (but see Burstein [1999] for an interesting application of these ideas stressing the role of public opinion in determining political outcomes). With the exception of the literature on war and state making in historical sociology (Tilly, 1985, 1990; Ertman, 1997; Kiser and Linton, 2000), sociologists have shown little interest in the causes and consequences of warfare. Therefore, although there is a great deal of interesting rational choice work in political science on this topic (Bueno de Mesquita, 1981; Bueno de Mesquita and Lalman, 1992; Fearon, 1995), we do not address it here. We ignore work on voting, in spite of the fact that there has been a great deal of it in political science, because we believe the small costs and benefits associated with voting make it beyond the scope of rational choice theory (see below).

[6] It is no coincidence that the increased focus on institutions has been coupled with the revival of political economy, the core of classical economics.

[7] In extensive form games, actors move sequentially. The game is thus depicted as a series of branching actions and reactions, in a decision tree.

[8] Focal points are basically shared understandings of what is obvious and are generally produced by shared culture, history, or personal experience.

explains both its stability and its extremely cumbersome administrative procedures. He noted that politicians creating bureaucratic agencies face an intertemporal control problem – the next administration may have different policy goals and thus attempt to change the way the agency works. In order to prevent this and make their policies more durable, creators of the EPA enacted a series of complicated and rigid procedures that decreased the efficiency of the agency somewhat, but made it much more difficult to alter its functioning in the long term.

Another set of models of institutional change focus on the role of incomplete information. For example, Arthur Stinchcombe (1999) showed that organizations grow toward areas of uncertainty, in an attempt to reduce it. Keith Krehbiel (1991) and Kenneth Shepsle and Barry Weingast (1994) demonstrated that committees are important to Congress in part because they provide incentives to some actors to gather costly but useful information, and Susanne Lohmann (1995, 1998) developed interesting models of the informational functions of lobbying.

As rational choice models of institutions moved from economics to political science and sociology, analyses of their aggregate efficiency effects (often based on functionalist logic in neoclassical models)[9] have been supplemented by models focusing on power and distributional effects. Through a consideration of the distributional effects of institutions, rational choice theorists have developed a class of models that explicitly incorporate power. William Riker's (1962) analysis of distributive politics, focusing on the formation of "minimum winning coalitions," is an important early move in this direction. More recently, Robert Bates et al. (1998) began their discussion of "analytic narratives" by assuming that "coercion is as much a part of... life as are production, consumption, and exchange." Geoffrey Garrett and Barry Weingast (1993:185–6) also incorporated power into their argument, in order to determine which of multiple possible equilibria are chosen. Edgar Kiser and Joshua Kane (2001) showed that the power of aristocrats and tax farmers often blocked administrative reforms in early modern states – revolutions often broke the power of entrenched aristocrats and thus facilitated some bureaucratizing reforms. Jack Knight (1992; see also Knight and Sened, 1995) developed a general model of the formation of institutions focusing mainly on how power is used to control distributional outcomes.

George Tsebelis (1990:246) developed these arguments further by specifying the conditions in which institutions will be based more on efficiency or more on distributive factors. He argued that when little information about the future is available, actors will attempt to construct institutions that maximize efficiency, whereas good information about the future leads to the creation of redistributive institutions. These theoretical developments provide a strong response to critics who claim that rational choice theory ignores the role of power in politics (Oberschall and Leifer, 1986). They may also be useful in providing more detailed causal mechanisms for traditional sociological arguments focusing on power and conflict, such as Marxism (for a start, see Elster, 1985; Roemer, 1986).

Another area in which rational choice models of institutions have made substantial progress is in understanding the management of jointly owned ("common pool") resources. Garrett Hardin's (1968) analysis of the "tragedy of the commons" suggested that there is a strong tendency for collectively shared resources to be overexploited by self-interested individuals. This will lower the productivity of the resource, in some cases exhausting or ruining it. Although this argument was theoretically compelling, it was soon confronted by a host of anomalies – many common pool resource situations were both long-lasting and efficient. These anomalies were resolved by focusing on the role of institutions. Most importantly, Elinor Ostrom (1990) analyzed the wide variety of institutions that have been used to solve problems of common pool resources. She used game theory and extensive empirical research to show that privatization and state regulation are not the only

[9] The validity of this type of functionalism depends on the extent to which the existence of strong selection mechanisms can be demonstrated.

two solutions to "commons" problems. Voluntary self-organization often works – as the case of early modern peasant communities illustrates. This work lays the foundation for analyses of the increasingly important international conflicts over the control and protection of natural resources that cross state boundaries.

Rational choice theorists in sociology have extended analyses of institutions to many diverse spheres of society, including, but not limited to, political institutions.[10] Instead of treating the state as a unitary actor, as state-centered theory has often done, the multilevel character of rational choice models allows for the state to be disaggregated and analyses to consider interactions between different political actors. Therefore, they are in a position to further develop the insights of state-centered theory (Evans et al., 1985).

AN ILLUSTRATION OF THE NEW INSTITUTIONALISM: AGENCY THEORY

The implementation of state policy, a classic issue in Weberian political sociology (and one of Weber's main concerns), has recently been addressed by rational choice theorists using agency theory. This allows us to assess the extent to which contemporary rational choice models improve on Weber's work. There is now a fairly large literature, mostly in political science, applying agency theory to a Weberian question: How can rulers (usually democratically elected officials) control the bureaucratic agencies to which they have delegated the power to implement state policies?[11] The focus has been on institutional responses to the problem of "bureaucratic drift" – the tendency for the actions of a bureaucratic agency to "drift away" from the goals of politicians. The form of many of the arguments is partly functionalist: Existing institutional structures (procedures, monitoring systems, etc.) are explained by the agency problems they presumably mitigate (Moe, 1990:224; Fiorina, 1990:256).

William Niskanen's (1971) *Bureaucracy and Representative Government* is the classic rational choice analysis of agency problems in state policy implementation. He argued that one of the main threats to contemporary democracy is that elected politicians are losing power relative to appointed bureaucrats. He assumed that bureaucrats want to maximize the budget of the agency they control. They can use the fact that they have better information than politicians to get inflated budgets for their agencies, so the state becomes larger than either politicians or voters want it to be.

Because the central problem in all agency relationships is information asymmetry, the bureaucrats have better information about both the environment and their actions than politicians do – agency analyses naturally tend to focus on politicians monitoring bureaucrats. It is thus surprising that there seems to be very little direct monitoring of bureaucratic agencies by their political principals (Weingast and Moran, 1983; Hammond and Knott, 1996).[12] This discovery led some to conclude that Weber (1968) and Niskanen (1971) must be right, that bureaucracies are indeed beyond the control of politicians. However, this still leaves a critical question unanswered: Why are politicians hardly even trying to monitor them? The main answer offered by "congressional dominance" arguments (Weingast and Moran, 1983; Weingast, 1984) is that Congress is in fact able to adequately control bureaucratic agencies, but that they use means other than direct monitoring. Matthew McCubbins and Thomas Schwartz (1984:166) noted that direct monitoring is very expensive, so principals have strong incentives to find less

[10] For another example, Rosemary Hopcroft (1999) drew on Douglass North's (1981) model of institutions to analyze the importance of different types of agrarian social relations for economic development.

[11] Roberto Michels's (1915/1959) argument about the "iron law of oligarchy" is another classical analysis of an agency problem – in this case, party members (principals) are unable to adequately control their leaders (agents) as the party grows larger and more organized.

[12] There is of course some direct monitoring of bureaucratic agencies, by organizations including the Congressional Budget Office and the General Accounting Office (using hearings, investigations, evaluation research, and budget reviews).

costly strategies. One way to compensate for poor monitoring is to use stronger sanctions (Becker and Stigler, 1974). Because any decision to deviate from the interests of the principal will combine the probability of getting caught and the punishment if caught (as well as the likely rewards), increasing the severity of sanctions can be used to compensate for a low probability of being caught (as in deterrence theory in criminology). Therefore, several scholars (Weingast, 1984; Weingast and Moran, 1983; McCubbins and Schwartz, 1984) have argued that the use of strong ex post sanctions (adjusting budgets using appropriations and reauthorizations bills) are key components of congressional control over bureaucracy.[13]

Even with strong sanctions, some monitoring is still necessary – how does Congress know whose budgets to cut? Because most types of bureaucratic "drift" harm some interest groups or other citizens, these third parties have strong incentives to monitor bureaucracies and report problems to politicians. This type of reactive "fire alarm" oversight is much cheaper for politicians than direct monitoring because the costs are paid by the third parties. It is also often more effective, as these third parties usually have better information about the actions of bureaucratic agents than Congress does (Weingast, 1983; Keiweit and McCubbins, 1991:27–34). However, Weingast and Moran (1983:767) also noted that third parties can hinder monitoring. For example, interest groups may collude with agencies to serve their mutual interests, which may include hiding some agency actions from politicians. This argument provides an important addition to pluralist theory, indicating that interest groups can be important not just in policy making, but in implementation as well.

Administrative procedures can also be used to mitigate monitoring problems. Several political scientists (McCubbins, 1985; McCubbins, Noll, and Weingast, 1987:254–5) have argued that various types of administrative procedures can mitigate informational disadvantages with reporting requirements ("red tape" thus serves a monitoring function) and can facilitate third-party monitoring by giving particular constituencies access to the agency. However, Kathleen Bawn (1995) noted that there is often a trade-off between technical efficiency and political control. Administrative procedures can enhance control, but they often decrease efficiency (thus the common complaints about the proliferation of red tape). Overall, using administrative procedures to control agents will be effective when the gains in controlling corruption outweigh the losses due to red tape.[14]

Although early versions of agency theory tended to ignore the role of power and dependence (Emerson 1962), this is not true of more recent models. For example, Julia Adams (1996) used agency theory to model the relationship between metropolitan principals and colonial "company men" in colonial trading companies in the Netherlands and England. Given the problems principals in the Netherlands and England faced gathering information about the activities of their agents in Asia due to the distance involved, how were they able to control them? In the Dutch hierarchy, the Batavian outpost (contemporary Jakarta) maintained a middleman or brokerage position between the metropolitan principals and company agents, allowing them to illegally extract some of the surplus by collusive corruption with other agents. In spite of this, the level of corruption initially was limited. To account for this, Adams made an argument that was stressed often by Weber (1968:1007, 1015–18): The level of corruption is inversely related to the level of agent dependence on principals. Agents of the Dutch initially had no alternative opportunities, and this dependence limited their corruption. The situation changed when the English company moved

[13] This relationship holds in a wide variety of historical contexts. For example, Kiser (1994) showed that tax farming was used in early modern states when strong sanctions were necessary to compensate for poor monitoring capacity.

[14] Another way of mitigating monitoring problems is by attempting to hire loyal agents. Andrew Walder's (Walder, Li, and Treiman, 2000; Li and Walder, 2001) work on the ways that party membership (a loyalty signal) affect recruitment and mobility in communist states provides a good example.

in, because they provided not only direct competition but also more opportunities for collusive corruption for agents of the Dutch (Adams, 1996:23). The ultimate result is the one predicted by Weber: By the end of the eighteenth century, patrimonial principals had almost totally lost control of their colonial agents.

Kiser also used agency theory to address classic Weberian questions. For example, Kiser and Schneider (1994) addressed Weber's claim that the efficiency of Prussian tax administration was due to its early bureaucratization. In contrast to Weber's claim, they demonstrated that particular variations from the bureaucratic ideal type that increased the dependence of agents or strengthened their incentives were the primary causes of efficiency in this case. For example, Prussian rulers used a unique system of caring for injured military veterans. Instead of giving them welfare payments, they gave them positions as collectors of indirect taxes (what we would now call a "workfare" program). Because these officials had poor alternative employment opportunities, they were very dependent on rulers and thus less corrupt. By creating a high level of dependence, this way of selecting officials was more effective than bureaucratic selection on the basis of merit.

RATIONAL CHOICE MODELS OF CULTURAL ASPECTS OF POLITICS

Rational choice and cultural theories are generally seen as polar opposites, and many traditional criticisms of rational choice fault it for ignoring culture. Like many other standard criticisms of rational choice, this one is rapidly becoming outdated. Some of the most interesting recent developments in rational choice have been in the area of culture broadly defined, including work on information, signaling, norms, focal points, legitimacy, and reputations.

As functionalist theories stress (Parsons, 1963), politics are not just about conflict, but also involve coordination around shared interests ("power to" as well as "power over"). Rational choice work on focal points and common knowledge develops this insight further by outlining the causal mechanisms that produce coordination. One of the first attempts to incorporate culture in a rational choice framework is Thomas Schelling's (1978) work on how focal points are used to solve coordination problems. Focal points come from shared expectations derived from cultural common knowledge,[15] which allow the coordination of behavior in the absence of explicit communication between actors. In situations of multiple equilibria, focal points can determine which particular solution is chosen. Garrett and Weingast (1993) suggested that shared beliefs can act as "constructed focal points" around which actors can converge.[16] They used this to explain the institutional structure of the internal market created by the European Community. Steve Pfaff and Guobin Yang (2001) provided a great example, showing how important political anniversaries and landmarks, usually used to legitimate regimes, can also serve as focal points that coordinate collective action by groups opposed to the regime.

One of the most important moves in the transition from neoclassical economics to broader forms of rational choice theory was dropping the assumption of perfect information. Models of agency relations, property rights, and transactions costs (the costs of creating, monitoring, and enforcing contractual agreements) were all developed to deal with situations in which information is incomplete and unequally distributed across actors. Because information is one of the key components of culture, analyses of the effects of the amount and distribution of information available to actors provide one important part of a rational choice theory of culture

[15] People have common knowledge when they all know something and they all know that they all know it. Pluralistic ignorance is thus the absence of common knowledge, as the second criterion is not met (Chwe, 2001:17).

[16] This notion of constructed focal points may provide a way to develop a rational choice model to address one of the classic critcisms of social contract and market formation arguments in Thomas Hobbes and Adam Smith–Emile Durkheim's (1893/1964) argument about the importance of the "precontractual bases of contract." These precontractal understandings that are the necessary foundation of trade and institution building could be understood as constructed focal points.

(with implications for political issues such as legitimacy and public opinion).

Beginning with Herbert Simon's (1958) work on bounded rationality and satisficing,[17] a focus on the complexity of many choice situations and the lack of complete information (or the cognitive capacity to process it) has led to a reconceptualization of the microfoundations of rational choice models. Although there have been many moves in this direction, the most significant is what has come to be called behavioral economics (Thaler 1991). Building on Daniel Kahneman and Amos Tversky's (1979) famous experiments, behavioral economics is an attempt to construct more realistic microfoundations for rational choice theory. It began as an attempt to explain a large body of anomalies in standard neoclassical theory,[18] and has evolved into a nascent (as yet not fully unified) set of alternative microfoundational assumptions.

Because it is not possible to even list all of the anomalies and explanations here, we focus on one with important implications for politics – fairness norms.[19] Behavioral economists have shown that people are willing to pay costs to punish others who act unfairly. They often reject "unfair" offers in ultimatum games, thus imposing costs on themselves in order to punish the other actor.[20] This suggests that they might do the same thing when states act unfairly toward them. If so, collective action (especially high-risk collective action like revolts and revolutions) would be more frequent than neoclassical rational choice theory predicts.

Rational choice theorists have also begun to study legitimacy. Following Weber (1968), Margaret Levi (1988, 1997) argued that things like paying taxes and serving in the military cannot be explained by coercion alone. Instead, compliance is "quasi-voluntary" and based on "contingent consent." The legitimacy of the state (and thus the granting of contingent consent) is based essentially on two factors: (1) does the state provide public goods as promised; and (2) can the state ensure that other citizens comply with their obligations (so those who do comply do not feel like "suckers"). These two conditions are the basic terms of the implicit contract between the state and its citizens, and when they are met the state will be legitimate and compliance by citizens will be high. She used this to explain variations in the structure and effectiveness of systems of taxation (ranging from Republican Rome to contemporary Australia) and military organization over the past three centuries.

One of the most interesting elaborations of Schelling's work on coordination problems and focal points, Michael Chwe's (2001) argument about the rationality of (political and other) rituals, also has important implications for the study of legitimacy. Submitting to a political authority is in part a coordination problem, because everyone will be more willing to do so if others do (this is true for both existing states and challengers). Because coordination problems are

[17] When actors maximize, they examine all of the alternative actions in the choice set and select the best one (the action with the highest net benefit). Simon (1958) argued maximizing is rare – due to the limited cognitive capacities of actors and the complexity of the world, actors usually use a much simpler and quicker procedure. Satisficing refers to a choice process in which alternative choices are only explored until one that is "good enough" (satisfactory) is found, at which point that actor stops the search and selects that alternative.

[18] To take just a few examples: (1) why don't people ignore sunk costs?; (2) why do they often choose to eliminate options from their choice sets?; (3) why are things like Super Bowl tickets and great wine always underpriced?; and (4) why don't people treat losses and gains symmetrically?

[19] For a different substantive political example of the use of ideas from behavioral economics, Randall Calvert (1986) moved beyond the assumption of fixed preferences by using learning models of how voters form beliefs about candidates and parties, and "voter heuristics" models to look at how voters use ideology to predict more complex policy preferences of candidates.

[20] An ultimatum game is a situation in which two players divide a fixed amount. Player 1 gets to specify a particular division of the pie, and player 2 can either accept or reject the offer. If the offer is accepted, the players split the sum as offered; if it is rejected, both players get nothing. For example, if the total sum to be divided is a dollar, neoclassical theory predicts that player 1 will make an offer of 99 cents for herself and 1 cent for player 2, and that player 2 will accept that offer. However, the experiments almost never work out that way. Offers of 1 cent (and other very low offers) are almost always rejected, leaving both players with nothing.

solved by common knowledge, Chwe explored the social processes that create common knowledge. He argued that one of the main ways that common knowledge is generated is by public rituals. The purpose of public political rituals is neither to indoctrinate individuals ideologically (as Marxist theories suggest) nor to create prostate emotions (Durkheim's "collective effervescence"), but to show individuals that others participating in the ritual support the state. Because these rituals make it more likely that individuals will think others support the state, they make support of the state a stable focal point. Therefore, states (and groups opposing them) are expected to use rituals to try to create the common knowledge that will facilitate coordination.

Another recent example of a rational choice analysis of culture is Michael Hechter's (2000) work on nationalism. He argued that the rise and decline of nationalism is primarily a consequence of changes in the nature of the state. When states were decentralized and ruled indirectly (through local notables), the interests of different national groups within states were not threatened because they controlled important policies locally. This changed when states began to centralize and rule directly. When states were able to make and enforce uniform policies, they often infringed on particular group interests and led to the development of nationalist movements. This explains why nationalism is mainly a modern phenomenon, as centralized direct rule was rare prior to the French Revolution. Moreover, it implies that containing nationalism usually requires decentralization or some form of federalism to return local control to nationalist minorities.

Norms are another aspect of culture traditionally ignored by rational choice theorists. That changed with the seminal work of James Coleman (1990) on the development and effects of different types of norms. Coleman argued that the demand for norms is a function of the externalities of behavior. Behaviors with negative externalities for others will increase the demand for norms proscribing them, and behaviors with positive externalities will increase the demand for norms encouraging them. However, demand will not ensure the supply of norms, as that will depend on the willingness of people to sanction noncompliance. When can this second-order free rider problem (free riding on the collective responsibility to sanction the noncompliance [first-order free riding] of others) be overcome? Coleman argued that tight networks (multiple, overlapping ties) are necessary because they facilitate sanctioning. Thus norms are a joint product of the externalities of behavior and tight network relations.

Robert Ellikson (1991) also developed a compelling theory of informal norms of cooperation among cattle ranchers. Traditional neoclassical models expect disputes (such as those between ranchers about stray cattle) to be resolved "in the shadow of the law" – meaning that both parties know what the outcome would be if they went to court, so they use that as a guideline for resolving the dispute. He found instead that disputes are resolved "in the shadow of norms" governing interaction between ranchers (a fairly stable group in a repeated game situation) and that laws have very little effect.

More recently, two of the most prominent rational choice theorists in sociology collaborated on a book on norms (Hechter and Opp, 2001). Michael Hechter and Elizabeth Borland (2001) looked at the development of norms of national self-determination, showing that rational choice theory does a better job than cultural institutionalism of explaining their emergence and diffusion. Karl-Deiter Opp (2001) explored the emergence of "protest norms" out of personal networks and documented their importance in explaining collective action.

Another way in which rational choice theorists have begun to incorporate culture is by exploring the effects of reputation. Work on reputation emerged out of repeated game theory, as there are clear reputational costs for defection not present in one-shot games. Recent applications have been to areas as diverse as political party discipline and the dynamics of revenge. James Alt and Alberto Alesina (1996:653) argued that the main reason parties control appointments to committees is because the actions of committee members (especially chairs) can have important effects on the reelection chances of all party members through their effect on party reputation. The central prediction that follows from this, that parties will put members with views close to the mean of the party in important committee posts, has received strong empirical support. Denis Chong (1991) argued that the negative reputational effects of defecting in repeated game situations is one of the reasons that free riding in collective action is less frequent than Mancur Olson (1966) predicted. In a very different analysis of reputational effects, Roger Gould (2000) showed that a group tends to take revenge when its reputation for solidarity has been threatened. A reputation for taking revenge demonstrates group solidarity (because one member must take a risk to avenge another) and thus deters future attacks on group members.

As this short summary indicates, critics can no longer claim that rational choice theorists ignore culture.[21] The question now is how well rational choice models can explain the cultural aspects of politics relative to alternative theories. We explore this issue in the following section by analyzing the ways in which rational choice theory has incorporated cultural factors into the study of collective action.

THE EVOLUTION OF RATIONAL CHOICE WORK ON COLLECTIVE ACTION

Rational choice analyses of collective action began with Olson's (1965) seminal *Logic of Collective Action*. He showed that when goods are nonexcludable (it is difficult or costly to prevent anyone from consuming the good once it is produced) and characterized by jointness of supply (the consumption of the good by one actor does not significantly decrease the amount available to others), people will free ride on their provision and they will be undersupplied. This pathbreaking analysis of free riding in public/collective goods contexts showed why most sociological models predicted too much collective action. However, Olson's model predicted too little – collective action often occurs in the absence of his necessary conditions: selective incentives and small group size.

Some of the first and most important modifications of Olson's model from within rational choice theory came from game theory. Instead of looking at collective action as a one-shot prisoner's dilemma (Hardin [1971] showed that Olson's argument can be modeled this way), many instances of it might be more usefully modeled as repeated games (Axelrod, 1984) or different types of games (chicken, assurance, etc.) (Taylor, 1976).[22] The sociological findings that strong network ties facilitate participation in collective action (McAdam and Paulsen, 1993) could be modeled using assurance games. More recently, several scholars have broadened rational choice models of collective action by including more cultural components, such as norms, values, and shared information about the preferences of others (Chong, 1991; Opp et al., 1995; Kuran, 1995).

Chong's (1991) analysis of the civil rights movement combined standard game theoretic models with more cultural factors.[23] He (1991:235) argued that few movements will get off the ground without the actions of morally committed "unconditional cooperators." In addition to the value-based action in the early

[21] This is not to say that sociological rational choice theory has fully incorporated culture. As Adams (1999) noted in a compelling critique, emotions are generally ignored (but see Frank, 1988).

[22] A chicken game is one in which either of two actors could provide a public good unilaterally, but both would prefer that the other actor do it. This game has two equilibria, one in which the first actor provides the good and another in which the other actor does (because the costs of neither actor providing the good are greater to each than the cost to either one of them of providing the good themselves). An assurance game is one in which the joint efforts of two actors are necessary to provide a public good, and neither can provide the good alone. This game also has two equilibria, one in which both players contribute to the provision of the public good and one in which neither player contributes. Assurance games tend to produce conditional cooperation agreements – "I will if you will."

[23] Elster (1989:37) made a very similar proposal when he suggested that "when trying to explain individual participation in collective action, one should begin with the logically most simple type of motivation: rational, selfish, outcome-oriented behavior. If this proves insufficient to explain the phenomena we observe, we must introduce more complex types, either singly or in combination." Seigwart Lindenberg (1989) and Mark Lichbach (1996:236–9) have made similar arguments from a rational choice perspective.

stages of collective action, he suggested that successful campaigns generate social and psychological incentives that can turn a prisoner's dilemma game into an assurance game, making cooperation much more likely.[24] This composite model suggests that different games with different microfoundations occur at different stages of social movement development – but, most importantly, Chong showed the relationships between these stages (see also Lindenberg [1989] on revolutionary collective action). In another example of the use of composite models, Opp et al. (1995) developed a compelling account of the East German protests in 1989, showing that in addition to material incentives, both values and network ties were important causal factors.

Another example comes from Timar Kuran's (1995) work on the unpredictability of revolutions. One of the most interesting (and humbling) features of the revolutions of 1989 is that they came as a surprise to leaders, rebels, and academics alike. Kuran (1995) developed an argument about "preference falsification" to explain why this was the case, and more generally to specify a set of conditions in which we should not expect our theories to have much predictive power. Because people will systematically misrepresent their preferences in public in an autocratic setting (or even one in which their preferences are not socially desirable), it becomes very difficult for either participants or scholars studying them to know the actual level of discontent with the status quo and thus the potential for revolutionary collective action. The actual level of discontent only becomes apparent when some exogenous event decreases the cost of expressing true (antiregime) preferences. When this happens, revolutions often escalate very quickly, as people realize their grievances are widely shared.

It may also be possible to use Downsian optimal location models to study the strategies of social movements. Beginning with the assumption that politicians want to maximize the probability of winning elections, Downs (1957) developed elegant models predicting the optimal location of political parties (the policy platform that maximizes votes) in issue spaces (coninua of voters' opinions on an issue). Social movements may behave in the same way as political parties, choosing ideological positions to maximize members/participants, so it might be possible to use the Downsian model to explain the actions of social movement organizations. David Snow et al. (1986) developed a model of frame alignment (based on symbolic interactionist theory) to understand the techniques used by social movement organizations (SMOs) to recruit members. Basically, the argument is that when the frames (general worldviews) of potential members match those of SMOs, they will be more likely to join. SMOs thus use techniques to facilitate that matching. If we can think of these SMOs as analogous to political parties, it might be useful to model their positions relative to each other using Down's optimal location scheme. It then should be possible to make clear predictions about where SMOs should locate themselves relative to each other in the issue space and how many adherents they would be expected to attract as they move in that space – thus systematizing some of the insights in Snow's argument.

MODELING THE HISTORICAL DIMENSION OF POLITICS

The relationship between rational choice theory and history has been hotly debated recently (Gould, in press; Bates et al., 1998; Elster, 2000; Skocpol, 2000; Carpenter, 2000; Goldthorpe, 2000). Some critics of rational choice have argued that it is ahistorical and cannot incorporate particular details, temporal sequences, and narrative methods (Somers, 1998).[25] This section

[24] Another way to make this argument is to claim that there are benefits from the act of participation itself (Hirschman, 1982:86–7).

[25] One major proponent of rational choice theory (Goldthorpe 2000) has argued against historical sociology generally (based on the low quality of historical data), and thus against the use of rational choice in historical work (advocating instead a union of rational choice and quantitative data based on survey research).

shows that these are not valid criticisms of contemporary rational choice models, as contemporary rational choice theory is now doing all of these things.

Historical sociologists are no doubt correct that the temporal sequence in which causal factors occur often affects outcomes (Aminzade, 1992; Griffin, 1993). The fact that many rational choice models tend to be abstract and formal gives the impression that they are not well-suited to analyzing the messy details of history, such as complex narrative sequences. It is becoming increasingly clear that this superficial impression is incorrect. After all, it was rational choice theorists who first developed models of path dependence, in an attempt to explain the persistence of apparently inefficient outcomes (David, 1985; Arthur, 1994; for a good recent summaries, see Peirson, 2000; Mahoney, 2000). Rational choice work using game theory and models of agenda setting are intrinsically temporal – the sequence in which things happen always affects the outcome. Temporal sequences are explicitly modeled in extensive form games, a class of game theory models that explain outcomes as the consequence of temporally ordered strategic interaction (i.e., sequences of action and reaction). Game theory may prove to be an especially useful devise for the construction of theory-driven narratives that do not ignore the important roles of agency and particular events.

Peter Abell (1987, 1993), Kiser (1996), and Bates et al. (1998) offered general arguments about the utility of rational choice theory in historical analysis. *Analytic Narratives* (Bates et al., 1998) is especially useful because it provides five case studies illustrating their approach – just the sort of systematic empirical work Green and Shapiro (1994) claimed rational choice lacks. Both Avner Grief and Weingast focused on the determinants of institutional stability, using extensive form games to show how strategic interaction produced particular institutional equilibria. Grief showed that the *podesta* (foreigners hired to serve as political executives for short terms in several medieval Italian city-states) kept the peace and facilitated economic development in Genoa by protecting warring clans from each other. Weingast argued that the balance rule protected federalism (by providing both the North and South with the power to veto legislation contrary to their interests) and facilitated territorial expansion in antebellum America.[26] Both Levi and Jean-Laurent Rosenthal showed how differences in domestic political institutions shape the likelihood and nature of warfare. Levi looked at changes in conscription policy and Rosenthal showed how the frequency of war was determined by relations between monarchs and representative institutions in early modern France. Bates used a variety of models to analyze the rise and decline of a political institution that regulated international markets, the International Coffee Organization. In each case, their accounts combined detailed historical narratives with rational choice models.[27]

Game theory is not the only way in which rational choice models have incorporated temporality in political sociology. Yoram Barzel and Edgar Kiser (1997) demonstrated that the timing of factors affecting the insecurity of rule determines their effects on voting institutions – the Hundred Years' War disrupted the development of voting institutions in France more than in England because their prior development (and thus the ability to withstand shocks) was greater in the latter. Lindenberg (1989) outlined an ordered sequences of game structures that are likely to unfold as a revolutionary situation moves toward revolution – and then uses them to construct brief narratives of the French and Russian revolutions. As noted above, Chong (1991) argued that the timing of successful social movement activity is critical – early

This rejection of history is a minority position in contemporary rational choice theory.

[26] Weingast is not the only Americanist (the branch of political science most known for formal rational choice models) to turn to history. John Ferejohn (1993) analyzed the dynamics of the English Parliament in the Stuart era as in large part a consequence of changes in what he calls "non-verifiable beliefs."

[27] Elster (2000) criticized the "analytic narratives" project on several grounds: for assuming hyperrationality, for ignoring uncertainty, and for fitting their models to the historical evidence.

success is necessary to gain support and facilitate the development of emotional attachment to the group effort.

Rational choice work on agenda setting also incorporates temporality, generally by demonstrating how moving first allows certain actors to shape outcomes. Following Kenneth Arrow (1963), McKelvey's (1976) theory demonstrated that majority voting can be wholly cyclic, so whoever controls the agenda can lead the majority to any alternative (Lichbach, 1996:vii). One of the best recent examples of work on agenda setting is the "setter model" (Rosenthal, 1990). In this model, an executive individual or organization has exclusive power to set the agenda. Shepsle and Weingast (1987) applied this model to policy formation in Congress and viewed the congressional committee with jurisdiction over the issue as the "setter" with the power to shape the agenda. They showed that the agenda setting advantage of committees results in policies that reflect the interests of the committee more than those of Congress as a whole.[28]

Many historical sociologists, political scientists, and economists have begun to stress the path-dependent nature of social and political processes (David, 1985; Aminzade, 1992; Arthur, 1994; Peirson, 2000; Mahoney, 2000). One of the main problems with the concept of path dependence has been its vagueness – it has often been used to refer to any process in which temporality and sequence are important. Recently, that has begun to change. Drawing on the more precise definition of path dependence in economics (David, 1985; Arthur, 1994), Peirson (2000) clarified the concept and applied it to the study of politics. From a rational choice perspective, path dependence refers to processes that are characterized by increasing returns – the probability of further steps down a particular path increases (the costs of exiting from the path increase) because the relative benefits of the current path increase over time. The causal mechanisms generating increasing returns are high set-up/fixed costs (creating higher payoffs for future investments), learning effects (knowledge gained by operating a system increases the benefits of continued use), coordination effects (the benefits an individual gets from an activity increase if others do the same thing), and adaptive expectations (projections about future aggregate use affect current choices if coordination effects are important). The remaining debate mainly concerns whether path dependence is produced only by the mechanisms posited by rational choice theories (David, 1985; Arthur, 1994; Pierson, 2000) or by power and legitimation mechanisms as well (Mahoney, 2000).[29]

Paul Pierson's (1994) work on the welfare state provides a nice illustration of path dependence in politics. Although it is normal to look at how institutional structures and interest groups shape state policies, it is less common to explore the effects of policies on institutions and interest groups. Pierson did exactly this, tracing the "policy legacies" of the development of the welfare states in Britain and the United States. Because the welfare state created both institutional rigidities and supporting constituencies, attempts to dismantle it by both Reagan and Thatcher were largely ineffective. This is a classic case of path dependence – dismantling the welfare state is not simply the causal mirror image of creating it, because once it has been created it produces "increasing returns" processes

[28] Temporality is also important at a more micro level. Rational choice work on discount rates (the rate at which actors discount future costs and benefits relative to current ones) has contributed to our understanding of this. Most economists assume that discount rates are normally distributed in the populations they study, a reasonable assumption if one does not know what causes discount rates to vary. More sociological rational choice models have been attempting to discover the structural determinants of variations in discount rates. For example, Levi (1988) showed that discount rates increase with the insecurity of rule. Experimental work in behavioral economics suggests that discount rates will be lower when benefits are higher, when both choices are more distant in time, and when the choice is between negative outcomes (Thaler, 1991).

[29] Furthermore, Russell Hardin (1995:30) noted that all conventions have a path-dependent quality – their initial creation is often due to particular historical factors, but after that point, actors have little incentive to change them.

(working through both institutions and interest groups) that support its persistence.

CONCLUSION

Rational choice theory has recently made substantial contributions to our understanding of institutions, culture, and history. These developments have laid the foundation for a new, more sociological version of rational choice that should be very useful to political sociologists. Rational choice models of the emergence and the effects of political institutions have been used in a wide variety of substantive areas, facilitating the explanation of congressional policy making, the rise and decline of nationalism, "red tape" in bureaucratic administrations, and the management of common pool resources. Rational choice models of culture cover a diverse range of topics, including the politics of information, reputation, norms, and legitimacy. As yet, there has been no attempt to bring all of these strands of work together into a general rational choice model of culture, but that is clearly the next important step. Recent work has also begun to model the historical dimension of politics. Extensive form game theory now allows the construction of theoretically unified narrative histories. Work on path dependence is being applied to many political issues (Pierson, 2000; Mahoney, 2000). These models of institutions, culture, and history have allowed rational choice theorists to resolve the core problem of game theory, by allowing them to explain why one of many possible equilibria emerges.

We have stressed the virtues of rational choice theory throughout this chapter, but we do not intend to imply that it will ever be the only theory necessary to understand politics. Rational choice theory will not work well for all problems of interest to political sociologists, because noninstrumental bases of action are important in some situations. The scope of rational choice theory is determined mainly by two factors. Standard rational choice theory will probably not be effective when either: (1) the costs and benefits of actions are very low (Barry, 1978:40–6; North, 1990) or (2) uncertainty about costs and benefits of actions is very high. In the first situation, actors will not care much about acting instrumentally (because they will not "pay" much for acting on values, identities, etc.). This may explain the relative lack of success of rational choice theory in explaining low-cost activities like voting.[30] In the second situation, when uncertainty is very high, they will not be able to make rational choices. Uncertainty will be especially high when conditions change rapidly, creating many novel situations and choices. To put the point more positively, rational choice theory should work well in situations with high costs and benefits and that are often repeated.

Sociological versions of rational choice theory are developing a broad agenda for future research. However, because this theoretical perspective is currently still under construction, it is difficult to predict how it will evolve. As it has moved away from neoclassical economics, sociological rational choice theory has grown in two main directions: (1) developing better models of social structures and institutions and (2) developing more complex microfoundations. It is likely that both of these trends will continue, but which will be stressed and how far will the process go?

Sociological rational choice theorists currently disagree about which of these two strategies will be most fruitful. Some prefer to stick with the traditional microlevel assumptions while working on more sophisticated macrolevel models, whereas others pay little attention to the macro level and focus instead on elaborating more detailed microfoundations. In fact, one likely scenario is that rational choice theory will split into several related but competing theories – some stressing complex microfoundations that include values and emotions, and others retaining fairly simple

[30] Rational choice models have had some success in showing that marginal changes in the costs of voting lead to changes in turnout. However, they have been unable to explain why anyone ever votes (there is virtually no benefit because the odds of one vote affecting the outcome of an election are so low) or why people vote for particular candidates (especially these proposing platforms contrary to their material interests) (Green and Shapiro, 1994).

microfoundations but developing more elaborate models of structure and institutions. The latter group could revitalize versions of materialist structuralism, either by linking with some version of Marxism or by constructing a new synthesis. The former could draw on ideas from symbolic interactionism, experimental psychology, evolutionary psychology, or the four types of social action developed by Weber. Behavioral and experimental economists are just beginning to explore these issues. The further elaboration of the role of noninstrumental microfoundations (values, emotions) and their interaction with instrumental motives will no doubt be one of the most important growth areas in sociological rational choice.

If these trends toward broadening rational choice models at both the micro and macro levels continue, the eventual product may retain little more than a rough family resemblance to the old neoclassical version. At some point, it might make sense to give the new theory or theories new names – the current conceptual stretching of the label "rational choice" is already leading to some confusion, thus the use of "sociological rational choice" in this chapter.

Extrapolating from trends in the development of sociological rational choice theory leads to another question: How far can this transformation go without losing the positive features of standard rational choice theory? The danger here is that broadening the theory, especially if it is done simultaneously at both micro and macro levels, could make it less precise and more difficult to test. We should not forget that one of the main reasons neoclassical models produced so many anomalies is that they were parsimonious and precise enough to test. These virtues should not be given up lightly. The most difficult task facing sociological rational choice theory today is making it more sociological without making it less scientific.

CHAPTER NINE

Theories of Race and State

David R. James and Kent Redding

Popular notions of race have putative biological origins, but the mechanisms through which certain human characteristics come to represent categorical identities and differences have always been created by social, historical, and *political* processes. In the latter instance, we simply mean that racial signification is necessarily about power and, we might add, not simply the power of one group *over* another, but the power of any such group *to* collectively form a racial identity and organize in defense of it. In spite of this intimate connection between race and politics, the literature on race and the social construction of race on the one hand, and the literature on political sociology on the other, have largely developed independently and with little dialogue between them. This chapter explores the implicit and increasingly explicit connections between the two literatures with an eye to how race theory and state theory can inform one another.

First, we examine current constructivist theories of race and ethnicity, with special attention to issues concerning the political construction of race. Next, we argue that current research in the political sociology of race tends to ignore or deemphasize how states create and maintain racial identities. Race identities are typically viewed as the source of state-enforced racial policies, but are rarely seen as their effect. An examination of the social and political determinants of racial categories used by the U.S. Census provides a convenient illustration of how race identities are both causes and effects of state policies. We then examine the definition of the racial state proposed by Omi and Winant (1994) and argue that it has limited analytical power to explain the different ways that states create and/or maintain racial inequalities and identities. Racial states, according to Omi and Winant (1994) and the closely related work of Goldberg (2002), define racial states by their effects. Because all states have effects on racial inequalities, all states are racial states. We argue that a focus on the internal structure, rather than the effects, of states provides a stronger theoretical explanation of how states produce and maintain race inequalities and identities. In the last section, we develop a conceptual contrast between racial states, which enforce race-conscious policies, and liberal democratic states, which enforce equal citizenship rights for all regardless of membership in racial or other status groups. We review recent typological work on the variation in the extent to which race-conscious distinctions are institutionalized within state structures to illustrate how variation in state structures affects racial inequalities and identities.

THEORIES OF RACE AND ETHNICITY

Most sociologists agree that political processes and institutions shape race inequalities and identities and vice versa. Groups mobilize on the basis of race for the purpose of transforming political institutions, electing candidates who represent their interests, and shaping policies that affect the social distribution of symbolic and material goods. At the same time, policies are enforced by state agents within the context established by existing political institutions that assign race identities to citizens, influence the mobilization opportunities available to existing and potential groups, and distribute resources to citizens and groups in ways that have racial effects. Hence, political processes and institutions are dynamically linked to racial inequalities and identities in a process of mutual causation. The definition of race that we adopt here allows for the possibility that racial identities and inequalities can be politically constructed and can provide the motivation and resources to shape political outcomes.

All sociological definitions of race include some reference to the phenotypical characteristics of individuals that are thought to be decisive in assigning individuals to racial groups. For example, Cornell and Hartmann (1998:24) defined race as "a human group defined by itself or others as distinct by virtue of perceived common physical characteristics that are held to be inherent." The physical characteristics that serve as markers to distinguish races are selected by social processes and are in no way essentially determined by genetics or other biological processes. According to Omi and Winant (1994:55), racial categories are "created, inhabited, transformed and destroyed" through social and historical processes. Some of the most important of those processes are political. For example, the United States has assigned individuals to racial categories since its inception and enforced the assignments through political institutions at the state and federal level. The strength of the assignment process and the nature of the categories defining races varied dramatically over the past 200 years, of which more will be said below (Anderson, 2002; Lee, 1993; Rodriguez, 2000).

The transformation of race categories over time is shaped not only by the politically dominant race that assigns others to subordinate racial categories, but also by the resistance and agency of those who are so assigned. Constructivist theory claims that racial identities and inequalities emerge from the dynamic between assignment of individuals to categories and the assertion of group identities by members of racial groups. The identities of subordinate racial group members are shaped by their own actions as well as the actions of those who discriminate against them.

Omi's and Winant's (1994) influential theory calls this process "racial formation" and argues that it constitutes a process of "racial projects." A racial project, which may be produced by an individual or a group, is an "interpretation" of racial dynamics *and* an attempt to "reorganize and redistribute resources along particular racial lines" (Omi and Winant, 1994:56). In other words, a racial project contains both a *theory* of how race inequalities are created and maintained and a set of *actions or policies* that are designed to affect those inequalities in a manner consistent with the theory. A white supremacist racial project, for example, might be motivated by the theory that blacks are members of an inferior race and designed to disfranchise black voters for that reason. Resistance to the white supremacist racial project by blacks would constitute a rival racial project. The hierarchical structure of race inequalities and identities flows directly from the clash of racial projects. Omi and Winant located the motor of racial transformation in the purposive social actions of individuals who are divided into racial groups and act on the basis of group identities.

Omi and Winant viewed race and ethnicity as distinct concepts and argued that existing ethnicity theory – namely, U.S.-based explanations of the upward social mobility of Southern and Eastern European immigrants (and their descendents) as a consequence of cultural assimilation – cannot explain patterns of black–white disparities in the United States. Cornell and Hartmann agreed with Omi and Winant that theories of ethnicity and race are distinct, but argued that they are not mutually exclusive. They (1994:19) adopted Schermerhorn's definition of ethnicity, which is typical of most current definitions: "An ethnic group is a collectivity within a larger society having real or putative common ancestry, memories of a shared historical past, and a cultural focus on one or more symbolic elements defined as the epitome of their peoplehood" (Schermerhorn, 1978:12). Hence, an ethnic group is self-consciously ethnic; in-group members identify others as coethnics if they share the three general social claims specified in the definition regardless of whether the individuals are known personally or not.

Race identities are distinguished from ethnic identities by four factors (Cornell and Hartmann, 1998:25–35):

1. Race identities are based on perceived physical differences; ethnic identities are based on the three claims specified by the definition.
2. Race identities typically originate in the assignment of group members to the group by powerful outsiders; ethnic identities may originate in assertion by in-group members as well as assignment by others.
3. Race identities typically reflect power relations; ethnic identities may not.
4. Race identities are accorded different levels of social worth; ethnic identities may not be.

These four distinctions disappear under careful consideration. First, Schermerhorn (1978:12) included phenotypical characteristics explicitly among the possible symbolic elements that define ethnic groups. Somatic differences have often been used to distinguish groups typically identified as ethnic rather than racial or who were once considered racial and later regarded as ethnic (Collins, 2001; Isaacs, 1989). Consistent application of the definition of an ethnic group requires that racial groups be included if they are self-consciously ethnic. Second, Cornell and Hartmann noted that factor 2 does not apply to the dominant racial group that initially assigns others to subordinate race categories. For example, the white race in the United States is implicitly defined by the assignment of nonwhites to subordinate racial groups. Hence, some race definitions emerge through the assertion of dominant groups of their perception of inherent differences from other groups.

Third, factors 3 and 4 are conditional differences that may or may not apply in certain historical contexts and cannot be considered essential differences in defining the two concepts. Finally, Cornell and Hartmann (1998) argued that racial groups become ethnic groups when members of racial groups become self-consciously ethnic by thinking of themselves as members of racial groups. But when does this moment of self-conscious racialized identification occur? Evidence on this point is scant, but it makes little sense sociologically to view a racial group as a distinct race if most individuals assigned to the race do not view themselves that way. Treating individuals differently on the basis of perceived physical characteristics was the first step historically in the creation of new racial groups. But the process of racial group formation cannot be considered complete until those who are the objects of an assignment process recognize that fact and begin to push back. Once racial groups begin to resist the assignment process, they make the same three claims that define ethnic groups. Members of racial groups see themselves as sharing kinship ties, albeit often fictional ones, and may use familial terms (e.g., brother, sister) when speaking to others of their group. They claim a common history of discrimination and prejudice at the hands of the most powerful racial group, and they view certain physical characteristics (e.g., skin color) as the key symbolic elements that define membership in their racial group. Their view of themselves almost surely differs from that of out-group members, but that is characteristic of all ethnic groups. No substantive difference exists between the definitive claims of ethnic groups and those of racial groups.

The problems with Cornell's and Hartmann's treatment that led them to posit exceptions to the second factor for the dominant racial group are solved by Omi's and Winant's (1994) concept of the racial project. The idea of contending racial projects, which focuses the same theoretical lens on both dominant and subordinate groups, introduces a more powerful dynamic into the process of assignment and assertion of identities posited by current constructivist race and ethnicity theory. Claiming that race identities and inequalities emerge from a field of conflict and struggle over the meaning of race and/or the causes of racial inequalities removes the need to view identity formation of the dominant race as an exception to the theory of race making. Instead, white racial identities in the United States flow directly from the racial projects animated by the actions of whites as they clash with the racial projects of other races.

There is no fundamental obstacle to using the theory of racial formation to explain ethnic group formation. The major difference between ethnic projects and racial projects is the content of the symbolic elements selected to capture the core of group identity and the rhetorical differences among the sociologists who analyze those processes. We disagree with Cornell and Hartmann (1998) and Omi and Winant (1994) that *racial* categories and identities differ from *ethnic* ones in some fundamental way and share Collins's (2001) view that there is no "analytically important" difference between race and ethnicity.

POLITICAL INSTITUTIONS AND RACE

Most sociological research on the links between political institutions and process on the one hand and racial identities and inequalities on the other do not explicitly employ the constructivist theory of race discussed above. Instead, research typically takes one of three approaches. One is to take race inequalities as a given and view race identities and motivations as causal agents and determinants of political processes, political policy formation and implementation, and the like (e.g., Bensel, 1984; Blalock, 1967; James, 1988; McAdam, 1982; Valelly, 1995; van den Berghe, 1967, 1987; Wilson, 1978). A second approach examines the effects of state policies, social movements, and political institutional arrangements on race inequalities and ignores any impacts on race identities (e.g., Burstein, 1985; Kousser, 1999; Smith, 1997). A more common approach is to combine the second and the first with the causal path flowing from racial identities and motivations through state policies to impact race inequalities (Cell, 1982; Kousser, 1974; Massey and Denton, 1993; Quadagno, 1994).

Taking race identities and motivations linked to those identities as givens is an appropriate methodological strategy if it is reasonable to assume that the identities are stable during the period under investigation. The assumption of stable racial identities is usually valid if the data analyzed span a short period, but caution is required if race identities are transformed during the target period. Sometimes identities change rapidly. For example, the name preferred by blacks changed during the late 1960s as a result of the influence of the black power wing of the civil rights movement. The rapidity of change caught the U.S. Census Bureau by surprise, forcing it to scramble to allow "black" as one option for indicating race identity for the 1970 census tabulation.[1] Whether one preferred to think of one's race identity as "black" or "Negro" often indicated the person's position on the civil rights policies and practices advocated. Those who thought of themselves as "black" typically advocated more radical strategies. On the other hand, race identities are sometimes stable over long periods (Davis, 2001; Lee, 1993).

If constructivist theory is correct, race inequalities often reinforce the race identities that power the dynamic of racial politics (James, 1994). As Lieberman (1998:232) argued, "Race identity, constructed in and by politics, reshapes politics through institutions, which in turn reconstruct race." Increasingly researchers study how political institutions, processes, and conflict shape and influence racial identities. Scholars also utilize constructivist race theories to make sense of the dynamics of social movements, particularly with respect to the interactions between movements and political processes (Blee, 2002; Cornell, 1988; Redding, 2003; Williams, 1990). Nagel (1997), for example, identified

[1] The Census question for race in 1970, 1980, and 1990 treated "Negro" and "black" as two alternative but interchangeable choices for the same race category. In 2000, the option of choosing "African American" was allowed as an additional option as that label became increasingly popular (Farley, 2002; Snipp, 2003). Currently, "African American" and "black" are the two most popular names chosen for purposes of self-identification. "African American" tends to emphasize American ethnic status more than "black" does, but the political differences between those who prefer different race names has declined.

state policies as direct causes of changing identities of Native American groups. She found that the United States engaged in a variety of policies between 1880 and 1933 intended to force Native Americans to assimilate and to remove their access to Indian lands. As a result, Native Americans who migrated to urban areas began to form pan-Indian organizations. The U.S. policies shifted from the individual back to the tribes between 1933 and 1946, which spurred the growth of tribal identities, but as the tribe became more important as a link between individual Indians and the federal government, pan-tribal organization followed with a resulting weakening of tribal boundaries. Between 1946 and 1960, the United States again promoted the termination of tribal status and again pan-Indian identification and organization grew in urban areas. After 1960, different federal policies spurred all three forms of Indian identity formation and organization: tribal, pan-Indian, and pan-tribal (Nagel, 1982, 1995, 1997).

The formation of political parties within the context of electoral competition can have a marked effect on the institutionalization or deinstitutionalization of race categories within state institutions. Aminzade (2000) showed that competition between political parties was decisive in institutionalizing citizenship in Tanganyika on the basis of its national territory rather than the tripartite racial hierarchy (Europeans, Asians, and Africans) that it inherited from the colonial policy makers who governed the country before independence. A racial nationalism similar to that which triumphed in South Africa and the United States (Marx, 1998) was defeated by the party that championed a distinction between citizens and foreigners. In the more recent period, the ruling party in Tanzania[2] was able to win an ideological struggle with opposition parties to transform the meaning of "indigenous" to refer to the boundary between citizens and foreigners rather than the racially charged boundary between black Africans and Asians (Aminzade, 2003).

[2] Tanganyika joined with Zanzibar to form Tanzania in 1964.

AN ILLUSTRATION OF THE POLITICAL CONSTRUCTION OF RACE: CENSUS CATEGORIES

The creation of official race categories recognized by the state and used by the state for census tabulations and policy formulation and enforcement are the archetypal examples of the political institutionalization of race. As Starr (1992) pointed out, the state must create a multitude of categories among all kinds of people for all sorts of purposes ranging from tax collection to military service. Once created, official classifications become, over time, "impersonal cognitive commitments" for those who use them; the population counts based on them inform "countless decisions, private as well as governmental" (Starr, 1992). The creation of official race categories is a powerful force in the assignment of individuals to racial groups that increases the probability that some citizens will come to see themselves as members of that group (Cornell and Hartmann, 1998; Nagel, 1986; Nobles, 2000).

Race categories tend to persist over time, but the permanence of the classification system depends on the outcomes of the continuing clash of racial projects. The history of the creation of official race categories in the United States clearly illustrates the mutability of race categories and their link to competing racial projects. The United States recognized seven nonwhite races in 1890, and four of those (black, mulatto, quadroon, and octoroon) belonged to groups that were soon merged (Lee, 1993). Southern political influence at the federal level coupled with the concern of Southern whites to suppress black political power defeated the attempts of mulattoes to maintain an intermediate social status between whites and Negroes (Anderson, 1988; Davis, 2001; Starr, 1992). By 1930, the one-drop rule was adopted by both whites and blacks as the definition of "who is black" (Davis, 2001) and persisted for sixty years. Then, in the space of less than a decade, the rules for race classification in the United States changed.

Although the definition of and number of racial categories shifted over time, the view that individuals could be assigned to one unique race category (e.g., white, black, quadroon, etc.) persisted. This constant of race classification theory ended with the 2000 census. For the first time, the U.S. Census allowed individuals to select more than one race category to describe their race identity, a change that Farley labeled the "greatest change in the measurement of race in the history of the United States" (2002:33). Nearly 5 percent of those previously identified as black claimed more than one race, a figure twice as large as predicted, and the numbers selecting multiple races are likely to grow in the future (Hochschild, 2002:341).

The change in race classification was a bureaucratic response to an emerging movement for a multiracial category. The increasing rate of intermarriage between members of different racial groups since the civil rights victories of the 1960s produced a critical mass of citizens who felt that the existing system did not provide a place for them. State officials opposed changing the race classification system, but for reasons unrelated to the racist policies of the early twentieth century that used race classification as a basis for discrimination against nonwhites. State officials in the 1990s preferred administrative simplicity and cited the need to collect high-quality data for civil rights enforcement and the provision of social services (Robbin, 2000). The pressure for change was too great to resist, but the advocates for a multiracial race category did not get what they wanted. Powerful civil rights lobbyists representing the interests of African Americans supported the Office of Management and Budget's (OMB) suggestion that respondents be allowed to choose more than one race category in lieu of creating a new multiracial category. The clash of racial projects between those of the OMB, black civil rights organizations, and the new multiracial movement was resolved for the time being in favor of multiple race options rather than a multiracial category (Farley, 2002; Robbin, 2000).[3]

The number of racial groups recognized by the United States has expanded with each census between 1970 and 1990 (Lee, 1993). The new 2000 census multiple race options expand the number of officially recognized single and multiple race combinations to sixty three, which points to further proliferation of race categories; "there is no natural limit" to the number of races given this logic (Hochschild, 2002:356; Prewitt, 2002; Snipp, 2003). A consequence of the race classification system changes may be to delegitimize race classification altogether, a result that is consistent with the preference for color-blind policies by most whites, but that result is not imminent given the ardent support for major racial groups that continues to exist (see Perlmann and Waters, 2002 for other implications).

This brief account of the trends in the U.S. race classification system is consistent with a political constructivist theory of race. The mulatto category disappeared when the mixed-race racial project was defeated and disappeared at the beginning of the twentieth century (Starr, 1992). New multiple race options appeared in 2000 as a result of the clash of competing racial projects and especially with the emergence of mixed-race individuals and their advocates, who mounted a powerful challenge to the existing race classification system.[4]

[3] The political basis for the change in classifying people of mixed race was reflected in other changes as well. Native Hawaiians pressed OMB to be reclassified as "Native Americans" and were opposed by American Indians, who mounted a national campaign claiming that they were sovereign nations and that indigenous Hawaiians did not have that relationship to the United States although they had suffered many of the same injustices. In an attempt to please as many interest groups as possible, OMB removed Native Hawaiians from the "Asian or Pacific Islander" category, but placed them in a new category – Hawaiian or Pacific Islanders – rather than including them with Native Americans (Robbin, 2000). Other changes proposed by identity advocates included the addition of a special category for Middle Easterners and Arab Americans and including "Hispanic" as a race rather than an ethnic category. Both were rejected by OMB (Rodriguez, 2000:153–76). Hispanics, a supranational category that includes many Spanish language cultural groups, remain the only ethnic group officially recognized by the United States (Rodriguez, 2000).

[4] Sometimes states shape race identities for reasons having little to do with the pressure from social movements, political parties, or other factors typically associated with race, class, or interest group politics. In a study of state-level race policies, Williams (2003) found that a number of states adopted or seriously considered adopting multiracial category classification schemes for

THEORIES OF THE RACIAL STATE

Most research in the political sociology of race does not attempt to develop a theory of the state, even though understanding how variation in the political institutionalization of racial practices affects race inequalities and identities is a pressing practical and theoretical problem. Just as the heated debate on theories of the state subsided in favor of mid-level theories addressing issues of policy formation and implementation, few attempts to develop a theory of the incorporation of race into state institutions have been attempted. In fact, all of the classic works in the state theory debates essentially ignored the causes and effects of state enforced race discrimination (e.g., Barrow, 1993; Carnoy, 1984; Evans, Rueschemeyer, and Skocpol, 1985; Jessop, 1990; King, 1986; Laumann and Knoke, 1987; Miliband, 1969; Poulantzas, 1973; Skocpol, 1985).

Omi and Winant (1994) attempted to remedy the blindness of state theory to problems of race by devoting a chapter to the concept of the "racial state."[5] How should states be distinguished? Omi and Winant (1994) recognized that the clash of competing racial projects often transforms state institutions in ways that favor certain racial groups at the expense of others. The state is not a neutral, mediating body, but an institutional arrangement that shapes racial inequalities. Because of its power to distribute social resources unequally, the state is "increasingly the pre-eminent site of racial conflict" (1994:82). As a consequence, Omi and Winant argued that

> The state is composed of *institutions*, the *policies* they carry out, the *conditions and rules* which support and justify them, and the *social relations* in which they are imbedded. Every state *institution* is a racial institution.... (1994:83, emphasis in original)

Omi and Winant clarified the meaning of each of the italicized terms. Importantly for our purposes, they explained that state institutions organize and enforce the racial politics of everyday life through policies "which are explicitly or implicitly racial" (1994:83). What is meant by "explicitly or implicitly racial" requires a little digging. Omi and Winant argued that the civil rights movement of the 1960s accomplished a "great transformation"; voting rights drives, for example, led to black enfranchisement and created a new racial state in the process (1994:104–6). Even if the state extends the right to vote to all without regard for race, the state is still a racial state because it still affects racial inequalities. The overtly racist policies of the past have been replaced with "color-blind" policies that pay lip service to racial equality while preserving white privilege.

The "great transformation" of the 1960s was viewed in later decades by whites as enforcing racial injustice by extending group rights (e.g., affirmative action policies) to racial minorities. Whites came to view themselves as victims of the new racial state even though race inequalities and white advantages persisted (1994:117). Enforcing color-blind policies masks a defense of white advantage with the rhetoric of eliminating racist practices (Omi and Winant, 1994:104–18). Hence, Omi and Winant argued that a state is a racial state if it uses race as an explicit criterion to enforce race discrimination (e.g., segregated public schools) or if it allows race inequalities to continue without intervention by extending citizenship rights to all without regard to race. The failure to define different types of racial states makes it impossible to explain how the state's causal impact on racial inequalities changes as a result of the "great transformation" produced by the civil rights movement. If all states are racial states, knowing that a state

official purposes between 1992 and 1997. Surprisingly, multiracial category adoption did not occur as a result of pressure from a powerful movement; the multiracial movement was very weak or absent in some states. Nor did partisan party politics cause the new policy to be adopted. The policies were adopted because of the ways that some legislators perceived that the policies would be considered by their broader constituencies. Because the United States policy allowing individuals to have multiple race identities became official for all federal record keeping in 2003, the states are under great pressure to adjust their record keeping accordingly.

[5] The notion of a racial state is not new, but was used as a descriptive term for the explicitly racial policies of Nazi Germany (e.g., Burleigh and Wippermann, 1991; Jacoby, 1944) rather than a theoretical concept that could distinguish types of states. See also James (1988).

is racial provides no analytical leverage to understand how it creates racial inequalities and identities. Omi and Winant (1994:65–9) recognized this weakness implicitly by contrasting the "racial dictatorship" that existed before the "great transformation" to the "racial hegemony" that emerged afterward. How racial dictatorship and racial hegemony are linked to the racial state remains untheorized.

Goldberg (2002:195) implicitly adopted Omi's and Winant's definition: Racial states are "states that historically become engaged in the constitution, maintenance, and management of whiteness, whether in the form of European domination, colonialism, segregation, white supremacy, herrenvolk democracy, Aryanism, or ultimately colorblind-(ness) or racelessness" [sic]. Varieties of "raceless" states came into being around the world in the late twentieth century, and all mask white privilege and domination. Goldberg's cross-national comparison of race policies in Europe, the United States, Brazil, and South Africa concluded that in contrast to the racist policies of earlier periods, "racelessness" now represents "state rationality toward race" in modern states (2002:203). In the United States, racelessness is promoted under the banner of "color-blindness"; similar policies are called "racial democracy" in Brazil, "nonracialism" in South Africa, and "state multiculturalism" or "ethnic pluralism" in Europe (2002: 200–38). In all four cases, racelessness has racial effects. All four "raceless" states are "racial" states that protect white advantage, according to Goldberg, a claim that reproduces the weakness of Winant's definition of the racial state. Nevertheless, Goldberg's analysis recognizes that all racial states are not the same. Racial states differ in important ways that cause them to affect race inequalities in different ways. How racial states differ is developed further in the next section.

Winant's (2001) sweeping analysis of the role of race in making modernity overlaps considerably with that of Goldberg (2002), but contains broader claims (see Steinberg, 2003 for a review). Race is not just an epiphenomenon of state-making, capitalist development, modernity, or some other process. On the contrary, racial formation was crucial during the past 500 years in creating new forms of empire and nation, reorganizing new systems of capital and labor, and articulating new concepts of culture and identity (Winant, 2001:20–1). Winant claimed that he is not a racial determinist, but his work elevates race to a position of prominence, the most important cause among contenders.[6]

Omi and Winant (1994; Winant, 1994, 2001) and Goldberg (2002) provided a great service by presenting convincing accounts of how states in racially divided societies produce racially unequal effects whether the state policy being enforced is explicitly racial or not. That colorblind policies often create, maintain, or exacerbate racial inequalities is frequently overlooked by scholars as well as dominant racial groups that benefit from race-neutral policies (James, 2000; Kousser, 1999, 2000). Nevertheless, labeling all states "racial" does not provide the conceptual clarity needed to distinguish the racial impacts of states that enforce overtly racist policies from those that are ostensibly race-neutral.[7] Omi and Winant (1994; Winant, 1994, 2001) and Goldberg (2002) failed to conceptualize the state as an organization that has a multilevel relationship to status and class structures (Lehman, 1988).

THE ORGANIZATIONAL STRUCTURE OF LIBERAL DEMOCRATIC AND RACIAL STATES

Defining the state on the basis of its organizational structure provides four advantages

[6] Race is "a key causative factor in the creation of the modern world. Imperialism's creation of modern nation-states, capitalism's construction of an international economy, and the Enlightenment's articulation of a unified world culture... were all deeply racialized processes" (Winant, 2001:19).

[7] Goldberg apparently recognized this problem because he distinguished "raceless" racial states from those that explicitly enforce race discrimination by labeling the latter "racist" (2002:112–5). He pointed to the attack on affirmative action to illustrate the difficulty in using a racial state for antiracist purposes. Hence, Goldberg implicitly defined three types of racial states: racist states that use race explicitly to the disadvantage of subordinate races, antiracist states that use race explicitly to the disadvantage of dominant racial groups, and raceless states that do not use race explicitly to enforce racial state policies.

compared to the definition of the state preferred by Winant and Goldberg (Alford, 1975; Alford and Friedland, 1985; Lehman, 1988). First, the organizational features of the state are the usual targets of racially based social movements. Efforts to institutionalize racial advantages or to elide those advantages are a common goal (e.g., Jenkins and Brents, 1989). Second, focusing on the "supraorganizational" features of the state makes it possible to evaluate the effects of different organizational arrangements on race inequalities and identities. States are divided into different branches that are fragmented hierarchically, making for important variation in the racial impact on policy formation and implementation (James, 1988; Lehman, 1988; Omi and Winant, 1994).

Third, institutional arrangements constitute the practical context within which politicians and other officials of the state perform the actions that ratify and implement state policies. Understanding their impacts on racial inequalities and identities is a prerequisite to creating state institutions that make certain outcomes more likely. Transformative pressures on states are resisted by state officials, whose interests and conceptualizations of "the possible" are shaped by existing organizational features (Clemens, 2003; Skowronek, 1982).

Finally, the purposes of race-conscious policies enforced by racial states are apparent to those who benefit and those who suffer from them. Race-conscious policies have direct effects on race identities and race inequalities regardless of which races they are intended to favor. Liberal democratic state policies, by contrast, must be color-blind. Color-blind policies tend to protect the advantages of favored racial groups and prevent the state from taking direct action to redress race inequalities. Hence, how liberal democracies protect the race advantages of favored races is less transparent than are the results of racial state policies. We discuss how the ideological power of liberal democratic state policies legitimates race inequalities elsewhere (see Redding, James, and Klugman, Chapter 27 in this volume).

James's (1988) definition of the racial state distinguishes racial from liberal democratic states. Liberal states extend rights to citizens *qua* individuals whereas racial states protect the rights of citizens *qua* members of racial groups. Hence, the liberal democratic state, with its focus on individual rights, grants citizenship rights to each individual without regard to race, ethnicity, religion, social class, culture, language, national origin, sex, education, wealth, or any other group status.[8] To the extent that a democracy extends political, civil, or social rights to one, it must extend them to all if it is a liberal democracy. Racial states, by contrast, extend different citizenship rights to individuals according to their race status and therefore fall short of liberal democracy as classically defined (Bendix, 1964; Marshall, 1992, 1950; Starr, 1992).

Racial states are not defined by the outcome of state policies. The race nature of the state is defined by the incorporation of race criteria within the fabric of state institutions as the basis for enforcing state policies. For example, the racial state in the southern United States segregated public schools, public transportation, and public accommodations by race, disenfranchised black voters, and meted out more severe punishments to blacks than whites for equivalent crimes (James, 1988; Kousser, 1974; Lieberman, 1998; Perman, 1984, 2001; Quadagno, 1994). For the purpose of distinguishing racial states from liberal democracies, it matters not whether the policies increase or decrease race inequalities (Starr, 1992). Using race as a policy criterion to reduce race inequalities, for example, is also a racial state policy. Enforcing race advantage and disadvantage is the business of racial states.

The increasing drumbeat of state-enforced race and ethnic violence and discrimination

[8] Race is not the only status advantage that may be enshrined as official state policy and incorporated within the fabric of state institutions although it is the only status distinction considered here. We view race and ethnicity as equivalent concepts, but distinct from other social statuses that may form the basis of group identities. Any state that guarantees group rights in opposition to individual rights is a departure from the model of the liberal democratic state. For example, patriarchal states protect the group rights of men; theocracies defend particular religious groups; etc. Officially sanctioned state discrimination against women and religious minorities is more common today around the world than is officially sanctioned race discrimination (James and Heiliger, 2000).

since the disintegration of the Soviet Union has stimulated examinations of the various ways that racial and ethnic group rights are embedded in state institutions and how these arrangements affect race and ethnic mobilization and violence. Because we regard ethnic and race identity formation as manifestations of the same process, we view states that privilege ethnic groups as examples of racial states.

Smooha (2002a) distinguished five types of democracies according to the extent that they restrict individual rights in order to protect group rights. He distinguished the classical model of the liberal democratic state defined above from existing republican democracies (e.g., France) because they created a "nation" by enforcing brutal policies of homogenization and assimilation over a long period of time. Republican democracies (nation-states) impose a single language and culture and foster a community (nation) that shares a common identity. Republican democracies provide no state support for different racial groups. Distinguishing liberal democratic states from existing "republican democracies" provides no apparent conceptual advantage other than to draw attention to the historical processes that created modern nations.

Consociational democracies, a long-recognized third type (Lijphart, 1977), depart from liberal and republican democracies by recognizing ethnic differences; they provide state-enforced mechanisms for ensuring proportional allocation in resource allocation, power sharing, and veto power to the ethnic groups recognized by the state. Switzerland, Belgium, and Canada are typical examples.

Smooha (2002a) argued that two new types of democracies are emerging as a result of regionalization (e.g., the formation of the European Union) and globalization processes that weaken the autonomy of the nation-state. Multicultural democracies fall between liberal and consociational democracies because they recognize that ethnic and racial differences exist in society, but afford them no official recognition or special citizenship rights. He claimed that postapartheid South Africa and the Netherlands are examples of multicultural democracies (but note the criticism of multiculturalism by Goldberg and Winant discussed above).

Smooha's last type is labeled "ethnic democracy," which he locates between consociational democracy and nondemocracy. Ethnic democracies are "second-rate" democracies that extend some citizenship rights to all but deny other rights to nonprivileged ethnic groups. The level of democracy extended to subordinate groups is strongly conditioned by relationships with other states and the conditions of the state's founding. Estonia, for example, which was founded in the wake of the breakup of the Soviet Union, discriminates against Russians, the previously dominant group (Smooha, 2002a). Turkey's discrimination against Kurds is still strongly conditioned by its relationship to other states as it was during and after its emergence as a new state with the breakup of the Ottoman Empire (Saatci, 2002). Smooha (2002b) classified Israel as an ethnic democracy, a Jewish state that denies certain citizenship rights to non-Jews, and predicted that its long-term stability depends on its ability to move toward a more liberal democratic form. Israel's discrimination against its Israeli-Arab citizens is directly linked to the Israeli–Palestinian conflict. Rouhana and Bar-Tal (1998) showed that violence and conflict reinforce and valorize Palestinian and Israeli identities, thereby making peaceful reconciliation extremely difficult. Recognition of a Palestinian state, which would be a racial state and perhaps an ethnic democracy, would tend to legitimize Israel's ethnic democracy status and make transformation to more liberal democratic forms difficult.

Van den Berghe (2002) argued that ethnic democracies fall between consociational democracies and his concept of the "Herrenvolk democracy," which constitutes a sixth type (van den Berghe, 1967). Herrenvolk democracies provide democratic institutions to the dominant race or ethnicity but deny all citizenship rights to subordinate groups; South Africa under apartheid and the antebellum South in the United States are examples. Israel today and the postbellum South are examples of ethnic democracies. Of course, nondemocratic forms of racial or ethnic states have also existed. A common form of despotic regime that recognized ethnic (racial) differences is the "multinational" empire (Walzer, 1997). For example, the Ottoman Empire privileged Islam, but tolerated certain other religions under its millet system. Millets were allowed a certain amount of organization autonomy and all non-Muslims were required to belong to one. Group differences (but not individual differences) were tolerated so long as taxes were paid and the authority of the Ottomans was not challenged.

Different types of racial states have different impacts on the creation and maintenance of racial identities, the mobilization of contending racial groups, racial and ethnic violence, and the possibility of preserving state stability (e.g., Maiz, 2003; Marx, 1998; McGarry, 2002; Smooha, 2002b). For example, van den Berghe (2002) argued that multicultural democracies promote identity formation and group conflict by "unleashing a game of recognition-seeking between communities." Whereas van den Berghe (2002:437) provided evidence that consociational democracies are fragile, "clumsy and inflexible states that mainly benefit ruling elites" (see also Horowitz, 1985), McGarry (2002) claimed that Ireland tried Herrenvolk, liberal, consociational, ethnic, and multicultural democratic forms at different times in its history and that consociational democracy offers the greatest promise of peace and stability.

The attempt to develop taxonomies that describe how the organizational structure of the state affects race inequalities and identities, and therefore state stability, is an important step even if current efforts produce mixed results. Consociational, ethnic, and Herrenvolk democracies are all racial states by the definition that we propose because all depart from liberal democracy by using race categories to differentially allocate citizenship rights. No taxonomy can capture all of the past or present variation in racial states, but they illustrate the importance of analyzing how internal state structures shape racial inequalities and identities. But liberal democratic states have racial effects, too. That liberal democratic states protect existing race inequalities by putting them beyond the reach of policies that might ameliorate them has long been recognized (see, for example, Marx, 1978, 1843). By contrast, the impact of liberal democratic state policies on race identity formation and mobilization has rarely been examined, but is beginning to receive more scrutiny than in the past.

CONCLUSION

The emerging literature that links the construction of race identities and inequalities to political processes is encouraging. No longer do political sociologists take race categories and identities as givens, outside the domain of inquiry. This chapter reviewed critically a selection of important works from a huge and expanding literature and makes no claims of comprehensiveness. Nevertheless, we issue both a caution and a call based on our understanding of current trends in the political sociology of race.

First the caution. Serious scholarly attention to the role that race played and continues to play in political processes, state formation, and the institutionalization of citizenship rights is long overdue. Politics is central to race categorization and race identity formation and transformation. Nevertheless, there is a tendency in some strands of current research to view race as the chief determinant of social inequalities between and within states. State making and race making have been inextricably linked for 500 years and promise to continue their intimate association for the foreseeable future. Race is an important cause and effect of struggles for state power, but despite its ubiquity, it is not the sole cause or effect and may not be the most important cause in most cases. Race may be the face that class takes in shaping state making in many historical contexts. Or, more likely, race and class and gender may mutually constitute one another in complex ways in the context of capital accumulation and/or state building (Reed, 2002).

On the other hand, it is just as problematic to underplay the importance of race. The literature on the civil rights movement, for example, has typically not taken the issue of race making seriously as an object of analysis. Rather, race is seen largely as one mobilization identity among others, not as a social phenomenon with distinct characteristics. Political sociology needs to reconsider this omission. Just as race making and state making are causally linked, social movements are the engines of race and state making.

A political sociology of race that takes the construction of race and ethnic identities seriously may act as a corrective to a tendency to either exaggerate the importance of race or to fail to theorize its significance and distinctiveness. Sophisticated new studies of the interaction between state making and race making indicate that institutional arrangements matter. State structure must be theorized and linked to the collision of racial projects within and between states. Both racial states and liberal democratic states affect race inequalities within their territories, but in different ways. It is widely recognized that color-conscious policies vary dramatically in their impact on race inequalities. That the power of color-blind state policies to shape societal race inequalities varies with the organizational forms employed to implement them (e.g., Lieberman, 1998) is not widely recognized by either scholars or nonscholars. Studies that emphasize race need to better analyze the specific institutional and mobilization contexts in which race is made and remade; variations in state and organizational contexts of the sort discussed earlier in this chapter certainly shape both the degree as well as the kind of racializations that may occur. Careful, theoretically informed studies of the dynamic linkages between state making and race making promise to identify the institutional arrangements that emphasize the importance of race and those that do not.

We do not know much about the contexts that favor certain racial projects and make the success of others less likely. Aminzade's (2003) work is interesting in this regard because it shows that mobilization around racial divisions sometimes fails. Are there other such failures, and how do they compare to "successes"? Recent work by Gerteis (2002) is intriguing because it addresses the puzzle of why a movement pursued one racial mobilization strategy (including one racial group and excluding another) over others (including or excluding both groups) that seemed (at least in retrospect) to have been more likely.[9] We are beginning to accumulate enough studies of the political construction of race to allow fruitful comparisons, but more are needed. We need to investigate when and how racial identities become the vehicle of mobilization for the transformation of state institutions and why they are sometimes the mobilization vehicle of choice as political regimes crumble and decline (e.g., the rise of a racially motivated conservatism after the decline of the Great Society in the late 1960s/early 1970s, the Nazi takeover of the Weimar Republic, the replacement of communism with aggressive ethnonationalism in Yugoslavia and parts of the former Soviet Union).

A number of scholars have documented a trend away from color-conscious policies and toward a greater acceptance of color-blind policies in the United States, Brazil, South Africa, and the European Union. We characterize this trend as a movement from racial to liberal democratic states, but the trend is far from monolithic. Ethnic democracies, consociational democracies, and despotic states that privilege certain races or ethnic groups continue to emerge and persist as a result of state-building efforts in regions divided by race and ethnic conflict. In many contexts, appeals to race and nation are more powerful mobilization strategies than the ideology of liberal democracy. Granting equal citizenship rights to all without regard to race and ethnicity may be possible only in states in which no group is powerful enough to dominate all others or in those wealthy countries with long, albeit imperfect, liberal traditions. In the second case, color-blind policies consolidate the advantages of the privileged racial group by deflecting or delegitimizing the race-conscious appeals of those who suffer from the durable inequalities created by the color-conscious policies of the past.

[9] Gerteis (2002) shows that the Knights of Labor viewed Chinese workers, but not blacks, as lacking in civic virtue and therefore unsuitable for membership. Hence, Chinese workers were excluded, whereas blacks were recruited as members. We find Gerteis's analysis convincing, but wonder how the Knights of Labor developed this view given the monolithic racially exclusionary ideologies common among nineteenth-century white Americans.

PART II

CIVIL SOCIETY: THE ROOTS AND PROCESSES OF POLITICAL ACTION

CHAPTER TEN

Money, Participation, and Votes

Social Cleavages and Electoral Politics

Jeff Manza, Clem Brooks, and Michael Sauder

Democratic governance in the modern world presumes regular elections in which the rights of citizenship include, in principle, equal participation and collective influence over the composition of government. For individuals, "casting a ballot is, by far, the most common act of citizenship in any democracy" (Verba, Scholzman, and Brady, 1995:23). The right to vote also provides the foundation for other political and social rights of individuals and groups. At the aggregate level, election outcomes are an important causal factor behind national policy making (Castles, 1982; Blais, Blake, and Dion, 1996; Powell, 2000; Erikson, MacKuen, and Stimson, 2002:Chap. 7). For example, the institutional characteristics of welfare state regimes have been shown to be influenced by the share of the vote won by left-wing or other party families (e.g., Esping-Andersen, 1990; Hicks, 1999; Huber and Stephens, 2001).

Not surprisingly, given their importance in democratic capitalist societies, elections are also influenced by inequalities in the amount of power and status possessed by different groups. The impact of such inequalities on democratic governance has accordingly been a central topic of investigation in political sociology. Political divisions along class, religious, racial and ethnic, linguistic, national, or gender lines have often led to enduring patterns of conflict in party systems or political institutions. Indeed, the investigation of these divisions helped to define some of the central contributions of the post-World War II generation of political sociology (e.g., Berelson, Lazarsfeld, and McPhee, 1954; Lipset, 1960; Alford, 1963; Lipset and Rokkan, 1967a).

After the late 1960s, as part of a larger turn in political sociology toward research on the state and macrolevel political processes on the one hand and social movements and contentious politics on the other, scholarly debates shifted away from the study of voting behavior. With a few notable exceptions (Hamilton, 1972; Knoke, 1976; Form, 1985), relatively little work on the social influences on voting behavior and election outcomes appeared. The field of voting studies increasingly came to be dominated by the investigations inspired by the pioneering work on the social psychology of voting launched by the Michigan School (Campbell et al., 1960; Converse, 1964) and rational choice theories (beginning with Downs, 1957).

Since the early 1990s, however, there has been a renewed interest in questions regarding how, and under what conditions, social factors shape electoral outcomes. Beginning with the influential contributions of Anthony Heath and his colleagues in Britain (especially Heath, Jowell, and Curtice, 1985, 1991), research on voting behavior by political sociologists has accelerated, paying attention to both individual- and group-level factors (see Manza, Hout, and Brooks, 1995 for a comprehensive survey of research on class voting through the mid-1990s). This second generation of sociological work has revived the classical focus by introducing new methods and concepts. The results have underscored the enduring importance of social divisions while also pointing to the theoretical relevance of other factors relating to ideologies, economics, and institutions (see Manza and Brooks 1999, Brooks, Manza, and Bolzendahl, 2003).

In this chapter, we provide an overview of research on social cleavages in the study of electoral politics. To keep the discussion manageable, we focus on three hotly contested areas of research – the impact of cleavages on political participation, voting behavior, and campaign finance in U.S. elections – leaving aside considerations of important but related issues such as the role of social cleavages in shaping public opinion, party organizations, social movements, and political recruitment. Although our main empirical focus is on the United States, exclusively so in the case of campaign finance, we also draw on cross-national research and evidence.

Our approach is as follows. First, we introduce the cleavage concept in voting research as it developed, paying particular attention to some key postwar developments in survey research and analysis. Part two outlines a systematic model of social cleavages, distinguishing the *mechanisms* and *processes* through which cleavages influence elections. Part three applies insights from the model to explore in more detail the impact of cleavages in structuring political participation, whereas part four develops a similar analysis of voting behavior. We then turn (in part five) to the special case of campaign finance, examining debates over both who gives and with what substantive impact. A short conclusion summarizes the discussion while also suggesting some of the ways in which we expect future research on cleavages to intersect with other emerging research programs in political sociology.

SOCIAL CLEAVAGES AND ELECTORAL POLITICS: ORIGINS OF A RESEARCH PROGRAM

The concept of social cleavage can be traced to the intersection of Marxist and Weberian social theory as applied to the study of politics. Marx's class-centered model of history and social change and Weber's distinction between classes, status groups, and organizations in capitalist societies both suggest that political divisions are rooted in social structures. The possibility that a growing industrial working class could provide the foundation for an "electoral road to socialism" (Engels, 1895; Przeworski and Sprague, 1986) provided the earliest impetus for investigating the role of social cleavages in shaping voting behavior. Predictions about workers' preferences for socialism were based on the assumption that class interests inevitably lead voters to favor the political party most likely to advance those interests. The "class politics" thesis became the object of social science inquiry when political change did not unfold in the ways predicted by the theories put forward by Marxists and social democratic intellectuals, perhaps most famously in the question of "Why is there no socialism in the United States?" (Sombart, 1906; see also Lipset and Marks, 2000).

Many of the early claims about how social locations influenced voting behavior were based on largely impressionistic evidence. The earliest attempts to systematically investigate the impact of social cleavages drew upon ecological data (e.g., Ogburn and Peterson, 1916; Rice, 1928; Tingsten, 1937; Ogburn and Coombs, 1940). In this period, the best available sources of voting data were aggregate, district-level election returns, which could be combined with Census data to crudely estimate social group alignments. The nature of the available data, in fact, encouraged analysts to limit their attention to identifiable sociodemographic characteristics, usually class divisions, which could be measured at the district level with Census data (Dalton and Wattenberg, 1993:196).

Early Postwar Voting Research

The advent of the modern election survey from the mid-1930s onward encouraged social scientists to develop individual-level analyses of the sources of voting behavior. The rapidly developing tools of survey research made it increasingly possible to systematically test the impact of different kinds of social cleavages using multivariate models incorporating other political and ideological factors influencing voter alignments (although widespread use of multivariate analyses in voting studies would only develop after interest in the impact of social cleavages on elections had already begun to wane in the late 1960s). The first wave of studies – important and pathbreaking as they were – were based on cross-tabulations and relatively simplistic measurement strategies.

In the early postwar period, the most influential and pioneering work on political communication, social cleavages, and voting behavior was done by Paul Lazarsfeld, Bernard Berelson, and their students at Columbia University (Lazarsfeld, Berelson, and Gaudet, 1948; Berelson, Lazarsfeld, and McPhee, 1954). In developing a theory of the "two-step flow of political communication" and in highlighting the role of "opinion leaders," Lazarsfeld and Berelson made enduring contributions to the field of communication studies. They also developed pioneering understandings of the social factors influencing voting behavior. In their 1954 study of a panel of voters interviewed several times during the 1948 election campaign in Elmira, New York, for example, Berelson et al. identified nineteen distinct social characteristics that could be used to predict an individual's vote. Among the key findings of the Columbia investigations was the importance of social networks of friends, family members, and co-workers in reinforcing the political preferences of voters (helping to produce very high levels of stability even in the face of extensive campaigning). They also reported that "cross-pressured" voters, who had overlapping group memberships, were less enthusiastic and engaged participants in the political process.

The wide-ranging work of Seymour Martin Lipset probably did the most to focus attention on the role of social cleavages in structuring voting behavior (see especially Lipset, 1981, 1960, 1963; Lipset and Rokkan, 1967a, 1967b; see also Alford, 1963). In the essays gathered in his widely read 1960 book, *Political Man*, Lipset developed what he would later characterize – in the 1981 postscript to the reissue of the book – as an "apolitical Marxist" approach to explaining the social origins of democracy, fascism, communism, and the social bases of modern political parties. Lipset focused his investigations on the distinctive social bases of ideologies, social movements, and political parties that shape the larger political phenomena he sought to explain (fascism, communism, democracy). Democratic societies were said to be those with a large and stable bloc of middle class citizens. Fascism and communism, by contrast, were traced to the authoritarian politics of key groups or classes, including workers (Lipset's famous formulation of the thesis of "working class authoritarianism"), small business owners, and other economically threatened middle class segments.

The Development of Social Psychological Models of Voting

The most influential thrust of the postwar generation of research on voting behavior was the social psychological approach of the so-called Michigan School (see especially Campbell, Converse, Miller, and Stokes, 1960). Designers and first analysts of the early National Election Studies, Angus Campbell and his colleagues asserted that voters' alignments were best conceptualized as the product of long-standing emotional attachments and identification with a specific political party. Complementing this assumption, Campbell and his colleagues (1960: Chap. 10) reported further evidence that partisan voters were able to articulate general images of their preferred party as endorsing positions expected to benefit their social group. In this way, they extended the social cleavage model. In their famous "funnel of causality" metaphor of individual voting decisions, social structural attributes – including class origins and occupation – were viewed as operating at the large (back) end of the funnel, leading to the social–psychological attributes (primarily partisan identification and political attitudes) at the narrow front end of the funnel that ultimately predicted vote choice.

The *American Voter's* social psychological theory defined much subsequent research and debate over U.S. voting behavior (Brooks, Manza, and Bolzendahl, 2003). However, its emphasis on the stable sources of partisanship and the seemingly low capacity of voters to acquire either sophistication or factual information was (and is) not without controversy at the individual and aggregate level. (At the individual level, see Verba, Nie, and Petrocik, 1979 and Delli-Carpini and Keeter, 1996, At the aggregate level, see Page and Shapiro, 1992; Erikson et al., 2002:Chap. 3, and Green, Palmquist, and Schikler, 2002. See Niemi and Weisberg, 2001:Chap. 10, for an overview.)

Although hardly unproblematic, the Michigan model did provide a way of moving beyond the conceptual limitations of early cleavage-based approaches to studying voting behavior. Campbell and his colleagues noted that in no case did all of the members of a social group give their votes to one party: There were always plenty of defectors. One way of accounting for these defections was to consider the social–psychological factors mediating the relationship between social group membership and vote choice, pushing some voters away from voting their class or other group interest.

Economic Models

The third of the major postwar approaches developed an economic model of participation, voting behavior, and policy outcomes. Tracing its origins to Anthony Downs's influential (1957) work, these models emphasize the ways in which voters evaluate the expected utility of choices they are offered by candidates and parties. Downs's original thesis started with the assumption that "citizens act rationally in politics. This axiom implies that each citizen casts their vote for the party he believes will provide him with more benefits than any other" (1957:36). In this view, "groups" are aggregates of self-interested actors (albeit with possibly similar calculations of utility), and group-based voting is explained in terms of similar individual calculations.

Various extensions of the economic model have been introduced in a vast literature that has appeared since Downs. For example, the pioneering work of Fiorina (1981) developed an economic model of vote choice that distinguished between the *retrospective* versus *prospective* orientations of economic expectations and behavior. Kinder and Kiewiet (1981; see also Kiwiet, 1983) demonstrated the importance of conceptualizing and measuring the variable target of economic evaluations: Voters' evaluations are *egocentric* when they involve perceptions of economic conditions experienced by an individual; voters' evaluations are *sociotropic* when they involve perceptions of level of *national* economic prosperity.

CONCEPTS, MECHANISMS, PROCESSES

By 1960, with the publication of Lipset's *Political Man* and Campbell et al.'s *The American Voter*, following closely on the heels of Down's *An Economic Theory of Democracy* (1957) and Berelson et al.'s *Voting* (1954), much of the terrain of debate over social cleavages and voting behavior had been firmly established. These works identified social cleavages as important factors in studying voting, and taken as a group they also proposed a set of mechanisms – economic interests, social psychological factors, and social networks – to account for the effects of social cleavages on political behavior.

But the first generation of social science work on social cleavages in electoral politics did not, for the most part, develop systematic theories about the linkages between individual- or group-level factors, on the one hand, and organizational and institutional forces on the other (the early Columbia School work provides a partial exception). In general, the study of voting behavior developed as an individual-level enterprise, in which individual voters were viewed as having a set of attributes that allowed analysts to assign them to politically relevant groups. The subsequent attack on behavioral models in the social sciences by institutionalists was, at its core, a challenge to the isolation of research on voting from the broader political contexts in which elections occur and the feedback processes they generate (see Immergut, 1998).

In this section, we explicitly draw on later research to outline a multilevel model of social cleavages and elections. We begin by unpacking the *mechanisms* that give rise to, or reinforce, cleavage-based political divisions, and then present a model of the *processes* through which cleavages come to be manifest (to a greater or lesser degree) in the political system. This discussion points the way to a more systematic understanding of social cleavage impacts across the full spectrum of research on electoral politics.

Mechanisms

In the literature on social cleavages, three distinct though not exclusive mechanisms of the source of cleavage impacts have been proposed: *economic, social–psychological,* and *social networks*. We elaborate on each briefly in this section, beginning with economic factors.

The class models of voter preferences that underlay the socialist tradition assumed a straightforward economic logic in which working class voters would vote for socialist parties as a way of realizing their material interests (whereas middle and upper class voters were presumed to favor conservative parties). Such a rendering assumes that (class) voters evaluate the expected economic utility of the political choices offered by candidates and parties. In this view, "groups" are really aggregates of self-interested actors (albeit with similar calculations of utility), and group-based voting is explained in terms of calculations regarding which party will more likely bring about desired economic outcomes (see, e.g., Lipset et al., 1954:1136). For example, Hibbs's (1982, 1987) work on macroeconomic conditions and vote choice suggests group-specific applications: Working class voters prefer economic outcomes in which unemployment is low, whereas middle class voters prefer a low-inflation environment. Parties may adjust their policy priorities accordingly in order to best serve their electoral constituencies (see Haynes and Jacobs, 1994).

A second, quite different approach to analyzing the role of groups in shaping political behavior highlights the importance of subjective identification, or "group consciousness." Such affect models extend the original Michigan School approach by refining the notion of the social group beyond simple objective group memberships (such as one's religion, class, gender, race, or region of residence) to take into account the strength of feeling about membership in the group defining voters' overall identities. According to advocates of this approach, the underlying causal process is not to be found in the objective attributes of voters, but rather in the degree to which people identify with, or develop positive affect toward, a particular group. If *objective* group membership does not also involve a *subjective* component, it can be expected to have much less influence over attitudes and behavior.

At the heart of the social–psychological mechanisms accounting for group-based political differences are conceptions of the "linked fate" (Dawson, 1994:Chap. 4) of group members. Building from earlier arguments about the role of perceived interdependence in social groups (Conover, 1984, 1988; Gurin, Hatchett, and Jackson, 1989), Dawson argued that a strong sense of linked fate helps to explain why remarkable levels of political solidarity persist among African Americans even as class divisions have grown. On this account, middle class blacks see their own prospects as tied to the well-being of all blacks because "the historical experiences of African Americans have resulted in a situation in which group interests have served as a useful proxy for self-interest" (Dawson, 1994:77).

The third major mechanism that has been postulated concerns the role of social networks in shaping political participation and voting behavior. The basic idea is that social networks of family, friends, co-workers, and fellow participants in social or civic organizations influence voters' orientation toward politics. Huckfeldt and Sprague's (1995) work hypothesizes the importance of network-based information to voters' decision-making and voting behavior, arguing further that such information is routinely transmitted through both strong ties (e.g., involving friends) and weak ties (e.g., involving individuals acquainted solely through a common contact). For example, Weakliem and

Heath's (1994) analysis of the 1987 British Election Study found that a sizable portion of class differences in voting remain after controlling for income and economic policy preferences, suggesting that the operation of social networks accounts for the rest. Studies of the impact of social mobility on political preferences also point to the power of social ties to the class of origin in structuring the political identities of mobile citizens, whose political preferences tend to fall between those of their class of origin and those of their class destination (De Graaf, Nieuwbeerta, and Heath, 1995).

These three mechanisms – individual and group economic interests, group-based consciousness and a sense of linked fate, and social networks – are not mutually exclusive. For example, individual voters can simultaneously view the interests of their group in purely economic terms and be embedded in social networks that reinforce such perceptions. However, the analytical problem of separating out the respective influences of each is demanding, and few existing election study datasets contain fully adequate measures to carry out the appropriate tests. The American National Election Studies, for example, contain comprehensive batteries of items about economic views and social group identities but few measures of respondents' social networks.

Processes

In their macroanalysis of cleavage systems in Western Europe, Bartolini and Mair (1990) introduced a rich, multilevel approach that provides a useful starting point for any consideration of the processes through which cleavages come to be manifest in the political system. The analytical problem, as they put it, is that "the concept of cleavage lies in its intermediate location between the two main approaches of political sociology: that of social stratification and its impact on institutions and political behavior, on the one hand, and that of political institutions and their impact on social structure and change, on the other. . . . The concept of cleavage is often either reduced 'down' to that of 'social cleavage' or 'up' to that of 'political cleavage'" (1990:214). Their proposed solution to this dilemma was to suggest that any social cleavage capable of shaping political behavior will simultaneously exist on three different levels. First, it has an "empirical" component rooted in social structure. Second, it has a "normative" component, in that the social groups making up a cleavage adopt conflicting forms of consciousness. Third, it has a macroinstitutional component, expressed through "individual interactions, institutions, and organizations, such as political parties, which develop as part of the cleavage" (1990:214). We extend this model to note that social cleavages are also typically linked to the outputs of public policy (see Manza and Brooks, 1999:Chap. 10; Manza and Wright, 2003). Policies reflect both the capacities of particular groups to influence politicians and political parties and ultimately public policy, and the policy outputs of governments reinforce or reshape (depending on their content) the structural conditions giving rise to cleavage divisions in the first place.

In previous work, we have argued that politically significant social cleavages have impacts at all these levels; variation in their magnitude over time (or cross-nationally) can be explained by differences in how they manifest themselves at each level (Manza and Brooks 1999, Chap. 2). For example, the religious cleavage is often strongest in countries in which there is a pluralist religious market, competition between religious groups for access to desired goods, and/or a party system that includes religious parties. The force of class divisions will vary depending in part on the organizational capacities of labor unions and employer groups to mobilize and shape the political orientations of their members, as well as the extent to which the party system includes social democratic or labor parties making class-based political appeals.

We consider each of these processes across the four levels introduced in greater detail below.

Social Structure. "Social" cleavages are, by definition, grounded in the social structure of any society. Social structural divisions give rise to groups of people with shared interests or statuses. Major social structural divisions include those stemming from race/ethnicity, class, gender, religion, region, language, or national identity. Societies vary in the types of divisions embedded in social structure. Although class and gender may be universal, there is considerable variation on other social structural divisions. For example, in the case of religion there is wide variation in the types of divisions found in different countries. In some countries, a single denomination (the Catholic Church in Italy, Ireland, or Belgium; the Anglican Church in Britain; the Lutheran Church in Sweden) has the allegiance of most citizens who claim a religious identity. Here the social basis for a cleavage lies in the division between adherents versus secular or nominally affiliated church members. In other countries, however, there is much greater competition between distinct denominations or religious traditions with large memberships (e.g., Germany, the Netherlands, or the United States). Religion can, in such societies, provide a basis for social stratification and inequality, in which members of a "dominant" denomination have privileged access to valued positions (e.g., in the long dominance of mainline Protestant denominations in the United States).

Two points about social structural divisions are worth highlighting. First, because social structures change slowly, political change based on changes in social structure per se are typically cumulative, emerging over a period of time. Second, there are multiple ways in which social structural changes may alter political outcomes (Manza and Brooks, 1999:Chap. 7). Changes in the relative size of particular groups within a cleavage represents one such way. Changes in the internal composition of the group, irrespective of its relative size, provides another. If, for example, the proportion of working class voters declines, the overall impact of the class cleavage on party coalitions may decline even if the voting behavior of those who remain in the working class is unchanged. Conversely, the working class may change internally in ways that alter its political alignment. Either of these changes would reduce the importance of working class voters as a class, but they suggest very different analytical interpretations.

Group Identification and Conflict. The second level can be characterized as the cleavage "field," defined by the existence of two or more distinct groups whose members recognize themselves as both (1) distinct from and (2) in conflict with one another. In general, group identification is a crucial condition for social structural divisions to become politicized; without some clear recognition of group boundaries, social or economic inequalities are unlikely to become embedded in the organizational and institutional contexts in which political conflicts occur (Koch, 1993). One of the most powerful ways in which group-based consciousness may shape voting behavior is through group heuristics, in which voters make attributions about candidates or parties based on which group they think the candidate or party most closely represents (Brady and Sniderman, 1985; Sniderman, Brody, and Tetlock, 1991).

Macropolitical Factors. The third source of social cleavage impacts in a political system – and perhaps most important for its mobilizing impact – relates to the processes through which interest groups, social movements, political parties, or governing institutions explicitly draw upon or encourage group-based differences as a way of furthering their goals.

Let us consider these more specifically. The existence of organizations such as unions and business associations influences the political alignment of classes. Unions organize workers not only at the point of production but also in the polls (Asher, 2001). Similarly, groups or associations based on minority group memberships, as well as civil rights organizations, politically organize racial or ethnic group-based political action. In the United States, churches also have been particularly important in organizing African Americans politically (Rosenstone and Hansen, 1993:Chap. 6; Harris, 1999), as have the major organizations of the Christian Right (Layman, 2001; Brooks 2002).

Political parties vary widely in the degree to which they seek to organize on the basis of social cleavages, but some common patterns can be found (see Schwartz and Larson, Chapter 13 of this volume). Electoral systems shape the number and types of political parties and their general character (e.g., catchall parties versus parties organized around specific cleavages) (e.g., Mair, 1997). Parties may also shift the type of appeals they make, or the success of those appeals, in response to social and economic change or changes in the social structure of the electorate. An instructive example is the transformation of social democratic parties from class-based parties to parties that compete more broadly for middle class votes (see Przeworski and Sprague, 1986; Heath et al., 2001). This can also be a two-way process: Success in recruiting middle class voters changes the profile of a left party's electoral coalition and the balance of interests it represents (see Manza and Brooks, 1999b: Chap. 7).

Feedback Processes. A final, if underexamined set of processes, involves feedback dynamics in which social cleavages are reinforced by policy outcomes and politicians' strategic behavior. Policy outcomes skewed toward the benefit of some groups both *reflect* the existence of significant cleavages in the political system and *reproduce* those differences. Once in office, parties reward their supporters and attempt to make good on at least some of their campaign promises, thereby signaling in a manner that reinforces group-based loyalties.

There are three kinds of issues about feedback processes that relate to cleavages in electoral politics: (1) the impact of socioeconomic skews in the electorate on policy (the impact of who votes), (2) the impact of social cleavages on electoral coalitions (the combined impact of who votes and how they vote), and (3) the beneficiaries of the policy outputs of governments (who benefits). We discuss some of the key research findings relating to (1) and (2) below. With respect to (3), scholarship documenting bias in policy outputs is widespread, but it would go beyond the scope of this chapter to try to summarize it (on the United States, see, e.g., Weir, 1998; Page and Simmons, 2001; for comparative evidence, see, e.g., Lipjhart, 1997; Hicks, 1999; Esping-Andersen, 2001; Huber and Stephens, 2001). We do, however, consider one notable way in which American policy outputs are influenced by social cleavages – the system of campaign finance – in the fifth section of this chapter.

POLITICAL PARTICIPATION

In this section, we examine some of the recent contributions, interpretations, and controversies over the role of social cleavages in shaping political participation, focusing especially on the United States. One recent international survey shows that turnout in U.S. national elections ranks an extraordinary 138th among the 170 countries that hold elections, far lower than all similar capitalist democracies except Switzerland (which ranked 137th) (International Institute for Democracy and Electoral Assistance, 1997). The United States is also unusual for having a substantial cleavage-based skew in political participation: There is typically a turnout gap of some 25 percent or more between the highest turnout group within a cleavage and the lowest (such as professionals and unskilled workers in the case of class, Jews versus those with no religion in the case of the religious cleavage, and whites and Hispanics in the case of race/ethnicity) (Hout, Brooks, and Manza, 1995; Lijphart, 1997; Manza and Brooks, 1999: Chap. 7; Freeman, 2004). Such sharp socioeconomic-based cleavages are not generally found to the same degree in other countries, although cross-national research frequently finds that in those countries without compulsory voting, there are small to moderate effects of education on turnout (Powell, 1986, pp. 26–27; Font and Viros, 1995; Dalton, 1996; Lipjhart, 1997, pp. 2–3).

In the social science literatures on political participation, there are two broad streams of explanation that bear on cleavage-based differences: individual-level explanations and political and institutional explanations. Sociodemographic attributes of individuals such as education, race/education, income, gender, and religion are the ingredients of individual level explanations. Political and institutional explanations point to the role of mobilizing activities by parties and political organizations on the one hand, and institutional constraints such as voter registration requirements, the timing of elections, and the range of meaningful choices presented to voters through the party system, on the other. We consider both types of factors.

Social Structural Factors

It has long been understood that in elections where turnout is far from universal, resource-rich groups vote at higher rates than more disadvantaged groups (Lijphart 1997, pp. 1–2). For example, in his ecological study of voter turnout in Chicago during the 1924 presidential election, Gosnell (1927, p. 98) concluded that "the more schooling the individual has the more likely he is to register and vote in presidential elections." Other early research found similar results (Tingsten 1937), and it has remained a staple finding of participation research since that time (Wolfinger and Rosestone 1980, pp. 13–36; Teixiera 1992; Verba et al. 1995). Educational effects on turnout are often found to be mediated by other, associated factors: knowledge of the candidates and issues, newspaper reading to keep up on current events, a sense of political efficacy, and concern with the outcome of the election (Teixiera 1992; Conway 2000, pp. 25–28).

Other sociodemographic attributes of individual voters that influence turnout have also been widely documented (for overviews, see Abramson et al. 2000, chap. 4; Conway 2000, chap. 3). Whites vote at higher rates than blacks, although the gap has varied depending on electoral context and other factors (e.g. Tate 1993); and turnout among Latinos is lower still (Leighley 2001). For much of the 20th Century, men voted at higher rates than women, but that gap has disappeared in recent elections (Firebaugh and Chen 1995). Regional differences in turnout are more pronounced than is often recognized; for example, in the 2000 presidential election turnout ranged from a low of 40.5% in Hawaii to 68.8% in Minnesota. Younger people vote at lower rates than older voters (Wolfinger and Rosestone 1980:46–50; Highton and Wolfinger, 2001:202–9); whether the traditional pattern of increasing turnout with age will be true for more recent cohorts is less clear (Miller and Shanks, 1996:Chaps. 3–5).

Group-Level Factors

One of the most well-understood aspects of political participation is that social networks provide a key source of both information and motivation. The basic idea is straightforward: Interactions with others enhance one's likelihood of political participation, and the greater the degree of interaction, the greater the effect (Huckfeldt, 1986; Leighley, 1990; Kenny, 1992; Rosenstone and Hansen, 1993). Networks also provide incentives to participate; as Verba et al. (1995:16) pithily put it, one reason people do not participate is "because nobody asked." This finding appears to hold across both aggregate contextual measures of social environment and measures of individual networks, although Mutz (2002) produced new survey-based evidence suggesting that individuals with substantively cross-cutting and conflictual networks are less likely to participate, a point emphasized by the early Columbia School.

The identities of the candidates have also been shown to have significant group-level effects, especially with regard to race and gender and, to a lesser extent, religion. Racial differences are especially pronounced for African Americans (e.g., Bobo and Gilliam, 1990; Tate, 1993); a particularly dramatic example is the 1983 campaign for mayor in Chicago, in which an African American congressman, Harold Washington, surprisingly gained the Democratic nomination, prompting extraordinary levels of turnout among black voters in Chicago during the general election (Kleppner, 1985). White voters have similarly been shown to participate at lower rates in elections with black candidates (Reeves, 1997). The presence of a woman candidate influences the participation and voting behavior of women (Plutzer and Zipp, 1996). In the case of the religious cleavage, the group-specific mobilization of evangelicals Protestants caused by the presence of born-again Christian Jimmy Carter on the presidential ballot in 1976 and (to a lesser extent) 1980 increased turnout among evangelicals (see Manza and Brooks, 1997). The converse proposition – that when the candidate of one's party has a disliked social identity, participation frequently falls – has also found support. For example, Herron and Sekhon's (2002) study of voter roll-off (i.e., ballots containing invalid votes for some races) found significant declines in African American participation in election contests pairing only white candidates, and vice versa, in the 1998 election in Cook County (Harris and Zipp, 1999).

Organizational Factors

In attempting to explain why turnout is so much lower in the United States than in other comparable democracies, or why it is lower today than in earlier periods in American history, a great deal of attention has been paid to organizational and institutional factors. The underlying presumption in such research is that individual-level factors may not account for the full extent of low U.S. turnout. For example, Americans have as much or more education on average as the citizens of any polity (and far more on average than in earlier periods of American history with higher turnout). Furthermore, their lack of interest in politics, low levels of political efficacy, or apparent apathy toward election outcomes may reflect substantive views of the party system or the character of elite political conflicts (e.g., Burnham, 1982; Vallely, 1995; Piven and Cloward, 2000). Differences in levels of political mobilization in the United States promoted by social movements or party organizations, as well as institutional constraints on participation such as preelection registration requirements, also contribute to accounting for cross-national differences.

The level of mobilization efforts undertaken by social movements is especially important (e.g., Rosenstone and Hansen 1993; Wielhouwer and Lockerbie, 1994). The comparative weaknesses of mobilizing organizations in the United States, especially those targeted at lower-turnout groups such as workers, racial and ethnic minorities, and the poor, may thus account for some of the sociodemographic skew in the electorate, as low-turnout groups are potentially subject to more influence by mobilization efforts than higher-turnout groups (see Verba, Nie, and Kim, 1978; Powell, 1986; Radcliff and Davis, 2000). Leighley's (2001) examination of variation in the rate of mobilization and turnout of Latino voters in the United States found that higher levels of mobilization are associated with increased turnout (see also De La Garza, Menchaca, and DeSipio, 1994).

Mobilization may not always be successful, however. Over the past twenty years, for example, organizations of the Christian Right (CR), most notably the Christian Coalition and its predecessors, have consistently attempted to mobilize evangelicals to participate in the political process. Christian Right organizations have as their explicit goal the restoration of traditional values through public policy (Green, 1997; Layman, 2001). Employing a grassroots strategy of mobilizing supporters from below, the CR in the 1980s and 1990s built an extensive network of local organizations with perhaps as many as 200,000 members or more at their peak in the early 1990s (Persinos, 1994; Wilcox, 1994; Green, 2000). In each election, these groups claimed to have distributed millions of pamphlets, and survey data produced by Regnerus et al. (1999) found that over 20 percent of all voters reported receiving one of the pamphlets. In spite of these extraordinary mobilizing efforts, however, there is little evidence for any general increase in turnout among evangelical voters since these efforts began in the late 1970s (Manza and Brooks, 1997).

Although one case hardly undermines the entire mobilization thesis, other evidence suggests that electoral mobilization in the modern era rarely increases either aggregate or group-specific turnout *significantly*. For example, the sharp increase in mobilizing efforts of unions in the 1990s has produced only modest increases at best in turnout rates among union members or households (e.g., Abramson et al., 2002:82). Gerber and Green's (2000) field experiment comparing the effectiveness of nonpartisan appeals to participate using personal contacts, direct mail, and telephone contacts found a significant effect of person-to-person contacts, precisely the type of mobilization efforts that appear to have declined in recent years in favor of professional campaign techniques.

In specifying institutional factors, analysts have focused on the following sets of issues: (1) the difficulty of registering in the United States compared with other countries that use an automatic system of voter registration (Powell, 1986; Piven and Cloward, 2000); (2) the increased costs of voting, with national elections held on a working day in the United States versus on either a weekend or national holiday in most other countries (Crewe, 1981; see Freeman, 2001 for the extraordinary differences in turnout between Puerto Ricans voting in Puerto Rico, where elections are either held on Sunday or a national holiday, versus Puerto Ricans living on the U.S. mainland); (3) the role of negative campaign advertisements in the media in reducing voter participation (Ansolabehere and Iyengar, 1995), as well as the changing character of news media coverage of politics (e.g., Patterson, 1992); (4) societalwide trends of declining social capital reducing participation across a wide range of social institutions (Putnam, 2000), and specifically those related to social networks that promote political participation (e.g., Teixiera, 1992); and (5) the limited range of ideological choices available to voters in the U.S. two-party system (e.g., Burnham, 1982, 1987; but see also Jackman, 1987; Manza and Brooks, 1999: Chap. 1).

These mechanisms are not, of course, mutually exclusive; some or all may contribute to explaining the puzzle of low turnout. We do not have the space here to discuss all of the issues they raise, but it is important to comment briefly on the debate over voter registration laws because of their particular relevance to explanations about social cleavages in participation (see, e.g., Burnham, 1982; Powell, 1986; Piven and Cloward, 2000). It is well-known that registered voters participate at fairly high levels in American politics (with turnout rates over 80 percent in presidential elections) and that there is a substantial sociodemographic skew in terms of who is registered in the first place (with, for example, better-educated, more affluent voters being more likely to be registered than less-educated, less affluent voters) (Wolfinger and Rosenstone, 1980). This suggests that socioeconomic cleavages in participation are themselves rooted in voter registration requirements.

For the registration thesis to be supported, however, we would need systematic evidence that looser registration laws both increase turnout and reduce sociodemographic differences. There is some evidence that making registration easier encourages turnout, although the impact appears not to be as substantial as was often thought to be the case a decade ago (Teixeira, 1992:122). Cross-section comparisons show that states with easier registration requirements have higher turnout (e.g., Wolfinger and Rosestone, 1980; Teixera, 1992). The lowering of registration barriers in virtually all states after 1960 probably precluded an even greater decline in turnout (e.g., Rosenstone and Hansen, 1993:214), although most of the impact came from a single change: the removal of barriers to registration faced by African Americans in the South.

Against this evidence, however, is a wealth of counterevidence that raises substantial doubts about the impact of registration laws. For example, states with looser registration regimes might have had higher turnout even without reforming their registration laws; at least one fixed effects model found no evidence that changes in individual state registration laws increased turnout (Knack, 1995). At the aggregate level, increased registration levels after the passage of the motor voter law in 1993 has not increased overall turnout levels; turnout was lower in the presidential elections of 1996 and 2000 than in 1992, and these were among the lowest of the twentieth century, as were turnout levels in the 1994, 1998, and 2002 midterm elections. This does not mean, as Piven and Cloward (2000:Chap. 12) pointed out, that easier registration would not have an important impact in future movement-driven mass-mobilizing election contexts; but by themselves, changes in registration laws have had little impact on aggregate turnout levels.

Feedback Processes?

Writing in 1949, V. O. Key asserted that, "The blunt truth is that politicians are under no compulsion to pay much heed to classes and groups of citizens that do not vote" (Key, 1964/1949:527), and this argument has been frequently reasserted (Burnham, 1987; Rosenstone and Hansen, 1993; Piven and Cloward, 2000). Questions about *how* and *when* group-specific turnout may matter are, however, complicated and difficult to conclusively resolve. In this context, a reasonable initial hypothesis is that lower turnout among disadvantaged groups reduces the incentives for political parties to appeal to these groups (see Hill and Leighley, 1992), although those incentives likely vary depending on the institutional context (with multiparty proportional representation schemes producing higher levels of responsiveness to the shape of the electorate than single-member district systems).

Recent Trends in Political Participation

Between 1960 and 1988, official turnout figures in presidential elections fell from 62.8 percent to 50.3 percent, subsequently hovering within a narrow band between 49 percent and 53 percent since then (with a one-shot increase to 55 percent in 1992). Turnout in midterm congressional elections is far lower, sliding from 45.4 percent in 1966 to just 33.1 percent in 1990, rising to 37.4 percent in 1994, but back down to 32.9 percent in 1998, though up to 39.4 percent in 2002.

The implications of declining voter turnout in the United States, both in relation to recent downward trends and in comparison with other countries, have been subject to a great deal of discussion and scholarly concern (Putnam, 2000:Chap. 2). Turnout decline has also been viewed as something of a paradox, because steady increases in societalwide educational levels and declining barriers to participation (principally in terms of registration laws) should have combined to increase turnout during this same period (Brody, 1978).

Even determining the precise magnitude of turnout decline has proven a difficult challenge. Some analysts have questioned whether the actual extent of declining turnout has been exaggerated. The denominator used to calculate the "voting age population" includes legal immigrants and ineligible felons. Some of the fall in turnout is an artifact of the growing proportion of the adult population that cannot legally vote due to citizenship status, a felony conviction (Uggen and Manza, 2002), or other reasons. The most aggressive contribution on this issue is that of McDonald and Popkin (2001), who argued that, contrary to the conventional wisdom, all of the decline in turnout since 1972 is due to the rising proportion of ineligible individuals improperly included in the denominator of official turnout statistics or survey data (see also Burnham, 1987; Burden, 2000).

From the standpoint of the impact of social cleavages on turnout, the key question with regard to recent trends in turnout is how much, if any, group-based inequalities in participation have grown. In other words, is the turnout decline (whatever its precise magnitude) concentrated disproportionately among certain groups, most notably the working class or poor? The question is important if, as Rosenstone and Hansen (1993:248) warned, "the more recent decline of citizen involvement in government has yielded a politically engaged class that is not only growing smaller and smaller, but also less and less representative of American democracy."

The case for an increased skew in participation has been made using income and education to measure socioeconomic status (Reiter, 1979; Bennett, 1991; Rosenstone and Hansen, 1993) and occupation (Burnham, 1987). Most studies that have measured changes in turnout by educational level have also found a greater decline among better-educated groups (Teixeira, 1992; Leighley and Nagler, 1992; Abramson et al., 2002), even among analysts skeptical of any overall increase in social cleavage-related bias (especially Leighley and Nagler, 1992).

Explanations offered for an increased skew tend to focus on macrolevel attributes, although individual-level explanations have been proposed as well. Among the key organizational factors that have been identified, the most important has been declining levels of partisan mobilization by parties and social movements since the 1960s (see especially Rosenstone and Hansen, 1993; also Burnham, 1982, 1987; Piven and Cloward, 2000). These scholars have argued that the Democratic Party, and the social movements and organizations affiliated with the party, have generally lost the capacity to reach out to disadvantaged voters as part of a broader trend toward a more elite-oriented, money-driven party. Rosenstone and Hansen's (1993) widely cited analysis produced statistical evidence from individual-level survey data suggesting that declining mobilization accounts for half of the turnout decline between 1960 and 1988. However, since the late 1980s, both the Democratic and Republican Parties and their allies have significantly increased their efforts to mobilize voters; National Election Study (NES) data show that whereas 22 percent of voters were contacted by one of the parties in 1960 (the year with the highest postwar turnout), in 1996 29 percent of voters were contacted, and in 2000 fully 36 percent of voters were contacted (the highest total ever recorded) (Abramson, Aldrich, and Rohde, 2002:90; but see Gerber and Green [2000:653], who noted the shift from personal contacts to less effective telephone or mail contacts).

However, a number of other analysts have found less or no evidence of an increasing skew, emphasizing instead that turnout decline is the result of electoratewide trends. Leighley and Nagler (1992) argued that income is the best single measure of the class skewness of the electorate and that there is no change in the relative participation rates of different income groups (see also Shields and Goedel, 1997 on midterm elections). Utilizing a new dataset – the Roper Social and Political Trends Data – with overtime measures of participation across a range of political and charitable activities, Brady, Scholzman, Verba, and Elms (2002) found largely trendless patterns in the turnout ratio of upper to lower socioeconomic groups, concluding that although substantial participation inequalities remain, "the bowlers remain the same." Using an occupational measure of class, Hout, Brooks, and Manza (1995) found only very limited evidence that turnout fell among working class voters, principally among skilled workers (Brooks and Manza, 1999:Chap. 7).

Overall, the trend debate has proven difficult to resolve, in part because estimates based on self-reported turnout are subject to nonrandom reporting biases, and different model specifications produce sufficiently divergent results to permit alternative interpretations. These sources of uncertainty hold across the major datasets (the National Election Study and the Current Population Survey's Voter Supplement Module) and across different specifications of key social cleavages of interest, notably class. We conclude that there is at best only modest evidence for an *increase* in social cleavage impacts on turnout, but this should in no way obscure the fact that by any measure the *persisting* cleavage-based skews in participation rates in U.S. elections are substantial.

VOTING BEHAVIOUR

The impact of social cleavages on political participation provides one source of cleavage impacts, but it is through their impact on elections that their ultimate influence operates. In this section, we investigate issues relating to overtime trends in cleavage impacts on voting behavior, the question that has framed much of the recent controversy. Because the issues and key theories and evidence parallel the previous discussion about political participation, our discussion here is abbreviated. For a fuller account, see Manza and Brooks (1999) and Brooks et al. (2003).

Recent Controversies

At the center of recent debates is the question of whether or not cleavage impacts on voter alignments have declined. A wide range of scholars have argued that traditional group-based political alignments have eroded, often directly paralleling the decline of traditional left–right politics (Franklin, 1992; Franklin, Mackie, and Valen, 1992a, b; Van der Eijk et al., 1992; Dalton and Wattenberg, 1993; Dalton, 1996; Carmines and Huckfeldt, 1996). Ronald Inglehart and his collaborators' influential arguments about the emergence of a "new politics" rooted in a clash between materialist and postmaterialist values started from the assumption that there has been a decline in the impact of social cleavages such as class and religion (see, for example, Inglehart, 1990, 1997).

Comprehensive claims about the universal decline of social cleavages on voting behavior have, however, been challenged on several grounds. Persistent reassertions of class voting decline generally rely on simplistic measures of class and political outcomes whose flaws have been well-understood for a long time (Korpi, 1972; Heath et al., 1985, 1987). Recent work reconsidering the relevance of social factors for understanding vote choice has drawn upon more differentiated class schemas and better specifications of the party system (moving beyond simple polarizations to consider the full range of groups and party families). These studies also deployed statistical models that permit distinctions between over-time changes that affect the voting alignments of *all* groups from those changes that have *group-specific* impacts (a point first made by Heath, Jowell, and Curtice, 1985). This research has produced a mixed picture but no systematic evidence of universal decline (e.g., Heath, Jowell, and Curtice, 1985, 1991, 2001; Weakliem and Heath, 1994, 1999; Hout, Brooks, and Manza, 1995; Brooks and Manza, 1997; Evans, 1999, 2000; Manza and Brooks, 1999; Nieuwbeerta, Brooks, and Manza, 2004). Although it is sometimes assumed that these latter studies have reasserted old orthodoxies about the persistence of class or other social cleavages, there has been considerable recognition that changes in the patterning of groups and political alignment have occurred, including class and religious voting in some contexts (see Nieuwbeerta, 1996; Brooks and Manza, 1997a; Ringdal and Hines, 1999; Nieuwbeerta et al., 2004).

The lively debate concerning the fate of the class cleavage in British politics provides a good example of the increasingly complex overall picture. Early research by Heath et al. (1991) adjudicated competing models of British Election Studies data from 1964 through 1987, reporting a pattern of aggregate change with no net decline in the class cleavage. The most recent assessment of Heath et al. (2001), covering the period through the election of Tony Blair in 1997, however, reported evidence of the erosion in the overall level of class voting (Heath et al., 2001:Chap. 7; see also Goldthorpe, 1999:81–2). Nieuwbeerta, Brooks, and Manza (2004) found evidence of a significant decline in British class voting that developed in the 1970s. Although they analyzed different data and class schemes than other studies, Weakliem and Heath's (1999) analysis of election data from the 1930s onward suggests that British class voting was at its highest point in the early 1960s (preceded by lower levels in the 1930s and 1940s). This finding potentially reconciles contradictory findings in the literature.

Explaining Trends in Voting Behavior: Mechanisms and Processes

Debates over trends in the impact of social cleavages on voting behavior lead directly to a reconsideration of the underlying mechanisms and processes through which cleavage factors are expressed in elections.

Some of the most widely asserted claims about changes in the influence of social cleavages on electoral politics are linked to hypotheses about changes in social structure. Three key trends have often been invoked as factors producing declining levels of cleavage voting: rising levels of citizen affluence (e.g., Brooks and Brady, 1999) and increased upward intergenerational social mobility (Heath et al., 1995); increasing levels of education and cognitive capacities of voters (e.g., Nie et al., 1979; Inglehart, 1990:Chap. 10); and the changing size of key groups in the electorate (Manza and Brooks, 1999:Chap. 7; Heath et al., 2001:Chap. 7).

Taken together, these social structural changes tend not to lead to simple or unidirectional consequences. Social structural factors that push voters in one direction may be offset by other changes that pull in other directions. For example, rising affluence has frequently been accompanied by rising levels of class inequality (e.g., Danziger and Gottschalk, 1995; Fischer et al., 1996), which can result in class divisions (e.g., Greenberg and Skocpol, 1997). It is also likely that some social structural changes are producing new social cleavages. Consider the case of gender. Women, including those with small children, have become much more likely to hold full-time jobs in the 1990s than they were in the 1950s (Spain and Bianchi, 1996). The gender "wage gap" between men and women has, however, declined only modestly, mostly among younger cohorts in which women gained greater access to occupations (including opportunities in lower- and middle-level management and the professions) previously monopolized by men (e.g., Bernhardt, Morris, and Handcock, 1995). Greater exposure to workplace inequality contributes to a growing political cleavage between men and women (Manza and Brooks, 1998; Stryker and Eliason, 2002).

Next, group-level factors. A number of scholars have asserted that declines in group consciousness are important factors. There have been a number of arguments about the decline of class-consciousness (e.g., Pakulski and Waters, 1996; Kingston, 2000), old-fashioned racism (Sniderman and Carmines, 1997), and religious group (denominational) consciousness (e.g., Wuthnow, 1988, 1993). In the case of class and religion, most of the broad historical interpretations that have been advanced have emphasized the decline of homogeneous communities that helped to reinforce group consciousness (see especially Pakulski and Waters, 1996). The decline of such communities and the accompanying growth of social and religious mobility weaken the strength of group ties and the capacity of a cleavage to influence voting behavior.

Group consciousness in other cleavage fields may be increasing over time, or at least there may be more complex patterns emerging. Consider the case of race in shaping U.S. voting behavior. The larger debate extends beyond what we can cover in this chapter (for our previous analysis, see Manza and Brooks, 1999:Chap. 6; Manza, 2000; see also James and Reading, this volume). On the one hand, explicit racism has eroded (Schuman, et al. 1997), but a number of analysts have explored the rise and persistence of new forms of "subtle" or "symbolic" racism (Sears et al. 2000). At least with respect to U.S. voting behavior, there is relatively little reason to think that the main black–white divide has narrowed (e.g., Dawson, 1994; Manza and Brooks, 1999:Chap. 6), although the precise role of racial group interests and symbolic attitudes remains a fruitful topic for further research.

Finally, political and organizational factors. In the previous section, we discussed the role of organizations in reinforcing cleavage-based divisions in relation to turnout. Many of the same organizational factors that influence participation shape the vote. Unions, churches, interest groups, political organizations, and social movements push supporters and members of particular groups not only to turn out to vote, but also to support particular candidates or parties.

With respect to political parties, however, there are important differences between mobilization and vote-getting strategies. It is now clear that most of the parties that once sought to organize on the basis of a specific cleavage – especially class or religion – have tended to broaden their appeals over time; those parties that have not have tended to see their vote shares shrink drastically. Using a model of socialist parties as rational vote-seeking organizations, Przeworski and Sprague (1986) provide good reasons for understanding the logic of broadening party appeals. As the size of the working class electorate declines, incentives to launch class-based appeals decline in favor of cross-class appeals that will also win votes from middle class voters, in turn discouraging class-based voting. A similar model can be applied to religious parties (see Manza and Wright, 2003).

In analyzing the overall impact of social cleavages on major parties' electoral coalitions, bias in turnout must be combined with differences in group size and group-based political alignments. When these three components are combined, we can estimate the respective influence of any group of voters within the major party coalitions (Axelrod, 1972; Erikson, Romero, and Lancaster, 1989; Stanley and Niemi, 1993; Bartels, 1998). The approach of Manza and Brooks (1999:Chap. 7) and Heath et al. (2001:Chap. 7) developed such estimates for the electoral coalitions of U.S. and British political parties. The trend analyses undertaken by these authors showed extraordinary changes in the shape of the major left party coalition in each country: Both the Labour Party and the Democratic Party have undergone a major shift from a party with far more working class voters than professional and managerial voters, to parties with far larger representations of the latter (with the Democratic Party going from a 3:1 ratio of working class to professional/managerial voters in 1960 to a 1:1 ratio by 1996, and the Labour Party going from 5.2:1 ratio in 1974 to a 1.7:1 ratio in 1997). With such a vast shift in where the votes come from, it can hardly be surprising that these parties have altered their political appeals over the years.

SOCIAL CLEAVAGES AND CAMPAIGN FINANCE

Dramatic increases in the availability of money in the American political system in recent decades have prompted widespread concern, suggesting to many observers an important extension of the class cleavage in electoral politics. To be sure, the availability of large amounts of money to finance political campaigns is hardly a recent phenomena (e.g., Corrado, 1997). For example, in the first of her pioneering studies of campaign contributions, Overlacker (1932) found that nearly 70 percent of all money contributed to the 1928 federal election campaigns came from donations of over $1,000. But it is in the recent period that concerns about the increasing role of money in politics have erupted into widespread declarations regarding "the expanding corruption of money in all its pervasive ways" leading to "the debasement of American politics over the past twenty-five years," as one veteran political journalist recently characterized it (Drew, 1999:vii; see also Broder, 2000).

In this section, we consider the role of money and campaign finance in shaping elections and public policy. Consistent with the broader goals of the chapter, an examination of campaign finance shows how a cleavage-based analysis is usefully expanded beyond individual- and group-level dynamics to grasp the full range of the political impacts of money. In particular, as we will discuss below, vast disparities in the resources provided to politicians by different classes and interest groups constitute a potentially important component of the class cleavage in the organizational and institutional sphere of American electoral process. But at the same time, it is important to consider the causal force of money in relation to other social forces that shape the dynamics of elections and policy making; doing so suggests that some of the alarm over the impact of big money may be misplaced.

The Regulatory Context

Fears that wealthy corporate and individual campaign donors were buying government influence early in the twentieth century led to an initial attempt at campaign finance reform, the Tillman Act of 1907, which sought to ban corporate contributions to federal campaigns. The effectiveness of this legislation, however, was limited by lack of enforcement and its susceptibility to loopholes. Similar limitations have characterized the numerous attempts at campaign finance reform right up to the present (Corrado, 1997; Goidel et al., 1999; and Mutch, 2001).

The Federal Election Campaign Act (FECA) of 1971, along with key modifying amendments in 1974, 1976, and 1979, defines the landscape of money and politics today. The act put into place new requirements for the disclosure of money received by candidates while placing new limitations on contributions to candidates and political parties. Under the 1974 amendments to the act, each election individuals may contribute up to $1,000 to a candidate, $5,000 to a Political Action Committee (PAC), and $20,000 to national parties, but no more than $25,000 total; PACs are allowed to contribute up to $5,000 each election to a candidate, $5,000 to other PACs, and $15,000 to national parties. "Soft money" contributions were made legal in the 1979 amendment to the FECA; these contributions have no ceiling but are limited to party-building activities, such as get-out-the-vote drives and issue advertisements (see Potter, 1997; Magleby, 2002).

In a recent attempt to eliminate the influence of very large soft money contributions coming overwhelmingly (as we note below) from business sources, the Bipartisan Campaign Reform Act of 2002 prohibits (after the 2002 election) national party committees from accepting and spending soft money contributions, though it also allows for increased individual contribution limits. The legislation is unlikely to fundamentally alter the system of campaign finance, however, insofar as soft money is allowed for voter registration, get-out-the-vote efforts, and other allegedly nonpartisan activities. Further, the new legislation also does not set any limits on independent soft money for ideological or issue campaigns. In general, the use of proxies to funnel money to preferred candidates as a substitute for soft money donations can, if anything, be expected to increase.

Social Cleavages and Campaign Finance: Overview

Where does political money come from, and how can we characterize the overall division of funds? Contributions come from either individual donors or from PACs. PAC contributions can be divided into three broad categories: business-related, labor, and ideological PACs. Business PAC contributions are defined here as donations made by corporate PACs and nonlabor membership organizations such as trade, business, and health associations; labor PACs are those PACs generally associated with single unions, although the most prominent labor PAC is the AFL-CIO's Committee on Political Education (COPE); finally, ideological PACs are formed around single issues or explicit party support rather than sponsoring organizations. In addition to money given to PACs, individuals account for a large proportion of total donations, and a vast majority of the largest of these contributions are made by affluent individuals or families.

Table 10.1 presents a summary of the distribution of PAC contributions to congressional campaigns from the 1978 to the 2000 election cycle. Money contributed by PACs increased nearly eightfold during this period (from approximately $34 million to $260 million dollars), with business PACs increasing their giving from $20.7 million to $152.5 million. Although organized labor also increased its donations during this period, the relative share of business PAC contributions increased significantly, rising from just over twice that of organized labor in 1978 to more than three times as much in 2000. Total contributions doubled from the 1992 (the first year for which detailed reporting of soft money donations are available) to the 2000 election cycle, rising from approximately $591 million in 1992 to $853 million in 1996 to almost $1.4 billion in 2000 (Center for Responsive Politics, 2002).

In addition to these "hard money" contributions, an increasingly important source of campaign donations is reflected in "soft money" contributions. These are donations that are not regulated or limited by federal law and that may be used for party-building activities – such as voter registration drives and general campaigning for the party (e.g., bumper stickers and lawn signs) – as opposed to the direct, "hard money" election expenses that are regulated by the FECA. Before 1990, soft money contributions were not required by law to be reported, so systematic data on soft money contributions are only available beginning with the 1992 election cycle. During this ten-year span, however, there was a dramatic increase in total soft money contributions: from $75 million to $410 million dollars. Business soft money contributions completely dwarf those of labor and ideological groups. Consider, for example, the 2000 election cycle. Business organizations contributed a total of $368.9 million in soft money, whereas

Table 10.1. *Trends in Campaign Finance, 1978–2000*

Election Cycle	Business PAC contributions (in millions of dollars)	Business soft money contributions (in millions of dollars)	Labor PAC contributions (in millions of dollars)	Labor soft money contributions (in millions of dollars)	Ideological PAC contributions (in millions of dollars)[1]	Ideological soft money contributions (in millions of dollars)[2]	Total individual contributions (in millions of dollars)
1978	20.7		9.9		2.5		
1980	34.9		13.2		4.9		
1982	49.9		20.3		10.7		
1984	62.7		24.8		14.5		
1986	62.7		29.9		18.8		
1988	79.0		33.9		19.2		
1990	88.9		33.6		14.3		142.3
1992	115.3	69.0	39.4	4.3	17.4	1.3	322.0
1994	114.7	69.4	40.7	4.4	17.5	5.1	262.7
1996	125.6	193.0	46.6	9.5	22.0	4.2	419.2
1998	130.2	162.2	43.3	10.3	27.1	3.8	333.3
2000	152.5	368.9	50.1	30.4	35.7	10.4	698.3

[1] PAC data are from the Federal Election Commission. Data for the 1978 to 1984 election cycles are from Corrado et al. (1997); data for the 1986 to 2000 election cycles are from the Federal Election Commission Web site (www.fec.gov).

[2] Soft money donation estimates are from the Center for Responsive Politics (2002).

organized labor provided just $30.4 million (up from $4.3 million in 1992, although some of that increase reflects changed reporting requirements in which in-kind contributions are now required to be reported) and ideological groups $10.4 million. The ratio of business to labor contributions is thus vastly more skewed with respect to soft money donations: Business soft money contributions were twelve times greater than labor in 2000, fifteen times greater in 1998, and twenty times greater in 1996. The total share of campaign resources coming from business sources (PAC donations and soft money contributions) has steadily increased during the last twenty years. In 1978 the ratio of business to labor donations was 2.1:1; it had reached 6.5:1 by the 2000 election cycle.

Aside from business and labor PACs, the other two major categories of donors are "ideological" PACs (Clawson et al., 1998) and individual donors. As part of the larger trend toward increasing political donations, ideological PACs have also increased their giving in recent years, contributing almost as much as labor PACs in the 2000 election cycle in hard money (though much smaller amounts in the form of soft money donations). The largest share of ideological PAC money – approximately 40 percent of the total amount of hard money provided by these PACs in the 2000 cycle – is that given by so-called leadership PACs, organized by current or former political officeholders for the purpose of making donations to other candidates or PACs (Center for Responsive Politics, 2002). Among the other largest ideological PACs were single-issue groups such as the National Rifle Association, EMILY's List, and the National Committee to Preserve Social Security. Some ideological PACs associated with the major parties were also significant donors in this category; Americans for a Republican Majority (the third-largest ideological donor in this category during the 2000 election cycle) made all of its contributions to Republican candidates, while the National Committee for an Effective Congress (the sixth-largest donor in the category) gave 100 percent of its contributions to Democratic candidates (Center for Responsive Politics, 2002).

In addition to money coming from organizations, millions of Americans make campaign donations in their own names (or those of family members). Most of these donations are in small amounts, but when we consider larger individual contributions (over $200), the class disparity in donations is substantial. For example, the Center for Responsive Politics (2002) was able to categorize about 70 percent of such donations for the 2000 election cycle. They reported that individuals associated with business interests contributed a total of $533.7 million to election campaigns, compared with less than $1 million contributed by individuals associated with organized labor.

Burris (2001) cautioned against assuming that individual donations by corporate officers are likely to be identical to the giving of the corporation's PAC, because individual contributions, even those provided by individuals connected to corporate interests, tend to be motivated more by (usually conservative) ideology. He found evidence to this effect in a study of the 1980 campaign, finding a more strongly pro-Republican tilt of individual donors (see also Biersack, 1999). The fact that such donations may be connected to partisanship does nothing to reduce the disparity in overall resources, and may in fact tend to magnify the political consequences as Democrats receive a smaller share of such donations than they would from less partisan donor motivations.

Survey data on individual-level giving to political campaigns is consistent with this finding; patterns of significant giving are heavily skewed toward individuals from affluent households. For example, Verba et al. (1995:191–6) found that 56 percent of households with incomes over $125,000 (in 1989) donated to a political campaign, with the average amount of all donations being $1,183, compared with only 6 percent of households with incomes below $15,000 (who gave an average of $86). Surveying large ($200 or more) contributors to the 1996 congressional campaign, Biersack et al. (1999) reported that 79.5 percent of large donors had incomes over $100,000, and 42.4 percent had incomes over $250,000. These authors found that large donors are far more conservative politically than NES respondents (with only 29 percent identifying as Democrats, compared with 52.4 percent of the NES sample for that year), but they are more liberal on social issues than the entire NES sample.

We can now answer the question posed at the beginning of this section. Organized labor constitutes the main counterweight to business contributions, with contributions from ideological PACs and individuals scattered across the ideological spectrum. Labor's contributions are made almost completely through PACs and soft money donations, with very few donations coming from individuals connected to the labor movement. Estimating the contributions of business only through PAC and soft money donations, however, significantly underestimates the overall contributions of the capitalist class as a whole because of the large share of the total donations by individuals connected to business interests. A rough estimate of the total gap between business and labor sources suggests that in recent election cycles, the ratio of business to labor donations is more than ten to one.

Other Cleavages in Campaign Finance

Although class divisions in campaign finance are the most pronounced, other social cleavage impacts have been noted as well. For example, although data about the religious backgrounds of contributors are poorly documented (as contributors are not required by the FEC to list their religious affiliations) and much of the most visible activity of religious groups is more activist than financial, there is one particularly notable religious cleavage in campaign finance: clear evidence that Jewish contributors account for a significant proportion of Democratic contributions (see Domhoff, 1972, 1990:Chap. 9). Webber and Domhoff's (Webber, 2000; Webber and Domhoff, 1996) historical research on the New Deal showed that among religiously identifiable large contributions, Jews were overwhelmingly the largest bloc of Democratic donors. This pattern has continued in more recent elections (see Domhoff, 1990:245–7 for an overview). Allen and Broyles (1989) found, for example, that members of wealthy Jewish families contributed far more money to the Democratic Party than members of wealthy families in general; Cohen (1989) estimated that Jewish contributors have provided half of all individual Democratic Party donations outside of the South since 1960. Burris (2001:374) estimated that 60 percent of Jewish capitalists gave to the Democrats in 1980, compared to 24 percent for non-Jewish capitalists in his sample.

There is also evidence of a gender gap in campaign finance. The most systematic effort to compare rates of giving by men and women reported that in the 1990s, donations from women accounted for only a quarter of individual hard money contributions and one-seventh to one-eighth of individual soft money contributions (Biersack et al., 1999; Weber, 2002). Further, because some wealthy contributors, usually male, also donate money to candidates or PACs in their spouses' name to avoid donation limits, the gender gap in campaign finance, particularly with respect to hard money, may actually be even larger than these figures would suggest. A modest counterweight to the perception of male dominance in campaign finance is the increasing prominence over the past twenty years of women's organizations like EMILY's List, the Women's Campaign Fund, and Wish List, ideological PACs that contribute sufficient amounts to be visible. No comparable men's PACs exist.

A Note on In-Kind Donations

Although most of the literature on campaign finance focuses on direct giving, a second broad category of contributions has particular relevance for social cleavage impacts: in-kind contributions of voluntary activism provided directly or indirectly to political campaigns. Determining the precise value of such in-kind contributions is impossible (Alexander and Haggerty, 1985), but it is nonetheless frequently an important source of support for political campaigns. Survey data suggest that voluntary activity on behalf of political candidates is drawn much more evenly than financial contributions;

although poorer households are still underrepresented among all activists, far more hours are contributed by poor and middle income household than affluent ones (see Verba et al., 1995:191ff.). With respect to organized groups, business organizations have relatively little apparatus for providing in-kind contributions, but religious groups, unions, and organizations such as the National Rifle Association or pro-choice groups frequently work on behalf of particular candidates or political initiatives.

Of further note are the activities of religious and labor organizations. Perhaps recognizing the vast disparities in resources discussed above, AFL-CIO president John Sweeney has maintained that political activism, not money, is the key to labor's political influence (see, e.g., R. Gerber, 1999; Asher et al., 2001:107). Unions are especially well-equipped to generate manpower for political campaigns because of an organizational structure with paid staff at the national, state, and local levels to generate, maintain, and coordinate activity. The activities that union members have typically provided include distribution of voting literature, soliciting campaign contributions, working at phone banks, participating in voter registration drives, organizing and attending candidate meetings, putting up yard signs, and working at party headquarters (Asher et al., 2001:123). It has been estimated that during one particularly intense mobilization – on behalf of Walter Mondale's bid for the Democratic presidential nomination in 1984 – unions provided some $10 million to $20 million worth of in-kind contributions (Dark, 1999:132). (Note, however, that under current laws some of those in-kind donations, such as the use of office space, would now be officially recorded; see Alexander, 1992.)

Religious organizations have also provided important in-kind contributions in recent years. Although many mainline Protestant churches have long sponsored political action of various kinds among their laity (see Wuthnow and Evans, 2002), the most prominent type of in-kind contributions have been those of the Christian Right. As discussed previously, in-kind contributions by the Christian Right on behalf of Republican candidates have been especially significant in the past two decades.

Using Campaign Finance Data to Investigate Capitalist Class Influence

A recurring focus of the political sociological literature on money and politics has been to test various power-elite and business class segment theories using campaign finance data (e.g., Clawson, Neustadtl, and Bearden, 1986; Clawson and Neustadtl, 1989; Ferguson and Rogers, 1986; Burris, 1987; 2001; Boies, 1989; Mizruchi, 1989; Domhoff, 1990; Ferguson, 1995). In general, scholarship in the power-elite tradition has held that pluralist models (e.g., Ippolito and Walker, 1980; Malbin, 1980; Sabato, 1984) significantly understate the unity of business interests with respect to particular types of legislation or the pursuit of a broad pro-business agenda (e.g., Clawson, Neustadtl, and Bearden, 1986; Domhoff, 1990:Chap. 9, 2002; but see Smith, 2000). Beyond that, however, there is little agreement over the sources of business unity in spite of a wealth of attempts to formulate theories about capitalist class divisions along regional, industrial, or market sector factors.

A central issue concerning business political donations is whether they are motivated by pragmatic or ideological goals. Pragmatic donations are given in order to gain access to politicians, regardless of their party affiliation or ideological positions, and are most often measured by the percentage of donations given to incumbents (as they are obviously most likely to be reelected). The aim of ideological contributions, on the other hand, is to alter the composition of the government by giving money to politicians who share the contributor's political view; ideological behavior is usually measured by the similarity of donation patterns between a corporation's PAC and PACs explicitly oriented toward ideological issues. The distinction between these types of contributions has a long history in the literature (Gopoian, 1984; Clawson and Neustadtl, 1989; Clawson et al., 1998). Evidence from both quantitative and qualitative studies suggests that pragmatic giving is by far the more common form and that corporate PACs with ideological orientations are outliers. Clawson et al. (1998), for example, reported that during the 1996 election cycle, "almost 4 out of 5 large corporate PACs gave at least 70 percent of their money to incumbents, and a majority gave at least 80 percent to incumbents" (39). When business donations are ideological, they likely go to conservatives and to tight races (1998:39).

Analyzing pragmatic donations is important because it helps to explain why the results of past studies of corporate divisions in campaign finance have proven disappointing (see Burris, 2001:363). Two sets of findings stand out. Mizruchi's (1989, 1990) work on the political dynamics of corporate interlocks provided evidence in support of one version of power-elite theory (see also Useem, 1984; Mintz and Schwartz, 1985; Domhoff, 1990). In this work, interlocking directorates are hypothesized as providing network relations that foster similar patterns of political contribution. Mizruchi's results suggest that indirect ties among corporations – namely, shared relations with financial institutions – are positively associated with donation patterns (see Mizruchi, 1996 for a more recent overview). Second, studies exploring a range of explanatory factors to account for political divisions among the capitalist class, particularly in the context of a possible rightward shift in the late 1970s, found two factors that were important: the degree of governmental regulation in an industry and the extent of a firm's defense contracting (Clawson et al., 1985, 1986; Clawson and Neustadtl, 1989; Burris, 1987; Burris and Salt, 1990).

Skewed Outcomes? Assessing the Political Impact of Money in American Politics

The vast bulk of the scholarly literature on campaign finance focuses not on theories about the underlying cleavages among business donors, but rather on the overall impact of money on elections and public policy. We can organize the extensive debates over campaign finance in terms of a timeline, marking the respective points in which money might influence political outcomes. The main points along this timeline are the following: (1) the role of money in influencing who runs; (2) the role of money in affecting who is elected; (3) the role of money in shaping the voting patterns of those who are elected; and (4) related to the impact on legislative voting patterns, the impact of money in influencing other actions of legislators. At every stage of this process, there are arguments about the power of money to skew outcomes; but equally importantly, in no area is money universally viewed as a decisive factor.

Many of the recent debates turn on complex methodological issues, what two leading analysts have described as "the statistical morass that surrounds the study of campaign finance" (Ansolabehere and Gerber, 1994:1115). We do not have the space here to discuss the debates over competing statistical approaches, but several common issues appear repeatedly. Most notably, there are linked questions about simultaneity bias and assumptions about the exogeneity of money in the political process. For example, models that treat campaign contributions as an exogenous variable tend to ignore the possibility that PACs give legislators money *because* these legislators vote in a particular way. Such models are unable to distinguish between these two scenarios. The most sophisticated attempts to model the role of money at any of the four stages include parameters for capturing processes that may shape *both* the amounts of money received and their impact.

Who Runs. The debate over patterns of political recruitment primarily concerns the question of whether incumbent war chests (or war chests of one candidate in an open seat) deter potential challengers or, alternatively, encourage some types of challenges while discouraging others. On the question of deterrence, campaign funds may indirectly affect the quality of a challenger by signaling to potential rivals the commitment of the incumbent (or the front-runner) to winning the race, as well as the (large) amount of resources that will be needed to be competitive (see, e.g., Sorauf, 1992; Epstein and Zemsky, 1995; Box-Steffensmeier, 1996).

In the signaling process, early fund-raising plays a much greater strategic role than late fund-raising (Epstein and Zemsky, 1995). Because early fund-raising is much easier for candidates who already have access to elite money networks, some have argued that the early fund-raising process constitutes a "money primary" (Magleby and Nelson, 1990:58–61; Clawson et al., 1998:Chap. 1; Domhoff, 2002, Chap. 6). In the money primary, just as in the actual election, momentum and visible evidence of a high probability of ultimate success are key factors in being able to raise money; many affluent candidates also give or loan their campaigns substantial money from their own pocket to provide campaign start-up funds. The money primary is important because it serves to eliminate potential challengers who do not have access to the same types of resources as incumbents or front-runners (Magleby and Nelson, 1990:Chap. 4). In a more speculative vein, it may force challengers to tailor messages in ways that will appeal to potential donors.

There have been challenges to claims about the importance of money in influencing who runs for office. Large war chests rarely deter challengers who expect to have access to significant resources themselves. Critics of the money primary hypothesis have also asserted that because only "quality" challengers have a chance of defeating incumbents, and because "quality" challengers are rarely deterred by incumbent money, the true effect of war chests is very small (e.g., Krasno and Green, 1988; Bauer and Hibbing, 1989; Jacobson, 1990; Goodliffe, 2001). Goodliffe (2001), for example, argued that war chests provide little information that challengers do not already have about the incumbent. If past election performance and behavior in office are included in the model, the deterring effect of war chests falls significantly. Finally, the measurement of the relationship between war chests and deterrence is complicated by evidence that the fund-raising of incumbents is often tied to the real or anticipated quality of the challenger (Krasno and Green, 1988; Krasno, Green, and Cowden, 1994). Because the size of war chests is in some cases partially determined by the existence and quality of challengers, the effects of war chests on potential opponents are difficult to measure.

Who Wins. Aside from the impact of money on candidate selection, there are large controversies over the question of whether, once the major party candidates are selected, the amount of money involved in an election significantly influences the outcome. A striking feature of political money in the contemporary era is that there is usually relatively little overall difference between how much the major parties raise or even how much of that money comes from business sources. As a consequence, questions about who wins do not have clear partisan implications. Indeed, from the standpoint of resources, it is hard to resist the suggestion by Clawson et al. (1998) that the United States has only one major party: the "money party" (91). Those who are unable to raise substantial resources simply do not make it to this stage of the political process.

One important way in which this question has been framed is by reference to a policy-related controversy: Would setting limits on expenditures help or hurt challengers? Some analysts have argued that money plays a much bigger role in determining the success of challengers, whereas the marginal benefit for incumbents is fairly small (e.g., Jacobson, 1980, 1990; Abramowitz, 1991). Other analysts have argued that campaign spending is an important determinant of both incumbent and challenger success (e.g., Green and Krasno, 1988; Erikson and Palfrey, 1998; A. Gerber, 1998). The key to the latter set of findings centers around the endogenous role of money. Rational incumbents will raise and spend more money in close elections, that is, in elections they are more likely to lose, than those that are one-sided in their favor (e.g., A. Gerber, 1998). Because many incumbents spend little and win easily and those spending more have a greater likelihood of losing, it looks as if spending has little effect on outcomes for incumbents if spending is treated as an exogenous variable in a regression model. The policy implications of the latter set of findings are that spending limits would help to create more competitive elections by aiding challengers (see especially Green and Krasno, 1988; A. Gerber, 1998).

Legislative Voting Patterns. Does money influence legislative votes on policy, either for individual legislators or in the aggregate? Periodic scandals excite journalistic outrage. But what is the larger picture? With little, if any, direct evidence of systematic vote selling (see, e.g., Milyo, 1997; Milyo et al., 2000), much hinges on the assumptions of measures and statistical models. Early examinations treating political donations as an exogenous variable were split inconclusively between those finding that contributions influence voting patterns (Silberman and Durden, 1976; Frendreis and Waterman, 1985; Ginsberg and Green, 1986) and those finding no effect (Welch, 1982; Wright, 1985, 1989). The different findings were often attributed to the variance of issues on which votes were cast and competing approaches to measurement issues.

A related but more sophisticated version of the influence argument suggests the existence of a "spot market" in which votes are exchanged for contributions. Proponents of this approach (Austen-Smith, 1987; Baron, 1989; Stern, 1992; Stratmann, 1992, 1998) claim that contributions are short-term investments through which the donor will secure political favors (such as votes on relevant issues or the framing of legislation in ways that are beneficial to the donor) and/or ensure that legislators honor past agreements. Short of legislators admitting that their voting behavior was influenced by PAC donations, however, direct evidence of money buying votes is almost impossible to find except for explicit scandals. Members of Congress can always claim that voting behavior leads to contributions from like-minded PACs, rather than vice versa. In lieu of direct evidence, scholars have attempted to support the spot market hypothesis by showing that PAC behavior closely corresponds to behavior one would expect if votes were being exchanged for contributions. Stratmann's (1992) analysis of the behavior of PACs associated with the farming industry is illustrative, finding that these PACs tend to contribute more money to legislators whose voting decisions are uncertain than those who are expected to vote in the PAC's interest. This suggests that a relationship between PAC contributions and voting patterns cannot be solely attributed to shared political interests (i.e., PACs give money to certain candidates *because* they vote in accordance to the PAC's interest), but instead indicate attempts by PACs to sway undecided legislators.

Critics of the vote-buying thesis abound. A second generation of research on the influence of money on votes has introduced techniques for distinguishing how voting behavior influences PAC contributions as well as how PAC contributions influence voting behavior (e.g., Grenzke, 1989; Levitt, 1998; Wawro, 2001). This line of work suggests that contributions do not dictate voting patterns in a unidimensional fashion, that is, from money to votes. Other more recent critics of the view that money changes votes have further pointed out, plausibly, that the scholarly attention given to the influence of PAC contributions on voting patterns is exaggerated for the simple reason that PACs do not contribute enough money to be very influential. Legislators are, in this view, not capable of being bought off with contributions from a single PAC (even if the PAC gives the maximum $5,000). House incumbents are likely to spend upwards of $1 million on reelection (and Senate incumbents far more), amounts that rise in competitive races. Those holding "safe" seats should be even less subject to influence (see, e.g., Milyo et al., 2000).

The theoretical case for impact thus requires a more nuanced interpretation than a simple vote-buying thesis would suggest. Indeed, one model argues that the relationship between contributors and legislators is best understood as a long-term commitment. Neustadtl (1990), for example, reported that "PAC directors indicate that there is a long-term give-and-take established between interest groups and members and that, as a political player, one cannot be concerned only with legislative outcomes" (559). In explicitly theorizing this relationship, Clawson, Neustadtl, and their colleagues drew upon Mauss's famous analysis of the gift to argue that donations create a "gift" relationship in which periodic small favors are exchanged, but not any specific or immediate responses on the part of the recipient legislator (i.e., voting a particular way on a particular issue) (Clawson et al., 1998; see also Schram, 1995). Like a gift, the donation implies unnamed obligations and acts of reciprocity (i.e., legislators will attend, whenever possible, to the interests of contributors with whom they have a relationship) (e.g., Clawson et al., 1998:84–7).

One intriguing empirical test of this view is the contention that long-term gift relationships should skew the distribution of money given by PACs to the same members over and over, and that seniority should thus be a factor. Indeed, Snyder (1992) found that PACs tend to contribute to similar sets of legislators over time and that policy makers who have long careers in front of them (those with high electoral security, those who are relatively younger, and/or those whose career trajectories are ascendent) receive higher shares of PAC contributions than those who do not. Similarly, Grier and Munger (1991) and Romer and Snyder (1994) found that a disproportionate amount of money goes to committee chairs and legislators who are on committees relevant to the contributing PACs.

Access and Extravoting Influence. Although questions about the direct influence of PACs on votes remain, there is little disagreement among analysts that PAC money buys access (see, for example, Hall and Wayman, 1990; Austen-Smith, 1995; McCarty and Rothenberg, 1996; Clawson et al., 1998). The question is, what exactly does access provide? Critics of the proposition that access matters have questioned the lack of direct evidence of its influence on legislation (e.g., Milyo et al., 2000; Wawro, 2000).

The most straightforward claims about the role of access maintain simply that it provides a regular opportunity for interest groups/contributors to prime legislators with information or interpretations about specific policy issues; and that all else being equal, legislators are more than willing to listen to contributors when they are uncertain (Sabato, 1984; Langbein, 1986; Wright, 1990; Rothenberg, 1992). Because so much of what Congress does is not directly visible to the public or subject to media scrutiny, access may provide privileged opportunities for influence not easily available to noncontributing groups or individuals. Indeed, some research suggests that the influence of contributions on legislators' behavior is most apparent in cases of low public visibility (e.g., Frendreis and Waterman, 1985; Schroedel, 1986; Jones and Keiser, 1987; Neustadtl, 1990).

CONCLUSION

In this chapter, we have considered political sociological models of social cleavages, focusing on empirical implications for studying political participation, voting behavior, and campaign finance. We outlined a theoretical approach to cleavages that distinguishes the mechanisms through which cleavages are produced (specifically economic, psychological, and network factors) and the processes through which they become manifest (in social structures, group consciousness, political and organizational forms, and feedback processes). We believe this approach provides a coherent way of organizing a large set of scholarly debates concerning the connections between a diverse range of related topics in political sociology. It also suggests new questions and directions for research in this area. For example, future studies of social cleavages in voting should pay attention to how cleavages are organized by parties and/or other powerful institutional actors as well as simply documenting their existence in the political system as a whole. Studies of campaign finance would similarly benefit from linking institutional and organizational processes through which inequalities in funding are maintained to the core questions of who gives and with what impacts.

A multilevel approach incorporating individual, group, and political/institutional processes provides a useful check on premature dismissals of social cleavage impacts on political outcomes. It forces us to see, for example, that cleavages can persist in some domains even while they may be declining in others. For example, levels of class voting in recent American elections have eroded, but the class skew in turnout persists and has grown rapidly in the case of campaign finance. To say that class is a minor factor in American politics, as, for example, Kingston (2000:Chap. 6) does, thus requires an unduly restrictive focus. Viewed more broadly and taking into account the full range of processes through which class divisions become manifest (including feedback processes), we arrive at a much different conclusion.

Such considerations suggest that the investigation of social cleavages will remain an important part of any comprehensive assessment of political divisions in democratic polities. To be sure, sociological models that focus on social cleavages to the exclusion of other, more proximate forces shaping political behavior will generate little new knowledge about the linkages between inequality and political institutions. To make significant contributions to the study of electoral politics in the future, political sociology will have to engage a wider range of theoretical and empirical concerns in their work and build connections to related work in political science (see McAdam and Su, 2002; Brooks et al., 2003). But at the same time, we see no reason to conclude that social influences on electoral outcomes have become irrelevant to understanding election outcomes or the policy-making process.

CHAPTER ELEVEN

Public Opinion, Political Attitudes, and Ideology

David L. Weakliem

This chapter devotes roughly equal attention to recent research and work from the 1950s and 1960s. This dual focus is necessary because of the history of public opinion research. Political sociologists originally played a prominent part but tended to abandon the field after the late 1960s, for reasons that are discussed in the section on recent research. Hence, most contemporary public opinion research is oriented toward social psychology. The older research attempted to address macrosociological questions such as the sources of stable democracy or variations in the strength of socialist parties and hence remains relevant to the interests of political sociologists.

The chapter begins with a discussion of the distinction between sociological and political approaches to public opinion. Next, three strands of research from the 1950s and 1960s are reviewed: the Columbia voting studies, which focused on networks of communication and their role in creating and maintaining group differences; the Michigan studies, which focused on explaining short-term political change; and the "social cleavages" approach represented by Lipset (1960[1981]), which focused on long-term change and national comparisons. After discussing the reasons for the decline of public opinion research in political sociology, I then review four areas of contemporary research: the relationship between economic development and public opinion; framing and ideology; the effect of public opinion on policy, and "policy feedback" or the effect of policy on public opinion. Finally, the concluding section suggests directions for future research.

SOCIOLOGICAL AND POLITICAL RESEARCH

Research on public opinion developed rapidly after the appearance of sample surveys in the mid-1930s. Of course, the idea of public opinion was considerably older, and there had been some notable studies of the topic, such as those of De Tocqueville (1969[1850]), Dicey (1914), and Bryce (1897). However, the development of surveys greatly expanded the opportunities for systematic research. In fact, Osborne and Rose (1999) argue that survey research helped to create the modern sense of public opinion – as the aggregate of the views held by the entire adult population. Before the twentieth century, "public opinion" was often used in other senses, such as the opinions of knowledgeable or public-spirited persons or opinions that were expressed publicly. Some critics of public opinion research, including Blumer (1948) and Schlesinger (1962), have charged that surveys do not measure public opinion in the traditional sense. This issue is relevant to some contemporary research, and is considered in the section on ideology and framing but in general I use "public opinion" in the conventional modern sense. Opinions are sometimes distinguished from attitudes, with attitudes defined as predispositions that underlie specific opinions (Erikson and Tedin, 2001:6). Some observers distinguish a still deeper level, values, which can be defined as qualities that a person regards as desirable and important (Rokeach, 1968). For example, the value of equality will influence a wide variety of attitudes and opinions. However, even when these distinctions are made, the field of public opinion research is usually understood to include attitudes and values as well as opinions. In this chapter, no distinction is made between opinions and attitudes, but "values" is used in the sense given above.

The first major survey-based studies of public opinion were carried out by the Bureau of Applied Social Research at Columbia University (Berelson, Lazarsfeld, and McPhee, 1954; Lazarsfeld, Berelson, and Gaudet, 1944). Somewhat later, a group of social psychologists and political scientists at the University of Michigan began a series of national election studies, which culminated in a major work by Campbell, Converse, Miller, and Stokes (1960). The Michigan group had a great deal of influence on the subsequent development of public opinion research. The Columbia group did not continue beyond the mid-1950s, but a number of political sociologists, notably Seymour Martin Lipset, built on their work in the 1960s (Lipset, 1981[1960]; Lipset, 1970).

There is not much evidence of a rivalry between the Columbia and Michigan groups, although there were definite differences of emphasis. *Voting* (Berelson, Lazarsfeld, and McPhee, 1954) received enthusiastic reviews in the *American Political Science Review* and the *Journal of Politics*, and Campbell, Converse, Miller, and Stokes (1960:12–16) spoke of their own work and that of the Columbia school as sharing a common "behavioral" approach. Nevertheless, a conventional distinction between sociological and political approaches developed and persists to this day. As it is usually presented, the sociological approach holds that politics "reflects" social conditions and processes, whereas the political approach holds that politics and political thought are autonomous (Sartori, 1969). There are various ways in which this contrast can be applied. On the simplest level, the issue can be seen as the influence of demographic factors on individual opinions and voting choices: the sociological approach holds that demographic factors are a major influence, whereas the political approach denies this. Lazarsfeld, Berelson, and Gaudet (1944:27) stated "a person thinks, politically, as he is, socially. Social characteristics determine political preference." This passage has been quoted by a number of later authors as an exemplar of the sociological or "social determinist" approach (Cox and McCubbins, 1986:370–1; Pomper, 1978:620). Taken literally, the claim that social characteristics "determine" vote is clearly false. For example, 17 percent of the people in Lazarsfeld, Berelson, and Gaudet's "strongly Democratic" group voted Republican. In fact, just before the previously quoted passage, they made the much weaker claim that "a simple combination of three primary personal characteristics goes a long way in 'explaining' political preferences." Since that time, numerous empirical studies have shown that demographic characteristics virtually always have some predictive power. Different observers might disagree over whether a given association should be characterized as strong or weak, but there is clearly no objective standard for such judgments. Hence, at this level, the distinction between sociological and political views has no theoretical substance.

A related contrast between sociological and political approaches sometimes appears in debates about change in the association between opinions and demographic variables, especially social class. Beginning in the 1970s, a number of observers argued that there had been a decline in the predictive power of class and possibly of other traditionally important variables such as religious denomination. The change was sometimes characterized as a decline in the empirical relevance of a sociological model. According to Whiteley (1986:98), for example, "the sociological account of electoral behavior is clearly obsolescent." Other observers disputed the claim that the influence of class was declining, and the ensuing debate is reviewed in Evans (1999), Manza and Brooks (1999), and Clark (2001). Sociologists tended to be more skeptical about the claims of decline, so in a purely empirical sense the contrast versus sociological and political views has some validity. However, the debate does not easily fit into the framework of sociological versus political *theories*. In fact, Goldthorpe (in Mair, Lipset, Hout, and Goldthorpe, 1999:322) observes that many arguments about the decline of social cleavages are "sociological" in the sense of explaining this development as a reflection of general social changes. For example, Inglehart (1997) argues that economic growth leads to a decline of class conflict.

The political versus sociological contrast can also be applied at the societal level. For example, consider the classic question of the weakness of socialism in the United States. A sociological approach would hold that socialist parties and movements were weak because there was little popular demand for them. The lack of popular demand would be explained by some general conditions of American society such as mass affluence, ethnic divisions, or a high rate of social mobility. A political explanation, such as that proposed by Katznelson (1981), holds that the weakness of the socialist movement explains the subsequent lack of popular demand. The Democratic and Republican parties organized the public before socialist parties arrived on the scene. This initial advantage, combined with institutional factors that made it difficult for third parties to grow, meant that the socialist movement never gained a solid foothold in the United States. Hence, socialists were unable to communicate with a wide audience and cultivate class consciousness in the public.

At this level, the general issue is whether social conditions such as economic development, ethnic heterogeneity, or rates of social mobility have a uniform effect on politics. Sartori (1969) and Przeworski (1985) identify the assumption of uniform effects as the key flaw in the sociological approach. Przeworski (1985:101) asserts that "parties – along with unions, churches, factories, and schools – forge collective identities, instill commitments, define the interests on behalf of which collective actions become possible, offer choices, to individuals and deny them." Consequently, national differences in political alignments represent the accumulated effects of different strategies followed by various political actors.

To summarize, at the individual level the contrast between sociological and political approaches reduces to a question of the weight of various explanatory variables. At the societal level, the contrast has theoretical substance, although it does not correspond closely to disciplinary boundaries.

THE COLUMBIA STUDIES

The earliest major project of the Columbia group was a panel study of the 1940 presidential campaign. This study was primarily concerned with the flow of information and influence through social networks. The most notable finding was that the campaign had little effect on voting choices. The predominant influence appeared to be routine personal contact with family, neighbors, co-workers, and other acquaintances. Although everyday discussions rarely focused on politics, over the course of time people picked up a good deal of information about what other people were thinking. Because personal contacts tend to occur among people who resemble each other, personal influence reinforced voting tendencies within groups. An urban Catholic worker, for example, would talk mostly with other urban Catholic workers. Because the members of this group with strong political preferences would tend to be Democrats, the undecided members would hear opinions and information favorable to the Democrats and would gradually be won over. In between elections, voters might waver, but in times of enhanced political interest, most of the undecided people would return to the party of their friends and family. Despite the efforts of the parties, few voters were persuaded to change sides during the election campaign. As Lazarsfeld (1944:317) put it, "in an important sense, modern Presidential campaigns are over before they begin."

According to the Columbia studies, a small number of "opinion leaders" paid attention to politics and the media and then transmitted their views by personal contact (Katz and Lazarsfeld, 1955). Although these opinion leaders tended to have somewhat higher social standing than other people, they were not exclusively from the middle classes. Rather, different groups had their own opinion leaders. For example, manual workers would be influenced by the views of better informed or more articulate co-workers.

The second major work by the Columbia school was based on a study of the 1948 campaign (Berelson, Lazarsfeld, and McPhee, 1954). This work elaborated the theory of social cleavages implied in the earlier study. Berelson, Lazarsfeld, and McPhee proposed that political cleavages depended on three conditions: difference of interests, transmission to succeeding generations, and differential contact.[1] For example, class is a strong cleavage, not simply because it is related to material interests, but also because there is considerable stability across generations and a tendency to associate within classes. The conclusion was that class, race or ethnicity, and place met these conditions most fully and hence would generally be the most important political cleavages (Berelson, Lazarsfeld, and McPhee, 1954:75).

Subsequent research has confirmed the importance of social interaction in shaping political alignments, while adding some elaborations and qualifications (Huckfeldt and Sprague, 1993). For example, Finifter (1974) noted that tendencies to political uniformity could be mitigated if people with "deviant" views tended to form friendship groups, whereas Wald, Owen, and Hill (1990) found that conservative Protestant churches promoted cohesion on moral issues but that liberal churches did not. Like the original work of the Columbia school, the more recent studies emphasize the forces promoting stability. Although networks of social influence may help to explain the diffusion of new ideas, they do not explain why the ideas emerge in the first place. This weakness was quickly noted by critics of the Columbia school and was one of the factors that motivated a search for alternative models.

THE MICHIGAN STUDIES

A second research group formed around the American National Election Studies, which began with a pilot study in 1948 and a full-scale study in 1952. *The American Voter* (Campbell, Converse, Miller, and Stokes, 1960) was the major work of this group. For the purposes of this review, the Michigan group differed from the Columbia group in two important ways: they paid more attention to short-term change and they attempted to define and measure political ideology.[2]

As mentioned earlier, the explanation of change was a weak point in the Columbia model. If there are significant differences among demographic groups, then changes in the size of the groups will lead to change in the overall distribution of votes or opinions. However, demographic changes occur slowly, whereas the popularity of different parties often varies substantially from one election to the next. The Columbia researchers recognized this fact, but made little effort to explain it. Lazarsfeld (1944:330), for example, merely suggested that "elections are decided by events occurring in the entire period between the two elections," without saying what those events were or why they might have an effect. Authors from the Michigan school noted that there was also significant fluctuation in the strength of social cleavages (Key and Munger, 1959; Converse et al., 1960). For example, although social class continued to be associated with vote in the 1952 election, the connection was noticeably weaker than in 1948.

Campbell, Converse, Miller, and Stokes (1960) suggested that variation in the overall support for parties or opinions reflected the influence of factors that affected all people in roughly the same way. Thus, economic decline would tend to lead to demands for government

[1] Their reasoning suggests that continuity over the life course would also be relevant to the formation of cleavages.

[2] The Michigan group made many other contributions that cannot be discussed here. See Prewitt and Nie (1971) for a more extensive overview.

action, which would mean a move to the left in conventional terms. Variations in the strength of cleavages reflected changes in interest or focus. For example, during periods of international crisis, people might pay less attention to economic interests, so that class differences would decline. Furthermore, these changes in focus were not due solely to outside forces but could be influenced by the parties. For example, a party might choose to emphasize class issues more or less strongly in its appeals to voters. Although the social processes identified by the Columbia group governed the potential size of cleavages, historical or political factors influenced the degree to which this potential was realized (Campbell et al., 1960:369). The possibility of differences in the importance or "salience" of different concerns is an important component of many later accounts, as is discussed in the section on Economic Development and Public Opinion.

The Michigan researchers also attempted to measure political ideology. The Columbia studies had simply relied on the conventional spectrum of left and right, which were defined by class interests. The Michigan researchers, however, sought to discover the extent to which people actually thought in ideological terms. They found that few people offered any kind of ideological justification for their party preferences. Campbell, Converse, Miller, and Stokes (1960) classified only about 15 percent of their respondents as expressing an ideology, and even many of these seemed vague or confused. They concluded that "the concepts important to ideological analysis are useful only for that small segment of the population that is equipped to approach political decisions at a rarefied level" (Campbell et al., 1960:250).

Several subsequent researchers used other methods to measure ideology but came to similar conclusions. Butler and Stokes (1969) asked British voters to place the major parties on the right or left and found that many gave incorrect answers or said that they didn't know. Moreover, many of the people who placed the parties correctly could offer no definition of the terms. Converse (1964) considered ideology in terms of "attitude constraint" or the correlations among different political opinions. If people derived their opinions from some basic principles, opinions on different questions would be correlated because they shared a common cause. The advantage of this approach was that it did not require people to be able to characterize their principles in standard ideological terms, or even to realize that they were applying any principles. However, Converse found the correlations among opinions were generally low, suggesting that most people approached different issues in a piecemeal fashion rather than applying some general philosophy. Moreover, panel studies suggested that there was a good deal of change in opinions on specific issues. Converse (1964) argued that most of this instability did not reflect actual change in opinions but rather the absence of opinions: people answered at random rather than saying that they had no opinion. Thus, the overall conclusion of the Michigan studies was that most people had very low levels of political knowledge, interest, and sophistication. In general, people did not have ideologies but only collections of largely unrelated opinions, and even those opinions were often weakly held.

SOCIAL CLEAVAGES

Beginning in the late 1950s, a number of sociologists developed a synthesis that built on the Columbia school's analysis of cleavages while adding a psychological component. Lipset (1981 [1960]) was the most important figure in this approach, with other notable contributors including Alford (1963) and Kornhauser (1959). In this analysis, democratic politics were primarily a mechanism for responding to social inequality. In a well-known phrase Lipset (1981[1960]:230) called elections "the expression of the democratic class struggle." Democracy would not last if cleavages were too strong and persistent, because then there would be a permanent minority with no interest in abiding by the rules of the game. Conversely, if attachment to social groups were too weak, the result would be "mass politics," dominated by charismatic personalities (Korhnhauser, 1959). Moreover, given stable cleavages based on differences of interest, political leaders would learn to compromise. Hence, over time conflict would be routinized, resulting in what Lipset called the "politics of collective bargaining" (Lipset, 1970:277). In contrast, compromise would be difficult when movements were based on charismatic leaders or some grand vision of society.

The Columbia school had focused on differences of material interest as the major source of political opinions. Although they recognized the existence of noneconomic issues, they regarded them as secondary. Other researchers sought to analyze opinion in terms of psychology rather than material interests. The concept of authoritarianism proposed by Adorno, Frenkel-Brunswik, Levinson, and Sanford (1950) was particularly influential. These researchers sought to understand the origins of prejudice and antidemocratic ideologies. They argued that ideology could not be reduced to material interests. Rather, there was a distinct "authoritarian personality" that had an inclination toward racism, anti-Semitism, and rigid attachment to conventional morality. They argued that the existence of the authoritarian personality helped to explain why significant numbers of people in the lower classes had supported fascism.

Some observers criticized the assumption that the authoritarian personality was associated exclusively with support for the political right. In their view, authoritarianism should be treated as entirely distinct from the conventional division between left and right (Shils, 1954). Hence, political ideology had two distinct dimensions, which loosely could be described as involving economic and social affairs. Although both are conventionally described in terms of left and right, the two dimensions are essentially independent on the individual level – for example, views on economic redistribution do not predict views on crime. On the level of classes, there is actually a conflict between the two dimensions – the lower classes tend to have more conservative views on noneconomic questions. Lipset (1960:87–126) developed this observation into a model of "working class authoritarianism."

The two-dimensional model offered some potential for explaining political change. Variations in the relative importance of the two dimensions could affect political alignments and the success of the left or right. This general idea continues to be important in some contemporary accounts, particularly that of Inglehart (1990, 1997). However, several different interpretations of the second dimension were proposed. Hofstadter (1964[1955]:84) proposed a distinction between class politics and "status politics," which he defined as "the clash of various projective rationalizations arising from status aspirations and other personal motives." Hofstadter's definition suggests that status politics are irrational, in the sense that they are not directed against the true sources of discontent. This was close to the original view of Adorno et al. (1950), who regarded the authoritarian personality as a form of psychological ill health. Gusfield (1986 [1963]:16–19) proposed an alternative definition of status politics as conflict over the distribution of prestige among groups. In this definition, status politics are no less rational than class politics – they simply involve the rational pursuit of different goals. Gusfield's definition was closely connected to Weber's (1978[1920]:935–9) view of class and status as overlapping forms of stratification.

Hixson (1992:198–209) argues that Gusfield's definition of status politics has been more influential with later researchers. The suggestion that noneconomic conflicts are essentially projections of other concerns, however, still appears frequently: for example, Heath and Stacey (2002:667) state "the brutal volatility of globalized markets generates nostalgia for security that many associate with 'traditional family values.'" Hofstadter (1962:99) later suggested that his original definition had been too narrow and that status politics were part of a broader "cultural politics. . . . questions of faith and morals, tone and style, freedom and coercion, which become fighting issues."

Although there is still disagreement over the interpretation of the dimensions, later research has confirmed the general claim that there are at least two largely independent dimensions of political ideology. That is, describing people's views in simple left/right terms is inadequate even as a rough summary. Lipset's characterization of the lower classes as "authoritarian" may be exaggerated, but later research has confirmed that they are more conservative on social issues (Zipp, 1986). However, education rather than occupation seems to be the most important influence on social liberalism. Some observers have suggested that the apparent liberalism of more educated people may reflect social desirability bias and not real commitment to tolerance (Jackman, 1978). However, analysis of voting patterns indicates that parties that emphasize causes such as environmentalism and multiculturalism get most of their support from the middle classes (Heath et al., 1991; Weakliem, 1991). Thus, the class differences on social issues have real political consequences.

Another important aspect of the social cleavages approach was the extension of the Columbia school's model of cleavage formation. The core idea of this model was that communication within a group would reduce deviation from group norms, whereas communication across group lines would increase deviation. Because people simultaneously belong to a number of different groups, the extent of deviation would also depend on whether group boundaries overlaid or cut across each other. For example, if all working-class people were Catholic and all middle-class people were Protestant, class and religious divisions would reinforce each other. The lower the correlation between religious denomination and class, the more people would be subject to "cross-pressures." Such people might follow their class or their religion, arrive at some compromise, or avoid politics entirely. Cross-pressures were generally seen as enhancing the prospects of democracy by causing people to develop a degree of sympathy and understanding across group lines (Lipset, 1981[1960]:77–9).

The analysis implied that public opinion would be influenced by the composition of the population and the pattern of contact among groups. The effects of economic development received particular attention. The analysis in Lipset, Lazarsfeld, Barton, and Linz (1954) suggested that working-class support for the left would increase during industrialization. In the early stages of industrialization, many workers had grown up in rural areas and worked in small plants where they had personal contact with their employers. With the development of industrialization, workers experienced more homogenous environments – they grew up in working-class families, lived in working-class neighborhoods, and worked in large firms where they had little contact with the owners. Moreover, Lipset (1970:207–8; see also Lipset, Lazarsfeld, Barton, and Linz, 1954:1136) suggested that political knowledge and sophistication would make people more aware of the connection between government policies and their economic interests. This point implied that working-class consciousness would grow during industrialization because of increases in educational levels and exposure to the media.

This model was similar to the account of the development of class consciousness offered by classical Marxism but differed in that it did not predict the development of a commitment to socialism. The state to which economic development would lead was support for the "mixed economy" – capitalism with substantial regulation of business and income redistribution. In fact, Lipset (1981 [1960]:45–53) argued that "extremist" views would decline with industrialization as well, so that the moderate left would gain at the expense of both the revolutionary Left and the Right. The model could be taken to imply that national differences in politics would decline with economic development. For example, Alford (1963:333–5) found substantial differences in the influence of class on voting choices in different nations but suggested that the nations would converge toward a "normal" level of class voting as historical influences faded.

In later work, Lipset (1970:267–304) argued that class differences declined during the more advanced stages of industrialization. He suggested that even when workers continued to vote for socialist or social democratic parties, they had less commitment to their ideology. Conversely, the middle classes had moved toward the center, so that the political spectrum no longer ran between socialism and laissez-faire capitalism but only between a more or less extensive welfare state. Although Lipset never offered a comprehensive account of the relationship between industrialization and class differences, taken as a whole his writings suggest a nonlinear relationship – class divisions will increase with industrialization up to a point but then will decline.

The social cleavages model also implied that cross-pressures generally had more effect on the working classes than on the middle classes. Lipset, Lazarsfeld, Barton, and Linz (1954: 1136), for example, in reviewing factors affecting support for the left, state that "we shall discuss mainly variations on the lower income side, because the higher income groups show much less variation." One reason for this difference is that intraclass contact, particularly the exchange of political information and opinions, is greater among the upper classes (Lipset, 1970:205–7). Moreover, interclass contact has more influence on the lower classes, because the upper classes have greater prestige and resources. For example, the owner of a business may have a substantial influence on the way the workers vote, but the workers will have less influence over the owner. Hence, opinions among the lower classes are sensitive to the degree to which they are protected against influences from the upper classes. Working-class consciousness will therefore be strongly affected by factors such as the strength of labor unions and vigorous party organization. Middle-class consciousness, in contrast, will not need this kind of institutional support.

Two important implications follow from this point. First, national differences in average opinions will depend primarily on differences in the opinions of the working classes. To illustrate, suppose that average opinions in the middle classes are the same in all nations, whereas opinions in the working classes differ from one nation to the next. In that case, differences in national averages will depend entirely on the working classes – where they are farther to the left, the national average will be farther to the left.[3] Because average opinions in the working classes will virtually always be to the left of opinions in the middle classes, this means that larger class differences will be associated with greater support for the Left.

Second, working-class unity will be associated with more support for the Left. This is a familiar assertion, but it is not a logical necessity – in principle, the working class could be united around a moderate or conservative position. The social cleavages analysis, however, provides a rationale for this claim. In every society, some workers will be in homogenous working-class environments and will consequently be on the left. Other workers, however, will be in heterogeneous environments, and their position will vary depending on the extent to which they are influenced by their contacts with the middle class. Where middle-class influence is weak, these workers will tend to be on the left as well, and there will be little variation within the working class. Where middle-class influence is strong, only the "core" of the working class will be on the left, whereas "peripheral" workers will take more moderate positions.

Surprisingly, very little empirical research has been conducted on these issues. In fact, there are no studies that directly address them, although there are a few that provide relevant information. In a study of seven nations, Verba, Nie, and Kim (1978) find that working-class political participation is more variable than middle-class participation. They argue that working-class participation varies depending on the degree to which there is "*explicit* contestation on the basis of social class" (Verba, Nie, and Kim, 1978:307). Although they focus on participation rather than opinions, their findings support the general claim of greater variation in the working classes. Stephens (1979:411) conducted an empirical study of working class unity. In a comparative study of the working class in Britain and Sweden, he found that national differences are greater among peripheral workers.

[3] For the sake of illustration, it is assumed that the relative size of the classes does not differ among nations.

Core workers gave solid support to the left in both nations, but in Britain support was considerably lower outside of the core. Because his study included only two nations, however, it can hardly be regarded as conclusive.

RECENT RESEARCH

There is a significant gap between the research of the 1950s and 1960s and current work. Political sociologists turned away from public opinion research after the late 1960s for a variety of reasons. One was the growing interest in Marxism, particularly in its structuralist form. Structuralists regarded individual consciousness as relatively unimportant and were particularly critical of attempts to measure consciousness in the artificial setting of a survey or even a less structured interview. A second reason was the rise of resource mobilization and rational choice theories. After Olson (1965) demonstrated that shared interests did not provide a sufficient condition for collective action, social movement researchers shifted their attention to resources and incentives rather than grievances. Even sociologists who rejected a strict rational choice approach tended to accept the principle that actions should be explained by interests and resources rather than by values and beliefs. However, perhaps the most important reason for the loss of interest in public opinion was the resurgence of political and industrial conflict and the appearance of a variety of "new social movements." The Columbia, Michigan, and social cleavages approaches seemed to offer no promising explanation for these developments. The Columbia approach implied stability or gradual long-term change, whereas the Michigan approach implied short-term fluctuation within a constant framework. Hence, neither could account for the sudden appearance or growth of movements challenging the status quo. The idea of status politics did allow for relatively sudden change. However, it had usually been applied to declining groups that were trying to preserve their status; consequently, it did not provide a promising explanation of the new conflicts that emerged in the 1960s.

Hence, political sociologists made little contribution to the development of public opinion research during the 1970s and 1980s. There were a number of significant sociological studies of public opinion, but they were relatively specialized – there was no major work that set the agenda for later researchers the way that *Voting* or *Political Man* had. However, many political scientists and social psychologists continued to work on public opinion, and some of their work dealt with issues of relevance to sociology. Also, in recent years sociologists seem to have shown more interest in opinions, although often without drawing on the mainstream of public opinion research. The remainder of this chapter reviews four topics in recent work: the relationship between economic development and public opinion, political ideologies, the impact of public opinion on policy, and the effect of policy on public opinion.

ECONOMIC DEVELOPMENT AND PUBLIC OPINION

As discussed above, Lipset (1981 [1960]) held that economic development had consistent effects on public opinion. Specifically, he argued that it was associated with the development of attitudes conducive to stable democracy, such as tolerance and support for civil liberties, although his explanation for this relationship was sketchy. As historical studies emphasized complexity and variety, sociologists have become skeptical of general claims about the effects of economic development. A series of studies by Inglehart (1990, 1997; Inglehart and Baker, 2000), however, indicate that there is a correlation between economic development and public opinion in the contemporary world. In general, affluence is associated with more tolerance of differences in religion and lifestyle, increased acceptance of gender equality, and less respect for traditional authority (Inglehart and Baker, 2000). More broadly, one could say that affluence is usually associated with liberal views on social or cultural issues.

Of course, correlation is not proof of a causal connection – it may reflect the influence of some other factor that is associated with economic development. The most plausible alternative explanation is based on diffusion, where the opinions characteristic of the most developed nations spread to other nations. The influence might take place directly, as when people in other nations are exposed to American movies and television, or indirectly, as when the American or British educational system serves as a model for other nations. If one makes the additional assumption that the strength of Western influence is correlated with economic development, then one has an alternative explanation of the cross-sectional correlation. However, time-series data suggest that the same kind of changes have taken place within nations over time. For the United States, more than fifty years of data show a relatively steady growth in tolerance and support for gender equality (Page and Shapiro, 1992; Smith, 1990). Evidence for other nations covers shorter time periods, but also generally shows that the changes over time parallel the cross-sectional differences (Inglehart and Baker, 2000). If affluence affects opinions, economic growth will produce a gradual shift in opinions in all nations. In contrast, the diffusion argument does not predict a trend in affluent nations. Hence, whatever disagreements one might have with the specifics of Inglehart's argument, there is strong evidence for the general proposition that some factor related to economic development influences public opinion.

It should be noted that a claim that economic development influences opinions does *not* necessarily imply convergence among nations. In fact, Inglehart and Baker (2000) argue that there are persisting "cultural" differences among nations. Moreover, these cultural differences cannot be understood in terms of distance along a single path. For example, the United States has a number of distinctive features, including high religiosity and a strong sense of individualism. Hence, economic development does not mean that all nations will move in the direction of the United States or of any other specific nation.

There is considerable doubt about how the relationship between economic development and opinions should be interpreted. Inglehart (1990) holds that it reflects a shift in priorities: as material needs are satisfied, people pay more attention to "postmaterial" concerns. Drawing on Maslow's (1954) psychological theory, he argues that the postmaterial concerns involve freedom, aesthetics, and a sense of belonging and self-esteem. The distinction between materialism and postmaterialism is related to the idea of "status" or "cultural" politics discussed in the section on social cleavages. Hofstadter (1964[1955]) argued that cultural politics were essentially a luxury that people would pursue under conditions of prosperity and abandon under conditions of economic hardship. However, he understood prosperity in relative terms and hence saw the shift between cultural and economic politics as cyclical. Inglehart understands prosperity in an absolute sense and consequently argues that priorities will continue to shift as long there is economic growth.

A distinctive feature of Inglehart's account is that it links change in priorities to change in the content of opinions. Postmaterial values have an affinity with liberalism, as conventionally defined, so that a rise in the importance of cultural conflicts is accompanied by a shift to the left in most opinions. Previous discussions of cultural politics had treated salience and the content of values as distinct. That is, a rise in the importance of cultural politics did not generally go with a shift to the left on cultural issues. Another central feature of Inglehart's account is that it posits an inverse relationship between the importance of cultural and economic conflicts. Many accounts of cultural politics implicitly make a similar assumption, but as Parkin (1979:34) points out, it is not a logical necessity. That is, the importance of both economic and cultural politics could rise or fall together. Inglehart (1990) justifies the assumption by appealing to the economic principle of declining marginal utility. However, this principle is most relevant to the allocation of a fixed stock of resources such as income. One might say that value priorities involve the allocation of attention, but this is not a definite quantity in the same sense as money or time. This question deserves more attention from empirical researchers.

Inglehart's claim that affluence leads to a shift from economic to cultural conflict seems consistent with trends over the past few decades, but it is difficult to reconcile with a longer view. Although direct information on public opinion is very scarce before the middle of the twentieth century, examination of the historical record does not support the idea of a shift from economic to cultural politics over the whole period of the industrial revolution. During the nineteenth century, many countries saw controversies over religion, women's suffrage and the "woman question" more generally, and moral issues such as temperance. In fact, looking over the nineteenth and early twentieth centuries, one could make a plausible case that there was a shift from cultural to economic politics.

An alternative interpretation of the relationship between economic development and opinions is that it is a change in the content of values rather than priorities. For example, Inkeles (1983) argues that economic growth leads to increasing support for "modern" values, which include individualism, rationalism, and certain forms of egalitarianism. There is a corresponding decline in respect for traditional authorities. This model has the advantage of accounting for the trend toward liberalism without implying a steady growth in the importance of cultural politics. That is, the conflict between modern and traditional values is potentially important at all stages of economic development, but the center of gravity will be farther to the left at higher levels of development.

Although it is fairly apparent that economic development is associated with views on social issues, the relationship between economic development and economic opinions is much less clear. Using the assumption of an inverse relationship between economic and cultural conflict, Inglehart (1990:248–88) argues that the shift toward postmaterial values will lead to a decline of class differences in voting choices and opinions. This is a straightforward implication of his model – if people pay less attention to material interests, both the middle classes and the working classes will be more likely to deviate from their "natural" position. There has been a good deal of research on class differences in party choice, and there is some evidence that they have declined over the past few decades in most countries (Nieuwbeerta and De Graaf, 1999). However, there has been very little research on patterns of class differences in opinions. That is, we do not know whether class differences in opinions are smaller in more affluent nations, as Inglehart's account implies. We also do not know much about historical trends, but available information generally suggests that class differences on economic issues have remained steady (Shapiro and Young, 1989:74).

A related question is whether economic development leads to a general decline of the left. Inglehart (1997:263) argues that it does, noting that there is a substantial negative correlation between economic development and support for public ownership of industry. Moreover, nearly all socialist parties have retreated from programs of extensive public ownership and economic planning. Although this development has accelerated in recent decades, it was already visible in the 1950s. Thus, if the left is defined in terms of public ownership, there is strong evidence that support for the left declines with economic development. However, it is not clear that Inglehart's theoretical model actually helps to explain this pattern. That is, there is no obvious affinity between postmaterial values and opposition to socialism. One could argue that increased emphasis on the postmaterial value of freedom would lead to a decline in support for socialism. On the other hand, a major criticism of capitalism, dating back to the utopian socialists, is that it elevates economic accumulation over values such as community, leisure, and beauty. From this point of view, one would expect postmaterial values to be associated with support for socialism.

Moreover, most evidence about the decline of the left involves public ownership. There has been little research on the relationship between economic development and opinions about economic inequality, which has also been a central issue for the left. There is no substantial comparative study of the relationship between economic development and support for equality, but the scattered evidence that is available does not suggest any strong association. There is some evidence about changes over time in attitudes toward equality, particularly in the United States. The figures in Page and

Shapiro (1992:128–9) suggest that support for egalitarianism has fluctuated since the 1950s with no clear trend. Shapiro and Young (1989) review evidence about public opinion toward the welfare state and find a similar pattern. Moreover, Henderson (1998) notes that government regulation of business remains popular. More precisely, although most people support calls for less regulation in the abstract, they tend to be sympathetic to calls for particular kinds of regulation. For example, over 80 percent of the American public supported the provision of the Americans With Disabilities Act that required employers with more than fifteen employees to make "reasonable accommodations" for employees with disabilities. Similarly, there is overwhelming support for minimum wage laws and usually majority support for any proposal to increase the minimum wage.[4] Henderson (1998:81) concludes that "in most if not all countries, majority opinion remains hostile to ... what is termed 'leaving it to the market.' ... there is no sign that this situation, which historically has been the norm, is now about to change." Consequently, it is possible that what is often presented as a decline of the left is merely a decline in support for public ownership.

Although many aspects of Inglehart's model can be questioned, there is strong support for his basic claim that economic development affects opinions. This does not mean, however, that there is a universal, invariant effect. Rather, the effects of development might differ depending on circumstances. The general correlation, however, would still be meaningful in the sense of giving an average effect. In principle, it is possible to examine variation around the average – that is, to look for systematic differences in the effects of development. For example, one could compare the effects of economic development among Muslims and Christians or among traditionally Muslim and Christian nations. No studies of this type have yet appeared, but with the increasing availability of comparative survey data, there are promising opportunities for research.

Another question that deserves further investigation is the possibility that the relationship between economic development and public opinion reflects the effects of education. Research has found that education tends to be associated with liberal views on social issues (Hyman and Wright, 1979). Because there is a strong correlation between average levels of education and economic development, it seems possible that the changes in opinions that Inglehart ascribes to affluence are actually due to education (Davis, 1996). A natural counter to this claim is that the effects of education may vary substantially between societies. If the values taught in schools involve pluralism and tolerance, educated people will be more tolerant, but if they involve hierarchy and authority, they will be less tolerant. Weakliem (2002) examines the effect of education on a variety of opinions in about forty nations. Although the strength of the relationship varies among nations, it is almost always in a liberal direction for noneconomic issues. Because it appears that the liberal effects of education are relatively widespread, Davis's hypothesis remains plausible.

IDEOLOGY AND FRAMING

As discussed above, the Columbia, Michigan, and social cleavages schools gave little attention to political ideas. Ideology was seen as simply a classification along a scale of left to right, and the work of Converse (1964) suggested that even this assumed too much structure. Within mainstream public opinion research, there were very few efforts to think of ideology in terms of a system of thought. Even when considering the formation of specific opinions, the older research traditions gave very little attention to processes of thought. Opinions were taken as straightforward expressions of interest or as the direct result of social contact. When Lazarsfeld, Berelson, and Gaudet (1944:150–8) discussed the nature of personal influence, they emphasized the importance of trust rather than the content of arguments.

[4] These statements are based on searches using the iPOLL database of the Roper Center for Public Opinion Research.

Some observers objected to this picture on either theoretical or empirical grounds. Studies based on extended conversations generally suggested that people had meaningful principles and views of the world. Lane's (1962) interviews with working- and lower middle-class men, for example, gave a very different picture of political ideology than that suggested by the Michigan studies. Although Lane's subjects were not necessarily sophisticated thinkers, their political views seemed to be more than just a collection of unrelated opinions. Hence, some observers suspected that the apparent lack of structure reflected problems of measurement or analysis. Reinarman's (1987) more recent study addresses Converse's (1964) model of ideology as attitude constraint. He argues that people can often give reasonable justifications of apparent inconsistencies among their opinions (1987:215). Thus, low levels of attitude constraint do not necessarily demonstrate a lack of ideological sophistication. In his view, the apparent weakness of ideological thinking in the public is an artifact of the use of conventional structured surveys, which do not give people the opportunity to explain their reasoning.

The most ambitious attempt to observe political reasoning directly is the "deliberative poll" (Luskin, Fishkin, and Jowell, 2002). In a deliberative poll, participants first take a standard survey and then attend a weekend conference in which they hear briefings from experts representing diverse points of view and engage in small group discussions, after which they are surveyed again. The overall distribution of opinions remains about the same on some issues, but changes substantially on others. Although Luskin, Fishkin, and Jowell (2002) do not propose a theory of why change takes place, their results show that ordinary people are able to critically evaluate new information and arguments – they do not simply adhere to their prior beliefs or adopt the views of a trusted authority. Gamson (1992:175) assembled focus groups on various topics and came to similar conclusions: "one is struck by the deliberative quality of their construction of meaning about these complex issues . . . they achieve considerable coherence in spite of a great many handicaps . . . ."

A number of theoretical approaches to political reasoning have been proposed since the 1970s, but none has come to dominate. The idea of schemas, which draws from cognitive psychology, is popular among political scientists (Axelrod, 1973; Conover and Feldman, 1984). A schema is not just a set of beliefs but also includes rules for processing new information and arguments. Hence, people with different schemas could draw different lessons from the same events, as often seems to happen in reality. Given the scarcity of longitudinal data on opinions, however, it is difficult to examine this point. In empirical work, "schemas" often are no more than descriptive classifications of beliefs (Kuklinski, Luskin, and Bolland, 1991).

An alternative approach that has been more popular among sociologists is based on "framing." At its simplest level, the idea of framing is that changes in the way a question is presented may influence responses, even if the substance remains the same. For example, support for government spending to combat some problem may be higher if the question is preceded by questions about the severity of the problem and lower is preceded by questions about taxes. In this sense, framing has long been familiar to psychologists and survey researchers (Schuman and Presser, 1981). However, it may also have broader relevance to public opinion. There is usually room for disagreement concerning what a given political issue is "really about," and the way in which it is defined will change the attractiveness of the different answers. Hence, one would expect political actors to struggle over the definitions of issues. Snow, Rochford, Worden, and Benford (1986) argued that the concept of framing could be applied to the activity of social movements, and many later researchers have followed their lead.

Gamson (1992) argues that the concept of framing also helps to illuminate the formation of public opinion. He arranged for groups of people to have conversations on a variety of political topics. Although people did not necessarily begin with much information on the topics, they were able to have pertinent discussions by drawing on their own experience and frames that were current in the media or the general culture. The idea of framing is most naturally suited to actual conversations such as those analyzed by Gamson, but some authors have tried to extend it to include enduring structures of beliefs. Snow, Rochford, Worden, and Benford (1986:475) speak of a "master frame that interprets events and experiences in a new key." As Oliver and Johnston (2000) point out, in this sense a frame comes close to the traditional meaning of ideology. They argue, however, that the two concepts should be kept separate. In their view, "a frame lacks the elaborate social theory and normative and value systems that characterize a full-blown ideology, but instead is . . . an angle or perspective on a problem" (Oliver and Johnston, 2000:50). They argue that people with different ideologies can appeal to the same frame – for example, both opponents and supporters of abortion could frame the issue in terms of individual rights.

The idea of framing has most often been applied in studies of social movements rather than the analysis of opinions at the individual level. However, it is potentially relevant to the individual-level associations among opinions. Different ways of framing a question make some issues more relevant to a particular topic and others less relevant. Thus, changes in the prevalence of different frames might result in changes in the associations among individual opinions. That is, an opinion might become aligned with one set of issues and less closely aligned with others. For example, some observers of recent American politics argue that some issues that were once seen in terms of class are now generally seen in terms of race (Edsall and Edsall, 1991). This argument implies shifts in the associations among opinions. For example, views of welfare spending could shift from being associated with opinions about topics such as the minimum wage to being more closely associated with opinions about topics such as affirmative action. Also, the low levels of overall attitude constraint noted by Converse (1964) might be the result of competing frames. That is, different people might apply different frames, some seeing welfare primarily in terms of race, others in terms of gender, and others in terms of taxes and spending. When looking at the public as a whole, opinions on welfare would be correlated with opinions on race, gender, taxes, and spending, but all of the correlations would be relatively weak.

The idea of framing may also help to illuminate change in opinions. As Snow, Rochford, Worden, and Benford (1986) put it, some frames have high "resonance" with existing views. In this case, when confronted with arguments for change, many people will quickly accept them. For example, Zaller (1992:317) argues that after the American Psychiatric Association voted to remove homosexuality from its official classification of mental disorders, "the press began to employ a 'civil rights' frame of reference alongside the old 'vice' frame, thus offering the public an alternative way of conceptualizing the issue." Although information is scarce, he suggests that this change in coverage resulted in a substantial shift in public views.

Thus, one attraction of the idea of framing is that it potentially helps to explain cases of rapid opinion change. Many shifts in public opinion are slow and steady, with almost imperceptible changes from year to year adding up to substantial changes over longer periods of time (Page and Shapiro, 1992). However, there are some cases in which opinions change quickly without any obvious external cause. For example, support for President Clinton's proposed health care program declined from 57 percent to 47 percent between January and February 1994 and never rebounded after that time. Skocpol (1996) argues that this change occurred because opponents of the proposal successfully drew on popular distrust of government. A second attraction of the idea is that it may explain why certain changes precede or follow others. Historical accounts of change in opinions generally suggest that there is some logical sequence of change – that is, new ideas grow out of previous ideas. The civil rights frame referred to by Zaller (1992) is a familiar example, in which a concept that originally developed in the movement for racial equality was adopted for many other causes. Although not all efforts to frame questions as issues of civil rights were successful, the idea seems to have provided a useful resource for later movements.

There has been little effort to test these implications, and most applications of framing rely on case studies rather than analyses of opinion data. One reason for this situation is that framing has often been defined loosely, as Benford (1997) notes. A second reason is that relevant data are not always available. For example, Skocpol's (1996) account of the Clinton health care proposal implies that the shift of opinion against the proposal should have been larger among people with lower confidence in government. The surveys that contained the questions on health care, however, did not necessarily include questions on trust in government. In general, testing hypotheses about framing requires a good deal of continuity in repeated surveys and often requires longitudinal data on individuals. Moreover, the span of time that must be considered will vary depending on the question. For an analysis of a specific political controversy, it would be necessary to have frequent surveys over a short period of time. An analysis of efforts to apply a civil rights frame to various questions, in contrast, might require data extending over decades.

Finally, it should also be noted that the very characteristics that make the concepts of framing and ideology appealing to social scientists might make them less applicable to the general public. People who study politics are usually interested in political ideas and think about the connections between them. Ordinary people, however, may combine ideas in an eclectic way with little regard for consistency, as the work of the Michigan school suggested. Thus, it is possible that the efforts to take ideas more seriously will be relevant to the study of elite groups, but of little use in studies of general public opinion.

PUBLIC OPINION AND POLICY

If public opinion had no impact on events, it might still be of interest to social psychologists but not to political sociologists. Whether public opinion actually makes a difference is a classic question in the social sciences. Until recently there was very little systematic evidence, but in the last fifteen years or so the situation has started to change.

A variety of studies have looked at the match between public opinion and government policy on particular issues. Brooks (1985, 1987, 1990) examines policy and opinion in Canada, France, the United States, and Germany and finds that in all nations the policy favored by the majority was adopted in less than half of the cases. Other studies, however, have obtained more optimistic estimates (Monroe, 1998; Petry, 1999). An alternative approach relies on comparison of different units. Using data from the American states in the 1930s, Erikson (1976) found a significant correlation between average opinion and policies on several issues. Erikson, Wright, and McIver (1993) constructed general measures of public opinion and state policy, rating both in terms of liberal and conservative, and found a positive correlation. The cross-sectional correlation, however, might result from the influence of policy on opinion – people might come to accept whatever policies were in place. To establish the direction of causality, a number of studies have looked at changes in opinions and policy.

Stimson (1999) undertakes a comprehensive analysis of questions on government policy included in national surveys since the 1950s and finds that most of the change can be reduced to a single factor, which he calls "policy mood." That is, when opinions on one issue become more liberal, opinions on most other opinions do as well.[5] As noted previously, the individual-level correlations among opinions tend to be weak, and a one-factor solution does not fit well. However, because the units of analysis are different, there is no contradiction between these findings. In effect, most of the idiosyncratic factors that are relevant to individual opinions may cancel out when comparing aggregate opinion distributions over time. Stimson's (1999) estimates suggest that the public mood was at its most liberal in the late 1950s and at its most conservative around 1980. There were also several other

[5] There are some exceptions to this generalization. Erikson, MacKuen, and Stimson (2002) find evidence of a second dimension involving some issues of crime and poverty. They also report that opinions on a few issues, particularly abortion, move in a distinctive fashion.

striking movements, such as a gradual move to the right during the early 1960s and a shift back to the left in the second half of the decade.

Stimson, MacKuen, and Erikson (1995) and Erikson, MacKuen, and Stimson (2002) analyze the relationship between policy mood and several indexes of public policy, including congressional votes, the content of laws passed, and Supreme Court decisions. They find a substantial correlation – for example, the liberal mood of the early 1960s was followed by the passage of major civil rights laws and an extension of antipoverty programs, and the conservative mood of the late 1970s and early 1980s was followed by deregulation and tax cuts. The connection is only partly accounted for by party control of the presidency and Congress. For example, policy was relatively conservative in the late 1970s, despite a Democratic president and Democratic majorities in both houses of Congress. Thus, their results suggest that political leaders respond directly to public opinion. Their work, however, does not address the possibility that changes in both policy and public opinion reflect some other factor, such as the activities of organized groups. Burstein (1998) addresses this issue by reviewing a number of studies that take account of both social movement activity and public opinion. He concludes that public opinion has a direct effect on policy, but social movement activity does not. That is, any effect that social movements have on policy is an indirect one operating through their effect on public opinion. Given the difficulties of measuring social movement activity, his conclusion that it has no direct effect should not be taken as definitive. However, his work provides further evidence that public opinion does have an effect.

Given the general finding that public opinion influences policy, it is natural to ask whether the effect varies among nations, times, or types of issues (Manza and Cook, 2002). A few empirical studies have considered these questions. It appears that public opinion affects most types of policy, although there may be some differences in the strength of the influence. Smith's (2000) study of policies related to business is particularly important, because one might expect public opinion to be a weak force when matched against the financial resources and access of business. He limited his attention to policies on which business was united in support or opposition and found that public opinion continued to have an influence. His explanation of this finding is that policies that unite business tend to be visible and relatively easy to interpret in terms of interests, so that the public is easily mobilized.

There are very few studies of nations other than the United States. Soroka and Wlezien (2002) analyze the effect of public opinion on public expenditure in Great Britain. They find that spending generally responds to public opinion, as it does in the United States. In Britain, however, spending in specific areas is less closely tied to opinion about those areas – "it is as though policymakers receive cures for increased (decreased) spending ... but exercise discretion in deciding where spending increases (decreases) occur" (Soroka and Wlezien, 2002:23–4).

Systematic studies of change over time are also scarce. Jacobs and Shapiro (2000) argue that government responsiveness to public opinion has declined in the United States, whereas Quirk and Hinchliffe (1998) argue that it has increased. However, both rely on impressionistic evidence. The most systematic study finds that the correspondence between public opinion and policy was somewhat lower in 1980–1993 compared to 1960–1979 (Monroe 1979).

Another issue that deserves more attention is the relative influence of different groups. Blumer (1948:545) objected to the modern definition of public opinion as the opinions of the entire population and proposed that public opinion should be understood as only the "views and positions on the issue that *come to the individuals who have to act*." Even if political leaders pay attention to polling data, they will presumably give some attention to opinions expressed in letters, personal contact, and the media. This argument suggests that predictions could be improved by refining the measure of public opinion. One approach would be to construct measurements of other senses of opinion, such as the views expressed in newspaper editorials. Another approach would be to use survey data, but give different weights to the opinions of different people. In particular, because political participation and resources generally increase with socioeconomic status, one might expect influence on policy to do so as well. Another possibility is that political leaders focus on groups that are regarded as potential "swing voters." In this case, the opinions of these groups would have more weight than those of others.

In principle, it would be straightforward to conduct such an investigation: one would include average opinion in each group as an independent variable. For example, rather than regressing a measure of policy on average opinion, one could regress it on two variables – the average among people with high incomes and the average among people with low incomes. There are, however, several practical obstacles to this kind of research. First, surveys may not contain the necessary information on group membership. For example, some surveys do not ask about income, and those that do use a variety of response categories. Second, the opinions of all groups seem to move roughly in parallel over time (Page and Shapiro, 1992), so that the group measures of opinion will be highly correlated, making it difficult to distinguish their effects. That is, when opinions of high-income people are more liberal than usual, opinions of low-income people will be relatively liberal, too. Nevertheless, the question is important enough to deserve attention despite these difficulties.

POLICY FEEDBACK

In recent years, there has been considerable interest in "policy feedback" (Pierson, 1993). There are several different senses of policy feedback, but the one that is of interest here is the possibility that government policies shape public opinion. If public opinion affects policy, as the research discussed in the previous section suggests, that would mean that the policy choice at one time would influence the subsequent development of policy. There are some straightforward examples of this process. For example, leftist governments often enact policies that facilitate union organization. Because union membership affects a variety of opinions, such policies will affect public opinion, generally shifting it to the left. However, there may also be more complex effects. For example, the design of social policy may influence the way that people think of themselves – as members of a class, an ethnic group, an age group, or the general community. Also, it may influence the way that they draw group boundaries. If this is the case, policy decisions could have long-term effects that are not anticipated at their inception. A policy could lead the public to redefine their interests and identities in ways that undermine, enhance, or alter the bases of support for that policy. Moreover, the effect on public opinion could spill over beyond the policy in question. For example, if a policy encourages people to think of themselves in terms of social classes, it would ultimately influence a whole range of opinions.

Thus, the idea of policy feedback is a case of what I previously called a "political" approach on the societal level. Existing opinions depend not only on current structural conditions but also on past opinions. Also, rather than holding that national differences simply endure, as Inglehart and Baker (2000) do, policy feedback theorists hold that they can change based on the history of policy and opinions. For example, if class consciousness was initially stronger in one nation than another, governments might implement policies that were organized in class terms, strengthening class consciousness still further and increasing the gap between the nations.

The idea of policy feedback is connected to the popular but vague concept of political "coalitions." In a descriptive sense, a coalition is simply a collection of groups that gives relatively high support to a party or policy. However, the term is often used in a stronger sense – for example, it is sometimes said that a party was successful *because* it "forged" a particular coalition. In this explanatory sense, a coalition involves some sort of alliance – people do not simply happen to be on the same side but agree to work together. Of course, ordinary people do not make formal alliances in the way that organizations sometimes do. However, people may think of themselves as part of a common project which they will support even if they derive not immediate benefits. For example, a skilled manual worker in a secure job would not benefit from welfare spending, an increase in the minimum wage, or aid to farmers. However, he may support all of these programs if he thinks of them as benefiting "ordinary people" against the "big interests." Thus, in the explanatory sense a coalition would be a group of people who regarded themselves as sharing basic interests.

A decade ago, Pierson (1993:597) noted that studies of policy feedback usually focused on politicians, bureaucrats, and party organizations rather than the general public, and his observation remains true today. The most systematic attempts to study public reactions to policy have used a simple "thermostatic" model (Wlezien, 1995). In this model, the government responds to public opinion, but often overshoots it, causing the public to move in the opposite direction. For example, the conservative public mood of the late 1970s resulted in the election of Ronald Reagan in 1980. Once the direction of public policy shifted sharply to the right under Reagan, the public mood began to shift in a liberal direction (Erikson, MacKuen, and Stimson, 2002). Consequently, public opinion fluctuates around an equilibrium. In this model, the role of political leaders is very limited, because they cannot affect the equilibrium level. The implication of the policy feedback literature, however, is that there is no single equilibrium. The "final" state of public opinion will depend on previous choices of policy. For example, it has been claimed that reliance on means-tested welfare policies undermines support for welfare spending, whereas the reliance on universal policies enhances it (e.g., Korpi and Palme, 1998). This does not mean that means-tested programs are less popular at the start, but that they encourage people to think in terms of a division between a small group of beneficiaries and a large group of taxpayers and that this way of thinking ultimately leads to a loss of support. Hence, the decisions of political leaders can send initially similar societies down different paths. This kind of analysis has a strong appeal to people who are interested in politics, and many historical accounts contain suggestions about the long-term consequences of policy decisions.

Empirical analysis of claims about the effects of policy choices on public opinion is difficult, because it would require data from several nations covering substantial periods of time. Esping-Andersen (1985) analyzes voting patterns in Scandinavian countries, arguing that there was a stronger trend toward "decomposition" of the Social Democratic vote in Denmark and Norway than in Sweden. By this, he means that support became less stable and less uniform across the working class. He argues that the differences result from a combination of social and economic policies. However, Esping-Andersen's (1985) account is closely tied to the histories of these nations and offers no clear predictions that could be applied to other nations.

Some authors have made more rigorous attempts to model the effect of policy on opinions, although they have not tested them empirically. Lindbeck (1995) proposes a model in which norms against relying on state benefits decline as the size of the population receiving benefits increases. He finds that this model has two equilibrium values – a high or a low share relying on state benefits. He also suggests that there may be broader consequences: for example, if political debate focuses on the distributional implications of policies "the tolerance for income differences will gradually fall, and... social and political conflicts ... will rise in parallel with an equalization of disposable income" (Lindbeck, 1995:488).[6]

Although empirical study of these issues is likely to be difficult, the development of models would be helpful. Existing discussions are not very clear about exactly how policies are supposed to affect opinions: they generally appeal to some mix of self-interest, group interest, and psychological factors without specifying the role of each. It would also be particularly useful to

[6] This suggestion is reminiscent of De Tocqueville's (1850[1969]:673) analysis of equality: "it is therefore natural that love of equality should grow constantly with equality itself; everything done to satisfy it makes it grow."

consider implications that could be tested with comparative cross-sectional data. For example, if universalistic welfare policies create a sense of social solidarity, one might expect class or income differences in support for welfare policies to be smaller in nations with such policies. Alternatively, universalistic policies might win over parts of the middle classes without gaining support from the upper classes. In this case, one could not unambiguously describe the class differences as larger or smaller. Rather, one could say that there was a qualitative difference in the nature of the coalition supporting welfare policy.

Wright (1997) provides some evidence for the existence of national differences in class coalitions. He argues that in Sweden, the opinions of manual and white-collar workers are relatively close together, whereas in the United States they are more distant. As he puts it, "the bourgeois class formation penetrates the middle class to a much greater extent in the United States than in Sweden" (Wright, 1997:429). The pattern of class differences in Japan, meanwhile, is different from both the American and Swedish patterns. Wright explains the national differences as the result of differences in state employment and unionization. He also argues that the "shape" of class coalitions affects the prospects for future class conflict.

CONCLUSIONS

Compared to their counterparts from the 1950s and 1960s, contemporary researchers have far more information to work with. Public opinion data now extend over fifty years in some countries, and there are a number of international surveys that include nations from all parts of the world. Although having more information is obviously an advantage, it means that there is a great deal more to organize and assimilate. With more information and better models, it has been possible to make substantial progress on some questions, like the analysis of trends in class voting. However, there have been few general attempts to synthesize the new research, with Inglehart's (1997) work standing out as virtually the sole exception. Consequently, the major task for researchers is not choosing among theories but developing theories.

There is still much of value in the older work of the Columbia, Michigan, and social cleavage schools. As I argued previously, political sociologists turned away from public opinion after the late 1960s not primarily because of the failure of these approaches, but because their attention was attracted by other issues and theories. Many of their claims have been confirmed by later studies. For example, the evidence collected in the World Values Surveys (Inglehart, 1990, 1997) supports Lipset's (1960) claim that economic development generally leads to more tolerance and support for liberal democracy. It is still not clear why the relationship exists, but it is clear that there is something that needs to be explained. Moreover, there are a number of research questions suggested by older work, particularly in the social cleavages approach, that still have not received adequate study.

The work of the 1950s and 1960s did have two related weak points. One was that it did not take account of the processes of thinking and argument. A model in which opinions are simply transmitted by contact captures part of the truth but leaves something out as well. Similarly, the Michigan school's contention that people did not have worldviews but merely collections of largely unrelated opinions is difficult to square with the evidence of studies based on detailed observation such as those of Lane (1962) and Gamson (1992). A second weak point was the lack of a model of discontinuous change. The Columbia school saw change as the result of gradual changes in population and social structure, while the Michigan school saw it as a matter of fluctuation around an equilibrium level. These sorts of changes certainly do occur, but there are also occasions in which new ideas appear and spread quickly. The two weak points are related, because the rapid spread of an idea is likely to depend on some kind of intellectual appeal, such as the "resonance" spoken of by framing theorists.

There are several different attempts to take the process of thinking more seriously. The review in this chapter focused on framing but also mentioned work on schemas that is popular in political science. There are still other alternatives that were not discussed here. For example, from the perspective of rational choice theory, Riker (1984) proposes a model of "heresthetics" or political argument. It is not clear which, if any of them, will eventually be the most successful. However, this general area is likely to be the focus of considerable attention in the future.

To conclude, political sociology and public opinion research, after drifting apart during the 1970s and 1980s, may be moving closer together again. Public opinion is not likely to regain the preeminent position that it had in political sociology during the 1950s. However, as a result of the combination of better data and new research questions, it may be ready to move from the margins and enter a period of rapid progress.

CHAPTER TWELVE

Nationalism in Comparative Perspective

Liah Greenfeld and Jonathan Eastwood

THE STATE OF THE FIELD

The inclusion of a chapter on nationalism in a *Handbook of Political Sociology*, which introduces subjects fundamental to the profession in these early years of the twenty-first century, reflects the recognition, which has grown steadily in the past twenty-five years, of the political importance of nationalism. There has been considerable academic interest in nationalism before, but this interest wavered and at times seemed to disappear altogether. This faltering interest may be held responsible for the fact that our understanding of the phenomenon did not advance as much as one could have wished from the beginning of World War II, when its violent eruption took American social scientists by surprise, and even from the beginning of the twentieth century.[1]

The work of Hans Kohn is among the most useful early efforts in attempting to come to terms with the development of nationalism in historical perspective. Kohn was particularly notable for constantly stressing that nationalism is fundamentally an *idea*, rather than a static, structural phenomenon, echoing the argument that the French sociologist Ernest Renan made three-quarters of a century earlier.[2] However, Kohn (as well as Renan) can be criticized for being insufficiently rigorous in defining the idea of the nation. For him, the nation was fundamentally a sovereign community, but he failed to recognize the essentially *secular* quality of nationalism or the structural implications of national consciousness.

Between the late 1970s and 1980s, work on nationalism was largely dominated by several thinkers, whose works are often taken to be canonical, despite the many points of sharp disagreement between them. The most significant of these thinkers, most of whom began publishing on nationalism in that period, are Eric Hobsbawm, Ernest Gellner, Anthony Smith, and Benedict Anderson. Of these, the first two are ordinarily considered structuralists. By this it is meant that they judge nationalism (and the nation) to be fundamentally a "structural" or "material" phenomenon. That is, they approach nationalism from a theoretical point of view that owes a great deal to Karl Marx.

Perhaps the most influential of those theorists commonly identified as structuralists has been Ernest Gellner. Gellner takes the state to be the fundamental structural phenomenon, and he defines it as

> that institution or set of institutions specifically concerned with the enforcement of order . . . the state

[1] Those scholars who repeat the old prediction that so-called globalization is likely to lead to a reduction or elimination of nationalism evidence a similar lapse in judgment. There is little to indicate that nationalism is in decline, and global flows of capital, migrating labor, and the internet have not pushed it any closer to the brink of extinction.

[2] See Hans Kohn, *The Idea of Nationalism* (New York: MacMillan, 1946). See also Ernest Renan, *Qu'est-ce Qu'une Nation* (Leiden: Academic Press Leiden, 1994).

exists where specialized order-enforcing agencies, such as police forces and courts, have separated out from the rest of social life.

These order-enforcing agencies "*are* the state."[3] The state, in turn, is a function of the "industrial age," within which "the *presence*, not the absence of the state is inescapable."[4] Thus nationalism is dependent, for Gellner, on industrialization. Gellner attempts to define the nation itself as a form of consciousness. That is, for Gellner, a nation has a shared culture (he understands "culture" to refer to "a system of ideas and signs and associations and ways of behaving and communicating") and depends on the recognition of its members: "A mere category of persons . . . becomes a nation if and when the members of the category firmly recognize certain mutual rights and duties to each other in virtue of their shared membership in it."[5] There is a certain tension in Gellner's approach. On the one hand, the nation, for him, is a matter of consciousness which, as in the definition above, seems to be autonomous. On the other hand, it is inseparably tied to the state, which is understood as itself a function of industrial development. In other words, it is treated as Marx treated all consciousness: as epiphenomenal to the changing forces and relations of production. Later, Gellner offers an alternative definition of nationalism. It is "a very distinctive species of patriotism, and one which becomes pervasive and dominant only under certain social conditions, which in fact prevail in the modern world, and nowhere else" (as we've seen, the rise of industrial society and the state). The main characteristics of this "species of patriotism" are "homogeneity, literacy, [and] anonymity." He seems at times to identify it with "cultural chauvinism" as well.[6] These are, of course, not definitions, if we understand a definition to be something that brackets the thing defined off from everything else and that does not describe a set of things that includes items not meant to appear under that name. Gellner, despite his many laudable efforts, does not pinpoint what is *distinctive* about nationalism.

Eric Hobsbawm is a more unequivocal structuralist than Gellner and is very clear about the fact that he takes the nation to be an "objective" phenomenon (that is, he never even seems to suggest that nationalism is fundamentally a form of consciousness). For Hobsbawm, "defining a nation by its members' consciousness of belonging to it is tautological and provides only an *a posteriori* definition of what a nation is."[7] Moreover, Hobsbawm continues, the nation is "a social entity only insofar as it relates to a certain kind of modern territorial state, the 'nation-state', and it is pointless to discuss nation and nationality except insofar as both relate to it."[8] That is, the "modern" state (one wonders what, exactly, this "certain kind" of state is) is taken to cause nationalism. Ultimately, though, Hobsbawm rejects all possible definitions of the phenomenon under consideration and recommends "agnosticism" as "the best initial posture of a student in this field." As a result, his work "assumes no *a priori* definition of what constitutes a nation."[9] Critics would charge that one needs to define one's object of study to be reasonably assured of a consistent approach to the problem in question.

Anthony Smith, in contrast, provides us with a "working definition" of the modern nation wherein it is taken to be "a named human population which shares myths and memories, a mass public culture, a designated homeland, economic unity and equal rights and duties for all members." As such, nations have their roots in "ethnies," those "named units of population with common ancestry myths and historical memories, elements of shared culture, some link with a historic territory and some measure of solidarity, at least among their elites" that have "appeared in the historical record since at least the late third millennium."[10] Ultimately

[3] Gellner, *Nations and Nationalism* (Ithaca: Cornell University Press, 1983), p. 4. The italics are Gellner's.

[4] *Ibid.*, p. 5.

[5] *Ibid.*, p. 7.

[6] *Ibid.*, p. 138.

[7] Eric Hobsbawm, *Nations and Nationalism Since 1780: Programme, Myth, Reality* (New York: Cambridge University Press, 1992), pp. 7–8.

[8] *Ibid.*, pp. 9–10.

[9] *Ibid.*, p. 8.

[10] Anthony Smith, *Nations and Nationalism in a Global Era* (Malden, MA: Blackwell Publishers, 1995) pp. 56–57.

it is unclear exactly what separates ethnies from nations for Smith, leading to further definitional problems.

Benedict Anderson's *Imagined Communities* may indeed constitute the most influential account of nationalism produced to date. Anderson is typically identified as a "constructivist," meaning that he allegedly takes nations to be historically contingent products of human cultural construction. Indeed, such a conception is suggested by the very title of his book. Anderson stresses that the fundamental quality of the nation is that it is an "imagined community"; because the majority of inhabitants or members of any given nation do not know each other and do not meet face to face, they cannot be, presumably, a "real" community but can only constitute an imagined one. As he puts it, the nation is "*imagined* because the members of even the smallest nation will never know most of their fellow-members, meet them, or even hear of them, yet in the minds of each lives the image of their communion."[11]

This is most certainly the case, though, it should be pointed out, *all* human communities are imagined communities in precisely this sense. That is, as Emile Durkheim so clearly saw, social forces are ultimately moral (i.e., mental and not physical) forces.[12] Even the most organizationally simple societies cannot exist but through "collective representations," which are, though externalized through symbols, ultimately products of (and continue to reside in) the imaginations of individuals.[13] That is, even hunter-gatherer societies do not fundamentally constitute "real communities," if by that term we mean physical constellations of human beings, living in proximity to one another. They are not mere "populations," in the biological sense of the word, but instead depend on bonds that are essentially *symbolic* in nature.

What is important, as Anderson himself notes, is the "style" within which different political communities are imagined. It has been pointed out, however, that, as with Kohn, the definition of this style offered by Anderson is not sufficiently rigorous. That is, Anderson understands nations to be imagined communities that are "inherently limited and sovereign."[14] That is, they are limited because "even the largest of them, encompassing perhaps a billion living human beings, has finite, if elastic, boundaries, beyond which lie other nations."[15] It hardly needs pointing out that this is not a distinguishing characteristic of any particular type of human group. Anderson's understanding of sovereignty is relatively straightforward (he is referring, of course, to the notion of popular sovereignty), and he takes this aspect of national consciousness to be a function of the fact that "the concept [of the nation] was born in an age in with Enlightenment and Revolution were destroying the legitimacy of the divinely-ordained, hierarchical dynastic realm."[16] In other words, it seems that, in Anderson's estimation, the idea of popular sovereignty became attached to the nation because they (supposedly) happened to emerge at the same moment. It is also important to note Anderson's definition of the term *community*. For him, all communities, by definition, are based on "a deep, horizontal comradeship" that "makes it possible . . . for so many people . . . willingly to die for such limited imaginings."[17] Thus, nationalism, for Anderson, is an imagined form of human society that is taken to be sovereign and limited and that is based on a sense of egalitarian "comradeship." However, as with the other theorists considered above, this is insufficiently rigorous. This definition would include a number of things – for example, the city-states of ancient Greece (which,

[11] Benedict Anderson, *Imagined Communities: Reflections on the Origin and Spread of Nationlism* (New York: Verso, 1983/1991), p. 6.

[12] See Emile Durkheim, *The Rules of Sociological Method*, trans. Sarah Solovay and John Mueller (New York: The Free Press, 1966), pp. 1–13. See also Emile Durkheim, *The Elementary Forms of the Religious Life*, trans. Joseph Ward Swain (New York: The Free Press, 1965), pp. 237, 238, 260.

[13] See Emile Durkheim, *The Elementary Forms of the Religious Life*, *op. cit.*, pp. 21–2.

[14] Anderson, *Imagined Communities, op. cit.*, p. 6.

[15] *Ibid.*, p. 7.

[16] *Ibid.*, p. 7.

[17] *Ibid.*, p. 7.

incidentally, would contradict Anderson's claim that the nation is a modern phenomenon) – that are clearly not nations.[18]

The conclusion one draws from a review of the central texts in the field is that political sociology (and political science, more broadly) has not come to grips with nationalism as yet. Despite the broad ontological similarities between major theories (their convergence on fundamental structural materialism, for instance), there is no feeling in the profession that they have captured and sufficiently illuminated the phenomenon. In this sense, the inclusion of a chapter on nationalism in a section of this volume devoted to "the roots and processes of political action" in civil society may be taken as an indication of deepening understanding. Only recently, the preferred meaning of the term *nationalism* even in scholarly literature was pejorative, and civil society was emphatically absent among its immediate associations. In much of popular discussion, such pejorative meaning is still dominant[19], as is the belief that nationalism is a deep-rooted psychological, and therefore ancient and ubiquitous rather than culturally constructed, modern, and historically limited, phenomenon, essentially identical to ethnic, racial, and ultimately biological allegiances and groupings, which represent its earlier forms.[20] True, academic experts on nationalism since the early 1980s have leaned toward the "modernist" side of the "modernist/primordialist" or "modernist/perennialist" divide, postulated by Anthony Smith.[21] "Modernists," although admitting that nationalism was an outgrowth of ethnicity, nevertheless insisted that it was a strictly modern phenomenon that reflected specifically modern economic and political processes, such as the development of capitalism and/or industrialization and of modern bureaucratic state, and was inconceivable, or "unimaginable," out of their framework. As was noted above, the representative modernist theorists all subscribed to, and approached nationalism from, the Marxist perspective, dominant in the social sciences in regard to everything cultural; that is, they assumed the fundamental nature of "material" – specifically economic – processes, which, being fundamental occurred of themselves, and the epiphenomenal, reflective nature of "ideal" – that is, symbolic or cultural – processes.[22] As a result, the latter could always be explained by the former, while having very little independent influence to affect them in turn, so that the consequences of the cultural processes, however curious on the face of it, could be safely disregarded. Placing nationalism among the possible roots of political action in civil society, instead, forces us to focus on these consequences and represents a significant departure from the paradigm of the 1980s.

[18] For a more detailed discussion of these issues see Liah Greenfeld, "Etymology, Definitions, Types," in *Encyclopedia of Nationalism*, Vol. 1, ed. Alexander J. Motyl (New York: Academic Press, 2001), pp. 251–66.

[19] See, for example, William Pfaff, *The Wrath of Nations: Civilization and the Furies of Nationalism* (New York: Simon and Schuster, 1993).

[20] See, for example, Michael Ignatieff, *Blood and Belonging: A Journey into the New Nationalism* (New York: Farrar, Straus, and Girout, 1994).

[21] Smith, *The Ethnic Origins of Nations* (Cambridge, MA: Blackwell, 1986), pp. 7–12. Today, most versions of the "primordialist" or "perennialist" thesis recognize that, if they existed at all, prenational "nations" were not "objective" biological categories but were themselves socially constructed. See, for example, John A. Armstrong, *Nations Before Nationalism* (Chapel Hill: University of North Carolina Press, 1982). For alternative views see Steven Grosby, "The Chosen People of Ancient Israel and the Occident: Why Does Nationality Exist and Survive?" *Nations and Nationalism* 5(3), 1999, 357–80. See also Adrian Hastings, *The Construction of Nationhood* (Cambridge: Cambridge University Press, 1997); Donald L. Horowitz, "The Primordialists," in Daniele Conversi, ed. *Ethnonationalism in the Contemporary World* (New York: Routledge, 2002) pp. 72–82; and Walker Connor, *Ethnonationalism: The Quest for Understanding* (Princeton: Princeton University Press, 1994).

[22] All of the following "modernists" represent one or another version of this view. See, for example, Karl Deutsch, *Nationalism and Social Communication: An Inquiry into the Foundations of Nationality* (Cambridge, MA: The MIT Press, 1966) as well as Eric Hobsbawm, *op. cit.*; Ernest Gellner, *op. cit.*, and *Encounters with Nationalism* (Cambridge: Blackwell Publishers, 1998) – not to mention the collection of essays on Gellner's work in John Hall, ed., *The State of the Nation: Ernest Gellner and the Theory of Nationalism* (New York: Cambridge University Press, 1998); John Breuilly, *Nationalism and the State* (New York: St. Martin's Press, 1982); and Benedict Anderson, *op. cit.*

The authors of the present article take nationalism to be a "perspective or a style of thought," an image of the world, "at the core of which lies . . . the idea of the 'nation,'" which, in turn, we understand to be the definition of a community as fundamentally equal and sovereign. In the national world, the mass of the population – the people – is seen as the nation. Popular sovereignty signifies an essentially secular worldview: the living people, not a transcendental power, become the source of all law and authority. Because of the principles of popular sovereignty and equality, membership in the nation bestows dignity on the individual, in principle presuming everyone as a potential leader or a member in a leadership elite.[23] Such dignity, in turn, explains why people are willing to die for their nations. This definition meets the objections raised against the earlier attempts detailed previously. In other words, this definition does not fall to objections of either of the two following forms: (1) it cannot be said of it that phenomena that one "wants" to call nations are not captured by the definition and (2) the definition does not capture any phenomena that clearly are not nations. Like those definitions in the tradition of Ernest Renan, the approach is "voluntarist" or "constructivist," meaning that it is recognized that the existence of such nations is dependent on the imaginations of their members. However, unlike earlier proponents of such views, the type of "imagined community" or the "style of imagination" under consideration is here sufficiently specified. France, the United States, Russia, Japan, and so forth all clearly constitute nations, whereas ancient Greece and Rome do not. This definition does not involve the simple assertion that the nation is a modern phenomenon; it points to what separates this modern phenomenon from superficially similar phenomena that preceded it. Moreover, this is the only view that recognizes that nationalism is an essentially *cultural* phenomenon, not reducible to or derivative from some so-called structural factors.

On the most general level – apart from being an umbrella term for a series of related symbolic, psychological, legal, and geopolitical phenomena that are characterized as "national," such as national identity, national consciousness, national sentiment, national pride, national patriotism (i.e., sense of loyalty and devotion toward a national entity specifically), national membership, whether or not defined as citizenship (i.e., nationality and national communities, i.e., nations) – nationalism is a form of consciousness. It represents a comprehensive framework for seeing the world, both social and, in a somewhat vaguer way, natural, and thus constitutes the cultural blueprint for experiencing and constructing "reality." The image of reality nationalism projects lies at the roots of modernity, which, in turn, may be defined as the institutionalization or "embodiment" of nationalism in social, political, and economic structures, that is, in patterned relations and processes – patterned, indeed, by the dictates of this underlying form of consciousness.[24] Therefore, nationalism is most definitely to be included among the roots of political action in civil society: whatever else may inspire any particular movement or event, it is nationalism that both makes conceivable and generates modern political action – and civil society – as such.

THE POLITICAL EFFECTS OF NATIONALISM AS COMPARED TO THOSE OF OTHER FORMS OF CONSCIOUSNESS

As a comprehensive form of consciousness forming the cultural foundation of a distinctive type of society, nationalism is analogous to such broad forms of religion as monotheism, pantheism, or animism, from all of which it is simultaneously distinguished by its essentially secular character. Whatever prominence religion may be given in any particular nationalist discourse, it nevertheless exists on the latter's sufferance, reduced to a strictly subservient or at best

[23] Liah Greenfeld, *Nationalism: Five Roads to Modernity* (Cambridge, MA: Harvard University Press, 1992), pp. 3, 6–7, 12–14.

[24] Liah Greenfeld, *Nationalism, op. cit.* and *The Spirit of Capitalism: Nationalism and Economic Growth* (Cambridge: Harvard University Press, 2001).

marginal role, and in fact survives in every modern society as an atavism.[25] Nationalism is focused on this world, which it presents as ultimately meaningful and self-sufficient, rather than in any way dependent on grander transcendental forces, and this secular focus is reflected not only in the twin principles of the image of sociopolitical reality it projects – the principle of fundamental equality of national membership and the principle of popular sovereignty – but also in the awesome powers attributed in all modern societies to natural science. This does not mean, however, that nationalism should be regarded as a "civil religion." To identify this fundamentally secular form of consciousness in such a way does not do justice to the term *religion*, which, from a sociological point of view, is best understood as a cultural system oriented toward the transcendent. In other words, religion is, by definition, not secular.[26]

The essential secularism and the two principles of nationalism's image of the social world (popular sovereignty and the equality of membership in the nation) define this form of consciousness as such, and though its specific expressions, or particular nationalisms, are distinguished by numerous other qualities, it is these three general characteristics that explain the central political features of every modern society. The first of these central features to be listed is the democratization or universality of political action: the striking fact that in modern societies it may be found on any rung of the social ladder and in any corner of the national territory. It is this, dramatic by comparison to other types of societies, level of political participation that the term *civil society* as a rule describes.[27] Indeed, it would be absurd to talk of "civil society" or "political action" in the framework of the European feudal society or Indian caste society, to mention the two perhaps best known nonmodern types. The forms of consciousness prevailing in them did not allow for the existence of such political phenomena, and they still appear unimaginable to us, being logically incongruent with the two cultural frameworks. In distinction, the cultural framework, or foundation, of modern society – nationalism – not only allows for the proliferation of political action throughout the social system, but effectually calls "civil society" into existence. The focus of nationalism on this world as ultimately meaningful and the principle of popular sovereignty combine to render social reality changeable and place the responsibility for its shape in the hands of the earthly living community – the nation. The focus on the life in this world dramatically increases the value of this life to the individual and inevitably leads to the insistence on a good life, however defined. One is no longer expected to submit to suffering or deprivation, unless one has special reasons to do so, for the general reasons for such submission – the expectation of rewards in the beyond, transmutation and migration of the souls, the duty to serve witness to the glory of God wherever one is called, or the sheer impossibility to change one's condition – no longer apply. Religion, as Clifford Geertz noted so memorably, made suffering "sufferable," because it made it meaningful, and it made it meaningful because life on Earth was just a link, rarely a central link, in a great chain of being and drew meaning from its transcendental context.[28] In the framework of nationalism

[25] For a detailed discussion of the relationship between nationalism and religion see Liah Greenfeld, "The Modern Religion?" *Critical Review* 10:2 (Spring 1996), pp. 169–91. For alternative views, see Josep R. Llobera, *The God of Modernity: The Development of Nationalism in Western Europe* (Oxford: Berg, 1994) and Roger Friedland, "Religious Nationalism and the Problem of Collective Representations" *Annual Review of Sociology*, Vol. 27, August 2001, pp. 125–52.

[26] On the idea of "civil religion" see Robert Bellah, "Civil Religion in America," *Daedalus, the Journal of the American Academy of Arts and Sciences*, Winter 1967, Vol. 96 (1), pp. 1–21.

[27] This is what Edward Shils meant when he spoke of the spread of the center into the periphery in modern, mass society. As he put it, "in the modern societies of the West, the central value system has gone much more deeply into the heart of their members than it has ever succeeded in doing in any earlier society." See Edward Shils, "Center and Periphery" in Shils, *Center and Periphery: Essays in Macrosociology* (Chicago: University of Chicago Press, 1975), pp. 11–12.

[28] Clifford Geertz, "Religion as a Cultural System," *The Interpretation of Cultures* (New York: Basic Books, 2000), pp. 87–125.

one's earthly life became all one could ever have, fully meaningful in its own right, and this made suffering meaningless and therefore insufferable. Moreover, in a self-sufficient world, changeable and shaped by people, suffering is generally believed to be human-made. Even natural disasters are likely to be so interpreted: a famine, an earthquake, or an epidemic are as often as not attributed to some human agent's withholding of the needed but available resources or negligence; personal misfortunes, such as debilitating, life-threatening, and incurable illnesses, are blamed on artificially created environmental conditions (e.g., second-hand smoke and lead paint) or on doctors' incompetence. None of these natural disasters, it is said, "have to happen": they are no longer believed to be in the nature of things. Of course, the right to a life free of suffering is most clearly asserted when suffering is caused – as it is mostly, in modern societies – by social evils: war, economic or political conditions, competition for precedence, and so forth. Humiliation, rejection, thwarted ambition are felt as unjust – as contrary to expectations and thus resulting from illegitimate intervention of malicious others. As one's precious time on Earth is limited, the change in the conditions preventing the realization of one's right to a life of contentment, free of suffering, is experienced as urgent, and because those responsible for their creation are only human, any naturally active and temperamental individual who is not particularly timid easily gets engaged in whatever form the political process around him or her takes.

As a result, involvement in political action (or participation in civil society) under nationalism is a function not of the social position – as it was, let's say, in feudal and absolutist Europe or in Tokugawa Japan – but of character and personality.[29] Because temperament changes with age, and young people, for instance, are more likely to be impetuous and unthinkingly brave, it is also a function of age: it is noteworthy that all revolutionary movements of the past three hundred years, from the French Revolution (with the deservedly capital *R*) to the student one (with the small *r*) of the 1960s, were movements of adolescents and people in their twenties and, to a lesser extent, thirties. It is even more significant that in the past three hundred years – but never before – there were revolutionary movements, that is, explicit attempts at social change, movements oriented toward reshaping the world by human design. All forms of consciousness allow for revolts and rebellions, spontaneous eruptions of frustration and rage, essentially expressive collective actions, aimless – perhaps vaguely oriented to the righting of some tremendous, but ill-defined, wrongs – with goals and demands thought through, if at all, only after the fact. But revolutions are a modern form of political action: at their root always lies nationalism.

The present section of the volume being devoted to civil society, its focus is political action outside the state, but as the state is also a function of nationalism, a brief discussion of the connection between this, modern, form of government and this, constitutive of modernity, form of consciousness may be in order here. Formed under the profound influence of German Romantic thought, many of its fundamental concepts imported uncritically from the murky reservoirs of the latter, American political science often identifies the state with government as such. Thus numerous authors feel compelled to qualify their use of the term with such adjectives as *capitalist, modern,* or *bureaucratic.*[30] But to speak of *the* "modern state" or of *the* "bureaucratic state" is redundant, for the state is only a form of government, and this form is characteristically modern and necessarily bureaucratic. The concept of

[29] On political action in feudal and absolutist Europe see Marc Bloch's *Feudal Society: The Growth of Ties of Dependence* (Chicago: University of Chicago Press, 1988), esp. Part IV, "The Ties Between Man and Man: Vassalage and the Fief." Regarding political action in Tokugawa Japan, see Liah Greenfeld, *The Spirit of Capitalism, op. cit.*, pp. 227–98 and especially pp. 266–7.

[30] Works that treat the state in such terms include Bob Jessop, *State Theory: Putting the Capitalist State in its Place* (University Park: The Pennsylvania State University Press, 1990). See also Gianfranco Poggi, *The Development of the Modern State: A Sociological Introduction* (Palo Alto, CA: Stanford University Press, 1978), and Howard G. Brown, *War, Revolution, and the Bureaucratic State: Politics and Army Administration in France, 1791–1799* (Oxford: Clarendon Press, 1995).

"state" as a form of government appeared in the English of the sixteenth century – about fifty years after the entrenchment of the idea of the "nation" and well into the development of the nationalist discourse.[31] It obviously reflected a new reality, as it did later in other countries when the term migrated there in translation. This new reality was the new form of government, called forth by the new form of consciousness, which presented a new image of what a government should be. As nationalism first developed in Western Europe, this image contrasted most sharply with the then existing Western European ideal of government – the medieval ideal of kingship.[32] The distinguishing characteristic of kingship was its personality: the government was inseparable from a particular person, a person born at a certain time to a certain family, who needed no other qualifications in addition to this accident of birth (of course, never regarded as an accident and at a later stage explicitly reaffirmed as divine appointment) to assume power. In contrast, the distinguishing characteristic of the state became its impersonality.[33] Because supreme authority, in the framework of nationalism, resides in the body of the nation in accordance with principle of popular sovereignty, the authority of the state is necessarily delegated, representative (in the sense that it only represents the authority of the people), and, insofar as it is subject to recall, limited. Sovereignty is delegated to the office, not to any particular person, and any person exercises authority only as a holder of the office. The state is a government by officers, that is, a bureaucracy. In this sense, Adolph Hitler, the Führer who ardently believed that he represented the will of the German people, was but a bureaucrat, as was Joseph Stalin, the appositely referred to General Secretary, who did not believe in any such thing but made sure that everyone else did.

Finally, the principle of the equality of national membership lies at the root of the open recruitment for state offices, which obviously also exerts a most profound influence on the nature of politics in modern society.[34] It is through the principle of equality of membership – its core social principle – that nationalism affects the social structure most directly, because in modern society the system of social stratification – the nodal structural system, in which all social systems meet and connect – is based on this principle. In this case, too, the modern, or national, system of social stratification represents the very opposite of the stratification system characteristic of the European feudal society, which it replaced. In place of a rigid structure, sharply distinguishing between strata of which it was composed and, except by special dispensation, allowing no movement between them, we now have an open system with loosely and only theoretically defined compartments, in practice virtually indistinguishable and seamlessly flowing one into another via the numerous channels

[31] Liah Greenfeld, "Nationalism and Modernity," *Social Research* 62:4 (Winter 1996).

[32] Regarding the medieval conception of kingship, see Reinhard Bendix, *Kins or People: Power and the Mandate to Rule* (Berkeley: University of California Press, 1978). See also Ernst H. Kantorowicz, *The King's Two Bodies: A Study in Medieval Political Theology* (Princeton: Princeton University Press, 1957).

[33] Max Weber, *Economy and Society: An Outline of Interpretive Sociology*, eds. Guenther Roth and Claus Wittich (Berkeley: University of California Press, 1978), pp. 600, 998.

[34] The emphasis on the equality of national membership here should not be confused with an emphasis on citizenship. Different nationalisms conceive of membership in different terms (indeed, this is the essence of the civic/ethnic distinction noted elsewhere in this article) and only for some nations is membership coterminous with citizenship. Citizenship itself is not a function of nationalism. That is, other types of societies – consider Ancient Rome – have had citizens. *National* citizenship, however (like *national* patriotism), constitutes a subtype of citizenship more generally considered and signifies a particular set of relations with the state – the central political institution through which popular sovereignty is "made manifest." For a variety of views on the nature of citizenship, see T. H. Marshall, *Class, Citizenship and Social Development: Essays* (Garden City, NY: Doubleday, 1964); Bryan S. Turner *Citizenship and Capitalism: The Debate over Reformism* (Boston: & Unwin, 1986); and Thomas Janoski, *Citizenship and Civil Society: A Framework of Rights and Obligations in Liberal, Traditional, and Social Democratic Regimes* (New York: Cambridge University Press, 1998), as well as the essays in Bart van Steenbergen, ed., *The Condition of Citizenship* (Thousand Oaks, CA: Sage, 1994).

of social mobility.[35] One no longer has a social position and function, clearly defined by birth, which is supposed to serve one (or, rather, which one is supposed to serve) all of one's lifetime; instead, one is supposed to choose a function and to achieve a social position (which presupposes specifically upward mobility), moving from one social position to higher and higher ones as one grows older, "bettering oneself" or "getting ahead." In modern societies one does not talk of "usurpers," "parvenus," or, however great the temptation, "nouveaux riches": one is expected, even encouraged, to strive, to have ambitions, to be a proficient social climber. And so there is nothing strange in a poor seminarian from Georgia becoming the all-powerful ruler of the great Soviet Union, a son of elderly underpaid Leningrad parents rising through the ranks of foreign espionage to the presidency of only slightly less great Russia, a daughter of a modest greengrocer gaining recognition as the strongest premier of United Kingdom, and a child of a single mother, unhappily remarried to a garage mechanic from Arkansas, twice being elected to head the United States of America. Our form of consciousness, nationalism, makes this kind of mountaineering normal, respectable, and, in fact, necessary.

The combination of the principles of popular sovereignty and fundamental equality of membership implies democracy: government of the people by the people; therefore, political recruitment must be open to any member of the nation. The process of recruitment in the democratic, national, or modern societies differs drastically from those based on forms of consciousness different from nationalism, for, whatever the differences between nationalisms (which, as is argued in the section on "Types of Nationalism and their Implications for Political Action" may be very significant), it is in all nations essentially, rather than accidentally, a process of *self-recruitment*, always dependent (though not inevitably determined) by individual initiative, the nature of one's ambition and talent, whereas in other societies it follows strictly charted paths from certain initial social positions to specified political functions, which only extraordinary circumstances allow to circumvent.

TYPES OF NATIONALISM AND THEIR IMPLICATIONS FOR POLITICAL ACTION

Because of the fundamental dependence of all cultural processes on the individual mind, no form of consciousness is uniform by definition, and this applies in particular to comprehensive forms of consciousness that underlie broad types of social formations, such as nationalism. That is why nationalism is analogous to forms of religious consciousness, such as monotheism, rather than to specific religions, such as Christianity, for instance, and even less to specific secular ideologies, such as liberalism or conservatism (which cannot be considered comprehensive forms of consciousness), to which it is regularly compared.[36] As within monotheism one can distinguish Judaism, Christianity, and Islam, each one of which is a variety of monotheism interpreted and implemented in a distinctive way, so within nationalism one finds several types of this secular form of consciousness, distinguished by the manner in which they interpret and implement the twin principles of nationalism. The implications of these types for

[35] The authors do not mean to minimize enduring inequality in the modern world. Instead, we assert that modern, national societies are by definition devoted to the ideal of equality (however conceived, as there is indeed considerable variation in this regard) and that this tends to be reflected in the expanded possibilities of the majority of modern social actors. Indeed, it may very well be the case that discriminatory behavior is fundamentally a modern phenomenon, meaningful only in the national world. In premodern Europe, for example, the failure of a member of the lower social strata to rise would not have been regarded as unjust, given the absolute lack of expectation of social mobility. It is only because we live in a world where the expectation is widespread that if one works hard and applies oneself and is treated fairly one will rise that inequality, though less pronounced than in the past, is in some ways a more *apparent* feature of social life.

[36] For a recent example of this very old sort of confusion, see Ronald Beiner, "Liberalism, Nationalism, Citizenship: Three Models of Political Community" in Beiner, *Liberalism, Nationalism, Citizenship: Essays on the Problem of Political Community* (Toronto: UBC Press, 2003), pp. 21–38.

political action differ dramatically, as they do in all the spheres of social action generally defined,[37] and this explains singular features and characteristic tendencies in the political culture, process, and historical record of individual nations.

The character of a particular nationalism is a function of (a) the definition of the nation, which may be seen as a composite or as a unitary entity, and (b) the nature of membership criteria, which may be civic or ethnic. Three types of nationalism are created by the combinations of these possibilities.[38] Historically, the first type of nationalism to emerge was the *individualistic and civic* type, in which the nation is defined in composite terms, as an association of individuals (with plural pronouns corresponding to the concepts of "nation" and "people," as in "We, the people"), and the criteria of membership are civic, nationality being equated with citizenship. Nations such as United Kingdom, the United States of America, and Australia are nations of the individualistic and civic type. The type to follow was *collectivistic and civic*, represented, for example, by France and Israel. In this case a unitary definition of the nation, as an irreducible whole organized according to principles peculiar to itself, is combined with civic membership criteria. Both of these early types are quite rare. The few nations belonging to them have, by and large, recognized a deep affinity tying them together and treat each other as natural allies. For purposes of rough comparative analysis they may be discussed as one. The last to appear and the most widespread type of nationalism is the *collectivistic and ethnic* type, which combines a unitary definition of the nation with "ethnic," hereditary, or, in fact, genetic criteria of membership.[39] In its political implications, it represents a sharp contrast to the individualistic-civic type, the representative nations of the two types being traditionally found on the opposite sides of international political conflicts. The great ideological divide of the twentieth century was the divide between individualistic-civic and collectivistic-ethnic nationalisms, and collectivistic-ethnic nations were invariably parties and, as a rule, the aggressive parties, in all the many wars fought in it – from World War I to the almost permanent Arab–Israeli war – in which they either fought among themselves or opposed civic nations of the two other types.[40]

The type of nationalism affects every aspect of political conduct in a nation, beginning with the very manner in which political reality is constructed and embodied in various institutions, as these directly reflect the interpretation of the two core principles of nationalism. To start, it affects the type of democracy that prevails, for although every nation is a democracy by definition – government of the people by the people being implied in nationalism as such – it is well known that one nation's democracy is another one's nightmare.[41] Certainly, this is what, for instance, democracy in the Soviet Union or China of Chairman Mao's time ("popular" or "socialist" democracy) was for democracies of the American or British variety (that is "liberal" democracy) and vice versa. With the exception of a few pockets of resistance (particularly sophisticated societies such as the Dutch Republic of the Golden Age or Renaissance Italy), nationalism, similarly to monotheism at an earlier period, has spread quite easily throughout the world. But in its spread it has transformed into particular nationalisms, giving rise to particular forms of national organization, national

[37] Regarding social action, see Weber, *op. cit.*, pp. 22–6.

[38] A number of commentators, following Brubaker, have only distinguished between two types of nationalisms: ethnic and civic. See Rogers Brubaker, *Citizenship and Nationhood in France and Germany* (Cambridge: Harvard University Press, 1992).

[39] Ethnic criteria of membership are not necessarily tied to racialist thinking. The essential quality of an ethnic form of identity is that some *involuntary* ascriptive characteristic is taken to constitute the boundary marker of that form of identity. In other words, the essential quality of ethnic identity is that it is not taken to be a matter of choice. For an ethnic nationalist, one can neither acquire nor alienate one's national identity.

[40] Liah Greenfeld and Daniel Chirot, "Nationalism and Aggression," *Theory and Society* 23(1): 79–130.

[41] Liah Greenfeld, "Nationalism and Democracy: The Nature of the Relationship and the Cases of England, France, and Russia," *Research in Democracy and Society*, vol. 1, 1993, pp. 327–52.

consciousness, and national identity. In distinction to nationalism in general, these particular forms can be no more imposed one on another than can Islam on Christianity, Christianity on Judaism, and so on. (This, obviously, applies to societies, not to individuals; and societies under long-term occupation may represent an exception.) The type of democracy a nation develops (liberal or popular/socialist – a new phrase "managed democracy" has been coined to refer to this latter type in Mr. Putin's Russia), in distinction to democracy in general, which is implied in the nationalist principles of popular sovereignty and equality of membership, is a reflection of such particular forms of nationalism and therefore can no more be imported into and imposed on a nation than can a foreign national identity. In other words, it is as unlikely that an Arab, collectivistic-ethnic nation, such as Iraq, which until quite recently, anyway, was a socialist democracy (similar to the national socialist democracy in Germany in the 1930s, for instance) will transform into a liberal democracy as that the Iraqis *en masse* will redefine and consider themselves Americans or French. And, of course, it is a transformation of this kind that we care about, not the reaffirmation by nations hostile to us of their generally democratic character, truthful as it is.

To understand the political propensities of different types of nationalism, we have to consider the logical implications of the definitions of the nation and of national membership, on the basis of which these types are constructed. The composite definition of the nation as an association of individuals locates popular sovereignty – the will of the community – in the individuals who compose it, thus projecting an image of sovereignty as divisible and aggregate of separate sovereignties of each member. Members are thus viewed as interdependent but fully autonomous and self-governing. It is because they are essentially, that is, by their very nature, free and equal that the nation is free and egalitarian. The institutionalization, or implementation, of popular sovereignty, so interpreted, results in institutions (norms and routine practices) that safeguard individual freedom, equality, and autonomy. Everyone has the possibility to participate actively in the political process and have one's input counted through voting; the will of the nation, believed to be changeable within the broad value framework (of individual liberty and equality), is periodically operationalized as the will of the majority of individual members and always arrived at by induction, rather than being deduced from some first principles. Within institutions of government, or the state, members of the nation are represented by proxy by officials they have elected. This is the way one understands representative institutions in liberal democracies. But, of course, it is equally possible to understand them in a very different, if not wholly contradictory, way.

Political representation can be understood (or represented) as "representation to," rather than "representation of," the nation. In fact, this is precisely the function of specific – and distinctively modern – political role: that of the *ideologue*. Ideologues represent the nation, its nature, its interests, its will, to its members. Ideological politics reflect a unitary definition of the nation. The conceptualization of the national collectivity as an entity in its own right, irreducible to its elements, almost inevitably tends to abut in its reification, in imagining the nation anthropomorphically as a collective individual, which is particularly likely when the nationalism combines the unitary definition of the nation with ethnic criteria of national membership. This collective individual is then endowed with its own will, rights, and interests, independent of the wills, interests, and rights of human individuals who compose it and unalterable, because its essential nature does not change with natural changes in this composition. Human individuals are subsumed in the larger and so clearly more imposing collective individual similarly to the way in which cells are subsumed in the living organism and are to be considered only to the extent that they contribute to a life of the higher order; national membership loses its meaning of active participation and becomes something like a biological condition: one is a member in the sense in which a particular minor organ, say, a finger, is a member of a body.

Although in an individualistic nationalism, popular sovereignty is interpreted as the aggregate liberty of free individuals, in a collectivistic nationalism it is interpreted as the freedom of the nation from foreign domination. Liberty itself is redefined as a reflection of such national autonomy and is no longer seen as an innate human capacity. Equality is also reinterpreted. Members – nationals or citizens – of individualistic nations are equal specifically in their liberty: their capacity and right for self-government and political participation and, therefore, legal rights and obligations. In collectivistic nations they are equal only in that they equally share the essential nature of their nation, that which makes it a particular nation and them nationals of this particular nation. This equality is fundamental, but in everything else, including the nature of their political participation, they may be legitimately considered unequal.

When the nation is reified and believed possessed of its own, independent will, this will, which cannot be equated with the will of the majority, must be perceived by some other, nonempirical means. It is this need that creates the position of the ideologue. Ideologues – Rousseau's "great legislators" – are the natural rulers of collectivistic (especially ethnic-collectivistic) nations. They are the "aristocracy of intelligence (or) virtue" who know the will of the nation. They represent this will to the mass of the members (it is telling that members of the nation are in fact commonly referred to in collectivistic-ethnic nations as a "mass"), informing the people what it wants and needs and imposing these alleged wants and needs on them.

This profound distinction between those few who have (because they claim) direct access to the will of the nation and those multitudes who don't (because it is denied to them), itself a logical implication of the unitary definition of the nation, as a rule results in authoritarian politics. What is referred to as "popular," "socialist," or, in the case of Putin's new Russia, "managed" democracies are in fact authoritarian democracies of collectivistic nations, which represent the very antithesis of liberal democracies, characteristic of individualistic nations, such as the United States, and frequently equated in them with democracy as such. It is extremely dangerous to disregard the differences between these two types. Modern tyrannies have been invariably associated with collectivistic nationalisms, usually ethnic, from Jacobin France to the Russian Empire of the "official nationalism" period to Fascist Italy, National Socialist Germany, the Union of the Soviet Socialist Republics under "the Great Russian nationalism," and such late-twentieth-century/new millennium diehards as Ba'ath Iraq or Syria.[42] In the twentieth century these authoritarian regimes were often easily recognizable under the names of "socialist" or "communist" regimes. Since the early 1990s, such self-identification went out of fashion, which makes it more difficult for politicians who set great store by names to recognize these regimes for what they are. But, of course, a change of the name rarely, if ever, implies a change of nature.

Although at the root of distinctions between liberal and authoritarian regimes described previously lies the difference between the composite and unitary definitions of the nation, collectivistic nationalisms that are civic (namely when the unitary definition of the nation is combined with civic criteria of membership) may, but are unlikely to, develop authoritarian tendencies, because their civic character contradicts and neutralizes such development. Civic

[42] See Daniel Chirot, *Modern Tyrants: The Power and Prevalence of Evil in Our Age* (New York: The Free Press, 1994), pp. 267–308. The case of Iran after the revolution, so often taken by social scientists as an example of so-called religious fundamentalism, likewise seems to be closely related to, if not an instance of, collectivistic and ressentiment-laden nationalism. Khomeini, for example, so often taken as the religious ideologue *par excellence*, was clearly an Iranian nationalist. In response to the granting of capitulatory rights to the United States in 1964, Khomeini proclaimed that "Our dignity has been trampled underfoot; the dignity of Iran has been destroyed." Moreover, those responsible for the measure had "sold our independence, reduced us to the level of a colony, and made the Muslim nation of Iran appear more backward than savages in the eyes of the world!" He promised that "If the religious leaders have influence, they will not permit this nation to be the slaves of Britain one day, and America the next." See Imam Khomeini, *Islam and Revolution: Writings and Declarations of Imam Khomeini*, trans. and annotated by Hamid Algar (Berkeley: Mizan Press, 1981), pp. 181–3.

nationalism makes membership in principle voluntary, dependent on the will of the individual. As is made abundantly clear by the experience of the United States, Israel, and other immigrant nations, but may be observed in cases of non-immigrant civic national communities, such as, most notably, France, one can both acquire a civic nationality, if one is not born with it, and opt out of it if one is. Either of the two changes of identity and membership may be more or less difficult, depending on the laws of the particular nation, but both are possible. All that is needed to become a new member, in fact, is to convince the gatekeeping authorities (which in some cases may need more convincing than in others but are in all cases open to argument) that one is willing to adopt the fundamental values and practices – which may be linguistic, political, religious, or pertain to public behavior in general, such as not wearing a face-veil outdoors – of the nation in question and to assume the duties of membership in it. And very little indeed is needed to abandon membership one no longer wishes to have. This principled voluntarism makes the very existence of the civic nation dependent on the wills of its individual members, thus constantly affirming their autonomy and liberty, which the unitary definition of the nation constantly tends to deny. Collectivistic and civic nationalisms are ambivalent, conflicted, and conflictive nationalisms – which is daily reflected in their politics – because their two constitutive principles, equally capable of provoking political passion and devotion, are logically contradictory. No evidence of this is likely to be more familiar than the turbulent political history of France, the nation that invented political totalitarianism, while subscribing to the arch-individualist maxim "penser c'est dire non" and none better is needed.

Ethnic criteria of membership, in distinction, reinforce the authoritarian tendencies of collectivistic nationalisms. In the framework of ethnic nationalisms, nationality is regarded as an inborn trait, like those genetic characteristics that are also considered ethnic, such as physical type. In fact, physical type is usually believed to be the most reliable expression of nationality, less likely to be faked or claimed by outsiders, than its other common expressions: language, religion, traits of character, and territorial and political affiliation – thus the emphasis of ethnic nationalisms on blood. Physical type is transmitted genetically; nationality is presumably also so transmitted. This makes it indistinguishable from biological race and by extension turns national language, religion, traits of character, and territorial and political affiliations into racial characteristics. Biology becomes destiny. One can no more acquire a nationality, if one is not born with it, or give it up, if one is, than one can change one's blood type. Therefore, those who do are considered either impostors or traitors, that is, criminals of one degree or another. Individual will has nothing to do with the choice of nationality and language, religion, values, allegiance to a particular state, liking for a particular territory – whatever is counted among the national characteristics in the case – because there is no choice. The individual is determined by the nation into which he or she is born and is emphatically denied freedom. There is no need for freedom on the individual level – the individual is not defined as a free agent; the only freedom one may (and, as a matter of fact, should) wish for is the freedom of the nation from foreign domination. Nationality defined in ethnic terms, therefore, deprives the individual of what constitutes individuality, dissolving individual agency and making it logical indeed to talk of people as "a mass." At the same time, by attributing agency to the nation, its definition as a collective individual achieves the same result, or rather vastly reinforces the impression left by this result on the mind, and breaks whatever residual resistance to the submission of the human mass, dispossessed of its wills, to the crashing authority of the will of the nation and its self-appointed representatives.

Although ethnic nationalism (which is always collectivistic) is as open to individual ambition as are nationalisms of the two other types, it virtually excludes the population outside of the state institutions from participation in the government and policy formation: it is meaningless to speak of political process in this sense, or of public opinion, in its context. But, like nationalism in general, it still encourages political activism, and therefore political action, outside the state's sphere of action even when authoritarian democracies for which ethnic nationalism provides the cultural soil spawn, as they so often do, tyranny. Political activism, obviously, takes very different forms in ethnic nationalism and in individualistic and civic nationalisms that produce liberal nations. In liberal nations, it can be characterized as generally introvert (focused on the internal policies and domestic conditions); as directed by and large to the correction of, or improvement on, government actions and to their supplementation in instances where it is felt the government fails to take action; and as rational and instrumental in the sense of being oriented to specific and realistic goals. It is most emphatically goal-oriented. As a result, it expresses itself in constructive, methodical (which means unemotional, even when enthusiastic), organized action, which naturally ends when the goal is reached. By and large, individuals engaged in political action work with (i.e., seek to involve, inform, and secure the support of) governmental agencies and use channels provided for such action within political institutions: they lobby, they distribute petitions to be signed, and so forth.[43] Only exceptionally does political activism in liberal nations takes destructive, expressive, and emotional forms. Historically, this happens in times of major disorientation and exacerbation of *anomie* (a low-grade state of which is a systemic problem in modern – i.e., national – societies) and has to be taken as a symptom of these conditions.[44]

The political activism of ethnic nations, in contrast, is largely extrovert. To describe it as focused on foreign policies and conditions would not be accurate, because it is not at all a focused type of activism, because it leaves foreign policies to the authorities as much as it does domestic policies, and because foreign conditions are of no interest to the activists. But it is fired (as this activism expresses itself in sporadic outbursts of activity, rather than in systematic and organized action, *fired* is the proper descriptive term) by diffuse concerns with presumed foreign threats and by ever fomenting sense of collective injury and personal hostility toward the eternally unjust world somehow preventing the self-realization of one's nation. This sense of permanent siege is a function of *ressentiment*, which plays a central role in the formation of ethnic nationalisms[45] and shapes both the image of the particular ethnic nation itself and the attitudes toward the external world. Among its related functions is the dual vision in which the essential, the "really real," exists apart from the

[43] Examples of social movements relying largely on this sort of political action include the women's suffrage movement and the Civil Rights movement in the United States, as well as myriad local initiatives such as the establishments of Casinos on Native American Reservations and the building of new schools.

[44] Examples of such types of political action include the famous demonstrations by unemployed veterans of the First World War in Washington, DC, not to mention much of the political organization of the students' movements of the 1960s. This is not to say that such movements are necessarily "destructive," nor do the authors intend to praise or criticize, either implicitly or explicitly, their aims.

[45] The concept of ressentiment, which was developed by Friedrich Nietzsche and later Max Scheler, cannot simply be translated as *resentment* (it is, instead, a form of *existential envy*) and implicitly recognizes the significance of status in social life (a recognition to which, one might argue, recent work in political sociology has not been sufficiently attentive). *Ressentiment* can occur when a given actor (or set of actors) finds him- or herself in a position of fundamental comparability with another social actor (or set of actors) and discovers that, within the prevailing value scheme, he or she is of inferior status. There are three logically possible responses to such a state of affairs. One is to accept the prevailing value scheme and one's place in it – to resign oneself to a position of inferiority. In the modern, national world, with its tremendous emphasis on the importance of equality, this is a route seldom taken, because it is considered so important to be "as good" as everyone else. The second logically possible response is to accept the value system within which one seems to be inferior and to work to improve one's position in its terms. An example of such a response can be see in the Herculean works of propaganda of Friedrich List in nineteenth-century Germany. The third possible response, what is called the "transvaluation of values," involves attacking or inverting the value scheme in terms of which one appears inferior. This last option is consistent with ressentiment. On ressentiment and nationalism see Greenfeld, *Nationalism: Five Roads to Modernity*, *op. cit.*, pp. 15–17. Regarding Friedrich List's role in German economic development, including an analysis of his motivations, see Greenfeld, *The Spirit of Capitalism*, *op. cit.*, pp. 199–214.

empirical or the way things appear. This vision allows one to see one's nation as essentially and wholly good, whatever one's experience of reality and the nation's historical record, and to blame everything that is not good in these experience and record (usually there are plenty of things to blame) on malicious aliens. Because ethnic purity is an unattainable ideal, it is more than likely that aliens coexist with nationals as citizens of the national state or, if there is no state, inhabitants of the national territory. Political activists are likely to be suspicious and resentful of these aliens, seen as natural agents of the outside world (they carry treason in their blood in the same way in which members of the nation carry their nationality). As a result of all these representations, which are implicit in ethnic-collectivistic nationalism, political activism within its framework is largely expressed in more or less constant vociferation against others' wrongs and occasional outbursts of ethnic violence, both usually in accordance with the state-promoted line or ideology, even when the state, for reasons of diplomacy, abstains from explicitly supporting such vociferation and violence. This political action is not goal-oriented and, therefore, not rational and not organized. It is emotional and expressive (specifically of national identity, commitment, and solidarity). Its end is psychological gratification that is achieved in the process of expression, meaning that it has no end. Unlike political action inspired by individualistic and civic nationalisms, which comes in limited quanta, emitted, so to speak, in larger or smaller frequencies depending on the pragmatic requirements of the situation, political action within ethnic nations may be regarded as a wave, constantly simmering, and rising or falling in accordance with collective psychological dynamics.[46]

This has most serious implications for the understanding of the so-called national liberation movements. The very different understanding of liberty in individualistic and civic versus ethnic nationalisms implies that liberation, too, has different meanings and is likely to be sought for different reasons and by different means. These differences are obscured by the equation of the motivation behind all liberation movements with the desires for independence from foreign domination and the establishment of national state and the confusion between these two desires. The desire for a state of one's own is not necessarily related to the revulsion at, or even consciousness of, being governed by foreign powers. This is abundantly clear from that model case of liberation from colonial rule – the American War of Independence. It is not a mere coincidence that the American War of Independence is equally well known under the name of the American Revolution and that the confidently national political entity that came out of it remains until this very day a nation without a name. This curious asymmetry in nomenclature reflects the fact that the insurgents were a part of the British nation, in which they believed themselves to be mistreated by reason of the remoteness of their province, not at all because the European British were foreigners. Therefore, they decided to partially transform the political structure within their own – at the moment British – nation, turning its American part with which they were immediately concerned into a republic. This revolution was very much in the nature of limited, rational, specific-goal-oriented political actions characteristic of individualistic nations, of which the British nation was the prime example. Only the achievement of the goal inevitably resulted in abandoning the national name to the European kingdom that held it first. The actual reason the American British (whose descendents and fellow nationals are known today as Americans) craved independence was that the colonial structure of their nation prevented them from participating fully in the political process or, in other words, limited their individual liberty.

Only this liberty offers members of individualistic nations a sufficient reason to rise of their own will and risk their lives in a struggle against a government, if this government is not particularly brutal, does not starve people or subject them to physical and psychological conditions that cannot, by an impartial observer, be

[46] Liah Greenfeld, "Russian nationalism as a medium of revolution: an exercise in historical sociology," *Qualitative Sociology* 18:2, pp. 189–209.

considered tolerable (which does not, of course, apply to the "intolerable acts"). This would be so, whether the government in question is national or foreign, and this is likely to be so in nations which are strongly civic (i.e., when the individualistic element is strongly emphasized), even when they are collectivistic. The goal of national liberation or independence movements in all these cases is the protection of the human rights of the nation's individual members, and they result in the establishment of liberal democracies.

Israel presents an example of the movement of civic national liberation from foreign domination. In the case of the Jewish settlement in Palestine, the government of the British mandate, clearly, was not as mild as in the case of its own American colonies, but, though it was decidedly uncooperative with the Jewish community leadership and though its sympathies were generally pro-Arab, neither could it be considered particularly oppressive. Throughout the 1920s and 1930s, the concerns of the Jewish community, as earlier, focused on building on the spot of desert allotted to it by international largesse a liberal and socially just secular society, in accordance with the progressive ideals its founders brought with them from Europe, and on turning the dry barren earth of their "national home" into fertile ground, capable of sustaining flourishing agriculture and prosperous, growing, technologically sophisticated economy without any natural resources.[47] Independent statehood, however, became a central issue with the outbreak of World War II, when the world turned a blind eye on the tragedy of Jews in Europe and the British authorities closed to the straggling refugees the Jewish settlement in Palestine – the only community willing to take them in. The internationally sanctioned and officially designated Jewish "national home" was not allowed by its British landlords to open its doors to members of the nation who were thus condemned to death[48]; it was time to get rid of the landlord.

It is significant that despite the desperate urgency of the matter, the Israeli national liberation movement took the methodic, organized form political action takes in individualistic and civic nations under regular peace-time circumstances. The participants used the channels provided by, in this case, international legal and political institutions; they lobbied, petitioned, and argued. There was never violence against families of British officials; there was very little violence against British military violently implementing antiemigration policies of the mandate. The War of Independence broke, as is well known, only after the newborn, half-a-million-strong state of Israel, voted into being by the United Nations and barely declared, was attacked on all sides by five populous independent states of its Arab neighbors-to-be, who did not want to be its neighbors.[49]

In the case of ethnic nations, national liberation is motivated by different considerations and uses different methods.[50] The liberty of ethnic nationalism being the liberty of the nation from foreign domination, (ethnic) national independence movements are always oriented to the establishment of the state, the lack of which spells national – and therefore personal – indignity for the activists. Rather than being concerned with human rights (i.e., rights of individuals to life, liberty, and the pursuit of happiness), they are inspired by the sense of humiliation, which, in accordance with the reified, animistic

[47] Martin Gilbert, *The Dent Atlas of the Arab–Israeli Conflict* (London: J. M. Dent, 1993), p. 12.

[48] See Walter Lacquer, *The Road to Jerusalem: The Origins of the Arab–Israeli Conflict* (New York: The MacMillan Company, 1968), p. 7. See also Martin Gilbert, *Exile and Return: The Struggle for a Jewish Homeland* (New York: J. B. Lippincott Company, 1978), pp. 243–4.

[49] See Lacquer, *op. cit.*, pp. 11–13.

[50] This is not to suggest either that (a) nations that conceive of themselves in fundamentally ethnic terms are inevitably bound to pursue violent political action or (b) civic nations (whether individualistic or collectivistic) never engage in violent acts related to their nationalism. In the first case, it is argued that, for reasons specified in the text, there is a sort of built-in tendency toward collective violence in ethnic nationalism: but it is just that, a tendency. Regarding the second point, the participation of the United States in the Second World War, to take just one of many possible examples, cannot be understood but in relation to American nationalism. In general, the character, causes, and duration of political violence in different types of nations vary considerably.

imagery of ethnic nationalism, they believe to be intentionally inflicted on them by the evil other. This other is, usually, the nation from which ethnic nationalists in question seek independence, but not only and not necessarily; the decisive quality that creates the enemy is the latter's evident superiority over one's ethnic nation, which makes independence fighters resent the other's very existence. In other words, the motivation behind national liberation movements in the framework of ethnic nationalism is *ressentiment* responsible for the formation of the particular ethnic nationalism in the first place. Because foreign domination as such is experienced as an insult, it is never the specific actions or policies of the foreign authorities that are the cause of the liberation movements, but the fact of their foreignness. The foreign regime may actually be responsible for the improvement of conditions among the subject nation population, bringing them economic opportunities, medical care, and educational resources that they in its absence would not have; this would not change the attitude of activists in its regard. The activists are not concerned with the fates of individuals but with the dignity of the nation.

Still, if the foreign power owes its domination to accidental circumstances and is not seen as the superior eternally hostile other who is responsible for the sense of national inferiority and humiliation, the animus against it will be spent when statehood is achieved. Unfortunately, this is rarely the case, and therefore independence is only a stage (however necessary) in the process of liberation. The essential fault of the evil "superior" other is its very being – as long as it exists or as long as it remains "superior," it is seen as oppressive, and only its destruction or irreparable humiliation can bring the sense of freedom. This explains, among other things, why in the 1920s and 1930s, before the foundation of the state of Israel, when Palestinian Jews (incidentally identified in their documents as "Palestinians"[51]), as well as their Arab neighbors, were ruled by the British and exercised no authority at all over the Arabs, Arabs nevertheless repeatedly attacked the Jewish community and not the British officialdom, burning Jewish farms that offered them work and murdering people who nursed them when they fell sick and assisted their women in labor. The fault of the Jews was glaring: it was that in the short period of several decades since they were allowed to establish their "national home" in Palestine, they turned their sliver of desert into an orchard, which produced not only oranges (which were burnt with particular determination)[52] but also a bustling industry and world-class universities, whereas the vast stretches of land that Arabs possessed for centuries remained barren and kept their people hungry and dependent. Their presence was far more humiliating – thus far more of a foreign domination – than the British mandate.[53]

The methods employed in the fight for the national liberation of ethnic nations reflect the motivations and also represent logical implications of the ethnic nationalist consciousness and its essentialist and absolutist imagery. The struggles of ethnic nationalism are struggles to the ultimate end, to the death: ethnic nationalism brooks no compromise. Because the nation (every nation) is imagined as a collective, quasi-biological individual, and because nationality with all its characteristics is believed to be transmitted by blood, an entire nation, from newborn infants to elderly in nursing homes,

[51] Indeed, international documents similarly identified both the Jewish and Arab populations as Palestinians or residents of Palestine. See, for example, the declaration of the League of Nations concerning the British mandate from July 24, 1922 or the "Resolution on the Future Government of Palestine" of November 29, 1947. Both appear in Walter Lacquer and Barry Rubin, eds., *The Arab–Israeli Reader: A Documentary History of the Middle East Conflict* (New York: Penguin Books, 2001), pp. 30–6, 69–77.

[52] Regarding major attacks against Jewish-owned farms and orchards see Gilbert, *The Dent Atlas of the Arab–Israeli Conflict, op. cit.*, pp. 18–20.

[53] See Fouad Ajami, *The Arab Predicament: Arab Political Thought and Practice since 1967* (New York: Cambridge University Press, 1992) and *Dream Palace of the Arabs: A Generation's Odyssey* (Vintage Books, 1999) as well as Efraim Karsh, *Arafat's War: The Man and his Battle for Israeli Conquest* (Grove Press, 2003), *The Iran–Iraq War 1980–1988* (Osprey Publishing Co, 2002), and Efraim Karsh and Inari Rautsi, *Saddam Hussein: A Political Biography* (Grove Press, 2003).

is considered the enemy and a legitimate target for hostile action. Owing to its quasi-biological programming, the enemy is eternal, no concession on its part can turn it into a friend, and every unfriendly act on its part, no matter what the context, serves to prove its immutable fiendishness. For this reason the action against the oppressor regularly takes the form of violence against civilians. The preferred method of national liberation movements of ethnic nations is ***terrorism***: surprise peacetime attacks on members of the enemy population. The siege mentality of ethnic nationalism creates a siege reality for the unlucky nations chosen as the evil other. The goal of the "freedom fighters" in this case is to hurt the collective individual of the enemy nation wherever and whenever there is an opportunity. For this reason, they are likely to choose easy targets near at hand (such, for instance, as planting bombs in school buses or sending an individual suicide driver to a crowded street in a neighboring enemy center) more often than long distance ones and such that require careful and time-consuming organization (i.e., crashing American jets into the Twin Towers of the World Trade Center). This may create the impression that they are actually fighting for the liberation from foreign ***political*** domination and that the establishment of a national state would fully satisfy their demands and put an end to violence. But, of course, this is not so, and the fact of the attack on American soil (perpetrated as it was by individuals none of whom were stateless and the very same organizations, tacitly supported by several states, that fund and train the national liberation militants in what is now called Palestine) should have convinced us of that. International terrorism, carried by members of one nation against members of another, cannot be fought effectively without the understanding of its deep roots in ethnic-collectivistic nationalism and its connection and affinity to all the other types of political action to which this nationalism gives rise. Today, with our own country being made a target of terrorist attacks and placed in a state of siege, it would be dangerous to disregard these roots.

CONCLUSION

This chapter has focused largely on the nature of nationalism and its main implications for political action. To conclude, we take a slightly broader view of directions for future research. The scientific study of nationalism, like that of all social phenomena, must treat its object as an empirical problem. Like all cultural phenomena, nationalism is fundamentally a symbolic reality taking place in time. In other words, nationalism, though possessing a number of relatively static features, is a process. This is most readily grasped when one views the main contours of its initial (and ongoing) spread, from the site of its first imagining in late fifteenth or early sixteenth century England to its place today as the dominant mode of political discourse. The bulk of this process has, as of yet, not been explored in any detail. We know a good deal about nationalism's origins in England and its spread to France, Russia, Germany, Japan, and the United States (and, to a lesser extent, in Eastern and Southern Europe). The outlines of its spread elsewhere remain largely anecdotal at this point (despite a handful of truly illuminating studies of particular cases) and their clarification constitutes the foremost problem for future research.

At present, despite the considerable attention devoted to the study of nationalism since the early 1980s, the study of most of these cases constitutes more or less open terrain. Of the major theorists of nationalism cited in the section on "The State of the Field" most pay only passing attention (at most) to nationalism in Africa, the Middle East, Asia, or Latin America. A subset of the series of cases requiring further exploration includes what is often referred to as pan-nationalism. In general, examples of so-called pan-nationalism are nothing more than varieties of nationalism itself. Arab nationalism (or pan-Arab nationalism), for example, is a form of nationalism. What remains unknown at present, except, perhaps, to the most specialized researchers in the various cases, is the extent to which and how membership in multiple potential national groups is juggled by members or resolved within populations with competing and/or overlapping national affiliations. That is, to return to a timely example, to what extent is the population of Iraq devoted to an Iraqi nation as an object of loyalty and to what extent is that loyalty and identification reserved for a larger, Arab nation? It should be obvious, of course, that there is nothing inherently problematic about the overlapping existence of multiple identity groups in a given population.

In addition to the many empirical problems of nationalism remaining to be studied in depth, a number of theoretical problems remain. One involves the question of when, precisely, a given collectivity becomes a nation. In many cases, such as much of Latin America in the early nineteenth century, nationalism, after being imported, came to dominate elite political discourse relatively quickly and yet did *not* spread to the mass of the population for some time.[54] Logically, it is apparent that, given that nationalism is fundamentally an idea, it enters a society one mind at a time. Is there a critical threshold beyond which we ought to take a certain degree of national sentiment or self-identification to constitute a nation? If not, what sort of a "thing" do we take a nation to be?

[54] See Eric Van Young, *The Other Rebellion: Popular Violence, Ideology, and the Struggle for Mexican Independence, 1810–1821* (Palo Alto, CA: Stanford University Press, 2001). Indeed, as Eugene Weber famously showed, the idea of the French nation did not spread to the bulk of the French population until the late nineteenth century. See Weber, *Peasants Into Frenchmen* (Palo Alto, CA: Stanford University Press, 1979).

CHAPTER THIRTEEN

Political Parties:

Social Bases, Organization, and Environment

Mildred A. Schwartz and Kay Lawson

Political parties have long been the subject of opposing assessments. From a negative perspective, parties are criticized because they promote conflict and dissension. Lord Bolingbroke (1965), writing in the 1730s, saw parties as deserving suppression, to be replaced by a leader who could supply the moral authority to promote national unity. On the eve of World War I, perhaps viewing himself as such a leader, Kaiser Wilhem II announced that he no longer recognized parties, only Germans. In much less extreme fashion, James Madison's distaste for parties went along with a recognition that they were inevitable and hence needed to be controlled.

All the U.S. Founding Fathers, who, perhaps understandably, were uncomfortable with the kinds of rudimentary parties with which they were familiar, shared Madison's concerns in some form. It took another eighteenth-century Englishman, Edmond Burke, to recognize the value of parties when, removed from a milieu of paralyzing conflict, they could operate as civil competitors (Mansfield, 1965). At the birth of the United States, despite the ill-feeling toward political parties, the Founding Fathers soon found parties necessary to govern and, later, to peacefully transfer power (Hofstadter, 1972:viii).

It was not until the early twentieth century that political theorists began to give parties a central role in guaranteeing democratic government. In one such assessment, James Bryce (1921:119) wrote that, "parties are inevitable. No free large country has been without them. No one has shown how representative government could be worked without them." Outside of government, Lipset, Trow, and Coleman (1956) found that the presence of organized opposing interests, equivalent to parties, were the means to sustain internal democracy in the International Typographical Union.

Yet the relation between parties and democracy has not been settled to everyone's satisfaction. Part of the difficulty in finding a resolution stems from the many meanings assigned to democracy (e.g., Markoff, 1996:101–25). On one side are those who argue that one-party states can be "people's republics." Other critics, such as Ostrogorski (1970) and Michels (1962), stressed the ways parties foster corruption and resist needed changes. In the United States, we find those who feel confined by the overwhelming ascendancy of the Republican and Democratic parties. We offer no answers to such critics in this chapter – we, in fact, admit to believing that competitive parties are essential for democratic government. Yet these often negative perceptions continue to provide a context for more recent controversies present in the scholarly literature. As a result, it is important to recognize the difficulty in totally separating discussion about the nature of parties and how they operate from the normative judgments made about them. We therefore give attention to both normative and empirical concerns.

We divide our study of parties into four parts: the social bases of political parties, the structure and culture of political parties, parties' relations with the institutional environment, and remaining questions. The objective in each of the first three sections is two-fold. First, we seek to locate the study of political parties within the broader history of political sociology. Second, we offer a critical review of the literature, with a bias toward the past twenty years. That literature is evaluated in terms of continuities with earlier, influential traditions in the field as well as with regard to how effectively it breaks new ground. Accomplishing these two objectives permits us to address our final goal, making an informed assessment of where we are in understanding political parties, both with respect to what has been done and where significant gaps remain.

A political party is an organization that nominates candidates to stand for election in its name and seeks to place representatives in the government. Etymologically, party can be traced back to its roots in "part" and in "divide," implying that a party represents one side of a controversy. Yet in practice the word "party" is also used to refer to entities like the German Nazi Party or the Soviet Communist Party, where party and state were synonymous and no opposing parties were permitted. Furthermore, almost all parties claim that, if successful, they will exercise power on behalf of the general public, and some states with single-party systems may seek to build democracy rather than repudiate it (Wekkin, Whistler, Kelley, and Maggiotto, 1993). But some still insist that states with only a single party do not really have parties at all: "[A party is] an organization of society's active political agents who *compete* for popular support with another group or persons holding diverse views," says Neumann (1956:395), and Schlesinger (1968:428) claims a party is a "political organization which actively and effectively engages in the competition for elective office." Our own more generous definition includes both all-powerful single parties and hopelessly unpopular minor parties and is, we believe, more consistent with general usage. It is similar to that of Sartori (1976:64), who defines party as "any political group that presents at elections, and is capable of placing through elections, candidates for public office," although the word *capable* is a stumbling block for us – some parties are so very inept that capability seems out of their realm. At the same time, some parties, both in one-party states and where they are in competition for power, may engage in acts of violence and fraud that stretch the fabric of inclusion in a peaceful electoral process.

In searching for the broadest existing definition of political party, one unconstrained by national setting, degree of institutionalization, or electoral fortunes, there is a possibility of overlapping with social movements and interest groups (Clemens, 1997; Tarrow, 1995; Thomas and Hrebenar, 1995:1–2).[1] Moreover, not all definitions of parties confine them to actual or potential government roles. Weber (1978:939), for example, defined parties as contending groups that struggle for political control within corporate bodies. Lipset et al. (1956), as we have already noted, examined the internal workings of the International Typographical Union through the activities of two opposing organized groups or parties. Although these broader conceptions have contributed many insights to our understanding of how parties work, they do not form an essential part of our subsequent discussion. In this volume, interest groups and social movements are the primary subject of Chapters 14 and 16 respectively.

[1] In Tilly's model, a social movement offers "a sustained challenge to power holders" (1999:257), which, when coupled with electoral activity, can characterize a protest party, what Schwartz (2000, 2002) considers a "party movement." Keuchler and Dalton (1990:189–90) speak of a "movement party" as the partisan arm of a social movement and Yishai (1994:198–200) refers to "interest parties" as those that represent single-interest groups. Organizations like trade unions, farm organizations, and business interest groups, although they have nonelectoral goals that provide their primary rationale for existence, may, without having formal party status, also play an active role in elections and work exclusively on behalf of a single political party or its candidates. But when a movement or an interest group nominates candidates to stand for election in its own name and these candidates are accepted for placement on the ballot, then that organization is no longer "just" an interest group – it has become, however temporarily, a political party. Conversely, when a group does not place candidates in contention for office in its own name, it is not a party, no matter how active it may be in determining and supporting the candidates of existent parties.

THE SOCIAL BASES OF POLITICAL PARTIES

The social bases of political parties have three interrelated aspects – origins, ties with organized interests, and links with citizens. Under origins we treat the social structural roots from which parties emerge, an emphasis that gives weight to national histories while considering the extent to which history can be overtaken by contemporary changes. Ties with organized interests continue the theme of origins by linking groups with parties in a way that concentrates on active efforts at mobilization that take place after the founding experiences. Finally, links with citizens, although clearly an outgrowth of both origins and organized interests, need to be considered on their own terms, as ways even unorganized population categories are mobilized. It is this last kind of link that is generally associated with conceptions of "party in the electorate" (e.g., Beck and Sorauf, 1992; Dalton and Wattenberg, 2000). But the electoral or citizen component of parties are more than just ties with voters. Origins, whether remote or recent, and ties with organized groups, whether stable or changing, are also necessary in giving social meaning to political parties.

Party Origins

The originating circumstances of political parties remain important markers for their future development, comparable to the impact of childhood on an adult (Duverger, 1963:xxiii). For Duverger, a political scientist, the important question to ask is whether parties have formed inside or outside legislative bodies – those forming inside are, he says, more likely to be elite-based parties, whereas those forming outside tend to be open mass parties. Panebianco agrees that origins are important, but calls for a more complex "genetic model," one taking into consideration a party's specific construction and development, the presence or absence of an external "sponsor institution," and/or charismatic leadership (Panebianco, 1988:50–2).

What Panebianco calls a "sponsor institution" may simply be groups that turn themselves into a political party. Charlot (1967:37–8) shows how the French Rally for the Republic, known originally as the Union for a New Republic, was formed out of a collection of groups and individuals who supported Charles de Gaulle during the 1958 crisis produced by France's battle with Algerian rebels. Determined to place their hero (and themselves) in office, they found it necessary to form a party. More often, it is a single group that transforms itself into a political party, as did the African National Congress after the fall of apartheid in South Africa (prior to which it was an illegal movement) and the trade union-based movement of Solidarity in Poland after the fall of communism.

Sociologists have taken a different approach to the study of party origins, one based more on social than institutional factors. Unquestionably the most influential and far-reaching is found in Lipset and Rokkan (1967), who built on theories developed by Talcott Parsons to account for the kinds of parties that appear at particular stages of national development, depending on the cleavage structure. They array cleavages along two dimensions, the territorial-cultural and the functional. The first had its roots in the national revolution that led to the rise of nation-states; the second, in the industrial revolution. Each revolution, in turn, gave rise to two kinds of cleavages. The national revolution created tension between church and state and between a central nation-building culture and that of "peripheral" subjects distinctive in language, religion, or ethnicity. The industrial revolution created tension between the landed aristocracy and the new industrial entrepreneurs and between owners and landlords, on the one hand, and tenants and workers, on the other. They conclude that, "Much of the history of Europe since the beginning of the nineteenth century can be described in terms of the interaction between these two processes of revolutionary change: the one triggered in France and the other originating in Britain" (Lipset and Rokkan, 1967:14–15). Cleavages make up interrelated systems whose appearance under formative historical circumstances leads to the emergence of particular kinds of parties. Once established, these parties continue even under changing conditions – the party systems of the 1960s still reflected, they found, the underlying cleavages of the 1920s or even earlier. Politics may heat up and change, but party systems freeze at birth and do not alter much thereafter – what has come to be called the "freezing hypothesis."

Although often considered applicable to the United States and Canada, Lipset and Rokkan developed their model mainly to account for party origins in Western Europe. But even in Europe they found deviations. Where there is a "fully mobilized nation state" – that is, once all citizens have been incorporated – there can still be new forms of protest against elites stemming from conflicting conceptions of the nation and leading to the rise of "anti-system parties," exemplified by fascism and other authoritarian, right-wing movements (Lipset and Rokkan, 1967:23).

Limits to the Lipset–Rokkan model were apparent in the United States, where concern with party origins has focused on why it remained virtually the only industrialized country without a strong working-class party. Engels (1942:467) attributed U.S. backwardness to the absence of feudalism, which would otherwise have stimulated more differentiated classes. Sombart (1976) argued that U.S. workers enjoyed relatively better economic conditions, greater social equality, and opportunities for mobility, particularly to the West, which discouraged the kind of militancy experienced by German workers and required for a vibrant socialism. Lipset (1968) was motivated to write his dissertation on this topic in the 1940s, finding what was missing in the United States in the Canadian province of Saskatchewan, where socialism emerged among prairie wheat farmers.[2]

By using Saskatchewan as his source of comparison, Lipset allowed "agrarian socialism" to stand in for the more usual association between socialism and the urban working class (Schwartz, 1991). In contrast, other explanations for the absence of a viable socialist party in the United States focus on the weakness of the early labor movement. Despite its success in mobilizing large numbers of urban workers in the 1880s, the Knights of Labor soon lost its appeal with that population and hence its potential to form a working-class party. Voss (1993) blamed this failure on opposition from employers' organizations. Kaufman (2001) links the falloff in Knights of Labor support to its positioning as a fraternal association, putting it in competition with similar groups in a crowded organizational niche. Moving to the twentieth century, Katznelson (1982) finds the pull from ethnicity and community overpowering the potential for a unified working-class consciousness. Lipset's latest analysis gives greatest weight to the effects of the political system, antistatist and individualistic values, and working-class diversity. For example, the contention that immigrants made it difficult to sell socialism to workers is shown to apply only when the community was ethnically heterogenous (Lipset and Marks, 2000).

New questions about the origins of parties have arisen in Europe, where the durability of some parties in Western Europe has continued alongside rising electoral volatility and the creation of new parties. One of the first to document this trend was Pedersen (1979), stimulated by Denmark's "earthquake election of 1973" to analyze the phenomenon in Western Europe. Pedersen's observation that European party systems were steadily shifting was subsequently confirmed by others (Dalton, Flanagan, and Beck, 1984; Harmel and Robertson, 1985; Lawson and Merkl, 1988; Shamir, 1984; von Beyme, 1982; Wolinetz, 1979, 1988). As Rommele (1999:9) pointed out, "the new studies suggested the glacier was in retreat, and a great thaw had begun."

Consistent with Inglehart's (1977, 1990, 1997) work on value orientation and value change, Kitschelt (1989, 1990) found that the

[2] Lipset's explanation of how Saskatchewan differed from comparable regions in the United States has altered with time. Originally, he attributed it to social and ecological conditions in Saskatchewan that produced a rural class consciousness (Lipset, 1968:xiii). Later he would give more importance to political institutions, in particular, the nature of federalism and a parliamentary system of government (Lipset, 1968:xiii–xiv). In a third shift, he gave new significance to cultural factors, created by the impact of Canada's counterrevolutionary tradition (Lipset, 1990).

new parties were emerging from social movements concerned with lifestyle issues of the environment, racism, peace, and gender and labeled them "left-libertarian" parties. "They are 'Left' because they share with traditional socialism a mistrust of the marketplace, of private investment, and of the achievement ethic, and a commitment to egalitarian redistribution. They are 'libertarian' because they reject the authority of private or public bureaucracies to regulate individual and collective conduct" (Kitschelt, 1990:180). Characteristically, these parties are associated with economic affluence and appeal to the young and well-educated.

Were the old cleavages disappearing in this wave of political postmaterialism? Not according to Katz, for whom the new cleavages are strongly akin to the older ones, focused on disputes over the distribution of power between citizens and the central state and between employees, including employed professionals, and corporate enterprise. He argues that Lipset and Rokkan's evolutionary argument, in which class was the newest basis of party formation, overlooked the contemporary power of more primal cleavages of religion, language, origin, or location (Katz, 2001). Others have shown that these ascriptive characteristics show up as well in new parties of the right. In Canada, a significant basis for the formation of the Reform Party resides in the power of regionalism to mobilize discontent (Harrison, 1995:38–47). The anti-immigrant and politically disenchanted members of the French National Front, the Danish People's Party, the Italian Northern League, the Austrian Freedom Party, the Swiss People's Party, the Belgian Flemish Bloc, and the Norwegian Progress Party share the belief that democracy works best when there is a culturally homogenous population (Betz, 2001).

In other contexts, however, it is difficult if not impossible to find new parties based on the old cleavages identified by Lipset and Rokkan and this is particularly true in newly democratizing countries (Lawson, Rommele, and Karasimeonov, 1999). Yet successor parties in Portugal, after the passage from an authoritarian to a democratic regime, appear to have continued class cleavages, most readily from the left (Maxwell, 1986). The fall of the Soviet Union produced newly autonomous states and new opportunities for political parties. Parties in Russia appear to be based largely on shifting combinations of interests in the pursuit of capitalistic success (Barany and Moser, 2001; Pammett and De Bardeleben, 2000). In many Eastern and Central European states, old cleavages were brutally wiped out by successive Nazi and communist totalitarian regimes and the only consistent posttotalitarian cleavage has been that between current winners and losers. But more immediate history remains relevant. Kitschelt (1995a) classified communist regimes in Eastern Europe and the former Soviet Union to construct a typology of patrimonial, bureaucratic-authoritarian, and national consensus types that he then used to account for the character of communist successor parties.

Ties with Organized Interests

Many political parties exist in more or less close relationship with organized interests. Some ties arise at the formative stage, when a party is created as the political arm of an organized interest group. Past examples include the development of parties to defend the interests of particular religious denominations, which then continue to express positions reflecting the views of those churches. In the Netherlands, Calvinists formed two parties, the older Anti-Revolutionary party, which split through internal dissension, and the later Christian Historical Union (Daalder, 1955; Lijphart, 1968). Trade unions also have been both sources of parties and continuing influences on their policies and governance.

When the line dividing parties from related interest groups is unclear, it may lead to what Yishai (1994) calls interest parties, illustrated by the Poujadists in France, the Peace Party in Japan, and the Pensioners' Association in Israel. Or it may foster an uneasy relation, as illustrated by the Christian Right and its penetration of the Republican Party in the United States. Yet, although the Christian Right supplies important resources of money and support, its influence on the party's nomination process may lead to conflict with other interests within the party and to an inability to elect candidates it favors (Green, Rozell, and Wilcox, 2001).

Other ties have been instigated by parties themselves in efforts to ensure resources for their own continuity as well as to tap into the concerns of potentially important constituents. These efforts are often matched by those of organized groups seeking access to policy makers. One process through which such ties are formed is through co-optation, where new elements are given a voice in an organization to prevent them from causing disruption (Selznick, 1949:13). The expectation of those doing the co-opting is that the elements co-opted will become less fervid exponents of their original group's interests. The organizational literature suggests that co-optation is likely to take place as a means of managing interdependence (Scott, 1998:200), when the organization doing the co-opting would otherwise be hindered in its activities by opposition from competitors. And as Scott (1998:201) reminds us, co-optation "provides a two-way street, with both influence and support flowing sometimes in one direction, sometimes in the other." Rosenstone, Behr, and Lazarus (1996) describe how third parties in the United States may disappear through co-optation by one of the major parties yet still experience a kind of victory through their impact on the policies of the co-opting party.

In the United States, the amount and significance of interest group campaign contributions to, or on behalf of, candidates has grown exponentially in recent years (Goidel, Gross, and Shields, 1999). Efforts to keep the sums involved down to reasonable proportions have either failed altogether or resulted in such watered down legislation as to make little difference (Rozell and Wilcox, 1999:100–1). Although there is strong evidence for big business preference for the Republican Party and for legislation supporting a conservative agenda (Clawson and Su, 1990; Clawson, Neustadtl, and Scott, 1992; Clawson, Neustadtl, and Weller, 1998; Neustadtl, Scott, and Clawson, 1991; Su, Neustadtl, and Clawson, 1995), it has become more common for organized business interests as well as labor to distribute their contributions more evenly between both major parties. Because U.S. legislatures operate in a log-rolling fashion, not only will probusiness Democratic office-seekers be supported but so will others, perhaps not so sympathetic, yet in critically influential committee positions (Eisemeier and Pollock, 1988; Mizruchi, 1992; Schwartz, 1990:54–6).[3]

In other nations, where candidate dependency on private funds is less pronounced, the links between particular groups and parties have also weakened. In Canada, the Canadian Manufacturers' Association (CMA) has long been a strong supporter of the Conservative Party, but never to the exclusion of the Liberal Party.[4] On the Left, the New Democratic Party (NDP) began in 1961 with strong commitments from organized labor and formal provision for affiliation (Horowitz, 1968), but when the party gained office in the industrialized province of Ontario during an economic slow-down, labor did not hesitate to publicly criticize the government (Schwartz, 1994b:16–17).

Despite the fact that Socialist parties often owe their origin to organized labor, European trade unions have recently loosened their formerly strong ties with the left and have reached out to establish better relations with often-ruling conservative parties or, at least, as in the case of the relations between the French Parti Socialiste and the Confédération Francais de Travail (CFDT), to make it clear their support can no longer simply be taken for granted. Rivalry among trade unions, leading to competitive demands, is suggested as the cause for a loosening of ties with the Spanish Socialist Party (Ruiz, 2001). The British Labour Party (BLP), which grew out of the trade union movement, long encouraged "automatic" membership in the party through prior membership in affiliated trade unions, giving labor leaders, along with

[3] The relation between campaign contributions and social cleavages is dealt with in more detail in the chapter by Manza, Brooks, and Souder in this volume.

[4] However, when the two major parties lined up on diametrically opposed sides over free trade with the United States in the 1980s, the CMA's contacts with the Liberals became sidelined (Bashevkin, 1991).

elected party elites, influential roles in party decision making (McKenzie, 1956; Webb, 1992). However, under the leadership of Tony Blair, the BLP has moved to avoid being seen as merely a workers' party. In parallel, the trade union movement has worked to place its own eggs in more than one basket (Webb, 1994:115).

In the United States, in an analogous way, trade unions maintained relatively close relations with the Democratic Party. Unions are a significant source of campaign contributions, advisors, and party workers for the Democrats, especially in those geographic locations where unionized industry remains strong (Jewell and Morehouse, 2001:154). Yet the sharp drop in union membership has clearly reduced the overall presence of trade union leadership in the Democratic Party. The Clinton administration disappointed its union supporters time and again, perhaps most significantly by going forward with the North American Free Trade Agreement although unions kept up enough pressure to ensure the passage of a labor side-agreement, the North American Agreement on Labor Cooperation (Mayer, 1998). Unions now maintain better contacts than earlier with the Republican Party and can, at times, find individual candidates of that party they deem worth supporting (e.g., Schwartz, 1990:234, 237).

Citizen Linkage

The question of parties and linkage can be approached from two perspectives: we can assume that citizens who vote for a particular party are thereby linked to that party and, via it, to the political process and then seek to discover and track changes in voter alignment, asking which groups identify with which party and noting changes over time. Or we can, instead, ask how exactly political parties link citizens to the political process and whether there are different kinds of linkage, performed by different parties in different nations.

The first approach has been by far the most common, and here we begin by exploring sociological visions of linkage as the mobilization of population groups by political parties in competitive systems. In these studies "mobilization" means voting. Indeed, the connection between social cleavages and voter alignments is at the core of what is often thought of as the "sociological model" of politics (e.g., Dalton and Wattenberg, 1993:199–200).

In the United States, the most influential early studies of voting behavior, associated with what we can call the Columbia school (Lazarsfeld et al., 1948; Berelson et al., 1954) and the Michigan school (Campbell et al., 1954; Campbell et al., 1960), all agreed on the centrality of social characteristics in connecting voters to either the Democratic or Republican parties. Even without clearly class-based parties, it was possible to discern a strong connection between the working class and Democratic voting and the middle class and Republican voting. In addition, religion, race, urban or rural residence, and region of the country all played a prominent role in partisan mobilization.

By the 1980s, scholars were arguing that the social structural basis of partisan alignments was declining in the Americas and Western Europe (Dalton, 1988; Franklin, 1992; Wattenberg, 1996). Whatever had emerged in its place was now so fluid that patterns were no longer discernible. Reasons given for these changes, and conveniently summarized by Manza and Brooks (1999:20–33), rest on four theses:

> (1) changes in social structure, especially increased levels of affluence, upward social mobility, and declining marital homogamy; (2) increased levels of education and 'cognitive mobilization' in the electorate, which potentially provide voters with the tools to make judgments independent of social group loyalties; (3) the rise of new values and issue conflicts; and (4) changes in the party systems and the patterning of macro-level electoral alignments.

Given our focus on political parties, it is worth elaborating on this fourth theory, which argues that, because no party can muster a single cleavage-based constituency sufficient to give it office, parties must broaden their appeal to include other kinds of voters, thereby weakening ties with the original social base. First presented by Kirchheimer (1966), the "catch-all" theory of political parties found further support in an analysis of Western European social democratic parties (Przeworski and Sprague, 1986) and is buttressed by more recent changes in those parties in Britain, France, and Germany. It also finds support in the experiences of the Canadian New Democratic Party (Schwartz, 1994b) and in the shift to the center by the Democratic Party under President Bill Clinton. The result of these changes is to limit the options available to working-class voters. They can stick with their original party, though their influence is diluted by the inclusion of other kinds of voters, find an alternative party (generally a minor one), or withdraw from politics altogether. The likelihood of the latter possibility is supported by research that shows nonvoting to be higher among the poor and working class in the United States (Piven and Cloward, 1988; Verba, Schlozman, and Brady, 1997).

Yet not everyone is prepared to give up on the importance of social cleavages in providing links with particular parties. Manza and Brooks (1999) cover the field most thoroughly by first defining social cleavage according to whether it is rooted in social structure, associated with group consciousness, and mobilized for political action. Based on this definition, they identify four major cleavages in the United States: race, religion, class, and gender. Classifying religion and class more finely than by the usual dichotomous variables, they are able to find significant cleavages associated with partisanship as strong in the 1990s as in the 1950s. Among their relevant findings are the preeminence of race, followed by religion, then class, and finally gender. Class has fluctuated over the decades, showing sharpest decline in 1996. Professionals, once the most Republican, moved to be the most Democratic in 1996. The self-employed became more Republican and the nonskilled less Democratic. Liberal Protestants changed from being the most Republican to a centrist position, while Conservative Protestants remained unchanged as staunch Republicans. The gender gap has been growing since the 1960s, moving more women into the ranks of Democrats and reflecting the impact of increased labor force participation.

At one level, at least, Manza and Brook's analysis supports that of others who argue for the declining significance of class in U.S. politics, if by this is meant a decline in support from the working class for the Democratic Party. Growing unpopularity of the welfare state and countervailing pulls from race and ethnicity may account for some of this shift. At the same time, the increasing significance of race and ethnicity ensures that U.S. parties will remain distinct in composition, especially as more Latino voters enter the electoral arena.

What of other Western democracies? There too controversy remains over the declining significance of class as the underlying rationale for partisan behavior. Basing their argument on data analyzed by using an index first developed by Alford (1963) to dichotomize occupations into classes, Clark, Lipset and Rempel (2001) are among those who argue for decline most forcefully. Goldthorpe (2001), who works with a more complex index of class, represents those who, although abandoning any commitment to a straightforward Marxian analysis of class conflict, still see the salience of class to politics. In this second camp, researchers report decline in class voting as well but emphasize how it is tied to national differences, with Canada and the United States the lowest and Britain and the Scandinavian countries the highest (Nieuwbeerta, 2001). The division of postcommunist populations into winners and losers is another way of saying that class persists.

Nonetheless, as we noted earlier in our discussion of party origins and ties with organized groups, ascriptive characteristics also remain powerful in determining European partisan behavior, as they do in the United States. Dogan (2001), for example, who refers not only to the Western European drop in class but also in religious voting (which had remained very robust until the 1970s), sees new importance in ethnic factors as a result of immigration. Migrants, often visibly distinctive, unenfranchised, geographically concentrated, and working in low-skilled jobs, contribute to the erosion of working class solidarity and the attractions of right-wing parties to native-born workers (Kitschelt, 1995b).

Other writers are less concerned to discover linkages between particular groups and parties than to focus on the forms of linkage parties provide. Lawson (1980:13–19) takes the broadest view by identifying four possibilties. Parties can connect the public with government by serving as agencies for citizen participation, providing avenues for the representation of citizens' views, returning favors for votes, or manipulating and controlling constituents. From this perspective it is possible to view the linkage roles of parties even in noncompetitive and coercive political systems.

For some scholars the most fundamental linkage role is encouraging participation, regardless of how that participation is directed.[5] Here recent evidence of decline is considerable. Wattenberg (2000) looks at figures for nineteen industrialized countries, comparing the first two elections in the 1950s with the two most recent ones in the 1990s. Every country except Sweden and Denmark shows a drop in voting turnout, from as high as 39 percent for Switzerland to as low as 1 percent in Australia. Although acknowledging that these figures may represent only a temporary phenomenon rather than a long-term trend, because many countries did not demonstrate decline until the 1980s, Wattenberg is inclined to a pessimistic assessment. "The fact that voter turnout has declined indicates that there is less of a market for the parties' product and that party systems around the advanced industrialized world have fallen upon hard times" (Wattenberg, 2000:76).

Assessing Social Bases

Dividing our discussion of social bases into three has the virtue of revealing the distinct ways they operate. Origins give direction to party formation, indicating which social cleavages are sufficiently mobilized to take advantage of opportunities to emerge as parties. They also recognize the importance of national histories, including their capacity to create new tensions, sources of grievance, and cleavages that can take partisan shape. Attention to ties with organized groups picks up from origins to examine the possibilities of continuing interaction between parties and groups as well as the attenuation of those ties. Relations with the electorate are different in that they do not presume either a formal connection with parties or the organization of demographic groups. Each approach to these social bases remains important in its own right by demonstrating continuities, disjuncture, and new connections.

All three perspectives on social bases also point to interrelations and their consequences. At least as far as the literature is concerned, the most notable conjunction is between socialist parties and the working class. Socialist parties have emerged where there is a self-conscious working class, organized into trade unions. But they also appear in rural areas, where small landholders find, at least in some variant form, political solutions in socialism (Lipset, 1968:15–38; Schwartz, 1991). In either case, the existence of a class-conscious laboring group is a prerequisite for the emergence of a socialist party. Socialist parties that exist without this social basis, united solely by ideology, are not electorally viable. Genuine socialist parties must negotiate their relations with the organized constituencies that gave them birth. Yet even here the amount of influence that the latter will have on the day to day affairs of the party and on its policy making is now in question.

Our own assessment acknowledges both the reality of the declining relevance of class in advanced industrial societies, along with national variations, and the persistence of class as just one of the significant factors in the mobilization of the electorate. Overall, we see the continuing importance of social cleavages, not the homogenization of the electorate. At the same time, the size, salience, and mobilization of cleavages alter, supporting the need for ongoing research, as Katz (2001:89) convincingly argues. And to that research must now be added a new puzzle: to what extent do parties, especially those seeking power based on large majorities rather than the mere opportunity to speak out on behalf of cherished values, actually seek to mobilize cleavages?

[5] See the discussion by Manza, Brooks, and Sauder in this volume.

THE STRUCTURE AND CULTURE OF POLITICAL PARTIES

Classical Approaches and Influences

In the days before there were sharply drawn lines among social science disciplines, the organizational structure of political parties attracted the attention of a number of scholars who continue to influence both sociology and political science. The most preeminent were Ostrogorski, Weber, and Michels.

Ostrogorski (1970) viewed organization, which he equated with extralegislative party machines and caucuses, with suspicion. Using examples from U.S. urban politics, he worried that such organizations could manipulate the public and the political agenda through the use of patronage and outright corruption. Ostrogorski's warnings were supported by later exposés of party machines (Riordon, 1963) and fed the populist disdain for politics, leading to ever increasing legal restrictions on parties (Lawson, 1987; Winger, 1995), including their disbarment from competition in local elections (Hawley, 1973). Amenta (1998:252–3) argues that the continued existence of patronage-oriented parties in the United States was one of the barriers to the adoption of far-reaching social welfare policies. Others, however, take a more measured look at machines, finding virtues in them through their ability to integrate immigrants and provide local arenas for political participation (Gosnell, 1968; Merton, 1968:125–31). In addition, there is evidence that only rarely have machines actually been fully developed and dominant in American cities (Eldersveld, 1964; Key, 1964; Mayhew, 1986). Meanwhile, nonpartisan elections have been shown to depress voting turnout, advantage incumbents (Schaffner et al., 2001), and discourage working-class and minority participation (Winger, 1995).

Weber, who viewed parties broadly as groups that struggle for political control (1978:939), is most influential for his theory of legitimate authority and the administrative structures based on it (1978:212–45). Authority can stem from traditional, charismatic, or rational-legal roots but it is the latter, giving rise to bureaucratic structures, that best describe the modern world (1978:956–1002). Although Weber saw elections modifying the principle of rationality by introducing other, more personal factors (1978:266–9), he viewed competitive mass political parties, including those of England and the United States as well as the German Social Democrats, as essentially bureaucratic (1978:984).

When reference is made to organization it now often conjures the kind of bureaucratic structure described by Weber but with a negative image. Moreover, in the United States, the supposed absence of organization as a characteristic of political parties was perceived to be a positive virtue, captured in the sardonic tribute paid by Will Rogers, who said, "I belong to no organized party. I'm a Democrat." The result is that political parties have tended to escape the kind of study that has been addressed to a variety of other organized activities. Panebianco (1988) attributed the shift away from organizational analysis to new methods and theories that examined electoral behavior, social class, and public policy and led to an emphasis on party systems. But there has been a loss from this change, "namely the awareness that whatever else parties are and to whatever other solicitations they respond, they are above all organizations and that organizational analysis must therefore come before any other perspective" (Panebianco, 1988:xi).

Michels (1962) influential work, based mainly on his analysis of the pre–World War I German Social Democratic Party, argued that, even as social democratic parties formed to fight for greater democracy, they were destined to turn into oligarchies, with power concentrated in the hands of a small number of entrenched leaders. According to him, a viable political party, particularly one that sets out to challenge the existing distributions of power, must become organized. The result is a bureaucracy, where holding office becomes a full-time activity. Whether acting as functionaries or popularly elected leaders, officeholders acquire the kind of information that gives them power and reduces the role of rank-and-file members. In this model, internal democracy is not possible.

Michels's prediction about the inevitability of oligarchy has been a challenge to those who see political parties in more positive or nuanced terms (see Lipset, 1962:25–8). Duverger (1963:424) acknowledges that all systems of governance are necessarily oligarchic in the sense that it is virtually impossible for everyone to equally participate in decision making. Panebianco (1988:171–3), based on a more complex conception of organization, sees oligarchy as one possible outcome that results from the form of the dominant coalition (those who control and coordinate the party's activities) and the extent of institutionalization (closeness in the relation between the party and its environment). An oligarchy results when a small coalition exercises power under conditions of complete institutionalization. For Panebianco, such institutionalization is part of an evolutionary development that moves a party from expansive social movement-kinds of interests and organization to ones that are more limited, professional, and bureaucratic. Given that Panebianco (1988:165) offers the SPD as his prime example of an oligarchy, it is clear that he has not abandoned Michels but only added to his theory.

Variations in Organizational Structure

Perhaps the most radical statement about the significance of organization came from Duverger (1963:xv): "present-day parties are distinguished far less by their programme or the class of their members than by the nature of their organization. A party is a community with a particular structure. Modern parties are characterized primarily by their anatomy." From this position he went on to build a schema based on structural elements, kinds of membership and support, and leadership. Most relevant is his distinction between cadre and mass parties. Mass parties are based on members that contribute their resources to ensuring an ongoing operation, originally descriptive of Socialist parties. In cadre parties, a relatively small core is responsible for activities tied to elections and may be inactive at other times. There is a coincidence between these membership characteristics and party structure. "Cadre parties correspond to caucus parties, decentralized and weakly knit; mass parties to parties based on branches, more centralized and more firmly knit" (Duverger, 1963:67).

Duverger predicted that mass parties would become the dominant form of organization as cadre parties saw the advantages of greater member participation. He was soon opposed by, for example, Kirchheimer (1966), who instead saw the spread of "catch-all parties"; Epstein (1980:126–9), who disputed any "contagion from the left"; and, more recently, Katz and Mair (1995), who present an alternative model in the cartel party. Cartel parties loosen the boundaries between party and state and cooperate with each other to tap resources. Scarrow's (2000:92–5) empirical analysis of the eighteen OECD members concludes that the mass party was never widespread and was, in any case, more prevalent during the third quarter of the twentieth century, rather than in the first half, as Duverger argued. Even so, the mass party model has found some success in the postcommunist transition within the Hungarian Socialist Party and Social Democracy of the Polish Republic (Lewis 1996:16–17).

Structure can be evaluated differently when, in opposition to the Weberian model of bureaucracy, organizations are treated as coalitions of interests, sometimes cooperating and sometimes competing (Pfeffer and Salancik, 1978:36). In these situations, parts are more loosely coupled. With coordination no longer so important, it is possible for the organization to find areas of slack, where there are unused resources that can be mobilized at times of changing needs (Scott, 1998:234–5). In the United States, for example, field staff from the Local Elections Committee of the Republican National Committee often took the initiative in deciding which state legislative seats deserved their help, even when their choices did not coincide with those made by state-level party officials (Schwartz, 1990:32, 218–219). Loose coupling reduces interdependence among parts, an advantage where an organization operates in a diverse and segmented environment (Scott, 1998:268). In federal systems, like those in Canada and the United States, the weakness of a party at one level of government or in particular areas of the country does not then necessarily translate into overall weakness. Loose coupling within parties can also be associated with efforts to be broadly representative of a diverse electoral environment (Schwartz, 1990:257–9). Or, in the case of left-libertarian parties, loose coupling can also be present with more ideological coherence (Kitschelt, 1990:185).

One structural variation allowing loose coupling is a matrix form, where there are competing centers of authority based on vertical and horizontal lines. Vertical lines are usually tied to functions; horizontal lines, to projects, or geographic location (Hill and White, 1979). When political events occur at different geographic levels – local, provincial, and national – and when responsibilities are distinct (e.g., independent elections and unique activities) the kind of party organization that evolves will likely be of this matrix form. It should be noted that matrix is a label applied by an organizational analyst; it is not necessarily a form deliberately selected by party actors. The way in which a matrix emerges is illustrated by the Canadian New Democratic Party (NDP). In 1961, it was recreated from the Cooperative Commonwealth Federation (CCF) to better represent social democracy within urban, industrial Canada (Whitehorn, 1992). The NDP's structure and constitution made national politics crucial, yet the structure and culture of Canada ensured that regional/provincial interests would remain prominent. The results were illustrated by tensions between the national and Saskatchewan wings, where, provincially, the CCF had a history as the governing party. Formation of the NDP was unwelcome in Saskatchewan, still dominated by rural, farm interests rather than by the working-class concerns in more industrialized areas. To emphasize these differences, the party continued to call itself the CCF Saskatchewan Section of the NDP (Morton, 1986:22). It was not until 1968 that it officially changed its name to the New Democratic Party of Saskatchewan even while continuing to distinguish itself programmatically from its federal counterpart (Schwartz, 2002:160–1).

An analysis of the Republican Party of Illinois found the basis of a matrix organization in two dimensions subsuming how activities are organized – "central arenas of action in contrast to local ones, and efforts at centralization in contrast to those aimed at retaining autonomy" (Schwartz, 1990:84). The result is consistent with Epstein's (1982) characterization of U.S. parties as federations of individual and collective actors. Federations are "organized hierarchically, not in terms of dominance, but in the clustering of interdependent parts" (Schwartz, 1990:267).

Network structures that emphasize egalitarian and reciprocal ties among units are another organizational variant (Powell, 1990). Although egalitarianism may not be prominent in political parties, network imagery itself is broadly applicable to party structure. The network is not limited to a formal organizational chart but encompasses "individual and collective units sharing a party name whose activities have some recognized partisan purpose" (Schwartz, 1990:11). Components can range from public officeholders, at all levels of government; party functionaries, whether elected or appointed; official committees; unofficial influentials like advisors and financial contributors; representatives of allied interest groups; and members at specified levels of activism. This way of looking at party has been recognized by party functionaries such as Tom Cole (1993:61) when he was executive director of the National Republican Campaign Committee. "One of the blinders on political scientists is to think in terms of parties, not partisanship, which is much more important." Relations among network elements can be examined – for example, whether they are strong or weak – as well as with respect to sources of stability and change – for example, in so far as they are affected by the governing status of the party or the personal styles of individual actors.

A network approach supports new ways of looking at party membership. Mair (1994:16), for example, suggests that parties now are consciously distinguishing among categories of members by giving increased power to the supposedly more docile rank-and-file than to party activists. Even with overall membership decline, members remain important in intraparty struggles (Scarrow, 2000:100) and in selecting legislators and legitimizing elections (Scarrow, Webb, and Farrell, 2000). In Austria, membership is now fostered less to maintain a loyal electoral base than to enhance financial resources and sources for recruiting candidates (Müller, 1994:66–7). In Canada, the direct election of party leaders by all parties, not just by those that had a mass-type organization, has removed the old distinctions between members and nonmembers because now those choosing leaders need only pay a membership fee to be given this privilege without incurring any other responsibilities (Carty, Cross, and Young, 2000:227).

Abandoning rigid organizational models that focus solely on formal positions and conceiving of parties as network structures gives a place to professional advisors whose main loyalty is to party chiefs. Panebianco (1988:264) assesses the importance of professional staff in leading to the development of electoral-professional parties, where there is, concomitantly, a direct appeal to the electorate, emphasis on public representatives, and dependence on interest groups. The use of professional campaign staff contributes to party centralization and enhances the position of the party leader (Farrell and Webb, 2000). Professional staff is also given a critical role in Monroe's (2001) analysis of California parties. Schwartz's (1990, 1994a) network analysis of the Illinois Republican Party included elements whose influence in the party came from their status in the larger community, like business, trade union, or professional leadership.

There are, in effect, multiple ways for parties to organize. Bureaucracy remains a critical organizational form – it is just not the only one. Variations become apparent when parties are examined in different institutional contexts. For example, in the United States, there has been an inclination to think of party organization in terms of state or local bodies (for a summary, see Epstein, 1993). When the emphasis is on local machines, the model is a kind of fiefdom, based on personal loyalties and secured through patronage and other favors. Although using different terminology, this assessment is similar to Epstein's (1986:134–44) but differs from Ware's (1988:xii), who sees them as caucus-cadre types, with power concentrated in the hands of local elites. The decline of machines is matched by studies of individual cities where new kinds of organizations, with more bureaucratic structures, have emerged (see those included in Crotty, 1986).

Evidence suggests considerable variation and distinct differences between Republicans and Democrats at different levels, with county, and particularly state and national, levels of organization most elaborated among Republicans (e.g., Cotter et al., 1984; Herrnson, 1993; Ware, 1988). It is such differences that make it possible to plausibly argue either that parties as organizations are or are not declining. We feel most comfortable with a conclusion that party organizations are changing.

Organizational Culture

For Panebianco (1988:163–4), party organization has an importance that is independent of social base or ideological thrust. Our own agreement with this position is modified by the understanding that organizations are as much cultural systems as they are structures of relations. It is culture that provides the cognitive and symbolic bases for both constraining and enabling social action (Emirbayer and Goodwin, 1994:1436–42). Trice and Beyer (1993:2) distinguish the substance of culture as the emotionally charged ideologies developed for dealing with uncertainty. The expression of beliefs, values, and norms takes place through cultural forms manifested in symbols, language, narratives, and practices (Trice and Beyer, 1993:77–128).

Party culture operates in at least four ways. At one level, culture is expressed as ideology – the beliefs that identify a party as distinct from others and provide a rationale and identity for adherents, an explanation of political events, and a blueprint for action. Such cultures exist in the grand isms of modern political theory. Nationalism, fascism, socialism, and communism are all associated with major social movements that are (or were) also political parties, although not always in competitive party systems. Socialism retains its vitality in various workers, socialist, and social democratic parties at the same time as it is shaped and altered by national settings, electoral strength, and governing experience. Socialism also demonstrates how a single ideology can become fragmented, even within one country, through factional disputes over how it should be translated into actions and who are recognized as its genuine exponents (e.g., Bartolini, 2000). Nationalism also remains potent in the contemporary world, sometimes translated into specific regional or ethnic parties (Johnston, 1994). Examples include the Canadian Reform Party and the Italian Northern League. Meanwhile, new value orientations emerge, such as feminism and environmentalism, reshaping old parties or creating new ones, like the Green Party. Middle-of-the-road catch-all parties tend to suppress ideological currents. Yet, even so, in the United States, the Democrats and Republicans manifest clear differences along a right/left dimension, especially when viewed from the perspective of party leaders (Grofman et al., 2002).

Second, culture provides the organizing rationale by which members are incorporated. It is captured in Neumann's (1956) distinction between parties of representation and parties of social integration. The former are made up of cadre or catch-all parties that involve supporters mainly in their capacity as voters. The latter, descriptive mainly of democratic socialist parties that encompassed the social and cultural life of members through various auxiliary organizations, are now less common. The loosening of integrative ties has led to further inference about party decline.

Comprehensive social integration is often a feature of social movements that rely on solidarity incentives. To the extent that social movements and parties overlap, those kinds of incentives will create an integrative and committed culture. At the extreme, such a culture can preempt attachments to family, friends, or even the state. For example, a long-time Canadian Communist, Jack Scott, recounted how an organizer in the Communist Party of Canada – Marxist-Leninist exerted pressure on members' personal lives, dissuading the study of literature as a bourgeois pastime and demanding devotion to the movement to the point of driving one unfortunate person to suicide (Palmer, 1988: 219–21).

Third, culture is prominent in styles of action. Judgments that the two parties in the United States are indistinguishable are negated when culture is used to assess them (Freeman, 1985–6). Klinker (1994) describes competing cultural styles in which the Republicans display a business culture tied to the background of prominent activists and their treatment of the party as a business. He found the Democrats, at the time studied, to have a culture of democracy, premised on inclusiveness, internal democracy, and attention to constituencies. There is, of course, a difference between a culture that supports internal democracy and the practice of such democracy. The tension between ideals and performance was at the heart of Michel's critique of the German Social Democratic Party. It has been echoed as well in analyses of the Canadian CCF/NDP, whenever a preference for centralized organization and strong leadership comes in conflict with its commitment to member participation (Morley, 1984:173–200; Schwartz, 1994b:24–8; Whitehorn, 1992: 252–3).

Although culture, by definition, has considerable stability, styles can change. Clark and Hoffmann-Martinot (1998) relate how political policies of left-wing parties in Britain and Germany, as well as the Clinton Democrats, represent a "third way" (Giddens, 2000) in the sense of a new political orientation different from that of their predecessors. Yet it is exactly such cultural change that is interpreted as another sign of party decline.

Finally, party activities can be an expression of culture. Fine (1994) describes platforms as a way for parties to symbolically express their identity. Ideology is one of the factors that accounts for the direction of party policies (Amenta, 1998; Boix, 1998). Even in the United States, where ideology is thought to be a low-level influence, it enters into the policy preferences of legislators (Wright and Schaffner, 2002). Poole and Rosenthal's (1997) analysis of roll calls presents the most thorough historical study of how cleavages, ideology, and policy positions have changed over time.

The connection between party platforms and their effect on mobilization remains clouded. Although hard evidence in the form of governing party policies is not always clear, it has been argued that party platforms are treated as party mandates and do differentiate parties (Hofferbert and Budge, 1992; King, Budge, Hofferbert, Laver, and McDonald, 1993). But the sharpness with which party elites in the United States can now be distinguished along a number of policy dimensions appears not to be translated into parallel mobilization of the general public. That is, except for a hard core of party identifiers, public views have not followed leaders into similarly polarized ideologies (Layman and Carsey, 2002), suggesting that social cleavages may not be presented with compatible partisan choices.

By adding culture as an aspect of organization, we flesh out structural elements with symbolic and ideational ones. Culture is then not something separate but an integral part of organization and yet another way to assess the theme of party decline. The programs and policies associated with parties that rest on cultural factors become one of the outcomes of organization. Although party structures appear to becoming more similar, culture remains differentiating. However, the significance of cultural differences can also decline and become largely symbolic when detached from programs.

RELATIONS WITH THE INSTITUTIONAL ENVIRONMENT

Renewed Concern with Institutions

Contemporary concern with institutions and their analysis emphasizes the regulatory, normative, and cognitive forces that provide the context from which organizations emerge, flourish, and change (Scott, 1995:xiii–xix). To sociologists represented in the new institutionalism, institutions are distinct from individual actions, have rulelike qualities by virtue of being taken for granted, and are slow to change except under drastic circumstances (DiMaggio and Powell, 1991:8–11).

Curiously enough, although the institutional perspective encompasses systems of power, authority, and governance, it has led to little overt attention to the institutional basis of political parties. For example, even such political science luminaries as James G. March and Johan P. Olsen, who devote a volume to reinvigorating the application of institutional analysis to politics, have only a single reference to political parties. That one reference is itself to Lipset and Rokkan's (1967) paper on party origins, which March and Olsen (1989:169) use to demonstrate the stability of ineffective political forms.

Two decades ago, Skocpol (1985) and others began arguing that sociology had become neglectful of how state institutions played a role in both creating and restraining opportunities for action. Although Skocpol's plea led to a resurgence of work that is characterized as state-centered, among sociologists that work has stimulated only fairly narrow interest with political parties. Among political scientists, a greater variety of topics are considered. We try to take account of both disciplines in the following review.

Regardless of how much overt attention has been given to the institutional basis of political parties, there is little question that parties themselves have institutional qualities, operate in an institutional world, and influence the functioning of other institutions. Institutional analysis is present even if it is not labeled as such. Here we examine studies in which this institutional approach is explicit as well as those in which it is not, considering the exchange of power and influence between parties and the state, the media, and the global system.

Parties and the State

State institutions constrain parties through laws ranging from clauses embedded in national constitutions forbidding certain kinds of parties to municipal ordinances forbidding parties to run candidates in local elections. In the United

States some of the most significant restrictions on parties are a result of the direct democracy reforms at the beginning of the twentieth century. The establishment of primary elections took away a party's right to name its own candidates and placed that power in the hands of those whose only connection to the party was the label they gave themselves upon registering to vote, or not even that, in the case of open and blanket primaries (Cronin, 1989; Haskell, 1996; Lawson, 1999a; Reiter, 1993). Restrictive ballot laws have made it difficult for third parties to mount campaigns in the United States, though they have never been totally successful in suppressing them (Donovan, 2000; Lewis-Beck and Squire, 1995) and recent campaigns by Ross Perot and Ralph Nader have suggested to some that the pressure for changing such restrictions is mounting (Sifry, 2002). Changing constraints have been examined in Canada in the choice of national party leaders (Courtney, 1995) and in local constituencies (Carty, 1991) as well as in Europe in the rules governing candidate selection (Norris, 1997; Ware, 1987b). Subtle differences in constitutional structures also affect the ability of parties to govern: in some nations, narrow majorities are able to legislate despite resistance, whereas, in others, minority parties can sharply influence legislation (Huber, Stephens, and Ragin, 1993).

Other kinds of institutional constraint are often more indirect in their effects on parties. For example, a strong presidency has been shown to lead to an emphasis on winning, downplaying ideology, and fostering cadre-type parties (Linz, 1990). Similarly, the size of electoral districts affects how parties operate (Schlesinger, 1984), fostering mass-type communist successor parties where the average district size is larger (Ishiyama, 1999). More controversial are inferences about the effects of proportional representation and whether it leads to multiple parties and party innovation (Courtney, 2004; Duverger, 1963; Kim and Ohn, 1992; Kitschelt, 1988). Redding and Viterna (1999) find proportional representation one of the major factors contributing to the success of left-libertarian parties. Rule and Zimmerman examine its effect on the election of women and minorities to public office in the United States (1992).

Among political scientists, there is renewed attention to reforming the electoral system (Farrell, 1997; Lijphart, 1994). As states as diverse as Mexico, Russia, Germany, and Italy adopt mixed systems, scholars have begun to reassess the relative merits of single member districts, proportional representation, or some mixture (e.g, Amy, 1993). Lijphart (1999) and Powell (2000) expand these concerns to include how the number of parties, bicameralism, federalism, and other related institutional features contribute to greater democracy. At stake is the way such characteristics enable voters to influence policy-making and the part played by the relative strength of parties.

Another important theme focuses on the regulation of party campaign financing, both comparatively (Alexander and Shiatori, 1994; Ware, 1987a, 1987b) and in the United States (Goidel, Gross, and Shields, 1999; Reiter, 1993; Sabato, 1984; Sorauf, 1988; Thurber and Nelson, 1995; Wayne, 2000). Initially, questions about the need for such regulation produced conflicting answers, as did questions about the corrupting influences of money. But as technological changes made the need for money in campaigns so much greater (Magleby, 2002; Sabato, 1989; Selnow, 1994; Trent and Friedenberg, 2000), the effects of unregulated contributions raised troubling issues about the ability of large contributors to determine every stage of the electoral process: who is nominated, who wins, and what policy choices will be made (Medvic, 2001; Nelson, Dulio, and Medvic, 2002; West, 2000). Yet the kind of regulations that would be ideal is still far from clear (Mann, 2002; Ware, 1987a).

Parties and the state have a two-way relationship. As we have already seen, in working through the electoral process, parties link citizens to the state. They also provide political leadership in appointive as well as elective offices of governments and suggest programs of action to be followed. In the most positive assessment, parties lend legitimacy to government, ensuring that the people themselves choose the path government must follow. Because almost all legislative and executive officers in modern democracies wear partisan labels, government policies are policies made by parties (Castles, 1982). Indeed, according to Schattschneider (1942:1), "political parties created democracy, and . . . democracy is unthinkable save in terms of parties." More recently, Aldrich (1995), using a rational choice perspective, sees parties as the creation of ambitious politicians who can then accomplish their goals within parties. But they do so in ways that solve three problems intrinsic to democratic government: ensuring that the polity rests on popular elections, that legislatures enact public policies, and that issues are kept to a manageable number. By providing a basis for collective action, even if only imperfectly, parties encourage citizens to vote and politicians to cooperate while restricting the legislative agendas they must deal with.

Other, more limited assessments of the positive contributions of competitive parties find legitimacy flowing from the capacity of parties to channel dissent and maintain system stability (Epstein, 1980; Rose, 1980; Sartori, 1976; Ware, 1987, 1996). Wilensky's (2002) analysis of the nineteen richest democracies, for example, measures legitimacy by the vitality of political parties.

Not everyone is convinced of the connection between parties and legitimacy. In the United States, Mayhew (1974, 1991) has argued most forcefully that congressional candidates seek election independent of party positions, which he interprets as meaning that such candidates cannot be treated as exponents of unified party platforms. He concludes that government works just as effectively when parties are weak and levels of government divided.

Governmental institutions enable parties to enact policies, but do parties play their legislative role in ways that differentiate among them? Evidence of such partisan effects is provided by Boix (1998), whose examination of twenty countries shows that socialist governments invest relatively more heavily in education, labor market policies, and capital investment. Others who find an association between social democratic governments and generous social policies include Esping-Andersen (1990), Korpi (1978), and Stephens (1979). Marks, Wilson, and Ray (2002) find that parties, and especially party families (those linked by ideology), provide frames for new issues. When experts in thirteen countries were surveyed about the position of party leaders on European integration, they were able to reliably predict leaders' placement. There is, however, recent questioning of the link between policies and governing parties, primarily the result of economic retrenchments that have affected the welfare programs of social democratic parties (Hicks, 1999; Huber and Stephens, 2001; Swank, 2002).[6]

In the United States, it is also possible to see parties structuring issues (e.g., Cox and Poole, 2002). Wright and Schaffner (2002:377) argue that the apparently low level of ideological consistency in policy positions is the result of party actions to incorporate new issues and new voters. This assessment, we note, goes along with previous citations to evidence that there are sharp and growing ideological differences between the two parties. Examining policy making at the state level, Barrilleaux (2000:70) found that the ideological dispositions of the two parties interact with electoral competition so that "Democrats and Republicans differ when they are forced to." Even as contentious an issue as abortion policy, normally avoided by parties, became a source of opposing stands for the Democrats and Republicans (Halfmann, 2000). Cox and McCubbins (1993) trace how the majority party in the U.S. House of Representatives uses its rule-making power to ensure partisan outcomes to the legislative process.

Not all observers agree that partisan differences become apparent in policy. Rose (1980) showed years ago that British parties were largely in agreement with one another and so failed to offer seriously different choices to the voters. Although both major parties tended, by and large, to keep campaign promises, the policies adopted seldom had the effect promised in affecting unemployment, low wages, low growth, high public expenditure, and high interest rates.

[6] For a fuller discussion, see the chapter by Hicks and Esping-Anderson in this volume.

Such problems were created and changed by factors largely outside the control of government, such as the world economy. Furthermore, even when there was control, government effectiveness was limited by internal quarrels and administrative inertia. The rightward move of Tony Blair's Labour government has exacerbated these effects in more recent times.

Others debate whether parties actually do keep campaign promises; in such studies much seems to depend on what is meant by "promise" (Jacobs and Shapiro, 2000; McLaughlin, 2000). Lawson (1999b) points out that, in dissociating themselves from cleavages, majority parties tend to substitute less important (and less divisive) issues for those of deeper concern, a tactic which makes it easier to keep campaign promises. For Katz and Mair (1995) the strategic choices of cartel parties make them ever more remote from their supporters, both before and after elections.

The Media

Institutions other than the state also interact powerfully with parties, of which one of the most important are the media. Murray Edelman (1985, 1988) was perhaps the first to understand the profound implications of the growing relationship between media and party politics. Recent general studies include those by Dye, Ziegler, and Lichter (1992), Jamieson (1996), and Graber, McQuail, and Norris (1998). Here, as well, the relationship is two-way: the media influence what parties do; parties influence the media.

The first effect is often more apparent to voters. Several studies have stressed how the mainstream media – businesses that make a profit by attracting readers and viewers – seek to present political campaigns as entertainment, concentrating excessively on personalities and the "horserace" aspect of political competition, reducing serious discussion of issues, developing mere group fantasies about the nature of political reality and thus endangering the democratic process (Bennett, 1996; Jamieson and Waldman, 2003; McChesney, 1999; Newman, 1994; Nimmo and Combs, 1983; Perloff, 1998). According to some, the growing concentration of media ownership in the hands of giant corporations is another force compelling parties and candidates to distort their messages to reach their hoped-for publics (Alger, 1998). Picard (1998) has shown how far this process was taken by Italian Prime Minister Silvio Berlusconi, chairman of the multimedia Fininvest firm. Patterson (1998) demonstrates, in a broadly comparative study, that journalists do finds ways, nonetheless, to interject their own political values, but how reassuring that is to the parties obviously depends on the match between those biases and their own programs. And as in the question of campaign finance, it is not always clear what should – and can – be done to solve the problems of excessive mediaization of democratic politics: issues of free speech and questions of political feasibility are difficult to resolve (Lichtenberg, 1990).

Parties, however, should not be seen as helpless victims of the media. When in office, they may pass laws regulating the media that are designed to ensure fair representation of all points of view by preventing or seriously limiting the use of paid political advertising (or forbidding it altogether, as in France), by requiring the broadcast media to give equal or at least proportionate free coverage to all the parties, and/or by providing sufficient public funding so that even the smaller parties can buy the access they need (Kaid and Holtz-Bacha, 1995). Or they may, conversely, effectively block efforts to pass such laws, ensuring that the advantage continues to go to themselves, the well-financed majority parties.

Furthermore, party campaign strategists have learned to beat the media at their own game, securing favorable coverage by such "entertaining" tactics as sound bites, photo opportunities, and ever more aggressive and negative attacks on the opposition (Diamond and Bates, 1992; Maltese, 1994; Mickelson, 1989; Newman, 1994; Sabato 1996; Selnow 1994). They also use the Internet, direct mail, and the telephone to reach voters via media that are more difficult for others to control (Johnson, 2001). Finally, and most importantly, parties secure the media coverage they want by paying for it. The amount and cost of political advertising has steadily increased in every nation, although most dramatically in the United States (Diamond and Bates, 1992; Kaid and Holtz-Bacha, 1995; Magleby, 2002).

Globalization

Globalization is not only the internationalization of capital and capitalism but also the penetration of global institutions and processes into all parts of the world. With it come new constraints on the established ways in which national parties operate. For example, changing conditions in the global economy and the related decline in rates of unionization contribute to weakening ties between organized labor and parties. A study of sixteen industrialized countries finds that it is the decreasing importance of unions themselves that has reduced their influence on policy making in social democratic parties (Piazza, 2001). At the other end of the political spectrum Swank and Betz (2003) find that economic uncertainties affected by globalization have contributed to the success of right-wing populist parties in Western Europe.[7]

The role of parties at the international level is still a puzzle that studies are only now beginning to address. Changing conditions of globalization have led to assessments that nongovernmental organizations (NGOs)[8] will displace political parties in building links among a wide range of actors. This is because they can create advocacy networks that "multiply the channels of access to the international system" and make international resources available to new actors in domestic struggles, "blurring the boundaries between a state's relations with its own nationals and the recourse both citizens and states have to the international system" (Keck and Sikkink, 1998:1–2).

The evidence on this score remains mixed. In North America, where NGOs have been important in recent debates on free-trade treaties, political parties in their governing capacity remain important. Opportunities remain for parties to form transnational relations although these have barely begun (Macdonald and Schwartz, 2002). Europe has had most experience with transnational party links, going back to the first Socialist International. More recently, the move to the European Union stimulated parties to form ties across states (Gaffney, 1996; Hix and Lord, 1997). Meanwhile, the need for stronger involvement by both parties and NGOs to establish democratic procedures at the international level is argued by Etzioni-Halevy (2002).

In response to the formation of the European Union, the three most prominent families of parties, the Socialists, Liberals, and Christian Democrats, each formed its own federation in the 1970s – the Confederation of the Socialist Parties of the European Community (CSPEC), the European Federation of Liberal, Democratic and Reform Parties of the European Communities (ELDR), and the European People's Party (EPP, the Federation of Christian Democratic Parties in the European Communities). The degree to which these federations actually play party roles is, however, not clear, because their national components can have interests at odds with each other. The working of the European Parliament (EP), meanwhile, encourages national party representatives to seek coalitions outside the federations (Bardi, 1994).

The European Greens have differed from other party families by being less positive about the European Union and forming a federation with countries outside the EU. Still, they have been effective in presenting their positions to the EP. At the same time, their federation has been less effective than that of other parties in

[7] Stimuli to right-wing parties are mitigated by national policies with generous welfare provisions.

[8] NGOs may be voluntary associations, interest groups, or social movement organizations. Their separateness from government may be ambiguous where they are regulated by government or receive state funding. As we noted in the section on "ties with organized interests" the boundary between interest groups or social movement organizations and political parties may be blurred. NGOs make up what is termed civil society, a concept generally, though arguably, used to exclude political parties.

becoming unified. Dietz (2000:208) attributes this to

> Differing points of view concerning European integration in general, the reluctance to give up parts of the national sovereignty because of their decentralized, grassroots and anti-bureaucratic ideology, conflicts between more left and more center-oriented parties about the method and extent of cooperation with small left-wing parties and the permanently increasing number of member organizations.

Yet, to the extent that national ties remain strong among the Greens, they are not unusual among parties in the EP. From an examination of 1,000 roll call votes in the EP, Hix (2002) finds that national party policies are the strongest predictors of how members will vote.

The long-term effects of European integration on national cleavages remain unclear. National settings and their electoral environment remain important forces at the same time as integration arouses new foci for possible conflict and, with it, new alignments (e.g., Bartolini, 2001.

Globalization also goes along with renewed local and regional efforts to retain separate operations and identities (e.g., Di Muccio and Rosenau, 1992). Tossutti (2002) examined twenty-one countries with particularistic parties based on ethnic, religious, or regional interests. Yet rather than an expected direct reaction to globalization, she found the success of such parties greater in countries relatively more insulated from global forces. At present, the question is open on the extent to which global forces make partisan policies vulnerable to conditions that individual states will be unable to control (Scharpf, 2000).

In sum, relations with the institutional environment both allow political parties to operate and constrain what they can accomplish. In turn, parties actively influence the role other institutions are able to play. Here we have given most attention to the interaction between parties and governmental institutions, ranging over forms of governance, electoral systems, and campaigning. Parties link citizens to the state but debate continues over how effectively they do this. Although recognizing the growing relevance of institutions such as the media and the forces of globalization, we note that findings about relations with parties are often still tentative.

Missing from this discussion is the place of political parties in civil society, although some aspects of this were dealt with earlier, when dealing with the social bases of parties, and party scholars have always paid attention to the relationship between parties and groups.[9] Still unexamined is the extent to which political parties should be treated as components of civil society, completing the circle of institutional analysis.

REMAINING QUESTIONS

As subject matter for political sociology, the trouble with parties is that they arouse strong feelings pro and con. In earlier times, it was the conflicts that stemmed from opposing parties that produced negative reactions. Positive assessments, in contrast, assigned parties centrality in ensuring democratic government. Today's negativity is more often related to the failings of parties in bringing about a more perfect democratic governance, either of themselves or of the states where they operate. A mixture of normative concerns with a selective empirical agenda appears to affect the amount of emphasis that has been given to political parties by political sociologists. But if political sociologists take another look at political parties, unconstrained by concerns about what parties should be or by past findings that may have prematurely appeared to answer all our questions, they will find rich territory for study.

[9] Epstein (1986), for example, noted the ease with which interest groups and social movements could enter U.S. major parties, making the party system not only unique among competitive party systems but also commendably able to resist serious competition from third parties. Now authors are more likely to see nonparty groups as either a welcome alternative to disappointing parties (Putnam, 1995), as themselves one of the causes of the decline of parties as agents of democracy (Berman, 1997; Doherty, 2001), or just one of the crucial elements in modern democratic life (Foley and Edwards, 1996; Skocpol, Ganz, and Munson, 2000).

Among the most prominent questions that remain are ones about the continuing relevance of social cleavages, whether in countries with uninterrupted histories of democracy or in ones newly experiencing the struggles to achieve democratic government. Everywhere, the mobilization of specific cleavages continues to change. How do we anticipate which will become more prominent and how do we account for national differences? And to what extent are contemporary parties failing to mobilize cleavages altogether, focussing instead on issues that are less divisive?

Because the ways in which parties organize and the relation between culture and structure change over time, they need closer scrutiny. The transformations that come about as parties, both old and new, grapple with changing environments require an alertness on our part that is not constrained by preconceptions of what makes for organization. What is needed are alternate models of organization that take into account different ways of responding to structural problems and different opportunities for cultural expression.

Of the three general topics dealt with, the institutional environment received least coverage, a reflection of how political parties are perceived, especially within sociology. Most attention went to work on relations with the state, ranging from the particulars of policy making to the fundamentals of legitimacy. Under changing environments, we can expect the need to examine these issues in even more detail. As of yet, less well-studied are questions about the effects of the media, globalization, and the relation between parties and civil society.

Most of all, we need to be prepared to address the recurring predictions of party decline with more specific questions about the kind of decline involved. How do voters attach themselves to parties? What organizational adaptations do different parties follow? What is the current relation between the legitimacy of the state and the performance (and existence) of parties? In what ways do parties retain the ability to mobilize voters and produce policies?

We can, as well, find inspiration for further study in considering how well parties adapt and perform. For example, Lawson's (1999b:33) concern with the quality of linkage running from citizen to state via party leads her to ask: If winning parties, or coalitions of parties, are in fact campaigning on catch-all programs only marginally distinct from those of their nearest competitors, and then governing more and more in response to the demands of large donors (as is in the United States), and if increasingly large percentages of Western citizenries fail to exercise their right to vote altogether, then what difference does it make if those who do vote make their choices in terms of the cleavages or issues that separate them most from their fellows? Finding voters who characterize themselves in terms of old or new cleavages and pin their hopes accordingly to this or that party is not the same as finding parties that compete and perform accordingly.

CHAPTER FOURTEEN

Organized Interest Groups and Policy Networks[1]

Francisco J. Granados and David Knoke

What's thy interest in this sad wrack? How came it? Who is it? What art thou?

– William Shakespeare (1609, "Cymbeline," Act IV, Scene II)

INTRODUCTION

The organizational promotion of specific interests in public policy-making processes constitutes an important phenomenon of state-oriented politics. Theoretical and empirical analyses of interest groups are divided among two major themes. The first considers the formation and maintenance of organized interests groups, and the second theme considers their role and impact on public policy making. The latter investigates the patterns of relationships among governmental agencies and interest organizations, how interest groups and coalitions gain access to public policy makers, and the extent to which they exert advantageous influence over policy decisions.

We review fundamental elements of prior studies of organized interest groups and consider some relevant topics for advancing research in this area. We begin with basic conceptual issues in defining organized interest groups. We continue with an exposition of the main foundational approaches to investigating interest groups. Next, we briefly review some issues in the internal development of interest groups: organizational formation, resource mobilization, governance, and collective interest definition. We also briefly scrutinize policy research institutes, a particular and underanalyzed variety of interest organization. The following section investigates policy network approaches to examining the macrolevel dynamics of organized interest group efforts to influence public policies, especially by networking with other interest organizations. We then discuss the interest group systems of the European Union (EU) and the United States. We conclude with some suggestions for advancing the research agenda of interest organization studies.

DEFINING ORGANIZED INTEREST GROUPS

We restrict the term *organized interest group* to designate any political actor, usually consisting of a formally structured organization with a bounded membership and distinct leadership and participatory roles, whose goals include seeking to influence public policy-making activities of elected or appointed public officials. However, some organized interest groups may be informal cliques or coalitions consisting of politically active formal organizations and/or prominent families or persons. For variety, we also use the more common "interest group"

[1] The authors contributed equally to this chapter. We thank Jürgen Grote, Patrick Kenis, Jörg Raab, the handbook editors, and anonymous reviewers for their commentaries on previous drafts. Address all queries by email to: Knoke@atlas.socsci.umn.edu or Granados @socsci.umn.edu

label that appears throughout the literature, as well as the term *interest organization*. We prefer the organized interest group concept because it excludes status categories when they lack collective organization and political objectives, such as farmers, welfare recipients, consumers, or specific ethnic groups. Instead, we treat as theoretically problematic the relationships between a formal organization devoted to influencing public policy making and the latent identity constituencies from which it seeks to mobilize legitimacy, participation, funds, public support, and other politically valuable resources. For example, people with disabilities constitute subpopulations with diverse concerns about employment opportunities, health insurance, pensions, public services, medical research, and discrimination. A set of disability interest organizations seeks to represent these status groups in various policy-making processes.

Interest organizations are predominantly private-sector voluntary associations, whose members are natural persons or other organizations, that pool their members' financial and other resources for use in conventional political actions to affect policy making (Knoke, 2001:324). This definition excludes apolitical voluntary associations whose activities are restricted solely to religious, fraternal, philanthropic, self-help, or recreational purposes. But, many mass-membership voluntary associations pursue explicit political agendas, thus qualifying for inclusion in the organized interest group population.

Most private corporations do not independently engage in political influence activities, and thus we do not regard them as interest organizations. The prominent exceptions are large firms that try directly to influence public policy decisions affecting their economic goals (Hacker and Pierson, 2002; Swank and Martin, 2001; see Chapter 15). Peak business associations and sectoral trade associations are clearly organized interest groups that advocate for the economic policy objectives of their corporate members. Similarly, labor unions and federations behave as interest groups when lobbying for the labor market regulatory and social welfare redistribution policies favored by their constituencies (Bradley, Huber, Moller, Nielsen, and Stephens, 2003; Hicks, 1999).

We also exclude governmental agencies and public-sector policy-making bodies, such as city councils or state legislatures, whenever they are solely the targets of other interest organizations' influence efforts. But, governmental entities sometimes behave as interest organizations, whenever they engage in coalitional or direct lobbying of other governmental institutions. Examples of institutional lobbying include associations of subnational and local governments pressing national political institutions, as well as national governments promoting their interests to such transnational political institutions as the European Union or United Nations.

Most theorists treat social movement organizations (SMOs) as conceptually divergent from organized interest groups. SMOs consist of self-conscious groups of activists – more or less formally organized – who typically advance the claims of powerless and unrepresented constituencies to challenge powerholders and promote or resist social change (see Chapter 16). SMOs frequently resort to contentious extrainstitutional forms of political activity, such as street demonstrations. However, many SMOs become fully legitimated participants in public policy debates, such as civil rights, environmental, and women's organizations. And many conventional interest organizations participate in protests, for example, labor unions that marched against the recent World Trade Organization meetings in Seattle and Genoa. Some scholars indicate that SMOs engage in more-or-less institutionalized activities (public proclamation of grievances in the mass media, lobbying, hiring consultants to write impact reports, or litigation) depending of their resources and the structures of opportunities and constraints posed by specific political contexts (Marks and McAdam, 1999; McAdam, Tarrow, and Tilly, 1996). Burstein (1998) persuasively argued that treating SMOs as conceptually dissimilar to interest organizations is neither meaningful nor empirically useful and, because that dichotomy cannot stand up to close scrutiny, it should be abandoned. He noted that, although both types of organizations vary in their particular tactics, formal organization, numbers of members, resources, and goals, each still tries to influence political outcomes. We remain unpersuaded by theorists who conceptually exclude SMOs from the organized interest group category. Because analyses of political parties, corporations, and SMOs appear elsewhere in this volume, we deemphasize these types of organized interest groups. However, the policy research institute constitutes a distinct understudied subtype, with growing involvement in policy-making activities aimed at direct or indirect influence. An academic literature recently emerged that specializes in policy research institutes, as we note below.

FOUNDATIONAL APPROACHES TO INTEREST GROUPS STUDY

Since the 1950s, interest group studies within individual countries or cross-nationally have emphasized the relevance of several pluralist, Marxist, elitist, and corporatist theories for explaining issues of policy making, polity governance, and state-society relations (e.g., Berger, 1981; Cawson, 1985; Thomas, 1993). We assess these four foundational approaches from an historical perspective as prologue to discussing contemporary research on interest group networks.

Pluralism considers that interest groups play a central role in the political process, with significant power to influence policy outcomes (Bentley, 1949; Dahl, 1961; Finer, 1966; Truman, 1951; see Smith, 1990, for a critical review). This approach views political power as fragmented and widely dispersed among competing interest groups, with policy decisions resulting from complex interactions and bargaining within the different sets of groups, defined by specific matters or kind of personal traits. Pluralism describes the policy process in liberal democracies as analogous to a marketplace where many (plural) preferences on each policy issue are represented by organized interest groups that freely compete to gain governmental attention, hoping ultimately to win enactment and implementation of their preferred policy decisions. In this dynamic, elected and appointed government officials are depicted as accessible yet disengaged from interest-group rivalries and conflicts. The government's minor role in policy making consists of arbitrating the group competition without controlling it or trying to impose its own solutions. Especially in the United States, pluralism was elevated from a hypothesis about political behavior to an ideology about how the democratic system should operate (Lowi, 1967).

Pluralism maintains that certain institutional checks-and-balances prevent any group from becoming too powerful and dominating the policy-making process. In most instances, the constrictions imposed by these checks assure that political power is dispersed across diverse interest groups, and no single interest organization or set of organized interests always prevails. A primary check consists of matching political pressures from one group by a rival countervailing group. A latent interest group, which by definition was not previously mobilized, will formally organize if its constituent interests become threatened. Furthermore, given the potential mobilization of latent interests, governments anticipate and preemptively take unorganized interests into account despite complete absence of political pressures (Finer, 1966; Truman, 1951). A second check consists of politicians' propensities to listen to numerous interest groups in expectation of obtaining sufficient electoral support for reelection. Both mobilized and latent groups whose interests are ignored may threaten an electoral defeat. Therefore, inequality in economic resources is counterbalanced by interest-group voting strength (Finer, 1966). A third check is that governmental departments may develop close consultative relationships with different interest groups, providing every group with some political access (Wilson, 1977). Finally, internal disarray within very resourceful interest groups can weaken their political clout, further reducing power inequities among groups (Dahl, 1961; Truman, 1951). Although most pluralists acknowledge that pressure group power depends on political resources, and that resource variation may confer unequal power, access, and influence, they consider that all groups have some power resources and no singular asset, such as money, bestows special advantages (Smith, 1990).

The classical pluralist model is criticized for concentrating excessively on interest group resources and behaviors, paying insufficient attention to governmental interests and activities, and neglecting external constraints on governments such as international economic developments. It inadequately recognizes governmental capacity to make decisions independently of group influence (Nordlinger, 1981), and overlooks institutionalized organizational effects structuring the policymaking process (Hall, 1986). Classical pluralism also assumes a procedural consensus among all interest groups in the polity, without considering that actors who refuse to play by the policy game rules may be denied access to government officials and hence become politically disadvantaged (Smith, 1990, 1993). Moreover, relationships between government and some interest organizations can become very close and exclusive, conferring advantages on these favored groups (Finer, 1966). Checks-and-balances may be unrealistic in many cases and group access to officials might be less open than the model assumes. Pluralism fails to consider the impact of ideologies, which can shape policy content, group accessibility to policy makers, and variation in influence among groups possessing equivalent resources (Hall, 1986). If access is not completely open to all groups and some interests are excluded, pluralists erroneously assume that an absence of group activity implies political consensus, signifying widespread social agreement, acceptance of the policy processes and outcomes, and the peaceful conflict resolution benefiting most, if not all, contending interest groups. Instead, the apparent political consensus might be biased toward certain privileged interests, whereas silence and passivity might just reflect the effective exclusion of groups questioning the prevailing consensus and unwilling to conform to pluralist rules of participation. These groups are deemed irresponsible and unsuitable for policy consultations by the powers-that-be (Smith, 1990, 1993). Finally, some critics also argue that pluralism sustains socioeconomic inequality (Dahl and Lindblom, 1976).

Pluralists reacted to such criticisms and the theory's deviation from empirical evidence by modifying the original model (Smith, 1990; Manley, 1983). Thus, Richardson and Jordan (1979) acknowledged that perfect competition rarely exists because access to certain policy areas may be not completely open to all interest groups. Institutionalized relations between government and specific interest groups may exclude others. Policy events typically occur in oligopolistic or monopolistic power structures whose participants try to capture control of governmental units, resulting in situations of dependence, cooptation, and clientelism that blur distinctions between the public sector and private interest groups. Nevertheless, Richardson and Jordan insisted that sufficient countervailing power arises through interest group access and issue networks consulted by government. However, they disregarded the possibility that access and consultation differ from actual policy influence and that ideological constraints may block some group access.

Neopluralist scholars depart from classical pluralism by fully accepting that insufficient countervailing powers allow business domination of policy agendas and creation of structures of political patronage and privilege (see Chapter 2). These structures exclude the general public's interests, stabilize social inequalities, and harm democratic processes, institutions, and values (Lowi, 1967, 1969; McConnell, 1966). Business groups also attain a privileged policy position resulting from their structural power in the capitalist economy, given the government's need for a successful economy to survive politically. Policy makers adopt measures favorable to business interests, boosting "business confidence" to encourage economic investments, independently of any political actions that business groups might undertake, a point raised by Marxists such as O'Conner (1973) and Offe (1984). Consequently, government decisions mirror and reinforce existing social and political inequality. Neopluralists question the state's conventional image as fundamentally concerned with the welfare of the whole society, acknowledged that power inequalities rooted in the very structural organization of society privilege some organized interests more than others, and allowed for the role of ideology in policy making (Dahl, 1982; Lindblom, 1977). Lindblom and Dahl (1976) proposed incremental structural reforms to promote equality in the U.S. political economy, such as wealth and income redistribution, that imply just minor adjustments to the social structural foundations of capitalism. Despite significantly modifying the original model, neopluralists still fail to integrate the disproportionate power of business into the pluralist democratic framework (Manley, 1983), to specify the precise mechanisms connecting business to governments, and to consider sufficiently the state's political autonomy, which may explain why governments occasionally enforce policies harmful to some business interests (Smith, 1990).

Marxism explicitly emphasizes the effects of power inequality within the class structure and the state's policy-making biases. The capitalist state is extensively involved in resolving conflicts among contending interests by always championing capitalist class domination over the working class (Lukes, 1974; Miliband, 1969; Offe, 1975; Poulantzas, 1973, 1978). Marxists depict political power and class interests as fundamentally originating from the economic foundation of society; that is, from the ownership and control of the means of production and the consequent relations of production. They argue that control over the means of production confers massive political power advantages, regardless of the political party composition of the state, because capitalist society depends on economic production. The state is an instrument controlled by the dominant capitalist class to protect the rights of private property, thereby reinforcing that ruling class's power.

In Marxist theory, the state always does the bidding of capitalists and undermines democracy. The state acts to prevent or suppress class conflicts harmful to the interests of capital, coercively restricts working-class interests, and limits trade union influence in the polity. Marxists stress the powerlessness of many interest groups under capitalism (Miliband, 1969; Poulantzas, 1973). Although the capital class can be a pressure group, its policy influence is neither mainly a product of its organizational capacities nor its political activities, but results from capital's dominant structural position in the economy and its control of the state. Some Marxist conceptions portray the capitalist state in a semiautonomous relationship *vis-à-vis* the capitalist class whenever the state increasingly intervenes in the economy to deal with threatening market failures and negative economic externalities, accommodates the interests of different component parts of the electorate and political environment, acts to resolve conflicts among factions within the capitalist class, and responds to pressures from international economic and political context. Nevertheless, such relative autonomy does not reduce the class bias of the state but actually allows it to fulfill its class-subordinated role (Miliband, 1977; Prechel, 2000).[2]

Critics disagree with Marxism's overly simplified view of interest group systems in contemporary liberal democracies, noting that numerous noneconomic divisions permeate capitalist societies. Two differing neomarxist perspectives consider the existence of the capitalist class's internal unity. The first emphasizes intraclass consensus over conflict consisting of a class-wide rationality on general politicoeconomic interests (Miliband, 1969). Some scholars argued that consensus arises from bank hegemony over business corporations that supports politicoeconomic strategies to achieve general long-run economic profit (Bearden, 1987; Kotz, 1978; Mintz and Schwarz, 1985). Other studies

[2] These arguments about state autonomy parallel those of the state-centric perspective that conceives the state as an entity with its own economic and noneconomic agenda that results not merely from interest-group demands, but rather, a state's structures shape these groups' formation, operation, and influence on policy making (Skocpol, 1980, 1985; Block, 1977, 1980; Rueschemeyer and Evans, 1985; Weir and Skocpol, 1985; Prechel, 1990; Finegold and Skocpol, 1995). Under the state-centric perspective, the state's goals are also affected by its own organizational structure, and its own interests are carried out by state officials, with advice from policy experts, who tend to behave according to their roles as officials as well as pursuing their particular agency interests.

suggested that an inner circle, consisting of prominent members of interlocking corporate networks, have connections and organizational capacity to promote general business interests on behalf of the whole capitalist class (Useem, 1979, 1982, 1984; Stokman, Ziegler, and Scott, 1985). Conversely, a second neo-Marxist perspective maintains that the lack of a unitary economic trend produces divisions of interests among business sectors having differential and competing rates of capital accumulation (Aglietta, 1979; Offe, 1975; Poulantzas, 1978), depending on each sector's structural position in the economy (Baran and Sweezy, 1966; Mizruchi and Koening, 1986). Such production segmentation implies persistent conflicts over preferred state policies among the consequent capitalist class segments (Prechel, 1990; Zeitlin, Neuman, and Ratcliff, 1976).

Some Marxist analysts emphasize the cultural-ideological elements that sustain capitalist class hegemony, particularly intellectuals, professionals, and opinion leaders who help to develop and advance ideological positions supporting capitalist interests (Cockett, 1995; Connell, 1977; Gramsci, 1971[1934]; Sklair, 2001). Ideologies are important for shaping the premises of polity and the state's role in the economy and its crises (e.g., state fiscal crisis and crisis of the welfare state) (Gottdiener and Komninos, 1989). An important current cultural element of capitalist ideology is "consumerism," which encourages conspicuous and unrestrained consumption. The resulting economic demand, which is satisfied by enlarged corporate production, keeps the capitalist economy running at high levels. In addition to lobbying policy officials to obtain favorable legislation, corporations actively publicize and propagate cultural and ideological elements supporting their economic and political interests. Moreover, they disarticulate alternative ideologies threatening to their interests by co-opting adversary actors and counterculture ideas. Specifically, the capitalist class attempts to persuade public opinion of the close alignment between corporate and national economic interests (Ryan, Swanson, and Buchholz, 1987). It also advocates a "sustainable development" response to the global ecological crisis (Hoffman, 1997). Sustaining hegemonic capital interests by appropriate cultural-ideological activity is crucial for the "transnational capitalist class" undertaking global economic activities through multinational corporations (Sklair, 2001). This class participates in economic globalization struggles occurring within national and international political forums. It exercises direct control of strategic global localities and indirect control in other locations through alliances with local or national rulers and capitalists who favor basic aspects of globalization (Fennema, 1982; Sklar, 1987; Overbeek, 1993).

Elitist theories conceive elite interest groups whose top position holders are politically active while the nonelite citizenry remains politically passive. Hence, elitist policy analysts focus in activities undertaken by those elites. Authors disagree on reasons for the political apathy of average citizens in democracy, ranging from individuals' characteristics to political institutions and societal structures (Walker, 1966). Relevant studies of elite structures consider the relation between elite integration, political stability, and democracy (Dahrendorf, 1967; Higley and Moore, 1981). Elitist analysts tend to assume that social power is conferred by formal organizations (Domhoff, 1996; Mills, 1956). Several variants within the elitist perspective are identifiable according to the characteristics defining inclusiveness in elite groups (positional prominence in organizations, policy-making involvement, class membership, and social group attributes) and whether one elite group (e.g., business, trade union, political-governmental, mass media, military, and academic) dominates by possessing some resource conferring extraordinary power to rule the polity (Higley and Moore, 1981; Scott, 1990). Accordingly, from an elitist perspective, pluralism could be considered a variant of the elitist model in which no single group, defined by positional prominence and involvement in specific policy issues, dominates the polity; hence, denying the existence of a ruling elite. A second variant proposes a clear hierarchy of power and influence among elite groups, with business and political elites at its apex and other elites having lesser political power (Dye, 1976, 2002; Hunter, 1959; Mills, 1956; Porter, 1965).

A third variant is the class-dominance model, differing from the second variant in the interpretation of its analyses, which is based on economic relations between social classes, as well as in relying on social class as the key element to define elite inclusiveness (Connell, 1977; Domhoff, 1996, 1998; Therborn, 1978). Class-dominance and Marxism are highly compatible: both emphasize the extraordinary political power provided by ownership and control of the means of production, class conflict and dominance, and the issue of inequality pervasiveness in liberal democracies. The class-dominance model indicates that the state has little autonomy to promote its own interests and goals, although its institutional structure shapes the class-elite's exercise of policy influence. The class-elite is a well-defined, self-conscious, and tightly knit corporate community able to generate internal classwide consensus on the issues of greatest concern. Its great political influence usually ensures the dominance of its political preferences despite opposition from powerless groups. Domhoff (1996:18) asserted that the United States has "(1) a small social upper class (2) rooted in the ownership and control of a corporate community that (3) is integrated with a policy-planning network and (4) has great political power in both political parties and dominates the federal government in Washington." He identified three interlocking networks of the U.S. ruling elite: upper wealth-holding class members (identified through social networks of schools, clubs, and intermarriage); the corporate community (intercorporate network of upper-class members and executives sharing corporate boards); and policy-planning specialists (corporate experts and leaders of charitable foundations and policy research institutes). This power elite impacts government through four processes: seeking special-interest legislation by employing lobbyists, former government lawyers and politicians, and heads of trade associations; creating policy-planning networks to advocate preferred general policies; influencing the selection of candidates for public office; and attempting to shape public opinion (Domhoff, 1996).

Corporatist theories reacted to inabilities of other approaches to explain interest group activities in many democratic regimes, especially in European countries. Corporatism reached its peak in Europe during the mid-1970s and entered a decline starting in the 1980s, ironically at the moment scholars began to analyze corporatist systems (Lehmbruch and Schmitter, 1982; Schmitter, 1989; Schmitter and Lehmbruch, 1979; Williamson, 1989; see Chapter 22). In that period, most democratic European states relied on centralized national bargaining between institutionalized class, sectoral, or professional interest groups represented by peak associations that coordinated their constituencies. These negotiations were facilitated by social democratic governments willing to integrate their political systems after the social turmoil of the late 1960s, the deinstitutionalization of the capitalist world economy, and the international economic crisis after 1973. This crisis consequently inaugurated lower national growth rates and the fiscal crisis of the state, triggering impediments to reaching corporatist agreements to redistribute diminishing economic wealth.

Corporatism's distinctive feature is the state's leading role in orchestrating interest group participation in policy processes. Such political practice, referred to as "concertation," is characterized by explicit, officially recognized, and regular cooperation and reciprocity between these groups and the state, aimed at achieving harmony among special interests and participant obligations to promote the collective good and social solidarity. Not only are interest groups formally incorporated into the state policy system by representing their members' interests during consultations prior to legislative deliberation, but they also participate in decision making and assist the state to implement public policies to which they actively consent through delegated self-enforcement (Cawson, 1985, 1986). We focus on corporatist regimes allowing relatively free and plural interest groups, permitting widespread public participation, and sustaining a democratic state.[3] This corporatist variant (variously called "societal corporatism," "democratic corporatism," or "neocorporatism") is often based on an explicit constitution or series of contracts negotiated between the state and corporate interest groups spelling out mutual rights and responsibilities, thus giving corporatism a legal foundation. Such attributes differ from "state corporatism," where an authoritarian state imposes and strongly controls all interest group activities, thus verging on dictatorship or fascism (Schmitter, 1974). However, even neocorporatism can undermine democratic participation and representation. By granting monopolistic representation to certain interests and associations, the state excludes other, usually less powerful, groups. In this sense, not all interest groups are corporatized. A substantial number remain whose relations to the state more closely resemble the pluralist model or lack any effective political influence.

Interest groups under corporatism become explicitly incorporated into the state, that is, as agents that are no longer solely private enterprises but as public actors with responsibility to provide stability and predictability in deciding and implementing certain binding policies. Because corporatism has mainly concerned economic policies (income policies, employment, inflation, fiscal policy, working conditions, worker training, and productivity measures), most interest groups participating in corporatist arrangements are economic – business, labor, agriculture, and professions (Lehmbruch, 1979). The government grants a monopoly of representation to certain peak associations to speak for and negotiate on behalf of their constituents in exchange for their cooperation in developing and enforcing policy decisions. Therefore, corporatism requires large peak associations capable of representing large constituencies and compelling their members to abide by decisions negotiated through the policy process. It also involves governmental intervention in the economy and society to achieve policy goals regarding income distribution, welfare, and other socioeconomic issues. The exceptionally minimal state economic intervention and weak peak associations of the United States relative to European countries are largely responsible for scholarly disregard of corporatist theory in that country (Salisbury, 1979; Wilson, 1982).

Macroeconomic corporatist policies by European states decayed from the late 1970s into the 1980s as national governments lost economic sovereignty to implement effective Keynesian-expansionist economic policies. This trend came to a close with the creation of the European Central Bank in 1998. Moreover, fundamental aspects of nationally centralized collective bargaining faded by desegregation (Streeck and Schmitter, 1991). Market instabilities pressured firms to increase production and develop social organizational flexibility, resulting in increasing exclusion of centralized unions and employer associations from many workplace-specific negotiations and collective bargaining issues. One factor was the decreasing relevance, and at times counterproductivity, of negotiations aimed at establishing broad standard national solutions to regulate the employment relationship. Policies had to be tailored to improve the productivity and international competitiveness of specific sectors and individual enterprises. Another factor was the accelerating differentiation of social structures and collective interests within advanced capitalist societies that transcend the simple class polarization of capital and labor. Consequently, policy attention changed from a class-based cleavage toward many discrete dimensions such as consumer protection, gender and ethnic identity, environmental preservation, and other issues championed by social movement organizations (Streeck and Schmitter, 1991).

Although corporatism declined during the 1980s, it remained the practice at all government levels of most European states for negotiating diverse welfare-state issues (Schmitter, 1989). Some analysts detected a renaissance of national macrocorporatist policy making during the 1990s, perhaps motivated to ensure social

[3] See Williamson (1985) and Wiarda (1997:15–24) for different conceptions of the term corporatism.

peace by counteracting the negative social consequences of the economic adjustments required by the European Union (EU) processes of the Single European Market and monetary union (Grote and Schmitter, 1999). Finally, downgraded corporatist systems survived in some countries by shifting from national to sectoral industrial levels. This "meso-corporatism" involves policies agreements reached by the participation of sectoral capital, labor, and professional associations within one industrial sector (Cawson, 1985, 1986; Schmitter, 1989). Meso-corporatist studies usually compared policy-making process at different sectors within a country. Researchers investigated how interests enter into political arenas through the intermediation of organizations, considered the biases of that transformation, and analyzed the distinct potential to organize different interests. Still a third level of corporatism can be discerned, "micro-corporatism," referring to policy making between a government agency and an individual monopolistic firm, but implying neither "clientelism" nor a "franchise state" arising from weak state authorities lacking autonomy and dependent on serving a specific firm's interests (Wolfe, 1977).

The complexity national interest group systems allows researchers to find instances supporting some aspects of pluralist, Marxist, elitist, and corporatist perspectives. Thus, any interest group system explanation concentrating on one exclusive theory most likely will paint an incomplete picture. In this regard, analysts express divergent opinions about the relative presence of alternative features emphasized by the different perspectives in different countries and at different periods within a country (e.g., Lehmbruch and Schmitter, 1982; Streeck and Schmitter, 1991; Thomas, 1993; Wiarda, 1997). To obtain better descriptions and explanations of interest group systems, analyses should draw selectively from all four approaches. This selectivity is appropriate for advancing research programs on interest groups, as scholars too often fixate on identifying where each nation fits along some pluralist-corporatist continuum and thus marginalize more crucial issues about variations in political power and inequality among interest groups. However, attempts to construct a unitary theory capable of integrating all previous perspectives also seems difficult to reconcile with the idiosyncratic social, political, and cultural components among diverse national interest group systems. This agenda seems particularly ill-suited for investigating nonwestern democracies and other political systems found in African, Asian, Islamic, Latin American, and ex-socialist European countries (Wiarda, 1997; Zeigler, 1988).

ORGANIZATIONAL DEVELOPMENT OF INTEREST GROUPS

At the organizational level of analysis, an interest group pools financial and political resources contributed by its individual members and supporters, overcomes the weaknesses of isolated persons or organizations, and coordinates joint actions that seek to influence policy makers. We briefly discuss five problems that many interest groups confront during their development: organizational formation, resource mobilization, structural transformation, internal governance, and collective interest identification. Interest organizations also encounter other serious dilemmas that may impede collective action, such as opportunism (Williamson, 1981), loss-of-power (Coleman, 1973), loyalty and exit (Hirschman, 1970), and democratic accountability (Knoke, 1990a), which we cannot examine in depth. Many of these organizational-level issues also arise at the interorganizational network level, which we examine in later sections.

The historical trends over the past two centuries in many Western liberal democracies saw various interest organizations emerging at successive periods, encompassing ever-widening segments of society over time. In general sequence, the initial societal interests that politically mobilized were preindustrial religious and charitable organizations, followed by agricultural and industrial producer groups such as trade unions and employers' organizations, then professional associations, and more recently by identity groups such as those concerned with civil liberties, minority rights, and the environment. Interest organization formation seems to accelerate during periods of economic and political disturbances that create threats and opportunities, particularly when major ideological shifts in legislative, regulatory, and judicial decisions affect the interests of previously passive or unorganized social groups (Gray and Lowery, 1996; Scholzman and Tierney, 1986:74–82). To illustrate these dynamics with examples drawn from the United States, the National Grange in the late nineteenth century transformed itself from a service group for farmers into an advocacy organization demanding governmental regulation of unrestrained railroad prices (Browne, 1998:15; Clemens, 1997: 145–83). Rates of U.S. trade association creation increased dramatically as national markets expanded in the early twentieth century and business firms sought political influence in state and national capitals (Aldrich and Staber, 1988; Aldrich, Staber, Zimmer, and Beggs, 1994). During the 1970s and 1980s, numerous business advocacy groups took up permanent residence in Washington, seeking political redress from the newly created regulatory agencies that issued thousands of pages of federal regulations affecting business interests, from air pollution to pension funds to consumer product safety (Vogel, 1996). Similar expansions in interest organization populations occurred in the labor unionization struggles of the New Deal and the civil rights, antiwar, feminist, environmental, and sexual identity movements from the 1960s through the 1990s.

The creation of mass-membership interest organizations involves an exchange process between entrepreneurial leaders, who invest their social and economic capital in a set of benefits offered to potential supporters, and members who obtain those benefits by paying dues and participating in organizational activities. Mancur Olson's rational choice theory of group exchange depicted as illogical or irrational anyone who joined and provided resources to an interest organization that seeks only public goods from which no eligible recipient could be excluded (Olson, 1965; Salisbury, 1969). Utility-maximizing actors would refuse to pay for an interest organization's efforts to influence public policies from which they could benefit regardless of their individual contributions. That is, they would take a "free ride" on the group's political advocacy efforts. Olson deduced that most interest organizations would fail to mobilize their optimum potential supporters if they depended solely on public goods to attract member resources. Instead, membership organizations must offer nonpolitical "selective incentives," such as magazine subscriptions and social camaraderie, that could be received only by members in exchange for making contributions toward the organization's public-good advocacy efforts. The free-rider conundrum changed an organization's recruitment and resource mobilization strategies from emphasizing collective goals to satisfying its members' preferences for personal material and social benefits. Thus, the resources available organizational leaders to fight public policy battles were a "by-product" of selling selective incentives to politically disinterested members, creating a conspicuous "disjuncture between member goals and group goals" (Moe, 1980:74).

Despite the simple elegance of Olson's collective action theory, subsequent empirical research revealed that many members nevertheless desire policy solutions with little personal benefit and willingly contribute their money and time toward achieving interest organizations' public policy goals (Knoke, 1990a; Marwell and Oliver, 1993; Moe, 1980). The environmental conditions, internal organizational economies, and individual motivations that foster collective political action appear much more complex than Olson conceived. Several analysts proposed broader arrays of private- and public-good incentives to overcome the temptations for individuals to free ride on other members' efforts (Etzioni, 1975; Knoke, 1990a; Knoke and Wright-Isak, 1982; Oliver, 1980, 1984). James Q. Wilson (1973) attempted to shore up rational choice explanations of interest organization formation by positing a triad of material, solidary, and purposive inducements that mobilize members' resource contributions and engage them in collective political actions. Purposive incentives appeal to people's desires to feel connected to some highly valued larger purposes and to achieve altruistic goals. By explicitly stressing the importance of an interest organization's professed public policy goals, purposive incentives contradict the private-good dichotomy in Olson's selective incentive perspective. Membership organization leaders play a crucial role in resource mobilization by identifying prospective participants, recruiting members with diverse incentives, and persuading them to contribute toward public policy influence efforts despite the evident irrationality in maximizing their personal gains.

An important but relatively neglected corollary to the interest group formation problem is explaining the dynamic transformation of diverse organizational forms – including social movements, religious sects, professional societies, academic institutions, nonprofit foundations, for-profit businesses, and government agencies – into organized political interest groups. Social movements that successfully deploy disruptive mass protests, winning public legitimation and political acceptance from the established polity for their social change goals, may subsequently convert into conventional lobbying organizations, political parties, or nonprofit foundations. For example, the U.S. civil rights movement, after its major victory ending Southern legal segregation in the 1960s, spawned numerous specialized advocacy organizations that persevere today in legislative and regulatory politics in Washington and the state capitals (Garrow, 1989). Similarly, during the earlier Progressive Era, the sudden decay of mass political parties spun off activist factions into agrarian, women's, and labor associations that developed and disseminated innovative strategies and tactical repertoires for pressuring state and national governments on their narrowly focused policy interests (Clemens, 1997).

Less commonly, interest groups may change into nonpolitical organizations, for example, an environmental association that decides to make profits by publishing educational materials. Fluctuations in organizational forms may originate from external conditions, including seismic shifts in popular ideological climates and governmental policies that unintentionally engender new constituencies with vested policy interests. Internal factors can also transform organizational missions, particularly through the routinization of charismatic authority after the passing of a social movement's founding leaders (Glassman and Swatos, 1986). Organizational goal displacement occurs when oligarchic leaders lose sight of original public policy goals to concentrate on achieving greater organizational efficiencies or simply to feather their own nests. Although analysts have given organizational transformation scant theoretical and empirical attention, this theme should be pursued vigorously in future research agendas.

Analysts often pose the fundamental problem in interest organization governance as a choice between oligarchic or democratic alternatives. Entrenched leadership and staff cliques in labor unions, trade associations, fraternal organizations, professional societies, political parties, and social movement organizations allegedly demonstrate an inevitable "iron law of oligarchy" (Michels, 1958). Oligarchs not only capture control of organizational governance mechanisms but also typically pursue policy goals divergent from rank-and-file preferences. However, most voluntary membership organizations depend too heavily on their members for critical resources to enable officials to flout membership interests over the long run. Consequently, most interest organization constitutions provide an array of democratic institutions, including competitive elections, membership meetings, referenda, and committee systems (Berry, 1984:92–113; Knoke, 1990a:143–61). But actual practices of consulting members to formulate collective actions vary widely and researchers have little understanding of how democratic mechanisms shape organizational capacities to mobilize members for collective actions. The analytic task is complicated by the intricate interactions of formal governance processes with executive and leadership decisions, bureaucratic administrative practices, environmental conditions, and the internal economy of member incentives.

Organizational interests express collective preferences for specific processes or end-states. To assert that an organization holds a policy interest means that certain public policy decisions are consequential for its members and the constituencies it claims to represent. We do not attempt to classify the myriad objectives that interest organizations may pursue. Several typologies propose categorizing interest groups according to their primary economic, civic, recreational, or identity-group attributes (Baumgartner and Leech, 1998; Knoke, 1990a; Schlozman and Tierney, 1986; Smith, 2000).[4] Another important topic is the relationship between latent and manifest interests and alleged "false consciousness" arising when individuals' expressed preferences fail to reflect their class locations. Presumably, organizational interest formation results from internal power struggles, negotiation, and persuasion among factions that ultimately define the collective purposes and goals. Some analysts apparently assume that organizational interests are accurately revealed by explicit mission statements and leaders' expressed preferences for particular policy decisions. Others argue that such interests emerge through complex interactions between organizational properties and external actors. For example, business association interests are jointly shaped by attributes of the represented industries ("logic of membership") and by properties of labor unions and state institutions ("logic of influence") (Schmitter and Streeck, 1999). Unions confront similar dynamics, leading to distinct collective action problems for business and labor interest organizations (Offe and Wiesenthal, 1980). We urge that theorists give greater attention to specifying how members and leaders socially construct the collective interests of their organizations under uncertain environmental constraints. Empirical researchers should rely less on *ad hoc* interest group classifications and concentrate more on uncovering the substantive factors that create and transform interest group organizations.

POLICY RESEARCH INSTITUTES

Policy research institutes, also called think tanks, can be defined as organizations with expert members that study policy issues, actively seek to inform policy makers and other constituencies, and try to influence the policy-making process (Stone and Garnett, 1998). Policy research institutes typically are nonprofit organizations with relative autonomy from governments, universities, and political parties, although they may maintain formal and informal links – financial and personnel – with these organizations, and cooptation may occur in some cases. Their autonomy from other organizations varies from case to case and across countries, which complicates defining the line separating policy research institutes from university research centers, government research organizations, temporary governmental investigative commissions, party research departments, or for-profit consulting agencies. All these kinds of organizations, independently of any formal linkages they maintain with governments, parties, and universities, perform the same activities and have similar goals, an aspect that must be considered by researchers assessing the numbers and influence of organizations conducting policy research in different political systems (for a typology of policy research institutes see Weaver and McGann, 2000).

The members of policy research institutes conduct research and analyses that combine academic and policy-relevant features. Some institutes are mainly committed to advancing scholarly basic and applied political research and to evaluating government problems. In other cases, their primary goal is to engage in political advocacy and set the policy agenda, by influencing the content and decision making of public

[4] The Gale Encyclopedia of Associations, a prime source of information on more than 144,000 U.S. and international organizations, classifies them into seventeen categories reflecting their primary constituencies, beneficiaries, or goals; for example, trade and professional associations, social, welfare and public affairs organizations, religious, sports and hobby groups. The U.S. Internal Revenue Service tabulates tax-exempt organizations under two dozen headings, such as charitable, religious, educational, scientific, civic leagues, social welfare, local employees, labor, agricultural, horticultural, business leagues, chambers of commerce, real estate boards, social and recreational clubs, fraternal beneficiary societies, cemetery companies, and state chartered credit unions. For neither schema is any systematic theoretical principle evident.

policies or by shaping the ideas around political debates through different channels and at several policy-making stages. In their advocacy activity, some institutes pursue a more-or-less explicit ideology (e.g., neoliberal, social democrat, and ecological), whereas others try to give their analyses an objective scholarly character. Some institutes complement their research and analysis activities with education, training, and information dissemination programs. Their constituencies vary from governments, bureaucrats, political parties, international organizations, nongovernmental organizations (NGOs), SMOs, unions, businesses, churches, foundations, and any other consumers of research, policy analyses and ideological argument. In most occasions, these constituencies – together with individual donors – fund institute activities, which may constrain them to satisfy their funders' expectations. By remaining uncritical of their supporters' policies and political views, institute credibility as impartial policy analysts may suffer. When policy research institutes conduct research for nongovernmental constituencies, they may act as advocates between those groups and the policy makers.

Policy research institutes try to influence policy makers by presenting analyses and arguments in seminars, offering expert advice upon request or publicizing their research in the mass media, specialized publications, and conferences. These activities may help in socially constructing a common framework to improve communication among the diverse actors involved in policy debates, to inform the general public and broad scientific communities, and to enhance governmental transparency and accountability (Weaver and McGann, 2000). Some institutes also contribute to broadening the public debate on policy issues and communicating the views of diverse and underrepresented social groups. Given these emphases and their creation by nonstate entrepreneurs, policy research institutes often present themselves as civil society organizations. Nevertheless, these institutes do not always enhance societal democracy. They can actually restrict civil society pressures, participation, and access to the public debate. Moreover, in many cases, policy research institutes lack strong connections to the societal groups they claim to represent because they are rarely membership organizations, and their staff and administrators are usually social and political elites (Domhoff, 1998). Also, on some occasions, they are too closely tied to governments or specific interests (Stone, 2000).

The most relevant aspect for studying policy research institutes as components of specific interest groups consists of assessing their role in infusing ideas to advance the agendas of the groups they belong to, thus helping to develop and advance their ideological stances and policy interests (Domhoff, 1996, 1998; Sklair, 2001). Studies of these organizations' roles in promoting social and economic ideologies suggest that their activities may be a determinative factor in achieving the groups' political goals (Cockett, 1995; Ricci, 1993; Stefancic and Delgado, 1996). These studies reveal, especially in the United States but also globally as in cases of widespread neoliberalism, a typically unbalanced political struggle on the intellectual plane, with conservative, business-oriented, neoliberal think tanks having disproportional presence and impact in the polity compared to think tanks with other ideological orientations. That imbalance originates in the larger financial support those conservative think tanks receive from foundations, the constrictions that liberal foundations created by wealthy capitalists pose to criticisms of capitalism and their orientation toward action projects supporting the disadvantage rather than to ideological intellectual projects, and the fact that liberal and leftist intellectuals more often have full-time academic jobs and rarely write for policy purposes (Stefancic and Delgado, 1996).[5]

Although policy research institutes have existed for more than a century in some Western countries, they recently increased in number and variety of research interests, size, and resources. Some recent studies cataloging this type of organization estimated that more than 1,200 exist in the United States (Hellebust,

[5] About the role of foundations in public policy see Colwell (1980, 1993), Jenkins and Shumate (1985), and Allen (1992).

1997; about U.S. think tanks see Abelson and Lindquist, 2000; Ricci, 1993; Stefanic and Delgado, 1996) and more than 600 in Western Europe (Day, 2000). Policy research institutes can also be found in Asia (Langford and Brownsey, 1991; Yamamoto, 1995) Africa, the Middle East (CIPE 1997), Eastern Europe (Stryuck, 1999), Latin America (Levy, 1995), and other regions (see Stone, Denham, and Garnett, 1998, and McGann and Weaver, 2000, for analyses in several world regions and countries and of specific think tanks).[6] Although the research literature primarily investigates institute activities at the national level, either within specific countries or comparatively across nations (Stone, et al., 1998), since the late 1980s an increasing number of prominent think tank turned to regional and global policy issues such as foreign policy, national development, or environmentalism. Their constituencies can also be international governments and NGOs, multinational corporations, and other transnational actors. Some institutes are not nationally but regionally bounded. For example, at the European Union level, these organizations are typically concerned with European policy issues. Others participate in international networks and engage in research collaborations and scholarly exchanges and even establish subsidiaries outside their home countries that can provide political assistance to develop civil society, democratic, and economic institutions. Examples of international networks are the Global ThinkNet, which brings together directors of the world's leading think tanks, and the Global Development Network, which convenes many policy research institutes specializing in development (Stone, 2000).

[6] Prominent U.S. policy institutes include the American Enterprise Institute for Public Policy, Brookings Institution, CATO Institute, Heritage Foundation, National Bureau of Economic Research, and Rand Corporation, whereas examples from other nations include the Centre for European Policy Studies, Latin American Faculty of Social Science, Institute for Democracy in South Africa, Japanese National Institute for Research Advancement, and Australian Institute of International Affairs.

The impact, political status, and involvement of policy research institutes in policy-making processes vary across countries and among institutes. Although measuring their performance is difficult (some indicators are media citations and numbers of appearances before legislative committees), their effectiveness seems dependent on specific polity characteristics as well as institute features, strategies, and sociopolitical environments (Weaver and McGann, 2000; Weiss, 1992). Political systems with strong party unity, cabinet solidarity, permanent senior civil service, or a traditional high presence of interest-group representatives formally participating in the policy-making process may limit the opportunities for think tanks to participate apart from governmental and party activities. Highly decentralized and fragmented political systems allow greater access to policy makers, as in the United States, where presidential candidates usually hire think tanks to prepare policy position papers for their electoral campaigns (Abelson, 2000). The revolving-door phenomenon of staff experts moving from institutes to government offices and back again boosts governmental confidence and political legitimation of institute advice. Among institute characteristics, their endowments and funding resources, the quality of their staffs, and consequently of their research output, may all affect their influence over and demand from policy makers. Countries differ in appropriate political, legal, and intellectual-scholarly environments for policy research institutes to acquire optimal quantity and quality of financial and human resources. Also for institutes aiming to shape public policy debates, the potential for mass-media appearances is an indispensable influence activity, whereas actual media access depends on their recognition and acceptance as legitimate policy players. Overall, the ideological orientation of policy research institutes, their affiliation with powerful interest groups, or simply sharing common values with these groups, may be key factors differentiating which institutes have high access and impact on the public and the policy-making process, independently of specific characteristics of national political environments.

POLICY NETWORKS

One important perspective on interest group participation in public policy making, which seeks to transcend the arid debate over pluralism versus corporatism, is the application of sociopolitical network perspectives to policy domains characterized by multiple interorganizational relations (Börzel, 1998; John, 2001; Knoke, 1990b; Richardson, 2000; Thatcher, 1998). A policy domain comprises a set of interest group organizations, legislative institutions, and governmental executive agencies that engage in setting agendas, formulating policies, gaining access, advocating positions, organizing collective influence actions, and selecting among proposals concerned with delimited substantive policy problems, such as national defense, education, agriculture, or welfare (Burstein, 1991; Laumann and Knoke, 1987:10). Policy proposals may involve proactive solutions to solve perceived problems, such as reforming the U.S. national health care system (Skocpol, 1996), or reactive efforts intended to block or evade changing the status quo, such as restoring farm price subsidies. Social network theories make three basic assumptions about mutual influences between networks and actors in a domain: (1) the social structure of any complex system consists of the stable patterns of repeated interactions connecting actors to one another; (2) these social relations are the primary explanatory units of analysis, rather than the attributes and characteristics of the individual actors; and (3) the perceptions, attitudes, and actions of actors are shaped by the multiple structural networks within which they are embedded, and in turn their behaviors can change these networks' structures (Knoke, 2001:63–4). That is, actors can be strongly proactive agents who strategically manage their diverse network connections to reduce uncertainties arising from their pursuit of organizational advantage (Galaskiewicz, 1985).

Applied to policy domains, social network theory directs researchers' attention toward the causes of multiplex interorganizational ties and their subsequent effects on both the level of individual organizational behaviors and of the entire policy network (Brass, 1995; Knoke and Guilarte, 1994). Five basic types of interorganizational relations, which typically exhibit contrasting network structures, include resource exchange, information transmission, power relations, boundary penetration, and sentimental attachments (Knoke, 2001:65). Although many network ties involve voluntary resource exchanges, governmental mandates – such as legislation and administrative regulations – typically impose and enforce interorganizational arrangements on a policy domain.

Analysts seek to understand policy network formation, the persistence and change of network relations over time, and the consequences of policy network structures for interest group organizations, governmental agencies, and the policy domain as a whole. Comparative analysts examine the unique historical roots of national differences in the structural relations between state institutions and organized interest groups and their consequences for policy processes and outcomes (e.g., Baumgartner, 1996). An expanding volume of empirical policy network studies spans the levels of analysis ranging from cities (Melbeck, 1998; Stokman and Berveling, 1998), states (Mintrom and Vergari, 1998), regions (Ansell, 2000; Grote, 1998), and industries (Raab, 2002) to national (Maman, 1997; Schneider, 1992), multilevel (Benz and Eberlein, 1999), transnational nongovernmental (Keck and Sikkink, 1998, 1999), and global policy networks (Ronit and Schneider, 1999; Witte, Reinicke, and Benner, 2000). Because we lack space to review this vast empirical literature, we concentrate on conceptual and theoretical themes.

The earliest policy network schemes were criticized for metaphorical overkill, rampant terminological confusion, and typological proliferation (Dowding, 1995, 2002; Thatcher, 1998). Many initial conceptualizations simply described a policy network as a set of state and private-sector political actors. The theoretical challenge was to move beyond generic metaphors by using rigorous network principles to specify explanatory models that allow analysts "to understand what goes on within policy networks" (Raab, 1992:78; also Pappi and

Henning, 1998). Kenis and Schneider (1991) framed a useful definition involving three fundamental network elements as follows:

A policy network is described by its actors, their linkages and its boundary. It includes a relatively stable set of mainly public and private corporate actors. The linkages between the actors serve as channels for communication and for the exchange of information, expertise, trust and other policy resources. The boundary of a given policy network is not in the first place determined by formal institutions but results from a process of mutual recognition dependent on functional relevance and structural embeddedness.

Several analysts, particularly British scholars, tried to identify the key policy network dimensions typifying national network structures according to their differentiated pluralist and corporatist features (Atkinson and Coleman, 1989, 1992; Jordan and Schubert, 1992; Rhodes, 1985, 1990). One analyst constructed an especially complex typology, involving eight dimensions, that classified eleven types of relations between state agencies and organized interest groups (van Waarden, 1992). He concluded that policy networks had three primary dimensions: (1) the numbers and types of organizational actors involved (ranging from monopolistic to unlimited), (2) the major network functions (ranging from organizing lobbying to implementing public policies), and (3) the balance of power between state and private organizations. But, static typologies carry limited capacity to explain which conditions facilitate the emergence, development, and consequences of distinctive policy network configurations.

The rich variety of alternative policy network models proposed by British, American, and German researchers reflects several substantial changes in the polities of advanced industrial societies in the 1970s and 1980s. Common trends toward decreased governmental regulation, greater privatization, and more reliance on market transactions in various domestic policy domains generated remarkably open and fluid state interest-group relations (Feigenbaum, Henig, and Hamnett, 1998; Hulsink, 1999; Swann, 1988). The growing scope and technical complexity of many policy domains – such as environmental, health, energy, and science – compelled greater participation by professionals, consultants, and research experts. The variety of unique national institutional responses to these historical transformations spawned an array of policy network models designed to explain those developments. During the eighteen-year Conservative regime of Prime Ministers Margaret Thatcher and John Majors, British policy making shifted from entrenched subgovernments (i.e., policy domains at the national ministerial level) that tightly controlled the consensual policy agendas characteristic of corporatism, toward more fluid and unpredictable forms of interest group consultation and intermediation with government ministries (Richardson, 2000:1009–11). British political scientists elaborated a "policy community" concept to describe self-organizing groups drawing policy participants from government bureaucracies and related pressure organizations (Jordan, 1990; Marsh and Rhodes, 1992; Rhodes, 1990; Wilks and Wright, 1987). The rising power and influence of British interest groups to influence authoritative resource allocations and policy outcomes was evident from their increased political exchanges and informal relations within these policy communities. By the 1990s, the "hollowing out" of the state sector, new public management practices, and rising intergovernmental management had thrust networks into "a pervasive feature of [human] service delivery in Britain" (Rhodes, 1996). Rhodes concluded that policy network autonomy threatened to undermine reforms rooted in market competition and challenged governability by resisting central state guidance. Marsh and Smith (2000) proposed a dialectical model of policy network change involving mutual relations among structure, agency, contexts, and policy outcomes. They applied the model's causal and feedback relations to explain changes in British agricultural policy since the 1930s.

In the United States, the historic post–Watergate institutional reforms and the so-called Reagan revolution shattered the cozy "iron triangles," binding a captive federal agency and a subservient congressional subcommittee to corporate clients, that had long dominated the political agenda and policy decisions. In their place arose diffuse, malleable "issue networks" of experts and information brokers, where multiple streams of policy solutions chaotically competed in unpredictable "garbage can" processes (Gais, Peterson, and Walker, 1984; Heclo, 1978; Heinz, Laumann, Nelson, and Salisbury, 1993; Kingdon, 1984). Political sociologists analyzed policy networks from an explicit social exchange perspective on interorganizational relationships among governmental, corporate, and interest group organizations. Their structural analyses emphasized the patterns of multiplex ties across information, resource, and political support networks among organizations with overlapping policy interests. These interorganizational connections enable shifting organizational coalitions to mobilize their combined political resources in collective actions that attempt to influence the outcomes of public policy decisions (Browne, 1998; Hula, 1999).

This interorganizational approach to policy networks provided the theoretical and methodological foundations of the organizational state model that Laumann, Knoke, Pappi, and their colleagues developed from their comparative analyses of the U.S. national energy and health policy domains and the U.S., German, and Japanese labor policy domains (Knoke, Pappi, Broadbent, and Tsujinaka, 1996; Laumann and Knoke, 1987; see Knoke, 1998, for a detailed overview of these projects). The organizational state model conceptualizes national policy making as a process conducted by formal organizations rather than by individual elite persons who act as agents of their organizational principals. These core players are distributed across such broad public- and private-sector categories as labor unions, business associations, corporations, public interest groups, state and local government associations, executive agencies and ministries, and legislative committees. In every policy domain, some organizations may be involved in dozens of policy issues and dozens of legislative, executive, and judicial policy events. Given their divergent organizational interests and fragmented attention spans, no leading organization can control or even dominate a domain's policy making. Rather, most policy struggles involve short-term, shifting coalitions assembled to fight collectively to influence the formulation and outcome of authoritative policy decisions. The communication and resource exchange structures enable the domain's organizations to identify potential collaborators and opponents of a policy event. Typically, opposing *action sets*, consisting of subsets of domain organizations sharing common policy preferences, pool their political resources and pressure governmental decision makers to choose a policy outcome favorable to their interests. Once the policy decision occurs, these coalitions break apart as subsequent events give rise to new constellations of organized interest groups. The resulting patterns are fluid, continually changing network structures. Yet, despite this microlevel flux, national policy domains remain comparatively stable, socially constructed macrosystems whose boundaries and constituents persist over long periods (Burstein, 1991; Knoke, 2004).

The changing structural relationships between the German state and its civil society, especially following reunification, triggered analytic examination of "webs of relatively stable and ongoing relationships which mobilize dispersed resources so that collective (or parallel) action can be orchestrated toward the solution of a common policy problem" (Kenis and Schneider, 1991:21). The Germanic approach treats policy networks as a distinct particular form of governance that provides an alternative to hierarchical and market mechanisms for resolving conflicting policy preferences (Börzel, 1998:258–62). Functionally autonomous subsystems of mutually interdependent governmental and private-sector interest organizations jointly coordinate public policy making through their disaggregated problem-solving interactions. In the absence of central hierarchical authorities possessing sufficient legitimate power to impose political solutions, cooperative policy blocks (based on communication, trust, support, resource exchange, and other interorganizational relations) provide an informal institutionalized framework with the capacity to mobilize sufficient political resources for successful complex policy bargaining and collective decision making (Benz, 1995; Marin and Mayntz, 1991; Mayntz, 1993).

INTEREST ORGANIZATION SYSTEMS

European Union

The European Union produces a large amount of public policy, resulting in the emergence and institutionalization of stable policy communities and interest-group networks that establish regular relations with EU formal political institutions (Coen, 1998; Fligstein and Sweet, 2001, 2002; Greenwood, 1997).[7] The EU constitutes a new political structure for interest groups in addition to the national and subnational political institutions of each member state. And the relevant interest group systems at both these levels are altered by the presence of the EU system that, in some instances, provides a lobbying alternative for national and subnational interest organizations (Coen, 1998). Neofunctional theory of European integration predicted the creation of an interest-group system fostered by the EU institutions, especially by the European Commission (Haas, 1958). The Commission, as the primary initiator of policy making in the EU, depends heavily on consultations with interest group representatives, national government employees, and technical experts for drafting regulations and monitoring compliance. That system developed a character closer to pluralist than to corporatist: although interest group access to the EU was institutionalized, the system remains organizationally fragmented, nonhierarchically integrated, internally competitive, and with little control of peak associations over their affiliates or of associations over their members (Greenwood, Grote, and Ronit, 1992; Mazey and Richardson, 1993; Streeck and Schmitter, 1991). European peak associations that represent broadly encompassing industrial, commercial, and agricultural business interests began to form immediately after the Treaty of Rome in 1958, and peak groups representing workers and consumers were formed in 1973. But numerous more-specialized sectoral associations also formed (654 had already registered by 1985), which were rarely affiliated and never subordinated to the European peak associations. The Commission encouraged these specialized associations and established a procedure for recognizing their special European status, which implied privileged access to its deliberations. Initially, the Commission attempted to confine lobbying to certified European associations, but subsequently it permitted an increasing volume of direct contacts with national interest representatives.

For few years after 1968 and until the early 1970s, coincident with the accession to power of social democratic parties in major member countries, an ambitious program was inaugurated to extend supranational authority over a wide range of social policies. Macroeconomic and social policies were discussed in a series of Tripartite Conferences with European peak associations, national representatives of capital and labor, officials of national governments, and the Commission (Streeck and Schmitter, 1991). The labor movement seemed about to receive similar substantive concessions and institutional privileges at the European level, comparable to rights it was obtaining simultaneously in member countries. This expectation ended in 1978 when the strongest proponent of Eurocorporatism, the European Trade Union Confederation, withdrew its support due to lack of progress and rising dissent within its ranks fomented by ideological divisions and interest disparities across national labor movements (Visser and Ebbinghaus, 1992). Two other factors also contributed to prevent the anticipated breakthrough (Streeck and Schmitter, 1991). First, significant business factions interested in centralized negotiations with labor were absent. European businesses, represented in Brussels by both lobbyists for individual firms and sectoral trade associations, are primarily interested in the

[7] By 1992 the Commission estimated the presence of 3,000 interest groups in Brussels and up to 10,000 employees working in the lobbying sector (CEC, 1992:4). This estimation includes "listening posts" to gather information on funding opportunities or policy initiatives and did not include those individuals who visit Brussels to lobby without being based there. Many of those employees are experts on technical issues considered in the policies.

protection and regulation of their product markets. They have refused to support the transfer of social policy matters from national to European arenas by denying European peak associations the authority to negotiate binding commitments on behalf of their national business constituencies. Second, the unanimity principle, which guided most decisions of the European Council until 1986, enabled any interest group seeking to block a policy initiative to obtain the needed support of just one national government willing to cast its veto in the Council. Finally, for the foreseeable future the EU interest-group system seems unlikely to perform macrocorporativist policy making because it still lacks two necessary conditions to make it feasible: autonomous redistributive capability and a relative political equilibrium among class organizations (Schmitter, 1996; see Falkner, 1998, for an optimistic view in that regard).

Multiple lobbying venues exist within the multilevel political system of the European Union (Mazey and Richardson, 2001b) but the main interest group target has been the European Commission. Lobbying pressures on the national representatives in the European Council operate at the domestic level within each member state rather than at the EU level. National lobbying also influences the implementation of EU directives inside the states (Coen, 1998). The European Parliament has adopted a restrictive approach to lobbying as a result of criticisms about corruption, and the other EU institutions have only minor roles in policy making. Conversely, the European Commission recognizes the utility of a robust interest-group system and actively promotes its development by a clearly stated preference for open consultations with interest groups representing broad constituencies (CEC, 1992).[8] The system constitutes a source of information, support, and legitimacy for the Commission, contributing to a reduced risk of policy failures. The system also reduces risks for the interest organizations by enabling them to influence the policy process or, at least, to know what is going on (Mazey and Richardson, 2001a). Interests groups have an incentive to participate in the European policy processes to avoid adverse effects of new regulations. Interest groups also lobby to promote the creation of new legislation to regulate their activity, which can disadvantage nonparticipant rival groups unaware of the importance of the European policy process or less able or willing to mobilize the necessary resources to participate. In this sense, once a set of interest groups began to participate in European-level policy making, others were bound to follow to avoid the negative consequences of the resulting policy regulations (Coen, 1998; Fligstein and Sweet, 2001, 2002; Mazey and Richardson, 2001). Most interest groups engage in transnational European policies, but some participate to destabilize national rules and regulations that they oppose. The system also includes social movement organizations that usually engage in noninstitutional forms of pressure at the national level but some either accommodate their political activity at the European level to the institutional channels established by the EU institutions for lobbying (Marks and McAdam, 1999) or get their interests represented in the European institutions by pressuring their national political authorities (Tarrow, 1995).

Although the Commission prefers to deal with Euro-associations that aggregate national interests groups, and has encouraged NGOs to participate, in practice it cannot rely solely on such organizations for consultations because it must ensure the technical robustness of the policy proposals (the Commission decides much of the detail of policies). The Commission mobilizes all the stakeholders involved in a policy issue, which may prefer direct lobbying or forming *ad hoc* coalitions to mediation by Euro-associations.[9] Mazey and Richardson (2001a) distinguished between "thin" and "thick"

[8] The Commission has attempted to regulate the consultation process to manage more effectively the scattered interest-group system. The result has been a very basic set of guidelines and voluntary codes of practice supplemented with informal rules and norms (Greenwood, 1997). One goal of these regulations is to discourage corruption relations, which are sanctioned by exclusion from the policy process.

[9] Euro-associations on specific issues, about 800 by 2000, experience a complex and slow process of consensus building and usually lack internally the technical expertise required in many policy decisions.

institutional sites where consultations can occur. The former are open sites such as very large conferences, forums, or seminars, whose participants often have rather weak or no relationships. Thin sites allow the Commission to demonstrate an open and accessible policy-making style and facilitates legitimation of the policy process and the identification of key players and points of consensus. Thick sites consist of restricted locations involving only the key players. They have more intense and regular relationships over time and allow detailed technical negotiations about issues, and as a result Commission officials attempt to obtain practical and sound policy proposals within the wider parameters established in the thin sites.

Finally, as the set of topics of this section about the EU indicates, research has focused on the activity of interest groups on EU institutions, specially the European Commission, where more interest intermediation activity occurs. This approach to the issue of interest groups and EU has been one-sided. Until recently analysts have tended to disregard the study of other side, consisting of analyzing the effects of EU integration and policy making on the member states' interest group systems, as well as those of candidate countries seeking to join the EU. Research has recently started on these kinds of processes, suggesting the relevance of the penetration of national politics by issues defined at the EU level and the nation state polity as a still valid and necessary arena of interest intermediation that balances the lack of EU social policy (Grote and Schmitter, 1999).

United States

The policy influence actions and impacts of U.S. interest groups respond to political and institutional changes, particularly historical ideological shifts in legislative, executive, regulatory, and judicial conditions (Berry, 1977; Schlozman and Tierney, 1986; Vogel, 1996). In the New Deal, labor unions entered the Democratic Party's electoral coalition. Public interest groups and their liberal sociopolitical agendas flourished during the civil rights, antiwar, feminist, gay and lesbian rights, and other identity-group social movements that erupted during the 1960s and 1970s. Reacting to new regulatory agencies, such as the Environmental Protection (EPA) and Occupational Safety and Health (OSHA), business advocacy associations inundated Washington seeking political relief from mushrooming federal regulations. The numbers of registered lobbyists and advocacy groups increased dramatically in the last four decades of the twentieth century (Heinz et al., 1993). Post–Watergate reforms of the 1970s curtailed autocratic congressional committee chairmen while increasing subcommittee autonomy, giving interest groups numerous access points to press their policy claims and grievances.

Those reforms also vastly expanded the role of political action committees (PACs), which solicited, pooled, and dispensed electoral campaign donations by corporations, trade associations, labor unions, and interest groups. Many critics concluded that the ensuing deluge of political money, especially loosely regulated "soft money" contributions made directly to political parties, ultimately corrupted American policy making by allowing wealthy business donors unhindered access to and influence over elected officials whom they had financially backed (Clawson, Neustadtl, and Weller, 1998; Sabato and Simpson, 1996). However, evidence that connects campaign contributions directly to public policy outcomes is mixed, suggesting that any relation between donors and recipients operates more subtly than via an overt *quid pro quo* exchange of campaign money for congressional votes (Goidel, Gross, and Shields, 1999; Grenzke, 1989; Mizruchi, 1992; Wright, 1996).

Research on U.S. interest-group participation in policy making emphasizes the importance of organizational coalitions to influence the outcomes of specific public policy events. Interest groups with shared interests in passing or defeating particular legislative proposals coalesce into temporary coalitions that pool their political and financial resources and coordinate a lobbying campaign targeted at relevant public policy makers (Hula, 1999). Typically, short-term coalitions fight collectively over a specific policy event and then disband after the political authorities rendered their decision. Subsequently, new coalitions band together, composed of different participants lured by the substantive policy interests at stake in a new policy proposal. Many coalitions are assembled and led by an enduring set of core organizations, primarily the peak or encompassing organizations with broad mandates to defend and advance the policy interests of sizable constituency (Hojnacki, 1997). Examples of peak associations from diverse policy areas include the AFL–CIO, U.S. Chamber of Commerce, American Medical Association, and Sierra Club.

Network analysts revealed that global patterns of information exchange among political organizations were structured around their common interests in national policy domains. A policy domain comprises the set of organizations and institutions engaged in conflicts over specific proposals to solve substantive policy problems, such as national defense, education, agriculture, or welfare. Researchers applied an organizational-state conceptualization to investigate how interorganizational communication networks generated collective action campaigns by interest groups in the U.S. national energy, health, agriculture, and labor policy domains (Laumann and Knoke, 1987; Heinz et al., 1993) and in a comparison of U.S., German, and Japanese labor policy domains (Knoke et al., 1996). The latter study found that the more central an organization in both the communication network (measured by policy information exchanges) and the support network (measured by resource exchanges), the higher was its reputation as an especially influential player in labor policy. Similarly, greater centrality in both networks led to more involvement across numerous legislative events in six types of political influence activities, including coalitions with other organizations. In the U.S. and German cases, the communication centrality effect was much stronger than the support centrality effect on both organizational reputations and political activities, whereas the pattern in Japan was just the reverse (Knoke et al., 1996:120). Detailed analyses of specific legislative decisions showed that most national labor policy fights were conducted by relatively small action sets, defined as coalitions of organizations that hold the same preferred event outcome (passage or failure of a bill), communicate directly or indirectly with one another about policy affairs, and consciously coordinate their policy influence activities. Labor unions and business associations were the primary coalition leaders in all three nations, frequently taking opposing positions on legislative bills and almost never collaborating in the same action set even on rare occasions when they preferred the same policy outcome.

Debate continues to rage over the influence by business, labor, and public interest organizations on public policy outcomes. PAC donations, organizational resources, and lobbying coalition activities are just three factors in complex political calculations by Senators and Representatives, which also include these politicians' party affiliations, personal ideology, perceived constituency preferences, and instincts for self-preservation. By assisting public officials behind the scenes to shape technically arcane details of legislative and regulatory proposals, lobbyists reaped the fruits planted by campaign funds. This view of political money as mainly a door-opening device is consistent with John Wright's (1990) analyses of two controversial bills considered by the House Ways and Means and the Agriculture Committee in 1985. He concluded that the Representatives' committee votes were best explained, not by PAC money, but by the total number of contacts they had with groups on each side of the issue. "Consistent with the popular notion that money 'buys' access but not votes, campaign contributions influenced voting decisions indirectly through lobbying" (1990:433–4). Similarly, interest groups achieved greater subjective success in influencing federal agency rule making through formal procedures (e.g., commenting on proposed rules and participating at public hearings).

Information networking and coalition formation are indispensable tactics for organized interest groups to stay abreast of policy opportunities and to persuade policy makers to adopt to their preferred solutions. Disjointed policy struggles, in which no factions attain perpetual domination, are more consistent with pluralist theories of power structures than with corporatist or class-based explanations of the U.S. policy process. The centrifugal pulls of narrow industrial, occupational, ethnic, and geographic interests split fragile coalitions and dilute interests group capacities to achieve their political goals. Among the consequences of intensified lobbying by large numbers of interest organizations, in the context of party polarization and persistently divided government, was increased political overload, ungovernability, and policy gridlock – the inability to enact significant proposals on the national policy agenda (Rose, 2001; Skocpol, 1996). Chronic policy log jams plagued not only the United States but also Japan, South Korea, the United Kingdom and other European democracies as the twenty-first century dawned.

CONCLUSION

Future research should concentrate on constructing and testing more comprehensive theoretical explanations of the origin, development, and impact of organized interest groups on national policy-making systems. Various pluralist, Marxist, elitist, and corporatist theories could benefit from more rigorous specification, refinement, and modification of their original premises, as well as by integrating research from alternative approaches to power and political action. We urge interest-group theorists to incorporate perspectives paying greater attention to cultural, social constructionist, structural, and institutionalization processes, as analyzed by scholars with other research objectives in political sociology and in such related fields as economic sociology, organization studies, and political economy (e.g., Fligstein, 1990, 2001; Garret, 1998; Meyer and Jepperson, 2000; Meyer, Boli, Thomas, and Ramirez, 1997; Perrow, 1986, 2002; White, 2002). For interest-group research to flourish in the twenty-first century, its sociological practitioners must forge stronger intellectual ties to specialists studying interest groups, particularly social movement and state organization analysts. Our personal preference is to apply social network concepts, principles, and methods to investigate collective actions by interest organizations to influence state policy-making institutions. But, we recognize that the organizational state model of interorganizational networks in national policy domains currently remains theoretically underspecified as a logically coherent explanatory structure. It also ignores several central themes of alternative perspectives, such as class conflict, electoral constraint, governance institutions, and elite leadership.

We also consider that any research program mainly concerned with concluding about classifying interest group systems relative to a variety of models and overtime is a task of little benefit. Specially, because it requires an inductive simplification of political reality, whereas we rather contend the need of emphasizing its complexity by considering the possibility that insights of research made under different foundational approaches and of research in other fields show to be relevant to an accurate reflection of the different processes intervening in the cases analyzed. This call to accurate complexity rather than abstract simplification is especially pertinent in the study of conflicting interest among social actors, where unstated assumptions, misspecifications, and inaccurate statements about who benefits from pressure on state officials can be easily interpreted as fruit of *interested* research.

Some examples of complex aspects in the study of interest group activities that deserve consideration in further research are relationships (formal and informal connections, financial and personal support) among associated organized interest groups, social movements, and political parties acting collectively to achieve common goals; processes of transformation from interest groups to political parties or vice versa; effects of the changing ideological and structural political context on the formation and operation of interest groups (the EU case is an important example because of its dynamic development); variation in the political power of business groups resulting from the changing relevance of their activities (e.g., as a consequence of economic globalization) for states' economic objectives; organized policy disorganization (i.e., tacit intentional activity on the part of groups aiming to block the progress of policymaking initiatives they do not want to advance); and consideration of inclusions and exclusions (both of groups and ideas) in political processes as a result of "structural power" (i.e., the ability of actors to exert power without expression of rational individual decisions but rather through cultural institutions and routine behavior embedded in political or relational structures).

Another significant challenge ahead is to extend interest group research to the developing nations of Africa, Asia, Eastern Europe, Latin America, and the Middle East. Some countries in these geographic areas lack the full range of Western democratic norms and institutions, such as multiparty competitive elections and a free press, that both stimulate and respond to pressure-group actions. The alternative forms of linkage between these states and their civil societies undoubtedly means that interest-group theories and research methods created for advanced Western democratic nations must be substantially altered to fit other conditions. A closely related research issue is the impact that thousands of nongovernmental organizations, such as the World Trade Organization and Amnesty International, have on national and local interest-group systems. As NGOs proliferate, they become increasingly important players in influencing public policies in education, health, trade, justice, environmental, and other national policy domains. Eventually, emerging networks that closely connect transnational advocacy organizations to local interest groups may give credence to a new adage: "all politics is global."

CHAPTER FIFTEEN

Corporate Control, Interfirm Relations, and Corporate Power[1]

Mark S. Mizruchi and Deborah M. Bey

In a democracy, citizens possess an array of rights and privileges. Among these benefits is that all citizens are viewed as equal in the eyes of the law. No one is intrinsically endowed with a disproportionate set of political privileges. All citizens have a right to pursue their political objectives, as long as they do so in a legally sanctioned manner.

Although all citizens in a democracy have formal political equality, some are able to exercise more power than others. Sometimes this occurs within the confines of normal political action, when one group develops a position that garners widespread support. In other situations, some actors may have resources that provide them with an advantage independent of the quality of their ideas.

No observer of modern democratic societies denies that some political actors have significantly more power than others. The issue is how this power is distributed, both the extent to which it is concentrated among a relatively small group and the extent to which the structure is malleable. For several decades, beginning in the 1950s, social scientists engaged in a vigorous debate about the level of political inequality and its effect on the functioning of democracy. This debate began to lose steam in the early 1990s. By the turn of the twenty-first century, few sociologists or political scientists were writing on the topic.

Despite the apparent decline in attention given to the concentration of power, there seems to be no reason to doubt its relevance. A series of scandals swept the business world at the turn of the twenty-first century in the wake of a major stock market downturn and recession. Concerns about the role of money in politics, and the role of corporations in national political debates, remain strong. We believe that an assessment of theory and research on national power structures, especially in light of changing world conditions, is warranted.

In this chapter we examine the debates concerning the structure of power in developed capitalist societies. Because much of this debate involved the role of large corporations, we pay particular attention to the issues of corporate control and business political activity. We begin by briefly recapitulating the debates from earlier decades. We show that arguments about the concentration of political power ultimately hinged on conceptions of the role of corporations in capitalist societies. After discussing the relations among corporate control, corporate power, and democracy, we present four perspectives that have been proposed to account for these relations under current conditions. We conclude with an assessment of these perspectives and an agenda for future work.

[1] Research for this chapter was supported in part by the Werner Reimers Foundation and the Volkswagen Foundation. Please direct correspondence to Mizruchi at the Department of Sociology, University of Michigan, Ann Arbor, MI, 48104 phone (734) 764-7444, FAX (734) 763-6887, email mizruchi@umich.edu.

DEMOCRACY, CAPITALISM, AND CORPORATE POWER

All contemporary democratic societies are based on systems of representation. In a theoretical representative democracy, citizens form positions on issues and convey their views to elected representatives, whose job is to make policies consistent with those positions. In writing about American society in the early twentieth century, Joseph Schumpeter (1942) observed that most citizens were apathetic about politics and were not actively engaged in the political process. Instead, political elites were able to operate basically unimpeded, without significant input from their constituents. If democracy is based on representatives responding to the public, Schumpeter asked, then how could the system function if the public was largely inactive?

The answer, Schumpeter suggested, was that political elites were fundamentally divided. As long as one group of elites was without power, its members could appeal to the public to replace the incumbents with those presumably more favorable to their interests. Democracy, for Schumpeter and later observers (Galbraith, 1952; Lipset, 1962), was redefined as a system whereby elites competed for the votes of a largely passive electorate. This position, later known as "elite pluralism," became the dominant perspective among political scientists during the mid-twentieth century.

Elite pluralism was sharply challenged by some sociologists, most notably Floyd Hunter (1953) and C. Wright Mills (1956). Hunter, in a study of elites in a large Southern city, and Mills, in a study of national elites in the United States, both concluded that American society was dominated politically by a small group of leaders that included both the heads of major organizations as well as top political officials. These elites, according to Hunter and Mills, formed a largely cohesive community, unified not only through common interests in maintaining their privileges but also through common socialization experiences (including attendance at elite prep schools and universities), common membership in social clubs and policy-making organizations, and social and kinship ties. If accurate, this picture implied that the divisions among the elite – the precondition for democracy according to pluralists – were either nonexistent or, if they existed, insignificant. Much of the debate over whether the United States and other developed capitalist countries were democratic thus became a debate over the extent to which their elites were unified.

Two important questions flowed from this issue. First, of whom does the elite consist, and second, are some components of the elite more significant than others? Regarding the former, not all participants in this debate were explicit about exactly who were the elites about whom they were writing. Most members of Hunter's local elite were officials of major corporations and banks, but his elite also included noncorporate professionals (most of whom were lawyers), government officials, the idle rich, and even two labor leaders. For Mills, the national "power elite" consisted of the heads of leading corporations, the government (primarily the executive branch), and the military. Critics of Hunter and Mills did not dispute the existence of elite members of society nor did they take issue with the claim that these elites were primarily the leaders of major organizations. They argued instead that because the electorate had the ultimate say in who maintained office, office holders, regardless of their social background, must be responsive to their constituents.

On the question of whether some components of the elite were more important than others, some Marxist critics (see, for example, Sweezy, 1968[1956]) argued that despite the multiple institutional backgrounds of elites, ultimately it was business elites who played the dominant role. Interestingly, the early pluralists who addressed this topic were willing to concede that business elites had the potential to dominate. What prevented this from occurring, and allowed democracy to continue, according to these thinkers, was the fact that business itself was politically divided. In an early study, Galbraith (1952) acknowledged that corporations had the potential for enormous power. Because different industries had inherently conflicting interests (what Galbraith called "countervailing power"), however, business was unable to operate as a unified political actor. This was demonstrated in a subsequent study by Bauer, Pool, and Dexter (1972[1963]), who showed that members of different industries frequently held conflicting views (and acted in opposition to one another) with regard to protective tariff legislation. Dahl (1958) provided a theoretical expression of this position. As Dahl argued, for a group to be powerful it must have both a high level of resources and a high level of unity. Even groups whose members have enormous amounts of the former will not be an effective political force unless they also have the latter. Large corporations clearly have significant resources, but as long as conflicts of interest exist across industries, corporate elites will not operate as a unified political actor.

THE ROOTS OF BUSINESS DISUNITY: THE ROLE OF CORPORATE CONTROL

The acknowledgement that business, if unified, could constitute a threat to democracy shifted the focus of the debate toward the degree of business unity. A number of social scientists, including sociologists, had made observations on this topic, often in discussions of social change during the twentieth century. A widely held view among American sociologists was that during the rise of the large corporation at the turn of the twentieth century, American business was dominated by a powerful group of financiers, who controlled several corporations simultaneously, a system akin to the system of bank dominance then prevalent in Germany (Hilferding, 1981[1910]). Chief among this group in the United States were people such as J. P. Morgan, John D. Rockefeller, George F. Baker, and James Stillman. Morgan, for example, through his investment firm J. P. Morgan & Co. and a group of major banks, was widely believed to have effective control over several nonfinancial corporations, including U.S. Steel, International Harvester, and several railroads. Although histories of the time describe cleavages, such as that between Morgan and Rockefeller, they also describe a system of cross-cutting alliances and ultimate community of interest (see Mizruchi, 1982, for a discussion of these works). There is now some question about just how dominant the U.S. banks were during this period (Roe, 1994).[2] There was little controversy within the sociological community writing during the mid-century, however. If ever there was a period in American history when a unified capitalist class existed, these theorists argued, the period from 1890 to 1920 was it.

Many of the sociologists who acknowledged the high degree of business unity in the early twentieth century did so to argue that the capitalist class had disintegrated during the following decades. Much of the empirical basis of this argument rested on a single study, Berle and Means' classic work, *The Modern Corporation and Private Property* (1968[1932]).

The Berle and Means Thesis

The Modern Corporate and Private Property appeared in the early stages of the Great Depression, but it was more a product of the 1920s or, more generally, the period after 1890 that culminated in the stock market crash of 1929. Although the book is best known for the authors' focus on ownership and control, that is only one component of their discussion. Berle and Means began by arguing that capital in the United States had become heavily concentrated during the early 1900s, resulting in a relatively small number of highly powerful companies. Because of the large and increasing size of corporations, and because of the consequent difficulty of maintaining substantial family holdings in individual firms, stockholdings in large U.S. corporations gradually dispersed. The consequence of this dispersal, according to Berle and Means, was the usurpation, by default, of power by the firm's managers. These managers, whose interests were not necessarily identical to those of the firm's owners, were viewed as a self-perpetuating oligarchy, unaccountable to the owners who had elected them. In an analysis of the 200 largest U.S. nonfinancial

[2] Virtually all observers continue to believe that German banks had a high degree of power at the time.

corporations in 1929, Berle and Means found that 44 percent of them could be defined as "management controlled," meaning (based on their operational definition) that no individual owner held as much as 20 percent of the firm's stock. In only 11 percent of the firms did the largest owner hold at least a majority of the firm's shares.

Berle and Means were concerned about the separation of ownership from control in part because they believed that managers would increasingly lack accountability to investors. Of equal importance, however, was their concern about managers' lack of accountability to society in general. Berle and Means thus wrote of a small group, sitting at the head of enormous organizations, with the power to build (and destroy) communities, to generate great productivity and wealth, but also to control the distribution of that wealth, without regard for those who elected them (the stockholders) or those who depended on them (the larger public). Berle and Means, in the tradition of Thomas Jefferson, expressed considerable concern about this development. Their point that elected officials (the board of directors) could be far removed from and unaccountable to their voters (the stockholders) raised concerns similar to those raised by Schumpeter and Lipset about the possible lack of democracy in the political system.

Many postwar sociologists took a very different interpretation of Berle and Means, however. In these works, authored by scholars such as Daniel Bell (1960), Ralf Dahrendorf (1959), and Talcott Parsons (1960), the separation of ownership from control was viewed as a harbinger of increased democracy. In Dahrendorf's (1959) view, for example, the separation of ownership from control led to the "decomposition of capital." In Riesman's words (1953:242), "the captain of industry no longer runs business" and thus "no longer runs politics." Echoing this view, Bell (1960:42) suggested that "[n]o longer are there America's 'Sixty Families' [the title of a popular book from the 1930s]. . . . The chief consequence, politically, is the breakup of the ruling class." In Dahrendorf's words (1959:47), the business community in industrialized capitalist countries (in which he included Britain, France, and Germany, as well as the United States) had become "a plurality of partly agreed, partly competing, partly simply different groups." These authors thus conceded that something akin to a dominant capitalist class existed in the United States in the early years of the last century but that because of the separation of ownership from control, this class had dispersed, unable to realize itself as a unified block. Because, in the Berle and Means view, the owners of capital no longer controlled their enterprises and those who controlled did not own, Dahrendorf went so far as to claim that we had transcended capitalism altogether.

Rather than sharing Berle and Means' suspicion of managerialism as ushering in a dangerous era of concentrated economic power, American sociologists and other social scientists thus praised the new system as a further extension of democracy. This was reflected in statements about "peoples' capitalism," in which the widespread dispersal of stockholdings meant that corporations were, for practical purposes, publicly controlled, as well as in formulations about the "soulful corporation" (Kaysen, 1957), concerned as much about its position as a respected member of the community as with its pursuit of profit. In fact, the pursuit of profit was deemed no longer necessary, as great size, market power, and weak and disorganized stockholders allowed corporate managers to pursue alternative goals, including sales (Baumol, 1959), growth (Galbraith, 1967), or a combination of strategies (Marris, 1964). Corporate managers, freed from the dictates of stockholders (as well as bankers and other outside forces), were stripped of the entrepreneurial spirit, transforming instead into bureaucratic "organization men." To quote Dahrendorf once again (1959:46), "Never has the imputation of a profit motive been further from the real motives of men than it is for modern bureaucratic managers." Ownership of capital no longer even mattered for understanding peoples' life chances. As Blau and Duncan put it in the introduction to their classic analysis of occupational status attainment (1967:6), class, "defined in terms of economic resources and interests . . . , is no longer adequate for differentiating . . . [those] in control of the large capitalistic enterprises from those subject to their control because the controlling managers of the largest firms today are themselves employees of corporations."

IMPLICATIONS FOR BUSINESS POLITICAL UNITY

If corporations were controlled primarily by the bureaucratic managers who ran their day-to-day affairs, their leaders could now be concerned primarily with the interests of the firm rather than a set of larger class interests. It was for this reason that political scientists such as Bauer, Pool, and Dexter could find members of different industries falling on opposite sides of political issues. The identification with one's immediate firm thus created the precondition for countervailing power to flourish. Firms were like atoms, bouncing from issue to issue, finding common cause with some but disagreement with others. It was precisely the kind of condition that, according to Schumpeter, allowed democracy, however imperfect, to exist.

Critics of pluralism mounted several responses to this argument. Some critics rejected Berle and Means's empirical analysis. Others accepted Berle and Means's findings while rejecting the implications that later interpreters drew from them. Still others were either neutral on Berle and Means or were critical of selected parts of their discussion. In the following sections we describe several major responses to pluralism and their implications for the level of business unity.

Rejection of Berle and Means: The Social Class Model

Except for a handful of left-wing critics, virtually all observers of American society between the 1930s and early 1970s accepted Berle and Means' thesis of the separation of ownership from control. This relative calm ended with the publication of an article by Maurice Zeitlin (1974). Berle and Means had classified a firm as management controlled if no individual ownership interest held at least 20 percent of the firm's stock. In reexamining Berle and Means' data, Zeitlin found that of the eighty-eight firms (44 percent of the 200 largest U.S. nonfinancials) classified as management controlled, for nearly half of them Berle and Means were unable to locate the largest holder and thus classified the firms as management controlled by default. The prevalence of management control may have therefore been considerably lower than Berle and Means suggested.

A study during the 1960s by Larner (1970) might have rendered Zeitlin's point moot, however. Using a more conservative indicator of management control, 10 as opposed to 20 percent, Larner found that 84 percent of the largest 200 U.S. nonfinancials in 1963 could be classified as management controlled. Regardless of the validity of Berle and Means' findings, Larner's study appeared to demonstrate that the managerial revolution was now, as Larner put it, "close to complete." Zeitlin was unwilling to accept this conclusion, however, because of two other studies that appeared around the same time. In the first, an article published in *Fortune*, Robert Sheehan (1967) found a substantial ownership interest in approximately 30 percent of the 500 largest U.S. nonfinancial corporations, compared to the 19 percent that Larner had found for the full 500. In the second, Philip Burch (1972), through an exhaustive analysis of the business press between 1950 and 1971, argued that as many as 60 percent of the 500 largest U.S. manufacturing and mining firms could be viewed as owner controlled. Zeitlin argued that using an arbitrary cutpoint for ownership control, such as 10 percent, was invalid because detailed analysis of the history of firms often revealed substantial ownership interests that were not evident in company filings with the Securities and Exchange Commission.

Although some sociologists, most notably Michael Useem (1996), acknowledged a resurgence of stockholder activism beginning in the 1980s, few observers believe that owner control is a widespread phenomenon in the American economy. Even if Zeitlin has exaggerated the level of owner control in the United States, it is worth noting that the United States, is an anomaly internationally. A study by La Porta, Lopez-de-Silanes, and Schleifer (1999) indicates that the United States is virtually alone, accompanied only by the United Kingdom, in the extent of stock dispersal in its leading corporations. Ownership remains considerably more concentrated, even to the point of being fused with control, in nations such as France, Germany, Italy, and South Korea. At the same time, even if Zeitlin is correct that ownership and control are more fused in the United States than most believe, it does not follow that there is a cohesive capitalist class. The families that control particular firms are not necessarily linked and they may have directly conflicting interests. Zeitlin argued that members of a dominant social class transcend the individual firms they control and their kinship and other ties create an overarching unity. Zeitlin and Ratcliff (1988) provided some evidence of this in the Chilean context. That some capitalist families coalesce across firms does not necessarily mean that systematic conflicts are absent, however. Business historians of the United States have noted that Morgan and Rockefeller interests were generally opposed to one another, at least until the compromise reached after the 1901 struggle over the Northern Pacific Railroad (Cochran and Miller, 1961[1942]). Even if owner control is dominant, then, it does not ensure the existence of a cohesive capitalist class that acts as a unified political force.

Berle and Means without the Consequences: Managerial Marxism

A second response to Berle and Means, sometimes referred to as managerial Marxism, was most commonly associated with two Marxist economists, Paul Baran and Paul Sweezy (Baran and Sweezy, 1966).[3] Baran and Sweezy accepted Berle and Means' findings on the separation of ownership from control. They argued, however, that the large corporations now run by managers behave no differently from those run by owners. Both remain subject to the dictates of the market. The capitalist class still existed, according to Baran and Sweezy, but it was now lodged in corporations rather than in a social class that existed outside the firm.

The behavioral component of managerial Marxism had similarities with the neoclassical economic view of the firm. Neoclassical economists continued to assume the existence of competitive markets, whereas Baran and Sweezy assumed oligopolistic ones, but both saw firms as responding to market pressures. This meant that whether managers or owners controlled individual firms was irrelevant to the firms' behavior. Studies of firm profitability across ownership types seemed to support these claims. Although Monsen, Chiu, and Cooley (1968) and Palmer (1973) found some tendency for owner controlled firms to earn higher profits than management-controlled firms (which one would predict if, as managerialists argued, management-controlled firms were less profit-oriented), Kamerschen (1968) found no such effect, and the differences found in the first two studies were quite small. In the most comprehensive study on the topic, Larner (1970) found only negligible differences – slightly higher profits among the owner controlled firms, but differences of little substantive significance. In a study of chief executive firings among the 500 largest U.S. manufacturers in 1965, James and Soref (1981) found that the strongest predictor of dismissals was the extent to which the firm's profits had declined in the previous year. Whether the firm was owner or management controlled had no significant effect. Since that time, some authors have found ownership to have an effect on certain firm behaviors. Palmer and Barber (2001), for example, found that owner-controlled firms were less likely to engage in acquisitions during the 1960s than were management-controlled firms. There has not been widespread support for the idea that owner and management-controlled firms behave differently with respect to profit orientation, however.

[3] Although not explicitly within a Marxist framework, Edward S. Herman's *Corporate Control, Corporate Power* (1981) remains the most comprehensive expression of this position.

Although the managerial Marxist approach deviated from traditional managerialism, its political theory had an undeniable resemblance to pluralism. If corporations were now independent entities run by managers, would the business community not evolve to a series of "partly agreed, partly competing, partly simply different groups," as Dahrendorf had argued? What mechanism was there for capitalist class unity? The answer, according to Baran and Sweezy, was that class unity was built into the system. At the industry level, large corporations engaged in what the authors called "co-respective" behavior, in which they rarely engaged in serious competition. Across industries, corporations might differ on day-to-day issues, but all members of the corporate community were united on the basis of their shared support of the system. Any threat to capitalist domination would therefore result in a quick coalescence among firms. This shared interest may be genuine, but it is a weak basis on which to posit overall business unity because the vast majority of Americans, whether capitalist or not, accept the legitimacy of the existing system. Although Baran and Sweezy make a credible claim for how members of particular industries might share political interests, their model thus contains no clear structural basis for corporate political unity across industries. Without such a basis, members of different industries could as easily oppose as coalesce with one another. If so, the preconditions exist for business conflict, and hence pluralist democracy.

The Role of Mediating Mechanisms: Contemporary Elite Theory

Both the social class theory proposed by Zeitlin and the managerial Marxism suggested by Baran and Sweezy include mechanisms that could create political unity among some sectors of the business community. Neither perspective can handle the possibility that systemic sources of intercorporate conflict remain, however. On what basis is it possible for business as a whole to achieve a unified political position? What is needed, several observers have argued, is a series of mechanisms that allow for the mitigation of conflicts of interest. Mizruchi (1992) has referred to these as "mediating mechanisms." Several have been posited, including those internal and external to firms, industries, and the business community as a whole. Five in particular warrant discussion: elite social ties, interlocking directorates, policy-making organizations, financial institutions, and the inner circle.

Elite Social Ties. In addition to kinship ties, some theorists, dating back to Mills (1956), and including G. William Domhoff (1967) and Ralph Miliband (1969), have argued that members of the corporate elite hail disproportionately from privileged social backgrounds. This common set of experiences is presumed to give elites a similarity of outlook that leads them to develop a similar set of political interests. Common socialization experiences also create a degree of social connectedness that helps forge an elite unity in adulthood. This unity is then reinforced by common memberships in local elite institutions, including social clubs. Domhoff argues that these common social ties create a unity of outlook that brings those who do not have elite origins into the fold.

Although there is considerable evidence that members of the corporate elite have more advantaged origins than members of the general population, corporate CEOs in more recent decades are as likely to be drawn from professional and managerial origins as from elite society (Useem and Karabel, 1986). Moreover, as with kinship ties, common socialization experiences and social ties may contribute to a similarity of outlook, but they may not be sufficient to override structural conflicts of interest that occur between firms in different industries. Social connections may thus facilitate corporate political unity in some cases, but they are unlikely to be a sufficient basis for the unity of business as a whole.

Interlocking Directorates. No mediating mechanism has received more attention than that of the interlocking directorate (Mizruchi, 1996). The presence of individuals who sit on two or more corporate boards has been evident for more than a century. This presence has led to charges of interfirm collusion to fix prices (even leading to an outlawing of ties between firms competing in the same markets) as well as to suggestions that the heads of large corporations are part of a cohesive clique that runs the country. Members of a board of directors are bound by law to act in the interests of the stockholders who elected them. When a person sits on the board of two firms that do business with one another, the director faces a potential conflict of interest. If the two firms have a disagreement, in whose interest will the director act? One possibility is that the interlocked director can serve as a mediator in the event of a conflict.

Most interlocks, even those involving banks and nonfinancial firms, do not involve customer/supplier relations. Most outside directors of firms, who are likely to include lawyers and accountants as well as CEOs of other firms, are chosen because of their ability to provide advice. These individuals are often friends of the CEO, and interlock ties often reflect elite social connections (Mace, 1971). Because of this, even pluralist theorists such as Arnold Rose (1967) believed that interlocks facilitated cohesion among firms. Studies from the early twentieth century to the present have shown that the vast majority of large U.S. corporations are tied together into a single, connected network (Mizruchi, 1982; Davis, Yoo, and Baker, 2003). Similar results have been found for European (Stokman, Ziegler, and Scott, 1985), Latin American (Ogliastri and Davila, 1987), and East Asian (Lincoln, Gerlach, and Takahashi, 1992; Keister, 1998) countries. At the same time, individuals in interpersonal networks tend to be connected to millions of others within a relatively small number of steps (Watts, 1999). The fact that firms are connected through interlocks may therefore reflect only the natural patterns of social networks that occur in all settings. Even if, as Rose suggested, interlocks provide firms with a high degree of cohesiveness, most firms are neither directly nor indirectly interlocked with one another. Interlocks may in some cases be capable of facilitating corporate political unity. Whether they produce cohesion for the entire business community is less clear.

Policy-Making Organizations. Elite policy-making organizations such as the Business Roundtable have also received attention as a mediating mechanism. The goal of these organizations is to serve as a meeting place for corporate leaders, who often use them to develop positions on political issues that best reflect the views of the corporate community as a whole. Domhoff (1979) discussed in detail the ways in which these policy-making organizations generate ideas and disseminate them to political officials. In other cases, these organizations are involved in direct political activity. An example of the latter has been provided by Whitt (1982) in his study of mass transit propositions in California during the 1960s and 1970s. In the period after World War II, San Francisco business elites, especially those in the financial and real estate sectors, were increasingly concerned about congestion from automobile traffic, which threatened the value of property in downtown San Francisco. The Bay Area Council, an organization of local business elites, developed a plan to address this problem. Members of the financial and real estate community suggested a mass transit system that would feed people from suburban areas to downtown, thus allowing people to work downtown without driving. Leaders of major oil companies with offices in the Bay Area initially objected to the plan, fearing that it would divert people from their cars, leading them to consume less gasoline. Discussions within the Bay Area Council allowed members of both sectors to work out a compromise, to the point that the oil companies actually contributed funds for the proposition to support the mass transit plan. The business community was thus able to approach the state as a politically unified force.

To the extent that policy-making organizations are capable of forging a consensus, they could play a significant role in facilitating unity among corporations. The question is how often such groups are able to mitigate cross-industry conflicts. In the study by Bauer, Pool, and Dexter (1972[1963]) cited above, there was no organization capable of resolving disagreements between members of different industries.

Where they exist, therefore, policy groups may help forge a unity of outlook and behavior among members of the business community. It is less clear that such groups are always present or, even if present, able to accomplish this goal.

Financial Institutions. Based on data from the 1960s, Mintz and Schwartz (1985) argued that large commercial banks in the United States exercised a broad "hegemony" over the business community. Although the banks did not directly control nonfinancial corporations, as was common in the early part of the century, nonfinancial firms remained dependent on banks for financing, which allowed the banks to set limits on the firms' behavior. The banks' power in the business world was reflected, according to Mintz and Schwartz, in the fact that they tended to occupy the most central positions in networks of interlocking directorates. Bank boards typically hosted large numbers of CEOs from major nonfinancial firms, thus serving as meeting places for the leading figures in the business community. Politically, banks facilitate business political unity for two reasons, according to Mintz and Schwartz. First, given the huge capital needs of most major financing schemes, the banks typically act collectively and therefore are themselves unified. Second, because capital is a universal resource, the banks have no allegiance to any particular industry. If disputes arise between different segments of the nonfinancial community, the banks are thus in a position to resolve the dispute in a way that maximizes the benefit for business as a whole.

Mintz and Schwartz's argument about the dominant position of banks was supported by a considerable amount of evidence, both anecdotal (the plethora of cases of bank intervention into corporate affairs) and systematic (the repeated finding of high bank centrality in interlock networks). Moreover, their model provides a more explicit mechanism for business unity than do either the social ties or director interlocks arguments. The model has two shortcomings. First, there is little evidence that the banks in fact play a mediating political role. Mizruchi (1992) found that firms that were interlocked with the same banks were more likely to contribute to the same political candidates and support the same positions on issues than were firms without such links. It was unclear whether the banks played an active role in producing this similar behavior, however. Second, even if one accepts that banks were dominant during the period Mintz and Schwartz were analyzing, a series of changes have occurred since the early 1980s that significantly reduced the banks' power (Davis and Mizruchi, 1999). Rapid changes in technology and the regulatory environment led U.S. corporations to reduce their reliance on banks for capital and led individuals to reduce their deposits in commercial banks. Both the number of commercial banks and the proportion of corporate debt acquired from commercial banks declined by one-third between 1979 and 1994 (Davis and Mizruchi, 1999:220). Large commercial banks responded to the loss of their traditional franchise by changing their focus from lending to financial services, such as capital market services, foreign currency exchange, and derivatives. This change in bank strategies had the effect of altering the social role of commercial banks within the American business community: As Davis and Mizruchi (1999) document, the largest banks substantially reduced the number of executives of major corporations appointed to their boards, thus losing their place at the center of the interlock network. It is unlikely, as we enter the twenty-first century, that commercial banks are a primary mechanism for businesswide political unity.

The Inner Circle. An alternative to the bank hegemony model, but based on similar principles, was proposed by Useem (1984). Drawing on earlier arguments by Zeitlin and Domhoff, as well as concurrent work by Ratcliff (1980), Useem argued that the business community can be roughly divided into two segments. The vast majority of firms, Useem suggested, were relatively small and pursued their own interests, which, as pluralists suggested, were as likely to be opposed to one another as in concordance. At the top level of the corporate community, however, was a relatively small group of executives who spanned two or more firms simultaneously. This group, because of its exposure to multiple perspectives and the social cohesion resulting from its frequent contact, was able to develop a "classwide" interest, in which its members were conscious of the long-run interests of the business community as a whole. This "inner circle," which included both bankers and other leading corporate figures, thus performed for Useem a function similar to that played by banks in Mintz and Schwartz's model. Although the inner circle was not specifically concerned with capital allocation to particular industries, it was concerned with the overall health of business.

A considerable amount of evidence, both quantitative and qualitative, was consistent with Useem's argument. Useem (1979), Soref (1976), and Ratcliff, Gallagher, and Ratcliff (1979) showed that there was a group of heavily interlocked directors who were disproportionately represented on the boards of local and national policy-making, civic, cultural, and philanthropic organizations. Useem's (1984) interviews with CEOs from American and British companies revealed that those who sat on two or more boards were more likely than noninterlocked directors to express views commensurate with a "classwide" consciousness. Unlike most of the studies cited above, Useem also presented evidence on corporate leaders' interest and involvement in political activities on behalf of their firms. Several of the multiple directors interviewed by Useem explained that the political processes in which they were involved (such as providing advice on the appointment of top political officials) required the adoption of a communitywide, as opposed to a firm-centered, perspective. This study therefore extends Whitt's findings that demonstrated the possibility of collective action on the part of leading representatives in the business community.

One of Whitt's key findings was that even when it was unified, the business community did not always achieve its goals. Similarly, Useem does not demonstrate that the inner circle, either in Britain or the United States, constitutes a ruling class that regularly prevails. These studies do show the possibility of unified political action within the business community, however. This is significant because there are those who believe that the state acts in the interest of the capitalist class but that the class itself is incapable of taking a unified political initiative. We now turn to one such argument.

The Role of the State

The arguments presented earlier all show that at certain points, some businesses are capable of acting as a unified force. Yet none of them has yielded incontrovertible evidence that business as a whole is consistently able to reach such a consensus. Mintz and Schwartz's bank hegemony model contains a mechanism for systemwide unity, but the evidence on the declining power of banks in the past two decades makes it difficult to argue that the banks are capable of being a unified political force for business as a whole. If the business community is not capable of consistently acting as a unified political actor, are the pluralists not correct that countervailing power will reign?

One possibility is that there might exist an institution external to business that could play a mediating role. Several theorists, most notably Nicos Poulantzas (1973), made this argument. In Poulantzas' view, sectors of the business community are saddled with inherent, irreconcilable conflicts of interest. In this context, the role of the state is to act in the interest of the business community as a whole, to do for business what business is incapable of doing for itself. To fulfill this function, the state must have a certain autonomy because it is often necessary to act in the interest of one sector of business against another. The state thus plays a role analogous to that of the banks posited by Mintz and Schwartz.

Poulantzas provided a model for how the state in a capitalist society can operate in the interests of business even when business is not internally unified. He thus circumvented Dahl's argument that unity is necessary for a group to be powerful. The problem with Poulantzas' argument is his assertion that the state acts in the interests of business. Because this is the case by definition, the model is nonfalsifiable. Whatever action the state takes, even if it appears to run counter to the goals of various segments of the business community, is assumed to be in the interest of the capitalist class as a whole. This means that when the U.S. Congress passed social security legislation or pro-labor legislation guaranteeing the right to strike, this was done because it was in the long-term interests of business, despite the fact that the business community overwhelmingly opposed such measures. Certainly one could make a plausible case for such an interpretation. The possibility that Congress was responding to the wishes of the voters represents an equally plausible alternative, however. In addition to its nonfalsifiability, Poulantzas ignored the possibility that business has internal mediating mechanisms that enable it to resolve its own disputes. As we have seen, there is considerable evidence that such mechanisms exist, even if they do not operate in all cases.

Poulantzas' model set the stage for theorists to make even stronger claims about the autonomy of the state with respect to business. We discuss this in a subsequent section, but before doing so we must address Poulantzas' assumption that business is incapable of or unwilling to act as a unified political force. To what extent is this assumption warranted?

A Contingency Approach to Business Unity

The preceding discussion suggests that there are a number of mechanisms, including ones internal to the business community itself, that could generate business political unity. In none of these cases, with the possible exception of the finance hegemony model, is there a mediating mechanism that could plausibly be posited to encompass the entire capitalist class, even if it operated in the way its proponents suggested. The finance hegemony model, at least its suggestion about the role of banks in securing corporate political unity, lacks empirical support. We must reluctantly conclude that despite the significant efforts of a number of leading scholars, the evidence that business is politically unified remains inconclusive.

One possible solution to this problem is to treat business unity not as an either/or proposition but as a variable. Clearly there are situations in which business political unity occurs, but there are other situations in which it does not. Identifying the conditions under which unity and conflict occur might be preferable to continuing to argue over whether either phenomenon exists in the abstract. In a series of works culminating in a 1992 book, Mizruchi (1992) argued that business is neither inherently unified or divided but rather that unity is best treated as a contingent phenomenon. The focus should therefore shift toward identifying the conditions under which business unity occurs, he argued.

To do this, it was necessary to deal with one of the most vexing problems in this debate: the absence of systematic, behavioral data on corporate political activity. During the 1980s, data on the campaign contributions of corporate political action committees (PACs) in the United States became widely available for the first time. There is considerable debate over the meaning of these contributions and, as is well-known, there are several alternative forms of business political action. The weight of the evidence suggests, however, that corporations view PAC contributions as expressions of the firms' perceived political interests (see Mizruchi, 1992; Chapter 5; Clawson, Neustadtl, and Scott, 1992). In addition to examining corporate PAC contributions, Mizruchi also conducted a content analysis of corporations' positions on political issues, as reflected in their testimony before congressional committees.

If business unity is conditional, under what conditions is it likely to occur? The model that Mizruchi posited focused on two key mediating mechanisms: economic interdependence and interfirm social relations. Firms operating in industries that were heavily dependent on one another for sales and purchases might be assumed to have conflicting interests, as the auto and steel industries have historically experienced (Prechel, 2000). High levels of interdependence may be a source of unity, for two reasons: First, a unit upon which another is dependent may be able to coerce, either overtly or covertly, desired behavior out of its partner. In Whitt's study, for example, a group of banks that had originally agreed to support a proposal to divert highway funds to the building of mass transit subsequently changed their position. Whitt's interviews revealed that this change was a result of the banks' concern about how the oil companies, on which they were dependent, might react. A supplier may think twice about supporting a position opposed by one of its largest customers. A second reason that interdependent firms may exhibit political unity is that even when dependence is mutual, both parties are likely to have a stake in maintaining a smooth working relationship (Emerson, 1962:33), an example of what is called bilateral deterrence (Lawler, 1986; see also Keohane and Nye, 1977). This means that high levels of interdependence, even when relative symmetry is present, are also likely to lead to unity of action.

Firm political unity can also be forged by the mediating mechanisms described above, including interfirm social relations. The most widely used indicator of interfirm social ties is the presence of director interlocks (Mizruchi, 1996). If socially connected firms are likely to be politically unified, then we should expect firms that share board members to engage in similar political behavior. At the same time, if financial institutions play a mediating role in interfirm conflicts, then firms that share directors with the same financial institutions should also be disproportionately likely to engage in similar political behavior.

To test these hypotheses, Mizruchi examined the 1,596 dyadic relations among fifty-seven large U.S. nonfinancial corporations. Using PAC contribution data from the 1980 election and corporate testimony before Congress between 1975 and 1987, he found that pairs of firms (dyads) that operated in industries with high levels of interdependence were more likely to contribute to the same candidates and take the same positions on issues than were pairs without such interdependence. Although direct interlocks between firms had mixed effects on similar political behavior (not significantly positive with respect to PAC contributions but significantly positive with respect to positions on issues), indirect interlocks through financial institutions were consistently positively associated with similarities of both types of political behavior.

Mizruchi's study demonstrated that director interlocks and other types of interfirm ties had genuine consequences for political behavior. It raised a theoretical question, however: Simply because mediating mechanisms, where they exist, contribute to similar political behavior does not necessarily provide support for the business unity theorists. The problem is that mediating mechanisms are not ubiquitous. Where they exist they increase the probability of unified action. Where they are absent, unified action is often absent as well. Given the conditional existence of the mediating mechanisms, to what extent do Mizruchi's findings demonstrate anything beyond the fact that business represents a series of "partly agreed, partly competing, partly simply different groups" (Dahrendorf, 1959:47)? Mizruchi did find that instances of unified behavior greatly dwarf those in which firms politically oppose one another (see also Clawson, Neustadtl, and Bearden, 1986). That political unity is more common than opposition does not prove that business is *fundamentally* unified, however.

Is Business Unity Necessary?

The discussion in the previous section leads to two possible conclusions. The first is that the contingent nature of business unity provides support for pluralism: developed capitalist societies contain the preconditions for democracy after all. A second possible conclusion is to question whether business unity is a necessary condition for business power.

Virtually all theorists discussed above assumed that corporate political power is predicated on a unified and politically active business community. Those who did not, including Poulantzas, argued that the role of the capitalist state was to uphold the interests of business. Other than an assertion that this was the case, there was no mechanism in Poulantzas' model that explained why the state would operate in corporations' interests, especially if it had the degree of autonomy that Poulantzas assigned it. Without some demonstration of direct corporate influence, it was difficult to explain theoretically how business dominance could occur. A solution to this problem was proposed by Fred Block (1977). Block argued that the state did indeed operate in the long-run interests of business as a whole. It did this not because of its inherent function to uphold the interests of the capitalist class, however. Rather, the state had its own interests in maximizing its revenue. The best way to do this was to ensure that business continued to invest and procure profits, because the state's revenue was based not only in taxes placed on corporations but also on workers' wages. The latter would be forthcoming only to the extent that business continued to invest. A state that engaged too heavily in redistributive economic policies, Block argued, would be subject to a "capital strike." Businesses would simply refuse to invest, which would lead to an economic downturn, decreased revenue for the state, and vulnerability for elected officials.

The same year as the publication of Block's essay witnessed the publication of a major work by a pluralist political scientist, Charles E. Lindblom (1977). In observing American politics, Lindblom reluctantly concluded that corporate interests tended to dominate to an extent that was dangerous for a democratic society. In trying to explain business' power over the state, Lindblom independently reached a conclusion virtually identical to Block's. Because the state was ultimately dependent on business for its revenue, there was a built-in tendency for the state to favor policies that accorded with the general interests of business. Interestingly, Lindblom also saw the business community as strongly politically active, and successfully so. As with Block, however, the state's susceptibility to business influence was due to its dependence on business confidence for its revenue. The dominance of business, and the state's dependence on it, raised serious concerns about the viability of American democracy, Lindblom argued.

FOUR CONTEMPORARY APPROACHES

At this point we have come full circle. Business may not be unified but it may dominate nonetheless. The difficulty with assessing this argument, along with the others described previously, is that the topic of corporate political power has received little attention among sociologists since the early 1990s. There have been sociological analyses of corporate political activity (Clawson, Neustadtl, and Scott, 1992; Clawson, Neustadtl, and Weller, 1998), some excellent reviews of the area (Roscigno, 1992) and, more recently, studies of corporate leaders' individual participation in politics (Burris, 2001; Dreiling, 2000). Studies on the power structures of developed capitalist societies and the role of corporate influence have been few and far between, however. Meanwhile, potentially significant changes have occurred worldwide that cry out for assessment. To what extent are the theories discussed above relevant to understanding the world of the twenty-first century? What alternatives, if any, have appeared in their place?[4]

Our examination of recent literature yields four approaches, at varying levels of elaboration, that can be applied to understanding the nature

[4] One possible reason for the decline in attention to the topic of corporate and elite power was the rise, during the 1980s, of what became known as the "state-centered" model. This approach, usually associated with Theda Skocpol (1980), adopts a largely Weberian view of the state, viewing it as an entity with its own set of interests, able to set the parameters within which nonstate actors operate. External groups, including business, are thus viewed as, if not dominated, then heavily influenced by state actions. The emergence of this approach led to a debate between Skocpol and Jill Quadagno (writing from a perspective similar to that of Poulantzas) over the origins of Social Security legislation in the United States (see Skocpol, 1980; Quadagno, 1984; Skocpol and Amenta, 1985; Quadagno, 1985) and, subsequently, between Skocpol and Domhoff (see Domhoff, 1986/1987; Skocpol, 1986/1987) on the same topic. The state-centered approach brought a welcome acknowledgement that much of significance occurs within as well as outside the formal political apparatus. One possibility for its wide acceptance may have been that it was seen as the primary alternative to the Marxist-oriented theories that had begun to dominate political sociology following the discrediting of pluralism. The fate of the Clinton health care plan in the early 1990s served as a reminder that the state can still be dominated by powerful external interests, however. A fruitful alternative that acknowledges the reflexive relation between state and nonstate political actors has been presented by Laumann and Knoke (1987), who argue that the lines separating the two are often difficult to discern. We discuss this work in a subsequent section.

of corporate political unity and power in developed capitalist societies. These include the view proposed by Domhoff, which is an updated but essentially similar version of his earlier elite theoretic model; an approach that flows from recent work by Michael Useem, suggesting that institutional stockholders have become the primary centers of power in the American business community; a model, proposed by Gerald Davis, which suggests that there is no longer an identifiable group of power holders in the business community but rather that power now rests in the anonymous forces of the capital market; and an argument, developed by several theorists both in North America and (especially) Britain, suggesting that economic globalization has significantly affected the relations between business and the state in developed capitalist societies. We discuss each of these in turn.

An Elite Theory for the 2000s

Among contemporary proponents of an elite perspective, no one has been more prolific than G. William Domhoff. Through a series of books dating back to the original *Who Rules America?* (1967), Domhoff has continually refined his argument, taking into account criticisms, developments in scholarship, and changes in the larger society. His most recent statement is a 1998 revision of *Who Rules America?* Although his argument has become increasingly sophisticated over the years, Domhoff's model of the turn of the twenty-first century American power structure looks very much like the one he proposed more than three decades earlier. Domhoff argues that a power elite, drawn from the social upper class, corporate leaders, and officials of policy-making organizations, collectively dominates American politics. These elites are generally, if not perfectly, cohesive, sharing outlooks and political positions as a result of their similar backgrounds, social ties, and shared economic interests. They play a major role in politics through their funding of and (in some cases) participation in policy-planning organizations whose goal is to formulate ideas that are then conveyed to elected officials and that often form the basis of policies enacted by the state. The members of the power elite, especially those drawn from the social upper class, may be less visible in the contemporary world than in earlier years. Most of these leaders continue to come from relatively privileged backgrounds, however.

As in his previous works, Domhoff assembles a staggering amount of evidence, both quantitative and qualitative, to support his argument that the power elite dominate American politics. Although the argument is compelling, it raises questions as well. Domhoff has become increasingly sensitive to the fact that the dominance of the elite is not all-encompassing, that the elite suffers defeats, including ones driven by elected officials responding to public opposition. He does not address whether the power of the elite has varied over time, however. Vogel (1989) shows that during the late 1960s and early 1970s, when the consumer and labor movements were relatively strong, corporations suffered a series of political defeats, including the formation of the Environmental Protection Agency (EPA) and the Occupational Safety and Health Administration. By the late 1970s and early 1980s, business was far more successful politically, pushing through a series of measures and preventing others, including holding off the potential repeal of the Taft–Hartley Law that was vehemently opposed by the labor movement. Domhoff argues that the idea behind the EPA was actually formulated and initiated by the power elite. He acknowledges that business eventually came to oppose the agency, but Vogel presents equally convincing evidence that business opposed its formation from the start. Even if Domhoff is correct that such policies are formulated primarily by or at the behest of the power elite, his model does not explain why the business community was forced to develop such a plan in the first place. Domhoff's view that the elite perpetually dominates thus raises questions about nonfalsifiability not unlike those directed at Poulantzas' model of the capitalist state. As in previous versions of elite theory, Domhoff also does not demonstrate that the policies enacted by the state are opposed by the majority of the electorate. Unless one can show this, it is always possible to argue that elected officials are being responsive to their constituents. Despite its problems, it would be imprudent to reject Domhoff's model out of hand, especially because (as we discuss in a later section) corporations now place greater effort on lobbying the state than at any time in American history. Clearly, Domhoff's argument remains a major source of potentially useful empirical analyses.

The Role of Institutional Investors

A second approach for understanding the structure of corporate power has been advanced by Useem (1996). To understand Useem's position, it is worthwhile to return to the Berle and Means thesis about the separation of ownership from control. As we noted earlier, it seemed indisputable by the 1970s that, contrary to most developed nations, the United States had witnessed a significant amount of stock dispersal. In the 1980s things began to change. The U.S. stock market had performed poorly during the 1970s. Companies were in relatively weak equity positions. In the view of some finance economists (Fama and Jensen, 1983), firms were "undervalued," ripe for takeover by alternative management teams that would "right" the company, thus increasing its stock price. As Useem (1996) noted, managers began to come under increasing pressure from stockholders. Nearly one-third of the Fortune 500 received takeover bids during the 1980s (Davis and Useem, 2002).

Many of the ownership groups that launched takeover bids during the 1980s were individuals and members of firms devoted specifically to buying and selling companies. The largest single block of stockholders by the 1990s was not individuals, however, but institutional investors: mutual funds, pension funds, bank trust departments, charitable endowments, and other organizations. As of 1994, institutionals owned 57 percent of the stock in the 1,000 largest publicly traded U.S. companies, up from 43 percent in 1985 and just 16 percent in 1965 (Useem, 1996:25). Traditionally, stockholders who were dissatisfied with company managers would sell their stock. As the sizes of their holdings have increased, the ability of institutionals to sell when they are dissatisfied has become more limited. As a consequence, Useem suggests, institutional investors have become increasingly active in attempting to directly influence corporate policies.

Despite the potential power of institutional investors, Useem makes no claim that they constitute a cohesive elite such as that described by Domhoff, or even the "inner circle" described by Useem himself in his earlier work (1984). Those making the decisions, Useem suggests, are professional money managers, many of whom not only have no origin in the social elite but do not even belong to policy-making organizations or elite social clubs. Some leading institutional investors represent long-standing, powerful, and connected firms such as Citigroup and Bankers Trust (although the latter, as of this writing, is owned by Deutsche Bank). Those who manage company pension funds are increasingly tied to professional rather than intraclass networks (1996:267–9), however, and they often see themselves as having conflicting interests with the managers of the firms in which they invest. It seems a considerable stretch to suggest that the money managers of institutional investors have replaced either the owning families or commercial banks of earlier decades as the basis of a cohesive capitalist class. But as discussed in the following section, this does not necessarily mean that corporate power is any less pervasive.

Control Via the Capital Market?

An argument related to Useem's but more explicitly oriented toward accounting for the cohesion and power of business has been presented by Davis (1999). Drawing on the Davis and Mizruchi (1999) study described earlier, Davis argues that there is no longer a single, identifiable group of dominant economic actors in the U.S. economy. Rather, pressures for both firms and the state to conform emanate directly from the capital market, whose influence has increased significantly since the early 1980s. The absence of a single dominant group does not mean that managers are autonomous. In fact, pressures from the capital market render managers less powerful today than during the heyday of managerialism in the 1950s and early 1960s, Davis argues. The difference is that there is now no single, consciously organized interest that oversees business as a whole in the way that Mintz and Schwartz argued that the leading banks did. Not even institutional investors per se constitute such a group. Instead, corporate managers face pressure from an amorphous, but no less real, source. The implication is that this may leave them in an even more precarious situation than during the periods of family or bank control.

At the core of Davis's argument is his claim that the institutional and legal structure surrounding the American corporation makes control by owners, or a capitalist class in general, unnecessary. Although corporations in most developed countries are controlled by families, who transmit their control through inheritance, or banks, Davis accepts the Berle and Means argument and the evidence of more recent analysts (La Porta et al., 1999) in noting that U.S. corporations are dominated by managers. What is especially distinctive about U.S. firms, according to Davis, is that maximizing the share price is viewed as the firm's primary legitimating purpose, toward which the systems of corporate law and managerial compensation are devoted. Not only does the system not require large owners or banks to ensure that managers focus on share price, but such outside intervention is viewed as disruptive to such a focus. Here Davis differs from Useem, who notes the role of institutional investors in pressing managers to focus on the firm's share price.

Because the focus on share price is built into the system and because the process operates more smoothly when firms are management controlled, Davis suggests that the concept of class is irrelevant to the understanding of corporate behavior. "Whatever their class background, corporate elites are compelled to vow allegiance to 'shareholder value' and to accept the market's judgment" (1999:15–16) Davis argues. This point is by itself not new. It is consistent with discussions by several theorists discussed earlier, including Baran and Sweezy (1966), Useem (1984), and Mizruchi (1992), as well as Herman (1981), who suggest that firm behavior is driven by systemic constraints, which render the backgrounds of corporate officials irrelevant.[5] What makes Davis's argument unique is his stipulation that it is the capital market, the sum total of investors' assessments of firms, that drives corporate behavior. In tracing the larger implications of his view, Davis notes the similarity between his "capitalism without capitalists" conception of the economy and the earlier argument of Block (1977). "[T]he ruling class does not rule" (1999:20), Davis says, quoting Block. "[R]ather, structures and policies are driven by anticipations of their economic consequences, because those who manage the 'state apparatus' rely for their tenure on economic vibrancy" (1999:20–21).

Managerial Autonomy Redux

One of the most shocking business events of the past several decades occurred in 1970 when the Penn Central Railroad declared bankruptcy. This episode stunned the business community because only months earlier, the company had appeared to be on a strong financial footing. It was subsequently revealed that the firm's accountants had misled the board by providing an unjustifiably optimistic picture of the company's financial condition. This example became a textbook case for the dangers of unchecked managerial control, exactly what Berle and Means had warned of four decades earlier.

The models of Useem and Davis, despite their differences, are both based on an assumption that the managers of large corporations at the turn of the twenty-first century face external pressures beyond those experienced by managers of the Penn Central period. In Useem's case, managers are subjected to pressures from an

[5] See Bowman (1996:chapter 6) for a detailed discussion of this issue.

increasingly active group of institutional stockholders. For Davis, managers must be responsive to the investment community in general, regardless of how dispersed that community is.

Despite the increase in stockholder pressure posited by both Useem and Davis, the corporate world was rocked by several major scandals in the late 1990s, on a scale at least as large as the Penn Central bankruptcy. The most noteworthy of these was the collapse of Enron, but several others were significant as well. These cases appear to be examples of managers, unmonitored by outsiders, running amok. They call into question the arguments not only of Useem and Davis but of Domhoff as well.

In the case of Enron, the company's auditors, Arthur Andersen, were allegedly complicit in providing inflated views of the company's performance that caught the firm's investors and employees off-guard. Enron's board members have at this writing denied knowledge of the accounting improprieties, as had Penn Central's board members. It was the firm's inside officials, most notably its CEO, Kenneth Lay, who allegedly profited from them. At the same time, several aspects of the case suggest that both the firm's connections to other firms and its political activity may have insulated it from earlier detection and may yet insulate its managers from further sanctions. The largest accounting firms, of which Andersen may have been the best known, have moved increasingly into consulting as well as auditing. Andersen's consulting income from Enron amounted to half of its total business with the firm, and the firm may have had an incentive to avoid offending Enron's managers (*Time*, January 17, 2002). At the same time, Enron had contributed more than $5 million to federal elected officials and the firm had close ties to several officials in President George W. Bush's administration. This led to speculation that both the contributions and ties were sources of the Bush administration's relatively lenient stance toward the energy industry. Even if Enron benefited from these connections, however, it does not appear to have been at the behest of either its stockholders or another external group such as bankers. Enron appears to have been a clearly management controlled firm. Its insiders were the ones who gained the most from the government's largesse. In addition, the scandals as a whole and the stock market crash that accompanied them led to a loss of several trillion dollars of net worth. Certainly some individuals capitalized on the scandals, but they did so at the expense of other investors, many of whom were relatively small and powerless but some of whom, including a number of institutionals, lost significant amounts of money. If anyone in the capitalist class benefited from these scandals, it was a selective segment and not the class as a whole. Meanwhile, these events suggested that managers still had the ability to operate unaccountable to outside forces, including their own boards. The capital market and institutional stockholders certainly place constraints on managers, as Davis and Useem suggest, but these constraints are not all-encompassing.

Corporate Political Activity Redux

A further question must be raised against the neostructuralist view that the state is automatically responsive to business: If that were the case, why would corporations place such effort on lobbying and PAC contributions? That business is politically active is a staple of Domhoff's model. By positing the importance of business political activity, Domhoff implies that without such efforts, there would be no assurance that the state would act in the interests of business. That is tantamount to accepting the belief that the United States is a democracy. Yet the very domination of pressure by corporate interests raises questions about the effectiveness of democratic institutions.

The dominance of corporate interests in pressure group competition is not universally accepted. As we have seen, Vogel viewed business domination as a reality, but a contingent one. At various points, noncorporate groups have exercised considerable power, Vogel argued. A comprehensive study of health and energy policy by Laumann and Knoke (1987) yielded similar conclusions. Although corporate and industry interests were extremely active and highly influential, groups other than business, such as associations of health professionals, were also able to exercise influence. Moreover, as Laumann and Knoke argue, actors within the state often had their own agendas and entered into issues as one of several interested actors.

One fundamental issue does suggest the dominance of corporate interests, however: the sheer magnitude of their resources. In two major studies (Clawson et al., 1992, 1998), Clawson and his colleagues have shown the ways in which corporations use lobbying and PAC contributions to achieve their legislative goals. PAC funds are significant because fundraising requirements have now disqualified all but the most well-endowed candidates from seeking elective office. Clawson, Neustadtl, and Weller note that in 1996, the average major party candidate in House elections raised nearly five thousand dollars per week (and the average winning candidate raised nearly seven thousand dollars per week) over a two-year period. The only way to raise such sums, the authors argue, is to seek backing from large donors, most of which are major corporations. This renders it nearly impossible for a candidate strongly opposed to corporate interests to succeed.

Of course, even under these conditions there is still the issue of business unity. To return to the earlier arguments of Schumpeter, Galbraith, and Lipset, if corporate interests are split, do they not nullify one another? Perhaps firms are so active politically because they are competing with other firms, or industries. There is one important piece of evidence against the countervailing power argument, however: As Clawson et al. show, both in these works and in an earlier study (Clawson et al., 1986), corporations may pursue *different* interests but they rarely engage in head-to-head conflict. Similarly, Mizruchi (1992) found that in testimony before Congress, instances of corporations sharing a position on an issue outweighed cases of opposition by a four to one margin. In their PAC contributions, pairs of firms were more than nine times more likely to contribute to the same candidates as to candidates opposing one another. If corporations opposing one another is an important condition for the functioning of democracy, then, as both Lindblom (1977) and later Dahl (1982) warned, American democracy may be in serious peril.

Corporate Control and Power Outside North America

Although the empirical examples we have used in our discussion have focused primarily on the United States, the theories at the basis of this discussion were designed to apply to developed capitalist societies in general. Dahrendorf, in his discussion of the separation of ownership from control, referred to Great Britain, France, and Germany as well as the United States. Miliband's discussion of the backgrounds of government officials was based on an analysis of Britain. Poulantzas' model of the structural imperatives of the capitalist state was drawn from his study of the French bureaucracy. And Useem's examination of corporate political activity was based on a comparative analysis of the United States and Britain. It is not evident, however, that the theories developed in the United States, in particular the Berle and Means thesis and the reactions to it, apply to other parts of the world. To what extent have the various models tested on U.S. data been applied to non–U.S. settings, and what level of support have they received? A full answer to these questions would require at least a chapter of its own, if not a full-scale monograph. We can, however, offer a few general observations.

First, with perhaps the exception of Great Britain, the extent of stock dispersal outside the United States has been considerably lower than in the United States. The early data analyzed by Dahrendorf (1959) and a more thorough analysis by Scott (1979) indicated historical trends toward stock dispersal in all of the world's most industrialized countries. In a more recent study that we cited earlier, however, La Porta, Lopez-de-Silanes, and Shleifer (1999) found that the United States and the United Kingdom are outliers in terms of the relative levels of stock dispersal. To the extent that ownership and control remain more closely fused in nations such as Germany, Italy, and South Korea, the debates over the implications of stock dispersal become less relevant. This does not mean that families and individuals remain the dominant owners virtually everywhere outside the United States and United Kingdom. Variation remains, from the strong family influence in South Korea and Chile to the stronger institutional presence in France and Germany. LaPorta et al.'s findings do suggest the possibility that the nature of the business communities in many parts of the world cannot be accounted for in terms of the separation of ownership from control.

Second, although it is not fully determining, there is an evident connection between the theories of corporate power and the nationality of their proponents. The arguments developed by Domhoff and Miliband were almost certainly influenced by the relatively high level of elite representation in key government positions within the United States and United Kingdom. Similarly, Poulantzas' alternative perspective, which deemphasized the social backgrounds of state officials, was undoubtedly influenced by his focus on France, with its large civil service bureaucracy, staffed largely by those with middle-class backgrounds. The theorists' national backgrounds do not fully account for their perspectives. Both Domhoff and Miliband have been sharply criticized by their own compatriots, for example. A fuller account of exactly how the national backgrounds of various theorists have affected their analyses of relations between corporations and the state would be a fruitful area for further study.

Third, it is intriguing to observe the extent to which theories developed within the United States apply with greater relevance outside the United States than inside. Mintz and Schwartz's bank hegemony model was controversial in the United States even during the late 1970s and early 1980s, when nonfinancial corporations' use of external financing was at extremely high levels. Although its applicability to contemporary Germany may be limited as well, historically, the dominance of German banks was widely accepted. Mintz and Schwartz, Mizruchi, and others spent considerable effort, with only partial success, to identify coherent business groups in the United States. Yet business groups, in which the health of the group as a whole takes precedence over the well-being of particular firms, have been widely established in East Asia, as evidenced by the *keiretsu* in Japan (Gerlach, 1992; Lincoln et al., 1992), the *chaebol* in South Korea (Lee, 2000), and the *jituanqiye* in Taiwan (Hamilton and Biggart, 1988). Keister (1998), using data on Chinese business groups, found a positive effect of director interlocks on firm profits. Carrington (1981) found a positive interlock/profits association in Canada, as did Meeusen and Cuyvers (1985) in Belgium, but little evidence for such a link has been found in the United States.

Finally, the structures of corporate elite networks have been studied, with considerable success, in such nations as Chile (Zeitlin and Ratcliff, 1988) and Colombia (Ogliastri and Davila, 1987) and several European nations (Stokman, Ziegler, and Scott, 1985). The latter study revealed extensive structures of corporate interlocks in virtually all industrialized countries in Europe. These studies have in some cases posed challenges to widely held views. Ogliastri and Davila, in a study of the power structures of eleven mid-sized Colombian cities, found, contrary to an earlier argument by Walton (1976), that the more economically developed the city, the greater its concentration of power. Taira and Wada (1987) showed the ways in which the career life cycles of Japanese elites, beginning in the state bureaucracy, with subsequent movement into positions in private corporations, facilitate cooperative relations between business and government. Scott (1987) traced the varying systems of interfirm relations in Britain, France, and Germany to the distinct histories of the three nations; the prevalence of small, family-owned firms in Britain, alliances of large banks and companies in Germany, and financial and family-based "interest groups" in France. And more recently, Windolf (2002) has completed an extensive comparative study of corporate networks in ten countries, from Western and Eastern Europe to the United States, providing detailed analyses of the organizational and historical factors accounting for variation among them.

Less evident in these works, and still too rare in the United States, as well, are systematic analyses of the effects of corporate network structures on firm political behavior and the political consequences of such behavior. These data are admittedly difficult to identify, and where they do exist, such as PAC contribution data in the United States, their meaning and interpretation are not always clear. Even if there were data sources in non–U.S. countries analogous to corporate PAC contributions, and even if their meanings were clear within their national context, the ability to draw comparative inferences would be limited. It is perhaps for this reason that comparative discussions of the role of corporate power have tended to operate at a highly abstract level. Just as considerable attention has been paid to the development of comparative data sources for the cross-national study of social mobility, it might be useful for political sociologists to begin thinking about a similar effort to develop cross-national data on corporate political behavior.

Globalization

The level of international economic activity as a proportion of world GDP nearly tripled between 1953 and 1997 (Fligstein, 2001:196–7). The process spread especially rapidly after the deregulation of national financial markets brought on by the 1973 collapse of the Bretton Woods agreement, which had fixed international currencies to the dollar. Several scholars have suggested that with the increasing globalization of economic activity, national governments have lost the ability to regulate their own business communities (Cerny, 1997; Frieden, 1991; Strange, 1996). If these formulations are accurate, it would follow that business elites have become increasingly powerful with respect to individual capitalist states. The internationalization of economic activity also raises the question of whether elites have become intertwined cross-nationally over time. One possible outcome of this might be the disappearance, or at least the dispersal, of national corporate elites.

The extent to which corporations have the ability to move capital outside their borders certainly gives them leverage over their host states, in the same way that threatening to move to another location within a nation provides leverage over local governments. There is controversy regarding just how extensive and/or new the globalization process is, however. Although the relative frequency of cross-national economic activity increased significantly between the end of World War II and the 1990s, the level was approximately the same in 1997 as it was in 1914 (Fligstein, 2001). The proportion of economic activity occurring within national boundaries remained well above 80 percent even during the 1990s. Some institutions, such as American banks, moved overseas during the 1960s and 1970s but actually reduced their foreign operations after 1980 (Mizruchi and Davis, 2004).

If globalization has weakened the ability of capitalist states to regulate their domestic business communities, then corporate elites would have greater power with respect to their states at the turn of the twenty-first century than they did three decades earlier. This may be the case, but there is no evidence to demonstrate it. Those studying the process of globalization have focused on its effects on general domestic and foreign policies, such as welfare provisions. Whether globalization is the cause of reduced welfare expenditures in the West is a hotly debated issue. There is virtually no empirical work on the extent to which the political power of domestic business communities has increased during this period. Both this issue, and the degree of internationalization of corporate elites, are areas that clearly warrant greater scrutiny.

CONCLUSION

> The rise of the modern corporation has brought a concentration of economic power which can compete on equal terms with the modern state . . . ,where its own interests are concerned, it even attempts to dominate the state. The future may see the economic organism, now typified by the corporation, not only on an equal plane with the state, but possibly even superseding it as the dominant form of social organization. (Berle and Means, 1968[1932:313])

The period from the 1950s to the 1980s saw a ferocious debate among American social scientists over the concentration of political power in developed capitalist societies. This debate yielded scores, perhaps hundreds, of studies, and the sophistication of the work on all sides increased significantly over time. The debate began to lose steam in the early 1990s, however, and few sociologists any longer write about the role of economic elites or study such processes (for exceptions, see Dreiling, 2000; Burris, 2001). The world has changed since the heyday of the power structure debate. American firms (although not, as we have seen, American banks) have become more global, as have firms based in other developed nations. The banks' political position within the business community has declined. Older, visible families such as the Rockefellers have disappeared. Yet we do not know what, if anything, has arisen in their places. We outlined four current perspectives that have been advanced to account for the role of corporate power in contemporary developed societies. All four approaches require attention, and all four require empirical analysis.

We do not know what these new studies of corporate power will reveal. Although corporations face pressures from stockholders, and the capital market in general, that they did not face twenty-five years ago, they appear to be acting largely on their own rather than as members of a larger corporate community. Corporations are as politically active, through lobbying and campaign contributions, as they have ever been. This does not necessarily demonstrate that corporate power as a whole is increasing. As Robert Dahl noted many years ago (1958), for a group to be powerful requires not only resources, but also unity. Corporations pursuing their own interests, without an organized mobilization, may cancel each other out. Conversely, there is evidence for the diffusion of corporate behavior across networks that did not exist two decades ago, and even early pluralists such as Lindblom (1977) and Dahl (1982) eventually conceded that business was a disproportionately powerful actor. What implications do these networks have for corporate political power? Is business mobilized at anything approaching its level in the late 1970s? Is business less organized now because collective action is less necessary, because of the successes of the past? Can business be a powerful political actor without any organization at all, but simply by virtue of its structural position and the consequences, even inadvertent ones, that its behavior generates? What role, if any, has the globalization of economic activity played in this process? Can we develop systematic, cross-national comparisons of corporate political activity, and if so, what results will they yield? There is no shortage of important questions for sociologists, and other social scientists, to address.

CHAPTER SIXTEEN

Social Movements and Social Change[1]

J. Craig Jenkins and William Form

INTRODUCTION

Social movements have traditionally been defined as organized efforts to bring about social change (cf. Jenkins, 1983; McAdam and Snow, 1997:xviii–xxv; McCarthy and Zald, 1977:1217–18; Tarrow, 1998:4–6; Wilson, 1973:3–4). Yet, as several scholars have noted (Burstein, Einwohner, and Hollander, 1995; Giugni, 1998, 1999; Huberts, 1989; Lofland, 1993:347–8), whether and how they actually *cause* social change has received little attention. Social movement research has long focused on questions of emergence and participation. Some attention has been paid to immediate *social movements outcomes* but scant attention has focused of *social movement change*. By the latter, we mean the distinctive contribution of social movements to change net of ongoing changes and social processes. Many studies have examined the short-term or immediate outcomes of movements, for example, life course change (Fendrich, 1993; McAdam, 1988), policy enactment (Burstein, 1985; Burstein and Freudenberg, 1978; Costain, 1992), and policy implementation (Button, 1989; Handler, 1978), but few have placed these processes in a multivariate framework and controlled for the relevant societal influences. Most studies of movements have focused *inward* and have been "movement-centered" (Lofland, 1993:289–91), thus neglecting their possible impact on social change in the broader society. When movement outcomes have been studied, they have typically focused on immediate public policy effects and not the broader institutional and cultural changes central to long-term movement objectives. Understanding social movement change is central to political sociology because the field is defined as the study of social power (see chapter 1). Similarly, social movements are defined as organized efforts to bring about social changes in the distribution of power. This chapter reviews the current status of the social movement field and outlines a theoretical and methodological strategy for developing a theory of social movement change.

We use "social movement change" in preference to social movement "success" for several reasons. First, the question of "success" typically asks whether the outcomes were intended or in the interest of social movement actors. Not only are there frequent internal movement disagreements over desired outcomes, but movements may also have important unintended outcomes. The question also arises whether intended outcomes actually benefit the claimed beneficiaries of movements. As Amenta and Young (1999) argue, the central question is the creation of collective goods for movement beneficiaries, that is, those claimed to be primary to benefit from movement activity. We refer to these alternatives as *social movement outcomes*. Second, "success" is typically analyzed as a *social movement effect*, that

[1] We benefitted from the comments of Verta Taylor, Wayne Santoro, Joan Huber, and two anonymous reviewers as well as the assistance of Steve Boutcher.

is, in terms of specific immediate consequences of social movements, as in altered life courses or changed laws.

Analyzing *social movement change* requires a *causal* analysis that not only demonstrates an association between the movement and specific outcomes but also shows that movement processes contribute independently or in addition to other potential causes. Such an analysis also identifies the mechanisms involved in bringing about change. The analysis involves placing movements in a broader societal context that includes ongoing social changes, the structure of the state, prevailing political alliances, existing ideologies and cultural resources, and the structure of major social institutions relevant to the change in question.

What are relevant *social movement outcomes*? Gamson (1975[1990]) distinguishes two: (1) acceptance and (2) new tangible advantages. Some argue (Goldstone, 1980) that acceptance without tangible gains (i.e., cooptation) is a type of failure. However, Taylor (1989) has shown that organizational survival at some minimal level may eventually act as a catalyst to movement revitalization. The question arises, What constitutes a "tangible advantage"? Most studies focus on visible advantages, such as the enactment of favorable laws (Burstein, 1985; Santoro, 2002) or additional public expenditures (Albritton, 1979; Jaynes, 2002; Jennings, 1983), but they may ignore matters of policy implementation (Andrews, 2001), institutional and cultural changes (Chaves, 1997; Katzenstein, 1998; Staggenborg, 1998), and the distribution of socially valued resources (Eckstein, 1982; Kelley and Klein, 1980). As Weber (1946:chapter 8) early observed, tangible gains also include increased status or prestige, favorable cultural adaptations, and the reorganizations in lifestyles of everyday life. These changes reflect changes in the distribution of social power that may be brought about by social movements.

This essay begins by defining social movements and their potential contribution to political sociology. It then discusses the major theories of social movements and how they handle social change, arguing that they point to the need for an institutional analysis of the political system framed in terms of interorganizational networks and the interaction of collective action and political opportunities. We outline the major theories and then assess how movement strategies and tactics impact social change. The major impediment to such an approach has been the absence of a conceptual framework for identifying the relevant factors and a methodology for distinguishing social movement effects from other factors. We outline such a methodology and, in the conclusion, identify new directions for research.

SOCIAL MOVEMENTS: CONCEPTS AND CONTRIBUTION

We adopt Meyer and Tarrow's (1998:4) conception of social movements as "collective challenges to existing arrangements of power and distribution by people with common purposes and solidarities, in sustained interaction with elites, opponents and authorities." Two features stand out in this definition. First, social movements entail "collective challenge" (i.e., organized attempts to change institutional arrangements through contentious as well as conventional collective action). Such changes may center on public policies, which has been the major focus of study, or they aim at broader changes in the structure of social institutions, the distribution of social benefits, and conceptions of social rights and responsibilities. Although some movements create a single formal movement organization (SMO), most operate in multiorganizational fields (Curtis and Zurcher, 1973) of competing small groups knit together by interpersonal networks that have common goals, targets, and ideology (Diani, 1995; Gerlach and Hine, 1970). By using contentious as well as conventional tactics, social movements attempt to create uncertainty in the eyes of their targets and thereby pressure them to alter their practices. The second feature of social movements is their inherent political character. Movement goals typically include changing the distribution of power and authority and their impact depends on sustained interactions with other political actors, most notably political allies, opponents, and authorities.

Bringing social movements into the core of political sociology promotes a better understanding of the processes that generate social change. We argue that, in democratic polities, social movements are critical catalysts for social change. Recognizing this corrects a key problem with existing theories of social change. Since the early 1960s, standard social change theories (e.g. functionalist, evolutionary, conflict, and diffusion) have failed to provide a general explanation of social and political change. Some argue that a general theory is impossible and that a better approach develops contingency arguments about specific institutional mechanisms that operate in delimited contexts (e.g. Chirot, 1994; Tilly, 1995). In place of holistic change theories, the best we can develop are explanations that capture path-dependent and historically specific changes.

Whatever the merits of this position, we agree that social movement change is usually the product of specific sequences of political interactions between social movements, their allies, opponents, and authorities. For example, political revolutions are partially explicable in terms of the interactions among political contenders and the underlying networks and alliances that constrain these interactions (Tilly, 1978:chapter 7). Similar processes operate in democratic reform cycles (Tarrow, 1998:chapter 10). Drawing on political event data mapping of civil politics, Jenkins and Bond (2001) proposed an index of conflict carrying capacity based on the multiple interactions of civil contentions, state repression, and confrontational violence. They serve as "early warning" signals of political crisis in the onset of generalized political violence, violent regime change, and geno-politicides. These sequences depend on the mobilization and decisions of specific actors (most notably movement leaders and political authorities) and they reveal regular predictable patterns of interaction that may lead toward or away from political crises.

Movement goals and strategies are also critically shaped by political interactions. Goldstone (1998) argues that both reformist and revolutionary movements emerge out of similar grievances, resources, organization, and cultural solidarities, but their goals diverge due to interactions with political authorities. Where authorities resist mildly, cooperate or are neutral, and make no effort to eliminate the movement, a reform movement is likely to emerge. Where the state adopts a repressive exclusionary stance and is too weak and/or ineffective at repression, a revolutionary movement is likely, especially when it is reinforced by alliances with other political contenders (Goodwin, 2002).

Significantly, this type of political process explanation does not eliminate the need to analyze existing networks, the distribution of resources, and the structural limits of existing institutions and ideologies. The political processes shaping movement mobilization and its effects are embedded in institutions, a key point in functional arguments about system breakdown and equilibrium that social movement scholars often neglect. The same processes are also embedded in long-term evolutionary changes, including the changing population of organizations and the institutional selection mechanisms that favor the survival of specific types of SMOs (Edwards and Marullo, 1995; Hannan and Freeman, 1989; Minkoff, 1995, 1998).

A critical concern is whether social movements are working with or against the evolutionary trends in society. The societal contexts of movements must be considered to define the limits of existing institutions as well as their contradictions that may spark movements and the changes they bring about. Finally, it is important to understand the antagonisms and structural limits within the "parent structure" (Schwartz, 1975) or major the social institutions in which social movements are embedded. Such structures define not only the interests under contention but also the interinstitutional alliances and interdependencies that shape their power, interests, vulnerabilities, and their capacities to resist change. Drawing on geopolitical theory, Collins (1995) argues that the collapse of the USSR was structurally based and, at most, triggered by mass mobilization. Although he may have underestimated the importance of the mass protests (Bunce, 1999; Jenkins and Benderliglou, 2003), he correctly emphasized

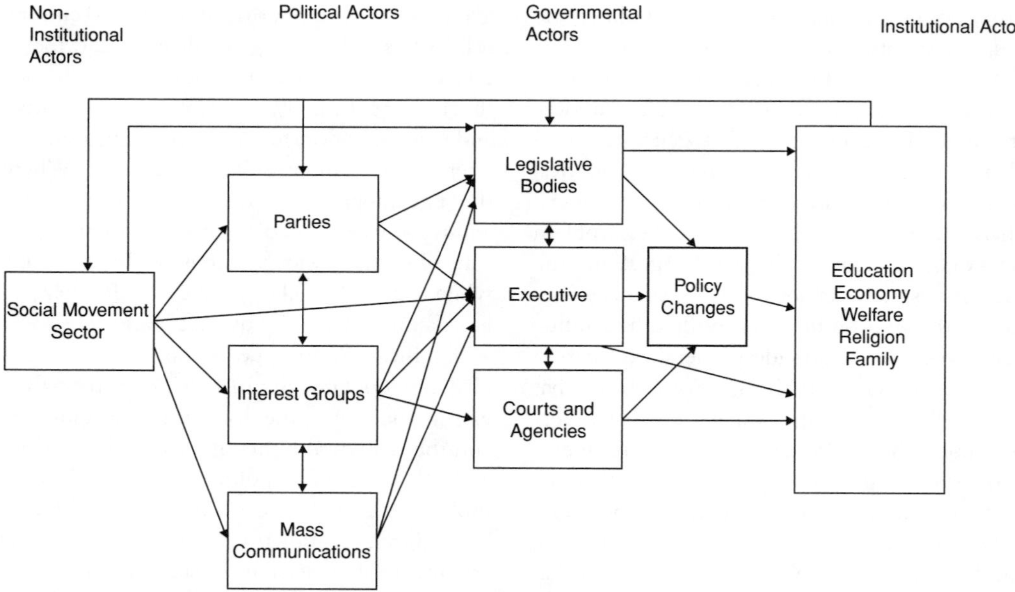

Figure 16.1. Sector Relations in the Public Policy System.

the importance of ongoing structural contradictions of the Soviet system and in *glasnost, perestroika*, and other internal reforms.

A MOVEMENT/SOCIETY FRAMEWORK

To understand movement/society interactions an interinstitutional network approach must be used. Figure 16.1 outlines a general framework of the social structures within which social movements are embedded. For the sake of simplicity, we divide society into four sectors: (1) social movements; (2) governmental institutions, such as legislatures, courts, chief executives, and agencies; (3) political interest organizations, such as political parties and interest groups; and (4) other social institutions of mass communication, education, economy, welfare, and religion. In open, democratic, pluralistic societies, these four sectors constitute an interactive system of interinstitutional bargaining, conflict, and change. In authoritarian regimes, the sectors are constrained by the extent of state control over other institutions. This sector framework does not provide a causal model for the study of movement impacts on change; rather, it is a scheme for identifying the major institutions and organizations with which movement interact when bringing about possible change.

For any given movement, the parent institution and the other three sectors constitute an external organizational environment in which the movement interacts in the process of advancing its aims, goals, and values. Our approach treats the macrosocietal structure as existing prior to social movements, defining the latter as emerging out of society (which must be specified) and responding to groups in this larger structure. The analysis proceeds from the societal system to the specific social movement (from the macro to micro) rather than the other way around (Blau, 1994:chapter 6). To analyze movement/society interaction and its outcomes, the appropriate methodology focuses on interorganizational bargaining treated as forced exchanges in bounded or constrained rational choices (Form, 1990). SMOs include both the formal organized structures as well as the diffuse informal networks that shape collective action. Unlike traditional exchange theory (Coleman, 1990), bargaining is neither individual nor voluntary but bounded by enduring externalities

(Form, 1990). Among them are institutionalized conflicts of interest that are embedded in unbalanced exchanges and define the major conflict lines of society (class, regional, others). In their attempt to bring about change, social movements get changed, shaped, and redefined by interacting with other groups in society as well as their political allies and opponents (Della Porta and Rucht, 1995).

In short, social movements are nested in an interinstitutional field defined by both the parent structure against which they have specific grievances and the other institutions with which the parent structures interact. Both shape the possible alliances among movements, their opponents (including countermovements), and other actors. Social movements are nested in an interorganizational field that the participants may or may not recognize (which itself has important consequences). Movement outcomes emerge out of multidimensional organizational bargaining that encompasses competing with some groups, cooperating with others, arriving at accommodations with still others, and even open antisystem activity.[2]

We do not adopt the simplistic functionalist position that all parts of the system in Figure 16.1 have equal power to change each other. In "postmodern" capitalist societies, institutional holders of economic, social, and cultural capital vary in their hegemony over subordinates as well as each other (Bourdieu, 1990; Collins, 1975). A multiplicity of potential conflicts impinge on the extent to which particular actors become mobilized and develop alliances with and against parent structures and their allies. The valid insight of functionalism recognizes institutional autonomy and that institutions vary in their independence, rules, logics, practices, and oppositions. Institutional autonomy is considerably reduced in authoritarian polities and in less developed societies. With this "society-centered" view of social movement change in mind, we now turn to specific social movement theories and examine the extent to which they consider and explain social change.

SOCIAL MOVEMENT THEORIES: THEIR LOGICS AND HOW THEY HANDLE CHANGE

We focus on five major theories: (1) early symbolic interactionist theories of collective behavior, (2) functionalist treatments, (3) resource mobilization, (4) political opportunity, and (5) newer ideas about framing and collective identity construction. All argue that social changes contribute to the rise of movements, creating strains, new resources, opportunities, and ideas about change, but only the last three actually discuss social movement change. In general, these discussions have gradually evolved from microexplanations of movement emergence[3] to analyses of how the institutions shape social movement outcomes and, most recently, to multivariate analyses of social movement change in a societal context.

Early Symbolic Interactionism

Early theorists advanced collective behavior explanations that focused on symbolic interaction and paid little attention to movement outcomes. Park's (1934) entry on "Collective Behavior" in the *Encyclopedia of the Social Sciences* (which had no entry for social movements) focused on the collective unrest and circular reaction processes that create contagion and bring individuals to join crowds. Blumer (1969) systematized these processes into stages: problematic situations, the breakdown of behavioral norms that

[2] A useful comparison is Giugni's (1998:388) "movement-centered" approach, which focuses on the interaction of the movement with its immediate environment in terms of how movement claims, actions, and their interactions with "outside events and actions" produce change. Our framework differs in that it starts from the larger interinstitutional system (or society) and specifies the effects of movement actions on the social change field. We term the first *movement-centered* in that it starts from the movement and its immediate environment, whereas ours is a "society-centered" framework that starts from the interinstitutional system within which a movement is embedded.

[3] Significantly, Heberle (1951) outlined a macro approach to social movements that put movements at the center of political sociology but, until the late 1960s, this challenge was not taken up by others.

lead to circular reaction, milling, collective excitement, and crowd action. Turner and Killian (1957, 1972, 1987) stripped this theory of the assumption that collective behavior is irrational by emphasizing the influence of symbolic interaction and information on defining problematic situations that in turn lead to the emergence of new norms. Such "emergent norms" (the process of emergence not explained) may eventually lead to the construction of social movements. Turner and Killian classified and described types of social movements, their stages of development, and leadership. Successful social movements become institutionalized and presumably bring about social change (Killian, 1964). However, the authors provided no analysis that distinguished successful from failed movements or dealt with difference in social movement outcomes and change.

Functionalism

Smelser (1962) outlined a functionalist approach that proposed a "value-added" framework to explain different types of collective behavior. Arguing that inconsistencies among the components of social action (values, norms, motivation, and situational facilities) create structural strain and the development of generalized beliefs, Smelser argued that six factors (structural conduciveness, strains, generalized beliefs, precipitating factors, mobilization, and social control) always operate to create collective behavior. Arguing that "any kind of strain may be a determinant of any kind of collective behavior" (1962:49), he argued that the form of collective behavior depends on the interaction of the other five factors. Yet, despite pointing to the importance of mobilization and social control (i.e., the interaction of movements and authorities), Smelser did not examine movement outcomes or change.

In sum, both of these early collective behavior theories focused on questions of movement emergence and participation but, apart from simplistic ideas about natural life cycles and the implicit assumption that institutionalized movements have some undefined impact, the theories ignored questions of social movement change. The analyses were interpretive and descriptive, typical of case studies of single SMOs.

Resource Mobilization and Political Opportunities

The social movements of the 1960s stimulated a reassessment of theories that led to the development of resource mobilization and political opportunity theories. They emphasized the role of movement strategies and political opportunities in bringing about social movement change. Although formally distinct, the two theories are typically used together. McCarthy and Zald (1973) argued that contemporary movements were becoming professionalized. They rely not only on paid professionals to mobilize transitory activists but also on discretionary time schedules, media events, and movement sponsorship by government agencies, private foundations, and social welfare institutions. Oberschall (1973) emphasized the importance of material and organizational resources in the mobilization process (especially preexisting solidarity networks and leadership). In an analysis of the southern civil rights movement, he documented the important role that sympathetic third parties (northern whites and political authorities) played in creating effective of civil disobedience. Barkan (1984) argued that this third party support was activated by the repressive violence of southern authorities against nonviolent protestors which, in turn, proved central to realizing the policy changes advocated by the movement. Specifying the idea of political opportunities associated with these arguments, Eisinger (1973) analyzed protests in U.S. cities. He found that closed or highly open city governments were less likely to encourage protests than cities with mixed or intermediate opportunities. An inverted U pattern operates. In closed systems (the left foot of the inverted U), repression and perceived lack of effects discourage protest; in open systems (the right foot of the inverted U), protest is unnecessary.

Defining "success" in terms of acceptance and tangible movement gains, Gamson (1975

[1990]) analyzed a sample of fifty-three "challenging groups" in the United States between 1800 and 1945 and found that the more successful movements (1) "think small" and pursue nondisplacement and single issue goals, (2) use selective incentives and enjoy external sponsorship, (3) employ unruliness (including violence) but are not targets of violence, (4) have centralized and formal structures that discourage fractionalization and provide combat readiness, and (5) are active during crisis periods (war and economic depression), and (6) have more radical competitors. Below we refer to this strategy of combining "thinking small" with unruliness as "radical reformism." Focusing on the importance of political allies and neutral elites, Jenkins and Perrow (1977) compared three farm worker union movements and demonstrated that third-party support from labor and liberal interest groups combined with governmental neutrality created successful unionization, whereas repression and weak allies led to failure.

The key variables in this discussion are resources and political opportunities. *Resources* include any capacity for carrying out collective action, ranging from tangible resources (money, space, publicity) to people resources (leadership, expertise, access to networks and decision makers, volunteer time and commitment) and societal resources (social status, legitimacy, name and issue recognition) (Freeman 1979:170–6). As Tilly (1978:7) argued, the key factors are "the ways that groups acquire resources and make them available for collective action." People and societal resources are central, especially the skills and networks of leaders and organizers who play a critical role in devising innovative strategies and tactics (Ganz, 2000). *Political opportunities* refer to "the probability that social protest actions will lead to success in achieving a desired outcome" (Goldstone and Tilly, 2001:182). Analysts distinguish between dynamic and structural opportunities as well as between cultural and institutional aspects (Gamson and Meyer, 1996). Important questions also arise about when and how potential supporters collectively perceive opportunities (see below) and whether threat or opportunities are more central to mobilization (Goldstone and Tilly, 2001; van Dyke, 2003; Jenkins, Jacobs, and Agnone, 2003).

Dynamic opportunities are centered in the immediate institutional environment of social movements and are "relatively volatile, shifting with events, policies and political actors" (Gamson and Meyer, 1996:277). Central to movement success are such factors as elite divisions, governmental control strategies (including excessive and erratic repression), support from political allies, and short-term crises (e.g., oil spills and airplane crashes) that create "policy windows" for political advocacy (Kingdom, 1984:173–4).

The general assumption here is that elites and polity members typically oppose the entry of new groups into the system, even those pursuing moderate change, because they threaten existing rules of political access and alliances. However, new developments may occur that lead elites and polity members to take neutral or even supportive stances toward movements. Analyzing the development of African American protests, McAdam (1999[1982]) argued that the mechanization of cotton production reduced the need for Jim Crow racism as a labor control device. Because United States Cold War foreign policy made the racial caste system a diplomatic liability, the Eisenhower administration supported domestic civil rights reforms. Party competition and a closely divided government led to relaxed repression and symbolic concessions that encouraged African American protest (Piven and Cloward, 1977:213–21, 231–5; McAdam 1999 [1982]:156–60, 169–72). Speaking of the opportunities behind the general protest wave in the late 1960s, Jenkins (1985:218) claimed that "In the context of a series of closely contested (Presidential) elections in which the margin of victory was often less than one percent, two swing voting blocs (African Americans and the new middle class) became increasingly decisive in the electoral calculations of political elites." Costain (1992:232–24) argued that close presidential elections and narrow margins of party control in Congress created bipartisan tolerance and thus support for the early women's movement. Jenkins et al. (2003) showed that divided governments and northern Democratic power created opportunities for African American protests. These opportunities influenced the emergence of movements, their goals and strategies, and the likelihood of social change.

Structural opportunities are more stable features of political institutions and culture that change only gradually over decades. "From the standpoint of social movements, these aspects are essentially fixed and given, barring dramatic and unforeseen changes beyond their control" (Gamson and Meyer, 1996:277). Comparing the strategies and policy impact of the antinuclear movements in four Western democracies (United States, West Germany, Sweden, and France), Kitschelt (1986) argues that the more accessible the state, the more moderate the movement, and the more likely the movement gains. Thus, antinuclear movements in the United States and Sweden relied on lobbying and litigation that were accompanied by little protest. Limited access to authorities in France and West Germany produced oppositional protest. Moreover, policy innovation seemed dependent on the capacity of the state to implement changes. In Sweden, a strong state was able to implement new energy policies that emphasized conservation and alternative fuels, whereas in the United States, a weak state produced a policy stalemate (i.e., the antinuclear movement imposed procedural obstacles to nuclear plant construction but had little effect on introducing innovation in energy policies). In France, limited access to authorities blunted movement influence and allowed a strong state to continue to expand its nuclear power industry. In West Germany, the combination of weak access with weak state capacity created oppositional protests and a stalemate in energy policy.

In sum, institutional structures channel interactions between movements and authorities and thereby shape movement goals and strategies. The structures also facilitate or impede a reactive learning process among elites. Movement impacts on policy are larger where political access is greater and policy capacities are strong (Sweden). Impacts are limited to procedural changes where political access is open but policy capacities are weak (United States). Finally, movement impact is minimal where input structures are closed (West Germany and France).

Opportunities need to be distinguished from *threats* that constitute "costs that social groups will incur from protest, or that it expects to suffer if it does not take action" (Goldstone and Tilly, 2001:183). The core argument of "prospect theory" (Quattrone and Tversky, 1988) is that negative sanctions are intrinsically more motivating than positive rewards. Some scholars use this theory to argue that threats (not opportunities) are central to protest (Berejikian, 1992; van Dyke, 2003) and that movements are more focused on preventing "bads" than securing "goods." Tilly (1978:134–5) makes the additional points that groups are more responsive to threats because they tend to inflate the value of resources already under control, overestimate the potential negative impact of threats, and can respond more quickly to threats by using existing networks and practices. In contrast, responding to new opportunities requires time-consuming mobilization.

Several studies have found that threats stimulate protest possibly more than do opportunities (Francisco, 1995; Rasler, 1996; van Dyke, 2003). The net impact of threats on social movement change is less clear. Meyer (1990) shows that the bellicose foreign policy rhetoric of the Reagan administration about "survivable nuclear war" stimulated the mobilization of the nuclear freeze movement but once the proposal was adopted by Democratic party leaders (an opportunity effect), it was watered down to a nonbinding congressional resolution, and the movement fizzled. Insofar as protests sustain mobilization, they may contribute to social movement change. However, in Jasper and Poulsen's (1993) comparative analysis of the animal rights campaign, the goals and mobilization of the protestors likely were less critical to the outcome than the vulnerability of the targets, their public relations blunders, and the mobilization of countermovements.

What is the relative importance of resources and opportunities with respect to social movement change? The evidence suggests that both are important. Cress and Snow (2000) found that both the organizational resources and political allies of homeless groups contributed to prohomeless policies in U.S. cities net of a range of other factors. In their study of the Townsend movement, Amenta, Carruthers, and Zylan (1992) coined the term *political mediation model* to depict how political opportunities mediate the impact of mobilization on policy change. The larger Townsend clubs gained larger old-age pensions but only in the context of the political opportunities afforded by liberal state Democratic parties and strong state agencies charged with protecting old-age recipients. Political opportunities provided the enabling context that made protest effective in bringing about changes.

Critics have pointed to several problems with resource and opportunity theories (Goodwin and Jasper, 1999; McAdam, 1996a; Zald, 2000). First, the often-exploratory studies have illustrated plausible causal processes but they lack conceptual clarity and methodological rigor in selecting control variables. Key terms such as *resource* and *political opportunity* have been used in ad hoc and inconsistent ways. McAdam (1996a) and Tarrow (1996) improved the situation somewhat by specifying multiple hypotheses about the impact of opportunities on social movement change. And several other studies (e.g., Amenta et al., 1992, 1994; Burstein, 1985; Burstein and Freudenberg, 1978; Cress and Snow, 2000; Jenkins and Perrow, 1977; McAdam and Su, 2002) have used systematic comparisons and multivariate techniques to show that both resources and opportunities are central to movement outcomes.

Second, much of this work has neglected subjective and cultural aspects of movements and has taken a narrow view of formal political processes. Opportunities and resources are often defined in terms of external objective situations that movement leaders activists may not perceive. That is, researchers have assumed that testing actions are ubiquitous and persistent in "everyday resistance" (Scott, 1991) and that activists will eventually discover the opportunities and resources. This may or may not be the case because cultural biases and information gaps may result in missed opportunities (Sawyers and Meyer, 1999) as well as overestimates of resources and opportunities. As our movement/society framework makes clear, bringing a broad range of processes to bear on movements is vital: changes in public opinion, the perceptions and practices of the protestors themselves, and their interactions with other institutions, such as the mass media, religious, and educational institutions. Finally, the theories share a rationalist bias in conceptualizing interests as given, fixed, and unproblematic. This has led to simplifying the process of collective decision making as nothing more than aggregated individual decision making (Ferree, 1992; Fireman and Gamson, 1979; Melucci, 1989). In response to these concerns, new interactionist arguments have been offered about the framing of grievances and the construction of collective identities.

Newer Symbolic Interactionism: Framing, Identity, and Ideology

The core framing argument (Snow and Benford, 1988; Snow, Rochford, Worden, and Benford, 1986) is that movement leaders and participants construct collective definitions of their immediate environment. They externalize blame by attributing grievances to the mutable policies and practices of institutional elites, and they propose concrete social changes to alleviate these problems. Cress and Snow (2000) showed that the framing activities by advocates for the homeless contributed to favorable city policies net of organization, opportunities, and protest tactics. Voss (1996) argued that limitations in the "working class republican" frame offered by the elites of the nineteenth-century Knights of Labor contributed to movement's collapse in the face of strike defeats. The framing limitations included opposition to state intervention (which could have countered employer organization and repression), overestimates of worker/middle-class alliances, and absence of "fortifying myths" (i.e., beliefs about the inevitability of success) to sustain member mobilization in the face of defeats. Although employer repression and organizational weakness were likely more critical factors in the union's collapse, these were intertwined with and reinforced by framing failures.

Framing contests need to be analyzed in the context of our movement/society framework (Figure 16.1). Movements, countermovements, the mass media, other third parties, and the state are constantly involved in competitive battles over the framing of grievances, issues, and the repackaging of cultural outlooks to get issues on the political agenda and to advance pet proposals (McCarthy, 1996). By honing news routines, "pegs," and other framing devices, and by adapting to them to issue-attention cycles, movements more likely gain media attention and thereby get their issues on the political agenda and influence public policy. This explains why professional public relations companies and political consultants who market political campaigns are often mimicked by SMOs involved in institutional advocacy (Berry, 1997).

Frames must be considered in conjunction with strategies and tactics. Analyzing the civil rights protests in the 1950s and 1960s, McAdam (1996b) argued that Martin Luther King's "radical reformist" frame worked to evoke predictable responses from five major audiences. It simultaneously provoked white segregationists (including local police and officials) into extreme racist violence which, in turn, mobilized sympathizers of the movement to nonviolent demonstrations. Both received sympathetic media coverage that outraged the general public, thereby compelling a reluctant federal government to intervene favorably. Effective frame management links grievance definitions and collective identities to specific tactics and strategies that target several audiences that may have discrepant views.

Resource mobilization theory's largest problem is its failure to deal with collective identity and ideology. Although some researchers have advanced cultural interpretations of collective identity while treating beliefs as arising simply from the minds of movement actors (Eyerman and Jamison, 1991), a more fruitful approach examines political interactions to identify how collective identities are constructed and reconstructed. The identities are not phenomenologically given. They are socially constructed out of interactions among movement leaders, potential supporters, targets, countermovements, the media, and political authorities. A major focus of in the production of collective claims is constructing collective identities for both actors and their targets, typically framed in dyadic "we/them" terms. Another focus refits existing cultural materials that emerge out of interactions with other actors in the larger sociopolitical environment (Figure 16.1). Although new identities and solidarities often emerge during contentious episodes (Fantasia, 1988), most of them are informally constructed in loosely integrated small networks of "critical communities" (Rochon, 1998) composed of informal leaders and organizers who debate grievance frames and collective identities, which they then test out in their recruiting and publicity. A leadership cadre with the ability to modify frames and collective identities helps in gaining immediate movement goals and perhaps eventually bring about social change.

Collective identities are enacted and maintained through identification rituals that provide movement activists positive self-identifications while attributing negative labels to opponents, dominant groups, and outsiders who seek to denigrate the movement (Taylor and Whittier, 1995). These identities also provide activists with a sense of movement history and continuity, thereby sustaining mobilization during periods of latency (Della Porta and Diani, 1999:89). At the same time, identities define political boundaries between supporters and others, thereby generating trust among movement actors. Marwell and Oliver (1993) demonstrate how collective identity is critical for addressing "free-rider" problems by generating a "critical mass."

It is nearly impossible to assess the independent impact of collective identity on movement outcomes because collective identity is interdependent with and inseparable from collective action. More difficult is the assessment of identity effects on social movement change. Yet some scholars have attributed identity effects on such life course outcomes as career choice, sustained movement involvement, and marital stability (Fendrich, 1993; McAdam, 1988). Importantly, tactics, identities, and frames of some social movements may spill over onto other movements and countermovements (Meyer and Staggenborg, 1996; Meyer and Whittier, 1993). On a collective level, it is impossible to disentangle the effects of identity construction from collective action because at this level they inseparably and simultaneously constructed. A more effective approach examines the construction of collective identity as a micro process where specific interactions and sequences can be isolated. In sum, the inclusion of collective identity construction and related arguments on the framing of grievances and ideological work are important correctives to an overly rationalistic approach to mobilization.

Because all social movement have their "perceptual frames" and collective identities, the social and cultural effectiveness of the messages that their leaders convey to potential participants affect their identification with and their support of the movement, thereby strengthening its survival and ability to achieve goals. This occurs when movement claims resonate with the traditions, daily experiences, and the social realities of potential supporters and third-party audiences (Babb, 1996). Presumably, when frames and collective identities converge, the probability of movements having an impact on change increases. When anomalies, contradictions, and nonaligned frames and identities appear, movements experience problems of morale, internal factionalism, and strategy disagreements. In short, social movement can bring about change when they develop frames and identities that resonate both with potential supporters and third parties (including the mass media) and when they map an effective strategy to exert leverage against opponents.

The relationship among framing, collective identity, and ideology is debated. Oliver and Johnson (2000) contend that framing and ideology are distinct and that framing is limited to the rhetoric used to conceptualize claims about grievances and social problems. Conversely, ideology provides a broader a map of movement goals, methods, strategies, as well as a collective identity. Snow and Benford (2000) respond that framing is best understood as a central component of ideological work that links grievance claims to broader movement goals as well as to specific strategies and tactics. McAdam (1996b) contends that ideational conceptions of framing are less relevant than analyses that link ideas about grievances and solutions to specific strategies and tactics. Thus, collective identity is an important construct that emerges from this process.

We underscore the irreducible interrelations among ideology, framing, and collective identity. Movements cannot be understood outside of some conception of their goals and understandings (Zald, 2000). As Dalton (1994) shows in his analysis of the West European environmental movements and Brulle (2000) in his analysis of the U.S. one, ideologies are fundamental to strategy and tactical choices as well as the interactions of movements with their societal environments. At the same time, there is the methodological challenge of how to separate objective and subjective aspects. Banaszak (1996) argues that the failure of the Swiss women's suffrage movement to secure women's suffrage earlier (1971 at the Federal level and 1991 in the last cantons) resulted from the movement's commitment to cantonal sovereignty and its refusal to consider pursuing a Federal amendment. Critically, this cultural belief that was shared by the movement, opponents, and bystanders was anchored in the decentralized structure of the Swiss state. A decision to "think outside the institutional box" likely would have spurred significant opposition. In short, analysts need to distinguish between institutional environments, situational resources, and opportunities of movements and their collective perceptions, beliefs, and identities. All of these need to be brought together in a single analysis.

Syntheses

In response to these arguments, several scholars have proposed integrating resource, opportunity/threat, and framing/identity/ideology explanations to account for social movement change (McAdam, McCarthy, and Zald 1988, 1996; McAdam, Tarrow, and Tilly, 2001). They are all needed to tap different aspects of social movements that may affect their outcomes. To be sure, this results in longer and more detailed description. It also requires more effort and imagination to bring together qualitatively different streams of data and a novel methodology that captures the interaction among the three explanations.

Two multivariate strategies have been suggested to bring about this analytic synthesis. Some researchers have used multiple regression and event history methods to assess the relative importance of the factors (Cress and Snow, 2000; McAdam and Su, 2002; Minkoff, 1997). This has the virtue of providing clearer causal inference by identifying the relative importance of various factors. Others have adopted a qualitative-comparative approach by using case studies to identify conjunctural combinations of factors that influence the likelihood of specific outcomes. Still others have used qualitative categorical analysis (Amenta et al., 1992, 1994; Cress and Snow, 2000) and historical comparative analysis (Goodwin, 2002; Wickham-Crowley, 1992). Both qualitative approaches appear to be fruitful, but the former seems to provide better inferential control.

In all approaches, it is critical to underscore the societal embeddedness of social movements. The task of accounting for changes brought about by social movements cannot be addressed without explicitly mapping their external organizational environment and testing the various theories of how social movements and other external factors contribute to the process.

SOCIAL MOVEMENT STRATEGY, TACTICS, AND OUTCOMES

Multiple criteria exist for gauging social movement impact. Most studies have focused on tangible gains linked to policy enactment, but others have dealt with policy implementation and institutional change. A growing literature is focusing on cultural change and everyday life and some attention is being given to broader distributional change. We begin with public policy studies and then address the need for a broader social change agenda.

Goals

Virtually all researchers agree that, at least in democratic polities, social movements that pursue reformist or incremental goals (as opposed to displacement and radical change) are more likely mobilize support (especially third parties) and confront less repression, thus increasing the probability of obtaining tangible gains (Derksen and Gartell, 1993; Gelb and Palley, 1981). This accords with Gamson's (1975[1990]) earlier findings on the advantages of "thinking small." In contrast, Schwartz and Paul (1992) argue that "consensus movements" (i.e., those that pursue moderate goals with broad public support) are less likely to generate significant social change than "conflict movements" aimed at structural change that have the support of determined minorities. However, empirical studies fail to support this argument. Movements with displacement goals that aim to revolutionize society are typically met with repression and hostility. A more effective movement stance is "radical reformism" (i.e., combining moderate goals with militant tactics). In many nondemocratic polities, movements may have no choice but to pursue structural changes, making this debate less relevant.

Tactics

The second component of "radical reformism" is tactics. Are protests and violence effective in the sense that they create disruptions and uncertainties, thereby spurring elites to make concessions? Several have argued that unruliness and violence contribute to tangible gains (Gamson, 1975[1990]; Piven and Cloward, 1977), whereas others point to backlash by third parties (Schumaker, 1975, 1978) and the importance of mobilizing public opinion through persuasive protests (Burstein, 1985; Burstein et al., 1995; Burstein and Linton, 2002). Although several studies have found positive effects of the 1960s urban riots on social welfare spending at the city and national level (Eisinger, 1973; Isaac and Kelly, 1981; Jennings, 1983; Jaynes, 2002), others have found negative effects (Welch 1975) and mixed and no effects (Albritton, 1979; Button, 1978; Feagin and Hahn, 1973; Kelly and Snyder, 1980). Button (1978) argued that the effectiveness of riots varied over time with short-term welfare benefits under Democratic rule, but once the Nixon administration was elected, positive welfare benefits disappeared and were replaced by a dramatic growth in the funding of federal police. This finding fits both the backlash proposition and the argument that disruptiveness has greater impact during the expansion phase of protest cycles (Brockett, 1991) and with favorable political alignments. At the same time, Button (1989) showed that protest and riots had short-term benefits (electing city governments more responsive to African American interests) but thereafter protest had little policy impact. Examining the allocation of city budgets in 1982, Jaynes (2002) showed that earlier levels of nonviolent protest contributed to greater investments in social welfare and housing net of population growth and budgets for core city functions, whereas riots stimulated greater police spending. Some of the effects may have been indirect and mediated through the election of more responsive officials.

One approach argues that unruliness is effective under favorable political opportunities but not in repressive or (perhaps) highly open polities. Thus, the interaction of unruliness with mixed or moderate opportunities produces policy benefits. Several reanalyses of the Gamson data are compatible with this, even though they did not test for the interaction effect of unruliness and mixed opportunities (Frey, Deitz, and Kaloff, 1992; Mirowsky and Ross, 1981; Steedly and Foley, 1979). Goldstone (1980) argues that, once one removes the "displacement" challengers from the Gamson data and focuses only on tangible gains, the sole factor influencing benefits is a crisis period. During crises, the direct antagonists are more vulnerable, whereas the likelihood of favorable allies and elite neutrality is greater. This finding resembles our "moderate opportunity context" argument and suggests that the strategy of unruliness and related factors is irrelevant. Yet, it is possible that unruly tactics are more effective in a context of moderate opportunity.

Another critical factor is public opinion. Lipsky's (1970) framework for discussing protest as a resource focused on media coverage and public opinion. Protest creates pressure on elites by mobilizing public opinion and sensitizing elites to it, thereby placing the issue on the political agenda. Lohmann (1993:319) advanced a "signaling" model in which elected officials use mass political activity to gauge the preferences of the electorate. Protest and unruliness can serve as information signals to policy makers, suggesting that vocal opinions may spread to others. Burstein and Freudenberg (1978) found that anti-Vietnam war protests stimulated congressional roll-calls on war issues up through 1970, but thereafter the mounting "costs" (battle fatalities and rising financial costs) of the war became central and protest had no effect. This suggests that protests had an agenda effect but no effect on policy enactment. Similarly, in a study of congressional floor motions on equal employment legislation, Burstein (1985) found that civil rights protest had no direct impact on policy enactment, but it did heighten the salience of the issue for the public and elites, thereby helping to get the issue on the political agenda.

A more complex argument focuses on the victimization of protestors by authorities and countermovements. In the southern civil rights movement, violence by police and white supremacists against "radical reformers" stimulated a favorable shift in public opinion that put civil rights legislation on the political agenda and pressured federal officials to overturn Jim Crow (Garrow, 1978; McAdam, 1999[1982]). Where police were restrained, protests were blunted and had little effect on public opinion and policy (Barkan, 1984). A final argument is Morris's (1993) thesis that mass disruption, not public opinion or third-party pressure, was critical to the desegregation and voting rights gains in the Birmingham civil rights campaign. This was, however, a single critical battle in a complex campaign and may not be generalizable to the overall process of overturning Jim Crow racism.

A key omission in this debate is the failure to distinguish forms of protest. It takes three major forms (1) conventional (i.e., legal demonstrations, marches, and petitions), (2) civil disobedience (i.e., sit-ins and occupying buildings), and (3) violence (Jenkins and Wallace, 1996; Tarrow, 1998:94–100). Most research focuses on conventional or on undifferentiated "protests," whereas much of the debates focuses on unruliness (i.e., civil disobedience) and violence. Schumaker (1978) offers the novel argument that violence and conventional protest are more effective, whereas civil disobedience, which lies in between in terms of militancy, is least effective. In contrast, Tarrow (1998:chapter 6) argues that civil disobedience is more effective because it creates uncertainty in the eyes of targets (e.g., authorities), whereas violence reduces uncertainty by polarizing conflicts and forcing other parties to choose sides. Violence often legitimize official repression and discourages third-party alliances. Thus, civil disobedience should be more effective, especially in the context of favorable political opportunities. In contrast, conventional protest lacks uncertainly because protest tactics increasing receive popular support (Meyer and Tarrow, 1998). Conventional protests often draw larger support and they often serve as "signals" to authorities that movement are gaining broad public opinion support.

To evaluate these various claims of protest effects, multivariate analysis is needed to capture all the major political processes involved. The most exhaustive test to date is McAdam and Su's (2002) analysis of protest effects on (1) congressional roll-calls and (2) propeace votes during the Vietnam war. They found quite different processes behind these two types of policy change. For the first, police violence against protestors and larger protests promoted roll-calls net of controls for antiwar public opinion and other "cost" factors. This supports the "functional victimization" and "signaling" theories and their importance for getting issues on the political agenda. But policy enactment (i.e., propeace votes) appears to have been driven by violent protests and smaller demonstrations. Antiwar public opinion was only weakly relevant. Signaling, as conventionally understood, did not hold; in fact, large demonstrations worked *against* propeace votes.

This suggests that large protests that use conventional tactics contribute to getting issues on the political agenda and that unruly protests (i.e., small violent protests) are central to policy enactment. Police violence against moderate protestors also promotes agenda access, but it reduces policy enactment. These results are net of controls for war costs (conscription and military deaths) as well as the number of conscientious objectors (another mobilization measure) and news coverage. Omitted was the fiscal cost of the war that Burstein and Freudenberg (1978) found was critical after 1970. The number of protests was also negatively related to antiwar shifts in public opinion, which suggests a popular backlash to the protests. Yet, violent protests had mildly positive effects, indicating that the intense demands associated with unruly protests did produce an antiwar shift in public opinion. At the same time, antiwar public opinion was positively related only to congressional attention to the issue (agenda setting), but it was unrelated (or weakly so) to the direction of congressional voting (policy enactment). Overall, these findings suggest that conventional protests had an agenda-setting impact on congressional action but unruly protests produced favorable changes in both public opinion and policy enactment.

Confronting this finding presents social movements strategists with a strategic dilemma: "To be maximally effective, movements must be *disruptive/threatening*, while nonetheless appearing to conform to a democratic politics of *persuasion*" (McAdam and Su, 2002:718). The early civil rights movement was able to balance this "disruptive/persuasion" dilemma with a stance of radical reformism, but the anti-Vietnam war movement did not. It splintered into "radical radicals" and more moderate conventional protestors. A similar split developed in the African American movement during the late 1960s. Rising urban riots and black nationalism led to diminishing policy impacts (McAdam, 1999[1982]:chapter 8; Meier and Rudwick, 1973). However, by this time the major policy gains of the civil rights movement had already been initiated, possibly accounting for the different political legacies of the two movements. The civil rights movement sustained itself through the present with significant African American and general popular support. The anti-Vietnam war movement, despite helping to halt the war, left little organizational or cultural legacy and had only a marginal policy legacy.

Other studies have examined whether protest effects depend on favorable public opinion. Costain (1992:132–5, 150–5) used structural equations to show that rising women's movement activities, interacting with favorable public opinion toward a female presidential candidate, resulted in the enactment of favorable women's policies. In a related study, Costain and Maksotoric (1994) showed that favorable media attention mediated the effects of movement actions to keep women's issues on the political agenda. Others, however, found that protests had direct effects on policy enactment. Santoro (2002) reported that the early civil rights protests served as "dramatic events" that, independent of public opinion, increased favorable federal civil rights policies, whereas later (post–1965) protests had less dramatic effects. Their impact was mediated by favorable public opinion.

Another option for social movement activists is to combine protests with insider tactics. In their study of city policies, Browning, Marshall, and Tabb (1984) showed that minority protests alone had little policy impact, but they did when they were combined with electoral mobilization strategies. Silverstein (1996) reported that the "double-barreled" threat of protests with high-profile litigation with heavy media coverage of animal rights campaigns, combined to force research labs and companies to alter their policies on animal experimentation. Apparently, the same formula extends to public policies. In a study of successful funding of a local Community Action Program in Mississippi in the 1960s, Andrews (2001) showed the effectiveness of combining strong protests by NAACP chapters with electoral support for the Mississippi Freedom Democratic Party. Local activists used a combination of lobbying and protests to promote CAP funding.

Other studies have also examined the interaction of protest and political opportunities. Jenkins and Perrow (1977) and Jenkins (1985) found that political allies with neutral or supportive elites enabled farm worker protests and strikes to be effective, thereby securing tangible gains in unionization. Likewise, the enactment of the major civil rights bills during the 1960s depended on partisan competition for the votes of Blacks and middle-class White liberals. These contributed to governmental neutrality and support along with tactical innovations by the movement and patronage from liberal foundations and advocacy organizations (McAdam, 1999[1982]). Similarly, Eisinger (1973) and Button (1989) found that mayor/ward forms of city governments created more favorable policies when Black protests were combined with electoral efforts. Amenta et al. (1992) argued that political opportunities provided by reformed political parties, strong legal protections of voting rights, and strong policy capacities of states contributed to Townsend movement influence on state old-age pensions during the New Deal. The authors labeled this process, the "political mediation model." Similarly, McCammon, Grambly, Campbell, and Mowery (2001) found that state ratification of the 19th amendment on women's suffrage was facilitated by state constitutions that had expanded women's rights and had previously passed legislation that permitted women to vote, as in school elections.

It is important to specify the opportunity context in which radical reformist strategies work best. Irish nationalists in the late 1960s initially modeled their protests on the U.S. civil rights movement, but they failed to rally Protestant workers to their cause. Instead, the latter supported the "unionists" and violent repression of the nonviolent protestors, which eventually led to an underground revolutionary movement by the Irish Republican Army (Maguire, 1993). Similarly, as Ghandi learned in his "Himalayan blunder" in Amritsar in 1919 (Mehda, cited by Tarrow, 1998:109), civil disobedience against a ruthless authoritarian regime may be politically disastrous. Potential support groups lacked sufficient autonomy to serve as effective allies and state repression destroyed the movement. Conversely, political democracy increases the supply of potential political allies, thus improving the probability of successful protesting.

However, even totalitarian regimes with strong incorporative institutions (government sponsored trade unions, professional societies, and sports clubs) may be vulnerable. Elite disagreements on how to deal with structural economic and other problems and widespread unrest may make nonviolent protests sustainable and effective. In East Europe during the late 1980s, elite disagreements over the need for internal reforms eventually led to a legitimacy crisis that fostered a receptive environment for nonviolent protests and a series of "velvet glove" revolutions (Bunce, 1999; Jenkins and Benderliglou, 2003; Oberschall, 1996).

The recognition that social movements operate in multisector fields (Figure 16.1) with different elite strategies, political alliances, and interorganizational networks calls for a more sophisticated analysis of their impact. Traditional analyses have focused on single SMOs dedicated to a single issue, thus limiting the scope of analysis to only the actors involved. But most social movements operate in multiorganizational fields and are involved in more than one issue. Individual activists are also typically involved in multiple issues. As Mueller's (1994) study of the early women's movement found, internal factions and schisms generated new ideologies and tactics that accelerated popular mobilization, political acceptance, and eventual policy victories. Moreover, the different SMOs with their diffuse informal networks make movements less vulnerable to repression (Gerlach and Hine, 1970). Due to "radical flank" effects (Haines, 1984), the agitation of "radical radical" movement actors may make moderate movement leaders more acceptable politically. They will have greater access to political elites and resources and greater influence on the enactment of favorable policies. There may also be spillovers effects of movement activity to other activists. So long as favorable prospects for policy change endure, intramovement rivalries and ideological differences typically are restrained, which allows mobilization and influence to grow (Diani, 1995). Yet, when very aggressive social movements appear to be achieving their goals, they may provoke countermovements (Meyer and Staggenborg, 1996) that interrupt the movement's agenda and blunt its impact on policy. The spiraling of movements and countermovements may result in stasis and no change. Because these processes are embedded in a complex interinstitutional context, the context must be taken into account to understands movement influence.

Together, the studies reviewed above have made a convincing case that social movements do have an impact on the political agenda, the enactment of public policies, and policy implementation. The evidence suggests that similar processes operate in changing social institutions, such as churches, the military, and families (Chaves, 1997; Katzenstein, 1998; Staggenborg, 1998). Finally, social movements may have some effects on the societal distribution of material and social rewards (Eckstein, 1982; Jaynes, 2002). Thus, Jacobs and Helms (2001) found that African American protests spurred changes in federal income tax rates, especially during Democratic presidencies that favored more progressive tax rates.

More studies are needed that address the broad institutional and structural impacts of movements. They will need to introduce multivariate controls and extend the historical period under study. The study of movements within the complex interinstitutional environment that they attempt to change will require a stronger methodology, an issue to which we now turn.

HOW TO STUDY SOCIAL MOVEMENT CHANGE

As stated in the section on a critical distinction must be made between *social movement outcomes* (i.e., the immediate consequences of movements) and *social movement change* (i.e., movement outcomes in a causal sense). Causation requires not only showing a correlation between movements and specific outcomes but also that the movements factor in causing change, net of other change factors. Indirect or mediated effects must also be examined, as well as moderated effects that appear only in specific contexts. Movement outcomes may take the form of acceptance, tangible gains, institutional changes, altered lifestyles, cultural change, as well as the redistribution of resources. When all of these have taken place, the movement may have actually caused change in the structure of social power.

Determining causal social change is a complex challenge (Giugni, 1998, 1999; Earl, 2000). We have stressed that social movement change cannot be explained if the researcher focuses solely or primarily on the movement. Past research has largely followed this "movement-centered" approach (Lofland 1993:346–7) by focusing on specific immediate consequences of movements. Such an approach cannot gauge the consequences relative to social changes already in progress. Nor does it control for the other factors bringing about change. Because movements as processes arise from social conditions, and because their outcomes are shaped by interactions with social institutions and other social processes, the researcher must also examine the sectors of society that have been involved and continue to be involved in the change. In short, as we have stressed, the study of social movement change requires probing the interaction between movements and their societal contexts.

The study of social movements is not for amateurs but for experts who have profound knowledge of the specific sectors of society that impinge on movements. Society is an abstraction. Thus, the expert is one who has concrete and comprehensive knowledge of the specific organizations, bureaus, and institutions involved with the movement under study. Focusing on the movement alone will not yield knowledge of the movement's historical and contemporary institutional environment. The researcher needs prior knowledge of that. For example, a student of the U.S. civil rights movement should know the history of race relations, the main movement organizations, sympathetic organizations that monitor the political and social environment, and organizations involved in advancing or blocking civil rights change. Concretely, this requires, among other things, prior knowledge of the institutional linkages between liberal foundations promoting civil rights change, religious leaders, government agencies involved with civil rights issues, and party ties with issue constituencies. On the opposition side, knowledge is required of the White supremacist countermovement opposing racial change, their political allies in business and labor unions, legal impediments, and local customs and institutions. To be sure, new organizations arise out of the interaction of movements with their immediate environment. Although these new organizations can be easily identified, other connections in the movement's broader institutional environment may be only dimly seen by the amateur. Yet, they may be critical to the eventual outcome of the movement campaign.

The major blind spot of social movement researchers has been the institutional embededness of social movement changes. By focusing solely on the movement, researchers may be able to draw inferences about the motives and behavior of activists, and immediate movement outcomes, but can say little about whether the movement contributes to social change. Movements rarely obtain their ideal goals, but yet they may still have a significant societal impact. Only experts know the interinstitutional environment of movements and the opportunities and constraints it provides. To capture changes beyond immediate movement effects, the researchers must consider the interinstitutional environment of the movement and examine how and if the movement has changed it in any way.

Stryker (1989), for example, showed that lawyers in the National Labor Relations Board promoted the growth of unions despite a hostile White House and independent of efforts of the labor movement. Governmental capacities also regulate the extent to which movement goals can be implemented. Courts, for example, may create movement access, but they have limited enforcement powers that enable movement victories to translate into social change (Handler, 1978).

Studies inspired by political opportunity/threat, political process, and political mediation theories seek to discover the allies and opponents of social movements. These studies can be evaluated and ranked in terms of their thoroughness in documenting the institutional environment in which movements operate. The best are longitudinal multivariate analyses that address the institutional environment within which movements act (e.g., public opinion, the activities of potential allies and opponents, as well as the interactions between movements and their immediate environments). Few studies consider the full set of criteria needed to draw valid inferences about social movement change. Research on social movement outcomes and change need to be cumulative, have an explicit research design, draw formal hypotheses, and rigorously test for the range of the relevant factors.

As in other areas of sociology, social movement research requires multivariate designs with relevant controls, especially for ongoing social changes in the arena under investigation. Only a longitudinal research design can capture the mechanisms, causes, and conditions of changes. Although cross-sectional and inductive studies are useful for developing hypotheses and illustrating them, one cannot infer change from traditional case studies. Sophisticated scaling may be required to measure the changes. Content analysis of documents may be needed to identify framing, changes in norms and laws, the creation of new organizations, and other institutional processes. Valid inference also requires attention to sampling. Many movement scholars are recruited from the movement they study or are research amateurs who support a movement and want to study it. Their easy access to movement personnel and organizations may yield good storytelling, but it discourages careful attention to research design. Although probability sampling may not be feasible in most social movement contexts, the sample that is drawn should have integrity and reasonably represent its universe. Because the relevant arguments on societal processes refer to different levels of aggregation, hierarchical linear modeling (HLM) may be needed to capture embedded processes. Some studies, such as McAdam and Su (2002) and McCammon et al. (2001), have met most of these requirements, but most studies have met only part of them.

Movement investigators must become more dedicated to constructing adequate research designs. Too many studies have been open-ended ethnographies or histories with little theoretical guidance or concern about making valid inference. Without prior consideration of the nature of the sample, the causal processes hypothesized (including an appropriate time duration), appropriate scaling, and analytic methods, a cumulative body of knowledge about social movement change cannot be attained. Lacking these attributes, even the best studies will yield only illustrative hypotheses about social movement outcomes and perhaps crafted stories about social movement heroism and defeats. Although moral story telling is a honorable profession, it is not to be confused with rigorous sociological analysis.

Several scholars have outlined additional methods that would strengthen social movement research (Earl, 2000; Lofland, 1993). We have little to add to their suggestions. Causal analysis and rigorous research design require understanding the societal context within which the movement operates, especially the interinstitutional relations that set the pattern of alliances and opposition that might lead to social movement change. In searching for change, we cannot be limited by the specific goals of the movement or by the immediate outcomes of its efforts, we must also search for the indirect and unintended consequences that flow from movement activities. Although the research findings may be useful to social movement leaders, our central concern it is to improve the quality of the methods and the theory of social movement change.

CONCLUSIONS

Our central message is simple. Social movement researchers need to confront the issue of demonstrating social movement change. This requires going beyond the study of social movement outcomes to look at the broader societal context within which these outcomes occur. If movement scholars fail to respond to this call, they risk being accused of trivial pursuits. Curiously, until recently, this issue has received little attention. Past failure to address this issue may be explained by the fact that many scholars have been personally identified with their favorite movement and neglected good methodological standards. To be sure, to meet them requires overcoming formidable difficulties, theoretical imagination, long-term studies to meet standards of longitudinal design, and multivariate controls that tap external societal factors.

Although social movement research should continue to focus on sustained collective challenges to the social order, these need to be examined in the context of the social system of support and opposition, the networks of interacting movements, other interest groups and political parties, governmental institutions, and other social institutions. It also requires focusing on multiple movement outcomes, including indirect and unintended consequences as well as assessing the contribution to ongoing social change. In addition to public policy change, this includes changes in institutions, culture, and everyday life. As Burstein (1998) points out, this is pure and simple politics, the grist of political sociology. This argues for treating social movements as core to political sociology.

Pursuing this research program risks conclusions that most social movements are marginal to social change. But recent studies strongly support the suggestion that certain features of movements actually move society. We predict that "radical reformism" effectively catalyzes social change, puts issues on the political agenda, moves public opinion and third-party actors to intervene, and prods elites and institutions to adopt changes. Movements may also alter cultural understandings and the organization of everyday life. Some of them are surely secondary agents that accelerate or decelerate the *rate* of social change already occurring in society. Others may initiate and monitor ongoing changes in the daily operations of institutions that respond to changes in their environment. Existing research also suggests that movements play a catalytic role in keeping issues alive and accelerate ongoing processes. They may not be the prime determinants of change (as supporters are prone to assume or wish) but they do contribute to social change by getting issues onto the political agenda, changing public opinion, and sensitizing elites to social problems and public opinion. Social movement effects may accumulate and, in combination with these other social processes, produce significant social changes. Such speculation can only be hardened into firm generalization when researchers construct reliable and empirically based causal models that capture the contribution of all participants in the change process.

What are the implications of these demands for future movement theory and research? Most importantly, the study of movements must be open to ideas from other parts of the discipline. Other subareas of sociology have pioneered most of the theories and methodologies that we have discussed. Resource mobilization theory came out of organization studies, stimulating the field to attend to the collective control over resources and the impact of movement strategies on outcomes. Organizational ecology theory has provided new insights into patterns of organizational structure, and framing theory drew on Erving Goffman's ideas about the social psychology of everyday life to analyze the construction of collective grievances and identities. The study of social movements lies at the intersection of many specialties, especially stratification, political sociology, and complex organizations. We should capitalize on this strategic position and open up dialogues with all these and other specialties. Surely, the production of new knowledge will deepen understanding of how new social movements arise, how public policy is determined, and how institutions get restructured. Obviously, students of social movements need to be more broadly trained than most students in other specialties, and practitioners need to undergo continuous retooling. In this process, although each subfield offers little, they accumulate into a bonanza.

CHAPTER SEVENTEEN

Toward a Political Sociology of the News Media

Michael Schudson and Silvio Waisbord

Sociologists have offered three different, if sometimes overlapping, responses to the question "how does journalism work?" Those who take a macroinstitutional approach argue that the structure of the state and the economic foundation of news organizations account for the process of news making and the content of news. Little can be understood about news, this position asserts, without addressing the political and economic conditions that underlie the workings of news organizations. A second approach stresses that microinstitutional practices and cultures shape how news is gathered, produced, and distributed. Understanding journalism requires an examination of occupational routines in the relations between reporters and their sources as well as a study of professional rules and values in the newsroom. Depending on the specific political and economic context, organizational and occupational demands may constrain journalists' daily job more than advertisers, securities analysts, corporate managers, or general political conditions. A third approach emphasizes the constraining force of broad cultural traditions and symbolic systems. In this view, news is storytelling, a form of cultural expression more than a market commodity or the product of an occupational practice. It is a structured set of genres of public meaning making that comes from and reaches out to enduring myths, narratives, values, and symbols. Journalism selectively taps into the cultural repertoire of societies as shown in journalists' penchant for drama, conflict, rituals of communion, and human interest events.

Macroinstitutional approaches typically, but not inevitably, minimize the role of human agency and imply that structural conditions alone account for most of the features of news content. Microinstitutional approaches stress the power of routines, convention, and social pressures on journalists but generally hold that journalists can resist, sabotage, bend, or challenge these constraints without normally losing their lives or their jobs. Cultural approaches may emphasize either a role for human agency, where individual reporters and editors can select for their own purposes from among a variety of cultural types, myths, and traditions, or they may stress the force of cultural archetypes, holding that journalists will not succeed in getting much notice for a story unless they link it to prevailing (and conservative) myths, archetypes, and narratives.

Our position is that these three approaches are complementary rather than mutually exclusive. Political, economic, social, and cultural dimensions need to be integrated to understand the production and distribution of news and its appropriation by audiences (Garnham, 1990:10). Reductionism, whether in its political-economic, organizational, or culturalist expression, fails to grasp the complexities of journalism. An approach that sees news as free-floating cultural formations needs to be sensitive to specific political and economic structures as well as to the procedures and norms that journalists follow in manufacturing news. By the same token, studies that see journalism as an unmediated reflection of state and market pressures and journalists as stenographers to economic interests miss how much the structures of journalistic work transcend different economic systems and political regimes. They also disregard how much news as a sense-making form is suspended in "webs of meaning" that likewise cut across economic interests and political regimes.

Only an integrated approach can account for changes and continuities in the relationship between journalism and society. An integrated or multidimensional approach is also an antidote to the functionalism that typically underlies reductionism. The idea that specific forms of news are functional to specific socioeconomic and cultural orders does not capture the dynamism and conflict that characterize journalism and societies in general. Yes, much of journalism is repetitive, predictable, and routine, but the press is hardly the mechanical cog that neatly fits or exactly meets the presumed needs of any political, economic, or cultural order. Moreover, functionalist studies conclude what they assume, that is, that journalism is the well-oiled conveyor belt of grand political-economic designs or deep-seated cultural forces. In doing so, they contribute little to understanding conflict and change both in journalism as an institution and in the varieties of news coverage it produces.

How does journalism work in relationship to and as a component of politics? It depends on what one means by politics. One might refer to political culture, to election results and policy outcomes, or to the ways in which the media stand inside political processes as a quasi-governmental institution. With respect to political culture, questions arise about the role of the news media as general tutors of popular attitudes toward politics. Is the press a force that speaks for political parties or is it a force that assumes a critical attitude toward partisanship? Does the press encourage attitudes of respect for law and procedure, government generally, and politicians in particular, or does the press stimulate cynicism about politics and public officials? Does journalism effectively relay information even if it does not change attitudes? Does it condition attitudes without necessarily influencing action or political engagement?

Or one might want to know how journalistic practices affect *election outcomes*, by influencing voters, or *policy outcomes* between elections, by affecting public opinion. (For a brief but authoritative review of the impact of media on public policy, see Paletz, 1998, but note his conclusion that media influence on policy "varies according to the type of issue, stage of process, time frame, and political and media systems" and depends on "what is covered, how often, and how it is framed.") Do the news media, perhaps by virtue of their corporate organization where the press is staunchly commercial, promote support for conservative candidates? Or do the news media, perhaps because of an organizational profit motive or because of a critical and adversarial news culture, stress scandal to the detriment of incumbents of any stripe? Or do the news media have a leftward or rightward political tilt? Do the media set the political agenda for the public? Media scholars for a long time took "agenda setting" to be a leading and powerful mass media influence – the capacity of the press not to tell people "what to think" but "what to think about" in Bernard Cohen's classic formulation (Cohen, 1963). Today, the agenda-setting hypothesis is treated more circumspectly, even by its advocates (Iyengar and Kinder, 1987); agenda-setting effects "are not necessarily powerful, consequential, and universal" (McLeod, Kosicki, and McCleod, 2002:227). In fact, news sources and events in the world the media cover, rather than the choices or slants the media independently and variably produce, account for the largest agenda-setting effects (McLeod et al., 2002:227) and substantial media efforts to define an agenda (like the emphasis of the British press on the European Monetary Union as a campaign issue during the 1997 elections) may have no measurable impact on the public (Norris, Curtice, Sanders, Scammell, and Semetko, 1999).

Or one might recognize that *the news media are a kind of quasi-official institution of government*, that is, an agency that, publicly owned or privately held, has become part of the daily operation of government because government officials are oriented to it and make plans, policies, and strategies in relation to it (Cook, 1998). In this case, how do the news media constitute contemporary governmental operations and, implicitly, how does that make the process of governing different from the past when the media may not have been so central to the governmental process? In many countries, an expanding array of news media outlets as well as increasingly powerful norms of publicity and democratic suspicions of decision making behind closed doors have encouraged a transformation of political styles and strategies that incorporate the press as an element of politicians' everyday work.

It is difficult to know how the media affect politics without recognizing that politics affect the media, too. Different political institutions and different political cultures constrain and contextualize the operations of journalism in different ways. It is also difficult to address the mediapolitics relationship in a general way because what counts as "media," like what counts as "politics," is variable. For the most part, we will assume that the media are newspapers, magazines, television, radio, and Internet organizations run by full-time professionals who identify themselves as journalists, whether or not they are formally trained or licensed as journalists. However, we note the lively discussion about the political influence of entertainment media, where practitioners do not claim to be journalists but do address political questions, and the growing discussion about the role of individual Internet news providers, who may be self-appointed pamphleteers.

A comprehensive review of the debates on questions about "media effects" is beyond our purview here. (For one useful recent review, see McLeod et al., 2002.) Most work in the "media effects" tradition in mass communication studies emphasizes social psychological and cognitive psychological generalizations based overwhelmingly on American research and pays little attention to cross-national differences or institutional or cultural variations in media organizations that might influence results. In any event, this research literature is maddeningly inconclusive. In part, this is because what may be the most important media effects are the least amenable to measurements of opinion change or information acquisition that are normally the dependent variables. If the larger influences of the media are to confer status on particular individuals and institutions, to disseminate the language and orientation for the construction of national and personal identities, and to provide a forum for and a model of reasoned debate in a "public sphere," then the media may have enormous political consequences without their being amenable to standard instruments of measurement (Schudson, 2003).

Moreover, "effects" studies overwhelmingly focus on the influence of the media on general audiences, not the effect of reporting on institutions. For instance, in the United States and increasingly elsewhere, "going public" has become a strategy of choice for politicians when they run for office, shifting their campaign spending to television advertising instead of supporting armies of people to walk precincts. It has also become a favored strategy for governing, with presidents seeking to influence legislation in Congress by rallying public opinion to their side rather than by directly negotiating with legislators (Kernell, 1986). Both European and North American observers insist that as the influence of political parties has receded, the news media have become power brokers or at least the forum in which struggles for power are waged (Mazzoleni and Schulz, 1999; Patterson, 1993:17). Still, the worldwide perception of "mediatization" suggests the kind of political and institutional shift that cannot be measured by attitude surveys or election results.

For our purposes, journalism is the practice of producing and disseminating information about contemporary affairs of general public interest and importance, usually on a regularly scheduled, periodic basis through newspapers, magazines, radio and television, or the Internet. The emphasis on "general" news practices excludes specialized news-gathering services, everything from the information that intelligence agencies gather and disseminate to strictly limited audiences to the tens of thousands of specialized newsletters and magazines for people in particular occupations, churches, or voluntary associations or people who pursue certain hobbies and so forth. We focus almost exclusively on news produced in organizations, such as newspapers, or units of organizations, such as news divisions of television networks, whose primary aim is news production. Other culture-producing organizations, notably entertainment-oriented television, may be important in disseminating news as part of comedy routines. There is indication that increasing numbers of people pick up news from entertainment programming such as, in the United States, "Late Night With David Letterman," "The Tonight Show With Jay Leno," or "Saturday Night Live." These programs, however, do not gather news, are not expected to be authoritative, and do not employ journalists. Nor, regrettably, is there much of a social science literature that examines them. The line that separates "news" programming from "entertainment" programming is surely more blurred than it used to be but, for all of its limitations, we employ it and focus on the "news" side of the distinction.

MACROINSTITUTIONAL APPROACHES TO NEWS

A set of studies has stressed the importance of macroinstitutional structures to understand news organizations, namely how political and economic forces affect the workings of media institutions.

The political economy scholars who have tended to dominate media studies since the 1970s generally hold that corporate ownership and commercial organizations necessarily compromise the democratic promise of public communication. They find either that there is an inherent contradiction between capitalism and democracy (Herman and Chomsky, 1988; McChesney, 1997) or that there is an invariable tendency of unregulated markets toward monopoly that in the marketplace for news reduces a democracy's multitude of perspectives to fewer and fewer voices (Bagdikian, 2000). Major media conglomerates control more and more of the world's media. Other observers note, however, that some countries with relatively critical media have very high concentrations of ownership, even higher than in the United States – as in Swedish broadcasting and Finnish cable television (Picard, 1998:201).

Where the news media are not controlled by corporations, they are generally voices of the state. Dominant media, whether commercial or state-sponsored, typically support political understandings that reinforce the views of political elites. No distinction is normally made between economic and state interests as, in Lenin's well-known formulation, the state is an instrument of the bourgeoisie to promote its interests. Drawing from Karl Marx's theorization of capitalism and neo-Marxist analyses of "the dominant ideology," political economy scholars have argued that the current media order serves highly concentrated corporate interests and reinforces the economic, political, and cultural status quo. This line of work was especially prominent and persuasive in a number of British studies that held that all kinds of media representations – on the BBC or in the British newspapers – expressed and reinforced the ideology of dominant classes and interests (Golding and Murdock, 2000; Miliband, 1973; Murdock, 1982). Media legislation legitimizes and consolidates media concentration. Mindful of not offending advertisers and politicians, corporate media produce bland coverage that simultaneously perpetuates existing power relations and hides conflicts or opposition and alternatives to the dominant system. The result is news coverage tailor-made to the goals of a powerful minority that helps to sustain inequalities in a capitalist system. Regardless of actual conflicts among a diversity of groups and interests in capitalist democracy, the fundamental structure and operations of the media system remain unchanged. This view, prominent in media studies beginning in the 1970s, later ran afoul of critics who doubted the coherence of a dominant ideology (Abercrombie, Hill, and Turner, 1984) and argued that ideologies are in any event "as fraught with contradictions as are any other historical phenomena" (Hallin, 1994:31). Critics denied that the media are effective in reinforcing dominant power structures and argued emphatically in a variety of "audience studies" that the mass audience in general and specific subgroups (notably women) in particular were not easy dupes of media propaganda but exercised choice, agency, and their own interpretive schemes in making sense of media fare (James Curran, 2002, provides a lucid and fair-minded history of these controversies).

Main tenets of this argument, sans the Marxist critique of capitalist media, are also found in the writings of critics of conglomerization, for whom cost-cutting measures and higher profit expectations, which corporations favor and Wall Street adores, eliminate critical, hard-hitting journalism that serves democratic ends. There is a kind of "market censorship" at work that leads media to minimize coverage of policy matters that might impinge directly on their economic interests (Picard, 1998:209). In view of increasingly rigorous, cost-conscious management in newsrooms and the mergers and buyouts in media corporations since the early 1980s, questioning the merits of corporate media is not the exclusive province of leftist critics. Mainstream critics in or close to the news business itself view recent technological and market changes with alarm. When a "new news" responds to corporate concerns and technological imperatives, the ethics of professional journalism seem increasingly under assault (Bagdikian, 2000; Downie and Kaiser, 2002; Fallows, 1996; Kalb, 1998; Roberts, 2000).

Still, free-marketeers and a variety of academic moderates find the anticorporate, things-keep-getting-worse argument analytically unconvincing and empirically wrong. In an era of media mergers, they observe, news has grown no more uniform nor has reporting embarrassing to big business diminished (Graber, 2002:47). Recent policies and technological innovations have made contemporary media markets more open than before (Compaine and Gomery, 2000). The availability of cheaper technologies for producing and distributing news content coupled with the deregulation of media markets has facilitated the entry of new companies. The current post-Fordist, Internet landscape, populated by megacorporations as well as a vast array of medium and small companies, is hardly a bleak, uncompetitive "media monopoly." Business responds to the preferences of audiences, and the result is a "brave new world" of unfettered competition and free expression or at least a loosening up of new communicative possibilities. There is considerable optimism in many quarters that the Internet offers a vast new location for dissent, diversity, and political activism (Jenkins and Thorburn, 2003; McCaughey and Ayers, 2003). Political economists respond by arguing that a multichannel environment may superficially suggest the coming of media choices, but new technologies (such as the Internet) have been swallowed into the corporate order. Markets do not effectively reflect audiences' preferences but rather business interests (McChesney, 2000). Others suggest that growing use of the Internet justifies neither utopian hopefulness nor glum despair that new media will be subjected to corporate control just like old media; instead, actual uses of the new technologies may suggest an acceleration or amplification of group-centered, pluralistic politics. As Bruce Bimber has argued, the new media may lead pluralism to "take on a fragmented and unstable character, through the rapid organization of issue publics for the duration of a lobbying effort, followed by their dissolution" (Bimber, 1998:156).

From a viewpoint that stresses the importance of political competition and conflict in developed democracies comes a different charge against political economic pessimism. Because the latter typically holds a rigid view of how powerful elites control news, they are insensitive to change and variation in news. An influential work in a political economy tradition, Edward S. Herman's and Noam Chomsky's *Manufacturing Consent* (1988), holds that the media "serve to mobilize support for the special interests that dominate the state and private activity" (1988:xi) and that the propagandistic role of the American press is not in any essential way different from the role *Pravda* played in the Soviet Union. Of course, the U.S. press as a whole is hardly antibusiness, or anti–law-and-order, or pro–gun control or strongly in favor of government environmental regulations over corporate prerogatives. However, sometimes it offers extensive critical coverage of greedy laboratories, corporate polluters, trigger-happy police, homophobic thugs, racist officials, domestic abusers, and pedophilic priests. It also provides criticism of the high salary levels of corporate executives, price gouging in the energy business, crude corporate grabs for tax breaks, and accounting industry collusion with the businesses they are supposed to assess. Nor is there evidence that such reporting has declined as corporate mergers have increased (Graber, 2000). One cannot approach journalism as a one-dimensional institution that obsequiously and inescapably collaborates in the maintenance of social order.

Still, it seems fair to conclude that the mainstream news media are generally establishment institutions and that even where they have relative autonomy from government control, either by commercial organization or arm's-length public ownership, they are willingly intertwined with the purposes and practices of government. "In sum," writes media scholar Gianpietro Mazzoleni, "the news media tend to take the side of the defenders of the status quo" (2003:11). Within this generalization are many variations of consequence for politics. Are the media more or less open to dissident voices and challenging perspectives? The general answer is that it depends less on the character of the media than on the degree of consensus in the political establishment. When political elites are relatively united, the media typically reproduce and reinforce their views. Where elites are sharply divided, the media reproduce and amplify the divisions. As Daniel Hallin puts it in his study of American news coverage of the Vietnam war, in a time of consensus the media are "consensus-maintaining institutions," but when consensus breaks down, they contribute to "an accelerating expansion of the bounds of political debate" (Hallin, 1994:55; see also Bennett, 1990).

Are the news media more or less engaged in reporting on politics in the first place? There is evidence that as commercial incentives in news institutions overtake professional commitments, political coverage declines. Conversely, some kinds of nonestablishment politics, like right-wing neopopulist movements, have been adopted and covered more by tabloid or popular media and radio talk shows than by establishment media – that is, media with more purely commercial incentives and less allegiance to the political establishment (Mazzoleni, Stewart, and Horsfield, 2003). The popular appeal of extreme rhetoric and personality-centered politics makes for symbiosis between neopopulist movements, commercial incentives, and what a study of news coverage of right-wing movements in Austria calls "newsroom populism" (Plasser and Ulram, 2003).

These complications and contradictions suggest that the claim that the press generally reinforce established power needs much greater precision and careful study in different political-economic contexts. For instance, outside of the United States and other developed democracies with large advertising and consumer markets, the balance between business and political forces is different. Applied to non-Western contexts, assumptions about the dangers of commercial media underestimate the state's role in media operations whether in authoritarian or liberal democratic regimes. In most Third World countries, the state has been the largest advertiser, partially due to the fact that governments have owned large and key businesses in the context of protected, inward-looking economies. Even as some economies have experienced a transition to the market since the early 1980s, government officials are still able to control resources that affect media economies and, despite privatization, remain in control of large advertising budgets. They dole out resources to lapdog media and punish critical news organizations through a variety of means (cutting advertising, inspecting accounting books, verbal and physical violence, favoritism in the allocation of state-owned bank loans). In fact, "too little market" has been responsible in some contexts for why states have had the upper hand in media dealings, particularly when controlled by military regimes or civilians oligarchies characterized by nepotism and corruption. State paternalism in media policies in the Middle East (Sreberny, 2000), clientelistic networks and practices (Hallin and Papathanassopoulos, 2002) or state depotism in many African media systems (Ette, 2000; Tettey, 2001) attest to the fact that states, not markets, continue to be the main opponents of media diversity.

Against this backdrop, it is not surprising that some studies (even those critical of the problems of market-dominated media) have concluded that the expansion of the market economy in some media systems has positive effects. In the case of Zimbabwe, Helge Ronning and Tawana Kupe argue that "the market can further media diversity, particularly . . . foreign media capital . . . provides the impetus for great media pluralism" (2000:171). In Latin America, large news organizations have investigated government officials in ways that state-dependent news organizations could not, partially because they attract substantial business advertising.

This does not mean that foreign capital is the key to a free press. In many Central American countries, the entrance of foreign capital (mainly, Mexican media barons) intensified the closeness between media organizations and dominant political powers (Rockwell and Janus, 2001). Nor does it mean that market-based media do not limit expressive freedom. Unchecked commercialism and growing conglomerization of newspaper and broadcast markets strongly limit the capacity of newsrooms to cast a wide net and cover issues fairly (Fox and Waisbord, 2002). Still, in state-dominated media systems, business-oriented media often usher in new possibilities. The strengthening of media organizations that are economically less dependent on the state introduces the possibility that some might take partial distance from government officials.

The analytical problem is that, particularly in underdeveloped countries, market and state interests are entangled in complex ways that are not captured by pure models of either market competition or state domination. This is the conclusion of a number of recent studies in regions and countries as diverse as China (Bin, 1999), Western Europe (Mancini, 2001; Papathanassopoulos, 2001), and Latin America (Jones, 2001; Waisbord, 2000). Contemporary media systems are experiencing a transition between partisan or state control and market control. In postcommunist Russia, too, business tycoons, politicians, and media personnel have struggled over power and jockeyed for position (Downing, 1996; Sparks and Reading, 1998). A similar case is post–Tiananmen Square China as Yuzhei Zhao (1998) demonstrates. Despite the tightening of party control after Tiananmen Square, there has also been a rapid commercialization of the popular press and a proliferation of sensational, entertainment-oriented tabloids that compete with the established press for advertising revenues. The audience for commercial media has grown rapidly at the expense of traditional party organs. Media outlets in the "commercial" sector still cater to the party's propaganda needs, but they try to "establish a common ground between the Party and the people" through covering popular topics (Zhao, 1998:161). The state continues to closely monitor political news, but with economic, social, and environmental issues the commercial press operates with relatively little constraint. In response to commercial competition, even Central China Television, the most influential station in the country, has tried new news formats that test the limits of orthodoxy to please the public.

Both state and market limit media content, but this does not make the comprehensiveness and severity of means, the coherence of motives involved, or the consequences of controls enacted just the same. Public criticism of state policy is invariably easier in liberal societies with privately owned news outlets than in authoritarian societies with either state or private ownership. The situation of the media in the Middle East and most African countries has been described in similar ways: watchdog journalism or any form of critical reporting faces an uphill battle when states directly control media outlets or influence coverage through a variety of formal and informal means (Downing, 1996; Koltsova, 2001; Tettey, 2001).

The distinction between "market" and "state" organization of media, or between commercial and public forms of broadcasting, masks important differences within each category. For example, in the United States, the First Amendment tradition inhibits government intervention in the news media more severely than in European democracies. In Norway, Sweden, France, and Austria, governments for several decades have subsidized newspapers directly, especially to strengthen newspapers that offer substantial political information but receive little advertising revenue. These policies have sought to stop the decline in the number of newspapers and so to increase public access to a diversity of political viewpoints. There is no indication that the subsidized newspapers are more likely to withhold criticism of the government than other newspapers; in fact, one Norwegian study indicates just the opposite (Morschetz, 1998; Skogerbo, 1997).

MICROINSTITUTIONAL APPROACHES TO NEWSWORK

News organizations may be constrained by political and economic structures of ownership and control, but daily reporting follows specific rules that define the practice of journalism even across different structures. News is not determined only by macroinstitutional conditions, but is the product of bureaucratic and occupational routines and rules. In fact, the definitions of news and the norms of professional journalistic practice are surprisingly similar across widely varying political-economic conditions for media operations. Even if powerful commercial or state interests have the upper hand in newsmaking, they do not operate in conditions of their own choosing. In particular, they must accommodate local constraints of the news-gathering and news-writing process.

A microinstitutional or social organizational perspective holds that news is less a report on a factual world than "a depletable consumer product that must be made fresh daily," as sociologist Gaye Tuchman put it (Tuchman, 1978:179). It is not a gathering of facts that already exist; indeed, as Tuchman has argued, facts are defined organizationally – facts are "pertinent information gathered by professionally validated methods specifying the relationship between what is known and how it is known... In news, verification of facts is both a political and a professional accomplishment" (1978:82–3).

One of the consistent findings in the sociology of the media is that in many media systems, including liberal Western democracies, government officials exercise considerable power in newsmaking and in the construction of reality. Whether at the national or local level, daily journalism is about the interaction of reporters and government officials, both politicians and bureaucrats. The center of news generation is the link between reporter and official, the interaction of the representatives of news bureaucracies and government bureaucracies. "News," as Leon Sigal put it, "is not what happens, but what someone says has happened or will happen" (Sigal, 1986:25).

The "someone" is usually a government official, whether a police officer or a politician. Government officials are informed. Their information is judged to be authoritative and their opinions legitimate. And they are eager to satisfy the cravings of the news organizations. They make information available on a regular basis in a form that the media can easily digest. As a Brazilian editor remarked, "All of us have been educated professionally according to the idea that the government is the main source of information, that everything that happens with it is important.... That's the journalistic law of the least effort. It's faster and easier to practice journalism based in the world of government than putting emphasis on what's happening in society" (Waisbord, 2000:95). Studies of media that see the process of news production beginning in the newsroom – rather than in the halls of power are too "media-centric" (Schlesinger, 1990). Sources matter.

Among government sources, routine government sources matter most. That is, most news comes to the news media through ordinary, scheduled government-initiated events like press releases, public speeches, public legislative hearings or deliberations, press conferences, and background briefings for the press. In some countries, reporter-official relations are especially routinized. The most famous case is that of the Japanese Kisha clubs. These clubs of reporters, which date to the early twentieth century, are maintained by the news organizations that provide their membership. They are formal associations of reporters from different media outlets assigned to a particular ministry and granted privileged – but highly controlled – access to the minister and other high officials. Because most clubs are connected to government agencies, news takes on an official cast. The daily association of reporters at the clubs contributes to a uniformity in the news pages; reporters are driven by what is described as a "phobia" about not writing what all the other reporters write (Feldman, 1993; Freeman, 2000; Krauss, 2000).

At the other extreme, consider Dutch foreign affairs journalists.

> They do not pound the halls and knock on doors in the Foreign Ministry, as American journalists do. Rather, they work for the most part at home, reading, thinking, perhaps phoning an officials whom they know, writing if the muse visits, and not writing if she does not. Since their output is personal and thus explicitly subjective, there is little basis among them for the competitive spirit that animates American coverage of foreign-affairs news and that results in a convergence of judgment of what that "news" is. (Cohen, 1995)

These correspondents are remarkably independent; they do not have much interaction with one another, do not generally know one another, and are generally ignorant of or indifferent to the work styles of their nominal peers.

Reliance on government officials does not guarantee progovernment news. Official wrongdoing is itself a form of government news and, as such, is more likely than other forms of wrongdoing to become the subject of journalistic investigations (Waisbord, 2000:94). It is difficult to muckrake the government without the government's cooperation. Journalists may have rumors, leads, leaks, or near-certain knowledge of a government misdeed, but normally they cannot go to print or air within the conventions of the craft without getting confirmation from a well-placed figure. Whether sources in the government are officials seeking to promote the government's position or other officials lobbying for alternative positions within the government and therefore seeking to discredit their superiors, sources use the press to their own advantage. In Latin American journalism, the practice of one insider using the press to spread scandal about another insider even has a name – *denuncismo.* From the reporter's perspective, this is quick and dirty journalism; from the source's perspective, it is a form of ventriloquism by which they dictate the news and advance their own interests through a reporter (Waisbord, 2000:108).

The capacity of journalists to write critically about government even when government is the primary source of information has grown in recent decades as government institutions become more open to public surveillance and more decentralized and democratic in operation, as the news media adopt a more professional and critical style, and as commercial incentives to produce shock and scandal overtake interpersonal pressures for collegial and congenial reporting. In the United States, campaign coverage of both Democratic and Republican contenders in newspapers, news magazines, and television grew significantly more negative in the 1980s and 1990s than it had been in 1960 (Patterson, 1993). In Britain, journalists conducting television news interviews were originally very deferential to politicians but in the 1960s and 1970s became more and more adversarial (Clayman and Heritage, 2002:55). A more alert, professional, cynical, and competitive press corps, observed in many countries around the world, has more eagerly sought out scandals and more readily taken advantage of accidents that discredit powerful institutions, both public and private (McNair, 2000; Tunstall, 2002). There has been what media scholar Regina Lawrence terms a shift from institution-driven to event-driven news (Lawrence, 2000) – and though this is a shift of degrees rather than a wholesale information of news making, it makes news more invasive and potentially unsettling.

The significance of studies of reporter/source interaction lies not only in detailing the dynamics of news production but in evaluating the power of media institutions as such. Media power looms large if the portrait of the world the media present to audiences stems from the preferences and perceptions of publishers, editors, and reporters unconstrained by democratic controls. However, if the media typically mirror the views and voices of established (and democratically selected) government officials, then the media are more nearly the neutral servants of a democratic order. To note a recent example, policy experts widely attacked American television news for pushing the United States to intervene with military force in Somalia in 1992 by showing graphic scenes of starving people. But the networks picked up the Somalia story only after seven senators, a House committee, the full House, the full Senate, a presidential candidate, and the White House all publicly raised the issue. When the networks got to it, they framed it very much as Washington's political elites had framed it for them (Mermin, 1997:397; see also Livingston and Eachus, 1995). This does not mean the TV stories made no difference; clearly they rallied public support for intervention. The so-called "CNN effect," even if it does not decisively influence a policy outcome, may shape the way policy decisions are made – for example, shortening response time or raising the salience of a particular foreign policy issue (Livingston, 1997). But where did the TV story on Somalia come from? From established, official sources. Similarly, the behavior of the American press in questioning the Vietnam War emerged precisely because official sources themselves were deeply divided. The press went about its normal business of citing official leaders – but at a time when officials were at odds with one another (Hallin, 1986).

There has been concern in the United States and increasingly in Europe that the dependence of journalists on sources has intensified in the past decade as candidates, parties, and officeholders grow more sophisticated in manipulating the news. There is no question that politicians have grown increasingly oriented to communicating with the public through the media. When politics is organized to give greater weight to public opinion, the news media obviously become a greater focus of concern for parties, candidates, and government officials. Campaigns, once dominated by old hands who knew the precinct leaders, has become dominated by media consultants, advertising and public relations specialists, and pollsters. More government bureaus and more government officials hire press secretaries and others to direct their relations with the news media. In the United States, for example, the work of legislation in Congress was once "an inside game" that since the 1960s has become increasingly mediated by publicity. More actors participated, more actions took place in public view, and more legislators were freed from internal hierarchies of legislative committees and individual seniority to behave as policy enterpreneurs (Cook, 1989; Zelizer, 2004). Although political systems generally have grown more media-centered, differences among them remain substantial. German and British politics, for example, remain notably more party-centered than the American media-centered system (Pfetsch, 1998). This is a good example of how politics affects media as much as media affect politics – where there is a presidential rather than a parliamentary political system, and where party organization and party loyalty is stronger, there is not so much of a vacuum for the media to fill.

The efforts of politicians today to control their coverage in the news is an effort to regain their footing in a newly open and uncertain political environment. In the U.S. Congress, for example, the old system – of committee meetings closed to the press, of the avoidance of roll-call votes and floor debates, of a relationship of "overcooperation" between press and politicians – is long gone, and it is no wonder that politicians resort to pollsters, media consultants, and "spin doctors" (Cook, 1989). Media scholar Raymond Kuhn suggests that recent British discussion of the dangers of spin doctoring stems from an effort of journalists themselves to reassert their own power in relation to the politicians they depend on (Kuhn, 2002:66).

The finding that official sources dominate the news is often presented as a criticism of the media. If the media were to fulfill their democratic role, they would offer citizens a wide variety of opinions and perspectives, not just the narrow spectrum represented by those who have attained political power. Herbert Gans issued a call for "multiperspectival news" in his classic *Deciding What's News* (1979) and has renewed that plea in *Democracy and the News* (2003). But there is an alternate view also consistent with democratic theory. What if the best to hope for in a mass democracy is that people evaluate leaders, not policies? What if asking the press to offer enough information, history, and context for attentive citizens to make wise decisions on policies before politicians act is asking the impossible? It may be a more plausible, if more modest, task for the media, consistent with representative democracy, that citizens assess leaders after they have acted (Zaller, 1994).

There has been more attention to reporter/official relations than to reporter/editor relations, despite some suggestive early work on the ways in which reporters engage in self-censorship when they have an eye fixed on pleasing an editor (Breed, 1955). Case studies of newswork regularly note the effects – usually baleful – of editorial intervention (Crouse, 1973:186; Gitlin, 1980:64-5; Hallin, 1986:22; Mortensen and Svendsen, 1980). But most research has focused on reporters' gathering of news rather than on its writing, rewriting, and "play" in the press. Some research suggests that the *play* of a story may matter a lot. Hallin (1986), Herman and Chomsky (1988), and Lipstadt (1986) all argue that in the press of a liberal society such as the United States, lots of news, including dissenting or adversarial information and opinion, gets into the newspaper. The question is *where* that information appears and how it is inflected.

If one line of research emphasizes the power of organizational constraints and professional values in news production, another insists they are no bulwark against a bias in news that emerges from the social backgrounds and personal values of media personnel. S. Robert Lichter, Stanley Rothman, and Linda S. Lichter (1986) made the case that news in the United States has a liberal "bias" because journalists at elite news organizations are themselves liberal. Their survey of these journalists finds that many describe themselves as liberals and tend to vote Democratic. (A 1992 national sample of journalists also finds them more liberal and more Democratic than the adult population as a whole, but not so liberal or Democratic as elite journalists in the Lichter survey. See Weaver and Wilhoit, 1996.)

The Lichter et al. approach has been criticized for failing to show that the news product reflects the personal views of journalists rather than the views of the officials whose positions they are reporting (Gans, 1985). American journalists, more than their European counterparts, are committed to an ideology of objectivity that emphasizes fair representation of the positions of the leading parties to a political dispute and keeping one's own political views from shaping the news account (Donsbach, 1995; Patterson, 1998:22). They are professionally committed to shielding their work from their personal political leanings. Moreover, their political leanings tend to be weak. Several close observers have found leading American journalists not so much liberal or conservative as apolitical (Gans, 1979:184; Hess, 1981:115).

Even so, the imputation of bias stemming from the social background of journalists does not go away. Critics and activists who advocate the hiring of more women and minorities in the newsroom share the intuition that the personal values journalists bring to their jobs color the news they produce. Did hiring practices adopted in the United States in the 1970s and 1980s, designed to develop a newsroom more representative of the population by gender and ethnicity, transform the news product itself? News should have become more oriented to groups often subordinated or victimized in society. Anecdotal evidence (Mills, 1989) suggests that a changing gender composition of the newsroom influenced news content, but other reports suggest that definitions of news have not dramatically changed (Beasley, 1993:129-30). There seems some reason to believe that more minorities and women in the newsroom make the press more responsive to a broader constituency. At the same time, in the United States there has been concern, even consternation, that the growing affluence of national journalists who increasingly report by accessing databases from their computers rather than walking city streets separates them from direct contact with ordinary Americans (Greider, 1992).

CULTURAL APPROACHES

Where a microinstitutional approach finds interactional determinants of news in the relations between people, a cultural perspective finds symbolic determinants of news in the relations between "facts" and symbols. A cultural account of news helps explain generalized images and stereotypes in the news media – of predatory stockbrokers just as much as hard-drinking factory workers – that transcend structures of ownership or patterns of work relations. Journalists write not news items so much as news "stories" and they follow, knowingly or not, conventions of storytelling that dramatize, simplify, and focus on individual character and responsibility (Schudson, 2003). Regardless of differences in the political-economic structure of media systems longitudinally or cross-nationally, what is defined as news across cultures shows remarkable similarities. Journalism taps into the cultural reservoir and imagination of specific societies, but similarities in news coverage of hard and soft news are noticeable. Journalism is a specific cultural form that, as Jean Chalaby argues, was born in nineteenth-century Britain and United States. More recently, however, journalistic cultures across regions have shown a number of similarities in the coverage of tabloid news (Sparks and Tulloch, 2000) and election campaigns (Swanson and Mancini, 1996).

One need not adopt assumptions about universal properties of human nature and human interest (although it would be foolish to dismiss them out of hand) to acknowledge that some aspects of news generation go beyond what sociological analysis of news organizations is normally prepared to handle. Why, for example, are violent crimes so greatly overreported in relation to their actual incidence? The overreporting has been documented not only in the United States (Katz, 1987) but in Britain, where it takes place not only in the popular press but also (to a lesser degree) in the midmarket and quality press (Schlesinger and Tumber, 1994:185). A deep fascination with violence and moral transgression crosses national political cultures.

Although it makes sense to assume that broad and long-lasting phenomena – such as heavy news coverage of crime over two centuries across many societies – will have deep cultural roots, it is also important to recognize fashions, trends, and changes in crime coverage. For example, some newly defined crimes receive only occasional or episodic press coverage and others, with better institutionalized support in a "victim industry," receive more systematic and ongoing treatment (Best, 1999). What is at stake here is the interaction of general cultural and specific social-organizational dimensions of news.

Consider also the role of the media in "moral panics" (Cohen and Young, 1973) in which the media heightens public anxiety and fears by devoting nonstop attention to rare occurrences that are thought to pose terrible dangers and risks to society. Rather than being a true reflection of reality, both the amount and the kind of attention the media devotes to specific fears respond to what journalists consider newsworthy and to issues that resonate with prevailing cultural fears (Glassner, 1999). Several studies have charged the media for recklessly and irresponsibly exaggerating the likelihood of certain events (e.g., specific types of crime, food poisoning) and demonizing certain groups and citizens (e.g., immigrants). It seems likely that the media normally follow prevailing cultural anxieties more than they invent them. When the broader culture changes, so do the media. In the United States and Britain, news coverage of homosexuality, for example, has changed enormously in the past generation, despite a universal cultural anxiety about anomalous social categories, categories of persons or things that disrupt standard cultural classifications. Gays and lesbians appear much more in the news today than fifty years ago and are covered much more "routinely" as ordinary news subjects rather than moral tales (Alwood, 1996; Gross, 2001).

With respect to politics, the "feeding frenzy" is a kind of media stampede rather than a general public neurosis. In the case of President Bill Clinton's affair with a young White House intern, Monica Lewinsky, Washington insiders and the news media were in full stampede while the general public, although titillated, did not find the President's marital infidelities changed their views of his capacity to govern (Zaller, 1999).

The cultural dimension of news concerns its form as well as its content. News is a form of literature. It draws on cultural traditions of narrative. Among the resources journalists work with are the conventions of storytelling, picture making, and sentence construction they inherit from their own cultures, with a number of vital assumptions about the world built in. For instance, television news in the United States typically presents information "thematically," whereas newspapers use an "inverted pyramid" structure that places the most important aspects of a story at the top and relates the rest in descending order of importance. This inverted-pyramid form is a peculiar development of late nineteenth-century American journalism that broke from a conventional chronological reporting and so implicitly authorized the journalist as an expert able to assess "importance" within a set of events. In political coverage, this helped redefine politics itself as a subject appropriately discussed by experts rather than partisans (Schudson, 1982).

Most research on news production takes it for granted that, at least within a given national tradition, there is one common news standard among journalists. This convenient simplification merits critical attention. Reporters who may adhere to norms of "objectivity" in reporting on a political campaign (what media scholar Daniel Hallin calls the "sphere of legitimate controversy") may report gushingly about a topic on which there is broad national consensus (the "sphere of consensus") or may write derisively on a subject that lies beyond the bounds of popular consensus (the "sphere of deviance") (Hallin, 1986:117) it is as if journalists were unconsciously multilingual, code switching from neutral interpreters to guardians of social consensus and back again without missing a beat. After September 11, 2001, television reporters and anchors spoke more quietly and somberly than usual, and moved from a normal to a "sacerdotal" journalism, a journalism of consensus and reassurance rather than of argument and information. Elihu Katz and Daniel Dayan have shown how television journalists in Britain, the United States, Israel, and elsewhere, in moments of high ceremony, such as a royal wedding, or high tragedy, like a state funeral, abandon a matter-of-fact style for "cosmic lyricism" (1992:108). This kind of code switching occurred in Israeli print journalism in covering the martyred Prime Minister Yitzhak Rabin. In life, Rabin was covered critically as journalists took his political moves to be within the sphere of legitimate controversy, but in death, Rabin was absorbed into the sphere of consensus (Peri, 1997).

How the storytelling styles of journalism affect policy debates of election outcomes has not been a topic of research, nor is it clear how it might be. Scholars who focus on narratives in the news and broad cultural influences on them emphasize either that news reproduces existing stereotypes (Entman and Rojecki, 2000; Gilens, 1999) or that journalism's competitive quest for audiences leads it to make use of the most accessible, popular, soap opera, melodramatic story lines or that particular political figures get quickly typecast in ways they are never able to escape – Gerald Ford as clumsy, Bill Clinton as slippery. These features of news are not divorced from the political economy of news or its social organization but would seem to be more easily understood in relation to a society's cultural presuppositions and requirements of the craft of storytelling.

CONCLUSIONS

None of the three perspectives by itself can account for what we might want to know about how journalism works. Take just one important example. There is a shift, reported in a number of studies from around the world, toward reporting styles that are more informal, more intimate, more critical, and more cynically detached or distanced than earlier reporting (McNair, 2000). British television interviewing changed from a style formal and deferential toward politicians to a more aggressive and critical style that makes politicians "answerable to the public through the television news interview" (Scannell, 1989:146). Japanese broadcasting changed in a similar direction under the influence of news anchor Kume Hiroshi, whose "alienated cynicism and critical stance toward society and government" appears to have charmed a younger, more urban, and more alienated generation (Krauss, 1998:686). The Swedish press grew more critical (Djerf-Pierre, 2000). Norway's most popular newspaper, *Verdens Gang*, has adopted the melodramatic framework of tabloid journalism in covering politics. "Politicians in a way become human beings, while the voters become customers" (Eide, 1997:179). New investigative aggressiveness in Latin American journalism may be related. In Brazil, Argentina, and Peru, revelation of government scandals emerges not from old-fashioned partisan journalism but from a new, more entertainment-oriented journalism that adopts stock narratives and a telenovela-style personality-focused moralizing style. Scandal becomes a form of entertainment and may contribute to political cynicism (Waisbord, 1997:201).

Meanwhile, in the tabloid press, talk radio, and elsewhere, unsubstantiated speculation and sometimes even blatant partisanship (particularly right-wing commentary) have become widespread and have even been rationalized (as more democratic, more responsive to popular taste, more free from a culture of deference and stiff respectability). This is especially significant because tabloid journalism has gained a measure of respectability and more than a measure of notice among mainstream journalists (Mazzoleni et al., 2003; Sparks and Tulloch, 2000; Thompson, 2000). Depending on ideological sympathies as well as beliefs about the role of the press in democratic governance, one could find these changes worrisome or encouraging – or both.

Normative judgments aside, how do we account for these changes? Are they linked to modifications in political-economic structures (including patterns of ownership, the coming of new technologies, transformations in political regimes, legal frameworks)? Did they happen because of changes in the process and culture of news making (the relations between reporters and sources, the personnel composition of newsrooms, the rise and consolidation of alternative sources of information, the affirmation of a competitive ethos among journalists)? Or did large cultural trends (post-Vietnam, post-Watergate, post-1960s, postfeminist distrust of authority, redefinition of gender roles, privatism, individualism) affect how news is reported?

All of these shifts are involved. A combination of macro- and microinstitutional developments coupled with broad cultural transformations have produced news that is not a stand-in for political-economic interests nor simply the perpetuation of cultural traditions. Just as some news stories reflect (or fail to question) dominant powers (whether they are defined in terms of class, gender, race, sexuality, geopolitics, culture), other coverage both articulates and interrogates social tensions and struggles.

Journalism is not simply an agent of domination in liberal societies nor of dissent, nor is it a forum that offers equal play to all views or all coherent views or even all views with substantial popular support. The vast universe of news is neither the result of one set of concurrent factors nor is it a standardized, unvarying product. It is the outcome of a messy dynamic that escapes a single logic and it cannot be understood as a neat response to systemic need.

An analytical approach that integrates macro- and microinstitutional factors as well as cultural trends would benefit from taking a historical and comparative perspective. Thinking about the media as political institutions has typically been ahistorical, ignoring possibilities for change in the nature of news. It has rarely been comparative. Comparative research is cumbersome, of course, and it is conceptually bedeviling. How can news be compared across countries when, in one country, the press is primarily national and in the next regional and local? How can comparison be made between the news media in a country where intellectual life is concentrated among a few media outlets in a capital city and another where it is highly dispersed? Media studies are genuinely linked to national political issues – they are an academic meta-discourse on the daily defining of political reality. The motive for research, then, is normally conceived in isolation from comparative concerns. If this strengthens the immediate political relevance of media studies, it weakens their longer-term value as social science. A nuanced understanding of "how journalism works" requires a historically situated, cross-national perspective to grasp the relations among the factors that shape the production of news.

Comparative research may take different forms. There is much to be gained from comparison across countries that share a political and cultural heritage (Waisbord, 2000) or across countries that share a set of liberal democratic institutions (Hallin and Mancini, 2004) or across similar news events in countries with similar press traditions (Pujas, 2002; Mazzoleni et al., 2003). The growth in recent years of comparative studies is encouraging, even though there is today no common paradigm or framework for comparative analysis of the media in political sociology. There is scarcely even a common vocabulary or a common set of intellectual icons (apart from Walter Lippmann, 1921), not even a common professional meeting ground with relevant journals and associations spread across the fields of political science, sociology, journalism, and communication. This domain of work at present is characterized by both a high degree of intellectual incoherence and at the same time a high degree of novel and ambitious exploration.

PART III

THE STATE AND ITS MANIFESTATIONS

CHAPTER EIGHTEEN

State Formation and State Building in Europe

Thomas Ertman

In political sociology, state building is usually understood to mean the process by which states are created and then establish and consolidate their monopoly of legitimate violence over a given territory by constructing a durable administrative, financial, judicial, and military apparatus. Though the first examples of state building in the widest sense may have occurred more than four thousand years ago in the ancient Near East and China, it was post-Roman state building in Western Europe, lasting from about the fifth century A.C.E. until the end of the Napoleonic period, that brought forth the modern state with a modern bureaucratic infrastructure at its heart. As the progenitor of a state form that has since been adopted or imposed on the rest of the globe, the case of European state building is of more than just historical interest. It reveals to those nations in Africa, Asia, and Latin America still grappling with problems of state consolidation the tremendous difficulty of erecting honest, efficient, and legitimate infrastructures while at the same time suggesting a variety of ways in which this may yet be achieved.

Sociologists and political scientists in the English-speaking world took up the task of explaining the process of state building in Western Europe in an intensive way beginning in the 1960's. A new concern to "bring the state back in" to the social sciences inspired a series of field-defining works by Reinhard Bendix, Barrington Moore, Stein Rokkan, Charles Tilly, Michael Mann, Perry Anderson, Immanuel Wallerstein, and others that were themselves inspired by the older writings of Max Weber, Otto Hintze, and Karl Marx. These works of the 1960s, 1970s, and 1980s above all pointed to the centrality of war and preparations for war as the key factor driving forward the expansion and rationalization of state capacities among European polities. In the 1990s a younger generation of scholars such as Brian Downing and Thomas Ertman refined and modified this key insight. More recently, approaches and questions derived from rational choice theory and the cultural turn within the social sciences have injected a renewed intellectual dynamisn into this field and opened up areas for future research.

THE "FOUNDING FATHERS" OF STATE BUILDING THEORY: OTTO HINTZE AND MAX WEBER

Together with his more famous contemporary Max Weber (1864–1920), the unorthodox German historian Otto Hintze (1861–1940) laid the groundwork in his many wide-ranging essays for much recent theorizing about European state building. Himself the son of a minor Prussian local government official, Hintze learned the historian's craft by spending twenty-two years editing a voluminous collection of administrative documents from the reigns of Frederick William I and Frederick the Great before writing the official history of the Hohenzollern dynasty (Hintze, 1915). Yet in addition to this mainstream academic research, which gained him a chair at Berlin University in 1902, Hintze also wrote a series of articles (1902, 1906, 1910, 1913) that sought to account for variations in outcome to the state-building process found across Europe during the eighteenth century. He groups these outcomes into two main categories: absolutist government with bureaucratic administration on the continent and parliamentary government with nonbureaucratic administration through local notables in England. How does Hintze explain these divergent outcomes? The clearest statement of his answer can be found in Hintze (1913:427–8) as follows:

> What then is the cause of this pronounced institutional differentiation? . . . The reason lies above all in the fact that on the continent compelling political imperatives held sway which led to the development of militarism, absolutism and bureaucracy, whereas such pressures were not present in England . . . . It was above all geographic position that had its effects.

Hintze argues in effect that it was military pressure – war itself – but also the threat of war – emanating from neighboring land forces – that drove rulers in medieval and early modern Europe to concentrate power in their own hands by eliminating or emasculating representative bodies and to construct professional bureaucracies to administer standing armies and the infrastructure needed to pay, equip, and provision them. Because England was protected from a direct land threat by the Channel, pressures toward absolutism and bureaucratization were less pronounced, thereby permitting Parliament to survive and eventually share executive power with the Crown. Put another way, Hintze's argument can be reduced to the following proposition: the greater the degree of geographic exposure to which a given medieval or early modern state was subjected, the greater the threat of land warfare, and the greater the threat of land warfare, the more likely an absolutist and bureaucratic outcome to state building.

After 1918, a marked change in Hintze's writings is clearly visible. Whereas before that date about two-thirds of his publications were devoted to Prussian history, this figure falls to only 10 percent during the Weimar period, to be replaced above all by works on state building and constitutional history. Furthermore, the model of European state building found in these works differs in key respects from the war-centered theory summarized above. Three reasons seem responsible for this shift in Hintze's interests away from Prussia and toward an almost exclusive concentration on comparative European political development and especially the development of representative institutions (Ertman, 1999a): his marriage in 1912 to a young academic and former student whose research area was ancien regime France; health problems that forced him by 1920 to give up both teaching and his editorship of the most important publication series on Prussian history; and the collapse of the Hohenzollern monarchy and the advent of democracy to Germany, which altered the intellectual concerns or *Erkenntnisinteresse* motivating his work in the direction of a greater interest in the geneology of parliamentarism as well as absolutism.

The fruits of Hintze's new thinking can be see above all in two articles (1924, 1930) in which he presents an argument to account for variations in medieval and early modern state building that differs in significant ways from that found in the pre-1914 essays. In those works it was principally the degree of threat from land forces resulting from relative geographic exposure that determined whether a given European polity developed in an absolutist or parliamentary direction. Hintze (1930) presents a far more complicated model, however (Ertman, 1999b). Here he claims that a tendency toward absolutism had been present in France, the German states, Naples and Sicily, and Aragon long before the great European conflicts of the sixteenth and seventeenth centuries, which in his earlier writings were presented as the principal reason behind that political outcome. The root cause of this tendency, Hintze goes on to argue, was that in France, Germany, southern Italy and northern Spain, the self-governing counties of the Carolingian period – which in other areas of the continent proved to be an effective barrier against absolutism – had been broken apart during the middle ages by the spread of feudalism. Rulers in these regions won back the authority lost during the feudal period and recentralized power by constructing bureaucratic infrastructures that took over the task of local administration. When these rulers called together representative assemblies during the thirteenth and fourteenth centuries, they could no longer be built around the now-dissolved counties. Instead, delegates were grouped according to their legal status into chambers representing the clergy, nobility, and the burghers of the towns. With the help of their new bureaucracies and the precepts of Roman law they employed, rulers were soon to gain the upper hand in relation to assembles deeply divided along status lines well before large-scale warfare finally engulfed the continent.

In other parts of Western Europe, by contrast – notably England and Scotland, Castile, Scandinavia, and Poland and Hungary – feudalism was either nonexistent or did not affect the pattern of local government. Hence in these areas self-governing counties and towns survived. Thus, when representative assemblies were created there during the central and later middle ages, rulers felt it politically expedient to group delegates from the counties and towns into a separate chamber to complement a first chamber composed of the bishops and members of the higher nobility who made up the monarch's council. Lacking a bureaucratic apparatus, Hintze argues, rulers in these regions on the periphery of Western Europe were ill-equipped to subjugate assemblies whose members fought vigorously to defend the autonomy of local government from which they derived their own political and social power. As Hintze summarizes (1930:139):

> ... [I]n the lands with the older, two-chamber type of assembly, the representative element was able to stand up to and often defeat rulers lacking in strong administrative staffs. Here the path of development clearly favored parliamentarism, just as it had absolutism [in those areas with tricurial, status-based assemblies]. The classic case of the former is England.... Also Poland with its aristocratic parliamentarism, and Hungary as well.

In a point of congruence with his earlier writings, Hintze claims that this tendency toward parliamentarism was further reinforced by the relative geographic isolation and hence lower level of threat from land armies to which those states with two-chamber assemblies were exposed, located as they were far from the Europe's principal battlefields in Germany, Italy, France, and the Low Countries. Though Helmuth Koenigsberger (1977), Thomas Ertman (1997; but see also Ertman, 1999a), and others have criticized Hintze's argument concerning assembly types in some details, it remains a brilliant and far-reaching attempt to account in a parsimonious way for the distribution of absolutist and nonabsolutist states across early modern Europe that too often has been overlooked in the English-speaking state-building literature.

If Otto Hintze concentrated in his later works on uncovering the historical roots of modern political regimes, his contemporary Max Weber devoted much energy to explaining the nature and origins of another product of European state building: modern bureaucracy. For Weber, the most common form of rulership in most times and places, including the medieval and early modern West, is *patrimonial* rulership in which the ruler exercises patriarchal authority over a staff that extends out beyond his or her private household (Weber, 1978:1013). From this perspective, then, the state-building process can be seen above all as a struggle between patrimonial rulers and their staffs over control of the "means of administration" such as rights to and income from offices. In the Near East and Asia, according to Weber, rulers were for the most part able to maintain control over the means of administration thanks to private mercenary armies and theocratic legitimacy and to introduce an "arbitrary" form of patrimonialism, best exemplified by sultanism, in which their personal will reigned supreme. Such oriental rulers often built extensive administrative staffs whose officials they could remove when they pleased, yet such patrimonial infrastructures differed fundamentally from modern bureaucracies because they lacked a rational, hierarchical organization of offices, professional training for officeholders, and established administrative procedures (Weber, 1978:231–2, 1020, 1040–1).

Western Europe, in Weber's view, experienced a very different pattern of development, one in which staffs were able successfully to appropriate the means of administrative from their sovereigns. First, an extreme form of "estate-based" (*staendische*) appropriation, feudalism, engulfed large areas of the West during the early and central Middle Ages. Although rulers successfully restored central authority with the help of newly constructed administrative staffs, the officials manning these staffs soon won strong rights over their offices, up to and including hereditary ownership. As Weber writes (1978:1028): "The typification (*Stereotypierung*) and monopolistic appropriation of the powers of office [in the West] by the incumbents as members of such a legally autonomous sodality created the *estate-type* (*staendischen*) patrimonialism [as opposed to the arbitrary type]." Thus although in Europe, unlike Asia, it was the staff rather than the ruler that gained control over the administration, that administration remained equally patrimonial, characterized by a lack of separation between office and officeholder, a typified rather than rationalized organizational structure and the tendency to exploit the revenues attached to the office for private gain.

Yet unlike rulers in the East, those in the West had by the eve of the French Revolution already begun to transform their patrimonial infrastructures into modern bureaucracies. This decisive step in the emergence of the modern state involved the appropriation of an appropriating officialdom by the ruler and its replacement not, as under sultanism, with an equally patrimonial staff fully beholden to the royal will but rather with a new corps of university-educated officials without rights to their offices organized in a functional hierarchy. Weber compares this monumental process to the separation of peasants and craftsmen from the means of production that ushered in modern capitalism (1946:82) as follows:

> Everywhere [in the West] the development of the modern state is initiated through the action of the prince. He paves the way for the expropriation of the autonomous and "private" bearers of executive power who stand beside him, and of those who in their own right possess the means of administration, warfare, and financial organization, as well as politically usable goods of all sorts. The whole process is a complete parallel to the development of the capitalist enterprise through gradual expropriation of the independent producers.

Weber implies that this transition from patrimonial administration to modern bureaucracy first took place in the early modern West because it was only there that two necessary preconditions of such a transition were met: the presence of centers of professional training in the form of universities and of autonomous cities whose burghers were willing to place their considerable financial resources at the disposal of the crown (Weber, 1978:240–1). Yet even given these favorable backround conditions, European rulers required a very strong incentive to undertake the arduous and politically costly task of replacing patrimonial with rational administrations. Where did this incentive come from? Weber's answer is very similar to that found in the pre-1914 writings of his contemporary, Hintze (1978:972): "In most cases, as mentioned before, the bureaucratic tendency has been promoted by needs arising from the creation of standing armies, determined by power politics, and from the related development of public finances." Hence it was geopolitical competition among Europe's polities that gave rise to the modern state.

Given the similarities that Weber invokes between the emergence of modern capitalism and of modern bureaucracy, it is surprising that he does not explore the possible religious roots of the latter phenomenon but falls back instead on a Hintze-like explanation highlighting the role of war and preparations for war. Ironically, such a religious hypothesis was taken up by none other than Otto Hintze himself in an article published in the *Historische Zeitschrift* (Hintze, 1931). Released after 1920 from all academic and editorial obligations, Hintze was free to read more widely than he had before, and among the fruits of this new freedom were three extended reviews of works by and about the recently deceased Max Weber and one on the writings of Weber's friend and Heidelberg colleague Ernst Troeltsch (Hintze, 1922, 1926, 1927a, 1927b). At about the same time, a collection of documents was published concerning the conversion of the Hohenzollern dynasty to Calvinism in 1613. This occasion provided Hintze with the incentive to investigate whether ascetic Protestantism might not have played the same revolutionary role in the political sphere that Weber had assigned to it in economic life (Ertman, 1999b).

In (1931), Hintze argues that reason of state is the "spirit of modern politics," the perfect pendant to Weber's "spirit of modern capitalism." Just like the latter, it possessed an elective affinity with the worldview of Calvinists, in this case those in the Netherlands and France rather than in the British Isles. The coolly realistic – and highly successful – power politics of the Dutch rebels and of the Huguenot leader Henri de Bourbon (the future king Henri IV) forced their competitors, according to Hintze, to adopt a similar approach to international relations. The ruthless dynamism of reason of state was alien to the conservative, peaceable Lutheranism of many seventeenth century German states. The new spirit was imported into Brandenburg, however, with the conversion of the Elector Johann Sigismund to Calvinism. Henceforth the Netherlands and their anti-Spanish ally, France, would serve as the models that would fire the ambitions of successive Hohenzollern rulers. It was above all, Hintze contends, the ascetic, methodical approach to work of the Great Elector and his grandson, Frederick William I, in both cases directly inspired by a pietistic variant of Calvinism, that would allow them to transform Brandenburg-Prussia from a minor German state into a great power in less then a hundred years.

Hintze's presentation of his broader argument is sketchy – most of "Calvinism" is taken up with a detailed discussion of the circumstances surrounding Johann Sigismund's conversion in 1613 and is of interest primarily to specialists. It was not the author's intention to provide convincing proof of his larger points but rather to revive and deepen, buttressed by the work of Weber, a claim about the possible relationship between Brandenburg-Prussia's special path of development and Calvinism that had once been put forward, to little effect, by Hintze's teacher, Gustav Droysen. How has more recent scholarship judged Hintze's efforts? Although Gerhard Oestreich in a number of articles (1970, 1981; see also Gorski, 2003) has confirmed the extensive exchange of ideas and personnel between Calvinist elites in the Netherlands and Brandenburg-Prussia during the reign of the Great Elector, he has also pointed to the importance of both the neostoicism of Justus Lipsius and of German pietism in shaping the reception of reason of state in Germany and in Europe more generally. The influence of religion and of other secular worldviews on European state building is a topic that remains woefully under-researched in political sociology, and a revival of interest in this area over the past decade (see below) represents one of the most encouraging trends in current research in the field.

THE RENAISSANCE OF STATE BUILDING THEORY IN THE 1960S, 1970S, AND 1980S

As Otto Hintze was composing his late essays in the 1920s and early 1930s, interest in the problem of European state building was already on the wane. That interest would revive again over four decades later among sociologists and political scientists in the English-speaking world and lead to a wave of new state-building literature that has not yet abated. This renaissance in state-building theory can be traced to three sources: first and foremost, a general turn back toward classical social theory, and especially the works of Marx and Weber, in reaction to the behavioralism, pluralism, and structural-functionalism dominant across the social sciences during the 1950s and 1960s; second, the Social Science Research Council's large-scale project on the comparative development of states and nations, which culminated in 1975 with the publication of the agenda-setting volume *The Formation of National States in Western Europe* edited by Charles Tilly, (Tilly, 1975); and finally, the discovery of the writings of Hintze thanks to the appearance of Felix Gilbert's collection *The Historical Essays of Otto Hintze*, also in 1975 (Hintze, 1975).

Significantly, it was a monograph by the Weber scholar and future cotranslator of *Economy and Society*, Reinhard Bendix, that reintroduced the study of European state building to the social science agenda. In his book *Nation-Building and Citizenship*, first published in 1964 and reprinted in an expanded edition in 1977, Bendix rechristens Weber's modern state as the "nation-state" and defines it in contrast to the patrimonial state of medieval and early modern Europe. He writes (1977:128) the following: "The modern nation-state presupposes that this link between governmental authority and inherited privilege in the hands of families of notables is broken . . . [T]he decisive criterion of the Western nation-state is the substantial separation between the social structure and the exercise of judicial and administrative functions." Thus Bendix in this work employs "nation building" principally to refer not to a state-initiated campaign of cultural centralization and standardization, as would Lipset and Rokkan (1968), Eugen Weber (1976), Eric Hobsbawm (1990), or Benedict Anderson (1991) but rather to the extension of a uniform central authority across the entire national territory through the construction of a modern bureaucratic infrastructure to replace patrimonial practices and personnel, a process that would be of fundamental concern to the subsequent state-building literature, just as it had been to Weber and Hintze. Like Weber, Bendix stresses the crucial role played by autonomous urban communes and Protestant sects in laying the groundwork for this breakthrough to the modern state in Western Europe (1977:194–5). Yet he lends even greater weight to the movement from below for equal citizenship, first in the form of equality before the law and then in demands for wider political participation.

Two years after the appearance of Bendix (1964/1977), Barrington Moore published his classic *Social Origins of Dictatorship and Democracy* (Moore, 1966). Though European state building was not the central concern of a book that sought to account for what it termed *three paths to the modern world*, the important role played by absolutist bureaucracies in propelling England and France toward democracy and Germany toward fascism nonetheless stimulated renewed interest in the early modern state. Thus for Moore it was the absolutist state's demand for taxes that led wool-producing English nobles to rent their land to tenant farmers, thereby laying the groundwork for the alliance between commercially oriented noble landlords and the urban bourgeoisie that, according to the author, defeated royal absolutism in the Civil War and set England down the road to capitalist democracy. Similar demands for taxes across the Channel in turn drove wine-growing French nobles to extract ever more revenue, often with the help of royal officials, from their beleaguered peasants. At the same time, the state's practice of selling offices and granting economic privileges to insiders alienated a significant portion of the bourgeoisie that was excluded from the royal bounty. Thus it was the particular (patrimonial) state-building strategy pursued by successive French governments that furthered the alliance between bourgeois outsiders and disadvantaged workers and peasants that was in turn responsible for the Revolution. Even clearer for Moore is the Prussian/German case, where the cooperation between the royal bureaucracy and a militarized aristocracy to maintain labor-repressive agriculture made possible the revolution from above that over the long run created favorable conditions for the triumph of fascism.

In a brilliant 1973 review, Theda Skocpol (1973) acknowledged that Moore attributes more significance to the state than is usual in works influenced by Marx, but she claimed that he ultimately "remains within the Marxist theoretical tradition," a tradition characterized by an inadequate political sociology that prefers "to explain political struggles and structures as functions of class structures and struggles" (Skocpol, 1973:36–7). To build on Moore's achievements and to move beyond him, Skocpol argues, it is necessary to modify his analytic framework to include "the independent roles of state organizations and state elites" (Skocpol, 1973:37) and to move away from an exclusive focus on "intrasocietal structures and practices" (Skocpol, 1973:36) toward one that incorporates the influence of the world economy and international state systems on individual polities.

A year later another major historical-comparative monograph in the Marxist tradition appeared that certainly did not limit itself to intrasocietal structures and practices: the first volume of Immanuel Wallerstein's *The Modern World System* (1974). A central theme of this book is the role that states played in the emergence and reproduction of what Wallerstein calls the "European world economy" beginning in the late fifteenth century. In a chapter entitled "The Absolutist Monarchy and Statism," he argues that "the development of strong states in the core areas of the European world was an essential component of the development of modern capitalism" (Wallerstein, 1974:134). Monarchs in the core were able to strengthen their states, according to Wallerstein, by employing four methods (Wallerstein, 1974:136, 157): bureaucratization through the sale of offices, the monopolization of force through the creation of standing mercenary armies, increased legitimation through the propagation of the doctrine of divine right, and the cultural homogenization of the subject population through the elimination of religious pluralism.

Although all of these mechanisms were undoubtedly employed across the continent from the fifteenth century onwards, the true test of any theory of early modern state building is its ability to account not only for similarities but also for *differences* in state structure found within this single economic and cultural area. Wallerstein contends that the strongest (Wallerstein, 1974:134) and most centralized (Wallerstein, 1974:162) states were found in the European core. Yet as Theda Skocpol has pointed out in her 1977 review of his book, this correlation does not appear to hold water. On the one hand, it would be difficult to classify the nonabsolutist core states England and the Netherlands as either strong or centralized compared to their absolutist neighbors France and Spain, and on the other, military powers Prussia and Sweden clearly were both strong and centralized although they belonged to Europe's semiperiphery rather than its economic core (Skocpol, 1977:64). As Skocpol explicitly mentions (Skocpol, 1977:65), the work of another theorist, Perry Anderson, does a considerably better job of accounting for this pattern of state development.

Anderson's *Passages from Antiquity to Feudalism* and *Lineages of the Absolutist State* (1974a, 1974b) were inspired above all by the works of Marx, but also by those of Weber and of Hintze, with whose writings Anderson had become acquainted in the original. In *Lineages* Anderson seeks to account for three outcomes to the state-building process in the West: a mild form of absolutism found in Western and Southern Europe (France, Spain), a harsher version of absolutism further to the east (Brandenburg-Prussia, Austria, Russia), and a few exceptional cases (England, the Dutch Republic) where absolutism was swept away by a precocious bourgeois revolution.

Anderson traces these divergent outcomes to what he calls the "uneven development of Europe" (1974a:213) rooted in the fact that some parts of the continent (latter-day Britain, France, Iberia, Italy and southern and western Germany) had been part of the western Roman Empire prior to the Middle Ages, whereas others (northern and eastern Germany, eastern Europe, Scandinavia) had not. In the former regions, feudalism emerged independently from a fusion of Roman and Germanic institutions, leaving a landscape characterized in the thirteenth century by parcelized sovereignty, autonomous towns, and serf-based agriculture. In the "colonial" East, however, royal authority was stronger, towns were weaker, and peasants were generally free.

The great economic and social crisis of the fourteenth century decisively deepened the division between Europe's two halves, according to Anderson. In the West, it weakened noble landlords but strengthened the towns and royal authority, thereby paving the way for the triumph of royal absolutism that protected the interests of an ailing aristocracy by creating standing armies that could be used both for foreign conquest and to enforce noble property rights. In England and Holland, however, the bourgeoisie proved strong enough to thwart this absolutist project. In the East, crisis undermined the position of the towns and peasantry rather than the nobility, thereby permitting the latter to introduce a "second serfdom." Meanwhile, rulers in seventeenth century Brandenburg-Prussia, Austria, and Russia were able to take advantage of the military pressure from Sweden to establish highly militarized bureaucratic-absolutist regimes to counter this threat.

Anderson's sweeping study is noteworthy for two reasons. First, it set a high standard for future research on European state building by choosing as his object of study the political development of the entire continent from the Roman Empire until the eve of the French Revolution. Second, although Anderson for the most part employs variations in socioeconomic structure (presence/absence of serfdom, relative strength of bourgeoisie/towns) to account for the contrasting trajectories of Western and Eastern Europe, he also assigns warfare a greater role in his model than one would expect from a neo-Marxist scholar. In so doing, he anticipated the centrality of war and preparations for war in the state-building literature of the 1970s and 1980s. For all of its eloquence and analytic acuity, however, Anderson's study suffers from a number of defects. First and foremost, he cannot explain how the same two factors that led to bureaucratic absolutism in Prussia and Austria – a serf-based economy and an acute security threat from an aggressive neighbor – resulted in nonbureaucratic constitutionalism in Poland and Hungary. Furthermore, it remains unclear why England and the Dutch Republic should have departed from the dominant path of development in Western Europe and installed constitutionalist rather than absolutist regimes.

One year after the appearance of Anderson's two volume study, *The Formation of National States* was published (Tilly, 1975). This work was the penultimate installment in the SSRC's monumental "Studies in Political Development" series, a series that had heretofore primarily focused on the dynamics of political change in the twentieth century outside of Europe and the United States. With this book, attention shifted toward the European past and the lessons it might hold for nations grappling with problems of state formation and state building today. Its most influential contributions proved to be the introduction and a concluding chapter by editor Charles Tilly and a piece by Stein Rokkan (Rokkan, 1975).

Rokkan's chapter was at least his third published version of his "conceptual map of Europe." A fourth was to appear two years after his premature death in 1979 (see Lipset and Rokkan, 1968; Rokkan, 1973, 1981). Precisely what these "maps" aimed to explain was never exactly specified: in some versions it was variations in Western European party systems and in others ease of transition to mass politics or the success or failure of democratic consolidation during the interwar years. In reality, the explicandum was something like the comparative political trajectories of the Western European states during the modern period. Although Rokkan does not specifically set out in his conceptual maps to account for variations in the process of state building in Europe, the framework he lays out there can equally well be applied to this problem.

In his contribution to Tilly (1975), Rokkan posits four "dimensions of variations" that can account for divergent patterns of development across the continent: distance northward from Rome (i.e., from the direct influence of the Catholic Church); distance east or west from the "trade-route belt," an area densely studded with cities running from the Low Countries in the northwest to northern Italy in the southeast; degree of concentration of land ownership; and degree of ethnic and/or linguistic homogeneity (1975:575–6). The underlying puzzle Rokkan is attempting to explain here is why state building, understood as the consolidation of central state power, appears to have been much easier on the periphery of Europe (Britain, Scandinavia) than in the older, more economically developed areas at the heart of the continent that remained highly fragmented until late in the nineteenth century. His answer is that consolidation was hindered by the presence of wealthy, autonomous cities and of the "rival power" of the Catholic Church, both of which had much to lose from successful centralization. At the same time, state consolidation was aided by concentrated landholdings and the existence of a strong ethnic/linguistic "core." As Rokkan says, "Paradoxically the history of Europe is one of center formation at the periphery of a network of strong and independent cities: this explains the great diversity of configurations and the extraordinary tangles of shifting alliances and conflicts" (1975:576).

The most telling criticism of Rokkan's "conceptual map" has come from his fellow contributor Charles Tilly (1981b:118–23; see also 1981a). Rokkan, in Tilly's view, has rendered an accurate understanding of European state building difficult by taking a retrospective view of this process, in other words by looking back into the past from the vantage point of those polities that survived into the late twentieth century rather than looking forward from the early Middle Ages. Furthermore, although he laudably focuses on the choices among various alternatives made by state-building leaders, he underplays the extent to which such choices were constrained and often resulted in unanticipated consequences. Finally, and most importantly, war and preparations for war play almost no role within Rokkan's scheme (Tilly, 1981b:123). Charles Tilly's own writings on European state building, beginning with his introduction and concluding chapter to *The Formation of National States in Western Europe* (1975), seek to correct these deficiencies while at the same time incorporating the unique insights found in Rokkan's work.

Tilly's contributions to the SSRC volume are above all important for the way they frame a bold new question about state formation and state building in Europe and for the preliminary answer they provide. Tilly asks how it was that one particular political form, a centralized, differentiated polity enjoying a monopoly of coercion over a well-defined territory that he calls the "national state" (1975:27) and others have termed the "sovereign, territorial state" (e.g., Ertman, 1997; Spruyt, 1994), defeated its competitors and became the dominant political form in the West and then in the rest of the world as well. For, as Tilly stresses, there certainly were competitors. From the perspective of the central Middle Ages, at least three other kinds of polities could have triumphed in Europe: a single empire, a "theocratic federation" centered on the Church, a trading network – presumably of city-states – without a strong center or a continuation of feudal patterns of rule (1975:26). To understand why the national state won out, we must, Tilly stresses, adopt a *prospective* rather than a retrospective approach, looking forward from a landscape crowded with perhaps five hundred autonomous political entities in 1500 and following their fate rather than beginning with the twenty-five states that survived until 1900 and tracing their origins. This prospective analysis is rendered somewhat easier by the fact that Western Europe around 1500 was characterized by a high degree of cultural homogeneity thanks to the presence of a single Church, a widely used written language (Latin), common legal, administrative and agricultural practices, similar family patterns, and a network of trade links spanning the continent (1975:14–19).

So why then did the national state prove victorious? Tilly's answer is simple and powerful: war. As he states (1975:74): "Preparation for war has been the great state-building activity." Or, in an even more famous formulation (1975:42), "War made the state and the state made war." A decentralized Europe of competing polities was a continent filled with armed conflict, and the national state proved better able to mobilize the resources necessary to fight wars effectively than any of its rivals. It did this by building bureaucratic infrastructures capable of recruiting and supplying armies and of collecting the taxes from an often recalcitrant population needed to finance those armies. A question that Tilly does not seek to answer directly in these pieces but will take up later is how one might account for variations *within* the dominant form of the national state, though he implies that such variations would be affected by, among other things, relative geographic position (isolated or open) and the ease with which resources could be extracted from the population (1975:40).

Tilly's next major contribution to the state-building literature (Tilly, 1985) also appeared in a volume sponsored by the SSRC, the agenda-setting collection *Bringing the State Back In* edited by Peter Evans, Dietrich Rueschemeyer, and Theda Skocpol and published in 1985. In her introduction to that volume, Skocpol invokes

Weber and Hintze's conception of the state as an autonomous actor as an alternative to the society-centered views of politics held by neo-Marxists and neopluralists alike. Her call to take historical cases and data seriously added further dynamism to the field of historical-comparative research initially stimulated by the appearance of Bendix, Moore, Anderson, and Tilly's studies, Gianfranco Poggi's elegant overviews *The Development of the Modern State* (1978) and *The State* (1990), and the world systems theory of Immanuel Wallerstein.

In his short but provocative contribution, Tilly takes up a number of themes touched upon in *Formation*. He repeats the dictum that "War makes states" (1985:170), but here his main argument centers on explaining differences among national states rather than why the latter triumphed over other kinds of polities. Tilly states (1985:172): "Variations in the difficulty of collecting taxes, in the expense of the particular kind of armed forces adopted, in the amount of war making required to hold off competitors, and so on resulted in the principal variations in the forms of European states." He later elaborates on what he means by "variations in the difficulty of collecting taxes" (1985:182):

> In the case of extraction, the smaller the pool of resources and the less commercialized the economy, other things being equal, the more difficult was the work of extracting resources to sustain war and other government activities; hence, the more extensive was the fiscal apparatus, . . . On the whole, taxes on land were expensive to collect as compared with taxes on trade, especially large flows of trade past easily controlled checkpoints.

Tilly illustrates this point by contrasting the case of Brandenburg-Prussia, a state that, he claims, built a large bureaucracy to extract scarce resources from a poor country in aid of its military efforts, with that of England, whose abundant commercial resources permitted it to get by with a much smaller state apparatus.

Like Hintze, Tilly sees war and preparations for war as the principal stimulus for "war making," yet he questions the tight link posited by the former in his pre-1914 writings between degree of military pressure and the size of the state apparatus built in response to that pressure. He argues instead that a polity might avoid bureaucratization and possibly absolutism as well despite intense military pressure if it possessed abundant resources that could be readily extracted. Thus in this piece Tilly puts forward a more sophisticated argument than that found in the early Hintze by bringing together geopolitical and economic factors (size and extractability of revenue sources, in turn determined by the relative weight of agriculture and commerce within a given economy) to explain differences in the size and character of early modern states.

Tilly expanded these ideas into a general theory of European state building in his monograph *Coercion, Capital and European States. AD 990–1990* (1990). He adopts the same prospective approach advocated in Tilly (1975), but is more specific in identifying three divergent paths of political development in late medieval and early modern Europe (1990:30): a "capital-intensive" path followed by the city-states and city-confederations of northern Italy, Switzerland, southern Germany and the Low Countries; a "coercion-intensive" path found on the continent's eastern and northern fringes (Poland, Hungary, Russia, Scandinavia); and finally an intermediate path of "capitalized coercion" exemplified by England, France, and later Brandenburg-Prussia. It was this third path that "produced full-fledged national states earlier" and beginning in the 1600s "proved more effective at war, and therefore provided a compelling model for states that had originated in other combinations of coercion and capital" (1990:30–1).

How can we in turn account for the existence of these three separate paths? Tilly argues that they come about because of the very uneven distribution of capital across Europe at the time during the central middle ages when large-scale warfare began to spread throughout the continent. Taking up Rokkan's idea of a "city belt," he claims that financial resources were heavily concentrated in a city-filled corridor running from northern Italy to the Low Countries. Rulers attempting to centralize coercive resources in this area were thwarted by city-states, city-empires, and urban federations jealous of their independence. These polities then employed their superior capital resources to purchase coercive means through military contractors and other entrepreneurs, thereby avoiding the necessity of building bulky administrative apparatuses to perform such tasks. By contrast, the polities of Eastern and Northern Europe were poor in cities and hence in capital. In response to military pressures, they first reacted with imperial expansion (cf. the Polish, Hungarian, Russian, and Swedish empires). To extract the meager resources found among the largely peasant populations under their control, they either constructed bulky bureaucracies (Russia) or, in a less effective strategy over the long run, relied on the direct coercive authority of powerful landowners (Poland and Hungary).

Because the regions just to the east and especially the west of the city belt were endowed with moderate concentrations of capital, states there could pursue a middle course, centralizing coercive power while at the same time encouraging further growth in the urban economies that they had to tax to pay for standing armies and bureaucracies. This mix of capital and coercion proved to be the most effective at extracting and organizing resources for war and hence polities employing either more capital-intensive or more coercion-intensive methods of mobilization were forced to imitate states like France or Prussia or to fall back into insignificance and possibly lose their independence as a consequence, as happened to Poland, Hungary, and, somewhat later, Venice (1990:130–60, 187–91).

As with Rokkan's "conceptual maps," the great strength of Tilly's approach is that he seeks to integrate the material development of the continent into his analysis of European state building in a way that does not simply reduce political to economic interests. Furthermore, he does this in a manner that goes beyond Rokkan because his perspective is generally prospective and, at least in Tilly (1990), he identifies a set of variations in outcome for which he hopes to account. The explanatory power of his model is weakened, however, by its difficulties in explaining variations in the form of government within each of the three trajectories. Thus, one might ask, even if the mix of capital and coercion in Britain and France, or in Poland and Russia were roughly similar, why did one polity in each pair become absolutist, whereas the other did not?

This was a question to which Michael Mann tried to provide an answer in the sections on European state building in the first volume of his *The Sources of Social Power* (1986). Here he acknowledges (p. 433) the inspiration provided by Tilly (1975) and up to a point his argument parallels that being developed by Tilly at about the same time. Thus Mann also sees state building in the period after 1500 dominated by the demands of warfare, and like Tilly he contends that the varying distribution across the continent of war's "raw materials" – money and men – led to alternative paths of development. He writes (1986:456) the following:

> Thus a very rich state could pay for and administer armed forces that were fairly separate from the rest of its civil activities .... Or a state that had some wealth but that was rich in manpower could generate large, competitive armed forces with a fiscal-manpower extraction system that was more central to its own overall administration .... Over the next centuries the major Italian republics .... Holland, and England were favored by their wealth, and Austria and Russia by their populations and relatively uniform state machineries. Spain and France enjoyed both advantages and, indeed, they came closest to military-led political hegemony over Europe.

This sounds very much like Tilly's capital-intensive, coercion-intensive, and capitalized coercion patterns of state building, though in this schema England is placed in the first category along with the polities of Rokkan and Tilly's "city belt" rather than in the third along with France and Spain. This key shift then allows Mann to identify these different "extractive regimes" with particular political outcomes (1986:456): "... we shall see that these "fiscal" and "mobilized" alternatives develop into "constitutional" and "absolutist" regimes." Poland is identified as a state that failed to adopt any effective extractive regime and hence was crushed, disappearing altogether from the map (1986:489–90). These suggestive ideas are not developed at any length in Mann's volume and hence retain the character of hypotheses. Attempts to account for divergent political outcomes (absolutist vs. nonabsolutist regimes) would, however, remain a major concern of the state-building literature over the coming decade.

RECENT TRENDS IN THE LITERATURE ON EUROPEAN STATE BUILDING

Since the early 1990s, three broad theoretical orientations have dominated the research on European state building within political science and sociology. The first of these, represented by the work of Brian Downing and Thomas Ertman, has continued to focus on the way warfare shaped divergent patterns of state development and hence might be called neo-Hintzean. A second orientation, which has gained in importance over the decade, derives its inspiration from rational choice theory and has been particularly interested in exploring issues of taxation, consent, and rent seeking in the state building process. Finally, the most recent trend to emerge in this field has been a "culture turn" found in the work of Julia Adams and Philip Gorski, who have brought a concern with gender, the family, and religion to the study of the medieval and early modern state.

Accounting for variations in political outcome to the state-building process in Europe stands at the heart of Brian Downing's monograph *The Military Revolution and Political Change* (1992). The starting point for Downing's argument is the fact, frequently noted by Weber and Hintze, that the medieval West was unique in possessing a whole array of institutional arrangements that checked royal power – the rule of law, a developed conception of rights, autonomous cities, decentralized military organization and above all representative institutions – institutional arrangements that Downing collectively terms *medieval constitutionalism*. The changes in military technology and the resulting explosion in the size and cost of armies generally known as the "military revolution" of the sixteenth and seventeenth centuries placed tremendous strain on these institutions as rulers sought to find the money and men necessary to defend themselves against – or attack – their neighbors. Downing summarizes his argument concerning the divergent impact of the military revolution as follows (1992:239–40):

> Countries faced with heavy protracted warfare that required substantial domestic resource mobilization suffered the destruction of medieval constitutionalism and the rise of a military-bureaucratic form of government. Second, where war was light, or where war needs could be met without mobilizing drastic proportions of national resources (through foreign resources, alliances, geographic advantages or commercial wealth), conflict with the constitution was much lighter. Constitutional government endured.... Third, where war was heavy and protracted, where domestic politics prevented military modernization and political centralization, and where the benefits of foreign resources, alliances, geography or economic superiority were not available, the country lost its sovereignty to strong expansionist states.

Thus the rulers of France and Brandenburg-Prussia, their states geographically exposed and forced to rely primarily on domestic taxation and recruits to feed their military machines, swept aside representative institutions and erected absolutist regimes with bureaucratic infrastructures, whereas the leaders of England, the Dutch Republic, and Sweden, protected by geography and enjoying access to substantial financial resources – in the first two cases due to domestic wealth and in the third thanks to foreign subsidies – could meet their military needs without eliminating representative institutions or constructing large bureaucracies. Finally, Poland is the best example of a state that, though under severe military threat, was prevented from meeting this challenge because of domestic politics and was eventually destroyed.

Downing's model is similar in many respects to Mann's, though it is presented and supported in much greater detail. It represents the most developed version of a "fiscal-military" alternative to the more narrowly "geopolitical" theory found in the pre-1914 works of Hintze, one that identifies both the (geographically determined) military threat from surrounding powers *and* the type and availability of financial and manpower resources as key causal factors in accounting for divergent state-building outcomes. As such, it can be seen as the culmination of a line of argument initiated by Tilly (1975).

Like Downing, Thomas Ertman in his *Birth of the Leviathan* (1997) seeks to explain variations in both political regime and in the character of state infrastructures found across Europe at the end of the early modern period. He contends that this problem is worth examining anew because research by historian John Brewer (1989) has undermined a central assumption of the state-building literature from Hintze and Weber to Downing: namely that eighteenth-century Britain with its strong Parliament, geographic isolation, small standing army, and abundant commercial wealth neither needed nor possessed a large, fiscal-administrative infrastructure of the kind associated in this literature with absolutist states like France and Brandenburg-Prussia. In fact, as Brewer and Geoffrey Holmes (1982) have shown, Britain possessed a fiscal-administrative infrastructure larger in both absolute and per capita terms than that of Frederick the Great's Prussia and just as bureaucratic (Ertman, 1997:12). Indeed, as Brewer has written (1989:68), the British Excise "more closely approximated . . . Max Weber's ideal of bureaucracy than any other government agency in eighteenth-century Europe." Although constitutionalist Britain and absolutist Prussia both possessed modern bureaucracies, a substantial literature on absolutist France and Spain as well as on constitutionalist Poland and Hungary has underlined the fact that the infrastructures of all these states most closely approximate Weber's category of "stereotyped" or appropriated patrimonial administration.

Ertman thus claims that, contrary to an assumption held by most of the literature on state building, political regime and infrastructural type did not covary in early modern Europe but instead cross-cut one another, thereby producing four kinds of outcomes to be explained – bureaucratic absolutism (German states), bureaucratic constitutionalism (Britain), patrimonial absolutism (France, Iberian, and Italian states), and patrimonial constitutionalism (Poland, Hungary), rather than the traditional two – bureaucratic absolutism and nonbureaucratic constitutionalism. In attempting to account for variations in infrastructure, Ertman agrees with the standard literature on the central causal role played by war and preparations for war. Yet what this standard literature overlooks, he maintains, is that although geopolitical competition may have had a crucial impact on the state-building process, the onset of such competition was "nonsimultaneous" – that is, it did not affect all states or regions at the same time. This mattered for the same reasons that the nonsimultaneous onset of industrialization mattered in the process of European economic development: because rulers who were not forced to expand their infrastructures until later (after about 1450) could take advantage of new institutions and "technologies of rule" not available to early state builders; because such late state-building rulers could draw from a larger pool of trained administrative, financial, and military personnel; and because they could learn from the mistakes of the early state builders. For all of these reasons, Ertman argues, late state builders (like Prussia's monarchs) were – other things being equal – able to win the battle with their staffs over control of the means of administration and construct protomodern bureaucracies, whereas earlier state builders (such as the kings of France or Spain) tended to lose the battle with their staffs and were saddled with patrimonial infrastructures (1997:25–8).

To explain variations in political regime, as opposed to variations in infrastructure, Ertman employs a different argument, one inspired by Hintze's lesser known work of the post-1918 period. Developing further the claim put forward by Hintze (1930), Ertman contends that because all rulers were interested in freeing themselves from the constraints of "medieval constitutionalism," especially given the intense geopolitical competition of the period after 1450, the key factor in determining whether they would succeed in this was the degree of resistance said rulers encountered from their representative assemblies. Two chamber assemblies with their roots in autonomous units of local government such as those found in England, Poland, and Hungary proved to be most durable, whereas tripartite estate-based assemblies with no such links to local government such as those in France, Iberia, Italy, and Germany invariably succumbed to rulers' attempts to concentrate legislative as well as executive power in their own hands. In addition, Ertman points out that if representative assemblies survived and remained vigorous throughout the early modern period, they could and did influence the character of the state infrastructures that collected and disbursed the taxes they voted and administered the laws they approved. Thus in England, parliamentary support made possible the efforts of reformers to replace a patrimonial infrastructure with a protomodern bureaucracy, whereas in Poland and Hungary noble-dominated representative institutions blocked rulers' attempts to build just such bureaucracies in the face of sustained military pressures, fearing that they would give rulers the upper hand in their struggle with the assemblies. At the same time, because such assemblies had either ceased to meet altogether or ceded all influence over legislation in France, Iberia, Italy, and the German states after the late 1500s, they could do little to either reform entrenched patrimonial administrations in the first three areas ("Latin Europe") or block the construction of protomodern bureaucracies across Germany (Ertman, 1997:19–25, 28–34; for critical discussions of Ertman, see Gorski, 1998, 2003, and Mahoney, 1999).

If Downing and Ertman carry forward, in their contrasting ways, an older, war-centered tradition of work on European state building, over the course of the 1990s research in this area has come to be dominated by two other theoretical orientations with quite different intellectual roots: rational choice and culture-centered analysis. Neither has as of yet sought to explain variation across the entire continent in the manner of Hintze, Rokkan, Tilly, or Ertman, but both have instead concentrated on single-country studies or comparisons involving a more limited number of cases. The foundations for a rational choice approach to the European past were laid in the 1970s and 1980s by the Nobel Prize-winning economist Douglass North and his political science colleague Margaret Levi. In his path-breaking writings on economic history beginning with *The Rise of the Western World* (North and Thomas, 1973) and *Structure and Change in Economic History* (1981; see also North, 1990) North highlights the centrality of establishing a system of equitable property rights to lower the transaction costs involved in negotiating and enforcing contracts and hence encourage economic activity. However, he also emphasizes the fact that, given the prevalence of inefficient property rights both in the European past and in the wider world, such a system is obviously very difficult to construct and institutionalize. A principal reason for this is the "predatory" behavior of rulers – whether individuals or collectivities – who will attempt to shape property rights to maximize their own income, most often to the detriment of economic growth more generally (North, 1981:21–31; Levi, 1981, 1988:10–40).

This basic framework has inspired two main strands of research on the medieval and early modern state by those employing a rational choice approach. One of these roughly corresponds to the problem of explaining variations in political regime in the neo-Hintzean literature, the other to the problem of explaining variations in infrastructural type. Thus both North and Levi have explored the conditions under which rulers might be willing to enter into durable bargains with representative institutions, leading to constraints on their predatory behavior and the creation of an efficient property rights system, by comparing the cases of late medieval England and France (Levi, 1988:95–121; see also Bates and Lien, 1985; North, 1981:147–57; North and Thomas, 1973:82–84, 98–101). They argue that the weaker bargaining position of English monarchs in the absence of a credible invasion threat, combined with the lower transaction costs associated with central bargaining in a smaller and more homogeneous country led the latter to enter into cooperative arrangements with Parliament (see also Kiser and Barzel, 1991). The subsequent breakdown in trust between the monarch and Parliament, and the establishment of parliamentary supremacy after 1688 have more recently been examined from a rational choice perspective by Ferejohn (1993) and North and Weingast (1989). Jean-Laurent Rosenthal (1998) has explored the reasons why seventeenth- and eighteenth-century French monarchs refused to revive the Estates

General despite the revenue gains this would have brought. He argues, echoing a point made earlier by Levi (1988:121), that they did not do so because they correctly perceived that this increased revenue would be purchased at the intolerably high price of a loss of autonomy in foreign and military affairs.

A second issue addressed in several rational choice contributions is that of administrative insiderism and inefficiency – patrimonialism, in Weber's terms. The predatory theory of rule explains this outcome by the tendency of rulers to trade rights, including monopoly rights to office, in exchange for revenue gains in the absence of constraints imposed by, for example, a permanent representative institution (North, 1981:149–50). North has subsequently stressed that dysfunctional institutional arrangements brought about by the granting of monopoly rights can reproduce themselves over long periods of time (1990:51–3, 92–104). In his monograph *Fountains of Privilege* (1994), Hilton Root shows how ancien regime France's pervasive "cronyism" – the allocation of rights to office and monopoly control over key state functions and economic activities to relatives and clients – led to dysfunctionality on such a scale that, under conditions of intense geopolitical competition, regime collapse was the inevitable outcome. Conversely, the pervasive electoral corruption in eighteenth-century England served to redistribute wealth to a wider, socially mixed electorate without impeding the wealth-creating function of a market economy largely free from state control (see also the critique of Root in Rosenthal, 1998:78–79).

Another way to conceive of the problem of patrimonialism is from the point of view of principal-agent theory. Rulers (principals) must delegate administrative duties to their staffs (agents), but controlling and monitoring these agents, especially under conditions of poor communication, is an extremely difficult task (North, 1981:25). Edgar Kiser (1994) has used agency theory to argue that rulers will employ tax farming when the size of the area from which taxes are to be collected is large and their existing administrative infrastructure provides poor capacities to control agents. Kiser and Joachim Schneider (1994) have also analyzed the tax collection system of early modern Prussia and claim that certain nonbureaucratic features of this system, including the use of royal spies to monitor tax officials and the right of arbitrary dismissal retained by the ruler, increased the overall efficiency of collection by heightening the control capacity of the principal.

Over the past decade, some of the most significant new contributions to the literature on European state building have come from sociologists Julia Adams and Philip Gorski, both of whom have called into question various features of the rational choice approach. Adams and Gorski were important contributors to the 1999 collective volume *State/Culture*, edited by George Steinmetz. This volume seeks to revitalize the study of state formation and state building by allowing it to partake of the fruits of the "cultural turn" now ongoing in sociology, anthropology, history, and, to a lesser extent, political science. In its ambitions Steinmetz (1999) strongly resembles Evans, Rueschemeyer, and Skocpol (1985). In Adams' piece (1999), she criticizes the rational choice model of wealth and power-maximizing predatory actors for neglecting the crucial role played by the pursuit of family honor and prestige among the elites of the early modern period. In her own work on the Netherlands, she has tried to elaborate an alternative model.

In two further articles, Adams (1994a, 1994b) contends that the driving force behind state development in the seventeenth-century Dutch Republic was the desire of the male heads of regent families to secure the future of their lineages by acquiring proprietary rights over public positions. Their success in this enterprise led to the kind of "familial" patrimonial state that resisted attempts to introduce rational-legal bureaucracy and eliminate damaging economic privileges. Adams implies that this type of patriarchal patrimonialism was not limited to the northern Netherlands but was in fact found across early modern Europe. This argument is developed in much greater detail in Adams (2005). The most original aspect of her work is the way it combines a contemporary gender-based perspective with an older analytic framework (Weber's concept of patrimonialism) that has been underutilized in the state-building literature.

One of Philip Gorski's first published pieces, "The Protestant Ethic and the Spirit of Bureaucracy" (1995), also involved a critique of rational choice, in this case of Kiser and Schneider's article "Bureaucracy and Efficiency" (1994). Here he maintains that the efficiency of the Prussian tax administration can be explained not by the use of patrimonial control mechanisms, as claimed by Kiser and Schneider, but by the largely Calvinist makeup of that administration. Prussian monarchs wisely chose their coreligionists for these sensitive bureaucratic positions because Calvinist congregations, with their intrusive examinations of their members, provided an extra check on the honesty and diligence of Calvinist officials. Though he echoes him in his title, Gorski's search for the religious roots of modern bureaucracy recalls Hintze (1931) more than Weber.

Gorski's larger project is to bring religion back into the study of European state building and he has been especially critical of Ertman for neglecting this causal factor. Although Gorski cites Weber and Foucault as his primary sources of inspiration, his project very much resembles that of the German scholar Gerhard Oestreich, who was also particularly influenced by Hintze's "Calvinism" essay. In several articles (1993, 1995, 1999) as well as in his book *The Disciplinary Revolution* (2003), Gorski, inspired by Weber and Foucault, has sought to show that religion was at the root of a "disciplinary revolution" during the early modern period that affected religious, social, and political and military behavior. Although Calvinism provided the main impetus for this revolution, it also spread as a result of imitation and post-Tridentine reforms to Lutheran and Catholic areas as well. However, this revolution was most intense in Calvinist-led states like the Dutch Republic and Brandenburg-Prussia and hence religious differences can go a far way toward explaining variations in social welfare regimes and in political and administrative mores across the continent.

CONCLUSION

What conclusions can we draw from the case of European state building for the state builders of today? At first glance, the European experience might seem of only limited relevance because, as theorists from Hintze to Anderson, Tilly, and Ertman have stressed, war was a decisive factor driving forward the expansion and reform of administrative, financial, military, and judicial infrastructures across the continent. Yet over the past two centuries, as over a hundred new states in Latin America, Africa, Asia, and Eastern Europe have come into being and sought to consolidate themselves, they have only rarely faced the kind of acute geomilitary pressure that was ubiquitous in Western Europe for over seven centuries, from the central Middle Ages until 1815 or, one might even argue, 1989. Only in the post-1945 Middle East have something like European conditions obtained. It seems reasonable to admit, then, that the portion of the state-building literature that explores the differential effects on state structures of long-term military pressures might be of only limited significance for most of today's developing polities.

There is, however, another side of that literature that is supremely relevant to contemporary state builders. A theme even more common than war links the writings of the neo-Weberians (Bendix), neo-Marxists (Wallerstein and Anderson), and neo-Hintzeans (Ertman) with those of rational choice and cultural theorists like Levi, Root, and Adams: the pervasiveness in the European past of patrimonial practices like proprietary officeholding, tax farming, and financial cronyism with their attendant inefficiency, arbitrariness, and large-scale diversion of public funds into private hands, a pervasiveness of which the endemic corruption and rent seeking in the public administrations of many developing states today is reminiscent. As the European case clearly illustrates, the creation and expansion of administrative and financial institutions represents a unique opportunity for personal and familiar enrichment and social aggrandizement because it involves the extraction of wealth from the tax-paying population and its concentration – ostensibly for the public good – in the coffers of the state. Once amassed, such wealth presents an inviting target to rent-seeking groups, be they government officials, local party bosses, the military, or employees of state enterprises. Further, such groups, whether in medieval and early modern Europe, nineteenth-century Latin America, or twentieth-century Africa and Asia, will attempt to structure the state apparatus in their own interest with little concern – especially in the absence of geomilitary pressure – for the consequences of their actions for their country's long-term defense capabilites or economic competitiveness and will fiercely resist all efforts at fundamental reform.

How might it be possible to resist the rent-seeking deformation of state institutions during and after the state-building process? The European experience as interpreted by Hintze, Ertman, Root, Kiser and Schneider, and Gorski suggests two answers. One of these is an authoritarian solution pioneered in Brandenburg-Prussia and, to a lesser extent, in other German states in which a monocratic executive closely monitors the activities of its administrators, using powers of arbitrary dismissal to impose honesty and efficiency. Such pressure from above may, as in Brandenburg-Prussia, induce a strong sense of corporate identity among these administrators, leading them to campaign for both education-based restrictions on entry and for basic rights like life tenure to protect themselves from the unbridled will of their employer. However, the shortcomings of this solution are clear. First, the degree of protection from cronyism and other forms of rent seeking depends on the consistency and high quality of the supervision emanating from the executive, a condition that is in no way assured. Second, monocratic regimes most often must enter into compromises with powerful socioeconomic groups to ward off liberalization or democratization, and such compromises may prevent the status leveling that Weber claims is a necessary prerequisite for any successful bureaucratization. Finally, the work of Hintze and Gorski implies that a certain ideational component (e.g., Calvinism or some functional equivalent) might be necessary for modern bureaucracy truly to take hold. Nonetheless, some contemporary states in Asia such as Singapore, Taiwan, and Hong Kong seem to have been able to build effective modern bureaucracies under different forms of authoritarian rule.

The alternative solution is the one first developed by seventeenth- and eighteenth-century Britain: the monitoring of administrators by an autonomous legislature. Such a legislature normally brings with it circumstances favorable to the expansion of financial markets, because it provides credible backing for government debt issues and to a relatively free press and the dynamic public sphere associated with it. Both financial markets and a vigorous investigative press possess strong incentives to concern themselves with the honesty and efficiency of state officials – and thereby act to reinforce direct monitoring by legislative committees – in the interest of taxpayers concerned about how their money is being spent. Yet this insight merely begs the question of what conditions allow for the creation of a durable, autonomous legislature. Here the classic answer of DeTocqueville, recently reiterated by Ertman, has lost none of its topicality: participatory local government. The management by citizens of their own affairs at the local level and the bonds of solidarity it creates still seems the best foundation on which to build strong legislatures and the honest and efficient state infrastructures that they can guarantee.

CHAPTER NINETEEN

Transitions to Democracy[1]

John Markoff

FROM STRUCTURES TO TRANSITIONS

Explaining the interest of social scientists like himself in democratic transitions, one eminent student of the subject recalls: "I'm Polish and I got involved with democratization for the first time by being beaten by police in 1957 at a student demonstration when the government closed a student newspaper. I left Poland; I came here; I went to Chile; saw democracy being destroyed there; and came back to the United States" (Przeworski, 1997:6). What is to be understood is a process – democrat*ization* – not a stable state of affairs. It may be undone (as in Chile). It involves serious conflict. It is shaped by parties in such conflict (such as troublemaking students and order-defending police), whose actions, achievements, and understandings eventually lead scholars to their own new understandings.

At the moment when government violence got our witness to thinking, and for a couple of decades after that, much scholarly reflection saw democracy resting on elements of social structure or culture not found in all countries. Places endowed with certain constellations of economic interests or imbued with certain kinds of values would be those likely to have democratic government, those less endowed or imbued less likely. Seymour Martin Lipset, for example, pointed out that the economically developed countries of the midtwentieth century were the democratic ones. He argued that growing national wealth reduced the stakes in social conflicts and made democratic compromise attractive to rich and poor alike at the same time as fostering a large middle class with tolerant values (Lipset, 1981[1960]:27–63).

Barrington Moore, to take a very different example, argued that when peasant majorities were able to participate in social revolutions at an early stage in economic development, democratic rights became secured early; when such revolutions had not taken place, economic development tended to produce two kinds of political outcome, neither of which boded well for democracy. In the first path, industrialization supported the interests of narrow agrarian elites and the highly conservative authoritarian states they favored (a variant of which led down the road to fascism). An alternate second path led to twentieth-century communist revolutions from below as revolutionary parties succeeded in mobilizing the large numbers of those left out from the benefits of economic growth. It was only the early opening up of the political system by revolution that avoided both options and laid the groundwork for democracy (Moore, 1966).

Both Lipset, in telling us that wealthy countries tended to develop democratic practices, and Barrington Moore, in connecting the outcomes of conflict between lords and peasants centuries ago to the functioning democracies of today, directed us to seeing democracy as a state of affairs, not as something made and unmade

[1] Thanks for valuable suggestions on an earlier draft: Thomas Janoski and Charles Tilly.

in the present. Lipset and Moore, different as their specific arguments are, encourage us to look for some set of conditions that provide the soil in which democracy will grow, but they tell us nothing about what growth is, nor about how human action brings democracy into (or out of) existence. So Przeworski (1997) suggests that anyone interested in making democracy would be led into a different kind of theoretical inquiry; one presumes the same would hold for anyone interested in unmaking democracy as well.

The general notion that democracy was significantly favored or retarded by some characteristics of national societies was a venerable one. In the midnineteenth century, John Stuart Mill was a great champion of self-government for the people of England and favored representative institutions. But he held self-rule inappropriate for some of Britain's colonies and wrote in considerable detail of the subtleties of providing decent government for a place like India that "is not fit to govern itself" (Mill, 1977[1861]:568). One can readily see in Mill a theory that some peoples are endowed with characteristics that make democracy likely to emerge and flourish, whereas others (particularly some of those ruled by Britain) are deficient in those essential traits. One could readily imagine one of his chapter titles being used in the social science writing of a century later: "Under what social conditions representative government is inapplicable" (Mill, 1977[1861]:413–21). Lipset sees the ancestry of his own variant of such theories to be a great deal more venerable still when he attributes to Aristotle the view that viable democracy is possible "only in a wealthy society in which relatively few citizens lived at the level of real poverty" (Lipset, 1981:31).

Scholars debated precisely which elements of culture or which constellations of economic interest were most favorable. Some took issue, for example, with Lipset's contention that a democratic culture tended to be rooted in the pragmatic values of the educated middle classes by interest inclined to cut deals and by education inclined to tolerance (Lipset, 1981:92–7). Did such formulations misunderstand the interests of the working classes and underrate their significance in forging democratic institutions (Collier, 1999; Houtman, 2001; Rueschemeyer et al., 1992)? Such questions have continued to engage scholars of democracy. But in the last quarter of the twentieth century or so, many turned from the question of favorable environments, whether conceived culturally or structurally, to the question of transition. How and why does one arrive at democracy from some other starting point?

This new vantage point was not primarily arrived at because scholars had exhausted the earlier questions (which they were continuing to debate), nor because of some major empirical flaw in the data upon which the earlier questions rested. Despite much arguing about detail, and about how it was to be explained, a recent reexamination of the contention that as a statistical tendency it is the richer countries that have democratic governments showed it holding up rather well (Diamond, 1992; see also Przeworski et al., 2000; Rueschemeyer et al., 1992).

It was the vivid demonstration of the dynamic aspects of democracy that brought the subject of transition to center stage: antidemocratic transition, first of all. The defeat of the fascist powers in World War Two was followed in short order by the restoration of democratic rule in Western Europe and the implantation of democratic rule in some new places as well. This was soon followed by the withdrawal of the European colonial powers from their colonies, many of which began independence with democratic constitutions.

By the 1960s, however, it had become apparent that more democratic practices in many poorer countries were giving way to less democratic practices, dramatically putting the collapse of democracy on the scholarly agenda. Although the geography of democratic collapse reinforced the weightiness of structural elements for some, and cultural elements for others, an imaginative group of scholars called attention to the undoing of democracy as a process. Instead of trying to locate the missing structural or cultural ingredients, such scholars tried to reconstruct the steps by which democracy was undone. The multivolume collection of case studies that Juan

Linz and Alfred Stepan (1978) put out in the late 1970s stressed the interplay of actors rather than the irresistibility of social forces, the contingent and often unexpected outcome of struggles rather than the determinism of structures and cultures.

When a new, quasi-global wave of democratizations began in the 1970s, they were observed by scholars many of whom had become intrigued by the dynamics of transitions *from* democratic rule and who readily turned to the dynamics of transitions *to* democratic rule. In the 1970s, Western Europe's remaining authoritarian states democratized; in the 1980s many South American militaries relinquished power to elected civilians; in 1989 one East European communist regime after another fell and the successors set about writing democratic constitutions; in the 1990s authoritarian orders fell in several Asian countries and by the beginning of the twenty-first century observers noted the frequency with which power was changing hands in African states holding multiparty elections for the first time (Bratton and van de Walle, 1997; Huntington, 1991; Markoff, 1996; Swarns and Onishi, 2002). Over that turbulent last quarter of the twentieth century, scholars' attention became increasingly drawn to the trajectories by which one regime gave way to another. Those with a comparative bent sought to identify recurrent processes and, in so doing, were rethinking what an appropriate theory ought to look like.

Transitologists, as some practitioners of this flourishing field of intellectual inquiry were calling themselves (e.g., Schmitter with Karl, 1994), were soon addressing a host of challenging issues.

TRANSITIONS FROM WHAT TO WHAT?

Starting Points

Were the prospects for democratization affected, and if so, in what ways, by the starting point? Nondemocratic political orders might unravel, but as many observers have long noted, that was hardly any guarantee of a democratic outcome. One important student of the subject in the 1970s indeed thought the dissolution of an "authoritarian" regime was far more likely to give birth to another authoritarian regime than a democratic one, a position he came to modify in light of the great democratic wave that followed (Linz, 2000:33, reflecting on work originally published in 1975).[2]

One early generalization drew on observation of the disappointed hopes that some democrats had placed in the abandonment of empire that followed World War Two. The European colonizers had been gravely weakened, the greatly strengthened United States was unenthusiastic about restoring European colonial domination, and a variety of national and revolutionary movements were making it very costly to try to restore the prewar order. The result was that in the quarter-century following the end of World War Two centuries of European colonial conquest were brought to an end. Although what were widely called the "new states" often started with democratic constitutions, it was not long before many of them experienced military coups, declarations of martial law, outlawing of opposition parties, or successful revolutionary movements with little inclination toward democratic politics. Many observers concluded that colonial rule was an inauspicious starting point (e.g., Shils, 1960). A more nuanced formulation noted that democratic politics seemed more likely to endure in former British colonies than others, from small Caribbean states to giant India (Weiner, 1987:18–21).

The Indian case alone occasioned a large literature, partly because it was the world's largest democratic state, and partly because its democratic character was in defiance of many a theory that made structure and culture determinative. It had vast poverty; much illiteracy; and enormous linguistic, cultural, and ethnic divisions – all widely held inimical to democratic practice.

[2] As originally formulated in 1975: "We therefore should be careful not to confuse the instability of authoritarian regimes with favorable prospects for competitive democracy. The alternative to a particular authoritarian regime might be a change within the regime or from one type of authoritarian rule to another, if not permanent instability or chaos . . . " (Linz 2000[1975]:269).

Its large population was for the most part not Christian and for those who might highlight with Huntington (1991:72–3) that "[a] strong correlation exists between Western Christianity and democracy" – which some might variously attribute to Christian respect for the individual or to its egalitarian strand – its religious mix would have seemed unlikely to provide needed cultural resources. The significance of caste inequalities, moreover, would not have seemed especially favorable, either.

India, therefore, was a particularly promising site for noting the importance of processes, of how democracy was forged and how it was sustained, and of how to get to democracy from somewhere else (Kohli, 2001). Its scholars have stressed such things as the mobilizational strategies pursued by the dominant independence movement and the forms of challenge mounted by that movement to British rule. The stress on unity against the British and the democratic aspects of the movement's internal decision making helped put in place the habits and institutions of negotiated compromise within the Indian National Congress; the choice of nonviolent confrontation helped avoid the large numbers of heavily armed independence fighters habituated to violence that have bedeviled a number of other cases. In addition, one could point to the ways in which the new Indian constitution provided for groups that might feel shut out of power at the national level to be weighty at the state level and thereby more inclined to be loyal to the overall structure.

Some scholars were less inclined to stress the particularities of the Indian movement for independence and the care with which its new constitution was crafted, setting this case instead among others that moved from British colonial domination to democracy. (By contrast, "[n]ot a single newly independent country that lived under French, Dutch, American, or Portuguese rule has continually remained democratic" Weiner, 1987:20.) Aspects of British rule that led to such an outcome were:

- The establishment of effective governing structures from courts to police to civil services that, after struggles, became indigenized and established national good government traditions; and
- Experiences with electoral and representative institutions at the local and regional levels that, despite limitations of suffrage rights and of the authority of those elected, created an elite socialized in democracy. (Weiner, 1987:19–20)

The problem with this theory is that many British colonies left colonial rule to travel down nondemocratic paths as in Nigeria, Kenya, or India's neighbor, Pakistan (the latter with a British administrative history in common with India's). Whatever role British as opposed to other colonial domination may have played, it must have been in interaction with other things. (I think there are some serious empirical difficulties about the benign administrative legacy as well.[3])

Some scholars aimed at developing taxonomies of nondemocratic regimes and hoped to identify favorable and unfavorable starting points for democratic transition. "Totalitarian" regimes would seem a good deal less promising than "authoritarian" ones to invoke one important distinction (Linz, 2000). Totalitarian regimes have dominating ideologies and great concentrations of power; authoritarian regimes are more pragmatic and more pluralistic. A public discourse of utopian goals would seem quite inimical to cultivating the habits of compromise and limited success that many hold part and

[3] Despite the frequency of claims that British rule left in its wake a modern, capable, and honest civil service, there is reason for skepticism about such adjectives. The most important systematic comparative rankings of corruption, for example, found that of ninety-one countries measured in 2001, four of the world's top five were former British colonies (Bangladesh, Nigeria, Uganda, and Kenya); in 2002 among a slightly larger collection of cases, these were still among the top nine with Bangladesh and Nigeria again at the very top. Although democratic India has not been quite at the pinnacle, its comparative location is still quite high, its administrative history is shared with top-ranked Bangladesh, and its citizens have a sense of widespread corruption. (See Transparency International 2001, 2002:264–5; Pavarala, 1996.)

parcel of the essential give and take of democratically managed conflicts. The absence of autonomously organized political actors, independent of the state, makes it difficult for a would-be democratic movement to negotiate a transition with those powerholders who might be open to change.

Postcommunist Europe provides an important naturally occurring social experiment for observing some theoretically very significant processes. By 1989, the states under Communist rule had moved away from totalitarianism to very different degrees and in different ways (Kitschelt, Mansfeldova, Markowski, and Toka, 1999). Despite widespread use of the totalitarian label to characterize the communist regimes of Eastern Europe, many of them had altered a great deal in many ways from the time of Stalin. Well before 1989, few in or out of power any longer believed in the foundational vision, for example, but the degree to which varied viewpoints could be openly expressed differed considerably from country to country. It will be interesting to observe how differences in postcommunist starting points are playing out: In different trajectories towards democracy? In different kinds of democracy? In different mixes of democracy and nondemocracy? As time passes since the great upheavals of 1989 we will increasingly be able to assess empirically whether such differences do lead to different end points, different paths, both, or neither.

Another type of nondemocratic regime is the highly personalistic pattern of rulership some were denoting as "sultanism," characterized by an extremely narrow ruling stratum cemented by loyalty to some leader subject to little constraint by interest groups, ideology, law, or organized bureaucracies. Supporters are granted personal rewards and others submit in fear. The building blocks of a future democratic order would seem in short supply. Such regimes may be particularly vulnerable to revolutionary overthrow (Goodwin, 2001) but this hardly makes a democratic outcome of such revolutions terribly probable (Stinchcombe, 1999). This is an important reminder that identification of actual and potential sources of instability in nondemocratic regimes is by no means identical to identifying the causes of democratization.

It would be difficult to make out that many very robust generalizations about starting points for political transitions had emerged from such classificatory activity. Consider the very plausible argument about the disadvantages to those seeking to construct democracy of working with the materials at hand in these highly personalistic regimes. Many observers would have agreed with Linz (2000[1975]:153) that the Dominican Republic in its decades under Rafael Trujillo was a good example of a sultanistic regime. Yet, as Jorge Domínguez (1993:3) points out, its "transit to democratic politics in the late 1970s preceded most of Latin America's democratic transitions of the decade that followed." And despite what another scholar calls "a troubled history," since that moment it "can be considered a political democracy" (Hartlyn, 1993:150, 159).

All this seems to suggest that there are many paths to democracy and ways to get there from diverse starting points and that the ways that starting points constrain possible paths is only very imperfectly understood.

End Points

By the beginning of the twenty-first century, very many more people in very many more countries than ever before in human history had governments that made claims to democratic rule. Yet although such regimes tended to have elections, they varied considerably in other important attributes, sufficiently so that observers were qualifying their democratic character. Some rulers, although validated by electoral victories, wielded power subject to very little of what U.S. citizens would call "checks and balances" and ruled over countries in which individuals were subject to arbitrary government actions. Those so subject might well include leaders of opposition movements who could be targets of violence by state authorities (sometimes semiconcealed, as when off-duty policeman or soldiers in civilian garb formed "death squads"), or potentially independent news media subject to government takeover, harassment, fines, or closings. The new country of Belarus that emerged from the breakup of the Soviet Union would provide many examples of such practices. Some observers began to speak of the rise of "illiberal" democracies as opposed to "liberal" ones to categorize such cases and might even suggest that it was primarily illiberal democracy that was on the rise (Diamond, 1999:24–63; Zakaria, 1997).

In still other cases, governments that were by many criteria democratic were profoundly deficient in supplying services that citizens had come to expect from any government, democratic or otherwise. In Brazil, for example, the restoration of civilian rule was followed by an extraordinary deterioration of citizen safety as crime rates soared. Brazilians who could afford it were making their homes into fortresses, police violence rose in tandem with criminality (Caldeira and Holston, 1999), and enthusiasm for democracy soured as large numbers of Brazilians responded to polls that they were indifferent as to whether Brazil was a democracy or not. In 1989, a few years after the Brazilian military relinquished power, 39 percent of a national sample "completely" agreed that "the police attack and kill innocent people" and another 39 percent "partially" agreed. (The main reason so many Brazilians were of this view was that it was quite accurate.) A rise in vigilantism suggests that for some, the problem was that the police were not getting the right people. It is not surprising that three years later, 24 percent of Brazilians held that "For people like me, a democratic and a nondemocratic regime are the same" and another 22 percent were of the view that "In some cases, a nondemocratic government could be preferable to a democracy" (Linz and Stepan, 1996:176, 172). To cover such cases of democratizing states that were failing to meet significant needs, some observers began to speak of "low-quality democracy."

A different sort of issue was posed by states in which democratic procedures did elect presidents and legislatures but in which those presidents had the authority, and used it, to insulate themselves from ongoing democratic debate. Students of several countries in South America in the 1990s took note of the frequency with which presidents formulated key aspects of their economic policies through secretive meetings of their chosen teams of advisors, with little input by business groups let alone labor, and shielded from public scrutiny and legislative debate. If need be, sweeping plans could be imposed constitutionally by emergency decree. Some presidents made use of such powers even when favored policies would have passed as ordinary law to bypass the normal wheeling and dealing of democratic politics or perhaps even just to demonstrate who was the boss. [The champion of this particular mode of governing was Argentina's Carlos Saúl Menem, who issued 244 such decrees between 1989 and 1993, eight times as many as had been issued in the previous 136 years (Linz and Stepan, 1996:200–4).]

Some scholars began to speak of "delegative democracy," in which vast powers are democratically delegated to powerful executives (O'Donnell, 1994). Others saw the ascent to power of unelected "technocrats," the bearers of the technical knowledge used in designing the president's policies (Conaghan and Malloy, 1994; Markoff and Montecinos, 1993). One fruitful direction of research was taking note of variation from country to country and from moment to moment in the relative power of presidents and congresses in order to try to tease out what was distinctive about the 1990s and beyond and what was simply a continuation of Latin America's long-standing patterns of powerful presidencies.

But one important observation suggested that there actually was a new form of legislative assertiveness. Faced with presidential power, the legislatures were no longer prone to look for military allies to overthrow the president by coup but to use such constitutional measures as impeachment as never before, and presidents (as in Brazil) might now sometimes be driven from office without any tanks driving up to the presidential palace. Congresses in turn were often being propelled into action by popular protest. If democratic politics includes executives seriously challenged by street demonstrations and congresses but not by the national armed forces, there is a case that in the 1990s

Latin American conflict patterns were looking in some ways, if pretty turbulent, more democratic than in the past (Pérez-Liñan, 2003). Although some were stressing the failures of such democracy, others saw things, on balance, as progress (Mainwaring, 1999).

Other observers took note of "hybrids" – significant democratic elements in combination with significant nondemocratic ones (e.g., Karl, 1995). Iran was a particularly notable instance. Following the overthrow of the Shah in 1979, the pull and tug of revolutionary forces with differing ideas about how the new Iran was to be governed led to a complex and evolving structure. A parliament and president are chosen by competitive multiparty elections. But there is also a Supreme Leader, a Council of Guardians, an Expediency Council, and an Assembly of Experts (who are predominantly Islamic clerics), who play a significant role in choosing each other, and who can both nullify acts of parliament and stymie presidential initiatives (Chehabi, 1995; de Bellaigue, 2002). Far from achieving institutional permanence, much about the Iranian political system is in tension, including tension between its more and its less democratic features. As a younger generation comes to maturity skeptical about continued clerical domination of daily life, Iranian voters are less and less prone to give electoral victories to clerical personnel. The postrevolutionary parliament began with a clerical majority; by 2002 clerics were only 12 percent of deputies (de Bellaigue, 2002:17) and a president supported by those who hoped for reform was in deep conflict with a Supreme Leader, who still had the upper hand.

The evident empirical reality was that recent transitions were not all transitions to the same place. Some scholars sharply distinguished "broken-backed" from "complete" democracy (Rose et al., 1998:200–1, 217–23). Others suggested that much being called democracy was better understood as an authoritarian variant (e.g., Linz, 2000:34). Still others thought "democracy" needed much adjectival qualification and that theoretical advance in understanding required more nuanced categorizations (Collier and Adcock, 1999; Collier and Levitsky, 1997). And others yet again thought the dividing line between democracy and authoritarianism was often blurry, with many regimes routinely thought of as democratic having significant authoritarian elements – and vice versa (e.g., Baretta and Markoff, 1987).

However formulated, one of the lessons some scholars took away from their study of transitions was that it was perfectly possible to create some sort of democracy that would disappoint the hopes of many democrats. As two of the most eminent students of transitions put it at the close of a magisterial survey: "We also unhappily acknowledge that some countries will consolidate democracy but will never *deepen* democracy in the spheres of gender equality, access to critical social services, inclusive citizenship, respect for human rights, and freedom of information. They might, indeed, occasionally violate human rights" (Linz and Stepan, 1996:457). Some thought that much of this was a symptom of the difficulties of democracy in the global circumstances of the early twenty-first century (Markoff, 2003a).

Paths

The realization that there was more than one path to democratization came early in the great wave that began in the 1970s, because two neighboring countries displayed strikingly different patterns. Samuel Huntington (1991:3), with some plausibility, actually dates the inception of "[t]he third wave of democratization of the modern world" from the launching of a coup by junior officers of the Portuguese army in April, 1974. A year and a half later, the death of Francisco Franco, head of the government of neighboring Spain for the three and a half decades since his forces triumphed in its Civil War, provided the challenges and opportunities that led to that country's democratization. The Portuguese process was marked by military conspiracy in the course of an African colonial war that was going badly, mass mobilizations in capital and countryside, and a Communist Party taking a radical stance under pressure from groups more radical still. The Spanish process was marked by initiatives from a governing establishment not under any of the delegitimating pressures of economic crisis or military failure commonly assumed to be the triggers of significant change, a great deal of out-of-sight negotiation, and two rival left parties making significant compromises with the parties of the right. The two cases came to be touchstones in the literature on transitions for many reasons:

- Markedly contrasting transitions in close geographic, cultural, and linguistic proximity was a powerful stimulus to comparative research and reflection
- They occurred so early in the global wave that scholars of later democratizing episodes elsewhere were likely to look at later cases with concepts developed in scrutiny of Spain and Portugal
- The Spanish case particularly struck many observers as "a miracle: one of a handful of countries that since World War I have escaped the economics, the politics, and the culture of poor capitalism" (Przeworski, 1991:8). The sense of the miraculous was all the greater in that Spain had acquired a reputation for a murderously violent political culture. That it was Portugal's transition that was the more troubled and its postauthoritarian social order also more troubled lent more force to the comparison of the two cases
- Although the great cluster of democratic transitions of the next decade were geographically far from Iberia, their concentration in South America probably made for easier diffusion across the south Atlantic of a conceptual apparatus honed in Spanish and Portuguese

The Iberian cases, and especially the Spanish instance, have by now generated a vast literature and a lot of ideas that have exercised considerable influence on scholars of transition processes elsewhere (e.g., Graham, 1992; Gunther et al., 1986; Linz and Stepan, 1996: 87–129; Maxwell, 1986; Maravall and Santamaría, 1986). Having noticed the importance of agreements among central political actors in Spain, for example, it was easy to recognize their significance in South America (e.g., Karl, 1986).

Or consider a more complex example. One of any number of things that apprehensive observers might well have thought endangered a democratic outcome in Spain – "the most dangerous" in the view of Linz and Stepan (1996:99) – was the potential challenge to the existing state on the part of Catalans and Basques, for many of whom a sense of regional and cultural distinctiveness was augmented by the bitterness of defeat by an alien Spanish state in the Civil War. Rather than accept a democratizing Spain as a superior homeland, in fact, Basque separatists who embraced violent tactics sharply increased their actions following Franco's death. The possibility of mutually reinforcing hostile identity claims producing escalating violent polarizations and the possibility of military attempts to derail democratization – the military were a particular target of separatist violence – loomed large.

Beyond Spanish particulars, some students of democracy have argued that conflicts defined in ethnonational terms are generally less amenable to democratic give-and-take than those defined in class terms (e.g., Diamond, Linz, and Lipset, 1995:42). For one thing, it is easier to imagine what a compromise on what wage policy, say, might look like than a compromise on acceptable symbols of national identity.

In light of such potential hazards, it is noteworthy that democratizing Spain held national elections at an early stage, not only giving democratic legitimation to its central authorities but inducing provincial political actors to become involved in forging alliances at the national level. Only after the creation of a nationally legitimated authority and national parties in which provincial actors were implicated were regional elections held. By considerable contrast, Linz and Stepan point to the Soviet Union. The March 1989 elections in that vast and powerful country reserved for the Communist Party a third of the seats in the Congress of People's Deputies, which in turn chose the Supreme Soviet, hardly a procedure that gave that body much democratic legitimation. When elections were held the following year in the Soviet Union's republics, not only were they not organized by Unionwide parties, but they endowed the new republic governments with a good deal more democratic legitimation than the Union's central government. This helps us understand how it was that Boris Yeltsin, based in the Russian Republic, could successfully challenge the Soviet Union (Linz and Stepan, 1996:370–400).

There is a good deal about this account worth further debate. Someone of a more structuralist bent might wonder whether more weight needs to be given to the Soviet policy which made nationality a matter of considerable significance, particularly by organizing job privileges in the republics for "titular nationalities" (thus Kazakhs would have advantages in Kazakhstan). This produced ethnically defined political actors all over the Soviet Union who hoped for change or who feared change. Others might wonder whether the Spanish case should be thought of as a blueprint foolishly missed in the failing Soviet Union or whether it was not possible to do likewise because of the entrenched strength of the Communist Party.

But even to discuss such issues is difficult without reference to that Spanish case, because it has become paradigmatic. If Iberian experience imparted a particular vocabulary into the discussion of transition, the next decade's varied South American experiences of military withdrawal enriched that vocabulary still further, as observers noticed the enormous differences between the step-by-step restoration of civilian authority in Brazil and the collapse of military rule in Argentina. What are some of the key concepts transitologists have extracted from Iberian experience or abstracted from Latin American political vocabulary?

In a first, rough approximation, a transition might be thought of as *ruptura* or a *reforma*. That is, new political actors might suddenly appear as established ones fled or were rudely shoved aside, new symbols of identity and legitimate authority might be invented or old ones that had been discarded brought back, mass mobilizations might be major components of a crisis, and the language of revolution might be invoked. Not all such elements might appear, but to the extent they did, those who lived through the transition would very likely experience it as a rupture, as a sharp break with the previous state of things. This is not a bad first approximation of Portuguese or Argentine experience.

On the other hand, powerholders within the old order might be central players, either finding a home within the new or at least negotiating their phased withdrawal from the scene; things might unfold for some time under the legal structures of the old with a new foundational document delayed; significant aspects of the transition might derive their legitimacy from the involvement of those identified with the old order rather than from their radical repudiation of the old order. In short, we might have something that some of those identifying with the old order would experience as a reform of that order, of its modification to fit new circumstances, rather than its overthrow.

On closer scrutiny, rupture and reform often turn out to be intertwined, and indeed the very claim that some ongoing process of political change is rupture or reform is itself something that might be deployed by actors in that conflict. Powerholders in the old order would not only tend to favor reform to the extent that they favored change at all but would very likely prefer to have whatever it is that was happening understood to be reform so that:

- There would be a place for them within the new order; or, failing that,
- They could be held to have played an honorable part in bringing about change, which would not humiliate them and repudiate all their works.

Those in opposition under the old order would very likely have a more complex set of preferences. Those favoring socially radical goals (of many imaginable sorts) might well prefer a rupture, in part for the sorts of mobilizational opportunities seen in the Portuguese case. For those Basque separatists for whom a successfully negotiated democratic transition threatened to limit the appeals of radical separatism by incorporating some Basque groups within the give-and-take of a democratized Spain, polarizing violence could seem a promising strategy to disrupt deals and derail reform. In other transition situations we might well find a moderate opposition that hopes to avoid the hazards of mass mobilization and cuts a deal to effect a negotiated transition, yet for its own legitimacy within the opposition camp tries to define that deal as a negotiated rupture.

In many of these processes, the pull and tug of various interests attempting to move the transition this way and that, would generate deals, and the Spanish case, with its explicit pact of Moncloa[4] provided a convenient paradigm. Transitologists came to speak of a "pacted" transition, rendering into something approximating English the Spanish *pactada*.

DEALS AND STRATEGIES

Armed with such concepts, the empirical antennae of transitologists were attuned to deals (and found them). This coincided with the flowering of "rationalist" modes of explanation in the social sciences. Having discovered pacts, whether explicitly formulated as in Spain or Venezuela, or tacitly adhered to, one could ask what sorts of things might lead a rational actor to embrace some particular pact and what sorts of strategies might that actor follow to induce other actors to do so. If a social scientist could construct some suitably simplified model of the actors involved, and pay due attention to their interests, one could think about democracy as a particular set of rules and then ask under what circumstances might rational actors be induced into playing by those rules. One could also ask under what circumstances might such rules constitute a self-locking process in which it was in the interests of actors who had at one point accepted those rules to continue to do so.

One rather frequent simplification was to treat collectivities as though they were a single actor writ large: "labor," for example, or "the establishment." One important line of debate about such models was whether this particular simplification did not bypass one of the central problematic issues of political life, namely the achievement of a political identity as itself a dynamic process (Lichbach and Seligman, 2000). A second very important set of issues swirled around the notion of interests – whether these were to be taken as somehow prior to the actions to be explained and thereby exogenous to the explanatory model or whether interests, like identities, might not be a dynamic product of interaction and conflict as much as an element in conflict.

O'Donnell and Schmitter (1986) get a good deal of mileage by imagining an authoritarian establishment confronting an opposition, with both establishment and opposition divided on the proper way to deal with the other. This particular simplification has been given an especially elegant formulation by Przeworski (1991). We may think of the authoritarian forces, currently in power, as composed of Hardliners and Reformers. These authoritarians confront opposition Moderates and Radicals. One might at first blush think that a reform process is most probable when authoritarian Reformers are far stronger than Hardliners and opposition Moderates far stronger than Radicals. Reformers and Moderates than make common cause and the outcome is democracy (at least if their common cause includes democracy). Were one to assume that Reformers and Moderates are more or less the same thing, this might be the case. In a position to ignore Hardliners and Radicals, they just join forces to do what they will.

If one makes what is no doubt a far more realistic assumption in many cases that the interests of Reformers and Moderates are significantly different, than matters are not nearly so simple. Reformers want to clean up the regime, not end it; Moderates want change, but do not care for radicalism. So what gets Reformers and Moderates together despite the gulf between them? Fear of Hardliners is one of the things that might get Moderates to give ground to less unacceptable Reformers. It may, therefore, be in the interest of Reformers not to squelch Hardliners but to support them from time to time. And it may be that fear of Radicals is one of the things inducing Reformers to accept more of the

[4] At Spain's Moncloa Palace, the major parties in 1977 formally agreed to a cluster of compromises on potentially explosive socioeconomic issues, an action widely taken to have made possible the following year's agreement on a democratic constitution.

position of less noxious Moderates. So a bit of radicalism may be very much helpful in getting the program of Moderates to win the support of Reformers.

It is an open question whether there is greater payoff in understanding democratic transitions through further elaboration of such (with luck) shrewdly crafted simplifications, or in carrying out the empirical research to provide us with rich and inherently far more complex accounts of actors in the process of *arriving* at strategies, *discovering* their interests, and *constituting* themselves as actors.

Although the two intellectual activities may (sometimes) be mutually supportive or (sometimes) in fruitful mutual tension, they are certainly not identical. No amount of thought on the situation confronting abstractly imagined Moderates and Radicals will tell you what actually happened as the Brazilian military, seeking to give itself a bit of democratic legitimation, organized elections whose rules were designed so as to have its supporters dominate and whose rules were continually redefined because (a) the supporters generally did not do well enough and (b) the supporters turned out to not be docile enough. The opposition, as in the abstract formulation, divided into those willing and those unwilling to participate in such elections – but the abstract formulation does not tell us at all about what was said, about which arguments prevailed, about what the oppositionists actually decided to do, about how the military and its civilian supporters reacted, or about how the oppositionists debated the next steps, let alone the climate of fears and hopes on all sides, and the sense of defeat, triumph, loyalty, and betrayal, also on all sides. (On all of which see Skidmore, 1989.) On the other hand without these or some other abstract formulation, no general principles will be discerned.

ELITES AND OTHERS

One matter that has occasioned some debate, but less debate than it should, concerns identifying the principal actors in democratizations. Several distinguishable trends in the democratization literature converged in suggesting a focus on the dealings of elites of various sorts.

- The paradigmatic Spanish case experienced important moments in which the leaderships of the major contending parties got together and worked out deals, imparting much impetus to the scholarly search for analogs in other cases.
- Beyond the Spanish case, the new empirical stress on deal making and pacts tended to focus on those who negotiated those pacts rather than on the collectivities for which they negotiated.
- Beyond the empirical particulars, the new theoretical taste for exploring the conditions for transition and for democratic stability in terms of small numbers of abstractly conceived actors also tended to replace complex and problematic collectivities by unitary actors who in turn could readily be identified with publicly recognized leaderships and at the limit, perhaps even preferably, with a single individual.

Political scientists developed refined analyses of the various ways in which elites negotiated settlements by research into the facts of individual instances. Students of Spain, for example, might write of the meeting in 1978 in a Madrid restaurant between representatives of several major parties as the moment "[a] new decision-making style was initiated" (Gunther, 1992:59). Apart from the advantages to theory building in thinking of the forging of democracy as primarily the outcome of the activities of a small number of actors, there were significant methodological advantages as well. An enterprising researcher, if blessed with adequate charm, could gather essential information by simply interviewing the participants in a rather small number of meetings. The empirical study of the achievement of solidary actions by shifting collectivities would generally be a more difficult matter. One may speculate that for U.S.-based researchers studying recent democratizations abroad, with limited budgets and constrained by the finitude of summer breaks and sabbaticals, looking for the evidence provided in talks with a dozen key participants would be extremely appealing. The same might well apply even to researchers from less well-funded universities in less rich countries, whose resource constraints – funds, libraries, time away from teaching – would often be substantially greater.

But the stress on elites may bypass many important issues. Why did representatives of Spain's Socialists get into that restaurant meeting in the first place – and why was it important that representatives of the communists (not at the restaurant) held prior discussions with the Socialists? To answer such a question requires the study of the forms of organization of Spain's workers, their relationships to left parties, the possibilities of disruption of elite plans should they not be included and a whole host of harder-to-research issues (Fishman, 1990).

Let me elaborate this point. Students of the Spanish process have called our attention to (as Linz and Stepan, 1996:92–3 put it):

> the moderating role of the king, the constructive leadership of Santiago Carrillo (the leader of the Spanish Communist Party), the prudence of Cardinal Tarancón (the leader of the Spanish Catholic Church), the support and courage of General Gutiérrez Melado (the chief of staff to the Spanish Army), the political astuteness of Josep Tarradellas (the exiled leader of the Catalan regional government), the parliamentary negotiating abilities of Torcuato Fernández Miranda, and the cooperation of the conservative leader Manuel Fraga . . . .

The abstractly imagined theorization of interests, situations, strategies and alliances may help shed light on the degree to which moderation, prudence, courage, astuteness, and negotiation were stable attributes of individuals or strategic options in relationships among these actors. But they will not tell us why these particular actors mattered, a question that takes us well beyond these individuals.

More broadly still, some would urge us to rethink the role of workers' movements in democratic episodes (Rueschemeyer et al., 1992; Collier, 1999) or the role of social movements and contentious politics in the entire history of democratizations (Markoff, 1996; McAdam, Tarrow, and Tilly, 2001). It is not even very plausible that there would be much democratization for us to be studying without a good deal of transgression by townspeople and villagers in many times and places (for an argument about one episode, see Markoff, 1995), but there is a good deal of room for thinking through the different kinds of weight of elites and others in different episodes as Collier's (1999) work suggests.

THE CHALLENGE OF DEFINITION

Although democracy is a very old word that referred to one among several imaginable forms of government in antiquity, in the late eighteenth century the word took on considerable new baggage. Europeans had generally used the term to refer to what was taken to be an undesirable and fortunately unworkable arrangement (at least for any large, modern state). The 1780s seems to be the moment that the word *democrat* came into use (Brunner, et al., 1972–84:821–99), an indication that there were people identified with the notion that democracy was to be created now.

It is quite a difficult matter to sort out what it was those late-eighteenth-century democrats understood democracy to be. As in many situations of conflict, it is a great deal easier to say what they were against than what they were for: they opposed the institutions of the monarchical, aristocratic, and corporate orders with which they were familiar. But they had little desire to recreate the institutions they, as educated Europeans, would have associated with "democracy," namely the institutions by which ancient Athens was governed. Nor were they staunch advocates of many of the practices most people at the onset of the twenty-first century would identify with democracy. Few among that first generation of democrats wanted voting rights for women, virtually none wanted election-contesting rival political parties, most were comfortable limiting voting rights to those of a certain income, many approved of significant restrictions on press freedoms, and many accepted slavery.

If we look through the various indexes that quantitatively inclined social scientists were using to measure democracy by the late twentieth century, we can be confident that as different as these indexes are from each other not a single one would classify as terribly democratic a country with women denied the right to vote, significant numbers of poorer men similarly denied, significant limits on press freedoms, and large numbers held in slavery. This simple imaginary act of measurement makes us realize that democracy has undergone considerable reconceptualization over the past two centuries or so. Most of the people involved in redefining democracy were not academic researchers, arguing with each other over the superiority of one classification scheme or another, but people involved in political struggles, including powerholders in government palaces and movements in town and countryside.

Because social movements have continued to be part and parcel of the fabric of democracy, just what it is that constitutes democracy will continue to be debated, and social scientists, like other citizens, will have different views from each other. The meaning of democracy will continue to be in flux. To study democracy is to study a moving target.

CONSOLIDATION AND INTERIM REGIMES

Some researchers hoped to identify some fixed state in the midst of, or perhaps at the end of, all this flux and attempted to distinguish a *consolidated* democracy from one in the process of construction. There is a general agreement among proponents of such a concept that a regime may be held to be consolidated when it is, in the memorable and much-quoted phrase of Giuseppe di Palma (1990:113), "the only game in town." In one particularly interesting effort at precision, Linz and Stepan (1996:5–7) explain that such a state may be said to exist when certain behavioral, attitudinal, and constitutional conditions are satisfied. Behaviorally, "no significant" actors are trying "seriously" to end democracy or break up the state; attitudinally, "a strong majority" embraces democratic procedures; constitutionally, "governmental and nongovernmental forces alike" carry on conflict within the "laws, procedures, and institutions" of democracy.

Some transitologists have debated the precise weight afforded to behavioral, attitudinal, or constitutional elements (Diamond, 1999:64–116; Mainwaring, O'Donnell, and Valenzuela, 1992). But one wonders how precision is to be achieved: to return to the Linz and Stepan specification, how do we know which actors are "significant," when do they "seriously" work to undo democracy, how much of a majority is "a strong majority," and so forth? The concept is supposed to help us find an island of at least some limited stability in the river of transformation, yet Linz and Stepan point out that even consolidated democracies can be overthrown (1996:6) and Diamond not only speaks of "deconsolidation" but suggests that it may be "easier to observe" (1999:67).

The point of the consolidation concept is to help us identify some conditions that are favorable for giving democracy a more than transitory quality (Schedler, 2001:67), but it is not obvious that current conceptualization has given us more than a comforting word that on scrutiny points us again in the direction of understanding change. We can expect that in response to such doubts, theorists hoping to get a handle on stability will be working to refine the consolidation notion, whereas others will balance di Palma's striking phrase with the equally striking observation of Charles Tilly (1997:213) that "sites of democracy always display the sign Under Construction."

One of the fruitful ways in which the concept of consolidation actually accentuates attention to processes as well as states is that it calls attention to governmental processes on the way to consolidation. Transitions do not only have a beginning and (maybe) an end, but there is a politics of transitional governance itself, of provisional, caretaker, interim regimes. These regimes are made up variously of people committed to democracy, people committed to heading somewhere else but claiming democratic commitments, people following the main chance of the moment, and beneficiaries of the old order who hope to find a place in the new. Such actors may find the state of the in-between to be itself highly rewarding and if they are powerful enough the interim regime may begin to acquire a permanence of its own. The claim of *making* democracy may provide its own form of legitimation. So it turns out that part of what is involved in explaining democratizations is not only how modern authoritarianisms and other forms of nondemocratic regime unravel but how provisional and interim regimes are superseded rather than drift toward permanence. The subject is beginning to receive some very insightful attention (Shain and Linz, 1995), and could use more.

MACROTRANSITIONS

The subject of transitions is not exhausted by the study of individual transitions. We need to consider the temporally clustered bursts of democratization in the world and the changing content of what was at issue in those clusters. In the twentieth century, we can identify three such democratic waves (Green, 1999; Huntington, 1991; Kurzman, 1998; Markoff, 1996).

Early in the twentieth century a significant number of countries became more democratic. In 1906 Finland became the first country in Europe to enfranchise women. The year 1911 brought an end to most of the powers of the British House of Lords, thereby increasing the powers of the elected House of Commons. In 1912 Italy ended restrictions on voting by men and Argentina enacted major suffrage reform. In 1913 Norway adopted universal suffrage, the United States shifted to direct election of senators, and France adopted an effective secret ballot.

Claiming participation in the rising tide, President Woodrow Wilson of the United States justified his country's entry into the First World War by proclaiming it a war for democracy. When only the democratic powers emerged from the catastrophe with their political systems intact, the new states that emerged on the ruins of empires in Central and Eastern Europe usually adopted constitutions that resembled those of the victors. The early twentieth century, in summary, was a moment when many transitions toward democracy were occurring: in some countries democratic constitutions were adopted for the first time; in other countries long-standing traditions were reinvigorated through significant change in political practice.

Most of the new, postwar democracies were overthrown in what many took to be the general collapse of democratic government in the 1920s and 1930s. By the time many of the remaining democracies were overrun by fascist armies, there was good reason for concern over whether democracy had much of a future. But the Second World War was not only followed by a restoration of democracy in Western Europe but also the implantation or reimplantation of democracy in places where it had been missing or had done poorly. The European restoration was followed by the independence of many European colonies that often marked that momentous event with a democratic constitution. Simultaneously a number of other states joined the democratizing tide (such as Costa Rica, Brazil, and Venezuela). Although this second democratic wave, too, was reversed by military coups and martial law proclamations, as we have seen, the last portion of the twentieth century saw a third wave, geographically the most extensive.

During this third wave, some students of democracy were examining the waves, not just specific national instances of transition. Many questions may be raised, few of which have been settled by existing research.

- Why have certain historical moments been those in which many democratic transitions are occurring?
- Why, at those moments, are democratizations occurring in some countries but not others?
- Why are some of those transitions longer lasting than others? (Some hardly get off the ground, others are derailed in short order, and still others endure for a very long time).
- What variants of democratization and what fusions of democratic and authoritarian

forms become institutionalized in particular places? And why?
- Does the nature of democracy alter from one wave to the next and, if so, in what ways?

This last question overlaps with the question of innovation: where and when were innovations in democratic practice created? And why did some innovations but not others come to be widely taken up – perhaps even redefining democracy?

We find, for example, that:

- Women's suffrage, although rejected at the onset of modern democracy in the late eighteenth and early nineteenth centuries, was gradually adopted in country after country, starting in places that were not world, regional, or national centers of power. The first national state with equal voting rights for women at the national level, for example, was New Zealand; the first country in Europe, Finland; the first U.S. state, Wyoming (Markoff, 2003b).
- The issues that were important differed from wave to wave. One study suggests that issues of human rights were not nearly as important in democratic transitions earlier in the twentieth century as they were at its end but "labor activism and leftist politics" were more important (Green, 1999:105). A second study argues that the first cluster of transitions was taking place in countries that had achieved effective national states with codified and enforced bodies of law, whereas the late-twentieth-century democratizations have often seen the institution of voting with broad suffrage rights but without the effective rule of law (Rose and Shin, 2001).
- Despite the very old argument that under democratic rules the very numerous voters with lesser incomes would effectively expropriate the fortunes of the better off, rights of poorer people to tax-based material benefits have in different countries developed on different timetables, have been organized in strikingly different ways and to remarkably different degrees. One of the notable distinctions of the third wave is the widespread contraction of social safety nets. Despite an extensive literature on innovations in this area, much remains in controversy among scholars, including the unusually limited nature of U.S. welfare measures (Huber and Stephens, 2001; Janoski and Hicks, 1994; Marshall, 1950; Piven and Cloward, 1997; Skocpol, 1992; Turner, 1993).

If there are such broad differences in processes that are typical of different waves, perhaps we need, theoretically, to think through how democratization might proceed differently given differing political, economic, or cultural contexts. This is quite a separate question from whether some contexts simply bar democratization altogether – barring some routes does not necessarily mean barring all routes. To follow one suggestion, for example, there may be both "strong-state" and "weak-state" trajectories. In the former, and far more common scenario, an effective but undemocratic state develops first and then is democratized. The less common weak-state scenario develops consultative institutions at an early point and only later brings an effectively functioning national government into being. This second case is no doubt considerably rarer because weak states are often gobbled up by rapacious neighbors or consumed by democracy-destroying civil warfare, but nineteenth-century Swiss history might offer a fair empirical approximation (McAdam et al., 2001:264–304).

CONNECTION ACROSS BORDERS

A focus on time entails attention to space. If democratizations are temporally clustered, then explaining that clustering will consider social processes that operate across national frontiers. Although it may be abstractly conceivable that similar social processes are unfolding in many separate national states separately, the likelihood that transnational connection has something to do with democratization would seem strong, even *a priori*. But a bit of history makes the point a great deal stronger. No one could sensibly study the democratization of European states at the end of the eighteenth century without taking into account the French armies and the reactions of worried or hostile powers to that threat. Nor could anyone usefully examine transitions from or to democracy in the 1940s without taking the actions of the German armies and then the American armies into account. Alfred Stepan surveyed the varying paths to "redemocratization" since World War Two and identified three variants "in which war and conquest play an integral part." He goes on: "The great majority of historical examples of successful redemocratization, most of them European, in fact fall into these first three categories" (Stepan, 1986:65).

Warfare is only one kind of transnational process with enormous consequences for the history of democracy. Let us think of democratizations as outcomes of the interaction of powerholders and of movements that challenge them, with a lot of variation in the significance of the powerholders (including divisions among them) and the movements (including divisions among them). Movements often and powerholders always exist in a web of social connection that crosses national frontiers. Movements take up ideas from elsewhere (ideas about goals, strategies, possibilities, threats, organization), sometimes involve participants who bring experience from elsewhere, sometimes make use of resources from elsewhere, sometimes enter into alliances with movements elsewhere, and occasionally form transnational organizations. Powerholders in one national state need to think about other states: about their military threats or vulnerabilities; about their successes worth imitating and failures worth avoiding; about their possible provision of resources, and about their relative prestige in a variety of transnational arenas. So it is not only foreign armies that may implant, nourish, deform, discourage, or destroy democracy. Foreign funds and foreign models may sometimes be weighty, too. And powerholders, operating in part in a transnational arena confront social movements that themselves are shaped by a variety of transnational processes (Markoff, 1996:20–36).

As the third wave focused researchers on transitions, some increasingly paid attention to such transnational dimensions (e.g., Huntington, 1991:31–46; Robinson, 1996; Whitehead, 1986).

CHALLENGES TO SCHOLARSHIP

Such considerations introduce challenges to scholarship at once *conceptual, theoretical, methodological*, and *historical*.

Conceptual Issues

In 1690, a century before the invention of the word *democrat* signaled that a new history of democracy was beginning, a learned French dictionary could define democracy with deceptive simplicity as "Form of government in which the people have all authority" (Furetière, 1970 [1690]). Because very few thought democracy either possible or desirable for large states, there was no need to specify precisely how such a government was to be organized, how the people were to exercise their monopoly on authority, or even how one would know who those authoritative people were. One hundred years later real people in the new United States, revolutionary France, and other places were struggling with how such a government might be organized, and people have been struggling over this question ever since.

Social scientists attempting to define democracy have pondered how to weigh various elements that since the late eighteenth century have been frequently been presumed by someone to be vital. Some of these suggested elements are:

- Some collection of personal rights on which even governments are not to infringe

- Some collection of personal rights on which even governments are not to infringe, except as provided by law
- A very large proportion of residents having rights to vote for the incumbents of state office
- A very large proportion of residents having a bundle of rights that are the same for all
- All offices exercising effective power being accountable to electorates directly or indirectly
- Military forces subject to civilian authority
- The right for those who so desire to form a political party to contest elections
- Credible vote counts
- A level of civil liberties sufficient for an election to be a genuine contest
- A high level of citizen participation in elections
- A high level of citizen participation in public life generally
- Sufficient substantive equality in wealth and other resources so that political contests take place on a level playing field

It would be easy enough to add to this list. Even a cursory study of the literature will readily demonstrate considerable difference among social scientists as to which of these elements they regard as essential to a good definition of democracy, which extraneous, which pernicious, and which suggest useful distinctions among subtypes of democracy. Much scholarly writing on democracy at the beginning of the twenty-first century is skeptical about the antepenultimate item and even more skeptical about the penultimate (e.g., Nelson, 1987), and most scholars reject the final item completely, preferring to define democracy as a set of formal procedures for the selection of incumbents.

Since the late eighteenth century, many governments have been inclined to evoke democratic legitimation even when they do not adhere to institutions and practices that many social scientists would call democracy. But even when they adhere to such practices, movements of many sorts often challenge such claims (and may sometimes find some social scientists to agree with the challenge). Under a political system with a claim to democracy, "This isn't democracy" is a common rallying cry for the aggrieved. The continual negotiation of challenging movements and powerholders continues to refine – and sometimes sharply alter – what democracy means in practice. Social scientists who study democracy are studying mutation. This is not merely because of the recent stress on studying a process, democratization, rather than a state, democracy, but because the point toward which democratization is tending keeps moving, sometimes a little bit and sometimes a great deal (Dahl, 1998; Markoff, 1996).

In a nutshell, democracy has been a concept of people engaged in political struggle at the same time that it has been a tool of analysis of social scientists. From the moment democrats came into the world at the end of the eighteenth century, "democracy" escaped from the philosopher's study. It has been a term of approbation and disapprobation in political struggles as people use or withhold the label to support or challenge a political program, a group of incumbents, a movement, or a regime. Social scientists were hardly immune. By many common definitions, a twentieth-century political system in which some significant group of adult citizens is excluded from the right to vote by force is not democratic (see, e.g., Linz, 2000[1975]:58) yet very few social scientists followed the logic of such definitions to conclude that the United States did not become a democracy until the 1960s. (For exceptions see Rueschemeyer, Huber, and Stephens, 1992:122; Therborn, 1977:17.)

Faced with this challenge, there are several ways to proceed. We might try to collect a wide variety of definitions of democracy and seek out some limited common core. We might, as is commonly done by social scientists in the early twenty-first century, agree to select only procedural elements, construct a multiplex set of procedures that approximates practice in the world's richer countries, and regard poorer countries as democratic if they approximate those procedures. We might choose a definition that approximates the political system we think desirable. We might think of the mutability of definition as a fascinating subject in its own right and make the study of the differing meanings of democracy in different times and places, and to different people, a subject of scholarly inquiry all its own. (It is surprising how little research has been done following this last option.)

Theoretical Issues

For many reasons, democracy is an invitation to change. These include:

- At the idea level, its legitimating formula of popular rule can readily be drawn on to challenge the democratic character of current procedures. People who believe in some abstract conception of democracy are frequently disappointed by democracy in practice (Hermet, 1984:137). The gap between dream and reality leads some to disown democracy in principle, others into cynicism, still others into pragmatically embracing existing procedures and downplaying the dream. But others yet again attempt to improve reality.[5]
- On the level of organization, its legitimating formula of popular rule is virtually an invitation to social movements to press their causes. When rulers claim to rule on behalf of the many and by their consent, it is difficult to prevent the many from speaking for themselves. Some of the movements will call for redefining political procedures, enlarging the rights of some whose rights are limited, or including some who are currently excluded. There is also the very important possibility that democracy will also open the way to antidemocratic movements, a subject beginning to receive the attention it deserves.
- The multidimensionality of notions of democracy often creates conflicts among those who seek to advance on one dimension at the expense of another that is more important to other people. From De Tocqueville on, many have recognized that big principles like "equality" and "liberty" may often be in contradiction. De Tocqueville (1990[1840]:93) tellingly titled one chapter in *Democracy in America* "Why Democratic Peoples Show a More Passionate and Enduring Love for Equality than for Liberty."

In the 1960s in the United States it was common on university campuses for some to denounce student demonstrators as undemocratic because they did not honor widely accepted procedures at the same time as the demonstrators denounced powerholders as undemocratic for not acting on a wide range of legitimate grievances. Such encounters often lead to change, sometimes very significant change.

The theoretical challenge is to get a handle on the many kinds of dynamism that democratization involves.

Methodological Issues

The comparative study of democratizing episodes has at least two difficult challenges to confront.

Measurement. The post–World War Two tradition of comparative inquiry into the conditions that favored democracy, when engaged in by the statistically inclined, demanded empirical indicators of "democracy" that could be systematically collected (Inkeles, 1991). It was readily recognized that this was not a simple matter, primarily for two reasons. First of all certain kinds of data were hard to come by in reliable form for large collections of countries. How, for

[5] Concern about the gap between many broad notions of democracy and the actuality of *all* existing political arrangements led Robert Dahl to favor the term *polyarchy* for political systems that meet certain democratic criteria while reserving *democracy* for political systems that meet more of them. Some existing systems, for Dahl, are polyarchic because mass electorates have an opportunity to choose the incumbents of office in competitive elections but none are democratic because all existing political arrangements are highly inegalitarian. If, to use this terminology, we ever manage to move beyond polyarchy toward democracy to any significant degree, the study of transition will acquire a whole new subject matter (Dahl 1971, 1998).

example, do you obtain good indicators of the extent of "freedom to organize parties" for a broad collection of cases? Second, and more perplexing, was the absence of consensus on what it was we needed good indicators of. Issue two would mean that even if there were no problem in obtaining reliable data there would remain differences among scholars on what the needed data were. A discussion of these issues on the eve of the late twentieth century democratic wave (May, 1973) shows how these issues were already appreciated.

Serious as these issues were, the measurement question became far more serious as scholarly attention turned to issues of transition. It would not be enough to have measures that might identify democracy with some institutions that could sharply distinguish democratic and nondemocratic states at some moment in time. We now needed measures that would track changes within particular national contexts but also that would be able to accomplish this for substantial numbers of national cases.[6]

Should we focus on relatively easy-to-assess practices in order to get comparable indicators for many cases? It would, for example, be far easier to get reliable indicators of whether opposition parties were legally tolerated than to be confident we knew the degree to which parties competed on a level playing field. For the former we only need to know the law, but for the latter we need to know a great deal about how electoral laws are applied, whether police and judges are following those laws, whether oppositions operate under a climate of nonlegal but real violence (which may only exist away from the eyes of reporters), whether incumbents have the capacity to falsify results, and whether the mass media are under the control or influence of the incumbents or (even more difficult to notice) their committed supporters.

But there are also very difficult questions about how even reliable information is to be joined to other information in forming an overall judgment to be compared to other cases or to be compared to the same national case at other moments. In considering the United States, for example, if we are measuring democracy before the 1960s how are we to weigh the severe limits on the right to vote of African Americans in one large region of the country? How are we to weigh the widespread limitations on the voting rights of the numerically far fewer Native Americans? How are we to weigh the rising numbers of people who since the 1980s have lost the right to vote as convicted felons (in some states for life)?[7]

These difficulties are pointed up in a fine review of noteworthy attempts at creating a large database for the comparative study of democratization. One annually collected body of data in the 1990s raised its standards for regarding various practices as moving in a democratic direction as well as assigned governments on the left lower scores than those on the right for comparable deviation from democratic practice. A second data set gives little weight to the extent of popular participation and none to civil liberties. A third is so narrowly focused on whether there are competitive elections that it classifies as democratic cases where political liberties were so restricted that the elections were a charade, including one where the head of government was actually chosen by the armed forces (Mainwaring et al., 2001:53–60).

It is a cause for methodological concern that differing measures of democracy might yield different results in particular studies. Pamela Paxton (2000) has shown, for example, that studies making claims about the dating of "democracy" wind up with very different results if they do or if they do not regard equal voting rights for women as part of their definition.

Although the focus on democratization as a process is bound to lead to continued efforts to develop superior measures and to refine

[6] Noteworthy data sets along these lines are described in Karatnycky (1998), Marshall and Jaggers (2000), "Polyarchy Dataset" (2000), and Przeworski et al. (2000).

[7] "Nationwide, 14 percent of black males are barred from voting because they are in prison or have been convicted of felonies. In Alabama and Florida, nearly one out of every three black men is disfranchised, and in Iowa, Mississippi, New Mexico, Virginia, Washington and Wyoming, the ratio is only slightly lower" (Keyssar, 2000:308; see also Uggen and Manza, 2002).

existing measures, it is not likely that there will ever be a consensus among researchers that some measure is so clearly superior that it drives inferior measures from the field. The so-called measurement problem is only in part a question of collecting good indicators. The difficulties surrounding definition are not simply failures of researchers to think clearly enough or to track down comparable measures for a variety of national cases. More fundamentally, it is because democratization is inherently a complex, debated, and mutating concept.

The Transnational Dimension. As usually conceived, comparative inquiry examines separate national experiences, identifies their points of similarity and difference, and attempts to identify (a) recurrent patterns that appear despite the diversity of cases, (b) distinctive patterns that appear despite the similarity of cases, or (c) the range of variation and the causes of that variation (Tilly, 1984). In light of the very important transnational connections, however, we can see that comparative studies when conceived as something like an experimental replication under varying conditions are not adequate to the task at hand. The study of transitions within national states demands attention to social processes that cross the frontiers of those states.

Historical Issues. Sociologists sometimes hope or even assume that historians have provided them with the raw materials which they can use to test theory or – for those of an inductive turn of mind – on which they can construct theory. Because the history of democracy involves very different sorts of actors (the powerful and the challengers, for example) and has unfolded in many places that are connected to each other, getting the history right is itself a major challenge. Examining social processes that brought, and bring, elites and plebeians into interaction across national frontiers will make demands on the practice of history, as it will on other social science disciplines (Markoff, 2002).

CHAPTER TWENTY

Revolutions and Revolutionary Movements

Jeff Goodwin

The sociological study of revolutions has made enormous explanatory strides during the past two decades. We now understand much better than previously both the "classic" revolutions in England, France, and Russia and more recent revolutions in so-called developing societies (e.g., China, Vietnam, Cuba, Iran, and Nicaragua). Some scholars have also fruitfully examined the collapse of communism in the Soviet Union and Eastern Europe as a peculiar type of revolution, and there is a growing literature on so-called Islamist movements as a revolutionary phenomenon. According to Randall Collins, "The most striking accumulation of knowledge" in the field of macrohistory "has taken place on Marx's favorite topic, revolution" (1999:3).

Sociologists have been especially interested in understanding "great" or "social" revolutions, that is, revolutions that bring about not only a change of political regime but also fundamental economic and perhaps cultural change (but cf. Tilly, 1993). Social scientists in the United States in particular have been especially fascinated with such revolutions – perhaps because of the often strenuous efforts by their own government to prevent or reverse such revolutions, or perhaps because the United States itself was borne of a revolution that some analysts consider "great" or "radical" (e.g., Lipset, 1988; Wood, 1992). Crane Brinton (1965[1938]), Barrington Moore (1966), Chalmers Johnson (1982[1966]), Ted Robert Gurr (1970), Samuel Huntington (1968), Eric Wolf (1969), Jeffery Paige (1975, 1997), and Ellen Kay Trimberger (1978) are just a few of the scholars who have made important contributions to this tradition.

Following the groundbreaking work of Charles Tilly (1978) and Theda Skocpol (1979), moreover, a veritable explosion of sociological studies of revolutions – much of it comparative as well as historical – has occurred. Works by John Walton (1984), Farideh Farhi (1990), Jack Goldstone (1991), Tim McDaniel (1991), Timothy Wickham-Crowley (1992), Eric Selbin (1993), Carlos Vilas (1995), John Foran (1997b), Mark Katz (1997), and Misagh Parsa (2000), among others, have further enriched our understanding of revolutions. And these works are just the tip of an intellectual iceberg that includes innumerable historical case studies of particular revolutions and revolutionary movements.

WHAT IS A REVOLUTION?

The word *revolution* has two general, "ideal-typical" meanings in the social sciences, neither of which is inherently more correct or accurate than the other, although each raises somewhat different questions for social analysts. According to the broader definition, *revolution* (or *political revolution*) refers to any and all cases in which a state or political regime is overthrown, supplanted, and/or fundamentally transformed by a popular movement in an irregular, extraconstitutional, and/or violent fashion. Revolution in this sense includes successful national independence and secessionist movements. This definition assumes that revolutions, at least those worthy of the name, necessarily require the mobilization of large numbers of people against the existing state – unlike, for example, coups d'etat or "palace revolutions." [Some scholars, however, have analyzed so-called "revolutions from above" that involve little if any popular mobilization prior to the overthrow of the state (see, e.g., Trimberger, 1978).] As Leon Trotsky (1961[1932]:xvii) once wrote, "The most indubitable feature of a revolution is the direct interference of the masses in historic events."

According to the other, narrower definition, a *revolution* (or *social revolution*) entails not only mass mobilization and regime change but also more or less rapid and fundamental social, economic, and/or cultural change during or soon after the struggle for state power. (What counts as "rapid and fundamental" change, however, is open to dispute.) Social revolutions in this sense are also called "great" revolutions.

Both of these definitions suggest that revolutions are the result, to a greater or less extent, of popular mobilizations and/or *revolutionary movements*. A *revolutionary movement* may be defined as that type of social movement which attempts to overthrow, supplant, and/or fundamentally transform state power. (Most social movements, by contrast, try to pressure existing authorities to enact social reforms.) The nature and extent of social, economic, and cultural change advocated by revolutionary movements varies greatly. Some revolutionary movements do not seek to change society much at all; they simply seek state power. Others seek very extensive and deep transformations of the social order, the economy (especially the distribution of property and wealth), and the culture. Of course, some revolutionary movements are much more successful than others; in fact, only a few such movements actually seize power. When revolutionaries fail to seize power, we may speak of a *failed revolution*. Other revolutionaries may succeed in taking power, but fail in realizing their broader goals of social transformation.

THEORETICAL APPROACHES

The theoretical literature on revolutions and revolutionary movements has grown quite extensive and complex. It encompasses numerous schools of thought and generations of analysts.[1] Instead of reviewing this entire literature, which simply cannot be done adequately in the space of a chapter, I will limit myself to an examination of the approaches that have most influenced sociologists: modernization theory, Marxist theory, and state-centered approaches. Modernization theory was most influential during the 1950s and 1960s and Marxist theory during the 1960s and 1970s. State-centered analysis has become more prominent during the past two decades.

Modernization theory links revolutions to the transition from "traditional" to "modern" societies, that is, to the very process of "modernization" itself. Traditional societies, in this view, are characterized by fixed, inherited statuses and roles; simple divisions of labor; social relations regulated by custom; local and particularistic attachments to the family, clan, tribe, village, or ethnic community; and thus very limited and localized forms of political participation. Modern societies, by contrast, are distinguished by social mobility and achieved statuses and roles, formal equality, complex divisions of labor, social relations regulated by legally enacted rules, broader collective identifications with "the nation," and mass political participation in national states.

Most modernization theorists argue that revolutions are especially likely to occur in so-called transitional societies, that is, societies undergoing very *rapid* (albeit uneven) modernization. Revolutions themselves, moreover, serve to push forward the modernization process. "Revolution," argues Samuel Huntington, "is thus an aspect of modernization. . . . It will not occur in highly traditional societies with very low levels of social and economic complexity. Nor will it occur in highly modern societies"

[1] Guides to this literature include Cohan (1975), Goldstone (1980, 2001, 2003), Zimmermann (1983: chapter 8), Kimmel (1990), Collins (1993), Foran (1993), and Goodwin (1994). This and the following section draw on Goodwin (2001).

(Huntington, 1968:265). In Walt Rostow's evocative phrase, revolutionaries are "the scavengers of the modernization process," and communism in particular "is best understood as a disease of the transition to modernization" (Rostow, 1967[1961]:110).

Why is this so? Modernization theorists have developed a number of explanations that link rapid modernization to the development of revolutionary movements. These explanations usually hinge on some sort of "lag" or lack of fit between different social institutions, which are putatively "modernizing" at different rates. Thus, Huntington argues that revolution, like "other forms of violence and instability, . . . is most likely to occur in societies which have experienced some social and economic development [but] where the processes of political modernization and development have lagged behind the processes of social and economic change" (Huntington, 1968:265).

More psychologically inclined theorists suggest that rapid modernization unleashes a "revolution of rising expectations" – expectations that a stagnant or suddenly depressed economy may prove unable to meet, thereby creating the widespread anger and sense of "relative deprivation" of which revolutions are made (see, e.g., Gurr, 1970). Still others have argued that rapid modernization may "dis-synchronize" a society's values and social structure. Accordingly, revolutionaries who offer an alternative set of values that better "fits" the social structure will become influential (see, e.g., Johnson, 1982[1966]; Smelser, 1962). And for still others, rapid modernization destroys the "integrative" institutions that held traditional societies together, creating a sense of meaninglessness (or "anomie") or uncertainty about one's place in society (or "status anxiety"); revolutionaries, in this view, may become influential in transitional societies because they are able to replace the institutions that modernization undermines. As Harry Benda (1966:12–13), an analyst of Asian communism, has written,

> it is not inconceivable that in Asia (as elsewhere) Communist movements as such provide a substitute for decayed or vanishing institutions – the family, the clan, the tribe, or the village community – that have suffered most heavily under the eroding onslaught of the new economic and political systems carried to Asia by the West in the course of the past century or so . . . . If iron discipline, rigid hierarchies, and unquestioning obedience are among Communism's most detestable features in the eyes of truly free men everywhere, they may yet spell security, order, and a meaningful place in the world for the social splinters of contemporary Asia.

During the 1950s, a large literature explained the "appeals of communism" and radical nationalism in much the same terms as Benda's (see, e.g., Almond et al., 1954).

Modernization theorists, however, generally do recognize that even very rapid modernization does not automatically lead to revolutions. It is at this point that many of them emphasize the role of politics: The success or failure of revolutionary movements, they claim, depends on how incumbent governments respond to revolutionary movements and to the broader social problems created by rapid modernization. More specifically, if a "modernizing elite" controls the government and responds flexibly and creatively to such problems – by "resynchronizing" values and the social structure, for example, through "conservative change" – then revolution will be avoided. Conversely, "elite intransigence," as Chalmers Johnson puts it, "always serves as an underlying cause of revolution" (Johnson, 1982[1966]:97). Huntington similarly argues that revolutions "are unlikely in political systems which have the capacity to expand their power and to broaden participation within the system." "Ascending or aspiring groups," he concludes, "and rigid or inflexible institutions are the stuff of which revolutions are made" (Huntington, 1968:275).

Having come this far, one might expect modernization theorists to discuss at some length the factors that explain the flexibility (or lack thereof) of different types or configurations of states and political regimes. Curiously, however, one finds little such analysis. Even Huntington, the most "state-centered" of modernization theorists, offers only a vague generalization in this regard:

> The great revolutions of history have taken place either in highly centralized traditional monarchies

(France, China, Russia), or in narrowly based military dictatorships (Mexico, Bolivia, Guatemala, Cuba), or in colonial regimes (Vietnam, Algeria). All these political systems demonstrated little if any capacity to expand their power and to provide channels for the participation of new groups in politics (1968:275).

Unfortunately, this formula is not altogether helpful. Not *all* colonial regimes, after all – in fact, relatively few – were overthrown by revolutions. Moreover, even if those colonial regimes that were so overthrown did indeed collapse because they lacked the capacity to incorporate new groups, what might explain this? Similarly, not *all* military dictatorships – even "narrowly based" military dictatorships – have been toppled by revolutionaries. Again, if those that were so toppled actually fell because they lacked the capacity to incorporate new groups, how can we explain this? To answer to these questions, we require an approach that examines states and state capacities more closely than does the modernization perspective.

Like modernization theorists, Marxists also view revolutions as occurring in "transitional" societies – only in this case the transition, which is seen as the result of class struggle, is from one economic mode of production to another. That said, the specific character of recent revolutions has come as something of a surprise, and poses a theoretical anomaly, to Marxists. To begin with, the socialist or communist orientation of many revolutions in the capitalist "periphery" has virtually "stood Marx on his head." As Ernest Mandel (1979:11) notes:

In general, traditional Marxism looked upon relatively backward countries – those of Eastern and Southern Europe, and even more those of Asia and Latin America – in the light of Marx's well-known formula: the more advanced countries show the more backward ones the image of their future development as in a looking glass. This led to the conclusion that socialist revolutions would first occur in the most advanced countries, that the proletariat would take power there long before it would be able to do so in more backward countries.

In fact, not only have a series of avowedly socialist revolutions occurred in the capitalist periphery, but the industrialized capitalist societies of the core have proven surprisingly immune to this form of social change.

One notable aspect of this historic reversal of Marxist expectations is that recent "Third World" revolutions have relied heavily on social classes deemed secondary (at best) to the classic socialist project, particularly the peasantry, rather than on the industrial proletariat. Instead of being built on the technological foundations of advanced capitalism, moreover, socialism has arguably been one of the means by which some relatively "backward" countries have attempted to "catch up" with the advanced capitalist core. In short, rather than being a *successor* to capitalism, socialism has been something of an historical *substitute* for it in many developing societies.

Moreover, the former Soviet bloc, China, and Vietnam have recently begun transitions from socialism to capitalism, thereby reversing the presumed course of history according to the traditional Marxist model. Indeed, this type of transition was virtually unthinkable to Marxists in the not-so-distant past. Even dissident Marxists and socialists who were harsh critics of authoritarian "state socialism" in the Soviet bloc by and large did not anticipate such a transition to capitalism. On the contrary, many expected, or at least hoped, that state socialism would be democratized from below by popular movements; the communist elite that had expropriated capitalist property would itself be expropriated, in this scenario, by the people. Instead, communism is now widely viewed, as the Eastern European joke goes, as the longest and most painful route from capitalism to ... capitalism.

How exactly have Marxists attempted to resolve the theoretical anomaly of socialist revolutions occurring in the capitalist periphery? Many (following the lead of Lenin, Trotsky, and Mao) begin by pointing to the weakness of the capitalist or bourgeois class in developing societies. Peripheral bourgeoisies – or "lumpenbourgeoisies," as Andre Gunder Frank has termed them – are small, only partially differentiated from feudal landowning elites, and, partly for these reasons, heavily dependent on the state for economic opportunities and protection from challenges from below. Consequently, capitalist classes in the Third World have proven unwilling or unable to play their "historic role" of leading antifeudal, democratic revolutions in the manner of their European counterparts. Ironically, "bourgeois" revolutions in Third World societies must thus be made by the working class – guided by vanguard parties – in a strategic alliance with the peasant majority in such societies. But because such antifeudal revolutions are made by worker/peasant alliances, they may, unlike Europe's bourgeois revolutions, more or less quickly attempt to initiate a transition to socialism. Third World revolutions, to use Trotsky's phrase, thus assume the form of "permanent" or "uninterrupted" revolutions that undertake socialist as well as antifeudal policies or "tasks" (Trotsky, 1961[1932]; see also Löwy, 1981). A similar line of argument about socialist revolutions has been introduced into academic social science by Barrington Moore's *Social Origins of Dictatorship and Democracy* (1966), which emphasizes the role of the peasantry in such revolutions.

Marxists do recognize, however, that strong revolutionary movements have not emerged in *all* developing or peripheral societies. This has been variously attributed to unexpectedly strong peripheral bourgeoisies, to a lack of revolutionary leadership, or to the fact that not all *types* of peasants are inclined to support revolutionary movements – although just what sort of peasants are revolutionary, and why, has been the subject of much debate.

For many Marxists, rural producers whose mode of life most closely approximates that of urban workers are, not surprisingly, the most likely stratum to ally with such workers. Consequently, landless rural workers and, to a lesser degree, poor peasants (especially tenants) with very little land have usually been considered by Marxists as the most revolutionary social strata in the countryside. These groups are seen as having irreconcilable conflicts of interest with landowners as well as an "objective" interest in socialism, understood as the collective self-management of production. These groups are revolutionary, in other words, or will eventually become so, by virtue of their economic class position. Landowning "middle" peasants, by contrast, are thought to waiver in their political allegiances, whereas rich peasants (not to mention landlords themselves), who hire wage labor, have usually been regarded as counterrevolutionary. Thus, developing societies with large middle and rich peasantries are not likely to generate strong revolutionary movements.

More recently, however, this general picture has been questioned in various ways by neo-Marxist or Marxist-influenced scholars of peasant politics. Eric Wolf (1969), for example, argues that landowning middle peasants, not rural workers or poor peasants, are in fact *most* likely to be revolutionary. Wolf, who examines peasant involvement in the Mexican, Russian, Chinese, Vietnamese, Algerian, and Cuban revolutions, views peasant rebelliousness as a reaction to the disintegrative effects of "North Atlantic capitalism" as it penetrates traditional societies (1969:276–82). He argues that landowning middle peasants, as well as "free" peasants who are outside landlord and state control, are most likely to rebel, both because their way of life is more threatened by capitalism compared to other social groups *and* because they are better able to act collectively to preserve their traditional ways.[2] As Wolf puts it, "it is the very attempt of the middle and free peasant to remain traditional which makes him revolutionary" (1969:292). Wolf does, however, recognize that poor and landless peasants have also become involved in revolutions when and insofar as they can be mobilized by "external" political and military organizations – organizations, moreover, that typically seek to do much more than preserve "traditional" ways of life (Wolf, 1969:290).

Wolf's arguments have been contested by Jeffery Paige, who argues that sharecropping tenants and migratory "semiproletarians," not middle peasants, are the most revolutionary rural strata. Like Wolf, however, Paige also links "agrarian revolution" to the penetration of world capitalism into preindustrial societies and, more specifically, to the creation of "export

[2] Craig Calhoun has argued that urban artisans have been more revolutionary than the urban proletariat for similar reasons (1982:chapter 6).

enclaves." (Paige's influential 1975 book, in fact, is subtitled *Social Movements and Export Agriculture in the Underdeveloped World*.) And Paige also agrees with Wolf – as against the traditional Marxist view – that landless rural workers are unlikely revolutionaries, being more inclined to support merely reformist political movements that seek better wages and working conditions. Unlike Wolf, however, Paige argues that revolutionary movements develop because sharecroppers and semiproletarians are wage-earning cultivators who face a dominant, noncultivating class that derives its income from more or less fixed landholdings (as opposed to capital investments), the control of which is nonnegotiable. And Paige, unlike Wolf, argues that revolutionary socialist movements in particular are "internally generated, not introduced by outside urban-based parties" (1975:62).

Thus, whereas modernization theorists view the development of revolutionary movements as a consequence of very rapid modernization, and their success as a consequence of intransigent elites, Marxists tend to explain recent revolutions in the periphery as a reaction to the incorporation of "backward" societies – or at least those with the "right" kinds of peasants – into the capitalist world economy. These revolutions, in other words, are ultimately a reaction to capitalist imperialism or globalization.

Are the Marxists right? Or rather, *which* Marxists are right in their search for the "really" revolutionary peasantry? All and none, I have argued (Goodwin, 2001). In fact, a wide variety of rural as well as urban strata – including poor, middle, and rich peasants as well as urban wage earners and middle strata – can and have played important roles in particular revolutionary movements. They have done so, however, not simply as exploited classes, but also and more directly as excluded and often violently repressed state subjects. For while class and economic grievances do often play an important role in revolutions, recent scholarship suggests that the roots of revolutionary movements are found in the specific type of political context in which class relationships and economic institutions (among other factors) are embedded.

Marxists have also said too little about the conditions that determine whether revolutionary movements, whatever their class composition, will succeed or fail in actually overthrowing the state. The failure of any particular revolution presumably indicates that class contradictions have not yet fully "matured" or that the revolutionary class or class alliance has not yet attained a critical mass. However, understanding the success or failure of revolutionary movements requires something rather less speculative and more specific: a close examination of the *states* that revolutionaries have sought to overthrow.

THE STATE-CENTERED PERSPECTIVE

If modernization theorists attribute revolutions to overly rapid modernization and Marxist theorists view revolutions as products of class struggles unleashed by capitalist globalization, state-centered analysts explain revolutions in terms of fluctuations in the nature and extent of state power. Sociological studies of revolution in this state-centered tradition include Chorley (1943), Skocpol (1979), Goldstone (1986, 1991), Snyder (1992, 1998), Collins (1993, 1999), and Goodwin (2001). According to Collins, this perspective has "created a paradigm revolution in the theory of revolution" (1999:3). But why "privilege" the state in this way when revolutions are obviously complex historical processes that involve multiple economic, social, cultural, social-psychological, and voluntarist factors (Emirbayer and Goodwin, 1996)? For two general reasons. First, successful revolutions necessarily involve the breakdown or incapacitation of states. Of course, revolutions obviously involve much more than this, and states do not break down in precisely the same way – although wars and fiscal crises induced by wars or geopolitical pressures are usually to blame. Still, there would be no revolutions to study (or to emulate or denounce) if states did not at least occasionally break down or were otherwise incapacitated, whether from the efforts of revolutionaries themselves or for some other reasons. This "state-centered" idea is now widely if not universally accepted not only among scholars of revolutions but also among large numbers of social scientists more generally (see, e.g., Collins, 1993).

There is, however, a second and perhaps more interesting reason for centering the state in a study of revolutions: Strong revolutionary movements of whatever social composition and ideological orientation, and whether they actually seize state power, only emerge in opposition to states that are configured and act in certain ways. There is a sense in which certain state structures and practices actively albeit unintentionally help to form or construct revolutionary movements as effectively as the best professional revolutionaries. State structures and practices invariably matter, in other words, for the very formation as well as the subsequent fate of revolutionary movements – and they generally do so in quite unintended ways.

Why is the development of revolutionary movements dependent upon particular state structures and practices? First, people will usually not join or support revolutionary movements when they believe that the central state has little if anything to do with their everyday problems. In other words, few people – even when they are poor and palpably exploited – seek to overthrow states (perhaps risking their necks in the process) that seem peripheral to their most pressing concerns. Second, few people join or support revolutionaries – even when they are more or less in agreement with their demands or ideology – if they feel that doing so will simply make them the targets of state violence or if they believe that they can obtain much or even some modicum of what they want, politically speaking, through some routine, institutionalized, and therefore low-risk channel for political claim making (e.g., voting or petitioning). Other things being equal, people, like electric currents, seem to take the path of least resistance. As Trotsky once put it, "People do not make revolution eagerly any more than they do war.... A revolution takes place only when there is no other way out" (1961 [1932], III:167).

More specifically, the formation of revolutionary movements has been unintentionally facilitated and even encouraged by that subset of violent and exclusionary authoritarian states that are also organizationally incoherent and militarily weak, especially in outlying or isolated areas of the national society. Other things being equal, the political context that is most conducive to the formation of strong revolutionary movements is found in those societies in which indiscriminately repressive *and* disorganized states possess geographically and socially delimited power, that is, *low-capacity authoritarian regimes* (Tilly, 2003). Revolutionary movements, for their part, have become especially powerful actors when they have been able to organize in opposition to such regimes broad multiclass (and, if necessary, multiethnic) coalitions with strong international support. The formation of such coalitions has been encouraged and facilitated (again, quite unintentionally) by especially autonomous – or socially "disembedded" (Evans, 1995) – authoritarian states that exclude and repress not only lower classes (i.e., peasants and workers) but also middle and even upper or "dominant" classes. In fact, such autonomous, exclusionary, disorganized, and weak states are particularly vulnerable to actual *overthrow* by revolutionary movements – and not necessarily by the largest or best organized revolutionary movements. This vulnerability derives in part from the fact that such states tend to preclude the sort of political openings that have elsewhere incorporated important social groups into institutional politics and thereby limited the appeal of revolutionaries. Revolutions are unlikely, in fact, where the state has institutional linkages with nonelite groups, is organized in a rational-bureaucratic fashion, and effectively governs throughout the territory of the national society. For these reasons, revolutions are unlikely in most democratic societies.

The preceding ideas can be figuratively represented. Figures 20.1 and 20.2 describe conceptual spaces in which empirical states may be located. Figure 20.1 provides a conceptual map of states as a function of their *organization* (bureaucratic/rational or patrimonial/clientelistic), on the one hand, and of the relative inclusiveness or exclusivity of the *political regimes*

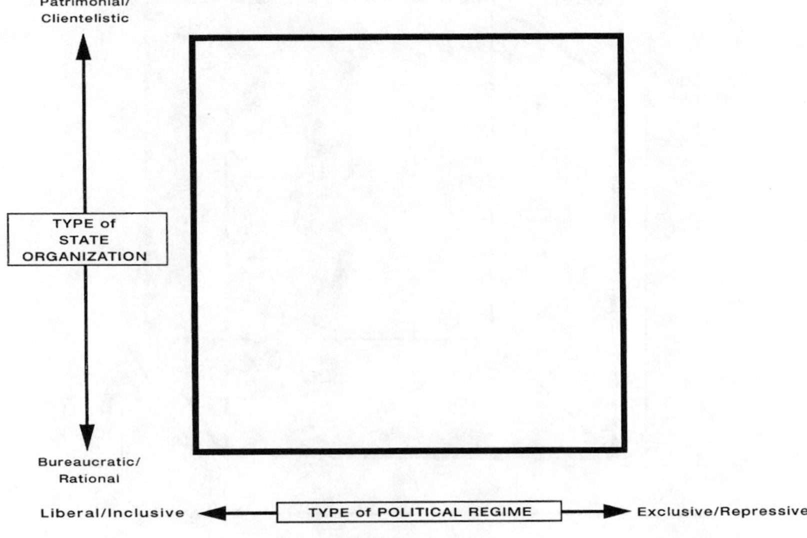

Figure 20.1.

to which they are attached, on the other – ranging from liberal/inclusive democratic regimes, at one extreme, to exclusionary/repressive dictatorships, at the other. Figure 20.2 adds an additional variable, namely the extent of the state's infrastructural power, that is, the state's capacity to enforce its will and to do so throughout the national territory.

Several basic claims about the relationship between states and revolutionary movements are represented in Figures 20.3 and 20.4. The shaded area in Figure 20.3 indicates the type of states that tend unintentionally to "incubate," or encourage the formation of, revolutionary movements, namely, those states that are especially exclusionary and yet infrastructurally

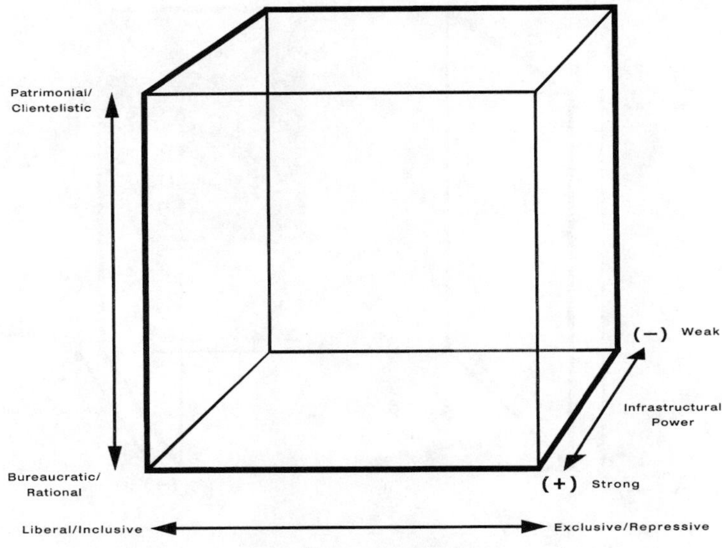

Figure 20.2.

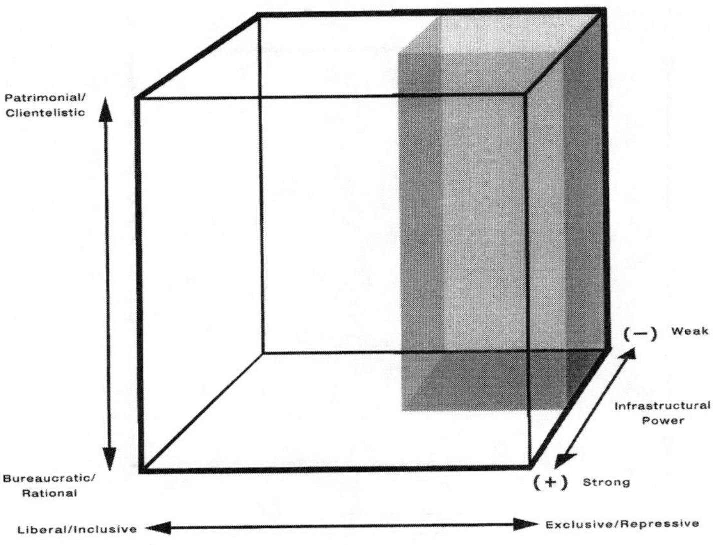

Figure 20.3.

weak. Political exclusion, especially indiscriminately violent exclusion, tends to "push" or channel excluded groups into revolutionary movements – and the state's weakness prevents it from destroying such movements. By contrast, more inclusionary states may confront considerable opposition, but this tends to be less radical in its ends and means; and infrastructurally strong states are generally able to repress disloyal opponents, even if political exclusion provides the latter with an incentive to rebel.

Not all states that "incubate" revolutionary movements, however, are necessarily vulnerable to actual overthrow by such movements. As Figure 20.4 indicates, only a subset of states that

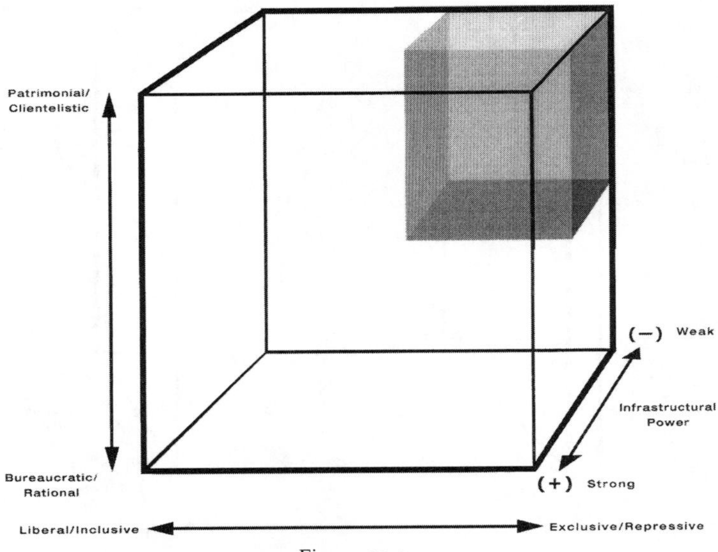

Figure 20.4.

unintentionally nurture revolutionary movements is especially vulnerable to being overthrown, namely, those exclusionary yet weak states that are also organized in a patrimonial or clientelistic as opposed to bureaucratic fashion. The key idea here is that patrimonial states do not easily allow for the sort of reformist initiatives that would successfully counter a popular revolutionary movement. Patrimonial states cannot easily jettison unpopular leaders, incorporate new groups into decision-making processes (or state offices), or prosecute a counterrevolutionary war in a rational or efficient manner.

Of course, these claims have a probablistic, "other-things-being-equal" quality. Revolutionary movements do not only or automatically form or seize power in the context of a specific type of state – although certain types of states are clearly much more vulnerable to revolution than others. Nor are states the *only* factor that matters for the formation of revolutionary movements; a very broad array of economic, cultural, and organizational factors may contribute to the development of such movements and influence their political fortunes. Still, there is a tendency among some scholars to view revolutionary movements as the products of rapid social change, intense grievances, certain class structures or land-tenure systems, economic dependency, imperialist domination, and/or the actions of vanguard parties abstracted from the political context in which each and all of these factors are embedded. (Still other scholars treat political context as a simple reflex of one or more of these factors.) The central claim of the state-centered perspective is that a close examination of states as a reality *sui generis*, to use Durkheim's expression, is invariably crucial for understanding the formation and fate of revolutionary movements. Political context is not simply one more variable to be examined by the conscientious scholar of revolutions (on the order of "educational attainment" or "median income"), but a "force field," so to speak, that mediates and powerfully refracts the effects of the wide range of factors that typically impinge on the development and trajectory of revolutionary movements.

WHY DO REVOLUTIONS – AND REVOLUTIONARY MOVEMENTS – OCCUR WHEN AND WHERE THEY DO?

The fact that state breakdowns, particularly the incapacitation of armies, create the type of political opportunities necessary for full-fledged revolutionary change is one of the best-known ideas to emerge from state-centered analyses of revolution; it is a point that is central, for example, to Theda Skocpol's influential state-centered study, *States and Social Revolutions* (1979). In fact, Skocpol explains not only why transformative, class-based revolts from below could occur in France, Russia, and China but also the origins of the political crises that created such opportunities in the first place. Indeed, one of the more interesting claims of Skocpol's study is that the political crises that made revolutions possible in France, Russia, and China were *not* brought about by revolutionaries; rather, conflicts between dominant classes and autonomous state officials – conflicts, Skocpol emphasizes, that were produced or exacerbated by geopolitical competition – directly or indirectly brought about such crises, thereby opening up opportunities that rebellious lower classes and self-conscious revolutionaries seized, sometimes years later.

By illuminating the origins of, and the political opportunities created by, these types of state crises and breakdowns, state-centered approaches help to explain the classic puzzle of why revolutions occur when and where they do. Indeed, it has become virtually obligatory for scholars to note that people are not often rebellious in the poorest of societies or during the hardest of times; and even where and when people are rebellious, and strong revolutionary movements form, they may not always be able to seize state power – *unless*, that is, they are able to exploit the opportunities opened up by state breakdowns. "It is the state of the army, of competing armies," Barrington Moore has noted, "not of the working class, that has determined the fate of twentieth-century revolutions" (1978:375). Of course, revolutionaries need not wait for such opportunities to appear. They often topple states, especially infrastructurally weak states, through their own efforts. Revolutionaries may create their own political opportunities as well as seize preexisting ones.

Indeed, state power and its breakdown cannot alone explain (or predict) revolutions; analysts also need to explain why and how specifically revolutionary movements are able to take advantage of these crises – or *create* such crises – and actually seize power. After all, an organized revolutionary movement simply may not exist or possess sufficient leverage within civil society to take advantage of (or create) a state crisis. In such cases, state power will be reconsolidated – if it is reconsolidated at all – by surviving factions of the old regime or by political forces that eschew any significant transformation of the state or society.

So why are groups with a revolutionary agenda or ideology sometimes able to attract broad popular support? Research suggests that at least five distinctive state practices or characteristics help unintentionally to engender or construct strong revolutionary movements; these practices and traits, moreover, are causally "cumulative," in the sense that a strong revolutionary movement is more likely to develop the more they characterize a given state.

1. *State sponsorship or protection of unpopular economic and social arrangements.* In certain societies, economic and social arrangements – particularly those involving people's work or livelihood – may be widely viewed as unjust (that is, as not simply unfortunate or inevitable). Yet unless state officials are seen to sponsor or protect those arrangements – through legal codes, surveillance, taxation, conscription, and, ultimately, force – specifically *revolutionary* movements are unlikely to emerge. People may blame their particular bosses or superiors for their plight, for example, or even whole classes of bosses, yet the state itself may not be challenged (even when the aggrieved are well-organized and the political context is opportune) unless there exists a widely perceived symbiotic or dependent relationship between the state and these elites (see, e.g., chapter 4; Tilly, 1993; Tarrow, 1998). Indeed, the fact that a despised state must actively protect certain institutions and groups will itself serve, in many instances, to delegitimate and stigmatize those institutions and groups.

For this reason, "ruling classes" that do not directly rule may be safer than those which do; other things being equal, that is, some measure of state autonomy from the dominant economic class may act as a bulwark against revolution. In such contexts, contentious, antielite actions may be chronic, in such forms as pilfering, malingering, sabotage, riots, strikes, and demonstrations; yet such actions are unlikely to escalate beyond a local or, at most, regional level in a way that would seriously and directly threaten a strong state.[3] And yet rebels are not revolutionaries, according to most definitions, unless they seriously contend for state power. Thus, if and when domination is widely perceived to be purely local, then revolution is unlikely, no matter how oppressive that domination is felt to be.

It follows that states that mitigate or even abolish perceived economic and social injustices are less likely to become the target of political demands (revolutionary or otherwise) than those that are seen to cause or perpetuate such injustices. On the other hand, a state that suddenly attempts to reform unpopular institutions that it has long protected may not be able to preempt thereby a revolutionary challenge; on the contrary, such reforms, or even attempted reforms, may be perceived as signs of the state's weakness and, accordingly, will simply serve to accelerate revolutionary mobilization. We might term this the "too-little-too-late syndrome." As De Tocqueville argued, "the most perilous moment for a bad government is one when it seeks to mend its

[3] As James C. Scott (1990) has emphasized, class struggles "from below" only very rarely break out of their localistic and necessarily disguised forms, even when inequalities, class identities, and oppositional subcultures are quite salient.

ways.... Patiently endured so long as it seemed beyond redress, a grievance comes to appear intolerable once the possibility of removing it crosses men's minds" (1955[1856]:177).

In sum, grievances may only become "politicized" (that is, framed as resolvable only at the level of the state), and thereby a basis for specifically revolutionary movements, when the state sponsors or protects economic and social conditions that are widely viewed as grievous (e.g., Tilly, 1986:chapter 9). State practices thus help to constitute both a distinctive *target* and *goal* for aggrieved groups in civil society, namely, the state itself and its overthrow (and reorganization), respectively.

2. *Exclusion of mobilized groups from state power or resources.* Even if aggrieved groups direct their claims at the state, they are unlikely to seek its overthrow (or radical reorganization) if they manage to attain some significant share – or believe they *can* attain such a share – of state power or influence. Indeed, even if such groups view their political influence as unfairly limited, their access to state resources or inclusion in policy-making deliberations – unless palpably cosmetic – will likely prevent any radicalization of their guiding ideology or strategic repertoire. In fact, the political "incorporation" of mobilized groups – including the putatively revolutionary proletariat – has typically served to *deradicalize* them (see, e.g., Bendix, 1977; Mann, 1993: chapter 18; Roth, 1963). For such groups often view this sort of inclusion as the first step in the accumulation of greater influence and resources; in any event, they are unlikely to jeopardize their relatively low-cost access to the state – unless that state itself is in deep crisis – by engaging in "disloyal" or illegal activities.

Political inclusion also discourages the sense that the state is unreformable or an instrument of a narrow class or clique and, accordingly, needs to be fundamentally overhauled. De Tocqueville emphasized how the exclusionary nature of French absolutism bred, by contrast, a political culture characterized by a utopian longing for total revolution – even though French social conditions were comparatively benign by European standards of the time (1955[1856]:part 3, chapter 1).

Accordingly, neither open, democratic polities nor authoritarian yet inclusionary (for example, "populist") regimes have generally been challenged by powerful revolutionary movements, although there are certainly exceptions (see below). By contrast, chronic exclusion of mobilized groups from access to state power is likely to push them toward a specifically revolutionary strategy – that is, extralegal, militant, and even armed struggle aimed at overthrowing the state (e.g., Seidman, 1994). Such exclusion, after all, serves as an object lesson in the futility of legalistic or constitutional politics (i.e., "playing by the rules"). Exclusionary authoritarian regimes tend to "incubate" radical collective action: Those who specialize in revolution tend to prosper under such regimes, because they come to be viewed by many people as more realistic and potentially effective than political moderates, who themselves come to be viewed as hopelessly ineffectual. Partly for this reason, virtually every powerful revolutionary movement of the past century developed under an exclusionary political regime, including the Bolsheviks in Russia (Kaiser, 1987), the communists in China and in Southeast Asia (Bianco, 1971; Pluvier, 1974; Young, 1991), Castro's July 26th Movement in Cuba (Pérez-Stable, 1998), the broad coalition that opposed the Shah in Iran (Arjomand, 1988; Parsa, 2000), and the guerrilla movements of Central America (Booth and Walker, 1993; Vilas, 1995; Wickham-Crowley, 1992).

3. *Indiscriminate, but not overwhelming, state violence against mobilized groups and oppositional political figures.* Like political exclusion, indiscriminate state violence against mobilized groups and oppositional

figures is likely to reinforce the plausibility, legitimacy, and (hence) diffusion of the idea that the state needs to be violently "smashed" and radically reorganized. For reasons of simple self-defense, in fact, people who are literally targeted by the state may arm themselves or join groups that have access to arms. Unless state violence is simply overwhelming, then (see the subsequent text) indiscriminate coercion tends to backfire, producing an ever-growing popular mobilization by armed movements and an even larger body of sympathizers (see, e.g., Gurr, 1986; Mason and Krane, 1989). Revolutionary groups may thus prosper not so much because of their ideology per se, but simply because they can offer people some protection from violent states. Many studies of revolutions emphasize that groups have only turned to extralegal strategies or armed struggle after their previous efforts to secure change through legal means were violently repressed (see, e.g., Booth and Walker, 1993; Kerkvliet, 1977; Walton, 1984).

Like political exclusion, indiscriminate state violence also reinforces the plausibility and diffusion of specifically revolutionary ideologies, that is, ideologies that envisage a radical reorganization not only of the state but of society as well. After all, a society in which aggrieved people are routinely denied an opportunity to redress perceived injustices, and jailed or even murdered on the mere suspicion of political disloyalty, is unlikely to be viewed as requiring a few minor reforms; such people are more likely to view such a society as in need of a fundamental reorganization. In other words, violent, exclusionary regimes tend to foster unintentionally the hegemony or dominance of their most radical social critics – religious zealots, virtuous ascetics, socialist militants, and radical nationalists, for example, who view society as more or less totally corrupted, incapable of reform, and thus requiring a thorough and perhaps violent reconstruction (see McDaniel, 1991: chapter 7).

4. *Weak policing capacities and infrastructural power.* Of course, no matter how iniquitous or authoritarian a state may be – or the society which it rules – it can always retain power so long as it is capable of ruthlessly repressing its enemies. Such a state may in fact have many enemies (including revolutionaries), yet they will prove quite ineffective so long as the state's coercive might remains overwhelming.

   Long before a state breakdown, however, revolutionaries may become numerous and well-organized if the state's policing capacities and infrastructural power more generally are chronically weak or geographically uneven. Guerrilla movements, for example, have typically prospered in peripheral and especially mountainous areas where state control is weak or nonexistent: The communist movement in China grew strong in the northwest periphery, Castro's movement in Cuba's Sierra Maestra, and El Salvador's guerrilla armies in that country's mountainous northern departments (see, e.g., Wolf, 1969:chapter 6, on Cuba; Pearce, 1985, on El Salvador). And revolutionaries are doubly fortunate if they confront states and armies that are ineffectual due to corruption or bureaucratic incoherence – traits that are often purposively fostered by ruling cliques or autocrats who fear palace coups (Snyder, 1992, 1998). In such situations, revolutionaries themselves may bring about or accelerate state breakdowns not only through direct military pressure but also by exacerbating conflicts between states (especially personalistic dictatorships) and dominant classes and between states and their foreign supporters. These types of conflicts, in addition to creating the general insecurity associated with revolutionary situations, may accelerate state breakdowns by creating economic downturns that bring on fiscal crises for states (see Foran, 1997b).

5. *Corrupt and arbitrary personalistic rule that alienates, weakens, or divides counterrevolutionary elites.* As these last remarks suggest, autocratic and so-called neopatri-

monial (or "sultanistic") dictatorships are especially vulnerable to revolution (see, e.g., Chehabi and Linz, 1998; Dix, 1984; Foran, 1992; Goldstone, 1986; Goodwin and Skocpol, 1989; Snyder, 1992; Wickham-Crowley, 1992). In fact, such regimes not only tend to facilitate the formation of strong revolutionary movements but also cannot easily defeat such movements once they have formed; examples of such regimes include the dictatorships of Díaz in Mexico, Chiang in China, Batista in Cuba, the Shah of Iran, Somoza in Nicaragua, and Ceauşescu in Romania. As especially narrow and autonomous regimes, such dictatorships tend to have few fervid supporters; their arbitrary exercise of power also tends to alienate certain state officials and military officers as well as vast sectors of society – including middle strata and even elites in addition to lower classes. In fact, because dictators often view economic and military elites as their chief foes, they may attempt to weaken and divide them in various ways, even though such groups share with dictators a conservative or counterrevolutionary orientation. By weakening counterrevolutionary elites, however, dictators may unwittingly play into the hands of revolutionaries, because such elites may thereby become too weak either to oppose revolutionaries effectively or to oust the dictator and reform the regime, thereby preempting revolution.

Of course, not all dictators are equally adept at controlling their armed forces and rival elites; their incompetence or incapacity in this regard does not bode well for them personally, but it may prove decisive in preempting revolution. For if civilian and military elites can remove corrupt and repressive dictators, and perhaps institute democratic reforms, they thereby undermine much of the appeal of revolutionaries. In fact, this is precisely what happened in the Philippines in 1986 with the ouster of the dictator Ferdinand Marcos (Parsa, 2000; Snyder, 1992).

In sum, certain types of states are not only liable to break down and thereby to create the sort of political opportunities that strong revolutionary movements can exploit; certain states also unintentionally foster the very formation, and indeed "construct" the hegemony or dominance, of radical movements by politicizing popular grievances, foreclosing possibilities for peaceful reform, compelling people to take up arms to defend themselves, making radical ideologies and identities plausible, providing the minimal political space that revolutionaries require to organize disgruntled people, and weakening counterrevolutionary elites, including their own officer corps. This is a sure recipe for social revolution.

WHY NO SOCIAL REVOLUTIONS IN THE POST–COLD WAR ERA?

The world has witnessed considerable ethnic conflict and several regime changes during the post–Cold War era, including popular revolts in Indonesia and Serbia that unseated dictators.[4] Yet not a single great or social revolution has occurred in the period since 1989, nor does one seem likely in the immediate future. How are we to explain this theoretically?

Of course, great revolutions have always been relatively rare and unexpected. Those who have planned (or simply predicted) revolutions have failed much more often than they have succeeded. During the two centuries prior to the Second World War, in fact, there occurred exactly three social revolutions: the French, Russian, and Mexican. Many more revolutions occurred during the Cold War era, but almost all of these were incubated by, and overthrew, three rather peculiar types of political order that have now almost completely passed from the scene: the rigidly exclusionary colonies of relatively weak imperial powers (Vietnam, Algeria, Angola, Mozambique); personalistic, "above class" dictatorships (Cuba, Iran, Nicaragua); and dependent, Soviet-imposed communist regimes (Eastern Europe) (see Goodwin, 2001).

[4] This section draws on Goodwin (2003).

Some have suggested that capitalist globalization has destroyed the very rationale for revolutions. According to this perspective, state power – that great prize of revolutionaries – has been dramatically eroded by the growing power of multinational corporations and transnational financial institutions and by the increasingly rapid and uncontrollable movements of capital, commodities, and people. These realities, according to Charles Tilly, "undermine the autonomy and circumscription of individual states, make it extremely difficult for any state to carry on a separate fiscal, welfare or military policy, and thus reduce the relative advantage of controlling the apparatus of a national state" (1993:247). In other words, the more globalization diminishes and hollows out state power, the less rational becomes *any* political project aimed at capturing state power, including revolution.

Historically, however, there has been a strong *positive* correlation between a country's exposure to external economic competition and the size of its public sector (Evans, 1997). Rather than uniformly diminishing states, in fact, globalization has been just as likely to spur attempts to employ and, if necessary, expand state power for the purposes of enhancing global competitiveness. Some have argued that globalization is itself a project of strong states (Weiss, 1997). Popular support for revolutionaries, in any event, is usually not based on estimations of their likely success in enhancing the autonomy of a country's fiscal policy or even its long-term global competitiveness. Rather, ordinary folk have typically supported revolutionaries when the latter have spoken up for them when no one else would (or could), provided for their subsistence, defended their traditional rights and, not least, protected them from state violence. As Jorge Castañeda has argued, mass support for revolution typically derives less from attractive visions of the future – although such visions have been important for intellectuals – than from a widely shared conviction that the status quo is simply unendurable:

> The rationale for revolution, from seventeenth-century England to Romania at the close of the second millennium, has always lain as much in the moral indignation aroused by an unacceptable status quo as in the attraction exercised by an existing blueprint for the future. The most powerful argument in the hands of the left in Latin America – or anywhere else – has never been, and in all likelihood will never be, exclusively the intrinsic merit or viability of the alternative it proposes. Its strong suit is the morally unacceptable character of life as the overwhelming majority of the region's inhabitants live it. (Castañeda, 1993:254)

There is no reason to believe that in the future people will accept the depredations of authoritarian states and shun revolutionaries on the grounds that state power "ain't what it used to be."

The current period has not exhibited the same scale of revolutionary conflict as the Cold War era primarily because of the wide diffusion of formally democratic and quasi-democratic electoral regimes throughout much of Latin America, Eastern Europe, and parts of Asia and Africa since the early 1980s. This is a development for which revolutionaries themselves can take considerable credit. And yet, be this as it may, these types of regimes are powerfully counterrevolutionary. It is not coincidental, in fact, that no popular revolutionary movement has ever overthrown a consolidated democratic regime. Certainly, no consolidated democracy is today even remotely threatened by a revolutionary movement – not in Western or Eastern Europe, Japan, North America, Costa Rica, Australia, or New Zealand. As one noted sociologist has written,

> There is now no substantial reason to believe that marxist revolutions will come about in the foreseeable future in any major advanced capitalist society. In fact, the revolutionary potential – whatever the phrase may reasonably mean – of wageworkers, labor unions and political parties, is feeble. This is true of the generally prosperous post–World War II period; it was also true of the thirties when we witnessed the most grievous slump so far known by world capitalism. Such facts should not *determine* our view of the future, but they cannot be explained away by references to the corrupt and corrupting "misleaders of labor," to the success of capitalist propaganda, to economic prosperity due to war economy, etc. Assume all this to be true; still the evidence points to the fact that, without serious qualification, wageworkers under mature capitalism do accept the system. Wherever a labor party exists in an advanced capitalist society,

it tends either to become weak or, in actual policy and result, to become incorporated within the welfare state apparatus. (Mills, 1962:468–69; emphasis in original)

These words were written in the early 1960s – although they require not the slightest revision – not by a conservative but by the radical sociologist C. Wright Mills.

Why is democracy so inhospitable to revolutionaries? First and foremost, democracy pacifies and institutionalizes – but does not eliminate – many forms of social conflict. Seymour Martin Lipset (1960:chapter 7) has aptly referred to elections as a "democratic translation of the class struggle." Indeed, democracy "translates" and channels a variety of social conflicts – including, but not limited to, class conflicts – into party competition for votes and the lobbying of elected representatives by "interest groups." Of course, this "translation" involves distortions and has sometimes taken violent forms, especially when and where the procedural fairness of electoral contests has been widely questioned. But the temptation to rebel against the state – which is rarely acted on without trepidation, given its typically life-or-death consequences – is partly quelled under democratic regimes by the knowledge that new elections are but a few years off and with them the chance to punish incumbent rulers.

Even more importantly, democracies have generally provided a context in which ordinary people, through popular protest, can win important concessions from economic and political elites, although this often requires a good deal of disruption, if not violence (Gamson, 1975; Piven and Cloward, 1977). But armed struggles that are aimed at *overthrowing* elected governments rarely win extensive popular support unless such governments (or the armies that they putatively command) effectively push people into the armed opposition by indiscriminately repressing suspected rebel sympathizers. As Che Guevara wrote:

> It must always be kept in mind that there is a necessary minimum without which the establishment and consolidation of the first [guerrilla] center [*foco*] is not practicable. People must see clearly the futility of maintaining the fight for social goals within the framework of civil debate.... Where a government has come into power through some form of popular vote, fraudulent or not, and maintains at least an appearance of constitutional legality, the guerrilla outbreak cannot be promoted, since the possibilities of peaceful struggle have not yet been exhausted. (1985[1960]:50–1)[5]

With very few exceptions, to paraphrase Alan Dawley (1976:70), the ballot box has been the coffin of revolutionaries.

Does the foregoing mean that political radicalism and militancy go unrewarded in democratic societies? Hardly. Democracy, to repeat, does not eliminate social conflict; in fact, in many ways democracy encourages social conflict by providing the institutionalized "political space" or "political opportunities" with which those groups outside elite circles can make claims on political authorities and economic elites (Tarrow, 1998). Not just political parties, then, but a whole range of interest groups, trade unions, professional associations, social movements, and even transnational networks become the main organizational vehicles, or "mobilizing structures," of political life in democratic polities. But these institutions of "civil society" are generally just that – civil. Their repertoires of collective action include electoral campaigns, lobbying, petitions, strikes, boycotts, peaceful demonstrations, and civil disobedience – forms of collective action that may be undertaken with great passion and militancy (and sometimes for quite radical ends), and which sometimes involve or provoke violence, but which are *not* aimed at bringing down the state.

Democracy, then, dramatically reduces the likelihood of revolutionary change, but *not* because it brings about social justice (although justice *is* sometimes served under democracies). Formal democracy is of course fully compatible with widespread poverty, inequality, racism, sexism, and social ills of all sorts, which is why Karl Marx criticized "political emancipation"

[5] Unwisely, Guevara later abandoned this view, claiming that even democracies could be toppled by revolutionaries.

and so-called bourgeois democracy in the name of "human emancipation." The prevalence of poverty and other social problems is precisely why extraparliamentary movements for social justice so often arise in democratic contexts. These movements, however, almost always view the state as an instrument to be pressured and influenced, not as something to be seized or smashed.

A new era of widespread revolutionary conflict will surely dawn, if this analysis is correct, if the most recent wave of democratization dramatically recedes – if, that is, the new democracies and quasi-democracies in Latin America, Eastern Europe, Asia and Africa are replaced by violent authoritarian regimes. (Revolutionaries are unlikely to overthrow such regimes, however, unless they are unusually weak or suddenly weakened; for even powerful revolutionary movements, we should recall, do not always succeed against strong states.) A widespread reversion to violent authoritarianism seems unlikely, however, if only because economic and political elites, including even army officers, seem increasingly aware of the growing costs of political violence in a globalized economy and of the unique vulnerabilities of narrow dictatorships in particular. The United States government has become increasingly astute at "sacrificing dictators to save the state" (Petras and Morley, 1990:chapter 4), that is, preempting revolution by abandoning or replacing dictators (e.g., Marcos, Duvalier, Noriega, Mobutu, Suharto, and Milosevic) in favor of more broadly based and even formally democratic regimes.

Democracy may be an especially powerful barrier to revolution in an age of capitalist globalization. And globalization, in turn, may help underpin democracy. Certainly, the unprecedented speed and mobility of capital in the current era hang like the sword of Damocles over those on both the left *and* right who would disrupt predictable business climates and "investor confidence." In the new world order, the fear of capital flight or boycott may stay the hand of would-be Pinochets as well as that of would-be Lenins. Globalization, in other words, notwithstanding its often disastrous socioeconomic effects on working people, may actually help undermine authoritarianism and preserve democratic and quasi-democratic regimes. This may explain the striking coincidence of globalization and democratization, which many analysts view as contradictory, since the early 1980s. Elisabeth Wood, for example, has shown how globalization facilitated democratization – and defused revolutionary challenges – in El Salvador and South Africa: the integration of domestic markets into the global economy and "the growing hegemony of neoliberal economic policies made it unlikely that postconflict states would have the capacity to implement confiscatory redistributive policies that would threaten elite interests. Deviation from the neoliberal model would be punished by capital movements" (Wood, 2000:15). Globalization thus provided an incentive for previously authoritarian economic elites to finally accept the full political inclusion of subordinate classes, because the latter would have limited means to threaten elite interests. In effect, elites accepted democracy, while their opponents accepted capitalism.

Revolutions, in sum, will undoubtedly continue to occur in those societies characterized by a combination of gross economic injustices *and* extreme political exclusion and repression by weak or suddenly weakened states. This combination of factors, however, is less prevalent than in the past and may become rarer still. The *political* contexts, especially, that new movements against global capitalism currently confront, and are likely to confront for the foreseeable future, are not nearly as conducive to revolution as during the Cold War era. As a result, most of these movements will attempt to enact reforms by winning a share of power through electoral means or through the pressure of nonviolent demonstrations.

RESEARCH FRONTIERS

Sociologists currently have a much better understanding than previously of the factors that explain why strong revolutionary movements emerge when and where they do as well as why some but not all of these movements are actually able to seize power. What, then, are the research frontiers in this corner of the social sciences? Any list is likely to be somewhat arbitrary, but four directions for future research on revolutions and revolutionary movements seem especially promising.

1. *Anomalous cases.* Trying to account for theoretical anomalies is always helpful for advancing a research program. Scholars of revolution will undoubtedly benefit from thinking harder about two particular sets of anomalous cases: first, cases in which theory and past research would seem to indicate that revolutions (or strong revolutionary movements) *should* have occurred, but none have; and second, cases in which theory and past research would seem to indicate that revolutions (or revolutionary movements) should *not* have occurred, but they nonetheless have. The former set of cases would include all those narrowly based, repressive regimes that have exhibited an unusual capacity to survive over an extended period, even in the face of intermittent opposition [for example, Saudi Arabia, Libya, Syria, Burma, China, North Korea, and Iraq (before the U.S. invasion of 2003)]. A key question here is whether the survival of such regimes – and the weakness or absence of revolutionary movements – is based mainly or solely on the state's infrastructural power or armed might or depends on different factors whose importance has perhaps been underestimated (for example, a state-backed ideology, including nationalism, a cult of the leader, or debilitating divisions among the regime's opponents).

   The second set of cases would include those contexts in which revolutionary movements have fared reasonably or even exceptionally well even though they confronted relatively liberal and/or democratic regimes (for example, Weimar Germany, Chile before 1973, France in May 1968, and Peru during the 1980s). How was the Nazi movement able to become so powerful during the Weimar period (Brustein, 1996; Luebbert, 1991)? Why did Chileans (albeit a minority) elect as president a radical like Salvador Allende (Sigmund, 1978)? Was France on the cusp of a revolution in 1968 (Singer, 2002)? Why did elections in which a range of leftist parties participated fail to defuse the Shining Path insurgency in Peru (Gorriti, 1999)? Were these regimes actually less liberal or democratic than they appeared? How were ordinary people radicalized in these contexts? Why exactly did democracy fail to "tame" revolutionaries? Did economic or cultural factors somehow "trump" political factors in these cases?
2. *Culture (including emotions).* For some years now scholars of social movements have been trying hard to synthesize structural and interest-based accounts of movements with perspectives that emphasize culture, including (increasingly) emotions (Goodwin and Jasper, 2004). Importantly, this work has generally *not* attempted to portray the ends and means of movements as arbitrary or irrational, but has rather forcefully challenged overly narrow conceptualizations of interests and rationality. A good deal of this work has influenced sociologists of revolution, but structuralist thinking remains especially powerful – arguably, too powerful – in this subfield. Thus, new insights into revolutions are likely to be generated by testing ideas that have been fruitfully employed by cultural sociologists (see, e.g., Gorski, 2003; Hunt, 1984; Sewell, 1985; Sohrabi, 1995). Among the questions that merit attention are the following: Are certain cultural contexts more conducive to collective action and revolution than others? Can certain cultural contexts derail or abort an incipient revolutionary movement in an otherwise propitious political context? Why do revolutionary movements – or at least their leaderships – exhibit particular ideological orientations and not others? And how do these orientations, and the cultural idioms of the movement's

rank-and-file, shape the outcomes or achievements of revolutions?

3. *Islamist movements.* If Marxism-Leninism was the dominant revolutionary ideology of the last century, Islam may be the dominant revolutionary ideology of the present. Since the Iranian Revolution of 1979, scholars have been curious about the conditions that encourage the dominance of militant Islamists in revolutionary movements or coalitions (Arjomand, 1988; Parsa, 2000). What factors have led Islamists, as opposed to other radical leaderships (including Marxists and radical nationalists), to dominate certain oppositional movements in the Islamic world (Esposito, 1999)? What are the specific appeals of Islam – and *to whom* exactly does Islam appeal – in these contexts (Wickham, 2002; Wiktorowicz, 2001)? And why have some Islamists rejected militant politics (Moaddel, 2002)?
4. *Strategy and tactics.* Some Islamic movements are attempting to revolutionize their societies "from below" (e.g., in Egypt), without seizing state power, by dominating or refashioning important social and cultural institutions in "civil society" (Berman, 2003). This strategy calls into question the very meaning of the concept of revolution. Is it possible to make a revolution *without* seizing state power? Can a movement be revolutionary that does not seek political power? How much and what kind of change can be effected through this strategy? Under what conditions might revolutionaries – if revolutionaries they be – opt for this "civil" strategy?

   Other Islamic movements have employed terrorism as a tactic, that is, the deliberate targeting of noncombatants for political ends (e.g., in Algeria, Israel/Palestine, and Kashmir). In fact, revolutionary movements of various ideological orientations have sometimes employed terrorism as part of a larger strategy of guerrilla warfare (e.g., in Northern Ireland, Sri Lanka, and Peru). But we still know relatively little about such tactical choices (but cf. Irvin, 1999). Why do some armed insurgencies employ terrorism but not others, and what difference does it make? Indeed, why have some revolutionaries turned to armed struggle in the first place? Why have others opted for nonviolent resistance or even the "parliamentary road" to revolutionary change? And what are the costs and benefits of these various strategic and tactical choices? Which strategies work in which contexts, and why?

These are just some of the questions, of course, that merit further inquiry by sociologists of revolution. If the past is any guide, scholars will continue to reexamine historical cases of revolutions and revolutionary movements with new theoretical ideas and hypotheses, and new revolutions may even come along – unexpectedly, as always – to provide new fodder for sociological analysis.

CHAPTER TWENTY-ONE

Regimes and Contention

Charles Tilly

How do diverse forms of political contention – revolutions, strikes, wars, social movements, coups d'état, and others – interact with shifts from one kind of regime to another? To what extent, and how, do alterations of contentious politics and transformations of regimes cause each other? Does virulent violence necessarily accompany rapid regime transitions? These questions loom behind current inquiries into democratization, with their debate between theorists who consider agreements among elites to provide necessary and sufficient conditions for democracy and those who insist that democracy only emerges from interactions between ruling-class actions and popular struggle. They arise when political analysts ask whether (or under what conditions) social movements promote democracy and whether stable democracy extinguishes or tames social movements. They appear from another angle in investigations of whether democracies tend to avoid war with each other. At least as context, they loom large in every historical account of popular politics. They figure centrally in any analysis of interactions between democracy and power.

The same sorts of questions recur in studies of industrial conflict, where one school of thought opines that strikes represent breakdowns in bargaining that could be pursued more efficiently by other means, another school of thought argues that strikes entail compromises of labor with capital and thereby integrate workers unwittingly into capitalism, whereas a third view treats strikes as rational, essential means of struggle in competitive capitalism but not elsewhere. They dog every analysis of revolution, which must consider whether certain kinds of contention regularly promote revolutions as well as whether revolutions regularly generate certain kinds of contention. Yet we have no coherent theory of links between regime change and contentious politics. We have, that is, no widely accepted and empirically defensible account of how prevailing forms of popular struggle vary and change from one sort of political regime to another, much less why such variation and change occur. At least two obstacles bar the path to coherent theory: first, that the relationship between regime change and contentious politics is surely complex, contingent, and variable; second, that no codification of variation in regimes has commanded wide assent.

This chapter will not unveil a general theory of regime change, of contentious politics, or of their interaction. It rests, indeed, on a set of premises denying the possibility of a general, lawlike theory in this domain:

although political change is causally coherent, it is also path-dependent

- as a consequence, it is crucial to trace effects of existing precedents, models, practices, and connections on any particular sequence of changes
- whole sequences and structures rarely or never repeat themselves
- smaller-scale causal mechanisms do, however, recur in a wide variety of settings
- explanation of changes in contention, in regimes, and in their interaction therefore has

two components: 1) identification of crucial causal mechanisms, 2) analysis of how preceding and existing conditions affect the concatenation and sequence of those causal mechanisms
- even at the unattainable limit of exhaustive explanation, a satisfactory account of interaction between regime change and contentious politics would not take the form of general laws for large sequences or structures but of constraints on combinations and sequences of mechanisms. (Tilly, 2001)

This chapter simplifies such an enormous agenda by singling out broad correspondences between regimes and forms of politics as indications of what must be explained. First, the chapter reviews some well-known classifications of regimes to draw out their implications for variation and change in contentious politics. Next, it synthesizes ideas from those schemes in a new map of regime variation and change. Then, it surveys likely correlates and consequences of regime change with an eye to identifying causal mechanisms deserving further attention. Throughout, it focuses on mechanisms embodied in political contention: discontinuous, collective, public claim making by political actors. Contentious politics runs the range from popular rebellion to strikes, electoral campaigns, and social movements (McAdam, Tarrow, and Tilly, 2001). The chapter ends not with answers, but with proposals for a research program.

How shall we map regimes? At first, Aristotle made it all seem vividly simple: "The true forms of government . . . are those in which the one, or the few, or the many, govern with a view to the common interest; but governments which rule with a view to the private interest, whether of the one, or of the few, or of the many, are perversions" (Barnes, 1984:2030). This reasoning led to a straightforward typology of all governmental forms:

True		**Perversion**
Monarchy	⟶	**Tyranny**
Aristocracy	⟶	**Oligarchy**
Constitutional Government	⟶	**Democracy**

Thus if a single ruler (a monarch) promoted his own self-interest instead of the common good, he became a tyrant; if an aristocracy similarly used governmental power exclusively for its own advantage, the regime became an oligarchy; and if the majority in a constitutional government likewise sought only their own benefit without regard to the commonwealth, their regime became a democracy.

According to Aristotelian principle, proper monarchy rested on rule by the best man, aristocracy on rule by the richest and best men, and constitutional government on rule by free men. (For Aristotle, ineluctable nature condemned women, like slaves, to inferiority.) Because the rich are usually few in number and the free poor many in number, reasoned Aristotle, as a practical matter aristocratic regimes generally mean rule by the few in the common interest, constitutional government rule by the many, likewise in the common interest. Perversions into tyranny, oligarchy, and democracy arise where rulers – one, few, or many – place their own interest above the common good. Democracy's characteristic perversion, in this Aristotelian view, consists of discrimination by the governing poor against both the state's collective interest and the interests of the rich.

To be sure, Aristotle recognized distinctions within his major types of regime, for example five types of democracy, of which the fifth

> is that in which not the law, but the multitude, have the supreme power, and supersede the law by their decrees. This is a state of affairs brought about by the demagogues. For in democracies which are subject to the law the best citizens hold the first place, and there are no demagogues; but where the laws are not supreme, there demagogues spring up. For the people becomes a monarch, and is many in one; and the many have the power in their hand, not as individuals, but collectively . . . this sort of democracy is to other democracies what tyranny is to other forms of monarchy. (Barnes, 1984:2050–1)

In these circumstances, furthermore, demagogues often stir up the rabble to attack the rich and thereby seize power for themselves. In this way, democracy turns into tyranny. When he got to details, Aristotle allowed for plenty of transitions and compromises among his three pure types.

Aristotle proceeded repeatedly from ostensibly static categories to dynamic causal processes. In thinking through the effects of different military formats, for example, he offered a shrewd causal account:

> As there are four chief divisions of the common people, farmers, artisans, traders, labourers; so also there are four kinds of military forces – the cavalry, the heavy infantry, the light-armed troops, the navy. When the country is adapted for cavalry, then a strong oligarchy is likely to be established. For the security of the inhabitants depends upon a force of this sort, and only rich men can afford to keep horses. The second form of oligarchy prevails when a country is adapted to heavy infantry; for this service is better suited to the rich than to the poor. But the light-armed and the naval element are wholly democratic; and nowadays, where they are numerous, if the two parties quarrel, the oligarchy are often worsted by them in the struggle. (Barnes, 1984:2096–7)

In the *Politics*, Aristotle confined his systematic discussion of political contention to revolutions, which meant forcible overthrow of regimes by ostensible subjects of those regimes. In passing, however, he also mentioned factional struggles, conspiracies, and collective resistance to governmental demands. In each case, he treated the form of regime as an outgrowth of the balance among local forces (notably among the rich, the middle class, and the poor) tempered by historical circumstance. He then explained contention as a joint outcome of that balance and the regime type, again tempered by historical circumstance.

Without developing his observations at length, Aristotle clearly saw regimes as having their own characteristic forms of contention, and changes of regime as resulting largely from political contention. In contrasting regimes, different ruling coalitions pursued distinct strategies of rule, which altered the incentives and capacities of various constituted groups within the state to defend or advance their own interests by acting collectively. Aristotle explained struggles of his time by combining the perspectives of rationalists and structuralists, millennia before anyone used those labels (for those labels, see Lichbach and Zuckerman, 1997).

Broadly speaking, recent analysts of relations among regime types, regime transitions, and forms of public politics have arrayed themselves along a continuum whose two ends we might call Principle and History. Despite employing historical illustrations, Aristotle situated his analyses fairly close to the continuum's Principle end: regardless of their proximity or distance in space and time, one regime differed from another to the extent that their rationales, premises, or organizing principles differed. Historical encyclopedias, in contrast, frequently place themselves at the continuum's other end, treating regimes as different to the extent that they operate in different times and places (see, e.g., Stearns, 2001). At both extremes, accounts of regimes become quite descriptive – at the Principle extreme, attempts to capture the internal coherence of fascism or state socialism, at the History extreme, attempts to identify the particularities of Ming China or Tokugawa Japan. The extremes do not much interest us here, but location of competing regime classification regimes along the continuum matters. For explanatory strategies vary systematically along the continuum. Toward the Principle end concentrate inquiries into necessary and sufficient conditions for different types of regimes (Dogan and Higley, 1998; Dogan and Pelassy, 1984; Held, 1996; Spruyt, 2002). Toward the History end, we find searches for recurrent processes – notably including path-dependent processes – that regularly cause regime changes without producing identical outcomes (Collier and Collier, 1991; Mahoney, 2001, 2002; Mahoney and Snyder, 1999).

Consider Marxist accounts. Beginning with Marx's own work on precapitalist economic formations (Marx, 1964), Marxists have usually taken positions near the midpoint, but on the History side modes of production generate each other in well-defined historical sequences, with struggle that emerges from a given mode's internal contradictions driving the transition to the next mode (see, e.g., Anderson, 1974a, 1974b). But within each mode, the logic of productive relations shapes a political regime that implements the power of the mode's dominant class. Thus in the communist manifesto simplification bourgeois revolution destroys feudal regimes and replaces them with parliamentary regimes implementing bourgeois interests. My great teacher Barrington Moore criticized the classic Marxist account, but replaced it with another account located at almost precisely the same position on the Principle/History continuum (Moore, 1966). A specialist in Russian politics and a close student of Russian history, Moore attributed more importance to class relations within agriculture than have most Marxists. Although sharing with Marx the idea that parliamentary democracy resulted from bourgeois predominance, Moore argued that commercialization of agriculture, elimination of great landlords, and proletarianization of the peasantry (rather than the rise of industry itself) together opened the way toward bourgeois predominance. Yet for Moore, as for Marx, changing configurations of class generated regime transitions through struggle.

Moore's analysis inspired a great deal of subsequent work on regime transitions (e.g., Andrews and Chapman, 1995; Collier, 1999; Downing, 1992; Rueschemeyer, Stephens, and Stephens, 1992; Skocpol, 1979; Stephens, 1989). More than anything else, analysts in Moore's lineage have sought to explain how democratic regimes replace nondemocratic regimes. There they confront a host of theorists who operate closer to the Principle end of the continuum, looking for necessary and sufficient conditions of democratic regimes. In a convenient if risky simplification, many students of contemporary democratization distinguish two main types of regime: authoritarian and democratic (e.g. Przeworski, Alvarez, Cheibub, and Limongi, 2000). Their work ranges from close comparison of particular cases in a search for crucial differences to quantitative comparisons of many regimes in which authoritarianism and democracy become the low and high ends of the same variable: degree of democracy (Anderson, Fish, Hanson, and Roeder, 2001; Arat, 1991; Bratton and van de Walle, 1997; Burkhart and Lewis-Beck, 1994; Dawisha and Parrott, 1997; Lijphart, 1999; Linz and Stepan, 1996; Vanhanen, 1997; Yashar, 1997).

A similar distribution of analyses appears in the comparative study of welfare states. Although often departing from the relatively historical account of British welfare policy formulated by T. H. Marshall (Marshall, 1950; see also Barbalet, 1988; Turner, 1997), recent efforts have concentrated on two largely unhistorical questions: what conditions promote the development of different degrees and kinds of social provisioning? What effects do different systems of social provisioning have on the actual social lives of citizens in different types of regimes? Once again, the range runs from close comparison of particular cases in a search for crucial differences to quantitative comparisons of many regimes in which different levels or aspects of provisioning or social experience turn into variables to be explained by a variety of theoretically motivated predictors (Esping-Anderson, 1990; Goodin, Headey, Muffels, and Dirven, 1999; Hage, Hannemann, and Gargan, 1989; Janoski and Hicks, 1994; Ruggie, 1996).

Thomas Janoski offers a complex version in his *Citizenship and Civil Society*, which compares liberal, traditional, and social democratic regimes with regard to their delivery of citizenship rights and obligations. (Although Janoski compares many countries, the United States exemplifies the liberal type, Germany the traditional type, and Sweden the social democratic type.) After specifying how to recognize the three types of regimes, Janoski traces their origins to different combinations of prevailing class and status ideologies with the interests that they represent. He then dares to relate regime types to forms of contention:

> Social democratic regimes with the franchise as an organizing issue, trade union strength, left party power, strong self-administration, and proportional representation have high rights and low demonstrations in an open system. Traditional regimes are similar to social democratic regimes except that they bottle up discontent in what tends to be an elitist political system creating more riots and demonstrations. On social closure they are split into colonizers with more open naturalization and mobility who develop greater tolerance and rights, and non-colonizers with closed naturalization and little social mobility who develop more authoritarian regimes. And liberal societies who never had the franchise as a labor organizing issue,

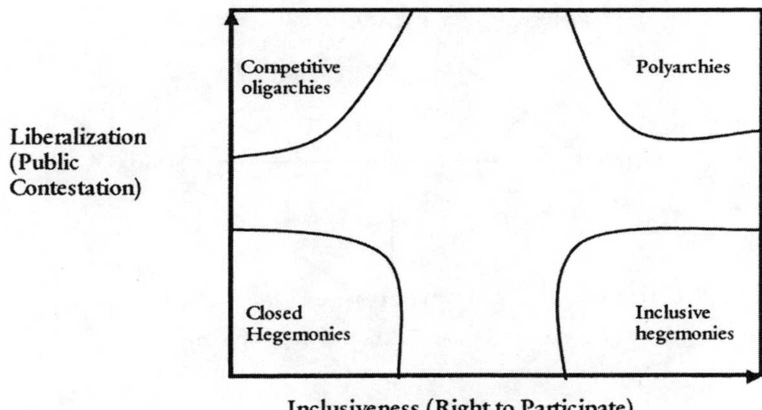

Figure 21.1. Robert Dahl's Classification of Regimes.

developed weak trade unions, have much less left party power, and in general have a weak state. The results are a low level of rights and obligations in a society that is open to integrating immigrants, and the highest amounts of social mobility. (Janoski, 1998:222–3)

Although his book contains plenty of historical material, this passage shows us Janoski organizing his explanations around a search for necessary and sufficient conditions behind different sorts of citizenship.

Rather than criticizing, codifying, or synthesizing these various approaches to typification of regimes and regime transitions, let me reconstruct just two exemplary analyses, one on the Principle side of our continuum, the other closer to the History end of the continuum. For Principle, take Robert Dahl. For History, take S. E. Finer.

Robert Dahl's treatment of approximations to democracy has a distinctly Aristotelian air. As summarized in Figure 21.1, Dahl's useful scheme distinguishes two dimensions of variation: *inclusiveness*, the extent to which people under a given regime's jurisdiction have the right to participate at all, and *liberalization*, the extent to which participants in the regime have rights to contest conditions of rule. Dahl adds to Aristotle recognition of very inclusive regimes that allow little public contestation, which Dahl calls inclusive hegemonies. He also leaves a large open space among his four corner types, where we might locate a great many other regimes – for example, the thinly ruled nomadic empires, urban federations, composite dynastic states, and city-empires that governed much of Europe five hundred years ago.

What Dahl calls contestation enters his classification as a bundle of rights; at the liberal extreme (1) freedom to form and join organizations, (2) freedom of expression, (3) the right to vote, (4) eligibility for public office, (5) competition by political leaders for support, (6) alternative sources of information, (7) free and fair elections, and (8) institutions for making government policies depend on votes and other expressions of preference. Regimes vary enormously, as Dahl declares, "in the extent to which the eight institutional conditions are openly available, publicly employed, and fully guaranteed to at least some members of the political systems who wish to contest the conduct of the government" (Dahl, 1975:119; see also Lindblom, 1977). His closed hegemonies accord such rights to no one, his competitive oligarchies extend them to a small elite, his inclusive hegemonies entertain no such rights, and his polyarchies open them to much of the population. Note that under the label *contestation* Dahl is speaking about institutionalized rights to opposition, not about the character or frequency of contention.

Noninstitutionalized public contention enters Dahl's story incognito, as demands (of

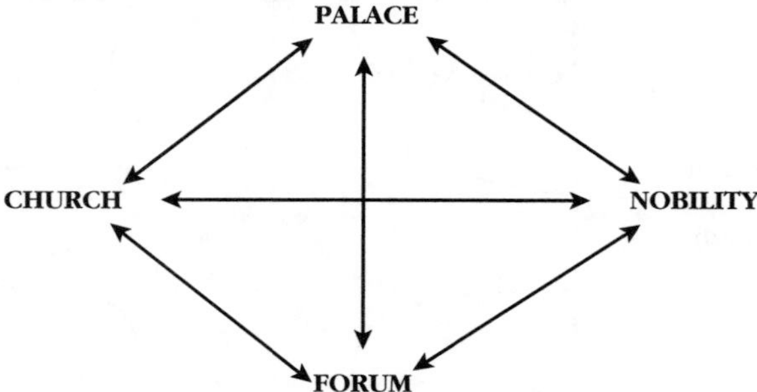

Figure 21.2. Samuel Finer's Typology of Regimes.

unspecified form) that regimes remove causes of extreme inequality, as disputes in which one segment of the population appears to threaten the survival of another, as the formation of revolutionary oppositions, and as foreign conquest. His scheme therefore challenges us to specify the interaction between regimes and the rights embedded within them, on one side, and contentious politics that sometimes adopt rightful means and sometimes defy them, on the other. The work at hand includes relating regimes and regime change to prevailing distributions of (1) actors, actions, and identities in contentious politics, (2) conditions for emergence of contentious politics, and (3) trajectories and outcomes of contentious politics.

Samuel Finer's posthumous *History of Government* provides another neo-Aristotelian handle for the classification of regimes. After stipulating that one can classify regimes along a territorial dimension (city, national, or empire), divide decision-making personnel into elites and masses, and distinguish decision implementation by bureaucracies and armed forces, Finer ultimately settles, like Aristotle, for a focus on the social character of a regime's ruling personnel. As represented in Figure 21.2, Finer identifies four pure types: Palace (monarch and following), Nobility (privileged class), Forum (segments or representatives of populace), and Church (priesthood). The diagram's double-headed arrows portray likely paths of movement from one regime type to another and likely locations of mixed regime types.

Contention thrusts its way repeatedly into Finer's accounts of particular regimes. Speaking of Italian city-states, for example, Finer observes that thirteenth-century patriciates often closed their ranks to newcomers. "But as they did so," he remarks,

> They came under pressure from the less wealthy or newly wealthy elements demanding a due share in office; the so-called 'democratic' movement. These elements, characteristically, used their guild organizations to channel their pressure, so that the struggle looks like craft-guilds trying to break the political monopoly of the wealthier and more prestigious merchant-guilds. In Italy . . . these excluded elements formed themselves into sworn associations and called themselves the 'People' – the *popolo* – and tried to assert their claims by revolt. But what happened in Italy is but the paradigm case of what was occurring in much of urbanized Europe as the thirteenth century began to close: resistance to the oligarchy, violence, even revolution. (Finer, 1997:954)

Pursuing other ends, however, Finer does not examine relationships – empirical or causal – among regime types, political transitions, and forms of contentious politics. This chapter concentrates, in contrast, on asking how and why political contention varies from one regime type to another, and how contention interacts with movement from regime to regime.

Following the premises laid out earlier, let us approach that pair of questions here in profound skepticism about the existence of neat correspondences between regime type A and action X, emergence process Y, or trajectory Z. On the contrary, we should search for rough empirical regularities in hope of accomplishing two distinct objectives: first, to specify what theoretically telling similarities and differences must be explained by any causal account of contention; second, to place firmly on the agenda how historically accumulated models, memories, understandings, and social relations – for example, residues of the Mongol empire's previous hegemony in a given region – affect the operation of contentious politics. The challenge is therefore to create two rough conceptual maps – one of regimes, the other of contentious politics – whose similarities and differences pose crucial questions of causation.

In meeting this challenge, we have deplorably little systematic analysis to build on. Analysts commonly recognize the concentration of social movements (narrowly defined) in parliamentary democracies, the vulnerability of weakened despotic regimes to revolution, the greater frequency of coups d'état where military forces exercise great autonomy, and a miscellany of near-tautologies such as the prevalence of strikes under industrial capitalism or the concentration of peasant revolts in large-landlord systems. But we have no well-established general mapping of variation in the forms and dynamics of contentious politics across the multiple types of governmental regime. Existing formulations, furthermore, suffer major weaknesses: first, little insight into interactions between contentious political processes and their settings, for example, in the ways in which contentious politics incited by certain sorts of regime transforms those regimes; second, no effective account of interpretation, for example, in the interplay between understandings that pervade routine noncontentious politics and those that inform contentious claims. Much less, then, do we possess a dynamic causal account that explains interconnections between regimes and contention.

Let us therefore take a leaf from Aristotle, creating a simple taxonomy of regimes on the way to reasoning about variations, trajectories, and transformations of contentious politics. The term *regime*, in this context, refers to any distinctive configuration of a polity: connections among a government, members of the polity defined by their routine access to agents of that government, challengers consisting of constituted actors lacking routine access to governmental agents, and intermittent actors – outside governments, international organizations, third parties, and so on – based outside the zone of the government's jurisdiction.

To make such a model fit the complexities of real political processes, we must complicate it: show the government as less like a unitary star and more like a galaxy, with multiple centers and hierarchies, often competing, rather than a single unitary point; vary the sharpness of the polity's boundary; allow for jagged or blurred edges to the government's jurisdiction; recognize that contenders (both members and challengers) vary in strength and coherence; note that a given individual or group within a government's jurisdiction may belong to multiple contenders or none at all.

We must also put the model into motion, with the government shifting, contenders changing, and claim making fluctuating. Finally, we must place polities within their historical and cultural settings, recognizing at a minimum that previous and adjacent forms of government provide powerful templates for the creation of new governments; as a consequence, history and culture constrain the operation of ostensibly general processes such as repression and political mobilization. We are dealing with mutual claim making and responses to claim making among unequally powerful contenders in the presence of at least one government.

The simple polity model opens the way to a taxonomy of all regimes since Aristotle's era. The taxonomy shifts away from the Aristotle/Finer emphasis on the identity of ruling classes to the Dahlian emphasis on political relations between rulers and ruled. The classification concentrates on relations between governments and polity members. It operates as a function of five dimensions:

1. **Governmental capacity** (actual impact of governmental action on activities and resources within the government's jurisdiction, relative to some standard of quality and efficiency): low (0) to high (1)
2. **Breadth** of polity membership: ruler alone (0) to every person under a

government's jurisdiction belonging to at least one polity member (1)

3. **Equality** in polity membership: radically unequal (0) to every person who belongs to a polity member has equal access to governmental agents and resources (1) strength of collective
4. **Consultation** among polity members with respect to governmental personnel, policy, and resources, considered as a multiple of (a) how binding that consultation is, and (b) how effectively that consultation controls governmental personnel, policy, and resources: from nonbinding and ineffectual (0) to binding and determining (1)
5. **Protection** of polity members and persons belonging to them from arbitrary action by governmental agents: no protection whatsoever (0) to complete protection (1)

Thus 10011 (high capacity, narrow polity membership, unequal polity membership, strong consultation, extensive protection) describes an idealized powerful oligarchy, or perhaps even a valid aristocracy in Aristotle's view. The figures 11100 (high capacity, broad polity membership, equal polity membership, no consultation, no protection) describe an idealized totalitarian state, Aristotle's worst dream of tyranny. The series 00000, finally, designates utter anarchy. All real governments fall somewhere between, with the average Western capitalist country, relative to all states that have ever existed, scoring perhaps .75 on capacity, .80 on breadth, .75 on equality, .70 on consultation, and .85 on protection. Translated into Janoski's regime types, the relative scores of democratic regimes might run as follows (Janoski, 1998:33–8):

Element	Liberal	Traditional	Social Democratic
Capacity	.80	.85	.90
Breadth	.80	.85	.90
Equality	.85	.80	.95
Consultation	.80	.90	.85
Protection	.75	.80	.95

Although I make no effort at deriving precise measures of these five elements here, we can imagine history since Aristotle's time as unfolding before an immense scoreboard that displays five fluctuating numbers for each state. The explanatory problem is then to identify and explain connections between those fluctuations, on one hand, and changes in the character, intensity, and trajectories of contention, on the other.

The five dimensions are logically distinct: to some extent we can analyze variation within each dimension independently. Nevertheless, they (or rather the causes embedded in them) interact so strongly that much of the logical space they imply is empirically empty. Low-capacity governments, for example, rarely or never provide their polity members with extensive protection from arbitrary action by governmental agents. Nor do very broad polity membership, very unequal polity membership, and binding consultation of polity members long (if ever) cohabit. In general, it looks as though substantial increases of governmental capacity propel broadening of polity membership when the essential resources for the government's operation come from the population within the government's jurisdiction, because struggle over those resources lead to provisional bargains that establish mutual rights and obligations between governmental agents and providers of resources. Thus a whole theory of governmental transformation awaits articulation in the form of causal propositions linking the five dimensions. For now, however, the salient questions concern variation in contentious politics as a function of a regime's location with respect to the five dimensions taken singly.

Governmental capacity does not enter the definition of democracy, yet it strongly affects the chances for democratic processes. In principle, one could imagine broad political participation, relative equality of individuals or other social units, binding collective consultation, and protection in the absence of an enforcing government. Anarchists and utopians have often taken the relative democracy of some crafts, shops, and local communities as warrants for the feasibility of stateless democracy on a large scale. The historical record, however,

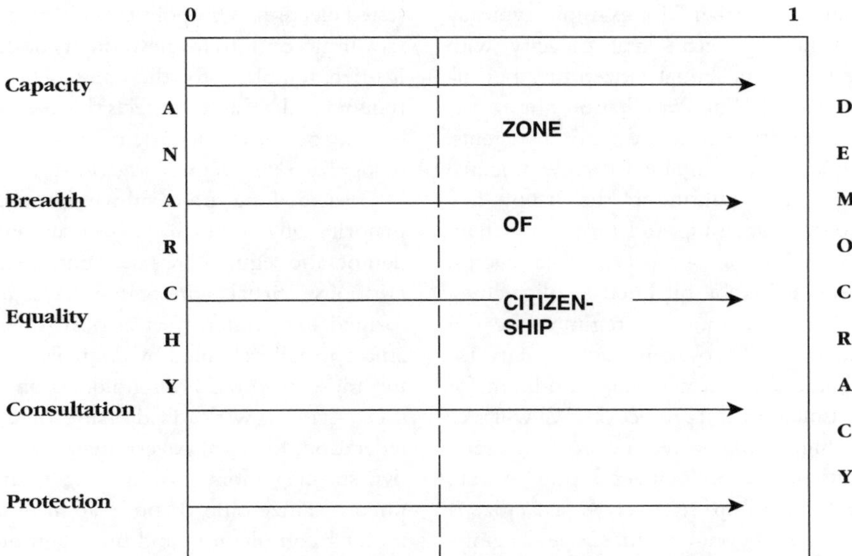

Figure 21.3. A Five-Dimensional Taxomony of Regimes.

suggests another conclusion: where governments collapse, other predators spring up. In the absence of effective governmental power, people who control substantial concentrations of capital, coercion, or commitment generally use them to forward their own ends, thus creating new forms of oppression and inequality. If high governmental capacity does not define democracy, it looks like a nearly necessary condition for democracy on a large scale.

We cannot, however, draw from such an observation the comforting inverse conclusion that expansion of governmental capacity reliably fosters democracy. In fact, expanding governmental capacity promotes tyranny more often than it causes democracy to flower. In the abstract calculation that sums over all governmental experiences, the relationship between governmental capacity and democracy is no doubt asymmetrically curvilinear: more frequent democracy from medium to medium-high governmental capacity, but beyond that threshold substantial cramping of democratic possibilities as governmental agents come to control a very wide range of activities and resources.

Citizenship, in this view, forms only on the higher slopes of the five continua. Only where governmental capacity is relatively extensive, polity membership involves some significant share of a government's subject population, some equality of access to government exists among persons who belong to polity members, consultation of those persons makes a difference to governmental performance, and persons belonging to polity members enjoy some protection from arbitrary action can we reasonably begin to speak of mutual rights and obligations directly binding governmental agents to whole categories of persons defined by their relation to the government in question – that is, of citizenship. Although citizenship of a sort bound elite members of Greek city-states to their governments and elite members of many medieval European cities to their municipalities, on the whole citizenship at a national scale only became a strong, continuous presence during the nineteenth century. Figure 21.3 sums up the five dimensions, showing the locations of anarchy, democracy, and citizenship.

Democracy builds on citizenship, but does not exhaust it. Indeed, most Western states created some forms of citizenship after 1800, but over most of that period the citizenship in question was too narrow, too unequal, too nonconsultative, and/or too unprotective to qualify their regimes as democratic. The regimes we loosely call "totalitarian," for example, typically combined high governmental capacity with relatively broad and equal citizenship, but afforded neither binding consultation nor extensive protection from arbitrary action by agents. Some monarchies maintained narrow, unequal citizenship while consulting the happy few who enjoyed citizenship and protecting them from arbitrary action by governmental agents; those regimes thereby qualified as oligarchies. In searching for democratic regimes, we can take relatively high governmental capacity for granted because it is a necessary condition for strong consultation and protection. We will recognize a high-capacity regime as democratic when it installs not only citizenship in general, but broad citizenship, relatively equal citizenship, strong consultation of citizens, and significant protection of citizens from arbitrary action by governmental agents.

Both consultation and protection require further stipulations. Although many rulers have claimed to embody their people's will, only governments that have created concrete preference-communicating institutions have also installed binding, effective consultation. In the West, representative assemblies, contested elections, referenda, petitions, courts, and public meetings of the empowered figure most prominently among such institutions; whether polls, discussions in mass media, or special-interest networks qualify in fact or in principle remains highly controversial.

On the side of protection, democracies typically guarantee zones of toleration for speech, belief, assembly, association, and public identity, despite generally imposing some cultural standards for participation in the polity; a regime that prescribes certain forms of speech, belief, assembly, association, and public identity while banning all other forms may maintain broad, equal citizenship, and a degree of consultation, but it slides away from democracy toward populist authoritarianism as it qualifies protection. At the edge of the five-dimensional space that contains democratic regimes, furthermore, previous historical experience has laid down a set of models, understandings, and practices concerning such matters as how to conduct a contested election. This political culture of democracy limits options for newcomers both because it offers templates for the construction of new regimes and because it affects the likelihood that existing powerholders – democratic or not – will recognize a new regime as democratic.

Over the long run of human history, the vast majority of regimes have been undemocratic; democratic regimes are rare, contingent, recent creations. Partial democracies have, it is true, formed intermittently at a local scale, for example in villages ruled by councils incorporating most heads of household. At the scale of a city-state, a warlord's domain, or a regional federation, forms of government have run from dynastic hegemony to oligarchy, with narrow, unequal citizenship or none at all, little or no binding consultation, and uncertain protection from arbitrary governmental action. Before the nineteenth century, large states and empires generally managed by means of indirect rule: systems in which the central power received tribute, cooperation, and guarantees of compliance on the part of subject populations from regional powerholders who enjoyed great autonomy within their own domains. Seen from the bottom, such systems often imposed tyranny on ordinary people. Seen from the top, however, they lacked capacity; the intermediaries supplied resources, but they also set stringent limits to rulers' ability to govern or transform the world within their presumed jurisdictions.

Only the nineteenth century brought widespread adoption of direct rule, creation of structures extending governmental communication and control continuously from central institutions to individual localities or even to households, and back again. Even then, direct rule ranged from the unitary hierarchies of centralized monarchy to the segmentation of federalism. On a large scale, direct rule made substantial citizenship, and therefore democracy, possible. Possible, but not likely, much less inevitable: instruments of direct rule have sustained many oligarchies, some autocracies, a number of party- and army-controlled states, and a few fascist tyrannies. Even in the era of direct rule most polities have remained far from democratic.

Of course, we could array regimes along other dimensions than capacity and democracy – size, multiplicity of internal governments, and directness of central control immediately come to mind. Let us retain our grip on the problem, however, by following the leads drawn from Aristotle, Dahl, and Finer. We concentrate on two sorts of regime variation: from undemocratic to democratic regimes and from low-capacity to high-capacity governments. We concentrate on these two aspects of regime variation for several reasons: (1) because they have attracted more theoretical and empirical attention from students of popular politics than have such aspects as uniformity of governmental administration or multiplicity of governmental units; (2) because within recent centuries they have made very large differences to the character, trajectories, and dynamics of contentious politics; and (3) because even over the longer run the position of a regime with respect to capacity and democracy has (as any good Aristotelian would expect) profound effects on the quality of its contentious politics.

Let us return to the democratic pentagon: capacity, breadth, equality, consultation, and protection. I spell out a line of reasoning about regime variation in contentious politics as a dimension-by-dimension set of arguments – call them conjectures, hypotheses, or speculations. The arguments rest on knowledge limited mainly to recent Western experience. I offer no conjectures that I know to be contradicted by substantial evidence. The conjectures therefore invite refutation from specialists who know better.

Why and how should we expect variation in governmental capacity to affect contention? Most generally because higher capacity means (a) governmental agents have the incentive and means to intervene in a wider range of social interactions within the government's zone of action, (b) governmental actions, for whatever ends undertaken, affect a wider range of actors and interactions, hence stimulate the interested parties to make offensive, defensive, or deflecting claims of their own, (c) whatever projects contenders and third parties undertake, governmental agents, government-controlled resources, and likely governmental reactions become more crucial to those projects. Conversely, in the presence of weak governmental capacity, most contentious politics occurs with little or no governmental involvement, and a high proportion of governmental intervention meets concerted resistance. A number of empirical inferences follow from these arguments, for example:

1. The greater governmental capacity, the larger share of all resources and activities within a polity affected by governmental action, hence the more likely claims directed at government agents.
2. The less governmental capacity, the higher the proportion of all claim making consisting of violent competition between nongovernmental groups.
3. The less governmental capacity, the more popular direct action against renegades, moral reprobates, and agents of central authority.
4. The less governmental capacity, the more clandestine retaliatory damage, the more concerted resistance to outside threats, the more localized action, the closer ties of claim making to embedded (rather than detached) identities, and the more variation in claim making's cultural content.
5. The less governmental capacity, the higher the proportion of governmental interventions that consist of violent predation and/or exemplary punishment, hence the greater probability of violent resistance.
6. Beyond some threshold, governmental capacity correlates with directness of rule, hence with the likelihood that claim makers and objects of claims will be governmental agents rather than empowered intermediaries or essentially autonomous powerholders.
7. Higher governmental capacity, on average, depends on greater extraction of resources from the subject population, hence produces a greater frequency of contests over extraction of resources that

subjects have committed to nongovernmental enterprises.

All these hypotheses lead to concrete comparisons among regimes and forms of contentious politics. They have the advantage of straightforward research implications, but the disadvantage of focusing on static high/low comparisons.

What about breadth of polity membership? At the narrowest, no one who is subject to the authority of a given government enjoys any rights or mutual obligations binding them to governmental agents and governmental agents to them. At the broadest, everyone who is subject to that authority enjoys citizenship. Categorical citizenship is then either identical to or highly correlated with polity membership. With that understanding, we might expect to find a strong difference in means of contentious claim making between narrow and broad polities, with (a) claim makers (especially nonmembers of the polity) in narrow polities tending to approach governmental power indirectly and/or covertly through informal networks, corruption of governmental agents, external power-holders, terror, or subversion and (b) challengers in broad polities frequently adopting means similar to those employed by polity members – although just different enough to call attention to their distinctness and disruptive potential.

Here are some more specific hypotheses that follow from this line of reasoning:

8. Broadening polity membership incites alliance-formation and claims of recognition, satisfaction, and membership by still-excluded actors.
9. Narrowing polity membership incites anticipatory resistance and alliance formation by threatened polity members.
10. The narrower is polity membership, the more frequently subjects will approach governmental power indirectly and/or covertly through informal networks, through corruption of governmental agents, through external powerholders, through terror, or through subversion.
11. The narrower is polity membership, the higher the share of all open contention that directly defies authorities, hence occurs at a distance from the forms of claim making prescribed or rewarded by authorities.
12. The broader is polity membership, the higher the share of all open contention that occurs at the immediate edges of prescribed political forms, for example as social movements or diversion of authorized public ceremonies.
13. A curvilinear relationship exists between the breadth of polity membership and the frequency with which dissident polity members bid for support of nonmembers by promoting their inclusion: rarely in the case of extremely narrow or extremely broad polity membership, more frequently in between.
14. The greater a split within a polity, the more frequent such coalitions. Thus a dynamic of inclusion, exclusion, and contention begins to emerge. Once again, the hypotheses lead to fairly crisp static comparisons, but fall short of specifying dynamic cause/effect relations.

And equality of polity membership? Perfect equality of polity membership does not require equality of wealth, power, or well-being, but absolutely identical relations of all to governmental agents. Absolute inequality of polity membership does not require deep inequality of life condition, but person-to-person and group-to-group differentiation of relations to governmental agents. (It is nevertheless probably true, as Aristotle suggested, that great inequality of material condition promotes inequality of polity membership because affluent actors use their means to influence the political process and the performances of governmental agents, thus increasing inequality of polity membership itself.) No government has ever extended perfect equality of polity membership, if only because all exclude certain segments of the subject population – notably children, felons, and certified incompetents – from full benefits of governmental power. Even very democratic governments with extensive rights of citizenship differentiate benefits and obligations of citizenship by gender, age, military service, penal status, and officeholding.

These arguments have strong implications for contention-by-regime maps. The more equal polity membership is, for example, the more the polity will respond to challengers' effective displays of WUNC: worthiness, unity, numbers, and commitment. (This should be the case because WUNC signals a contender's capacity to intervene effectively in routine consultation and to attract support of other contenders in doing so.) The more unequal polity membership, on the other hand, the greater the differences among channels by which distinct segments of the population make claims, hence the greater the variability in conditions for effectiveness of a given actor's claims. ("Channels" means not only the course of claim making itself but also coalition formation, characteristic interactions with authorities, centripetal vs. centrifugal orientations, and repertoires.) Other related hypotheses include the following:

15. The more equal polity membership, the greater the frequency with which losers in binding consultation accept the outcome, hence the rarer contentious outcomes to such consultations, including violence.
16. The more equal polity membership, the greater the resemblance among the claim making repertoires of different contenders. (This despite incessant efforts at marginal innovation differentiating one claimant or claim from the next: variety within an extremely limited compass.)
17. Equality of polity membership, net of other effects, bears a curvilinear relationship to size of polity: greater for intermediate sizes than for very large and very small polities.
18. The more extensive exploitation and opportunity hoarding (hence categorical inequality) in the base population, the greater the inequality of polity membership (see Tilly, 1998:chapter 7).

Thus, according to this line of argument, both equality and equalization have strong impacts on the character of contentious politics. To move into dynamic territory, however, we would have to look much more closely at actual processes that alter patterns of inequality.

Binding consultation? Democratic theorists often focus on elections as the critical institutions. Popular elections have, indeed, served as a crucial technology for consultation – binding or otherwise. But note that even in strongly electoral regimes an interplay typically occurs among electoral campaigns as such and (a) displays of potential electoral strength by collective actors outside of electoral campaigns, (b) legislative performance, (c) candidate-selection processes, including payment for campaign costs, and (d) payoffs to supporters. In any case, some degree of binding consultation also occurs in various sorts of regimes through operation of patron/client networks, virtual representation, plebiscites, recall, referendum, consultative assemblies, polls, petitions, lobbying, payoffs, public rituals, and weapons of the weak. Let us concentrate here relatively public, transparent, and institutionalized forms of binding consultation.

This reasoning suggests strong interactions between contentious politics and binding consultation. The more extensive and binding is consultation of polity members, for example, the more shared interpretations arise from public discussion. Conversely, the less extensive and binding is consultation, the more shared interpretations emerge from unofficial, underground conversations and bifurcate between (a) subversive indirect discourse of the sort that James Scott (1985) calls "weapons of the weak" and (b) public dramaturgy drawing on unmistakable references to widely known symbols, legends, events, dates, and persons. More detailed hypotheses follow:

19. Predominant forms of consultation (e.g., elections vs. audiences at court) strongly

affect the location and forms of contentious politics, especially in the presence of democracy and extensive governmental capacity. Parapolitical and contentious claim making shadow routine politics.

20. The more extensive and binding the consultation of polity members, the greater the clustering of contention around perimeters of institutionalized consultation.
21. The more extensive and binding is consultation of polity members, the greater the prominence of detached (rather than embedded) identities in collective claim making.
22. Presence of civil liberties – freedom of speech, assembly, association, and belief as well as due process with respect to government agents' seizure of persons and property – enhances consultation and channels contention toward perimeters of institutionalized consultation.
23. Extensive binding consultation promotes adoption of claim making forms that depend on extensive organization and preparation rather than springing from noncontentious daily routines such as marketing, working, drinking, or attending religious services.
24. Extensive binding consultation promotes forms of claim making that broadcast capacity, threat, and/or intentions to act – both individual and collective – rather than immediately engaging the actions in question. Such forms dramatize the worthiness, unity, numbers and commitment both of direct participants and of populations they claim to represent.
25. Extensive binding consultation promotes targeting of regional or national power holders, including governmental agents.
26. Extensive binding consultation promotes activation of detached collective identities: identities broader than or separate from those that inform routine social relations (e.g., workers in general rather than machinists in this particular shop).
27. The more uniform is consultation across an entire population (obviously a function of breadth and equality of polity membership) the more similar are claim making repertoires across that population.
28. Claim making increases with social, temporal, and geographic proximity to major consultations.
29. Mobilized contenders excluded from major consultations commonly act to disrupt, counter, or intervene in those consultations.
30. The less binding consultation, the more sensitive the response of contenders to fluctuations in opportunity and threat on two fronts: change in their relations to the current regime, change in relations between the regime and outside actors.

What about protection of polity members against arbitrary action of governmental agents? Here we enter a conceptual and theoretical thicket for two reasons: first, because "arbitrary" implies a standard of even-handed due process that is extremely difficult to state generally and a priori, and, second, because even more so than binding consultation, protection involves incessant negotiation of particular arrangements with governmental agents, as when demonstrators clear their planned marches with police or welfare administrators bend their rules to mitigate hardship. Nevertheless, we can persevere by thinking of a rough scale including positive elements such as publicity of governmental claims on citizens, routine availability of review and redress, and uniformity of agents' practice across social categories. We can also consider negative elements such as absence of government-protected paramilitary forces, secret forms and loci of detention, or extensive domestic espionage. This general approach suggests strong hypotheses concerning interconnections between protection and contentious politics, for example:

31. The more protection, the greater the clustering of contention around perimeters of institutionalized politics, and the less the

employment of forbidden means of claim making.

32. The less protection, the higher the proportion of claim making directed to seizures of governmental power, fragmentation of governmental power, or establishment of autonomy from governmental power.
33. The less protection, the greater the centrality of patron/client relations in contention.
34. The less protection, the greater the propensity of all contenders to acquire their own coercive force.
35. The less protection, the higher the proportion of claim-making events involving violence.
36. The less protection, the greater the reliance of claim-making challengers on protected social locations and on identities grounded in everyday social relations – that is, embedded identities.
37. The more differentiated protection by social category, the greater the differentiation of contentious repertoires.

This long string of hypotheses is, of course, no more than that: a set of reasoned conjectures about what we might expect close examination of regime variation in contentious politics to show us, constrained by whatever I know (or think I know) about actual variation in contentious politics within Western regimes over the past few centuries. It therefore constitutes an agenda for inquiry, not a set of firm conclusions. My inquiry, furthermore, does not aim at empirical generalizations linking types of contentious politics to types of regime, much less general laws from which such empirical generalizations might follow. Instead, I am trying to (1) establish rough empirical regularities specifying what sorts of variation valid theories of contentious politics must explain, (2) formulate partial but powerful causal analogies that cross boundaries of regimes and contentious political forms, (3) use the map of variation to promote study of contentious episodes differing significantly in setting and form, thereby demanding analytical finesse and requiring robust analogies, and (4) use it again to specify scope conditions for robust analogies when they appear.

To bring some of these scattered arguments together and confirm the utility of concentrating on governmental capacity and democracy/undemocracy, let us explore implications of the scheme for a crucial problem in contentious politics: similarity in repertoires among different forms of contentious and noncontentious political interaction. By contentious repertoires I mean collective claim-making routines that characterize any pair of politically constituted actors. The theatrical metaphor conveys the sense in which such claim making generally consists not of bureaucratic form filing but of improvisatory and contingent performances, based on previous experience, drawing on existing understandings, social relations, and known practices. Contentious repertoires always include limited numbers of such performances, far fewer and far narrower than the interactions of which the parties would be technically capable.

Let us generalize the idea of repertoire to designate all the claim-making performances commonly employed within a given regime. In general, we should expect high-capacity governments to feature more uniform means of claim making (whether contentious or otherwise) than low-capacity governments for several reasons: high-capacity governments connect dispersed actors, including challengers, more effectively with each other, thus promoting their mutual learning and collaboration in the formulation of claims; obtrusive high-capacity governments themselves generate higher proportions of all contention, hence imprint their own rhythms and structures on claim-making routines; and such governments also tend to create uniform administrative organization throughout their territories as compared with the regional particularism of low-capacity governments, a circumstance that increases the similarity of situations stimulating and channeling claim making in different segments of the population under a high-capacity government's control. For these reasons, modular repertoires – bundles of performances easily transferred from

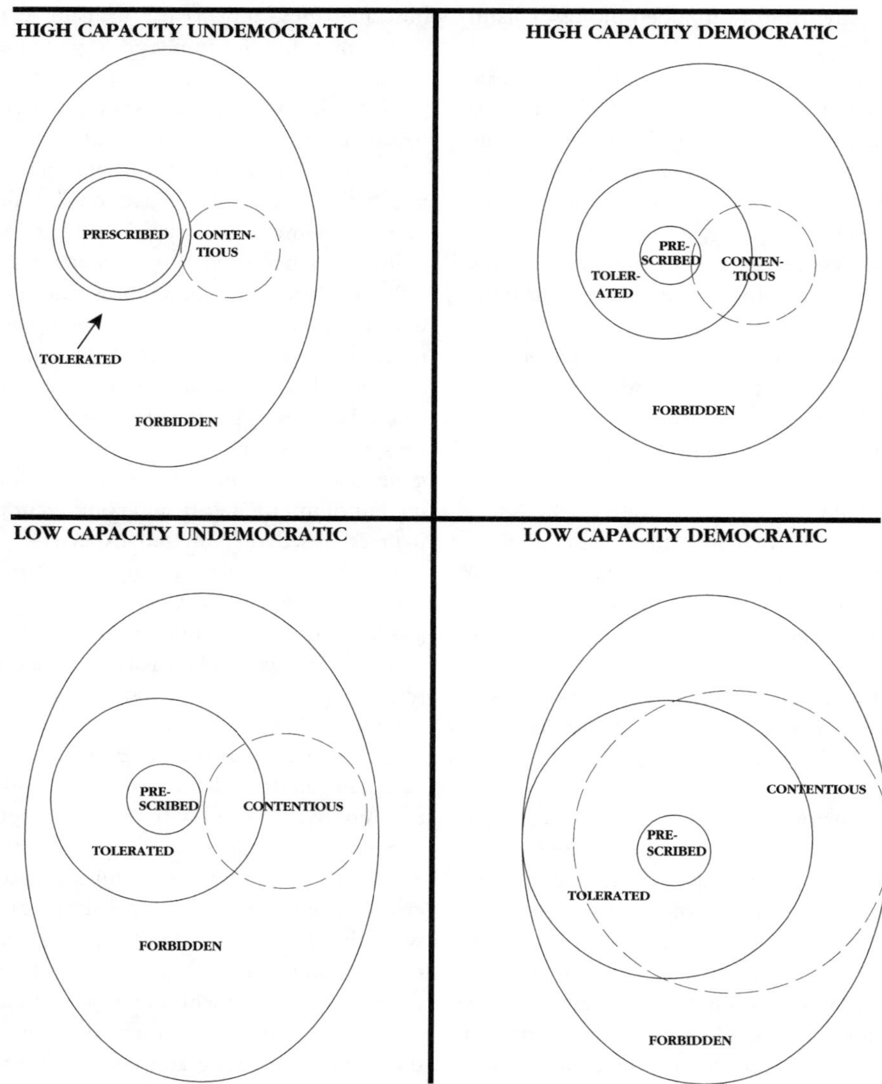

Figure 21.4. Configurations of Political Interaction under Different Types of Regimes.

one locality, population, issue, or organization to another – should prevail in high-capacity governments.

What about differences in repertoires between democratic and undemocratic regimes? Figure 21.4 schematizes a crude first cut. It argues that both governmental capacity and democracy affect overlaps among prescribed, tolerated, forbidden, and contentious public political performances. How? First, democratic regimes absolutely prescribe relatively few such performances, but they tolerate quite a range; whereas military conscription, tax payments, and replies to censuses come close to being compulsory for affected parties in democracies, even registering to vote remains voluntary in most democratic regimes. Conversely, high-capacity nondemocratic regimes commonly prescribe a wide range of public political performances while tolerating few others. They also forbid a much wider variety of claim-making performances.

Second, democratic regimes draw contentious claim making toward their prescribed and tolerated forms of expression because access to power and recognition regularly pass through effective uses of those forms; thus electoral campaigns and sessions of legislative assemblies become foci of claim making, even on the part of contenders that currently exercise little or no power. High-capacity nondemocratic regimes, in contrast, typically exclude contentious issues and actors from prescribed and tolerated forms of claim making, with the consequence that dissidents make their claims either by covert use of tolerated performances such as public ceremonies or by deliberate adoption of forbidden performances such as armed attacks.

But governmental capacity matters as well. According to the arguments embedded in Figure 21.4, low-capacity undemocratic regimes tolerate a relatively wide range of contentious claim making, for three reasons: (1) they lack the means to prescribe many performances, and therefore settle for tribute, ritual obeisance, and a few other services from subjects; (2) they also lack the means to police small-scale contentious claim making throughout their nominal jurisdictions; (3) their efforts to impose cultural and organizational uniformity throughout their jurisdictions remain weak and ineffectual, with the consequence that actions, emergence processes, and trajectories of contentious politics vary greatly from region to region and sector to sector.

On the democratic side, similar arguments apply. Low-capacity democratic regimes have rarely formed in history and even more rarely survived; most have taken no more than a local scale. When they have existed, however, they have typically prescribed few performances, tolerated a great many, and passed a great deal of their public life in contention among conflicting claims, factions, and forms of action. From long Mediterranean experience with city-states, Aristotle recognized the vulnerability of low-capacity democratic regimes to takeover by factions and to external conquest. They also appear to fragment easily into polities organized around rival – or at least distinct – governments. Because many of today's emerging democracies build on relatively low-capacity governments, any leads we can find to the operation of low-capacity democratic regimes should illuminate struggles going on in the contemporary world.

These conjectures about variability of repertoires require refinement and empirical verification. They nevertheless fit recent Western history well enough to encourage us in thinking that regimes varying along the two major axes – governmental capacity and undemocracy/democracy – generate significantly different qualities of contentious politics. Governmental capacity and democratization therefore get much more attention than other aspects of regimes. But we break down the analysis of democratization into four dimensions: breadth of polity membership, equality of polity membership, strength of consultation, and protection. At our most general, then, we are asking how a regime's position within the five-dimensional space interacts with the character, trajectory, and dynamics of contentious politics within that regime.

Here is the first question that emerges from such an agenda: How does the character of a regime affect (a) the forms of contentious politics that occur within its perimeters and (b) the dynamics of contentious politics within its perimeters? Our second question follows: How do changes in a regime's character affect changes in forms and dynamics of contention? Translation: how do "changes in (1) governmental capacity, (2) breadth of polity membership, (3) equality of polity membership, (4) strength of collective consultation, (5) protection of polity members from arbitrary action by governmental agents" affect changes in "(6) repertoires of contention, (7) paths of claim making, (8) parties to claims?"

Which leads effortlessly to the third question: How do changes in repertoires of contention, paths of claim making, and parties to claims affect characteristics and trajectories of regimes? More particularly, we are searching for partial causal analogies in these respects that cut across considerable ranges of regimes and contention. Those sought-for causal analogies three main clusters of phenomena: actors, actions, and identities in contentious politics; the emergence of contention; and trajectories of contentious struggle.

Most of the answers I have proposed here cling to comparative statics: they say what sorts of political contention we might expect to find at different positions along the five continua or at best what sorts of changes we might expect to see as a regime moved along the continua. That happens partly because taxonomic reasoning invites comparative statics, partly because the causal arguments in and behind these conjectures remain gross or poorly articulated.

Nevertheless, reflection on regime variation and contention opens a promising program for research. The comparative program locates different contentious processes along the five dimensions of regimes and the trajectories of change they imply; those static relations deserve closer empirical attention. In a partly separate enterprise, we should be examining such change processes within well-defined historical settings where we can identify available models of political practice as well as current international constraints on regimes and contentions, for example, in the turbulence of Eastern Europe's postcommunist political change. A third somewhat different research line follows particular mechanisms such as brokerage and identity formation across different regimes and varieties of contention, for example, by looking for causal analogies between their operation in nationalism, ethnic conflict, and nonethnic social movements. The agenda will keep students of comparative politics and political contention busy for quite a while.

CHAPTER TWENTY-TWO

Theories and Practices of Neocorporatism

Wolfgang Streeck and Lane Kenworthy

The modern territorial state and the capitalist market economy superseded a political–economic order that consisted of a plethora of corporate communities endowed with traditional rights and obligations, such as churches, estates, cities, and guilds. Organized collectivities of all sorts, more or less closely related to the economic division of labor, regulated cooperation and competition among their members and negotiated their relations with each other. While themselves changing under the impact of modernization, they often resisted the rise of territorial bureaucratic rule and the spread of market relations, sometimes well into the twentieth century. But ultimately they proved unable to prevent the victory of the state form of political organization and of the self-regulating market as the dominant site of economic exchange. Modern liberalism, both political and economic, in turn aimed at abolishing all forms of intermediary organization that intervene between the individual and the state or the market. In the end, however, it failed to eliminate collectivism and had to accommodate itself to both political faction and economic cooperation.

Twenty-first-century political communities are all organized by territorial nation-states. But these had to learn to incorporate organized collectivities and elements of a collective–associative order in their different configurations of bureaucratic hierarchy and free markets. Variation among modern types of government, between the utopian extremes of anarcho-syndicalism and Rousseauian radical liberalism, rotates around the relationship between territorial and associative rule (Table 22.1). In the *Ständestaat* (state of estates) conceived in the constitutional debates of nineteenth-century Germany as a conservative alternative to liberal democracy, territorial rule is exercised by delegates of corporate groups, which are the principal constituents of the state. Later, in the twentieth century, dictatorial state rule often used state-instituted corporate bodies as transmission belts of a governing party; this is what Schmitter (1974) referred to as "state corporatism." In European postwar democracies, by comparison, territorial rule, which now took place through parliamentary representation, shared the public space with social groups organized on a more voluntary basis and entitled to various forms of collective participation and self-government, provided they recognized the primacy of parliamentary democracy. This, in essence, is what the literature is called in "neocorporatism" or "liberal corporatism" (Schmitter, 1974; Lehmbruch, 1977). Finally, in more strictly liberal political systems, organized groups are tolerated by the constitutional order on condition that they limit themselves to lobbying the parliament and refrain from claiming rights, however circumscribed, to authoritative decision making. As a type of governance, this configuration of

Table 22.1. *Type of Government as a Result of Interaction Between Territorial State and Associative Order*

Territorial State	Type of Government	Associative Order
Does not exist	Anarcho-Syndicalism Guild Socialism	*Prevents state formation*
Constituted by associations	*Ständestaat*	Controls territorial rule
Controls associations	State Corporatism	Constituted by the state
Sharing public space with associations	Liberal Corporatism Neocorporatism	Group self-government under parliamentary democracy
Tolerates associations	Pluralism	Parliamentary lobby
Outlaws associations	Radical Liberalism	*Does not exist*

territorial state and associative order is here referred to as "pluralism" (Schmitter, 1974).[1]

Our discussion is divided into five sections. The first describes the origins of neocorporatism and its conceptualization in political thought, and the second does the same for the early post-World War II period. The third section addresses the distinction between corporatism and pluralism and then discusses corporatist organizational structure, concertation, and private-interest government. Section 4 reviews theory and research on the impact of corporatism on economic performance. In the fifth section we address current tendencies that undermine democratic corporatism.

CORPORATISM AND THE POLITICAL CONSTITUTION OF MODERN SOCIETY

In the French Revolution, modern politics began as a revolt against a political order that recognized people, not as individuals, but only as members of established social groups. The revolution abolished the estates and postulated a direct, unmediated relationship between citizens and a state conceived as a republic of individuals. A law passed by the Assembly in 1791 – the *Loi le Chapelier*, named after its author – declared illegal any intermediary organization that represented subsections of the citizenry and thereby interfered with its direct relationship with the state.

In the spirit of thinkers such as Rousseau (1964) and Madison (1973), nineteenth-century liberalism remained suspicious of collective organization below the nation-state, holding on to an atomistic image of political life in which autonomous individuals were the only legitimate constituents of the political order. Subnational collectivism of all sorts, including religious organization, was suspected of diverting loyalty from the national state and was seen as a threat to both political unity and individual liberty. Similarly in the emerging capitalist market economy, collective organization and cooperation were perceived as conspiracy against free competition. Not surprisingly, the political and economic strands of liberal anticollectivism easily blended into each other.

When faced with political or economic organization among its citizenry, the liberal state felt called upon to suppress factionalism or conspiracy in restraint of trade. However, state intervention in the name of political unity, individual freedom and economic liberty, to safeguard the proper individualism of the republic and of the marketplace, may have paradoxical implications. A political doctrine that relies on a strong state to make society fit its premises borders on totalitarianism. In societies in which collectivism and factionalism are deeply rooted, enforcement by a strong state of a liberal political and

[1] For a differing use of "pluralism" that encompasses corporatism and specifies the above type of pluralism as "hyperpluralism," see Dahl (1982:chap. 4). On "organizational pluralism," see Hicks and Lechner (this volume).

economic constitution may require considerable repression. Not only may this infringe on the very liberty it is claimed to protect, but it may also become too demanding on the state and result in an overturn not just of the government, but of the republic as well.

The paradoxes of liberalism become particularly obvious where collective organization is related to social class. Working class collectivism in nineteenth-century Europe was partly a remnant of premodern feudal society. But it also offered protection against a liberal economy that subjected sellers of labor power to the same self-regulating markets as owners of capital. Trade unions and mass parties enabled the working class to take advantage of freedom of contract and of democracy and share in the benefits of the new order (Marshall, 1964). That they interfered with the free play of market forces and intervened between the individual and the state mattered less for them.

A state attacking working class organization in the name of either political individualism or free labor markets risked being perceived by a sizeable number of its citizens as an instrument of class rule. As the nineteenth century went on, then, the question became how to accommodate organized collectivities in a liberal polity and free-market economy. Apparently national societies were too large and too heterogeneous for the state to be their only focus of social integration and political loyalty – just as the market was too anonymous and unpredictable for individuals, especially those who had nothing to sell but their labor power, to have confidence in it without additional protection. The stubborn persistence of collectivism inside the nation-state and the market indicated that the Rousseauian program of atomistic republicanism was in need of amendment.

If factions were unavoidable, and rooting them out was either impossible or possible only at the price of liberty or domestic peace, what status to assign to them in a modern political order? In Germany and the countries where German intellectual influence was strong, Hegel's *Philosophy of Right* (1983 [1820]), which described corporate associations – *Korporationen* – as the "second moral root" of the state alongside the family, was read by some as a call for a return from egalitarian parliamentarism to a corporatist *state of estates*. Thus Adam Mueller (1922 [1809]) developed for Metternich the concept of a *Klassenstaat* (class state) in which organized groups would jointly regulate production and coordinate their interests through negotiations, in ways radically different from French liberalism and Adam Smith's market economy. Although this never became more than a constitutional blueprint, it later provided the background for a search for a synthesis between liberal and traditional elements of political order. Given that countries like Germany had not gone through a radical–liberal Jacobine revolution, the inclusion in the modern state of group-based forms of nonmajoritarian governance seemed less paradoxical there than in France, where this required the overthrow of a revolutionary tradition (Lehmbruch, 2001).

By the end of the nineteenth century, the liberal program was challenged by various sorts of collectivism in the name of a need for social reconstruction after what was widely regarded as a failure of the "liberal experiment" (Polanyi, 1944). To the European Right, a corporatist *Ständestaat* remained an alternative to liberal democracy well into the interwar period of the twentieth century. Corporatist thinking deplored the disorder and social conflict brought about by party competition and the market economy. Catholic social doctrine, in its attempt to limit the power of the national state with its liberal–secular tendencies in general, and its antagonism toward Roman Catholic "internationalism" in particular, favored political representation on the basis of professional groups, sometimes with and sometimes without independent trade unions. It also insisted on the "natural" right of subnational, or prenational, social groups to an autonomous conduct of their affairs, mainly in defense of Catholic charities and schools against being absorbed in compulsory national social security and educational systems. In countries with a significant Catholic community, this issued in a constitutional principle of "subsidiarity," under which the state must refrain from activities that smaller social entities can perform by themselves and indeed is obliged to help them independently to govern their affairs.

More radical corporatists proposed to resolve the social and economic crises of modernity by compulsory organization of society along the lines of industrial sectors and producer groups, which were to serve as the modern equivalents of the guilds and estates of the past. Joint organization of workers and employers as "producers" in "vertical" sectoral corporations was to put an end to class conflict and replace it with cooperation in production. Represented by hierarchical organizational structures, the relations of cooperation, competition, and exchange that made up the industrial economy were to be returned to political control. Mussolini in Italy, Franco in Spain, and Salazar in Portugal conceived of the political organization of the corporatist state as reflecting the organic structure of society and its economic organization, thus providing for superior governability in the national interest compared to the conflict and disorder caused by the abstract formalism of parliamentary democracy and by the vagaries of free markets. Whereas traditional corporatists had called upon organized groups to limit the power of the modern state, the state corporatism of the twentieth century tried to use corporatist organization as an instrument of state rule.

Antiparliamentarism was not confined to the Right, and neither was the idea of a political and economic order based on corporate associations instead of individuals (Table 22.1). Syndicalism, anarcho-syndicalism, guild socialism and similar movements, which survived in different strength in a number of countries until World War II, strove for a polity of self-governing "producer groups" that had neither place nor need for capitalists, state bureaucrats, parliaments, and political parties. Workers councils – *Räte* in German and *Soviets* in Russian – freely elected and easily recalled by their constituents, the "associated producers," were to take the place of both the market and the state. Councils were to plan the economy democratically from below, overcome the "anarchy of the market" by consensually adjusting production to the needs of society, end the extraction of surplus value, and as a result make organized repression by a bureaucratic state apparatus unnecessary. Left syndicalist corporatism shared with the corporatism of the Right its collectivism and its rejection of the liberal state and the market economy, while it differed from it in its anticapitalism, antinationalism, and antistatism, as well as in its progressive culture and politics (Korsch, 1969 [1922]).

Why did both Left and Right versions of a corporatist political order fail to become a viable alternative to the modern nation-state? One reason was that a polity based on organized producer groups tended to be incompatible with the social and economic dynamism of a modern economy and society. As Max Weber (1964:221 ff.; 2002 [1918]) had already pointed out, a *Ständestaat* presupposes a static social structure that makes it possible to assign each individual to one of a small number of broad but still internally homogeneous social categories. The more dynamic a society becomes, Weber argued, the more frequently individuals have to be reassigned, new categories created and others abolished, while the total number of groups would be continuously rising with growing functional differentiation. A polity modeled after the group structure of a modern society would therefore be ultimately unmanageable. Similarly, economic corporatism, such as syndicalism or any other form of "producer-based democracy," would be governed by producer conservatism resisting adjustment of production to changing demand. Ultimately it must amount to a dictatorship of producers over consumers, acceptable only in a world of stable technology and static, traditionalist demand for a narrow range of elementary products and services. Indeed in the real world, no corporatist order, whether rightist or leftist, ever survived for more than a few years. In the Soviet Union as well as in the right-wing corporatist regimes of the interwar period, the councils and syndicates that were supposed to be the ultimate authority soon came under the control of a dictatorial state party sufficiently detached from the social structure to override static group interests in the name of economic progress or military mobilization. What on the surface remained a corporatist constitution soon became a facade for dictatorial state rule.

An alternative to liberalism on the one hand and syndicalism, the *Ständestaat*, and state corporatism on the other were attempts to accommodate organized groups in liberal democratic polities and find some form of coexistence of territorially and functionally based political representation. In the United States in particular, but to differing degrees also in the other Anglo–American countries, this involved recognition of organized collectivities as *interest groups*, with constitutional rights to lobby the democratically elected parliament. "Pluralist" admission of organized interests was conditional on acceptance by the latter of a strict division between themselves and state authority. To prevent organized interests from "capturing" the state, membership in them had to be strictly voluntary and their organizations preferably small, specialized, internally homogeneous, democratic, and in constant competition with each other and with other organizations undertaking to represent the same interests (Truman, 1951).

In Continental Europe by comparison, Roman Catholic and social democratic traditions merged to give rise to various forms of "sharing public spaces" between states and organized social groups (Crouch, 1993). Subnational communities that the rising nation-state had been unable or unwilling to break up were conceded semipublic authority to make binding cisions for and enter into commitments on behalf of their members, in exchange for coordinating their core activities with the government. Social groups that were allowed various forms of self-government in the public domain, typically under de facto obligatory if not compulsory membership, included churches, farmers, unions, employers, small business, and the liberal professions. The resulting blurring of the boundary between the state and civil society involved a delicate balance between individualism and collectivism, individual rights and group rights, and competition and cooperation. The integration of organized groups into both liberal parliamentary democracy and the market economy reached its high point in a number of European countries after World War II. In the 1970s, it came to be referred to as neocorporatism or liberal corporatism.

One of the first to provide a coherent rationale for a liberal corporatist political order was the French sociologist Emile Durkheim (1858–1917). In the Preface to the 1902 second edition of his *Division of Labor in Society* (1893) – titled "Some Notes on Occupational Groups" – Durkheim reminded the reader of the main result of his investigation, namely that the progressive functional differentiation of modern society is a source of both disorder and order, of anarchy and anomy as well as of social integration. Anomy, according to Durkheim, is caused by the rise of "industrial society" and the increasing importance in social life of a highly differentiated economy, whereas integration may result from mutual interdependence of actors specializing on different activities. For interdependence to result in cooperation, however, mutual trust is required, which in turn presupposes reliable rules. These a liberal state cannot on its own provide: "Economic life, because it is specialized and grows more specialized every day, escapes (the state's) competence and . . . action" (Durkheim, 1964 [1893]:5). This is no longer so if "professional associations" organized to reflect the structure of economic relations are charged with elaborating the general rules made by the state to fit their special circumstances (Durkheim, 1964 [1893]:25). Corporate associations are also optimally suited to enforce professional codes of conduct, provide mutual assistance, regulate professional training, and so on. "A society," Durkheim concluded, "composed of an infinite number of unorganized individuals, that a hypertrophied state is forced to oppress and contain, constitutes a veritable sociological monstrosity . . . A nation can be maintained only if, between the state and the individual, there is intercalated a whole series of secondary groups near enough to the individuals to attract them strongly in their sphere of action and, in this way, drag them into the general torrent of social life . . . " (Durkheim, 1964 [1893]:28).

DEMOCRATIC STATE BUILDING, FREE COLLECTIVE BARGAINING, AND NEOCORPORATISM AFTER 1945

The "postwar settlement" in the European countries under American influence after 1945 was a successful attempt to reconcile a capitalist economy with mass democracy and prevent a return of the political and social divisions that had destabilized Europe in the interwar period. Central to it was the neocorporatist inclusion of worker collectivism in the liberalized political economies of the reconstructed European nation-states. Like in World War I, labor inclusion was prefigured by wartime policies of national unity. It was also a consequence of the leading role of the Left in antifascist resistance movements, the collaboration of traditional elites with right-wing governments or the German occupation, and the presence of a communist alternative to capitalism in Eastern Europe. Where the institutionalization of national systems of industrial relations involved the extension of collective rights to organized labor at the level of the national polity, it followed the model of other nonmajoritarian constitutional provisions in countries whose cohesion depended on protection of ethnic or religious groups from being overruled by natural majorities ("consociational democracies"; Lehmbruch, 1974; Lijphart, 1984; Rokkan, 1966).

The incorporation of labor in postwar democratic capitalism as a separately organized group – unlike the vertical corporations of state corporatism that also included capitalists – had developed out of the institution of "free collective bargaining." Rooted in nineteenth-century Britain, free collective bargaining emerged where states recognized their inability to suppress the collective action and organization of workers, short of civil war with uncertain event. Where trade unions, like British craft unions in the mid-eighteenth century, were prepared to pursue their interests primarily in the economic sphere, governments were happy to abstain from direct intervention in a class conflict they found difficult if not impossible to pacify. Instead they let unions and employers set the terms of employment between themselves, increasingly under legal immunities, protection, and even facilitation. As T. H. Marshall (1964) pointed out, collective industrial agreements could be regarded by governments as economic contracts negotiated in the market, and thus as an outflow of civil rights rather than as coercion by illegitimate political force. Whereas private compulsion would have challenged the territorial state's monopoly of force, private contracts were in a liberal order properly left to themselves.

Free collective bargaining became widely established immediately after World War I, only to be eliminated again in the 1920s and 1930s in many countries in the name of national unity, individual liberty, free competition, economic planning, or all of the above. Its worldwide return after 1945 was part of the complex political compromise that was the postwar settlement. Using different legal instruments, democratic states exempted unions from conspiracy and anticartel laws and accepted national collective wage bargaining as a major element of the machinery of public economic policy. In return, unions in the tradition of social democratic reformism recognized private property, free markets and the primacy of parliamentary democracy, limiting themselves to the direct pursuit of economic goals through collective bargaining and to the indirect pursuit of political goals through lobbying the parliament and supporting sympathetic political parties. Whereas government refrained from direct intervention in wage setting – let alone enforcing free price formation in the labor market – unions gave up previous ambitions to put themselves in the place of the government or the state, in exchange for being recognized as legitimate co-governors of the emerging postwar democratic welfare state. The successful integration of the trade union movement in the liberal political order was indicated by its gradual abandonment of the political strike and its more or less explicit concession to use the strike only for economic purposes.

Although the legal and political forms in which free collective bargaining became institutionalized differed between countries, from the perspective of the state the new group rights were granted on condition that they were responsibly exercised. Unions, for their part, insisted that their autonomy in representing their members was not derived from the state, but reflected rights that preceded the modern state and its constitution. Even for more reformist unions, conceiving of free collective bargaining as a conditional privilege granted by the state was no more than legal fiction. In their view, collective bargaining ultimately resulted, not from the state, but from the capacity of workers collectively to withdraw their labor and bring the economy to a halt. Generally in neocorporatist arrangements, whether collective rights are original or delegated by the state often was deliberately left open to avoid conflict.

What exactly the status of unions was in the postwar settlement – part of the state, or "state in the state" – was not just a legal subtlety. In most European countries, responsible behavior of unions in collective bargaining could not effectively be enforced on them by hierarchical means. As states had to respect free collective bargaining – for constitutional reasons, for reasons of political expediency, or both – union responsiveness to the needs of national economic policy became a matter, not of authority, but of *political exchange* (Pizzorno, 1978), in which government paid for union cooperation with a wide range of political side payments. The stability of the postwar political economy thus depended on a precarious give-and-take between government, business, and the organized economic interests of the working class, in which social and political integration were purchased by the provision of material benefits rather than enforced by coercive state authority.

Postwar democratic corporatism involved the inclusion of organized labor not only at the workplace, but also in national politics. Also, the "corporations" on which neocorporatism is based are not large firms – as the concept might suggest especially to speakers of American English – but intermediary associations of groups of individuals or firms in similar positions and, as a consequence, potentially competing with one another. Reference to the Japanese case as one of "corporatism without labor" (Pempel and Tsunakawa, 1979) is therefore to be qualified in two respects at least. First, with the abortive general strike of 1949 and the firm establishment of enterprise unionism in the 1950s, Japanese trade unionism had become effectively eliminated as a national political force. Second, inclusion of labor at the enterprise level only, although it is inclusion in "corporations" and may also give rise to extensive labor–management cooperation, is not corporatism as it is not based on associations capable of suspending market competition. It is therefore better referred to as enterprise paternalism (Streeck, 2001).

In Western postwar democracies, unions that used their autonomy responsibly became recognized, in practice if not in law, as performing a public function that the liberal democratic state found difficult to perform: the creation of social order and the provision of social peace at the workplace. With time, what had originally been a struggle for power between workers associations and the modern state could thus be redefined, in a Durkheimian way, as a matter of an efficient allocation of functions between private and public organizations together governing the public domain. To compensate unions for wage and political moderation, states granted them legal privileges and institutional guarantees, again to different degrees and in different ways in different countries. Unions were also invited to share in a wide range of economic policies in tripartite arrangements that included them together with employers and the government, making trade unionism part of the public policy machinery and of the implicit constitution of postwar democracy. In this way, the organized collectivism of the working class became integrated in liberal democracy and the market economy, conditional on its political and economic moderation as well as on the ability of the reconstituted nation-state to provide for material prosperity and organizational support.

NEOCORPORATISM: ORGANIZATIONAL STRUCTURE AND POLITICAL FUNCTIONS

In the 1970s, political science and sociology discovered neocorporatism as a European anomaly from the perspective of what had in the meantime become a predominantly American, pluralist theory of interest politics. Authoritarian state corporatism of the Portuguese and Spanish sort, and various Latin American dictatorships modeled after it, were still around. They provided the backdrop for the observation that in many, now perfectly democratic, European countries, interest groups were organized and behaved in ways reminiscent of corporatist systems. Research on interest-group corporatism in liberal democratic polities centered on two subjects in particular: on the organizational structure of interest groups and on the way these were made to act in line with more general, public interests. A central topic became the relationship between, on the one hand, the organization of group interests in established intermediary associations (the *structural* aspect of neocorporatism) and, on the other, the political coordination between interest associations and the state (the *functional* aspect; Lehmbruch and Schmitter, 1982).

As a system of interest organization, democratic neocorporatism has been conveniently described in relation to interest-group pluralism, sometimes as its polar, ideal–typical opposite and sometimes as a variant of it (Hicks and Esping-Andersen, this volume). In *structural* terms, pluralist theory most commonly conceives of interest politics as free competition among a variety of organizations in a market for political representation, whereas in corporatist systems selected organizations enjoy a representational monopoly. Organizational autonomy under pluralism contrasts with direct or indirect state intervention in the internal affairs and the structural makeup of interest organizations under corporatism, favoring members over leaders or leaders over members depending on who is expected to be more reasonable from the perspective of state policy.

With respect to *function*, under pluralism organized interests are tamed by competition and the primacy of public legislation, whereas corporatism depends on political incentives and sanctions to make interest groups cooperate with public purposes. Unlike the sharp division in liberal democratic theory between hierarchical state authority and the voluntary organization of civil society, corporatist theory and practice blur the boundary between state and society as the state shares authority with private interest associations, using the latter as agents of public policy by coordinating their behavior or delegating public functions and decisions to them. In a corporatist context, private interest representation thus shades into public governance. In the pluralist view, organized interests are relegated to the input side of the political process, where they may have a right to be heard before decisions are made. Under corporatism, by comparison, social interests participate not only in the making of binding decisions but also in their implementation. As corporatist associations assume responsibility for the compliance of their members with public policies, they help the state overcome inherent limits of legal regulation and direct intervention.

The pluralism–corporatism distinction may be read either as one between two types of government or between the ideal world of liberal theory and the real world. It is often taken to signify the extreme ends of a continuum on which extant regimes of interest politics in liberal democracies can be located. Whereas originally there was a tendency to classify entire societies, or polities, in terms of their being more or less corporatist, later on the discussion became more subtle and allowed for different sectors in a society to be differently corporatist in their organization and policy making ("macro" vs. "meso" corporatism; Cawson, 1985). The same applied at the regional level where corporatist governance arrangements and practices were claimed to have emerged without the support of the national state. Moreover, in addition to the coexistence of different types of state–society relations in a given country, it was realized that even interest groups that were organized in a corporatist fashion sometimes relied on pluralist pressure tactics in pursuit of their objectives, or used pluralist and corporatist strategies simultaneously. Vice versa, interest groups were found to behave responsibly and cooperate with state policies even in the absence of corporatist organizational structures. Over time, research also began to extend to organized groups representing less vested interests than unions and business associations, such as charities and social movements concerned with issues like the environment. These, too, were studied in terms of the more or less pluralist or corporatist character of their structures and relations with the state.

As to the functional aspects of corporatist arrangements, it is helpful to distinguish between *concertation* and *self-government*. Concertation refers to efforts by national governments to make unions and employers exercise their right to free collective bargaining in such a way that it is not at odds with national economic objectives; it turns collective bargaining and its agents into instruments of macroeconomic management coordinated between the state and organized social groups that command independent political capacities. The principal example is tripartite incomes policies, first under Keynesianism and, in the 1990s, in national employment pacts. Concertation achieves moderation of wage demands through extended or "generalized" political exchange, offering unions in particular a variety of material or institutional concessions to make them behave "in concert" with government policies.

Self-government, by comparison, involves diverse forms of collective participation of organized groups in public policy at the national or subnational level. It may result from accommodation by the state of powerful group interests or from technically expedient devolution of state functions to organized civil society. It may also result from social groups cooperatively producing collective goods for themselves that state and market fail to provide, or from any mixture of the above. Collective self-government, with varying degrees of state facilitation and legal formalization, may relieve the state from demands for regulation or services that it would find difficult to satisfy, but it also may amount to particularistic capture of public authority. It can therefore be analyzed from both a power and a problem-solving perspective. Self-government is often found in the cooperative – "third" – sector of the economy where groups operating between the hierarchy of the state and commercial markets provide themselves with collective goods, or where – like at the regional level – hierarchical state authority is not present. Generally, whereas concertation regulates the relationship – the terms of exchange – between economic groups differently located in the economic division of labor, self-government involves cooperation between competitors in pursuit of common objectives, sometimes on the basis of explicit bipartite agreements with the state. Whereas concertation serves to contain distributional conflict, self-government mobilizes the economic benefits of cooperation.

Unlike pluralism, democratic corporatism lacks a coherent normative justification. The memories of antidemocratic, authoritarian state corporatism linger on and make corporatist ideas suspect. Catholic advocacy of the subsidiarity principle carries with it a traditional communitarianism that conflicts with the modernist and statist tradition of social democracy. Leftist support for collective bargaining, in turn, is often accompanied by fears of loss of union autonomy due to incorporation in government economic policy, and by rejection of "class collaboration." Social democratic hopes for state intervention to bring about greater equality also stand in the way of unambiguous support for corporatism. Liberals eschew corporatism for its anticompetitive, monopolistic institutions and its inherent collectivism. Conservatives, often together with the republican Left, fear for the unity and integrity of the state. Whereas the former associate corporatism with a "trade union state," the latter are afraid of state capture by special sectoral or business interests using privileged institutional positions to block majority decisions. Democratic theory warns of a "cartel of elites" rendering the parliament powerless, while economic theory deplores the rent-seeking and the allocative inefficiency allegedly caused by suspension of competitive markets. Fears of a totalitarian state takeover of civil society exist alongside fears of the conflicts inherent in the latter tearing apart the state or making it subservient to democratically illegitimate special interests.

In the following subsections we first discuss neocorporatist organization, that is, the *structural* dimension of corporatism. Following this we turn to the *functional* aspects of neocorporatism, addressing concertation and self-government in turn.

Structure: Organization

Regarding structure, neocorporatist interest organization differs from its pluralist counterpart in that collective interests are organized in few rather than many organizations, which are broad instead of narrow in their domain and centralized and broadly based instead of specialized and fragmented (Schmitter, 1974). Interest differences between constituent groups are as much as possible internalized in encompassing organizations, and the management of interest diversity becomes in large part a matter of the internal politics of associations instead of the public political process. Charging associational leaders with the aggregation and transformation of diverse special interests into more broadly defined common, *adjusted* interests, corporatist organization allows them considerable discretion in selecting which interests to represent and act upon as those of their members. Corporatist associations can therefore be seen as active producers instead of mere purveyors of collective interests.

Corporatist organizational form affects the substance of collective interests in a variety of ways. The higher discretion enjoyed by the leaders of encompassing associations enables them to observe technical considerations in addition to political ones. Technical perspectives are injected in the internal deliberations of associations, especially by professional experts based in staff departments that smaller organizations cannot afford. Experts are crucial in defining collective goals more instrumentally, making them more acceptable to the organization's interlocutors (more "moderate") and thus more likely to be accomplished (more "realistic"). Leadership autonomy also makes it possible for corporatist associations to take a long-term view of collective goals and postpone the gratification of demands, for example, in the hope of expanding the resources available for distribution. This enables associations to enter into stable relations of "generalized political exchange," where present concessions may be traded for as yet undetermined and legally not enforceable future rewards. It is these and similar processes of interest definition and adjustment that distinguish *corporatist interest intermediation* from *pluralist interest representation* and indicate the transformation of a pluralist interest group into an *intermediary organization*.

The rise of interest intermediation may in part be attributed to *internal factors*, such as the interests of professional staff in safe jobs, career advancement, and acceptance by a larger professional community. This mechanism figures prominently already in the writings of Max Weber (1964:841ff.) and Robert Michels (1989 [1911/1925]). Staff interests represent the economics of organization, such as the need to protect past investment in collective action capacities by regularizing the existence of the organization. In addition, the literature on neocorporatism also points to *external factors* contributing to what Schmitter and Streeck (1999 [1982]) call organizational development, in particular incentives held out and supports provided by the state and other interlocutors. The reason why the latter might favor corporatist intermediation over pluralist representation is the *political moderation* they can expect to come with large size, encompassingness, professionalization, organizational continuity, and centralization. Large and stable organizations not only develop powerful interests in their own survival that militate against political adventures, but they can also negotiate on a broader range of issues, which increases the variety of possible package deals. Moreover, as Mancur Olson (1982) has explained, encompassing organizations internalize not only a diversity of special interests but also much of the damage they do if they stray too far from the general interest.

There are several inducements and supports the state and other actors can offer interest groups to persuade them to assume corporatist organizational forms. To help overcome pluralist fragmentation, interlocutors may talk only to organizations that exceed a certain size or qualify as majority representative of their constituency. Privileged access strengthens the position of the leadership in relation to the members, as these cannot hope to be effectively represented if they join a competing organization. Elimination of competition may also contribute to political moderation as it relieves leaders of the need to outbid each other in militant demands potentially more appealing to the membership than moderate policies. Interlocutors furthermore may provide associations with material support, to enable them to build a strong bureaucracy and offer their members "outside inducements" (Olson, 1971) – services that unlike their political achievements they can withhold from nonmembers to increase the appeal of membership.

External support for organizational development and political moderation may include tacit or open assistance in recruiting or retaining members, which can take a variety of forms from moral suasion to compulsory membership (like in Chambers of Commerce and Industry in some Continental European countries). Assistance with recruitment helps associations deal with the "free rider" problems that increase as their policies become more compatible with general, public policies. Here in particular neocorporatist interest organization becomes reminiscent of traditional corporatism, also because organizational assistance may be accompanied by – more or less subtle – intervention in an association's internal process, in the name of associational democracy or political moderation. Unlike state corporatism, however, intermediary organizations in liberal democracies remain ultimately free to refuse cooperation with the government, regardless of the extent to which the state may help them with their organizational problems.

In a simplified model, the organizational dynamics of intermediary organizations derives from their simultaneous involvement in two environments, the social group from which they draw their members *(membership environment)* and the collective actors in relation to which they represent these *(influence environment;* Figure 22.1). The two environments are governed by different "logics" (Schmitter and Streeck, 1999 [1982]). Interaction between an interest organization and its *constituents* is shaped by the interest perceptions and demands of the latter, by the willingness of the members to comply with decisions made on their behalf, by the means available to the organization for controlling its members, and by the collective benefits and outside inducements the organization has to offer. Together these constitute an organization's *logic of membership*. The interaction between an interest organization and its *interlocutors* is governed by the demands the organization makes on the latter, the support it has to offer to them, the compromises it is willing and able to negotiate, and the extent to which it can "deliver" its constituents – as well as by the constraints and opportunities inherent in the relevant political institutions, especially for the establishment of lasting relations of political exchange, the concessions offered to the organization, and the degree to which the organization is granted privileged access and status. This interaction reflects the organization's *logic of influence*.

As the demands made on intermediary organizations by their members and interlocutors may be contradictory, their leaders typically confront difficult choices. Interest representation in a pluralist mode is controlled by the logic of membership and emphasizes the authentic representation of members' interest perceptions and articulated demands. Political influence, however, often depends on a capacity to moderate and compromise member demands, and so may a stable supply of organizational resources. However, if interest associations adapt to the logic of influence, they are drawn away from their members and into their target environment, in the process assuming corporatist traits. For example, whereas the logic of membership speaks for the formation of homogeneous and, by implication, small ("pluralist") organizations, the logic of influence tends to place a premium on interest organizations being broadly based and representing more general instead of highly special interests. To build lasting relations of political exchange with their interlocutors and thereby enhance their own stability and security, interest organizations may have to acquire organizational characteristics that make

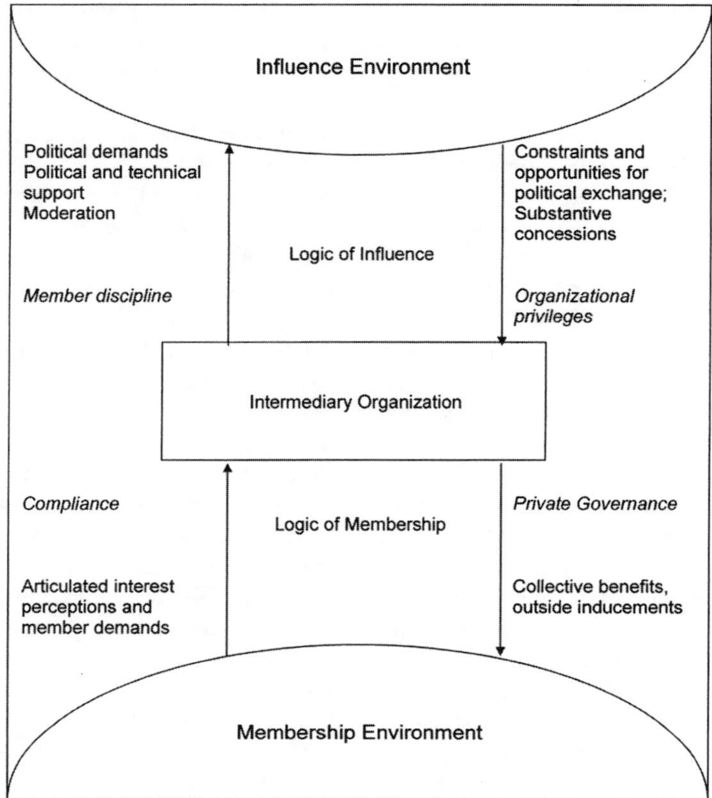

Figure 22.1. The Logics of Membership and Influence.

it more difficult for them to procure legitimacy for themselves under the logic of membership. In fact, intermediary organizations that become too distant from their members and too closely involved in the logic of influence may turn into extended arms of the government (i.e., into quasi-governmental agencies) or become representatives of interests opposed to those of their constituents ("yellow unions").

Striking a balance between member-responsive but weakly organized, fragmented, and competitive pluralism on the one hand and corporatist institutionalization in their target environment on the other is the central political and organizational problem of neocorporatist interest intermediation. Successful intermediation requires stable relations of exchange with environments subject to different and sometimes contradictory logics of action; in a sense it may be seen as arbitrage between markets for membership and influence. Pluralist interest representation transforms the interest perceptions of its clients into political demands and extracts concessions from its interlocutors to provide its constituents with collective benefits (Figure 22.1). Neocorporatist interest intermediation *in addition* exchanges member discipline for organizational privileges under the logic of influence, and private governance for member compliance under the logic of membership. In this it uses the compliance of its members as a resource in its dealings with its interlocutors, just as it relies on its organizational privileges in turning its constituents into members, trying to keep an equal distance between the different dictates of the logics of membership and influence by drawing on one to stay clear of the other.

Function: Concertation

The literature on national neocorporatist "concertation" reached a first peak in the late 1970s and early 1980s. It focused on the management of national economies after the wave of worker militancy in the late 1960s and the oil shocks of 1973 and 1979 (Cameron, 1984; Crouch, 1985; Katzenstein, 1985; Lange and Garrett, 1985; Pizzorno, 1979; Scharpf, 1987; Schmidt, 1982). The issue was what government and employers could do to make unions that had become stronger than ever moderate their wage demands in the context of a negotiated incomes policy, where statutory incomes policies were impossible for constitutional, technical, or political reasons. Tripartite national policies agreed between government, employers, and unions were to safeguard macroeconomic objectives such as low inflation, low unemployment, a stable exchange rate, and high growth while respecting the right of unions and employers to free collective bargaining. Neocorporatist concertation efforts reflected a Keynesian political economy in which full employment was a responsibility of the government that it had to live up to if it wanted to survive politically, and for which it had in principle the necessary tools available in the form of fiscal and monetary intervention. Politically guaranteed full employment, however, increased union bargaining power and thereby gave rise to inflation, unless unions could be persuaded not to use their bargaining power to the fullest.

The neocorporatist literature of the time identified a variety of concessions governments and employers offered to unions in tripartite package deals, including tax relief for low-income earners, more progressive income taxes, improved pension benefits, active labor market policies, increased educational spending, growth-promoting infrastructural investment, expanded rights to workplace representation, and organizational security. Comparative research explored whether countries that succeeded in negotiating tripartite national agreements performed better economically than liberal or pluralist countries with more adversarial institutions and practices. Research also tried to specify the conditions under which tripartite deals were achieved, such as the political complexion of the national government, the degree of independence of the central bank, or the size of the country. Much attention was paid to the organizational structure of unions and employer associations, especially whether they conformed to a corporatist pattern or not and whether concertation and cooperation between the state and organized groups was possible also with a more fragmented and pluralist structure of industrial relations.

For a while, neocorporatist concertation seemed a generally applicable recipe for the joint management of a Keynesian political economy by a democratic state and independently organized social interests. It soon turned out, however, that concertation was difficult to transport to countries like the United Kingdom with traditionally fragmented and adversarial interest groups. Moreover, the concessions that had to be made to unions became more expensive with time and more often than not only moved inflation forward into the future or caused an accumulation of public debt. Not least, unions frequently failed to deliver on their promises of wage moderation as they came under pressure from their members. In other cases, cooperative unions suffered a loss of confidence on the part of their constituents, which ultimately forced them to withdraw from concertation.

In the early 1980s, the neoconservative governments of the United States and Great Britain proved that labor-exclusive monetarist methods of bringing down inflation were not only effective but also politically sustainable, even though they involved high rates of unemployment. As inflation rates in OECD countries declined and converged at a historic low, research on corporatism shifted from incomes policy and demand management to collective infrastructures, like support for vocational training and technological innovation, that both free markets and state hierarchies seemed to have difficulty providing on their own. Again the question was whether corporatist organization of social groups and cooperation between them and the state resulted in better economic performance than a pluralist separation of state and society that left the economy to the free play of market forces. Although requisite organizational forms remained an issue, most of the research on "supply-side corporatism" looked at subnational regional, sectoral, or workplace-level institutions promoting cooperation between state and society or between competitors, rather than the national arrangements and macroeconomic policies that had been at the center of early research on corporatism (Streeck, 1984, 1992).

Research on national incomes policies revived in the 1990s in the context of efforts of European governments to bring down persistent unemployment and meet the strict criteria for accession to European Monetary Union (Pochet and Fajertag, 2000). National employment and stability pacts were proposed and negotiated that aimed at bringing union wage-setting behavior in line with the imperatives of a monetarist macroeconomic policy and the need, resulting not least from the neocorporatist bargaining of the 1970s, to consolidate public budgets (Ebbinghaus and Hassel, 2000). Pacts also involved sometimes far-reaching reforms of social security (Baccaro, 2002). Union cooperation with governments seemed to depend on a variety of factors. Unlike in the 1970s, however, governments of the Left were not significantly more successful than conservative governments in negotiating national pacts. Moreover, whether the organizational structure of national unions was corporatist or not seemed to be largely irrelevant (Regini, 2000).

Function: Self-Government

Much of the political science literature of the 1980s was concerned with the limits of state intervention and of the problem-solving capacity of governments. Whereas traditionally attention had focused on the input side of political systems, it now shifted to the technical difficulties facing legislators and state bureaucracies on the output side: for example, in fine-tuning policies to meet increasingly differentiated needs and in ensuring that programs were correctly implemented. In Europe it was in the context of rising disillusion with social democratic pretensions at political planning – the end of the "planning euphoria" of the 1960s and 1970s – that debates began to revolve around a need for *Staatsentlastung*, or relief of the state from an overgrown policy agenda (Scharpf, 1992).

Perceptions of state failure coincided with a tendency in Western societies at the time toward privatization of state activities and deregulation of markets. The latter was based on an emerging presumption that a free play of market forces was better suited to resolve complex issues of allocation and production than state intervention. There were also, however, attempts to develop an alternative response to the deficiencies of state intervention, one that avoided the risk of market failure succeeding state failure. In this context, a variety of forms of collective participation in policy making were rediscovered that extended far beyond collective bargaining and the concertation of incomes policies. Some involved an explicit delegation of governance functions to parapublic institutions and agencies offering opportunities for participation to affected social groups. Others licensed organized groups to regulate matters of common interest themselves and free from state interference.

Like incomes policy, the incorporation of interest groups in public policy making may be explained in terms of both power politics and functional expediency. From the former perspective, institutions of self-government are a concession of the state to the independent power of social groups and are therefore liable to turn into private bridgeheads in the public sphere. From a functional or policy perspective, self-government increases a society's problem-solving capacity as it makes for a better interface and more efficient cooperation between state and civil society – in a Durkheimian sense drawing on subgroup solidarity as a public resource and mobilizing the productivity advantages of cooperation between competitors. Rather than imposing its policies on society from above or turning them over to the market, a state in a neocorporatist system governs in part through negotiations with and devolution to organized social groups, using them for public policy functions they are better able to perform than a public bureaucracy.

Taking off from the literature on concertation, the writings in the 1980s on neocorporatist devolution of governance to organized civil society emphasized the potential contribution of interest associations to social order (Streeck and Schmitter, 1985). Especially in European countries with corporatist or Catholic traditions, interest associations were observed to share in public responsibility in policy sectors such as product standardization, quality control and certification, vocational training, environmental regulation, research and development, and welfare provision. Here, group interests as defined and acted upon by firmly institutionalized associations seemed to be compatible with general, public interests, so that associations could be given both autonomy and authority. Arrangements of this sort were often bilateral, involving the state and a particular organized group; they involved groups with ideal interests, such as churches or new social movements, no less than economic interests like those of farmers or of firms in particular sectors; and they tended to be concerned with market regulation or the supply of services or infrastructural facilities, rather than with the management of demand.

Group self-government through associations – the "public use of private organized interests" (Streeck and Schmitter, 1985) – enriches the repertoire of the state and expands the toolkit of governance. Public recognition and organizational support are to transform pluralist interest groups into disciplined "private interest governments," both inducing and enabling them to define the interests of their members with a view to their compatibility with the public interest. By enlisting the support of associational self-interest, the state mobilizes expert information that it would be unable to build and maintain itself. As association members usually have more confidence in their representatives than in state bureaucrats, private interest government also tends to have fewer problems of legitimacy and greater powers of persuasion than direct state regulation.

Self-governance also benefits the involved associations. By assuming responsibility for regulating the behavior of their members, associations achieve institutionalization in the public sphere and gain in status and security. They and their members may also prefer self-regulation over potentially heavy-handed state intervention. Groups may furthermore be afraid of incompetence on the part of state bureaucracies, making it unpredictably more costly to be policed by them than by themselves. Governments, for their part, must be able to identify situations when the organized private interest of a social group can be made compatible with the public interest of society. They also must have at their disposal organizational incentives and material compensations by which to move group interests close enough to the public interest for the independent pursuit of the former to contribute to the latter. In particular, states must find ways to prevent a decay of self-government through "agency capture" by rent-seeking interest groups and to ensure that the power of organized interests can for the practical purposes of public policy be treated as devolved and delegated public power, even if it is in fact not derived from the state. Domesticating group interests in this way requires, among other things, reserve state capacity enabling the government credibly to threaten direct intervention in case self-government fails to meet its public responsibilities.

Moving beyond narrower concepts of private interest government through associations, the mainly American literature on "associative democracy" explores decentralization of decision making to local actors and facilitation of cooperation between them as an alternative to centralized state intervention (Cohen and Rogers, 1995; Cohen and Sabel, 1997). With corporatist theory, this literature shares an emphasis on self-organization below and within the state performing functions of rule making and collective goods production that liberal states cannot satisfactorily perform. Informed mainly by research on regional economies drawing on informal social capital for better economic performance (Trigilia, 1990), theories of associative democracy attribute less significance than the corporatist literature to formal organizational structures. Instead they rely mostly on the cultivation of informal social relations between a variety of local actors united in a search for comparative advantage in competition with other regional economies.

THE ECONOMIC EFFECTS OF CORPORATISM

A substantial part of the empirical research on neocorporatism since the late 1970s has consisted of quantitative comparative analysis of corporatism's economic impact. Numerous attempts have been made to score the eighteen or so most affluent OECD countries on a corporatism scale (for detailed discussion see Kenworthy, 2001; Kenworthy and Kittel, 2002). Early measures focused on *interest group structure*, of which there are three chief dimensions: representational coverage (e.g., union density), organizational centralization, and organizational concentration. Since roughly the mid-1980s, measures of *concertation* have played a more prominent role. These have focused primarily on the degree of centralization or coordination of wage setting. Fewer attempts have been made to measure interest-group participation in public policy in general – that is, apart from wage setting. Many researchers have created composite corporatism measures that combine information about various aspects of interest-group structure and/or concertation.

Research on the economic effects of corporatism has focused chiefly on macroeconomic performance, especially unemployment and inflation. Most heavily studied has been the impact of centralized or coordinated wage setting. Three causal mechanisms have been hypothesized.

First, centralized or coordinated wage setting may yield low unemployment or inflation by engendering *wage restraint*. The general logic is simple, although specific applications can be complex (Franzese, 1999; OECD, 1997). If employees bargain aggressively for high wage increases, employers can do five main things in response: raise productivity, raise prices, reduce profits paid out to investors, reduce investment, and/or reduce the number of employees. When wages are bargained separately for individual firms, none of these responses will necessarily have an adverse short-term effect on employment or inflation-adjusted wages, which are the principal concerns of union negotiators. For instance, if a firm raises prices, this is likely to have little impact on the living standard of its workers. Even if the firm chooses to reduce employment, those laid off should be able to find work elsewhere as long as wage increases and layoffs are not generalized throughout the economy. Thus, where bargaining is decentralized and uncoordinated, there is an incentive for unions to pursue a strategy of wage militancy.

By contrast, if wage negotiations cover a large share of the workforce, union bargainers can be reasonably sure that a large wage increase will have an adverse impact on their members. When firms representing a sizable share of the economy raise prices, the resulting inflation offsets or nullifies the wage gains of most workers. Similarly, if layoffs are economy-wide, employment opportunities will diminish. Centralized or coordinated wage setting thus generates an incentive for wage moderation, as interest groups are forced by their size and structure to internalize the negative impact of aggressive bargaining.

Many researchers have assumed a linear relationship between wage-setting centralization or coordination and wage restraint. However, some have proposed that the effect is hump-shaped, with high and low levels of centralization best at generating labor cost restraint (Calmfors and Driffill, 1988). Others contend that corporatist wage setting yields superior performance outcomes only in combination with particular types or levels of central bank independence (Hall and Franzese, 1998), leftist government (Lange and Garrett, 1985), unionization (Kittel, 1999), or public sector unionization (Garrett and Way, 1999). Still others hypothesize that the effect is both hump-shaped and interactive with central bank independence or the monetary regime (Cukierman and Lippi, 1999; Iversen, 1999).

One glaring weakness of research in this area is the limited empirical investigation of the assumed causal mechanism. Only a handful of studies have actually examined the relationship between wage setting and labor cost developments (Bruno and Sachs, 1985; Kenworthy,

1996, 2002; Layard et al., 1991; OECD, 1997; Traxler et al., 2001; Traxler and Kittel, 2000). Most have looked only at the statistical correlation between wage setting and macroeconomic performance and have simply presumed that the link between wage setting and labor cost restraint, and also between labor cost restraint and performance outcomes, is as hypothesized.

A second potential link between corporatist wage setting and unemployment is *economic growth*. One of the outcomes of centralized or coordinated wage determination, achieved either informally or explicitly in corporatist pacts, may be greater investment, which in turn tends to spur more rapid growth of economic output (Lange and Garrett, 1985). Faster growth, in turn, increases employment.

A third hypothesized link is *government policy*. Policy orientations are seen as a key determinant of cross-country differences in unemployment. Policy makers in countries with centralized or coordinated wage setting are likely to feel more confident than their counterparts in countries with fragmented bargaining that labor cost increases will be moderate. Thus, they should tend to worry less about wage-push inflation. This may increase their willingness to adopt an expansive monetary or fiscal policy, an active labor market policy, or other policies that reduce unemployment. By contrast, policy makers in nations with less coordinated wage arrangements may feel compelled to resort to higher levels of unemployment in order to keep inflation in check (Hall and Franzese, 1998; Kenworthy, 1996; Soskice, 1990).

Although much of the research on the impact of corporatism on economic performance centers on wage setting, some studies have emphasized union participation in economic policy making. Unions desire low unemployment. The more input unions have in economic policy decisions, the more likely it would seem that government policies will give priority to fighting unemployment (Compston, 1997). To the extent that the respective policies are effective, the result should be lower rates of joblessness.

Although there are some dissenting findings (OECD, 1997; Smith, 1992; Therborn, 1987; Western, 2001), most studies have discovered an association between corporatist wage setting and low unemployment or inflation in the 1970s and 1980s (Bruno and Sachs, 1985; Calmfors and Driffill, 1988; Cameron, 1984; Garrett, 1998; Hall and Franzese, 1998; Hicks and Kenworthy, 1998; Iversen, 1999; Janoski, McGill, and Tinsley, 1997; Kenworthy, 1996, 2002; Layard, Nickell, and Jackman, 1991; Scharpf, 1991 [1987]; Soskice, 1990; Traxler et al., 2001). In the 1990s, however, inflation rates converged across affluent OECD nations, and restrictive monetary policy coupled with growing employer leverage led to substantial wage restraint in traditionally noncentralized and uncoordinated countries such as Canada, France, the United Kingdom, and the United States. Consequently, at least one recent study finds no effect of corporatist wage arrangements on unemployment in the 1990s (Kenworthy, 2002). Empirical analyses of the macroeconomic impact of interest-group participation in policy making have been considerably less common, but findings have tended to be favorable, even into the 1990s (Compston, 1997; Kenworthy, 2002; Traxler et al., 2001).

The bulk of research on the effects of corporatism has dealt with macroeconomic performance, but a number of studies suggest that its impact may be no less important, and perhaps more so, for the distribution and redistribution of income. Unions tend to prefer smaller pay differentials, and centralized or coordinated wage setting increases unions' leverage over the wage structure. Because differentials are more transparent if wages are set simultaneously and collectively for a large share of the workforce, centralization may reinforce union preferences for low pay differentials. Furthermore, low pay inequality may be one of the things unions ask from employers in exchange for pay restraint. Empirical findings have tended to yield strong support for the hypothesis that corporatist wage setting is associated with lower pay inequality (Alderson and Nielsen, 2002; Iversen, 1999; OECD, 1997; Rowthorn, 1992; Rueda and Pontusson, 2000; Wallerstein, 1999).

There also is reason to expect a link between corporatism and the redistributive efforts of government. Unions may demand more generous redistributive programs in exchange for wage moderation, and regularized participation by unions in the policy-making process may heighten their influence. Here, too, there is empirical support in the literature (Hicks, 1999:chap. 6; Hicks and Kenworthy, 1998; Hicks and Swank, 1992; Swank and Martin, 2001), though it is difficult to disentangle the impact of concertation from that of related factors such as social democratic government.

THE FUTURE OF NEOCORPORATISM

In the span of two decades, corporatism was hailed as an effective model of governance in affluent countries (Katzenstein, 1985; Schmitter, 1981), dismissed as irrelevant in an era of internationalization and restructuring (Ferner and Hyman, 1998:xii), and rediscovered by policy makers and scholars as a potentially superior way of managing rapid economic and political change (Auer, 2000; Hassel and Ebbinghaus, 2000; Pochet and Fajertag, 1997; Regini, 2000; Visser and Hemerijck, 1997). What lies ahead?

The future of neocorporatism is bound up with the ongoing transformation of *social structure* on the one hand and of the *nation-state* on the other. Social groups in advanced societies, certainly the producer groups of the industrial age, have become less cohesive and more difficult to organize into centralized, monopolistic, and hierarchical associations. For example, with the decline of Fordist industrial organization and Keynesian economic policy and the growing prominence of the service sector, unionization has fallen almost everywhere and the degree of union centralization has declined in many countries (Traxler et al., 2001; Western, 1997). Generally social structures today seem to generate less stable group identities and give rise to more individualistic perceptions of interest that may make an encompassing association's "logic of membership" intractable. Moreover, the producer groups that formed the principal constituency of postwar democratic corporatism are shrinking in size while other groups with distinct political interests have emerged, such as women or immigrants, who are not well represented within traditional corporatist arrangements.

The nation-state, once the opponent and later the sponsor of organized group interests, is being transformed by economic and social internationalization. Exactly to what effect is, however, far from clear. Heightened capital mobility has rendered firms less dependent on the domestic institutions of any one country, increased the desire of employers for flexibility of labor and labor costs, and impaired the capacity of governments to deliver on political deals. The breakdown of centralized wage bargaining in Sweden in the early 1980s, and the elimination of formal interest-group representation on the boards of several public agencies in the early 1990s, are frequently cited as an example for the decline of labor-inclusive democratic corporatism in its historical connection with Keynesianism and the social democratic welfare state.

On the other hand, observers have expressed skepticism about the degree to which globalization is likely to alter national institutional structures and policy choices (Berger and Dore, 1996; Garrett, 1998; Hollingsworth and Streeck, 1994; Kitschelt et al., 1999). Nonmarket institutions can offer competitive advantages to firms that may outweigh their costs. Quantitative analyses by Traxler et al. (2001) suggest little if any convergence in interest-group organization, wage-setting arrangements, and interest-group participation through the late 1990s. However, they do find evidence of a trend toward "organized decentralization" of wage bargaining, whereby wages are set largely at the sectoral level but coordinated informally across sectors (see also Iversen, 1999; Thelen, 2001). Meanwhile, neocorporatist pacts dealing with issues such as wage restraint and labor market and social security reform have played a prominent role in the Netherlands and Ireland – two countries widely viewed as European economic success stories over the past decade. Similar pacts have been forged or renewed in Norway, Finland, Belgium, and Italy (Auer, 2000; Hassel and Ebbinghaus, 2000; Molina and Rhodes, 2002; Pochet and Fajertag, 1997; Regini, 2000; Visser and Hemerijck, 1997).

Generally, changes in the capacities of the nation-state in the course of internationalization seem to have different and partly contradictory consequences for neocorporatism. Where national states lose control to international markets, they become unable to underwrite tripartite bargains, in which case a decline in state capacities is associated with a decline in associational capacities. At the same time, where governments can no longer keep capital captive, they may depend on organized groups to create institutional conditions and infrastructures attractive to investors. Also, states that come under international pressure to balance their budgets, like the member states of the European Union, may need the cooperation of still powerful trade unions for institutional reform and wage restraint. In such instances, state weakness may enhance rather than diminish the role and power of associations.

On the other hand, most nation-states today have embarked on a strategy of liberalizing their economies. Liberalization implies a greater role for markets and regulatory authorities, at the expense of both discretionary state intervention and corporatist bargaining. In part liberalization responds to pressures exerted by internationalization for increased competitiveness and openness of national economies; the latter may require replacement of corporatist self-government, for example of financial markets, with more transparent and internationally accountable state regulation. There also, however, may be domestic reasons for liberalization, among them certain long-term effects of neocorporatism after its peak twenty years ago. These include overblown social security systems, rigid labor markets, high and persistent unemployment, a widening gap between a shrinking group of well-represented insiders and a growing group of disenfranchised outsiders, and the defense by trade unions of a social policy and labor market regime that reflects the social structures and economic conditions of the 1970s rather than of the present. Especially in countries where trade unions and, to an extent, employers use their institutional position to veto change, governments have felt challenged to limit the influence of corporatist interest groups and replace self-government with more publicly accountable state control. In this they have followed a spreading liberal discourse that suspects any form of organized collectivism of particularistic rent-seeking and places its hope on a strong state recreating free markets and defending them against interference by "distributional coalitions" (Olson, 1982).

Although internationalization may make national states part with neocorporatism, it may simultaneously open up new opportunities for group self-government by "nongovernmental organizations" in state-free international settings. Prospects for a transnational renaissance of prenational corporatism are, however, uncertain. Group cohesion beyond the nation-state tends to be weak. Also, the very absence of state authority that might empower organized groups deprives them of institutional support. (In addition it makes it impossible to hold them accountable to a public interest.) Internationally there are only few organized groups capable of making binding rules for themselves, not to mention correcting international market outcomes by negotiated redistribution. Other than competing states, the main actors in the international arena are large firms, increasingly transnational in character, with ample resources to pursue their interests individually, unconstrained by union or government pressure forcing them into international class solidarity, and indeed with a growing capacity to extricate themselves from associative governance at the national level (Streeck, 1997).

Where there is something resembling neocorporatist interest intermediation above the nation-state, it seems heavily dependent on the sponsorship of international organizations like the European Union. In its effort to develop statelike properties, the European Union has long cultivated a substructure of organized interests from which it hopes to draw increased legitimacy. But although the European Union attracts a great deal of lobbying, this is far from congealing in a corporatist system. Most of it continues to be nationally based, as national interest organizations hesitate to transfer authority to their European peak associations. Although the European Commission relies and indeed depends greatly on information and expertise furnished by organized interests, devolution of decision-making powers to organized interests is rare. Nor has the "social dialogue" between the Commission, the European trade union confederation, and European business developed into tripartite concertation, mostly because national actors, including national governments, jealously defend their autonomy. All in all, even in the European Union international interest-group politics is as a rule far more pluralist than in national systems (Streeck and Schmitter, 1991).

The same holds for corporatist arrangements at the regional level within and, sometimes, across national borders. Much of the literature on "industrial districts" stresses the commonality of interests held by workers, employers and policy makers in a number of subnational areas, and the advantages of negotiated decision making in pursuit of those interests. Yet the long-term sustainability of such arrangements is open to question. Regions, not being states, are unable to insert coercive power in the voluntary relations between their citizens. In particular, they may lack the capacity to provide the kind of support required to transform unstable, voluntaristic, pluralistic interest groups into mature ones capable of attending to the larger sectoral, regional, or national interest. For example, regionally based unionism would have to do without external sources of associational monopoly, without authoritative stabilization of bargaining arenas, and without recourse to a public sphere balancing the manifold advantages employers enjoy in the marketplace.

If the twentieth century that witnessed the ascendancy of the modern nation-state was "still the century of corporatism" (Schmitter, 1974), the same may not be true for the postnational twenty-first century.

CHAPTER TWENTY-THREE

Undemocratic Politics in the Twentieth Century and Beyond[1]

Viviane Brachet-Márquez

Unser National Sozialismus ist die Zukunft Deutschlands. Trotz diese Zukunft wirtschaftlich rechts-orientiert wird, werden unsere Herzen links orientiert bleiben. Aber vor allem werden wir niemals vergessen, dass wir Deutschen sind.[2]

– Adolf Hitler, 1932 Annual Congress of the National Socialist Democratic Party

Socialement je suis de gauche, économiquement je suis de droite, et nationalement je suis de France![3]

– Jean Marie Le Pen, 2002 presidential campaign speech for the Front National

To write about undemocratic politics after the fall of the Berlin Wall and in the midst of widespread democratization in Central Europe and Latin America may look like a vain effort to revive a fast-dwindling subject. Yet, even if the age of Soviet or Nazi totalitarianism seems over and many autocracies are fast being propelled – by financial necessity if by anything – toward democratic openings, we are now experiencing a period in which undemocratic politics are manifested as much in sundry dictatorships, fundamentalisms, and bloody civil wars as in antidemocratic ideologies, parties, and tolerated practices outside and within established democracies. Instead of clearly characterized "regimes," to which we may unambiguously assign a democratic or undemocratic label, we often find a patchwork of mixed democratic and undemocratic ideologies, mentalities, rules, and entrenched practices. This is especially true of countries that have only recently emerged from colonial rule and those recently returned to elected civilian government after bloody dictatorships. But it is also true of more established democracies, to wit the astounding success of Haider in Austria and Le Pen in France.

All these manifestations have stimulated an active and fast-expanding beehive of research, but one also extremely fragmented: by disciplines, geographical areas, periods, and, inevitably, languages. As a result, we are confronted by a series of geographically restricted debates that speak to relatively small groups of specialists. This chapter is an attempt to pull different threads out of this fast-growing literature so as to establish possibilities of dialogue between them. It should also help us to better understand the political dynamics of recently redemocratized countries. In that sense, the debate on undemocratic politics is inseparable from that on democracy.

Rather than shoulder the impossible task of reviewing thoroughly this extremely broad and heterogeneous field, this chapter maps out the main research programs and issues that have guided work on undemocratic politics in the

[1] My heartfelt thanks to Guillermo Alonso, Eugenio Anguiano, Flora Boton, Cas Mudde, Tony Tillett, and my anonymous reviewers for their critical comments on the first draft of this chapter. This chapter is dedicated to my uncle Freddy Staehling, who faced totalitarian fascism in Buchenwald.

[2] Our national socialism is the future of Germany. Although this future economically leans to the Right, our heart will stay on the Left. But above all, we will never forget that we are German.

[3] Socially, I stand on the Left, economically, on the Right, and nationally, I stand for France.

past half century. Due to its importance in initially defining the field, the lion's share is given, in the first part, to the regime approach to undemocratic politics. The second part deals with movements against authoritarian and sultanistic regimes and the extreme reaction on the Right that has come in their wake. The third part focuses on movements and parties that show strong undemocratic tendencies yet function within established democratic contexts.

UNDEMOCRATIC POLITICS FROM A REGIME PERSPECTIVE

Regime categories and types are taxonomical devices that order polities according to sets of abstract categories and then serve as summary statements to refer to empirical cases. Although few analysts would ever claim that regimes are unchanging, typification carries implicitly a belief in the relative stability over time in the characteristics singled out for any given type. (And indeed, without such an assumption, why typify at all?) Up until the 1980s, students of undemocratic politics made extensive use of regime types, pairing them up with countries in ways that have underplayed change and emphasized essence. Since then, they have been used more flexibly to refer to families of regimes with common grounds despite important differences (Kershaw and Lewin, 1999) and to characterize phases or episodes through which polities evolve, allowing for a shift of our attention from essential characteristics and stable structures to differences, transitions, and change.

Following Juan Linz's initial typification, undemocratic polities have often been classified as either totalitarian or authoritarian (Linz, 2000). Such a division, however, either forces many cases into the wrong camp or leaves them out altogether.[4] There have been, de facto, three relatively distinct debates using the regime approach: the first over totalitarianism versus fascism involving interwar Europe; the second over authoritarianism focused on Southern Europe and Latin America; and the third on sultanistic regimes, referring to Asia and Africa as well as some countries in Latin America.

The Totalitarian–Fascist Debate

In totalitarian regimes, Linz (2000) wrote, the state asserts its monopoly over power and imposes exclusively one ideology on the basis of which it attempts the total mobilization of the population through a single party and various organizations controlled by the same. This definition points to a structural institutional view of totalitarianism (as also in Mann, 1997), as opposed to one emphasizing culture and ideology (Ahrend, 1968; Marcuse, 1967; Burrin, 2000) or origins (Korchak, 1994). Despite wide differences, most authors recognize three major components of totalitarian regimes: (1) an all-encompassing ideology setting forth a program of radical transformation of society and calling for the extermination of all people suspected of incompatibility with or enmity toward said program; (2) a centrally controlled state bureaucracy at the service of this ideology, with virtually unlimited authority and modern means of communication, propaganda, surveillance, and repression; and (3) a mass party controlled by the state to implement this transformation, involving the willing or forced participation of the whole population. Some authors also include the leader principle (Friedrich and Brzezinski, 1965; Burrin, 2000), the presence of state terrorism (Ahrend, 1968; Friedrich and Brzezinski, 1965), and militarist expansionism (Friedrich and Brzezinski, 1965). Needless to say, important differences opposed Stalinist USSR to Nazi Germany in many of these respects. Whereas the socialist ideology was highly codified and inscribed in policy, Nazi shibboleths came closer to millenarist statements (Friedrich and Brzezinski, 1968). Whereas the Nazi Party was relatively successful in mobilizing the population from the base up, the distrust generated by Stalinist propaganda and the terror its police methods inspired are said to have pushed the rank and file toward withdrawal and depolitization.

[4] At the height of the Cold War, all communisms and fascisms were commonly considered "totalitarian," but such views have been revised since then.

Taken in its strictest definition, totalitarianism would seem to refer only to Stalin's purges and Nazi Germany's implementation of the "Final Solution." Yet should our conception of this phenomenon be less historically or culturally limited, other examples come to mind. Can China's 1957–8 Hundred Flowers[5] period be classified as totalitarian? The ideologically based purge of those intellectuals and students who had responded to Chairman Mao's appeals to self-crititicism would suggest that it can. The violence of the criticism that erupted out of this opening (especially, and surprisingly for Mao, from young students educated under communism) led to the rectification campaigning whereby officials were made to do regular spells of manual labor. Yet because this repression targeted a limited number of people and no wide popular mobilization was engineered by the state to justify its actions, a good case can be made that this period should remain under the general label of authoritarianism.[6] By contrast, totalitarianism seems appropriate to characterize China's 1966–76 Cultural Revolution, during which the masses (especially the adolescent Red Guards) were ideologically radicalized and mobilized by the state in order to serve as instruments to purge a very wide cross-section of close to 100 million people (Fairbank, 1992:383).[7] After Mao's death in 1976, the regime veered back to authoritarianism in the context of a commodity economy (Bragger and Reglar, 1994), offering estranged elites and minority factions token presence in the legislature in exchange for their unconditional support of party rule (O'Brien, 1990:155). In this light, the 1989 Tienamen Square massacre and subsequent repression of protesting students can be interpreted as a manifestation of authoritarianism rather than totalitarianism, bearing in mind that even "limited" pluralism is not to be found in the Chinese brand of that regime type.

Like totalitarianism, fascism[8] has been defined in a number of ways, from so general as populist ultranationalism (Griffin, 1995)[9] to so specific as to fit only the Italian case, as by Gentile – the regime's official philosopher – (from Payne, 1995:5, or Gentile, 1975). Some definitions focus on origins (Paxton, 1995; Korchak, 1994), others on cultural–ideological characteristics (Ahrend, 1968; Burrin, 2000; Sternhell and Sznajder, 1994) or structure (Linz, 2000; Mann, 1997). Some have restricted the term to the interwar period (Rémond, 1982), whereas others apply it to a wider range of periods and cases (Sternhell et al., 1994).

From the Marxist camp, rather than definitions, we have interpretations as to the origin and purpose of fascism. For the Third International, fascism is understood to emerge in the context of the monopolistic and imperialist stage of capitalist society, being simultaneously the product of its contradictions and the

[5] The name came from a sentence in a 1956 unpublished speech by Mao: "Let a hundred flowers bloom, let a hundred schools contend." The first referred to the literary field, though it later took on a wider connotation, whereas the "hundred schools" referred to the flourishing of philosophical debates during the third and fourth centuries B.C. (MacFarquhar, 1960).

[6] The regime's rigid policy of forced reeducation toward intellectuals and artists is said to have "thawed" when, following the Hungarian 1956 rebellion, Mao started pondering how his rule might be made less oppressive. The ideological basis for such an opening could be found in the "mass line" which established that information must be gathered from the masses before decisions were taken, so that the latter must, in turn, accept said decisions as their own. However, the twin principle of "democratic centralism" also established that all issues must be discussed within the CCP, so that whatever critique emerges from the grassroots could be conveniently condemned as deviationist if it failed to meet with the approval of the center, as happened in 1957. For information on the Hundred Flowers period, see Macfarquhar (1960) and Fairbank (1992). On the Cultural Revolution, see MacFarquhar (1974) and Fairbank (1992).

[7] Such purges, unlike their Russian or German counterparts, fell short of executing their victims. Although a large number of purged leaders committed suicide under the pressure of the treatments they were made to endure, many survived. Deng Xiaoping, for example, was purged twice during the Mao era.

[8] The word fascism comes from the Latin *fasces*, which designated the insignia of official authority in Ancient Rome. It consisted of an ax head projecting from a bundle of rods. Mussolini adopted this symbol in 1919 as the emblem of the Italian fascist movement to represent the union of the masses with the head of the state.

[9] "A genus of political ideology whose mythic core in its various permutations is a palingenetic form of populist ultra-nationalism" (Griffin, 1991:4).

particular form it takes in its antiproletarian reaction (Milza, 2001; Beetham, 1983). For Thalheimer, however, rather than the final phase of capitalism, fascism expressed the greater power held by capitalist relations on political forms leading to bonapartism (1967:15). Closer to the ground, Gramsci held that Mussolini's fascism was only partially a class phenomenon that nevertheless served the interests of the bourgeoisie by destroying the organizational links forged between workers, thereby making them into a fragmented helpless mass incapable of recovering their power with the return of democracy (Gramsci, 1924).

Despite the multiplicity of definitions, interpretations, and historical forms, fascist regimes or periods have displayed similar characteristics: the absolute primacy of the state and its chief; the submission of the individual to the state understood as the unified will of the people; and a rejection of democracy, bourgeois values, and rationalism in favor of martial virtues, combat, and conquest. On paper (and in many writings), fascism appears to have differed little from totalitarianism, including its mystical fervor for remaking the nation and conquering beyond its borders. Yet in historical fact, it has departed from totalitarianism first in falling short of pursuing its ideological program with the same ruthlessness as Stalinism or Nazism and second in the necessity it faced of negotiating clientelistic relations with preexisting elites and institutions in the de facto absence of absolute state power over them.

Who were the nontotalitarian fascist states? Although everyone agrees on placing Mussolini's Italy in that category, considerable disagreement reigns when dealing with Spain, Austria, or Central Europe. Preston (1990) argued that Franco's record, which in the case of the repression of the working class is said to have been worse than Germany's,[10] should place him squarely in the fascist camp, forgetting that authoritarianism can be every bit as murderous as fascism (to wit, many Latin American authoritarian regimes discussed later). It is still arguable that Spain was fascist during the early part of Franco's rule due to the closeness to the caudillo of the fascist *Falange*, but it soon became clear that the Catholic conservative oligarchy held the reins and that Franco had to govern with their approval and little mobilization from below. Spain thus failed to fulfill three major requirements of fascism – state supremacy, population mobilization, and a strong ideology. Likewise, Salazar's Portugal, while using some fascist slogans, as did Austria's conservative governments under Englebert Dollfus and Kurt von Schuschnigg, also remained within the traditional conservative camp. Radical fascist movements also developed in most Central European countries in the interwar period[11] – especially in Hungary, Croatia, Bulgaria, and Romania (Payne, 1995) – but did not succeed in installing fascist governments (except in Croatia), which led analysts to conclude that traditional conservatism was as inhospitable for fascism as established democracy. Fascist movements also developed in interwar Western Europe, particularly in France (Soucy, 1986), but by 1938, they had lost much of their impetus (Winock, 2001:266) and not even German occupation could breathe new life into them. As for the Vichy government under Nazi-occupied France, analysts have concurred to give it mere traditional conservative credentials (Milza, 2001; Burrin, 2000; Winock, 1990; Soucy, 1999).

The single most disputed and unresolved issue is the origin of fascism, beginning with the insistent "why Germany" question. The belief in German exceptionalism dominated early debates, projecting, as Eley (1995) argued, a culturally and historically deterministic view explaining triumphant Nazism as the inevitable outcome of a backward society held back by preindustrial authoritarian traditions (as in Moore, 1966; Dahrendorf, 1968; Gerschenkron, 1943).

The last decades have thrown doubt on diehard commonplace explanations of the rise of fascism in Germany and Italy as either caused by the Depression, revanchist resentment against

[10] Franco's rule claimed hundreds of thousands of lives and forced hundreds of thousands more into exile. The dictatorship is said to have executed a quarter-million people, maintained concentration camps, and sent troops to fight for Hitler on the Russian front. On the evolution of Franco's regime, see Linz (1970b).

[11] See Wippermann (1983).

the Versailles Treaty settlement, or the atavistic racism of the German nation. It has been shown that in the Depression years, industrial production dropped more sharply in Czechoslovakia (61%) than in Germany (39%), and that Germany's sharper drop in relation to Norway's and Denmark's (15%) or Sweden's (11%) was explained by lower predepression levels of industrial activity in these countries (Luebbert, 1991:307–8). Unemployment between 1929 and 1933 was just as high in Scandinavia as in Germany, and hyperinflation affected Poland as much as Germany. Even in Austria, a country as burdened as Germany by an imperialist and conservative past and a strong fascist movement, no fascist regime took power during the prewar period despite a 38 percent decline in industrial production. As for Italy, where fascism took power in 1922, long before the Depression, its industrial activity actually rose by 11 percent during the 1929–33 period (Luebbert, 1991: 307–8). By contrast, in Spain, where industrial production fell by only 18 percent, a fascist-dominated coalition did rise, eventually destroying Spain's fledgling democracy, admittedly with some help from Nazi Messerschmidts.

The thesis of military revanchism (Milza, 1987; Collins, 1995; Linz, 1976; Macherer, 1974) has fared no better. Granted that Spain's military may still have been smarting from their 1921 defeat against Kabyl rebels in Northern Morocco and from the Spanish–American War of 1894,[12] but Austria and Hungary had also suffered defeat in 1918 yet did not become fascist regimes.[13] Lastly, in Portugal, where the preconditions for the rise of fascism had all seemed present,[14] the fascist movement was unable to take power. As for racism, it is well-known that far from being restricted to Germany, anti-Semitism was so widespread in Central Europe (especially Poland and Croatia) that the populations of these countries virtually delivered the Jews into German hands. Hamilton (1995) has also shown the weakness of cultural explanations of Nazi success in Germany.

Equally in dispute is Moore's view of the road to democracy versus fascism (Moore, 1966)[15] and its recent revival by Stephens (1989) and Rueschemeyer, Stephens, and Stephens (1992).[16] They propose to relax Moore's thesis on the rise of fascism to state that the presence of a large landed class blocks the development of democracy or facilitates its eclipse by limiting the kinds of alliances which other classes can make. Accordingly, the alliance between the Junker class, capitalists and the Nazi Party in interwar Germany, and the failure of the middle and working classes to form the alliance that would have saved the Weimar Republic, is explained by the sheer presence of a powerful agrarian class. Capitalists, allegedly too dependent on the state for industrial policy, are said to have absorbed the authoritarian politics of the agrarian elites, a view strongly disputed by Blackbourne and Eley (1984), whereas the German working class, although one of the best organized in Europe, is said to have been too "isolated" to defend its interests.[17] Furthermore,

[12] General Sanjurjo, veteran of the Spanish–American War, was the initial head of the military conspiracy against the democratic government. His accidental death in an airplane crash allowed Franco to take leadership.

[13] This is not to say that the use of fascia as emblems or anti-Semitism were not widespread in these countries as in most Central European countries.

[14] These conditions were: modernism and futurism, nationalism, traumas resulting from World War I, a worker offensive, anticommunism, young army officers politicized by the extreme Right, the fascia *avant la lettre* of Sidonio Pais, the emergence of mass politics, and the crisis of legitimacy of liberalism (Pinto, 1995).

[15] Stephens (1989) summarized Moore's thesis of the fascist road in the following way: (1) the landed upper class must be strong and retain considerable power in a democratic interlude; (2) agriculture must be labor-repressive, but employ political rather than market control over peasant laborers; (3) there must be sufficient industrialization so that the bourgeoisie is a significant political actor; and (4) the bourgeoisie is kept in a politically dependent condition as industrialization is aided by the state.

[16] Regarding Europe, Stephens, 1989 and Rueschemeyer, Stephens, and Stephens, 1992 will be used interchangeably, as the chapter on Europe in the latter is identical with Stephens, 1989.

[17] Rather than this cryptic argument that the German working class was "isolated," the fact that German communists at the time were divided between the "deviationist" social democratic wing and die-hard adherents to the Third International may partially explain their relative weakness in the face of early attacks by the Nazi Party. Equally credible is Gramsci's position

rather than attempt to explain the rise of fascism, as Moore did, Rueschemeyer et al. (1992) limited their forecast to an "authoritarian path," so that in the end, they leave unanswered the questions of why agrarian conservative forces in Germany, Italy, and initially, Spain, should have allied with fascism rather than followed a straight authoritarian path. Using the same set of data[18] but measuring the strength of the landowner class as percent agricultural laborers, Luebbert (1987) found no correlation between agrarian social structure and fascism.

Breaking with a straightforward class view, Luebbert (1991) has proposed instead that where liberal parties overcame middle class cleavages and attracted working class support before 1914, liberal democracy emerged, as in France, Great Britain and Switzerland, but where they did not, "the only coalition that could provide an adequate political majority would be one that joined an urban class with a rural class under either social democratic or fascist leadership.... When the family peasantry sided with urban workers, the result was a social democratic regime. When it sided with the urban middle classes, the outcome was fascism" (Luebbert, 1991:10–11). This interpretation puts perhaps too much weight on party politics, which, in the absence of universal male suffrage (that came after World War I for countries that took the fascist path), were oligarchical in nature. Following Payne (1995), the explanation behind the pattern found by Luebbert may have been that the road to democracy represented "broad political participation relatively early in the era of modern politics, [while] for those societies in which universal male suffrage arrived only in 1919, it would turn out to have come too late, at least for the interwar generation" (Payne, 1995:130). Also in agreement with Luebbert's findings is the fact that "in the surviving parliamentary regimes, alliances of liberals and moderate social democratic labor forces were established before or soon after WWI" (Payne, 1995:130).

This interpretation also somewhat clears up the puzzle of the alliance between agrarian aristocrats and fascists that the simple "presence of agrarian elites" does little to explain: Where a long parliamentarian and universal male franchise tradition had existed, conservative forces could rely on established conservative parties to defend their interests and obtain benefits without having to question the republican framework. The temptation to incorporate fascist forces into the conservative alliance in order to reestablish a conservative tradition interrupted by the democratic interlude occurred in contexts with little experience in parliamentarian politics or voting among the masses. Once the alliance was established, what happened is not something that can be deduced from any set of structural variables.

Unsatisfied with either Luebbert's or Payne's explanations, Brustein (1996) answers the 'why Germany' question by focusing on the 37.3% vote in favor of the nazi party in 1932 which led to the fateful conservative-nazi coalition that put Hitler in the Chancellor's seat in 1933. Based on a classification by economic interest groups of nazi party members, he argues that German voters responded rationally to the nazi program of economic recovery more than to the anti-semitic and xenophobic appeals which it shared with most other conservative parties. Granted that too much weight has been put on the ideological aspects of nazi appeal, it is questionable that the whole answer to German exceptionalism can be found in a sudden surge of voters' preference. Such vote was only crucial because it was followed by Hindenburg's single decision to form a coalition government with the Nazi party, which opened the door for what happened later, but even then did not completely determine it.[19] Apart from history, the social

(1924) that fascism in effect destroyed working class organization.

[18] The countries included were Sweden, Denmark, Norway, Switzerland, Belgium, Netherlands, France, Finland, Britain, Austria–Hungary, Spain, Italy, and Germany.

[19] To recall a more contemporary example of a similar scenario, but a different outcome, in 2000, Jacques Chirac, head of the France's center Right, *refused* to form an electoral coalition with Le Pen's ultraconservative *Front National*. Whereas Hindenburg's decision plunged Germany into a national and world tragedy, Chirac's probably avoided one.

sciences have had so far little to say about such radical historical switchpoints.

The present tendency is a more contingently constructed view of Germany's or Italy's fates (Eley, 1995; Burrin, 2000; Furet and Nolte, 1998), which leaves some space for nonsociological factors and for the unexpected.

A safe conclusion from this whole body of research is that Germany, although undoubtedly burdened by a heavy authoritarian past, shared conditions pointing to a traditional authoritarian future with most of Central and Southern Europe.[20] But only in Germany and Italy did fascism develop into full-blown regimes, something so far left unexplained by social science that should perhaps be catalogued among the accidents of history.

Authoritarianism

Although, as we have seen, authoritarianism was widespread in Europe and elsewhere early in the twentieth century, it had not been precisely defined until Linz characterized Spain under Franco as belonging to a class of "political systems with limited, not responsible, political pluralism, without elaborate and guiding ideology, but with distinctive mentalities, without extensive, nor intensive political mobilization, except at some points in their development, and in which a leader or occasionally a small group exercises power within ill-defined limits but actually quite predictable ones" (Linz, 1970a:255).

This new perspective was soon to acquire relevance with the widespread eruption of a new kind of undemocratic rule in Latin America, which abruptly ended the era of protodemocratic populist mobilizations in Argentina, Uruguay and Brazil, and that of democratic socialism in Chile. To some analysts, this suggested a conservative reaction to such upheavals, despite the fact that the same kind of political mobilizations in Mexico (under Cárdenas in 1934–9) had had no such consequence, and that neither Chile nor Uruguay had gone through any previous populist era yet had also fallen into the authoritarian mold. Guillermo O'Donnell named this new phenomenon "Bureaucratic Authoritarianism" (BA) in *Modernization and Bureaucratic Authoritarianism* (1973), a book that built upon Linz's concept, yet took it further by merging it with the debate on dependent capitalism[21] and Stepan's work on the professionalization of the military (1971, 1973). The concept was immediately heralded as a major turning point, providing, so it seemed, just the key to the puzzle over the cascading breakdown in the 1960s and 1970s of Latin American populist protodemocracies.[22] The importance of Linz's and O'Donnell's work on authoritarianism and that of others following (O'Donnell, 1979; Malloy, 1977; Collier, 1979) also lies in their questioning of the then still dominant ideas on modernization, which had predicted imminent democratization for the relatively advanced industrialized countries of Latin America. Together with the ongoing debate on dependent capitalism, these works opened an extremely rich and fruitful debate.

The conceptual birth of authoritarianism also had important policy repercussions, insofar as in their strategic alliances against potential Soviet/Cuban expansionism, U.S. policy makers found authoritarian governments politically more acceptable allies than other undemocratic rulers, a fact that in no small part contributed to the legitimation and consolidation of these regimes. With the change of policy in the Carter administration, however, and the generally dismal

[20] In Hungary, a revolutionary Marxist dictatorship was replaced by the rightist opposition; in Bulgaria, Stomboliski's progressive government was overrun in 1923 by a radical right alliance; in Romania the genuinely fascist *Legion of the Archangel Michael* became very powerful by the mid-thirties; in Spain, Primo de Rivera instituted a right-wing dictatorship from 1923 to 1930, followed by Franco from 1936 to 1976; right-wing coups took place between 1926 and 1929 in Greece, Poland, Lithuania, and Portugal.

[21] On dependence theory, see the works of Francisco Weffort, Octavio Sunkel, Theotonio Dos Santos, Gunder Franck, Celso Furtado, Anibal Quijano, Immanuel Wallerstein, James Cockcroft, Edelberto Torres Rivas, José Nun, Ruy Mauro Marini, and Cardoso and Falleto.

[22] In Brazil in 1964, in Argentina in 1966, and again in 1976 after a brief respite; in Uruguay in 1973; and in Chile in 1973.

economic performance of these regimes,[23] they lost internal as well as external support, thereby preparing the grounds for the third wave of democratization that began in 1983 with Argentina.

At first glance, little discrepancy between Linz's and O'Donnell's ideas on authoritarianism is apparent if we focus on regime structures only. In contrast to Linz, however, O'Donnell gives primary importance to the social base of regimes: BA regimes are said to rest on a coalition of high-level military and business technocrats working in close association with foreign capital. They exclude subordinate classes (outlawing any kind of political organization thereof and persecuting labor, peasant, or urban popular leaders with Dirty War techniques) and are therefore "emphatically antidemocratic" (Collier, 1979:24). The "limited pluralism" included in Linz's definition is hereby given an important corrective: Because BA regimes included only a very small elite, their politics can hardly be "plural"; if anything, factional. Equally absent from O'Donnell's BA is the notion of "mentality," a somewhat obscure concept in Linz's definition that is difficult to understand except as a somewhat run-down ideology.

The most important difference between the two authors is that Linz aimed at typifying the structural characteristics of authoritarianism regardless of origin or policies, whereas O'Donnell was theorizing on a particular historical sequence of regimes ending up in the birth of BAs in Latin America. At stage one, oligarchic democracies, which ruled in Latin America from the nineteenth century to the Depression, were supported by economic elites (mostly landed, but also mining) whose power was based on the export of primary products to industrialized countries. At stage two, these oligarchies were overthrown by protodemocratic populist leaders,[24] based on multiclass coalitions of urban elites and popular sectors and sustained by import substitution industrialization (ISI). Finally, at stage three, the rise of BAs was said to have coincided with the end of the easy phase of import substitution (of light consumer industry), leading to domination by a military–technocratic elite and based on a phase of capitalism excluding popular sectors from the benefits of new capital-intensive industrial growth.

O'Donnell's economic explanation of the rise of bureaucratic authoritarianism had a mixed reception, particularly his hypothesis of the "deepening" and "exhaustion" of import substitution industrialization alleged to have caused it (Serra, 1979; Cardoso, 1979), with calls for a more actor and ideology mediated view of the transition from populist to orthodox market-oriented economic policies (Hirshman, 1979). A second kind of critique concerned the overextended use of the concept of BA, which came to describe almost any Latin American nondemocratic regime in the 1970s, whether populist and inclusionary, as postrevolutionary Mexico, or elitist and exclusionary, as Chile under Pinochet or Argentina under the military *junta* from 1976 to 1983.[25] To palliate this problem, analysts resorted to appending a wide variety of qualifiers in order to distinguish between various kinds of authoritarianisms, particularly "inclusionary" or "populist" versus "exclusionary" or "bureaucratic."

Despite the relative narrowness of the BA scheme, however, O'Donnell's concern for the alliances and coalitions backing up these kinds of regimes has been crucial to understanding the latter's logic and evolution, easily translat-

[23] Except in the case of Chile where steady growth was eventually achieved, but at a very high cost to the majority of the population that has been excluded from the new prosperity.

[24] It is important to note that the term "populist" in the Latin American context connotes inclusionary regimes with some authoritarian traits, but basically allowing policy demands for social welfare and progressive labor legislation to be met.

[25] In the case of Mexico, the term was applied despite three glaring contradictions with the definition of BA: the inclusion of the popular sectors (via state corporatist mechanisms) since the 1930s, the presence of a more populist than technocratic governing elite until the 1980s, and the preservation of import substitution well into the 1980s. Even in the 1990s, when neoliberal policies were at their zenith, a facade of inclusion of the masses via tailored welfare programs was preserved. Above all, Mexico's military was nowhere on the political map at any time since the 1910 revolution (or even before then).

ing into today's concern for the social composition supporting or weakening the stability of newly reestablished democracies. In fact, as O'Donnell, Schmitter, and Whitehead's volumes on democratic transitions (1986) have shown, we owe the demise of these dictatorships to the dissolution of the unholy alliances that had made BAs possible – between *blandos* and *duros*[26] within the military and between the military and capitalists.

The debate on authoritarianism was soon to be interrupted *sine die* when Argentina returned to civilian rule in 1983, following the Malvinas military fiasco,[27] shortly followed by Uruguay (1984), Brazil (1988), and Chile (1989). These transformations were immediately (and somewhat hastily) heralded as "democracy," despite the enduring presence of the military in several countries (conceptualized as military guardianship by Loveman, 1994; Agüero, 1992; and Mainwaring, Brinks, and Pérez-Liñán, 2000) and the absence, in many cases, of constitutional guarantees of democracy, basic citizens' rights, or the rule of law, all of which were expected to eventually appear with democratic consolidation. As a result, the potentially enduring overlap between authoritarianism and democracy received little attention.[28] The tendency to think of authoritarian regimes as indivisible units had left relatively little room for the study of subregime forces at work, alternately making such regimes more extreme than Linz's definition warranted or working toward their future dissolution. In the first case, virtually totalitarian institutional enclaves that had given the military unlimited power to disregard all human rights in the fanatical pursuit of anticommunism and national security ideology (Barahona de Brito, 1997:25) have tended to be overlooked. In the second, the importance for redemocratization of both overt and covert antiregime popular mobilizations during the dictatorships received too little attention.

As a result, democratization was overwhelmingly attributed to top-down elite negotiations and deliberate "crafting" from above (Di Palma, 1991).[29] Likewise, the nondemocratic ways displayed by some of the new democracies (as in Argentina under Menem or in Peru under Fujimori) were given short shrift. But more than anything, what failed to develop as a central debate is the growth of extreme right-wing movements capable of establishing themselves as legitimate interest groups and parties in the new democracies. As we shall see below, such phenomena are also found in old democracies, and important work is currently underway to understand the reasons for their growth.

Sultanistic Regimes

A category of undemocratic regimes that fits neither the totalitarian nor the authoritarian mold is *sultanism*, a term Linz originally borrowed from Weber to signify an extreme form of patrimonialism in which authority is solely based on personal rulership exercised without restraint, unencumbered by law, values, ideology or custom, and where loyalty to the ruler signifies total submission based on a mixture of fear and greed (Chehabi and Linz, 1998a). In such contexts, corruption is the golden rule and human rights abuse a key instrument to maintain the status quo (Chehabi and Linz, 1998a). The same phenomenon has been diversely coined as "patrimonial praetorianism" by Rouquié (1984 and 1987), "mafiacracy" by Wickham-Crowley (1992), "kleptocracy" by Evans (1995), or simply "neopatrimonialism," each term emphasizing a different facet of the phenomenon. As for

[26] Literally, soft and hard.

[27] In which the military junta confronted Britain's claims over the Falkland Islands (or Malvinas Islands, as called by the Argentines) and lost dismally.

[28] Important exceptions are characterizations of countries (including old democracies) as patchworks of "rule" and "unrule" of law (see O'Donnell, 1993; Mendez, O'Donnell, and Pinheiro, 1999; Fox, 1994 on the persistence of the enduring mixtures between authoritarianism and liberalism; and Fatton Jr., 2002 on the persistence of sultanism in Haiti). Also, as some regimes in Central America have failed to pass even the light test of minimal shumpeterian democracy, they have been recognized as permanent hybrids (Karl, 1990; Schmitter, 1991).

[29] For a critical review of the theorization on democratic transition in Latin America, see Brachet-Márquez (1997).

all typifications, this definition designates a family of regimes rather than a prototype against which cases can be measured, so that in fact, many variants are included, such as the presence in some cases of remnants of democratic institutions (although not functioning as such), as in Batista's Cuba or under the Shah in Iran. Other typical cases are Haiti under both Duvaliers, the Somoza dynasty in Nicaragua, Zaïre under Mobutu, the Dominican Republic under Trujillo, the Philippines under Marcos, or Uganda under Idi Amin. In sultanistic regimes, all autonomous institutions and organizations disappear, becoming the personal property of the ruler, so that these regimes are, in some sense, stateless. As in totalitarianism, all forms of social organization, save the most elementary ones (e.g., the family, the shop, the neighborhood), are banned and destroyed, thereby reducing society to a shapeless mass.

Sultanistic regimes usually evolve from other forms of rule: Duvalier was democratically elected in 1957, as was Ferdinand Marcos in 1965. They can also emerge from the breakdown of clientelistic democracy or the decay of totalitarian or authoritarian regimes, as in Ceaucescu's Romania (Chehabi and Linz, 1998b). Some of the conditions that facilitate the rise of sultanism parallel those of totalitarianism: modernization in transportation, communications, military and police techniques, and the development of a minimal civil bureaucracy to provide a base of financial administration (although nowhere near the organizational capacity of the totalitarian state). Other conditions – the isolation and extreme poverty of the masses to ensure passivity and massive doses of foreign aid – are peculiar to this form of despotism.

Snyder (1998) asserted that structural conditions are insufficient to explain the rise or decay of sultanism, proposing instead a combination of strength of opposition with what he calls "structural conditions," but may be more properly understood as events or circumstances. For example, opposition may be weak, but the regime can be toppled by a combination of unforeseen events, such as an earthquake (as in the case of Nicaragua) or a U.S. invasion (as in the case of Panama under Noriega). Vice versa, opposition may be strong, but the regime endures because circumstances are favorable, which dovetails with Przeworski's (1986) claim that extremely illegitimate regimes will survive as long as key actors do not perceive alternatives. Actors may also mistakenly perceive alternatives and launch rebellions that are crushed (as the Kurds under Sadam Hussein in the 1980s).

Although most authors acknowledge the importance of external support for sultanistic regimes, they usually gloss over it as just another variable among many representing favorable conditions for the rise of that type of rule. It is perhaps time that we give this component the importance it deserves, acknowledging that sultanistic regimes arise and remain viable for decades precisely because such support is forthcoming, with a virtually unlimited source of wealth, such as oil revenues (as in the case of Iraq and Iran). Without such resources, armies and militias cannot be trained or armed, intelligence services and informers cannot be paid, [30] supporters cannot be bought, and imports cannot compensate for the ransacked economy. In other words, left to their own devices, sultanistic regimes simply devour their own until no supporters are left standing. Hence they can only be maintained in power artificially.

From 1945 to the 1970s, sultanistic regimes were the scourge of Africa, Latin America and Asia, surging and waning in tune with the willingness of respectable democracies (France, Great Britain, Belgium, the United States) to continue supporting them despite the atrocities they openly committed. In the McCarthy era, liberal nationalists in Iran led an initially successful coup against the Shah, immediately followed by a CIA-engineered countercoup, after which the regime turned sultanistic and SAWAK, the newly created intelligence agency, began to torture and execute presumed opponents (Parsa, 2000). Likewise, 1954 marked the end of democratic rule for Guatemala when the CIA sided with the most extreme right-wing forces of the country to unseat the democratic Jacobo Arbenz administration, guilty of having carried out a land reform in a country where

[30] Mobutu had a multiplicity of intelligence services that terrorized the population and fought among themselves for turf and revenue (Willame, 1992).

debt peonage was still the rule. By contrast, the Carter administration's policy of nonsupport toward regimes perpetrating human rights violations was paramount in limiting the Shah's use of military force against his people in the 1970s.[31] Subsequently, the Reagan and Bush administrations had no objection to the slaughter of the opposition in Iraq and Syria (Katouzian, 1998).

Seen in this light, sultanistic regimes are not just old-fashioned authoritarian regimes that somehow take a bad turn all on their own, but a phenomenon that owes its existence to the configuration of international relations. Far from disappearing with the end of the Cold War, they have acquired new strategic importance in the war against terrorism and extremism, so that neopatrimonial regimes in Saudi Arabia, Kuwait, Azerbaijan, Pakistan, or Nigeria can still count on the full support of Western democracies. Nevertheless, it is noteworthy that such regimes are more likely to take hold in prelegal virtually stateless societies with a long history of arbitrary rule and the absence of rights of any kind, exemplified by Iran, Haiti, and countless postcolonial African and Asian countries.

What happens to sultanistic regimes when they break down? It is no great surprise that they are less likely than other undemocratic regimes to evolve into democracies (Chehabi and Linz, 1998b:37), due to the virtual absence of autonomous institutions, the social disorganization wreaked by terror, and elite manipulation of democratic procedures. This may explain why revolutionary upheavals are more likely to arise and be successful in sultanistic than other kinds of nondemocratic regimes (as in Pahlavi's Iran, Somoza's Nicaragua, Batista's Cuba, or the Saigon regime in South Vietnam). In cases of negotiated transitions to democracy, the best that can be expected are resistant hybrids of democracy and authoritarianism (as in present-day Central America) or military guardianships (as initially in Chile and Argentina). The regimes emerging from revolutions against sultanism can be socialist in all its variants of authoritarianism (as in Vietnam or Cuba), left radical (as the Sandinista governments in Nicaragua), or clerical guardianships (as in Iran and Afghanistan).

[31] Following the success of the Iranian social revolution led by Khomeini in 1978 and the 1979 Sandinista victory in Nicaragua, however, both the Carter and the Reagan administrations made the prevention of yet another revolution a policy priority (Goodwin, 2001:203). For an assessment of Iran's evolution since its revolution, see Esposito (2001).

MOVEMENTS AGAINST AUTHORITARIAN AND SULTANISTIC REGIMES

Insofar as democracy shuns the use of violence, armed insurgency, even against totalitarianism or authoritarianism, is inevitably undemocratic.[32] As such, the study of armed movements cannot be altogether omitted from a broad debate on undemocratic politics as defined in this chapter. Armed rebellion is defined here as the extralegal ideologically justified use of violence in the name of a greater common good (socialism, territorial independence, or some brand of radical welfare state), which in turn may trigger violent repression.[33]

Rather than fight injustice at home, the first wave of armed insurgents in Latin America (1959–67)[34] followed Guevara's path, as analysts have generally agreed (Castañeda, 1993; Wickham-Crowley, 1992). Contrary to their model, however, these insurgents quickly lost all contact with the moderate Left despite the fact that they were fighting neither unrelenting military or sultanistic regimes (excepting Guatemala), nor wars of national liberation,

[32] A democratic way of preparing for the demise of a dictatorship would be exemplified by the clandestine organization of antiregime social movements and parties, as in Chile during the Pinochet dictatorship and Poland under communist rule. This is not to say that undemocratic action is not needed in order to force undemocratic regimes out of power. But should such action fail to be underwritten by democratic activists, the regime that ousts undemocracy from power is likely to be undemocratic itself.

[33] We should note that the qualifier of "totalitarian" as applied by some to armed insurgent movements is inappropriate insofar as these lack a state, and therefore the dimensions of state organization (bureaucracy, party, military, police) and state terror that are essential to the concept of totalitarianism.

[34] This first wave started in 1959 with the Cuban revolution and ended in 1967 with Guevara's death (Wickham-Crowley, 1992).

as Fidel Castro and his allies initially had (Wickham-Crowley, 1992).

This first wave of insurgents were radicalized university-educated young men,[35] scornful of the moderate Left or their respective governments' accommodations with the center or the Right. The political situations they faced represented a broad gamut from radical populism (as the government that followed Bolivia's 1952 revolution) to moderate Left (as Romulo Betancourt's social democratic government in Venezuela);[36] to conservative authoritarian (as Peru under Belaunde)[37] all the way to extremely violent military regimes as in Guatemala. Despite these differences, the revolutionary repertoire was virtually the same in every country: Bourgeois democracy was a sham, and armed insurgency the only means to build socialism.

Although it failed militarily, the first wave of insurgency began winding up the enormous machinery of repression that would carry to power four military dictatorships in the Southern Cone (Uruguay, Argentina, Brazil, and Chile) and further entrench those already in power in Central America. This reaction boosted the rolls of the Army School of the Americas in the Panama Canal Zone,[38] where officers from Latin American countries were trained in methods of guerilla warfare, counterinsurgency, and intelligence; taught the doctrine of national security; and warned against the dangers of world communism.[39]

After the first wave of insurgency seemed to die down and the urban guerillas briefly following from it had quickly been decimated,[40] a new wave of rural armed insurgency, less amateurish and more deadly, took hold in Latin America. The repression also turned more vicious, as paramilitary groups and death squads multiplied, clandestinely paid by various sources, among others their own governments. In this period again, the only successful guerilla war was that aiming at national liberation against the universally hated (even in business circles) sultanistic regime of Anastasio Somoza in Nicaragua.[41] Thereafter, however, the U.S.-supported conservative military "Contra" response to the victorious Left-oriented Sandinista regime led to the latter's demise and a negotiated transition to parliamentary democracy.

Rather than try to win militarily, a second kind of armed insurgency, as exemplified in El Salvador, managed to maintain a stalemate against government forces until the peace accords of 1992, thereafter agreeing to disarm in order to participate in democratic elections. In Colombia – the only country in which armed insurgency antedated the Cuban revo-

[35] Estimated from the number of the dead, between 1964 and 1978, 64% of the guerillas were educated upper middle class, 33% manual workers, and 3% technical. Among the officially tortured (i.e., not counting the "disappeared"), 55% were college educated, 12% technical, 25.9% students, and 10% university professors (Castañeda, 1993:93).

[36] In 1947–8 Betancourt had headed a government that had carried out social reforms without heeding the conservative backlash, which led to a military coup that ousted him from power. During his 1959–64 administration, he carried out a substantial agrarian reform and repelled three (right-wing) military rebellions.

[37] Belaúnde carried out a largely cosmetic agrarian reform in 1964 that distributed infertile jungle sections to landless peasants rather than the arable land held by oligarchic families (Seligmann, 1995).

[38] According to Wickham-Crowley's sources (1992: 77), between 1950 and 1973, close to 30,000 men were trained in Panama and the United States and over 40,000 in other countries (probably their own). By contrast, the estimated number of guerillas trained in Cuba is around 3,000. The elites trained by the United States are reported to have been exceptionally strong in their antiguerilla feelings. In addition to their indoctrination against communism, they had been convinced that the victory of the "subversives" would signify their downfall, in the same way as Castro had executed 600 officers of the Batista army.

[39] To this day, officers accused of violating human rights during the Dirty War claim that they were saving their country from the communist scourge and doing their patriotic duty when torturing their prisoners to death (Payne, 2000).

[40] The *Tupamaros* in Uruguay, *Mir* in Chile, *Montoneros* in Argentina (the surviving Left wing of Peronism), and *Marighellas* in Brazil.

[41] Yet after achieving the only successful revolution in Latin America after the Cuban revolution, the *sandinistas* proceeded to impose Soviet-style land collectivization and forced conscription on peasants and Miskito indigenous people (many of whom had sided with the revolution), who then engrossed the files of the *contras* fighting the revolutionary government with the help of the Reagan administration (Payne, 2000).

lution[42] – the stalemate has continued uninterrupted, leading to de facto territorial division between the two camps. In Peru, the extremely authoritarian Maoist *Sendero Luminoso* (Shining Path) – born in Ayacucho in 1969 – was initially backed by substantial popular support (Degregori, 1990) but met its final defeat in the mid-1990s through a combination of military reprisal and peasant self-defense (Degregori et al., 1996).[43] As for Guatemala, where guerilla warfare grew throughout this period, especially in the mostly indigenously populated highlands, it was decimated by the especially violent government military forces, estimated by the Catholic Church to have killed some 200,000 people – most of them unarmed civilians – between the early 1960s and the signing of the peace accords in 1996 (Goodwin, 2001:198).

The newest outbreak of armed insurgency, in this case wholly indigenous except for its military chief (the *subcomandante* Marcos), took place in Mexico in January 1994, in the poorest and most densely indigenous state of Chiapas. In this case, however, the military phase lasted only a few weeks, followed by a tenacious (but so far unsuccessful) attempt on the part of the *Ejército Zapatista de Liberación Nacional* (EZLN) to negotiate with three successive governments constitutional changes in the status of indigenous Mexicans. The movement has accused the government(s) of failing to respect indigenous people's citizenship and local self-government rights, so that it represents, paradoxically, demands for more democracy than the ruling regime has been willing to grant its native population, despite the end of one-party rule in 2000.[44]

The history of military violence against the status quo in Latin America would not be complete if it did not include Juan Velasco Alvarado's military coup in 1968 that unseated Peru's oligarchic patrimonial regime (Stepan, 1976). Rather than represent conservative forces, however, the military government that followed (1968–75) carried out a vast agrarian reform and radical industrial and mining reforms. But it also imprisoned its opponents, closed dissenting radio stations and newspapers, and suspended civil liberties.

Although repression was the first reaction to armed insurgency, it was not invariably the only one, as noted by Goodwin (2001:199). In the 1980s, semidemocratic elections were undertaken by the military in El Salvador and Guatemala in which Christian democratic (centrist) and moderate social democratic parties were able to take part. The reasons for such openings were, first, the absence of any clear military victory after years of fighting, and, second, the U.S. demand that some form of democratic process be instituted as the condition for continuing to finance counterinsurgency effort, evidencing once again the influence of the support or nonsupport of democracy by the United States.[45] These elections, although highly unsatisfactory from a strictly democratic viewpoint, can nevertheless be credited for having

[42] From 1949 to 1965, Colombia underwent a period known as *La Violencia*, in which various insurgent groups confronted government forces and peasants formed independent republics in order to protect themselves. In 1965, these first groups were destroyed by the military. Thereafter, the Colombian Communist Party (one of the very few to have participated in insurgency) declared that all forms of struggle should be undertaken, thereby exposing even civilian nonviolent groups to paramilitary assassinations (Castañeda, 1993:90).

[43] The war period was extremely violent, as reflected in a net population loss of 23.3% in the Ayacucho region and mass migration from isolated villages in the Highlands (Degregori et al., 1996:16). An important change occurred when armed and trained peasant civilian defense committees (or *Rondas Campesinas)* were formed. This approach substituted the previous policy of treating the indigenous population a priori as suspect of collaboration with the *Shining Path* (not unlike the United States in Vietnam during the 1970s). Peasants, on the other hand, were motivated to collaborate with the army after Sendero's leadership started substituting their own cadres for local peasant leaders via assassination.

[44] For more detail on the religious origin in liberation theology of this most unusual movement, see Womack (1998), Harvey (1998), and Legorreta Díaz (1998). For the question of democracy in *zapatismo*, see Harvey (1998). For an overall view of the movement from guerilla to political movement as stated by subcomandante Marcos, see Le Bot (1992, 1995, 1997). For the problem of regional autonomy for indigenous groups, see Diaz Polanco (1991).

[45] Nevertheless, in 1982 the Reagan administration decided to remove Guatemala from the list of human rights offenders, after which money from international donors could pour into the country unimpeded by any legal obstacle (Goodwin, 201:203).

interrupted the upward spiral of violence that had approached genocidal levels in both countries, and therefore to have prepared for peace negotiations. Thereafter, the notorious "intelligence" branches of the police were disbanded both in Guatemala and El Salvador, and death squad violence abated (Goodwin, 2001:201). But the extreme Right also took advantage of the opportunity to organize its own political parties and democratically take up positions in the system, so that they were able to effectively veto the reformist legislation proposed by victorious centrist forces (Goodwin, 2001: 202).

Finally, although armed rebellion and paramilitary terrorism has been far less common in postwar Europe than in Latin America, we should mention the separatist Basque ETA, which has fought for independence from Spain throughout the authoritarian period and down to the present,[46] and Ireland's IRA, a seemingly permanent feature of politics in the United Kingdom. To these must be added the recent alarming growth of neo-Nazi armed groups in Germany and Sweden despite (or perhaps because of) their lack of political representation in these countries (Mudde, 2002) and the accumulation of terrorist military and paramilitary actions during the civil war in the former Yugoslavia (Mudde, 2000a), without omitting the ongoing bloody struggle between Russian troups and Chechnia nationalist rebels in the former Soviet Union.

DISCONTENTS AND DISSIDENTS

The last two decades, as many analysts agree (Betz, 1998; Hainsworth, 2000b; Merkl and Weinberg, 1997; Plotke, 2002:xxix), have seen a general shift toward the Right in most democracies, old or new. As a result, the Right and extreme Right have come to overlap, giving the latter a patina of democratic respectability and, in some cases, substantial electoral successes. The variety of contexts and forms of right-wing politics that have developed in the last two decades has led to important definitional disagreements among specialists, divided between those typifying the extreme Right as *old* traditional versus *new* postindustrial (Ignazi, 1997); populist, neopopulist, or national–populist (Betz and Immerfall, 1998; Mudde, 2001); "radical" or "ultra" Right in terms of its distance from the center; or conservative antistatist (economically liberal) versus nationalist populist and state-centered (Mudde, 2000b). Overarching these classifications, a broad category of "extreme" parties and movements has been defined as "opposing in terms of ideas or action the fundamental values or institutions of democratic regimes" (Mudde, 2002:135), contrasting with conservative or radical Rights that accept democratic rules of the game.[47]

For the purpose of this discussion, a broad four-way distinction is drawn between right-wing parties and movements oriented on the one hand toward the market, or *neoliberals*, and those oriented toward the state as an instrument for the redefinition of politics and society, or *neopopulists.* On the other hand are *ultraconservatives* that keep their actions within the confines of democratic politics (although calling for a radical revision of such politics), and the "*extreme Right,*" which resorts to extrainstitutional violence (Figure 23.1). Although these distinctions come close to those advocated by Mudde (2000b), they encompass more right-wing formations than he envisages. Nevertheless, it does not imply a clear divide in every case, as some ultraconservatives cumulate a liberal view of economics and a neofascist view of how the state should act, whereas other groups implement a double strategy of clandestine violence and loyal participation in democratic competition.[48] Some groups also move strategically between ultraconservatism and extreme right

[46] ETA *(Euzkadi Ta Azkatasuna)*, founded in 1959, grew out of the Basque Nationalist Party and survived throughout the Franco regime despite severe repression. From 1975 on, despite the granting of regional autonomy and pardon offered to ETA members renouncing terrorism, the number of killings and assassinations multiplied tenfold over what had existed during the Franco regime.

[47] For a further discussion of Western extremist groups, see Hewitt (2002), Abedi (2003), and Eatwell and Mudde (2003).

[48] As Ireland's IRA and its political party Sinn Fein, or Basque country's ETA and its party Herri Batasuna.

	Ultraconservative	Extreme Right
Neoliberal	***Unión Nacional de Propietarios*** (Brazil)	***Carapintadas*** (Argentina)
Neopopulist	***Front National*** (France) ***Freiheitliche Partei Österreichs*** (Austria)	***Pro-Life*** (USA) **Socialist Party Of Serbia** (Yugoslavia)

Figure 23.1. A Taxomony of Undemocratic Movements and Parties

categories, depending on available opportunities and constraints. Finally, we find cases, particularly in Central Europe, in which the previous communist past and populist nationalist present are so mixed that it is difficult to place them along a Left–Right continuum.

Movements in all four categories have in common a capacity to mobilize resentment and fire their respective constituencies into relatively long-term electoral and/or violent action. Ultraconservative neoliberals such as Brazil's *Unión Nacional de Propietarios* (UNP), made up of large landowners, have opposed any kind of agrarian reform, first by force and then electorally (Payne, 2000). Ultraconservative neopopulist parties such as France's *Front National*, led by Jean Marie Le Pen,[49] or Jörg Haider's xenophobic nativist *Freiheitliche Partei Österreichs* (Austria's Freedom Party) (Morrow, 1998; Antidefamation League, 2001) capitalize on popular disillusionment with mainstream politics, crises of representation in old party systems, antielitism, and xenophobic feelings toward immigrants (variously blamed for economic decline, falling welfare coverage and standards, unemployment, or rising crime) (Hainsworth, 2000a:9). Given their association with neoliberal military dictatorships, paramilitary groups such as Argentina's *Carapintadas*[50] would fit into the extreme right/neoliberal cell, whereas several fundamentalist groups such as Pro-Life or communist–nationalist parties such as Milosevič's Socialist Party of Serbia (*Socijalistička Partija Srbije*) could be counted among neopopulist extreme right movements.[51]

For Western Europe (Germany, the Netherlands, and Flanders), Mudde (2000) has codified the ideological profiles of extreme right parties in four points: *nationalism* (including monoculturalism); *xenophobia* (also including homophobia, antileftism, and antifeminism); the "*strong state*" of law and order; and *welfare chauvinism* (i.e., only for the truly national population). To these, some parties also add *exclusionism* (often defined as the "separation" of races) and historical *revisionism* (revising the past in the case of German or Flemish extreme right parties).

This four-point list, although arguably reflecting the cases under study, is bound to lose some of its validity outside of Western (and

[49] On *Front National*, initially created in 1972 with former collaborationists and fascists, see Mayer (1990), Camus (1996), and Hainsworth (2000b).

[50] *Carapintadas* (literally, "painted faces") is an extreme right clandestine military organization that has perpetrated assassinations of individuals considered "subversives" (i.e., communists) even after the Cold War had ceased. They paint their faces in order to both disguise themselves and advertise for their group when carrying out their "missions."

[51] Although it might seem counterintuitive to place Pro-Life and Milosevic's party in the same category, it illustrates that these say nothing about the severity of the breaking of democratic rules. Pro-lifers bomb abortion clinics in defiance of democratically enacted law making abortion permissible, whereas Serbian nationalists have used fascist methods (hiring paid mobs to stir up ethnic conflict, perpetrating ethnic cleansing, etc.).

probably also Eastern) Europe,[52] where extreme right movements share a certain nostalgia for the fascist past, clearly reflected in three out of the four key values (excluding welfare chauvinism) selected by Mudde. But it is doubtful that we could find a general list of unifying myths and cultural narratives globally shared by all groups. We should, however, be able to build matching value lists and group typologies for the United States, where racism and anticommunism have defined the identity of right-wing groups for decades, starting with McCarthyism, continuing with the John Birch Society (Bell, 2000), and moving to ever-novel forms of religious fundamentalism (Christian Coalition), paramilitary groups (the Militias), or white supremacism (The New Order, Liberty Lobby).[53] Another grouping may be achieved with postdictatorship Latin American countries where the immense and advancing mass of the poverty-stricken in need of redistribution and the demands for the prosecution of Dirty War crimes constitute major rallying points for the Right. Finally, a fourth cluster might group Mid-Eastern and Asian countries where fundamentalist Islamics have been the only dissident groups to have survived the repression of modernizing authoritarian or sultanistic regimes, and whose religious traditional values have in some cases been incorporated into the official discourse in an effort by states to expand their power over society (Macfarquhar and Resa Narr, 2001).[54]

The list could be further expanded. Yet more than the variety of issues regionally and historically clustered extremist groups may raise or the specific ideological rallying points they may define, their most important family resemblance may lie in the tactics they use to mobilize their membership and gain access to political power. Payne (2000) sees what she calls "uncivil movements" as mobilized through "political agents," who "frame" contemporary events in ways that echo the concerns and fears of their intended audience by drawing on cultural symbols and legitimating myths that connect movements with recognized villains and heroes. Framing is said to involve *naming*, which transforms given events into political threats, and hence catalysts for political action; *blaming*, which identifies a commonly held scapegoat that takes the blame for named problems; *aiming*, which convinces the intended audience that the severe threat which the blamed group represents for the nation "leaves the movement no alternative save radical political action" (Payne, 2000:23); and finally *claiming*, which asserts the possibility of defeating the named culprit, thereby convincing the intended audience that it can be defeated, provided that the movement is vigilant and that its members take action.

Far from being peculiar to the Right, such patterns show the ways in which relatively marginalized (civil or uncivil) social movements of all creeds are able to create and maintain their base of support in society, so that their actions can be seen as prompted by the prior organizational necessity of "inventing" and crystalizing symbolic communities via the continuous succession of framing processes. What actions are actually undertaken, rather than directly flow out of a set of preestablished values, are the contingently and circumstantially-constructed consequence of the interaction between leaders and members as played out within the structured political frameworks in which these take place.

CONCLUDING REMARKS

In this chapter, I have defined the major research programs and debates that figure prominently in a broad field of inquiry on undemocratic politics. As we have seen, major old unresolved issues (e.g., the class versus cleavage nature of

[52] In Central Europe, where a few extreme right parties took power right after the fall of the Berlin Wall, many more have achieved continuous minority presence in parliaments and usefulness as legitimate coalition partners, in contrast with Western Europe where conservative parties have shunned them. On Eastern Europe post-communist politics, see Kopecký and Mudde (2003). For a list of major ultraconservative and extreme right political organizations, see Camus (1999) and Mudde (2000a, 2002).

[53] On the extreme Right in the United States, see Bell (2000), Plotke (2000), Hewitt (2003), and Michael (2003).

[54] On extremism in Muslim countries, see Macfarquhar and Resa Narr (2001), Dekmejian (1995), Faksh (1997), Marty and Appleby (1995), Kepel (1984), Willis (1996), and Wickham (2002).

the path to democracy or fascism, the "why Germany" question, the origins and economic underpinnings of authoritarianism) are still being debated and new evidence brought in the balance. But new ones have also been created by the entry of formerly authoritarian regimes into the democratic camp, thereby raising new questions and opening up new areas for inquiry.

Rather than summarize the literature and arguments reviewed, these concluding remarks aim at pointing out some key proposals and directions for inquiry, out of which new research programs can emerge or old ones further develop to produce important scholarship in the future.

Are Fascism and Totalitarianism a Thing of the Past?

Totalitarianism, as narrowly defined, is circumscribed to two countries and periods – Nazi Germany and Stalinist USSR. Efforts to stretch the concept to other cases have failed or amounted to mere Cold War propaganda. These two cases are therefore to be clearly distinguished from nontotalitarian ones of either communist or fascist regimes. In other words, the two (rather distinct) totalitarianisms that sprang to life in the interwar period were both unique and rare clusters of antecedents, circumstances, ideological currents, agents, and events never to be repeated. Yet, new totalitarianisms with their own nonreproducible specificities have subsequently emerged (and may continue to do so in the future), as the example of China's Cultural Revolution suggests. Moreover, some extreme left or right movements have waited in the wings but failed to win politically. For example, Peru's *Shining Path* had all the markings of a Maoist-style totalitarian regime to-be and in fact enforced totalitarian rule over a good part of Peru's territory in its late period. Likewise, fascist elements are still lingering or new neofascist regimes waiting for the appropriate circumstances and alliances of today's neopopulist parties with ultraconservatives and/or the military. Totalitarian practices have also appeared in resistant institutional enclaves, such as the military and paramilitary in Latin America, which have proven difficult to extirpate and therefore constitute permanent threats of return to undemocratic rule. Perhaps, then, the concept of totalitarianism would be more useful as a qualifying than as a substantive term, so that communist or fascist regimes can be labeled as totalitarian in specific cases and periods only. In that way, we would avoid the forced comparison between the substantive aspects of regimes as distinct as Stalin's USSR, Hitler's Germany, or Mao's China.

All this means that both totalitarianism and fascism continue to have some heuristic value in the examination of current undemocratic politics, but only as long as they are used both precisely and flexibly. Revisiting Russia's and Central Europe's precommunist and communist pasts in that light, for example, is an opportune and important task, not only to set the record straight on how those regimes really functioned from 1945 to 1989, but also to better understand the variety of cultural and structural departure points in the transition to democracy found in that region. In short, totalitarianism and fascism as they have existed in the twentieth century were unique and therefore unrepeatable, but the concepts constructed to capture these phenomena continue to be useful if properly unpacked and judiciously applied to new situations.

Should We Continue to Speak about Authoritarianism?

Despite Linz's and O'Donnell's efforts to systematize the concept authoritarianism has proved so protean that it can hardly refer to a single family of regimes, hence the many qualifiers usually appended to the term. Nevertheless, Linz's original typification of the postfascist phase of Franco's Spain continues to function as a useful conceptual beacon insofar as it clearly distinguishes authoritarianism from traditional autocracies on the one hand, and from fascism or totalitarianism on the other. Contrasting with traditional domination, authoritarian governance relies on modern bureaucracy and technologically advanced means of surveillance and repression, and is therefore a thoroughly modern phenomenon. In contrast with fascism and totalitarianism, it does not mobilize the masses into action based on a transforming ideology (or does so only in earlier phases, as most postfascist or postrevolutionary regimes). In every case, however, it cripples the capacity of civil society to organize itself independently of the state, and as such creates obstacles to democratic citizenship for decades after its demise.

A major task for future research, and one so far neglected in favor of characterizing regimes *in toto*, is to investigate the survival or reappearance in democracies of authoritarianism in given groups and subnational regions and within specific institutional niches. In doing so, we may discover that far from being alien to democratic practices, such authoritarian standards as clientelism, regional bossism, and the selective application of the law plague new as much as old democracies.

Another major research program to be developed is the investigation of the dynamics of transitions from different varieties of authoritarianism to democracy, while finding a good balance between theorization and case studies. Case studies will keep us in contact with the unique historically constructed nature of the ways in which people and leaders transform their particular authoritarian structures into democratic ones (or fail to do so), and will put some meat on such concepts as quickly negotiated (Spain) versus delayed "natural" transitions (Mexico), transitions from territorially balkanized situations (e.g., Central America, Colombia) versus those from situations of strong central state hegemony, or unplanned transitions from military disasters (as Argentina's) or economic collapse (Warsaw Pact countries) versus planned ones (Brazil, Chile). In other words, far from being a task for the past, the study of authoritarianism will continue to be an important aspect of the study of democratic as well as undemocratic politics, whose development should lead to a more nuanced view of the differences as well as connections between the two.

Exit Cold War Sultanism, Enter Post-Cold War Sultanism?

Although sultanism has not occupied the limelight in the study of undemocratic politics, the research carried out has done much to clear the way for the work that is now urgent if global terrorism and rogue sultanistic and authoritarian states continue to take center stage in international politics. This initial work has established that far from being a variety of authoritarian regime, sultanism is a peculiar form of patrimonial rule distorted by access to international alliances and modern means of repression. In the Weberian sense, whereas authoritarianism is a rationally organized form of autocracy (especially in its bureaucratic–authoritarian form) that must include some plebiscitarian elements (especially in its more inclusionary form), sultanism is a profoundly irrational and disorganized form of despotism devoid of any rule limiting state power or social base of legitimacy, which sustains itself by terror. In sum, it is modern in its means of repression and irrational in its form of organization.

Broadening the stage within which sultanism has been studied, we might ask whether this kind of extreme undemocratic rule is the inevitable consequence of global international politics as dominated by the United States, as opposed to largely home-grown phenomena. In the Cold War era, the answer given by Western powers was a clear yes, insofar as sultanistic allies were considered preferable to communist enemies. In the name of that principle, these powers (especially the United States) have not only tolerated, but also outright supported, regimes perpetrating untold atrocities as well as helped them to crush many a genuine national rebellion, in order to check the potential creation of communist strongholds on the international checkerboard. In the post-Cold War era, however, the answer is no longer so clear, as past experience with former "allies" such as Panama's Noriega or Iraq's Sadam Hussein has failed to bear the anticipated fruits.

At the opening of the new century, a new phenomenon calling for research has been emerging in some Muslim countries: Islamic movements in Algeria, Morocco, and Turkey have been electorally marginalized in favor of moderate Muslim leaders who are nevertheless critical of U.S. policy in their region.[55] Should such independent-minded leaders be forcibly removed from power in favor of despots more closely alined with NATO powers as in the past, are we likely to see more extremist Islamic movements gaining popularity and electoral strength? Iran's postrevolutionary trajectory suggests that stigmatizing unfriendly regimes may entrench more deeply their clerical theocratic elements and destabilize their reformists, while Panama's and Iraq's cases show that supporting despotic and corrupt sultanistic power can backfire. In the future, understanding the rise and fall of sultanistic regimes in the context of international politics will contribute to a better understanding of such phenomena and show the close relation between politics in established democracies and undemocratic politics in the Third World.

Did Left Rebellions and Right Reactions Ease or Block the Way to Democracy?

The historical itinerary of Latin America's two successive waves of Marxist insurgency and their repression may be significant for an understanding of the dynamics of undemocratic politics. First, it is clear that armed insurgencies, whatever the good intentions of their initiators, were no midwives to peace or prosperity in the region, let alone political liberty, even in the two cases where they were successful. It is recognized that international forces were paramount in either defeating (Nicaragua) or hardening (Cuba) the regimes that followed upon these revolutions, so that not all the responsibility should be laid at the door of the movements that launched them. Yet in both cases, the insurgency started as national revolutions backed by multiclass coalitions, so that the option to evolve toward some form of democracy was not irremediably closed.

Second, unsuccessful armed rebellions coalesced the political forces necessary to either establish or further consolidate extremely harsh and exclusionary authoritarian regimes, something that represented a huge step back for democracy in a region where progressive coalitions of urban middle classes, popular masses, and new industrial elites had established early in the twentieth century protodemocratic populist regimes willing to extend the benefits of industrialization to the masses.[56]

Third, and most importantly for the future of democracy, as these new bureaucratic authoritarian regimes outlawed and mercilessly pursued all forms of independent political representation and participation (while experimenting with exclusionary neoliberal policies on the disenfranchised masses), the apprenticeship of peaceful adversarial politics that, for some countries, had started as far back as the 1830s was violently interrupted, thereby setting back the clock of democracy for decades.

It does not follow, however, that we should consider authoritarianism the necessary consequence of leftist uprisings. For example, the reaction of the French government to the May 1968 student uprising in Paris can in no way compare to the savage treatment of the very similar student uprising of October 1968 in Mexico, where hundreds were mercilessly machine-gunned by the police and thousands remained political prisoners for years. The interaction between leftist uprisings and authoritarian reaction must therefore be historically contextualized. Perhaps, then, the main reason that revolutions rarely breed democracy has less to do with the intrinsic nature of these social convulsions than with the fact that they can look back to nothing better in their past than ruthless patrimonial, sultanistic, or colonial rule (as in Iran, Afghanistan, Nicaragua, or Vietnam) and therefore lack any familiarity with the essential ingredients of democracy.

[55] Information of recent elections in Muslim countries such as Algeria, Morocco, and Turkey was taken from Samaha (2002).

[56] Both in Argentina during the Peronist eras (1946–55 and 1973–4) and in Mexico during the Cárdenas years (1934–40), important social reforms were carried out, such as social security for industrial labor and civil servants. Cárdenas also distributed more land to the landless peasants than all of his antecessors put together.

Is the Electoral Participation of Extreme Parties a Threat to Democracy?

In old as well as new democracies, the existence of ultraconservative or extremist groups and parties must be tolerated as long as they do not step outside of democratic rules. From examining their electoral record in Western and Central Europe, they appear as little more than marginal and ineffective rabble-rousers. There are two reasons for taking such reassuring conclusions with some skepticism, however. First, most available analyses base their conclusions on national elections, thereby disregarding the importance of subnational processes. Territorial extremist movements such as the Basque and Irish nationalists are still the exception rather than the rule, but new ones are emerging (in Chechnia, among Turkish and Iraqi Kurds) and old ones being rekindled (as in Corsica). Research must therefore assess the more local and regional dimensions of the territorial entrenchment of extremist and ultraconservative politics within democracies. A second reason for skepticism is that we cannot predict from electoral results obtained in normal conditions the role some of these groups may play in alliance with others in the aftermath of some national emergency comparable, for example, to what occurred in the United States on September 11, 2001. So far, the extreme Right in Western Europe has maintained friendly relations with Middle Eastern leaders shunned by the West,[57] but given the right circumstances they could easily take electoral advantage of any widespread Islamic terrorist activity on their respective national territories.

FINAL CONSIDERATIONS ON THE RELATION BETWEEN DEMOCRATIC AND UNDEMOCRATIC POLITICS

As suggested by various works reviewed in this chapter, undemocracy and democracy are not only opposed in principles and juxtaposed in fact, but also closely intertwined in ways that are still to be systematically spelt out and evidenced. It follows that advancing in the task of explaining undemocracy is inextricably connected with that of finding approaches to democracy that do not treat undemocratic manifestations as accidental, epiphenomenal, or destined to disappear as democracy gradually becomes "the only game in town." In these final considerations, I outline the ways in which we may build research programs around two broad postulates: (1) democratic and undemocratic politics are linked within democracies; and (2) democratic and undemocratic politics are linked internationally.

Democratic and Undemocratic Politics are Linked within Democracies

This may happen in a number of ways. I will restrict these last comments to two typical situations: (1) when democratic procedures are used as legitimate cover in order to send out undemocratic messages or carry out undemocratic deeds; and (2) when democratic procedures are made to systematically misfunction for some groups (blacks, immigrants, women, the poor), thereby covering up for prejudice, exclusion, or downright aggression. In the first case, democracy lets in undemocracy by extending its legal mantle too far, whereas in the other, it fails to extend it far enough.

An example of the first kind is the use of democratic elections by some parties in order to establish an undemocratic regime, as when Islamic parties participate in democratic elections with the explicit intention, should they win, of denying full citizenship to women and giving overriding authority to unelected clerics. At the subnational level, we may exemplify the overextended use of democratic principles when child pornography is legally tolerated in the name of freedom of speech and therefore without regard for the rights of minors, when a party includes undemocratic principles in its platform or forms an electoral coalition with one that does, or when a democratically elected body enacts laws violating democratic principles. A third kind of example is the inclusion

[57] Jörg Haider visited Sadam Hussein in 2002, and Jean Marie Le Pen made pronouncements in favor of Palestinian nationalism on several occasions.

of undemocratic principles in democratic constitutions such as the provision that the military may lawfully take power when they judge the national interest to be in danger (as in present-day Argentina, Chile, and Brazil).[58]

Undemocracy resulting from the failure to provide equal protection of the law to all is illustrated every day when the police fails to adequately protect the poor from crime, when municipal sanitary trucks somehow "miss" low-income areas, or when ghetto schools produce little more than functional illiterates. It is also illustrated when the law is enforced so selectively that some ethnic groups are overprosecuted while others are underprosecuted, when the police stand by while extremists attack defenseless citizens, or when illegal and life-threatening activities go virtually unchecked. We are all familiar with most of these examples but unaccustomed to treating them as manifestations of undemocracy, as opposed to inefficiency, resource scarcity, or individual misconduct.

Undemocratic and Democratic Politics Are Linked Internationally

As seen in the review of sultanistic regimes, undemocratic politics of the worst kind taking place in the Third World are often created and nurtured by established democracies that are wont to prefer unconditional submission to a respect for human rights or democratic principles as criteria for selecting their allies.[59] We are also familiar with such facts as well as accustomed to attributing them either to the myopia of individual statesmen or to the zero-sum game calculus these make, ostensibly in the national interest.

Democratic elections, for example, require funds in ever-growing amounts. Yet national sources are often scarce. What kind of regimes are more likely to make "deals" with candidates in such contests and be handsomely rewarded should these win? Authoritarian and sultanistic regimes with a long history of deals with democratic regimes (arms deals, drug deals, money laundering deals, aids deals, etc.), who therefore can be trusted not to blow the whistle. Should the candidate who has benefited from such contributions win, undemocratic politics have entered democracy through the back door, so to speak: The elected government is committed to sustaining the benefactor's undemocratic regime.[60] Democratic countries have also knowingly hired criminals, as when the postwar U.S. government found it necessary to hire recognized Nazi criminals as spies against the Soviet Union.[61]

Rather than exceptions unworthy of our sociological attention or objects offered for our self-righteous disapproval, such cases represent opportunities for analizing undemocratic principles and realities not as phenomena distinct from and opposed to democracy, but as part and parcel of the dynamics of democracy (and undemocracy).

[58] For more illustrations of these principles, see Zakaria (1997).

[59] As a recent example, Human Rights Watch reports that Iraqi dissident Nizar Al-Khazraji, favored by the United States against Sadam Hussein, has been prosecuted by the Sorö tribunal in Denmark (where he resides) for failing to protect civilians in wartime and committing grievous crimes against the Kurds during the war between Iraq and Iran (from *Le Monde*, November 28, 2002).

[60] An empirical example that has come to the author's attention may serve as an illustration. The context is a presidential election in an established Western democracy in which X, a candidate, has successfully negotiated a $30 million medical aid package for Isthmus, a recently democratized ex-sultanistic regime. Only $15 million worth of aid material have arrived at its destination (although invoiced for $30 million), some of it not medical, because Y, the health minister, was involved in an arms deal. The loop has been closed: Democracy feeds upon undemocracy, which in turn thrives on democracy.

[61] These facts have recently been revealed with the opening of U.S. postwar archives. Among those hired was Hermann Höfle, who organized the deportation of all Jews from Warsaw, Dublin, Radom, Cracovia, and Lvov; supervised the construction of extermination camps in Sobibor, Treblinka, and Belzec; and was the mastermind behind the construction of gas chambers in these camps. In 1983, when Barbie (alias Lyon's Butcher) was arrested in France, the U.S. Justice Department apologized to the French government for having hired in 1947 the man responsible for the deportation of French Jews and assisting in his flight to Bolivia in order to evade French justice. For more details, see *Le Nouvel Observateur*, July 11–17, 2002.

CHAPTER TWENTY-FOUR

State Bureaucracy

Politics and Policies

Oscar Oszlak

The present chapter will analyze the theme of public bureaucracy in politics and implementing policies from the perspective of the power relations in which the bureaucracy intervenes as an actor in the political process and the institutional arrangements established for implementing public policies and attaining their goals. The involvement of bureaucracy in politics raises the question of its relative power vis-à-vis other actors, whereas its intervention in the process of public policy implementation is related to its performance (or productivity) in achieving policy goals.[1]

The subject of bureaucratic power has been treated in the literature from several perspectives. Rourke (1984), for example, considered that the power of bureaucracies derives mainly from two sources: "(1) their ability to create and nurse constituencies and (2) their technical skills that they command and can focus on complicated issues of public policy" (1). At the same time, bureaucracy is seen as the one permanent institution in the executive branch and for that reason "it enjoys a certain degree of autonomy" (Cayer and Weschler, 1988:67). In Ripley and Franklin's (1982:30) synthesis, "bureaucrats are not neutral in their policy preferences; nor are they fully controlled by any outsider forces. Their autonomy allows them to bargain – successfully – in order to attain a sizeable share of preferences." Hence, limitations on their power are a central issue. Rourke (1984) argued that its limits stem not only from the competitive pressures from outside but also from factors related to the way in which organizations operate and bureaucrats behave within their own habitat (competition among bureaucracies, internalized restraints, ethical codes, internal procedures, testing performance, representativeness).

In turn, bureaucratic productivity (i.e., efficiency plus effectiveness, in Ilchman and Up-

[1] Productivity and power constitute the variables most frequently treated in the literature (Jacob, 1966; Ilchman and Uphoff, 1969; Ilchman, 1984; La Porte, 1971; Rourke, 1984; Shafritz and Russell, 1996). Garvey (1995:65) referred to these two variables in terms of a "dilemma of democratic administration" when he suggested that "administrative action in any political system, but especially in a democracy, must somehow realize two objectives simultaneously. It is necessary to construct and maintain administrative capacity, and it is equally necessary to control it, in order to ensure the responsiveness of the public bureaucracy to higher authority." The author would probably agree that building administrative capacity has to do with increasing productivity, whereas control from, and deference to, higher authority involves mainly a power relationship. In a similar vein, Przeworski (2002:212) suggested that "one cannot eliminate politics from public administration: this is a project with authoritarian overtones. One can only control its forms and moderate its magnitude." In another recent study, it was held that no matter what types of reform have been implemented or attempted and no matter in what political, economic, and social context, civil service reform in general aims at improving performance of the civil service and the legitimacy of government action. Again, performance is another name for productivity, whereas legitimacy can be viewed as one of the manifestations of power (see, for example, Cleaves, 1974; Ilchman and La Porte, 1970; Wilson, 1989; Rama, 1997; Coplin et al., 2002).

hoff's view) has been related to the extent to which this institutional apparatus is able to successfully achieve the goals and policies that justify its existence – an outcome that generally depends on a complex combination of idiosyncratic and historical circumstances.

These issues will be tackled from both historical and theoretical approaches. In the first section, public bureaucracy will be presented as an outgrowth of public policy. In this analysis, I will introduce some remarks about the process of state formation, of which the emergence and development of bureaucratic organizations is one of its main features. In the second section, I will present a framework for interpreting the internal dynamics of bureaucracy, by identifying a number of variables and dimensions that may explain different levels of efficiency and effectiveness. Finally, section three will reexamine the old politics–administration dichotomy in the light of our main question: the involvement of bureaucracy in politics and in implementing public policies. A few concluding remarks will summarize the main points raised in this chapter.

BUREAUCRACY AS AN OUTGROWTH OF STATE POLICIES

Let us begin with a few general propositions. Instead of being an ideal type doing or not doing various tasks, a public bureaucracy is what it does. It is an outgrowth of politics and it is shaped by the nature and contents of public policy. It is, at the same time, the material expression of the state[2] – viewed as a concrete institutional apparatus – and the executing arm for implementing its policies. It is also one of the state attributes and the main instrument for achieving and maintaining its other attributes of "stateness."[3] It is not the outcome of a rational process of structural differentiation and functional specialization, nor does its development follow a planned and coherent design. Rather, its formation generally describes a sinuous, erratic and contradictory pattern, in which remnants of various strategies and programs of political action can be observed.

Public bureaucracies are the concrete counterpart to the ideal–abstract notion of state seen as the main instance for the articulation of social relationships, or as the conjunctive tissue that holds a society together. Most modern bureaucracies were formed as part of the process of state building, which occurred in Europe, the United States and Latin America mainly during the nineteenth century, except for England and France, where this process took place earlier. In turn, state formation can be viewed as a component of a more encompassing process of social building, in which several other components gradually come into being as well: nation building (understood as widespread and shared feelings of belonging within a territory), a citizenry, a system of production relationships, a marketplace, the structuring of social classes, and the consolidation of a "pact" of political domination.

To some extent, the state embodies this complex social formation. When fully developed, it exhibits a number of features that may be labeled "stateness," that is, the set of attributes featuring a "national state." Following Nettl (1968) and Oszlak (1982), the main traits of "stateness" are: (1) the externalization of power, (2) the institutionalization of authority, (3) the diffusion of control,[4] and (4) the capacity to reinforce a national identity. The first attribute implies acquiring external recognition of sovereignty

[2] As distinct from the state seen as the ideal–abstract instance of social articulation.

[3] In this sense, the bureaucracy is not coterminous with the state: It is simply its material embodiment. The notion of "state" also includes external recognition by other states, a legal order, a monopoly of coercion, a power of taxation, and a capacity to create symbols of nationality as attributes that clearly exceed the concept of an institutional apparatus. The subject will be discussed in detail later, when considering the formation of national states.

[4] Diffusion of control is a correlate of centralization of power. To be effective, state power at the central level must rely on various forms of *presence* within a national territory. For example, the establishment of a territorially based army corps was an early mechanism whereby new national states deployed military forces to control rebellions and upheavals against their authority, conquer land in the hands of Indians, or fight wars against foreign powers. Similarly, the building of physical infrastructure or the creation of a centrally managed school system within the entire territory constituted other ways in which the national state made its presence felt within the nation's borders.

by other nation-states. Most Latin American, African, and Asian countries gained recognition from the United States and Western European countries immediately after, or even during, their wars of independence, without having acquired most of the other attributes of stateness. The second one implies achieving a monopoly of the use of coercion within a given territory, as the Weberian definition suggests.[5] The third trait has a twofold composition: (1) attaining a capacity to extract fiscal resources from society on a regular basis, both for reproducing the bureaucracy itself and for performing its role in achieving law and order, economic progress, and social equity; and (2) developing a professionalized body of civil servants, able to conduct the ever-increasing business of governing.[6] Finally, the fourth attribute requires the state apparatus to produce symbols that reinforce a people's sense of belonging, feelings of nationality, and beliefs in a common destiny.

A national state can emerge and develop insofar as, in its still embryonic form, it begins to demonstrate a capacity to solve social issues that transcend parochial demands and are concerned with (1) the very creation of a capitalist mode of production and (2) the welfare of the people embraced by this social formation. In his edited volume on *The Formation of National States in Western Europe*, Tilly (1975:71) indicated that "the extractive and repressive activities of states" was one of the original biases of his book, adding that "[T]he bias was deliberate. The singling out of the organization of armed forces, taxation, policing, the control of food supply, and the formation of technical personnel stresses activities which were difficult, costly, and often unwanted by large parts of the population. All were essential to the creation of strong states; all are therefore likely to tell us something important about the conditions under which strong or weak, centralized or decentralized, stable or unstable, states come into being."

Historically, the expansion of capitalism has found a decisive impetus in the increasing capacity of national states to undertake and surmount developmental obstacles. To a large extent, their growing ability to mobilize resources for this purpose had an immediate effect on the scope of its institutional domain. This process implied the expropriation from civil society and subnational governments of a series of functions that came to form part of its own operational realm.[7] Those functions were related to the satisfaction of societal needs in such areas as defense, justice, transportation, infrastructure, public health, and the like. The issues thus incorporated into the state's agenda represented a selective portion of the social problematic, the functional terrain opened as the national state came into existence, thereby creating a new division of labor. The state agenda was multiplied and expanded as it further incorporated new issues required by the very functioning and progress of society.

In some cases, the new division of labor implied a definitive functional transfer from subnational to national states, as in the case of monopoly of coinage, armed forces, foreign relations, and the like. In other cases, the state and the market shared a common area of services, as in school and health services or in transportation. Finally, the new capacities acquired by the nation-states as they developed allowed them to intervene in other critical areas, such as the building of infrastructure or the negotiation of international funding. Along this process, the national and subnational states, the market, and the nongovernmental organizations of society

[5] There are recent examples of countries that have lost, at least in part, this attribute. Former Yugoslavia disappeared as a state federation as a result of a bloody civil war; Colombia is heavily involved in fighting *narcos* and paramilitary irregular forces that control part of the national territory. The American Civil War stands as a nineteenth-century illustration of a national state in which the pretense of monopolizing coercion by a central government was overtly questioned.

[6] No national state can survive without attaining a capacity to ensure a regular source of income through taxation. Tax collectors have been the first and main bureaucratic cadres of the newly created states. In turn, the creation of a more extended and professionalized civil service marked the beginning of modern state bureaucracies (cf. Raadschelders and Rutgers, 1996).

[7] This expropriation process was originally observed by Karl Marx in his *Critique of Hegel's Philosophy of the State*. For further references on the process of state formation, see Tilly (1975), Skocpol (1979), and Oszlak (1982).

drew up new boundaries and changed the contents of their respective agendas.

Obviously, without an agenda, the state – and its bureaucracy – would become meaningless. It would imply that its role is needless, that society can handle community problems on its own and can be self-administered – as was envisioned by anarchism, communism,[8] or even some ultraconservative positions calling for a minimal state.

The formula that symbolized the process of state formation and gave essential content to the public agenda was expressed in the motto "order and progress," which, on the one hand, signaled the need to establish (1) who would become legitimate members of (and who would be excluded from) the new mode of capitalist organization that was taking shape; and (2) what rules of the game ought to be institutionalized so that economic transactions became stable and foreseeable, thus promoting the development of productive forces through the articulation of the classical factors of production (land, labor and capital) and, therefore, according to the vision of the time, making indefinite progress possible.[9]

Attention to the multiple macro and micro manifestations of these two issues gave content to a policy agenda that began to expand at the pace of the very advancement of society and the state. Toward the end of the nineteenth and early twentieth centuries, both in Europe and in America, the unequal opportunities provided by capitalism to different social sectors revealed that economic progress was obtained at the expense of increasing social inequity. The so-called social question and the fights conducted around it at the political level "completed" a trio that was destined to maintain a permanent place in the state agenda.

In their more updated versions, the trio is composed of governance (order), development (progress), and equity (the social question) – in other words, the formidable challenges facing most underdeveloped and many developed societies. This continuing presence is nothing but the manifestation of a permanent tension among its components, observable in capitalist systems incapable of establishing a stable formula for reconciling the conditions of democratic governance, sustainable growth, and equitable distribution of income, wealth, and opportunities. Under these circumstances, the state agenda becomes ever more complex and contradictory, as the issues contained turn out to be much more difficult to solve, given rising social expectations and scarce resources.

It has already been indicated that, as the process of state (and social) formation advanced, the resolution of the issues constituting the social agenda was distributed among the state (at its various jurisdictional levels), the market, the organizations of civil society (NGOs), and a number of noninstitutionalized and solidarity social networks. Figure 24.1 illustrates this functional distribution, providing some examples of goods and services contained in the various sectors' agendas.

Although the frontiers separating these different sectors moved over time, through successive expansions or contractions, there is little controversy about the fact that the state territory showed a growing expansion that only seems to have come to a halt recently, involving new forms of intervention in society's affairs. This new role of the state, which acquired different "incarnations" over time (i.e., as entrepreneur, employer, subsidizer, regulator), began to be questioned about two decades ago, giving way to a new displacement of the frontier lines that revealed a greater protagonism of the other three sectors (the market, the NGOs, and the informal social networks) as well as a transfer of state responsibilities from the national to the subnational levels of government (see arrows in Figure 24.1). Privatization, decentralization, demonopolization, deregulation, and contracting out appeared as the main manifestations of this process. Taken as a whole, these policies were

[8] In a famous statement, Lenin (1971) held that the state would wither away in the transition from socialism to communism.

[9] In the 1968 presidential campaign, Richard Nixon was still referring to this formula in their old original terms when he pointed out that "[S]ome people say progress comes before order. Some say order comes before progress. Both miss the mark. The point is that in a free society, order and progress must go together."

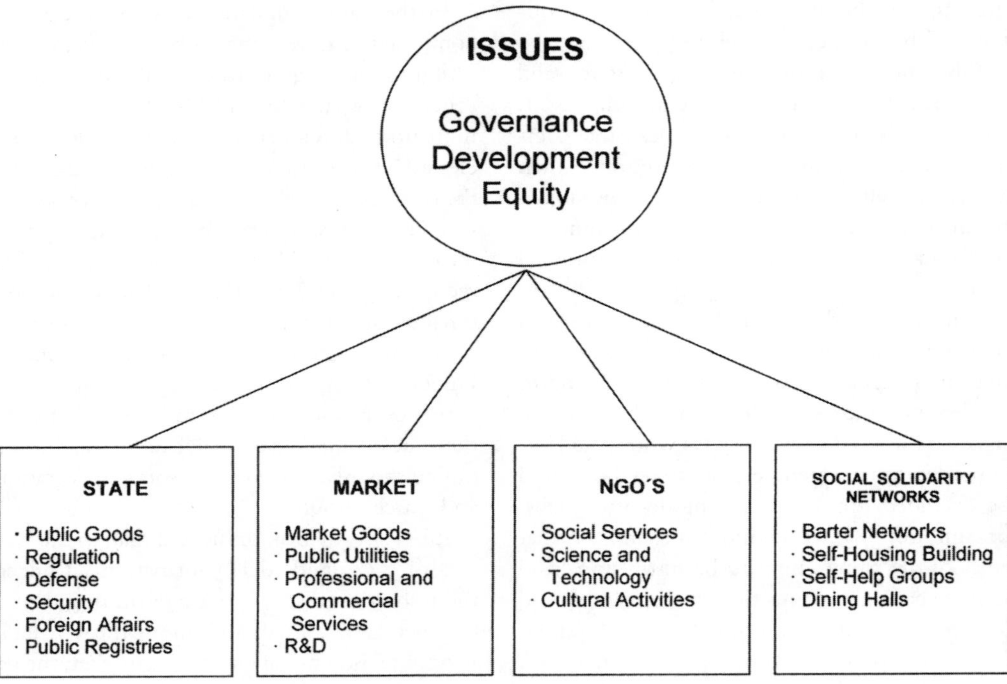

Figure 24.1. Social Division of Labor.

part of the so-called first generation of state reforms based on the Washington consensus.[10]

Does this mean that the state is no longer necessary?[11] Societies would probably be better off had they not to confront the myriad of needs, demands, perils, and contingencies facing their evolution. As suggested, the state is a major – if not the main – institution capable of deploying the human, organizational, and technological resources needed to meet most of those challenges. Other economic and social actors do play a more or less important role in solving many of these issues, but there is little question that the state exerts a role that cannot be delegated. As a matter of fact, if judged by most indicators (i.e., budget and personnel size, number of agencies, percentage of state employment with respect to the economically active population), the state shows almost no signs of disappearance.

Returning to our main line of argument, every issue included in the state agenda creates

[10] This reform movement originally developed under President Reagan and Prime Minister Thatcher, whose governments made strong structural adjustments and carried out several changes in the administration mainly to surmount their fiscal crises. Later on, in 1989, the Washington consensus approved John Williamson's ten-point proposal for restructuring Latin American states (1) fiscal discipline, (2) reordering public expenditure priorities, (3) tax reform, (4) liberalizing interest rates, (5) a competitive exchange rate, (6) trade liberalization, (7) liberalization of inward foreign direct investment, (8) privatization, (9) deregulation, and (10) property rights extension to the informal sector. Despite its targeted goals (i.e., introduce reforms in Latin American countries), this philosophy of state reform was also applied in many other developed and underdeveloped countries.

[11] In his book *The End of the Nation State*, Ohmae (1995) presented the provocative thesis that the nation-state is becoming superseded by a regional (supranational) state because it no longer generates real economic activity, having lost its capacity to function as a critical participant in a globalized world. The twin contradictory forces of regional integration and decentralization are, to many observers, a clear trend in this direction.

a "tension" that only disappears when it is removed from the agenda, either because the underlying problem has been "solved" or the issue was temporarily deferred to be handled sometime in the future. In any case, the state must take a stand or position on the subject before any issue is somehow solved or postponed for future resolution. So do other political actors having something to do with the values or interests at stake (i.e., political parties, business corporate organizations, labor unions, international organizations, public opinion, the media, NGOs, and so on). Public policies are simply the sequence of stands or positions taken by governmental and bureaucratic institutions (i.e., legislature, the presidency, central government agencies, public enterprises) acting in the name of the state regarding the issues included in the public agenda. The particular choices made for solving those issues end up generating a social dynamics featured by conflicts and confrontations among actors holding different and often contradictory views.

The courses of action adopted imply, at least, two different things: (1) that solutions to the issues have been identified, involving a cause–effect relationship between employing certain instruments and obtaining the results sought; and (2) that there is a commitment to create agencies or governmental units that may contribute to solve the issue or, in case they already exist, to allocate the resources needed for fulfilling their respective mission. Hence, (1) the incorporation of issues or social problems that the state chooses or is forced to take on as part of its responsibilities, and (2) the stands taken by individuals or agencies assuming the representation of the state, are the main generators of bureaucratic organizations, which are created and/or endowed with resources to handle and solve these issues.

The process of institutional development of the national state (i.e., the formation of a bureaucracy) has not been fortuitous. It always has responded to a particular interpretation of certain needs or social demands and has resulted in resource allocation patterns and institutional arrangements grounded upon the latter's alleged efficacy to satisfy those needs or demands. From a static point of view, one may "freeze" and classify the functions of bureaucracy in terms of relatively permanent features. For instance, Ripley and Franklin (1982) suggested that bureaucracies have been created for the following different purposes: (1) to provide certain services that are the natural province of government responsibility; (2) to promote the interest of specific economic sectors in society such as farmers, organized labor, or segments of private business; (3) to regulate the conditions under which different kinds of private activity can take place; and (4) to redistribute various benefits, such as income, rights, and medical care, so that the less fortunate and less well-off in society get more of these benefits than they ordinarily would have (cf. Oszlak and O'Donnell, 1976; Meny and Thoening, 1992; Aguilar Villanueva, 1996).

However, bureaucracies evolve: New functions may be assigned to or removed from their domain; their structures may become more differentiated and complex; new coordination mechanisms may be required; and they may gain or lose resources. These dynamics may be viewed in terms of a deliberate process intended to adapt a given resource combination to the achievement of certain ends.[12]

This reasoning may be plausibly extended to any field of public management. In each of them will be observed an intimate relationship between the issues contained in the state agenda, the stands taken in the process of "alternative-specification" (Barzelay, 2002), and the institutional mechanisms (including resource allocations) established for handling and solving them. The particular configuration of bureaucracy at each time will be a historical product resulting from confrontations and disputes around "who will get what, when, how," as

[12] Downs (1967:10) considered that "[T]he major causes of growth and decline in bureaus are rooted in exogenous factors in their environment. As society develops over time, certain social functions grow in prominence and others decline (...) the interplay between external and internal developments tends to create certain cumulative effects of growth and decline."

Lasswell once put it. Very often, bureaucracies become a conflict arena for settling these disputes, whereby the agencies involved (and other political stakeholders) take stands, build alliances, develop strategies, and put into play various types of resources in order to make their respective positions predominant.

For the time being, I will present a brief summary of the points discussed so far:

1. State emergence and formation are intimately related to the development of other components of the overall social building process, namely nationhood, capitalism, a class structure, and a system of political domination, as abundantly proven by the European and the Americas' experience.
2. Along this process, the state acquires a series of attributes (stateness) of which the gradual formation of a professional machinery (a civil service, a public bureaucracy) becomes of special interest for our analysis.
3. This institutional apparatus is formed and grows as an increasing number of social issues are incorporated into the state agenda. Partly, this incorporation requires the expropriation of functional domains from subnational states or civil society organizations previously in charge of satisfying social needs; and partly it entails the development of a previously inexistent capacity to assume more demanding responsibilities, made possible by the very formation of the state and its new, expanded possibilities for resource mobilization.
4. The particular composition of the agenda and the positions taken by the state (public policies) determine the type of solution devised to solve the agenda issues and, therefore, the configuration and characteristics of the resulting bureaucracy. For example, a military bureaucracy (armed forces and defense institutions) may be central in the present-day agenda of certain states, such as the United States or North Korea, or totally nonexistent in others, such as CostaRica. Or it may have been critical in earlier times (as it occurred in most Latin American countries during the nineteenth century). A revenue service has been established as a direct result of the need to sustain the state apparatus itself, allowing it to play its public management role. Regulatory agencies of private business or public agencies may have a key relevance in the state agenda of interventionist governments or may be totally insubstantial in more liberal ones. More generally, the relative importance of welfare, education, science and technology, or domestic security, as illustrations of issues composing the state agenda, may be estimated by the size and resources allocated to the agencies in charge of solving the corresponding issues within the bureaucratic apparatus.
5. Hence, the state bureaucracy can be conceived of as the institutional crystallization of public policies and state activity, manifested through bureaucratic agencies that, along the implementation process, end up defining the nature of the state they embody.
6. From this vantage point, the state (and its bureaucracy) is what it does – a proposition that takes us back to my initial statement in this section.

This *interim* conclusion-cum-proposition should be explored further by presenting an analytical framework that may serve to examine the internal dynamics of bureaucracy and its effect on its productivity.

BUREAUCRATIC PRODUCTIVITY: AN ANALYTICAL FRAMEWORK

In a most general way, public bureaucracy has been defined as "the totality of government offices or bureaus that constitute the permanent government of a state . . . (it) refers to all of the public officials of government – both high and low, elected and appointed" (Shafritz and Russell, 1996:215).[13] Similarly, Lindblom and Woodhouse (1993:57) considered that "bureaucracy is the largest part of any government if measured by the number of people engaged or by fund expended." Jacob (1966:34), in turn, argued that "bureaucracy may be thought as a complex system of men, offices, methods and authority which large organizations employ in order to achieve their goals." Finally, Downs (1967) established as primary characteristics for defining bureaucracy: large size, full-time membership and economic dependency of members, personnel hiring, and promotion and retention on a "merit" basis.

Basic similarities can be observed among these definitions, but in terms of its structural arrangements, Weber's conceptualization of bureaucracy remains as a more abstract and compelling characterization. His ideal type is featured by a number of well-known traits: (1) bureaucrats are arranged in a clearly defined hierarchy of offices; (2) they are compelled by the impersonal duties of their offices; (3) units and positions are arranged in a chain of command; (4) the functions are clearly specified in writing, so there is a specialization of task and a specified sphere of competence; and (5) the bureaucrat's behavior is subject to systematic control.[14]

From a different standpoint, Weber also considered bureaucracy as the form of organization most compatible with the requirements of a capitalist system, but at the same time, as a threat or stumbling block along the process of democratization. Ever since his ideal type came to scholarly attention, the literature on the sociology of organizations and public administration has developed many different theoretical models that have tried to capture and explain the main features of bureaucracy; its manifold organizational forms; and its performance, power, behavior, and other like attributes. For heuristic, rather than explanatory purposes, I will present an analytical framework that will be used to examine the most significant dimensions and variables related to our subject.[15]

We may characterize bureaucracy – the institutional state apparatus – as a system of production formally invested with the mission of satisfying certain goals, values, expectations, and social demands. According to its normative framework, the bureaucracy employs resources (human, material, financial, technological) and combines them in various ways in order to produce a variety of results or products – expressed in the form of goods, regulations, services, and even symbols – somehow related to its defined goals and targets. The nature of the normative framework, the way resources are structured, and their volume and quality will elicit certain behavior patterns that, in turn, may affect the quantity and quality of the products obtained.

Let us consider the basic elements of the proposed model in greater detail.

Productivity

Bureaucratic productivity may be defined as the capacity of bureaucracy to generate public value.

[13] Lane (1999:1) underlined the inexistence of a unique organization: "In actuality, there are many administrative agencies rather than a single government bureaucracy, and these organizations have difficulty coordinating activities and sometimes even compete with each other." Instead Cayer and Weschler (1988:57) point out that "bureaucracies are dynamic organizations which permeate our governmental system. While they have features that facilitate their ability to accomplish the purposes of government, they also have features that inhibit their effectiveness and especially their responsiveness to elected leaders and the general public."

[14] We can see a peculiar tension between the reference and the meaning of the concept of bureaucracy. On the one hand, if it is taken for granted that "bureau" refers to existing organizational entities within the public sector, then there hardly exists any single theory that adequately portrays the distinguishing characteristic of such entities. On the other hand, if we start from a specified concept of bureaucracy, then we must try to specify what is its range of application. It could be the case that their various properties are not generally true of existing bureaus (Lane, 1999).

[15] This model was originally developed in my unpublished doctoral dissertation (*Bureaucracy and Environment: on bureaucratic productivity in Uruguay*, University of California, Berkeley, 1974). See also Oszlak (1972).

Moore (1998) identified success in the public sector with carrying out state activities in such a way as to increase their value for the public, both in the short and the long run.[16] *Ceteris paribus*, the generation of public value will be higher the greater the degree of alignment and congruence between the goal function (or combination of objectives and targets) pursued and the production function technically required to achieve them. Two elements may be distinguished in this definition: (1) the degree of goal achievement, that is, the relationship between goals and outputs (effectiveness); and (2) the employment of the least quantity of inputs by product unit or the highest level of production at a given level of inputs (efficiency).[17]

This definition carries serious operational problems, particularly concerning what and how to measure, because its two elements – effectiveness and efficiency – have as a common referent a highly abstract and heterogeneous "product" (cf. Rourke, 1984; Lindblom and Woodhouse, 1993; Beetham, 1993; Yarwood and Nimmo, 1997; Allison, 1999; Blau and Meyer, 1999; Coplin et al., 2002).[18] There are, to be sure, clear similarities between the services provided by state-owned and privately run public utilities companies (i.e., fuel, electricity, telephone services). In fact, there should not be many differences between state and private companies in terms of measuring their levels of productivity in providing similar goods or services.

But services and regulation have never been measured well in economics or elsewhere. For example, there are many underdeveloped countries in which public schools provide a free lunch to their poor students, besides the routine educational programs. If measured exclusively on the basis of the latter, their efficiency would surely fall below schools not offering such services. Or, as a different example, regulatory agencies find it difficult to evaluate their performance regarding the control of prices, degree of security, compliance with investment plans, service quality, market competitiveness, and other aspects related to the activity of their regulated enterprises. In any case, recent efforts at identifying benchmarks and indicators of bureaucratic productivity have brought considerable progress in this area.[19]

Environment

Our model assumes that the physiognomy of the state apparatus and its levels of performance are intimately related to the characteristics of the social and political contexts that frame its activity. This information is concretely referred to the existing policy agenda and the nature of the social structure at the historical juncture under analysis (Pfeffer, 1982; Allison, 1999; Knack, 2000; Provan and Brinton, 2001; Considine and Lewis, 2003).

As the government takes stands vis-à-vis socially relevant issues contained in its agenda, it is likely that a new agency will be created to solve a given issue or additional resources will be allocated to already existing agencies (Oszlak and O'Donnell, 1976; Rama, 1997; Wilson, 1999). Efforts at carrying out government projects, initiatives, and priorities lead, within the state apparatus, to multiple organizational arrangements and operational styles, the nature of which is, to

[16] The author points out that sometimes this may imply increasing the efficiency, efficacy, or impartiality in the missions presently defined, whereas at other times, it may take introducing programs that respond to new political aspirations or redefining the organizational mission.

[17] Admittedly, this is just *one* possible way of conceiving efficiency and effectiveness together, under the common label of productivity. I would not take issue at other possible conceptualizations, and would rather use my approach to advance the argument further.

[18] In this sense, Allison (1999:18), following Dunlop, affirmed that "there is little if any agreement on the standards and measurement of performance to appraise a government manager." In turn, Beetham (1993:34) indicated that "the 'product' of government is not specific and readily measurable" and concluded that "decisions about how to define or measure 'effectiveness' are thus themselves qualitative or political judgments."

[19] Compare the conclusions reached in Oszlak (1973) and other articles in the same journal with those arrived at in more recent contributions (Ruffner, 2002; Heinrich, 2002; Helgason, 1997).

a large extent, the result of how social conflicts are settled within this institutional arena.

To specify the impact of these forces requires the consideration of: (1) the nature of the political regime; (2) the level of economic development, the patterns of capital accumulation and distribution of social output, and the degree of the country's external vulnerability; (3) the relative weight of sectorial interests, the strength of their corporate organizations, and the degree of control they exert on the state apparatus; (4) the prevailing social conditions (in terms of human development, welfare, educational level, social mobility, people's expectations, and degree of consensus or social warfare); and (5) the weight of tradition and cultural traits, such as the extension of clientelism and political patronage, or the diffusion of values compatible with democracy and efficiency of public management.

Resources

Next, we must consider the resources employed by the bureaucracy (probably the most tangible expression of its existence) in achieving its mission. Variables under this analytic dimension include the nature of the diverse resource components, their volume, capacity, adaptability, pertinence, and possibilities of articulation, taking into account the goals pursued. Thus, the state apparatus can be conceived of as a production system that combines its resources in varying ways and proportions, which defines a given "production function" deemed to meet a particular "goal function."[20] In budgetary terms, this means that the possibility of achieving certain levels of productivity will depend, in part, on the allocation of right combinations of personnel, material goods (i.e., infrastructure), and services, aligned with the goals sought which, at bottom, are expressed in certain specific targets.[21]

For example, several years ago, the Argentine government owned three ships that conducted research on fishery. These ships were at sea around 200 days per year. The Chilean government, in turn, owned two ships navigating a total of 300 days per year. Obviously, Chilean ships performed much better than the Argentine ones in terms of actual research done. The reason for the low level of performance in the latter case was mainly due to the lack of professional personnel, the low level of maintenance of the ships, and the difficulties in providing the necessary material inputs (fuel, special research instruments, etc.) for doing the job. Hence, the Argentine ships remained safely docked and idle.

Therefore, there are two ways in which the inconsistency between a goal function and a production function may occur. The first way is when the factors of production (i.e., infrastructure, personnel and operating expenses) are inadequate for the task at hand. The second way is when the composition of human resources (i.e., the combination of managerial, professional, technical, and nonspecialized personnel) is not the right one. In Oszlak (1972), I have coined the expression "excess-lack syndrome" to refer to this simultaneous existence of supernumerary workforce (usually for certain routine tasks) and insufficient personnel for performing other critical functions, thus creating bureaucratic deformity.

[20] The notion of "production function" has been borrowed from classical economics, where land, labor, and capital were considered as the basic factors of production. Land can now be equated to infrastructure, labor to human resources, and capital to nonpersonal goods and services required for maintenance and operation.

[21] Both at the global state apparatus or at that of specific bureaucratic agencies, there is a frequent lack of accord between the bureaucracy's goals and the resource combinations employed to reach them. The causes are manifold: incongruent normative frameworks, agencies purposely devoid of a mission, outdated or unnecessarily complex procedures and practices, lack of coordination, weak planning and control systems, unbalanced allocation of human resources, and demoralized personnel with few incentives and low self-esteem. These situations are more common the higher the country's political instability and, consequently, the more contradictory or antagonistic the nature of the political projects held by successive governments or regimes. To a great extent, this lack of fit is reflective of a persistent, invisible, and, perhaps, involuntary violation of a golden rule of public management: A goal function and a production function should be congruent.

Norms

Resource combinations are not fortuitous but respond to a set of norms that establish guidelines for action and provide the legitimate instruments to ensure that the activities carried out by bureaucratic agencies are in line with those criteria. Basically, this system operates through three mechanisms that follow an analytic (but not a temporal) sequence, because they keep a certain hierarchical relationship where more concrete norms translate more abstract and diffuse directives.[22]

The first mechanism is aimed at ensuring that the output of bureaucracy corresponds to social demands and is congruent with the institutional goals. By applying this mechanism, goals are set, priorities are established, targets are approved, and this normative set is trasmitted to the overall organizational structure. In essence, it provides action guidelines for deciding which activities will be required to produce the type, volume, or scope of government's output. Examples are the type and volume of services to be provided, the incursion into entrepreneurial activities, the degree of intervention in the regulation of social and economic activities, or the scope of its repressive function.

The other two mechanisms have a more instrumental character. One of them serves to assess different strategies of political action and to formulate policies and plans that would translate, at the operational level, the broad guidelines and options giving contents to the normative system. Planning, administrative methods and procedures, and resource allocation policies are some of the main instruments of this type. The third, and last, mechanism is the sanctions system, which sets the domain for the exercise of authority, providing the means to ensure its application and thereby regulate superior–subordinate relationships. It therefore represents the instrument that those in authority apply to ensure that activities will be conducted in accordance with predetermined goals and procedures.

The normative framework may also comprise the cultural patterns in which the bureaucracy operates, which may prevail within the society at large or in specific agencies or units. Given this dual nature of culture, I consider it as a contextual constraint and treat it as such in the next section.

Structures

Bureaucratic productivity is strongly conditioned by the relative complexity and adequacy of the organizational structures. Three main features define this analytic dimension: (1) the *degree of structural differentiation*, namely the extent to which the hierarchical structure is disaggregated in terms of relatively autonomous units and the resulting stratification; (2) the *degree of functional specialization*, that is, the technical specificity required at the operational level and the resulting scheme for the division of labor (or management structure); and (3) the *degree of interdependence* – the extent to which the effectiveness of any organizational unit is subordinated to, or depends on, the performance of other units.

Structural differentiation and functional specificity may give way to duplication or overlapping of organizational units and functions. Under democratic regimes, in which the functioning of the political system becomes more open and competitive, the tendency toward duplication and overlapping is heightened, because the mechanisms of political representation are firmly embedded within the bureaucratic arena.

The greater the differentiation, specialization and interdependence, the higher the degree of complexity and uncertainty of public management and, consequently, the greater the need to establish proper mechanisms for articulation and integration. Interdependence may be of (1) a *hierarchical* type, where individuals receive orders from superiors and/or give orders to subordinates, constituting a network of authority relationships; (2) a *functional* type, defined as the

[22] "How these rules work together to allow individuals to realize their productive potential is a question of importance in resource management in particular, and public administration in general" (Evans, 1997:187).

network of technical and normative relations resulting from the exchange of information or the application of knowledge to material goods; or (3) a *budgetary* (or *resource-exchange*) kind, where interdependence is based on competitive allocation among units of material and financial resources originating from a common source.

A fluid information and communication system is an asset of the most effective mechanisms for articulation and integration. It tends to reduce bureaucratic isolation and makes monitoring, control, and performance evaluation possible. Another asset is coordination, which exists when the activities and behavior of individuals and organizational units are guided by criteria of complementarity in the satisfaction of common objectives. A basic condition for achieving coordination is convergence of ends (identity, congruence, compatibility). Otherwise, efforts to achieve consensus among the intervening parties would prove fruitless. Another condition is that actors have sufficient degrees of autonomy to make adjustments or adaptations required by interdependence. Mintzberg (1999:121) observed that the defining element of the bureaucratic structure is that "coordination is obtained through internalized norms which predetermine what should be done."

Given bureaucratic fractioning, resulting from functional decentralization and autonomization, coordination of activities among organizational units often turns out to be either unnecessary or impossible. Hence, each unit tends to function within close compartments, even when its activity is technically linked to that of other units. To a great extent, this fragmentation of bureaucracy may be explained by symbiotic relationships between bureaucratic agencies and organized sectors of society. In their search for legitimacy and resources, these agencies try to mobilize influential clients, although the relationship often may lead to bureaucratic capture of the agencies by their clienteles. On the other hand, the functioning of an institutional system so loosely integrated, so reluctant to subordinate its activity to the directives of "articulating" units, raises serious problems of uncertainty requiring diverse forms of redundancy in order to maintain an acceptable level of confidence in the system (Landau, 1969).

Integration mechanisms help establish a more expeditious decisional process and facilitate the coordination of activities. In turn, coordination is conditioned by the relative effectiveness of the authority structure that regulates the legitimate exercise of power within the bureaucratic organization, clarifies the hierarchy of roles, and allocates the means of control and execution of the decisions attributable to each specific role.[23] As may be observed, all of these variables belonging to the structural level of our model maintain complex, mutually determining relationships regarding norms and resources, indirectly affecting the levels of bureaucratic productivity.

Behavior

Administrative behavior is the last significant dimension for our analysis. The characteristics of the resources employed and allocated by the public sector, the demands and norms orientating state activity, and the various structural arrangements that constrain the integration or coordination of resources set the coordinates for administrative behavior. In other words, the conduct of public servants is not totally unexpected or random: It is highly influenced by their personal traits (age, experience, level of instruction); by their individual goals and their degree of compatibility or conflict with the institutional objectives; by the material resources at their disposal; by the nature of the norms and the type of external demands to which they must respond; by the opportunities for interaction and the kind of relationships they establish with their peers, superiors, and subordinates; or

[23] One possible way of articulating interorganizational relationships requires submitting the units involved to some form of compulsion – based on impersonal principles, charismatic leadership, or threat of coercion – in order to guide their actions in the direction of the goals pursued. This is the essence of authority, that is, the formal capacity to decide and achieve that other execute actions aimed at certain ends.

by the evaluation and control procedures they may face.[24]

In the final analysis, it is the activity of human beings, manifested through behaviors, that determines the level and quality of the products resulting from their organized action. Hence, the efficiency and effectiveness of bureaucratic activity will depend, in an immediate sense, on the conduct of civil servants, but such behavior will be just exteriorizing the aggregate of environmental, normative, and structural variables that stimulate certain perceptions, generate attitudes, and determine differentiated orientations toward action.

Among the variables integrating this analytical dimension, the following should be mentioned: (1) the degree of identification or motivation evidenced in the performance of the civil service (Perrow, 1986; Cook, 1999);[25] (2) the level of existing conflict in intrabureaucratic relationships (Thompson, 1967; Lane, 1999); (3) the predominant orientations toward authority, action, or time (O'Dwyer, 2002); (4) the presence of legitimate leadership in public management (Rourke, 1984; Lee, 2002); or (5) the levels of morality and accountability in performance (Romzeck and Dubnick, 1987; Hellman et al., 2000; Roberts, 2002).

A depiction of the theoretical dimensions, variables, and relationships involved in the model just described can be seen in Figure 24.2. To summarize the points made regarding the internal dynamics of the state bureaucracy, the figure shows that demands, supports, and constraints comprise the environmental variables operating at the input side of the bureaucracy. Demands express social preferences and authoritative policy decisions; supports include empowerment for public management and resource allocation; and constraints involve all sorts of variables impinging on the autonomy and scope of bureaucratic activity (i.e., legal bindings, social structural conditions, financial deficit, clientelistic pressures, cultural barriers).

Resources stand at the center of the triangle-shaped bureaucracy. Resource combinations determine the production function, but a production function can only exist insofar as its counterpart, a goal function, is set. The normative dimension, at the top of the triangle, is what provides sense and orientation to the activity of the bureaucracy, including decisions as to how resources should be spent to create public value. Norms (including legislation, culture, policies, and organizational rules) also determine how the bureaucracy is structured to perform its institutional role. Structural variables (differentiation, specialization, integration), in turn, bear on how resources are organized and assigned to various bureaucratic units, giving way to a certain pattern of division of labor. Both normative and structural variables, in turn, affect bureaucratic behavior, whereas all three dimensions (and their interplay) end up impinging on productivity.

However, we may also observe that in countering normative beliefs and expectations in the sense that norms determine structures, and norms and structures determine behavior, we find that in some cases, norms ↔ structures ↔ behaviors ↔ norms may function as mutually

[24] It may be objected that personal values also play a fundamental role in determining behavior, but our concern here is the modal behavior of civil servants. Therefore, from this perspective, they tend to become socially shared values, which in turn constrain bureaucracy's normative system.

[25] This subject has given rise to several typologies of employees' identification and attitudes. For example, Presthus (1962) pointed out three patterns of accommodation that seem to occur in an organization: (1) *upward-mobiles*, the values and behavior of whom include the capacity to identify strongly with the organization, permitting a nice synthesis of personal rewards and organizational goals; (2) *indifferents*, who tend to reject the organizational bargain that promises authority, status, prestige, and income in exchange for loyalty, hard work, and identification; and (3) *ambivalents*, creative and anxious, whose values conflict with bureaucratic claims for loyalty and adaptability. In turn, Ripley and Franklin (1982) found four types of bureaucrats in the implementation process: (1) *careerists*, employees who identify their careers and rewards with the agency that employs them and whose main aim is to maintain the agency's position and their own position within it; (2) *politicians*, who expect to pursue a career beyond the agency and whose aim is to maintain good ties with a variety of sources external to agency; (3) *professionals*, a group which derives satisfaction from the recognition of other professionals; and (4) *missionaries*, who are motivated primarily by their loyalty to specific policy or social movements that suggest certain configuration of policies as desirable.

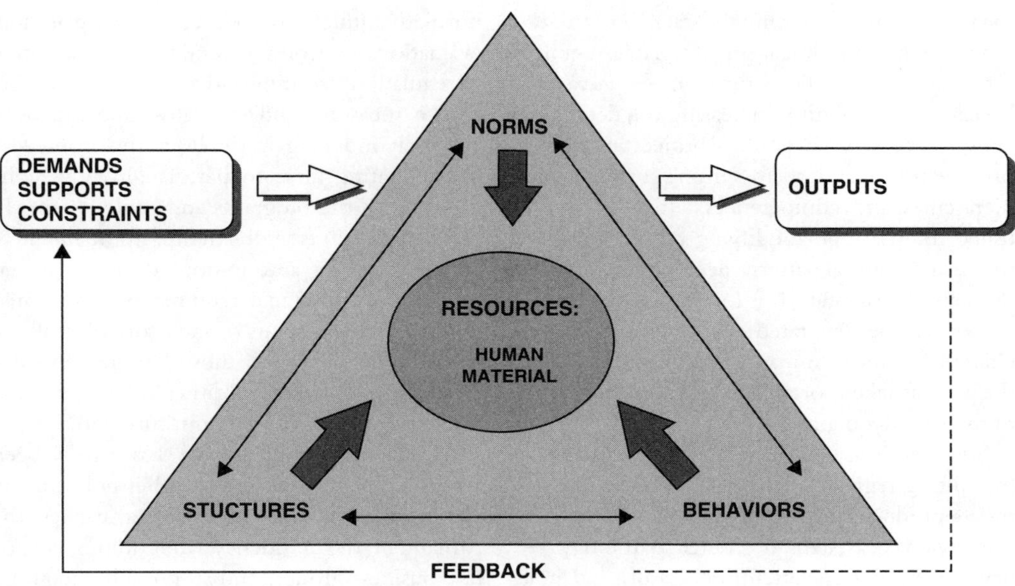

Figure 24.2. Dynamics of Bureaucracy.

dependent and independent variables. For example, the organizational structure of a governmental agency will depend, in the first place, on the mission and objectives (norms) guiding its activity. And the behavior of its personnel will depend, in turn, on what are they supposed to do (again, norms) and in what position of the organization (structure) they are placed. "Reverse arrows" are usually identified with signs of bureaupathology. Goal displacement may be seen as a situation in which behavior modifies norms, whereas unnecessary redundancy can be interpreted as behavior modifying structures. The extent of this phenomena varies widely depending on the specific context considered. In the next section I will introduce additional elements for understanding these perplexing dynamics.[26]

BUREAUCRACY, POWER, AND PUBLIC POLICY

Most academic work on the sociology of public bureaucracy originates in national contexts where the regular succession of governments through elections, the legitimate representation of society through institutionalized mediations, the prevailing incremental decision-making style, or the generalized recourse to bargaining and compromise constitute assumptions – rather than variables – of the political process. These traditions are so pervasive that speculation about other possible scenarios cannot be mirrored in, and hence, stimulated by, local circumstances.

However, the alternation of political regimes exhibiting widely opposed ideologies and orientations and their respective impacts on – among other aspects – the policy framework, the fate of the mechanisms of representation, or the style of state management raise a number of issues and research questions that are complex enough to render most current models and conceptualizations inappropriate for capturing the complexity of these other realities. This is especially the case when political instability and regime shifts become not simply a short-lived "abnormality," but rather the current state of affairs.

Every new regime attempts to alter not only the power relationships within civil society, in line with its political conception and the need of strengthening its social bases of support, but also

[26] This kind of analysis is akin to Philip Selznick's (1949) analysis of the TVA, in which the focus is placed on the structural conditions that influence behavior in formal organizations, with a special emphasis on constraints.

the power structure within the state apparatus itself. To make a political project viable requires action upon – as well as through – a *preexisting* bureaucratic structure. Increasing the degree of congruence between political project and public organization may lead to shifting jurisdictions, hierarchies and competences, affecting established interests and modifying power arrangements and cultural patterns deeply rooted inside the state bureaucracy. It is foreseeable that resistances will be generated and behavior will be elicited tending to impair the decisions made or the actions taken, or at least, to attenuate some of their consequences.

Such tensions created inside the bureaucracy by shifting regime orientations and the adjustments produced by changing policies – sometimes viewed as signs of "bureaupathology" – have received scant attention. Casuist, ad hoc explanations abound. Yet, a crucial question remains open to continuing controversy: What relevant dimensions and variables may explain and predict congruence or conflict in the processes of policy implementation? A systematic treatment of this subject confronts a fundamental difficulty, namely the sheer number of intrabureaucratic and environmental factors intervening in such processes. However, progress in this field calls for a conscious effort at integrating existing knowledge while keeping in mind the substantive, contextual, and historical specificity of the public and private actors involved in the policy process.

The implementation of most public programs and policies demands the intervention of a complex governmental structure and several decision units in the society. The performance of this network will depend on whether the succession and articulation of individual behavior turn out to be congruent with a given normative framework or a policy direction. Each decision unit will be subject to the conflicts inherent in the decisions taken at each level (i.e., degree of antagonization produced) and to the uncertainty derived from lack of knowledge of the impact of decisions. Indeed, a good deal of the organizational mechanisms will be destined to eliminate sources of conflict and uncertainty. Those organizations in charge of normative functions (i.e., legislation, planning, evaluation, control) will tend to design a system of regulations, administrative structures, performance measures and standards, and sanctions aimed at inducing lower level and front-desk implementing units to perform in ways consistent with the programs and goals sought. In turn, these units will attempt to maintain a certain space of autonomous decision power, so that the functional requirements associated with the achievements of their formal goals are made compatible with those requirements derived from the need to satisfy other goals and interests (i.e., clientelistic, institutional).[27]

The power of bureaucracy has usually been compared to that yielded by other political and economic actors, be they political parties, the parliament, the presidency, labor unions, corporate business groups, and so on. The literature has given this subject a great deal of attention, ever since Marxists in the 1970s–80s rediscovered Karl Marx's notion of the "relative autonomy of the state" in his *18th Brumaire* of *Louis Bonaparte*, and neo-Weberians started giving a more political interpretation to Weber's ideal type of bureaucracy and his warnings of "iron cages." For example, the Comparative Administration Group (CAG)[28] underlined this variable as a key factor for political development in developing countries;[29] Olson (1965) and Downs (1967) viewed it from the standpoint of collective action; and another current of research turned its attention to the study of bureaucratic capture (especially in cases of regulatory agencies) or, more recently, the theme received a renewed interpretation by Evans (1996), who

[27] On the simultaneous and conflicting interests pursued by bureaucratic institutions and the true role thus played by the state, see Oszlak (1977).

[28] The CAG emerged in the late 1950s as a new approach for the study of public administration, aimed at explaining the role and performance of bureaucracy in less developed countries. Initially sponsored by the Ford Foundation and the United Nations, the group conducted research in many different countries, particularly in Asia. It gained importance during the 1960s and maintained its momentum until the early 1970s.

[29] See, for example, La Palombara (1963) and Riggs (1964, 1971).

introduced the concept of "embedded state autonomy."

As a rule, each bureaucratic unit possesses a certain volume of power resources, which may be composed of coercion, information, legitimacy, and economic goods. Access to the use of ideological mechanisms is usually considered a powerful resource as well. Coercion may or may not be applied legitimately, depending on the nature of the incumbent government and the extent to which governance is based on social consensus. Information is another important source of power and the basis of bureaucratic activity at the functional level. Interaction within bureaucracy entails a permanent exchange of information or the application of knowledge (an elaborate form of information) to material goods. Economic goods are mainly the material resources that bureaucratic units receive through the budget, for hiring personnel, investing in infrastructure, and making the necessary maintenance and operation expenditures. Finally, legitimacy is a source of power that may derive from one or a bundle of variables: authority, status, leadership, consensus, and capacity to manipulate symbolic and ideological instruments. The legitimacy of bureaucracy is a major resource to substantiate its claim to continue to obtain the resources and supports that allow its existence.

These various power resources are unequally distributed throughout the bureaucracy both in terms of absolute power possessed by different agencies or units and in the particular composition of those resources in each case. For example, monopoly of coercion by military bureaucracies has historically been a major source of power for ousting democratic regimes. In turn, asymmetry of information between regulatory agencies and private companies in charge of formerly state-owned enterprises has often caused the incapacity of the former to control tariffs. Low budgetary allocations to certain welfare programs may lead to critical reductions in social work, health, and education services. In other words, the quantity and composition of power resources may or may not support the bureaucracy's capacity to settle social conflicts and allocate values in a legitimately authoritative fashion. Power resources are vital for reinforcing institutional legitimacy and securing survival. Both goals are intimately related: The more the legitimacy, the greater the chances of survival.

From a different perspective, Peters (1999) observed that bureaucracy enjoys other important resources: (1) its great agility, as compared with legislature, to act quickly on multiple issues, as it is free from following the legislature's strict procedural rules for debate and decision;[30] (2) its capacity to mobilize political affiliates in demanding greater budgetary allocations; and (3) the relatively high degree of autonomy of its organizations and agencies. However, I would argue that (1) these are not resources of power but rather outcomes deriving from the ones previously discussed, and (2) these outcomes may or may not be forthcoming depending mainly on the nature of the political system being considered. For example, under authoritarian and patrimonialist regimes, or even in weak democracies, decisions may be highly centralized in the executive, while legislature and the bureaucracy may play an insignificant or merely formal role.

In view of these contingent outcomes, is it possible to explain or predict the turn of events in a process of policy implementation? What power balances favor success in bureaucratic performance and productivity? In a most immediate sense, and given a certain level of power resources, performance will largely be explained by the behavior of those in charge of managing the organizations – what Thompson (1967) called "the variable human." No doubt, the degree of motivation, the existing leadership, the level of training, the orientation toward conflict, the search for power, or the formation of coalitions are, among others, the kind of factors affecting the quality of the available human resources and their probable action orientation. But in turn, these expressions of bureaucratic behavior are subject to four different types of

[30] The existence of a fluid network of formal and informal contacts that public administration services maintains with both the outside and with the top decision-making levels is seen by Subirats (1994) as an important resource for getting access and exerting influence on important policy actors.

constraints: *technological, cultural, clientelistic,* and *political.*

Technological and Cultural Constraints

Technological and cultural variables subsume most of the immediate determinants of bureaucratic behavior. The joint consideration of these variables is frequent in the specialized literature, in view of the increasing concern with the transfer of administrative technologies whose criteria of rationality are incongruent with those prevalent in the recipient countries.

Technological variables affect the functioning of a public bureaucracy in two ways. First, there is a type of technology intimately associated with the nature of the organization's core activity, for example, more or less standardized processes for the production of electricity, the supply of transportation services, or the public registry of certain transactions. Hence there is a technology which may present variations according to scale or degree of innovation but responds to a basic process of production of the good or service that is inherent to the activity, demands a given type of cooperation, and constrains the way the organization is structured. Usually, it is called the *core technology.*

Second, any complex organization will attempt to eliminate the sources of uncertainty operating on its technological core, because the legitimacy and survival or the organization strongly depends on the steady and efficient functioning of its core technology. In other words, under norms of rationality the organization will seek to seal off its core technologies from environmental influences, through the appropriate management of input (i.e., preventive maintenance, supplies, personnel) and output (i.e., disposition of products, marketing policy) activities (Thompson, 1967). To carry out these managerial activities, the organization must observe certain rules and principles dealing with the integration of human resources and professional expertise within a given technological system. Such aspects as span of control, departmentalization, hierarchy, relationship between coordination and size, or patterns of administrative career fall within these organizational support activities I will refer to as *managerial technology.*

Core and managerial technological components[31] may explain why organizations performing similar activities are likely to present similar technical and managerial features (Powell and Di Maggio, 1991).[32] Hospitals, schools, steel plants, or planning boards, operating in widely different environments, may possess for that reason a number of common traits. Certain professional norms and standards contribute to reinforce these similarities, by conforming a sort of technological subculture that tends to prevail beyond geographical or cultural barriers.

Also, cultural variables exert a homogenizing influence on bureaucratic behavior. The ways of perceiving and categorizing reality, the beliefs of the efficacy of certain instruments for achieving goals, the prevailing criteria of legitimacy, the attitudes toward authority, or the orientations toward time are elements that concur to standardize interpersonal perceptions as to what should be done or expected in a given situation – thus reducing uncertainty in the interaction. Of course, a distinction between organizational culture within bureaucracies and societal culture should be made because they often differ. Indeed, each culture has its own vision as to how public officials should behave, and the legitimacy of their roles is strongly pervaded by this cultural element.[33] Nepotism, venality, absenteeism – for example, practices that Parsons would have called particularistic – are part and parcel of certain cultures, or perhaps are more widespread in some cultural milieus than in others. In this respect, culture operates as an homogenizing factor but, at the same time, as a differentiating element vis-à-vis other cultures.

[31] In fact, these two kinds of technology are related to what are better known as substantive versus support organizational functions or as outside versus inside production.

[32] These are core issues in the recent bibliography on the sociology of organizations. For instance, isomorfism among organizations has been discussed in Powell and Di Maggio (1991).

[33] French and German bureaucrats, for instance, have high status, pay, and privileges; U.S. bureaucrats have low status, moderate pay, and few privileges.

A great number of administrative reform programs are precisely designed to operate upon these cultural traits, departing from a supposedly universalistic conception which, at bottom, is anything but a transplant of foreign cultural patterns disguised under the shape of neutral organizational technologies.

Already in 1964, Stinchcombe observed that cultures in transitional societies often do not incorporate the skills required for the operation of complicated technologies. Later on, this same author offered a provocative contrast between public organizations with different technological requirements, similarly subject to the Latin American cultural influence (Stinchcombe, 1964, 1974). In these societies, therefore, the homogenizing influences of culture tend to become constraints upon the organizations, that is, factors retarding or interfering with organizational action. In industrialized societies, on the other hand, the homogenizing effect of culture goes almost unnoticed given the high degree of congruence between technology and culture. In other words, the technological contents of culture are compatible with the cultural assumptions of technology.

The foregoing observations present administrative reformers with some crucial questions. What is the degree of tolerable incongruence between managerial technology and cultural patterns? How do incongruences affect bureaucratic efficiency and effectiveness? To what extent can reform activities force, or else overlook, the prevailing cultural patterns? These questions have no direct or easy answers. Bureaucratic units operating under different technological and environmental constraints will exhibit varying degrees of tolerance. In many cultures, the symbolic value or ceremonial nature of certain organizations, their consequent functional sterility, or their utilization as mechanisms for absorbing the unemployed are acceptable criteria of institutional legitimacy. Thus, in traditional contexts, technologically sophisticated units, such as a planning board or a public administration institute, may sometimes survive as curious islands of modernization embedded in a bureaucratic machinery whose dominant culture is eminently adscriptive and particularistic.

Clientele and its capacity for articulating demands will entail different exigencies in terms of compatibility between technology and culture. In traditional societies, in which individuals and organizations do not participate in narrow-interest networks that control their behavior, ideology, tradition, or attachment to normative imperatives may be much more important than self-control and self-determination. Feedback from society is very low; consequently, individual bureaucrats need to be told what should be done instead of for what purposes. The normal behavior pattern is likely to follow "bureaucratic–normative" criteria rather than "professional–clientelistic" criteria (Mayntz, 1979). This indicates the important role played by bureaucratic clienteles and political conditions as additional sources of constraints of public organizations, a theme to which I now turn.

Clientelistic and Political Constraints

In the late 1950s, Dill (1958) distinguished four environmental groups potentially relevant for defining and achieving organizational goals for private sector firms: (1) customers (both distributors and users); (2) suppliers of materials, labor, capital, equipment, and work space; (3) competitors for both markets and resources; and (4) regulatory groups, including governmental agencies, unions, and interfirm associations.

State bureaucracies, however, differ from this pattern of functioning in some important respects. First, the overall state apparatus may be considered as one large and single organization, with few or no competitors, rather than heterogeneous clients and "regulatory groups" with varying capacity of control, depending on the political context being considered. Second, the division of labor within this apparatus tends to parcel out functions, jurisdictions, and competences in such a way that virtual monopolies are created over the production of goods, regulations, or services. Third, the normative frameworks of these organizational units tend to rely, at least formally, on criteria and directives somehow external to the organization, in line with the division of labor previously mentioned. Fourth, clienteles tend to be "captive," given the monopolistic nature of most public bureaucracies' outputs and the interest networks generated around their supply. Hence, the consideration of environmental actors in the case of state bureaucracies needs a differing approach.

Two contextual dimensions appear particularly relevant to the case of bureaucratic units "linked" by processes of policy implementation: the specific character of the bureaucratic clienteles and the nature of the political regime. The former are important in view of the demands, supports, and legitimacy they may provide to the various agencies according to their performance. In turn, different political regimes may also entail different normative frameworks and management styles, with high probabilities that certain policy areas – and consequently certain agencies – will be favored at the expense of others. Let us take a closer look at the way these parameters constrain the internal dynamics of state agencies – hence impinging on productivity.

Every state agency struggles to gain positions within the policy space; in this process, it defines a "territory" or "functional domain." A sharp "territorial" sensibility usually affects bureaucratic behavior and the level of conflict among agencies. As a result of interagency struggle for domain building and maintenance, the physiognomy of the public sector becomes permanently transformed by borderline expansions and contractions. As a source of agency power and legitimacy, clients play a fundamental role in defining the terms and outcomes of this struggle. How effective their role may be will depend, among others, on several circumstances: their social origin, their sheer number, their interest articulation capacity, their proximity and control of the bureaucratic agencies, and their significance in terms of the prevailing patterns of capital accumulation and political domination. In this respect, clients may resort to similar power resources as those discussed earlier in this section.

A public agency may simultaneously occupy different policy spaces. These various locations would help placing the organization within a functional – or public policy – map. The hierarchy defines levels of authority and responsibility, introducing a "vertical" dimension in the policy space. Under normal circumstances, the higher the hierarchical level, the larger the functional "territoriality"; but at the same time, the more diffuse the kind of interests linking the organization with its clientele. In the policy space, a ministry of agriculture occupies a larger territory than a rural extension agency. But the former's clientele is constituted by second- or third-level corporate organizations whose interests are surely much more aggregate and diffuse than those claimed by rural producers dealing with the extension agency of our example.

This observation has important consequences, because it is often asserted that the state lacks a defined position in this or that policy area. In studies carried out in two state technological institutes in Argentina, the "lack of public policy" (i.e., agricultural or industrial) appeared as a recurrent theme (Oszlak et al., 1971; Oszlak, 1984). The possibility of policy formulation in the area of research and extension was thus automatically subordinated to the previous formulation of a global policy for the overall sector, within which the more specific policy would presumably become meaningful. In this conception, each policy area would resemble a system of "Chinese boxes," with policies keeping internal consistency among themselves and gaining in specificity as the operational levels are approached. Symmetrically, both the public agencies responsible for a functional area and their respective clienteles would also form a system of "Chinese boxes" through diverse structural combinations somehow shaped as a pyramid.

Although this conception is not totally mistaken, as it finds support in the formal organization of both the state and the corporate organizations, the underlying assumptions may not always be valid. In a study of the National Institute of Industrial Technology of Argentina, we found that the most successful industrial research centers were those in which the clientele was more actively involved in the promotion and management of the centers, and in which the policy framework for the sector favored (or at least was not openly contradictory with) the projects and action programs of the centers

(Oszlak, 1976). But the promotion of technology in a given branch of industry was not necessarily part of a global conception of technological policy, nor did it assume consistency with some definition of the "general interest" of society. Contrarily, in other situations we found that the lack of articulation between the output of an organization and the effective demand of its expected clientele led to situations in which the initiative of the members of the organization, the influence of professional fashions, or the requirements of financial or technical assistance from international organizations played a much more determining role in the definition of the institution's normative framework (Oszlak, 1972; Oszlak et al., 1971).

These illustrations suggest that, along with the distribution of the policy space (e.g., the division of labor within the state apparatus) and the hierarchical structure that creates another form of bureaucratic articulation and interdependence, an invisible stratification can be imagined which has a direct bearing on the role played by the clienteles of state agencies and the type of regime in power. For example, a study carried out in Guatemala (Martínez Nogueira, 1978) established a typology of bureaucratic agencies based on the relationship between the nature of the demands made by the clienteles and the level of knowledge and the capacity shown by the agencies for processing information. The degree of specificity and articulation of demands emerged as a critical variable for differentiating three types of state organizations. First were those attending to demands related with areas or activities considered as dynamic within the development model given their capacity to generate surplus, their links with foreign markets, and the productivity resulting from the technologies employed.[34] Second were units facing scarcely organized clients or, related with more traditional sectors or branches, weakly linked with external markets.[35] Third were agencies with similarly widespread, unorganized clients facing equally diffused demands as those of the second type but whose requirements of skills and technologies were scarce.[36] At a different level of abstraction, this invisible stratification of the public sector somehow replicates the very social structure of the country and the prevailing patterns of power relationships. It also suggests the existence of a close correspondence between social demand and bureaucratic productivity.[37]

[34] State agencies related to these sectors revealed great flexibility to adapt their internal structures, modes of operation, and resources to the requirements of changing circumstances. Their staff was composed of young, dynamic members, frequently shifting between the private and the public sectors. The critical value and the strategic character of their interventions assured the support of their clienteles. These institutions included, among others, those engaged in the formulation and implementation of economic policies, the regulation of economic behavior, and financial activities. They also included certain units that satisfied demands from the public sector itself, such as planning agencies or regional and local development agencies.

[35] Their functions benefited the community at large (i.e., educational or sanitary programs, infrastructure with no external economies for dynamic activities). These organizations somehow reflected the technologically backward, static, and unproductive character of the economic and social sectors served. Although the knowledge required to carry over their functions was high, their capacity to process information was extremely low. The demands from society did not promote organizational innovations, and the available and installed technology exerted a strong inertia. Among others, institutions in this category included those in the areas of education, social welfare, foreign affairs, and certain public utilities, such as telephone and gas.

[36] All organizations of this sort were heavily staffed at the operational level, showing very weak – or lacking altogeather – internal differentiation in terms of policy formulation, planning, and programming of activities. Many institutions used to outsource the elaboration of projects or the execution of public works. But they exhibited a reduced capacity of analysis and fiscalization of the technical resources provided by the contractors. They faced a high permanent turnover of their qualified personnel, who were attracted by the higher prestige and dynamism of other public or private organizations. Very often, these units were utilized as instruments of political clientelism. This category included units of the presidency, agriculture, public works, communications, ports, and some agencies working in the rural area.

[37] Casuistic explanations often preclude this broad proposition. To illustrate the point, consider the area of road maintenance, a favorite World Bank example. In general, highway development projects operated by the World Bank have not met with great success. As in the cases examined before, the demand for this type of

Regime Constraints

The intrabureaucratic dynamics is also affected by the nature of the existing political regime. What is the specific weight of this explanatory dimension, and how does it influence the policy process? Without falling into teleological or conspirative reasoning, it can be safely assumed that any incoming government or political regime, in attempting to implement its governmental program, will try to control the policy options and the resources needed for their achievement. For this purpose, it will try to increase the degree of congruence between political project and bureaucratic apparatus through: (1) modifications in the priorities and contents of substantive policies, thereby affecting (positively or negatively) the various sectors of society and, consequently, the state agencies and the bureaucratic clienteles related with such policies; and (2) changes in the support activities of the public sector (i.e., managerial technologies, cultural patterns). Put another way, the regime will try to act upon the technological, cultural, and clientelistic dimensions previously examined.

Regarding policy contents, Lowi (1972) distinguished four types of policies (i.e., distributive, redistributive, regulatory, and constituent) whose adoption or relative emphasis varies directly with the political regime. For example, by their very nature, populist regimes will give priority to programs of rural development, low-cost housing, public health, and mass education. In general, these types of redistributive policies tend to strengthen the position of the state agencies in charge of their execution and that of the social sectors benefiting from them. Under these regimes, the popular sectors normally enjoy greater capacity of organization and interest articulation. The failures of the state bureaucracy regarding social welfare programs may be partially compensated by voluntary organizations, labor unions, parastate agencies, and social solidarity networks, that is, by institutions which under these political circumstances play a significant role as mechanisms of social articulation. The situation is inverted under most antipopular authoritarian systems, in which regulatory policies and attempts at "regenerating" certain older patterns of social relations bring into prominence state units in charge of repression and control of social activities.

However, beyond differences in the substantive policy sector considered (i.e., defense, education, energy), it is likely that the orientations and propensities of the regimes in terms of reforming the "support" units and activities of the public bureaucracy will also differ. Changes in authority structures, redefinition of domain boundaries, or reallocation of resources are typical measures designed to reinforce or transform deeply rooted practices. The programs of downsizing, decentralization, and budgetary reform or changes in the ministerial organization charts or in procedural rules should be observed as conscious attempts of the government at controlling its bureaucracy.

Modernizing authoritarian regimes exhibit a strong tendency toward using highly sophisticated administrative techniques. The opposite is true of traditional authoritarian (or neopatrimonial) regimes, in which the dominant culture is mainly prebendalist. In sum, political regime and bureaucratic machinery may present varying degrees of compatibility in their cultural and technological orientations and practices; but in most cases the former will try to impose changes on the latter, in line with its values and preferences. Hence, in revolutionary situations – as has been the case of Nicaragua or Cuba, where the patrimonialist regimes of Somoza and Batista were succeeded by manifestly socialist regimes – the transformation of the public sector has involved actions at the political level (i.e., orientations and beneficiaries of state policies) as well as at the cultural and technological levels.

service is scarce and inarticulate. Most of the benefits are enjoyed by motor vehicle operators and, indirectly, by the population living within the area of influence of the road. The demands, therefore, do not easily reach those in charge of maintenance. Community pressure is low, particularly because awareness of road deterioration is gradual and almost imperceptible. There are instead much more incentives to direct the scarce resources available to highway construction, where the benefits are immediate, tangible, and, therefore, elicit the adherence of governments and clienteles alike.

In order to counteract the initiatives of the regime, the government agencies may resort to several, more or less institutionalized, mechanisms and practices. In the older agencies, there is a sort of ministerial or departmental ideology as to how certain matters should be dealt with. In the more specialized ones, the management of technical information often constitutes a powerful resource. The support of relevant clients, the establishment of informal relationships, or the existence of norms reducing the scope of the regime attributes (i.e., ability to remove personnel, civil servants' right to strike) operate as additional resources at the agencies' disposal.

In turn, the organizations and civil servants most directly related with the regime usually resort to various tactics and mechanisms for increasing their control over the agencies. The creation of integrating and supervising units – as in the areas of planning, science and technology, public enterprises –; the establishment of parallel hierarchies – either the military corporation, as in most bureaucratic–authoritarian regimes, or the ruling political party – as until recently in Mexico –; the creation of counter-staffs – such as a general secretariat of the presidency, personal advisors, trustworthy personnel – ; the passing of legislation allowing the government to get rid of public officials; or the setting up of ad hoc units, outside the formal bureaucracy, are some of the instruments available to the regime in power for overcoming bureaucratic obstacles and inertia.

Keeping in mind this complex interaction, the regime–bureaucracy relationship should be specified in terms of different national settings and historical circumstances. I have argued that there is a causal relationship between political regime and bureaucratic organization. Or, more specifically, the various forms of bureaucratic interdependence (or intrabureaucratic dynamics) are differently affected by the nature of the political regime. The transformations of the public sector as a new regime takes power can partly be explained by the kind of interactions occurring once the incumbent powerholders try to make the state machinery compatible with their political designs.

In considering political regimes, two questions should be clarified: (1) What are the criteria for categorizing political regimes as a variable? and (2) How much of the variance in the intrabureaucratic dynamics can be attributed to this variable? To answer the first question, the literature provides a full stock of labels to designate different regimes (i.e., liberal, authoritarian, patrimonialist, socialist, theocratic), but consensus has not been reached. Sometimes, different categories are used to refer to similar cases (i.e., fascism, corporatism, bureaucratic authoritarianism, totalitarianism). In addition, there are problems in constructing typologies that reasonably cover the universe of political regimes. Finally, no category is capable of comprehending the essentially dynamic and changing character of any regime; this has often led to qualifications that attempt to account for a regime's phases or "moments": that is, implantation, tensions, transformation, transitions, "exit."[38]

The second question demands making reasonable assumptions about the proportion of the variance in bureaucratic interdependence that is explained by the nature of the regime or, for that matter, by interactions with clients. The main difficulty here lies in the fact that many of the features these relationships present are – as has already been discussed – culturally or technologically determined. Put differently, interdependence is altered not only by exogenous variables but also by traditions and technical requirements of the relationship itself. In this sense, the intrabureaucratic dynamics would have a logic of its own, independent of the fluctuations and odds of politics. Therefore, it is difficult to establish the "specific weight" of these permanent elements of bureaucracy and to isolate them from those whose variation may be explained by alternative types of political regimes or by the nature of interactions with clients. However, these observations should not preclude further efforts at building typologies and advancing propositions about the way political regimes constrain

[38] On the problems and limitations of concept building in the social sciences, see Oszlak (2001).

bureaucratic dynamics – an exercise I tried several years ago (Oszlak, 1984).

To round out this section, a few final remarks should be added. First, on a closer analysis of the constraints mentioned, it appears that the technological and cultural ones seem to be more strongly related to the performance and productivity of a bureaucracy, whereas clientelistic and political constraints have as a common concern the subject of power. Clearly, technology and culture directly affect the way the production function of bureaucracy is arranged – a central issue when trying to identify the reasons for its low performance. In turn, the concern with power is inherent in its relationship with clients, where bureaucratic capture appears as a main outcome; and in the interactions with the political regime, where the problems of policy orientations and management styles are of central importance. I would pick up this hypothesis, and the next observations, as topics for further research.

Second, if typologies of bureaucracies' management styles (derived from political regimes–bureaucratic dynamics matrices) are to be developed, it should be considered that some features may well be observed in all sorts of regimes. For example, diplomatic personnel tends to behave as a closed stratum with clearly defined hierarchies and high deference to authority, whichever regime is in power. Or a common pattern of resource appropriation and allocation, based on a centralized treasury, has become the current practice of governments facing stringent financial difficulties, regardless of the ideological or political orientations.

A third important point is the increasing homogeneity of countries with widely disparate historic and sociopolitical environments, as a result of widespread diffusion of models and formulas for public sector institutional strengthening promoted by multilateral financial organizations and bilateral cooperation agencies.

Fourth, in those countries with high political instability and frequent changes in the nature of the political regimes, institutional "lags" in the recurrent readaptation process tend to become chronic. Very often, their influence is such that the resulting configurations are mixed, falling quite apart from the "pure" cases suggested by a particular typology.

A fifth point, closely related to the previous one, is that even the characterizations of political regimes should be carefully qualified before comparisons with discrete national experiences are drawn. It can hardly be contended that the democracies established in Latin America, Eastern Europe, Asia, or Africa all belong to the same type. The differences are manifold: degree of consolidation of a party system, remaining influence of the military, relative hegemony of the executive vis-à-vis other powers and political actors, diffusion of prebendalism, political strength of irregular military forces (i.e., narcos or guerrillas), and political weight of the civil service labor unions, among others.

SOME FINAL NOTES

My introductory remarks were intended to provide justification as to why the involvement of public bureaucracies in politics and policy implementation can be adequately captured by a systematic analysis of power and productivity as the main variables. For this purpose, the first section proposed an examination of the historical roots of bureaucracy as one of the main attributes of "stateness" and, in turn, as a component of the broader process of societal building. This analysis revealed why and how a national state originates and develops, its agenda (and contents of issues that await decisions) is formed, public policies (or stands on issues) are formulated, resources are assigned, and institutional arrangements are established for policy implementation. The conclusion was that bureaucracy can be viewed as an outgrowth of public policies inasmuch as it *is* what it *does*.

The second section presented a model that attempted to explain the internal dynamics of bureaucracy in terms of the main analytical dimensions and variables intervening in the processes of resource allocation, particularly the constrains posed by the bureaucracy's normative framework, structural arrangements, and behavioral patterns. Some relevant contextual variables and the way they may impinge on the internal dynamics of bureaucracy were also considered in broad terms. The main purpose of this model was to make tentative propositions about the way the interactions among these variables end up affecting the productivity (i.e., the efficiency and effectiveness) of bureaucracy. One of the main conclusions of this section was that productivity is strongly hindered by incongruence between political and technical rationality in the organization of bureaucracy activity, leading to various manifestations of bureaupathology.

In the third section, the model was developed further by incorporating several aspects related to the power relationships that bureaucratic agencies and units maintain with political actors outside their domain, especially with the incumbent regime. An examination of different sorts of power resources in the hands of bureaucratic agencies and other political actors appeared to provide some clues regarding how each source of power may affect the implementation of public policies. To this effect, it was suggested that bureaucratic activity and performance may be differently affected by technological, cultural, clientelistic, and regime constraints. Each of them was then explored in some detail.

A final dynamic element is the adaptation of state bureaucracies (at the national and subnational levels) to the changes brought about by the processes of decentralization, privatization, and deregulation.

By their very nature, the conflictive behavior patterns within and between bureaucracies and regimes tend to alter formal relations of interdependence presented in my analytic model, without observing any formal rational scheme. Once adopted, they become institutionalized and exist side by side with prescribed behavior. It is this coexistence that introduces an element of permanent contradiction and induces a counterpoint of "formal prescription–adaptive behavior" in which certain patterns of interaction, truly guiding expectations, attitudes and behavior, get settled. To find out and explain these behavioral patterns (i.e., why bureaucracies act the way they do; how do they use power) and to incorporate them as a datum of reality without assuming pathology may lead to processes of policy formulation and implementation perhaps less ambitious, although probably more sensitive to the complexity of the intrabureaucratic dynamics and to the constraints of the political environment. The prospects of institutional development for effective policy implementation largely depend on this increasing awareness.

PART IV

STATE POLICY AND INNOVATIONS

CHAPTER TWENTY-FIVE

Comparative and Historical Studies of Public Policy and the Welfare State

Alexander Hicks and Gøsta Esping-Andersen

The welfare state and sociology grew up in tandem. The cornerstones of the modern welfare state were erected in the late nineteenth century, first in Germany and soon thereafter across most of Western Europe. This was during the same era in which sociology, as an academic discipline, was founded. Such coincidence is hardly accidental. Both evolved out of prevailing controversies on how to address the 'social question'; how to ensure order and consensus in an increasingly individualized, atomized, and seemingly polarizing society; how to respond to the commodification of both needs and labor; and how to manage the changing balance of political power that, predictably, would result from democratization.

The Western welfare states did not evolve uniformly as industrialization and democratization unfolded. Indeed, the beginnings of modern social policy appear to belie any connection at all. The pioneers were autocratic Germany and Austria, and the laggards *par excellence* were the democratic and industrial leaders, such as the United States and Great Britain (Rimlinger, 1971). Furthermore, today's prototypical examples of highly advanced welfare states – the Scandinavian – would, until the 1930s, have appeared comparatively undeveloped. This apparent paradox has stimulated an especially long-standing and intense sociological debate over welfare state development. Certainly, an explanation of the social origins of a phenomenon may not be a good guide to later development. Nonetheless, the very fact that nations, one after the other, eventually converge in adopting and expanding social policies suggests that, yes, there exist common underlying causal forces behind the modern welfare state. These may, as Wilensky (1975) emphasizes, be largely "nonpolitical," namely long-term economic growth, demographic aging, and the emergence of modern bureaucracy. But most political and historical sociologists argue otherwise.

The chief contribution of historical sociology lies in its careful differentiation of the causal logics pertaining to the *epoch* in question. Rimlinger (1971), followed by Flora and Heidenheimer (1981), Alber (1982), Ashford (1986), and Baldwin (1990), show convincingly that the first steps toward social legislation came in conservative, indeed authoritarian, polities bent on perpetuating the reign of absolutism against the double onslaught of laissez-faire liberalism and socialism. In the first phase of welfare state development, what scant democracy marked innovators could not have played a very large role in welfare state emergence (Esping-Andersen, 1990). In such authoritarian states as Bismarck's Reich, fledgling, politically estranged workers' movements and parties might set the stage for autocrats by raising the specter of socialism but could have none but indirect effects on welfare policy (Esping-Andersen, 1990; Hicks, 1999).

This brings us to the second major phase in welfare state development – the so-called Golden Age of Capitalism, spanning the 1940s–1960s. Indeed, this was the era in which the concept of the welfare state was coined (by Gustav Moller in Sweden and Lord Beveridge in Britain) and in which modern democracy became fully institutionalized. The main political protagonists of social reform were now social democratic parties (in Northern Europe and Britain) or Christian Democrats (in Continental Europe).[1] The political sociology of the welfare state has taken its lead not so much from history as from contemporary variations in "welfare stateness," that is, from international differences in comprehensiveness, generosity, or egalitarianism. Its main question is not what drives broad historical or comparative convergence but the opposite: How do we explain the vast differences in the welfare states of today?

WHAT IS THE WELFARE STATE?

The welfare state has, for decades, been a truly controversial topic in the social sciences. Yet, it is not wholly clear that sociologists are always debating the same phenomenon. What do we mean by the "welfare state"? Definitions basically condense into three types. Wilensky (1975) provides one widely shared definition, emphasizing a basic guaranteed social minimum for citizens, or income maintenance. In order to distinguish between welfare states, he simply adopts social expenditure levels (in his words, "welfare effort") as a percent of GDP. Therborn (1983) takes this logic one step further, arguing that a state is only a welfare state if more than half of its outlays are destined to citizens' welfare. A second, unquestionably far more influential, view takes its cues from T. H. Marshall's (1950) theory of social citizenship, by which he means an explicit social contract between government and citizens very analogous to civil and political rights. His basic idea is that citizenship has evolved historically around a progressively expanding sets of entitlements, all interdependent. When, in the seventeenth century, civil rights began to crystallize, it soon became evident that these needed to be safeguarded by effective political rights – hence the eighteenth-century battles for political democracy. Once again, according to Marshall, the conquest of political citizenship soon provoked calls for social rights simply because political rights are only really effective if *all* citizens command adequate economic resources and security. In brief, Marshall sees the welfare state as a centuries-long fruition of the fight for equality of citizenship and rights. In this respect, his theory is a modern echo of Thomas Paine's revolutionary call for "*the rights of man*," which was written (1791) just after the American and French Revolutions.

Marshall's concept of the welfare state has been hugely influential in modern sociology, both because it is historical (albeit faintly teleological) and because it implicitly identifies criteria for judging "welfare stateness." Social rights imply a double negation of the pure market economy. On the one hand, rights imply *decommodification*, that is, a relaxation of the pure commodity status of both labor and goods.[2] Social policy means that individual social risks are recognized as a common responsibility, that citizens' well-being is at least partially made independent of the marketplace, of charity, or of familial support. Welfare guarantees imply that workers need not accept any job at any price. On the other hand, still according to Marshall, social citizenship promotes new *social solidarities*, a more collective social community. If all citizens enjoy identical entitlements, regardless of social class, status, color, or gender, the welfare state de facto reconfigures the prevailing social stratificational order, implanting a modicum of universalism and equality where, otherwise, atomization, individualism, class, or narrow corporate loyalties would prevail.[3] It follows that Marshall's concept of the welfare state is useful both as a guide to interpret the history of social

[1] Roosevelt's New Deal in the United States can be regarded as an American version of European social democracy (Amenta, 1998; Hicks, 1999).

[2] This admittedly awkward concept derives from Karl Polanyi's (1944) classical analysis of the commodification of labor in the rise of capitalism and has been incorporated into sociology by Offe (1984) and Esping-Andersen (1990).

[3] For an extensive discussion of the doubly egalitarian and emancipatory meaning of Marshall's concept, see Esping-Andersen (1990:chap. 1). For a wide-ranging theoretical and empirical study of social citizenship, see Janoski (1998).

policy and to analyze international differences in welfare state goals and accomplishments.

The third type of definition is primarily influenced by the writings of Richard Titmuss (1958, 1974), who was the first to develop a framework for welfare state comparisons. Writing just after World War II, he was already then struck by the noticeable differences in welfare state evolution. At that time Britain, along with the Nordic countries, seemed to be moving toward a very comprehensive idea of the welfare state, emphasizing equal and universally shared rights to all citizens as well as a broad notion of social entitlements. Other countries, the United States in particular, were heading toward a more minimalist, ungenerous, targeted, and market-biased approach to social protection. To capture these differences, he distinguished between the *institutional* and *residual* welfare state models, respectively.

Much recent scholarship has been devoted to the specification of salient welfare dimensions, by and large following the leads of Marshall and Titmuss. Decommodification is one such key dimension, usually measured as the strength of social entitlements and citizens' degree of immunization from market dependency. It should therefore capture levels of benefit generosity, conditions of entitlement, and durations of eligibility (Esping-Andersen, 1990). All told, unconditional benefits with high income replacement rates are potentially more decommodifying. In contrast, if entitlements depend on lengthy contribution records or on means-tests or if they are targeted narrowly to the poor, their potential for decommodification is clearly circumscribed. To exemplify, welfare states like the Scandinavian with universal and free health services, guaranteed income replacement during illness; and Scandinavian unemployment or maternity/paternity benefits are more decommodifying than, say, those of the United States, where neither universal health care nor legislated sickness and maternity benefits even exist – a clear demarcation of its residual character.

A second key dimension has to do with social solidarities. The literature usually distinguishes between three main (and, as presented here, rather stylized) approaches to risk-pooling. One is universalism, particularly stressed in the Nordic countries, in which eligibility and rights are shared equally by all citizens regardless of prior earnings, employment, or other status. A second, prevalent in the United States and other Anglo-Saxon nations, seeks deliberately to limit benefits to the demonstrably needy alone, assuming that the majority can satisfy its welfare needs in the marketplace. A third organizes social protection around occupational status groups in the form of contributory social insurance schemes. This approach is especially diffused among the Continental European nations with their long-standing "corporatist" legacies, distinctions based on social rank and hierarchy, and the strong link between employment record and social entitlements.

The concept of decommodification is premised on the assumption that citizens in market economies are already "commodified." This, as a large feminist literature has argued, is a problematic assumption as far as women are concerned (Orloff, 1993; O'Connor, 1996; Sainsbury, 1994). In order to establish greater gender equality, the major welfare state challenge might simply be to aid women's employment chances and ability to pursue careers – which would call for policies to *commodify*. Indeed, because family obligations traditionally are the main impediment to women's emancipation, policies that help commodify women are simultaneously *defamilializing*, that is, they externalize familial welfare responsibilities, such as care for small children or the elderly. Similarly, many potential workers are separated from the employment relationship due to exclusion, unemployment or handicaps, and here the objective would be to help *re-commodify* citizens. In these terms, we may compare welfare states in terms of their support for working mothers ("women-friendly policy"), their accent on "active labor market policies" (worker retraining, placement, or direct job provision), or, more generally, services aimed at strengthening people's market power (Janoski, 1994; Supiot, 2000).

The sociological conceptualization of welfare states is now dominated by the idea of distinct real-world models, thus rejecting the notion that they can be compared simply along a single linear dimension – such as social spending levels. The *locus* of welfare provision is key to many typologies, mainly because it prefigures the nature of social rights, levels of decommodification, and also models of "solidarity." Welfare state scholars are often myopically focused on government welfare provision, forgetting that markets are normally the principal source of well-being for most citizens throughout most of their lives, and that the family, albeit waning, does remain a principal source of welfare responsibilities. How social welfare provision is allocated between the three pillars is what demarcates any given *welfare regime*.

In this vein, Esping-Andersen (1990, 1999) distinguishes between, first, a "conservative" (mainly Continental European) welfare regime, one that gives primacy to families' responsibility to see after their own. Its "familialistic" bias goes hand-in-hand with a continued adherance to the conventional male-breadwinner model, meaning undeveloped family- and "women-friendly" policy. In addition, this model is largely based on social insurance schemes, typically organized according to narrow corporatist, occupation-based solidarities. A second – "liberal" – regime stands out for its promarket bias and residual definition of government welfare obligations. The Anglo-Saxon countries, with the United States their prototype, exemplify this regime. Its chief characteristics include a limited array of governmental social obligations (for example, the absence of universal health care, family, or maternity benefits in the United States), generally modest social benefit levels, strict criteria for eligibility, a preference for targeting public money very narrowly to the "needy" rather than the citizenry at large, and active encouragement of market solutions (such as stimulating employer-provided occupational- or individual savings plans). A third major regime, epitomized by the long-standing role of social democratic parties in the Nordic countries, promotes Titmuss's idea of the institutional welfare state by defining the scope of public welfare responsibilities extremely broadly, by giving high priority to social equality and redistribution, by actively attempting to secure citizens' welfare "from cradle to grave," and by striving toward broad universalism in coverage and eligibility. Paradoxically, it is in this regime that we find a maximum effort to both decommodify and to "re-commodify" workers: Very powerful income guarantees go hand-in-hand with efforts to facilitate employment for all. The Nordic countries stand out internationally in terms of their commitment to "defamilialize" welfare obligations as a means to further gender equality.

The indicators discussed so far measure public welfare constituent aspects of welfare regimes. Predictably, many of these should correspond to systematic differences in welfare "outcomes," such as rates of income redistribution or poverty reduction. Table 25.1 provides a synthetic comparison of the world's advanced welfare states, utilizing both welfare regime types (which define columns) and elements and outcomes of welfare regimes (in rows). To give a more concrete idea of the main differences, means-tested benefits account for almost 20 percent of all social transfers in the United States, but for only 1 percent in Sweden. Private pension plans account for more than a fifth of total pension spending in the United States, compared to 6 percent in Sweden and a low of 2 percent in Italy (Esping-Andersen, 1990). The Scandinavian welfare states manage to reduce poverty levels by over 40 percent, compared to only 15 percent in the "liberal" cluster (Hicks and Kenworthy, 2003). The most recent data (mid-1990s) show a postredistribution poverty rate for the United States at 19 percent, compared to about 6 percent for Scandinavia and 8–10 percent for Continental Europe (Esping-Andersen, 2002:Table 2.3). Most telling, perhaps, are figures on (re-) commodification, that is, facilitating the employment of all citizens. Recent data show that the share of households with *no* person employed is about 18 percent in the United Kingdom, while less than half that in Denmark (Esping-Andersen, 2002:Table 2.5).

POLITICAL SOCIOLOGICAL ANALYSES OF WELFARE STATES

Sociologists have examined welfare states from two distinct angles. On one side there exists a

Table 25.1. *Welfare State Models and Welfare Policy Indicators*

Regime Elements and Outcomes	Conservative	Regimes Liberal	Social Democratic
Population coverage	occupational	selective	universal
Role of private market for welfare	low	high	low
Target population	(male) employed	the poor	all citizens
Decommodification	medium	low	high
Defamilialization	low	low	high
(Re-)commodification	low	medium	high
Redistribution poverty reduction	low	low	high
Reduction	medium	low	high

Note: Conservative regimes includes Austria, Belgium, France, Germany, Italy, Japan, Portugal, and Spain. The liberal regimes includes Australia, Canada, Ireland, New Zealand, the U.K., and the U.S. The social democratic regime includes the Nordic countries. The Netherlands is the most difficult case to classify, combining universalistic traits and strong redistribution (with low poverty reduction), yet remaining strongly familialistic. Also, Canada deviates from the liberal model (as the UK once did) because of strongly universalistic program coverage – a trait also once prevalent in the U.K.

long tradition of explaining the causes of welfare policy and cross-national welfare state variations. On the other side, there is a vast literature examining how social policies in turn affect social inequalities. The former is primarily interested in establishing the long-term root causes of welfare state development; the latter is primarily concerned with what kinds of outcomes any given welfare model engenders.

The Political Sociology of Welfare States

Inevitably, the welfare state will have major implications for income distribution. Hence, it lies at the heart of the age-old issue of "Who gets what from government?" (Lasswell, 1950; Page, 1983). Not surprisingly, the welfare state has become a major test case for theories of democracy and power. The theoretical origins go back to turn-of-the-century controversies over parliamentary democracy and reform, especially as they were played out in labor movements. On one side, Marxist–Leninists saw parliamentarism as little more than a "talking shop," an unlikely source of democratic popular power. Real power, in this view, lay in the control of private property. On the other side, reformist socialists and liberals believed that progressive parliamentary majorities could effectuate genuine change. Sociological theory, likewise, sees a direct link between political democracy and social citizenship, most famously formulated by T. H. Marshall (1950). As discussed earlier, he saw the modern welfare state as the latest expression of a centuries-long process of democratization that began, in the eighteenth century, with the struggle for civil rights, continued in the nineteenth century with the extension of political citizenship, and progressed in the twentieth century with social citizenship rights. Marshall shied away from pinpointing exactly how such progressive democratization came about. This, however, has been a leading question in postwar political sociology of the welfare state.

In other words, most sociological debate has been about the role of political power in explaining welfare state evolution and variation, especially in the rich and stable democracies. The welfare state emerges as a focal point across the entire array of theoretical perspectives in political sociology, be it in the pluralist tradition (Lipset, 1983 [1961]), in elite theory (Heclo, 1974), in class analytical perspectives (Korpi, 1979, 1982), in the institutionalist tradition (Lowi, 1964), or in gender-centered writings (Orloff, 1996; Skocpol, 1992). The centrality of the welfare state is especially evident in comparative and historical sociology (Bendix and Lipset, 1966; Amenta, Bonastia, and Caren, 2001; Myles and Quadagno, 2002; Green-Pedersen and Haverland, 2002).

The theories that guide the comparative history of welfare states range from the relatively unidimensional to more complex synthetic accounts. In most cases, the welfare state has been characterized either in terms of overall social spending levels or in terms of the emergence, adoption, and evolution of core social protection programs, like pensions or unemployment insurance.

Modernization Theory. One of the single most influential perspectives comes from modernization theory, which, in structural-functionalist terms, stresses the impact of industrialism (Giddens, 1973:217–19). In this theory, new needs for security emerge due to the transition from agriculture to industry, which, in turn, fosters urbanization and the shift from small communities and close personal relations to impersonal exchange. This transition creates imperatives for adaptation (such as social protection), but also the administrative and economic means to do so (Kerr et al., 1964). Wilensky and Lebeaux (1964), Wilensky (1975), and Stinchcombe (1985) represent this theoretical tradition, arguing that the modern welfare state is to be understood in terms of industrialization and economic growth. Because population aging accompanies growth, it is to be expected that pension expenditures (and general expenditures in which pension spending figures large) are strongly correlated with levels of economic development. Empirically, it has been shown that social spending correlates with GDP, levels of industrialization, and demographic variables (Wilensky, 1976; Pampel and Williamson, 1989; Usui, 1991; Williamson and Pampel, 1993; Collier and Messick, 1975). Examining longer historical periods, Hicks (1999) shows that economic development is a necessary (but hardly sufficient) condition for early program adoption. Hicks (1999) also demonstrates that politics – class mobilization in particular – is most crucial for early program consolidation in relatively developed nation-states.

More recently, Wilensky (2002) identifies eight convergent tendencies of rich democracies that he attributes to the broadly common experience of industrialization. These are changes in kinship systems (including declining birthrates and increasing female labor-force participation), improvements in the relative social standing of interest groups, the spread of mass education, the emerging prominence of experts and intellectuals, increasing social mobility, convergence in production systems (from the erstwhile Fordist model toward "flexible specialization"), the adoption of a set of core social programs (such as old-age pensions, unemployment protection, and health care), and a fall in civil violence (Wilensky, 2002:70–3).

Marxism represents a second, long-standing developmental theory, albeit one of "modes of productions" rather than society, and, within Marxists' currently dominant mode of production, of capitalist society rather than industrial (and postindustrial) society, and, finally, of "capital accumulation" rather than economic development. Stressing structural constraints built into capitalist economies, Block (1977) argues that the limits of possible reform are overdetermined by a tacit understanding among political actors that the capitalist economic structure cannot be transgressed. Hence, reform becomes limited to a narrow repertoire of policy that is consistent with the reproduction of the system. Quadagno (1988) has applied this perspective to the empirical case of New Deal social-security pension legislation.

Ruling Class Theory. Some studies stress the direct causal force of capitalist actors in public policy making. Domhoff (1970), Quadagno (1984), and Jenkins and Brents (1989, 1991) all argue that capitalist agenda setting prefigures social policy agendas and, through them, policies. Yet, Skocpol and Amenta (1985) and Amenta and Parihk (1991) argue that the case for capitalist determination of New Deal policy flies in the face of observable and decisive capitalist opposition. Swenson (1997) presents a more hedged argument, suggesting that key capitalist representatives appeared dominant in New Deal reforms primarily because they had been incorporated into policy making by New Deal politicians. That is, he builds a case for the structural power of capitalists in policy reform by identifying the micromechanisms at play in the process of accommodating powerful potential resistance. However, in a comparison including Swedish postwar welfare policy, Swenson, (2002) argues that leading capitalists here played a more direct and active role. This is contested by Huber and Stephens (2001), who argue that his case confuses strategic accommodation with an underlying opposition to extant policy. Swenson does not generalize the argument to welfare states in general, but quantitative comparisons by Swank and Martin (2001) provide some evidence for prowelfarist effects of organized business communities.

Pulling these studies together, the evidence suggests that welfare state development may be merely limited, or even promoted, by a politically organized business community. However, further investigation seems mandated by the contrary view of business and welfare policy that emerges from Huber and Stephens (2001) and other studies that link business interests to anti-welfare secular centrist and conservative parties (Huber, Ragin, and Stephens, 1993; Castles, 1998). According to Hacker and Pierson (2002), any strong conclusions are made difficult by such basic theoretical and methodological problems as a failure to distinguish and investigate multiple mechanisms of exercising influence, a failure to distinguish between business power in systems more or less open to unfettered capital flight, a misspecification of class preferences, and the inference of influence from *ex post* correlation between actor preferences and outcomes. According to these authors, once one corrects for these deficiencies, neither business dominance nor weakness appears clear-cut. Instead, marked variation in business influence over time and across institutional settings emerges.

Class Mobilization Theory. To the extent that welfare states imply more equality and social security, one would expect that working class movements and Left parties have played a major role in their rise and development. In fact, the "Left party" or "working class mobilization" thesis has come to dominate the political sociological debate. Its theoretical underpinnings are closely associated with the work of Korpi (1982), in particular with his notion of resource mobilization as the key to effective power. Basic to his argument is the inherent asymmetry in power that comes from capitalists' control of the means of production. But, Korpi argues, this asymmetry can be rectified to the extent that wage earners are capable of translating their numerical majorities into de facto power. To Korpi, this primarily depends on a simultaneous process of electoral and associational mobilization and of worker political unitification. His argument helps identify the more precise mechanisms that may or may not produce strong correlations between Left party rule and welfare state development.

Studies of the role of Left party influence provide only scattered and unsystematic evidence for the period up to World War II (Rimlinger, 1971; Luebbert, 1990; Hicks, 1999). As previously mentioned, the early phase of social policy development was mainly one of predemocratic, authoritarian rule. We must also recall the extreme rarity of any stable Left government prior to the Great Depression 1930s – indeed, the rarity of sustained Left rule outside of Scandinavia and the antipodes before the 1950s (Mackie and Rose, 1982; Flora, 1983; Hicks, 1999). Still, Hicks (1999) provides some evidence of more indirect effects through pre-Depression worker mobilization into trade unions and in electoral action; and occasional participation in governments seems also to have yielded prowelfare effects. His study documents a strong correlation between the consolidation of all major social programs in the 1950s and strong interwar and immediate postwar unionization rates.

Evidence for the *entire* postwar era is far more extensive, although not unambiguous. Some, like Castles and McKinlay (1978), Korpi (1982), Huber, Ragin, and Stephens (1993), Huber and Stephens (2001), and, to an extent, Franzese (2002), find support for a Left-support/Right-opposition interpretation of welfare state development, but other studies find only spotty evidence, or no evidence at all (Pampel and Williamson, 1989; Hicks, 1999; Iversen, 2001; Swank, 2002; Williamson and Pampel, 1993). The correlations appear to be period-sensitive. When we limit our perspective to the 1960s and early 1970, evidence in favor of a Left-effect seems quite strong (Hewitt, 1977; Cameron, 1978; Stephens, 1979; Korpi, 1982; Swank, 1988; Esping-Andersen, 1990; Huber, Ragin, and Stephens, 1993; Castles, 1999; Huber and Stephens, 2001:chap. 6), and this effect may extend into the early 1980s (Huber and Stephens, 2001:chap. 6). By the late 1980s and 1990s, however, one tends to see an erosion of consistent Left–Right partisan differences. Perhaps this erosion pertains because Left governments began to embark on (usually limited) welfare retrenchment. Perhaps it is an artifact of strong post-World War II leftist reform (Hicks, 1999) or the result of a statistically misconceived focus on levels of, rather than changes in, welfare policy (Kwon and Pontusson, 2002) and poor specification of time lags. In any case, there is no doubt that recent recalibrations of welfare state programs that define comparative welfare regimes reflect the pattern of ideological dominance with far more radical retrenchment and privatization occurring in "liberal" welfare states, such as the United Kingdom and New Zealand. In contrast, there has been very little in the way of free-market reform in the "conservative" continental welfare states (Scharpf and Schmidt, 2000; Pierson, 2001). Interestingly, the configuration of regime ideology and welfare reform in this age of "retrenchment" appears to situate social democrats, cautious rationalizers of the welfare state, in the center of a continuum anchored by liberal "reformers" at one pole and conservative guardians of the old welfarist order at the other pole.

Unionization represents an important complementary dimension within the class analytical interpretation – particularly in terms of neocorporatist policy making (which reflects degree of union bargaining coordination and confederational centralization and monopoly). Stephens (1979) and Hicks (1999:chaps. 2, 4) find strong cross-sectional correlations between social spending and prior union strength. Although temporally sensitive evidence that union density accounts for welfare effort is less than definitive, there is ample evidence that neocorporatism promotes welfare spending, both in simple cross-sectional models (e.g., Stephens, 1979; Korpi, 1982; Cameron, 1984; Swank, 1988; Lijphart, 1999). Moreover, a number of more complex and temporally sensitive models offer evidence of positive neocorporatist effects on welfare policy. (Lijphart and Crepaz, 1991; Crepaz and Lijphart, 1992; Hicks, 1999; Swank, 2002). Moreover, though the neocorporatist–welfare nexus appears quite robust in a range of studies that simultaneously estimate effects of Left partisanship (Hicks and Swank, 1992; Hicks, 1999; Swank, 2002), definitively gauging the balance of Left party and neocorporatist findings is hampered by multicolinearity between measures of neocorporatism and Left party power (Huber and Stephens, 2001; Hicks, 2002).

It has also been suggested that less institutional forms of mobilization, such as strikes and protests, might put pressure on the political system to promote social welfare. This has been argued with reference to movements of the poor (Piven and Cloward, 1971) and also of workers (Korpi, 1982; Huber, Ragin, and Stephens, 1993). This line of argument has lost centrality in the comparative literature, but retains some importance in studies of particular nations and periods (Isaac and Kelly, 1981; Fording, 2001). In fact, comparative studies have produced only inconsistent support for the thesis.

Most of the studies we have reviewed so far have focused mainly on social insurance programs and, in particular, on social insurance spending shares of GDP. Some studies have attempted to disaggregate the welfare state in order to arrive at more fine-grained measures of welfare effort and outcomes, including, for example, indicators of the strength of entitlements, the universality of coverage, and degrees of income redistribution or poverty reduction. Indeed, there are good reasons for this because overall spending levels may prove to be ambiguous measures of a welfare state. To give two examples: One, some countries (e.g., Austria) spend a very large amount on benefits to privileged civil servants, and this will naturally weigh substantially in overall spending data; two, heavy spending levels do not necessarily capture welfare effort and can even represent a poorly functioning welfare state, unable to stem a tide of social problems (especially, but not solely, unemployment). The latter problem is amply illustrated by the Thatcher era in Britain, when spending continued to rise notwithstanding deliberate efforts to weaken the social safety net: Spending rose because social problems rose.

A number of studies suggest that such disaggregated specifications of the welfare state give added support for the class mobilization thesis, in particular for the impact of Left party or trade union power. Examples include analyses of the generosity and universalism of pension, unemployment, and sickness insurance (Palme, 1990; Kangas, 1991; Esping-Andersen, 1990; Carroll, 1994).

As regards recommodification or public enhancement of workers' employability, Janoski's (1992) study of active labor market policy (or ALMP) in Germany, the United States, and Sweden found evidence for a strong association between the strength of social democratic parties and the share of ALMP spending in GNP, a finding replicated by Hicks and Kenworthy (1998). There is similarly evidence that the enhancement of female employment levels is positively related to social democratic power, while negatively related to Christian Democratic rule (Hicks and Kenworthy, 2003).

Studies of income redistribution tend to provide quite strong support for a Left power hypothesis, but also for the salience of labor unions and neocorporatism (Von Arnheim, Corina, and Schotsman, 1982; Hicks and Swank, 1984; Bradley, Huber, Moller, Nielsen, and Stephens, 2003; Moller, Bradley, Huber, Nielsen, and Stephens 2003; Hicks and Kenworthy, 2003). Studies of the taxation side of redistribution (such as tax progressivity) are few and far between (but see Alt, 1983; Campbell and Allen, 2001; Myles and Pierson, 1997; Kenworthy and Pontusson, 2002; Swank and Steinmo, 2002).

Although studies that adopt aggregated and more differentiated welfare state measures often conclude in favor of a Left power theory, the debate remains far from settled. Comparative analyses are hampered by limited sample sizes and pervasive colinearity between variables. Hence, they have so far fallen short of definitively adjudicating among competing class-linked (and nonclass) explanations.

State-Centered Approaches. Many authors trace welfare state development to the workings of the state itself, emphasizing the self-interested propensities of state personnel, the centrality of public bureaucracies in framing the political agenda and in driving policy development and implementation, as well as the state's historical role in the process of nation building.

The latter is, indeed, a key theme in studies of early welfare development, and many studies emphasize how central states, often controlled by aristocratic and monarchical elites, adopted social policy for the purpose of stabilizing or aggrandizing absolutist rule (Rimlinger, 1971; Flora and Alber, 1983). Many studies have also emphasized the key role that public bureaucracies have played in the policy-making process. Heclo's (1974) comparison of postwar social reform in Britain and Sweden stands as a landmark study within this tradition of early welfare policy innovations. Overall, there exists a rather broad and diverse specification of what exactly are the mechanisms at work as bureaucracy shapes policy. Some studies stress the state personnel's capacity for sophisticated diagnoses and prescriptions for social problems (Weir and Skocpol 1985); others, the role of administrative precedents and policy legacies (Skocpol, 1985; Ashford, 1986); and still others point to the central state's role in reforming clientelistic and patronage systems (Orloff and Skocpol, 1984).

Another group of studies put the emphasis on constitutional structures, such as the existence of majoritarian parliamentary government (Lijphart, 1984); the degree of centralization of policy administration (Hage, Gargan, and Hanneman 1989; Amenta and Carruthers, 1989); or the degree of federalism as opposed to centralized, unitary statehood (Lijphart, 1984; Hage, Gargan, and Hanneman, 1989; Hicks and Swank, 1992; Mann, 1993). Huber, Ragin, and Stephens (1993) have, additionally, emphasized how constitutional structures with many inbuilt veto points may help obstruct social spending and reform. They suggest that federal (as opposed to unitary) systems disadvantage working class movements (see also Dahl, 1982; Lijphart, 1984, 1999; Immergut, 1989; Skocpol, 1992). A somewhat similar impediment to welfare state growth has been traced to bicameral legislatures (with twice the legislative hurdles) and presidential systems. A major problem with this literature is the unclear causal connection between, say, federalism and inequality. It may, as most studies assume, be that federalist polities produce greater interregional inequalities. But it may also be that it is regional inequalities which, in the first place, spur political decentralization. It is not unlikely that the entire process is endogenous, as Alvarez-Beramendi (2003) shows.

Pluralist Theory. Pluralist (and neopluralist) theory, as the name suggests, assumes that politics and power derive from a plurality of sources, be they cultural (e.g., ethnic, religious, regional, linguistic) as well as "classes" (Lijphart, 1984), or more narrowly defined economic interests and associations (Dahl, 1982; Williamson and Pampel, 1993).

Because this tradition is open-ended as far as cause is concerned, its empirical emphasis is oriented toward the preferences of political actors in very specific settings (Alford and Friedland, 1985:22). It does not assume that there exists – as the class analytical tradition often does – a set of inherent and relatively impermeable collective interests that drive social history.

Pampel and Williamson's (1989) work represented a revival of the pluralist tradition in welfare state research. In it they highlighted the political importance of citizen groups with vested interests in welfare programs, such as retirees. Such groups act as organized voting blocks and, predictably, as their numbers swell so does their lobbying power – hence the seminal rise in pension benefits, and hence the difficulties of reforming pension systems. The evidence in favor of this argument is quite strong, especially in terms of explaining social benefit generosity and growth (Pierson, 1994, 1996; Huber and Stephens, 2001).

Different versions of pluralist theory emerge in the literature that stresses the multiple ideological and political roots of welfare state growth. Many studies show, for example, that centrist – and especially Christian Democratic – governments are as likely as Left governments to promote social spending (Castles and McKinlay, 1978; Pampel and Williamson, 1985, 1989; Esping-Andersen, 1990; Hicks and Misra, 1993; Huber, Ragin, and Stephens, 1993; Ragin, 1993b). Indeed, many heavy-spending welfare states were primarily developed by either liberals or by multiclass-based Christian Democratic movements, in particular in the Netherlands and in Southern Europe (Van Kersbergen, 1995; Berghman, Peters, and Vranken, 1987; Roebroek and Berben, 1987; Baldwin, 1990; Huber, Ragin, and Stephens, 1993).

Basic to the pluralist view is the idea that the political agenda is set by groups able to wield "swing votes," by the lobbying activities of interest organizations more generally, and by the routine administration of statutorily encoded entitlements (Pampel and Williamson, 1989; Franzese, 2002). It has also been argued that newly mobilized voters (disproportionately low status and prowelfarist) tend to augment welfare outlays (Dye, 1979; Pampel and Williamson, 1989; Mahler, 2001).

Welfare "Regimes." The literature we have reviewed so far typically is focused exclusively on the welfare *state* and its programs or expenditure commitments. The concept of welfare regimes seeks, on the other hand, to specify the welfare state's relative position within the broader welfare mix – in particular in relation to market and family provision of welfare (Esping-Andersen, 1990, 1999).

Although theoretical development remains unsystematic, there has been a visible growth in the application of the regime concept within comparative research. Comparatively speaking, there is strong evidence that advanced democracies cluster around three (or arguably four) basic welfare regime models. Indeed, these end up pretty much identical to the distinct welfare state models discussed above. Considering the qualitatively different constellation of welfare provision that characterizes the "social democratic," "liberal," and "conservative" regimes, it also easily follows that we may require a different set of explanations to account for each. Put differently, the long historical process that has resulted in apparently orthogonal welfare models, most likely, is not computable with one common explanation. As a matter of fact, the very labels that describe the different regimes were deliberately chosen so as to highlight what, in each model, appeared to be the dominant political impulse – and explantory root. Hence, in Esping-Andersen's (1990) analyses, the Continental European welfare regime is largely the historical product of strong absolutist legacies combined with a dominance of Christian Democratic rule in the postwar democratic era. In turn, the "social democratic" regime arose primarily out of a long and sustained rule by social democratic parties, combined with an unusually unified and powerful trade union movement. Of particular importance here has been the chronic weakness of the political right (Castles, 1978). The "liberal" regime, finally, represents countries in which neither labor movements nor predemocratic conservative forces ever managed to hold sway, thus ensuring a lasting dominance of liberal (if often "reform-liberal") policy. This dominance has been additionally advantaged by the absence of strong and unified trade union movements (except, perhaps, in the cases of Australia and, for a time, New Zealand.[4]

There has also evolved a fairly voluminous literature that examines the second-order policy consequences within specific welfare regimes (Scharpf, 1999; Scharpf and Schmidt, 2000; Pierson, 2001; Huber and Stephens, 2001, Swank, 2002; Pontusson, 2003). Pierson's (1994, 2001) work, for example, has highlighted how specific regimes, once consolidated, produce unique policy path dependencies that, in turn, overdetermine solutions to new problems as well as strategies of welfare reform. Scharpf (1999) and Scharpf and Schmidt (2000) have investigated how emerging new employment and welfare trade-offs take very different forms depending on the characteristics of a nation's welfare regime.

Yet another literature has emerged that stresses a more dichotomous conception of international political economies. For example, Iversen (1999) and Hall and Soskice (2000) identify two distinct "production regimes," and Hicks (1999) suggests a bimodal distribution of nations in terms of neocorporatist policy making. Much of this work draws directly on Esping-Andersen's analyses of regimes. Linking the concept of production and welfare regimes, De Beer, Vrooman, and Schut (2001) suggest that differences in welfare state perfomance are well captured by a simpler welfare regime dichotomy that coincides with a social and liberal production regime, and simultaneously with neocorporatist policy making.

Evidence in favor of a simpler two-regimes view comes also from Hicks and Kenworthy (2003), who stress welfare dimensions rather than regime categories. They argue that a dimension arraying welfare states along a continuum ranging from "social democratic" to "liberal" better explains redistributive and labor market policy outcomes than does Esping-Andersen's three-regime classification.

There is one final point that needs to be stressed. Because the literature is dominated by cross-sectional comparisons at one point (or within one period) in history, welfare state (or regime) classifications tend to become ahistorical and may very easily miss out on important shifts and historical volatility. As Hicks (1999) argues, the basic logic of social policy within one regime may change character from one era to another. Similarly, countries that once formed part of one type of regime may end up very differently as time passes. As we noted earlier, Britain stands as an epitomy of "regime shifting," starting out in the postwar era as strongly "social democratic" in terms of its universalistic ideals of social citizenship, only to end up as a nearly prototypical example of "liberalism" as privatization accelerated and as universal rights

[4] For additional (and often critical) assessments of the political roots of welfare regimes, see Castles (1993), Huber and Stephens (2001), Swank (2002), and Hicks and Kenworthy (2003). There has been substantial controversy about the precise number of distinct welfare regimes. Castles (1993) argues that the antipodean countries, Australia in particular, simply do not fit. Ferrera (1996) insists that Southern Europe constitutes a distinct "fourth" welfare regime, in particular due to pervasive clientelism and a very incomplete welfare state.

eventually were transformed into targeted assistance programs.[5]

THE SOCIAL STRATIFICATION OF WELFARE

Welfare state policies affect social inequalities and therefore also the overall system of social stratification. Child allowances diminish economic inequalities among families; mass education has been promoted as a vehicle for eliminating inherited class privilege; maternity leave and child care are meant to equalize gender relations.

Sociological analysis has always combined its interest in isolating the causes of welfare state evolution with a focus on whether, indeed, welfare states "make a difference." To sociologists this is primarily a question of distributional results, of inequalities.

Until the postwar years, the main issue had to do with the social class divide. There is substantial disagreement as to how welfare states affect class inequalities. Orthodox Marxists have always claimed that the welfare state, despite appearing to level inequalities is, in practice, designed to reproduce class domination (Muller and Neususs, 1973; O'Connor, 1973). But most sociologists favor the view that social policy is genuinely instrumental in diminishing class differences. As a hypothesis, this idea dates back to early social democratic thought. Eduard Heimann (1929), a major exponent of reformist socialism in the Weimar Republic, believed that social reforms push the frontiers of the socialist ideal forward even if such reforms are implemented with other motives in mind. Similarly, the first Swedish socialist government in the 1930s was firmly convinced that social policy is a first step toward a more classless and egalitarian society. Such views found their way into mainstream postwar sociological theory. T. H. Marshall (1950) saw the postwar welfare state as the bearer of the social citizenship ideal that, to him, implied a frontal attack on the class divide. Lipset (1960) went even further, arguing that economic prosperity, coupled to social reform, transformed the "workers' question" into a democratic class struggle – by which he meant a society in which class perhaps remained a lingering source of collective identification but of little else, since such important correlates of class as poverty, insecurity, or unequal life chances had been eradicated sufficiently to diffuse revolutionary class conflict.

Recent research in social stratification suggests that such optimism was exaggerated. Studies of comparative class mobility as well as educational attainment show consistently that the opportunity structure has not become more equal, that social origins matter as much today as they did in the past (Eriksson and Goldthorpe, 1992; Shavit and Blossfeld, 1993; Solon, 1999). This may seem surprising considering the massive postwar expansion and democratization of education systems everywhere. The chief explanation is that formal education by and large replicates prevailing social inequalities, despite greater seeming equality of access to educational resources than to economic and social rewards. Hence, the mechanisms of class inheritance must lie elsewhere. But where? One important clue comes from the consistent finding that Sweden (with Denmark and possibly the Netherlands) *does* exhibit a decline of social inheritance effects among the young cohorts. Eriksson and Goldthorpe (1992) as well as Shavit and Blossfeld (1993) speculate that this may be explained by Sweden's extraordinarily egalitarian welfare state, in particular its effective abolition of child poverty. Because Denmark and the Netherlands also stand out internationally

[5] Large, principally descriptive literatures on the welfare state in less developed nations, newly industrializing nations, and the welfare states of these nations are bypassed here. These literatures are too extensive for brief inclusion, too emergent at this moment on Web sites around the world for timely treatment right now. However, it is important to note that Williamson and Pampel (1992) provide an excellent entree to the literature on former British colonies in South Africa and Asia, Mesa-Lago (1978) provides a necessary introduction to Latin American welfare states, whereas Brown and Hunter (1999) and Kaufman and Segura-Ubiergo (2001) document the emerging analytical sophistication of this Latin American literature around the millennium. On Asian and post-Soviet welfare states, the reader is referred to Aspalter (2002), Deacon (2000), Lipsmeyer (2000), and Ost (2000).

in terms of very little child poverty, the causal link appears credible. But there is an alternative welfare state-based explanation, namely that the equalization of opportunities is primarily the result of universal, high-grade day care for preschool children. This arguably helps equalize cognitive abilities, especially to the benefit of those children who come from disadvantaged families (Esping-Andersen, 2004).

During the 1960s, social scientists were on the forefront in discovering the "new poverty" (Harrington, 1962; Fermen, 1965). They pointed to what appeared as a fundamental paradox: The welfare state had grown immensely and, yet, widespread poverty remained. This provoked a major sociological reassessment of the link between social policy and the quest for equality, and in hindsight we can see a major redirection of social scientific research as a result. The "class question" faded into the background and questions of persistent poverty and unequal life chances came to the fore. In the United States, Lyndon Johnson's War on Poverty was very much inspired by social scientists such as Moynihan and economists associated with the Institute for Poverty Research in Wisconsin. In Europe, likewise, there emerged a new breed of social scientists closely linked to social democratic renewal, such as Walter Korpi (1979) in Sweden or Peter Townsend (1979) in the United Kingdom, all attempting to understand why ostensibly mature welfare states failed miserably to eradicate the most simple and evident expression of inequality, namely abject poverty.

As it happened, postwar economic growth and full employment, coupled with a major upgrading of social benefits and coverage, did eventually bring down poverty rates in all advanced countries – especially among the elderly (Atkinson et al., 1994; Kenworthy, 1999; Kenworthy and Pontusson, 2002). Nevertheless, comparative research on income redistribution and poverty shows quite consistently that international variations remain enormous. For example, although pretax and redistribution income inequality or poverty rates are quite similar in North America and Scandinavia, the redistributive impact of the Nordic welfare states is far greater than the North American, resulting in final levels of both inequality of disposable income and of poverty that are each about half of those in the United States (Smeeding et al., 1990; Gottschalk and Smeeding, 1997).

Why exactly this is the case is the source of some controversy. The first, and most obvious argument, is that less generous and comprehensive welfare states leave large welfare gaps unmet. Thus, the absence of family benefits and universal health care in the United States is frequently cited as a major reason for very high poverty rates, especially in families with children. Second, all else being equal, one would have assumed that a more targeted approach to poverty, as in the United States or Britain, would be far more redistributive than a universal approach with equal benefits more or less across-the-board, as in Scandinavia. However, this is not the case. One answer lies in what Korpi and Palme (1999) call the "paradox of redistribution." The argument is that welfare states which target benefits heavily to the poor enjoy scant public support and, hence, the result is meager benefits. In contrast, universalistic programs gain universal support and as a consequence benefits are far more generous across-the-board. This, they argue, is a more effective strategy for eliminating poverty. A third answer is that the real mechanism of poverty elimination lies not so much in public transfer payments to households, but more in securing that men *and* women have well-paid and stable employment. Mothers' employment is, for example, the single most effective assurance against child poverty (Esping-Andersen, 2002). Put differently, we would do well in broadening our analytical lens to the interplay between social and employment policies when we analyze welfare states' impact on inequalities. We might also do well in the wake of the Clinton-era contraction in welfare entitlements in the United States and New Zealand and the Bush-era increases in unemployment to look to refining the analytical lenses with which we address the political forces behind income security and jobs policy (for example, Huber and Stephens, 2001; Swank and Georg-Betz, 2003; Hicks, 2003).

Research on welfare states and social stratification has recently moved in three new directions, in particular focusing on gender inequalities, the new social exclusion, and, more generally, on the nexus between social protection and employment. Early feminist writings, such as Pateman (1989) and Hernes (1987), argued that the welfare state institutionally reproduces patriarchy in the public realm. As Hernes saw it, women's dependency on men undoubtedly declines as women also acquire individual social entitlements, but this merely implies a shift in the locus of dependency toward the state. To feminist scholars, decommodification through social policy might apply to men, but not to most women whose integration in the wage relationship was marginal or non-existent – women were traditionally "precommodified." The chief question had come to do with the conditions under which welfare states actively helped women become "commodified" and economically sovereign, at which stage social policy would then "decommodify" women and men on a parity basis (Orloff, 1993; O'Connor, 1996). In the past years, we have seen a cumulation of research on gender, family, and labor market policy (Wilensky, 1990; Wennemo, 1992, 1993; Sainsbury, 1994, 1996; Lewis, 1994; Oppenheimer and Jensen, 1995; Misra, 2003, 1996; O'Connor, 1996; Gornick, Meyers, and Ross, 1997; O'Connor et al., 1999; Misra, 2003; Huber, Stephens Bradley, and Moller, Nielsen, 2001). The literature demonstrates how welfare policy, in particular parental leave schemes and daycare provision, is key to women's economic independence.

There has evolved a large literature on how different welfare states promote "women-friendly" policy, in particular with regard to programs that reduce or eliminate the incompatibilities between motherhood and careers. Put differently, the issue became to what extent welfare states actively "defamilialize" welfare responsibilities (Saraceno, 1997; Esping-Andersen, 1999). Logically, research also examines how social policies might help to create more gender equality in the distribution of both paid and unpaid domestic work. Comparatively speaking, this research suggests that the most gender egalitarian welfare states – the Nordic countries, with Belgium and France – are those in which the traditional emphasis on income maintenance has been replaced by a greater concern for servicing families (Gornick et al., 1997; Sainsbury, 1994, 1996). The evidence also points to a major second-order effect of gender egalitarian social policy, namely that the creation of labor-intensive public social services jobs engenders occupational segregation. Hence, the irony is that purportedly egalitarian policy helps reinforce gender-segregated employment (Esping-Andersen, 2002).

The debate on social exclusion derives from two concomitant structural trends in advanced societies. On one side, labor markets are giving rise to new "atypical" employment forms that, coupled to rising wage disparities, seem to create a "two-speed" society in which a growing proportion of workers are relegated to precarious and low-paid jobs that, additionally, do not permit adequate accumulation of social entitlements. This trend is further reinforced at the household level, where one detects a potential polarization between "work-rich" and "work-poor" households. On the other side, technological change is driving up skill requirements and this is especially to the detriment of less skilled workers. In a sense, the "ante" for good life chances is rising. All this implies that research needs to change its focus from its erstwhile rather static "snapshot" view of equality (how many poor are there at any given moment) to life chances and welfare *dynamics*.

Over the past decade we saw a spectacular growth in research on how welfare states affect long-term dynamics, such as entrapment in poverty and exclusion (Gottschalk, 1997; Duncan and Brooks-Gunn, 1997; Goodin et al., 1999). As regards the state and poverty reduction, one chief finding is that durations of poverty, low pay, and exclusion (such as unemployment) seem to be powerfully correlated with poverty levels. That is, countries where poverty or exclusion is widespread tend also to be those where long-term entrapment is more likely (Gottschalk et al., 1997). Put differently, welfare states like the Scandinavian not only boast low overall levels of poverty but, simultaneously, also pose few risks of entrapment. Gottschalk's (1997) data suggest that the incidence of long-term entrapment is five times higher in the United States than in European countries. This has profound implications for how we understand inequality. If most citizens' experience of poverty is short-lived (relieved by upward mobility), the experience of poverty is unlikely to be harmful for overall life chances. Long-term entrapment, however, is much more likely to have negative repercussions throughout life. The long-term effects of poverty and welfare deficiencies have also been documented in recent research on child poverty. Duncan and Brooks-Gunn (1997), for example, show that poverty in early childhood leads to substantially less schooling, higher dropout risks, lower earnings in adulthood, and, worst of all, to high risks of reproducing the poverty syndrome once they form families. Herein lies most probably a key mechanism that helps explain a curious finding from comparative educational stratification research. In the most authoritative study so far, Shavit and Blossfeld (1993) find that the impact of class inheritance on children's educational attainment remains as strong as always in Western countries, *except* in Sweden (and possibly also Denmark and the Netherlands), where one identifies a noticeable weakening of the social origins effect. The explanation given is that Sweden's welfare state has been doubly effective in equalizing the social conditions of childhood: first by virtually eliminating poverty in families with children, thus strengthening parental resources; second by universalizing early child care provision, thereby helping to compensate for unequal cognitive and cultural resources among families of different class position (Erikson and Jonsson, 1996). Danziger and Gottschalk (1997) provide a rich review of related issues in the United States.

The literature on poverty reduction points to what may be the single most crucial stratification dimension of social policy, namely the extent to which welfare states can indeed help create genuinely more equal life chances and bridge the traditional class divide. If one were to sum up what we so far know from comparative research, the answer would be a cautious yes, it is possible, but certainly far less than early welfare state theorists (and social democratic reformers) optimistically believed. The key conditions that emerge from the literature would seem to include an effective eradication of income poverty, especially in families with children, the employment of mothers (which implies a comprehensive, service-intensive welfare state), and, more generally, low unemployment.

Also, the debate on social exclusion and employment trends has increasingly been linked to second-order welfare state effects. Esping–Andersen (1990:part II) and also Kohli et al. (1991) show that welfare policy became central in the management of deindustrialization and mass unemployment after the 1970s. For example, the Nordic countries' expansion of social services generated a female-driven growth of the service economy and overall employment levels, whereas the Continental European welfare states reinforced a low-employment equilibrium by utilizing early retirement as a vehicle for clearing labor markets.

Similarly, Iversen (1999), as well as Scharpf (1998) and Scharpf and Schmidt (2001), have emphasized the dysfunctional aspects of social insurance financing (associated with heavy contributory burdens on employers) and of overly generous pension benefits in terms of promoting high unemployment and of limiting governments' financial ability to expand public services. There is also a growing literature on how public labor market regulation interacts with social policy to produce divergent employment and wage outcomes (Traxler, 1996; Traxler and Kittle, 1999; Traxler, Blaschke, and Kittle, 2001; Esping-Andersen and Regini, 2001; Streeck, 1992). Indeed, one very important insight is that employment regulation and social security policy are often rival alternatives to the same underlying problems, namely worker insecurity. Broadly speaking, the Nordic countries (with the Netherlands) have favored fairly unregulated labor markets while placing security guarantees within the welfare state. In contrast, countries like France, Germany, and Italy stand out in terms of highly regulated ("rigid") labor markets, primarily intended to safeguard the earnings and jobs of the prime age male breadwinner.

CONCLUSIONS

If we view the comparative political sociology of welfare states in historical-analytical terms, a number of principal empirical conclusions stand out quite sharply. One is that different historical epochs were guided by different sociopolitical actors. It is, for example, evident that early social reform was primarily guided by conservative actors, however varied the forces pressuring their action. Likewise, it is largely after World War II – entirely after the onset of the Great Depression – that working class movements emerged as central and decisive players. But it would be erroneous to view postwar welfare state development as a simple contest between "labor" and "capital" or between Left and Right. In many countries, the leading impulse behind social reform has been Christian Democratic parties (and their associated unions). What the comparative "welfare regime" literature informs us is that social democratic and Christian movements are far from simple functional equivalents. Welfare states ends up being qualitatively different, depending on which kind of political force has spearheaded social reform.

If we move from a broad sweep of welfare state history toward a more fine-grained examination of specific periods, the causal logic seems also to change. During the 1930s and 1940s, welfare state development was hardly a pervasive outcome of Left governments, but the ascendance of these along with labor movements and worker protests did pressure upgrades of welfare states during these decades and made worker mobilization a force to be reckoned with. The importance of Left rule becomes even more evident when we turn to the post-World War II "golden age." Yet, in this epoch new causal forces undeniably gained importance, chief among them demographic change, but also the rise of neocorporatist systems of interest intermediation in some countries. Again, we should also be cautious not to exaggerate the postwar influence of Left parties, considering that Christian Democratic movements have been key in a large number of countries. We should also be very cautious not to adopt a too one-dimensional causal interpretation of welfare state growth. Political actors (of all colors) promoted policy under constraints and in nation-specific institutional contexts. Thus, the impact of political parties is conditioned by government and constitutional structures. For example, what is feasible for Left governments in a unified state may not be so in a federal system.

Many also believe that globalization is changing the conditions for welfare state policy, particularly in terms of putting downward pressures on social spending and taxing. Although systematic research on such effects is still nascent, the belief seems to enjoy rather limited empirical support (Garrett, and Mitchell, 2001). Indeed, there is evidence to the contrary, namely that the heightened risks of the new economy find response in terms of augmented social spending as welfare states strive to indemnify and recompense increasingly vulnerable populations (Rodrik, 1997, 1998; Garrett, 1998a, 1998b). However, there is also evidence that welfare states have begun to restrict entitlements and reduce benefit generosity, although so far at the margins (Pierson, 2001; Huber and Stephens, 2001; Swank, 2002). Whether changes in spending and generosity are driven by globalization, or by other parallel forces such as population aging, remains unclear. It may be that we are entering a new epoch in which, once again, the causal connections between politics and welfare policy are being rewritten. If we are, we are unlikely to know so for years or perhaps even decades. As the title of this chapter itself suggests, the comparative, *historical* political sociology of welfare states can only arrive at firm causal inferences by examining data out of the historical past. What we can continue to count on is that the welfare state shall persist for some time as a major nexus in the determination of "Who gets what from government?" and, thus, as a major focus in the politics of social stratification, especially of stratification by the state. We can also expect that welfare states will remain key sites of conflicts over social citizenship, over who has it fully and over what social citizenship entails. For example, will women have parental leave rights and public child care? Will gay partners' survivors have entitlements?

We began by referring both to the early development of the sociology "in tandem" with the welfare state and to the orientation of early sociologists to "the social question" in the age of commodification. Today the sociological focus on "Who gets what from government?" entails a major component of the sociological subfields of social stratification and political sociology, indeed also involves a major portion of political economy in economics and political science as well as in sociology. Today sociologists are increasing concerned with the "social questions," old as well as new. To touch on relatively old ones, how are welfare policies related to citizenship and citizenship to welfare policies (Esping-Andersen, 1990, 1999; Janoski, 1998)? How do we sustain social safety nets in a world of increasing demographic strain on public budgets due to societal aging, high and intransigent unemployment, and globally intensifying economic competition (Esping-Andersen, 1999, 2002; Huber and Stephens, 2001)? These questions motivate much sociological work and help inform the policy making and, thus, the politics of the age (e.g., Green-Pedersen and Haverland. 2002). To touch on the new, attention is being directed to the role of business and the business class that is beginning to bring to it the same kind of empirical attention that had been concentrated upon welfare states in the last decades of the twentieth century (Swank and Martin, 2001; Hacker and Person, 2002; Swenson, 2002; Hicks, 2003). On these matters, sociologist are addressing governments as well as each other (Esping-Andersen, 2003; Myles and Quagagno, 2002). In the current era, as in the nineteenth century, sociology – indeed social science – and the welfare state mature in tandem.

CHAPTER TWENTY-SIX

Women, Gender, and State Policies

Joya Misra and Leslie King

Gender is about power. Norms, traditions, and values concerning gender have served to maintain a system of inequality in virtually every society. From the moment a person is born, the state is involved in upholding and maintaining gender as an institution: Birth certificates always include the sex of the child (typically allowing for only two possibilities), sending a message that this is an important axis of difference. State policies often reflect patriarchal norms and may constrain both men's and women's choices. Yet states also may serve as arenas for challenging traditional gender norms (Gordon, 1990). Feminist political sociologists have called attention to both the gendered impact of state policies and structures and how gender ideologies and gendered social patterns shape politics (Wilson, 1977; Gordon, 1990; Ward, 1990; Orloff, 1993; Bose and Acosta-Belén, 1995).

Feminists[1] tend to view states and state policies with some ambivalence. Although some feminists view the state as an agent of change and use the state to create legislation that may equalize women's and men's opportunities, others view the state as antithetical to feminist goals (MacKinnon, 1989; Sharp and Broomhill, 1988; Brown, 1992). Ambivalence about the role of the state in gendered policies may discourage some types of feminist mobilization (Miller and Razavi, 1998). But as Sainsbury (1999:270) suggests, "Irrespective of whether the state is conceived of as a structure or a terrain, the state is a crucial site in regulating and constructing gender relations. It is too important an arena not to enter because of ideological antipathy or fears of co-option."

Feminist work underscores the complex, dynamic, and fluid nature of the state (Alvarez, 1990). Lynne Haney (1996:759) argues, "The state is not simply an abstract, macro-level structure; it is also a complex of concrete institutions. . . . " There is not only variation across states – within one country, policies may both reinforce and challenge traditional gender norms. Indeed, one policy may empower certain groups of women and limit the opportunities of other groups of women (Misra and Akins, 1998). Rather than seeing states as either simply reinforcing traditional gender norms or serving as a site for challenging gender norms, we must view states as complex institutions, situated in a larger societal context, and composed of elements that are *both* patriarchal *and* empowering to various constituents.

In our analysis, we focus on gender and on women. An ideal approach to an analysis of gender and state policy would focus on how state policy affects and constructs women, men, and transgendered people. But whereas our understanding of the gendered content of state

[1] The term "feminist" here refers to people working to alleviate gender inequalities; by "feminist goals" we refer to efforts to reduce gender inequality, broadly defined.

policies derives in large part from an understanding of gender as a social construct and a social structure, much of the scholarly work on policy implications focuses on how *women* are affected by state policy. In the area of mobilizing for policy change too, scholarship focuses mostly on women as opposed to "gender." Women have often organized and sought to affect state policy as "women" or "feminists." Men obviously organize to affect state policy; however, they rarely do so explicitly as "men" but rather as "gay men" or "workers" or any number of other affiliations or identities, even while norms of masculinity are embedded in their efforts and the resulting policy.

We begin by discussing the politics of gender. Women serve as political actors in a variety of interest groups – for example, as members of religious groups, women's movements (both formal and informal), or labor movements – as well as in their roles as state actors – for example, as party officials, political leaders, and bureaucrats (Bock and Thane, 1991; Skocpol, 1992; Koven and Michel, 1993; Stetson and Mazur, 1995; Misra, 2003). We then move from this discussion to focus on state policy and gender in three policy areas: labor market policies, social welfare policies, and population policies. We limit ourselves to these three in order to provide a certain level of depth in our analyses of these areas.[2] These policy areas have generated the greatest levels of comparative feminist research; trends in these policies are also mirrored in many other policy areas. In addition, these areas are often not presented together (but see O'Connor, Orloff, and Shaver, 1999), and the links between them have not been fully explored. We show how policies vary across regions and countries, as well as within countries, which serves to illuminate the roles states play in policy making vis à vis gender.

GENDER AND POLITICS

Orloff (1996:52) defines gender relations as "the set of mutually constitutive structures and practices that produce gender differentiation, gender inequalities, and gender hierarchy in a given society." Gender roles exist as powerful social constructs, which shape policies in a variety of ways, such as when policies are based on the idea that men are primarily breadwinners and women are primarily caretakers. In addition, state policies have "gender-specific consequences," even when they do not appear to have a "gender-specific content" (Alvarez, 1990:260). However, state policies regarding gender have a variety of outcomes. As Orloff (1996:56) argues, there is "variation in the effects of social policies on gender: Male dominance is not necessarily reproduced; indeed it is often transformed. Some amielioration is possible, although it is sometimes coupled with greater regulation by the state."

The types of policies adopted and the gendered content and/or implications of those policies vary enormously both between and within states. At least five important factors affect the gendered implications of state policies: (1) political resources and institutions, including the political parties in power, and the responsiveness of government to interest groups, social movements, and other elements in civil society; (2) the strength of interest groups and social movements; (3) the ideologies prevailing among policy makers and other powerful players; (4) the degree of state autonomy and capacity to make and enforce policies; and (5) cultural, legal, social, political, and economic histories and traditions. These factors all influence each other as well as state policy, yet we believe it is instructive to separate them out for heuristic purposes.

First, political institutions, including specific political parties, influence the gendered content and impact of social policies. Powerful political parties influence the content and approach taken to gender. For example, conservative religious parties may emphasize policies that uphold traditional gender roles and/or limit reproductive

[2] We leave out discussions of many other policy areas, including other health care policies, educational policy, marriage and divorce law, criminal justice, credit, housing, tax policy, etc. For thoughtful analyses of these issues, we encourage readers to turn to the existing literature (Sainsbury, 1996; Staudt, 1998; Conway, Ahern, and Steuernagel, 1999; Mazur, 2002).

rights. In addition, women's representation in government may influence policy outcomes, although it is by no means a predictor of feminist policy making.

In most political systems, women are vastly underrepresented (Peterson and Runyan, 1993). Women on average comprised only about 14 percent of national parliament members worldwide in 2002 (UNIFEM, 2003:40).[3] Women are similarly underrepresented in nongovernmental organizations, both national and international, governmental bureaucracies, and other important institutions. Indeed, women rarely make up more than 5 percent of officeholders and decision makers in unions, political parties, special-interest organizations, and bureaucracies (Peterson and Runyan, 1993:55).

Many states (as varied as Chile, Italy, Poland and China) have developed women's policy machineries ("state feminism"), which connect feminist movements to state actors (Alvarez, 1990; Stetson and Mazur, 1995, 2000; Matear, 1997; Waylen, 1997; Howell, 1998; Sawer, 1998; Mazur, 2001). Stetson and Mazur (2000:618) find that women's policy machineries may advocate for feminist proposals, but are most likely to be effective when allied with the Left, and while the Left is in power, and when there is a vibrant context of autonomous radical and reformist women's organizations (Stetson and Mazur, 1995; Randall, 1998). Not surprisingly, state feminism is often only symbolic or may work in contradictory ways (Alvarez, 1990; Valiente, 2001; Mazur, 2001).[4]

The responsiveness of government to social movement organizations and civil society as a whole also explains a great deal. Where states are more permeable to social movements, these movements, including feminist movements, will have more dramatic effects. States may, however, be open to certain social movements, such as religious groups, but not to others, such as feminist groups (Meyer, in press; Costain, 1992).

Second, interest groups and social movements can profoundly affect the gendered nature of state policies. Women's movements have made considerable progress toward effecting social change and are engaged in shaping a wide array of economic and social policies (Basu, 1992, 1995a, 1995b; Jaquette, 1994; Stetson and Mazur, 1995; Afshar, 1998; Jaquette and Wolchik, 1998). Yet there are differences in the organization and approaches of women's movements. Women's strategies for mobilizing differ based on their needs, resources, and experiences as well as the openness of state institutions (Gordon, 1990).[5] Even where women have been engaged in policy making and policy development, the resulting policies do not necessarily support all women (Lewis, 1992; Pedersen, 1993; Gordon, 1994; Mink, 1995; Misra, 1998a). Indeed, women may mobilize in right-wing, fundamentalist, and nationalist movements (Moghadam, 1994; Basu, 1995a, 1999). For example, Power (2000) shows how conservatives mobilized an anti-Allende women's movement in Chile by using essentialist gender ideologies about women's roles as mothers, although these ideologies cut against the class interests of many of the participating women.[6]

[3] The Beijing Platform for Action suggested that countries should pursue a benchmark of 30% women's representation, but by 2002 only eleven countries (as varied as Mozambique, Costa Rica, Germany, and Sweden) had attained this target; all of these nations had legislated or adopted quotas (UNIFEM, 2003).

[4] In Chile, SERNAM (Servicio Nacional de la Mujer) incorporates gender into public policy but has been fairly limited in its ability to empower women (Matear, 1997; Waylen, 1997). Howell, (1998:181) notes that state feminism in China has promoted women's rights and reduced gender inequality, but has also "often subordinated gender interests to national economic development goals."

[5] For example, in the United States Gordon notes that white women relied upon their "wealth and connections" to lobby for welfare legislation whereas minority women's welfare activism "was often indistinguishable from civil rights activity" (Gordon, 1990:24).

[6] Alvarez (1990:20) notes that throughout Latin America, upper and middle class women have organized to demand women's rights, but that incorporating women and gender issues into policy making has reproduced rather than overturned existing gender inequalities. Although in some cases, such as Peronist Argentina and socialist Cuba, women's movements have significantly improved the conditions of women's lives; in many

Many women's movements have helped create policies supportive to (at least some) women. However, these movements also shape, reflect, and use existing gender ideologies. For example, women's movements have at times fought for suffrage by appealing to notions of women's ability to bring nurturing and morality to politics – a strategy that may emphasize women's *difference* from men in ways that limits women's opportunities. Similarly, women's movements have supported the development of family policies at times by emphasizing the importance of supporting women's caretaking roles over workforce participation (Pedersen, 1989, 1993). These strategies do not always lead to emancipatory outcomes, as they may reinforce essentialist views of gender.[7] As Gordon (1994:8) argues, to understand this "apparent paradox," we should recognize "feminism as a historically and contextually changing impulse." Policies shaped by women reformers may still reflect classist, racist, nationalist, and paternalistic ideologies.

Of course, women's movements are not the only movements explicitly concerned with gender-related issues. Conservative fundamentalist or nationalist movements, such as Le Pen's National Front Party in France, may focus on upholding the "traditional" family and push for policies supportive of family wage models and/or abortion bans (King, 2002). Historically, some labor movements have secured rights for male workers to the detriment of women workers (see Milkman, 1990).

Third, the prevailing ideologies among political leaders and policy makers also matter. Policy makers in countries with strong socialist-oriented ideologies, such as Sweden, may favor social spending, thus providing a safety net for the poor, a disproportionate number of whom tend to be women. Policy makers in countries with a dominant ideology of individualism and free-market capitalism may conversely avoid social spending. In some countries religion is a dominant ideology linked to the state. For example, policy makers in Catholic countries (e.g., Poland) or countries drawing on Islamic legal systems (e.g., Iran) may support certain types of policies that limit women's choices. Similarly, in the United States government leaders influenced by conservative Christian ideology may oppose abortion.

Fourth, some states have greater resources and thus have a greater financial capacity for providing certain services or programs in response to citizen needs or demands. Limited funds and/or a dearth of appropriate bureaucratic structures might limit a state's capacity, whereas relationships with corporations, international lending agencies, other nongovernmental organizations, and/or other national governments may also limit a state's autonomy (see Bello, 1994). For example, although many state leaders may recognize the challenge that families face in balancing work and home, only certain states may have the autonomy and the capacity to provide universal free child care for children over three. Developing countries may have fewer resources for expensive social programs or may be limited in the level of social provision they can provide by lending requirements imposed by organizations such as the World Bank.

Finally, cultural, legal, social, political, and/or economic histories of specific locations may affect state policies (Ferree, 1994). For example, Saguy (1999, 2000) explains how feminists in France have had difficulties convincing lawmakers to pass strong sexual harassment legislation. Lawmakers and others often see sexual harassment as an "American" and a "puritan" idea that conflicts with their notions of France as a sexually tolerant society. In Romania, abortion was banned as part of former dictator Nicolae Ceausescu's pronatalist program. The abortion ban was extremely unpopular and was one of the first laws overturned when Ceausescu was deposed. Subsequently, due to this history, abortion has remained legal in Romania even as some other Eastern European countries restrict access to the procedure (Verdery, 1996).

cases women's movements have been co-opted by dominant groups.

[7] For example, Marilyn Lake (1993:393) argues that Australian women were unsuccessful in using the ideology of motherhood to pursue a radical change in social policy, because "within the confines of a patriarchal state, in which citizen and worker are defined in masculine terms, neither 'sameness as' nor 'difference from' men will produce a genuine democracy for women."

These factors help explain the gendered variation in state policies around the globe. Political structures and opportunities, social movement organizing, ideologies, state capacities and autonomy, and the specific historical contexts of countries all matter in explaining how gender has been incorporated into state policy making and how gender relations have been affected by these policies.

In addition to these factors, we wish to highlight three major global trends that are currently affecting state policies as they pertain to gender: (1) the growing impact of neoliberalism, an ideology that promotes state retraction from social policy in favor of market reliance; (2) the rise of both religious and nationalist conservative movements, which often promote state support for traditional gender roles; and (3) international feminist organizing.

The growing power and prevalence of neoliberal ideology promotes state retrenchment (Razavi, 1998). Neoliberalism is deeply centered around free-market ideology, seeing state interventions in markets as problematic and encouraging states to limit provisioning. As a result, industrialized countries have undergone a process of "welfare state restructuring" while developing countries have responded to "structural adjustment" – both rolling back the state's role in social welfare (Daly and Lewis, 1998; Della Sala, 2002). Such restructuring has helped reinforce and reconstitute gendered (and other) patterns of inequality across a wide range of nations through a decline in both social spending and social care services. Sparr (1994:17) notes, "In cutting back on public services . . . governments have implicitly relied on a quiet army of wives, co-wives, mothers, daughters, aunts, grandmothers, sisters, female friends and neighbors to pick up the slack."

In addition to the rise of neoliberalism, the rise of conservative religious and nationalist movements also affects the gendered nature of state policy. Fundamentalist religious and nationalist movements often have agendas that include specific notions about gender relations. The rise of these movements often relates to tensions due to economic and political globalization within a capitalist world-system, such as increased economic insecurity, greater secular state power, global cultural homogenization, changes in education, increased migration, as well as the growth in women's rights (Keddie, 1998). Conservative movements may then use changing gender roles (such as an increase in divorce) as a symbol for many others types of social change; targeting women's rights may be simpler than targeting the larger political and economic changes in society. (Mernissi, 1988; Feldman, 2001; Moghadam, 2002; Afkhami, 2001). Both nationalists and fundamentalists may press for regressive reproduction policies, such as outlawing or limiting abortion (Vuolo, 2002). Such movements may also work to uphold patriarchal norms among families and limit women's rights regarding marriage and family law (Haeri, 2001).

Finally, international feminist organizing actively shapes and attempts to change international and state policies regarding economic development, employment policy, social welfare, and population policy, as well as many other policies (e.g., those addressing violence against women) (Walby, 1997; Keck and Sikkink, 1998). For example, women's international NGOs have played a crucial role in placing gender-related issues on the agenda of a wide variety of organizations, including the United Nations Development Programme, the International Labour Organization, and the World Bank, which have then played important roles in shaping not only international but also national-level policies (Miller, 1998). In addition, international women's conferences, such as the U.N. conferences, have set agendas for redressing gender inequalities at the state level.

In the next several sections of the chapter, we describe how employment policies, welfare policies, and population policies reflect and shape gender relations in a wide range of countries, including relatively wealthy industrialized countries and a broad array of developing contexts.[8] Examining these policies reveals both ideas and assumptions about gender

[8] "Developing" is a term imbued with many meanings. Although we use the terms "development" and "developing" in a very broad way to characterize

as well as certain gendered implications of policies, whether such policies are gender-specific or technically "gender-neutral."

GENDER AND EMPLOYMENT

States play an important role in shaping the workplace for men and women. Scholarship on gender and work grapples with a number of issues, including how state policies both support workers and contribute to their exploitation in gendered ways. Additionally, scholars address the reconciliation of work and family caregiving. In this section, we begin by describing gendered employment patterns and then discuss several sets of policies related to gender: policies related to economic development, antidiscrimination policies, and policies oriented toward balancing unpaid care and labor force participation.

Employment patterns vary significantly across countries and across a number of other factors, such as region, age, class, race, and ethnicity. Currently, women are more likely than men to be engaged in agricultural work or "informal" sector manufacturing and services (UNIFEM, 2003). Women's share of "formal" nonagricultural employment varies from 8 percent in Pakistan to 53 percent in Lithuania and the Ukraine; however, in most nations, women's share of formal nonagricultural employment is 30 to 40 percent (UNIFEM, 2003:Table 4, 33).[9] Of course, these statistics underestimate women's work in a number of ways. In addition to participation in formal employment captured by government statistics, women often play critical roles in the economy through their domestic labor and caregiving work, subsistence agricultural work, and/or informal sector work. In addition to demographics, culture, and traditions, state policies also shape these different levels of labor force participation. Indeed differences across countries may reflect differences in a variety of political factors, including state institutions, the strength and pressure of women's movements, religious movements, and particular political parties, as well as existing gender and religious ideologies.

Women play a central role in the global economy. Jobs throughout the world have been affected by the "feminization of labor," as women have increasingly joined the labor force (Moghadam, 1999). In addition to women's increasing employment in low-paid manufacturing and service sector work, the number of well-educated professional women workers (particularly in public sector jobs) has been increasing throughout the world (Moghadam, 1999). Yet, in every type of work, from banking to manufacturing computer chips, women tend to occupy the lowest positions in the hierarchy, in sex-segregated jobs with less pay and job security (Acevedo, 1995; UNIFEM, 2003).

Although women have gained opportunities in the labor market, they remain responsible for household work and child care. On average, women receive lower wages than men and often are employed in occupationally segregated jobs. In addition, women are more likely than men to be involved in home-based work, part-time work, casual, and temporary employment (Moghadam, 1999). These troubling trends may result from a lack of policies that protect women against gender discrimination and provide adequate job-protected leaves and child care. In the last several decades, more antidiscrimination policies and work–family reconciliation policies have been adopted, as we discuss below. These policies have in many cases been adopted in response to the pressure of women's movements.

Women's Employment and Economic Development

Gender is deeply intertwined in the structure of labor markets and development strategies. Although women have always been involved in productive work, state development strategies have created and recreated certain gendered models of work. Women workers often experience low wages, in many cases below

extremely diverse nations, we recognize the problems inherent in these terms.

[9] These data are limited as they rely on governmental indicators of formal employment for a subset of countries.

subsistence, justified by employers by the notion that women workers are not "breadwinners." In addition, many women face poor working conditions and little or no opportunity for advancement (Ward and Pyle, 1995).

For many decades development policies assumed women's economic dependence on men, despite clear evidence of women's productive contributions. Economic development policy initially emphasized incorporating men into new forms of agriculture and industry, without recognizing the independent roles of women in production (Boserup, 1970). For example, policies providing small loans for agricultural upgrades targeted men, assuming that women would benefit through their relationships with their husbands and were not directly involved in agriculture (e.g., India) (Lisk and Stevens, 1987; Sen and Grown, 1987; Ward and Pyle, 1995). Similarly, development policies disadvantaged women by supporting men's involvement in the large-scale production of goods, to the detriment of the women left out of production or those involved in small-scale production (e.g., Sierra Leone) (Lisk and Stevens, 1987). Involving men in large-scale production both diminished women's status and forced women into working more hours in order to replace men's former roles in subsistence activities (Acosta-Belén and Bose, 1995). However, in recent decades, development policies more explicitly consider women's roles as workers and how to engage women in workforce participation.

Although women have been incorporated into many different types of work, including a wide variety of professional occupations, many scholars have concentrated attention on women's incorporation into manufacturing, particularly export production. Historically, women in countries such as England and the United States found jobs in textile factories, piecework shops, and coal mines (Gordon, 2002). Employers paid women workers lower wages than men, using gender ideologies about the centrality of women's roles as caretakers, rather than workers, to justify low pay. More currently, many developing states, including Malaysia, Thailand, South Korea, and Mexico, to name but a few, seek to attract foreign investment by creating an economic environment appealing to business, with low-wage workers and limited tax and tariffs. These states recognize women workers as ideal participants in low-wage labor-intensive export production (Fernandez-Kelly, 1983; Sassen, 1998). In many cases, state actors, as in Taiwan, deliberately use existing gender ideologies and inequalities to create a low-wage labor force of presumably "docile" women as part of their attempt to lure companies to their shores (Gallin, 1990; Hsiung, 1996). For example, to try to attract companies some governments have advertised the idea that women in their countries are hard workers with "nimble fingers," perfect for working in electronics or clothing factories (Mies, 1998).

Export-oriented production receives significant attention, in part because the numbers of these jobs have grown dramatically and because, worldwide, women make up the majority of workers in export-processing zones (Staudt, 1998).[10] States support these gendered patterns of employment by leaving many forms of work unregulated, by not enforcing certain labor regulations (e.g., minimum wages) for jobs in which women are the primary employees, and by encouraging women to do home-based subcontracted work through government programs and loan programs (Lim, 1990; Ward, 1990; Ward and Pyle, 1995; Hsiung, 1996).[11] In addition, states may limit the organization of workers (particularly women workers) into labor unions and in other political forums (e.g., South Korea) (Enloe, 1989; Gallin, 1990; Hsiung, 1996).

With trends toward subcontracted work and the increasing "informalization" of work in many countries, state regulations now provide even less support for many workers than in the past (Beneria and Roldán, 1987; Ward and Pyle, 1995).[12] Global corporations subcontract

[10] As export-oriented jobs become less labor-intensive and increasingly mechanized and automated, men are winning back these positions in some regions of the world (Sklair, 1993).

[11] Some scholars suggest that these jobs are always exploitative to women; others suggest that women use these jobs and their wages to empower themselves (Ong, 1987; Ward, 1990; Lim, 1990; Safa, 1993; Kabeer, 2000).

[12] Informal work refers to work that is not regulated by the state, often untaxed, and without benefits

to local factories and home-based workers, in part because subcontracting allows corporations to "pay lower wages than in factories, bypass provision of benefits, and avoid protective legislation" (Ward and Pyle, 1995:45). States and corporations from Sri Lanka to England draw upon existing gender ideologies about women's place in the home, encouraging women to take these low-paying and insecure jobs because they allow women to combine caregiving and work (Boris and Prugl, 1996). Even where labor laws are established, they do not apply or are not enforced for this work.

An example of state involvement in informalizing the work process is the Taiwanese state program "Living Rooms as Factories," which provides small loans to families purchasing machines for women to do home-based work and establishes day care centers for home-based workers (Hsiung, 1996). Taiwanese state-sponsored programs enforce women's "traditional" role in the home by encouraging women to do home-based work, along with reinforcing women's traditional gender roles by offering classes on applying cosmetics and childrearing. Although corporations profit from such arrangements, spending less on overhead and wages, the state's role "is sometimes in direct conflict with women's interests; more generally it fails to protect women against capitalist exploitation" (Hsiung, 1996:53–4).

Informal sector work also includes women's involvement in low-paid jobs in clerical or telemarketing services, domestic service, the sex trade and tourism, and agriculture. As part of their development strategies, various governments have used gender ideologies and inequalities in promoting specific types of informal work. The Filipino government, for example, has a program focused on exporting women around the world to work as domestic workers and sex workers, as well as nurses and caretakers (Chang, 2000). Some governments, including Thailand, have been complicit in promoting sex tourism (Enloe, 1989).

Neoliberal policies (often imposed in developing nations by international lending agencies such as the International Monetary Fund and World Bank) have also impacted development strategies and women's employment. Neoliberal structural adjustment includes trade liberalization measures, cutting subsidies on products and services (e.g. food, water, electricity, etc.), limiting labor market policies such as wage restraints, as well as cutting, privatizing, or severely limiting social welfare programs (Laurell, 2000; Sparr, 1994). As a result, poverty and income inequality have increased in many developing nations. In response, women have increased their roles in subsistence production and informal work activities (due to changes in agricultural, employment, and trade policies) and caregiving (due to cutbacks in health services, education, and child care) (Folbre, 1994; Sparr, 1994; Dewan, 1999; Laurell, 2000).[13] The Egyptian state, for example, has cut back on paid maternity leave and child care services, which may limit some women's access to the paid labor force and strengthen conservative Islamic forces that emphasize women's place in the home (Hatem, 1994).[14]

Clearly, then, state policies, including those influenced by international organizations, have

(Karides, 2001). The expansion of informal work has occurred in both industrialized and developing countries. For example, Del Boca (1998:127) estimates that the informal economy makes up 20–30% of the Italian GDP.

[13] In her analysis of the effects of structural adjustment across the globe, Sparr (1994) discusses: increasing numbers of poor women; increasing numbers of women looking for income-generating work, including informal sector work; increasing levels of women's unemployment; increasing gender differentials in wages, working conditions, and types of work; increasing domestic and caregiving responsibilities and subsistence farming work for women; slowing of progress in girls' education; lower levels of food consumption for girls and women, worsening rates of girls' health and mortality rates and changes in women's fertility rates; women's greater reliance on credit; greater levels of domestic violence and stress; and increasing numbers of women-headed households and other changes in household structure.

[14] However, Moghadam (1997, 2003b) argues that women's access to the Egyptian labor market has been limited less by changes in maternity leave and more by low wages, high unemployment, traditional gender ideology, and the gender division of labor.

helped shaped gendered patterns of employment in developing contexts. In many cases, states still reinforce traditional gender norms regarding women's place in society. Even when they wish to increase women's labor force participation, states do not always necessarily provide adequate supports for women workers.

Antidiscrimination and Equalization Policies

Women compose ever-larger proportions of the workforce, in a wide variety of occupations, but at the same time women continue to be relegated to low-paying, gender-segregated jobs (Moghadam, 1999). Even where women and men share similar educational achievement levels, there are still important differences between men's and women's perceived and actual caregiving responsibilities, which shape women's and men's employment opportunities. However, many states (particularly, industrialized countries) have attempted address gender disparities in employment, although these policies do not eliminate gendered labor market patterns.

Women provide a fairly flexible low-cost supply of labor (Hantrais, 2000). However, there are significant variations in women's labor force participation rates, levels of part-time employment, and wages relative to men (UNIFEM, 2003; Acevedo, 1995; Gornick, 1999; Van Doorne-Huiskes et al., 1999; den Dulk et al., 1999; Daly, 2000). Women's movements and pressure from international organizations, such as the United Nations and the International Labour Organization, have encouraged a number of countries (such as the United States and Denmark) to adopt policies focused on antidiscrimination, sexual harassment, affirmative action, and comparable worth (Gornick, 1999), and broaden women's employment opportunities.

These laws are both meant to correct for employment discrimination on the basis of gender and address patently unfair gendered differences in wages and working conditions. For example, in the absence of antidiscrimination legislation in the United States through the 1960s, women could be denied access to managerial positions or fired if they married or became pregnant (Huckle, 1988; Conway et al., 1999). Many countries adopted equal pay and equal treatment policies by the end of the 1970s (van Vleuten, 1995; Määttä, 1998; Mazur, 2002). Sexual harassment and affirmative action policies were put into place primarily in the late 1980s and 1990s, whereas comparable worth policies have been more selectively adopted. Yet countries have implemented these policies inconsistently.

Antidiscrimination policies target unequal access and treatment or discrimination in hiring (e.g., a man considered for a child care position) or promotion (e.g., a woman considered for a managerial position), and strike down previous discriminatory legislation. Other policies focus on equal pay for equal work by gender or equal treatment by gender. Sexual harassment policies also address discrimination on the basis of gender, usually focusing on conduct that may affect employment, interfere with a worker's performance, or create a hostile work environment (Conway et al., 1999). Affirmative action or "positive action" policies redress inequalities by giving preferential treatment to women applicants who have the same qualifications as men applicants.[15] In Europe, these policies have had a wider scope, addressing issues of public awareness and diversifying occupational options (de Jong and Bock, 1995).

Yet despite the adoption of these policies in a number of nations, occupational gender segregation continues to exist in all countries. Gender segregation not only separates women and men in the labor force, but also supports wage disparities, as jobs dominated by women generally pay less.[16] Although some women have made inroads into jobs previously dominated by men, there has also been an increased feminization of female-dominated occupations, which

[15] These policies may also provide opportunities for racial and ethnic minority workers.

[16] For example, in the United States, child care workers (jobs dominated by women) are paid less than parking lot attendants (jobs dominated by men), even though caring for children requires greater skill and responsibility (Folbre, 2001).

means that overall, little progress has been made (Plantenga and Tijdens, 1995; Anker, 1998; Budig, 2002). For example, Den Dulk et al. (1999:13) estimate that 60 percent of working women in the European Union are employed in three broad occupational groupings – secretaries and clerks, service workers, and care-workers. Comparable-worth policies and job classification systems address the wage disparities created by occupational gender segregation, by ensuring that jobs requiring the same level of skills, education, and responsibility earn the same wages (Schippers, 1995). Although such policies do not abolish occupational gender segregation, they challenge the norm that women-dominated occupations should pay less simply because the work is done by women (Van Doorne-Huiskes, 1995). However, comparable-worth policies do not deal with the problem of women's involvement in part-time and otherwise "atypical" employment – often jobs with lower wages, limited benefits, and which rarely allow for advancement. These positions allow women greater flexibility to continue labor force involvement and also provide care for their families, but also carry significant disadvantages (McRae, 1998).

Gender, Care, and Employment

Gender is apparent in the complex of policies that address the needs of workers with care obligations. States increasingly address the issue of balancing care and employment through "reconciliation" policies, such as family leave and child care. As Hantrais (2000:2) argues, these policies go beyond "measures designed to bring women into line with men as workers, to gender policy aimed at tackling socially constructed inequalities at work and in the home." Simply put, women will only reach equality with men in employment when men reach equality with women in caregiving (Lohkamp-Himmighofen and Dienel, 2000).

Although many countries around the world (such as Morocco and Colombia) provide maternity leave and benefits (Social Security Administration, 1999, 2002, 2003), these policies are not always enforced or only apply to some working mothers.[17] Maternity benefits may serve as a disincentive to hire women workers (Alvarez, 1990; Folbre, 1994; Griffith and Gates, 2002) or may be "implemented and financed in ways that [restrict] women's employment opportunities and [reinforce] a traditional division of labor in the home" (Folbre, 1994:223), in part because they are not provided as "parental" leaves for both men and women, but as leaves for women.

Almost all wealthy industrialized states provide maternity leaves that include time off from work and protections from job loss as well as cash benefits of up to 100 percent of usual earnings (SSA, 1999, 2002, 2003; Daly, 2000; Meyers et al., 1999).[18] Paid paternity leave policies exist in a few countries, usually for only a brief time after the birth of a child (Plantenga and Hansen, 1999; Lohkamp-Himmighofen and Dienel, 2000; Daly, 2000), and some nations also provide family leaves for caretaking for other family members. Parental leave varies in significant ways. For example, in Sweden, parental leave can be taken as a block or in short periods until the child reaches the age of eight. In many countries, parental leave can alternate between parents, and in Sweden and Austria, some of the leave is lost if men do not take it. Parents are most likely to take advantage of parental leave policies where leaves are well-compensated (Lohkamp-Himmighofen and Dienel, 2000).

Child care policies also play an important role in reconciling family and work life. Whereas maternity and parental leave may help guarantee women's return to employment, child care

[17] In many developing countries, eligible women can take a maternity leave and receive a certain proportion of their earnings for a period before and after the birth (often about four months around the birth), although these programs usually only include women working in a formal nonagricultural position and rely on employee contributions as well as employer and state contributions (SSA, 1999, 2003).

[18] The United States has the least generous policy, although it recently adopted the Family and Medical Leave Act, which allows *some* employed men and women to take up to twelve weeks of *unpaid* leave to care for a family member, including women who wish to take maternity leave (Conway et al., 1999).

allows women to remain fairly continuously employed. Again, there are significant differences cross-nationally in the public provision of or support for child care. Several countries, notably Belgium, Denmark, Sweden, Norway, France, and Finland, offer publicly provided child care to infants and toddlers; many more wealthy states offer publicly provided child care to children over three (Plantenga and Hansen, 1999; Michel, 1999; Meyers et al., 1999; Daly, 2000; Marchblank, 2000). Women's groups in a variety of developing contexts have recently made demands for child care programs and policies (Alvarez, 1990; Matear, 1997; Wazir, 2001; Sorj, 2001). Yet successful child care policies must address the wide diversity of experiences in most developing countries (rural versus urban, factory versus informal work). For example, Matear (1997:104) found that Chilean child care policies were not developed "in response to women's gender-specific needs to be replaced in their reproductive, nurturing role to enter the labor market," but simply to "allow employers in a certain export-oriented sector central to state development strategies greater profit by drawing in mothers as low-paid, temporary workers."

Although other policies also shape gendered patterns in employment, we have highlighted a number of the most central employment-related policies. In the next section, we examine social welfare policies, which are inextricably bound up with employment policies. The feminization of poverty can primarily be explained by women's lower wages in the labor market and the effects of women's care responsibilities on labor force participation. Employment policies play a key role in ensuring the welfare of the population. However, almost all states have various forms of safety net programs for those who need it.

GENDER AND SOCIAL WELFARE POLICIES

Welfare generally provides assistance for those who are unable to support themselves through earnings. Welfare programs insure families against loss of earnings due to old age, disability, or death, sickness and maternity, injuries due to work, and unemployment. Other programs exist to provide health care as well as funds and services for families living in poverty. Such policies may be universal (providing flat-rate benefits to all citizens regardless of need), employment-related (providing benefits based on the length of employment and earnings), and/or means-tested (providing benefits for those who drop beneath a certain benchmark of economic need) (SSA, 2003).

Welfare policies are rich sites for exploring how gender ideologies affect policy and how policies differentially affect men and women. Gender ideologies have been central to the construction of these polices and due to lower earnings and greater caregiving duties, women are also more likely to live in poverty and require the assistance of welfare policies. Welfare provision may reinforce gender biases by covering men workers more often than women workers or by expecting women to provide care for family members. Yet social welfare policies also help ameliorate needs such as poverty and may at times also work to create greater levels of gender equity between men and women (Misra and Akins, 1998; Borchorst, 1999; Sainsbury, 1999). These policies have complex and sometimes contradictory effects, transforming but not necessarily ending male dominance, and often regulating women's lives in exchange for meeting certain needs (Orloff, 1996; Hernes, 1984). The effects of these policies also vary based on the class, race, ethnicity, nationality, immigration status, age, sexuality, marriage status, and ability status of the recipients. While some policies may advantage certain groups of women, they may disadvantage other groups (Boris, 1995; Gordon, 1994; Mink, 1995; Misra and Akins, 1998; Lewis, 2000). In addition, although some welfare policies have been adopted in keeping with pronatalist and/or religious aims, women's movements have also played a major role in putting welfare policies on political agendas.

Social Welfare Policies

Some variant of a welfare state exists in almost all countries, but developing nations generally cannot boast extensive welfare states, in part due to requirements imposed by lending agencies and limited state budgets. The wealthiest countries – Western European nations, Japan, Canada, the United States, Australia, and New Zealand – generally have the most developed welfare states. Eastern European, Latin American, and the newly industrializing Asian countries tend to provide the next best level of social welfare programs. Eastern European policies reflect earlier expansive protections, although without appropriate funding levels, these protections are often ineffective (Lakunina, Stepantchikova, and Tchetvernina, 2001; Makkai, 1994; Kapstein, 1997). Many Latin American nations offer significant social welfare policies, but these policies often benefit only more privileged sectors of society (Folbre, 1994). Industrializing Asian nations provide limited welfare states that tend to accentuate economic policy over social policy (Holliday, 2000). Poorer countries in Asia and Africa may provide pensions and other work-related policies, but often cover only employees at firms with five or more workers. Extremely poor countries, particularly in Africa, generally only provide policies covering work-related injuries for certain workers and pensions for public employees (SSA, 1999, 2002). However, there remains significant variation beyond these simple descriptions. For example, public sector workers in many developing countries, for example, throughout the Middle East and North Africa, have received very generous benefits, including free health care, paid maternity leaves, and child care. However, such programs exclude many workers, including farmers, homeworkers, domestics, and informal sector workers (Moghadam, 2003a).

In many nations, social welfare policies reflect assumptions that each family has a male breadwinner in a job that pays high wages and provides benefits. Almost all countries assume a model of partnerships between men and women, gendered divisions of labor, and gendered employment systems (Lewis, 1992; Sainsbury, 1996; Orloff, 1996). Benefits through social insurance are often targeted toward men workers, assuming that they provide for needy women and children. Indeed, many families headed by women are not reached through employment-related social welfare programs, either because women are not employed or not employed in the right types of jobs (e.g., formal work in settings with many employees) (Folbre, 1994). For example, domestic workers, who are mostly women, are not covered by pensions in many nations.

One example of gender-differentiated policy exists in survivor benefits. In many nations, widows automatically receive survivor benefits, whereas widowers only receive such benefits if clearly dependent (usually aged or disabled) on a wife's earnings (Folbre, 1994). Widows are often more likely to receive benefits if they are caring for children or are older, but younger and childless widows (or those who remarry) still usually receive a lump-sum payment (SSA, 1999, 2002). Widowers caring for children do not receive survivor benefits or receive lump payments when they remarry. Such policies clearly assume a male-breadwinner model of earnings, while also encouraging women's roles in caregiving and women's remarriage after the death of a spouse. Although these gendered assumptions may support women who may not have other economic opportunities, they reflect and reinforce a system that limits women's opportunities and ties women to caregiving roles.

States may also use social welfare policies to achieve greater levels of gender equality. Three strategies aimed at gender equity include the universal breadwinner strategy (equal employment opportunities for men and women), the caregiver-parity strategy (compensating and supporting caregivers), and the earner–carer strategy (enabling both men and women to be both earners and carers) (Sainsbury, 1999). The first strategy may come at the expense of caring, as in the United States, where men and women are both engaged in the labor force but where there is little state support for caregiving. The second may reinforce a gendered division of labor, as in the Netherlands, where until recently policies encouraged women to focus on caregiving. The earner–carer strategy, pursued by countries such as Sweden and France, may be the most effective at achieving gender equity, though it is not without its challenges (as Joan

Acker [1994] suggests, Swedish women still look very tired). It is clearly difficult to disentangle labor market policies from social welfare policies.

Policies oriented toward single mothers, seen as transgressing traditional gender roles, can be particularly illustrative of gendered norms and expectations. For example, poverty is often high for families headed by lone mothers, because women earn less in the labor market than men and their caregiving duties may also preclude employment or full-time employment. In Sweden and France, employment-related policies such as child care and parental leave, along with transfers for single-parent families, help prevent many lone mother families from falling into poverty. In the United Kingdom and the Netherlands, transfers to lone parents have played a key role in addressing poverty. In Germany, where tax and child care policy have discouraged many married mothers from working, policy has reinforced the employment of lone mothers (Misra, 1998b; Lewis and Hobson, 1997; Ostner, 1997; Hobson and Takahashi, 1997; Kilkey and Bradshaw, 1999). Lone mother families stave off poverty most successfully when benefits and services are universally available and labor market participation is high, as in Sweden and France (Lewis and Hobson, 1997; Sainsbury, 1996; Borchorst, 1999).

Neoliberal restructuring has profoundly affected social welfare across a variety of nations. Industrialized states have increasingly privatized care (sending care provision to private, nonprofit, and voluntary sectors) while also marketizing state provision of care (contracting out specific services and providing funds to families to negotiate care) (Knijn, 2000). For example, in France, restructuring has meant a weakening of state-provided care for young children in favor of subsidies to families hiring individual caregivers. Such changes have disadvantaged poor and working class families and increased disparities between families. Driven by the requirements of structural adjustment policies, developing countries have similarly privatized care, expecting families and nongovernmental organizations to meet care needs once met by the state. As a result of these changes in countries across the globe, from Jamaica to Indonesia, women are more likely to be involved in caring for family members, at times at the expense of their labor market participation, and are more likely to be hired in low-paying caregiving positions.

All in all, social welfare policies both reinforce and challenge traditional gender roles. Although social welfare policies have reinforced gendered norms, particularly in the gendered division of work and care, in recent years policies have shifted toward creating greater gender equality. Yet neoliberal restructuring may lead to greater levels of gender inequality, particularly when restructuring relies on women to meet social welfare needs.

GENDER AND POPULATION POLICY

Most states seek to engineer their populations, mainly through migration and/or fertility policy. Although all types of population policies have implications for gender, we restrict our discussion to fertility policy, which seeks to lower or raise birthrates. Sixty-eight percent of all national governments have explicit fertility policies (United Nations, 2003). These state attempts to alter fertility reinforce and reshape gender relations, first, by shaping reproductive rights, and second, by affecting the structure of social welfare policies that support families. We begin by discussing antinatalist efforts, examining population control and reproductive health in developing countries, and then we delineate attempts to raise fertility. Finally, because of its centrality to women's reproductive autonomy, we examine state policy as it pertains to abortion.

Antinatalist Policies

Currently, eighty-six countries (45 percent of the world's nations) have policies to reduce fertility (United Nations, 2003). Many developing governments have received Western (especially U.S.)[19] support for population control

[19] Three main ideas influenced international policy on population growth – that high fertility limits eco-

programs, and aid has often been contingent on the institution of family planning programs. However, many state leaders institute policies without international pressure because they are convinced that population growth needs to slow in order for economic development to occur (Jain, 1998).

Until the mid-1990s, when a new paradigm emerged from the United Nations Conference on Population and Development, population control policies relied almost exclusively on the provision of contraception, sterilization, and sometimes abortion. Teresita De Barbieri (1994:261) contends that "the design of population policies and family planning programs has been dominated by a male perspective and cut from a technocratic cloth . . . . " Population control programs have typically targeted women and ignored men's role in reproduction. Often numerical targets have been established, which seek to attain specific rates of contraceptive usage (Bandarage, 1997). According to Dixon-Mueller (1993:52), "Within most family planning programs, the *quality* of reproductive health services was sacrificed to the *quantity* of family planning acceptors, the safety of contraceptive methods sacrificed to efficiency and technical effectiveness."

Throughout the 1980s and 1990s, a strong feminist critique of these policies emerged. Although feminist researchers diverge on the need for population control,[20] most agree that women have borne a disproportionate share of the burden of such efforts. Access to birth control may provide men and women with more reproductive choices – indeed family planning programs have been beneficial to millions of people worldwide. However, policy makers and researchers have often failed to closely examine the social contexts in which various birth control devices might be used or whether they enhance women's health and well-being (Hartmann, 1995). Many women, especially poor women (in both wealthy and poor countries), have suffered negative health consequences from approaches to birth control promoted by family planning workers, including dangerous medications and some devices that have caused disabling side effects (Hartmann, 1995). In addition, birth control no longer marketable in wealthy countries (such as high-estrogen oral contraceptives and the Dalkon Shield IUD – known to pose serious health risks) has been sold in poor countries (Dixon-Mueller, 1993).

Governments have sometimes allowed researchers to do clinical trials on contraceptives without ensuring that women were fully informed (such as Norplant trials in Brazil – see Barroso and Corrêa, 1995). In addition, some family planning workers, intent on achieving their target number of contraceptive acceptors, have failed to describe common side effects of contraceptives or sterilization. Coercive practices have been documented as well. Bandarage (1997:71) notes that "coercion does not pertain simply to the outright use of force. More subtle forms of coercion arise when individual reproductive decisions are tied to sources of survival like the availability of food, shelter, employment, education, health care and so on." Sterilization abuse has occurred in many parts of the world as part of population control programs (Bandarage, 1997; Hartmann, 1995). For example, in Puerto Rico a mass sterilization program took place from the 1950s to the 1970s; many women were sterilized without their knowledge (Hartmann, 1995). Other countries, among them India, have also engaged in mass sterilization campaigns, sometimes offering financial incentives for sterilization to desperately poor people. China's "one-child policy" has subjected some women to forced abortions (Greenhalgh, 2001). Most coercive practices have been targeted at women. One of the few instances of coercive practices aimed at

nomic development, hurts the environment, and could lead to social instability. U.S. interest in population control derives from these ideas and the various movement groups and NGOs espousing them (see Hartmann, 1995; also see Demeny, 1998).

[20] Some feminist researchers and activists believe population growth impedes development and that fertility reduction is a worthy goal (Dixon-Mueller, 1993; also see Presser, 1997). Others take issue with the notion that population growth must impede development and view population control programs of any ilk with suspicion (see Hartmann, 1995).

men – the mass sterilization campaigns of India in the early 1970s – resulted in mass riots and, some claim, led a temporary collapse of the ruling party; since then, policies in India have generally targeted only women (Corrêa, 1994).

A second critique of population control policies is that they have ignored existing inequalities and power structures or, in some cases, even sought to control population growth among the poor, fearing social turmoil. Population control may do little to reduce inequalities; instead, it simply serves as a distraction from more pressing economic inequalities (see Hartmann, 1995). Fertility control projects may also fail to consider the social and cultural contexts in which fertility decisions occur. For example, women may bear many children because children, especially sons, add to their status and well-being. Fertility control policies often do little to address unequal gender arrangements. De Barbieri (1994:260) explains that, "the inequality between men and women globally, at the family level, and in interpersonal relationships has gone unquestioned. Quite the contrary: Population policies seem to aim to preserve the existing social order, with its hierarchies and divisions."

In recent decades, researchers have linked gender inequalities to fertility control, arguing that family planning policies might better achieve their goal of lowering fertility if existing power structures changed (Dixon-Mueller, 1993). In the absence of educational and employment-related opportunities for women, fertility may remain high even when broad access to contraceptives exists. At the 1994 United Nations Conference on Population and Development in Cairo, "feminist activists succeeded in essentially rewriting the script for international population policy, transforming the agenda from the achievement of demographic targets to the enhancement of women's sexual and reproductive health, choice, and rights (Greenhalgh, 2001:852). Feminists at Cairo succeeded in bringing about a paradigm shift – away from "population control" with its narrow emphasis on fertility reduction, to reproductive health and women's education and empowerment. Hodgson and Watkins (1997) claim that, in asserting that population stabilization depends on the elimination of discrimination against women, the Cairo Program represents a joining of feminist and neo-Malthusian goals. The new paradigm called on states to "empower women to actively participate at all levels of social and economic activity, a change that would result in lowered fertility and improved survival for women and their children" (Mundigo, 2000:323). The program recommends that governments work to expand the educational opportunities of girls and women; reduce violence against women; address gender-based income disparities; and reduce infant, child, and maternal mortality (United Nations, 1994, 2003). Such an approach requires integrating economic and social welfare policies, as well as others, into reproductive planning. An important component was the call to integrate family planning with other reproductive health services (United Nations, 2003).

In addition, the role of men in reproduction, previously ignored by researchers and policy makers, was made explicit in the Cairo Program of Action:

> Men play a key role in bringing about gender equality since, in most societies, men exercise preponderant power in nearly every sphere of life, ranging from personal decisions regarding the size of families to the policy and programme decisions taken at all levels of government. (United Nations, cited in Mundigo, 2000:324)

The program also cited the need to "assign high priority to the development of new methods of fertility regulation for men (United Nations, 2003:17). Since the conference, more research investigates men's role in reproductive decision making (Mundigo, 2000) and many governments report having introduced programs aimed at involving men in reproductive health (Sadik, 1997).

The Cairo Program was a victory for feminists (although see Hartmann, 1997 for a critical discussion of Cairo Consensus); however, implementation has been uneven. Barriers include "social and cultural influences, infrastructure and accessibility problems, and economic constraint" (Sadik, 1997). Neoliberal structural adjustment policies, for example, have hindered some governments from expanding maternal and child health care or even girls' education. Whereas some population control programs have moderated their activities, others have changed little. For example, China's government has softened its approach to population control, exploring ways to improve the quality of care (Greenhalgh, 2001). India's family planning program abolished targets in 1996. However, Indonesia's program merely gave targets another name – "demand fulfillment" (Hartmann, 1997). Jocelyn DeJong (2000:948) reviewed national case studies (covering forty countries) of implementation of the Cairo Program and found that these studies "share the consistent finding that the progress in implementing the far-reaching reforms advanced by the ICPD has depended very much on the political situation of the countries in question." More progress has been made in open and democratic rather than closed political contexts. Despite the uneven implementation, the program agreed upon at the Cairo Conference is significant. Nations and NGOs charted a new direction for reproductive health and family planning with emphasis on redressing institutionalized gender inequalities and human rights.

Pronatalist Policies

Though far more national governments have policies to lower fertility rates than raise them, ever-increasing numbers of states express concern that their birthrates are too low, for both nationalist and economic reasons. Countries with generous health care and social security programs are especially worried that these systems will become unstable as an ever-increasing proportion of the workforce enters retirement. Pronatalism has emerged as a dominant political ideology at various historical moments. Responding to downward trends in birth rates, many Western European countries – including Germany, France, Sweden, Italy, and Spain – instituted pronatalist-inspired family policies in the late nineteenth and early twentieth century. At the center of these policies was a system of family benefits. Some countries outlawed abortion and contraception for pronatalist reasons as well. In the 1960s and 1970s, many newly independent countries adopted pronatalist stances. For example, Moghadam (2003a:95) explains that, in the 1960s, the Algerian government's demographic policy "was predicated on the assumption that a large population is necessary for national power." Currently, twenty-six states have explicit policies to increase fertility (United Nations, 2003), and most of these policies rely on various types of incentives.

A central feminist question on pronatalism focuses on whether nationalist ideologies lead states to encourage births to members of a specific collectivity. Some scholars argue that pronatalist policies spring from conservative nationalist ideologies which, because they tend to advocate "traditional" gender roles, conflict with feminist goals of gender equality (Hamilton, 1995; Heng and Devan, 1992; Yuval-Davis, 1989).[21] Nationalist leaders often oppose abortion for pronatalist reasons and advocate "traditional" family values (e.g., Jean Marie Le Pen in France – see King, 2002). Yuval-Davis (1989:93) argues that, in Israel, "pressures to define and reproduce the national collectivity . . . have constituted Israeli Jewish women as its national reproducers." Yuval-Davis argues that in Israel women's roles and, ultimately, legal rights have been constructed and defined through debates surrounding various demographic policies. Bracewell (1996) explains that pronatalism in Serbia has been oriented toward restoring a precommunist view of the family, where women were primarily homemakers and mothers. In the Serbian discourse, Albanian women become "baby machines."

Just as women have borne most of the burden of antinatalist policies, women have also tended to be more affected than men by pronatalist efforts, especially when reproductive rights are curtailed. Historically some states have outlawed abortion and contraception – or made them

[21] In some instances, population policies influenced by nationalist ideologies have historically affected members of racial and ethnic minority populations differently from the dominant population.

difficult to obtain – for pronatalist reasons (King, 2002). More recently, women's access to abortion and even contraception has sometimes been affected by state pronatalist agendas. For example, Israeli women seeking abortion face numerous obstacles, including expense, bureaucratic hurdles, and the necessity to prove need for the procedure to a hospital committee, due to the state's interest in increasing birthrates (Portugese, 1998). In 1995, the Serbian government instituted a more restrictive abortion law for pronatalist reasons. In addition, state interest in raising birthrates has occasionally resulted in severely repressive reproductive policies, such as those instituted in Romania in the 1970s and 1980s that "turned women's bodies into instruments to be used in the service of the state" (Kligman, 1992:365). Abortions were outlawed and contraceptives made unavailable. Women were unable to mobilize politically against these pronatalist measures; they resisted by seeking clandestine, often dangerous, abortions.

However, states mostly rely on incentives, including a variety of employment and social policies, including family allowances, housing subsidies, tax breaks for dependent children, and/or paid family leave, to attempt to coax citizens to bear more children. Such programs have the potential to be helpful to both women and men who have children. Gender ideologies invariably influence the construction of such incentives and the extent to which policies correspond to feminist principles varies. For example, leave programs that allow parents to spend time at home with young children may (implicitly or explicitly) encourage more women than men to do so. Such policies may, however, encourage men to spend more time on carework if, for example, family leave programs provide such incentives (as in Austria and Sweden).

Historically, women have had relatively little impact on government decisions to create fertility policies and little input as to the shape of those policies (Maroney, 1992; Yuval-Davis, 1989). Often, such policies have resulted from nationalist concerns or state interest in economic development. More recently, feminist movements in many countries have influenced reproductive policy by helping to secure access to contraceptives and abortion and (indirectly) by achieving social, political and economic opportunities, such as the right to participate freely in the labor force or even, as in France, the right to more equal representation in government (parité). Increasingly the overall trend in many low-fertility countries seems to be toward policies that are more gender-neutral than in the past (King, 2002), though this does not necessarily translate into a transformation of existing gender roles.

A key question for feminists is whether the state's desire for more children can be translated into "women-friendly" social policies. Some argue that pronatalism has led lawmakers away from family policies that would truly advance feminist goals (Jenson and Sineau, 1995). But the earliest comprehensive family policies owe their existence in large part to the desire of some government leaders to increase national fertility rates (Pedersen, 1993; Ohlander, 1991). Alena Heitlinger (1991, 1993) argues that, although not all pronatalist policies help women, there is no inherent incompatibility between pronatalism and feminism. Indeed, women's equity could serve as the impetus for states to institute social policies broadly defined as pronatalist.

The extent to which the goal of greater gender equality can be merged with pronatalism may turn out to be an important question. Fertility is declining around the world and in welfare states fertility rates are at all-time lows. While the number of states claiming their fertility is too high is leveling, the number of states expressing concern over low fertility continues to rise (from sixteen states in 1976 to thirty-four in 2001 – United Nations, 2003). But because such efforts have too often been associated with ethnonationalist, racist and antifeminist ideologies, many feminist researchers and activists will likely continue to be wary of any state efforts to regulate fertility.

Abortion and State Policy

Because of its centrality to women's ability to control their fertility, feminist researchers have paid particular attention to abortion policy

(Brand, 1998). In some countries, abortion has been linked to government attempts at population engineering. In such instances, the desires of state leaders may take precedence over the needs and desires of individual citizens. A glaring example is China, where abortion has been a tool of state-sponsored fertility control.

In other countries, abortion is less closely linked to state desires to raise or lower fertility; in those locales where abortion is legal, the right to abortion has often been the result of long, hard struggles, typically led by feminist activists. In such cases, women's groups and their allies have sought from the state the right to legal and safe abortion and, in some cases, for state funding of abortion. State regulations vary dramatically and abortion policies tend to change over time in response to pressure groups, changes in political leadership, technological innovation, and so on. For example, abortion became legal in the United States in 1973 as a result of a Supreme Court ruling (*Roe v. Wade*), which, while legalizing abortion throughout the country, left open the possibility for the states to regulate the procedure. Thus, in the United States, access to abortion has become more restricted since the mid-1970s. In France, by contrast, feminists lobbied the state for legislation to legalize abortion. Policy makers sought to construct a policy that would be a compromise between religious groups, women's groups and other parties, including pronatalist groups (see Glendon, 1987). The result was a law, passed in 1975, that made abortion legal under fairly restricted circumstances; since then, those circumstances have become more broadly defined (King and Husting, 2003). In Poland, the ascendance of the Catholic Church in the postcommunist era has led to restrictions on the right to abortion, which was previously available on demand. Poland now has one of Europe's strictest abortion laws.

As this discussion of population policy shows, states have used population policies to pursue a variety of goals; yet these policies have had strongly gendered effects. In many cases, policies in both pronatalist and antinatalist contexts have become more aligned with feminist goals, in large part due to feminist organizing. However, almost everywhere hard-won reproductive rights are threatened by conservative nationalist and/or religious forces.

DISCUSSION AND CONCLUSIONS

Using examples from three policy arenas – employment, social welfare, and population – we have shown how state policies may reinforce and/or reshape gender roles. Some state policies are explicitly gendered in that they presuppose differences between men and women. These policies may exploit existing gender inequalities, such as policies to create an inexpensive female workforce. Some seek to redress gender inequalities, such as antidiscrimination and affirmative action policies. Other policies are technically gender-neutral but have gendered effects, such as parental leave policies that allow parents to take unpaid time off of work to spend time with children. Within the current social context, these policies may reinforce existing gender roles because women tend to earn less and are thus more likely to forgo their salary to engage in care work at home. In addition, reproductive policies may more profoundly affect women, who must bear the most of the cost of unwanted pregnancies or unwanted fertility control. Finally, *lack* of state involvement often has gendered implications as well. For example, if states fail to institute or enforce laws to address sexual harassment or gender discrimination, existing inequalities continue. If states fail to provide assistance with child care, lone mothers may fall into poverty. If states neglect to address disparities in income, such gender inequalities may persist.

Employment, social welfare, and population policies are inextricably woven together. Employment policies oriented toward giving women greater economic opportunities within the labor market may be related to limiting social welfare benefits for women and their families. Reproductive policies also shape women's workforce participation, as women's disadvantages in the labor market are in part due to their role in reproduction, but women may also be encouraged to bear children (future workers)

(Pyle, 1997). Indeed, social welfare and employment policies aimed at reconciling family and work life may have significant effects on women's reproductive choices. Social welfare policies may also stigmatize women who cannot provide for their families through employment or who are viewed as breaking societal norms regarding reproduction within stable marriages. Some population policies (such as the U.S. selective antinatalist policy that seeks to lower the birth rates of unmarried teenagers) instituted with the idea that lower birth rates will ultimately reduce poverty may draw attention away from underlying problems of poverty and lack of educational and employment opportunities (see Luker, 1996). In addition, policies such as parental leave and subsidized child care, for example, can support higher birth rates, promote employment, and help reduce poverty, especially among lone mothers. Although no two countries take the exactly same route, in every nation, countries combine population, employment, and social welfare policies to respond to perceived needs, including the needs of the state, the needs of capital, and the needs of men and women.

In this chapter, we have illustrated how state policies have gendered implications. Yet although the state poses structural constraints to women, it also acts as an arena in which women may seek to redress gender-based inequalities or to address gender-based need. The complex of factors we discussed at the beginning of this chapter – political resources and structures; the strength of interest groups and social movements; prevailing ideologies; the degree of state autonomy and capacity to make and enforce policies; and cultural, legal, social, political, and economic histories and traditions – shape gendered policy choices. Intersecting with these factors are global trends including the increasing power of neoliberal ideology, the growing power of conservative nationalist and/or religious movements, and increased feminist organizing.

Perhaps the most positive sign for the future has been the global alliances that have brought feminists together from around the globe to share tactics and information and demand certain cultural, political, and economic changes (Vuolo, 2002). As Moghadam, (2000, 2002) points out, women's movements now must be understood as global, including supranational goals, strategies, organizations, and constituencies. Transnational feminist movements help develop new criteria for women's rights and have significantly affected employment, social welfare, and population policies at both national and international levels (Bock and Thane, 1991; Koven and Michel, 1993; Basu, 1995a; Stetson and Mazur, 1995; Rupp, 1997; Ali, Coate, and Goro, 2000; Bull, Diamond, and Marsh, 2000; Moghadam, 2000, 2002).[22] In an increasingly globalized world, women's movements shape not only local and national governance, *but also* international governance, which then reinforces local and state policy making. Although the political and economic processes of globalization have led to the increased dispersion of neoliberal ideologies and to conservative fundamentalist ideologies that may undermine and disempower women, globalization has also led to an increase in transnational feminist organization that provides women with resources, strategies, and support. Future research should further explore the impact of these global alliances on policy.

Future research should also focus greater attention on how policies shape men's lives and men's roles in society. State policies shape men's roles as workers, citizens, and fathers just as they shape women's roles as workers, citizens, and mothers (Hobson, 2002). In addition, more research needs to explain why policies differ (or do not) across a range of contexts. Much research on gender and social policy focuses on particular cases; other research explores only a range of similar nations. However, as we try to

[22] Women's movements must also remain located within specific local political and economic contexts (Basu, 2000). However, transnational feminist movements can reflect the vitality and richness of grassroots organizing (Alvarez, 2000; Sperling, Ferree, and Risman, 2001; Thayer, 2001). Thayer (2001) shows how participants in a rural Brazilian women's movement create their own meaning within a transnational feminist context, defending their autonomy from the larger movement and appropriating and transforming transnational feminist discourses.

point out, there are similarities that cut across very different nations, even while there are differences that cut across similar countries. We need more comparative and cross-national research that does not overgeneralize, but develops contextualized explanations for the patterns that occur.

Both in their development and impact, states and their policies are simply not gender-neutral. Gender is reinforced and reconstructed through the variety of policies that states enact. Some of these policies may be very explicit in their gendered approaches, as when policies address gender discrimination or abortion. Other state policies are gendered more implicitly, as when states provide employment-related pensions for full-time workers, without recognizing that women workers are less likely to be covered and that such a pension scheme simply reproduces gender stratification. Indeed, almost all policies have been created with certain gendered assumptions about men's and women's roles in society; resulting policies then support these assumptions. By examining how policies and gender relations are intertwined, political sociologists can develop a better and more thorough understanding of both policy making and the nature of states.

ACKNOWLEDGMENTS

We appreciate the research assistance of Jessica Cichalski, Penelope Dane, Sabine Merz, and Jonathan Woodring, and the excellent comments of the anonymous reviewers and editors, Amrita Basu, Betsy Hartmann, Ivy Kennelly, Madonna Harrington Meyer, Valentine Moghadam, Stephanie Moller, Sarah Wilcox, and Millie Thayer. This material is based upon work supported by the National Science Foundation under Grant #SES-0095251, the Social and Demographic Research Institute, and the Center for Public Policy and Administration at the University of Massachusetts-Amherst.

CHAPTER TWENTY-SEVEN

The Politics of Racial Policy

Kent Redding, David R. James, and Joshua Klugman

Politics and race have been intimately intertwined since the inception of notions of racial difference and the beginnings of race-based slavery at the dawn of the modern era. Moreover, race-conscious public policies constructed and reflected racial identities and inequalities since that time, creating what we have called "racial states" (James and Redding, this volume). The color-conscious policies of the past created race inequalities that are durable (Brown, 2003; Tilly, 1998). The current rush toward "race-neutral" or "color-blind" policies that tend to mask race inequalities emphasizes the importance of understanding how politics and race affect each other.

This chapter examines the literature on the causal linkages between race and public policy from the beginnings of race-based slavery to the present. Different theoretical understandings of the interactions between race and politics are important not only because of how they explain racial politics and policies of the past, but because they also shape our understanding of the racial dilemmas of the present. If one thinks that racism has been the primary motivator of racial exclusions and consequent racial inequalities, it may be easier to believe that eliminating racism and state-enforced color-conscious policies will cause racial inequalities to disappear as well. An allied or complementary perspective that views intraclass conflict between workingclass blacks and whites as the prime motivation for black exclusion and race inequalities may lead to color-blind policies that seek to mend intraclass divisions on the basis of universalistic, nonracial policies that serve working class interests as a whole. If, on the other hand, one finds that political elites used racial mobilization strategies and race-conscious public policies to win and maintain state power, then a different set of policy prescriptions may be in order. If the past enforcement of race-conscious policies created durable race identities and inequalities, then racially specific state remedies become much more plausible, even necessary, in certain circumstances. The hard choice between color-conscious policies that reduce inequalities but reinforce identities and color-blind policies that leave inequalities intact must be understood and considered carefully.

Our aim in this chapter is not only to consider how racial state politics and policies were erected on the basis of divergent racial identities and inequalities, but also how politics and policies are implicated in the creation of race identities and inequalities. Suffrage is a primary focus because without it, excluded groups have no institutionalized mechanism to promote and defend their civil and social rights. Without the vote, excluded groups remain excluded.

We begin by examining U.S. policies concerning civil and political rights in the pre-Emancipation era. Next we review the politics of postslavery enfranchisement and disfranchisement before examining how the civil rights movement provoked the dismantling of racial state structures in the United States (see James and Redding in this volume) and the passage of civil rights legislation including the Voting Rights Act of 1965 and its subsequent emendations. We then consider the literature on two core policy areas of the modern welfare state, welfare policies and public education as well as research on public opinion regarding these policies, especially those that are race-conscious. Finally, we examine the power of color-blind policies to legitimate white advantage and black disadvantages in liberal democracies, especially those with white majorities.[1]

RACE AND SUFFRAGE IN THE UNITES STATES

Disfranchisement before 1865

From the fifteenth through the nineteenth centuries, expanding commodity markets in Europe for sugar, cotton, tobacco, coffee, and other products stimulated the demand for greater supplies of servile labor to work the plantations and mines of the Americas. Weak states throughout large areas of sub-Saharan Africa left large populations vulnerable to the armed predations of stronger states that supplied the expanding markets for slaves. Just as political factors have always shaped the freedoms enjoyed by laborers as their interests conflicted with those of landowners, large-scale slave labor systems required states to defend the power of slave masters to discipline slave labor, capture and return runaways, and quash slave rebellions.

White servile labor was replaced by black slavery in much of the Americas between 1600 and 1800, but it is by no means clear that preexisting racial prejudice of white against black explains the shift (Morgan, 1975). Fredrickson's (2002:30–1) recent masterful survey of racism argued that a fully developed antiblack racism developed much later and that enslavement of Africans in the early colonial period "could easily be justified in terms of religious [whether they were converted Christians] and legal status without recourse to an explicit racism." Surely economic and even epidemiological factors were key factors in this transition to African enslavement, but political factors associated with the legal status of persons were particularly important (Engerman, 1986; Galenson, 1981). As British citizens, indentured servants retained state-protected natal rights, which their masters were obliged to respect. For example, masters could beat servants and slaves to enforce work discipline, but colonial courts protected servants against unfair punishment (Smith, 1947). Importantly, Europeans could choose the place of their servitude and most refused transportation to the plantation regions from the eighteenth century on. African slaves could not avoid the plantation regions and were citizens of no state in Africa or America that would defend their interests.

By the time of the American Revolution, African slavery was well-established in the United States. Even though some of the nation's founders recognized the hypocrisy of arguing for political liberty on the one hand while simultaneously subjugating Africans on the other, postrevolutionary state building actually resulted in the further institutionalization of slavery. At the Constitutional Convention, white Southern slaveholders refused to even debate the future of slavery and achieved most of their aims regarding it, most notably the three-fifths rule that counted slaves as three-fifths of a white citizen with respect to representation and taxes in the Constitution. Only on the question of the slave trade did the convention leave open the door for strong congressional intervention at a later date, a result possible because the Southern states were divided on the issue (Cooper and Cooper, 1991:106–7).

In the wake of the revolution, some slaveholding states allowed manumission of slaves, a practice which was more common in the upper

[1] A caveat: The literature on the political sociology of racial policy is vast, covering some 500 years of history, spanning the globe, and covering a gamut of topics that runs virtually as wide as the study of politics in general. Our review is necessarily selective. Throughout, we focus primarily on the literature on black–white racial politics as it applies to the United States, but we make references and comparisons to analyses of race and politics in other areas of the world. Even with this focus, our attempt to cover the literature reflects our judgments as to key issues and developments rather than any effort to be exhaustive.

South states of Virginia, Maryland, Kentucky, and Delaware. Free blacks were allowed to vote in many states (including some in the South) in the immediate postrevolutionary period; however, those rights were increasingly revoked such that by 1855 only five states, all in New England (excepting Connecticut), allowed free blacks to vote. Further, the federal government did not allow black suffrage in U.S. territories. In 1857, the Supreme Court ruled that neither free nor slave blacks could be citizens of the United States (Keyssar, 2000:54–8 and appendix A.4).

As such low numbers suggest, nowhere in the Americas was slavery in danger of withering away economically at the time that it was abolished (Eltis, 1983). Strong states with dynamic economies based upon free-wage labor where abolitionist ideologies flourished imposed abolition on weaker states. Britain played the dominant role in abolishing the transatlantic slave trade and, finally, in the worldwide abolition of slavery. Britain outlawed the slave trade in 1808 and freed the slaves in its West Indian colonies in 1833 over the strenuous objections of slave owners. The United States prohibited the importation of slaves after 1808 and the Civil War led to abolition in 1865. By the 1870s, all of the major European and American maritime and commercial powers had acquiesced to British pressure and outlawed the slave trade. Brazil became the last state in the Americas to abolish slavery in 1888.

Enfranchisement and Disfranchisement after 1865

If the brutal legacy of slavery remains the foremost reason for the stubborn persistence of racial inequality, prejudice, and discrimination in the twenty-first century United States, the spectacular failure of post-Civil War Reconstruction and the subsequent development of disfranchisement and segregation may rank a close second. This failure not only delayed American efforts to reckon with race, but also played its own role in deepening racial rifts.

Three constitutional amendments, and statutory laws to implement them, such as the Civil Rights Act of 1875, were at the core of Reconstruction. The amendments abolished slavery (Thirteenth); established due process and equal protection of the laws (Fourteenth); and barred suffrage restrictions on the basis or race, color, or previous condition of servitude (Fifteenth). These first attempts to address race inequalities with what we now call color-blind policies made possible an extraordinary political mobilization by African Americans in the late 1860s and early 1870s that resulted in high rates of participation and office-holding. Estimates of black turnout put black voting rates at above 50 percent in most Southern states during the 1880s and into the 1890s (Kousser, 1974; Redding and James, 2001). Black office-holding in Southern states during Reconstruction was also substantial, and included virtually every office but that of governor. An average of 268 black men served in the state legislatures of ten Southern states in the sessions between 1868 and 1876; moreover, two black senators and fourteen black representatives served in the U.S. Congress during the same period. More than 1,000 served in some local capacity. Though still hardly representative of population proportions, the numbers of officeholders are truly amazing when considered against the backdrop of recent history; moreover, they compare favorably, for example, to estimates of the numbers of women voters and officeholders in the wake of the adoption of the Nineteenth Amendment to the Constitution (Valelly, 2004:chap. 4). Though the national Republican Party and the affiliated, social movement-like Union League provided important resources for black political mobilization, much recent research has emphasized the self-organization of African Americans themselves.

This unprecedented political incorporation of a new racial group in the wake of its enslavement suffered early setbacks even as it advanced. Those setbacks included Supreme Court decisions that weakened Republican efforts to restrict the southern white electorate through loyalty oaths and undermined and greatly narrowed the scope of the statutory implementation of the Fourteenth and Fifteenth Amendments (Valelly, 2004). Other early setbacks included large-scale white resistance from groups such as the Ku Klux Klan in the form of violent intimidation, lynching, and electoral fraud, and the recession of 1873 that sapped Republican resources and will. The compromise of 1877, an oft-used marker for the end of Reconstruction, made Garfield the president in the disputed election of 1876 in exchange for the final withdrawal of troops from the South.

In spite of these setbacks and some de facto disfranchisement and segregation, race relations in the Southern states remained fluid in significant ways. Black suffrage (and, to a lesser extent, black office-holding) persisted, with average black turnout rates estimated at greater than 60 percent in 1880 and still above 40 percent in 1892 (Redding and James, 2001). Nonetheless, beginning in the late 1880s, Southern states adopted poll taxes, literacy, and other suffrage restrictions. Those laws, among other factors, virtually eliminated black voting by 1904. Accompanied by the adoption of rigid Jim Crow segregation measures, disfranchisement had devastating effects and marked the final death knell for efforts to reconstruct racial politics in the wake of the Civil War and Emancipation (Valelly, 1995).

Different accounts have been offered to explain the failure to incorporate African Americans into the American polity. Though they overlap and combine in many cases, we consider four accounts of this failed incorporation: racial attitudes, class exploitation, war and the international context, and institutionalist–constructionist approaches.

Racial attitudes have long been thought by many to lie at the core of racial conflict and discrimination. If, as Sumner suggests, "stateways cannot change folkways," then racial inequality will persist absent changes in attitudes. Historians such as Williamson (1984), Donald (1981), and Litwack (1998) all suggest that Southern race relations deteriorated as the turn of the century approached. In this view, younger blacks born in freedom asserted themselves more forcefully against de facto discrimination and segregation and white paternalism was displaced by a much more radical form of white supremacy that sought black deference in every aspect of life and imposed *de jure* measures to ensure that subordination.

Others focused on more general status and economic interests in accounting for hardening white racism (Stampp, 1965). William Julius Wilson (1978) saw poor white fears of economic competition with blacks as the key motive force behind racial oppression, which segued with his claim about the declining significance of race in the late twentieth century. Perman (2001) also found racial motivations as a central impetus to disfranchisement in the South during the 1890s.[2] The racial explanations of the failure of Reconstruction and the resulting racial disfranchisement and segregation dovetail with more contemporary accounts of racial politics that trace the changes in policy associated with the so-called second reconstruction of the civil rights movement era to shifts in the attitudes of whites toward blacks (Chong, 2000; Page, 1992).

The tendency to make racial attitudes the "deus ex machina that independently explain. . . the course of events" (Foner, 1988:xxvi) has been criticized on the grounds that "historic prejudices, however powerful and pervasive, do not by themselves do the work of political organization" (Kantrowitz, 2000:3).[3] Poor whites, sometimes seen as the key source for such racism, were profoundly unorganized prior to the late 1880s. The exceptions were the Southern Farmers' Alliance and Populist Party, which did succeed in organizing a large number of smaller white farmers. By and large, however, the Populists initially opposed rather than led efforts to restrict suffrage. Any account of race must show how it worked as a vehicle for power in a particular social context.[4]

[2] This line of argument emphasizing race as the key to southern history has a long history. See also Phillips (1928), Cash (1991 [1941]), Key (1984 [1949]), and Degler (1972).

[3] See also Harold D. Woodman (1987:259–60), who more broadly surveyed race arguments and concluded: "The explanation is potent, ubiquitous, and timeless. But it is just this universality that some insist weakens racism's explanatory power; anything that explains everything in the end explains nothing."

[4] Barbara Fields (1982:146, 156) in particular argues that scholars must analyze racial ideologies and attitudes

Du Bois (1935) was among the first to develop a class-based analysis of Reconstruction, developing Beard's and Beale's arguments that the Civil War and its aftermath was, among other things, an economic revolution which marked the triumph of Northern business interests. Among the recent class-based explanations, some research adapts Barrington Moore's (1966) argument that the dominant landed upper class, in alliance with a dependent middle class, produced a conservative industrialization. This "Prussian road" to modernization did not allow for the development of the bourgeois social structures and values necessary to support a democratic capitalist system. To make this thesis work for the South required showing the persistence of the landed elite through Emancipation, war, Reconstruction, and the instability of the last two decades of the nineteenth century. This persistence fatefully determined how modernization and politics developed (Billings, 1979; Wiener, 1978). The continued prevalence of planter elites and labor-repressive agriculture doomed both poor whites and blacks to an extremely lopsided economy and an elitist, repressive political system (James, 1986; 1988; Rueschemeyer, Stevens, and Stevens, 1992: 127–9).

Class analyses solve at least one problem associated with the race arguments – that of mobilization capacity. In contrast to poor whites, planter elites were, of course, very organized. Even the Ku Klux Klan terror activities were in the late 1860s and early 1870s largely organized and led by white elites.[5] The same can be said of the massive disfranchisement white supremacy campaigns of the 1890s. Both campaigns could be said to have resulted from class interests (Keyssar, 2000; Kousser, 1974).

While downplaying society-centered explanations based on race and class, a third line of argument focuses on states within the international arena, especially in the context of wars. Wars or the threat of war can induce states to extend suffrage rights and/or policy concessions to previously excluded groups in the name of national unity or as an inducement or reward for national service (Markoff, 1996). Whereas the late nineteenth century provided no international impetus for the ongoing incorporation of blacks into the American polity,[6] the 1950s were a much different time. The Cold War, in particular, has been found to have spurred the federal government, especially the executive branch, to side increasingly with the civil rights movement's quest for full civil and political rights for African Americans. As Dudziak (2000:100) succinctly put it, "racial segregation interfered with the Cold War imperative of winning the world over to democracy."[7]

In the previous three types of explanations, political institutions and mobilization are derivative, a product of preexisting social structures or configurations of states. Institutionalists are less apt to see classes and races as ready-made political actors than as contingent factors whose form is shaped by the institutional arenas (the type of electoral system, the traditions of the party system, the degree of state centralization, etc.) in which actors vie for power. In this view, stateways can and do change folkways associated with race and also can shape how classes form as they vie for political power.[8]

Kousser (1974) provides one means of getting around disputes about race and class by putting political institutions at the core of his understanding the failed incorporation of blacks at the end of the nineteenth century. In his account, dominant southern white planters used their overwhelming power and the racism of the white majority to mobilize blacks out of politics. They did this, he argues, once the threat of Northern intervention diminished after 1890, after putting down the strong internal political

within specific historical contexts in order to understand them. See also Frederickson (2002:75), who argues that "racism is always nationally specific."

[5] See Allen W. Trelease (1971:51–3, 115, 296, 332, 354, 363) and Paul Escott (1985:156–7).

[6] The Civil War itself, of course, was a crucial impetus toward emancipation as blacks soldiers played an important role in the Union victory. That role, in turn, became an important argument for extending suffrage to black males via the Fifteenth Amendment.

[7] See also Klinkner and Smith (1999), Plummer (1996), and Von Eschen (1997).

[8] In that sense, these more political and institutional accounts are not far from work on class that stresses the contingent nature of class formation, such as work in Katznelson and Zolberg (1986).

opposition of blacks and Populists through the use of large-scale fraud and often violent intimidation at election time. The disfranchisement of blacks was only fully achieved when white elites changed the rules of politics, using institutional mechanisms such as poll taxes and literacy tests to shut out black and poor white voters.[9] Kousser takes race and class positions and interests as given to explain how political institutions were used to incrementally disfranchise blacks and solidify racial divisions.

By contrast, Anthony Marx (1998) stresses the ways that state building is deeply implicated in race making in the United States, Brazil, and South Africa. In Marx's view, ethnic, regional, and class divisions among whites may threaten state-building efforts and therefore encourage elites to generate racial exclusionary laws that unify whites by subordinating blacks. Such laws in turn generate black political identity, which can then be used as mechanisms of mobilization to threaten social stability and force the relaxation of such laws. Thus, state making and race making are dynamically linked.

Though Marx is somewhat vague on how divisions among whites generate enough white unity to make blacks into scapegoats and implement racially exclusionary laws, recent work tackles issues of identity formation and mobilization more directly. Kantrowitz (2000), for example, focuses on the ideological manifestations of such mobilizing processes through an examination of the "reconstruction" of white supremacy by South Carolinian white supremacist Ben Tillman. Gilmore (1996) looks at the way in which class, race, and gender intersect in the generation of power. Finally, like Smith (1997), Redding (2003) argues that race making is a by-product of efforts toward political mobilization in unstable democratic systems. He examines the complex interplay between elites' manipulation of political and racial identity and the innovative mobilizing strategies marginalized groups adopted to combat disfranchisement. These latter innovations, along with changes in social relations wrought by postwar economic transformations, subverted the dominant hierarchical or vertical organization of politics by the Democratic Party and generated a significant degree of black political solidarity. White elites, however, were able to regain the upper hand by using their superior resources to co-opt and trump such innovations and embed their power in racially exclusionary laws. In these accounts oriented toward institutions and mobilization, politics are seen as an inventive and constructive struggle within the constraints and opportunities created not only by societal forces but also by formal and informal institutions.

The implementation of a one-party racial caste system in the South at the end of the nineteenth century, combined with the less formal but still sharper drawing of the color line in the North and West, was brutal, rigid, and thoroughly institutionalized. Once established, the Southern racial state persisted for more than half a century. It took no less than the disappearance of labor-intensive cotton agriculture, the great migration of blacks to Northern and Southern cities, and the power of the civil rights movement to change the way race was institutionalized within U.S. state institutions.

ENFRANCHISEMENT ONCE AGAIN: THE CIVIL RIGHTS MOVEMENT AND THE STATE

The civil rights movement ranks among the most important social movements in U.S. history. It not only directly led to the demise of the Southern Jim Crow state system and dramatically extended democracy in the United States, but it also served as a model and stimulus for many other domestic and international social movements of liberation (Morris, 1999). The political sociology of the civil rights movement has reflected and also led the general trajectory of the social movement literature itself over the course of the past three to four decades.[10]

[9] See Kousser (1974), generally and especially chap. 9 and Table 9.4, p. 244. See also his (1999) *Colorblind Injustice*, chap. 1.

[10] This review of the civil rights movement focuses on the social science literature. For reviews of the rather large historical literature on the topic, see Fairclough (1990), Lawson (1991), and Engles (2000).

Early sociological analyses of the civil rights movement parted ways with tendencies of the collective behavior tradition by emphasizing the essential rationality of the actors' grievances and their efforts to address them as well as the political nature of the struggle. Nonetheless, such studies often maintained an emphasis on the spontaneous (rather than the planned and organized) nature of movement mobilization and tactics (Killian, 1968; Matthews and Prothro, 1966; Meier and Rudwick, 1973; Zinn, 1964). Theorists more closely associated with mobilization approaches also argued that some parts of the movement were not very organized (Oberschall, 1973; Piven, 1977), which fit with a notion that marginalized groups lacked sufficient resources to develop organizational capacity. Instead, the success of the civil rights movement was linked to its ability to be spontaneously disruptive or garner strategically placed (usually elite) allies that bolstered the group's power.

McAdam (1982) and Morris (1984) produced studies of the civil rights movement that attacked a number of the central claims of both resource mobilization and classical collective behavior theory. Those two studies, now twenty years old but still among the most widely read political sociological analyses of the civil rights movement, and perhaps of movements in general, developed different but still largely complementary accounts.

Arguing for what he called a "political process" model, McAdam put organizational capacity and political opportunities at the core of his analysis of the generation, successes, and eclipse of the civil rights movement. The organizational capacity of the movement was strengthened by the decline of the Southern cotton economy; by the subsequent migration of blacks to cities and the North; and by the growth of the black church, black colleges, and the NAACP. Such changes, along with the shift in black political preferences to the Democratic Party and favorable federal government action (coming largely at the end of World War II), opened up opportunities for black insurgency that had not been there before, according to McAdam.

Morris's account focused more singularly on the organizational side, developing an account that zeroed in on black agency as central to both the origins and the outcome of black insurgency. To be sure, Morris stressed the changes in structural conditions (especially urbanization and growth of the black church) that made such agency possible. Nonetheless, Morris was much more skeptical than McAdam and others (Barkin, 1984; Garrow, 1978) about the importance of factors external to the movement, be they political opportunities, outside resources and allies, the media, or the federal government (Morris, 1984, 1993). Instead, Morris focused on what he called "indigenous" factors such as the mobilization of internal resources; strong linkages to mass-based secondary associations, especially black churches and the culture and charisma lying within them; and the use of innovative tactics and strategies.

As noted previously, a number of recent studies have cited the importance of the international context, especially postwar anticolonial struggles and the Cold War, in creating allies for the movement and inducing greater federal involvement in the South in the 1950s and 1960s (see Dudziak, 2000; Plummer, 1996; Skrentny, 1998; Von Eschen, 1997).

Other scholars turned (with the more general movement literature itself) to neglected issues of gender, culture, and movement outcomes. Black women such as Rosa Parks, Fannie Lou Hammer, Diane Nash, and Ella Baker as well as countless female activists of lesser renown played a crucial role in the movement, but only recently have scholars begun to fully analyze the interaction between gender and race in shaping movement mobilization and success. Robnett (1997) examined how high levels of patriarchy could both shunt the contributions of women to the background and also facilitate the development of black women as crucial "bridge" leaders between the mass of local activists and the more formal (male) leadership. In this interstitial position, women were often more radical given their proximity to the grassroots and freedom from interactions with state authorities (see also Herda-Rapp, 1998).

Coinciding and overlapping with work on gender by Robnett, Ling, and Monteith (1999), and Irons (1998) has been a more general recognition of the importance of cultural factors. Although neither McAdam (1982) nor Morris (1984) ignored culture, more recent works put culture at the core of the analysis. Chappell, Hutchinson, and Ward (1999), for example, examined the importance of dress and the presentation of "respectable" images that shaped movement activities whereas Platt and Fraser (1998) examined movement frames and discourses. Still other recent studies examine the importance of music and its influence on the construction of ideas and identities in the movement (Eyerman and Jamison, 1998; Ward, 1998) that keyed the movement's political successes.[11]

One of the more interesting lacunae in the literature on the civil rights movement involves how little we know about the opposition to the movement. There are exceptions touching on institutional- and class-oriented opposition (Bloom, 1987; James, 1988) as well as works by historians such as Roche (1998), and Chappell (1994) and early work by Bartley (1969) and McMillan (1971). As Engles (2000:842) has pointed out, "the failure to explore the segregationists would certainly disappoint Gunnar Myrdal, who argued more than fifty years ago that the real racial problem was in the white mind."

There is little doubt that the civil rights movement had a dramatic impact on U.S. politics and policy. Civil rights protests, urban riots, and segregationist violence have typically been seen as the main catalysts for breakthrough legislation and court rulings with respect to voting rights, equal employment opportunity, fair housing, and school desegregation. Because of their capacity to sow social disorder, create electoral instabilities, open the United States to international criticism in the context of the Cold War, and shift public perceptions, movements generated policy concessions from political elites and helped produce changes in public opinion with respect to racial inequality and public policy concerning it (Garrow, 1978; McAdam, 1982; Morris, 1984; Morris, 1993; Piven, 1977). This "dramatic events approach" (Santoro, 2002) sees the widespread sit-ins and the Birmingham and Selma protests of the early 1960s, and the dramatic media coverage of them, as leading directly to the early presidential executive orders dealing with racial discrimination, the 1964 Civil Rights Act, and the 1965 Voting Rights Act. Burstein (1985) focuses less on the movement events themselves than on liberalizing public opinion as being key to such legislative changes. Recent research by Santoro (2002) attempts to reconcile these two claims by arguing, at least with respect to fair employment laws, that dramatic movement events explain the first wave of racial policy responses. Movement events, since they subsided in number and intensity in the early 1970s, however, cannot explain subsequent policy developments such as the 1972 Equal Employment Opportunity Act as well as fair housing laws and subsequent extensions of the Voting Rights Act. Here more conventional political processes, especially public opinion, come into play.

Skrentny (1996), on the other hand, takes a different view, at least with respect to affirmative action. His evidence suggests that this policy developed not because of demands from the civil rights movement (which was initially wary of race conscious policies) or shifts in public opinion (which was solidly against such policies). Rather, one of the many ironies of this policy was that it was incrementally developed and then promoted by white government and business elites (many of them Republicans) as a form of "crisis management" to quell urban riots and burnish the American image abroad during a time of Cold War.

ANALYSES OF PUBLIC POLICIES

The dramatic social movement activity of the 1960s produced transformations of political

[11] See also McAdam's (1999) new introduction to the second edition of his (1982) book. Newer studies are increasingly examining the ways in which the cultural content of black churches may facilitate and sometimes inhibit civil rights movement mobilization (e.g., Calhoun-Brown, 1998; Patillo-McCoy, 1998).

institutions in the United States and stimulated a rich body of public policy research that continues to grow. A comprehensive review of the literature on public policies focused on racial inequalities is beyond the scope of this chapter (see Brown, 2003). Instead, we provide a selective review of important works that we believe are illustrative of the breadth of the issues addressed and then discuss the political forces that undermined support for such policies and produced an impetus toward color-blind policies. The critique of the racial state (James and Redding in this volume) provides the critical framework for evaluating the nature of the policies adopted and enforced in different contexts. A strong tendency away from color-conscious policies and toward color-blind policies is apparent, but the multilayered and fragmented U.S. state structure produces a variety of impacts on race inequalities. We focus first on policies that affect political and civil rights and then turn to a variety of social welfare policies that are impacted by political and civil rights (Marshall, 1992 [1950]).

Voting Rights

Matthews' and Prothro's (1966) classic analysis of the denial of voting rights to African Americans ended in 1960 just before the passage of the 1965 Voting Rights Act. Compared with the huge amount of research on the politics of black disfranchisement during the period from about 1877 to 1910, research on the reenfranchisement of blacks and other minorities has been limited. Historical accounts analyze the forces leading to the passage of the Voting Rights Act and the effects of increasing levels of black voter turnout immediately thereafter (e.g., Keech, 1968; Lawson, 1976; Lawson, 1985, 1990). James (1988) found that the areas of greatest resistance to black enfranchisement were governed by local state structures serving areas where labor-intensive cotton agriculture persisted and depended on black agricultural labor. Alt (1994) found that the elimination of state-enforced registration obstacles (e.g., literacy tests and poll taxes) and allowing federal examiners to intervene at the local level to register black voters increased black registration rates dramatically. Black registration rates apparently approached those of whites as white mobilization stimulated black countermobilization (Alt, 1994). The disadvantage of "agricultural labor dependence," so prominent earlier, disappeared by 1971 (Alt, 1994). Black voter turnout still lags white turnout nationally, but continued to increase slightly between 1994 and 1998 (from 39 to 42%) as white turnout declined (from 51 to 47%) (Gaither and Newburger, 2001). As expected, legislators are more receptive to the interests of minority groups if they are enfranchised and vote (e.g., Kousser, 1999; Lawson, 1985, 1990; Lublin, 1995).

As the enfranchisement of racial minorities appeared complete, scholarly attention shifted to the electoral representation of minority group voters. Because racially polarized voting persists, the election of black candidates depends heavily on the black proportion of the electorate. Furthermore, candidates continue to mobilize constituencies by making racial appeals (Mendelberg, 2001). Black candidates for public office seldom win elections in districts that do not have black majorities (Grofman and Davidson, 1994; Handley and Grofman, 1994). The Voting Rights Act of 1965 (VRA) prohibited changes in the boundaries of electoral districts if those changes would dilute black voting strength. In 1982, the VRA was amended to strengthen the protection of minority voting rights and enhance their ability to elect representatives of their own race if they chose to do so (Davidson, 1994). As a result of Justice Department actions and private litigation in the early 1980s to enforce the new provisions of the VRA, the number of black majority districts grew and the number of black elected officials increased appreciably (Grofman and Davidson, 1994; Handley and Grofman, 1994). The Democratic Party traditionally supported the creation of black majority districts because black voters vote overwhelmingly for Democrats. On the other hand, Republicans have been able to turn this initial Democratic advantage in black voting into a disadvantage. By concentrating black voters in black majority districts, Democratic strength in other districts is diluted, making Republican victories there more likely (Kousser, 1999; Lublin, 1995; Thernstrom, 1987).

Deliberately redrawing electoral district boundaries to create black majority districts is an example of a racial state policy (James and Redding in this volume) and has been subjected to heavy criticism for that reason. Thernstrom argues that the VRA, a law originally intended to prevent the racist disfranchisement of Southern black voters, has been turned into "a means to ensure that black votes have value – have the power, that is, to elect blacks" (1987:4). Nevertheless, the trajectory of recent U.S. Supreme Court decisions is moving toward color-blind criteria for drawing electoral district boundaries. Kousser's massive study documents this trend in detail and concludes that the Court's motivation for weakening the protection for black majority districts is a thinly disguised attempt to enforce white supremacy rather than equal rights (1999).

Another voting rights issue that is beginning to draw greater attention is the larger number of blacks who have been disfranchised by virtue of a felony conviction. Uggen and Manza (2002) estimate that nearly 2 million blacks, more than 7 percent of the black voting age population, have been disfranchised in this way. They also estimate that felon disfranchisement laws and high rates of crimination punishment may have altered the outcomes of numerous elections since the 1970s.

With the increase in black voting brought by the Voting Rights Act and other political reforms, black office-holding grew dramatically. In 1970 there were fewer than 1,500 black elected officials in the United States; by the year 2000 there were close to 9,000. The U.S. Congress had only twelve black members in 1970 but nearly forty in 2000. Still, in terms of percentages, the overall numbers remain quite low for the most part. While blacks make up more than 12 percent of the U.S. population, the 9,000 blacks in office represents less than 2 percent of all elected officials. At the state legislative level, the figure is closer to 7 percent, whereas representation in Congress is nearly 9 percent (U.S., 2000; U.S., 2002). There is strong evidence that black elected officials and whites elected with the support of large black constituencies support policies that are more consistent with the stated interests of blacks than is otherwise the case (Canon, 1999; Kousser, 1999; Thernstrom, 1987).[12] Such evidence on black representation has led some to argue for changing the winner-take-all U.S. representational system in ways that will make greater black office-holding more likely (Guinier, 1994).

While incorporation of African Americans into U.S. politics remains today a contentious issue, in Britain (which is, among European countries, closest to the United States in terms of having a settled ethnic minority where skin color – as opposed to nationality, culture, or religion – is a major marker of distinction), political rights for its ethnic minority never required the national government's intervention, as in the United States. As Hansen (2000) points out, due to the prerogatives of the British Empire, immigrants from Commonwealth societies like Jamaica and India were, until 1962 (when Britain severely restricted immigration from the Commonwealth), defined as British subjects who had the right to vote in elections. Ironically, British racial minorities have less political power at the national level than do African Americans – they do not have a major organization at the national level, nor have they been allowed to have racial caucuses within the political parties or in Parliament (Layton-Henry, 1992; Lieberman, 2002; Teles, 1998). Frederickson (1998) and Teles (1998) also suggest that racial identity among minorities is weaker in Britain than in the United States, making it a less suitable basis for political mobilization.

Social Welfare and Housing Segregation

William J. Wilson and his colleagues provided a voluminous and influential stream of research on the continuing high levels of poverty among

[12] See also Frymer (1999), Swain (1993), Whitby, (1997), and Whitby and Krause (2001) for recent research on this issue.

African Americans in the United States (1987, 1996, 1999). His recent research identifies a variety of causes of poverty among African Americans (e.g., loss of jobs in black residential areas, poor qualifications among black job seekers, residential segregation, white racism and discrimination, etc.), but none attribute any continuing causal impacts to state institutions. Rather than enforcing racial oppression, the state now promotes "racial equality" (Wilson, 1978). Wilson's underdeveloped theory of the state coupled with an understanding of the white electoral majority's widespread opposition to color-conscious policies designed to eliminate race inequalities (e.g., affirmative action) led him to advocate color-blind policies to reduce class inequalities. Because blacks are disproportionately poor, they would benefit disproportionately from any federal program designed to reduce poverty. Hence, politically possible color-blind antipoverty policies are preferred over color-conscious policies that alienate whites and tend to help middle class blacks more than "truly disadvantaged" whites and blacks (Wilson, 1987, 1996).

Douglas Massey and his colleagues also produced a massive volume of research on the causes of African American poverty (e.g., Massey and Denton, 1993). Their research establishes the links between residential segregation and the asymmetry in the concentration of poverty for whites and blacks (Massey, 1990). Racial segregation concentrates poor African Americans in high poverty areas at high rates and, by contrast, disperses poor whites to more affluent areas. As segregation concentrates black poverty, it also concentrates blacks in neighborhoods with higher crime rates and myriad other social problems (Massey, 1990, 2001; Massey and Denton, 1993). Racial segregation is an obstruction to black residential mobility, which, in turn, inhibits black social mobility.

Color-conscious state policies in the past are prime contributors to racial differences in the concentration of poverty in the present (Massey and Denton, 1993). Continuing patterns of labor market and housing market discrimination also exacerbate the disadvantages of the depressed neighborhoods that are home to large numbers of African Americans. In addition, residential segregation is perhaps the most powerful cause of the creation and maintenance of racial identities in the United States today (James, 1994; Tilly, Moss, Kirschenman, and Kennelly, 2001). By shaping racial identities, residential segregation reproduces the motivation that perpetuates race discrimination. Perhaps recognizing the liberal state's inability to force people to live in racially integrated neighborhoods, Massey recommends that more resources and commitment of will to the enforcement of fair housing laws as the principal instrument of desegregation. Massey joins with Wilson in recommending color-blind solutions for current problems of race inequality. Schill (1994) points out that antidiscrimination enforcement alone is ineffective in dismantling the racial concentration of poverty and argues that federal policies of locating low-income housing in white suburban areas are essential. Nevertheless, Schill also advocates a color-blind, class-based policy. Wilson and Massey show that the legacies of color-conscious policies linger in the race inequalities of today, but have difficulty devising color-blind policies that will correct them.

Studies that theorize the state show that color-blind policies have different impacts depending on the organizational structure of the state. The political scientist Robert Lieberman (1998) covers some of the same territory as Quadagno (1988, 1994), but provides a nuanced model of the state that reflects the multilevel, hierarchical model of organizational structure advocated by Lehman (1988). As did Quadagno, he identifies the difference between programs that are federally administered according to universal criteria and national programs administered through racially biased organizations shaped by locally powerful parochial interests. In addition, Lieberman claims that the organizational institutionalization of who pays and who benefits shapes political support for the social welfare programs and the political identities of contributors and beneficiaries.

> Policies with egalitarian benefits and contributory financing will produce self-generating, perpetual, and unified constituencies, whereas discretionary, noncontributory policies will have constituencies that are more fragmented and separated politically from the

> general population. The structure of benefits and financing also influences the relationship of beneficiaries to other elements of the political system, particularly their status in the public mind as "deserving" or "undeserving," "honorable" or "dishonorable." (Lieberman, 1998)

Lieberman analyzes the historical trajectory of three social welfare programs to evaluate the adequacy of his claims. Old Age Insurance (OAI) was nationally administered and funded by contributions from beneficiaries who were selected according to egalitarian criteria. Aid to Dependent Children (ADC) was a noncontributory program administered locally according to the discretion of state and local officials who discriminated against blacks. Unemployment Insurance (UI) provided an intermediate case between OAI and ADC.

Because agricultural and domestic workers were originally excluded from OAI and because blacks were disproportionately employed in agriculture or domestic work, few blacks benefited from OAI during the 1930s. Amendments during the 1950s finally extended OAI to agricultural and domestic workers, and blacks were brought into the system without stigmatizing the program. OAI is still the most popular and most fairly administered welfare program in the United States. By contrast, political struggles surrounding ADC stigmatized it as an entitlement program for blacks that they had not earned. Discriminatory administration of ADC through parochial local institutions eventually became the target of black protest politics, which ratified the racial stigmatization of the program in the minds of many whites. Without the protection of national political institutions, the racial politicization of ADC at the local level led to the "political degeneration of welfare" and the "political construction of the urban underclass" (Lieberman, 1998).

The intermediate case of Unemployment Insurance produced intermediate results as expected. UI was administered fairly across racial lines and did not become mired in racial politics as did ADC. Nevertheless, because UI was administered through parochial local institutions and because it was largely funded through employer rather than employee contributions, it tended to reinforce racial divisions in the workforce. UI provided an honorable link to the welfare state for the black middle class, but had little to offer poor African Americans who were isolated and cut off from the labor force (Lieberman, 1998).

Lieberman's analysis of social welfare policy in the United States provides three important qualifications to the theory of the racial state. First, all color-blind policies are not the same. The way that social policies are institutionalized within the organizational structure of the state has a profound impact on the maintaining or exacerbating of racial inequalities. Second, the administration of social welfare policies through local political institutions that have discretionary power in determining program eligibility and benefits produces unequal provision of social benefits. If locally powerful interests are motivated by racial bias, social provision will be racially biased. Third, locally administered, need-based, social welfare policies tend to reinforce racial politics and identities. Racial polarization tends to stigmatize the target welfare program and its beneficiaries.

Other Policies

The trend toward color blindness in policy formation and implementation is apparent in other social policy areas. For example, color-conscious policies such as busing to desegregate public schools are being abandoned even though many public school systems, especially those in the largest cities, have disproportionate numbers of white or blacks students assigned to them. Supreme Court decisions increasingly release public school districts from within-district mandatory desegregation policies that were imposed as a remedy for the racially discriminatory policies of the past (e.g., Armor, 1995; Orfield and Eaton, 1996). Cross-district remedies are not required unless it can be shown that the boundaries between districts were drawn with discriminatory intent, an almost impossible standard to prove.

The administration of public schools in the United States is fragmented into thousands of public school districts. The forces that created the patterns of residential segregation in urban areas contribute to the racially unequal assignment of students to schools (Massey and Denton, 1993; Orfield, 1978; Orfield and Eaton, 1996). The network of school districts creates a decision environment that allows whites with sufficient resources to escape sending their children to schools with substantial black enrollments if they choose. Thus, the fragmentation of metropolitan schooling into many independent districts increases segregation between districts (James, 1989; Orfield, Bachmeier, James, and Eitle, 1997). Political boundaries between districts insulate white majority districts from desegregative policies and shape the residential housing choices of whites by serving as markers that distinguish "good" neighborhoods from "bad" (Weiher, 1991; Wells and Crain, 1997). As in the case of social welfare programs, the fragmented, multilevel institutional structure that provides public schooling in the United States also provides racially unequal schooling environments for students and contributes to the maintenance of racial identities. Similar patterns are typical of studies of affirmative action, labor market discrimination, and racial inequalities in criminal justice (e.g., Brown, 2003; Hawkins, 2001; Kennedy, 2001; Moss and Tilly, 2001; Skrentny, 1996, 2001; Swain, 2001; Walker, Spohn, and DeLone, 2004).

Nonetheless, scholars have noted the paradox that antidiscrimination policies are stronger and more "race-conscious" in America, the epitome of being a "weak state," than in stronger states with antidiscrimination laws such as Britain. Lieberman (2002) argues that the fragmented nature of the U.S. government proved to be an unexpected strength for antidiscrimination enforcement. The U.S. Equal Employment Opportunity Commission (EEOC) was able to use its power of publicity, the courts, and its alliance with the NAACP to overcome weak White House support and congressional hostility and pursue a "collective, race-conscious enforcement of Title VII [of the 1964 Civil Rights Act]" (Lieberman, 2002:148). In Britain, the weak support, if not outright hostility, of the British national government – which is more centralized and has a stronger executive than in the United States – was a constraint that the Commission for Racial Equality (the British counterpart to the EEOC) could not overcome (see also Teles, 1998). Both Lieberman (2002) and Teles (1998) also highlight the importance of the lack of political power of British minorities at the national level compared to that of African Americans.

The moves away from race-conscious policies and toward color-blind policies discussed earlier reflected broader events and trends in U.S. class and racial politics. As noted previously, both the Johnson and Nixon administrations pushed affirmative action programs; those programs, however, presented both difficulties and opportunities for the two parties. For Democrats, promulgation of such policies could solidify black support for the party. However, to the extent that policies such as the Philadelphia Plan attacked racially exclusionary hiring practices in predominantly Democratic building trade unions, they could cause intramural fights in the Democratic coalition. The Nixon administration, in spite of its surprisingly strong early support of affirmative action, changed its rhetoric rather quickly when it saw it could use "quotas" as a wedge issue between labor unions and minorities (Skrentny, 1996; Edsall and Edsall, 1991).

A number of research studies that address these concerns have yielded mixed results. In their (1999) book, Manza and Brooks trace the roles of social cleavages (race, class, religion, and gender) in voting during presidential elections from 1952 to 1992. Although they find that the aggregated impact of class cleavages (i.e., differences between managers, professionals, the self-employed, the skilled and nonskilled working classes, and people outside the labor force in vote choice) has fluctuated with no apparent trends, they do find evidence that skilled and unskilled workers showed a sharp decreases inDemocratic support in the late 1960s and late 1970s, respectively (although both groups are more likely than not to vote Democrat). The consequence of these shifts is that the class compositions of Democratic and Republican voters have converged over time.

Meanwhile, differences between blacks and nonblacks in vote choice have increased over time, with African American support for the Democrats jumping to over 90 percent starting with the 1964 presidential election, whereas white Democratic support has tended to hover between 40 and 50 percent. Moreover, Manza and Brooks show that during elections when black/nonblack differences in vote choice are heightened, the impact of an individual's class position is muted, suggesting a zero-sum relationship between class and race cleavages. Weakliem (1997) also finds that the impact of class on vote choice is depressed in states with a high proportion of African Americans (although this negative effect of black population on class voting decreases over time). This zero-sum relationship between class and race cleavages, as well as the fact of declining working class support for the Democrats, suggests that Democratic support for the civil rights agenda has alienated the white working class. However, the evidence is not wholly consistent with this claim. Manza and Brooks (1999) find that racial attitudes do not explain all of the working class shift toward the Republicans. Instead, workers' evaluations of the national economy and their increased hostility toward welfare policies were the major factors leading to their alienation from the Democrats.

Frymer (1999) details how the cross-pressures of increased black and declining white working Class support affected the Democratic Party. Due to the civil rights movement and Cold War pressures (discussed previously), the Democrats were able to pass landmark civil rights legislation such as the 1964 Civil Rights Act, the 1965 Voting Rights Act, and the 1968 Fair Housing Act. After Nixon's election and the fiasco of the 1968 Democratic Convention, the Democratic Party became the major vehicle for the civil rights agenda. The party reformed its nominating process, giving grassroots movements more influence over which candidate would be nominated. Black Democratic Congresspeople formed the Congressional Black Caucus (CBC) in 1970 and worked to draw attention to issues of employment, poverty, civil rights, and human rights in Latin America and Africa (interestingly enough, Frymer finds that the CBC dedicated more of its efforts to economic and welfare policies that would benefit both blacks and whites than to civil rights).

However, as a result of ensuing Democratic defeats in presidential elections, white Democrats began to accept the political necessity of distancing their party from African American interests, a strategy epitomized by Bill Clinton, whose commitment to civil rights rarely went beyond symbolic gestures (Frymer, 2002). In the legislative realm, the Democratic Party also refused to support legislative initiatives by the CBC, such as its attempts to pass full employment legislation during the Carter administration (despite the fact that the Democrats were the majority party in Congress). When white Democratic congresspeople did ally with the CBC, it was usually on issues that had bipartisan support, such as the 1982 Voting Rights Act. Black Democrats have been instrumental in promoting contract set-asides for minorities and blunting domestic spending cuts in behind-the-scenes committee work, but their success in crafting legislation in committee depends on congressional rules that thwart the majority will, such as the seniority system for committee chairs (Frymer, 1999).

Even though African Americans provide the highest support for the Democratic Party of any racial group, Frymer (1999, 2002) argues the Democratic Party takes its black constituency for granted and will rarely support policy initiatives that would benefit minorities (or the poor in general, for that matter), in an effort to win white support. He concludes that the effective exclusion of minorities from the agenda-setting process is an inevitable outcome of a two-party, majoritarian electoral system, and that nothing less than major electoral reform will fully incorporate blacks in American politics.

PUBLIC OPINION AND RACE

We now turn our attention to the public reaction to these policy efforts to ameliorate racial inequality. After justifying the study of public opinion on racial issues, we describe the trends in whites' and blacks' support for government action to ensure racial equality and then review the contending interpretations of these trends.[13]

Studying individuals' opinions on racial issues is important for two reasons. First, individuals' stands can influence broad political outcomes such as policy. Some scholars are skeptical of racial attitudes having an independent role in long-term shifts in racial politics and view changes in whites' sentiment toward blacks as reflections of political actors maneuvering in institutional arenas. However, even if one believes that racial attitudes are epiphenomena, it is plausible that aggregate public opinion can spark or facilitate short-term changes in racial politics. This can occur through individuals voting (Brooks 2000), policy makers heeding public opinion (see Manza and Cook, 2002 for the case that public opinion does influence state actors, albeit contingently), or people thwarting policies after their formulation (e.g., Northern whites forming antibusing social movements and fleeing to the suburbs in response to federal desegregation efforts).

Another reason for studying racial attitudes is that they are a barometer of group relations. Jackman (1994), for example, argues that intergroup attitudes reflect the messages and ideologies that not only percolate within groups, but are also the messages that are transmitted to the other group in a drawn-out process of intergroup negotiation and persuasion. Thus, intergroup attitudes are not, as Jackman (1994:60) puts it, "naively expressive," but rather "communicative and political" as well.

Trends and Patterns[14]

The most remarked-upon finding in research on racial attitudes is that since the civil rights movement, whites have increasingly endorsed principles of equal treatment for blacks, which is the sentiment that blacks should be able to go to the same schools, live in the same neighborhoods, enjoy the same public accommodations, and work at the same workplaces and jobs that whites do. Support for some of these principles approaches 100 percent. Usually, however, white support for government intervention to enforce rights for blacks lags behind their support for the principles in question. For example, although over the years white Americans have told surveyors that whites should not keep black families out of white neighborhoods, whites are less disposed to favor open housing laws. This has led Schuman et al. (1997) to coin the phrase "the principle-implementation gap" to describe white endorsement for general principles of racial equality but reluctance to support government implementation of those principles.

Affirmative action-like policies that require preferential treatment in jobs and university admissions elicit very low support from white Americans (usually less than 30 percent of whites support such policies). Studies using split ballot survey experiments show that whites oppose preferential treatment regardless if the beneficiaries are blacks or another disadvantaged group, like women; but whites are more likely to oppose preferential treatment benefiting blacks than similar policies benefiting women. Whites are much more amenable to "opportunity-enhancing" policies for blacks, such as job training, educational assistance, and companies' outreach efforts to attract minority applicants, but again they show greater support for policies when the beneficiaries are not specifically black, such as low-income individuals or women (Bobo and Kluegel, 1993; Steeh and Krysan, 1996).

[13] This section follows the public opinion and race research agenda's focus on whites and blacks. For work that examines attitudes about Latinos and Asians or the racial attitudes of Latinos and Asians, see Bobo and Hutchings (1996), Bobo and Johnson (2000), Bobo and Massagli (2001), Citrin et al. (2001), Huddy and Sears (1995), Kluegel and Bobo (2001), and Sears et al. (1999). For recent work on public opinion toward immigrants (who are usually considered ethnic outgroups) in European societies, see Coenders, Scheepers, Sniderman, and Verbeck (2001), Lubbers, Scheepers, and Billiet (2000), McLaren (2003), Meertens and Pettigrew (1997), Pettigrew and Meertens (2001), and Scheepers, Gijsberts, and Coenders (2002).

[14] Much of this section is based on Schuman, Steeh, Bobo, and Krysan's (1997) *Racial Attitudes in America*.

Blacks show much higher support for principles of equal treatment, government implementation of those principles, and opportunity-enhancing and affirmative action policies than whites do. Black Americans also show greater support for social welfare policies not related to race than whites (Bobo and Kluegel, 1993; Kinder and Winter, 2001; Schuman, Steeh, Bobo, and Krysan, 1997). Black support for most of these policies has remained at high levels throughout the years with no clear trend, although there is some evidence that black support for preferential treatment declined in the 1990s (Steeh and Krysan, 1996). Interestingly enough, the principle–implementation gap also exists for blacks, although the gap is much smaller than for whites.

THEORIES OF PUBLIC OPINION AND RACIAL POLITICS

For the past two decades, social scientists have debated interpretations of the changes in Americans' opinions on race policies and why so many white Americans oppose state efforts to ensure black–white parity in social status and economic resources. Although there are many contending answers, at its core this debate boils down to the extent of white hostility toward racial equality. On one side, scholars taking a "politics-centered approach" (Sniderman, Crosby, and Howell, 2000) argue that this hostility is limited to Americans with little education and that much of white disapproval of government intervention to help African Americans is grounded in commitments to meritocracy or laissez-faire principles. Researchers in a race-centered framework, however, believe that white antipathy to racial equality is the key element for understanding the changes in white support for racial policies.[15]

Sniderman and colleagues (1997, 1996, 2000, 1993) argue that contemporary racial politics represent a sharp break from the past. Whereas politics during the Jim Crow era revolved around whether one was in favor of racial equality or not – indeed, whether one viewed blacks as equal to whites – current politics over racial issues hinge on broader political values and less on evaluations about blacks per se. While Sniderman and Piazza (1993) agree that prejudice continues to exist among whites, its effect on whites' stands on racial policies is confined to the less educated. Among the well-educated, Sniderman argues, political views – namely, about the extent to which government should intervene in market processes – motivate positions on racial issues. Research bears out Sniderman's general claim that political values not directly related to race do substantially influence whites' support or opposition to race-targeted policies (Kinder and Sanders, 1996; Sears, Laar, Carrillo, and Kosterman, 1997; Tuch, 1996).

Generally speaking, authors in the race-centered approach believe that hostility toward racial equality has survived the social changes brought about by the civil rights movement, but this animus has changed form in the face of the empowerment of African Americans.[16] According to Jackman (1994), groups involved in expropriative, unequal relationships (including blacks and whites) benefit by avoiding open conflict that risks whatever stake they have in the status quo. When the civil rights movement successfully forced the state to extend the franchise to blacks, they gained enough political leverage to make blatant, Jim Crow racism costly and self-defeating. Where Jim Crow racism was premised on categorical and inherent differences between whites and blacks, new forms of racism treat black–white differences as more differences of degree than of kind and do not attribute these differences to inherent qualities of whites and blacks. This new racism views black disadvantages as problems largely of African Americans' own making, and not so much due to discrimination. It combines universalistic principles like individualism to indifference toward existing black–white

[15] For more extensive overviews of this debate, see Krysan (2000) and Sears, Hetts, Sidanius, and Bobo (2000).

[16] Due to space limitations, we try to present a coherent synthesis of various race-centered works; for more information on disagreements among the race-centered approaches, consult the references in note 15.

inequalities, and thus provides a powerful justification for whites to oppose remedies for black-white inequality in wealth, power, and status (Bobo, Kluegel, and Smith, 1997; Jackman, 1994).

A number of researchers have offered their own versions of new racism; currently the most prominent are symbolic racism (Kinder and Sears, 1981; Sears, 1988), racial resentment (Kinder and Sanders, 1996), and laissez-faire racism (Bobo, Kluegel, and Smith, 1997). Usually, the new racism is measured by survey items asking respondents their agreement with statements that are tinged with either sympathy toward African Americans or moral condemnation (e.g., "Over the past few years, blacks have gotten less than they deserve" and "It's really a matter of some people not trying hard enough; if blacks would only try harder they could be just as well off as whites").

The new racism has powerful effects on whites' policy opinions. Research shows that it is the most powerful predictor of whites' opposition to various racial policies, such as enforcing antidiscrimination employment laws, spending money to assist blacks, and affirmative action (Kinder and Sanders, 1996; Sears, Laar, Carrillo, and Kosterman, 1997). Scholars have also found that new racism and similar measures also temper support for other domestic policies not directly related to race, such as welfare (Gilens, 1999; Kinder and Sanders, 1996).[17]

Other research in the race-centered framework focus on black–white cleavages in support for racial policies and argue that these divisions represent the contrary group interests of blacks and whites. These policies may not necessarily help the individual blacks who support them or hurt the individual whites who oppose them; the race cleavages occur because of perceptions that the policy would help or hurt the racial groups as a whole (Bobo, 1988; Bobo and Kluegel, 1993; Jackman, 1994; Kinder and Winter, 2001). Besides examining black–white differences in opinion, Bobo (1983, 2000; Bobo and Johnson, 2000) has also examined how perceptions of group conflict vary among racial groups and how they motivate support or opposition to various racial policies, showing mixed results.

The race-centered approach makes a persuasive case that white opposition to racial policies is not reducible to political principles and values and that white hostility to racial equality is still a potent political force. Though this perspective offers provocative insights on contemporary U.S. politics, more work is needed to refine its ideas about group conflict and negotiation into falsifiable hypotheses (Schuman, 1995; Sniderman, Crosby, and Howell, 2000).

THE POWER OF COLOR-BLIND POLICIES TO LEGITIMATE WHITE ADVANTAGE

A crucial turn in the worldwide process of racial formation occurred after World War II (Goldberg, 2002; Winant, 2001). White supremacy is gradually giving way to "racial dualism" in which overt expression of racism is opposed, but the inequalities created by centuries of white supremacy are viewed as largely corrected. At the state level, this process is reflected in the abandonment of explicit racial policies in favor of race-neutral policies. Winant (2001) argues that protecting and extending race inequalities no longer needs "explicit state enforcement" as it did in the past because race is hegemonic. Members of racial minority groups consent to persistence of race inequalities because liberal democratic political institutions hide their causes. Explicit enforcement of white supremacist policies now undermines white supremacy; racial hegemony protects whites' racial advantages by denying that they exist (Winant, 2001).

Studies of race policy trends in the United States concur with Goldberg and Winant (Brown, 2003; Kousser, 1999; Lublin, 1995). For example, Brown et al. (2003) argue that whites fail to see the durable pattern of race inequality that accumulated over the decades

[17] Research using new racism concepts have been criticized on both conceptual and measurement grounds – see work by Sniderman and colleagues (2000, 1993) and Schuman (2000). For the defense of the concept and its measures, see Sears et al. (1997) and Kinder and colleagues (2000, 1996).

to their advantage and to the disadvantage of nonwhites. The cumulative advantage enjoyed by whites is the direct result of color-conscious state policies that discriminated against blacks in the past. Whites who agree with the liberal principles enshrined in the civil rights laws view themselves as having no direct responsibility for the disadvantages suffered by blacks. Whites are convinced that they are not guilty of racism because they do not engage in or support race-conscious policies that discriminate against blacks. Bonilla-Silva (2003) argues that liberalism's emphasis on equal opportunity makes it possible for whites to "appear 'reasonable' and even 'moral,' while opposing almost all practical approaches to deal with de facto racial inequality." Whereas color-blind ideology was once a powerful tool for racial justice because it attacked state-enforced race discrimination, it is now a "near-impenetrable shield, almost a civic religion, that actually promotes the unequal racial status quo" (Brown, 2003).

Policy makers who wish to reduce racial inequalities face a dilemma. Color-blind policies tend to protect white advantage by prohibiting policy tools that would use race criteria to redistribute resources from whites to nonwhites. Color-conscious policies, even modest ones like most affirmative action programs, reinforce white race identities and white opposition to the policies. Advocates of color-conscious policies to reduce race inequalities (e.g., Bonilla-Silva, 2003; Brown, 2003; Kousser, 1999) may be correct that some whites, perhaps most, hide their preference for white advantage behind a convenient mask of liberal values. Nevertheless, advocates do not confront directly the claims of critics (e.g., D'Souza, 1995; Sleeper, 1997; Thernstrom, 1987; Thernstrom and Thernstrom 1997) that color-conscious policies anger whites and reinforce white-identity politics that the color-conscious policies are intended to ameliorate. In some policy areas such as public school and residential segregation, white withdrawal or refusal to participate reduces or destroys the effectiveness of color-conscious policies (e.g., James 1989; Massey and Denton, 1993; Peterson, 1981). In other policy domains such as wealth inequalities, the normativity of whiteness[18] interprets white advantage as entitlement and renders invisible the cumulative disadvantage suffered by nonwhites (Brown, 2003). In every policy area, color-blind policies tend to leave inequalities unchanged, whereas color-conscious ones reinforce white racial identities and stiffen white resistance to change. When whites are in the majority, they may be able veto color-conscious policies that threaten their advantages or sense of entitlement.

But color-blind policies are also popular in Brazil and South Africa, where whites are not a numerical majority. Widespread belief in the legitimacy of individual citizenship rights are reinforced by the institutions of liberal democracies. The exercise of individual citizenship rights legitimizes racial inequalities by disguising them as the effect of individual choices. Just as Lenin (1943) argued that democracy is the "best possible political shell" to legitimate capitalist exploitation, liberal democracy is also the best possible shell to mask racial inequalities. (See Anderson, 1976 on the power of liberal democracies to legitimate social inequalities.)

CONCLUSION

This review of the political sociological literature on race reveals an increasing appreciation of the ways that race identities and inequalities are both causes and effects of state making. The disruption and turmoil caused by the civil rights movement during the 1960s was the engine of change in the United States that drove state policies from an overt defense of white supremacy and white advantage toward color-blind policies and institutional arrangements typical of liberal democratic states. The trend toward color-blind policies in the United States, which is mirrored in other countries around the world,

[18] Brown et al. (2003:34) describe the inability of whites to see the cumulative advantage of whiteness and the durability of black disadvantage as analogous to the blindness of fish to the water that surrounds them. Whites "cannot see how this society produces advantages for them because these benefits seem so natural that they are taken for granted, experienced as wholly legitimate."

has significant power to disguise race inequalities, making them appear natural rather than the result of color-conscious policies of the past or the direct race discrimination in the present.

In this chapter we have traced the trajectory of social policies bearing on race in the United States. We argue that, due to the maneuvering of white elites in political arenas, local, state, and national governments enforced both race-conscious and ostensibly race-neutral laws that perpetuated racial hierarchy and inequality up until the civil rights movement. The civil rights movement tactically used dramatic events to pressure the U.S. federal government to attack white supremacy in elections, housing and labor markets, and schools. The general trend in all these domains was for the federal government to initially formulate race-neutral policies banning discrimination. Although these reforms probably reinforced whites' growing appreciation for equal treatment of African Americans and discredited blatant racist politics, the reforms ultimately could not overcome racial discrimination that occurs in a white-dominated economy and polity. While the civil rights movement had exhausted itself by the early 1970s, the intervention of the courts and the bureaucratic logic to obtain measurable results led the United States to implement more race-conscious policies (such as majority–minority districts, school busing, and affirmative action) intended to eliminate black disadvantage. We suggest these policies had an unanticipated side effect: the retrenchment of white racial identity hostile to efforts to ameliorate black–white inequalities. Consequently, as the Supreme Court has ruled against racial gerrymandering and as the Democratic Party has been strategically inactive on racial inequalities, the U.S. government has retreated from its color-conscious policies.

In our reading of the literature on the politics of race and racial policy, four themes emerge. First, racial inequalities are, in Charles Tilly's apt phrase, "durable." Once created, they are perpetuated by a variety of formal and informal social mechanisms that are resistant to change. Second, whatever its roots in cultural and economic processes, race has always involved politics as both cause *and* effect. From the beginnings of the New World, racial inequalities and identities were created and sustained by political processes involving, on the one hand, the mobilization of democratic electorates and, on the other, the building of states and state policies. Third, the durability of race inequalities continues to give life and meaning to racial identities with asymmetric stakes in those inequalities.

Fourth, so-called color-blind policies affect race inequalities, although in different ways than do color-conscious ones. Sometimes the implementation of color-blind laws has the opposite effects of those intended. Constitutional language providing for color-blindness in the enforcement of equal protection of the laws, due process, and equal access to the ballot was turned into poll taxes, literacy tests (on their face, both color-blind), and the separate but equal doctrine, exacerbating and deepening racial divisions for some eighty years past their adoption. Of course, the white supremacy movement in the American South that succeeded in disfranchising blacks used color-blind laws in a color-conscious fashion. But even in the current era, color-blind laws have impacts on race inequalities in ways not recognized by many.

A trend toward color-blind policies in the United States is apparent, but the United States is not a unique case. Similar patterns are evident in other countries that have many of the institutionalized organizational features that define liberal democratic states. We suggest that liberal democratic institutional forms may be more effective in legitimizing racial inequalities than are racial states and, therefore, more stable. Racial states use race classification systems to differentially allocate citizenship rights and, therefore, create race identities consistent with the race inequalities produced. States that produce and defend white supremacy by protecting white advantages and denying full citizenship rights to blacks are unable to disguise the political power needed to accomplish those ends. Whites are sometimes aware that their advantages stem from their control of state power. Blacks realize that their disadvantages were and are imposed on them by enforcement of racially biased state policies. Using state power to reduce rather than increase race inequalities is contradictory because such policies reinforce the race identities that make the policies necessary in the first place. Enforcing race-conscious laws to overcome the effects of race identities makes the identities of those involved more salient rather than less.[19] Hence, state policies that reduce race inequalities motivate whites to oppose the policies. Liberal democratic states, by contrast, tend to disguise race inequalities as the natural result of the exercise of freedom. By denying policy makers the use of color-conscious tools to reduce race inequalities, liberal democratic states protect and legitimate white advantages, even those that were accumulated over a long history of racially discriminatory policies against blacks.

[19] Reed (2000; Reed and Bond 1991) suggests one way out of this impasse – a social movement that mobilizes a working class identity cutting across racial lines. Such a transracial movement would push the state to reduce economic inequalities and by doing so defang a white racial identity invested in white advantage. Of course, this solution assumes that white workers and black workers can overcome the racial barriers that divide them.

Current public opinion research appears consistent with the claim that color-blind policies legitimate race inequalities, especially among whites, but more research is needed. Why are color-blind policies also popular in countries with nonwhite majorities? The historical legacy of past discrimination should tend to delegitimate color-blind policies among those who were the victims of that discrimination. More attention also needs to be paid to the role of social movements in the policy formation process and, simultaneously, to their impact on categorical identities. As Omi and Winant (1994) and Tilly (1998) argue, social movements can also create or reinforce categorical identities that, in turn, have implications for policies. As we have suggested before, race-conscious policies such as school desegregation and affirmative action have resulted in the retrenchment of white identity and white racial resentment. State policy and state institution's influence on racial identities is not only direct, but is also sometimes mediated by social movements. Further research is needed to understand this interaction of policy and social movements and the consequences for racial inequalities and identities.

CHAPTER TWENTY-EIGHT

War, Militarism, and States

The Insights and Blind Spots of Political Sociology

Gregory Hooks and James Rice

Had this chapter been written a quarter of a century ago, it would have been a lengthy lament over the silence of political sociology on the topic of war. But such a focus would ring hollow at this time. It is now taken for granted that states wage war and that war making has molded the histories of states and politics more generally. This is more than a grudging and half-hearted acknowledgment. In fact, war figures prominently when leading sociologists paint with a broad brush. Consider these examples:

1. In a sweeping history of social power, Michael Mann (1986, 1993) distinguishes the military from other networks of power and explains how military power has been interwoven with cultural, economic, and political power throughout human history. Among other insights, Mann points out that states, not classes and not firms, declare and wage war. As war is waged, the state is transformed as are other social institutions and the relations among them.
2. Charles Tilly (1975, 1990) points out that the twentieth century was the bloodiest in human history – and provides little reason to assume that wars will decline in ferocity or importance. Moreover, if political sociology is to come to terms with (let alone anticipate) historically important political transformation, wars are a central issue.
3. Randall Collins (1981, 1995) focused on the geopolitical to assess the durability of states. Based on this assessment, especially its unmanageable strategic liabilities, he was one of few social scientists to predict the collapse of the Soviet Union. He emphasizes that political sociology offers unique insights because it can weave together a concern with the geopolitical and the domestic political processes (Collins, 1995).
4. In the realm of culture, Elias ([1939] 1982) is known for the study of the civilizing process – a process in which the nobility and then all of European society was transformed. This transformation was set in motion by a change in the strategic balance that tilted to the advantage of the royalty, and away from the aristocracy. It is notable that the civilizing process was set in motion and contributed to a transformation of military power. It began as a pacification of warlords – and subsequently transformed European culture more generally. Arguably, Meyer et al. (1997) discern a present-day civilizing process. In this instance, it is not autarkic warlords who are becoming civilized – it is the state.
5. Wallerstein (2000) is not optimistic about the state becoming more peaceful. In fact, he believes that the first half of the twenty-first century will be a "black period" as the world system undergoes fundamental change and the decline of U.S. hegemony accelerates. In the past, devastating and global wars have been integral to such

a transition. Warfare and transformation of the world system constrain and mold social reform and inequality.

Given the importance of the issues addressed and the prestige of those raising the issue, the study of war is clearly on political sociology's agenda. Nevertheless, for political sociologists, the study of war remains compartmentalized and incomplete. This compartmentalization persists despite the bloody wars of the twentieth century – and the twenty-first century is dawning with spectacular terrorist attacks, several wars in Central Asia, civil wars in several nations, ongoing bloodshed between Israelis and Palestinians, and the United States pursuing an aggressive military policy in the Middle East. Moreover, due to their nuclear arsenals and the deteriorating relationship between India and Pakistan, the *Bulletin of Atomic Scientists* has moved the "doomsday clock" to seven minutes before midnight (*Bulletin of the Atomic Scientists*, 2002). Although it has examined and provided insights into the great wars of the past, political sociology has very little to say about contemporary wars.

This chapter begins by documenting sociology's tendency to focus on domestic politics and processes. Because war making is international by definition, this domestic focus has made it difficult for sociology to fully consider war making and its interplay with the domestic processes at the center of sociology's agenda. That said, the study of war making has reentered the sociological debate over the past quarter century. The consideration of war and militarism has been pronounced in prominent books that have examined state making, revolution, and social movements (Giddens, 1985; Mann, 1986, 1993; Skocpol, 1979; Tilly, 1990). In turn, wars and militarism have received great attention by students of social movements, democratization, and the welfare state. Given the influence of these authors and the wide acceptance of the importance of war, it comes as a surprise how rarely political sociological articles reflect this intellectual shift. We examined each article published in the *American Sociological Review, Social Forces*, and *American Journal of Sociology* from 1990–9. Although political sociology was well-represented in these journals, we found surprisingly few articles addressing the issue of war – and those articles discussing war rarely followed through on the larger historical and theoretical issues raised in prominent books.

We close this chapter by arguing that this compartmentalized study of war leaves political sociology largely silent on some of the most important substantive and theoretical issues of the twenty-first century. Political sociologists rarely contribute – and certainly not in the articles published in sociology's core journals – to discussions of human rights, genocide, and other issues that are beyond the scope of individual nation-states. Nor have political sociologists figured prominently in debates over the impact of globalization on the state – and whether or not states will continue to be the dominant political entity on the planet. By deepening the consideration of war and the international dimensions of war, political sociology can bring its insights to bear in these important debates – and its understanding of domestic political processes will be enriched.

AN EMPHASIS ON THE HOMEFRONT

Wallerstein (2000:112–13), relying on the *Oxford English Dictionary* (OED), offers an insightful discussion of the etymology of "society." Of the twelve definitions presented in the OED, two first emerged at the beginning of the modern era: (1) "the aggregate of persons living together in a more or less ordered community" (circa 1639); and (2) "a collection of individuals comprising a community or living under the same organisation of government" (circa 1577). Shortly after the state had established its primacy in early modern Europe, society is defined in terms of a state. The state became the dominant political entity because of its singular ability to wield the means of violence. "Eventually, the personnel of states purveyed violence on a larger scale, more effectively, more efficiently, with wider assent of their subject populations, and with readier collaboration from neighboring authorities than did personnel from other organizations" (Tilly 1985:173). During the modern era, society refers to the peoples and territory controlled by states; and wars are a means of negotiation and conflict specific to states. Thus, Tilly (1985:181) defines war making as efforts by states to eliminate or neutralize rival states "outside the territories in which they have clear and continuous priority as wielders of force."[1]

Sociology – including political sociology – has worked with a definition that assumes the boundaries of states and societies coincide; it has maintained a focus on the interactions of people within a territory controlled by a state. As a subfield, political sociology examines the relationships between people and the state, paying special attention to challenges to the state emerging from within the polity. Because they involve military contests internal to a state, civil wars and revolution conform to these unspoken assumptions, and political sociology has produced insightful analyses. However, interstate wars involve relations among states; on this front, political sociology's contribution has been halting and uneven. And this unevenness extends to issues related to war and militarism, including human rights, and to the (mis)treatment of women and ethnic minorities (Enloe, 1990).

States and Societies

Reflecting on the rise of the state in early modern Europe highlights political sociology's omissions. From the decline of Charlemagne's empire (circa 900 A.D.) until the rise of protostates in the fourteenth century, the dominant political entity in Europe was the fiefdom. The hegemony of the aristocracy was based on military power. Each fiefdom was largely autarkic; civilian and military resources were extracted and controlled locally. Alliances of aristocrats did make possible relatively large military campaigns. But the lords on the victorious side were rewarded with control over larger land holdings, reinforcing centrifugal tendencies (Elias [1939], 1982:17). From 1000–1500 A.D., the return of long-distance trade and the increased circulation and use of money tilted the balance of power toward the crown and away from local aristocrats. As titular kings and queens became actual sovereigns, they extracted resources from the commercial activities concentrated in cities across a relatively large geographic area – but aristocrats were constrained by the limited geographic reach of their fiefdoms and their economic assets were concentrated in land. States outflanked the aristocracy because they exercised dominion over a much larger area and were able to extract more flexible resources than aristocratic rivals (Elias [1939], 1982; Mann, 1986, 1993; Tilly, 1990).

The rise of the state sets the stage for the "civilizing process." With the French state leading the way, emergent states disarmed and pacified the warlords of feudal Europe – aristocrats became civilized. In contrast to their autonomy at the height of the feudal era, the power of warlords became increasingly dependent on their relationship to the crown and delegations of royal authority to them. As the pacification of the warlords proceeded, "courtly forms of conduct" eschewed the overt violence and intimidation of an earlier era, replacing this with an elaborate set of customs and manners. In turn, courtly manners and sensibilities diffused throughout society – influencing manners of eating, sexuality, household arrangements, and interpersonal interaction (Elias [1939], 1982).

Elias's account makes sense to contemporary readers because his unit of analysis was the emergent states of early modern Europe. That is, Elias accepted and worked creatively with the definition that defines societies in terms of states. Imagine for a moment that his unit of analysis was the fiefdom. From the vantage point of the early twenty-first century, this is an obvious mistake. Had Elias lived and worked during the several centuries in which states were emergent but feudalism remained the dominant mode of organizing political and economic life, it would certainly be an understandable mistake. Nevertheless, instead of seeing the state's strategic

[1] We drew on Tilly when defining war because our focus is on war making of and between states. Although this focus is broad, it nonetheless pushes to the margins or ignores altogether a variety of conflicts (e.g., guerilla, colonial, and private war).

advantage and the erosion of the aristocracy's power due to a changing strategic environment, Elias would have been left to exaggerate the processes and structures internal to fiefdoms that contributed to the "civilizing process." In all likelihood, Elias would have explained the emergence of "courtly forms of conduct" in terms of a collective shift among the aristocracy – and would have devoted little attention to the changes in the strategic balance of power.

Elias is not the only author to have examined this process (for accounts that stress political and military phenomena, see Mann, 1986, 1993; Tilly, 1990; for an emphasis on the rise of the capitalist world system, see Wallerstein, 1989). But reflecting on Elias's account is worthwhile because it highlights several troubling silences of contemporary political sociology. For a discipline that strives to give voice to the marginalized and to shed light on injustice, political sociology (especially U.S. political sociology) is surprisingly silent on the military interventions and atrocities committed by the United States. Nor has political sociology contributed prominently to the study of international human rights, including the (mis)treatment of women and ethnic, racial, and religious minorities around the world. Instead, political sociology's focus has been internal to the nation-state. The central issues have revolved around the distribution of power and social resources within a nation-state. Thus, despite the recognition that wars are important, the sociological study of war has maintained an overriding concern with the domestic consequences. Too often, the study of militarism and war has been left to other disciplines, for example, history and political science (Hooks and McLauchlan, 1992).

Ignoring War

From its inception in the nineteenth century and for most of the twentieth century, sociology assumed that peace is "normal" and wars were temporary and reversible. Even when war could not be ignored, sociology maintained a focus on domestic and endogenous processes. For example, the most notable war-related sociological study of the World War II era was *The American Soldier* (Stouffer et al., 1949). This was the initial work in the behavioralist tradition and, as was characteristic of the genre, this work was quantitative and expansive, involved the collaboration of social scientists in leading universities and think tanks, funded by leading foundations (e.g., Ford and Carnegie) and justified by national security (Robin, 2001). Prominent sociologists, including Louis Guttman and Paul Lazarsfeld, promoted behavioralism, and the discipline of sociology, especially social psychology, was heavily influenced by it. Arguably, although rarely mentioned by contemporary political sociologists, the behavioralist tradition should be counted as political sociology. The behavioral sciences examined attitude formation and stability, with an emphasis on political attitudes and attitudes salient to a nation at war. But these studies did not study social organization or the state, nor did behavioralism focus on social transformation wrought by war. Stated simply, the study of war was isolated from the classical foundations of sociology. Instead of examining the macrosocial phenomena that concerned Marx, Durkheim and Weber, the most visible efforts of sociologists centered on the attitude formation of individuals, with political sociologists playing a marginal role in this endeavor.

There have been notable exceptions to this domestic focus of sociology. For instance, Raymond Aron (1959) provided a broad overview of war in the twentieth century and was very concerned with states and with the relations among them. During and after World War II, Harold Lasswell (1941) theorized about the "garrison state." Drawing on Spencer's notion of a militant society, Lasswell made the case that mid-century Japan was a "garrison state" consumed with war and war making. More provocatively, Lasswell raised the specter that an unforeseen consequence of the World War II mobilization may be that the United States would become a garrison state. Although Lasswell's works and his concept of a garrison state continue to resonate among historians and political scientists (see, for example, Friedbeg, 2000), there is no sustained investigation of this topic in political sociology.

For U.S. sociology, Morris Janowitz is the most visible sociologist who studied war. In a wide range of works, Janowitz examined the profession of soldiering. Moreover, Janowitz promoted an interdisciplinary study of war and played an instrumental role in the formation of the Inter-University Seminar on Armed Forces and Society and the journal *Armed Forces and Society*. Janowitz's work extended to topics of concern to political sociology. Most notably, he was concerned with when and why the military, especially in developing societies, would "leave the barracks" to exert direct control of a government (Janowitz, 1988; for a recent and insightful examination of military–civilian relations, see Desch, 1999).

By pointing to inequalities and the unseemly side of the polity, C. Wright Mills disrupted the American post-World War II celebration. He also broke sociology's silence on war and war making. Mills (1956) identified the military high command as one of the three pillars of the power elite. In defending this claim and explaining the ascent of the military elite, Mills explored the social origins of military leaders and the transformation of military institutions. Mills (1958) also wrote *The Causes of World War Three*, an insightful examination of strategic planning and preparations for nuclear war in the late 1950s. Although Mills is widely respected by political sociologists, his views of militarism and war making have been set aside (Hooks, 1992). Even William Domhoff, an outspoken champion of Mills, rejects Mills's views on the military. Whereas Mills thought military elites ascended to become peers with economic elites during and after World War II, Domhoff (1967:257) believes that "[e]vents and data of the years since Mills wrote have made clear the subordinate role of military men within the power elite."

In another vein and for other reasons, E. P. Thompson (1982) examined the issue of war. Thompson's antiwar activism emerged from his deep concern over the Reagan-era nuclear arms race. Thompson placed stress on the U.S.'s insulated military bureaucracies and the dangers they pose in the nuclear missile era. Although an historian, Thompson's study of the working class and his incisive criticism of structuralist Marxism have been well-received and quite influential in sociology. However, because war making does not fit into the domestic focus of sociology, his timely and insightful studies of militarism and nuclear warfare attracted little attention.

War Reenters the Discussion

When the state reclaimed its centrality to sociological debate, the study of war reemerged as well. Although a number of authors contributed, the works of Moore, Skocpol, Giddens, Mann, and Tilly were pivotal. In *Social Origins of Dictatorship and Democracy*, Moore (1966) emphasized the decisive war that cemented the demise of a landed aristocracy and the ascent of the bourgeoisie. Where the bourgeoisie won, the nation-state was on a path toward political democracy. When the landed aristocracy proved resilient, especially if agriculture was based on coercive labor relations, the nation was likely to be fascist in the middle of the twentieth century. In her *States and Social Revolutions*, Skocpol (1979) emphasized wars at home and abroad. Her study of vulnerable states – French (circa 1789), Russian (circa 1917), and Chinese (circa 1945) – demonstrated that net of domestic political processes and structures, these states were crippled by failures in international wars. In each case, the ensuing revolutionary regime was consolidated by civil war – and this war permanently stamped the postrevolutionary state.

Charles Tilly's impact has been striking. Few authors have placed greater emphasis on the manner in which states and wars are intertwined – and fewer still have brought this issue to the forefront of political sociology. Tilly (1975:42) provides compelling evidence to sustain his assertion that "war made the state, and the state made war." The symbiosis between states and wars was central to his 1990 book, *Capital and Coercion*. In a project that resonates with Moore's, *Dictatorship and Democracy*, Tilly charts the paths to modernity taken by various European polities. He concludes that the availability of the means of production and the means of coercion in the area over which a state exerts dominion molds the approach to war making and domestic governance. That is, European states with control over the means of coercion – but without a sizeable concentration of capital – often exerted sweeping control over society and postponed a democratic transition until well into the twentieth century (e.g., Spain). Conversely, such a state waged war by strengthening its ability to coerce, but lacked the ability to promote economic expansion and technological innovativeness. The ultimate winners in this competition among European states were those that exercised sovereignty over a region with both the means of coercion and capital (e.g., France and England). These states were able to harness economic resources and technological dynamism to further war aims. But in so doing, a state compromised with leading economic institutions and elites – and it negotiated with the citizenry to serve as soldiers. Due to their approach to waging war, these nations tilted toward a democratic and pluralistic polity – and these domestic political bargains stamped the strategic choices when these states waged war. For future inquiry, Tilly's (1995) insistence that sociology must look to the relations among social actors can help push political sociology toward a greater emphasis on the relations among states and transnational political actors – and away from a focus on dynamics internal to nation-states.

In the early 1980s, British sociologists made a deliberate effort to rethink social theory with recognition that war and warfare have stamped human history (see Shaw [ed.], 1984). In *The Nation-State and Violence*, Anthony Giddens (1985) stressed that war is not an aberrant phenomena that influences society temporarily and at the margins. Instead, states are based on the ability to wage war; nation-states are forged through violence. Moreover, violence remains central to states and their activities. Michael Mann made several contributions to the call for renewed consideration of war (1988), and he has maintained a concern with war in both volumes of his study of social power (1986, 1993). Mann's approach is notable because he sees military power as one of four major networks of power, the others being political, economic, and cultural. In the contemporary era, with nation-states the principal political entity, political and military power are concentrated in the state. However, for much of human history – and by implication, in the future – the boundaries of political and military power may no longer coincide.

By the 1990s, the association between war and state making was well established and uncontested, providing fertile ground for further refinement and extension. Goldstone's work is notable in this regard. Building on Skocpol's account of social revolutions, Goldstone (1991) incorporates a concern with demographic and other domestic pressures on states. Thus, Goldstone's revised explanation of state breakdown couples a concern with the geopolitical and the traditional (domestic) issues of concern to sociology. Randall Collins has touched on the issue of war and violence throughout his career (see, for example, Collins, 1981). His recent works have drawn on the works cited above to advance geopolitical theory. On the basis of this theory, Collins (1995) predicted the collapse of the Soviet Union (within a fifty-year window) and makes the case that political sociologists cannot afford to ignore war and geopolitics if we are to understand the processes of political transformation and revolutionary change.

War Examined, But Compartmentalized

Political sociology has begun to address an issue that had been overlooked. But the consideration of war remains compartmentalized and incomplete. The works highlighted in the previous section were books – and the authors of these books drew on and contributed to a literature in which historians and political scientists have been primary contributors and consumers. Our examination of the three leading journals in the discipline over a ten-year period revealed that there is little evidence that political sociologists publishing articles have been influenced by the books that have examined war.

Table 28.1 summarizes the number of political sociology articles, including those dealing with war, relative to all other journal articles in

Table 28.1. *Political Sociology Articles 1990–1999*

1990–94	All Articles	Political Soc. Articles	Articles on War
ASR	301	57	7
AJS	222	47	5
SF	260	36	4
1995–99			
ASR	293	51	3
AJS	224	50	3
SF	275	46	1
1990–99			
ASR	594	108	10
AJS	446	97	8
SF	535	82	5
TOTAL	1,575	287	23

the *American Journal of Sociology, American Sociological Review, and Social Forces* between 1990 and 1999.[2] We employed expansive criteria when classifying articles as political sociology and those addressing war. With that in mind, we determined that 287 articles addressed political sociological concerns and twenty-three articles examined war. From 1990–4, sixteen articles examined war; from 1995–9 there were only seven articles. These twenty-three articles represent but a handful of the 287 political sociology articles and less than 2 percent of all articles published between 1990 and 1999. A closer reading of these twenty-three articles reveals that war is rarely examined as an important sociological dynamic in and of itself but rather indirectly or as a context in which other issues of sociological interest are played out. The result is a striking lack of consideration of the interdependencies, conflict, and cooperation among nation-states in lieu of domestic issues internal to a nation-state.

Examining these twenty-three articles reveals an eclectic and varied approach. For example, Schuman and Rieger (1992) test Mannheim's theory of generational effects by analyzing debates over initiating the Gulf War with Iraq in 1991. Using survey research, they discovered individual attitudes toward the Gulf War were contingent on which of two historical analogies proved most salient: World War II or the Vietnam War. Individuals growing up during or in the aftermath of World War II were more likely to find this experience as a relevant analogy to the Gulf War and, hence, support the Gulf War. Those who grew up in the Vietnam War era were more likely to select this analogy and display opposition to the Gulf War. Shavit, Fischer, and Koresh (1994) utilize the Gulf War as a context in which to examine social network patterns in Haifa, Israel in coping with external threats, discovering Israelis relied more on kin as opposed to nonkin, everyday networks in coping with the threat of missile attack.

Schwartz (1996) analyzes the invocation of cultural memory to elicit and maintain support during World War II, arguing images of Abraham Lincoln were used by local and federal agencies to clarify, legitimate, inspire, and rationalize the experience of war. The effect of World War II on divorce rates is the object of analysis by Pavalko and Elder (1990). When compared to nonveterans, veterans of World War II were more likely to divorce, although marriages established during the war were no more likely to end in divorce than marriages begun at other times. Studying a sample of economically disadvantaged young men, Sampson and Laub (1996) find evidence that overseas duty during the World War II era, in-service

[2] We focus on *The American Sociological Review, American Journal of Sociology*, and *Social Forces* because these journals are prominent outlets for generalists. We recognize that a number of other journals provide an outlet for scholars specializing in the study of the war and the military. If the concern were on the publishing outlets of specialists, *Armed Forces & Society, Theory & Society, Politics and Society*, and most notably, *The Journal of Political and Military Sociology*, are important outlets. These journals have provided a space for articles on these topics, many of which follow through on themes of state making and macrosociological inquiry (see, for example, Kourvetaris, 1991). Whereas the study of war and militarism is one among many topics considered by political sociology, these issues are central to the "Peace, War and Social Conflict" section of the American Sociological Association (for additional information, see the section's homepage: http://www.la.utexas.edu/research/pwasa/index.htm). The Peace, War and Social Conflict Web page also provides links to several journals that make the study of war and militarism a central concern: *Peace Review, Peace and Change, Journal of Conflict Resolution*, and *Mobilization*.

schooling, and G. I. Bill training serve as social mechanisms promoting long-term socioeconomic achievement. Gross (1994) examines the motivations behind the rescue of Jewish individuals in Holland and France during World War II. He argues people were motivated by religious and social norms and considerations of social justice. Infrastructural variables such as level of organization, social networks, and material support were also important determinants.

Wagner-Pacifici and Schwarz (1991) highlight the tension and ambiguity encountered in creating the Vietnam Veterans Memorial in Washington, D.C. They reveal the process of memorializing this event pitted different social constituencies against each other in a struggle to articulate the meaning of a still much contested and controversial war. Addressing the question of who fought in Vietnam, Gimbel and Booth (1996) search for the determinants of combat exposure risk among U.S. servicemen. They conclude that biosocial predispositions toward aggression and stress management are associated with degree of combat exposure, and time-specific war conditions and battlefield strategies also structured the selection of individuals for combat. Bearman (1991) sets out to explain desertion among Confederate soldiers during the U.S. Civil War. Challenging individual-level variables of social class, occupation, status, and age, he argues men deserted because their identity as Southerners was eroded by an "emergent localism." Soldiers replaced their "Southern" identity with their old local identity and no longer felt obligated to fight for the Confederacy.

Several articles regarding war do address the issues of state making and political transformation that figure prominently in books authored by political sociologists. Kowalewski (1991) utilizes a world system perspective to investigate the association between core country intervention and revolution within peripheral countries from 1821–1985. He argues there is a positive correlation between intervention and revolution and that this relationship became stronger during times of world system restructuring and hegemonic decline. Challenging the assertion that war making builds states, Centeno (1997) provides contradictory evidence from eleven Latin American countries. Due to differing historical circumstances, the experiences of Latin American nations contrast with those of European nations. Without the prior establishment of political authority and without a link between such organization and relevant social actors, war is not likely to contribute to institutional development, he argues. Sohrabi (1995) suggests revolutions occurring from 1905–8 in the Ottoman Empire, Iran, and Russia were inspired and legitimated by the idea of constitutional systems of rule. He argues this "paradigm" or ideology of constitutionalism did not emanate from each country's respective social structures but was shaped by conceptions of politics and appropriate goals that can be traced back to the French Revolution of 1789.

With a focus on the United States, Hooks (1990, 1993) examined the relationship between war and state making. He investigated the manner in which the state pursued a distinctive agenda relative to powerful economic actors during World War II and the Cold War era. This research highlights the important role the state has played in directing and shaping industrial policies in the post-World War II era as a consequence of national security efforts. Across the World War II planning agencies, outcomes asserted by middle-range formulations of business dominance, structural Marxism, and state-centered theory find utility in varying institutional contexts depending on state goals and needs (Hooks, 1993). In addition, Hooks and Bloomquist (1992) highlight the cumulative legacy of federal industrial investments during World War II for regional growth and decline of manufacturing in the United States from 1947 to 1972. Hooks (1994) examined the regional distribution of military bases, steel factories, and airframe plants. This study examined the regional impact of the U.S.'s rise to hegemony during the middle decades of the twentieth century.

The relationship between the state and levels of lethal conflict, as embodied in war, rebellion, homicide, and execution, is examined by Cooney (1997). In contrast to a Hobbesian perspective that predicts a negative relationship between state development and lethal conflict, Cooney discovers cross-national conflict rates appear to follow a U-shape. Lethal conflict is high in the absence of state structures and when the state is extremely strong or centralized, but declining between these extremes. Moaddel (1994) investigates the relationship between levels of political instability and conflict in less developed countries relative to their differing structural relations with developed countries. Cross-national evidence between 1970 and 1981 reveals political conflict in less developed countries is indirectly correlated with position in the world system, mediated by income inequality and vulnerability to the destabilizing effects of the world economy. In addition, the effects of modernization on political conflict are found to be linear and indirect, mediated by income inequality and regime repressiveness.

Military coups in postcolonial Africa can be traced to ethnic antagonism stemming from cultural plurality and political competition and the presence of a strong military with a factionalized officer corps and access to state resources, Kposowa and Jenkins argue (1993). However, foreign capital penetration, they assert, deterred coups by strengthening states. Examining black African states between 1957 and 1984, Jenkins and Kposowa (1990) provide further evidence of the structural influence of ethnic diversity and competition, military centrality, debt dependence, and political factionalism as predictors of military coup activity. Boswell and Dixon (1990) argue economic and military dependence promotes domestic rebellion cross-nationally by influencing domestic class and state structures. Their research highlights the argument that dependency in the world economy and international state system shapes domestic political control. Barkey (1991), in addition, finds large-scale peasant rebellions within France in the seventeenth century gained momentum by fostering allies among other societal groups, particularly the formation of strong peasant–noble alliances in reaction to the absolutist state. The absence of peasant rebellions in the Ottoman Empire in the seventeenth century, however, can be traced to the failure of peasant–landowner collaboration.

Despite the extensive treatment of war by political sociologists writing books, the political sociology articles appearing in the three leading sociology journals between 1990 and 1999 are only intermittently concerned or influenced by these debates. War and war making are often analyzed indirectly. In the following paragraphs, we make the case that the failure to sustain the discussions of war constrains the theoretical, empirical, and substantive advances political sociology can contribute to better understanding war and the impact of war on society.

THE STATE OF KNOWLEDGE CONCERNING WAR AND POLITICS

The preceding discussion highlighted the extensive examination of war as it relates to state building and social revolution – typically appearing in books that draw on and contribute to multiple disciplines. However, the articles generated by political sociologists and published in leading sociology journals have displayed far less concern for war and war making. Political sociology has examined several issues related to war making in some detail. Still, the uneven and compartmentalized study of war leaves a number of questions unasked and answers incomplete.

Topics Addressed by Political Sociologists

War and militarism has been considered when their impact on domestic politics and economics have been visible. For the most part, sociologists have not dominated debate on these topics and the issues of war and militarism have been side issues in the larger sociological debate. Nevertheless, war and militarism have crept into the sociological understanding of economic growth, enfrachisement, welfare state, gender, and environmental degradation.

Economic Growth and Planning. States spend a great deal of money to wage war, and the firms that deal with the state are often enriched. Although this empirical observation is not controversial, there has been a great deal of debate over why states prosecute wars in this fashion and whether economic benefits are restricted to a handful of contractors – or if these benefits extend to the entire society. Prominent economists (especially Keynesians) argued that the stimulus of twentieth-century wars provided stimulation to the entire economy and that waging war induced planning and technological innovation that extended far beyond defense contractors (Galbraith, 1967). Beginning in the 1950s and legitimated by Eisenhower's warning of the military–industrial complex in 1961, a number of authors have called into question the claims that militarism was beneficial (Melman, 1970; Kaldor, 1981; Markusen and Yudken, 1992; Tirman [ed.], 1984). While acknowledging that selected firms have benefited, these critics provide evidence that militarism diverts economic resources toward unproductive purposes, bidding up the cost of (and at times monopolizing) physical and human capital, especially in high-tech sectors. Working from Marxist assumptions, military-Keynesianism has been the focus of several studies (Baran and Sweezy, 1966; Griffin et al., 1982; O'Connor, 1973). These works acknowledged the aggregate stimulus of the defense program and investigated the timing of increases in defense spending over time. The central conclusion was that the countercyclical tendencies in defense spending were more closely tied to the needs of the monopoly sector than they were to the overall dynamics of the economy.

Over the past quarter century, a number of quantitative and cross-national studies have explored the trade-off between guns and butter. In this literature, data have been collected on a sample of nations with the goal of evaluating the relationship between military spending (guns) and measures of economic growth and quality of life (butter). There is mixed evidence of an inverse relationship – and several studies point to a positive relationship between militarism and economic growth in developing nations (Bullock and Firebaugh, 1990; Chan, 1985; Mintz and Stevenson, 1995). However, no studies suggest defense spending has stimulated growth among the developed nations (see Mintz and Stevenson, 1995) – and several studies provide evidence that defense spending is inversely related to economic growth (Rasler and Thompson, 1988; Smith, 1980). This inverse relationship observed in developed nations is explained by opportunity costs. Nations investing less in national security are able to allocate resources to alternative uses – civilian governmental programs or nonmilitary commercial uses – and these alternatives are associated with a significantly higher rate of economic growth. This emphasis on the opportunity costs has figured prominently in studies of the military–industrial complex in the United States (Chan, 1985; DeGrasse, 1984; Dumas, 1984).

Specific to the United States, Hooks (1990, 1993; Hooks and Luchansky, 1996) provides evidence that the defense program was oriented toward strategic objectives. By the same token, there can be little doubt that defense spending has played a decisive role in molding regional processes (Markusen et al., 1991). As concerns political sociology, these regional investments did not follow the extant civilian industrial and scientific infrastructure – these investments were guided by military priorities and reordered America (Kirby [ed.], 1992; Markusen et al., 1991; Hooks, 1994). Finally, during and after the Cold War, the defense program became increasingly reliant on science and high-tech weaponry. To a large extent, military planners created "big science" in the Manhattan Project that produced the first atomic bomb. Since World War II, science and technology have been harnessed and in important respects controlled by national security planners (McLauchlan and Hooks, 1995).

Political Enfranchisement and Welfare States. The association between war and political enfranchisement has been a recurrent theme in accounts of state making. For the most part, political sociology has concentrated on the role of wars in the expansion of enfranchisement. The inverse of this relationship – that is, the tendency for democracies to defeat less democratic foes – has also been a focus of inquiry. Reiter and Stam (2002) offer a novel account that challenges explanations based on the greater economic might of democracies or battlefield advantages associated with liberty and freedom. Instead, because elected leaders are ultimately held accountable to voters, Reiter and Stam make the case that democracies are less likely to go to war than authoritarian regimes – they enter wars when the likelihood of success is high.

Downing (1992) sets out to explain the origins of both liberal democracy and absolutism in Europe. He focuses on predispositions to medieval constitutionalism or the system of decentralized government and the subsequent role of state relations and war in undermining such institutional structures. He argues medieval constitutional arrangements predating modernization and military conflict in the burgeoning state system provided institutional, legal, and ideological bases for the subsequent rise of liberal democracy. Clearly weak or absent constitutional predispositions hampered emergence of liberal democracy. He further examines how war among major European states in the seventeenth century impacted constitutional arrangements. Under pressure to mobilize militarily, countries with weak constitutional structures and requiring extensive domestic resource mobilization were more likely to experience the emergence of military–bureaucratic absolution and the decline of constitutionalism. Conversely, countries with stronger constitutional arrangements and the opportunity to mobilize foreign resources, enter into alliances, and possessing domestic commercial wealth were less likely to experience the undermining of constitutional form when faced with military conflict in the seventeenth century.

Over the past 500 years, states have repeatedly sparked and often directed an expansion of the manufacturing base to support ever-larger armies and navies. To wage war, states needed to accommodate leading economic and financial institutions – they were also obliged to develop the means to recruit armed forces that represented a sizeable portion of the population (Tilly, 1990). In the wake of a mobilization for war demands for citizenship and fuller citizenship rights are "pressed by veterans and civilians who have risked life and limb for the country" (Janoski, 1998:146).

War and its aftermath also influenced the consolidation of democracy in the United States. As Mann points out (1993), the Founding Fathers were probably the richest and best-educated revolutionary band in world history. When drafting the Constitution, a strong case was advanced that only the propertied classes – like those who drafted the Declaration of Independence and Constitution – should be allowed to vote and hold office. Eventually the property requirement was sharply reduced, granting political enfranchisement to nearly all white males. Clearly, the combination of a transnational discursive community and an entrenched commitment to democracy among these revolutionaries influenced this debate (Mann, 1993; Markoff, 1996). However, the victorious faction also placed great stress on the contribution that the landless made to the Revolutionary Army – and that fairness and political stability required the young nation to recognize the sacrifice made by the landless. During World War II and the Cold War, national security institutions exerted a significant and sustained influence on the lives of Americans and other societal institutions (Segal, 1994). The G.I. Bill, for example, provided educational support for millions and facilitated a massive expansion of human capital and higher education, and educational benefits continue to provide an incentive for military service (Segal, 1994). In addition, affordable G.I. mortgages provide families with the opportunity to own a home (Segal, 1994).

World War I enhanced the effectiveness of both the workers' and the women's movements in seeking voting rights in a number of countries (Markoff, 1996). Following World War I, the victors embraced opportunities to reshape many European countries and assert greater democratic structures. Mobilization for World War II across numerous countries in turn laid the institutional and economic policy foundations necessary for the reordering of state–society relations and the creation of the postwar welfare state in Europe (Klausen, 1998; Markoff, 1996). The enormous mobilization of men created chronic labor shortages and increased demand for factory workers, a demand that necessitated the incorporation of women into the industrial workforce. Powerholders became increasingly aware of the requisite cooperation and sacrifice of workers, both and men and women, and soldiers who suffered or died during the war. Possibly motivated by a perceived obligation, moral responsibility, or the fear of social revolution, particularly in the defeated countries, the idea of extending the right to vote gained momentum within political institutions (Markoff, 1996).

Sustained war often facilitates the reshaping of state institutions and political relationships between the state and social groups (Kryder, 2000). African Americans benefited from the World War II mobilization through reduced poverty rates and increased employment opportunities, largely a by-product of the central state's pursuit of other war-related primary goals (Kryder, 2000). During World War II, African Americans increasingly gained employment in semiskilled positions in urban industrial areas (Wilensky, 1975). The war provided a mix of social order concerns and opportunity within which African Americans could press their collective advantage, though in the postwar years much of this leverage evaporated and the advantageous political effects of the war lessened (Kryder, 2000).

The U.S. military has advanced the expansion of citizenship rights to excluded groups, particularly in regard to racial integration (see, for example, Moskos, 1988), but we should not adopt too sanguine a view regarding gender relations, Segal (1994) argues. He notes the U.S. military has lagged behind other societal institutions in terms of internalizing principles of gender equality. Women in the U.S. military, for example, have historically been barred from access to many roles available to men. The relationship of U.S. military activities on women's opportunities has been termed "problematic, tense, and often abrasive" (Booth et al., 2000:319). A study of the impact of active-duty armed forces personnel and women's employment and earning in local labor markets, for example, reveals that in labor markets where the military is prominent, women, on average, experience lower annual earnings and higher rates of unemployment (Booth et al., 2000).

Just as wartime mobilizations have been associated with an extension of political enfranchisement, so too they have lent momentum to an expansion of the welfare state. Skocpol (1992) documents the generous Civil War pensions for Union Army veterans and their surviving dependents that placed the United States at the forefront of social provision in the late nineteenth century. Civil War veterans' assistance marks an important turning point in the political origin of social policy in America and, for a time, the potential groundwork for the development of a "paternalist" welfare state in which social provision is provided to protect families headed by a male wage earner (Skocpol, 1992). Although the maternalist aspects of the U.S. welfare state are distinctive, the association in timing between the growth of the welfare state and military mobilization has been common throughout the industrialized world. After World War I, and even more decisively after World War II, the welfare state was extended and enriched throughout Europe (for a discussion of the importance of war on the British and American cases, see Amenta, 1998).

Contentious Politics and State Breakdown. Skocpol's (1979) pathbreaking investigation of social revolutions was innovative because it simultaneously examined the geopolitical and domestic pressures on states – and their interplay. In her account of the French, Russian, and Chinese Revolutions, wars were pivotal. Specifically, in each instance, a spectacular geopolitical failure set in motion a decisive set of challenges to vulnerable states. Whereas constrained extractive capacities and an anachronistic class structure left these states vulnerable, disastrous wars and ruinous domestic consequences were of decisive importance. Although his work complements Skocpol's, Goldstone (1991) places less emphasis on military failure in explaining state breakdown. His work places greater weight on intraelite conflict and fiscal strains (unrelated to war). While successfully demonstrating that military defeat is not a necessary condition for state breakdown, Goldstone also provides evidence of a number of instances in which military defeat was of decisive importance (Collins, 1995). In the essay included in this volume, "Regimes and Contention," Charles Tilly lays the groundwork for further consideration of the relationship between regimes and contentious politics, including not only peaceful but violent protest as well.

While social revolution and state breakdown provide vivid examples, issues of peace and war have figured prominently in the social movement literature more generally. The resource mobilization literature, especially works by Charles Tilly (1978) and Sydney Tarrow (1994), make this connection most forcefully. A state's geopolitical context, especially its engagement in an international war, plays a direct role in the mobilization of resources and the political opportunity structure available to social movements. Although there is no assertion that wars necessarily give rise to social movements, wars and related policies of mobilization are among the most important events to spark and lend energy to contentious politics (McAdam, Tarrow, and Tilly, 2001:51). Whether wars enhance solidarity and or give rise to a cycle of protest and contention depends on the attribution of threat and opportunity, how the war and its outcome are framed, and the intersection with ongoing politics of protest. Clemens (1996:218–21) offers an interesting account of Coxey's Army, a late-nineteenth-century labor organization that drew on the Civil War experience to mobilize workers into an egalitarian movement modeled on the image of the militia. Although effective in mobilizing activists, the image of an army challenging the social order heightened the sense of threat and the repressiveness of the response by employers and the state. Directly and indirectly, the study of social movements and contentious politics has been sensitive to the study of war and war making because very important protest cycles and revolutions have been set in motion by wars and their aftermath.

The preceding discussion of political enfranchisement and the welfare state placed little emphasis – too little emphasis – on the social movements that demanded these reforms. In instance after instance, war both provided a boost to social movement formation and transformed the political opportunity structure to the advantage of a social movement. Indirectly, the changes wrought by war and mobilization can have important consequences for social movements. For instance, the World War II migration of blacks out of the Southeast and towards Northern and Western cities sustained the U.S. civil rights movement in the postwar era. Urban blacks played a decisive role in the 1960 presidential election – and the black vote was certain to figure more prominently in future elections. In turn, urban blacks provided financial (often channeled through churches) and other forms of support to embattled activists in the South. The outmigration of blacks preceded World War II and continued after the war – but the sharp increase in migration during the war was unparalleled and its legacy for the civil rights movement unmistakable.

Political Sociology's Blind Spots

Despite the progress, political sociology's understanding of war and militarism remains incomplete and uneven. In discussing these oversights, we start with specific topics that have been overlooked. We end with a discussion of larger theoretical and methodological issues. Sociology strives to see below the surface of society to shed light on dynamics that are hidden from view and operate according to a logic that is often counterintuitive. C. Wright Mills (1959) referred to this as the sociological imagination (see also Portes, 2000). Moreover, "sociology's complicated vocation" calls on the discipline to be a "field of moral and political concern for the world's troubles" (Lemert, 2002:111). War and militarism have been studied to the extent they are "seen" to impact on the established debates in political sociology (see above). But other important issues – including those that reside below the surface and are demonstrably related to issues of injustice and inequality – have been ignored because they do not fit into established categories and concerns.

The Overlap of Military and Political Power. As Wallerstein notes (see above), society has been defined in terms of a state – and states have carved up (with modest exceptions) the entire planet into mutually exclusive geographic areas. Thus, states are the quintessential containers of modernity (Giddens, 1985). Their very real power and importance notwithstanding, social theory has in important respects reified states. Mann (1986) provides a useful corrective because he documents that the geographic reach of networks of political, economic, cultural, and military power do not coincide. A reified view of the state assumes that these four power networks are contained by a nation-state and controlled (if indirectly) by the state (or by the nation's dominant class or elites). But this has never been the case. Taking Europe 1000 to 1300 A.D. as an example, economic power was quite localized and concentrated in fiefdoms, whereas cultural power (in the form of the Catholic Church) transcended fiefdoms and states. States claimed dominion (political and military power) over expansive areas, but this power was diluted, with the aristocracy largely autarkic within their fiefdoms. Problems persist if one moves forward several centuries. Long after states usurped the power of the nobles, the networks and dynamics of power continued to be messy and uneven. Christendom continued to transcend all of Europe, and discursive networks that reached across Europe and North America challenged absolutism in the seventeenth and eighteenth centuries (Mann, 1993).

For those emphasizing the world capitalist system (Wallerstein, 1989) and for students of international politics, states were never the appropriate unit of analysis, not even when states were unrivaled as the pinnacle of political organizations. With increasing evidence of globalization (Dunne and Wheeler [ed.], 1999; Hirst and Thompson, 1999; Sassen, 1998), a number of scholars are questioning the state's centrality and viability. Castells (1997) makes a forceful case that new information technologies and processes of globalization undermine the autonomy and sovereignty of states. Many economic transactions are no longer physically located in one place but are instead enmeshed in a global financial and economic network (Castells, 1997:245; Held, 1996:343). Of course, states were never able to dictate to corporations – but the rapid shift toward a global, networked, and information-based economy impedes the state from translating its ability to coerce and administer into de facto economic power. The nation-state no longer contains the economy, but the nation-state is constrained and dependent on a global economy. Although states may survive, they will lose power if they are unable to control political, economic, and cultural processes (Castells, 1997). Held (1995) spells out the dilemmas for polities under these circumstances. Democracy allows the enfranchised to exercise a measure of control over political decisions. However, as globalization proceeds, many important issues are beyond the control of any state, for example, environmental problems created beyond a nation-state's borders, global economic processes.

Of course, states have never completely contained "their" society (Held, 1996:350–1). Waging war is the quintessential action of the state and a major contributor to state building. But wars have also contributed to state breakdown and have undermined the ability of individual states to control their own borders. When a state loses a war, it loses a measure of its own sovereignty and may well experience a crisis of legitimacy. Even when states win, waging war opens the borders and brings the nation-state into contact with other polities and economies (Kolko [1994] recounts a number of the unanticipated transformations brought by war). Tilly (1995) makes an analogy to the study of hydraulics. In this analogy, the state is a basin and the various pressures on the state are comparable to fluids flowing into the basin. The stability of this basin *does not* rest on its ability to keep water out – its stability is in successfully channeling fluids in and out of a basin, that is, avoiding a catastrophic collapse and rapid outflow. Building on this analogy, the durability of states is *not* first and foremost their ability to close off "their" society from outside contact; their durability resides in an ability to channel flows and dynamics across national frontiers. The increasing permeability of nation-state borders under conditions of globalization implies that states must adapt to unanticipated inflows and outflows. Given that war making has been one of the most important processes that has accelerated flows across national frontiers – the study of political stability and state transition must pay careful attention to war making and to its transnational dimensions.

For our purposes, the uneven overlap of political and military power is of special interest. It is a testament to the state's power that it has been taken for granted that political and military power are controlled by a state and coincide with the nation-state's frontiers. But this taken-for-granted assumption has never been accurate – and is certainly not the case now. The military reach of a powerful state extends beyond its official geographic boundaries; this powerful state can constrain, guide, and at times directly control political decisions in weaker states. Conversely, weak states do not exercise full control over their own military forces, and their political authority is compromised. History provides scores of examples; we discuss several recent and contemporary instances.

1. *Europe 1950–90:* In the wake of World War II, the United States grudgingly accepted the Soviet Union's sphere of influence in Eastern Europe. The Soviet Union directly intervened in the political reconstruction of Eastern European nations and formed (and controlled) a diplomatic and military alliance among these nations (Warsaw Pact). In several instances, Soviet troops were deployed – most notably in Hungary (1953) and Czechoslovakia (1968) – to impose Soviet preferences. During the Cold War, the United States played the role of great power in Western Europe. Although not as overt as the Soviet Union, the United States intervened to influence electoral processes in several European nations. Through the Marshall Plan and the Bretton Woods accords, the United States helped to revive Western Europe and imposed its preferences for liberalism (Block, 1977). On the diplomatic and military front, the United States promoted the creation of the North Atlantic Treaty Organization and was the dominant voice in this alliance (Leffler, 1992).
2. *Iraq and Afghanistan:* Both Iraq and Afghanistan are nation-states, but relative to standard definitions of states, neither controls military and political decisions. The United States was in the forefront of nations that defeated Iraq in 1991 and overthrew Saddam Hussein in 2003. Throughout the 1990s, the United States and its allies patrolled Iraqi airspace and demanded international inspection of suspected military production centers. Moreover, the United States repeatedly bombed Iraq and maintained an embargo that has resulted in tens of thousands of deaths from disease and malnutrition. After removing Saddam Hussein from power, the United States molded the postwar reorganization of the polity. As of 2000, Afghanistan had endured decades of civil war, Soviet occupation, and years of Taliban rule. In 2000, with thousands of well-armed international Islamic warriors encamped, many suspected that control of Afghanistan resided with Al Qaeda – and not the Afghan state. The United States and its allies removed the Taliban from power in Afghanistan. In the wake of the military intervention by the United States and its allies, neither the Afghani nor the Iraqi state exerts sovereignty in the manner the sociological definition of the state assumes.
3. *U.S. interventions in Latin America:* On dozens of occasions and for a variety of reasons, the United States has intervened in Latin America. Some of the more notorious examples include: supporting Panamanian secession from Columbia to facilitate the construction of the Panama Canal (1903), assisting the overthrow of Chile's democratically elected Allende and assisting the installation of the Pinochet dictatorship (1973), mining Nicaragua's harbors (in violation of U.S. and international law) to destabilize the Sandinista regime (1984), and assisting the overthrow of Guatemala's democratically elected government in 1954 followed by decades of support for nondemocratic regimes perpetrating a genocidal war on that nation's indigenous peoples (see Chomsky, 1993).

We have presented a number of examples in which a state's actual military power does not extend to its own frontier, and with this compromised military control, a state's control over political decisions is likewise compromised. The near silence of political sociology on these issues may be the result of the mismatch between de facto military and political power with official geographical boundaries of states. This mismatch flies in the face of Weber's classic definition of the state: "A compulsory political organization with continuous operations will be called a 'state' insofar as its administrative staff successfully upholds the claim to the monopoly of the legitimate use of physical force in the enforcement of its order." When a state is subject to external influence and control (e.g., Latin America, Iraq, and Afghanistan that have experienced U.S. interventions), what does this imply about the "stateness" of the political organizations that govern these nation-states? Does contemporary Iraq exercise a monopoly over the legitimate means of violence within its territory? Conversely, how does the contemporary United States and its assertion of military power across national boundaries fit with the classic definition of the state?

The examples we have selected highlight the reach of the United States beyond its geographic boundaries. No doubt, political sociologists are well-aware of Cold War politics, developments in Iraq and Afghanistan, and U.S. interventions in the Western Hemisphere and beyond. Nevertheless, as an intellectual enterprise, political sociology has had next to nothing to say about these developments. We return to these topics in the conclusion and make the case that examining war is essential to understanding states and polities in general. For now, we build on this discussion of the mismatch between de facto political and military power and the geographic boundaries to discuss human rights – a topic that political sociology has overlooked.

Human Rights. There has emerged a lively and important literature on human rights (for a sampling, see Dunne and Wheeler [eds.], 1999; Hesse and Post [eds.], 1999; Ishay [ed.], 1997; see also *The Global Site* [http://www.theglobalsite.ac.uk/] for useful links to discussions of human rights and globalization that makes links to political and social theory). The Peace, War, and Social Conflict section of the American Sociological Association routinely promotes the study of human rights, genocide, and related issues. But political sociologists have not played a prominent role. This marginal role is surprising because political sociology has been concerned with the expansion of rights – a rich theoretical and research tradition has examined the public sphere, establishment and enrichment of democracy, and the welfare state (Janoski, 1998). Nevertheless, because political sociology – like sociology more generally – has accepted the nation-state as the unit of analysis, political sociology has difficulty examining the transnational expansion of rights, especially when this expansion erodes the sovereignty of the state.

Founded in the wake of World War II and its many atrocities, one of the first agreements passed by the United Nations was the Universal Declaration of Human Rights (1948). But this declaration was founded on a contradiction. The members of the United Nations were states – and states committed the most serious violations of human rights. Moreover, as the Commission on Human Rights observed, it had "no power to take any action in regard to any complaints concerning human rights" (in Donnelly, 1999:73). There is much to criticize about the halting and ineffective interventions in support of human rights, with Bosnia, Rwanda, Afghanistan, and Iraq offering recent examples. Large and powerful nation-states have jealously protected their sovereignty – and have resisted the imposition of a supranational definition of human rights. The United States and China retain extensive reliance on capital punishment and high rates of incarceration despite international condemnation. Russia's brutal tactics in Chechnya have been the subject of international criticism – but this remains a national issue, as does China's treatment of Tibet. Due to their extensive military and geopolitical power, the sovereignty of these major powers remains robust – and there is little likelihood that a supranational force will intervene to guarantee human rights in the foreseeable future.

Still, even if the dream of human rights guarantees remains elusive, states are now operating in a very different environment. At a discursive level, even the world's major powers are under greater scrutiny and do feel some pressure to comply with international norms of human rights (Skrentny, 2002). The discursive context has been transformed by the presence and action of the transnational human rights community (including the U.N. Commission on Human Rights and a host of nongovernmental organizations), the ubiquity of televised news coverage, and the ability of endangered populations to document human rights abuses in real time over the Internet (Castells, 1997; Kaldor, 1999; Shaw, 1999).

Collins (1995) argues convincingly that sociology has made a significant contribution to the study of revolution because it brings a robust understanding of the domestic structures and processes that impinge on states. By simultaneously considering the domestic and the geopolitical, sociology has made an important contribution to the study of revolution. With Collins's advice in mind, political sociology has much to offer to the study of human rights. There are insightful studies of global civil society and of the role nongovernmental organizations play in diffusing cultural idioms and in challenging individual regimes (Meyer et al., 1997). But the study of human rights will require a careful consideration of states and war making. By and large, the transnational effort to expand human rights is directed toward the protection of individuals from the police and military of their home states. Moreover, enforcing human rights requires the existence of a supranational power capable of controlling states. Thus, we return to a variation on Elias's question. Whereas Elias examined the process of pacifying and civilizing the aristocracy, we must examine the degree to which states are becoming civilized. If there is evidence of a global civilizing process, the question is if this is largely a cultural process (a continuation of a process of rationalization that has a long history) or will there emerge a supranational authority with the power and authority to supervise and discipline abusive states. These issues and the implications are the focus of the conclusion.

DISCUSSION AND CONCLUSION

We believe that political sociology has been on the sidelines of debates that are of great importance because it has failed to come to terms with issues of war and militarism. Political sociology has contributed a rich and insightful research tradition that has examined the expansion of citizenship, class struggle, democracy, gender and racial injustice and struggles to eliminate them, welfare states, and the politics of criminal justice. But this research has concentrated on the world's richest and most powerful polities – ignoring peoples and places in which citizenship is constrained, class differences are sharpest, democracy is diluted or nonexistent, gender and racial injustice is manifest, welfare states are stunted (if present), and the system of criminal justice systematically violates human rights. Because political sociology has been quite concerned with the human rights of citizens in the world's dominant polities but unconcerned about the most obvious instances of inequality and injustice, an uncharitable but reasonable explanation would suggest that political sociology is encumbered by ethnocentrism (Connell, 1997). We believe that this explanation is ultimately incorrect. Instead, we believe that the reification of the nation-state generates political sociology's blind spots – and that coming to terms with war and militarism is a necessary step in ameliorating this situation.

In raising this criticism, we risk slighting important efforts that lay a solid foundation and others that have begun to fill this gap. Given that we defended this assertion by reviewing the articles appearing in the three most visible sociology journals, we are especially likely to overlook work that has appeared in other outlets. With this in mind, we close by identifying recent efforts to lay a foundation for the study of war in the twenty-first century.

The world systems literature and the neoinstitutionalist school have been asking the right questions. Both schools assert that a global dynamic sharply constrains the range of options for individual states – but they disagree sharply about the dynamics at work. For neoinstitutionalists, this global process is fundamentally cultural. For example, Meyer et al., (1997:150–1) argue that "nation-states are more or less exogenously constructed entities – the many individuals both inside and outside the state who engage in state formation and policy formulation are enactors of scripts rather than they are self directed actors" (Meyer et al., 1997:150–1). Specifically, states are molded by "global models of rationally organized progress and justice" resulting in rhetorical support for human rights declarations – even if these pronouncements rarely translate into a dramatic change in state behaviors. The world systems literature identifies a global division of labor, including the challenges and impediments confronting individual states (Wallerstein, 1989). Although there is hope for a dramatically more just and peaceful world in the medium to long run, Wallerstein believes the first half of the twenty-first century will witness the decline of U.S. hegemony and the ascent of a new hegemon. In the past, these transitions have been dangerous, violent, and turbulent. During such transition, states did not display a commitment to progress and justice (not even rhetorically) – instead states marshaled forces, waged war, and committed atrocities on a grand scale. Wallerstein (2000) anticipates the current transition to be equally violent. Collins's (1981, 1995) views on the barbarity of states during high-stakes wars lend support to Wallerstein's sober assessment.

Students of human rights and international politics are examining the prospects for the creation of a transnational polity capable of enforcing human rights treaties around the globe. States are responsible for many of the atrocities and human rights abuses in the twentieth century, and the defense of state sovereignty undermines international enforcement mechanisms. Still, as Falk observes (1999:181), "statism, like democracy, is a normative failure unless it is compared with likely alternatives!" Globalization is "weakening state structures, especially in their capacity to promote global public goods, their traditional function of enhancing the quality of life within the boundaries of the state, and their most recent role of assisting and protecting the vulnerable within their borders. Such trends, in turn, encourage disruptive ethnic and exclusivist identities that subvert modernist secular and territorial commitments to tolerance and moderation" (Falk, 1999:181). Long before an international polity can enforce human rights declarations across all states, it is probable that the processes of globalization, the weakness of state structures, and neoliberal policies guiding international politics will give rise to horrific regional wars and brutal ethnic and civil wars internal to nation-states. Indeed, the recent wars and atrocities in Africa, Columbia's ongoing civil war, and the strife in Indonesia bear witness to these tendencies.

As noted, Elias examined the transformation of the dominant polities and the relations among them. This transformation propelled the pacification of the aristocracy and the diffusion of the civilizing process throughout Europe. Elias had the benefit of 500 years to gain insight into the transformation of European polities. Although the pronouncements of the state's irrelevance are premature, we may be living through the dawning of an era in which the geographic reach of states is surpassed by global economic, cultural, political, and military processes. The civilizing process that Elias examined was in large measure a consequence of (and a contributor to) a changing strategic balance in Europe. States commanded the military resources to outflank the aristocracy – in this new strategic context, the politics, economics, and cultural context transformed.

Although it has been notoriously difficult to predict which states would be stable and which would experience wrenching transformation and breakdown, Randall Collins is optimistic about sociology's potential: "The macrodynamics of political change is one of the longest standing research interests in sociology; the passion and energy it has attracted over the years has given it a core of theory that can provide increasingly good service as more refined theory is elaborated in the future" (Collins, 1995:1589). The questions before political sociology are daunting. Our most important question is no longer to identify which states will be stable and which will collapse; the task is to anticipate whether or not states will survive as the world's dominant political organization – or if global or transnational entities will supercede them. If the past is any guide, such a transformation will be a violent and confusing one, marked by instability in a large number of polities. Should there be a shift away from the state as the dominant political organization, this shift will undoubtedly be difficult to discern and marked by apparent reversals. Given that states were built on war making and one of their decisive advantages remains in this realm, wars and war making will play pivotal roles in the survival or the eclipse of the state. Stated otherwise, should it focus on domestic politics and endogenous political processes, political sociology will remain on the sidelines for one of the most exciting and important debates of the twenty-first century. But if political sociology fully considers militarism and war making – throughout the world – it would bring its unique insights and rich tradition to bear on questions that are of central concern to the peoples of the world and rich with theoretical conundrums.

PART V

GLOBALIZATION AND POLITICAL SOCIOLOGY

CHAPTER TWENTY-NINE

Globalization[1]

Philip McMichael

Globalization is widely perceived as the defining issue of our times. Exactly what "globalization" means, however, is unclear. Some commentators argue that the world is not necessarily more integrated now than at the turn of the twentieth century (Hirst and Thompson, 1996), whereas others grant globalization only epiphenomenal significance in an era of transition to a postmodern world system future (Wallerstein, 2002:37). Positive definitions can take several forms, in which globalization is viewed as a process, an organizing principle, an outcome, a conjuncture, or a project. As a *process*, globalization is typically defined, in economic terms, as "the closer integration of the countries and peoples of the world . . . by the enormous reduction of costs of transportation and communication, and the breaking down of artificial barriers to the flows of goods, services, capital, knowledge, and (to a lesser extent) people across borders" (Stiglitz, 2002:9). As an *organizing principle*, it can be conceptualized as "deterritorialization" (Scholte, 2000:46), that is, as the *explanans* in accounting for contemporary social change, as "the 'lifting out' of social relations from local contexts of interaction and their restructuring across indefinite spans of time–space" (Giddens, 1990:21).[2] Related to this is the notion of globalization as the compression of time/space (Harvey, 1989; Castells, 1996; Helleiner, 1997), expressed for example in biopolitical disciplines (Hoogvelt, 1997:125). And there is the political angle, emphasizing the global transformation of the conditions of democratic political community, as "effective power is shared and bartered by diverse forces and agencies at national, regional and international levels" (Held, 2000:399), challenging conventional, state-centered accounts of world order. As an *outcome*, globalization is usually understood as an inexorable phase of world development, in which transnational economic integration takes precedence over a state-centered world (e.g., Radice, 1998; Robinson, 2001).[3] As a *conjuncture*, globalization has been viewed as an historically specific ordering of post-Bretton Woods international relations, structured by the "financialization" of strategies of capital accumulation associated with a posthegemonic world order (Arrighi, 1994), or as a form of corporate management of an unstable international financial system (Amin, 1997; Panitch, 1998; Sklair, 2001). And as a *project*, globalization has been viewed as an ideological justification of the deployment of neoliberal policies privileging corporate rights (Gill, 1992; Cox, 1992; McMichael, 2004).

Any attempt to define the term, especially in a handbook such as this, needs to be clear about

[1] The author is grateful to Alicia Swords for background research on the MST and to Dia Mohan, Raj Patel, the editors, and reviewers for comments on earlier drafts.

[2] For an extended and incisive critique of this theoretical abstraction, see Rosenberg, 2000.

[3] See Block, 2001; Goldfrank, 2001; and McMichael, 2001 for cautionary responses to Robinson's call for transcending a state-centered paradigm.

its orientation. The above distinctions represent emphases, which are not unrelated to one another, and concern how to represent current transformations. How to do that is the key question, perhaps underlining the directional and compositional indeterminacy of globalization, as a discursive reordering of the world. Globalization has such institutional force as a discourse that we need historical specification of why and how this is so. Problematizing contemporary globalization as a form of corporate rule helps to situate it historically and clarify its relational political dynamics. This requires two steps: first, understanding globalization as a *general* condition of the capitalist era (initiating world history) and *particularizing* its contemporary form;[4] and second, demystifying globalization's phenomenal, or empirical, forms (e.g., economic integration measures) by examining it through its political countermovements – as globalization's historical and relational barometer. Because globalization is realized at various scales (global, national, regional, subregional), it can be examined effectively through its multilayered processes, registered in movements that operate on different (but often interrelated) scales.

This chapter attempts to capture the contradictory relations of corporate globalization through an analysis of the movements that reveal its politics, rather than its broad and everyday trends. In order to demonstrate this fundamental property of corporate globalization, I draw on Karl Polanyi's (1957) exemplary account of the formation of the modern nation-state. In interpreting state formation through the prism of the double movement of political resistance to the institution of market relations, Polanyi provides a dual legacy. First, his method of distinguishing substantive from formal economics identifies the social dimension of such representations of material relations. And second, Polanyi's use of this method to interpret the crisis of market rule at the turn of the twentieth century conceptualizes modern institutions as embedded in, and ultimately subject to, political relations. In other words, the trajectory of an institution like the market is only comprehended through an interpretation of its cumulative social and political consequences. Beyond an economic process, market construction is a historical process of governing resistances to social transformation via conceptions of sovereignty and rights. This is also the case with corporate globalization, a successor episode of instituting market relations on a world scale. Polanyi provides a link between the two episodes, not only historically but also methodologically, in his formulation of the "double movement" of instituting and resisting market relations.

The link between the formation of the European nation-state system and corporate globalization is that the latter emerges in opposition to the protective shell of the nation-state – what economists term "artificial barriers" to material flows across national borders. The ideology of corporate globalization champions "free" exchange, the logic of which is to reduce the historic frictions to global market relations in state regulations (sovereignty) and economic subsidies (rights). In this sense, corporate globalization represents a sustained challenge to the citizen state, rolling back the political and social gains of the countermovements of the last century and a half (the "citizenship" bundle of economic, political, and social rights). The state itself is transformed, as an instrument of privatization, and its evident complicity in decomposing modern citizenship fuels an alternative politics, informing a global countermovement.

THE *GLOBAL* COUNTERMOVEMENT[5]

This chapter argues that the global countermovement both resembles and transcends the

[4] Examples of the use of the method of historicizing forms of capitalist globalization include Arrighi and Silver et al.'s multifaceted analysis of a series of hegemonic/posthegemonic moments in the history of world capitalism (1999); Arrighi's "systemic cycles of accumulation" associated with Dutch, British and U.S. hegemony (1994); and analysis of U.S. hegemony as a resolution to the crisis of British hegemony (McMichael, 2000b).

[5] I use the singular "countermovement" to replicate Polanyi's usage, which portrayed the double movement as instituting and resisting market rule, across the nineteenth and early twentieth centuries. As then, today's

Polanyian double movement of implementation of and resistance to economic liberalism. By emphasizing the discontinuity with Polanyi's double movement, I identify a distinctive dimension of the politics of the global countermovement, namely the rejection of the universalisms of the project of modernity, that is, the linking of the inevitability of progress to the necessity of science in the service of the industrial state.[6] The World Social Forum (WSF) slogan of "another world is possible" challenges the neoliberal world vision, but from the perspective of strategic diversity. That is, another world would respect diversity, understood here as crystallizing through imperial relations constituted by asymmetrical forms of power and differential forms of exclusion (quite distinct from "development/underdevelopment" relations). This variation, expressed in ethnic, class, gender, racial, and sexual relations of inequality across the world, informs an overriding solidarity, as expressed in the WSF. The WSF unifies those diverse resistances to global empire, articulated thus: "We are fighting against the hegemony of finance, the destruction of our cultures, the monopolization of knowledge, mass media and communication, the degradation of nature, and the destruction of the quality of life by transnational corporations and anti-democratic policies" (World Social Forum, 2001).

The global countermovement nurtures a paradigm shift.[7] Transcending the politics of "underdevelopment," it draws attention to the choice facing the world's peoples: between a path of exclusion, monoculture, and corporate control or a path of inclusion, diversity, and democracy. Baldly put, this is a historic choice in two senses. First, the discourse of diversity confounds the universalisms of modernity, through which powerful states/cultures have sought to colonize the world with their singular vision. And second, the historic attempt to impose the logic and force of market rule on the world appears to be reaching its apogee. A protective movement is emerging, viewing markets not simply as objects of regulation but as institutions of corporate rule and espousing alternative social forms.

These alternative social forms draw on cultural and ecological traditions and radical interpretations of democratic politics. While embodying a vision of another world, these diverse social forms are strategic in sharing their rejection of neoliberalism. Whether the global countermovement adopts a political superstructure remains to be seen (Wallerstein, 2002:37).

countermovement is quite heterogeneous – in political goals, identities, scales, tactics, etc. – nevertheless its multiple networks, organizations, and movements increasingly harbor a sensibility of connection (through strategic diversity) to a common world-historical condition, as is evident in the politics of the World Social Forum and as is noted by participating activist/analysts, for example: "Whether located in obscure third world cities or the centers of global commerce, the struggles of the Global Justice Movements increasingly intersect because they focus on virtually identical opponents: the agencies and representatives of neoliberal capitalism – global, regional, national and local" (Bond, 2001:7; see also Starr, 2000).

[6] Although modernity is an unfinished project, it embodies the separations of nature and society and culture and society, reason, secularization, sovereignty, specialization, instrumental or functional rationality, a scientific imperative, bureaucratization, and so forth. Historically, these properties have come to define, or be identified with, industrial capitalism. Early modernity's idea of progress conceived of the possibility of domination of nature and the desirability of rational change versus traditional eternities and divine rights, but in the modernity of the age of high colonialism, progress as such became *inevitable*. Given the context, the project of modernity now became the imperative condition of the West and its colonial empire – all societies were to follow the path of urban–industrial capitalism governed by nation-states legitimated by popular sovereignty and universal legal codes (see Araghi and McMichael, 2004).

[7] David Held, although unprepared to view the nation-state as an institution of Western hegemony, considers this turning point as an indeterminate transformation of the question of sovereignty and rights: "globalization . . . has arguably served to reinforce the sense of the significance of identity and difference . . . One consequence of this is the elevation in many international forums of non-Western views of rights, authority and legitimacy. The meaning of some of the core concepts of the international system are subject to the deepest conflicts of interpretation, as illustrated at the UN World Conference on Human Rights in Vienna (June 1993) . . . If the global system is marked by significant change, this is perhaps best conceived less as an end of the era of the nation-state and more as a challenge to the era of 'hegemonic states' – a challenge which is as yet far from complete" (1995:94–5).

Ideally, a superstructure drawing on emergent WSF networks among grassroots movements, NGOs and unions, and respecting the principle of multiple overlapping jurisdictions (Cox, 1994; Held, 1995:137), would embody the distinctive cosmopolitan sensibilities of countermovement politics. These sensibilities reflect its world-historical foundations and/or the growing prominence of transboundary issues, creating "overlapping communities of fate" where "the fortunes and prospects of individual political communities are increasingly bound together" (Held, 2000:400).

The connections among movements as diverse as labor, feminist, peasant, environmentalist, and indigenous organizations may not be immediate, but the power of the movements lies in shared circumstances and reflexive diversity. In this sense, corporate globalization has distinctive faces, places, and meanings, concretizing it as a complex, diverse, and contradictory unity conditioned by its multiplicity of resistances. This relationship is evident in the World Bank's tactical embrace of social capital and "voices of the poor" (Narayan, 2000), fuels the tensions within the Washington Consensus[8] over the legitimacy or efficacy of globalization's policy apparatus (cf. Stiglitz, 2002), and leads UN Secretary-General Kofi Annan to encourage "globalization with a human face."

In short, this chapter's specification of globalization as corporate power highlights the process by which its contradictory relationships form it as an ongoing discursive project of market rule. From this perspective, globalization is a formative (and thereby unresolved) process. Although analysis may not resolve the question of what globalization is, it can usefully situate this question diachronically and synchronically. Diachronic analysis considers globalization's *contextual* (historical) dimensions, whereas synchronic analysis considers its *compositional* dimensions. Both aspects lend themselves to incorporated comparison,[9] which views forms of globalization as successively related instances of an historic world ordering in the modern epoch (see note 4), and interprets corporate globalization as a product of its contradictory political relations – in particular the historical dialectic of sovereignty and rights.

MODERNITY, RIGHTS, AND SOVEREIGNTY

As perhaps the touchstone of modernity, sovereignty is institutionalized in the process of nation-state formation and the construction of citizenship rights. The rise of the modern state is premised on the emergence of civil society, the realm of private property and individual rights. How individual rights are translated into citizenship rights (and vice versa) and what those rights entail depend on the transformation of property relations and state trajectories. The classic formulation of this evolutionary modernist view of citizenship was that of T. H. Marshall (1964).

Marshall defined citizenship as comprehensive membership in the national community – a historical resolution of the tensions between political equality in the state and economic inequality in the marketplace. As the political expression of the development of civil society, citizenship derives from a process of formalizing substantive rights in the state, from political, through economic, to social rights. Political rights (as limited as they were to propertyholders in the state) provided the precondition for economic rights (arising from labor organization), which enabled the institutionalization of social rights in the twentieth-century

[8] The Washington Consensus refers to that collection of neoliberal economic policies (trade and financial liberalization, privatization, and macrostability of the world economy) uniting multilateral institutions, representatives of the international arm of the U.S. state, and associated G-7 countries enabling corporate globalization and, arguably, U.S. hegemony.

[9] Incorporated comparison is geared to dereifying the social world as a relational process rather than a set of categorical constructs; collapsing the externalist categorization of social entities as discrete, independent cases to be compared; and collapsing metaphorical binaries like global/local (McMichael, 1990). The comparative juxtaposition of relational parts (such as rules and resistances) progressively constitutes a whole, as a formative construct: here, a world-historical conjuncture, the "globalization project."

welfare state (cf. Stephens, Rueschemeyer, and Stephens, 1992).[10]

This interpretation of citizenship as the social democratic achievement informed much of the post-World War II political sociology literature and its search for a progressive model in the shadow of totalitarian regimes (cf. Polanyi, 1957; Bendix, 1964; Moore, 1965). The key shortcoming of this interpretation was its state-centered understanding of political outcomes, discounting imperial relations and their recursive impact on Western states and citizens (Cooper and Stoler, 1997). Remarking on the "institutionalized racism" in states in the post-colonial era, Bryan Turner notes that the rise of citizenship was intimately associated with nationalism, where citizenship involved "(1) an inclusionary criterion for the allocation of entitlements, and (2) an exclusionary basis for building solidarity and creating identity" (2000:135, 137), discriminating against traditional peripheral cultures in Europe (cf. Hechter, 1975) and reproducing this inclusionary/exclusionary relation in colonial states.

Corporate globalization clarifies the world-historical and exclusionary dimensions of citizenship as it erodes social entitlements and redistributes people across national boundaries, complicating the question of sovereignty and citizenship. As David Held remarks: "there is a fundamental question about whether the rights embodied in citizenship rights can any longer be sustained simply within the framework that brought them into being" (1995:223). New conceptions of citizenship have emerged: from cosmopolitan citizenship (Held, 1995) through mobility citizenship (Urry, 2000) to global citizenship (Muetzelfeldt and Smith, 2002), and in the notion of the "multilayered citizen," where "people's rights and obligations to a specific state are mediated and largely dependent on their membership of a specific ethnic, racial, religious or regional collectivity, although they are rarely completely contained by it" (Yuval-Davis, 2000:171).

The concept of global citizenship invokes the possibility of a global civil society (cf. Cox, 1999), and whether (and in what sense) movements aimed at containing global market rule are today reproducing the Polanyian protective impulse to secure social rights (cf. Bienefeld, 1989; Bernard, 1997). Polanyi offers a world-historical understanding of the derivation of rights: through the differential "discovery of society" across Western states embedded within a world market managed by international financiers. Polanyi's account of the challenge to the market ideology of economic liberalism remains state-centered. It is framed by the contemporary belief in the instrumentality of the nation-state as the vehicle of social protections. In his (modernist) account, the question of rights is overdetermined by the question of state sovereignty.

Corporate globalization generates the circumstances in which the modern form of sovereignty, although still relevant to counter-movement politics, is challenged by alternative forms of sovereignty, referred to variously as "globalization from below" (Brecher et al., 2000), "the anticapitalist resistance," "global social justice movements," or "democratic globalization." Many of these forms embrace, substantively, the idea of "subsidiarity," situating decision-making power at the lowest appropriate levels/*loci*, transforming sovereignty into a "relative rather than an absolute authority" (Brecher et al., 2000:44). Although it is impossible to detail the range of such movements, this chapter draws on the examples of the regional Mexican *Zapatista*, national Brazilian *Sem Terra*, and transnational *Via Campesina* movements to identify such alternative social forms practicing a politics of subsidiarity that is, significantly, cosmopolitan.

Explication of the tension between the conventional, Polanyian countermovement (reasserting national sovereignty against neoliberalism) and the emergence of a decentralized transnational, "network movement" (Brecher et al., 2000; Hardt, 2002) suggests a crisis in the

[10] Marshall's legalistic conception of rights obscures the participatory dimension of citizenship, rooted in civil society discourses of rights and obligations (see Janoski, 1998:17). These discourses inform the principle of autonomy (structured self-determination) that underpins the democratic project – whether in nation-states or in cosmopolitan political arrangements (Held, 1995:147).

paradigm of modernity. While there is a variety of reform and/or advocacy networks and nongovernmental organizations (from Amnesty International through Oxfam to Friends of the Earth), loosely defined as an emergent "global civil society" or an incipient organic "world parliament" (Monbiot, 2003), we consider here the discourse of three political movements, with active constituencies, that reformulate conceptions of sovereignty and rights reflexively – that is, in critical relation to *extant* global power relations. Social science conventions may view these as "peripheral" movements, but I regard this designation inappropriate in a global economy whose foundations rest firmly on a dialectic of exploitation/marginalization of the world's majority population. I focus on two features of modern sovereignty addressed by these movements: first, the limits of formal sovereignty, institutionalized in the liberal–modern binary of state/market (political/economic); and second, occlusion of imperial relations as the historic crucible of the modern state.

LIMITS OF THE PROJECT OF MODERNITY

We begin with an account of Polanyi's contribution, as it presages the politics of globalization. *The Great Transformation* (1957), constructed around the process of the "discovery of society," locates the question of rights in the social regulation of the market. Polanyi termed the commodification of land, labor, and money a fiction of economistic ideology, because these social substances are not produced for sale – rather, they embody social relations. Their subjection to market relations is a political act. The fictitious nature of these commodities was revealed in the overwhelming social reaction to the rule of the market at the turn of the twentieth century. Landed classes mobilized against the pressures of commercial agriculture, workers organized against exploitation of their labor as a mere commodity whose price depended only on its supply and demand and whose employment depended on business fortunes beyond employee and employer control, and whole societies struggled over the financial austerity imposed by the gold standard on national economies experiencing trade imbalances. These various mobilizations formed a historic countermovement to the idea of the "self-regulating market."

Under sustained popular pressure, governments intervened in the market, abandoned the gold standard (the mother of all commodities), and the early-twentieth-century world resorted to socialism, fascism and New-Dealism. Out of these experiments, at the end of a period of world wars, the Cold War divided the industrial world between variants of social democracy (First World) and communism (Second World). While the former turned services like unemployment relief, health care, and education into public rights through a measure of decommodification and as a complement to market society, the latter abolished the separation of economics and politics through central planning, representing an "enormous political challenge to the social form of the modern states-system" (Rosenberg, 2001:134).

For Polanyi, the movement of resistance to the ideology of the self-regulating market turned on a public vision of society, based in social protections, civil rights, and modern citizenship. That is, the countermovements revealed the social character of rights and equality in the state. But Polanyi's conception of the great transformation as the "discovery of society" betrays an essentialism of modernity, in a primordial social interest recovered through the double movement, obscuring the class, gender, ethnic, and imperial relations constituting the state. State-sanctioned citizenship may be a universal ideal, but its historic practice has been marked by relational strategies of alterity, privilege, and exclusion (Isin, 2002). Although the state is represented formally as the site of sovereignty (politics), its substantive dimensions include the class and cultural politics of the relations of power, production, and consumption.[11] That is, the

[11] The conventional understanding of the state as a one-sided and artificial "superstructure" of politics, distinguished from an equally artificial and depoliticized "base" of economics, stems from the fetishism

state itself is, in part, a relation of production (Sayer, 1987) and reproduction (cf. Bakker and Gill, 2003) and therefore part of the constitution of the thought and practice of civil society.

The modernity paradigm represents the state as the realm of political sovereignty, linked to civil society via national forms of citizenship, but historically states were constituted within imperial relations. That is, the substantive history of the state system is embedded in a complex of global and regional, class, racial, and ethnic power relations (cf. Wallerstein, 1974). The modern state's discriminatory modes of rule contradict the rhetoric of European civility and modernity (see, e.g., Davis, 2000). Racism was integral to settler states, formed through genocidal relations with indigenous peoples, and colonial states – where, in Africa, exploitative apparatuses were often based in state patronage systems formed through artificial tribal hierarchies and land confiscation (Patel, 2002; Davidson, 1992:206, 257). With decolonization, independence formally abolished racial discrimination and affirmed civil freedoms, but it often divided power within the new nation-states according to the tribal relations (ethnic, religious, regional) established via colonial rule (Mamdani, 1996:17–20). Similarly, the states in the Indian subcontinent were constructed through the politics of partition in the moment of decolonization, at the same time as the state of Israel occupied and subdivided Palestine. Whereas the modernity paradigm proclaims formal equality in the state, assimilating minorities and deploying civil rights to correct historic inequities of access to the state and market, most modern states embody historic tensions between formal secularism and historical layering of race, class, and ethnic political relations.

What is so distinctive about contemporary globalization is that it exacerbates these tensions through state transformation. Under the guise of formal sovereignty, states author the deregulation of financial flows and the privatization of public capacity, decomposing national political–economic coherence (Chossudovsky, 1997) and elevating ethnic and racial hierarchies within and across states. At the global level, historic north–south relations shape currency hierarchies and multilateral institutional power in such a way as to distribute the costs of structural adjustment to the weaker and more vulnerable states and populations (Cohen, 1998). Under the resulting austere conditions, states become the site and object of class, ethnic, and religious mobilizations based in regional or national politics. The insecurities and forced deprivations attending corporate globalization are expressed in myriad ways, from food riots through land occupation to indigenous and fundamentalist movements demanding rights in the state. These tensions express the historic inequalities within a global states system constituted through the uneven and incomplete project of postcolonial sovereignty and development, to which we now turn.

MODERNITY AND DEVELOPMENT

Development emerged as part of the modernity paradigm, as a political response to the depredations of the market. Its centerpiece was the problem of dispossession and displacement of populations (both rural and industrial), through the consolidation of private property relations (in land or money–capital). As a result, "development" was reproduced on a broadening scale as governments sought to accommodate (and discipline) the expropriated to paid labor systems within industrial capitalist relations (Cowan and Shenton, 1996). This intervention informed, on a world scale, a discourse of international development in the mid-twentieth-century era of decolonization, targeting Third

surrounding exchange relations. Social relations among people *appear* as exchange relations between commodities, extinguishing the interdependence among people and elevating their dependence on "economy" (cf. Marx, 1967). The phenomenal independence of the economy is matched by the phenomenal independence of the realm of politics. Polanyi's critique of the commodity fetishism of economism as simply *unnatural* accepts the fetishized social form of the state, occluding its origins in the property relation, precluding an historical (and cultural) understanding of the phenomenon of market rule, and perhaps obscuring the inevitable return of what he referred to as "our obsolete market mentality" (1971).

World poverty (Escobar 1995), clearly enunciated by U.S. President Harry Truman on January 20, 1949:

"We must embark on a bold new program for making the benefits of our scientific advances and industrial progress available for the improvement and growth of underdeveloped areas. The old imperialism – exploitation for foreign profit – has no place in our plans. What we envisage is a program of development based on the concepts of democratic fair dealing" (quoted in Esteva, 1992:6).

The discourse of development, as a "fair deal," offered a vision of all societies moving along a path forged by the Western world – a path constituted by dispossession (cf. Davis, 2000). It was liberal insofar as it rejected colonialism and promoted self-determination, envisioning a national popular mobilization in the project of modernization and improvement of living standards. But it ignored the contribution of colonial peoples, cultures, and resources to European development; it forgot that the postcolonial states could not repeat the European experience of development through colonialism (other than through further dispossession of rural and minority peoples via internal colonialism); and it denied the intrinsic merit of non-European cultures.

As an ideal, the development paradigm erases the relation between the rise of modern citizenship in Europe and the horror of slavery and colonialism, and offers the world a single vision that flattens its diversity and sponsors an increasingly unsustainable monocultural industrial system. The development paradigm embodies a contradictory logic: It offers self-determination at the same time as it suspends self-definition (Rist, 1997:79). That is, it frames self-determination as a property of the nation-state: an imposed Western discipline (cf. Mitchell 1988). Here, "development" rehearses the duality of modernity, which at once celebrated the progressive Enlightenment principle of self-organization but contained it through the device of state sovereignty (Hardt and Negri, 2000:74). Political sovereignty was thus constructed as a relationship of power, channeling citizen and subject sovereignties through the state. In short, modernity is expressed in the state form, as a *relation* with national and international dimensions.

In world-historical terms, citizenship, democracy, and development – all universal visions implying political, social, and economic rights – were forged, as attributes of states, within the colonial relationship and its disorganizing impact on the non-European world. The colonial relation conditioned these discourses, enabling their projection as universal conditions charting the future of the non-European world (cf. Cooper and Stoler, 1997:37). Together they informed the post-World War II "development project," a discursive vehicle for the ordering of world political–economy under U.S. hegemony (McMichael, 2004). The U.S. strategy, representing development as a historic entitlement of the community of (new) nations, was, as Immanuel Wallerstein (1995) put it, New Dealism writ large. Development was instituted as a regime of "embedded liberalism," premised on the deliberate organization of the world market around national economic priorities (Ruggie, 1982). In other worlds, it was a globally instituted market, anchored in a now complete states system.

As the projection of the Anglo–American welfare state into the postcolonial states system, the development project combined aid with responsibility, especially adherence to the principle of the freedom of enterprise (Arrighi, 1994:68; Karagiannis, 2004). But the development project was an unrealizable ideal in an asymmetrical world order. Its four pillars combined national and international forms of regulation. First, it responded to, and sponsored, the completion of the nation-state system via decolonization and the institutionalization of the principle of self-determination in the United Nations.[12] Second, the 1944 Bretton Woods conference (creating the IMF and the

[12] This principle anticipated the post-Westphalian inclusion of individuals (rather than just states) as subjects of international law and codification of human rights. Held, noting the potential paradigm shift, suggests the logical conclusion of this vision is to challenge "the whole principle that humankind should be organized as a society of sovereign states above all else" (1995:89).

World Bank) institutionalized the regulation of monetary relations on a world scale. Unlike the nineteenth century, when world money was produced through private financial houses, post-World War II world money was produced through a combination of the U.S. Federal Reserve (the U.S. controlled 70 percent of gold reserves) and an allied coalition of central banks (Arrighi, 1994:278), with an IMF/World Bank loan system designed to stabilize currency exchanges (aided by capital controls) and to incorporate postcolonial states into the development project. Third, national political–economies, with considerable variation, regulated wage relations with combinations of Keynesian macroeconomic policy and Fordist strategies to stabilize expanding production and consumption relations. Fourth, the Marshall Plan and other foreign aid programs driven by Cold War concerns infused the world economy with military, technological, and financial relations privileging U.S. corporate and geopolitical interests. These four pillars instituted a world market within an ideal discourse of development, in which states were responsible for managing national economic growth. Postcolonial states sought to transcend the structural dependency of the colonial division of labor by pursuing strategies of "import substitution industrialization" to build domestic manufacturing capacity, financed by continued patterns of exports of primary goods and/or by bilateral technical and food aid and multilateral loans.

The development project, as an attempt to universalize the model of the citizen state, remains unrealized. First, the nation-state was essentially a West European institution (cf. Davidson, 1992). It has had a troubled history in Eastern Europe and the postcolonial world, where state boundaries intersect cultural groupings and where the in-migration of ex-colonials has accelerated the erosion of civil rights associated with neoliberal reforms. Second, geopolitics has conferred privilege on some states at the expense of others. Industrialization of showcase, or strategic, states of the Cold War (e.g., South Korea, Taiwan, Chile, South Africa) served to confirm the development project while most of their erstwhile Third World partners have been hard-pressed to replicate the First World development path (cf. Grosfoguel, 1996). And third, the institutional structure of the development project promoted transnational economic integration through aid programs and foreign investment. Freedom of enterprise encouraged transnational corporate activity and generated an offshore dollar market that ballooned in the 1970s with the recycling of petrodollars. A global money market arose, and, with rapid developments in information and communication technology, global banks gained prominence and an era of financialization ensued (Arrighi, 1994). Colin Leys (1996:7) captures the transition to the "globalization project":

> By the mid-1980s the real world on which "development theory" had been premised had . . . disappeared. Above all, national and international controls over capital movements had been removed, drastically curtailing the power of any state wishing to promote national development, while the international development community threw itself into the task of strengthening "market forces" (i.e., capital) at the expense of states everywhere, but especially in the Third World.

Ultimately, the globalization project represents an attempt to resolve the crisis of development, which appears as the crisis of state sovereignty. This crisis was immanent in the contradiction between the ideal of national development and transnational economic integration (cf. Friedmann and McMichael, 1989). The development project premise, that states were supposed to organize national economies, was undercut by the geopolitical and corporate relations ordering the "free world" as an international hierarchy of political and technological relations. Transnational firms deepened the "material integration of social reproduction across borders" (Rosenberg, 2001:134–5), compounding the differentials among Third World states as global production chains fragmented national economic sectors, preempting nationally driven forms of capital accumulation and wealth redistribution, and new forms of global finance exacerbated indebtedness among Third World states. These circumstances clarified the paradox of formal sovereignty: first, in the austere conditions imposed on overexposed Third

World states via the debt regime of the past two decades; and second, in the subsequent participation of governments in implementing market rule, via the institutions (WTO) and protocols (FTAs) of the globalization project.

GLOBALIZATION AND DEVELOPMENT: RECYCLING THE DOUBLE MOVEMENT?

Arguably, globalization is the politics of instituting a corporate market on a global scale. There are two sides to this coin: the restructuring of states to facilitate global circuits of money and commodities (conventionally termed "opening economies"), and the construction of multilateral institutions and conventions securing this global "market rule." It involves a reconfiguration of priorities and power within states, typically expressed in the ascendance of globally oriented financial and trade interests over national developmentalist coalitions rooted in labor and peasant unions and institutionalized in urban welfare, education, and agricultural ministeries (Canak, 1989). States are not disappearing; rather, they undergo transformation to accommodate global corporate relations and the requirements of sound finance, as interpreted by the multilateral agencies. Thus the condition for the Mexican state signing on to the North American Free Trade Agreement (NAFTA) was the sale or dissolution of 80 percent of its 1,555 public enterprises, the reduction of average tariffs on manufactured imports from 27 to 8 percent, wage reductions of up to 50 percent, a shift from husbanding a national agricultural and food sector to encouraging foreign investment in agro-exports, reducing rural credit and food subsidies, promoting food importing, and liberalizing access to the financial and transport sectors for foreign investors (McMichael, 2004:135, 192). In these ways and more, the transformation of the Mexican state facilitates the global deepening of relations of social reproduction. The paradox of sovereignty is exposed in the state's performance of its historic task of organizing the (now global) market.[13]

Formal political sovereignty enables the enforcement of market rule. The management of the debt crisis by the Bretton Woods institutions illustrates this proposition. Bailouts of indebted states in the 1980s, and beyond, mandated government enactment of austerity measures under market-enabling conditions laid down by the IMF and World Bank crisis managers. Structural adjustment loans require combinations of currency devaluation, wage reductions, removal of social subsidies, privatization of the state, and liberalization of foreign trade and financial markets. Whereas these measures were implemented on a case-by-case basis in the 1980s, they were institutionalized in the 1990s as universal rules applying to a collective sovereignty, although not without some (continuing) resistance (Chossudovsky, 1997; McMichael, 2000a).

With the collapse of the Cold War in 1991, the stage was set for a universal application of liberalization, under the leadership of the United States and its G-7 allies. In the GATT Uruguay Round (1986–94), plans were afoot for extending trade liberalization measures from manufacturers to agriculture, services, and intellectual property. A powerful complex of transnational firms, including GM, IBM, and American Express, formed a multinational trade negotiations coalition to lobby GATT member nations (*New York Times*, November 11, 1990). The outcome of the Round was the creation of the World Trade Organization (WTO) with over 130 member states. Unlike the GATT, a trade treaty only, the WTO has the power, through its dispute settlement body, to enforce its rulings onto member states. Should states refuse to comply, the WTO can authorize the plaintiff to take unilateral action. The ambit of the dispute settlement mechanism is wide: covering trade, investment, services, and intellectual property.

[13] In observing that financialization has reduced the options of even powerful nation-states regarding economic policy instruments, Held accentuates the ambiguity of sovereignty: "While this alone does not amount to a direct erosion of an individual state's entitlement to rule its roost – sovereignty – it leaves nation-states exposed and vulnerable to the networks of economic forces and relations which range in and through them, reconstituting their very form and capacities" (1995:134).

Member states can lodge complaints against states deemed in restraint of trade with the WTO, whose ruling holds automatically unless every other member state votes to reverse it.

Consistent with the moderns conception of political sovereignty, the role of the WTO is ostensibly to enforce market freedoms, by depoliticizing the global economy. This implies a *general* challenge to national laws and regulations regarding the environment, health, preferential trade relations, social subsidies, labor legislation, and so on. Although the challenge does not eliminate all laws, it seeks to harmonize regulation across the state system and to lower the ceiling on democratic initiatives within the national polity, especially those involving subnational jurisdictions (Tabb, 2000:9). That is, instituting a self-regulating market on a global scale reformulates and redistributes, rather than removes, sovereignty, simultaneously generating resistances.

The current challenge to national laws – and currencies – invokes a second cycle of Polanyian countermovements in a rediscovery of society. But instead of a historic *movement*, the discovery of society now appears to have been a historic *moment* rooted in the political history of the West. This was the moment of consolidation of the nation-state. The maturing of social rights (and, therefore, of social protections) was conditioned by the maturing of movements for decolonization – ignored by Polanyi, but, arguably, just as significant in the process of completion of the nation-state system. The significance of this conjuncture lay not only in the proliferation of new nations (and the creation of the United Nations), but also in the possibility of a sovereignty crisis, contained in the terms of the development project. Here, while the postcolonial world of the UN enshrines the individual sovereignty of states, the institutionalization of a global states system occurs in a world structured by an international division of labor and a hegemonic order premised on integration via corporate, military, and financial relations.

The crisis of sovereignty is revealed through Justin Rosenberg's concept of the "empire of civil society" (the formal duality of public and private political realms *across* the modern states system). He suggests that the public/private disjuncture "explains part of the paradox of sovereignty: why it is both more absolute in its 'purely political' prerogatives than other historical forms of rule, and yet highly ambiguous as a measure of actual power" (Rosenberg, 2001:131). Thus, the moment of consolidation of national sovereignty as a universal form via the development project simultaneously spawned a powerful counterpoint in the state-sponsored corporate integration of economic relations on a world scale. It is this dialectic that sparks debates about the fate of the state under globalization and underlies current tensions within the WTO, as the agency now responsible for instituting the self-regulating market. And it is this tension that reveals the crisis of sovereignty.

The crisis of sovereignty is expressed formally in declining state capacity to protect (all) citizens as well as in the substantive challenge by countermovements to modern understandings of sovereignty, both spurred by corporate globalization. As Charles Tilly (1984) suggests, historically capital inherited the state as a protection racket, subordinating peoples and cultures across the world to territorial administration and refashioning the state via civic representation as a legitimizing and/or empowering relation with its subjects. Arguably capital now owns or seeks to own the state, via privatization and the disciplines of deregulated monetary relations, and has a diminishing need for substantive forms of democracy associated with the twentieth-century "discovery of society" (cf. Hardt and Negri, 2000). In the twenty-first century, the citizen state is "de/reregulated" as a market state in the service of global capital circuits, unleashing a protective movement that is compelled to rethink the meaning of civil society and social rights. That is, the significance of corporate globalization lies in the trajectory of the state and the related question of rights.

GLOBALIZATION AND ITS COUNTERMOVEMENTS

In this era of globalization, we find a curious tension embedded in the discourse of universal rights. Globalization, as a discursive corporate project, portrays the world's future in singular, universalist, and abstracted terms – as moving toward a market culture enabled by Western science and technology and promoting expanding freedoms of capacity and choice. This is a particular vision of the world, presented as a universal. However, after fifty years of development, only 20 percent of the world's population has the cash or access to consumer credit to participate in this market, and the remaining 80 percent do not all necessarily aspire to Western consumerism (Barnet and Cavanagh, 1994:383). In fact, we find a proliferation of social movements proclaiming the universal right to be different.

Instead of a politics of participation in the centralizing marketplace of development, countermovements pose alternative, decentralized conceptions of politics governed by locality (place, network, diaspora) and/or situated identity (where relations of class, gender, race, ethnicity, and environmental stewardship are specified world-historically). This is not a wholesale rejection of modern relationships (technical, financial, landed) so much as a reformulation of the terms and meanings of these relationships. The countermovements may seek to subsume market relations to their particular politics, but, "post-Polanyi," these alternative forms of sovereignty are governed not by the universals of the states system but by the particulars of locality/identity-based relations (which may inform global network organizations, such as Fairtrade Labelling Organizations International and *Via Campesina*). Although this politics is distinguished as locality/identity-oriented politics, it is not *postmodern* in the sense of eschewing a material politics. It is a politics born of modern world-historical circumstances, of corporate globalization: It is only at the point at which national sovereignty is *universally* called into question that the artificial separation of politics from economics is fully revealed, encouraging alternative conceptions of political–economic sovereignty.

The unclothing of the "empire of civil society," so to speak, is precisely the moment of transition between the development project and the globalization project, as the sovereignty of the nation-state yields to the sovereignty of monetary relations.[14] This transition was effected by two, related, world events. First, the 1970s deregulation of financial relations subordinated all currencies and, therefore, states, to the rationality of global money markets.[15] The second transitional event was the puncturing of the "developmentalist illusion" (Arrighi, 1990) by the 1980s debt regime, preparing the ground for the project of globalization. The devastating devaluation of southern economies and societies, imposed by the multilateral agencies on behalf of finance capital, exposed the growing autonomy of global economic relations and the structural and institutionalized *necessity* of state sponsorship of these relations.[16]

The potential erosion of individual national sovereignties was formalized in 1995 in the establishment of the WTO. In redefining development as a global corporate project, the WTO *collectivizes* the sovereignty of its member states as a general vehicle of market rule (McMichael, 2000a). Joseph Stiglitz confirms this in distinguishing the WTO from the Bretton Woods institutions thus: "It does not set rules itself; rather it provides a forum in which trade negotiations go on and it ensures that its agreements are lived up to" (2002:16). The recomposition of sovereignty involves abstraction: Just as the global economy reduces production sites across the world to competitive replicates of one

[14] For an extended discussion of this, see Arrighi, 1998 and McMichael, 2000b. In this sense, Polanyi's claim that "the currency is the nation" was prescient.

[15] Thus: "When interest and currency rates are no longer determined politically by legitimate institutions of the nation-state but rather are formed by global markets, the market dynamic can no longer be politically regulated according to directives which are incompatible with it . . . Politics does not disappear, but its rationality is synchronized with the economy" (Altvater and Mahnkopf, 1997:463).

[16] As Jeffrey Sachs observed of IMF management: "Not unlike the days when the British Empire placed senior officials directly into the Egyptian and Ottoman finance ministries, the IMF is insinuated into the inner sanctums of nearly 75 developing-country governments around the world . . . (which) rarely move without consulting the IMF staff, and when they do, they risk their lifelines to capital markets, foreign aid, and international respectability" (1998:17).

another, so state organizations surrender their particularity to the competitive relations of the global money market.

In this recomposition of sovereignty, the corporate empire reveals that the economic is political (and vice versa), spawning countermovements no longer captured by the abstractions of modernity, development, state, and economy. The global countermovement, in resisting privatization and the conversion of social life into the commodity form, reformulates the political terrain in which reembedding of the market can occur, producing a radical redefinition of political economy. This is not just about infusing a moral economy into an existing political economy of nation states, which, under mid-twentieth-century circumstances became the Polanyian *realpolitik*, for better or for worse (cf. Lacher, 1999). It is about reformulating conceptions of civil/human rights, the state, and development (cf. Mohan, 2004).

PROPERTY RIGHTS VERSUS THE COMMONS

When welfare systems and other public services are privatized, the meaning of citizenship switches from membership of the public household with rights to social protections, to membership of the market with rights to produce, exchange, and consume. Citizens are regarded increasingly as "bearers of economic rationality" (Drainville, 1995:60), and access to goods and services (some of which were once public) is determined less by need and more by merit. As states restructure, rights to public goods dwindle, replaced by uneven access to the market. Neoliberal policies accentuate the individual (as opposed to the civic) content of citizenship, subordinating social rights to economic rights, which enables corporate claims on the state: "an aggregation of economic rights . . . constitutes a form of economic citizenship, in that it empowers and can demand accountability from government." Thus investors rather than citizens "vote governments' economic policies down or in; they can force governments to take certain measures and not others" (Sassen, 1996:39).

The aggregation of economic rights is not so defining of this form of globalization as the attempt to *institutionalize* property rights on a global scale. Sheer size or scale may distinguish the twenty-first-century corporation, but the privileging of corporate rights over citizens' rights via institutional transformations is more profound. Nowhere is this more dramatic than in the participation of states in the elaboration of global market rule. Citizens understand this threat – from the 146 IMF food riots in thirty nine countries, protesting the austerity policies of the debt regime as social rights to food subsidies shrunk (Walton and Seddon, 1994), through broad civic protest over privatization schemes to the exploration of alternative local forms of government (e.g., Argentina's neighborhood assemblies).

The successful resistance to the attempt to privatize Cochabamba's water system was a turning point for popular mobilizations in Bolivia, formerly touted by the multilateral agencies as a model for other low-income countries (Farthing and Kohl, 2001:9). The corporate consortium that purchased the city's water doubled prices and charged citizens for rainwater collected on rooftops. Poor families found food was now cheaper than water. The depth of public outcry forced the city to resume control of the water system. Citizen action thus decommodified a public good. However, if the WTO's proposed General Agreement on Trade in Services (GATS 2000) had been in place, such a reversal would have been practically impossible. GATS, described by the WTO as "the world's first international investment agreement," targets the privatization of basic services such as health care, education, and water supply; infrastructures such as post, public transport, and communications; cultural services such as broadcasting, films, libraries, and museums; as well as finance and tourism. Whereas GATS may exclude services provided "under the exercise of government authority," it does apply if services have a commercial dimension or compete with the private sector, and, because governments can liberalize more, but not less, under GATS, an *expansion* of regulation or public assets is ruled out (Coates, 2001:28).

Privatizing public goods is also enabled by the intellectual property rights protocol in the WTO, known as Trade Related Intellectual Property Rights (TRIPs). As a relational feature of corporate globalization, it is premised on the elimination, or incorporation, of the commons and at the same time crystallizes resistance around the protection of indigenous knowledges and practices. The intellectual property rights regime originated in stemming pirating of Western products such as CDs, watches, and so forth in the global south, but it now sanctions a reverse biopiracy on a disproportionate scale, threatening cultural rather than simply commodity rights. Patenting microbiological organisms, via TRIPs, protects monopoly rights to seeds, plants, and plant products where they have been genetically modified. By appropriating plant varieties developed over centuries, TRIPs' protection of Western scientific innovation invisibilizes alternative sciences of indigenous agriculture and biodiversity management (Shiva, 1997:8).

Within the WTO, the TRIPs protocol privileges governments and corporations as legal entities and disempowers communities and farmers whose rights to plant their crops are subject to claims of patent infringement. One model of resistance emerged in 1996 in the Indian village of Pattuvam in the southern state of Kerala, when it declared its ownership over all genetic resources within its jurisdiction (Alvares, 1997). This preemption of corporate genetic prospecting is protected by the Indian constitution, which decentralizes certain powers to village-level institutions. By registering local plant species and cultivars in local names, the village claimed collective ownership of genetic resources, denying the possibility of corporate patents applying to these resources and removing the property from intellectual rights.[17] As Shiva observes: "The seed is, for the farmer, not merely the source of future plants and food; it is the storage place of culture and history" (1997:8).

The Pattuvam resistance exemplifies the significance of place in countermovement politics against the spatial abstraction inherent in the commodity relation and the monoculture of modern scientific rationality. Vine Deloria Jr.'s claim that modernity's obsession with time (as money) contrasts with the place-based epistemology of nonmarket cultures (in Starr, 2000:189) echoes Marx's observation that the logic of commodity circulation is the destruction of space by time. Arguably, the global south offers a multiplicity of examples of place-based epistemology – whether ecologically and/or cosmologically driven peasant and indigenous cultures. Attempts to revalue local space through constructing alternative currency relations or community-supported agricultures, especially in the north, pursue a similar goal but within a different historical relationship to capitalist modernity (cf. Hines, 2000). By extension, transnational networks, such as environmental, fair trade, human rights, unions, and farmers' movements, address concerns rooted in localities that, together, unify their diversity. Counterposed to the uniform market culture of corporate globalization, resistance is heterogeneous in time and space and yet well aware of its world-historical context.

GLOBAL COUNTERMOVEMENT POLITICS

Corporate globalization generates a range of resistances, those highlighted here developing a counterhegemonic politics based in the right to live by values other than those of the market. Grassroots movements assert cultural diversity as a world-historical relation and human right, embodying what Sachs calls "cosmopolitan localism" (1992:112). The antimarket rule movement is most evident in the global south, where the tradition of the commons is more recent and/or where the empire has no clothes.

Revealing the nakedness of empire is decidedly postcolonial, in the sense that the crisis of development includes its (and the state's) demystification. As the *Zapatistas* commented, in resisting the Mexican state's embrace of NAFTA (1994):

"When we rose up against a national government, we found that it did not exist. In reality we were

[17] This notion comes from Raj Patel.

> up against great financial capital, against speculation and investment, which makes all decisions in Mexico, as well as in Europe, Asia, Africa, Oceania, the Americas – everywhere" (quoted in Starr, 2000:104).

Having confronted the paradox of state sovereignty, the *Zapatista* uprising significantly unsettled regional financial markets, contributing to a 30 percent devaluation of the peso at the end of 1994. Arguably, the *Zapatista* political intervention revealed the contingency of development (as registered by Mexico's 1994 admission into the OECD), implying that it was a confidence trick of the globalization project:

> "At the end of 1994 the economic farce with which Salinas had deceived the Nation and the international economy exploded. The nation of money called the grand gentlemen of power and arrogance to dinner, and they did not hesitate in betraying the soil and sky in which they prospered with Mexican blood. The economic crisis awoke Mexicans from the sweet and stupifying dream of entry into the first world" (quoted in Starr, 2000:104).

The power of the *Zapatista* movement lies precisely in its ability to situate its political intervention in cosmopolitan, world-historical terms – relating its regional condition, through national, to global, relationships. This includes linking the Mexican state's participation in NAFTA, which Subcomandante Marcos declared to be "a death sentence for indigenous people," to the historic colonization of Chiapas; and linking *Zapatismo* to resistance movements across the world: "we are the possibility that (empire) can be made to disappear... tell it (empire) you have alternatives to its world" (quoted in Starr, 2000:104–5).

The *Zapatista* uprising, timed to coincide with the implementation of NAFTA, was revelatory rather than simply programmatic (Harvey, 1999:199). It linked a powerful and symbolic critique of the politics of globalization with the demand for civil rights linked to regional autonomy. When the Mexican government tried appeasement through a National Commission for Integral Development and Social Justice for Indigenous People and injecting funds into Chiapas, the *Zapatistas* rejected this as "just another step in their cultural assimilation and economic annihilation" (Cleaver, 1994:50). *Zapatismo* asserted a politics of rights going beyond individual or property rights to human and community rights, resonating with indigenous rights movements elsewhere. As Neil Harvey observes: "If citizenship in Salinas' Mexico was contingent on the economic competitiveness of each individual, the indigenous had little hope of surviving either as citizens or as peoples" (1999:200). That is, *Zapatista* politics are not about inclusion per se, but about redefining citizenship, calling for: "A political dynamic not interested in taking political power but in building a democracy where those who govern, govern by obeying" (quoted in Harvey, 1999:210).

The durability of the *Zapatista* resistance stems from a lengthy process, undertaken by Marcos and a small cadre band, of blending the *Zapatista* critique of Mexican political history with the "indigenous peoples' story of humiliation, exploitation and racism" (Harvey, 1999:166). It exemplifies a world-historical sensibility in bringing a cultural politics to the question of civil rights. The more substantive notion of collective rights grounds the civic project in place-based mobilization, based on "historical memory, cultural practices, and political symbols as much as on legal norms" (Harvey, 1999:28). As a regional movement against empire and its state form, the *Zapatistas* particularize a universal notion of rights in blending ethnic, gender, and class relations into a process, rather than a structure, of democracy.

The particularization of rights, in a self-organizing movement addressing and redressing tangible historical relations, is simultaneously a universal claim to substantive forms of democracy, which I am arguing is the root of the global countermovement. The conception of rights makes no prior claim to content, as movements and communities reserve the right to define for themselves appropriate political and ecological relations. Some movements consciously invert the problematic of capitalist modernity, understood here as a European universal legitimizing global empire. Contemporary indigenous movements, from the Ecuadorian movement (CONAIE) to the North American Inuit, affirm citizenship as a basic national and human right but view it as the vehicle for respecting the differential rights of minorities, creating plurinational states with varying degrees of autonomy. Within the *Zapatista* movement, women have questioned the premise of official indigenous state policies that dichotomizes modernity and tradition, insisting on "the right to hold to distinct cultural traditions while at the same time changing aspects of those traditions that oppress or exclude them" (Eber, 1999:16). This involves blending the formal demand for territorial and resource autonomy with the substantive demand for women's rights to political, physical, economic, social, and cultural autonomy.

Another compelling social experiment crystallizing in the crucible of neoliberalism is the Brazilian landless workers' movement, the *Movimento dos Trabalhadores Rurais Sem Terra* (MST). The Cardoso government's neoliberal experiment (1995–2002) subordinated Brazilian political economy to global financial capital in a late-twentieth-century context where 1 percent of landowners own (but do not necessarily cultivate) almost 50 percent of the land, while 4.8 million families are landless. Between 1970–85, agricultural subsidies cost Brazil US $31 billion. Since 1985 they have disappeared, even as OECD member states' agricultural subsidies continue at US $360 billion a year. As the MST Web site claims: "From 1985 to 1996, according to the agrarian census, 942,000 farms disappeared, 96% of which were smaller than one hundred hectares. From that total, 400 thousand establishments went bankrupt in the first two years of the Cardoso government, 1995–96." Between 1985–96 rural unemployment rose by 5.5 million, and between 1995–9 a rural exodus of 4 million Brazilians occurred. While in the 1980s Brazil imported roughly US $1 million worth of wheat, apples, and products not produced in Brazil, from "1995 to 1999, this annual average leapt to 6.8 billion dollars, with the importation of many products cultivable . . . in Brazil" (www.mstbrazil.org/EconomicModel.html).

Since the mid-1980s, the MST has settled 400,000 families on more than 15 million acres of land seized by takeovers in Brazil. The MST draws legitimacy from the 1988 Brazilian constitution's sanction of the confiscation of uncultivated private property, not performing its social function. The method of direct occupation, met with state military and legal force, has exposed the inequality of landed relations and the complicity of the state in the centuries-old Brazilian system of landed rule. National polls confirm popular support of seizure of unproductive land, and government administrators have recognized that the cost of maintaining the same people in urban *favelas* is twelve times the cost of legalizing land occupation (*Food First,* Winter 2001). The priority given to producing staple foods for low-income consumers (rather than foods for affluent consumers in cities and abroad) led to an agreement with the da Silva government, for direct purchase of settlement produce for the national Zero Hunger campaign (Jardim, 2003).

The power of the movement resides not only in its practice of securing landed "spaces of hope," but also in its sponsorship of demonstrations, marches, occupation of government buildings, and negotiations through which it has managed to seize strategic moments in national politics. The MST pursues a program called "Project Brazil," using alliance-building to develop a national alternative to the global corporate project. In articulating its agrarian struggle with urban-based struggles (such as the Movement of Homeless Workers and various *favela* organizations), the MST draws on several themes in Brazilian political history: liberation theology and Marxism, the "new unionism" of urban social movements of the basic church communities, and the Peasant Leagues. Through an initial alliance with the church, "the only body that had what you might call a capillary organization across the whole country" (Stedile, 2002:79), and its Pastoral Commission on Land (1975), the MST developed a national, but decentralized, organization spanning twenty-seven states (concentrated among descendants of European immigrants in the south and *mestizos* in the northeast). Dispossessed farmers comprise the majority of its membership, but in the more urban south in particular the MST includes unemployed workers and disillusioned civil servants. Originally autonomous of the Worker's Party (PT), the MST has supported it electorally and developed closer ties. Following the PT's recent success in the presidential elections, President da Silva created a new Ministry for Economic Solidarity, headed by an ex-seminary student active in liberation theology and in the founding of the MST and supportive of its agrariant agenda.

The formation of cooperatives (sixty by 2003) follows land seizures (large-scale for security). The MST Settlers Cooperative System differs from traditional cooperatives through social mobilization "transforming the economic struggle into a political and ideological struggle." Over and beyond the (often unforgiving) task of settling hundreds of thousands of families on recovered land, the political–economic novelty of this movement lies in "linking up what it calls the struggle for the land with the struggle on the land" (Flavio de Almeida and Sanchez, 2000). The model of social appropriation includes democratic decision making to develop cooperative relations among workers and alternative land use patterns, and participatory budgeting, financed by socializing some settlement income (Dias Martins, 2000). The social project of the MST connects production and pedagogy, informing its work and study method of education.[18]

The MST's 1,600 government-recognized settlements include medical clinics and training centers for health care workers; 1,200 public schools employing an estimated 3,800 teachers serving about 150,000 children at any one time. A UNESCO grant enables adult literacy classes for 25,000, and the MST sponsors technical classes and teacher training. Cooperative enterprises produce jobs for thousands of members, in addition to foodstuffs and clothing for local and national (nonaffluent) consumption. Although more recently the MST has linked its prospects to the success of the PT, it continues a regenerative political culture based in agroecology, continuous learning, and community self-reliance. In a transitional moment such as this, global justice movements reach beyond the nation-state to more complex, and uncertain, ideas of sovereignty, even as they position themselves as transformative movements within the states system.

MST politics exemplify the mushrooming movement across the world for "food sovereignty": a material and discursive counterpoint to the concept of "food security," linked in the 1980s to global agro-industries and breadbaskets supplying food through "free trade."[19] Food sovereignty insists on cultural and ecological integrity, and food quality, counterposed to the agro-industrial fetish of quantity, which has produced "scarcity in abundance," expressed in the marginalization of local farming on a world scale (Araghi, 2000). Marginalization is a by-product of the corporate pursuit, via WTO rules, of comparative advantages via farm sector liberalization. This involves exploiting north/south asymmetries, where the average subsidy to U.S. farmers and grain traders is about a hundred times the income of a corn farmer in Mindanao (Watkins, 1996). Conservative estimates are that between 20 million and 30 million people have recently lost their land due to the impact of trade liberalization (Madeley, 2000:75). Global food insecurity stems from the appropriation of land for the exports to affluent markets and by world market dumping of heavily subsidized but artificially cheap food by the grain-rich countries undermining peasant agricultures (McMichael, 2003).

[18] João Pedro Stedile, president of the MST, observes: "Under the objective economic conditions, our proposal for land reform has to avoid the oversimplification of classical capitalist land reform, which merely divides up large landholdings and encourages their productive use. We are convinced that nowadays it is necessary to reorganize agriculture on a different social base, democratize access to capital, democratize the agroindustrial process (something just as important as landownership), and democratize access to know-how, that is, to formal education" (Orlando Pinassi et al., 2000).

[19] The trade principle justifying this global reconfiguration of agriculture informed the 1995 WTO Agreement on Agriculture, enunciated by the U.S. delegation during the Uruguay Round: "The U.S. has always maintained that self-sufficiency and food security are not one and the same. Food security – the ability to acquire the food you need when you need it – is best provided through a smooth-functioning world market" (quoted in Ritchie, 1993:25).

The food sovereignty countermovement seeks to revitalize cultural, ecological, and democratic processes in protecting local farming. It anchors its political–economy in alternative, agro-ecological models producing substantially higher, more diverse, and more sustainable outputs of food than high-input industrial agriculture (Norberg-Hodge, Goering, and Page, 2001:61). The Charter of Farmers' Rights issued by the international Seed Satyagraha Movement for biodiversity asserts the rights to land; to conserve, reproduce, and modify seed and plant material; to feed and save the country from food insecurity; and to information and participatory research (Nayar, 2000:21). Expressing the global solidarities of this countermovement, MST National Committee member Joâo Pedro Stedile claims:

"It's not enough to argue that if you work the land, you have proprietory rights over it. The Vietnamese and Indian farmers have contributed a lot to our debates on this. They have a different view of agriculture, and of nature – one that we've tried to synthesize in Via Campesina. We want an agrarian practice that transforms farmers into guardians of the land, and a different way of farming, that ensures an ecological equilibrium and also guarantees that land is not seen as private property" (2002:100).

The several-million-strong transnational movement, *Via Campesina* (the MST is one of its eighty-seven national members), asserts "Farmers Rights are eminently collective" and "should therefore be considered as a different legal framework from those of private property." Uniting landless peasants, family farmers, agricultural workers, rural women, and indigenous communities, *Via Campesina* claims that:

"biodiversity has as a fundamental base the recognition of human diversity, the acceptance that we are different and that every people and each individual has the freedom to think and to be. Seen in this way, biodiversity is not only flora, fauna, earth, water and ecosystems; it is also cultures, systems of production, human and economic relations, forms of government; in essence it is freedom." (http://www.ns.rds.org.hn/via/)

Via Campesina privileges food sovereignty over agricultural trade as the path to food security, noting that "the massive movement of food around the world is forcing the increased movement of people." The precondition of food sovereignty, in this vision, is access to credit, land, and fair prices to be set via rules negotiated in UNCTAD, not at the WTO. And, as a political alternative to the current corporate regime, "the active participation of farmers' movements in defining agricultural and food policies within a democratic framework is indispensable." The specificity of these politics is that, while the consumer movement has discovered that "eating has become a political act," *Via Campesina* adds: "producing quality products for our own people has also become a political act . . . this touches our very identities as citizens of this world" (http://ns.rds.org.hn/via/).

Via Campesina enriches the Polanyian sensibility for agrarian reform, declaring not only that it is "an instrument to eliminate poverty and social differences," but also that "peasants' access to land needs to be understood as a form of guarantee of the value of their culture, autonomy of community, and of a new vision of preservation of natural resources for humanity and future generations. Land is a good of nature that needs to be used for the welfare of all. Land is not, and cannot be, a marketable good." Instead of simply regulating land and food markets, this perspective embodies the alternative principles of autonomy, sovereignty, and political–ecology common to the global countermovement. The enactment of this principle in communities (e.g. across Africa)[20] or mass movements like the MST[21] emerges most dramatically in the global

[20] Fantu Cheru documents the variety of "organized struggles for subsistence" in Africa, where "peasants now market their produce and livestock through their own channels, disregarding political boundaries and marketing boards," and self-organizing village development groups create physical and educational infrastructures, including cereal banks, grain mills and local pharmacies, concluding that "Locally based co-operative movements are the only ones that can realistically articulate an alternative vision of world order by creating new avenues of social and political mobilization" (1997:161–3).

[21] Settlers do not automatically embrace the vision of the leadership (Caldeira, 2004). While movements are never single-minded, the reflexive goals of the global countermovement tend to consolidate the vision (Wright and Wolford, 2003).

south where the complicity of the political in the corporate empire has the starkest consequences.

The ecological principle stems from two sources: the critique largely from within northern, market societies of the social and environmental devastation from economic monocultures; and the critique largely from southern cultures that practice principles of biodiversity and agro-ecology, through custom and/or necessity. Insofar as the global countermovements' common object is to resist corporate globalization and state sponsorship of commodity relations that threaten human communities and habitats, it includes the tactical goal of social protection. However, in addition to regulating market relations, countermovements champion nonmarket polycultures and new forms of subsidiary political representation, asserting a new strategic right to diversity, in and across cultures.

CONCLUSION

As a discursive project of market rule, globalization enlists the instrumentality of the modern state in increasingly unaccountable policies with profound, crisis-ridden consequences for the politics of rights. This chapter argues that the crisis of sovereignty stems from three dimensions of corporate globalization: first, the erosion of citizenship rights in modern states via broad strategies of privatization and dismantling of social protections; second, the increasingly evident "citizenship gap" associated with, for example, more than 50 million political and economic refugees, displaced indigenous peoples, the 100 million unregistered domestic migrant workers in China, 1 million to 2 million modern-day slaves, and even subjects of southern countries in context of an exploding tourist industry (Brysk, 2002:3, 10–11); and third, the rising political claims for participatory alternatives within the global countermovement.

In delineating these three dimensions, I draw attention to the temporal layering of political responses to globalization. The immediacy of responses to current abuses of rights and human victimization ("globalization with a human face") may be distinguished from the more visionary responses by movements to develop alternatives ("globalization from below"). The first set of responses includes the "struggle to promote the subaltern discourse on human rights," for example, to operationalize the "sleeping provisions" (Articles 25 and 28) of the Universal Declaration of Human Rights, which link rights to the elimination of poverty and to humane governance of the social and international order. The 1990s saw several conferences on environment, women's rights, development, population, and human rights address these concerns, culminating in the UN Social Summit of 1995 (Falk, 2002:71). Because globalization is a power relation, we also find the multilateral agencies, the Davos economic forum, and their spokespeople proposing to reform the G-7's monopoly of financial power by imposing a "Tobin tax" on cross-border financial transactions and adopting the language of poverty alleviation and improving transparency in governance in an attempt to close the legitimacy gap (e.g., Stiglitz, 2002, Narayan, 2000). In other words, the double movement constitutes the politics of globalization.

As I have argued, the twenty-first-century double movement is different and links immediate protective goals with transitional, visionary practices exemplified in the mass movements of the global south. One such linkage is evident in postcolonial politics, where the "African Alternative Framework for Structural Adjustment Programs for Socio-Economic Recovery and Transformation," adopted by the United Nations Economic Commission for Africa, critiqued the neoclassical assumptions of the development paradigm and offered a participatory model of collective development goals rooted in the specificity of African political cultures (Ake, 1996:36–8). Although these institutional responses are vulnerable to the G-7 development establishment's disproportionate financial and discursive power to appropriate its critics, nevertheless they register the participatory and cosmopolitan politics maturing across global communities in countless contexts, stimulated by the political deficits and social depredations of corporate globalization.

Many of these contradictory circumstances stem from the crisis of development and its global extension via the neoliberal project, posing as a neutral market-driven solution. In this world-historical conjuncture, resistances reveal capitalist modernity as an imperial project, privileging corporate rights and depending on geopolitical and currency hierarchies. Contrary to the early-twentieth-century dress rehearsal for global development, today's countermovements reach beyond the formula of national market regulation and wealth redistribution to develop an alternative politics rooted in an ecological paradigm, rejecting modernity's separations of politics and economics, natural and social worlds, and rulers and ruled. Instead of the singular worldview associated with the modern state, this politics asserts the right to multiple worldviews regarding democratic organization and the securing of material well-being through cultural and environmental sustainability.

The specificity of corporate globalization is that in universalizing a particular vision on a diverse world, it crystallizes that diversity in increasingly reflexive resistance movements marked by a strategic solidarity. More than a global process of integration, globalization is a contradictory set of relations conditioning its politics, and recurring crises, with no necessary linear movement or outcome. The social experiments of the countermovements and the "cosmopolitan project" (Held, 2000), exemplified in the European Union, will continue in tension with a WTO increasingly hamstrung by the inherent disorder of an asymmetrical states system (e.g., the conflict between the United States and the EU regarding GMOs, the intractability of the question of agricultural reform) and the global north's overbearing treatment of the global south. The collapse of the WTO Ministerial in Cancun (2003) revealed this power differential. A renewed solidarity within the global south (forming the Group of 21, led by Brazil, India, and China) and a parallel solidarity among global justice groups converged decisively to stall the meeting, exposing undemocratic WTO proceedings and unequal agricultural trade rules, GATS, and TRIPs protocols.

Although grassroots movements will by necessity develop their resistance, the short-term direction of the world order is complicated by the geopolitics of oil, U.S. unilateralism, and reactive terrorism (Achcar, 2002). In addition, the 1999 "global compact" (the "corporatization" of a financially strapped UN) and the politics of the 2002 UN resolution on weapons inspections in Iraq have deeply compromised the UN's ability to anchor an agenda of international law dedicated to advancing social and human rights reflecting multilateral rather than unilateral interests. For the foreseeable future, then, globalization and its analysis will be overdetermined by a resurgence of bilateralism and questions concerning the militarization of the corporate empire, the elevation of the rights of consumer–citizens in this new world disorder, and equations of resistance with terror – sharpening and clarifying the contradiction between this world and "another world" projected by the World Social Forum.

CHAPTER THIRTY

State Economic and Social Policy in Global Capitalism

Evelyne Huber and John D. Stephens

Across the capitalist world in countries of varying levels of development, the 1980s and 1990s witnessed a retreat of the state from intervention in the economy, reversing a trend that dates back to the Great Depression. In the advanced capitalist countries, countries led by parties of varying political colors privatized state enterprises, reduced state regulations, liberalized capital markets, and, to varying degrees, cut welfare state entitlements. In the Latin American and Caribbean economies, as in much of the rest of the less developed world, countries turned from import substitution industrialization (ISI) with high tariffs, capital market regulation, and high levels of state intervention to neoliberal open, export-oriented models.

The dominant interpretation among political and journalistic observers has been that trends toward greater reliance on the market were both products and manifestations of "globalization," the increasing economic openness of the national economies and integration of the world economy. The academic version of this view, the "hyperglobalization thesis," argues that the emergence of a single global market and global competition has eliminated the political latitude for action of national states and imposes neoliberal policies on all governments. Proponents contend that as markets for goods, capital, and, more recently, labor have become more open, all countries have been exposed to more competition and the liabilities of state economic intervention and deviation from market-oriented "best practices" have become more apparent because these raise the cost of production. As capital markets have become more open and capital controls increasingly unworkable, capital in these countries moves elsewhere in search of lower production costs. Thus, governments must respond and reduce state intervention to stem the outflow of capital. The hyperglobalization thesis has Marxist (e.g., Amin, 1997) and neoliberal (e.g., Ohmae, 1995) proponents. For the neoliberals, traditional social democratic policies are the targets of globalization; for the Marxists, they are the victims.

In the literature on advanced industrial societies, proponents of the hyperglobalization thesis are rare outside open economy macroeconomics and business schools, as Hay (2002) points out. Although it is commonplace to note that economies have become more open in the past three decades, the effects of this increased openness are highly disputed. Garrett (1998) stakes out the diametrically opposed position that globalization is positively related to welfare state generosity, resurrecting the thesis that economic openness generates demands for "domestic compensation" and for productivity-enhancing public goods characteristic of an earlier generation of writings on comparative political economy, particularly the work on corporatism (e.g., see Cameron, 1978; Katzenstein, 1985). In his comprehensive review of the experiences of twelve advanced industrial societies, Scharpf (2000) takes the middle ground, arguing that countries' ability to shape macroeconomic policy and intervene in the economy has been reduced in large part due to international economic integration, but that this has had a much more modest impact on countries' ability to pursue full employment, social security, and social equality. With regard to the welfare state, Esping-Andersen (1999), Pierson (2001a, 2001b), and Myles and Pierson (2001) contest the thesis linking globalization to retrenchment, particularly the neoliberal version of it, citing other more important causes of stagnation and retrenchment such as changing demographic patterns, changing gender roles, the changes in the rates of return on capital relative to wage growth, and changing sectoral and occupational compositions of the economy (also Stephens, Huber, and Ray, 1999; Huber and Stephens, 1998, 2001).

In Latin America, the economic transformation has been much more dramatic than in advanced industrial countries. In addition, it took place in the midst of an economic crisis, which caused tremendous economic and social dislocations. At the level of political and journalistic debate, the hyperglobalization thesis is popular also. It certainly provides a convenient way to legitimize painful measures taken by governments in the process of economic opening. Academic explanations of the trend toward greater openness and reliance on markets, however, center around a combination of three factors, with different emphasis put by various authors on one or the other of these factors. First are the problems with ISI, particularly the chronic balance of payments problems, which began in the 1950s and were glossed over because of easy access to massive amounts of recycled petrodollars in the 1970s in the form of loans at floating interest rates. Second, when international interest rates began to rise in the early 1980s, at the same time as commodity prices fell, and the large international banks reacted to solvency problems of major debtor countries with a full stop of new lending, Latin American and Caribbean countries found themselves in a profound debt crisis. This debt crisis then gave heavy leverage to the international financial institutions (IFIs) that demanded stabilization and liberalization of the economies. Third, as the reforms progressed, they created their own beneficiaries and thus strong political supporters for further liberalization and privatization, mainly among the largest entrepreneurs and in the financial sector. The reactions to these pressures for reform, however, were not uniform but rather heavily shaped by domestic power distributions and political institutions.

The debate about the effects of economic opening, deregulation, and privatization is still in its beginning, given the relatively short period of time that has passed since their implementation. The record shows that Latin American and Caribbean countries experienced renewed economic growth in the 1990s, but with high volatility because of vulnerability to external shocks. Most countries made some progress in reducing poverty, but not inequality. Moreover, progress in poverty reduction in the 1990s did not even fully repair the damage done in the 1980s. Given this modest record, the main argument of the proponents of reform is that Latin America still is confronting deep structural problems of long standing and that things would be much worse without the reforms. Critics point to the high social costs of the reforms in terms of increased inequality, low human capital formation, and lack of employment in high productivity sectors. Unlike in advanced industrial countries, there is also much concern about the impact of the structural reforms on the quality of the emerging democracies.

In this chapter, we examine the evidence on the extent of economic internationalization, the interaction between domestic and international causes of policy change, and the nature of changes in state economic and social policy in advanced industrial countries and Latin America and the Caribbean. We begin by documenting, quantitatively where possible, the extent of the increase in economic internationalization in the past four decades and then proceed to an analysis of the experience of advanced industrial countries and then Latin America and the Caribbean.

DIMENSIONS OF ECONOMIC INTERNATIONALIZATION

In this chapter, we limit ourselves to examining the economic aspects of globalization. Economic internationalization can be broken down into four dimensions: increasing integration of markets for goods and for capital, growing internationalization of production, and growing strength of supranational bodies. Both trade and capital market openness can be indexed by the flows of capital or goods and services and by the barriers to flows (Tables 30.1 and 30.2). For capital markets, we have data on both controls and flows. The data on tariff and nontariff barriers are spotty for the earlier period so we have not included them. This is unfortunate because variations in trade volume across countries are not very good indicators of trade barriers, as size of the domestic market is such an important determinant of volume of trade. Due to economies of scale, small countries cannot produce a full range of goods for domestic producers and consumers and must import goods to satisfy these needs. Thus, small countries may have very high trade barriers and nonetheless have high trade flows. For instance, in the 1970s Jamaica had very high tariffs, nontariffs barriers, and quantitative restrictions on trade, yet exports and imports were still over 70 percent of GDP, far higher than most European countries in the 1990s when trade barriers there were quite low (Stephens and Stephens, 1986). Fortunately, we do have data on trade barriers for the EEC and six South American countries (Bulmer-Thomas, 1994:280), which, though not completely comparable to the available World Bank Data for the 1990s, do allow us to sketch variations through time and across regions.[1]

Table 30.1 presents the trade and capital market data for advanced industrial countries. The index of capital controls (columns 1 and 2) varies from 0 to 100, with 100 denoting complete absence of capital controls and 0 denoting the presence of all controls coded by the creators of the index (Quinn and Inclan, 1997). As one can see, many countries maintained significant capital controls in the Golden Age of postwar capitalism but by the 1990s only a few countries retained any controls. The change in actual flows of capital is even more dramatic, with both flow measures increasing more than eightfold from the 1960s to the 1990s. By contrast, the trade flows increased modestly, by 30 percent. The change in tariff protection was also less dramatic than in the case of capital controls, with EEC/EU external tariffs varying from 1 to 19 percent depending on the sector circa 1960, to 1 to 5 percent in 1999. Across all sectors, the advanced industrial countries imposed average tariffs of 4 percent in 1999. Our spotty evidence indicates that the corresponding figure would have been around 10 percent in 1960.

Table 30.2 presents similar data for Latin America and the Caribbean. With regard to trade, most countries register significant increases in trade flows, though there are some notable exceptions. Tariff barriers were very high, especially in the six countries that fully adopted an inward-oriented ISI model (Argentina, Brazil, Chile, Colombia, Mexico, and Uruguay). In those countries, average tariffs were typically over 100 percent. The remaining countries, while continuing to depend on exports from a few primary products, did eventually turn to ISI to develop a domestic consumer goods industry and thus also imposed tariffs that were very high by industrial country standards, though not as high as in the six inward-oriented countries (Bulmer-Thomas, 1994:297). The abandoning of ISI by both groups resulted in impressive reductions in tariffs: The average tariff level in the region in 1998 was only 10 percent. Latin American and Caribbean countries also liberalized capital flows, but on average not nearly as dramatically as advanced industrial countries, at least not by the mid-1990s. Whereas the average Quinn/Inclan index of liberalization increased from 65 to 92 in advanced industrial countries from the 1960s to the 1990s, it only increased from 68 to 77

[1] The World Bank data are available at http://www.worldbank.org/data/databytopic/trade.html.

Table 30.1. *Indicators of Economic Openness: Advanced Industrial Countries*

	1	2	3	4	5	6	7	8
	Degree of Liberalization of Capital Controls		Outward Direct Foreign Investment		Borrowing on International Capital Markets		Trade Openness	
	1960–73	1990–94	1960–73	1990–94	1960–73	1990–94	1960–73	1990–94
Sweden	60	95	0.5	6	0.17	10.54	46	59
Norway	37.5	100	0.1	1.9	1.37	5.01	82	72
Denmark	75	100	0.2	1.6	1.01	3.91	60	65
Finland	25	87.5	0.2	1.5	0.92	9.63	45	54
Austria	55	87.5	0.1	0.8	0.39	4.16	53	77
Belgium	75	100	0.3	3	0.35	2.77	77	138
Netherlands	75	100	1.3	6.6	0.41	4.01	92	99
Germany	100	100	0.3	1.2	0.05	1.85	40	62
France	72.5	90	0.2	1.9	0.09	2.69	27	44
Italy	72.5	90	0.3	0.7	0.42	1.91	31	39
Switzerland	97.5	100	0	4.4	0.06	2.21	61	69
Japan	50	70	0.2	0.7	0.09	1.46	20	18
Canada	93.75	100	0.3	0.9	1.69	4.91	40	56
Ireland	50	82.5	0	0.7	0.73	7.15	78	119
UK	46.4	100	1.1	4.5	0.45	4.61	41	51
USA	92.5	100	0.6	1.4	0.1	1.81	10	22
Australia	57.5	75	0.2	0.9	0.35	3.7	30	37
New Zealand	37.5	87.5	0.1	6.5	0.67	4.12	46	58
Mean	65.15	92.50	0.33	2.51	0.52	4.25	48.83	63.28

(1–2) Liberalism of capital controls. Quinn and Inclan (1997).
(3–4) Outward foreign direct investment as a percentage of GDP. Provided by Duane Swank (see Swank, 2002), originally coded from IMF, *Balance of Payments Statistics*, various years.
(5–6) Total borrowing on international capital markets as a percentage of GDP. Provided by Duane Swank (see Swank, 2002), originally coded from IMF, *Balance of Payments Statistics*, various years.
(7–8) Value of exports plus imports as a percentage of GDP. Huber, Ragin, and Stephens (1997) based on OECD data.

Table 30.2. *Indicators of Economic Openness: Latin America and the Caribbean*

	1	2	3	4	5	6
	Degree of Liberalization of Capital Controls		Outward Direct Foreign Investment		Trade Openness	
	1960–1973	1990–1997	1967–73	1990–98*	1960–73	1990–98
Argentina	71	86	.00	.63	12.69	18.42
Brazil	41	47	.02	.27	13.89	17.56
Mexico	80	75	n.d.	n.d.	17.49	47.55
Bolivia	96	89	.00	.03	59.22	48.88
Chile	53	58	.00	1.43	27.09	59.19
Colombia	53	59	.04	.36	27.05	34.79
Ecuador	77	89	.00	.00	36.1	57.26
Paraguay	76	81	.00	.03	29.96	86.43
Peru	77	92	.00	.03	36.5	25.89
Uruguay	88	100	.00	.01	26.77	43.42
Venezuela	90	72	n.d.	.64	41.01	52.78
Barbados			.44	.09	126.85	116.35
Costa Rica	92	88	.00	.05	57.43	85.91
Dominican Republic	46	55	.00	.00	43.87	67.86
El Salvador	27	84	.00	.00	51.85	54.02
Guatemala	71	100	.00	.00	33.78	43.21
Jamaica	50	81	.05	1.14	72.54	122.18
Nicaragua	89	69	.00	.00	57.6	87.2
Trinidad and Tobago	42	64	.00	.00	102.18	86.71
Mean	67.7	77.2	.03	.26	45.99	60.82

*1992–98 for Argentina, 1994–98 for Jamaica.

(1–2) Liberalism of capital controls. Dennis Quinn (personal communication).

(3–4) Outward foreign direct investment as a percentage of GDP. Coded from IMF, *Balance of Payments Statistics*, various years.

(5–6) Value of exports plus imports as a percentage of GDP. World Bank, *World Development Indicators* CD–ROM (2000).

in Latin America and the Caribbean. There is also much greater variation among countries in the region than among advanced industrial countries, with the larger countries (Brazil, Mexico, Colombia) tending to maintain more controls. Outward direct foreign investment remained at a very low level; only Chile, Jamaica, Venezuela, and Argentina surpassed .5 percent of GDP.[2]

The third dimension of economic internationalization is internationalization of production: the growth of transnational corporations (TNC) and development and growth of "global commodity chains" in which the manufacture and distribution of a product occurs in different countries organized by a single enterprise and produced by either that enterprise or subcontractors (Gereffi and Korzeniewicz, 1994). Although there are no hard figures on the growth of the proportion of total world production accounted for by TNCs and global commodity chains, case studies suggest that it is substantial. Because a large proportion of the expansion of these global production networks must occur through direct foreign investment, the figures for the increases in DFI in Table 30.1 are probably a good indicator of the increase in the internationalization of production.

The fourth dimension of economic internationalization is the growth of the role of supranational governing bodies: the international financial institutions (IFIs), such as the International Monetary Fund (IMF) and World Bank, and international organizations, such as the European Union (EU) and the World Trade Organization (WTO). The growth in the influence of IFIs in developing countries in the wake of the debt crisis is extraordinary. In the case of the advanced industrial countries, the expansion and deepening of the EU is without historical precedent, shifting vast areas of decision making from the national state to the EU (Schmitter, 1996:125). We document the extent of the influence of these organizations below.

[2] We were unable to obtain satisfactory data for borrowing on international capital markets. The data were not comparable across countries and spotty in coverage.

DEVELOPMENTS IN THE ADVANCED INDUSTRIAL COUNTRIES

Economic and Social Policies up to 1980

In order to situate the retreat of the state and increase in market regulation in advanced capitalist societies, it is necessary to characterize the political economies of these countries about a decade after the close of the Golden Age of postwar capitalism, a point at which the degree of state regulation was at its pinnacle. Beginning with the relationship between welfare state and production regimes, we take Soskice's (1999) distinction between coordinated market economies and liberal market economies as the point of departure for our conceptualization. Soskice emphasizes employer organization and relationships between companies and financial institutions as defining characteristics of production regimes. Employer organization takes three distinctive forms: coordination at the industry or subindustry level in most continental and Nordic economies (industry-coordinated market economies – CMEs), coordination among groups of companies across industries in Japan and Korea (group-coordinated market economies), or absence of coordination in the deregulated systems of the Anglo–American countries (uncoordinated or liberal market economies – LMEs). In coordinated economies, employers are able to organize collectively in training their labor force, sharing technology, providing export marketing services and advice for R&D and for product innovation, setting product standards, and bargaining with employees. The capacity for collective action on the part of employers shapes stable patterns of economic governance encompassing a country's financial system, its vocational training, and its system of industrial relations.

A central characteristic of the coordinated economies is the generalized acceptance by all major actors of the imperative of successful competition in open world markets for tradable goods. Successful competition in turn requires a high skill level of the labor force and the ability of unions to deliver wage restraint to the extent needed to preserve an internationally competitive position. In the industry-coordinated market economies of Central and Northern Europe, initial labor skills are effectively organized in companies or with strong company and union involvement in public schools. Unions are organized mainly along industrial lines and play an important cooperative role in organizing working conditions within companies and in setting wage levels for the economy as a whole. Banks and industries are closely linked, providing industries with preferential sources of long-term credit, or the state plays a major role in bank ownership and performs a similar role in preferential credit provision for industry. In uncoordinated market economies, in contrast to both types of coordinated economy, training for lower level workers is not undertaken by private business and is generally ineffective. Private sector trade unions are viewed as impediments in employer decision making, have little role in coordinating their activities, and are weak. Bank–industry ties are weak and industries must rely on competitive markets to raise capital.

Following Esping-Andersen (1990), within the industry coordinated market economies, we can distinguish two subtypes on the basis of their welfare state: The Nordic social democratic welfare states and the continental European Christian democratic welfare states. Although both have very generous transfers systems, the social democratic type is more redistributive (Bradley et al., 2003). The greater degree of centralization of bargaining in the Nordic countries which results in lower levels of wage dispersion reinforces this highly egalitarian pattern (Wallerstein, 1999). The continental countries' intermediate degrees of bargaining centralization still result in more wage equality than in the liberal welfare states, which are characterized by enterprise level bargaining and weak unions. The main difference in the welfare state configuration is the very high level of public health, education, and welfare services delivered in the Nordic welfare states and the low level in the continental welfare states. The difference in public social service employment results in very high levels of female labor force participation in the social democratic welfare states and low levels in the Christian democratic welfare states.

The liberal market economies can be divided into two groups based not on their welfare states, which in both cases are residual, but on the basis of wage regulation systems and tariff regimes. Following Castles (1985, 1988), we distinguish the "wage earner welfare states," Australia and New Zealand, from the liberal welfare states, the remaining Anglo–American countries. Similar to the Latin American countries discussed below, the antipodes followed an import substitution policy of high tariff barriers on manufacturing goods, with primary product exports financing the cost of importation of consumer goods and inputs for the manufacturing sector. The high tariffs were part of an explicit compromise in which workers received high wages delivered by the compulsory arbitration systems.

Outside of Australia and New Zealand, none of the advanced industrial countries maintained high tariffs on goods. As previously mentioned, the CMEs, particularly the smaller countries, were dependent on exports and defended open trade in international fora (Katzenstein, 1985). Otherwise, the state was highly interventive, the area of intervention varying by the particular political economy configuration of the country, although all had generous welfare states.[3] Some countries had large state sectors (Austria, Finland, France, Italy, and Norway), and the state often subsidized investment and employment in the enterprises. Most countries maintained capital controls (Table 30.1) and heavily regulated internal capital markets. This allowed them to set interest rates below international interest rates and offer lower interest rates domestically to business investors. Some countries (Finland, Italy, and Sweden, as well as Australia, Britain, and New Zealand among the LMEs) resorted to politically determined devaluations in order to restore competitiveness. Almost all countries pursued Keynesian countercyclical demand policies, and a number of countries incurred large fiscal deficits in the fight against economic stagnation in the 1970s.

[3] See Huber and Stephens (2001) and Scharpf (2000) and the contributions to Scharpf and Schmidt (2000) for a more detailed country by country description.

Some countries (Austria, France, Germany, and Norway) used state-owned banks to subsidize investment in both private and public industries whereas in others the state budget was used for the same purpose. In all of the CMEs and most of the LMEs, public interest services such as telecommunications, mass transportation, energy supply, and public utilities were provided primarily by state monopolies insulated from both domestic and international competition (Héritier and Schmidt, 2000). And finally, many countries used nontariff barriers, such as product regulations, to protect domestic producers.

Changes in Economic Policies and Globalization

As Scharpf (2000) points out, the policies just outlined had been greatly reduced or abandoned by the turn of the century. Many state-owned enterprises had been privatized, even by social democratic governments. Those which were not privatized were directed to operate by market, profit-seeking principles; operating without subsidies and no longer supporting employment. Capital controls were eliminated and domestic capital deregulated. Devaluation was abandoned as a policy tool and twelve European countries adopted a common currency, completely eliminating even the possibility of using currency adjustment as a policy instrument. The combination of the elimination of capital controls and the fixing of currencies meant that international markets set national interest rates, effectively eliminating monetary policy as a countercyclical tool and cheap interest rates as a measure to stimulate investment. External financial decontrol also limits a government's ability to employ fiscal stimulation as a tool, as fiscal deficits are considered risky by financial markets and either require a risk premium on interest rates or put downward pressure on foreign exchange reserves. For European Union countries, the deepening of European integration after 1990 further limited monetary and fiscal policy latitude and prohibited nontariff trade barriers and subsidies to support investment and employment. Finally, with the possible exception of Switzerland, almost all countries reluctantly retrenched welfare state entitlements, though the cutbacks were modest in all but a few cases.[4]

The fact that there are parallel trends toward globalization and reduction of state intervention in the market does not, of course, establish that they are causally linked. Let us first take increased exposure to trade where, outside of Australia and New Zealand, the effects of increased economic internationalization have been most limited because, other than in those two countries, the advanced industrial economies were very trade open at the beginning of the globalization era and increases in trade openness have been modest (Table 30.1). The one area in which one does detect a significant impact of increased trade openness is the trend toward privatization and "marketization" of state enterprises. Even here the process is complex and the lowering of tariff barriers does not figure strongly in the picture. Perhaps the most dramatic change is the public service monopolies, particularly telecommunications. Here rapid technological change made what were once natural monopolies into enterprises exposed to international competition. With the advent of satellites and cell phones, governments could only prevent private alternative providers from offering their services with increasingly draconian measures. The cost of using state enterprises to support employment, a common response to the crisis of the 1970s, forced government after government to abandon the practice in the course of the 1980s and attempt to put state enterprises on a profit-making basis. Once this was accomplished, the logic of even having the enterprises in the state sector disappeared and privatization was often the next step. The large budget deficits faced by many governments made this a yet more attractive option.

Another pressure toward privatization was growth of the scale of enterprises, as the optimal size for competitiveness in sectors such as manufacturing outgrew the scale of the national

[4] There have been cutbacks in the 1990s in Switzerland, but these were overshadowed by the expansion over the whole of the last two decades (Bonoli and Mach, 2000).

enterprises and the search for partners through merger or absorption resulted in the dilution of the state-owned portion of the resulting enterprise or outright privatization. Finally, the spread of neoliberal ideology primarily in parties of the secular right but also of other political tendencies, most notably New Zealand Labor, further spurred on privatization. Neoliberal ideological commitments led governments to push privatization and marketization even to sectors that remained natural monopolies or that were widely perceived by the public to be public services which should not be governed by market principles, such as education and health care. In such cases, the results of privatization/marketization were often less satisfactory as in the privatization of British rails (Héritier and Schmidt, 2000) and the marketization of health care in New Zealand (Kelsey, 1995).

With regard to increased capital mobility, there is compelling evidence that the opening of capital markets and the very large increases in capital flows shown in Table 30.1 have had a large constraining influence on macroeconomic policy. As Simmons (1999:41–3) points out, whereas the early popular accounts stress technological innovation, the revolution in electronic transfer, as the impetus for removing capital controls, later more nuanced academic analyses add market competitive, political, and ideological factors. The technological innovations and the growth of the offshore dollar market in the 1960s and the collapse of the Bretton Woods systems of fixed but flexible exchange rates in 1971–3 set the scene for a round of competitive deregulation led by the United States in 1974, then Canada and the Netherlands in the same year, and then by Germany and Switzerland later in the decade (Simmons, 1999:41). Note that all of these countries were characterized by relatively liberal foreign capital regulations in the 1960s already (Table 30.1). Leftist governments tended to resist this movement but by the mid-1980s, the ability of multinational businesses and financial institutions to circumvent national controls and to exploit them for arbitrage influenced most governments to abandon controls. The final vestiges of controls were eliminated in European Union countries under the provisions of the Single European Act of 1987 by the beginning of 1993.

As a result of the elimination of controls on capital flows between countries, governments cannot control both the interest rate and exchange rate. If a government decides to pursue a stable exchange rate, it must accept the interest rate that is determined by international financial markets. The absence of capital controls makes the option of setting low interest rates while accepting a depreciating currency unattractive as it results in inflation, which greatly complicates wage bargaining (see below). As a result of the decontrol of financial markets, competition from non-OECD countries for investment funds (Rowthorn, 1995) and the worldwide debt buildup in the wake of the two oil shocks, real interest rates increased from 1.4 percent in the 1960s to 5.6 percent in the early 1990s (OECD, 1995:108). As a result of decontrol of domestic financial markets (which was in many cases stimulated by international financial deregulation), government's ability to privilege business investors over other borrowers also became more limited. Countries that relied on financial control to target business investment were particularly hard-hit as businesses moved from a situation in which real interest rates offered to them via government subsidies, tax concessions, and regulations were actually negative to a situation in which they had to pay the rates set by international markets. In addition, in the pivotal German economy, the increase in capital mobility weakened the bank–industry link, with capital becoming less patient, less willing to wait for the long-term payoff (Seils and Manow, 2000; Streeck, 1997). External financial decontrol also limits a government's ability to employ fiscal stimulation as a tool, as fiscal deficits are considered risky by financial markets and either require a risk premium on interest rates or put downward pressure on foreign exchange reserves. Finally, because of the interest rate penalty that international currency markets made countries with a history of devaluation pay, countries effectively dropped competitive devaluation as a policy tool and the twelve European Monetary Union countries went so far as to completely eliminate the possibility of currency adjustment.

These developments put great pressure on wage bargaining systems in countries where unions were at least moderately strong, at the same time as they pushed huge responsibilities for maintaining macroeconomic balance and external competitiveness onto these systems. With EMU membership or fixed exchange rates, the wage gains above the European norm are translated immediately into loss of export markets and thus into higher unemployment. In this environment, inflation is the number one enemy of the bargaining system because nominal, not real, increases in wages undermine export competitiveness. Without the fiscal and monetary tools once available to combat unemployment, the responsibility increasingly falls on the wage bargainers.

With containing inflation as the central policy goal and interest rates set by international markets, it is not surprising that countries with central banks dependent on government authority moved to increase the independence of their central banks, because such a move could increase the credibility of government policy in the eyes of international money markets and thus reduce interest rate premiums. The monetary policy and institutional arrangements favored by the German Bundesbank and conservative economists became the norm.

The remaining question in the area of macroeconomic management is the extent to which these outcomes were products of inescapable processes of economic internationalization or were partly or even largely products of voluntary choices to deepen European integration, as Hay (2002) contends, or of political decisions guided by neoliberal ideology. There is little doubt that fixed exchange rates/common currency, independent central banks, macroeconomic policy targeting inflation, no capital controls, and so on are all policy commitments of the European Union and that meeting the criteria for entry into the EMU, particularly the deficit, debt, and inflation targets, imposed economic austerity on many of the prospective entrants. However, it is clear that the process of decontrol of capital markets, which was so critical in constricting the latitude for macroeconomic management, substantially predated the decision to deepen European economic integration. The average index of capital market openness shown in columns 1 and 2 of Table 30.1 was 2.5 in 1973 and had been stable for a decade. It moved to 3.1 by 1985, the year of the announcement of the Single European Act, and then to 3.7 by 1993, the year than the act came into force. In Sweden in 1985, five years before the Social Democrats reversed their stand to favor entry into the European Community, the Swedish social democratic government made the decision to decontrol domestic capital markets because the development of "gray," that is, not quite illegal, credit markets had made the existing controls unviable (Feldt, 1991:260, 281–2).

The economic thinking that underlay the U-turn of the French Socialists after their first eighteen months in office in the early 1980s and the Swedish Social Democrats' "Third Way" between Keynesian expansion and monetarist austerity introduced on their return to office in 1982 is consistent with the constrained macroeconomic choices outlined earlier. Thus, while it is possible that the neoliberal commitments of social democratic policy makers, such as Swedish finance minister Kjell-Olof Feldt, led social democrats to abandon policies that were still viable – the countercyclical investment funds come to mind here (see Pontusson 1992:75–9) – it is probably the case that changes in the broad parameters of macroeconomic policy were the inevitable result of the decontrol of capital markets by the early liberalizers which then forced such moves on others. Whether the early liberalizers' hand was forced by the development of offshore dollar markets and technological innovations is a matter of dispute (e.g., see O'Brien, 1992; Helleiner, 1994).

Welfare State Retrenchment and Globalization

There is very little evidence from recent scholarly studies, including our own (Huber and Stephens, 2001), supporting the neoliberal thesis that strongly and directly links welfare state retrenchment to globalization. The recent quantitative work on social spending shows a very modest positive relationship between variables measuring various aspects of economic internationalization and welfare spending (e.g., see Garrett, 1998; Swank, 2002). However, social spending data are particularly unsuited for the study of retrenchment as spending can increase substantially due to the increase in recipients; the unemployed, disability pensioners, early pensioners, and the retired.[5] The few analyses of data that directly measure welfare state entitlements (e.g., replacement rates in various programs) come to different conclusions about the determinants of retrenchment (Allan and Scruggs, 2002; Hicks and Zorn, 2006; Korpi and Palme, 2001), perhaps because they differ in both the statistical methodology and dependent variables. All three studies agree that there are no statistically significant positive effects of globalization on retrenchment, and Hicks and Zorn (2006) actually find negative effects of trade openness and capital account openness on welfare state cutbacks. Both Hicks and Zorn (2006) and Korpi and Palme (2001), which, unlike Allan and Scruggs (2002), are true studies of retrenchment,[6] find that fiscal deficits and/or unemployment are related to retrenchment, which squares with the results of comparative case studies.

Based on our analysis of nine advanced industrial countries (Huber and Stephens, 2001), the twelve case studies in Schmidt and Scharpf (2000), and Myles's (1996, 2002) studies of North America – that is, sixteen of the eighteen advanced industrial countries in Table 30.1 – we find that rollbacks in welfare state programs have been a universal phenomenon in the past two decades. Our case studies indicate two different dynamics: ideologically driven cuts, which occurred in only a few cases, and unemployment driven cuts, which were pervasive. It is the timing and severity of the latter type of rollbacks that argues that they were largely unemployment driven. The countries where unemployment rose early (Denmark and the Netherlands) initiated cuts in the mid-1970s; the countries where unemployment rose late (Sweden, Norway, Finland) continued to expand welfare state entitlements until the late 1980s. The countries where unemployment levels remained very high for a long time (e.g., the Netherlands) made deeper cuts than the countries where they remained more moderate (e.g., Norway). This is not to say that all the policy changes were somehow dictated by economic constraints; perceptions and beliefs about the effectiveness of different policies in achieving certain goals did play a role. Thus, the rising hegemony of neoliberal doctrines certainly contributed to the rollbacks.

These rollbacks in most cases did no more than reduce the increase in welfare state expenditures. In fact, if one looks at the aggregate data for the different welfare state types, the average annual increase in most indicators of welfare state expenditures in the 1970s was higher than it had been in the Golden Age, and it continued to increase in the 1980s, though at a slower pace than in the previous two periods. Essentially, in the 1970s governments countered the deteriorating economic situation with traditional Keynesian countercyclical policies, but by the 1980s they had all realized that the rules of the economic game had changed and demanded new approaches. Still, the increase in claimants of benefits kept pushing up expenditures.

Our data and case studies show a sharp decline in partisan effects on welfare state expansion/retrenchment.[7] Curtailment of entitlements, or at best defense of existing entitlements, was

[5] See Huber and Stephens (2001) and Allan and Scruggs (2002).

[6] The dependent variable in Allan and Scruggs (2002) is annual change in various replacement rates in the period 1975 to 1999. Although the study is clearly a study of the retrenchment era, part of the results are certainly products of *increases* in replacement rates that occurred in many countries, especially early in the period.

[7] Our data analysis is based on social spending, which is fraught with difficulties as noted above, and thus we consider the case studies which do show a narrowing of partisan differences to be more reliable evidence. The three quantitative studies of entitlements mentioned above come to differing conclusions on partisan effects: Allan and Scruggs (2002) find that right government is negatively associated with replacement rate changes, and Korpi and Palme (2001) find that left government is negatively related to retrenchment, while Hicks and Zorn (2006) find that Christian democratic government is most negatively associated with retrenchment.

on the agenda everywhere. As Pierson argues (1996, 2001; also see Huber and Stephens, 1993, 1998), the politics of retrenchment are different from the politics of welfare state expansion. The Right was constrained in its ability to cut by the popularity of most of the large welfare state programs, and the Left was constrained in its ability to raise taxes to keep the programs on a sound financial basis by the economic slowdown. This is not to say that there have not been significant differences in the rhetoric of political parties with regards to desirable welfare state reforms, but simply that electoral constraints worked against radical departures from established welfare state models.

There were only a few cases of large-scale ideologically driven cuts. The most dramatic were Thatcher in Britain, the National (conservative) government in New Zealand, and the Reagan administration in the United States. In the case of the Reagan administration, the cuts were focused on cash and in kind benefits to the poor, a small but highly vulnerable minority, while Social Security was preserved by a large increase in the contributions. In any case, the United States cannot have been said to have made a "system shift" if only because it already had the least generous welfare state of any advanced industrial democracy. Only in Great Britain and New Zealand could one speak of an actual system shift from welfare state regimes that used to provide basic income security to welfare state regimes that are essentially residualist, relying heavily on means-testing. Although the radical changes in these two countries were certainly facilitated by the fact that they had experienced the lowest growth rates of any two advanced industrial countries for the period 1950–79, thus leading to a widespread view in the publics of both countries that a fundamental change was necessary, the changes in social policy, as opposed to neoliberal economic reforms in other sectors, were deeply unpopular in both countries and did not have the support of the median voter. We argue that the exceptional nature of these two cases can be traced to their political systems, which concentrate power (unicameral or very weakly bicameral parliamentary governments in unitary political systems) and make it possible to rule without a majority of popular support (single member districts and plurality elections that allow parties with a minority of votes to enjoy large parliamentary majorities).

Given the crucial role that the rise in unemployment has had in stimulating welfare state retrenchment, we have to seek to understand the reasons for the dramatic increases in unemployment in the 1980s and early 1990s. Here we can only summarize the arguments we make elsewhere at length (Huber and Stephens, 1998; Huber and Stephens, 2001a:chap. 6–7). Let us begin by dispensing with the standard neoliberal argument on trade openness, that is, with increased trade openness, the countries with generous welfare states and high wages were increasingly exposed to trade competition and their generous social provisions made them uncompetitive in ever more open world markets. First, increased trade openness is not a good candidate for explaining dramatic change as it has increased only modestly (see Table 30.1).

Second, as we pointed out above, the generous welfare states of Northern Europe were developed in very trade open economies in which the performance of the export sector was pivotal for the economic welfare of the country. Moreover, retrenchment was unrelated to export performance. For instance, the export sectors of countries such as Sweden and Germany were performing incredibly well in the mid-1990s at precisely the same time when the governments of those countries were cutting social benefits (Huber and Stephens, 1998; Pierson, 2001b; Seils and Manow, 2000). As Scharpf (2000:76–8) points out, there is no relationship between total tax burden and employment in the exposed sector in advanced industrial societies, strong evidence that generous social policy does not make countries uncompetitive in world markets.

The question then becomes what caused the increases in unemployment?[8] Let us begin by observing that it was not the low level of job creation, because employment growth after 1973

[8] The following few paragraphs summarize our arguments in Huber and Stephens (2001a:chap. 7; 2001b). See those writings for more detailed discussion and statistical documentation.

was as rapid as before (Glyn, 1995). Rather, rising labor force participation due to the entry of women into the labor force is one proximate cause of the increase in unemployment. The inability of the Christian democratic welfare states to absorb this increase either through an expansion of low-wage private service employment as in the liberal welfare states or through the expansion of public services as in the social democratic welfare states is one reason why the unemployment problem in these countries has been particularly severe. The other proximate cause is the lower levels of growth in the post-1973 period. This in turn can be linked in part to lower levels of investment, which in turn can be linked in part to lower levels of savings, to lower levels of profit, and to higher interest rates. High interest rates is where globalization comes in because, as outlined previously, they can be linked in part to deregulation of capital markets. Moreover, because decontrol of capital markets made countercyclical economic management more difficult, it certainly raised unemployment in that regard also.

Although we do think the evidence supports the view that financial deregulation has contributed to the rise in unemployment, it is important to recognize the importance of political decisions and conjunctural developments in explaining the current high levels of unemployment in Europe. Though it almost certainly was not a conscious decision, or at least not seen in these terms, the Christian democratic welfare states, faced with a growing supply of (female) labor, rejected the alternatives of creating a low-wage market in private services along American lines or expanding public services (and thus raising taxes) along Nordic lines. As we pointed out previously, the combination of the debt buildup in the 1970s and the policies required for accession to the EMU imposed austerity on European countries in the 1990s. The mismanagement of the process of financial deregulation led to a consumer boom and then real estate bust, which was the primary cause of the unemployment crisis in Finland, Sweden, and to a lesser extent, Norway.

Nor do we want to overstate the importance of the increases of unemployment (whatever their causes) for welfare state retrenchment. Pierson (2001a, 2001b) succinctly summarize other pressures on the welfare state. The shift from manufacturing to services has slowed productivity growth and contributed to the slowed economic growth noted previously. The growth of spending on programs legislated in the past, most notably pensions and health care, stresses national budgets. Population aging pushes up spending, particularly on these two programs. The decline in fertility, which has been dramatic in Christian democratic welfare states, threatens to greatly aggravate this problem in the future (Esping-Andersen, 1999). The change in family structure, the decline in male breadwinner families and increase in single mother and dual earner families, creates new demands for day care, maternity leave, and related programs (Esping-Andersen et al., 2002). The decline in wage growth and increase in returns on capital along with demographic change undermine the PAYGO pension systems and make funded systems more attractive, yet present the public with a double payment problem in financing a transition to a funded system (Myles and Pierson, 2001). In sum, the rise in unemployment has been only one contributor to welfare state stress, and globalization in all of its manifestations has been only one contributor to unemployment. Thus, the contribution of economic internationalization to welfare state retrenchment is modest.

For Australia and New Zealand, it would appear that a case can be made for the globalization thesis in that changes in the international economy did compel both countries to deregulate markets and fundamentally change their systems of social protection. In these "wage earner welfare states," social protection was delivered primarily by the compulsory arbitration system, which assured the family of an adequate living standard by providing a male breadwinner family wage and a number of social benefits from the employer to the wage earner. The formal welfare state, that is, transfers and services delivered by the state, was rather underdeveloped by European standards. This distinctive Australasian political economy became unviable as a result of long-term secular changes in commodity prices and the entry of the United Kingdom into the European Community, with a consequent loss of preferential markets for Commonwealth exports. In both countries, the wage regulation system, which was the core of the system of social protection, was changed substantially – in New Zealand altered completely – and this, along with the rise in unemployment, exposed workers to much higher levels of risk of poverty than had earlier been the case. Add to this other marketizing reforms (see Castles et al., 1996; Schwartz, 1994a, 1994b, 1998), and it becomes apparent that the political economy of the antipodes has converged on the liberal type. Thus, in these two countries, it is accurate to say that changes in the international economy forced them to abandon policies which had protected an uncompetitive manufacturing sector.

LATIN AMERICA AND THE CARIBBEAN

Economic and Social Policies up to the 1980s

The first argument to make when discussing Latin America and the Caribbean is that the countries in the region are extremely diverse, much more so than OECD countries. There are very small, extremely poor, still largely agricultural countries like Haiti, Nicaragua, and Honduras, along with upper–middle income countries with partly advanced industrial sectors like Argentina, Chile, Brazil, and Mexico. So, any generalizations are extremely hazardous. Nevertheless, it is possible to point to some important economic characteristics that are shared by most of these countries. Starting with colonization, they were all shaped into raw material export economies. The effects of the Great Depression then generated incentives for ISI, and the more advanced countries – Brazil, Chile, Mexico, Argentina, Colombia, and Uruguay – began to implement pro-ISI policies; other countries, such as Peru, Venezuela, and Jamaica, followed much later on this path. Pro-ISI policies entailed high protective tariffs and nontariff barriers to imports, preferential interest and exchange rates for industrial investment and thus regulated capital markets, state investment in strategic sectors of the economy, regulation of DFI, and a host of other regulatory activities.

As industrialization progressed, these countries faced the problem of integrating labor as an economic and political actor. The political integration took different forms, in some cases under leadership of the state and in others through party–union alliances, but in all cases the state played an active role (Collier and Collier, 1991). State corporatism was prevalent; in more inclusionary and more exclusionary versions, and even where state/ capital/ labor relations were more pluralistic, there was a high degree of labor market regulation. With industrialization and as part of the process of labor incorporation came the expansion of social insurance schemes to the urban working class. Social insurance schemes had been introduced earlier for the most important pressure groups, such as the military, civil servants, and the judiciary, and then slowly expanded to middle class groups and strategic sectors of the working class (Mesa-Lago, 1978; Huber, 1996). As a result of this process of gradual expansion, the systems of social insurance were highly fragmented and generally quite inegalitarian. What is crucial, however is that the entire edifice of social protection, from pensions to family allowances and health care, was built around employment and the male breadwinner model, not citizenship rights. Women and children were covered as dependents. This meant that coverage remained restricted to those employed in the formal sector. Even where the self-employed were included on a compulsory basis, their evasion rate in paying contributions was very high, as contribution rates for them were set high. Employer contributions to social security reached in many cases comparatively high levels, but given the high tariff wall, employers were able to pass the costs on to consumers.

Only six Latin American countries had built up a system of social protection that might be called a welfare state, covering more than 60 percent of the economically active population with some form of social security as of 1980. These countries are Argentina, Brazil, Chile, Costa Rica, Cuba, and Uruguay; at least three Caribbean countries, Bahamas, Barbados, and Jamaica, also belong to that category.[9] Another group of six countries had expanded coverage to between 30 percent and 60 percent of the economically active population by 1980 – Colombia, Guatemala, Mexico, Panama, Peru, and Venezuela. Coverage in the remaining countries had remained below 30 percent of the economically active population, with the lowest being the Dominican Republic, El Salvador, and Paraguay, with 12 percent, 12 percent, and 14 percent, respectively.

As noted above, ISI strategies began to run into a variety of problems, which in turn manifested themselves in recurring balance of payments crises from the 1950s on. Still, with a variety of coping strategies the model was kept alive and then received a new, albeit short-lived, lease on life due to the easy availability of loans from international banks in the 1970s. The debt crisis of 1982, however, forced a reorientation. Since that time, every single country in Latin America and the Caribbean has been exposed to pressures for reform. Yet, there are significant differences in the extent to which countries have complied with these pressures.

The austerity measures used to deal with the recurrent balance of payments crises also put pressure on the social security systems. In addition, the pension components of social security in the more advanced countries were experiencing severe financial pressures of their own (Mesa-Lago, 1989). The pension systems had matured and thus the ratio of working to retired people was deteriorating. The reserves that should have been built up in the maturation phase typically had been used for other state expenditures, often for the health care component of social security. During periods of high inflation, there was often decapitalization of the pension systems. Benefits in the privileged systems in some countries were very high, as were administrative expenditures of the systems. Employers attempted to evade payment of contributions or delayed payment for long periods, particularly during high inflation. Thus, there was a Consensus on the need for reform, but again the types of reforms chosen have varied significantly.

Reforms in Economic and Social Policy

The main points of the reform agenda, what Williamson has aptly called the Washington Consensus, are reduction of fiscal deficits, to be achieved mainly through cuts in expenditures, particularly in subsidies of all sorts; tax reforms that cut marginal rates and broaden the tax base; market determination of interest rates; market determination of exchange rates, with possible intervention to keep them competitive; import liberalization; liberalization of foreign direct investment; privatization of state-owned enterprises; deregulation of all kinds of economic activity; and protection of property rights (Williamson, 1990:7–20). To this one should add the agenda for second-generation reforms, that is, reforms in labor market policy, social policy, and political institutions, which was developed by the IFIs in the 1990s. The main points of this agenda are liberalization of labor markets; privatization of social security systems, primarily pensions but also provision of health care; targeting of social expenditures on the neediest groups; decentralization of responsibility for the provision of social services; and reforms of the judicial system.

On average, the countries in the region moved far in trade liberalization and financial liberalization; they advanced less in privatization, tax reform, reforms of social security systems, and decentralization of social services; and least in deregulation of labor markets and judicial reform. The average tariff rate was lowered from 49 percent in the mid-1980s to 11 percent in 1999, and nontariff restrictions were reduced from a coverage of 38 percent of imports in the prereform period to 6 percent of imports in the mid-1990s (Lora, 2001). Now, as

[9] These figures are drawn from Mesa-Lago (1994:22); he does not provide figures for Trinidad and Tobago or for any of the small Caribbean countries. Coverage figures vary widely among different sources, depending on whether legal entitlements or actual contributions are taken as the criterion. Mesa-Lago is the most prolific researcher and writer on social security in Latin America, and his figures can be accepted for the purposes of classification here.

we discussed above, in comparative perspective these tariff levels remain higher than in advanced industrial countries. Nevertheless, the lowering had a dramatic impact on many Latin American economies, particularly where it was done in a very short period of time. Many enterprises went bankrupt, which meant that many formal sector jobs were lost.

The decrease in the gap between the black market and the regulated market exchange rate is one indicator of relaxation of foreign exchange regulations. Deregulation in this area, along with fiscal and monetary stabilization policies and the renewed flow of capital to Latin America, led to a drastic reduction in this gap between 1988 and 1997, from over 100 percent in some cases to around 5 percent. In the area of financial regulation, controls on interest rates were abolished in all countries by 1995 and reserve requirements were reduced, but most countries retained some forms of intervention in lending agreements (Lora, 2001).

In tax reform, a replacement had to be found for revenues previously coming from taxes on foreign trade, which fell from 18 percent of total tax revenue in 1980 to 14 percent in the mid-1990s. Most countries adopted or substantially increased value-added taxes, but collection rates have remained lower than the statutory rates (Lora, 2001). Marginal tax rates on personal income and taxes on corporate profits were reduced in virtually all cases. However, average tax revenue has remained low; taxes made up only 72 percent of total government revenue in Latin America in 1990–4, compared to 90 percent in the OECD countries. Nontax revenue included items such as natural resource rents and income from state-owned enterprises. Income taxes and social security contributions accounted for 44 percent of government revenue compared to 67 percent in the OECD countries. Total government expenditure was on average slightly below 25 percent of GDP, roughly half of the level of OECD countries (IADB, 1997:104–6).

The extent of privatization has varied considerably among countries; the cumulative value of privatizations between 1988 and 1999 reached 5 percent or more of GDP in ten countries, whereas other countries hardly privatized anything. Most of the privatizations affected infrastructure, particularly energy and telecommunications, and in some countries the banking system (Lora, 2001).

Reforms of the social security system are generally categorized into structural and nonstructural reforms, the former involving elements of privatization and the latter changing rules on financing and entitlements. Nine Latin American countries have implemented and a tenth has legislated full or partial privatization of the pension system. In five cases, privatization was total, with the public system being closed down; in five cases it was partial, with the private system being supplementary or a parallel option (Muller, 2002). In the cases where the public system survived, it typically underwent reforms as well to strengthen its financial basis. Reform of the health insurance and delivery systems has been very heterogeneous, which makes a summary assessment very difficult. In many cases, private insurance and delivery have expanded their share, sometimes by design and sometimes by default. Generally, public resources have been targeted at the neediest sectors of the population, but even these sectors are expected to pay user fees.

Decentralization has been high on the reform agenda and most countries did transfer some responsibilities and revenues to lower levels of government, particularly in the area of social services, but again the actual reforms that have been implemented are very heterogeneous (Willis et al., 1999). On average, the share of state and local governments in total government spending increased from 16 percent in 1985 to almost 20 percent in the mid-1990s (IADB, 1997:99). However, the variation is large, ranging from 49 and 46 percent in the federal systems of Argentina and Brazil to less than 5 percent in small unitary countries, such as the Dominican Republic, Panama, and Costa Rica (IADB, 1997:157). Even among the more decentralized countries, there is considerable variation in the amounts of actual autonomy enjoyed by subnational governments in decisions on expenditure and revenue generation (Garman et al., 2001).

In the areas of labor law reforms, the IFIs have been pressing for reduction of costs associated with laying off workers, relaxation of restrictions on the hiring of temporary workers, and a lowering of social security contributions. They have been arguing that these policies restrict employment creation in the formal sector. Yet, only six countries implemented significant reforms in these areas between the mid-1980s and 1999 (Lora and Panizza, 2002). This is understandable in light of the fact that unemployment insurance is virtually nonexistent in Latin America, and that virtually all social transfers and services are tied to formal sector employment. Thus, loss of a formal sector job is a catastrophic event and labor has strenuously opposed such reforms.

Reform of the judicial system is important to the IFIs because of protection of property rights and predictability of decisions in case of a dispute between investors, particularly foreign investors, and the government or private actors. Accordingly, the World Bank, the Inter-American Development Bank, and USAID have been supporting reform projects in a majority of countries in the region. However, the concentration on reforms favorable for economic activities entailed a neglect of reforms in the area of human rights in general, and specifically of access for the underprivileged to the justice system for protection from police abuse. Overall, not much progress has been made in improving the independence, efficiency, and accessibility of the justice system (Prillaman, 2000; Jarquín and Carrillo, 1998).

Depending on the criteria and time points used, analysts come up with somewhat different classifications of countries' reform efforts. For instance, the Inter-American Development Bank, looking at their structural policy index in 1985/86 and 1995, lists Argentina, Chile, and Jamaica as early reformers (above the average in both 1985 and 1995); Bolivia, El Salvador, Nicaragua, Paraguay, and Peru as intense reformers (below in 1985, above in 1995); Colombia and Uruguay as gradual reformers (above in 1985, below in 1995); and Brazil, Costa Rica, Ecuador, Guatemala, Honduras, Mexico, and Venezuela as slow reformers (below at both time points) (IADB, 1997:50). In contrast, Stallings and Peres, in a study sponsored by the United Nations Economic Commission on Latin America and the Caribbean (ECLAC), only look at the nine countries with the longest history of implementing economic reforms in the region and divide them into aggressive and cautious reformers, the former including Argentina, Bolivia, Chile and Peru; the latter Brazil, Colombia, Costa Rica, Jamaica, and Mexico (2000:14; 48). In general, Chile is regarded as the prototype of the early and radical reformer and Argentina of the late and radical reformer, the former being highly successful and the latter experiencing economic chaos in 2001–2. There is also consensus that Peru, Jamaica, and Bolivia have introduced far-reaching reforms and that these reforms were implemented rather rapidly in Peru and Bolivia. In contrast, Brazil, Costa Rica, Uruguay, and Venezuela are clearly regarded as slow and cautious reformers.

Explanations of Reform Trajectories

Three main types of explanations have been advanced to account for the differences among countries in the depth and speed of reforms: insulation of technocratic political leaders and/or centralization of political power in the hands of the executive, depth of the economic crisis and consequent leverage of IFIs and readiness of leaders and the public to accept radical reforms, and coalitions of political leaders with winners from initial reforms for further reforms or changes in the balance of power between proponents and opponents of reforms. These explanations are certainly not mutually exclusive; rather, they can be combined to some extent, and to some extent they explain different phases of the reform process. Haggard and Kaufman (1995) argue that in the early phases of stabilization and adjustment, centralized executive authority is crucial because winners are not defined yet but losers perceive the threat or reality of losses more clearly. Thus, the reforms have to be imposed against opposition and with little support from internal allies. For consolidation of reforms, then, and progress in second-generation reforms, executive behavior needs to become more predictable and new support coalitions have to be formed. The formation of support coalitions is particularly crucial in the case of social sector reform, where there are many stakeholders.

Many authors have argued that depth of preceding crisis is a good predictor of support for reforms, but Weyland (1998, 2002) has offered the most theoretically coherent version of this explanation. He uses prospect theory, which holds that when people are in the domain of losses they are more ready to accept the risks of reform, whereas being in the domain of gains makes people, both leaders and the mass public, risk-averse and thus opposed to far-reaching reforms. Indeed, this explanation fares well in explaining both cross-national differences and the timing of reforms. Depth of crisis has another crucial effect which then tends to propel reforms forward. The deeper the crisis, the greater is the leverage of the IFIs and thus the probability that they will be successful in pushing their reform designs.

Chile is a special case, as it was the first country to adopt radical neoliberal reforms, beginning in the mid-1970s. Certainly, executive power was extremely centralized in Pinochet's hands and opposition to the reforms was simply not tolerated. In the Chilean case, the economic reforms went way beyond what the IFIs prescribed, as the reforms followed a political agenda as well, to remove the state from the center of decisions about distribution and thus as a target for collective action, and to atomize civil society (Garretón, 1989). Chile moved very rapidly in trade and financial liberalization and in privatization. The speculative boom created by these reforms ended in a spectacular financial crash in the early 1980s, even before the general debt crisis in Latin America. In response, the government expanded its role in the economy again temporarily, but at the same time it proceeded with a full privatization of the pension system and a very significant expansion of the private sector in health care. The sustained high economic growth rates experienced by Chile from the mid-1980s to the mid-1990s, and the comparatively low degree of volatility turned the country into a poster child for advocates of neoliberalism. The fact that the democratic governments did not attempt to change the basic parameters of the model in the 1990s further enhanced its legitimacy.

Argentina is an interesting case of radical reform carried out by an unlikely candidate, the leader of the historically labor-based Peronist party, Carlos Menem, who became president in 1989 after running a vaguely populist campaign. Clearly, in this case the disastrous experience with heterodox stabilization programs introduced by his predecessor, Alfonsín, who resigned early in the midst of hyperinflation and a deep fiscal crisis, strengthened Menem's resolve and his capacity to obtain support for his reforms from his own party. Because the Peronists for the most part controlled both houses of congress, he faced little effective legislative opposition. He used various strategies to neutralize opposition from the unions, and with varying success, from giving some of them participation in ownership of privatized enterprises, compensating workers who lost their jobs, and allowing unions to run private pension funds, to weakening others with simple dismissal of their members, thus exacerbating divisions in the union movement that had deep historical roots (Murillo, 2001). The price stabilization brought about in part by the convertibility plan, which tied the peso to the dollar, along with renewed capital inflows and economic growth enabled Menem to win a second term in 1994. However, exchange rate parity and financial deregulation over the longer run led to a rising foreign debt and severe balance of payments problems. Internally, these problems were aggravated by fiscal indiscipline, particularly among provincial governments. Inaction on the part of Menem and his successor, de la Rua, ultimately led to a profound financial crisis and a default on Argentina's foreign debt.

Fujimori in Peru is another leader who campaigned on a vague but clearly anti-IFI platform, only to make a 180-degree turn right after his election to embark on a radical reform course. Like Menem, he followed a predecessor who had pursued populist, nationalist, expansionist policies and presided over a spectacular economic disaster. Unlike Menem, he did not have a strong party base and faced strong legislative opposition. His solution was to close congress in a self-coup and thereafter continue to rule in a semiauthoritarian fashion, which was facilitated by the fact that his supporters gained a majority of seats in the new constituent assembly and then the new legislature.

All three of these cases of rapid and profound reform share the characteristics of a profound crisis preceding the accession to power of an executive enjoying high power concentration, albeit through different means. In Argentina and Peru, leaders who had come to power on an alternative platform were confronted with disastrous economic conditions that left them few alternatives to adopting IFI prescriptions. In Argentina, Menem was able to implement the reform program through legal means combined with heavy political maneuvering due to high party discipline and virtual control by his party over the legislature, whereas Fujimori in Peru dealt with political opposition through unconstitutional means. In Chile, the military regime ruthlessly repressed any opposition and embarked on a process of economic and social engineering to destroy the chances for any possible reemergence of a mass movement of the Left, their equivalent of a profound crisis.

Among the slow and cautious reform cases, the combination of profound crisis and high power concentration was not present, with the result that either no far-reaching reform package was presented by the executive or the package was blocked in the legislature or by popular referenda. In Brazil, the fragmentation of the party system and the lack of party discipline stymied reform efforts of presidents, and in Uruguay popular referenda played that role in the case of pension reform.

Globalization and Reforms

Certainly, globalization was the key driving force behind the economic and social policy reforms in Latin America and the Caribbean, much more so than in the OECD countries. In fact, Kaufman and Segura (2001) found consistent statistically significant negative effects of both a short- and a long-term nature of trade openness on social spending in Latin America, and they also found a significant negative effect of an interaction term of trade increase and capital openness. They interpret these effects as reflecting producer interests in lower tax burdens, an interpretation with which we would agree. However, if we want to go beyond expenditures and understand the nature of reforms, we need to look for additional mediating mechanisms that translate the growing integration of world markets into concrete policy changes and that can explain differential responses to market dynamics. The essential mediating mechanisms were the debt crisis of the 1980s, the growing power of the IFIs, and the spread of specific educational and career patterns. The causes of differential responses to world market dynamics are domestic political institutions and power distributions between opponents and proponents of reform.

At the root of the reforms is clearly the debt crisis, and the debt crisis in turn is a result of the growth of international financial markets. The growth and integration of international financial markets facilitated overborrowing in the 1970s, put pressure on debtor countries through rising interest rates in the early 1980s, and served as catalyst for a general crisis when the large private banks all decided to stop new lending to Latin America. It then propelled the IFIs into a very powerful role, because agreements with the IMF were generally a precondition for any debt rescheduling agreements with private lenders and any bilateral or multilateral rescue packages. However, it is important to emphasize here that international financial markets were backed up by the power and interests of economically powerful nations. The governments of these nations decided that the burden of solving the debt crisis was to fall exclusively on the shoulders of the debtor countries. Defaults were to be prevented and debt relief was initially not even considered.

A further mediating mechanism between globalization and economic policy reform in Latin America is the growth of educational and career circuits that bring technocrats with neoliberal world views into powerful political positions. These circuits bring promising Latin American graduate students in economics to

Ph.D. programs in the United States, where they absorb neoliberal economics. After graduation, these economists often circulate between positions in the IFIs and in leading administrative positions in their home countries. Thus, the IFIs find domestic supporters for their reform programs who share a common worldview and help to convince politicians of the necessity of neoliberal reforms (Teichman, 2001).

Globalization then had an indirect effect on the systems of social protection via the austerity and structural adjustment policies implemented in the wake of the debt crisis, and a direct effect via the influence of the IFIs. Social expenditures were reduced as a percentage of GDP and in absolute terms in the 1980s, and they recovered slowly in the early 1990s. Bankruptcies and privatizations led to layoffs in the formal sector and thus to loss of social security coverage of a large number of employees and their families. Though the IFIs had developed a clear concern with the political sustainability of the economic reforms by the late 1980s, their reform plans did little to alleviate the plight of these employees. The approach of the IFIs was to privatize pensions and large parts of health care and to concentrate resources in targeted programs on the poorest sectors in the form of preventive health and nutrition programs and social emergency funds. These funds were to provide loans to the poorest communities for economic and social infrastructure, social services, and sometimes production ventures. In the 1990s, the IFIs added a concern with human capital and began to promote investment in primary education.

Effects of the Reforms

The most cited achievements of the reform efforts are a reduction of inflation through macroeconomic stabilization measures and a strengthening of fiscal discipline, visible in smaller budget deficits. Also, after the lost decade of the 1980s, growth resumed in the 1990s as did capital flows to Latin America, increasingly in the form of direct investment. Renewal of capital flows is attributed to economic liberalization insofar as these reforms strengthened investor confidence. However, Latin American economies have suffered from great volatility and vulnerability to external shocks, and various financial crises, such as the Mexican peso crisis, the East Asian financial crisis, and the Argentine crisis of 2001–2, had ripple effects throughout the area. The boom and bust pattern can clearly be linked to the reforms. Strong inflows of capital in the context of liberalized capital markets and trade led to an appreciation of the real exchange rate, increasing trade deficits, excessive expansion of the financial system, and increases in private and public spending. When investor confidence and capital inflows declined precipitously due to some external shock, the booms were followed by busts and governments were forced into new rounds of austerity measures. Average growth performance was far from sufficient to generate enough jobs to absorb the growth in the labor force, and growth rates fell from an average of 4.1 percent in the first half of the decade to 2.5 percent in the second half (ECLAC, 2002:23).

Defenders of the reforms argue that Latin America's main problems – insufficient export performance, high concentration of wealth and income, high un- and under-employment, high poverty, and low tax revenue – are of a long-standing structural nature. However, not only did the reforms not fulfill the promise of alleviating these problems, but at least in the case of concentration of wealth and income they also aggravated the problem. The largest firms, with access to foreign financing and markets, were in the best position to take advantage of the liberalized markets and of privatization of public enterprises, and thus to expand their holdings, while many smaller enterprises went bankrupt. Among the many unfulfilled promises of the reforms is the sluggish response of export production; indeed, export increases have been lagging behind import increases (Baumann, 2002; Stallings and Peres, 2000:20–1). Unemployment increased from 4.6 percent of the labor force in 1990 to 8.6 percent in 1999. Also, most of the jobs that have been created since the early 1990s are in low-productivity and thus low-wage sectors, principally in the informal sector (Tokman, 2002).

Most countries increased their social spending in the 1990s in both absolute terms and as a percentage of GDP; on average, social expenditure rose from 10.4 percent in 1990 to 13.1 percent in 1999. This increase, however, even combined with economic growth, was far from sufficient to lower poverty effectively and undo the damage done in the 1980s. Poverty did decrease from 48.3 percent of the population in 1990 to 43.8 percent in 1999, but this figure remained above the 40.5 percent of the population who had been poor in 1980. In absolute terms, the number of poor people increased by 11 million in the 1990s (ECLAC, 2002:14–15). Nor was there any progress in reducing inequality; Latin America remains the region with the most unequal income distribution. Indeed, in some countries inequality continued to increase. What is crucial to point out here is that the two countries that performed clearly best in protecting the lowest levels of inequality were Uruguay and Costa Rica (ECLAC, 2002:18), where structural reforms had been carried out slowly and cautiously and the structural reform index in 1999 was below the regional average (Lora and Panizza, 2002).

Given these experiences with two decades of reform in economic and social policies, critiques of the Washington Consensus are assuming a higher profile in policy-making circles in some Latin American governments and even in some IFIs. Most simply urge greater attention to human capital formation and to state capacity for implementing reforms properly, but others are beginning to ask whether the reforms have not restricted the state's role excessively. In particular, the recurrent financial crises and their ripple effects are putting the question of deregulated capital markets squarely on the table.

CONCLUSION

Advanced Industrial and Latin American and Caribbean Societies Compared

The extent of liberalization and privatization has clearly been greater in Latin America and the Caribbean than in advanced industrial societies, in both economic and social policy realms. Just to take a couple of dramatic examples: no advanced industrial society completely privatized its pension system, whereas five Latin American countries did so; no advanced industrial country slashed its government expenditure in half, as did Argentina between 1983 and 1989. Three main factors account for these differences. First, state intervention in the economy, particularly protection of domestic production, had been more extensive, so there was more to liberalize. Tariff levels in the early 1980s were still at an average of 45 percent, and average maximum tariff levels at 84 percent (Baumann, 2002). Second, Latin America's dependence on foreign capital had been an incentive for overborrowing in the 1970s, which in the context of the debt crisis of the 1980s gave great leverage to the IFIs to push the agenda of austerity and liberalization. The rising debt burden greatly aggravated government deficits, which climbed above 5 percent in the early 1980s in many countries and reached into the double digits in some. The IMF response was a slashing of public expenditures. Indeed, total government expenditures as a percentage of GDP declined between 1983 and 1989 from 20 to 10 percent in Argentina, 35 to 26 percent in Chile, 26 to 23 percent in Mexico, and 19 to 13 percent in Peru; the decline in Uruguay and Costa Rica was smaller, from 20 to 18 percent and from 20 to 19 percent, respectively (IADB, 1991:284–5).

Third, domestic opponents of liberalization, particularly labor unions and leftist political parties, have been weaker than in advanced industrial societies, and the democratic political institutions through which they might have resisted have been weaker also. Labor had been greatly weakened through repression under the military regimes, and the economic crisis added to its weakness (Drake, 1996). There are no reliable data on union density in Latin America, but even if we take the higher end of McGuire's (1999) estimates, there is no doubt that density is much lower than in advanced industrial countries, with the exception of the United States and France. Political divisions with long historical roots further diluted the collective action potential of the union movement. With some important exceptions, parties as institutions are rather weak in Latin America (Mainwaring and Scully, 1995), and parties of the democratic Left are among the weakest. Only in Costa Rica and

Chile can one speak clearly of effective participation of democratic Left parties in national governmental power in the 1980s and 1990s.[10] Relatedly, legislatures as institutions have often been too weak in the newly established democracies to oppose overbearing executives in the implementation of radical austerity and liberalization policies.

Reflections on the Nature of Globalization

In the visions of neoliberal academics and popular journalism, the root cause of globalization is the inexorable operation of impersonal market forces assisted by advances in communications and transportation technology. By contrast, our account has emphasized how political the process has been, with the decisions of governments, international organizations, and powerful economic interests figuring centrally in the onward march of globalization. Although it is disputed whether the hands of the early capital market liberalizers were forced, as we mentioned above, it is indisputable that these governments, all large actors in the international economy, made these decisions to secure their own economic advantage. By sociological accident not yet fully understood, the size of the domestic market is inversely related to union density and by extension to the strength of the Left (Stephens, 1979, 1991; Wallerstein, 1989, 1991; Western, 1997). Thus, countries where the Left was strong and had employed capital controls as a tool to pursue its economic ends were not in a position to resist decontrol once the large countries had liberalized their internal and external capital markets. As a consequence, even Nordic social democracy favored entry into the EU under the conditions of the Single European Act by the end of the 1980s. However, with the exception of New Zealand and Britain, pro-welfare state forces were able to resist radical retrenchment, so the edifice of the postwar welfare state stood intact as of 2002, and poverty and inequality did not rise significantly except in New Zealand, Britain, and the United States with its traditionally minimalist welfare state. The Latin American countries, as we have seen, were not so fortunate due to both more unfavorable internal balances of power, greater influence of the IFIs, and the differing posture of the relevant international organizations (IMF and World Bank versus EU) on the appropriateness of neoliberal solutions in the area of social policy. Moreover, the reality of political power and interests continues to support globalization: Though the economic costs of currency speculations have been repeatedly demonstrated, the political will to reintroduce modest controls, such as the Tobin tax, is lacking, particularly in the United States, one of the chief beneficiaries of the free flow of capital.

Agenda for Further Research

In order to identify the relative impact of the severity of the economic crisis, the leverage of the IFIs and private capital, the weakness of democratic institutions, and the distribution of political power on the types of reforms implemented, we need more systematic comparative studies of countries at different levels of development, in different positions in the world economy, and with different historical experiences of democracy. For instance, one could hold the degree of consolidation of democratic institutions constant and vary the level of economic development and position in the world system (e.g., Australia and New Zealand versus Costa Rica and Jamaica as democratic systems with considerable longevity, or Spain and Portugal versus Chile and Uruguay as cases with relatively recent democratization), or hold the level of economic development constant and vary the degree of consolidation of democratic institutions (e.g., Spain versus Australia and New Zealand) in order to identify the effects of these variables on economic and social policy formation.

In order to gauge the room for policy choice that remains open to governments within the

[10] In Chile the reforms had been implemented under the military dictatorship; the civilian governments of the 1990s left the new structures unchanged but significantly increased social expenditures.

constraints of the new international economic order, we need more systematic comparisons of countries with similar structural conditions and political legacies but different reform trajectories and outcomes in terms of growth, poverty, and inequality. For advanced industrial democracies, there is a significant body of research on these questions (e.g., Scharpf and Schmidt, 2000; Huber and Stephens, 2001; Swank, 2002), but not for developing countries. Within the Latin American context, Uruguay and Costa Rica should be given special attention in comparative analyses, as they have done better than other countries in protecting comparatively low levels of poverty and inequality.

Finally, we need a better understanding of the consequences of neoliberal reforms for human capital formation. We know that low skill levels at the bottom, as measured by literacy tests (OECD/HRDC, 2001), are associated with higher degrees of inequality among advanced industrial societies (Huber and Stephens, 2001:95). We also know that inequality has increased over the past two decades in many Latin American and Caribbean countries. What we do not know is whether the reforms in social policy that have emphasized targeting the poorest groups have been able to counter the effects of this growing inequality on the quality of human capital. Given that investment in human capital is now recognized as crucial for economic development, it is clearly essential to understand whether the economic and social components of policy reform packages are mutually supportive or are working at cross-purposes.

CHAPTER THIRTY-ONE

The Politics of Immigration and National Integration[1]

Thomas Janoski and Fengjuan Wang

In the United States the baby boom generation will officially enter into retirement in 2010 as massive numbers of retirees will leave the labor force for the next twenty years until 2040. Europe and Japan's baby boomers will retire about ten years later. As a consequence, massive labor needs will make immigration an issue of intense political scrutiny and debate in the first half of the twenty first century. Even before these demographic shifts, immigration has proven to be an explosive issue, with antiimmigrant parties and attacks on foreigners in Europe and the withdrawal of welfare benefits and new forms of human smuggling in the United States. Whether shielded or exacerbated by the business cycle, the politics of immigration will be a cauldron of emotions and wills for the next half century.

But sociological theories explaining the politics of immigration and naturalization are not well-developed. Kingsley Davis calls explanations of international migration "opaque to theoretical reasoning in general" (1988:245) and Barbara Heisler states that "we still lack a formal theory of immigration and immigrant incorporation" (1992:638). Randall Hansen says that the "study of Commonwealth immigration and UK migration policy has been theory poor; many if not most accounts are descriptive" (2000:10). And in a recent review of theories of immigration policy, Eytan Meyers says that immigration policy "lacks . . . attempts to debate the relative merits of various schools of thought" (2000:1246). Unlike the theory-rich welfare state literature, political sociology has largely ignored the politics of immigration. But in the late 1990s, a number of more explicit political sociological explanations of immigration emerged (Brubaker, 1992; Soysal, 1994; Favell, 1988; Freeman, 1995; Fitzgerald, 1996; Gimpel and Edwards, 1999; Carter et al., 1987; Hansen, 2000; Hollifield, 1992, 2000; Schmitter Heisler 2000; Tichenor, 2002; Geddes 2003). This chapter reviews many of these theories and argues that political parties and their supporters will become more intensely involved in immigration politics, and that more theoretically integrated theories of immigration based on sending and receiving countries will be needed with increasing globalization.

Because receiving and sending countries are often vastly different in development – most receiving countries are rich and democratic; most sending countries are neither – theoretical approaches to the politics of immigration must begin to recognize these differences. Consequently, this chapter examines both the immigration politics in receiving democracies and emigration policies in sending countries, and then moves to naturalization and integration politics. In a final section, we consider a framework of transnational theory that can include

[1] We appreciate the critical readings made by Robert Alford, Alexander Hicks, and Mildred Schwartz in the development of this chapter. Research assistance was provided by Karen Diggs, Darina Lepadatu, and Chrystal Grey. Support was received from NSF Grant SES 01-11450.

both sending and receiving countries in a more unified theory.

POLITICS OF RECEIVING COUNTRIES TOWARD IMMIGRATION

Four explanations delineate immigration to receiving countries: (1) power resources or power constellation theories, (2) state-centric and institutional theories, (3) cost–benefit or economic theories, and (4) cultural and racial/racialization theories. A section will follow these theories to discuss how public opinion fits into the equation.

Power Resources and Constellation Theories

Power resources theory explains immigration politics on the basis of political party power, ethnic organization, and the balance of business and trade union power. More recently, it has added how parties or coalitions shape and react to public opinion. Power constellation theory builds on power resources theory but goes beyond class to emphasize status groups (race, ethnic, and gender) and state structures (Huber and Stephens, 2001).[2] The addition of these status factors is certainly useful in a cross-national topic like immigration.

Many views of Britain, France, Germany, and the United States considered immigration politics to be low in salience and political conflict, but in the last thirty years this view has given way to a recognition of contention and party polarization. Marion Bennett (1964:170) says that "If it must be said that the criticisms of the McCarran-Walter Act of 1952 were bipartisan in nature, it must also be said that the defense of the law from its conception has been equally bipartisan." The beginnings of the French approach were forged in the French Revolution, but subsequent amendments and changes were relatively subdued (1992:35–49, 50–72). W. Rogers Brubaker's description of nineteenth- and early twentieth-century German immigration and naturalization politics is mostly uneventful. Hansen found British policy before 1962 to be based on "bipartisan ideological commitment" (2000:17). However, after the loss of empire, slow economic growth, and two oil crises, the politics of immigration in Britain heated up as Margaret Thatcher helped pass one of the most restrictive immigration laws in the developed world. Contentious politics followed in the United States, France, and Germany in the next two decades.

Consequently, more recent work emphasizes conflict. Daniel Tichenor (2002:35–40) indicates that even earlier American politics were more contentious than previously thought. To some extent, a lack of direct party conflict until the 1970s concealed conflicting coalitions that cut across party lines. First, "immigration expansionists" collected largely Democratic "cosmopolitans" who wanted an expansion of citizenship rights (e.g., Jane Addams, Edward Kennedy, Immigration Protective League, American Jewish Committee, Mexican-American Legal Defense Fund or MALDEF, National Immigration Forum) and largely Republican "free-market expansionists" who were more interested in easing labor shortages and less interested in citizenship (e.g., William Howard Taft, Ronald Reagan, American Farm Bureau, National Association of Manufacturers, CATO Institute). These two groups opposed each other on most issues, but they both supported increased immigration. Second, immigration restrictionists included egalitarians who wanted to expand citizenship rights but wanted to do it for labor and African Americans first (e.g., Frederick Douglass, Samuel Gompers, Barbara Jordan, and the AFL) and exclusionists who wanted to protect American–European culture and deemphasize new citizenship rights (e.g., Henry Cabot Lodge, Patrick Buchanan, Peter Brimelow, the Immigration Restriction League, Federation of American

[2] For reviews of power resources theory and immigration, see Fitzgerald (1996:56–64) and Ireland (1994:5–7). For power resources or class theory, see Castles and Kosack (1974, 1973/1985); Castles, Booth, and Wallace (1984); Castles, Cope, Kalantzis, and Morrissey (1992); Phizacklea (1980); and Miles (1982). On power constellation theory, see Huber and Stephens (2001), Janoski (1998, 1990), and van den Berg and Janoski (Chapter 3 in this volume).

Immigration Reform). These two internally diverse coalitions opposed each other with considerable conflict despite the oblique positions within each political party.

In Europe, party positions also split on immigration. On the Right, the foreign office faction has been strongly in favor of immigration from the Commonwealth to the United Kingdom when the empire was an issue (Hansen, 2000:26). The Right's connections to employers have been important, especially during labor shortages. But traditional or Tory-oriented factions sometimes see immigrants from diverse backgrounds as a threat to native cultural and religious traditions (e.g., the inflammatory Enoch Powell of the 1960s).[3] On the Left, social democratic and labor parties have often favored keeping the labor supply low to reduce competition among workers. But on the other hand, poor immigrants have often entered into the class and ethnic cleavages that have pushed workers to the Left. The development of Green parties in the 1990s brought support for immigrants due to their humanitarian orientations (Kitschelt, 1994: 164–5). Consequently, parties appear to be quiescent, but cross-party coalitions pressed their claims.

James Gimpel and James Edwards's extensive empirical study (1999:152) concludes that by 1982 U.S. immigration policy had become highly divisive, moving political party positions from cross-cutting alliances to strong and intense party polarization. Conservative parties have unified around an unfriendly position toward immigrants in order to stop or cap welfare state benefits for immigrants. In Europe, far-left parties have often been in favor of international free movement, though in practice where communist parties have had power as in France, this may dissolve in strategic maneuvering (Schain, 1990:262). Far-right parties often endorse a nationalist line. The National Front in France, *Vlams Blok* in Belgium, and *Republikaner* party in Germany are examples of large-scale anti-immigrant parties that have become popular in the last few decades.[4] In comparison, anti-immigrant political movements have been slower to develop in America.

Two factors increase interest among political parties and cause political polarization. First, recessions and depressions create unemployment and support for immigration wanes. Citizens complain and ask for less immigration. When the economy booms, the issue becomes defused and immigration decisions are made in the relatively quiet halls of power. But when the business cycle, which has been around for a long time, is coupled with asylum, there is a strong effect.

Second, as immigration has increasingly involved asylum and refugee issues since the 1980s, welfare state supports and services have increased greatly. This has brought traditional Left and Right divisions out of oblique coalitions, and party clashes on immigration policy have become commonplace and increasingly bitter. For instance, Gimpel and Edwards (1999) show that political party membership in the Congress was weakly correlated with votes on immigration bills before the 1980s, but thereafter political party membership was not only significant but also the strongest factor when regressed against legislative votes (1999:appendices 4–6). The debates over new immigration laws in France, Germany, and the United Kingdom have brought bitter resentments and threats for further partisan battles (TWIG, 2002; Hansen, 2002; Janoski, forthcoming; Feldblum, 1999). Party polarization on immigration has made it a much more contentious issue as immigrants, refugees, and asylum seekers have penetrated the welfare state. It also brings power constellation theory to the fore.

The two strongest interest groups in favor of immigration come from opposite ends of the class spectrum. Business federations and interest

[3] The Republican Party in the United States has been a site of anti-immigrant politicians from the nationalist Pat Buchanan to the more moderate governor of California, Pete Wilson. However, recently President George W. Bush has actively courted the Hispanic vote with some small success.

[4] France and Germany have also banned racist political parties like Ordre Noveau in 1973 and the Schmierwellen in 1960, but Fennema concludes that efforts to fight intolerance by banning parties and speech undermine a multicultural and democratic consensus (2001:140).

groups favor immigration because an increase in the labor supply lowers wages, promotes flexibility, and may provide employees with specific skills. For instance, since 1996 the Business for Legal Immigration Coalition in the United States has worked hard for skilled worker immigration, especially in the computer industry (Gimpel and Edwards, 1999:46–7). High-tech firm managers often testify before congressional committees on these issues. From the opposite direction, ethnic and some religious groups representing immigrants have favored increased immigration. In the United States the National Council of La Raza, MALDEF, the League of United Latin American Citizens, and the Organization of Chinese Citizens have lobbied for increasing immigration (Gimpel and Edwards, 1999; Virgil, 1990). Church and humanitarian groups have asked for more refugees and asylum seekers, but they have been less influential than the business lobby and immigrant associations. Also, the American Immigration Lawyers Association has a small amount of political power, but mainly through its high expertise and credibility.[5]

Some European countries have encouraged immigrant groups, while others have ignored them. In Soysal's regime approach, the corporatist countries have subsidized and then integrated ethnic interest groups into larger immigrant advisory councils (1994:79–83). As a result, the National Association of Finnish Associations and National Yugoslav Federation, in Sweden, and the National Cooperation of Foreign Workers Organizations (LSOBA) and Turkish Islamic Cultural Federation in the Netherlands have been strong and effective players in molding integration policies. Switzerland, the United Kingdom, France, and Germany have not subsidized immigrant groups; however, unassisted groups have formed and are active such as the Federation of Associations of Solidarity with Immigrant Workers (FASSTI) in France and city organizations in Germany (e.g., Turkish Union of Berlin) (Soysal, 1994:84–118).

The politics of business interests are fairly straightforward, but those of ethnic groups can be quite tricky for politicians. Beyond direct lobbying, offending an ethnic group can have serious consequences for a politician who has a significant number of their citizens in his or her home district or state. Representatives from nonimmigrant areas are relatively immune to this source of pressure (e.g., Senator Alan Simpson from Wyoming). On the other hand, vociferous protest against immigrants may also come from areas with many immigrants (e.g., Governor Pete Wilson of California). The resulting offense done to second- and third-generation immigrants may be long-lasting. As a result, the decision to support or oppose immigration and to what level of intensity may be hazardous and fraught with future implications.

On the opposing side, labor unions tend toward restrictions on immigration due to labor competition, but also eventually see immigrants as future recruits for their movement. Labor unions prefer a labor shortage to a glut of lower-wage workers (Mink, 1986; Briggs, 1992, 2001) because it protects their standard of living and job security.[6] In the United States, Samuel Gompers as the longtime head of the AFL (1886–1924) and Dennis Kearney of the San Francisco-based Workingmen's Party (1878–82) were labor leaders who strongly opposed immigration. While immigration was very low during the Depression, the CIO embraced immigrants when it started its industrywide rather than narrow skill recruitment drives. However,

[5] By 1900, important groups included: the AFL, Workingmen's Association, and Immigration Restriction League. By 1947, these groups included: Citizens Committee to Repeal Chinese Exclusion, American Committee for Protection of the Foreign Born, Common Council for American Unity, and Chinese Consolidated Benevolent Association (Olzak, 1989; Riggs, 1950).

[6] Ethnic competition creates real or imagined economic threats along with cultural fears. In Olzak's (1992) model of ethnic competition, she finds that strikes and union resource mobilization lead rather indirectly to ethnic violence. What is tragic in the American case is that immigration may have threatened wages and job security for native workers, but labor violence was often redirected against African Americans. Also, the native workers who were threatened by immigration moved West during the 1800s and supplied the pressure for taking lands from the indigenous tribes through a series of broken treaties and the Trail of Tears.

Briggs (2001) maintains that successful unionization drives only occurred in the United States when immigration was cut back from 1921 to 1965. There has also been local African American sentiment in opposition to immigration, but black opposition tends to fade in the Congress (Lim, 2001; Borjas, 1995; Gimpel and Edwards, 1999).

In a major shift of position, the AFL-CIO has recently courted legal and illegal immigrants, especially Hispanics, who they see as potential union recruits. Thus, labor unions, like Left parties, were torn between protecting wages by opposing immigration and recruiting immigrants into their base, but they are now favoring alliances with immigrant workers. Haus (2002) and Watts (2002) show how labor unions in France, Italy, Spain and the United States have moved decisively in this new direction.

Groups that oppose immigration for more general reasons are much less influential. The Federation for American Immigration Reform (FAIR) and Zero Population Growth (ZPG) claim public-interest backing. In the United States, think tanks are relatively balanced with the CATO Institute for and the Center for Immigration Studies against unlimited immigration (Gimpel and Edwards, 1999:45–55).

States in general must be committed to economic growth to provide tax revenue for services and to accumulate capital and achieve the industrial capacity to wage war. This requires both business and labor support. States often respond to the needs of firms with low-wage and/or highly skilled workers with open immigration policies. In economic "pull" theories, labor shortages in the wealthier country produce a need for workers (Ritchey, 1976:364–75; Petersen, 1978:554–6; Stahl, 1989; Molho, 1986; Massey, 1988). In economic "push" theories, the poverty of the sending country produces a strong incentive to emigrate to a wealthier country with high wages, public assistance, and perhaps more equality (Ritchey, 1976:375–8).[7] Applying push and pull to politics adds a reflexive pressure factor – the more immigrants who enter the country and the longer they stay, the more immigrants will naturalize to full-citizen status. This leads to a lobbying group for these new citizens and their families, and these people often need services and they are channeled toward labor and Left parties. Although push–pull theories are not political sociological theories, they fit into power constellation theory and national interests quite well.

States may develop specific policies for highly skilled workers. The Prussian government invited the Mennonites and other dissenting groups because of their reputation for farming to clear swamps and rocky lands. The Russian government under Catherine the Great did the same when the Mennonites encountered religious difficulties with the Prussians (Stumpp, 1973). In the 1990s, Canada (and other countries) actively recruited wealthy Hong Kong capitalists to become citizens of Canada after the communist government's recent assumption of power in Hong Kong that made private capital vulnerable. The United States has pursued similar policies with such singularly high-skilled workers as Albert Einstein and Werner von Braun, and has offered special immigration status to computer programmers and media moguls. Australia and New Zealand have had such policies for a very long time, but in the 1980s they began to realize that cultural diversity might produce economic growth (Freeman, 1994).

States also develop policies for low-wage workers. Migratory and guest worker programs have been instituted in Germany (Castles and Kosack, 1973, 1985) and a number of other countries, including the United States with its Bracero Program (Calivita, 1992; Craig, 1971). Sometimes governments set up recruitment offices in the sending countries. If they do not, there may be internal pressure to regulate the abuses of private or informal recruitment mechanisms. And low-wage workers have often been vulnerable to global human smuggling networks (Kyle and Kozlowski, 2001). Thus, whether as parties or coalitions that cross party lines, power constellation theory explains the pressure and resistance of immigration policies.

[7] Recent immigration can even be seen as a solution to the North–South problem of inequalities of resources (Hein, 1993).

State-Centric and Institutional Theories

State-centric theories concern both the structure of bureaucracies to the prominence of the empire and nation building where the state plays an important strategic role (Ireland, 1994; Fitzgerald, 1996; Hansen, 2000). Nation-building or empire-maintaining factors are an important aspect of state autonomy and interests. Freeman (1979) looks at the political economy of immigration and racism, but this political economy argument combines with a long-term state-centric position on immigration. Freeman indicates that three aspects of colonialism vary in importance. First, how much does the colonizer portray its culture as universalistic (available to natives) or particularistic (available only to colonizers)? Second, was the colony part of the colonizing country? This ranges from full incorporation (direct rule by the French state, for example), confederation (indirect rule via British Commonwealth), to direct but distant rule (the Germans and Belgians) (Albertini, 1971). Third, what bureaucratic mechanisms were put into place to manage economic and service production? This may range from creating new bureaucracies (the British railroads, for example) to using tribal organization to control agricultural production.

The closer the colonies are geographically and culturally to the colonizer, the greater the state's promotion of immigration. The British enshrined open immigration from their colonies in the British Nationality Act of 1948 and did not even begin to restrict the entry of colonial subjects until 1962 (Freeman, 1979; Hansen, 2000). Freeman explains much of post-World War II immigration policy "as an attempt to remove rights of citizenship too generously extended during the colonial period" (1979:38). In French nationality law, Senegalese and Algerians were treated as French citizens with privileges to migrate to France. Other Africans were not treated as generously, but some had opportunities to become French citizens (Suret-Canale, 1971:83–6; Johnson, 1971; Headrick, 1978).

Castles and Miller (1998:39–45) have presented four ideal types of citizenship that shape immigration and naturalization: the "imperial approach" that is liberal as the United Kingdom and France described above, the "folk approach" that tries to protect the native citizens from foreign incursions, the "republican approach" that is based on individual rights and obligations, and the "multicultural models" that recognize the cultural rights of immigrants. This is a useful typology, but they do not provide an underlying causal mechanism.[8] The theory discussed by Freeman fits the imperial control model (the United Kingdom) and the folk model (Germany). But France seems to fit both the imperial and the republican model, and in some ways it is difficult to differentiate between these two models except for the French preference for direct political incorporation of the colonies into the nation as opposed to the Commonwealth approach of the British.

What Freeman does not discuss is Castles and Miller's "multicultural model" (1998:43–4) or what Janoski and Glennie (1995a) refer to as the "settler country" approach. Settler states have both a national security problem with indigenous people and foreign colonial powers (i.e., they need soldiers), and a labor market shortage caused by the subsequent subjugation and near-genocide of indigenous peoples (i.e., they need workers and mothers). In the short term, the state actively promotes immigration for political economy purposes to solve these problems, but in the longrun these interests become state-centric features of each country or model. However, the settler countries break down into several subtypes. The United States has often been portrayed as a country of assimilation and its language policy is a notable feature that distinguishes it from Canada's multicultural or mosaic policy that promotes immigrant language rights and some self-governance (e.g., Quebec and Nunavit). Australia, New Zealand, and South Africa have been unique in their long-term restrictions on non-European immigrants, which at the same time has reduced their immigration

[8] Their multicultural model is more under discussion than concrete policies adopted by any particular country. Australia, Canada, and Sweden certainly do not accept all cultural difference and the formation of ethnic communities.

levels and population growth. Recently, these white-only policies have changed considerably and they are coming closer to the assimilating or multicultural models (Janoski and Glennie, 1995a; Freeman, 1994; Kymlicka, 1995; Joppke, 1999).

States through their foreign policy and subject to some humanitarian and religious pressures will sometimes accept refugees, asylum seekers, and other immigrations who are fleeing persecution by the sending state. After the St. Bartholemew's Day and other massacres (1572–1629), the Huguenots fled from France to Britain, Germany, and many other countries in Europe. Mennonites from the Netherlands and Switzerland fled to Prussia and then Russia, only to flee again to the New World (1700s). The Puritans fled from England to the United States (1600–1700s); the European Jews and gypsies from Germany (1870–1940s) and Russia (1860s–present) to the United States, Israel, and other countries; the Bosnians to Germany and much of Europe (1980s–90s); and the list goes on and on. States also create emigrants through their own policies in failed wars (e.g., Moluccans went to the Netherlands and the Hmong, Vietnamese, and Montangards entered the United States).

Immigrants often flee political persecution only to find new religious and economic discrimination. The West had strong ideological and propaganda reasons for accepting Russian and Warsaw bloc refugees, and the United States has been particularly open to Cubans because of Castro's communist regime. But the United States is not particularly welcoming to Salvadoran, Guatemalan, and Haitian refugees. Immigrants fleeing noncommunist but equally authoritarian regimes, whom the American government labels "economic" refugees, have not been accepted despite evidence of death squads.

A variety of approaches examine the structures of states using the core hypotheses of institutional theory. Ruth Rubio-Marin (2000) focuses on U.S. and German law and constitutions, showing that each country has different constitutional protections for refugees or immigrants. Hansen indicates that the UK's strong executive and lack of a formal constitution hinders the protection of immigrant rights (2000:237–42). Patrick Ireland's institutional channeling theory (1994:10) argues that political opportunity structures are constructed from immigration laws with social and political rights, naturalization procedures, social policies (e.g. education, housing, labor market and social assistance policies), and trade union, religious, and political participation. Keith Fitzgerald's (1996) sectoral theory of the state, which shows how policies differ by the ministries and administrations that implement them, explains the different outcomes of laws on legal immigration, refugees, and illegal immigration that result from the different state structures (e.g., foreign office, border police, labor ministry, integration committees, etc.) at work in each policy domain or sector. He puts forward an especially complex version of state-centric theory that he calls "improvisational institutionalism." For instance, the American state is neither strong nor weak, but each particular policy sector of the state differs tremendously in terms of how much it affects and in what way it molds each policy (1996:60, 81–9). The recent transfer of the Immigration and Naturalization Service to the Homeland Security Department in the United States demonstrates how this theory works. Finally, the state's judicial system has largely steered clear of immigration in many countries, but increasingly these "plenary powers" are being taken back by the courts in the United States and other Anglo-Saxon countries (Spiro, 2002).

Although state-centric theories are useful in explaining aspects of immigration politics, they beg the question on causality because many state organizations are created out of power resources and elite participation in the first place. More often than not, current state structures were created in earlier bouts of power resources. Power constellation theory incorporates their additional power without resort to a near tautology that the state causes state structure.

Cost–Benefit and Economic Theories

Gary Freeman (1995, 1998) and Jeannette Money (1999) have applied James Q. Wilson's

Table 31.1. *The Cost/Benefit Distribution Theory of Politics*

	Benefits	
Costs	*Concentrated*	*Diffuse*
Concentrated	Interest Group Politics: Groups A and B are both equally for or against the policy and they fight it out in high-profile battles determined by who has the most resources. *Examples*: Illegal Immigration Reform & Immigrant Responsibility Act of 1996, Immigration Reform Act of 1990	Entrepreneurial Politics: Group A benefits, though being in the minority, and imposes all the costs on Group B. Group A is led by a strong entrepreneur. *Examples*: Chinese Exclusion Act of 1882
Diffuse	Clientelist Politics: Group A benefits a great deal from the policy and does not encounter much opposition because the policy costs do not generate opposition because they are so diffuse. No Group B of any importance tends to form. A small interest group takes advantage of specific benefits. *Examples*: Immigration & Nationality Act Amendments of 1965, Immigration & Nationality Act Amendments of 1976, Refugee Act of 1980	Majoritarian Politics: Groups are in agreement with most of society, and everyone expects to gain and pay. As a result, interest Groups A and B have little incentive to form around such issues because no particular segment of society will pay for such a diffuse benefit. Nonpartisan politics prevail. *Examples*: Immigration Act of 1924, Immigration & Nationality Act of 1952

interest-based theory of costs and benefits to immigration as the third major type of theory. Wilson (1980) posited that the costs and benefits of a policy fall into four combinations: "majoritarian politics" where overall consensus causes the policy to be passed because it affects everyone and everyone benefits, "clientelist politics" where a strongly organized but narrow group of interests enacts their policy because no one really opposes its diffuse costs, "interest group politics" where both sides are fully mobilized and partisan, and "entrepreneurial politics" where policies are least likely to pass because the opposition is strong (i.e., the powerful bear the costs) and most people remain uninterested (i.e., the masses receive diffuse benefits). (Please see table 31.1).

Freeman's purpose is to explain why countries seem to pursue immigration policies contrary to the majority's interests to avoid labor market competition. His clientelist model postulates that the legislative process is captured by proimmigration interest groups, but the costs are diffused to the whole population to whom immigration is not salient. Examples of proimmigration groups are agricultural growers in Texas and California, the software industry in Oregon and Washington, and the construction industry in Germany. As a result, nonsalient policies are passed to benefit specific groups and political competition between parties is largely avoided.

But this model also helps explain historical changes in many countries. First, in the late 1800s, "majoritarian" politics largely prevailed. Political parties passed immigration laws that allowed massive amounts of immigration. Despite the Know-Nothing Party and some initial labor opposition, these laws were not controversial because large majorities believed in allowing a great deal of immigration to settle the land. The same political process produced the opposite result when the Depression led to immigration quotas to prevent further unemployment. The issue was not very controversial because the public wanted it.

Entrepreneurial politics operated in the 1880s when the costs of immigration were concentrated on the working class in California, while the benefits were diffused throughout the country. Many workers felt that they were facing declining wages and poor working conditions due to Chinese immigration fueled by the 1868 Burlingame Treaty and the Southern Pacific's pro-Chinese hiring policy. Social movement leaders like Dennis Kearney and Frank Roney developed a form of "entrepreneurial" politics. Kearney's Workingmen's Party was quickly fused with general anticapitalist feelings throughout the Democratic Party as the Philadelphia unions, who had not seen Chinese immigrants, mustered a demonstration of 3,000 workers against Republican President Arthur's veto of the first Chinese Exclusion Bill. Arthur soon signed an amended bill in May 1882. Thus, to avoid concentrated costs, diffuse benefits require an entrepreneurial leader (Mink, 1986:71–112; Hutchinson, 1981:73–84).

The "interest-group" model with political polarization revived itself in the 1980s–90s (Gimpel and Edwards, 1999). With concentrated benefits for immigrant groups and refugees through welfare benefits and family reunification, and concentrated costs in the border states from Texas to California, the battle between political parties heated up. One can conclude that immigration policy falls into all four areas – majoritarian, entrepreneurial, clientel, and interest group – depending on the context and historical period.[9]

While costs and benefits in a microeconomic or rational choice theory provide some interesting insights, there are two additional problems. First, the actor in the mixed situations in the typology may be uncertain. The entrepreneur is assumed to act for the diffusely interested majority against the concentrated industry insider. But in clientelist politics, a nationalist leader like La Pen is also an entrepreneur who tries to impose costs on employer groups that need immigrants. So two entirely different models may apply to the same law. Low-wage employers in France may get concentrated benefits with diffuse costs, but entrepreneurial nativists may organize diffuse benefits to impose a concentrated cost on low-wage employers. The same situation predicts diffuse and concentrated costs, and concentrated and diffuse benefits. Second, rational choice logic requires tightly constrained situations. In the passage of many laws, the situation is simply not tight enough. This defect makes it difficult for the theory to explain cross-national results. For instance, why do employers in clientelist politics prevail in the United States but not in Germany? The reason may be that Germany has more powerful labor groups that are not thrilled about increasing the numbers of low-wage workers. Cost–benefit analysis does not help explain this international difference.

Joppke (1999:18–22) also questions Freeman's cost–benefit theory: (1) the legal process with judges and courts is largely ignored in making decisions that vitally affect immigration law, (2) resistance to immigration in Europe is not explained by clientelist politics, (3) the theory does not distinguish well between nonimmigrant European nations and settler countries, and (4) the theory does not handle guest worker and postcolonial immigration well. Point one is largely a state-centric criticism whereas the others question the theory's ability to consider widely differing institutional contexts, which interacts with the point made above about tight constraints. Nonetheless, this approach may be appropriate when the costs and benefits of immigration appear to be diffuse and the issue has low salience. When the battles become more pitched, the theory tells us little about events better explained by power constellation theory.

Cultural and Racialization Theories

Cultural and race theories see racial bias in many largely white societies. Culture and race are, of course, not the same thing, but race has frequently been tested as an indicator of culture. We deal here with two types of theory – racial/ethnic conflict theories and racialization theories (Ireland, 1994:7–8) – and leave cultural idiom theory for the section on naturalization, where it has the greatest impact.

First, a number of scholars have viewed race or ethnicity as central to the passage of immigration laws and implementation of immigration policies. After World War II, the United States

[9] For other critiques of Freeman's theory, see Perlmutter (1996) and Brubaker (1992).

intended to reward its allies and aliens who actually served in the military by making them "racially eligible for naturalization" (Hutchinson, 1981:275). In these theories, racism may be defined by ethnic, cultural, or religious attributes that are attacked from both the political Right and the mainstream (Solomos, 1995:43; 1993). Racism may affect public opinion, interest groups, and political parties. Thus, race can be one of many variables affecting political outcomes as racial prejudice and discrimination may be deeply embedded in a country's culture (Layton-Henry, 1984, 1992, 1996; Layton-Henry and Wilpert, 1994; Mason, 1995; Miller, 1981; Moore, 1975; Heisler and Schmitter Heisler, 1986, 1991; Huttenback, 1976; Park, 1922, 1928; Rex, 1979; Rex and Moore, 1967).

Second, racialization theories go beyond previous more societywide theories of race (Omi and Winant, 1994). Racialization theories place the state in a central role in creating racist reactions to immigrants of different racial and ethnic groups. The citizenry as a whole is neutral toward immigrants, but the government racializes immigration in order to justify controls on immigration and the prosecution of crime and other factors (Carter, Harris, and Joshi, 1987, 1993, 1996; Dummett and Dummett, 1982; Dummett and Nicol, 1990; Katznelson, 1973; James and Harris, 1993; Paul, 1996; Solomos, 1993, 1995; Solomos and Back, 1995). In this view, the state plays a central role in creating racism in order to justify its policies to control crime, reduce unemployment, and alleviate crowding in housing. A number of sociologists have explained the politics of immigration by racialization, but Hansen (2000; see also Dean, 1992) has argued strongly against it because the theory must show that state elites cause immigration policy in a form of top-down racism, and he shows that this was not the case in the United Kingdom.[10] Racialization theory works much better with the "white Australia Policy" of immigrant exclusion, where it may be shown that the process was state- rather than interest group-led (Castles and Davidson, 2000:chap. 3).

[10] A more cultural approach comes from Shanks (2001), who focuses on the structure of public interest, policy, and causal arguments in U.S. immigration history. Although this is embedded in a larger question of international political economy and state sovereignty, her approach is very much connected to cultural narratives.

The Puzzle of Public Opinion about Immigration

Since the advent of polling, public opinion in the United States and other countries has been largely opposed or at least lukewarm about immigration. Simon and Lynch conclude (1999:458) that in "no country – those with long histories of admitting immigrants, those with more restrictionist policies, and those who have consistently kept a lock on their doors – does a majority of citizens have positive feelings about their current cohort of immigrants." Joel Fetzer find that opposition to immigration in the United States has ranged from a low of 43.8 percent in 1953 to a high of 71 percent in 1982 (2000:165–6).[11] Lahav finds that 54% of European Union citizens in fourteen countries find that immigrants are a "big problem," and 84% of the members of the European Parliament say that problems of immigration are greater today than in the past (2004:83, 85). And these same citizens feel that immigration is "one of the most controversial issues on the political agenda" and that "they want it controlled" (2004:106). Simon and Alexander conclude that it is "something of a miracle that so many immigrants gained entry to the US between 1880 and 1990" (1993:244) because immigration has been unpopular.

The public's opposition to immigration does not work well with power constellation or cultural theories, though it falls into Freeman and Money's theory of nonsalience and interest-group domination of immigration politics. We would like to pursue the various class, cultural,

[11] In Germany it has ranged from 50.3% in 1991 to very recent lows of 26.0% in 1993 (Fetzer, 2000:171–2). This contrary result helped cause the major reversal in German laws that occurred in the last ten years in Germany.

and political explanations of the public's opposition to immigration. In a national study of the United States, Citrin et al. (1997) found that better-educated persons (i.e., often cosmopolitan liberals) are more likely to favor immigration and benefits for immigrants than less well-educated persons. Otherwise, current economic status does not add much to the explanation. Instead, more generalized opinions about the nation's economy, the impact of immigration on taxes, and a belief that immigration will impact national culture have more impact. They concluded that "enduring values and identifications" about immigration have more impact than "narrow self interest" on opinions (1997: 874). This could be interpreted as long-term class and status (i.e., nation or ethnic) interests.

Fetzer interprets his findings of substantial opposition to immigration to support a cultural theory of marginality (i.e., immigrants tend to be of dissimilar religious and cultural backgrounds) as well as often of low status (2000:20, 95–102, 112–16, 125–31).[12] Most new immigrant groups were initially charged with being impossible to assimilate, but some have suffered more than others from that stigma (i.e., Catholics and Jews in the United States in the 1800s, Asians and Africans in the 1900s, and Muslims in most European and American countries today). Using zero-order correlations, Fetzer's study found that cultural threats (e.g., Protestant religion) were more important than economic threats (e.g., low education) in France and Germany, but economic threats are nearly twice as important in the United States (2000:101–7). However, in regression equations, being poor and African American in the United States, having a financial decline in France, and being old or unemployed in Germany all create an economic threat that is strongly opposed to immigration. In effect, multivariate analysis reversed the original finding that in Europe, cultural factors were more important than economic ones.

[12] Perhaps the reason that the cultural theory does not work as well in the United States has to do with the major immigrant group being Christian in the United States (i.e., Hispanics) and the major groups being Muslim in France and Germany (i.e., Algerians and Turks).

Citrin et al. (1997) found that Republicans wanted increased immigration but delays in providing benefits, and Democrats were more in favor of benefits but only slightly in favor of increased immigration. In three election-year surveys from 1992–6, Gimpel and Edwards found that 3 to 5 percent more Republicans were in favor of reducing immigration, but 50 to 60 percent of people in both parties, depending on the year, were opposed to immigration (1999:35–7).

The jury is still out on explaining attitudes toward immigration, especially because these results can be interpreted in three ways. In one view, the differences between parties are small and can be attributed to an "absence of partisan divisions" (Citrin et al., 1997:34). In another view, public opinion clearly wants to restrict immigration when times are tough, (1919–65), but overlooks immigration during better times when expansive legislation is passed and elites have their way. As with national health insurance plans, the American public often does not get what it wants. Yet a third view sees the Left, especially recently, pursuing immigration and naturalization expansion, while the Right pursues restrictions. In terms of theories, these results bolster Freeman's theory, which says that special-interest groups have largely co-opted public opinion, mainly due to low salience, but they also support power constellation theory with recent party competition and battles over immigration laws.

POLITICS OF SENDING COUNTRIES TOWARD IMMIGRATION

The politics of immigration in sending countries is much understudied (but see Schmitter Heisler, 1985). Most studies focus on how emigrants engineer their travels, with some study of transnational return and communication occurring more recently. But sending countries find themselves in four basic geopolitical situations that affect their policies. First, senders that are close to a receiver are most often in a relationship of dependence due to weaker economic and political positions. They may or may not have been a colony. Mexican emigrants are attracted to the strong economy in the United States, and some Mexicans and Central Americans may be attracted to more political freedom. In Europe, economic opportunity attracted the Irish to the United Kingdom, Poles to Germany, and Finns to Sweden. Immigrants may also have cultural, nationalist, or nation-building sentiments. For the most part, these sending countries and their cultures are well-known to the receiving countries and there may be considerable cultural diffusion between them. Emigrants can easily return, and remittances facilitate continued contact. Because regulations are easy to evade, illegal immigration will always be a problem. Nonetheless, the relationship between these countries will be relatively positive; there will be less persecution and greater immigration.

Second, sending countries that were former colonies fall into a category of their own. Much depends on the relationship between the receivers and senders. Residents of the former British colonies had privileged status in emigrating to the United Kingdom and the Dominions (i.e., Canada, Australia, New Zealand). They were equal citizens throughout the Commonwealth with extensive rights (Hansen, 2000). Since 1962 that privileged status has been reduced, but nonetheless, there are many economic, linguistic, and cultural connections from Jamaica to Calcutta. The former colonies of France have a rather complex legal situation that ultimately favors emigration and the maintenance of some commonwealthlike arrangements. Citizens/subjects of the colonies were technically part of France (Algeria, Tunisia, Morocco, Martinique, and Vietnam). While this is no longer the case, many persons from these areas could still choose to be citizens of France after independence.

Colonial participation in the colonizer's wars has an impact on immigration. The French integrated many colonial soldiers into their armed forces as early as 1868, when Senegalese regiments fought against the Germans in the Franco–Prussian War (Headrick, 1978; Mellors and McKean, 1984). In the Netherlands, emigrants from Indonesia and Surinam have found a similar situation as that in the United Kingdom. Molluccans form a special group based on colonial military service. After 1947, they emigrated to the Netherlands intending to receive Dutch assistance in retaking the Mollucan Islands. When this promise went unfulfilled, resistance movements and kidnapings followed. The Philippines exhibit a similar relationship with the United States. Many Filipino immigrants have served as stewards in the U.S. Navy and other branches of the service. During nursing shortages, American hospitals ship or fly thousands of Filipino nurses to the United States, as the British did with West Indian nurses in the 1950s. Former colonial situations are complex, but for the most part, they promote further immigration.

Third, migrants from sending countries at some distance from receiving countries who were not colonized will be unfamiliar with the receiving country's language and culture. Emigrants will often find themselves stranded and in difficult positions because the passage to the receiving country is long and arduous. The economic and political impetus to stay in the receiving country is often stronger due to the distance traveled. As return is linked to support, remittances may also decline due to distance. Because of the lack of information, recruiter abuses will tend to be stronger and scandals may erupt, with the receiving countries putting pressure on the senders to control their emigrants. In the 1800s, German, Swedish, Japanese, and Russian immigration fit this pattern, and more recently, Thailand and Turkey. Some receiving countries have had colonies with little emigration, mainly due to the shortness of the colonizing period. For example, it is estimated that fewer than 100 immigrants from Namibia (German Southwest Africa) and the Cameroon ever set foot in Germany, much less settled there (Stoecker, 1985, 1986; Walker, 1964). A similar situation prevails in Belgium with Zaire and in Japan with Korea and China.

A fourth category is really a subset of the third as it only refers to China and Russia. These are noncolonies at some distance from the receiving country that have been or still are empires. The main country here is China, which is a good candidate to consider separately. Because it is so large and potentially powerful, it continues to supply large numbers of immigrants. Russia could also fall into this category, but the case is a bit weaker. The reason we consider it separately is that the sending country in this case is clearly poor, otherwise it would not be sending emigrants outside its borders in such large numbers, but it is also or has greater potential to become a world power. This creates some national security issues for receiving countries and complicates sending country immigration interests.[13]

Sending Country Policies Toward Emigration

Direct and unintended governmental policies toward emigration in sending countries range from allowing large waves of immigration to imposing heavy restrictions. While unintended policies result from revolutions, civil wars, famines, and other calamities, these policies usually do increase emigration. But in this chapter, we are mainly concerned with sending country policies that are directly oriented toward emigration.[14]

Before World War II, sending countries pursued three policies toward emigration. First, governments have tried to alleviate the plight of their nationals taken advantage of during the emigration process. For instance, during the wave of German emigration from 1814 to 1869, German governments were continually embarrassed by scandals. Many poor emigrants found themselves stateless and stranded in the Netherlands waiting to cross the Atlantic (Walker, 1964). Other scandals erupted like the Delrue Affair, when thousands of German emigrants were sold off into indentured servitude in Brazil (Walker, 1964:97). Although Germany was under intense pressure from receiving countries to control emigration, it was unable to do so and only passed a few licensing laws to control the recruitment of emigrants. Governments may also protest human rights violations of their former citizens in the receiving country, as Japan did in the 1920s with the United States. From 1946 to 1970, France, Germany, and Belgium concluded twenty-two bilateral agreements to protect the rights of migratory workers from Spain, Portugal, Turkey, Morocco, Algeria, Tunisia, and other countries (Schmitter-Heisler, 1985:474). Such agreements continue to be negotiated.

Second, governments may promote emigration by expelling dissidents, criminals, and paupers. From 1572 to 1598, the Catholic French persecuted and then expelled the Protestant Huguenots, forcing their emigration throughout Europe and the Americas. In the 1800s, the Grosszimmern Affair emptied the Starkenburg jails in Hesse and the prisoners were sent to America (Walker, 1964:85–7). Russia and Germany expelled radicals and Jews westward toward Europe and to the New World (Gatrell, 1999). Though not as direct as these policies, the coolie trade that replaced many of the labor needs after the end of slavery required at least some cooperation from the sending countries to function. The Mariel emigration from Cuba allegedly fell into this category.

Third, many sending states tried to prevent emigration, especially for skilled and highly educated workers (Cervantes and Guellec, 2002; Saxenian, 2002; Zolberg, 1978, 1981). In the 1600s, France prohibited emigration without passports and would not issue them to the persecuted Huguenots; however, that did not forestall their mass emigration throughout Europe and to the Americas (Fahrmeir, 2000:101). In the late 1800s, many German states required that emigrants give up German citizenship upon leaving the country (Walker, 1964:17), which made emigrants stateless and highly vulnerable during their travel to the receiving country. But these policies fluctuated: In good times, politicians railed against the loss of skilled workers; but in bad times, emigration was a safety valve for the unemployed and political dissidents. After the

[13] The two-by-two classification of distance and colonial status implies: colony–border, independent–border, colony–nonborder, and noncolony–nonborder countries. We have collapsed the first two categories and divided the last by potential power.

[14] On how the international community may deal with the resulting refugee flows from these problems, see Brown, Cote, Lynn-Jones, and Miller, 2001, and Loescher, 1993.

unification of Germany in 1871, Bismarck expressed the opinion that "to immigrate was to betray the Fatherland, and the Fatherland had no responsibility" to protect emigrants (1964:178). Somewhat reluctantly, Bismarck engaged in a colonial policy that was a partial solution to emigration (i.e., emigrants could go to German colonies in Poland, Africa, or Samoa). But Bismarck knew that Prussia could not easily control emigration by direct legislation (1964:196).

Before World War II, Jewish emigration from Germany constituted a brain drain, but the ideologically driven Nazi government was not particularly concerned. In many ways, Jewish emigration functioned as an unemployment reduction program because many Germans moved into higher-paying jobs, took over business properties, and otherwise prospered as a result. Hence many Germans viewed emigration as positive rather than negative. But as World War II drew closer, Germany sought to forbid emigration to protect the size of the labor force and military, a policy somewhat different from the previous century. Similar controls were enacted in Japan as war approached.

After World War II, sending nations pursued a wider variety of policies to protect, promote, or prevent emigration. First, the Turkish government passed laws to protect immigrants by requiring labor contracts and other stipulations. While the German government established recruitment offices in Turkey to negotiate contracts, the Turkish government also established offices in Germany to protect Turkish guest workers. These policies tended to be relatively formal in some cases (guest worker programs in Europe) and informal in others (general immigration to the United States and Canada). As institutions of international civil society have developed, interest groups and the UN have increasingly tried to protect immigrants, refugees, and asylum seekers (Zolberg et al. 1989).

Second, preventing emigration was more common during the Cold War than before or after. The USSR and the communist satellite nations were among the few countries that tried to stop or heavily penalize emigration (Simon, 1987). Most citizens were prevented from emigrating, and many sports and entertainment stars often feared for the safety of their families remaining in the country if they defected. Controls over external emigration were strengthened by preventing the internal migration of rural workers to urban areas. In East Germany, the communist government sought to prevent emigration despite spectacular and often tragic escape attempts at the Berlin Wall. Nonetheless, many young adults still emigrated, leaving the demographic structure of the country seriously tilted toward the aged. In Maoist China, emigration was severely constrained because of national security and communist ideology as the state controlled internal migration through internal passports and job assignments by use of labor market planning, which made external emigration all the more difficult (Biao, 2003:23–7). Nonetheless, many emigrants flooded into Hong Kong (Tu, 1996).

Two other factors prevented emigration from communist countries. First, since unemployment did not technically exist, it could not be used to justify emigration. Second, political dissidents were not expelled but were more effectively silenced by sending them to prison in Siberian Gulag or rehabilitation in northwest China. Further, emptying out jails and receiving remittances from emigrants were totally ruled out for ideological and publicity purposes. To reinforce this, nationality laws prior to the 1980 reform made the overseas Chinese throughout Southeast Asia (and the rest of the world) Chinese citizens by descent (Chen, 1997). Consequently, the combination of communism and the Cold War led to more intense control of emigration than in other sending countries.

Another prevention policy was directly connected to the brain drain – repaying the state for one's education. In the USSR, sometimes dissident religious groups including Jews could obtain permission to leave. But the government often required that they pay back the costs of their education, which could be expensive according to Soviet accounting practices. In recent-day China, potential emigrants have the choice of serving the country for five to eight years after receiving a university degree or paying 10,000 RMB for a bachelor's degree, 12,000 RMB for a masters, and 18,000 RMB for a Ph.D. The value of this amount of money varies according to one's job, but it roughly translates into five months' pay, which may take years to save, but it is much less than the 30,000 RMB payments often made to "snakeheads" for illegal immigration to the United States (China, 1993; Kyle and Kozlowski, 2001).[15] Since 1996, the government has increased the cost of tuition by 500 percent, and those who paid the higher tuition do not have to reimburse the government or work inside the country for five years. Although most sending countries do not have explicit laws concerning emigrating professionals and highly skilled workers, they may have other general laws. For example, the Turkish constitution states that "a citizen's freedom to leave the country may be restricted on account of the national economic situation, civic obligations, or criminal investigation or prosecution" (Turkey, 1987, see also Saxenian, 2002).

Third, some sending countries have recently adapted dual nationality policy to promote emigration and possible return to their country, as well as to increase remittance payments. This promotes transnational migration because dual nationals are more likely to return compared to emigrants who must give up their original citizenship. For example, the Mexican nationality law of 1998 allows dual nationality for the first time since the 1857 and 1917 constitutions forbade it (Ramirez, 2000). In addition, Turkish guest workers in Germany tended not pursue German citizenship because they would lose access to family lands and inheritances in Turkey. In 1995, Turkey removed all restrictions on acquiring or inheriting property for its former citizens (Joppke, 1999:205; Münch, 2001:107; Hammar 1985). And as Turkey has increasingly allowed dual nationality, especially concerning its constitution, Germany has become much more lenient in its own practices (Turkey, 1987; Joppke, 1999). Although not offering dual citizenship, China has increased incentives to return including offering skilled emigrants higher salaries, special tax rates, business loans, housing subsidies, educational subsidies for children, and even a "first meeting present" (Biao, 2003:30). One province will give 100,000 RMB as a "first meeting present" to returning emigrants with advanced technology projects, and another province will give a two-year income tax waiver and reduced taxes for their companies (Sun, 2002, Tianjin City, 1998).

Because most sending countries are not democratic, they do not have open media that publicize or reveal the reasons that various policies have been created. Nonetheless, one may refer to a "submerged power resources theory" whereby factions within the government press for one or another policy position. Since sending countries often have surplus population, they are not so much interested in restricting emigration as a whole, but rather maintaining technical and profession employees whose loss may critically affect their economy and businesses. Consequently, business and economic development elites will place restrictions on the emigration of skilled employees.

However, since the fall of communism in Europe and Russia and the loss of faith in autarky and import substitution policies, many less developed countries have shifted their policies toward the free movement of nationals. Globalizing coalitions based on the market with entry into trade groups such as the EU (for Turkey), NAFTA (for Mexico), and the WTO (for China) have replaced traditionalists or nationalizing leftists.[16] The "globalizing coalition" must accept market principles and privatization in order to enter these transnational organizations. The free emigration of workers inside and outside the country, whether highly expert or less skilled, and increased protection of human rights are part of the bargain to gain large capital

[15] Jobs vary considerably in pay. English majors can easily start at 2,000 RMB per month working as an interpreter for a foreign or even domestic company. However, engineering majors work for government construction companies, and they often start at only 800 RMB. Note that RMB refers to Ren Men Bin.

[16] The EU's rejection of Turkey's bid for membership in December of 2002 was a considerable blow to their economic aspirations, especially as many other countries were admitted and Turkey had instituted many human rights reforms (Sciolino, 2002). Nonetheless, their EU efforts continue.

investments from advanced industrialized countries. Not all the bargains will, of course, be the same because some countries will continue to exert more control than others. Nonetheless, free emigration is likely to become common for sending countries.

THE POLITICS OF NAURALIZATION, INTEGRATION, AND NATIONALISM

Nativist organizations who oppose integration and naturalization have existed for a long time in the United States (e.g., the "No Popery" and "Know-nothing" movements of the early 1800s), and the Ku Klux Klan after the 1870s engaged in terror, murder, and other types of violence. Nativist efforts to restrict immigration through legislation are obviously legal, yet scholars and various ethnic and immigrant organizations are quick to label the legislative activists of nativist organizations as "racist" (Hingham, 1965, Tatalovich, 1995). Freeman (1985) and Briggs (1992) ask if countries do not have the right to rationally pursue their interests and exercise their sovereignty. Fitzgerald (1996) points out that immigration policies create new national identities and have great consequences for culture, whether it involves language, religion, or the "national" way. Thus, immigration policy also provides a playing field for national identity and culture, and nativist and labor groups may play their political hands in legislatures as they see fit.

After World War II, welfare state and social policies have been available to immigrants in Europe for a long time. In fact, the availability of social assistance and medical care rights along with legal rights led to the claims that citizenship through naturalization had lost its *raison d'etre* (Brubaker, 1992; Soysal, 1994; Joppke, 1999). Proposition 187 in California and subsequent amendments to immigration laws at the national level have led to restrictions on these social rights. However, those restrictions have been successfully challenged in the American courts. Nonetheless, special assistance programs for refugees and asylum seekers have provided automatic supports and special services, which are sometimes quite generous. They are most needed among the Hmong, who come from hill tribe backgrounds, but less so for urbanized and educated Vietnamese. But how much these immigrants integrate into society often depends on attaining legal status as a citizen through naturalization rather than simply consuming social benefits.

Although single-nation studies abound (Schuck, 1998; Aleinkoff and Klusmeyer, 2000, 2001; Hansen and Weil, 2002), naturalization and integration laws have received little attention from political sociology when compared to immigration policies, especially in cross-national studies (but see Groot 1989, Rham 1990, and Weil 2001). There have been two basic theories: one culture and the other power constellations. First, Brubaker's cultural idiom theory (1992, 1989) focused on citizenship and nationhood in France and Germany. "Cultural idioms" are ways of thinking and talking about nationhood. His two cases demonstrated that cultural idioms were either quickly forged in the crucible of the French Revolution or developed gradually over centuries in Germany.

The French Revolution transformed "belonging" to French society into active participation based on rights and obligations within a nation-state. Prior bases for membership came from the cosmopolitan aristocracy in the *ancien regime*, and then in a new cosmopolitan world of citizenship in the early revolution when even Tom Paine and George Washington were made French citizens. Modern citizenship began with closure upon the French nation-state, especially when political dissidents were executed and citizens were conscripted as part of their duty to protect the republic. Aristocrats could no longer be cavalier in their allegiance to the nation-state. This cultural crucible created the French universal approach that allows immigrants to become a citizen if they assimilate to French cultural and political norms. Consequently, French naturalization rates are relatively high for a densely populated country, and until recently the legal principles of *jus soli* citizenship derived from birth in the country according to "the law of the soil" have equaled those of *jus sanguinis* citizenship based on one's parents through the law of blood or descent (Brubaker, 1992:35–49).[17]

Germany did not have such a leveling revolution, and the development of citizenship was connected to the estate or *Stand*, which is a highly particularistic rather than a universalistic institution (Brubaker, 1992:50–72). As the *Stand* evolved into the *Ständestaat*, multiple legal communities developed rather than a single state, which continued to carry community- and group-based notions of belonging to a state. The focus was inward rather than outward, and the most extreme example can be found in the German "hometowns" where membership meant livelihood (Walker, 1971). Although legal development took place within and between numerous German states, the eventual laws developed with the exclusion of the poor (often migrating Jews from Russia), and later, of the "Slavic" Poles. The end result was an immigration system based on *jus sanguinis* that has brought millions of dispersed German ethnics (*Aussiedler*) back from a Central or Eastern European diaspora as full-fledged citizens. But until recently the system lacked principles of *jus soli*, and this caused great roadblocks to citizenship for long-term guest workers and their children.

Brubaker's cultural idiom argument is the first macrosocial explanation of naturalization and how the long-term development of citizenship laws in the two countries occurred. It has a number of difficulties, however. First, the search for the genetic code of citizenship policies relies on unique events to have a continuous effect over centuries. One may easily look to other historical periods for different cultural idioms. In the search for cultural idioms, one may go back to the earliest foundings or later refoundings of the state. For instance, rather than focusing on the French Revolution, one may go back to Clovis and the earliest nation-building processes in France.[18] Second, this nation-forging position fails to provide guidance in exploring the unique cultural idioms of other countries. Only the French had the French Revolution; what explains the more open citizenship policies in the United Kingdom and incredibly closed policies in Japan? Cultural idioms are by nature idiographic and thus provide little guidance in formulating hypotheses for many other countries.

Third, naturalizing divergent neighbors differs from naturalizing distant strangers. Poles were a long-standing cultural competitor to the Germans not only on their border but also within their territories. The Algerians and Moroccans were at arm's length from the French across the Mediterranean Sea. Fourth, political economy arguments discounted by Brubaker are much more important than he indicates. The French decline in births was early and severe, and military conscription was a major problem. Weil makes this point quite conclusively in his history of French nationality (2002). Neither was a serious problem in Germany despite successive waves of emigration to the Americas. Fifth, the labor market for poor people and the invitation of rich people is as different as Canada's solicitation of rich Hong Kong businessmen and the avoidance of boat people (e.g., the Vietnamese in Japan and Haitians in the United States). Clearly, the race, class, and religious characteristics of immigrants do make a difference.

The second approach to naturalization comes from the power constellation approach. Janoski and Glennie (1995a, b), somewhat based on the early Freeman, put forward a regime theory based on long-term state interests in integrating

[17] Usage of these two Latin legal terms is common, but they do not form a typology that covers all naturalization law. For instance, the terms do not refer to immigration of nonethnics and their subsequent naturalization.

[18] Some French historians speak of the struggle of the nobility descended from the Frankish aristocracy who conquered Gaul at the beginning of the Middle Ages, and then claim that the vanquished Gauls emerged victorious over the Franks in the French Revolution (Noiriel, 1996:72). The Teutonic knights or new Prussians intermingled territories with the Poles and other groups, and even in the areas that they controlled, native nobility complained of their isolation from the population and importation of German peasants and townspeople (Carsten, 1954:10–27, 52–72; Graus, 1970; Bosl, 1970; Bade, 1983, 1990, 1992, 1994; Schumacher, 1958). Are the French are a product of fusion, the Germans the result of segregation? On nations before nationalism, see Armstrong (1982) and Smith (1988).

foreigners. Long-term power resources explain the direction of state policy in three contexts: colonial powers, settler countries, and nonsettler countries. In extending Freeman's political economy approach (1979), former imperial powers have fashioned an approach to immigration and naturalization that promotes their empires. France and Britain had open naturalization policies because they made promises to their colonies. If natives acculturated, learned the language of the colonial power, became educated even in the mother country schools, and served in the empire's military forces, then colonial natives were promised citizenship and the right to immigrate to the core nation. Britain tried to maintain the Commonwealth with such wide-open passports within the empire. In a different way, black troops from Algeria and Senegal fought the Germans on French soil in the Franco–Prussian War, World War I, and World War II (Echenberg, 1991). Institutions were created to maintain these long-term political economic goals, and they had a half-life of two to four decades as the empires receded.

Settler countries have immigration needs for two reasons. First, they frequently repressed an indigenous people causing 50 to 90 percent of the indigenous majority population to be decimated through fighting and/or disease, which created a labor shortage that must be filled through immigration. Second, they have national security needs to continue the subjugation of the indigenous enemy and defend themselves against colonizing and other foreign powers. Consequently, settler countries then established recruitment programs, easy naturalization, and promise social mobility and opportunity. The United States, Canada, New Zealand, Australia, and even South Africa have fit this pattern (Janoski and Glennie, 1995a; Janoski, 1998:165–71; Çinar, 1994; Waldrauch and Hofinger, 1997).

Noncolonizers have no particular interest in immigration. Their institutions have been oriented toward emigration over long periods of time, and often, these states have been rather authoritarian. Emigration may also induce feelings of cultural doubt and nationalism. These countries will enact laws that have high barriers to naturalization. For instance, residency periods are five to seven years longer than in the settler countries, and naturalization may be a privilege rather than a right (e.g., German residency requirements have been ten years and the Swiss require twelve). Immigrants are often strictly defined as guest workers, which means that their status is temporary. Quantitative analysis of naturalization rates shows that a barrier index composed of eight components of nationality laws is a strong deterrent to naturalization rates within these countries (Janoski and Glennie, 1995a, b; Janoski, 1998).[19]

Yasemin Soysal provides an explanation of immigrant assimilation where politics plays a critical role. Soysal (1994:29–44) develops the concept of "incorporation regimes" that draws on aspects of immigration and naturalization law. She focuses on the organizational responses of immigrant communities to discrimination and the state, and their subsequent incorporation into liberal, corporatist, and statist regimes.[20] In corporatist regimes like Sweden, immigrant interest groups have received state

[19] The components of this barrier index are: (1) good conduct as measured by convictions and signing a statement, (2) willingness to integrate based on an oath, (3) language skills, (4) application complexity, (5) naturalization fees, (6) naturalization as a right, (7) residency requirement, and (8) *jus soli* for children born in the receiving country (Janoski and Glennie, 1995a; Janoski, Lepadatu, and Diggs, 2003).

[20] Soysal's approach to incorporation regimes is particularly revealing because work had not been previously done on immigrant associations in Europe. However, she does not put her theory to the test with concrete measurement of incorporation regimes. In a preliminary extension of her work, we have coded the following variables, with each being standardized with a range of 1 to 0 (i.e., dividing by the highest score or other standardizations). The seven variables in the regime scale are: (1) years to 2002 that the central state has had an agency directly responsible for immigrants, (2) central and local channels by which immigrants can be represented, (3) a dummy variable for state funding of ethnic associations, (4) the years necessary for permanent residence, (5) the time required for unlimited work permits, (6) being able to vote in local elections, and (7) being represented in works councils or other advisory forums. Corporatist regimes were easy to delineate, with Sweden scoring 6.01 and the Netherlands 5.65 out of a possible 7. Liberal regimes were somewhat easy to identify, with the United States scoring 2.13. However, statist regimes

aid, protected the immediate interests of their ethnicity through services, and promoted their longer-term interests through lobbying. She claims that the different strategies of these ethnic and immigrant groups have resulted in distinctive policies in the countries that she studied. Statist regimes like France expect assimilation. But France is not open to immigrant associations because the French state provides little funding to them, keeps them at arm's length, and minimizes their influence (Kastoryano, 2002). Liberal regimes like the United States and Canada neither encourage nor discourage group formation, but when groups form, they can influence the political process just like other associations.

Types of immigrant incorporation regimes are similar to the types of welfare regimes (Esping-Andersen, 1990). James Hollifield (1992) suggests the guest-worker, assimilationist, and ethnic-minority. Hans Etzinger (2000) suggests a six option approach to incorporation with cross-classification of individual versus group approaches, and political, cultural, and social/economic regimes. This yields individual approaches with equal rights, liberal pluralism, and equal opportunity. Based on group rights, multiculturalism, and the equality of results, the group approach has been heavily advocated in the political theory literature, especially concerning indigenous peoples, and applied to immigrants in the multicultural approach in Canada (Etzinger, 2000:107; Kymlicka, 1995; Lipset, 1990). However, group rights of various sorts have existed to some degree for a long time (Janoski and Gran, 2002).

Rob Witte (1996) traces the development of ethnic and racial integration policies in the United Kingdom, France, and the Netherlands. He provides data on violence against foreigners with an explanatory focus on the organizations protecting and representing them. His stage theory explaining integration consists of: stage A – racist violence is an individual problem, stage B – society sees such violence as group-based, stage C – the state initially responds to racist violence, and stage D – violence against foreigners becomes a state priority (1996:12–21). Witte's stage theory provides detailed information on the interaction of the state, political parties, ethnic organizations, and integration councils.

In comparing the United Kingdom, France, and the Netherlands, Soysal's work can be tied to Witte in developing a theory of civil society where frequent interactions between groups in civil society and with the state create different integration regimes. In keeping the deaths of immigrants at the lowest level, the most effective response to racist acts emerges in the dense corporatist network of the state and groups in civil society in the Netherlands. Without these same networks in the public sphere, France's reliance on statist conceptions of citizenship leads to many more immigrant deaths per capita. The United Kingdom is in between with its race relations acts. Thränhardt (2000) adds Germany into this four-country comparison as a country that clearly pursued an arm's-length or statist guest-worker model. The Dutch state approached integration by creating and then bringing an immigrant elite into all political parties so that they will have immigrant leaders within their ranks (2000:171, 180). Dutch policies formed an elite consensus after some discussion with many groups throughout civil society, and created a virtuous circle that kept many ethnic minority issues out of the media (Thränhardt, 2000). Though Witte and Thränhardt do not make use of Soysal's regime theory, it can be extended from her network evidence in both an elite and group-based perspective.[21]

were more difficult, with France scoring 3.55. This score was hard to differentiate from the United Kingdom with 4.48 and Switzerland and Germany with 3.66 and 2.41. It would appear that Soysal's attempt to delineate incorporation regimes is useful, but the category of statist regimes needs more directly relevant variables to adequately separate it from the other two regime types.

[21] This regime theory and its overall characterization of the Netherlands having less racial violence than the other countries is backed up by public opinion. While not definitive and in need of further study, Meertens and Pettigrew find that Dutch levels of blatant prejudice toward Turks and blacks are much less than German (toward Turks), French (toward North Africans and Asians), and British (toward Asians and West Indians) prejudices in the 1988 Euro-Barometer study (1997:66).

As the European discussion implies, the American discourse on integration is much less group-focused. It looks less at regimes and more at identity, networks, and local politics. Assimilation with its new variant of segmented assimilation, including ethnic enclaves and ethnic resilience theory, are central to American discourse (Portes, 1997; Massey et al., 1998; Waldinger, 2001). Assimilation theory has long stressed differences in education, occupation, and family status as important explanations of behavioral (i.e., learning norms and values), structural (i.e., social mobility), marital (i.e., intermarriage with native spouses), and self-identification assimilation. The closer immigrants are embedded in socioeconomic, family, and identity positions – work with natives, speak the language, marry a native, interact with natives and upwardly mobile immigrants, and internalize native culture – the more likely they will assimilate. This theory has been connected to social networks of immigrants who engage in chain migration processes through their kin networks from their country of origin. The more immigrants leave their ethnic enclave, the more they will integrate and assimilate to the dominant culture (Liang, 1994; Massey et al., 1998). Although segemented assimilation theory challenges some aspects of process and depth, assimilation is the dominant American political value.

As opposed to assimilation theory, ethnic resilience theory proposes that ethnic groups resist naturalization and integration. Not only do immigrants gain sustenance from social networks and cultural maintenance in ethnic enclaves, but they also prosper economically through ethnic and more general business activities (Waldinger, 2001). For example, Cuban immigrants in Miami have established an important economic and political base. Resilience theory argues that ethnics may then have conflicts with natives in residential neighborhoods and at work (Bélanger and Pinard, 1991) and that they may resist naturalization and assimilation. As societies move more and more in a multicultural direction, ethnic resilience may gain strength with sending country language instruction and traditional religious practices.

Despite an impressive body of research, assimilation/resilience theories have little to say in terms of macropolitical sociology. These theories center on the United States and are based on individual and social network phenomena, and avoid the causes of different naturalization laws and integration policies, although they criticize laws for their ineffectiveness. Assimilation is useful in explaining neighborhood and local politics, but it does not explain cross-national variations in policy. Thus, assimilationist and ethnic resilience perspectives are protopolitical theories that explain immigrant identities that may then lead to interest-group organization and lobbying for particular types of policies.

TRANSNATIONAL THEORIES AND UNIFYING RECEIVER AND SENDER THEORY?

Transnational theories will further impact political sociology in combining theories of sender and receiver countries. First, under globalization, immigration theory faces two trends. In one direction, the power of states and their sovereignty have lessened because of the rise of international organizations.[22] Second, a transnational civil society has developed apart from states and governmental federations. In one major statement of this approach, Soysal combines increasing immigration with a growing international civil society to claim that there is a postnational citizenship developing with transnational membership principles independent of

[22] While we are arguing for transnational theories, we recognize that there are limitations. For example, the European Union (EU) is creating a new country, though few want to call it that and some deny it. The EU has gone beyond economic unity (e.g., free trade and a common currency) to create a new form of European citizenship with political and social rights within a common legal system (Richardson, 2001; Brah, 2001; Leontidu and Afouxenidis, 2001). Immigration between EU countries is now internal migration without passports or even reporting. A European identity is forming with German citizens tending to be the leader, and the United Kingdom the laggard (Kostakopoulou, 2001; Kastoryano, 2002; Guild, 1996; Münch, 2001). Consequently, immigration within the EU is not strong evidence of transnational behavior in the world.

any one state. The transition from national citizenship to postnational membership has four aspects (1994:139–56). First, national citizenship existed in a nation-state until about 1945, but postnational citizenship is a new phenomena with fluid boundaries that downplay the nation-states. Second, national citizenship tied membership to a distinct territory, but postnational membership has multiple statuses and locations. Third, membership was based on citizenship rights in a state where national rights are grounded in positive law. Transnational membership views universal personhood as rooted in human rights without regard to national boundaries. Finally, the nation-state was the source of legitimacy and organizer of membership. Although the nation-state still provides services and rights, the transnational community now provides legitimacy, and international civil society supervises it through a network of nongovernmental agencies that lobby and make exposés, and supranational governments that organize and enforce human rights treaties. Thus, Soysal (1994), Bauböck (1994), Ong (1999), and Held et al. (1999) have made claims that have captured many scholars' imaginations.

Transnational membership is pressured by the global interest groups and international human rights organizations that both report on and lobby for the rights of refugees, asylum seekers, and denizens of different racial and ethnic groups (Welch, 2001a). As reporting organizations, Amnesty International (2002) and Human Rights Watch (1999) have published summaries of the condition of rights in most countries in the world, and lobby offending governments through the press and electronic media so that receiver countries will cut off aid, assistance, and even trade. Direct action has also been initiated with consciousness-raising groups and activities similar to Witness for Peace, who has sent observers to be in harm's way, which generates information and alters behavior to some degree (Welch, 2001b; Keck and Sikkink, 1998). Many other international organizations have been involved in human rights work and in developing other aspects of global civil society (e.g., the International Labor Organization, International Human Rights Law Group, Foodfirst Information and Action Network, and Greenpeace). Soysal (1994) and Bauböck (1994) have considered these organizations' influence to be large, whereas other scholars are much more cautious (Joppke, 1999).

One target of these nongovernmental advocacy and action groups has been supranational government, such as the UN, NATO, WTO, the World Bank, and so on. The United States and NATO have been somewhat effective in activating international human rights accords and protecting rights (Janoski, 1998:40–1). The WTO and World Bank have been targets for protest groups due to their adverse effects on human rights. For example, Human Rights Watch initially focused its activities around the rights outlined in the Helsinki Accord. Even as global treaties constrain the activities of the private economy and the state sector, many of these human rights treaties and accords also constrain the treatment of immigrants and refugees. The trials of Slobadan Milosevich, Rawandan leaders, and Augusto Pinochet serve as examples of how human rights violators can be brought to trial in various tribunals. On the other hand, although the Zapatista rebellion brought the adverse affects of globalization to the world's attention, the trials of corporations and the WTO are unlikely to happen.

Another focus on transnational and postmodern identity looks at the increase in dual nationality and multiple identities, increasing remittances and investments in the sending or home country, and flexible citizenship or even superfluous citizenship. Both receiver policies (encouraging French Islam as a nonradical and national alternative to international Islam) and sender policies (promoting Arabization to Berbers and even Arabs in Algeria) have proven to be hazardous (Naylor, 2000:258–73). Nonetheless, composite identities are often held together with a "segmented assimilation" (Portes, 1997), and "flexible citizenship" (Ong, 1999) allows immigrants to partake of many cultures during a time when travel becomes a minor consideration. Another aspect of this research focuses on indigenous peoples and their land and other rights in the face of European immigrants (Tully, 1995; Kymlicka, 1995, 1996).

While recognizing that identity is important to interest-group and social movement activities, much of the focus of this research has remained at the local and personal level (Appadurai, 1996) and as yet is somewhat protopolitical.

Critics of these theories of transnational membership challenge both the existence and the consequences of globalization. Joppke explicitly criticizes Soysal's transnational membership theory (1999:268–80) because human rights are not yet legally or politically institutionalized. Even with external moral constraints, states really react to the pressures and power resources of internal groups (1999:268). Joppke claims that the evidence for declining sovereignty exists neither for nation-states giving up control of immigration policy to supranational states, nor for the claim that the ability of nation-states to control immigration is waning (this is where considering the EU evidence of transnational trends rather than nation building confuses the issue). In fact, he says that technology is providing even greater resources to create "Fortress Europe" (1999:270). Another criticism is that international regulation of nation-states and human rights has existed to various degrees since the Treaty of Westfalia (1648). Berman (2001) indicates that an international law of nationality long existed (e.g., the Treaties of Berlin of 1878 and Versailles after World War I, the Geneva Convention, and UN General Assembly Resolution 1514 on colonial independence).

But transnational arguments often exaggerate sovereignty claims. Weak states have never escaped influence from stronger states, and even strong states existed within the constraints of a myriad of other states' actions. One strong argument against transnational membership is that rights require enforcement. For the vast majority of cases, enforcement still depends on the law and police forces of nation-states. Despite some recent developments mentioned above concerning crimes against human rights, international law is still weakly institutionalized. Most of its legitimacy is through voluntary adherence, and some nation-states can pull out of treaties just as easily as they sign them (e.g., George W. Bush withdrawing from treaties).

Our main point is that given the emphasis on globalization in sociological and other theories, one might easily see how a theory that unifies the actions of sender and receiver countries would be needed. World systems and globalization theories have a little bit to say about this in that immigrants flow from the sender to the receiver countries and that they are often exploited. But this is not enough for a theory of immigration. What one might expect from a more developed theory would be the meshing of different sender and receiver regime types. In this last section, we can only sketch out the beginnings of such a theory. In Figure 31.1, we put the regime types of the receiver countries and the sending countries together.

Past transnational organizations of empire and colonization (item 1) lead to different pairs of receiver and sending regime types (items 2 and 3), which produce some interesting matches between different state structures (items 4 and 5) with their associated factional or interest groups (items 6 and 7) including public opinion. For example, Mexico and Turkey have reacted to U.S. and German policies against dual nationality by relaxing their requirements that only Mexican and Turkish citizens could own land and be entitled to inheritances (as discussed previously). In the opposite direction, the United States and Germany have also relaxed their naturalization policies or embraced amnesties. In the past, immigration and naturalization policies were contextualized by empires and commonwealths, but now they critically depend on whether the sending country belongs to the receiving country's transnational organization (e.g., see item 8 with the EU, NAFTA, and WTO). At the same time, international civil society (i.e., see Amnesty International and UN Declarations of Human Rights, also in item 8) has an impact on human rights within both the sending and receiving countries. The result is a relational creation of policies between receiver and sender countries. This framework and its subsequent theoretical development, we believe, will increasingly replace much of the current focus on one country, one law, and one society's agglomeration of immigrants.

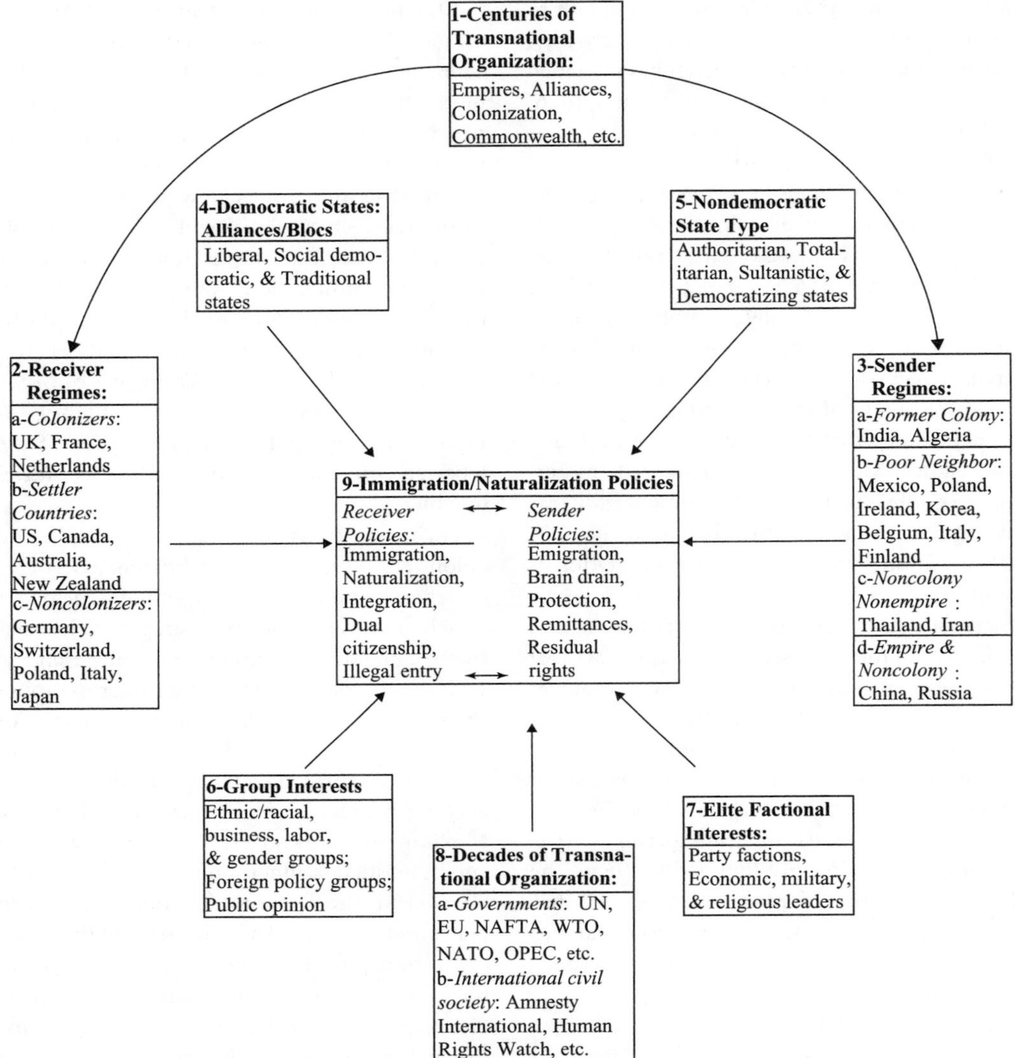

Figure 31.1. The Matching of Receiving and Sending Country Regimes and Policies.

CONCLUSION

Political sociology has been strongly focused on explaining revolutions, dictatorship and democracy, race and gender politics, and the rise of welfare states, but not very much on immigration and naturalization politics. However, in the last decade, immigration, citizenship, and integration policies have come to worldwide attention. And as welfare costs, terrorism concerns, and increasing globalization increase, the politics of immigration is getting more attention and will become more central as labor shortages occur from 2010 to 2050. It is now clear that immigration research has now penetrated into political sociology.

In the past, state-centric, cost–benefit, and cultural theories have been fairly popular theories explaining immigration politics. But as this chapter has attempted to show, a power constellation theory that includes critical insights from state-centric, institutional, and status-group theory can also provide a complex explanation of immigration and naturalization laws. It will become increasingly important to explain the interests of ethnic and racial groups, human rights, labor, and business groups in domestic and international politics, that is, in both societal and international civil societies. The relational dance among sending and receiving countries will reveal a conducive approach to obtaining a better explanation of the politics of immigration and naturalization throughout the world.

Cultural idiom theory needs work in the sense of being a theory in and of itself, but one can envision a "strong cultural argument" such as the one Philip Gorski provides concerning "pietization" driving the new structures of the seventeenth-century state (1999, 2003), and perhaps we might have such a major change with Muslim immigration or in the further explanation of the politics of multiculturalism. This would be as welcome as Weber's view of culture as the track changer that reroutes the locomotive of political economy. But such reroutings, though they may occur every few centuries, do not provide the more track-laying explanations of decades or half centuries that are needed. And as the face of immigration politics has changed in the last few decades with fiery debates and polarized parties, power constellation theory will have even more impact. Identity studies may also develop more in a political sociological direction with their movement into the politics of interest groups and social movements.

With this theoretical orientation in mind, where might the political sociology of immigration go in the next decade? First of all, more comparative work in the area needs to be done to test various theories. For this to happen, theories of immigration and naturalization need to do more in bringing receiver and sender country interaction into focus. Too much research in this area has been either case-study material or descriptive studies of various state policies masquerading under the title of "the politics of immigration." We present a framework to start the process. Rather than saying globalization and transnational citizenship are affecting immigration, one needs to come up with specific hypotheses about the interaction of these various combinations of regimes (e.g., colonizer–former colony, settler–poor neighbor, noncolonizer–former colony, settler–empire/noncolony, etc.). This framework is not a theory, but we offer it here as a suggestion about where studies of immigration should be going in the next twenty years. Theories would emerge out of the combinations of sender and receiver countries developing particular policies, politics (i.e., immigrant social movements and interest groups interacting with parties, labor, and management), and international civil society. This would require the matching of sender country immigration and receiver country emigration, which may be a daunting prospect because sender country data are much worse than receiver country data, which leads to the next point.

Second, in order to do this, immigration and naturalization data must be strengthened from their surprisingly poor state. Although the OECD-SOPEMI reports (1983–2002) have increased the reporting of immigration and naturalization data, they still rely on somewhat idiosyncratic national correspondents, and there are major gaps (e.g., Ireland still fails to report naturalization data and Austria does not publish many immigration figures). At a microlevel, something like the Luxembourg Income Studies would be a boon to the microprocesses and comparisons of immigration and politics in many countries. As Fitzgerald (1996) indicates, countries recreate and mold their identities through immigration policies. Finding out how this may be operating requires decent comparable data in a more consistent and cross-national form. Current ethnographic studies of immigration can often be excellent, but presently, it is difficult to aggregate them into a national reporting system.

Sociological questions concerning the politics of immigration will be most prescient in the next few decades. When declining fertility rates in the West (Spengler, 1979; Massey et al., 1998) are coupled with globalization, receiving countries may very well undergo massive denativization and reculturation by immigrants. Will the United States will become increasingly Catholic as Hispanic immigrants come in large numbers? Will Europe become a society based on Christian/Islamic cleavages, perhaps similar to the Protestant/Catholic divisions of the past? Do receiving countries have rights of self-determination to protect their own cultures as they have overrun the cultures of sending countries through the global economy and media? In effect, ethnic nations cannot claim cultural dominance when they cannot reproduce their culture with sufficient birth and fertility rates. The end result will provide exciting grounds for research in political sociology as receiving and sending countries make critical decisions about their futures in the next half century.

CHAPTER THIRTY-TWO

Counterhegemonic Globalization

Transnational Social Movements in the Contemporary Global Political Economy

Peter Evans

When people invoke "globalization," they usually mean the prevailing system of transnational domination, which is more accurately called "neoliberal globalization," "corporate globalization," or perhaps "neoliberal, corporate-dominated globalization" (cf. McMichael, 2000: chap. 29). Sometimes they are referring to a more generic process – the shrinking of space and increased permeability of borders that result from falling costs of transportation and revolutionary changes in technologies of communication. Often the two are conflated.[1]

Implicit in much of current discourse on globalization is the idea that the particular system of transnational domination that we experience today is the "natural" (indeed inevitable) consequence of exogenously determined generic changes in the means of transportation and communication. A growing body of social science literature and activist argumentation challenges this assumption. Arguing instead that the growth of transnational connections can potentially be harnessed to the construction of more equitable distributions of wealth and power and more socially and ecologically sustainable communities, this literature and argumentation raises the possibility of what I would like to call "counterhegemonic globalization." Activists pursuing this perspective have created a multifaceted set of transnational networks and ideological frames that stand in opposition to contemporary neoliberal globalization. Collectively they are referred to as the "global justice movement." For activists and theorists alike, these movements have become one of the most promising political antidotes to a system of domination that is increasingly seen as effectual only in its ability to maintain itself in power.

Although the growth of membership and political clout of transnational social movements is hard to measure, the burgeoning of their formal organizational reflections – transnational NGOs – is well-documented. Their numbers have doubled between 1973 and 1983 and doubled again between 1983 and 1993 (Sikkink and Smith, 2002:31). Perhaps even more important than their quantitative growth has been their ability to seize oppositional imaginations. From the iconic images of Seattle to the universal diffusion of the World Social Forum's vision that "another world is possible," the cultural and ideological impact of these movements has begun to rival that of their corporate adversaries.

As these movements have grown, an equally variegated body of social science literature has begun to analyze, empirically and theoretically, the possibilities of a global countermovement

[1] Stiglitz's (2002:9) definition is an interesting case in point: "Fundamentally, it is the closer intergration of the countries and peoples of the world which has been brought about by the enoromous reduction of costs of transportation and communication, and the breaking down of artificial barriers to the flows of goods, services, capital, knowledge, and (to a lesser extent) people across borders." By seeing new commercial rules as simply removing "artificial barriers," he naturalizes globalization. Later in his analysis Stiglitz goes on to decry some of the new rules – e.g., capital account liberalization – as "unnatural" and indeed economically dangerous.

that would take advantage of the technological capacities associated with generic globalization and turn neoliberal globalization's own ideological and organizational structures against itself, subverting its exclusionary rules of governance and logic of allocating resources. Yet, as is to be expected, the scholarly literature lags behind the growth of the movements themselves.

Any adequate theorization of contemporary globalization must include an analysis of antisystemic oppositional movements. Yet, with a few exceptions (e.g., Boswell and Chase-Dunn, 2000; Gill, 2002; McMichael, this volume), discussion of oppositional movements is usually "tacked on" to the end of an analysis that is theorized primarily in terms of the logic of neoliberal globalization. From novel analyses of contemporary globalization, such as Hardt and Negri (2000), to encyclopedic treatments like Held et al. (1999), structure and dynamics of countermovements are afforded only a fraction the theoretical attention given to dominant structures.

A careful analysis of countermovements is essential to our understanding of the dynamics of contemporary politics. Without an analysis of the organization and strategies of transnational social movements, our understanding of the politics of global governance institutions like the WTO, the Bretton Woods twins, and the UN system is incomplete (see, for example, Fox and Brown, 1998; Evans, 2000; O'Brien, 2000; Wade, 2001). Correspondingly, nation-states must increasingly take into account the reactions of transnational countermovements when they operate in global arenas.

The analysis of transnational movements has also become increasingly important to the understanding of what might have earlier been considered "domestic" politics. Contentious politics at the national level is increasingly contaminated by global issues and movements, whether in the North or in the South. Theorization of social movements cannot proceed without full consideration of the implications of transnational experiences (cf. McCarthy, 1997; Tarrow, 2001, 2002; Khagram, Riker, and Sikkink, 2002; Smith and Johnson, 2002). Concepts like "frame alignment" and "resource mobilization" take on a different meaning when the "society" involved consists of an interconnected congeries of national political units varying dramatically in their material resources and cultural foundations (cf. Snow, 1986; Benford, 1997; McAdam, Tarrow, and Tilly, 2001).

Analytical, practical, and political motivations for focusing on oppositional transnational social movements are all intensified by growing disillusionment with the currently hegemonic version of globalization. Margaret Thatcher's admonition "there is no alternative" becomes increasingly difficult to accept and the idea that there might be something like "counterhegemonic globalization" correspondingly more attractive.

HEGEMONIC VERSUS COUNTERHEGEMONIC GLOBALIZATION

Despite the visibility and fervor of its supporters (e.g., Tom Friedman), neoliberal globalization has proved a disillusioning disappointment to ordinary citizens, not just in the global South but in the rich industrial core as well. More surprisingly, prominent development economists, who might be expected to be its most fervent promoters (e.g., Rodrik, Sachs, Stiglitz), are sharp critics of neoliberal globalization and its governing institutions. McMichael's discussion sets out these disappointments at length in Chapter 29 and there is no need to reiterate them in detail here, but a quick reminder is in order.

Neoliberal globalization has delivered global financial volatility that regularly destroys productive capacity (without stimulating the creativity that Schumpeter considered definitive of capitalist progress). Instead of accelerating the improvement of living standards for the majority of the world's population, it has been associated with slowing growth rates (cf. Easterly, 2001). It has often jeopardized the delivery of essential collective goods like public health, education, and a sustainable environment and it has exacerbated inequality within and between nations to a degree that is destructive of the basic social solidarity.

While generating a proliferation of electoral regimes and celebrating "democracy" in the abstract, neoliberal globalization has undermined the possibility of democratic control over state policies and insulated the most fundamental policy decisions from even the fiction of democratic control. It has had pervasively corrosive effects on any sense of self-worth that is based on local culture, difference, and identity. Finally, it is now associated with a return to military adventurism whose potential future destructive effects are frightening to contemplate.

Despite its failures, few would deny that neoliberal globalization remains "hegemonic" in the Gramscian sense of combining an ideological vision of "what is in everyone's interests" that is largely accepted as "common sense" even by subordinate and disprivileged groups with the effective ability to apply coercion when necessary to preserve the existing distribution of privilege and exclusion. To call movements "counterhegemonic" therefore implies that they have the potential to undermine the ideological power of existing hegemony and threaten the established distribution of privilege (and exclusion).[2] Likewise, "counterhegemonic globalization" would entail building a global political economy that used the shrinking of space and facility of cross-border communication to enhance equity, justice, and sustainability rather than to intensify existing forms of domination.

For anyone who shares, even partially, disillusionment with neoliberal globalization, the prospect of a "counterhegemonic" globalization is alluring. It is hardly surprising that analysis of transnational social movements and their theoretical implications has growing appeal among both political sociologists and activists. Unfortunately, preoccupation with discovering new agents of social change also creates temptation to exaggerate the virtues and power of existing groups and networks and their ideologies.

Avoiding inflated and unrealistic assessments of either the virtues or efficacy of those who oppose neoliberal globalization is the first step toward real understanding of their potential power. It must be admitted that the "antiglobalization movement" contains its share of irresponsible nihilists. It must also be acknowledged that some alternative visions may be worse than the currently dominant one. It is entirely possible to oppose Western-dominated global capitalism with a vision that is more oppressive, authoritarian, and intolerant than neoliberalism, as Al Qaeda illustrates. Likewise, "antiglobalization" provides a handy "modern" gloss for a multitude of old-fashioned, reactionary nationalist agendas.

Nor is "counterhegemonic globalization" a label that applies to the whole of the "global justice movement." Some groups with goals grounded in a vision of equity, human dignity, and a sustainable relation to the environment may reject the possibility of a progressive version of globalization. Instead of counterhegemonic globalization, these groups would reverse the effects of generic globalization and somehow retrieve a world in which power and values could be defined on a purely local basis.

Yet, ironically, even the celebration of local power and culture cannot escape the necessity of constructing some form of "counterhegemonic globalization." Even those most committed to escaping the domination of modern universalisms often end up using global networks and global ideologies. Universal citizenship rights are invoked to protect headscarves (Soysal, 1994). Transnational networks are mobilized to preserve local feastdays (Levitt, 2001). The Internet played a key role in the Zapatista's defense of their local autonomy (Schulz, 1998).

The reverse is also true. Just as the defense of difference and quests for local power

[2] This is not to say that my use of the term "counterhegemonic" should be taken to imply a commitment to complete dismantling of the current global market system. Although one can imagine that successful pursuit of the changes these movements espouse might ultimately lead to a "revolutionary" break, their immediate demands are for "reforms," including the recapture of earlier modes of capitalist market regulation. My use of "counterhegemonic" is, therefore, quite different from the way in which Gramsci might have used the term, which, of course, he did not (see Gramsci, 1999).

require global strategies and connections, likewise transnational social movements must have local social roots. Without the promise of redressing the grievances of ordinary people where they live, transnational social movements have no base and their capacity to challenge established power is limited. If global corporate strategies depend on creating deracinated consumers incapable of collective action, counterhegemonic strategies depend on the reverse. It is, therefore, hardly surprising that participants in transnational campaigns are often what Tarrow (2003) calls "rooted cosmopolitans" – people whose activism begins with ties to local communities and is driven by the desire to improve the lot of members of those communities. A constant dialectic between strategies that speak to local roots and strategies that leverage global connections is fundamental to counterhegemonic globalization.

The most powerful and challenging form of the local–global dialectic are the North–South divisions that have been inscribed in the structure of the global political economy for 500 years and exacerbated by contemporary neoliberal globalization. This divide is built into global structures of power, both public and private, economic and cultural. If transnational social movements cannot find a way to transcend it, their political effectiveness will be fatally compromised.

There are then some minimal caveats for any useful analysis of the transnational social movements that are involved in counterhegemonic globalization. It must be about local political motivations and social structural foundations as much as it is about transnational strategies, structures, and actions. It must recognize that local conditions of life are fundamentally different depending on where they are located in our abysmally divided world. Most important, the desire to discover potent new agents for social change must be balanced with dispassionate skepticism.

Exaggerating the transformative power of those groups whose efforts to build antisystemic global networks do appear grounded in a vision of equity and dignity is as bad a mistake as pretending that the antiglobalization movement is innocent of sinister and reactionary projects. It would be a disservice to the transnational movements themselves, as well as to ordinary citizens looking for relief from the disappointments of neoliberal globalization, to exaggerate their power. Sometimes "soft power" (Sikkink, 2002) can indeed successfully confront "hard" domination, but the current hegemony of corporate globalizers is supported by a full array of cultural and ideological machinery as well as a very solid set of coercive instruments. It will not be easily dislodged by even the most creative and well-organized transnational social movements. To have real effects, transnational movements must first be able to generate powerful cascades of normative change and then use this ideological advantage to transform the hard structures of established political and economic (and ultimately military) power. It is a tall order.

Even after we fully accept their flaws and limitations, the proliferation of transnational social movements with an agenda of counterhegemonic globalization is still one of the substantively exciting and theoretically provocative topics in contemporary political sociology. Whether or not the current global justice movement is capable of making "another world" possible, analyzing its nature and implications, in both practical and theoretical terms, must be part of the core agenda of contemporary political sociology.

THE NEW ORGANIZATIONAL FOUNDATIONS OF COUNTERHEGEMONIC GLOBALIZATION

Here I will focus on three broad families of transnational social movements aimed at counterhegemonic globalization: labor movements, women's movements, and environmental movements. Each of these movements confronts the dilemmas of using transnational networks to magnify the power of local movements without redefining local interests, of transcending the North–South divide, and of leveraging existing structures of global power without becoming complicit in them. Looking at the three movements together is useful because it highlights the ways in which surmounting these challenges might produce common strategies and possibilities for alliances among them.

Before embarking on an analysis of these three families of movements, however, I will briefly focus on two prominent organizations that are plausible would-be agents of "counterhegemonic globalization" – ATTAC and the World Social Forum (WSF). If Seattle and the subsequent demonstrations that have plagued the WTO, IMF, G-7, and World Economic Forum are the favorite media images of "antiglobalization," ATTAC and the WSF are paragons of organizations explicitly designed to build omnibus transnational networks aimed at transforming neoliberal globalization into a social protection-oriented, market-subordinating, difference-respecting mirror image.

Looking at these groups underlines the organizationally novel forms whose emergence has been stimulated by neoliberal globalization. At the same time, it highlights the degree to which counterhegemonic globalization draws on long-established social movements and ideological "tropes." In both respects it provides the ideal backdrop for analyzing the way in which the labor movement, transnational women's movements, and the global environmental movement provide both an interwoven infrastructure for reshaping globalization and a challenge to the existing political sociology literature.

No examination of counterhegemonic globalization can avoid examining ATTAC. Perhaps more than any other single organization it embodies the proposition that agency in the face of the purported power of neoliberal globalization requires only ideological and organizational imagination. Yet, ATTAC is a curious and, on the surface, very unlikely organization to fill this role. Its name – "Association pour la Taxation des Transactions Financières pour l'Aide aux Citoyens" (Association for the Taxation of Financial Transaction for the Aid of Citizens) – suggests an organization doomed to obscurity. Even worse, the name does indeed reflect ATTAC's initial focus on support for the Tobin tax (itself a relatively arcane idea embedded in the mechanics of neoliberal globalization). Its homeland – France – an archetypically "antiglobalization" political milieu, characterized much more by chauvinism than global solidarity, makes it even an even more unlikely candidate to be a paradigmatic promoter of "counterhegemonic" globalization. If ATTAC's origins make it a very peculiar candidate to typify organizations aimed at "counterhegemonic globalization," its success at spawning a network of politically active sister organizations around the world is undeniable (cf. http://attac.org/indexen/index.html). Hence a quick look at ATTAC is one way of illuminating the ideology and strategies of counterhegemonic globalization.

The best analysis of ATTAC is provided by Ancelovici (2002). In Ancelovici's view, ATTAC's ideology is essentially one of "associational statism," which essentially entails two strategies of trying to reassert the primacy of political/social decision making in the face of the growing dominance of global markets. On the one hand it has a very traditional (French) affection for the regulatory power of the nation-state. At the same time it rejects bureaucratic/representational/party control of public/political decision making in favor of locally based participatory structures.

In short, analysis of ATTAC suggests that the political foundations of "counterhegemonic globalization" involve a combination of Ruggie's (1982) "embedded liberalism" (with its emphasis on social protections rooted in the structures of the nation-state) and "New Left" forms of participatory democracy. The World Social Forum – one of the most important organizational forms of South-based "counterhegemonic globalization" – confirms this perspective.

It is only a partial caricature to propose that the origins of the World Social Forum, which now arguably represents the largest single agglomeration of South-based organizations and activists, began as a sort of joint venture between ATTAC and the Brazilian Workers Party (Partido dos Trabalhadores or PT). Because the founding vision of the PT's organizers was of a classic Marxist socialist mobilizational party, the party's involvement in the World Social Forum is further confirmation of the extent to which "counterhegemonic globalization" has its roots in both quotidian struggles for dignity and economic security in the workplace and classic agendas of social protection (*à la* Polanyi, [1944] 2001) in which the machinery of the nation-state is heavily implicated (see McMichael, 2000:chap. 29).

Even unsystematic participant observation of the meetings of the World Social Forum in Porto Alegre, Brazil confirms this hypothesis. The fact that the Workers Party controls the municipal administration of a major city and has (until the 2002 elections) controlled the state government as well has been essential to enabling the infrastructural investments that make a global meeting of thousands of participants and hundreds of oppositional groups from around the globe possible. At the same time, in part because of Workers Party sponsorship, both local and transnational trade unions play a major role in the WSF.

All of this suggests that counterhegemonic globalization is not as "postmodern" as its adherents (and detractors) sometimes argue. To the contrary, rescuing traditional social democratic agendas of social protection, which are otherwise in danger of disappearing below the tide of neoliberal globalization, is a significant part of the agenda of both ATTAC and the World Social Forum. At the same time, it would be a mistake to dismiss counterhegemonic globalization as simply "old wine in new bottles." The gamut of variegated transnational social movements that must be dealt with in any account of counterhegemonic globalization includes movements with organizational forms and ideological propositions that are novel and refreshing in relation to the old agents of "embedded liberalism" (indeed ATTAC and the World Social Forum are among them).

This blend of novelty and persistence is one of the most interesting features of counterhegemonic globalization, whether one is most concerned with a substantive analysis of the movement or with its implications for existing theoretical frameworks and conceptualizations. And, if one is interested in the blend of novelty and persistence, there is no better place to start in analyzing "counterhegemonic globalization" than with the transformation of the international labor movement.

LABOR AS A GLOBAL SOCIAL MOVEMENT[3]

Having been tagged by nineteenth-century socialists as the preeminent agent of progressive social change, the labor movement was abandoned by most social movement theorists of the mid-twentieth century as primarily concerned with defending the privileges of a Northern aristocracy of labor in the face of challenges from the South and hopelessly sclerotic in any case. Now the tide seems to be turning again. Recent analysis of the U.S. labor movement has begun to argue for renewed appreciation of the potential importance of labor as a progressive actor (e.g., Clawson, 2003; Fantasia and Voss, 2004).

Curiously, the literature on transnational social movements still seems to reflect earlier disenchantment. With few exceptions (e.g., Kidder in Khagram et al., 2002), the case of labor has not been well-integrated into this literature. A typical collection on transnational social movements focusing on European cases (della Porta, Kriesi, and Rucht, 1999) offered individual chapters on the campaign against international trade in toxic wastes, farmers protest movements, abortion rights movements, and indigenous peoples movements, but only two quick references to labor: one noting that "the labor movement seems to be particularly disadvantaged by the developing European institutions" (19) and the other asserting that "European labour unions are not taking advantage of the possibilities for contentious politics at the European level" (118).

Why has labor not been seen as a promising candidate for becoming a transnational social movement? Conventional ways of framing labor's relation to the global political economy are central to the answer. The current framing of the transnational politics of labor is dominated by what I would call a "geography of jobs" perspective. In this perspective, "Workers of the World Compete!" replaces

[3] This section draws heavily on Anner and Evans, 2004.

admonitions for transnational solidarity in the neoliberal mantra. Even those hostile to neoliberalism tend to assume that geographic competition for jobs precludes possibilities for transnational solidarity (cf. Rodrik, 1997). In the "geography of jobs" frame, preventing the movement of jobs to the global South becomes the prime aim of workers in the North, erasing possibilities for North–South solidarity.

The "geography of jobs" perspective does capture one important facet of reality. The increasing ease with which capitalists move high-productivity technologies around the globe does intensify the potential for cross-border competition among workers (cf. Shaiken, 1994). Nonetheless, as Miller (2003) points out, the "geography of jobs" perspective is flawed even within an economic framework. Once political and ideological dynamics are included, a creative reframing of labor struggles at the global level, similar to the one that analysts like Ganz (2000) and Voss and Sherman (2000) have described at the national level, becomes an intriguing possibility.

I will analyze the possibilities for transnational labor solidarity by looking at three ways of framing contestation: "basic rights," "social contract," and "democratic governance." All three share one fundamental characteristic. They employ what I have called elsewhere (Evans, 2000) "political jujitsu," exploiting ideological propositions universally acknowledged as basic to the hegemonic ideology of contemporary global neoliberalism and utilizing transnational organizational structures that neoliberal globalization has helped create (cf. Risse-Kappen, Ropp, and Sikkink, 1999; Risse-Kappen, 2000; Smith and Johnson, 2002).

Global corporate networks built around labor-intensive, "sweatshop" manufacturing in the South and brand-name marketing in the North create political opportunities along with profits. Imbuing their brands with cultural value is vastly more important to the profitability of the overall corporation than production costs attributable to manufacturing labor. At the same time, the normative and ideological hegemony of "basic human rights" makes it almost impossible for a brand to retain its value once potential customers become convinced that basic human rights are being violated in the production of the goods that bear its name. The trick, of course, is building the mobilizational structures required to take advantage of such political opportunity (see Fung et al., 2001).

Looking at paradigmatic cases like the now famous Kukdong case (Anner and Evans, 2004) illustrates the point. The original revolt of the Kukdong workers was the product of the usual miserable local working conditions combined with unusual local courage and combativeness. Sustaining the struggle depended on an intricate transnational network that included local and U.S. NGOs as well as U.S. unions. Each organization in the network brought different but complementary capacities to bear, creating a robust and powerful braid of alliances. For example, USAS (United Students Against Sweatshops), which fits the Keck and Sikkink model of an organization whose leadership and members are driven primarily by "principled ideas or values," was able to provide campus mobilization and publicity (see Featherstone, 2002). Workers' Rights Consortium (WRC), a "monitoring" NGO also a product of the antisweatshop movement, was able to credibly invoke the technocratic standards of "objective" investigation.

Most interesting in terms of undercutting the "geography of jobs" perspective is the role of North American trade unions in the network. The AFL-CIO's Solidarity Center provided key expertise and international connections. UNITE, which organizes textile and apparel workers in the United States, was also deeply involved. Why were North American trade unionists involved? Certainly not because UNITE was hoping to bring the Kukdong jobs back to the United States. Many of the individual trade union activists within these organizations were, of course, driven by the same sort of "principled ideas or values" that motivated NGO activists. More important, North American unions saw Kukdong workers as key allies in their own domestic struggles to delegitimate corporate adversaries by exposing them as violators of basic human rights, and generating the kind of political advantage that is critical to the success of the strategic campaigns that are the focus of contemporary labor contestation in the North.

Despite their importance, the industries in which effective transnational alliances are built around basic rights framings are a limited set. For labor to become a global social movement, a broader range of industries and workers must be involved. The idea of "social contract" provides one basis for expanding organizational range.

Emblematic of the post-World War II "golden age of capitalism" was the hegemony of the idea that relations between employers and employees were more than a simple exchange of labor for wages. The employment relation came to be seen as embodying a social contract, one in which competent, loyal employees could expect to be rewarded from the firm over the long term. Employees also came to expect auxiliary benefits that were less tightly tied to job performance – primarily retirement, disability, and health benefits, provided in combination by employers and the state.

Emblematic of the contemporary global neoliberal regime is the effort to reconstruct employment as something closer to a spot market in which labor is bought and sold with only the most minimal expectations regarding a broader employment relationship. Around the globe – from Mumbai to Johannesburg, Shanghai to the Silicon Valley – jobs are being informalized, outsourced, and generally divorced from anything that might be considered a social contract between employer and employee.

Precisely because the attack on the idea of labor as a social contract is generalized across all regions of the world, it creates a powerful basis for generating global labor solidarity. I illustrate the point with two examples: the emerging relations of effective mutual support that join metalworkers in Brazil and Germany and the successful leveraging of transnational solidarity by the International Brotherhood of Teamsters (IBT) in the 1997 UPS strike. In addition to demonstrating again that the "geography of jobs" perspective cannot explain transnational relations among labor movements, these cases also further illustrate how the corporate structures that form the carapace of the global economy contain political opportunities as well as threats.

The long-term collaboration between IG Metal in Germany and the Brazilian Metalworkers affiliated with CUT (Central Unica dos Trabalhadores) provides a good example. In 2001, when IG Metal was starting its spring offensive in Germany, the members of the Brazilian Metalworkers union (CUT) working for Daimler–Chrysler sent their German counterparts a note affirming that they would not accept any increased work designed to replace lost production in Germany. This action grows out of a long-term alliance between the two unions that exploits transnational corporate organizational structures for counterhegemonic purposes and has proven to be of practical value to the Brazilian autoworkers in their struggle to maintain some semblance of a social contract in their employment relations. For example, in the previous year when workers at Volkswagen's biggest factory in Brazil went on strike trying to reverse job cuts, Luiz Marinho, president of CUT VW, was able to go to VW's world headquarters and negotiate directly with management there, bypassing the management of the Brazilian subsidiary, and producing an agreement that restored the jobs.

The successful 1997 UPS strike offers a North–North example of how transnational alliances can be built around the idea of social contract. One element in the victory was a very effective global strategy, one that took advantage of previously underexploited strengths in their own global organization – the International Transport Workers Federation (ITF) (Banks and Russo, 1999). Through the ITF, a World Council of UPS unions was created – which decided to mount a "World Action Day" in 150 job actions or demonstrations around the world. A number of European unions took action in support of the U.S. strikers (Banks and Russo, 1999:550).

Why were the Europeans so willing to take risks for the sake of solidarity with the IBT in the United States? The answer was summarized in one of the ITF's leaflets, "UPS: importing misery from America." UPS was seen as representing the intrusion of the "American Model" of aggressive antiunion behavior, coupled with the expansion of part-time and temporary jobs with low pay and benefits and the use of subcontracting (Banks and Russo, 1999:561). The Europeans also knew that they had a much better chance of reining in UPS operating in concert with the 185,000 unionized UPS workers in the United States than they would ever have alone. Solidarity made sense and the logic of competition based on the geography of jobs made no sense.

Although defending the idea of the employment relation as a social contract is a project that will draw broad sympathy, the actual organizational efforts remain largely internal to organized labor. Other global social movements may be ideologically supportive, but not likely to be mobilized. Given the fact that those who enjoy the privilege of a formal employment relationship with union representation is a shrinking minority of the global population, the success of labor as a global social movement depends on being able to complement "social contract" and "basic rights" campaigns with other strategies that have the potential of generating broad alliances with a range of other social movements. Contestation framed in terms of "democratic governance" offers just such an opportunity.

The hegemony of "democracy" as the only acceptable form of governance is as pervasive a part of contemporary neoliberal ideology as "basic human rights." However substantively undemocratic the operation of the global neoliberal regime may be in practice, invocations of the principle of democratic governance are politically powerful. Global governance institutions, whether in the form of organizations like the WTO or in the form of international agreements like the FTAA (Free Trade Area of the Americas), are politically vulnerable targets precisely because their procedures so often contradict neoliberalism's supposed commitment to democratic governance.

The FTAA is a good case in point (Barenberg and Evans, 2004). In its fight to restructure the FTAA, the labor movement has been able to move beyond a "geography of jobs" perspective to one that focuses on range of social issues, democratic governance prominent among them.[4] The organizational reflection of this politics is the Alianza Social Continental/Hemispheric Social Alliance (ASC/HSA), a coalition of national umbrella organizations each of which represents a coalition of NGOs or labor organizations. Headquartered first in Mexico and then in Brazil, the ASC/HSA brings women's groups and environmental groups together with ORIT (Organización Regional Interamericana de Trabajadores – the hemispheric trade union organization to which the AFL-CIO and most other major national trade union confederations belong).

The ACS/HSA is only one of the possible mobilizational structures that might be created to democratize the creation of the hemisphere's new "economic constitution" (which is what the FTAA is in reality), but it is an excellent illustration of labor's potential to become not just a global social movement, but a leading element in the broadest possible coalition of social movements. To understand the possibilities and challenges of connecting the labor movement with other transnational movements, there is no better place to start than with global feminism.

Building a Feminist Movement Without Borders

While the transnational women's movement also has a long history, global neoliberalism has brought issues of gender to the forefront of transnational social movement organizations in a dramatic way. Until there has been a revolutionary transformation of gender roles, the disadvantages of allocating resources purely on the basis of market logic will fall particularly harshly on women. The UNDP talks of a global "care deficit," pointing out that women spend most of their working hours on unpaid care work and adding that "the market gives almost no rewards for care" (1999:80). Others have pointed out the extent to which "structural adjustment" and other neoliberal strategies for global governance

[4] For an analysis of an earlier evolution away from the geography of jobs perspective in the case of NAFTA, see Armruster, 1995, 1998; Kay, forthcoming.

contain a built-in, systematic gender bias (e.g., Cornia, Jolly, and Stewart, 1987; Elson, 1991; Afshar and Dennis, 1992; Staudt, 1997). Consequently, it is almost impossible to imagine a movement for counterhegemonic globalization in which a transnational women's movement did not play a leading role.

At first glance, women's organizations have an advantage over transnational labor movements in that they do not have to transcend a zero-sum logic equivalent to that of the "geography of jobs" which would put the gendered interests of women in one region in conflict with those in another region. Perhaps for that reason, the transnational women's movement has been in the vanguard of transnational social movements in the attention that it has devoted to struggles over how to bridge the cultural and political aspects of the North–South divide and how to avoid the potential dangers of difference-erasing universalist agendas.

Like the labor movement, the women's movement's ideological foundations are rooted in a discourse of "human rights" (cf. Keck and Sikkink, 1998; Meyer, 2001), but transnational feminism, much more than in the labor movement, has wrestled with the contradictions of building politics around the universalistic language of rights. Although no one can ignore the ways in which demanding recognition that "women's rights are human rights" has helped empower oppressed and abused women across an incredible gamut of geographic, cultural, and class locations, any earlier naïve assumptions that there was a single "one size fits all" global feminist agenda have been replaced by appreciation that the goal is much more complex (see Basu and MGrory, 1995; Alvarez, 1998, 1999; Barlow, 2000; Bergeron, 2001; Naples and Desai, 2002; Vuola, 2002).

On the one hand, the adoption of CEDAW (Convention on the Elimination of All Forms of Discrimination Against Women) by the UN might be considered the normative equivalent of the environmental movement's victories in the Montreal Accord to limit CFCs and the Kyoto Accord on global warming. On the other hand, critical feminists have examined UN activities like the 1995 Beijing World Conference on Women and accused them of perpetuating colonialist power relations under the guise of transnational unity (Spivak, 1996). Mohanty (2003:226) summarizes the conundrum nicely: "The challenge is to see how differences allow us to explain the connections and border crossings better and more accurately, how specifying difference allows us to theorize universal concerns more fully."

One of the consequences of this debate is to force Northern-based women's organizations to develop a much more sophisticated perspective on development of "collective action frames" than the treatment normally found in the social movements literature. They have been forced to reflect on the ways in which supposedly universal agendas can become ideological impositions that erase the specific interests of less-privileged participants in the movement. This awareness has, in turn, had the effect of strengthening the hand of local organizers in the South in their bargaining for greater autonomy and fuller recognition of their locally defined interests and agendas.

Millie Thayer (2000, 2001, 2002) provides one of the most vivid and nuanced analyses of the debate "on the ground" within the transnational women's movement. In her study of the relations between transnational feminist NGOs and local women's groups based in the backlands of rural Northeast Brazil, Thayer (2001) shows, first of all, that "global scripts," in this case an article by Joan Scott on the concept of gender, can in fact "make sense" to local women embedded in families and involved in class as well as gender struggles. Because the concept of gender made sense for these women, and because of their creative ability to transform and reinterpret the concept to fit local circumstances, it helped them to advance their local struggles.

Thayer's work also illustrates how the goals and ideologies of the transnational women's movement (including their awareness of the possibilities of "colonialist attitudes") limit the dominance of Northern NGOs, despite the enormous differences in resources between the local Brazilian group and its Northern allies. Access to the resources that are channeled through transnational networks does depend on the ability of locals to conform to more standardized administrative procedures that transnational support networks can understand and evaluate (Thayer, 2002). At the same time, Thayer's analysis also makes it clear that the ideology and goals of Northern-based transnational NGOs give local social movement organizations important political advantages in internal negotiations. Northern-based transnational NGOs not only know that their legitimacy in the eyes of funders and Northern supporters rests on their ability to transform the lives of local groups in the South for the better. They themselves see service to these groups as their goal. Consequently, when a legitimate local group questions whether their local interests and goals are being met, the question cannot simply be dismissed or suppressed. The "soft power" of norms and values is even more important within transnational movements than it is in their relations to dominant global structures, and this works to the advantage of the South.

If its explicit and persistent confrontation of dangers posed by the North–South divide within the movement makes the women's movement an exemplar for other transnational social movements, its potential influence in the transformation of other movements is equally important. The potential impact of closer alliance between the women's movement and the labor movement offers a good example. Patriarchal organizational forms and leadership styles continue to divide the labor movement from the women's movement (cf., for example, Bandy and Bickham-Mendez, 2003), but the survival of the labor movement globally clearly depends on its ability to become more feminist. Women are not just important to the labor movement because both genders are now thoroughly incorporated into the labor market: they are also important because they occupy the positions in the global labor force that are most crucial to labor's organizational expansion.

The numerically predominant situation of women in the global economy is one of precarious participation in the "informal economy" – a vast arena in which the traditional organizational tools of the transnational labor movement are least likely to be effective. Women in the informal sector experience the insecurity and lack of "social contract" that appear to be the neoliberal destiny of all but a small minority of the workforce, regardless of gender. If members of established transnational unions like the metalworkers are to succeed in building general political support for defending the "social contract" aspects of their employment relation, their struggles must be combined with an equally aggressive effort to expand the idea of the social contract into the informal sector. Insofar as the women's movement's campaigns around livelihood issues have focused particularly on the informal sector, it might be considered the vanguard of the labor movement as well as a leading strand in the movement for counterhegemonic globalization more generally.

One response to the challenge of the informal sector has been the diffusion of the "Self-employed Women's Association" (SEWA) as an organizational form, starting in India and spreading to South Africa, Turkey, and other countries in Latin America, Southeast Asia, and Africa, and eventually creating incipient international networks such as "Homenet" and "Streetnet" (Mitter, 1994). This is not only a novel form of labor organization. Because the archetypal site of informal sector employment is among the least-privileged women of the global South, it is simultaneously an organizational form that should help build the kind of "feminism without borders" that Mohanty (2003) argues is necessary to transcend the contradictions that have divided the international women's movement in the past.

Global and Local Environmentalism

In the last decades of the twentieth century, organizations that focused on environmental issues were the most rapidly expanding form of transnational NGO (Sikkink and Smith, 2002:30). Starting as an almost nonexistent category in the 1950s, by the 1990s they had become the most prevalent form of transnational NGO outside of human rights groups. A case can be made that the global environmental movement has also been the most effective of any set of transnational social movements at changing both the global discursive and regulatory environment. In short, the global environmental movement offers one of the best examples of "counterhegemonic globalization" available. By the same token, the arena of environmental politics becomes one of the best sites for measuring the limits of counterhegemonic globalization.

Environmental stewardship is almost by definition a collective issue and therefore an issue that should lend itself to collective mobilization. Even neoclassical economic theory recognizes that environmental degradation is an externality that markets may not resolve, especially if the externalities are split across national political jurisdictions. Thus, environmental movements have advantages, both relative to mobilization around labor issues, which neoliberal ideology strongly claims must be resolved through market logic if welfare is to be maximized, and relative to women's movements, which are still bedeviled by claims that these issues are "private" and therefore not a appropriate target for collective political action (especially not collective political action that spills across national boundaries).

The obstacles to trying to build a global environmental movement are equally obvious. To begin with, there is the formidable gap that separates the South's "environmentalism of the poor," in which sustainability means above all else sustaining the ability of resource-dependent local communities to extract livelihoods from their natural surroundings, and the "conservationist" agenda of traditional Northern environmental groups, which favors the preservation of fauna and flora without much regard for how this conservation impacts the livelihoods of surrounding communities (Friedmann and Rangan, 1993; Guha and Martínez-Alier, 1997; Martínez-Alier, 2002). The North–South divide in the global environmental movement may be less susceptible to being portrayed as "zero-sum" than in the "geography of jobs" perspective on the labor movement, but the logic of division appears more difficult to surmount than in the case of transnational feminism.

Even aside from the difficulties of superseding North–South divisions, integrating local and global concerns appears more daunting in the environmental arena. Some issues – such as global warming and the ozone layer – seem intrinsically global, whereas the politics of others, such as the health consequences of toxic dumps, can be intensely local. The challenges of building a global organization that effectively integrates locally focused activities with global campaigns would seem particularly challenging in the case of the environmental movement.

Despite the structural challenges it faces, the global environmental movement is usually considered among the most successful of the transnational social movements. How do we explain the relative success of transnational movements with environmental agendas? The first point to be made is how strikingly parallel the political assets of the global environmental movement are to those of the labor and women's movements, despite the obvious differences among them. This is true both of ideological resources and institutional ones. Once again, we see a counterhegemonic movement leveraging the ideas and organizational structures implanted by hegemonic globalization.

As in the case of the labor and women's movements, political clout depends on the global diffusion of a universalistic ideology affirming the value of the movement's agenda. As the labor and women's movements are able to leverage the ideological power of abstract concepts like "human rights" and "democracy," environmentalists can claim an impeccable universal agenda of "saving the planet" and invoke "scientific analysis" as validating their positions. As in the other two cases, these ideological resources are worth little without organizational structures that can exploit them and without complementary mobilization around quotidian interests. Nonetheless, the point is that once again, hegemonic ideological propositions are not simply instruments of domination; they are also a "toolkit" that can be used in potentially powerful ways for "subversive" ends.

The possibility of using governance structures that are part of hegemonic globalization also applies in the case of the environmental movement. Even more than in the case of the women's movement, the UN system has proved an extremely valuable institutional resource. As in the case of the women's movement, global conferences organized by the UN have played a crucial role both in helping to solidify transnational networks and to promote and diffuse discursive positions. Pulver's (2003) research on climate change negotiations provides one of the most sophisticated analyses of how the institutional resources provided by the UN system can be leveraged by transnational environmental movements (see also Lipschutz and Mayer, 1996; Betsill and Corell, 2001; Caniglia, 2000).

In Pulver's view, the UN climate policy process, including the 1992 Framework Convention on Climate Change (FCCC) and the annual Conferences of the Parties (COPs) organized to review and assess the implementation of the FCCC, provides an institutional arena that works to the advantage of transnational environmental NGOs in three ways, even though the negotiations are formally between national delegations. First, negotiations take place in an atmosphere of "public-ness" – not only in the sense that proceedings are for the most part open to public scrutiny but also in the sense that positions must be justified in terms of the "public good" rather than simply presented as reflecting particular interests which must be taken into account because of their proponents' power. This kind of discursive context lends itself naturally to arguments about stewardship and the promotion of sustainability while it is much more awkward to introduce corporate concerns with managerial prerogatives and profitability.

Second, and equally important according to Pulver, the "public" actors who manage the process on behalf of the UN system tend to be drawn from "epistemic communities" (Haas, 1992) in which "science" and "stewardship" are valued. (Indeed, even the national delegations that end up at the COPs are more likely to be sympathetic to these values.) Third, both prevailing ideology and the preferences of meeting managers give environmental NGO representatives a degree of influence on the negotiations between national delegations that rivals or surpasses that of business and industry representatives. In this case at least, global governance institutions have given transnational social movements an opportunity to shape an emerging regulatory regime, which has the potential to substantially modify the market logic of neoliberal globalization.

One might argue that climate change is a special case, that because climate change is an intrinsically global issue, it was possible to mount a global campaign without strong local foundations that transcend the North–South divide. This may be correct. Nonetheless, other examples suggest that transnational environmental networks can still make effective use of global governance institutions, even when local foundations and North–South solidarity are crucial.

Chico Mendes and his Amazonian rubber tappers, as chronicled by Keck (1995, 1998) and Keck and Sikkink (1998), are the classic case. Transnational environmental NGOs interested in preserving Amazonian forests and an organized local peasantry desperate to preserve their extractive livelihoods in the face of the depredations of local ranchers were able to jointly use the transnational connections that linked the Brazilian government, the World Bank, and parochial but powerful U.S. politicians to generate leverage that neither the transnational NGOs nor the rubber tappers could have dreamed of separately. Despite Mendes's assassination, the fruits of his fight were institutionalized in important ways in the subsequently environmentalist Workers' Party Government in Mendes's home state of Acre (Evans, 2000).

Such successes depend on combinations of circumstance that are still unusual (as Keck and Sikkink's [1998] comparison of Acre and Sawarak illustrates). Nonetheless, they are not aberrations. The worldwide movement to limit the development of large dams also brings local communities with immediate quotidian livelihood interests at stake (saving their homes from inundation) together with transnational environmental NGO networks. As in the rubber tapper case, the political vulnerability of the World Bank has made it possible to use the machinery of global governance for counterhegemonic purposes and both ideology and practice at the global level have been shifted (see Khagram, 2004).

Closer alliance with the women's movement could help bridge the global–local divide. The issues of urban "livability" that are becoming increasingly central environmental issues in the South are gendered in their impact. As in the case of the gendered impact of structural adjustment programs, the fact that women shoulder a disproportionate share of the responsibilities for caring for children and families forces them to bear the brunt of bad urban sanitation, precarious water supplies, and pollution-related disease. To the extent that prominent transnational environmental organizations like Greenpeace, Environmental Defense, or the WWF were willing to focus more attention on such issues, it would help bridge both North–South and global–local divides.

Unless such opportunities are seized, the transnational environmental movement could move in a direction that will undercut its potential contribution to counterhegemonic globalization. The intensive, widespread, decades-old debate over how to make sure that the women's movement fully reflects the perspectives and interests of its largest constituency (disprivileged women in the global South) rather than its most powerful members (elite women in the global North) appears to have a harder time getting traction in the transnational environmental movement.

The fact that the "scientific analysis" paradigm provides significant advantage to environmentalists in battles against degradation by corporate (and state) polluters may become a disadvantage when it comes to engaging in internal debates over competing visions within the transnational environmental movement, making it easier for Northern activists to assume that the solutions to environmental issues in the South can be "objectively" defined from afar rather than having to emerge out of debate and discussion with those immediately involved (cf. Li, 2000; York, 2002). None of this is to suggest that the environmental movement is doomed to go astray or end up fragmented. The point is that just as there is no "natural logic" that dictates the inevitability of a corporate neoliberal trajectory for globalization, even the most successful counterhegemonic movements have no functionalist guardian angels that will prevent them from undercutting their own potential.

The Potential and Pitfalls of Counterhegemonic Globalization

I have focused here on positive examples, first in the form of the general organizational advances represented by ATTAC and the World Social Forum and then in the form of successes drawn from the transnational labor, womens', and environmental movments. Efforts at counterhegemonic globalization do help shift the balance in local struggles in favor of the disprivileged. From apparel workers, to poor rural women, to rubber tappers, there are numerous examples of how creating transnational connections can put new power into the hands of groups that face insurmountable odds at the local level. Counterhegemonic globalization has also made some headway with respect to global regulatory regimes. Nonetheless, any progress at the level of the global regulatory regime in what are defined as "noneconomic" areas has been more than counterbalanced by the deepening institutionalization of neoliberal rules with regard to trade, investment, and property.

If discounting the potential of counterhegemonic globalization would be a serious analytic error, exaggerating its potential or discount the pitfalls that lie in wait for these movements as they develop would be, as I underlined in the beginning of this chapter, an equally serious error. Now, with a better sense of the organizational and ideological structure of counterhegemonic globalization, it is time to revisit the issue of limitations and pitfalls.

The most basic limitation is that none of the successes discussed here offers a direct prospect of shifting the basic trajectory of current struggles over the shape of global trade and property rule. As the September 2003 WTO ministerial in Cancan indicated, putting sand in the gears of the neoliberal global project depends on new creating political alliances that involve states as well as social movements. Future battles of this type over everything from the FTAA to the completion of the Doha

Round will be crucial to any future possibility for building counterhegemonic globalization. Transnational social movements, even in alliance with each other, cannot reshape these negotiations without collective action on the part of national delegations from the global South. Constructing a globally inclusive version of "embedded liberalism" (Ruggie, 1982) – a reasonable minimal measure for the success of counterhegemonic globalization – is an even more distant goal. Ruggie's (1994:525) assessment that "[c]onstructing a contemporary analog to the embedded liberalism compromise will be a Herculean task" has not been substantially changed by the more recent successes of transnational social movements.

Current limitations should not, however, be discouraging in themselves. The politics of counterhegemonic globalization are a politics of institution building and alliance formation, ideological innovation and reframing, of the accretive accumulation of "soft power," leading, if successful, to "normative cascades" and real shifts in the balance of power. If a long succession of small victories (inevitably intermingled with defeats) leads eventually to major transformation, the process will only make sense to skeptics well after the fact, much as the abolition of slavery and women's suffrage seem plausible (perhaps even "inevitable") after the fact (cf. Keck and Sikkink, 1998).

Pitfalls are a more immediate concern than apparent limitations. The kind of creative reframing that has allowed the labor movement to shift from preoccupation with the geography of jobs to a focus on fighting for basic rights, the social contract, and democratic governance is always vulnerable to being overwhelmed by immediate defensive concerns. Transnational environmental organizations are always in danger of slipping back into a traditional conservation/preservation perspective that leaves little space for building bridges to the resource-dependent poor of the global South. Despite its continual efforts at self-reflection, steering a course between false universalism and unreflective particularism continues to challenge the transnational women's movement. In all three cases, finding ways to embody unifying framings in concrete organizational alliances is an even tougher challenge. Unless they can avoid the pitfalls that lie in their own organizational paths, superseding their current macropolitical limitations is a utopian dream.

Realistic awareness of limitations and pitfalls must be balanced against the basic point established in the initial rendition of optimistic examples. Global neoliberalism is not just a structure of domination; it is also a set of ideological and organizational structures vulnerable to being leveraged by oppositional movements. Global neoliberalism's aggressive efforts to spread the dominion of market logic make it easier for diverse movements to mount a common program. As the gap between the formal hegemony of global neoliberalism's ideological program and its substantive manifestations grows more stark – most obviously in the case of "democracy" – shared opportunities for leveraging these ideological presuppositions increase.

Ideologically neoliberal globalization generates a transnational ideological toolkit that counterhegemonic movements can draw on in parallel ways from a variety of different social locations. Structurally, global neoliberalism helps promote possibilities for alliance by different groups situated in divergent national contexts in similarly disadvantaged positions. Organizationally, contemporary transnational opportunities reinforce the point, made by Tilly (e.g., 1991, 1995) and Tarrow (1998) among others at the national level, that just as oppositional movements can turn dominant ideological repertoires to their advantage, they can also take advantage of existing governance structures. In some cases, such as the environmental and women's movements' leveraging of the UN system to help build transnational links and gain access to public space, the possibilities are obvious. In other cases, such as the use of the World Bank by the rubber tappers or the leveraging of corporate structures via brand names and basic rights, they are only obvious after the fact.

Acknowledging the potential for use of dominant governance structures brings us back to the cases with which we began – ATTAC and the World Social Forum. Leveraging dominant structures will work only when there are comparable oppositional organizations and networks available to do the leveraging. Ultimately, the scope of these mobilizational structures must transcend issue-specific and group-specific organizations. "Global civil society" (Lipschutz and Mayer, 1996; Wapner, 1995) requires an organized agent of equivalent scope if it is to dislodge the highly organized system of domination that sustains global neoliberalism. A new (post)modern prince in the form of a "World Party" as advocated by Gill (2002) and Chase-Dunn and Boswell (2003) is probably too much of a leap, but trying to develop some kind of omnibus transnational form still makes sense.

The end result is likely to look more like a network than a bureaucratic tree and, by definition, will require unexpected organizational innovations. ATTAC and the World Social Forum are encouraging precisely because their unexpected organizational forms have been so successful. They have created new possibilities for concatenation among existing transnational networks as well as adding organizational innovations of their own. Novel organizational forms like these are reassurance that, whether or not the possibility of another world has been demonstrated, the potential for a more robust and politically formidable movement for counterhegemonic globalization is a social fact.

ACKNOWLEDGMENTS

I would like to acknowledge the support and patience of the editors and the invaluable comments of Michael Burawoy, Hwa-jen Liu, Simone Pulver, Sarah Staveteig, Millie Thayer, Anna Wetterberg, Jodi york, and two anonymous reviewers. The errors of omission, commission, and misconception that remain are entirely of my own making.

References

Abbott, Andrew. 1992. "From causes to events: notes on narrative positivism." *Sociological Methods & Research* 20:428–55.

Abdullah, Rashidah. 1993. "Changing population policies and women's lives in Malaysia." *Reproductive Health Matters* (1):67–77.

Abedi, Amir. 2003. *Antipolitical Establishment Parties*. London: Routledge.

Abell, Peter. 1987. *The Syntax of Social Life*. Oxford, UK: Clarendon.

______. 1993. "Some aspects of narrative method." *Journal of Mathematical Sociology* 18(2–3):91–184.

Abelson, Donald E. 2000. "Do think tanks matter? Opportunities, constraints and incentives for think tanks in Canada and the United States." *Global Society* 14:213–36.

Abelson, Donald E., and Evert A. Lindquist. 2000. "Think tanks in North America." Pp. 37–65 in J. G. McGann and R. K. Weaver (eds.), *Think Tanks and Civil Societies*. New Jersey: Transaction.

Abercrombie, N., S., Hill, and B. Turner. 1984. *The Dominant Ideology Thesis*. London: Allen & Unwin.

Abramowitz, Alan. 1991. "Incumbency, campaign spending, and the decline of competition in the U.S. House." *Journal of Politics* 53:34–57.

Abrams, Philip. 1984. *Historical Sociology*. Ithaca, NY: Cornell University Press, 1984.

Abramson, Paul R., John H. Aldrich, and David W. Rohde. 2002. *Change and Continuity in the 2000 Elections*. Washington, D.C.: CQ.

Acevedo, Luz del Alba. 1995. "Feminist inroads in the study of women's work and development." Pp. 65–98 in Christine E. Bose and Edna Acosta-Belén (eds.), *Women in the Latin American Development Process*. Philadelphia: Temple University Press.

Achcar, Gilbert. 2002. *The Clash of Barbarians. Sept. 11 and the Making of the New World Disorder*. New York: Monthly Review.

Acker, Joan. 1988. "Class, gender, and the relations of distribution." *Signs* 13:473–97.

______. 1994. "Women, families, and public policy in Sweden." Pp. 33–50 in E. N. Chow and C. W. Berheide (eds.), *Women, the Family, and Policy: A Global Perspective*. Albany: State University of New York Press.

Acosta-Belén, Edna, and Christine E. Bose. 1995. "Colonialism, structural subordination, and empowerment: Women in the development process in Latin America and the Caribbean." Pp. 15–36 in Christine E. Bose and Edna Acosta-Belén (eds.), *Women in the Latin American Development Process*. Philadelphia: Temple University Press.

Adams, Julia. 1994a. "The familial state: Elite family practices and state-making in the early modern Netherlands." *Theory and Society* 23:505–39.

______. 1994b. "Trading states, trading places: The role of patrimonialism in early modern Dutch development." *Comparative Studies in Society and History* 36(2):319–55.

______. 1996. "Principals and agents, colonialists and company men: the decay of colonial control in the Dutch East Indies." *American Sociological Review* 61(1):12–28.

______. 1998. "Feminist theory as fifth columnist or discursive vanguard: some contested uses of gender analysis in historical sociology." *Social Politics* 5(1):1–16.

______. 1999. "Culture in rational-choice theories of state formation." Pp. 98–122 in George Steinmetz (ed.), *State/Culture: State Formation after the Cultural Turn*. Ithaca, NY: Cornell University Press.

______. 2003. "The rule of the father: patriarchy and patrimonialism in early modern europe." Working Paper #208, Russell Sage Foundation, New York.

______. 2005. *The Familial State: Ruling Families and Merchant Capitalism in Early Modern Europe*. Ithaca, NY: Cornell University Press.

Adams, Julia, and T. Padamsee. 2001. "Signs and regimes: Rereading feminist work on welfare states." *Social Politics* 8:1–23.

Adams, Julia, Elisabeth Clemens, and Ann Shola Orloff (eds.). 2004. *Remaking Modernity: Politics, History and Sociology*. Durham, NC: Duke University Press.

Adorno, Theodor W. 1978/1938. "On the fetish character in music and the regression of listening." in Andrew Arato and Eike Gebhardt (eds.), *The Essential Frankfurt School Reader.* New York: Urizen Books.

Adorno, Theodor W., Else Frenkel-Brunswik, Daniel J. Levinson, and R. Nevitt Stanford. 1950. *The Authoritarian Personality*. New York: W. W. Norton.

Afkhami, Mahnaz. 2001. "Gender apartheid, cultural relativism, and women's human rights in Muslim societies." Pp. 234–45 in Marjorie Agosin (ed.), *Women, Gender, and Human Rights: A Global Perspective*. New Brunswick, NJ: Rutgers University Press.

Afshar, Haleh (ed.). 1998. *Women and Empowerment*. New York: Macmillan.

Afshar, Haleh, and Carolyne Dennis. 1992. *Women and Adjustment Policies in the Third World*. New York: St. Martin's.

Agger, Ben, and Tim Luke. 2002. "Politics in postmodernity: the diaspora of politics and the homelessness of political and social theory." *Research in Political Sociology* 11:159–95.

Aglietta, Michel. 1979. *A Theory of Capitalist Regulation*. London, UK: New Left Books.

Agüero, Francisco. 1992. "The armed forces, democracy and the limits to democratization in South America." Pp. 153–98 in Scott Mainwaring et al. (eds.), *Issues in Democratic Consolidation: The New South American Democracies in Comparative Perspective*. Notre Dame: University of Notre Dame Press.

Aguilar Villanueva, Luis. 1996. *La hechura de las Políticas*. Mexico DF: Porrua.

Aiken, Michael, and Paul E. Mott (eds.). 1970. *The Structure of Community Power*. New York: Random.

Ajami, Fouad. 1992. *The Arab Predicament: Arab Political Thought and Practice since 1967*. New York: Cambridge University Press.

______. 1999. *The Dream Palace of the Arabs: A Generation's Odyssey*. New York: Vintage Books.

Akard, Patrick. 1992. "Corporate mobilization and political power." *American Sociological Review* 57:597–615.

Ake, Claude. 1996. *Democracy and Development in Africa*. Washington, DC: Brookings Institute.

Alber, Jens. 1982. *Von Armenhaus zum Wohlfartsstaat*. Frankfurt: Campus Verlag.

Albertini, Rudolf von. 1971. *Decolonization: The Administration and Future of the Colonies, 1919–1969*. Garden City, NY: Doubleday.

Albritton, R. B. 1979. "Social amelioration through mass insurgency." *American Political Science Review* 73:1003–11.

Alderson, Arthur S., and François Nielsen. 2002. "Globalization and the great U-turn: Income inequality trends in 16 OECD countries." *American Journal of Sociology* 107:1244–99.

Aldrich, Howard E., and Udo Staber. 1988. "Organizing business interests: Patterns of trade association foundings, transformations, and death." Pp. 111–26 in Glenn Carroll (ed.), *Ecological Models of Organizations*. New York: Ballinger.

Aldrich, Howard E., Udo Staber, Catherine Zimmer, and John J. Beggs. 1994. "Minimalism, mutualism, and maturity: The evolution of the American Trade Association population in the twentieth century." Pp. 223–38 in Joel A. C. Baum and Jitendra V. Singh (eds.), *Evolutionary Dynamics of Organizations*. Newbury Park, CA: Sage.

Aldrich, John H. 1995. *Why Parties? The Origin and Transformation of Party Politics in America*. Chicago: University of Chicago Press.

Aleinikoff, T. Alexander & Douglas Kusmeyer (eds.). 2000. *From Migrants to Citizens: Membership in a Changing World*. Washington, DC: Carnegie Endowment for Peace.

______. 2001. *Citizenship Today: Global Perspectives and Practices*. Washington, D.C.: Carnegie Endowment for Peace.

Alexander, Herbert E. 1992. *Financing Politics*, 4th ed. Washington, D.C.: Congressional Quarterly.

Alexander, Herbert E., and Brian A. Hagerty. 1987. *Financing the 1984 Election*. Lexington, MA: Lexington Books.

Alexander, Herbert E., and Rei Shiratori. 1994. *Comparative Political Finance among the Democracies*. Boulder, CO: Westview.

Alexander, Jeffrey C. 1983. *Theoretical Logic in Sociology, Vol. Four: The Modern Reconstruction of Classical Thought: Talcott Parsons*. Berkeley: University of California Press.

______(ed.). 1985. *Neofunctionalism*. Beverly Hills, CA: Sage.

______. 1988a. "Three models of culture and society relations: towards an analysis of Watergate." Pp. 153–74 in *Action and Its Environments: Toward a New Synthesis*. New York: Columbia University Press.

______. 1988b. "Culture and political crisis: 'Watergate' and Durkheimian sociology." Pp. 187–224 in Jeffrey C. Alexander (ed.), *Durkheimian Sociology: Cultural Studies*. Cambridge, UK: Cambridge University Press.

______. 1990. "Core solidarity, ethnic out-groups, and social differentiation." Pp. 267–93 in Alexander Jeffrey C. and Colomy Paul (eds.), *Differentiation Theory and Social Change.* New York: Columbia University Press.

______. 1995. *Fin de Siècle Social Theory*. London: Verso.

______. 1998. *Neofunctionalism and After*. Oxford, UK: Blackwell.

______. 1998a. "Introduction. Civil society I, II, III: constructing an empirical concept from normative controversies and historical transformations." Pp. 1–19 in Jeffrey C. Alexander (ed.), *Real Civil Societies: Dilemmas of Institutionalization*. London: Sage.

______. 1998b. "Citizen and enemy as symbolic classification: on the polarizing discourse of civil society." Pp. 96–114 in Jeffrey C. Alexander (ed.), *Real Civil Societies: Dilemmas of Institutionalization*. London: Sage.

Alexander, Jeffrey C., and Paul Colomy (eds.). 1990. *Differentiation Theory and Social Change: Comparative and Historical Perspectives*. New York: Columbia University Press.

Alford, Robert R. 1963. *Party and Society*. Chicago: Rand McNally.

______. 1973. *Party and Politics: The Anglo-American Democracies*. Greenwood, CN: Greenwood Press.

______. 1975. *Health Care Politics: Ideological and Interest Group Barriers to Reform*. Chicago: University of Chicago Press.

______. 1975. "Paradigms of relations between state and society." Pp. 145–60 in L. N. Lindberg (ed.), *Stress and Contradiction in Modern Capitalism: Public Policy and the Theory of the State*. Lexington, MA: Lexington Books.

______. 1998. *The Craft of Inquiry: Theories, Methods, Evidence*. New York: Oxford University Press.

Alford, Robert R., and Roger R. Friedland. 1985. *Powers of Theory: Capitalism, the State, and Democracy*. New York: Cambridge University Press.

Ali, Suki, Kelly Coate, and Eangui Wa Goro. 2000. *Global Feminist Politics: Identities in a Changing World*. New York: Routledge.

Allan, James, and Lyle Scruggs. 2002. "Political Partisanship and welfare state reform in advanced industrial societies." Unpublished paper, University of Connecticut.

Allen, Michael. 1991. "Capitalist response to state intervention: theories of the state and political finance in the New Deal." *American Sociological Review* 56:679–89.

______. 1992. "Elite social movement organizations and the state: The rise of the conservative policy-planning network." *Research in Politics* 4:87–109.

Allen, Michael Patrick, and Philip Broyles. 1989. "Class hegemony and political finance: Campaign contributions of wealthy capitalist families." *American Sociological Review* 54:275–87.

Allison, Graham Jr. 1999. "Public and private management: Are they fundamentally alike in all unimportant respects?" Pp. 14–29 in Frederick Lane (ed.), *Current Issues in Public Administration*. 6th ed. Boston: Bedford/St. Martin's.

Allison, Graham T. 1971. *Essence of Decision: Explaining the Cuban Missile Crisis*. Boston: Little, Brown.

Allison, Graham, and Philip Zelikow. 1999. *Essence of Decision: Explaining the Cuban Missile Crisis*, 2nd ed. New York: Addison Wesley Longman.

Almond, Gabriel A. 1990. *A Discipline Divided: Schools and Sects in Political Science*. Newbury Park, CA: Sage.

Almond, Gabriel A., and James Coleman. 1960. *The Politics of the Developing Areas*. Princeton, NJ: Princeton University Press.

Almond, Gabriel A., and Sidney Verba. 1963. *The Civic Culture: Political Attitudes and Democracy in Five Nations*. Princeton, NJ: Princeton University Press.

Almond, Gabriel. et al. 1954. *The Appeals of Communism*. Princeton, NJ: Princeton University Press.

Alt, James E. 1983. "The evolution of tax structures." *Public Choice* 41(1):181–222.

______. 1994. "The impact of the voting rights act on black and white voting in the South." Pp. 351–77 in C. Davidson and B. Grofman (eds.), *Quiet Revolution in the South: The Impact of the Voting Rights Act, 1965–1990*. Princeton, NJ: Princeton University Press.

Alt, James E., and Alberto Alesina. 1996. "Political economy: An overview." Pp. 645–74 in Robert E. Goodin and Hans-Dieter Klingemann (eds.), *A New Handbook of Political Science*. New York: Oxford University Press.

Alt, James E., and Alec Crystal. 1983. *Political Economics*. Berkeley, CA: University of California Press.

Althusser, Louis. 1969/1965. *For Marx*. London: New Left Books.

______. 1971. *Lenin and Philosophy and Other Essays*. New York: Monthly Review Press or London: New Left Books.

Altvater, Elmar, and Birgit Mahnkopf. 1977. "The world market unbound." *Review of International Political Economy* 4, 3:448–71.

Alvares, Claude. 1997. "An Indian village bucks GATT over control of genetic resources." *Resurgence* 84:11–12.

Alvarez, Sonia E. 1990. *Engendering Democracy in Brazil: Women's Movements in Transition Politics.* Princeton, NJ: Princeton University Press.

______. 1998. "Latin American feminisms 'go global': Trends of the 1990s and challenges for the new millenium." Pp. 293–324 in Sonia Alvarez, Evalina Dagnino, and Arturo Escobar (eds.), *Cultures of Politics/Politics of Cultures: Re-visioning Latin American Social Movements.* Boulder, CD: Westview.

______. 1999. "Advocating feminism: The Latin American feminist NGO 'boom'." *International Feminist Journal of Politics* 1(2):

______. 2000. "Translating the global: Effects of transnational organizing on local feminist discourses and practices in Latin America." *Meridians: Feminism, Race, Transnationalism* 1:29–67.

Alvarez-Beramendi, P. 2003. *Decentralization and Redistribution.* Ph.D. thesis, Nuffield College, Oxford.

Alwood, Edward. 1996. *Straight News: Gays, Lesbians, and the News Media.* New York: Columbia University Press.

Amenta, Edwin. 1998. *Bold Relief: Institutional Politics and the Origins of Modern American Social Policy,* Princeton, NJ: Princeton University Press.

______. 2003. "What we know about social policy: comparative and historical research in comparative and historical perspective." Chapter 3 in Dietrich Rueschemeyer and James Mahoney (eds.), *Comparative and Historical Analysis in the Social Sciences.* New York: Cambridge University Press.

Amenta, Edwin A., and Bruce G. Carruthers. 1989. "The formative years of U.S. social security spending policies." *American Sociological Review* 53:661–78.

Amenta, Edwin, and Michael P. Young. 1999. "Democratic states and social movements: theoretical arguments and hypotheses." *Social Problems* 57:153–68.

______. 1999. "Making an impact." Pp. 22–41 in Marco Giugni, Doug McAdam, and Charles Tilly (eds.), *How Social Movements Matter.* Minneapolis: University of Minnesota Press.

Amenta, Edwin, and Sunita Parikh. 1991. "Capitalists do not want social security, etc.?" *American Sociological Review* 56:891–909.

Amenta, Edwin, Bruce Carruthers, and Yvonne Zylan. 1992. "A hero for the aged? The Townsend movement, the political mediation model, and U.S. old age policy, 1934–1950." *American Sociological Review* 98:308–39.

Amenta, Edwin, Chris Bonastia, and Neal Caren. 2001. "U.S. social policy in comparative and historical perspective: concepts, images, arguments, and research strategies." *Annual Review of Sociology* 27:213–34.

Amenta, Edwin, Kathleen Dunleavy, and Mary Bernstein. 1994. "Stolen thunder? Huey Long's share the wealth, political mediation and the second New Deal." *American Sociological Review* 59:678–702.

Amin, Samir. 1997. *Capitalism in the Age of Globalization.* London: Zed.

Aminzade, Ron. 1992. "Historical sociology and time." *Sociological Methods and Research* 20:456–80.

______. 2000. "The politics of race and nation: Citizenship and Africanization in Tanganyika." *Political Power and Social Theory* 14:53–90.

______. 2003. "From race to citizenship: The indigenization debate in post-socialist Tanzania." *Studies in Comparative International Development* 38:43–63.

Aminzade, Ron, and Doug McAdam. 2001. "Emotions and contentious politics." Pp. 14–50 in Ronald R. Aminzade et al. (eds.), *Silence and Voice in the Study of Contentious Politics.* Cambridge, UK: Cambridge University Press.

Amnesty International. 2002. *Amnesty International Report 2002.* Washington, D.C.: Amnesty International.

Amy, Douglas J. 1993. *Real Choices/New Voices: The Case for Proportional Representation in the United States.* New York: Columbia University Press.

Ancelovici, Marcus. 2002. "Organizing against globalization: The case of ATTAC in France." *Politics & Society* 30(3):427–63.

Anderson, B. 2000. *Doing the Dirty Work?: The Global Politics of Domestic Labour.* London: Zed.

Anderson, Benedict. 1983. *Imagined Communities.* London: New Left Books.

______. 1991. *Imagined Communities,* 2nd ed. London: Verso.

Anderson, Elijah. 1999. *Code of the Street: Decency, Violence, and the Moral Life of the Inner City.* New York: W. W. Norton.

Anderson, James E. 1994. *Public Policy-Making.* New York: Houghton Mifflin.

Anderson, Margo J. 1988. *The American Census: A Social History.* New Haven, CT: Yale University Press.

______. 2002. "Counting by race: The antebellum legacy." Pp. 269–87 in J. Perlmann and M. C. Waters (eds.), *The New Race Question: How the Census Counts Multiracial Individuals.* New York: Russell Sage Foundation.

Anderson, Perry. 1974a. *Passages from Antiquity to Feudalism*. London: New Left Books.

______. 1974b. *Lineages of the Absolutist State*. London: New Left Books.

______. 1976. "The antinomies of Antonio Gramsci." *New Left Review* 100:5–78.

______. 1976. *Considerations on Western Marxism*. London: New Left Books.

Anderson, Richard D., Jr., M. Steven Fish, Stephen E. Hanson, and Philip G. Roeder. 2001. *Postcommunism and the Theory of Democracy*. Princeton, NJ: Princeton University Press.

Andrews, George Reid, and Herrick Chapman (eds.). 1995. *The Social Construction of Democracy, 1870–1990*. New York: New York University Press.

Andrews, Kenneth. 2001. "Social movements and policy implementation." *American Sociological Review* 66:71–95.

Ang, Ien. 1985. *Watching* Dallas: *Soap Opera and the Melodramatic Imagination*. London: Methuen.

Anker, Richard. 1998. *Gender and Jobs: Sex Segregation of Occupations in the World*. Washington, DC: International Labour Office.

Anner, Mark, and Peter Evans. 2004. "Building bridges across a double-divide: Alliances between U.S. and Latin American labor and NGOs." *Development in Practice* 14(1–2):34–47.

Ansell, Chris. 2000. "The networked polity: Regional development in western Europe." *Governance* 13:303–33.

Ansolabehere, Stephen, and Alan Gerber. 1994. "The mismeasure of campaign spending: Evidence from the 1990 U.S. House elections." *Journal of Politics* 56:1106–18.

Ansolabehere, Stephen, and Shanto Iyengar. 1995. *Going Negative: How Attack Ads Shrink and Polarize the Electorate*. New York: Free Press.

Antidefamation League. 2001. "Jörg Haider. The rise of an Austrian extreme rightist." http://www.adl.org/backgrounders/joerg_haider.asp.

Appelbaum, Richard P. 1979. "Born-again functionalism? a reconsideration of Althusser's structuralism." *The Insurgent Sociologist* 9(1):18–33.

Araghi, Farshad. 2000. "The great global enclosure of our times." Pp. 145–60 in Fred Magdoff, Frederick H. Buttel, and John Bellamy Foster (eds.), *Hungry for Profit. The Agribusiness Threat to Farmers, Food and the Environment*. New York: Monthly Review.

Araghi, Farshad, and Philip McMichael. 2004. "Contextualizing (post) modernity: a world-historical perspective." Paper presented to the annual meeting of the American Sociological Association, August. San Francisco.

Arat, Zehra F. 1991. *Democracy and Human Rights in Developing Countries*. Boulder, CO: Lynne Rienner.

Arato, Andrew, and Jean Cohen. 1984. "Social movements, civil society & the problem of sovereignty." *Praxis International* 4(3):266–83.

Archer, Margaret S. 2000. *Being Human: The Problem of Agency*. Cambridge, UK: Cambridge University Press.

Arendt, Hannah. [1951] 1968. *Totalitarianism, Part III: The Origins of Totalitarianism*. 4th ed. New York: Harcourt, Brace, Jovanovitch.

Aristotle. 1962. *The Politics*. (T. A. Sinclair. trans.). Baltimore, MD: Penguin Books.

Arjomand, Said A. 1988. *The Turban for the Crown: The Islamic Revolution in Iran*. New York: Oxford University Press.

Armbruster, Ralph. 1995. "Cross-national labor organizing strategies." *Critical Sociology* 21(2): 75–89.

______. 1998. "Cross-border labor organizing in the garment and automobile industries: The Phillips Van-Heusen and Ford Cuautitlan cases." *Journal of World-Systems Research* 4(1):20–51.

Armor, David J. 1995. *Forced Justice: School Desegregation and the Law*. New York: Oxford University Press.

Armstrong, John A. 1982. *Nations Before Nationalism*. Chapel Hill: University of North Carolina Press.

Aron, Raymond. 1959. *The Century of Total War*. Boston, MA: Beacon.

Arrighi, Giovanni. 1990. "The developmentalist illusion: A reconceptualization of the semi-periphery." Pp. 11–42 in William G. Martin (ed.), *Semiperipheral States in the World-Economy*. Westport, CT: Greenwood.

______. 1994. *The Long Twentieth Century. Money, Power and the Origins of Our Times*. London: Verso.

______. 1998. "Globalization and the rise of East Asia: Lessons from the past, prospects for the future." *International Sociology* 13, 1:59–78.

Arrighi, Giovanni, and Beverly Silver. 1999. *Chaos and Governance in the Modern World System*. Minneapolis: University of Minnesota Press.

Arrow, Kenneth. 1963. "Uncertainty and the welfare economics of medical care." *American Economic Review* 53:541–67.

Arthur, Brian. 1994. *Increasing Returns and Path Dependence in the Economy*. Ann Arbor: University of Michigan Press.

Asher, Herbert, Eric S. Heberlig, Randall B. Ripley, and Karen Snyder (eds.). 2001. *American Labor Unions in the Electoral Arena*. Lanham, MD: Rowman and Littlefield.

Ashford, Douglas E. 1986. *The Emergence of the Welfare State*. Oxford, UK: Basil Blackwell.

Aspalter, Christian (ed.). 2002. *Discovering the Welfare State in East Asia*. Westport, CT: Praeger.

Atkinson, J. Maxwell, and John Heritage. 1984. *Structures of Social Action*. Cambridge, UK: Cambridge University Press.

Atkinson, Anthony B., Lee Rainwater, and Timothy M. Smeeding. 1994. *Income Distribution in OECD Countries*. Paris: OECD.

Atkinson, Michael M., and William D. Coleman. 1989. "Strong states and weak states: Sectoral policy networks in advanced capitalist economies." *British Journal of Political Science* 19:47–67.

______. 1992. "Policy networks, policy communities and the problems of governance." *Governance* 5(2):154–180.

Auer, Peter. 2000. *Employment Revival in Europe: Labour Market Success in Austria, Denmark, Ireland, and the Netherlands*. Geneva: International Labour Organization.

Austin-Smith, David. 1987. "Sophisticated sincerity: Voting over endogenous agendas." *American Political Science Review* 81:1323–30.

______. 1995. "Campaign contributions and access." *American Political Science Review* 89:566–81.

Axelrod, Robert M. 1972. "Where the votes come from: An analysis of electoral coalitions." *American Political Science Review* 66:11–20.

______. 1973. "Schema Theory: An Information Processing Model of Perception and Cognition." *American Political Science Review* 67: 1248–66.

______. 1984. *The Evolution of Cooperation*. New York: Basic Books.

Benford, Robert D. 1997. "An Insider's Critique of the Social Movement Framing Perspective." *Sociological Inquiry* 67:409–30.

Babb, Sarah. 1996. "A true American system of finance: Frame resonance in the U. S. labor movement, 1866–1886." *American Sociological Review* 61: 1033–52.

Baccaro, Lucio. 2002. "The construction of 'democratic' corporatism in Italy." *Politics and Society* 30:327–57.

Bacchi, Carol. 1990. *Same Difference: Feminism and Sexual Difference*. Sydney: Allen & Unwin.

Bacharach, Samuel B. and Edward J. Lawler. 1980. *Power and Politics in Organizations*. San Francisco, CA: Jossey–Bass.

______. 1981. *Bargaining: Power, Tactics and Outcomes*. San Francisco, CA: Jossey–Bass.

Bachrach, Peter, and Morris S. Baratz. 1962. "The two faces of power." *American Political Science Review* 56:947–52.

Bade, Klaus J. 1983. *Vom Auswanderungsland zum Einwanderungsland? Deutschland 1880–1980*. Berlin: Colloquium Verlag.

______. 1990. *Ausländer-Aussiedler-Asyl in der Bundesrepublik Deutschland*. Hannover: Verlag der Landeszentrale für politische Bildung.

______. 1992. "German transatlantic emigration in the nineteenth and twentieth centuries." Pp. 121–56 in P. C. Emmer and M. Mörner (eds.), *European Expansion and Migration*. New York: Berg.

______. 1994. *Ausländer, Aussiedler, Asyl*. Munich: Beck.

Bagdikian, Ben H. 1983. *The Media Monopoly*. Boston: Beacon.

______. 2000. *The Media Monopoly*, 6th ed. Boston: Beacon Press.

Bailey, F. G. 1991. *The Prevalence of Deceit*. Ithaca, NY: Cornell University Press.

______. 2001. *Stratagems and Spoils: A Social Anthropology of Politics*. Boulder, CO: Westview.

Baker, Keith Michael. 1990. *Inventing the French Revolution*. Cambridge, UK: Cambridge University Press.

Baker, Kendall L., Russell J. Dalton, and Kai Hildebrandt. 1981. *Germany Transformed: Political Culture and the New Politics*. Cambridge, UK: Harvard University Press.

Bakker, Isabella, and Stephen Gill (eds.) 2003. *Power, Production and Social Reproduction*. Hampshire: Palgrave Macmillan.

Baldwin, Peter. 1990. *The Politics of Social Solidarity: Class Bases of the European Welfare State 1875–1975*. Cambridge, UK: Cambridge University Press.

Banaszak, Lee Ann. 1996. *Why Movements Succeed or Fail: Opportunity, Culture and the Struggle for Women's Suffrage*. Princeton, NJ: Princeton University Press.

Bandarage, Asoka. 1997. *Women, Population and Global Crisis*. London: Zed Books.

Bandy, Joe, and Jennifer Bickham Mendez. 2003. "A place of their own? Women organizers in the maquilas of Nicaragua and Mexico." *Mobilization: An International Journal* 8(2):173–88.

Banfield, Edward C. 1958. *The Moral Basis of a Backward Society*. New York: Free Press.

Banks, Andy, and John Russo. 1999. "The development of international campaign-based network structures: A case study of the IBT and ITF World Council of UPS Unions." *Comparative Labor Law & Policy Journal* 20:543–68.

Baran, Paul A., and Paul M. Sweezy. 1966. *Monopoly Capital*. New York: Monthly Review Press.

Barany, Zoltan, and Robert G. Moser (eds.). 2001. *Russian Politics: Challenges of Democratization*. Cambridge: Cambridge University Press.

Barbahona de Brito, Alejandra. 1997. *Human Rights and Democratization in Latin America*. New York: Oxford University Press.

Barbalet, J. M. 1988. *Citizenship*. Minneapolis: University of Minnesota Press.

______. 2002. "Secret Voting and Political Emotions." *Mobilization* 7:129–140.

Bardi, Luciano. 1994. "Transnational party federations, European parliamentary party groups, and the building of Europarties." Pp. 357–72 in Richard S. Katz and Peter Mair (eds.), *How Parties Organize: Change and Adaptation in Party Organizations in Western Democracies*. Thousand Oaks, CA: Sage.

Barenberg, Mark, and Peter Evans. 2004. "The FTAA's impact on democratic governance." Pp. 755–89 in A. Estevadeordal, D. Rodrik, A. M. Taylor, and A. Velasco (eds.), *FTAA and Beyond: For Integration into the Americas*. Cambridge, MA: Harvard University Press.

Baretta, Silvio, R. Duncan, and Markoff, John. 1987. "Brazil's Abertura: A transition from what to what?" Pp. 43–65 in James Malloy and Mitchell A. Seligson (eds.), *Authoritarians and Democrats: The Politics of Regime Transition in Latin America*. Pittsburgh: University of Pittsburgh Press.

Barkan, Steve. 1984. "Legal control of the civil rights movement." *American Sociological Review* 49:552–65.

Barker, Colin. 2001. "Fear, laughter, and collective power: The making of solidarity at the Lenin Shipyard in Gdansk, Poland, August 1980." Pp. 175–194 in Jeff Goodwin, James M. Jasper, and Francesca Polletta (eds.), *Passionate Politics: Emotions and Social Movements*. Chicago: University of Chicago Press.

Barkey, Karen. 1991. "Rebellious alliances: The state and peasant unrest in early seventeenth-century France and the Ottoman Empire." *American Sociological Review* 56:699–715.

Barlow, T. 2000. "International feminism of the future." *Signs* 25:1099–105.

Barnes, Jonathan. (ed.). 1984. *The Complete Works of Aristotle*. Princeton, NJ: Princeton University Press.

Barnes, Samuel, and Max Kaase. 1979. *Political Action: Mass Participation in Five Western Democracies*. Beverly Hills, CA: Sage.

Barnet, Richard J., and John Cavanagh. 1994. *Global Dreams: Imperial Corporations and the New World Order*. New York: Touchstone.

Baron, David. 1989. "Service-induced campaign contributions and the electoral equilibrium." *Quarterly Journal of Economics* 104:45–72.

______. 1994. "Electoral competition with informed and uninformed voters." *American Political Science Review* 88:43–57.

Barrett, M. 1980. *Women's Oppression Today: Problems in Marxist Feminist Analysis*. London: Verso.

Barrilleaux, Charles. 2000. "Party strength, party change and policy-making in the American states." *Party Politics* 6:61–73.

Barro, Robert. 2002. *Nothing Is Sacred*. Boston, MA: MIT Press.

Barroso, Carmen, and Sônia Corrêa. 1995. "Public servants, professionals, and feminists: The politics of contraceptive research in Brazil." Pp. 292–306 in Faye D. Ginsburg and Rayna Rapp (eds.), *Conceiving the New World Order*. Berkeley: University of California Press.

Barrow, Clyde W. 1993. *Critical Theories of the State: Marxist, Neo-Marxist, Post-Marxist*. Madison: University of Wisconsin Press.

Barry, Brian M. 1970/1978. *Sociologists, Economists, and Democracy*. Chicago: University of Chicago Press.

Barry, Brian. 2001. *Culture and Equality: An Egalitarian Critique of Multiculturalism*. Cambridge, MA: Harvard University Press.

Bartels, Larry. 1998. "Where the ducks are: Voting power in a party system." Pp. 43–79 in John Geer (ed.), *Politicians and Party Politics*. Baltimore, MD: Johns Hopkins University Press.

Barth, Fredrik. 1959. *Political Leadership among Swat Pathans*. London: Athlone Press.

______. 1969. *Ethnic Groups and Boundaries: The Social Organisation of Cultural Difference*. Oslo: Universitetsförlaget.

Barthes, Roland. 1972/1957. *Mythologies*. New York: Farrar, Straus, Giroux.

______. 1982/1970. *Empire of Signs*. New York: Farrar, Straus, Giroux.

______. 1983/1967. *The Fashion System*. New York: Farrar, Straus, Giroux.

Bartley, Numan V. 1969. *The Rise of Massive Resistance: Race and Politics in the South During the 1950s*. Baton Rouge: Louisiana State University Press.

Bartolini, Stefano. 2000. *The Political Mobilization of the European Left, 1860–1980: The Class Cleavage*. Cambridge, UK: Cambridge University Press.

______. 2001. "A integracao europeia provocara uma reestrutacao dos istemas de clivagens nacionais?" ["Will European integration lead to the restructuring of national cleavage systems?"] *Sociologia – Problems e Practicas* 37:91–114.

Bartolini, Stefano, and Peter Mair. 1990. *Identity, Competition and Electoral Availability*. New York: Cambridge University Press.

Barzel, Yoram, and Edgar Kiser. 1997. "The development and decline of medieval voting institutions: A comparison of England and France." *Economic Inquiry* 35:244–60.

Barzelay, Michael. 2002. "Diseñando el proceso de cambio en las políticas de gerenciamiento público (resumen ejecutivo)." *Boletín Virtual TOP,* No. 3. (www.top.org.ar/publicac.htm).

Bashevkin, Sylvia B. 1991. *True Patriot Love: The Politics of Canadian Nationalism.* Toronto: University of Toronto Press.

Basu, Amrita. 1992. *Two Faces of Protest.* Berkeley: University of California Press.

______. (ed.). 1995a. *The Challenge of Local Feminisms.* Boulder, CO: Westview.

______. 1995b. "Introduction." Pp. 1–21 in Amrita Basu (ed.), *The Challenge of Local Feminisms.* Boulder, CO: Westview.

______. 1999. "Women's activism and the vicissitudes of Hindu nationalism." *Journal of Women's History* 10:104–24.

______. 2000. "Globalization of the local/llocalization of the global: Mapping transnational women's movements." *Meridians: Feminism, Race, Transnationalism* 1:68–84.

Basu, Amrita, and C. Elizabeth McGrory. 1995. *The Challenge of Local Feminisms: Women's Movements in Global Perspective, Social Change in Global Perspective.* Boulder, CD: Westview.

Bates, Robert H., Avner Greif, Margaret Levi, Jean-Laurent Rosenthal, and Barry Weingast. 1998. *Analytic Narratives.* Princeton, NJ: Princeton University Press.

Bates, Robert, and Da-Hsiang Lien. 1985. "A note on taxation, development, and representative government." *Politics and Society* 14(1):53–68.

Bauböck, Ranier. 1994. *Transnational Citizenship.* Aldershot, UK: Edward Elgar.

Bauer, Monica, and John R. Hibbing. 1989. "Which incumbents lose in house elections? a response to Jacobson's 'Marginals Never Vanished.' " *American Journal of Political Science* 33:262–71.

Bauer, Raymond A., Ithiel de Sola Pool, and Lewis Anthony Dexter. 1972[1963]. *American Business and Public Policy: The Politics of Foreign Trade.* New York: Atherton Press.

Bauman, Zygmunt. 1989. "Hermeneutics and Modern Social Theory." In David Held and John B. Thompson (eds.), *Social Theory of Modern Societies: Anthony Giddens and his Critics.* Cambridge, UK: Cambridge University Press.

Baumann, Gerd. 1996. *Contesting Culture: Discourses of Identity in Multi-Ethnic London.* Cambridge, UK: Cambridge University Press.

Baumann, Renato. 2002. "Trade policies, growth, and equity in Latin America." Pp. 53–80 in Evelyne Huber (ed.), *Models of Capitalism: Lessons for Latin America.* University Park: Pennsylvania State University Press.

Baumgartner, Frank R. 1996. "Public interest groups in France and the United States." *Governance* 9:1–22.

Baumgartner, Frank R., and Beth L. Leech. 1998. *Basic Interests: The Importance of Groups in Politics and in Political Science.* Princeton, NJ: Princeton University Press.

Baumol, William J. 1959. *Business Behavior, Value, and Growth.* New York: Macmillan.

Bawn, Kathleen. 1995. "Political control versus expertise: Congressional choices about administrative procedures." *American Political Science Review* 89:62–73.

Bearden, James. 1987. "Financial hegemony, social capital and bank boards of directors." Pp. 48–59 in M. Schwartz (ed.), *The Structure of Power in America: The Corporate Elite as a Ruling Class.* New York: Holmes & Meier.

Bearman, Peter S. 1991. "Desertion as localism: Army unit solidarity and group norms in the U.S. Civil War." *Social Forces* 70:321–42.

Beasley, M. 1993. "Newspapers: Is there a new majority defining the news?" Pp. XX–XX in P. J. Creedon (ed.), *Women in Mass Communication.* Newbury Park, CA: Sage.

Beaulieu, Jill, and Mary Roberts (eds.). 2002. *Orientalism's Interlocutors: Painting, Architecture, Photography.* Durham, NC: Duke University Press.

Beck, Paul Allen, and Frank J. Sorauf. 1992. *Party Politics in America,* 7th ed. New York: HarperCollins.

Becker, Gary. 1976. *The Economic Approach to Human Behavior.* Chicago: University of Chicago Press.

Becker, Gary, and George Stigler. 1974. "Law enforcement, malfeasance, and compensation of enforcers." *Journal of Legal Studies* 3:1–18.

Becker, Gary S. 1991. *A Treatise on the Family.* Cambridge, MA: Harvard University Press.

______. 1995. *The Essence of Becker.* Stanford, CA: Hoover Institution Press.

Beetham, David (ed). 1983. *Marxists in Face of Fascism. Writings by Marxists from the Interwar Period.* Manchester: Manchester University Press.

______. 1993. *Bureaucracy.* 2nd ed. Mineapolis: University of Minnesota Press.

Beiner, Ronald. 2003. *Liberalism, Nationalism, Citizenship: Essays on the Problem of Political Community.* Toronto: UBC Press.

Beisel, Nicola. 1997. *Imperiled Innocents: Anthony Comstock and Family Reproduction in Victorian America.* Princeton, NJ: Princeton University Press.

Bélanger, Sarah, and Maurice Pinard. 1991. "Ethnic movement and competition model: Some missing links." *American Sociological Review* 56:446–57.

Bell, Daniel. 1960. *The End of Ideology*. New York: Free Press.

______. 1973. *The Coming of Post-Industrial Society*. New York: Basic Books.

______. 2000. *The Radical Right*. 3rd ed. New Brunswick, NJ: Transaction.

Bell, Robert. 1985. *The Culture of Policy Deliberations*. New Brunswick, NJ: Rutgers University Press.

Bellah, Robert. 1967. "Civil religion in America." *Daedalus, the Journal of the American Academy of Arts and Sciences* 96(1):1–21.

Bellah, Robert N., Richard Madsen, William M. Sullivan, Ann Swidler, and Steven M. Tipton. 1984. *Habits of the Heart: Individualism and Commitment in American Life*. Berkeley: University of California Press.

Bello, Walden. 1994. *Dark Victory: The United States, Structural Adjustment and Global Poverty*. Oakland, CA: Institute for Food and Development Policy.

Benda, Harry J. 1966. "Reflections on Asian communism." *The Yale Review* 56:1–16.

Bendix, Reinhard. 1960. *Max Weber*. Berkeley: University of California Press.

______. 1964. *Nation-Building and Citizenship; Studies of Our Changing Social Order*. New York: Wiley.

______. 1970. *Embattled Reason: Essays on Social Knowledge*. New York: Oxford University Press.

______. 1977a. *Nation-Building and Citizenship*, 2nd ed. Berkeley: University of California Press.

______. 1977b. *Max Weber: An Intellectual Portrait*. Berkeley: University of California Press.

______. 1978. *Kings or People: Power and the Mandate to Rule*. Berkeley: University of California Press.

______. 1984. *Force, Fate and Freedom*. Berkeley: University of California Press.

Bendix, Reinhard, and Seymour M. Lipset (eds.). 1966. *Class, Status, and Power: Social Stratification in Comparative Perspective*. New York: Free Press.

Bendor, Jonathan and Piotr Swistak. 2001. "The Evolution of Norms." *American Journal of Sociology.* 106:1493–1545.

Beneria, Lourdes, and Martha Roldán. 1987. *The Crossroads of Class and Gender*. Chicago: University of Chicago Press.

Benford, Robert D. 1997. "An insider's critique of the social movement framing perspective." *Sociological Inquiry* 67(4):409–30.

Benhabib, Seyla. 1992. *Situating the Self: Gender, Community and Postmodernism in Contemporary Ethics*. Cambridge, UK: Polity.

______. 1998. "Models of public space: Hannah Arendt, the liberal tradition, and Jürgen Habermas." Pp. 65–99 in Joan B. Landes (ed.), *Feminism the Public and the Private*. Oxford, UK: Oxford University Press.

______. 2001. "Toward a deliberative model of democratic legitimacy." Pp. 67–94 in Seyla Behhabib (ed.), *Democracy and Difference: Contesting the Boundaries of the Political*. Princeton, NJ: Princeton University Press.

______. 2002a. *The Claims of Culture: Equality and Diversity in the Global Era*. Princeton, NJ and Oxford, UK: Princeton University Press.

______. 2002b. "Reversing the dialectic of enlightenment: the re-enchantment of the world." Pp. 341–60 in John McCormick (ed.), *Confronting Mass Democracy and Industrial Technology*. Durham, NC: Duke University Press.

Bennett, Marion. 1964. *American Immigration Policies: A History*. Washington, DC: Public Affairs Press.

Bennett, Stephen E. 1991. "Left behind: Exploring declining turnout among noncollege whites, 1964–1988." *Social Science Quarterly* 72:314–33.

Bennett, W. Lance. 1996. *The Governing Crisis: Media, Money, and Marketing in American Elections*. New York: St. Martin's.

Bensel, Richard Franklin. 1984. *Sectionalism and American Political Development, 1880–1980*. Madison: University of Wisconsin Press.

Bentley, Arthur F. 1949. *The Process of Government: A Study of Social Pressures*. Evanston, IL: Principia Press of Illinois.

Benz, Arthur. 1995. "Politiknetzwerke in der horizontalen Politikverflechtung." Pp. 185–204 in Dorothea Jansen and Klaus Schubert (eds.), *Netzwerke und Politikproduktion: Konzepte, Methoden, Perspektiven*. Marburg, Germany: Schüren.

Benz, Arthur, and Burkard Eberlein. 1999. "The Europeanization of regional policies: Patterns of multi-level governance." *Journal of European Public Policy* 6:329–48.

Berejikian, Jeffrey. 1992. "Revolutionary collective action and the agent-structure problem." *American Political Science Review* 86:649–57.

Berelson, Bernard R., Paul F. Lazarsfeld, and William McPhee. 1954. *Voting: A Study of Opinion Formation in a Presidential Campaign*. Chicago: University of Chicago Press.

Berezin, Mabel. 1997. *Making the Fascist Self: The Political Culture of Interwar Italy*. Ithaca, NY: Cornell University Press.

Berger, Peter L., and Thomas Luckmann. 1966. *The Social Construction of Reality: A Treatise in the Sociology of Knowledge*. Garden City, NY: Doubleday.

Berger, Suzanne (ed.). 1981. *Organizing Interests in Western Europe*. New York: Cambridge University Press.

Berger, Suzanne, and Ronald Dore (eds.). 1996. *National Diversity and Global Capitalism*. Ithaca, NY: Cornell University Press.

Bergeron, S. 2001. "Political economy discourses of globalization and feminist politics." *Signs* 26(4):983–1006.

Berghman, Jos, Jan Peters, and Jan Vranken. 1987. "Belgium." Pp. 751–810 in P. Flora (ed.), *Growth to Limits*, Vol. IV. New York: de Gruyter.

Berle, Adolf A., and Gardiner C. Means. 1968[1932]. *The Modern Corporation and Private Property*. New York: Harcourt, Brace & World.

Berman, Edward H. 1983. *The Ideology of Philanthropy: The Influence of the Carnegie, Ford and Rockefeller Foundations on American Foreign Policy*. Albany, NY: State University of New York Press.

Berman, Nathaniel. 2001. "The international law of nationalism: Group identity and legal history." Pp. 106–38 in Robert Beck and Thomas Ambrosio (eds.), *International Law and the Rise of Nations*. New York: Chatham.

Berman, Sheri, 1997. "Civil society and the collapse of the Weimar Republic." *World Politics* 49:401–29.

______. 2003. "Islamism, revolution, and civil society." *Perspectives on Politics* 1:257–72.

Bernard, Mitchell. 1997. "Ecology, political economy and the counter-movement: Karl Polanyi and the second great transformation." Pp. 75–89 in Stephen Gill and James H. Mittelman (eds.), *Innovation and Transformation in International Studies*. Cambridge, UK: Cambridge University Press.

Bernhardt, Annette, Martina Morris, and Mark Handcock. 1995. "Women's gains, men's losses? the shrinking gender gap in earnings." *American Journal of Sociology* 101:302–28.

Bernstein, Basil. 1975[1971]. *Class, Codes and Control*. New York: Schocken.

Bernstein, Eduard 1909. *Evolutionary Socialism*. New York: Huebsch.

Bernstein, Mary. 1997. "Celebration and suppression: The strategic uses of identity by the lesbian and gay movement." *American Journal of Sociology* 103:531–65.

Berry, Jeffrey M. 1984. *The Interest Group Society*. Boston: Little, Brown.

Berry, Jeffrey. 1997. *The Interest Group Society*, 3rd ed. New York: Longmans.

Berry, Jeffrey, Kent Portney, and Ken Thomson. 1993. *The Rebirth of Urban Democracy*. Washington, DC: Brookings Institute.

Best, Joel. 1999. *Random Violence: How We Talk About New Crimes and New Victims*. Berkeley: University of California Press.

Betsill, Michele, and Elisabeth Corell. 2001. "NGO influence in international environmental negotiations: A framework for analysis." *Global Environmental Politics* 1(4):65–85.

Betz, Hans Georg, and Stefan Immerfall (eds.). 1998. *The New Politics of the Right: Neopopulist Parties and Movements in Established Democracies*. New York: St. Martin's.

Betz, Hans-Georg. 2001. "Exclusionary populism in Austria, Italy, and Switzerland." *International Journal* 56:393–420.

Bhabha, Homi K. 1994. *The Location of Culture*. London: Routledge.

Bhaskar, Roy. 1975. *A Realist Theory of Science*. Leeds, UK: Basic Books.

Bianco, Lucien. 1971. *Origins of the Chinese Revolution: 1915–1949*. Stanford, CA: Stanford University Press.

Biao, Xiang. 2003. "Emigration from China: A sending country perspective." *International Migration* 41(3):21–47.

Bienefeld, Manfred. 1989. "The lessons of history and the developing world." *Monthly Review* July–August:9–41.

Biersack, Robert, John C. Green, Paul E. Herrnson, Lynda W. Powell, and Clyde Wilcox. 1999. "Individual congressional campaign contributors: A preliminary report." Prepared for the annual meeting of the Midwest Political Science Association, Chicago, IL, April 15–17.

Billig, Michael. 1987. *Arguing and Thinking: A Rhetorical Approach to Social Psychology*. Cambridge, UK: Cambridge University Press.

Billings, Dwight. 1979. *Planters and the Making of the "New South."* Chapel Hill: University of North Carolina Press.

Bimber, Bruce. 1998. "The Internet and political transformation: populism, community, and accelerated pluralism." *Polity* 31:133–60.

Bin, Z. 1999. "Mouthpiece or money-spinner: The double life of Chinese television in the late 1990s." *International Journal of Cultural Studies* 2:291–305.

Birchfield, V., and Crepaz. M. M. L. 1999. "The impact of constitutional structures and collective and competitive veto points on income inequality in industrialized democracies." *European Journal of Political Research* 34(2):75–200.

Blackbourne, David, and Geoff Eley. 1984. "Introduction." Pp. 1–38 in David Blackbourne and Geoff Eley (eds.), *The Peculiarities of German History. Bourgeois Society and Politics in Nineteenth Century Germany*. New York: Oxford University Press.

Blais, Andre, Donald Blake, and Stephane Dion. 1996. "Do parties make a difference? a reappraisal." *American Journal of Political Science* 40:214–20.

Blalock, Hubert M. 1967. *Toward a Theory of Minority-Group Relations*. New York: Wiley.

Blau, Peter. 1964. *Exchange and Power in Social Life.* New York: Wiley.

______. 1994. *Structural Contexts of Opportunities.* Chicago, IL: University of Chicago Press.

Blau, Peter, and Otis Dudley Duncan. 1967. *The American Occupational Structure.* New York: Free Press.

Blau, Peter, and Peter Meyer, 1999. "Why study bureaucracy?" Pp. 3–13 in Frederick Lane (ed.), *Current Issues in Public Administration.* 6th ed. Boston: Bedford/St. Martin's.

Blauner, Robert. 2003. "Remembering Bob Alford: A Friend for Fifty Years," 2003. Pp. 3–8 in *Remembering Bob Alford 1928–2003.* Ph.D. Program in Sociology. The Graduate Center, the City University of New York, September 12th.

Blee, Kathleen. 1991. *Women of the Klan: Racism and Gender in the 1920s.* Berkeley, CA: University of California Press.

______. 2002. *Inside Organized Racism: Women in the Hate Movement.* Berkeley: University of California Press.

Bloch, Marc. 1988. *Feudal Society: The Growth of Ties of Dependence.* Chicago: University of Chicago Press.

Block, Fred. 1977a. "The ruling class does not rule: notes on the marxist theory of the state." *Socialist Revolution* 33(7):6–27.

______. 1977b. *The Origins of International Economic Disorder: A Study of United States International Monetary Policy from World War II to the Present.* Berkeley: University of California Press.

______. 1980. "Beyond Relative Autonomy: State Managers as Historical Subjects." In R. Miliband and J. Saville (eds.), *The Sociologist Register.* London: Merlin Press.

______. 1996. *The Vampire State.* New York: New Press.

______. 2001. "Using social theory to leap over historical contingencies." *Theory and Society* 30, 2:215–21.

Bloom, Jack M. 1987. *Class, Race, and the Civil Rights Movement.* Bloomington: Indiana University Press.

Blumer, Herbert. 1948. "Public opinion and public opinion polling." *American Sociological Review* 13: 542–54.

______. 1969. "The Field of Collective Behavior." Pp. 65–122 in Alfred McClung Lee (ed.), *Principles of Sociology.* New York: Barnes & Noble.

______. 1978. "Social Unrest and Collective Protest." In Norman K. Denzin (ed.), *Studies in Symbolic Interaction,* v. 1, Greenwich, CT: JAI Press.

Blumler, May G., and Michael. Gurevitch. 1986. "Journalists' orientations to political institutions: The case of parliamentary broadcasting." In Peter Golding, Graham Murdock, and Philip Schlesinger. (eds.), *Communicating Politics.* Leicester, Leicester University Press.

Boas, Franz. 1940. *Race, Language and Culture.* New York: The Macmillan Company, 1940.

Bobo, Lawrence D. 1983. "Whites' opposition to busing: Symbolic racism or realistic group conflict?" *Journal of Personality and Social Psychology* 45:1196–210.

______. 1988. "Group conflict, prejudice, and the paradox of contemporary racial attitudes." Pp. 85–114 in P. A. Katz and D. A. Taylor (eds.), *Eliminating Racism: Profiles in Controversy.* New York: Plenum.

______. 2000. "Race and beliefs about affirmative action: Assessing the effects of interests, group threat, ideology and racism." Pp. 137–64 in D. O. Sears, J. Sidanius, and L. Bobo (eds.), *Racialized Politics: The Debate about Racism in America.* Chicago: University of Chicago.

Bobo, Lawrence, and Franklin Gilliam. 1990. "Race, sociopolitical participation, and black empowerment." *American Political Science Review* 84:377–93.

Bobo, Lawrence D., and Vincent L. Hutchings. 1996. "Perceptions of racial group competition: Extending Blumer's theory of group position to a multiracial social context." *American Sociological Review* 61:951–72.

Bobo, Lawrence D., and Devon Johnson. 2000. "Racial attitudes in a prismatic metropolis: Mapping identity, stereotypes, competition, and views on affirmative action." Pp. 81–166 in L. D. Bobo, M. L. Oliver, J. H. Johnson, and A. Valenzuela (eds.), *Prismatic Metropolis: Inequality in Los Angeles.* New York: Russell Sage Foundation.

Bobo, Lawrence D., and James R. Kluegel. 1993. "Opposition to race-targetting – self-interest, stratification ideology, or racial-attitudes." *American Sociological Review* 58:443–64.

Bobo, Lawrence D., and Michael P. Massagli. 2001. "Stereotyping and urban inequality." Pp. 89–162 in A. O'Connor, C. Tilly, and L. D. Bobo (eds.), *Urban Inequality: Evidence From Four Cities.* New York: Russell Sage Foundation.

Bobo, Lawrence D., James R. Kluegel, and Ryan A. Smith. 1997. "Laissez-faire racism: The crystallization of a kinder, gentler, antiblack ideology." Pp. 15–41 in S. A. Tuch and J. K. Martin (eds.), *Racial Attitudes in the 1990s: Continuity and Change.* Westport, CT: Praeger.

Bock, Gisela, and Susan James. 1992. *Beyond Equality and Difference: Citzenship, Feminist Politics and Female Subjectivity.* London: Routledge.

Bock, Gisela, and Pat Thane. 1991. *Maternity and Gender Policies.* New York: Routledge.

Bohman, James. 1996. *Public Deliberation: Pluralism, Complexity and Democracy.* Cambridge, MA: MIT Press.

Boies, John L. 1989. "Money, business, and the state: Material interests, *Fortune* 500 corporations, and the size of political action committees." *American Sociological Review* 54:821–33.

Boix, Charles. 1998. *Political Parties, Growth and Equality: Conservative and Social Democratic Economic Strategies in the World Economy*. New York: Cambridge University Press.

______. 1999. "Setting the rules of the game: the choice of electoral systems in advanced democracies." *American Political Science Review* 93(3):609–624.

______. 2001. "Democracy, development, and the public sector." *American Journal of Political Science* 45(1):1–17.

Bolingbroke, Henry St. John, Viscount. 1965. *The Patriot King*. S. W. Jackman (ed.). Indianapolis: Bobbs–Merrill.

Bond, Patrick. 2001. "Strategy and Self-Activity in the Global Justice Movements." *Foreign Policy in Focus Discussion Paper #5*. www.fpif.org/papers/gjm_body.

Bonilla-Silva, Eduardo. 2003. *Racism without Racists: Color-Blind Racism and the Persistence of Racial Inequality in the United States*. Lanham, MD: Rowman & Littlefield.

Bonoli, Giuliano, and André Mach. 2000. "Switzerland: Adjustment politics with institutional constraints." Pp. 131–74 in Fritz Scharpf Scharpf and Vivien A. Schmidt (eds.), *Welfare and Work in the Open Economy. Volume II. Diverse Responses to Common Challenges*. Oxford, UK: Oxford University Press.

Booth, Bradford, William W. Falk, David R. Segal, and Mady Wechsler Segal. 2000. "The impact of military presence in local labor markets on the employment of women." *Gender & Society* 14(2):318–32.

Booth, John A., and Thomas W. Walker. 1993. *Understanding Central America*, second ed. Boulder, CO: Westview Press.

Booth, William James, Patrick James, and Hudson Meadwell (eds.). 1993. *Politics and Rationality*. New York: Cambridge University Press.

Borchorst, Anette. 1999. "Feminist thinking about the welfare state." Pp. 99–127 in Myra Marx Ferree, Judith Lorber, and Beth B. Hess (eds.), *Revisioning Gender*. Thousand Oaks, CA: Sage.

Boris, Eileen. 1994. *Home to Work: Motherhood and the Politics of Industrial Homework in the United States*. Cambridge, UK: Cambridge University Press.

______. 1995. "The racialized gendered state: Constructions of citizenship in the United States." *Social Politics* 2:160–80.

Boris, Eileen, and Elisabeth Prugl (eds.). 1996. *Homeworkers in Global Perspective: Invisible No More*. New York: Routledge.

Borjas, George. 1995. "Do blacks gain or lose from immigration?" Pp. 51–74 in Daniel Hamermesh and Frank Bean (eds.), *Help or Hindrance? The Economic Implications of Immigration for African Americans*. New York: Russell Sage.

Börzel, Tanja A. 1998. "Organizing Babylon: On the different conceptions of policy networks." *Public Administration* 76:253–73.

Bosl, Karl. 1970. "Political relations between East and West." Pp. 43–82 in F. Graus, Karl Bosl, F. Seibt, M. Postan, and A. Gieysztor (eds.), *Eastern and Western Europe in the Middle Ages*. London: Thames & Hudson.

Boswell, Terry, and Albert Bergesen. 1987. *America's Changing Role in the World System*. New York: Praeger.

Boswell, Terry, and Christopher Chase-Dunn. 2000. *The Spiral of Capitalism and Socialism: Toward Global Democracy*. Boulder, CD: Lynne Rienner.

Boswell, Terry, and William J. Dixon. 1990. "Dependency and rebellion: A cross-national analysis." *American Sociological Review* 55:540–59.

Bottomore, Tom. 1979. *Political Sociology*. New York: Harper & Row.

Boudon, Raymond. 2003. "Beyond rational choice theory." *Annual Review of Sociology* 29:1–21.

Bourdieu, Pierre. 1977. *Outline of a Theory of Practice*. Cambridge, UK: Cambridge University Press.

______. 1984. *Distinction: A Social Critique of the Judgement of Taste*. London: Routledge & Kegan Paul. Cambridge, MA: Harvard University Press.

______. 1988. *Homo Academicus*. Cambridge, UK: Polity Press.

______. 1988. *Homo Academicus*. Stanford, CA: Stanford University Press.

______. 1990. *In Other Words: Essays Towards a Reflexive Sociology*. Cambridge, UK: Polity Press.

______. 1991. *Language and Symbolic Power*. Cambridge, MA: Harvard University Press.

______. 1994. "Rethinking the state: genesis and structure of the bureaucratic field." *Sociological Theory* 12(1):1–18.

______. 1996. *The Rules of Art*. Stanford, CA: Stanford University Press.

______. 1998a. *Acts of Resistance: Against the New Myths of Our Time*. New York: New Press.

______. 1998b. *On Television*. New York: New Press.

______. 2001. *Masculine Domination*. Stanford, CA: Stanford University Press.

Bourdieu, Pierre, and Jean-Claude Passeron. 1971. *Reproduction in Education, Society and Culture*. Beverly Hills, CA: Sage.

______. 1979. *The Inheritors: French Students and Their Relation to Culture*. Chicago: University of Chicago Press.

______. 1990 [1977]. *Reproduction in Education, Society and Culture* (Richard Nice, trans.). Newbury Park, CA: Sage.

Bourdieu, Pierre et al. 1999. *The Weight of the World: Social Suffering in Contemporary Society*. Stanford, CA: Stanford University Press.

Bowman, Scott R. 1996. *The Modern Corporation and American Political Thought*. University Park: Penn State University Press.

Box-Steffensmeier, Janet. 1996. "A dynamic analysis of the role of war chests in campaign strategy." *American Journal of Political Science* 40:352–71.

Bracewell, Wendy. 1996. "Women, motherhood, and contemporary Serbian nationalism." *Women's Studies International Forum* 19(1/2):25–33.

Brachet-Márquez, Viviane. 1997. "Democratic transition and consolidation in Latin America: Steps toward a new theory of democratization." *Current Sociology* 45(1):15–53.

Bradley, David, Evelyne Huber, Stephanie Moller, François Nielsen, and John D. Stephens. 2003. "Distribution and redistribution in postindustrial democracies." *World Politics* 55:193–228.

Brady, Henry E., Kay Lehman Scholzman, Sidney Verba, and Laurel Elms. 2002. "Who bowls? the (un)changing stratification of participation." Pp. 219–42 in Barbara Norrander and Clyde Wilcox (eds.), *Understanding Public Opinion*. Washington, D.C.: CQ.

Bragger, Bill, and Stephen Reglar. 1994. *Politics, Economy and Society in Contemporary China*. Stanford, CA: Stanford University Press.

Brah, Avtar. 2001. "Re-framing Europe: Gendered racisms, ethnicities and nationalism in contemporary Western Europe." Pp. 207–30 in Janet Fink, Gail Lewis, and John Clarke (eds.), *Rethinking European Welfare*. London: Open University and Sage.

Brand, Laurie A. 1998. *Women, the State, and Political Liberalization: Middle Eastern and North African Experiences*. New York: Columbia University Press.

Brandon, Robert. 1998. *Making It Explicit: Reasoning, Representation and Discourse Commitment*. Cambridge, MA: Harvard University Press.

Brass, Daniel J. 1995. "A social network perspective on human resources management." *Research in Personnel and Human Resources Management* 13:39–79.

Bratton, Michael, and Nicholas van de Walle. 1997. *Democratic Experiments in Africa*. New York: Cambridge University Press.

Braungart, Richard. 1981. "Political sociology: history and scope." Pp. 1–80 in Samuel Long (ed.), *Handbook of Political Behavior*. New York: Plenum.

Brecher, Jeremy, Tim Costello, and Brendan Smith. 2000. *Globalization from Below. The Power of Solidarity*. Boston: South End.

Breed, Warren. 1955. "Social control in the newsroom: A functional analysis." *Social Forces* 33:326–355.

Brents, Barbara. 1992. "Class political organizing and welfare capitalism." *Critical Sociology* 19:69–101.

Breuilly, John. 1982. *Nationalism and the State*. New York: St. Martin's Press.

Brewer, John. 1989. *The Sinews of Power*. London: Hutchinson.

Bridges, Amy Beth. 1974. "Nicos Poulantas and the Marxist Theory of the State." *Politics and Society* 4(2):161–90.

Briggs, Vernon. 1992. *Mass Immigration and National Interest*. Armonk, NY: Sharpe.

______. 2001. *Immigration and American Unionism*. Ithaca, NY: Cornell University Press.

Brinton, Crane. 1965[1938]. *The Anatomy of Revolution*, revised ed. New York: Random House.

Brinton, Mary. 1998. "The social-institutional bases of gender stratification: Japan as an illustrative case." *American Journal of Sociology* 94:300–34.

Brinton, Mary, and Victor Nee. 1998. *The New Institutionalism in Sociology*. New York: Russell Sage Foundation.

Brockett, Charles D. 1991. "The structure of political opportunities and peasant mobilization in Central America." *Comparative Politics* 23:253–74.

Broder, David S. 2000. *Democracy Derailed*. New York: Harcourt.

Brody, Richard. 1978. "The puzzle of nonparticipation." Pp. 291–9 in Anthony King (ed.), *The New American Political System*. Washington, D.C.: American Enterprise Institute.

Brooks, Clem. 2000. "Civil rights liberalism and the suppression of a Republican political realignment in the United States, 1972 to 1996." *American Sociological Review* 65:483–505.

______. 2002. "Religious influence and the politics of family decline concern: Trends, sources, and U.S. political behavior." *American Sociological Review* 67:191–211.

Brooks, Clem, and David Brady. 1999. Income, economic voting, and long-term political change in the U.S., 1952–1996. *Social Forces* 77:1339–74.

Brooks, Clem, and Jeff Manza. 1997a. "Class politics and political change in the United States, 1952–1992." *Social Forces* 76:379–408.

______. 1997b. "Social cleavages and political alignments: U.S. presidential elections, 1960 to 1992." *American Sociological Review* 62:937–46.

______. 1997c. "The social and ideological bases of middle-class political realignment in the United

States, 1972 to 1992." *American Sociological Review* 62:191–208.

Brooks, Clem, Jeff Manza, and Catherine Bolzendahl. 2003. "Voting behavior and political sociology: Theories, debates, and future directions." *Research in Political Sociology* 12:137–73.

Brooks, Joel E. 1985. "Democratic frustration in the Anglo-American polities." *Western Political Quarterly* 38:250–61.

______. 1987. "The opinion-policy nexus in France." *Journal of Politics* 49:465–80.

______. 1990. "The opinion-policy nexus in Germany." *Public Opinion Quarterly* 54:508–29.

Brown, David S., and Wendy Hunter. 1999. "Democracy and social spending in Latin America, 1980–1992." *American Political Science Review* 93:779–90.

Brown, Michael K., Martin Carnoy, Elliott Currie, Troy Duster, David B. Oppenheimer, Marjorie M. Shultz, and David Wellman. 2003. *Whitewashing Race: The Myth of a Color-Blind Society*. Berkeley: University of California Press.

Brown, Michael, Owen Cote, Sean Lynn-Jones, and Steven Miller (eds.). 2001. *Nationalism and Ethnic Conflict, Revised Edition*. Cambridge, MA: MIT Press.

Brown, Howard G. 1995. *War, Revolution, and the Bureaucratic State: Politics and Army Administration in France, 1791–1799*. Oxford, UK: Clarendon Press.

Brown, Wendy. 1992. "Finding the man in the state." *Feminist Studies* 18(1):7–34.

Browne, William P. 1998. *Groups, Interests, and U.S. Public Policy*. Washington, DC. Georgetown University Press.

Browning, Rufus, Dale Marshall, and David Tabb. 1984. *Protest Is Not Enough: The Struggle of Blacks and Hispanics for Equality in Urban Politics*. Berkeley: University of California Press.

Brubaker, William Rogers. 1989. "Citizenship and naturalization: Policies and politics." Pp. 99–127 in W. R. Brubaker (ed.), *Immigration and the Politics of Citizenship in Europe and North America*. Lanham, MD: University Press of America.

______. 1992. *Citizenship and Nationhood in France and Germany*. Cambridge, MA: Harvard University Press.

Brulle, Robert J. 2000. *Agency, Democracy, and the Environment: An Examination of U.S. Environmental Organizations From the Perspective of Critical Theory*. Cambridge, MA: MIT Press.

Brunner, Otto, Werner Conze, and Reinhart Kosseleck. 1972–84. *Geschichtliche Grundbegriffe: Historisches Lexikon zur politisch-sozialen Sprache in Deutschland*. Stuttgart: Klett Verlag.

Bruno, Michael, and Jeffrey D. Sachs. 1985. *Economics of Worldwide Stagflation*. Cambridge, MA: Harvard University Press.

Brush, Lisa D. 1991. "The Red Menace and the rise of Italian fascism." *American Sociological Review* 56(5):652–64.

______. 2003. *Gender and Governance*. Walnut Creek, CA: AltaMira.

Brustein, William. 1996. *The Logic of Evil: The Social Origins of the Nazi Party, 1925 to 1933*. New Haven, CT: Yale University Press.

______. 2003. *Roots of Hate: Anti-Semitism in Europe before the Holocaust*. New York: Cambridge University Press.

Bryce, James. 1897. *The American Commonwealth*, Volume 2. London: Macmillan.

______. 1921. *Modern Democracies*. New York: Macmillan.

Brysk, Alison. 2002. "Introduction, transnational threats and opportunities." Pp. 1–16 in Alison Brysk (ed.), *Globalization and Human Rights*. Berkeley: University of California Press.

Bryson, Valerie. 1992. *Feminist Political Theory: An Introduction*. Houndmills, Basingstoke, Hampshire: Macmillan.

______. 1999. *Feminist Debates: Issues of Theory and Political Practice*. Basingstoke, Hampshire [England]: Macmillan.

Brzinski, J. B., Lancaster, T. D., and Tuschhoff, C. 1999. "Federalism and compounded representation: Key concepts and project overview." *Publius Journal of Federalism* 29(1):1–17.

Bubeck, D. E. 1995. *Care, Gender and Justice*. Oxford, UK: Clarendon Press.

Budig, Michelle Jean. 2002. "Male advantage and the gender composition of jobs: Who rides the glass escalator?" *Social Problems* 49(2):258–77.

Bueno de Mesquita, Bruce. 1981. *The War Trap*. New Haven, CT: Yale University Press.

Bueno de Mesquita, Bruce, and David Lalman. 1992. *War and Reason: Domestic and International Imperatives*. New Haven, CT: Yale University Press.

Bulbeck, C. 1998. *Re-orienting Western Feminisms: Women's Diversity in a Postcolonial World*. Cambridge, UK: Cambridge University Press.

Bull, Anna, Hanna Diamond, and Rosalind Marsh (eds.). 2000. *Feminisms and Women's Movements in Contemporary Europe*. New York: St. Martin's.

Board of Directors of the *Bulletin of the Atomic Scientists*. 2002. *Bulletin of the Atomic Scientists*. http://www.thebulletin.org/media/current.html.

Bullock, Brad, and Glenn Firebaugh. 1990. "Guns and butter? The effect of militarization on economic and social development in the Third World." *Journal of Political and Military Sociology* 18:231–66.

Bulmer-Thomas, Victor. 1994. *The Economic History of Latin America since Independence*. New York: Cambridge University Press.

Bunce, Valerie. 1999. *Subversive Institutions.* New York: Cambridge University Press.

Burawoy, Michael. 1979. *Manufacturing Consent: Change in the Labor Process under Monopoly Capitalism.* Chicago: University of Chicago Press.

Burawoy, Michael, and Erik Olin Wright. 2002. "Sociological marxism." Pp. 459–86 in Jonathan Turner (ed.), *Handbook of Sociological Theory.* New York: Kluwer.

Burch, Philip H., Jr. 1972. *The Managerial Revolution Reassessed.* Lexington, MA: D. C. Heath.

Burden, Barry C. 2000. "Voter turnout and the National Election Studies." *Political Analysis* 8:389–98.

Burke, Edmund. 1973/1790. *Reflections on the Revolution in France.* Garden City, NY: Anchor Books.

Burke, Kenneth. 1941. "The rhetoric of Hitler's 'battle.'" Pp. 191–220 in Burke (ed.), *The Philosophy of Literary Form.* Baton Rouge: Louisiana State University Press.

Burkhart, Ross E., and Michael S. Lewis-Beck. 1994. "Comparative democracy: The economic development thesis." *American Political Science Review* 88: 903–10.

Burleigh, Michael, and Wolfgang Wippermann. 1991. *The Racial State: Germany, 1933–1945.* Cambridge, UK: Cambridge University Press.

Burnham, Walter Dean. 1982. *The Crisis in American Politics.* New York: Oxford University Press.

______. 1987. "The turnout problem." Pp. 97–133 in James A. Reichley (ed.), *Elections American Style.* Washington, D.C.: Brookings Institute.

Burrin, Philippe. 2000. *Fascismo, Nazism, autoritarisme.* Paris: Editions du Seuil.

Burris, Val. 1979. "The structuralist influence in marxist theory and research." *The Insurgent Sociologist* IX(1):4–17.

______. 1987. "The political partisanship of American business: A study of corporate political action committees." *American Sociological Review* 52:732–44.

______. 1992. "Elite policy-planning networks in the United States." *Research in Politics and Society* 4:111–34.

______. 2001. "The two faces of capital: corporations and individual capitalists as political actors." *American Sociological Review* 66:361–81.

Burris, Val, and James Salt. 1990. "The politics of capitalist class segments." *Social Problems* 37:601–19.

Burstein, Paul. 1985. *Discrimination, Jobs, and Politics: The Struggle for Equal Employment Opportunity in the United States, 1940–1980.* Chicago: University of Chicago Press.

______. 1991. "Policy domains: Organization, culture, and policy outcomes." *Annual Review of Sociology* 17:327–50.

______. 1998. "Interest Organizations, Political Parties, and the Study of Democratic Politics." Pp. 39–56 in Anne Costain and Andrew McFarland (ed.), *Social Movements and American Political Institutions.* Lanham, MD: Rowman & Littlefield.

______. 1998. "Bringing the public back in: Should sociologists consider the impact of public opinion on public policy?" *Social Forces* 77:27–62.

______. 1998. "Interest organizations, political parties and the study of democratic policies." Pp. 39–56 in Anne Costain and Andrew McFarland (eds.), *Social Movements and American Political Institutions.* Boulder, CO: Rowman and Littlefield.

______. 1999. "Social movements and public policy." Pp. 3–21 in Marco Giugni, Doug McAdam, and Charles Tilly (eds.), How Social Movements Matter. Minneapolis: University of Minnesota Press.

______. 2003. "The Impact of Public Opinion on Public Policy: Review and Agenda." *Political Research Quarterly* 56(1):29–40.

Burstein, Paul, and W. Freudenberg. 1978. "Changing Public Policy." *American Journal of Sociology* 84:99–122.

Burstein, Paul, and April Linton. 2002. "The impact of political parties, interest groups and social movement organizations on public policy." *Social Forces* 81:380–408.

Burstein, Paul, Rachael Einwohner, and Jocelyn A. Hollander. 1995. "The success of political movements: A bargaining perspective." Pp. 275–95 in J. Craig Jenkins and Bert Klandermans (eds.), *The Politics of Social Protest.* Minneapolis: University of Minnesota Press.

Burstyn, Varda. 1983. "Masculine Dominance and the State," Pp. 45–89, in R. Milibend and J. Saville (eds.), *The Socialist Register.* London: Merlin Press.

Bussemaker, J., and R. Voet. 1998. "Citizenship and gender: Theoretical approaches and historical legacies." *Critical Social Policy* 18:277–307.

Butler, David, and Donald Stokes. 1969. *Political Change in Britain.* New York: St. Martin's.

Butler, Judith. 1990. *Gender Trouble: Feminism and the Subversion of Identity.* New York: Routledge.

Butler, Judith, Ernesto Laclau, and Slavoj Zizek. 2000. *Contingency, Hegemony, Universality.* London: Verso.

Button, James. 1978. *Black Violence: The Political Impact of the 1960s Riots.* Princeton, NJ: Princeton University Press.

______. 1989. *Blacks and Social Change: The Impact of the Civil Rights Movement in Southern Communities.* Princeton, NJ: Princeton University Press.

Caldeira, Rute. 2004. "A house and a farm or social transformation? Different modes of action and one dominant utopia." Paper presented at workshop

'Poverty, Inequality and Livelihoods,' University of Reading, June.

Caldeira, Teresa P. R., and James Holton. 1999. "Democracy and violence in Brazil." *Comparative Studies in Society and History* 41:691–729.

Calhoun, Craig (ed.). 1992. *Habermas and the Public Sphere*. Cambridge, MA: MIT Press.

______. 1994. *Social Theory and the Politics of Identity*. Cambridge, UK: Blackwell.

Calhoun, Craig. 1982. *The Question of Class Struggle*. Chicago: University of Chicago Press.

______. 1993. "New social movements of the early nineteenth century." *Social Science History* 17:385–427.

______. 1997. *Nationalism*. Minneapolis: University of Minnesota Press.

Calhoun-Brown, Allison. 1998. "While marching to Zion: Otherworldliness and racial empowerment in the black community." *Journal for the Scientific Study of Religion* 37:427–39.

Calivita, Kitty. 1992. *Inside the State: The Bracero Program, Immigration and the INS*. London: Routledge.

Calmfors, Lars, and John Driffill. 1988. "Bargaining structure, corporatism, and macroeconomic performance." *Economic Policy* 6:14–61.

Calvert, Randall L. 1986. *Models of Imperfect Information in Politics*. New York: Harwood.

Camerer, Colin F. 2003. *Behavioral Game Theory: Experiments in Strategic Interaction*. New York: Russell Sage Foundation.

Cameron, David R. 1978. "The expansion of the public economy: A comparative analysis." *American Political Science Review* 72:1243–61.

______. 1984. "Social democracy, corporatism and labor quiescence: the representation of economic interests in advanced capitalist societies." Pp. 143–78 in John H. Goldthorpe (ed.), *Order and Conflict in Contemporary Capitalism*. New York: Oxford University Press.

Cameron, Maxwell, and Brian Tomlin. 2000. *The Making of NAFTA*. Ithaca, NY: Cornell University Press.

Campbell, Angus, Gerald Gurin, and Warren E. Miller. 1954. *The Voter Decides*. Evanston, IL: Row Peterson.

Campbell, Angus, Philip E. Converse, Warren E. Miller, and Donald E. Stokes. 1960. *The American Voter*. New York: Wiley.

Campbell, John L. 2002. "Ideas, politics, and public policy." *Annual Review of Sociology* 28:21–38.

Campbell, John L., and Michael Allen. 2001. "Identifying shifts in policy regimes: Cluster and interrupted time-series analyses of U.S. income taxes." *Social Science History* 25(2):37–65.

Campbell, John L., and Ove K. Pedersen (eds.). 2001. *The Rise of Neoliberalism and Institutional Analysis*. Princeton, NJ: Princeton University Press.

Camus, Jean Yves. 1996. *Le Front National. Histoires et analyses*. Paris: Ballan.

______. 1999. *Extremism in Europe. 1998 Survey*. Paris: Editions de l' Aube/CERA.

Canak, William L. 1989. "Debt, austerity and Latin America in the new international division of labor." Pp. 153–69 in William L. (ed.), *Lost Promises: Debt, Austerity and Development in Latin America*. Canak. Boulder, CO: Westview.

Caniglia, Beth Schaefer. 2000. "Do elite alliances matter? Structural power in the environmental TSMO network." Ph.D. Dissertation, Department of Sociology, University of Notre Dame.

Canon, David T. 1999. *Race, Redistricting, and Representation: The Unintended Consequences of Black Majority Districts*. Chicago: University of Chicago Press.

Cappella, Joseph, and Kathleen Hall. Jamieson. 1997. *Spiral of Cynicism: The Press and the Public Good*. New York: Oxford University Press.

Cardoso, Fernando Henrique. 1979. "On the characterization of authoritarian regimes in Latin America." Pp. 33–60 in David Collier (ed.), *The New Authoritarianism in Latin America*. Princeton, NJ: Princeton University Press.

Carmines, Edward G., and Robert Huckfeldt. 1996. "Political behavior: An overview." Pp. 223–54 in Robert E. Goodin and Hans-Dieter Klingemann (eds.), *The New Handbook of Political Science*. New York: Oxford University Press.

Carmines, Edward G., and James Stimson. 1989. *Issue Evolution: Race and the Transformation of American Politics*. Princeton, NJ: Princeton University Press.

Carnoy, Martin. 1984. *The State and Political Theory*. Princeton: Princeton University Press.

Carpenter, Daniel. 2000. "What is the marginal value of analytic narratives?" *Social Science History* 24(4):653–67.

Carrington, Peter J. 1981. *Horizontal Co-optation through Corporate Interlocks*. Unpublished Ph.D. dissertation. University of Toronto.

Carroll, Eero. 1994. *Emergence and Structuring of Social Insurance Institutions*. Stockholm: Swedish Institute for Social Research.

Carruthers, Bruce C., and Sarah Babb. 1996. "The color of money and the nature of value: Greenbacks and gold during postbellum America." *American Journal of Sociology* 101:1556–91.

Carson, M. 2004. *From Common Market to Social Europe? Paradigm Shift and Institutional Change in European Policy on Food, Asbestos and Chemicals, and Gender Equality*. Stockholm: Almqvist & Wicksell Phd Stockholm Studies in Sociology, NS 22.

Carson, Rachel. 1962. *Silent Spring*. Greenwich, CT: Fawcett Crest Books.

Carsten, Francis Ludwig. 1954. *The Origins of Prussia*. Oxford, UK: Clarendon.

Carter, B., C. Harris, and S. Joshi. 1987. "The 1951–1955 Conservative government and the racialization of black immigration." *Immigrants and Minorities* 6(3):335–47.

______. 1993. "The 1951–1955 Conservative government and the racialization of black immigration." Pp. 55–71 in W. James and C. Harris (eds.), *Inside Babylon: The Carribean Diaspora in Britain*. London: Verso.

______. 1996. "Immigration policy and the racialization of migrant labor: The construction of national identities in the USA and Britain." *Ethnic and Racial Studies* 19(1):135–57.

Carty, R. Kenneth. 1991. *Canadian Political Parties in the Constituencies*, Vol. 23. Royal Commision on Electoral Reform and Party Financing and Canada Communication Group. Toronto and Oxford: Dundurn Press.

Carty, R. Kenneth, William Cross, and Lisa Young. 2000. *Rebuilding Canadian Party Politics*. Vancouver BC: UBC Press.

Carver, Terrell, and Paul Thomas. 1995. *Rational Choice Marxism*. University Park, PA: Pennsylvania State University Press.

Cash, W. J. 1991 [1941]. *The Mind of the South*. New York: Vintage.

Castañeda, Jorge. 1993. *Utopia Unarmed: The Latin American Left After the Cold War*. New York: Alfred A. Knopf.

Castells, Manuel. 1996. *The Rise of the Network Society*. Oxford, UK: Blackwell.

______. 1997. *The Power of Identity*. Malden, MA: Blackwell.

Castles, Francis G. (ed.). 1982. *The Impact of Parties: Politics and Policies in Democratic Capitalist States*. London: Sage.

______. 1985. *The Working Class and Welfare*. Sydney: Allen and Unwin.

______. 1988. *Australian Public Policy and Economic Vulnerability*. Sydney: Allen and Unwin.

______. 1993. *Families of Nations*. Aldershot: Dartmouth; Berkeley: University of California Press.

______. 1998. *Comparative Public Policy: Patterns of Post-War Transformation*. Chaltenham: Edward Elgar.

Castles, Francis, and Robert McKinlay. 1978. "Public welfare provision and the sheer futility of the sociological approach to politics." *British Journal of Political Science* 9:157–72.

Castles, Francis G., and Deborah Mitchell. 1993. "Worlds of welfare and families of nations." Pp. 93–128 in Francis G. Castles (ed.), *Families of Nations*. Aldershot: Dartmouth.

Castles, Stephen, and Alastair Davidson. 2000. *Citizenship and Migration*. London: Routledge.

Castles, Stephen, and Godulka Kosack. 1973. *Immigrant Workers and Class Structure in Western Europe*. Oxford, UK: Oxford University Press.

______. 1974. "How the trade unions try to control and integrate immigrant workers in the German Federal Republic." *Race* 15(4):497–514.

______. 1985. *Immigrant Workers and Class Structure in Western Europe, Second Edition*. Oxford, UK: Oxford University Press.

Castles, Stephen, and Mark Miller. 1998. *The Age of Migration, Second Edition*. New York: Guilford.

Castles, Stephen, H. Booth, and T. Wallace. 1984. *Here for Good: Western Europe's New Ethnic Minorities*. London: Pluto.

Castles, Stephen, B. Cope, M. Kalantiz, and M. Morrissey. 1992. *Mistaken Identity: Multiculturalism and the Demise of Nationalism in Australia, Third Edition*. Sydney: Pluto.

Cawson, Alan (ed.). 1985. *Organized Interests and the State*. London, UK: Sage.

______. (ed.). 1986. *Corporatism and Political Theory*. Oxford, UK: Basil Blackwell.

Cayer, N. Joseph, and Louis Weschler. 1988. *Social Change and Adaptative Management*. New York: St. Martin's.

CEC (Commission of the European Communities). 1992. An Open and Structured Dialogue between the Commission and Interest Groups. SEC (92) 2272 final. Brussels: Commission of the European Communities.

Cell, John Whitson. 1982. *The Highest Stage of White Supremacy: The Origins of Segregation in South Africa and the American South*. Cambridge, UK: Cambridge University Press.

Centeno, Miguel Angel. 1997. "Blood and debt: War and taxation in nineteenth-century Latin America." *American Journal of Sociology* 102:1565–605.

Center for Responsive Politics. 2002. http://www.crp.org.

Cerny, Philip G. 1997. "International finance and the erosion of capitalist diversity." Pp. 173–81 in Colin Crouch and Wolfgang Streeck (eds.), *Political Economy of Modern Capitalism*. London: Sage.

Cerulo, Karen, (ed.). 2002. *Culture in Mind: Toward a Sociology of Culture and Cognition*. New York: Routledge.

Cervantes, Mario, and Dominque Guellec. 2002. "The brain drain: Old myths, new realities." *OECD Observer*, January 230:40–3.

Chaftez, J. 1997. "Feminist theory and sociology. Underutilized contributions for mainstream theory." *Annual Review of Sociology* 23:97–120.

Chalaby, Jean. 1996. "Journalism as an Anglo–American invention." *European Journal of Communication* 11:303–26.

Chambliss, William J. 1964. "A Sociological Analysis of the Law of Vagrancy." *Social Problems* 12:66–67.

______ 1975. "Toward a Political Economy of Crime." *Theory and Society* 2:149–70.

Chan, Steve. 1985. "The impact of defense spending on economic performance: A survey of evidence and problems." *Orbis* 29:403–34.

Chang, Grace. 2000. *Disposable Domestics*. Cambridge, MA: South End.

Chappell, Marisa, Jenny Hutchinson, and Brian Ward. 1999. "Dress modestly, neatly... as if you were going to church": Respectability, class and gender in the Montgomery bus boycott and the early civil rights movement." Pp. 69–100 in Peter J. Ling and Sharon Monteith (eds.), *Gender in the Civil Rights Movement*. New York: Garland.

Chappelle, David L. 1994. *Inside Agitators: White Southerners in the Civil Rights Movement*. Baltimore, MD: John Hopkins University Press.

Charlesworth, Simon J. 2000. *A Phenomenology of Working Class Experience*. Cambridge, UK: Cambridge University Press.

Charlot, Jean, 1967. *L'UNR*. Paris: Armand Colin.

Chartier, Roger. 1991. *The Cultural Origins of the French Revolution*. Durham, NC: Duke University Press.

Chase-Dunn, Christopher. 1983. "The kernel of the capitalist world economy: three approaches." Pp. 35–78 in W. Thompson (ed.), *Contending Approaches in World System Analysis*. Beverly Hills, CA: Sage.

Chase-Dunn, Chris, and Terry Boswell. 2003. "Transnational social movements and democratic socialist parties in the semiperiphery." Paper presented at ASA meetings in Atlanta, GA, August 19.

Chaves, Mark. 1997. *Ordaining Women: Culture and Conflict in Religious Organizations*. Cambridge, MA: Harvard University Press.

Chehabi, H. E. 1995. "The provisional government and the transition from monarchy to Islamic republic in Iran." Pp. 127–143 in Yossi Shain and Juan J. Linz (eds.), *Between States: Interim Governments and Democratic Transitions*. Cambridge, UK: Cambridge University Press.

Chehabi, H. E., and Juan Linz. 1998a. "A theory of sultanism 1. A type of nondemocratic rule." Pp. 3–25 in H. E. Chehabi and Juan J. Linz (eds.), *Sultanistic Regimes*. Baltimore, MD: Johns Hopkins University Press.

______. 1998b. *Sultanistic Regimes*. Baltimore, MD: Johns Hopkins University Press.

Chen, Tung-Pi. 1997. "The nationality law of the People's Republic of China and the overseas Chinese in Hong Kong, Macao and Southeast Asia." Pp. 193–202 in Tahirih V. Lee (ed.), *Foreigners in Chinese Law*. New York: Garten.

Cheru, Fantu. 1997. "The silent revolution and the weapons of the weak: Transformation and innovation from below." Pp. 153–169 in Stephen Gill and James H. Mittelman (eds.), *Innovation and Transformation in International Studies*. Cambridge, UK: Cambridge University Press.

China. 1993. "The regulation of People's Republic of China on self-sponsored overseas study." Beijing: Ministry of Education, People's Republic of China.

Chirot, Daniel. 1986. *Social Change in the Modern Era*. New York: Harcourt Brace Jovanovich.

______. 1994. *Modern Tyrants: The Power and Prevalence of Evil in Our Age*. New York: The Free Press.

______. 1994. *How Societies Change*. Thousand Oaks, CA: Pine Forge Press.

Chodorow, Nancy. 1999. *The Power of Feelings*. New Haven, CT: Yale University Press.

Chomsky, Noam. 1993. *Year 501: The Conquest Continues*. Boston: South End.

Chong, Dennis. 1991. *Collective Action and the Civil Rights Movement*. Chicago: University of Chicago Press.

______. 2000. *Rational Lives: Norms and Values in Politics and Society*. Chicago: University of Chicago Press.

Chorley, Katharine. 1943. *Armies and the Art of Revolution*. London: Faber and Faber.

Chossudovsky, Michel. 1997. *The Globalization of Poverty. The Impacts of IMF and World Bank Reforms*. Penang: Third World Network.

Chwe, Michael. 2001. *Rational Ritual*. Princeton, NJ: Princeton University Press.

Çinar, Dilek. 1994. "From aliens to citizens. A comparative analysis of rules of transition." Pp. 49–72 in Rainier Bauböck (ed.), *From Aliens to Citizens*. Aldershot, UK: Avebury.

CIPE. 1997. *Improving Public Policy in the Middle East and North Africa*. Washington, DC: Center for International Private Enterprise.

Citrin, Jack, David O. Sears, Christopher Muste, and Cara Wong. 2001. "Multiculturalism in American public opinion." *British Journal of Political Science* 31:247–75.

Citrin, Jack, Donald Green, Christopher Muste, and Cara Wong. 1997. "Public opinion toward immigration reform." *Journal of Politics* 59(3):858–81.

Clark, T. J. 1973. *Image of the People: Gustave Courbet and the 1848 Revolution*. London: Thames and Hudson.

Clark, Terry N. 2001. "What have we learned in a decade on class and party politics?" Pp. 9–38 in Terry Nichols Clark and Seymour Martin Lipset (eds.), *The Breakdown of Class Politics*. Washington, DC: Woodrow Wilson Center Press.

Clark, Terry Nichols, and Vincent Hoffmann-Martinot (eds.). 1998. *The New Political Culture*. Boulder, CO: Westview Press.

Clark, Terry Nichols, Seymour Martin Lipset, and Michael Rempel. 2001. "The declining political significance of social class." Pp. 77–104 in Terry Nichols Clark and Seymour Martin Lipset (eds.), *The Breakdown of Class Politics: A Debate on Post-Industrial Stratification*. Washington, DC: Woodrow Wilson Center Press.

Clawson, Dan. 2003. *The Next Upsurge: Labor Fuses with Social Movements*. Ithaca, NY: Cornell University Press.

Clawson, Dan, Allen Kaufman, and Alan Neustadtl. 1985. "Corporate PACs for a new pax Americana." *The Insurgent Sociologist* 13:63–78.

Clawson, Dan, Alan Neustadtl, and James Bearden. 1986. "The logic of business unity: Corporate contributions to the 1980 congressional elections." *American Sociological Review* 51:797–811.

Clawson, Dan, Alan Neustadtl, and Denise Scott. 1992. *Money Talks: Corporate PACs and Political Influence*. New York: Basic Books.

Clawson, Dan, Alan Neustadtl, and Mark Weller. 1998. *Dollars and Votes, How Business Campaign Contributions Subvert Democracy*. Philadelphia: Temple University Press.

Clawson, Dan, and Alan Neustadtl. 1989. "Interlocks, PACs and corporate conservatism." *American Journal of Sociology* 94:749–73.

Clawson, Dan, and Tie-ting Su. 1990. "Was 1980 special? A comparison of 1980 and 1986 corporate PAC contributions." *Sociological Quarterly* 31:371–87.

Clayman, Steven, and John. Heritage. 2002. *The News Interview*. Cambridge, UK: Cambridge University Press.

Cleaver, Harry. 1994. "The Chiapas uprising." *Studies in Political Economy* 44:141–7.

Cleaves, Peter. 1974. *Bureaucratic Politics and Administration in Chile*. Berkeley: University of California Press.

Clemens, Elisabeth S., and James Cook. 1999. "Politics and institutionalism: explaining durability and change." *Annual Review of Sociology* 25:441–66.

Clemens, Elisabeth. 1996. "Organizational form as frame: Collective identity and political strategy in the American labor movement, 1880–1920." Pp. 206–26 in D. McAdam, J. McCarthy, and M. Zald (eds.), *Comparative Perspectives on Social Movements*. New York: Cambridge University Press.

______. 1997. *The People's Lobby: Organizational Innovation and the Rise of Interest Group Politics in the United States, 1890–1925*. Chicago: University of Chicago Press.

______. 2003. "Rereading Skowronek: A precocious theory of institutional change." *Social Science History* 27:443–53.

Coates, Barry. 2001. "Big business at your service." *Guardian Weekly*, March 15–21:28.

Coates, David. 2000. *Models of Capitalism*. Oxford, UK: Polity Press.

Cochran, Thomas C., and William Miller. 1961 [1942]. *The Age of Enterprise*. New York: Harper & Row.

Cockett, R. 1995. *Thinking the Unthinkable: Think-Tanks and the Economic Counter-Revolution, 1931–1983*. London, UK: Harper Collins.

Coen, David. 1998. "The European business interest and the nation state: Large-firm lobbying in the European Union and member states." *Journal of Public Policy* 18:75–1000.

Coenders, Marcel, Peer Scheepers, Paul M. Sniderman, and Genevieve Verberk. 2001. "Blatant and subtle prejudice: Dimensions, determinants and consequences; some comments on Pettigrew and Meertens." *European Journal of Social Psychology* 31:281–98.

Cohan, A. S. 1975. *Theories of Revolution: An Introduction*. London: Nelson.

Cohen, Benjamin. 1998. *The Geography of Money*. Ithaca, NY: Cornell University Press.

Cohen, Bernard C. 1963. *The Press and Foreign Policy*. Princeton, NJ: Princeton University Press.

______. 1995. *Democracies and Foreign Policy: Public Participation in the United States and the Netherlands*. Madison: University of Wisconsin Press.

Cohen, Jean L. 1995. "Critical theory and feminist critiques: The debate with Jurgen Habermas." Pp. 57–90 in Johanna Mehan (ed.), *Feminists Read Habermas: Gendering the Subject of Discourse*. New York: Routledge.

Cohen, Jean, and Andrew Arato. 1992. *Civil Society and Political Theory*. Cambridge, MA: MIT Press.

Cohen, Joshua, and Joel Rogers. 1995. *Associations and Democracy*. London: Verso.

Cohen, Joshua, and Charles Sabel. 1997. "Directly-deliberative polyarchy." *European Law Journal* 3: 313–42.

Cohen, Stanley. 1972. *Folk Devils and Moral Panics: The Creation of the Mods and Rockers*. London: MacGibbon and Kee.

Cohen, Steven Martin. 1989. *The Dimensions of American Jewish Liberalism*. New York: American Jewish Committee.

Cole, Tom. 1993. "Comments." Pp. 60–63 in Michael Margolis and John Green (eds.), *Machine Politics, Sound Bites and Nostalgia*. Lanham, MD: University Press of America.

Coleman, James S. 1966. "The possibility of a social welfare function." *American Economic Review* 56:1105–1132.

______. 1973. "Loss of power." *American Sociological Review* 38:1–17.

______. 1986. "Social theory, social research, and a theory of action." *American Journal of Sociology* 91: 1309–35.

______. 1990. *Foundations of Social Theory*. Cambridge, MA: Harvard, Belknap Press.

Collier, David. 1979. "Overview of the bureaucratic–authoritarian model." Pp. 19–32 in David Collier (ed.), *The New Authoritarianism in Latin America*. Princeton, NJ: Princeton University Press.

Collier, David S., and Richard E. Messick. 1975. "Prerequisites versus difussion: testing alternative explanations of social security adoption." *American Political Sciennce Review* 69:1299–315.

Collier, Ruth Berins. 1999. *Paths toward Democracy: The Working Class and Elites in Western Europe and South America*. Cambridge/, New York: Cambridge University Press.

Collier, Ruth Berins, and David Collier. 1991. *Shaping the Political Arena. Critical Junctures, the Labor Movement, and Regime Dynamics in Latin America*. Princeton, NJ: Princeton University Press.

______. 1991. *Shaping the Political Arena*. Princeton, NJ: Princeton University Press.

Collingwood, R. G. 1942. *The New Leviathan*. Oxford, UK: The Clarendon Press.

Collins, Patricia Hill. 1991. *Black Feminist Thought: Knowledge, Consciousness, and the Politics of Empowerment*. New York: Routledge.

Collins, Randall. 1971. "Functional and conflict theories of educational stratification." *American Sociological Review* 36:1002–19.

______. 1975. *Conflict Sociology: Toward an Explanatory Social Science*. New York: Academic Press.

______. 1979. *The Credential Society*. New York: Academic Press.

______. 1981. "Does modern technology change the rules of geopolitics?" *Journal of Political and Military Sociology* 9:163–77.

______. 1986. *Weberian Sociological Theory*. Cambridge, UK: Cambridge University Press.

______. 1988. *Theoretical Sociology*. New York: Harcourt Brace Jovanovich.

______. 1990. "Conflict theory and the advance of macro-historical sociology." Pp. 68–87 in George Ritzer (ed.), *Frontiers of Social Theory*. New York: Columbia University Press.

______. 1993. "Maturation of the state-centered theory of revolution and ideology." *Sociological Theory* 11:117–128.

______. 1995. "Prediction in macrosociology: The case of the Soviet collapse." *American Journal of Sociology* 100(6):1552–93.

______. 1998. *The Sociology of Philosophies*. Cambridge, MA: Harvard University Press.

______. 1999. *Macrohistory: Essays in the Sociology of the Long Run*. Stanford, CA: Stanford University Press.

______. 2001. "Ethnic change in macro-historical perspective." Pp. 12–46 in E. Anderson and D. S. Massey (eds.), *Problem of the Century: Racial Stratification in the United States*. New York: Russell Sage Foundation.

Colomy, Paul (ed.). 1990a. *Neofunctionalist Sociology*. Aldershot: E. Elgar.

______. 1990b. "Strategic groups and political differentiation in the antebellum United States." Pp. 222–64 in Jeffrey C. Alexander and Paul Colomy (eds.), *Differentiation Theory and Social Change*. New York: Columbia University Press.

Colwell, Mary. 1980. "The foundation connection: Links among foundations and recipient organizations." In R. F. Arnove (ed.), *Philanthropy and Cultural Imperialism*. Boston: Hall.

______. 1993. *Private Foundation and Public Policy*. New York: Garland.

Compaine, Benjamin, and Douglas Gomery. 2000. *Who Owns the Media?: Competition and Concentration in the Mass Media Industry*. Mahwah, NJ: Erlbaum.

Compston, Hugh. 1997. "Union power, policy making, and unemployment in Western Europe, 1972–1993." *Comparative Political Studies* 30:732–51.

Conaghan, Catherine M., and Malloy, James M. 1994. *Unsettling Statecraft: Democracy and Neoliberalism in the Central Andes*. Pittsburgh: University of Pittsburgh Press.

______. 2002. *Gender*. Cambridge, UK: Polity.

Connell, R. W. 1977. *Ruling Class, Ruling Culture: Studies of Conflict, Power, and Hegemony in Australian Life*. Cambridge, UK: Cambridge University Press.

______. 1987. *Gender and Power*. Stanford, CA: Stanford University Press.

______. 1990. "The State, gender and sexual politics." *Theory and Society* 19:507–44.

______. 1995. *Masculinities*. Berkeley: University of California Press.

______. 1997. "Why is classical theory classical?" *American Journal of Sociology* 102(6):1511–57.

Connor, Walker. 1994. *Ethnonationalism: The Quest for Understanding*. Princeton, NJ: Princeton University Press.

Conover, Pamela Johnston. 1988. "Feminists and the gender gap." *Journal of Politics* 50:985–1010.

Conover, Pamela Johnston, and Stanley Feldman. 1984. "How people organize the political world: A schematic model." *American Journal of Political Science* 8:95–126.

Considine, Mark, and Jenny Lewis. 2003. "Bureaucracy, network or enterprise? comparing models of governance in Australia, Britain, the Netherlands, and New Zealand." *Public Administration Review* 63(2):131–40.

Converse, Philip E. 1964. "The nature of belief systems in mass publics." Pp. 75–169 in David A. Apter (ed.), *Ideology and Discontent*. New York: Free Press.

Conway, M. Margaret. 2000. *Political Participation in the United States*. Washington, D.C.: CQ.

Conway, M. Margaret, David Ahearn, and Gertrude A. Steuernagel. 1999. *Women and Public Policy, 2nd edition*. Washington, DC: CQ.

Cook, Garth. 1999. "Working for the government is cool?". Pp. 30–36 in Frederick Lane (ed.), *Current Issues in Public Administration*. 6th ed. Boston: Bedford/St. Martin's.

Cook, Terrence. 2002. *Nested Political Coalitions*. Westport, CT: Praeger.

Cook, Thomas D., and Donald T. Campbell 1979. *Quasi-experimentation: Design and Analysis Issues*. New York: Houghton Mifflin.

Cook, Timothy E. 1989. *Making Laws and Making News: Media Strategies in the U.S. House of Representatives*. Washington, DC: Brookings Institution.

______. 1998. *Governing With the News*. Chicago: University of Chicago Press.

Cooley, Charles Horton. 1902. *Human Nature and the Social Order.* New York: Scribner's.

Cooney, Mark. 1997. "From war to tyranny: Lethal conflict and the State." *American Sociological Review* 62:316–38.

Cooper, Frederick, and Ann Laura Stoler. 1997. *Tensions of Empire. Colonial Cultures in a Bourgeois World*. Berkeley and Los Angeles: University of California Press.

Cooper, William Jr., and Terrill Cooper. 1991. *The American South: A History*. New York: McGraw–Hill.

Coplin, William, Astrid Merget, and Carolyn Bourdeauz. 2002. "The professional researcher as change agent in the government-performance movement." *Public Administration Review* 62(6): 699–711.

Cornell, Stephen E. 1988. *The Return of the Native: American Indian Political Resurgence*. New York: Oxford University Press.

Cornell, Stephen E., and Douglass Hartmann. 1998. *Ethnicity and Race: Making Identities in a Changing World*. Thousand Oaks, CA: Pine Forge Press.

Cornia, G. A., R. Jolly, and F. Stewart. 1987. *Adjustment with a Human Face*. Oxford, UK: Clarendon.

Corrado, Anthony. 1997. "A history of campaign finance law." Pp. 27–35 in Anthony Corrado, Thomas E. Mann, Daniel R. Ortiz, Trevor Potter, and Frank J. Sorauf (eds.), *Campaign Finance Reform: A Sourcebook*. Washington, D.C.: Brookings Institution.

Corrêa, Sônia. 1994. *Population and Reproductive Rights*. London: Zed Books.

Coser, Lewis (ed.). 1956. *The Functions of Social Conflict*. New York: Free Press.

______. 1966. *Political Sociology*. New York: Harper Torchbook.

______. 1976. "The Notion of Power: Theoretical Developments." In Lewis Coser and Bernard Rosenberg (eds.), *Sociological Theory: A Book of Readings*. New York: Macmillan.

Costain, Anne N. 1992. *Inviting Women's Rebellion*. Baltimore, MD: Johns Hopkins University Press.

Costain, Anne N., and Steven Majstorovic. 1994. "Congress, social movements and public opinion." *Political Research Quarterly* 47:111–35.

Cotter, Cornelius P., James L. Gibson, John F. Bibby, and Robert J. Huckshorn. 1984. *Party Organizations in American Politics*. New York: Praeger.

Courtney, John C. 1995. *Do Conventions Matter? Choosing National Party Leaders in Canada*. Montreal and Kingston: McGill–Queens University Press.

______. 2004. *Elections*. Vancouver: UBC Press.

Cowan, M. P., and R. W. Shenton. 1996. *Doctrines of Development*. New York: Routledge.

Cox, Gary W., and Mathew D. McCubbins, 1986. "Electoral politics as a redistributive game." *Journal of Politics* 48:370–89.

______. 1993. *Legislative Leviathan: Party Government in the House*. Berkeley: University of California Press.

Cox, Gary W., and Keith T. Poole. 2002. "On measuring partisanship in roll-call voting: The U.S. House of Representatives, 1877–1999." *American Journal of Political Science* 46:477–89.

Cox, Robert W. 1992. "Global perestroika." Pp. 21–45 in Ralph Miliband and Leo Panitch (eds.), *Socialist Register 1992*. London: Merlin.

______. 1999. "Civil society at the turn of the millennium: Prospects for an alternative world order." *Review of International Studies* 25, 1:3–28.

Craig, Richard. 1971. *The Bracero Program: Interest Groups and Foreign Policy*. Austin: University of Texas Press.

Crane, Diana, (ed.). 1994. *The Sociology of Culture*. Cambridge, MA: Blackwell.

Crenshaw, K. 1995. *Critical Race Theory: The Key writings That Formed the Movement*. New York: New Press.

Cress, Daniel M., and David A. Snow. 2000. "The outcomes of homeless mobilization: The influence of organization, disruption, political mediation, and framing." *American Journal of Sociology* 105:1063–1104.

Critchley, Simon. 1998. "Metaphysics in the dark: A response to Richard Rorty and Ernesto Laclau." *Political Theory* 26:803–17.

Cronin, Thomas E. 1989. *Direct Democracy: The Politics of Initiative, Referendum and Recall*. Cambridge, MA: Harvard University Press.

Crotty, William (ed.). 1986. *Political Parties in Local Areas*. Knoxville, TN: University of Tennessee Press.

Crouch, Colin. 1985. "Conditions for trade union wage restraint." Pp. 105–39 in Leon N. Lindberg and Charles S. Maier (eds.), *The Politics of Inflation and Economic Stagnation*. Washington, DC: Brookings Institution.

______. 1993. *Industrial Relations and European State Traditions*. Oxford, UK: Oxford University Press.

______. 1997. *Industrial Relations and the European State Tradition*. Oxford, UK: Clarendon.

Crouch, Colin, David Fiengold, and Maro Sako. 1999. *Are Skills the Answer?* Oxford, UK: Oxford University Press.

Cukierman, Alex, and Francesco Lippi. 1999. "Central bank independence, centralization of wage bargaining, inflation, and unemployment: Theory and some evidence." *European Economic Review* 43:1395–1434.

Curtis, Russell, and Louis A. Zurcher. 1973. "Stable resources of protest movements: The multi-organizational field." *Social Forces* 52:53–61.

Daalder, H. 1955. "Parties and politics in the Netherlands." *Political Studies* 3:1–16.

Dahl, Robert A. 1958. "A critique of the ruling elite model." *American Political Science Review* 52: 463–9.

______. 1961. *Who Governs? Democracy and Power in an American City*. New Haven, CT: Yale University Press.

______. 1967. *Pluralist Democracy in the United States: Conflict and Consent*. Chicago, IL: Rand McNally.

______. 1971. *Polyarchy: Participation and Opposition*. New Haven, CT: Yale University Press.

______. 1975. "Governments and political oppositions." In Fred I. Greenstein and Nelson W. Polsby (eds.), *Handbook of Political Science. Volume 3: Macropolitical Theory*. Reading, MA: Addison-Wesley.

______. 1982. *Dilemmas of Pluralist Democracy: Autonomy vs. Control*. New Haven, CT: Yale University Press.

______. 1989. *Democracy and Its Critics*. New Haven, CT: Yale University Press.

______. 1990. *After the Revolution?: Authority in a Good Society*, rev. ed. New Haven, CT: Yale University Press.

______. 1998. *On Democracy*. New Haven, CT: Yale University Press.

Dahl, Robert A., and Charles E. Lindblom. 1976. *Politics, Economics and Welfare*. Chicago, IL: University of Chicago Press.

Dahlerup, D. 2003. "Three waves of feminism in Denmark." Pp. 341–50 in G. Griffin and R. Braidotti (eds.), *Thinking Differently: A Reader in European Women's Studies*. London and New York: Zed Books.

Dahrendorf, Ralf. 1959. *Class and Class Conflict in Industrial Society*. Stanford, CA: Stanford University Press.

______. 1967. *Society and Democracy in Germany*. New York: Norton.

______. 1974. "Citizenship and beyond: the social dynamics of an idea." *Social Research* 41:673–701.

______. 1987. "Rights of citizenship: an interview with Ralf Dahrendorf." *Reporting from the Russell Sage Foundation* 10:6–7.

______. 1988. "Citizenship and the modern social conflict." Pp. 112–25 in Richard Holme and Michael Elliott *1688–1988: Time for a New Constitution*. London: Macmillan.

______. 1994. "The changing quality of citizenship." Pp. 10–19 in Bart van Steenbergen (ed.), *The Condition of Citizenship*. Newbury Park, CA: Sage.

Dalton, Russell. 1994. *The Green Rainbow: Environmental Groups in Western Europe*. New Haven, CT: Yale University Press.

______. 1996. *Citizen Politics: Public Opinion and Political Parties in Advanced Industrial Societies*. Chatham, NJ: Chatham House.

Dalton, Russell J. 1988. *Citizen Politics in Western Democracies*. Chatham, NJ: Chatham House.

Dalton, Russell J., and Martin P. Wattenberg. 1993. "The Not So Simple Act of Voting." Pp. 193–218 in Ada Finifter (ed.), *Political Science: The State of the Discipline II*. Washington, DC: American Political Science Association.

______. 2000. *Parties Without Partisans: Political Change in Advanced Industrial Democracies*. Oxford, UK: Oxford University Press.

Dalton, Russell J., Scott C. Flanagan, and Paul A. Beck. 1984. *Electoral change in Advanced Industrial*

Democracies: Realignment or Dealignment? Princeton, NJ: Princeton University Press.

Daly, Glyn. 1999. "Marxism and postmodernity." Pp. 61–84 in Andrew Gamble, David Marsh, and Tony Tant (eds.). *Marxism and Social Science*. Champaign. Urbana: University of Illinois Press.

Daly, Mary, and Jane Lewis. 2000. "The concept of social care and the analysis of contemporary welfare states." *British Journal of Sociology* 51(2):281–98.

Daly, Mary. 2000. "A fine balance: Women's labor market participation in international comparison." Pp. 467–510 in Fritz W. Scharpf and Vivien A. Schmidt (eds.), *Welfare and Work in the Open Economy, Volume II*. London: Oxford University Press.

Daly, Mary, and Jane Lewis. 1998. "Introduction: Conceptualizing social care in the context of welfare state restructuring." Pp. 1–24 in Jane Lewis (ed.), *Gender, Social Care, and Welfare State Restructuring*. Aldershot: Ashgate.

Danziger, Sheldon, and Peter Gottschalk. 1995. *Unequal America*. Cambridge, MA: Harvard University Press.

______. 1997. *America Unequal*. Cambridge, MA: Harvard University Press.

Dark, Taylor E. 1999. *The Unions and the Democrats: An Enduring Alliance*. Ithaca, NY: Cornell University Press.

David, Paul. 1985. "Clio and the economics of QWERTY." *Economic Review* 75(May):332–7.

Davidoff, L. 1998. "Regarding some 'old husbands' tales': Public and private in feminist history." Pp. 164–94 in J. B. Landes (ed.), *Feminism the Public and the Private*. Oxford, UK: Oxford University Press.

Davidson, Basil. 1992. *The Black Man's Burden. Africa and the Curse of the Nation-State*. New York: Times Books.

Davidson, Chandler. 1994. "The recent evolution of voting rights law affecting racial and language minorities." Pp. 21–37 in C. Davidson and B. Grofman (eds.), *Quiet Revolution in the South: The Impact of the Voting Rights Act, 1965–1990*. Princeton NJ: Princeton University Press.

Davis, F. James. 2001. *Who Is Black?: One Nation's Definition*. University Park: Pennsylvania State University Press.

Davis, Gerald F. 1999. "Financial markets and classes in late capitalism." Paper presented at the Annual Meeting of the Academy of Management. Chicago. August.

Davis, Gerald F., and Mark S. Mizruchi. 1999. "The money center cannot hold: Commercial banks in the U.S. system of corporate governance." *Administrative Science Quarterly* 44:215–39.

Davis, Gerald F., and Michael Useem. 2002. "Top management, company directors, and corporate control." Pp. 233–59 in Andrew Pettigrew, Howard Thomas, and Richard Whittington (eds.), *Handbook of Strategy and Management*. London: Sage.

Davis, Gerald F., Mina Yoo, and Wayne E. Baker. 2003. "The small world of the American corporate elite, 1982–2001." *Strategic Organization* 1:301–326.

Davis, James A. 1996. "Review essay: Value change in global perspective." *Public Opinion Quarterly* 60:322–31.

Davis, Joseph, ed. 2002. *Stories of Change*. Albany, NY: SUNY Press.

Davis, Kingsley. 1949. *Human Society*. New York: Macmillan.

______. 1988. "Social science approaches to international migration." Pp. 245–61 in Michael Teitelbaum and Jay Winter (eds.), *Population Resources in Western Intellectual Traditions*. NY: Cambridge University Press.

Davis, Mike. 2000. *Late Victorian Holocausts. El Nino Famines and the Making of the Third World*. New York and London: Verso.

Dawe, Alan. 1978. "Theories of Social Action." Pp. 362–417 in Tom Bottomore and Robert Nisbet (eds.), *A History of Sociological Analysis*. New York: Basic Books.

Dawisha, Karen, and Bruce Parrott (eds.). 1997. *The Consolidation of Democracy in East-Central Europe*. Cambridge, UK: Cambridge University Press.

Dawley, Alan. 1976. *Class and Community: The Industrial Revolution in Lynn*. Cambridge, MA: Harvard University Press.

Dawson, Michael C. 1994. *Behind the Mule*. Princeton, NJ: Princeton University Press.

Day, Alan. 2000. "Think tanks in Western Europe." Pp. 103–38 in J. G. McGann and R. K. Weaver (eds.), *Think Tanks and Civil Societies: Catalysts for Ideas and Action*. New Brunswick, NJ: Transaction.

De Barbieri, Teresita. 1994. "Gender and population policy." Pp. 257–66 in Amy Mazur (ed.), *Beyond the Numbers*. Washington, D.C.: Island Press.

De Beer, Paul, Cok Vrooman, and Jean Marie Wildeboer Schut. 2001. "Measuring welfare state performance: Three or two worlds of welfare capitalism?" Working Paper No. 276. Luxembourg Income Study. Available at http://www.lisproject.org/publications.htm.

de Bellaigue, Christopher. 2002. "Who rules Iran?" *New York Review of Books* 49(11):17–20.

de Gouges, Olympia. 1791/1986. "Déclaration des droits de la femme et de la citoyenne." Pp. 99–112 in Olumpia De Gouges (ed.), *Oeuvres*. Paris: Mercure de Francais.

De Graaf, Nan D., Paul Nieuwbeerta, and Anthony Heath. 1995. "Class mobility and political preferences: Individual and contextual effects." *American Journal of Sociology* 100:997–1027.

De Jong, Attie, and Bettina Bock. 1995. "Positive action in organizations within the European Union." Pp. 182–202 in Anneke van Doorne-Huiskes, Jacques van Hoof, and Ellie Roelofs (eds.), *Women and the European Labor Markets*. London: Paul Chapman.

De La Garza, Rodolfo O., Martha Menchaca, and Louis DeSipio. 1994. *Barrio Ballots: Latino Politics in the 1990 Election*. Charlottesville: University of Virginia Press.

De Tocqueville, Alexis 1969[1850]. *Democracy in America* (George Lawrence, trans., and J. P. Mayer, ed.). Garden City, NY: Anchor.

______. 1955[1856]. *The Old Regime and the French Revolution*. Garden City, NY: Doubleday.

de Tocqueville, Alexis. 1990[1840]. *De la Démocratie en Amérique*, Vol. 2. Paris: Librairie Philosophique J. Vrin.

Deaconz, Bob. 2000. "Eastern European welfare states: The impact of the politics of globalization." *Journal of European Social Policy* 10:146–61.

Dean, D. W. 1992. "Conservative governments and the restriction of Commonwealth immigration in the 1950s." *The Historical Journal* 35(1):171–84.

Degler, Carl N. 1972. "Racism in the United States: An essay review." *Journal of Southern History* 38:101–8.

DeGrasse, R. 1984. "The military and semiconductors." Pp. 77–104 in John Tirman (ed.), *The Militarization of High Technology*. Cambridge, MA: Balinger.

Degregori, Carlos Ivan. 1990. *Ayacucho 1969–1979. El surgimiento de Sendero Luminoso*. Lima: Instituto de Estudios Peruanos.

Degregori, Carlos Ivan, José Coronel, Ponciano del Pino, and Orin Starn, 1996. *Las rondas campesinas y la derrota del Sendero Luminoso*. Lima: Instituto de Estudios Peruanos/Universidad Nacional de San Cristobal de Huamanga.

DeJong, Jocelyn. 2002. "The Role and limitations of the Cairo International Conference on Population and Development." *Social Science and Medicine* 51:941–53.

Dekmejian, R. Hrair. 1995. *Islam in Revolution: Fundamentalism in the Arab World*. 2nd ed. Syracuse, NY: Syracuse University Press.

Del Boca, Daniela. 1998. "Labour policies, economic flexibility, and women's work: The Italian experience." Pp. 124–30 in Eileen Drew, Ruth Emerek, and Evelyn Mahon (eds.), *Women, Work, and the Family in Europe*. New York: Routledge.

Della Porta, Donatella, and Mario Diani. 1999. *Social Movements: An Introduction*. Malden, MA: Blackwell.

Della Porta, Donatella, Hanspeter Kriesi, and Dieter Rucht. 1999. *Social Movements in a Globalizing World*. Houndmills, Basingstoke, Hampshire, New York: Macmillan; St. Martin's.

Della Porta, Donatella, and Dieter Rucht. 1995. "Left-Libertarian Movements in Context: A Comparison of Italy and West Germany, 1965–1990." Pp. 229–72 in J. Craig Jenkins and Bert Klandermans (eds.), *The Politics of Social Protest*. Minneapolis: University of Minnesota Press.

Della Sala, Vincent. 2002. "'Modernization' and welfare state restructuring in Italy: The impact on child care." Pp. 171–90 in Sonya Michel and Rianne Mahon (eds.), *Child Care Policy at the Crossroads*. New York: Routledge.

DeMenil, George. 1971. *Barginaing: Monopoly Power versus Union Power*. Cambridge, MA: MIT Press.

Demeny, Paul. 1998. "International dimensions of population policies." Pp. 209–25 in Paul Demeny and Geoffrey McNicoll (eds.), *The Reader in Population and Development*. New York: St. Martin's.

Den Dulk, Laura, Anneke van Doorne-Huiskes, and Joop Schippers. 1999. *Work–Family Arrangements in Europe*. Amsterdam: Thela Thesis.

Derksen, Linda, and John Gartell. 1993. "The social context of recycling." *American Sociological Review* 58:434–5.

Derrida, Jacques. 1978. *Writing and Difference*. London: Routledge and Kegan Paul.

______. 1988. *Limited Inc*. Evanston, IL: Northwestern University Press.

______. 1994. *Spectres of Marx*. London: Routledge.

Desche, Michael. 1999. *Civilian Control of the Military*. Baltimore: Johns Hopkins University Press.

Deutsch, Karl. 1996. *Nationalism and Social Communication: An Inquiry into the Foundations of Nationality*. Cambridge, MA: The MIT Press.

Devine, Joel, A. 1985. "State and state expenditure: determinants of social investment and social consumption spending in the postwar United States." *American Sociological Review* 50(2):150–65.

Dewan, Ritu. 1999. "Gender implications of the 'new' economic policy: A conceptual overview." *Women's Studies International Forum* 22(4):425–29.

Dews, Peter (ed.). 1986. *Habermas: Autonomy and Solidarity*. London: Verso.

Di Muccio, R. B. A., and James N. Rosenau. 1992. "Turbulence and sovereignty in world politics: Explaining the relocation of legitimacy in the 1990s and beyond." Pp. 60–76 in Zdravko Mlinar (ed.), *Globalization and Territorial Identities*. Adershot: Avebury Ashgate.

Di Palma, Giuseppe. 1990. *To Craft Democracies. An Essay on Democratic Transitions*. Berkeley: University of California Press.

Diamond, Edwin, and Stephen Bates. 1992. *The Spot: The Rise of Political Advertising on Television*, 3rd ed. Cambridge, MA: MIT Press.

Diamond, Larry. 1992. "Economic development and democracy reconsidered." Pp. 93–139 in Gary Marks and Larry Diamond (eds.), *Reexamining Democracy*. Newbury Park, CA: Sage.

______. 1999. *Developing Democracy: Toward Consolidation*. Baltimore, London: Johns Hopkins University Press.

______. 1999. *Developing Democracy*. Baltimore, MD: Johns Hopkins University Press.

Diamond, Larry, Juan J. Linz, and S. M. Lipset. 1988. *Democracy in Developing Countries*. Boulder, CO: L. Rienner.

______. 1995. "Introduction." Pp. 1–66 in Larry Diamond, Juan J. Linz, and Seymour Martin Lipset (eds.), *Politics in Developing Countries. Comparing Experiences with Democracy*, 2nd ed. Boulder, CO: Lynne Rienner.

Diamond, Sara. 1995. *Roads to Dominion: Right-Wing Movements and Political Power in the United States*. New York: Guilford Press.

Diani, Mario. 1995. *Green Networks*. Edinburgh, UK: Edinburgh University Press.

Dias Martins, Monica. 2000. "The MST challenge to neoliberalism." *Latin American Perspectives* 27, 5:33–45.

Diaz-Polanco, Hector. 1991. *Autonomía regional: la autodeterminación de los pueblos indios*. México DF: Siglo XXI.

Dicey, A. V. 1914. *Law and Opinion in England*. London: Macmillan.

Dietz, Mary. 1985. "Citizenship with a feminist face: The problem with maternal thinking." *Political Theory* 13:19–37.

______. 1992. "Context is all: Feminism and theories of citizenship." Pp. 63–85 in Chantal Mouffe (ed.), *Dimensions of Radical Democracy: Pluralism, Citizenship and Community*. London: Verso.

Dietz, Thomas M. 2000. "Similar but different? The European Greens compared to other transnational party federations in Europe." *Party Politics* 6(2):199–210.

Dill, William. 1958. "Environment as an influence on managerial autonomy." *Administrative Science Quarterly* 2:409–43.

Dilthey, Wilhelm. 1976. *Dilthey: Selected Writings*. Cambridge, UK: Cambridge University Press.

______. 1989. *Introduction to the Human Sciences*. Princeton, NJ: Princeton University Press.

DiMaggio, Paul J., and Walter W. Powell. 1991. "Introduction." Pp. 1–38 in Walter W. Powell and Paul J. DiMaggio (eds.), *The New Institutionalism in Organizational Analysis*. Chicago: University of Chicago Press.

D. Muccro, R. B. A. and James N. Rosenau. 1992. "Turbulence and Sovereignty in World Politics: Explaining the Relocation of Legitimacy in the 1990s and Beyond." Pp. 60–76 in Zdravko Mlinar (ed.), *Globalization and Territorial Identities*. Aldershot: Avebury Ashgate.

Dix, Robert H. 1984. "Why revolutions succeed and fail." *Polity* 16:423–446.

Dixon-Mueller, Ruth. 1993. *Population Policy and Women's Rights*. Westport, CT: Praeger.

Djerf-Pierre, Monika. 2000. "Squaring the circle: News in public service and commercial television in Sweden, 1956–1999." *Journalism Studies* 1:239–60.

Dobbin, Frank. 1994. *Forging Industrial Policy: The United States, Britain, and France in the Railway Age*. Cambridge, UK: Cambridge University Press.

Dobratz, Betty, Lisa Waldner, and Timothy Buzzell (eds.). 2002a. *Research in Political Sociology, Vol. 10: Sociological Views on Political Participation in the 21st Century*. New York/Amsterdam: JAI/Elsevier Science.

______. 2002b. *Theoretical Directions for Political Sociology for the 21st Century. Research in Political Sociology, Vol. 11:* New York/Amsterdam: JAI/Elsevier Science.

______. 2003. *Political Sociology for the 21st Century Research in Political Sociology, Vol. 12:*. New York/Amsterdam: JAI/Elsevier Science.

Dogan, Mattei. 2001. "Class, religion, party: Triple decline of electoral cleavages in Western Europe." Pp. 93–114 in Lauri Karvonen and Stein Kuhnle (eds.), *Party Systems and Voter Alignments Revisited*. London: Routledge.

Dogan, Mattei, and John Higley. 1998. "Elites, crises, and regimes in comparative analysis." In Mattei Dogan and John Higley (eds.), *Elites, Crises, and the Origins of Regimes*. Lanham, MD: Rowman and Littlefield.

Dogan, Mattei, and Dominique Pelassy. 1984. *How to Compare Nations. Strategies in Comparative Politics*. Chatham, NJ: Chatham House.

Doherty, Ivan. 2001. "Democracy out of balance: Civil society can't replace political parties." *Policy Review* 106:25–35.

Domhoff, G. William. 1967. *Who Rules America?* Englewood Cliffs, NJ: Prentice Hall.

______. 1970. *The Higher Circles*. New York: Random House.

______. 1972. *Fat Cats and Democrats*. Englewood Cliffs, NJ: Prentice Hall.

______. 1974. *The Bohemian Grove and Other Retreats: A Study in Ruling-Class Cohesiveness*. New York: Harper & Row.

______. 1976. "I am not an 'Instrumentalist.'" *Kapitalistate* 4–5:221–4.

______. 1978. *Who Really Rules? New Haven and Community Power Re-Examined*. New Brunswick, NJ: Transaction Books.

______. 1979. *The Powers That Be: Processes of Ruling Class Domination in America*. New York: Random House.

______. 1983. *Who Rules America Now? A View for the '80s*. Englewood Cliffs, NJ: Prentice Hall.

______. 1986/87. "Corporate liberal theory and the Social Security Act." *Politics and Society* 15:297–330.

______. 1990. *The Power Elite and the State: How Policy Is Made in America*. Hawthorne, NY: Aldine de Gruyter.

______. 1996. *State Autonomy or Class Dominance? Case Studies on Policy Making in America*. Hawthorne, NY: Aldine de Gruyter.

______. 1998. *Who Rules America?: Power and Politics in the Year 2000*, 3rd ed. Mountain View, CA: Mayfield.

______. 2001. *Who Rules America? Power and Politics*. New York: McGraw–Hill.

______. 2002. *Who Rules America Now? Power and Politics*, 4th ed. Boston: McGraw–Hill.

Domínguez, Jorge I. 1993. "The Caribbean question: Why has liberal democracy (surprisingly) flourished?" Pp. 1–25 in Jorge I. Domínguez, Robert A. Pastor, and R. Delisle Worrell (eds.), *Democracy in the Caribbean. Political, Economic, and Social Perspectives*. Baltimore, MD: The Johns Hopkins University Press.

Donald, David. 1981. "A generation of defeat." Pp. 7–18 in W. J. Fraser and W. B. Moore (eds.), *Old South to the New: Essays on the Transitional South*. Westport, CT: Greenwood.

Donnelly, Jack. 1999. "The social construction of international human rights." Pp. 71–102 in T. Dunne and N. Wheeler (eds.), *Human Rights in Global Politics*. New York: Cambridge University Press.

Donovan, Todd. 2000. "Mobilization and support of minority parties." *Party Politics* 6:473–86.

Dosse, François. 1997. *History of Structuralism*. Minneapolis: University of Minnesota Press.

Douglas, Mary, and Baron Isherwood. 1979. *The World of Goods*. New York: Basic Books.

Douglas, Mary. 1966. *Purity and Danger: An Analysis of the Concepts of Pollution and Taboo*. London: Routledge and Kegan Paul.

______. 1973. *Natural Symbols: Explorations in Cosmology*, 2nd ed. London: Barrie and Jenkins.

______. 1989. *How Institutions Think*. Syracuse, NY: Syracuse University Press.

Dowding, Keith. 1995. "Model or metaphor? A critical review of the network approach." *Political Studies* 43:136–58.

______. 1996. *Power*. Minneapolis: University of Minnesota Press.

______. 2002. "There must be an end to the confusion: Policy networks, intellectual fatigue, and the need for political science methods courses in British Universities." *Political Studies* 49:89–105.

Dower, John W. 1986. *War Without Mercy: Race and Power in the Pacific War*. New York: Pantheon.

Downes, William. 1984. *Language and Society*. London: Fontana.

Downie, Leonard, Jr., and Robert G. Kaiser. 2002. *The News About the News*. New York: Knopf.

Downing, Brian M. 1992. *The Military Revolution and Political Change. Origins of Democracy and Autocracy in Early Modern Europe*. Princeton, NJ: Princeton University Press.

Downing, John. 1996. *Internationalizing Media Theory*. London: Sage.

Downs, Anthony. 1957. *An Economic Theory of Democracy*. New York: Harper and Row.

______. 1967. *Inside Bureaucracy*. London: Little, Brown.

______. 1999. *The Corruption of American Politics: What Went Wrong and Why*. New York: Overlook.

Dowse, Robert, and John Hughes. 1972. *Political Sociology*. New York: Wiley.

Drainville, Andre. 1995. "Of social spaces, citizenship, and the nature of power in the world economy." *Alternatives* 20:51–79.

Drake, Paul W. 1996. *Labor Movements and Dictatorships: The Southern Cone in Comparative Perspective*. Baltimore: Johns Hopkins University Press.

Dreiling, Michael C. 2000. "The class embeddedness of corporate political action: Leadership in defense of the NAFTA." *Social Problems* 47:21–48.

D'Souza, Dinesh. 1995. *The End of Racism: Principles for a Multiracial Society*. New York: Free Press.

Du Bois, W. E. B. 1935. *Black Reconstruction*. New York: Harcourt Brace.

Dudziak, Mary. 2000. *Cold War Civil Rights: Race and the Image of American Democracy*. Princeton, NJ: Princeton University Press.

Dumas, Lloyd. 1984. "University research, industrial innovation, and the Pentagon." Pp. 123–51 in John Tirman (ed.), *The Militarization of High Technology*. Cambridge, MA: Balinger.

Dummett, Ann, and Andrew Nicol. 1990. *Subjects, Citizens, Aliens and Others: Nationality and Immigration Law*. London: Weidenfeld & Nicolson.

Dummett, Michael, and Ann Dummett. 1982. "The role of government in Britain's racial crisis." Pp. 97–127 in C. Husband (ed.), *Race in Britain*. London: Hutchinson.

Dunaway, Wilma. 2001. "The double register of history: situation the forgotten woman and her household in capitalist commodity chains." *Journal of World-System Research* 7(1):2–31.

Duncan, Gorege, and J. Brooks-Gunn. 1997. *Consequences of Growing Up Poor.* New York: Russell Sage.

Duneier, Mitchell. 1999. *Sidewalk.* New York: Farrar, Straus and Giroux.

Dunne, Tim, and Nicholas Wheeler (eds.). 1999. *Human Rights in Global Politics*. New York: Cambridge University Press.

Durkheim, Emil. 1938. *Rules of the Sociological Method*. Glencoe, IL: Free Press.

______. 1957[1915]. *The Elementary Forms of the Religious Life* (Joseph Ward Swain, trans.). London: Allen & Unwin.

______. 1964[1893]. *The Division of Labor in Society* (George Simpson, trans.). New York: Free Press.

______. 1965. *The Elementary Forms of the Religious Life* (Joseph Ward Swain, trans.). New York: The Free Press.

______. 1966/1938. *The Rules of Sociological Method* (Sarah Solovay and John Mueller, trans.). New York: The Free Press.

______. 1984[1893]. *The Division of Labor in Society* (W. D. Halls, trans.), New York: Free Press.

Duverger, Maurice. 1963. *Political Parties: Their Organization and Activity in the Modern State* (Barbara and Robert North, trans.). New York: John Wiley and Sons. (Original published as *Les Partis Politiques*, Paris, 1951.)

Dye, Thomas R. 1976. *Who's Running America?: Institutional Leadership in the United States*. Englewood Cliffs, NJ: Prentice Hall.

______. 2002. *Who's Running America?: The Bush Restoration*. Englewood Cliffs, NJ: Prentice Hall.

Dye, Thomas R., and Harmon Zeigler. 2000. *The Irony of Democracy: An Uncommon Introduction to American Politics.* Fort Worth, TX: Harcourt Brace.

Dye, Thomas. 1979. "Politics versus economics: The development of the literature on policy determination." *Policy Studies Journal* 7:652–62.

Dye, Thomas, Harmon Zeigler, and S. Robert Lichter. 1992. *American Politics in the Media Age*, 4th ed. Pacific Grove, CA: Brooks, Cole.

Dyrberg, Torben Bech. 1997. *The Circular Structure of Power: Politics, Identity, Community*. London: Verso.

Dyrberg, Torben Bech, Allan Dreyer Hansen, and Jacob Torfing. 2000. *Diskursteori på arbejde*. Roskilde: Samfundslitteratur.

Eagleton, Terry. 1976. *Criticism and Ideology*. London: New Left Books.

Earl, Jennifer. 2000. "Methods, movements and outcomes." *Research in Social Movements, Conflicts and Change* 22:3–25.

Easterly, William. 2001. *The Elusive Quest for Growth: Economists' Adventures and Misadventures in the Tropics*. Cambridge, MA: MIT Press.

Easton, David. 1965. *Framework for Political Analysis.* Englewood Cliffs, NJ: Prentice Hall.

Eatwell, Roger, and Cas Mudde (eds.). 2003. *Western Democracies and the New Extreme Right.* Challenge. London: Routledge.

Ebbinghaus, Bernhard, and Anke Hassel. 2000. "Striking deals. The role of concertation in the reform of the welfare state." *Journal of European Public Policy* 7:44–62.

Eber, Christine E. 1999. "Seeking our own food. Indigenous women's power and autonomy in San Pedro Chenalhó, Chiapas (1980–1998)." *Latin American Perspectives* 26, 3:6–36.

Echenberg, Myron. 1991. *Colonial Conscripts: The Tirailleurs Sénégalais in French West Africa 1857 to 1960.* Portsmouth, NH: Heinemann.

Eckstein, Susan Eva and Timoth P. Wickham-Crowley (ed.). 2002. *Struggles for Social Rights in Latin America.* New York: Routledge.

Eckstein, Susan. 1982. "The impact of revolution on social welfare in Latin America." *Theory and Society* 11:43–94.

ECLAC. 2002. *Social Panorama of Latin America, 2000–2001.* Santiago, Chile: United Nations Economic Commission for Latin America and the Caribbean.

Edelman, Murray J. 1964. *The Symbolic Uses of Politics*. Urbana/Champaign: University of Illinois Press.

______. 1977. *Political Language: Words That Succeed and Policies That Fail.* New York: Academic.

______. 1985. *The Symbolic Uses of Politics*. Chicago: University of Illinois Press.

______. 1988. *Constructing the Political Spectacle.* Chicago: University of Chicago Press.

Edling, Christofe, and Charlotta Stern. 2003. "Scandinavian Rational Choice Sociology." *Acta Sociologica* 46(1):5–16.

Edsall, Thomas Byrne, and Mary D. Edsall. 1991. *Chain Reaction: The Impact of Race, Rights, and Taxes on American Politics.* New York: Norton.

Edwards, Bob, and Sam Marullo. 1995. "Organizational mortality in a declining social movement." *American Sociological Review* 60: 908–27.

Eide, Martin. 1997. "A new kind of newspaper? Understanding a popularization process." *Media, Culture and Society* 19:173–82.

Eisenstadt, S. N. (ed.) 1971. *Political Sociology: A Reader.* New York: Basic Books.

Eisenstein, Hester. 1996. *Inside Agitators: Australian Femocrats and the State*. Philadelphia: Temple University Press.

Eisenstein, Zillah. 1979. "Developing a theory of capitalist patriarchy and socialist feminism." Pp. 5–40 in Z. Eisenstein (ed.), *Capitalist Patriarchy and the Case for Socialist Feminism*. New York: Monthly Review.

Eisinger, Peter K. 1973. "The conditions of protest behavior in American cities." *American Political Science Review* 67:11–28.

Eismeier, Theodore J., and Philip H. Pollock III. 1988. *Business, Money, and the Rise of Corporate PACs in American Elections*. Westport, CT: Quorum Books.

Eldersveld, Samuel. 1964. *Political Parties: A Behavioral Analysis*. Chicago: Rand McNally.

Eley, Geoff. 1995. "The social construction of democracy in Germany, 1871–1933." Pp. 90–117 in Reid Andrews George and Herrick Chapman (eds.), *The Social Construction of Democracy 1870–1990*. New York: New York University Press.

Elias, Norbert. [1939] 1982. *Power and Civility: The Civilizing Process: Volume II*. New York: Pantheon.

______. 1978/1939. *The Civilizing Process*. New York: Urizen.

______. 1978. *What is Sociology?* London: Hutchinson.

Eliasoph, Nina. 1998. *Avoiding Politics: How Americans Produce Apathy in Everyday Life*. Cambridge, UK: Cambridge University Press.

Eliot, T. S. 1949. *Notes towards the Definition of Culture*. New York: Harcourt, Brace.

Elkins, David J., and Richard E. B. Simeon. 1979. "A cause in search of its effect, or what does political culture explain?" *Comparative Politics* 11:127–45.

Elman, R. A. 1996. *Sexual Subordination and State Intervention: Comparing Sweden and the United States*. Providence, RI: Berghahn Books.

Elshstain, J. B. 1992. "The power and powerlessness of women," Pp. 110–125 in Bock, G. and S. James (eds.), Beyond Equality and Difference: Citizenship, Feminist Politics and Female Subjectivily. London: Routledge.

______. 1981. *Public Man, Private Woman: Women in Social and Political Thought*. Princeton, NJ: Princeton University Press.

Elson, D. 1991. *Male Bias in the Development Process*. New York: St. Martin's.

Elster, Jon. 1982. "Marxism, functionalism, and game theory: the case for methodological individualism." *Theory and Society* 11(4):453–82.

______. 1985. *Making Sense of Marx*. Cambridge, UK: Cambridge University Press.

______. 1989. *The Cement of Society: A Study of Social Order*. Cambridge, UK: Cambridge University Press.

______. 2000. "Rational choice history: A case of excessive ambition." *American Political Science Review* 94(3):685–702.

Eltis, David. 1983. "Free and coerced transatlantic migrations: Some comparisons." *American Historical Review* 88:251–80.

Emerson, Richard M. 1962. "Power-dependence relations." *American Sociological Review* 27:32–41.

______. 1972. "Exchange theory, part II: exchange relations, exchange networks and groups as exchange systems." Pp. 58–82 in Joseph Berger, Morris Zelditch, and Bo Anderson (eds.), *Sociological Theories in Progress*. Boston: Houghton Mifflin.

______. 1976. "Social exchange theory." *Annual Review of Sociology* 2:335–62.

Emirbayer, Mustafa, and Jeff Goodwin. 1994. "Network Analysis, Culture, and the Problem of Agency." *American Journal of Sociology* 99:1411–54.

Emirbayer, Mustafa, and Goodwin, Jeff. 1996. "Symbols, positions, objects: Towards a new theory of revolutions and collective action." *History and Theory* 35:358–74.

Emirbayer, Mustafa, and Ann Mische. 1998. "What is agency?" *American Journal of Sociology* 103:962–1023.

Engels, Friedrich. 1942. "Letter to Sorge, February 8, 1890." P. 467 in *Karl Marx and Friedrich Engels: Selected Correspondence, 1846–1895* (Dona Torr, trans.). New York: International.

______. 1978 [1895]. "The tactics of social democracy." Pp. 556–73 in Robert W. Tucker (ed.), *The Marx/Engels Reader*. New York: Norton.

Engerman, Stanley L. 1986. "Servants to slaves to servants: Contract labour and European expansion." Pp. 263–94 in P. C. Emmer (ed.), *Colonialism and Migration*. Dordrecht, Netherlands: Martinus Nijhoff.

Engles, Charles W. 2000. "Toward new histories of the civil rights era." *Journal of Southern History* 66:815–48.

Enloe, Cynthia. 1989. *Bananas, Beaches, and Bases*. Berkeley: University of California Press.

Epstein, David, and Peter Zemsky. 1995. "Money talks: Deterring quality challengers in congressional elections." *American Political Science Review* 89:295–308.

Epstein, Edward J. 1973. *News From Nowhere*. New York: Random House.

Epstein, Leon D. 1980. *Political Parties in Western Democracies*. New Brunswick, NJ: Transaction. (Original published in 1967.)

______. 1982. "Party confederations and political nationalization." *Publius* 12:67–102.

______. 1986. *Political Parties in the American Mold*. Madison: University of Wisconsin Press.

______. 1993. "Overview of Research on Party Organizations." Pp. 1–6 in Michael Margolis and John Green (eds.), *Machine Politics, Sound Bites and Nostalgia*. Lanham, MD: University Press of America.

Erikson, Robert S. 1976. "The relationship between public opinion and state policy: A new look based on some forgotten data." *American Journal of Political Science* 20:25–36.

Erikson, Robert, and John H. Goldthorpe. 1992. *The Constant Flux*. Oxford, UK: Clarendon.

Erikson, Robert S., and Kent L. Tedin. 2001. *American Public Opinion*, sixth edition. New York: Longman.

Erikson, Robert S., and Thomas Palfrey. 1998. "Campaign spending and incumbency: An alternative simultaneous equations approach." *Journal of Politics* 60:355–73.

Erikson, Robert S., Michael MacKuen, and James A. Stimson. 2002. *The Macro Polity*. New York: Cambridge University Press.

Erikson, Robert S., Thomas D. Lancaster, and David W. Romero. 1989. "Group components of the presidential vote, 1952–1984." *Journal of Politics* 51:337–47.

Erikson, Robert S., Wright, Gerald C., and John P. McIver. 1993. *Statehouse Democracy: Public Opinion and Policy in the American States*. Cambridge, UK: Cambridge University Press.

Ermakoff, Ivan. 1997. "Prelates and princes: aristocratic marriages, canon law prohibitions, and shifts in the norms and patterns of domination in the central Middle Ages." *American Sociological Review* 62:405–22.

Ertman, Thomas. 1993. "The sinews of power and European state-building theory." Pp. 33–51 in Lawrence Stone (ed.), *An Imperial State at War*. London: Routledge.

______. 1997. *Birth of the Leviathan: Building States and Regimes in Medieval and Early Modern Europe*. Cambridge, UK: Cambridge University Press.

______. 1999a. "Explaining variation in early modern state structure: The cases of England and the German territorial states." Pp. 23–52 in John Brewer and Eckhart Hellmuth (eds.), *Rethinking Leviathan: The British and German States of the Eighteenth Century*. Oxford, UK: Oxford University Press.

______. 1999b. "Otto Hintze und der preussische Staat des 18. Jahrhunderts." Pp. 21–41 in Eckhart Hellmuth, Immo Meenken, and Michael Trauth (eds.), *Preussen um 1800*. Stuttgart: Frommann-Holzboog.

Escobar, Arturo. 1995. *Encountering Development. The Making and the Unmaking of the Third World*. London: Zed.

Escott, Paul D. 1985. *Many Excellent People: Power and Privilege in North Carolina, 1850–1900*. Chapel Hill: University of North Carolina Press.

Espeland, Wendy Nelson. 1998. *The Struggle for Water: Politics, Rationality, and Identity in the American Southwest*. Chicago: University of Chicago Press.

Esping-Andersen, Gøsta. 1985. *Politics Against Markets: The Social Democratic Road to Power*. Princeton, NJ: Princeton University Press/ London: Policy.

______. 1990. *The Three Worlds of Welfare Capitalism*. Cambridge, UK: Polity.

______. 1999. *Social Foundations of Postindustrial Economies*. New York: Oxford University Press.

______. 2002. *Why We Need a New Welfare State*. Oxford, UK: Oxford University Press.

______. 2003. "Why no socialism anywhere?" *Socio-Economic Review* 1:63–70.

Esping-Andersen, Gøsta, and Marino Regini (eds.). 2001. *Why Deregulate Labour Markets?* New York: Oxford University Press.

______. 2004. 'Equalizing opportunities: Money or cultural capital?' In M. Corak (ed.), *Intergenerational Income Mobility in America and Europe*. Cambridge, UK: Cambridge University Press.

Esping-Anderson, Gøsta, Roger Friedland, and Erik Olin Wright. 1976. "Modes of class struggle and the captialist state." *Kapitalstate* 4–5:184–220.

Esping-Andersen, Gøsta, and Walter Korpi, 1987. "From poor relief to institutional welfare states: the development of Scandinavian social policy." Pp. 39–47 in Robert Erikson, Erik Jørgen Hansen, Stein Rikgen, and Hannu Uusitalo (eds.) 1987. The Scandinavian Model: Welfare State and Welfare Research. New York, NY: M. E. Sharpe.

Esping-Andersen, Gøsta, Duncan Gallie, Anton Hemerijck, and John Myles. 2002. *Why We Need a New Welfare State*. New York: Oxford University Press.

Esposito, John L. 1999. *The Islamic Threat: Myth or Reality*?, third ed. New York: Oxford University Press.

Esposito, John L., and R. K. Ramazaniu (eds.). 2001. *Iran at the Crossroads*. New York: Palgrave.

Ette, M. 2000. "Agent of change or stability? The Nigerian press." *Harvard International Journal of Press/Politics* 5(3):67–86.

Etzinger, Hans. 2000. "The dynamics of integration policies: A multidimensional model." Pp. 119–44 in Ruud Koopmans and Paul Statham (eds.), *Challenging Immigration and Ethnic Relations Politics*. Oxford, UK: Oxford University Press.

Etzioni, Amatai. 1968. *The Active Society: A Theory of Societal and Political Processes.* New York: Free Press.

______. 1975. *A Comparartive Analysis of Complex Organizations*. New York: Free Press.

______. 1993. *The Spirit of Community Rights, Responsibilities and a Communitarian Agenda*. New York: Crown.

Etzioni-Halevy, Eva. 2002. "Political parties and NGOs in global environmental politics." *International Review of Political Science* 23:203–22.

Evans, Geoffrey. (ed.). 1999a. *The End of Class Politics? Class Voting in Comparative Context*. New York: Oxford University Press.

______. 1999b. "Class voting: From premature obituary to reasoned appraisal." Pp. 1–22 in Geoffrey Evans (ed.), *The End of Class Politics*? Oxford, UK: Oxford University Press.

______. 2000. "The continued significance of class voting." *Annual Review of Political Science* 3:401–17.

Evans, Peter B. 1995. *Embedded Autonomy: States and Industrial Transformation*. Princeton, NJ: Princeton University Press.

______. 1996. "El Estado como problema y como solución." *Desarrollo Económico*, No. 140: 529–62. Buenos Aires.

______. 1997. "The eclipse of the state? Reflections on stateness in an era of globalization." *World Politics* 50:62–87.

______. 1997. "Government action, social capital and development: Reviewing the evidence on synergy." Pp. 181–209 in Peter Evans (ed.), *State-Society Synergy: Government and Society*. Research Series, Vol. 94. Berkley: University of California Press.

______. 2000. "Fighting marginalization with transnational networks: Counter-hegemonic globalization." *Contemporary Sociology – a Journal of Reviews* 29(1): 230–41.

Evans, Peter B., Dietrich Rueschemeyer, and Theda Skocpol, eds. 1985. *Bringing the State Back In*. Cambridge, UK: Cambridge University Press.

Eyerman, Ron, and Andrew Jamison. 1991. *Social Movements: A Cognitive Approach*. University Park: Pennsylvania State University Press.

______. 1998. *Music and Social Movements: Mobilizing Traditions in the Twentieth Century*. Cambridge, UK: Cambridge University Press.

Fahrmeir, Andreas. 2000. *Citizens and Aliens: Foreigners and the Law in Britain and the German States 1789–1880*. London: Berghahn.

Fairbank, John K. 1992. *China. A New History.* Cambridge, MA: Harvard University Press.

Fairclough, Adam. 1990. "Historians and the civil rights movement." *Journal of American Studies* 24:387–98.

Fairclough, Norman. 1992. *Discourse and Social Change*. Cambridge, UK: Polity Press.

______. 1995. *Critical Discourse Analysis*. London: Longman.

Faksh, Mahmud A. 1997. *The Future of Islam in the Middle East: Fundamentalism in Egypt, Algeria, and Saudi Arabia*. Westport, CT: Praeger.

Falasca-Zamponi, Simonetta. 1997. *Fascist Spectacle: The Aesthetics of Power in Mussolini's Italy*. Berkeley: University of California Press.

Falk, Richard. 1999. "The challenge of genocide and genocidal politics in an era of globalisation." Pp. 177–94 in T. Dunne and N. Wheeler (eds.), *Human Rights in Global Politics*. New York: Cambridge University Press.

______. 2002. "Interpreting the interaction of global market with human rights." Pp. 61–76 in Alison Brysk (ed.), *Globalization and Human Rights*. Berkeley: University of California Press.

Falkner, Gerda. 1998. *EU Social Policy in the 1990s: Towards a Corporatist Policy Community*. London, UK: Routledge.

Fallows, James. 1996. *Breaking the News: How the Media Undermine American Democracy*. New York: Pantheon.

Fama, Eugene F., and Michael C. Jensen. 1983. "Separation of ownership and control." *Journal of Law and Economics* 26:301–25.

Fantasia, Rick. 1988. *Cultures of Solidarity.* Berkeley, CA: University of California Press.

Fantasia, Rick, and Kim Voss. 2004. *Hard Work: Remaking the American Labor Movement*. Berkeley: University of California Press.

Farhi, Farideh. 1990. *States and Urban-Based Revolutions: Iran and Nicaragua*. Urbana/Chicago: University of Illinois Press.

Farley, Reynolds. 2002. "Racial identities in 2000: The response to the multiple-race response option." Pp. 33–61 in J. Perlmann and M. C. Waters (eds.), *The New Race Question: How the Census Counts Multiracial Individuals*. Annandale-on-Hudson, NY: Russell Sage Foundation.

Farrell, David M. 1997. *Comparing Electoral Systems*. London: Macmillan.

Farrell, David M., and Paul Webb. 2000. "Political parties as campaign organizations." Pp. 102–28 in Russell J. Dalton and Martin P. Wattenberg (eds.), *Parties Without Partisans: Political Change in Advanced Industrial Democracies*. New York: Oxford University Press.

Farthing, Linda, and Ben Kohl. 2001. "Bolivia's new wave of protest." *NACLA Report on the Americas* XXXIV, 5:8–11.

Faulks, Keith. 1998. *Citizenship in Modern Britain*. Edinburgh: Edinburgh University Press.

______. 2000. *Political Sociology: A Critical Introduction*. New York: New York University Press.

Favell, Adrian. 1998. *Philosophies of Immigration: Immigration and the Idea of Citizenship in France and Britain*. New York: St. Martin's.

Feagin, Joe R., and Harlan Hahn. 1973. *Ghetto Revolts*. New York: Macmillan.

Featherstone, Lisa. 2002. *Students against Sweatshops*. London, New York: Verso.

Featherstone, Mike. 1990. *Global Culture: Nationalism, Globalization and Modernity*. London: Sage.

Federal Election Commission. 2002. <www.fec.gov>.

Feigenbaum, Harvey, Jeffrey Henig, and Chris Hamnett. 1998. *Shrinking the State: The Political Underpinnings of Privatization*. New York: Cambridge University Press.

Feldblum, Miriam. 1999. *Reconstructing Citizenship: The Politics of Nationality Reform and Immigration in Contemporary France*. Albany: SUNY Press.

Feldman, Ofer. 1993. *Politics and the News Media in Japan*. Ann Arbor: University of Michigan Press.

Feldman, Shelley. 2001. "Exploring theories of patriarchy: A perspective from contemporary Bangladesh." *Signs* 26:1097–127.

Feldt, Kjell-Olof. 1991. *Alla Dessa Dagar . . . I Regeringen 1982–1990*. Stockholm: Norstedts.

Fendrich, James Max. 1993. *Ideal Citizens*. Albany: State University of New York Press.

Fennema, M. 1982. *International Networks of Banks and Industry*. The Hague, Netherlands: Martinus Nijhoff.

Fennema, Meindert. 2001. "Legal repression of extreme-right parties and racial discrimination." Pp. 119–44 in Ruud Koopmans and Paul Statham (eds.), *Challenging Immigration and Ethnic Relations Politics*. New York: Oxford University Press.

Ferejohn, John. 1991. "Rationality and interpretation: Parliamentary elections in early Stuart England." Pp. xxx in Kristen Renwick Monroe (ed.), *The Economic Approach to Politics: A Critical Reassessment of the Theory of Rational Action*. New York: HarperCollins.

______. 1993. "Structure and ideology: Change in Parliament in early Stuart England." Pp. 207–31 in Judith Goldstein and Robert O. Keohane (eds.), *Ideas and Foreign Policy: Beliefs, Institutions, and Political Change*. Ithaca, NY: Cornell University Press.

Ferguson, Thomas. 1995. *Golden Rule: The Investment Theory of Party Competition and the Logic of Money-Driven Political Systems*. Chicago: University of Chicago Press.

Ferguson, Thomas, and Joel Rogers. 1986. *Right Turn: The Decline of the Democrats and the Future of American Politics*. New York: Hill and Wang.

Fernandez-Kelly, Maria Patricia. 1983. *For We Are Sold, I and My People*. Albany, NY: State University of New York Press.

Ferree, Myra Marx. 1992. "The Political Context of Rationality." Pp. 29–52 in Aldon D. Morris and Carol McClurg Mueller (eds.), *Frontiers in Social Movement Theory*. New Haven, CT: Yale University Press.

______. 1994. "'The time of chaos was the best': Feminist mobilization and demobilization in East Germany." *Gender & Society* 8:597–623.

______. 2000. "Patriarchies and feminisms: The two women's movements of post-unification Germany." Pp. 156–72 in Barbara Hobson (ed.), *Gender and Citizenship in Transition*. London: Macmillan.

Ferree, Myra Marx, and William Gamson. 2003. "The gendering of governance and the governance of gender: Abortion politics in Germany and the United States." Pp. 35–63 in Barbara Hobson (ed.), *Recognition Struggles and Social Movements: Contested Identities, Agency and Power*. Cambridge, UK: Cambridge University Press.

Ferrera, Maurizio. 1996. "Il Modello Solidarieta del Welfare State." *Revista Italiana di Sienzia Politica* 76:101.

Fetzer, Joel. 2000. *Public Attitudes Toward Immigration in the United States, France and Germany*. Cambridge, UK: Cambridge University Press.

Feyerabend, Paul K. 1975. *Against Method*. London: New Left Books.

Fichte, Johann Gottlieb. 1968/1807–8. *Addresses to the German Nation*. New York: Harper.

Fields, Barbara J. 1982. "Ideology and race in American history." Pp. 143–77 in J. M. Kousser and J. M. McPherson (eds.), *Region, Race, and Reconstruction: Essays in Honor of C. Vann Woodward*. New York: Oxford University Press.

Fine, Gary Alan. 1987. *With the Boys: Little League Baseball and Preadolescent Culture*. Chicago: University of Chicago Press.

______. 1998. *Morel Tales: The Culture of Mushrooming*. Cambridge, MA: Harvard University Press.

______. 2001. *Difficult Reputations: Collective Memories of the Evil, Inept, and Controversial*. Chicago: University of Chicago Press.

Fine, Terri Susan. 1994. "Proclaiming party identity: A view from the platforms." Pp. 265–73 in Daniel M. Shea and John C. Green (eds.), *The State of the Parties: The Changing Role of Contemporary American Parties*. Lanham, MD: Rowman and Littlefield.

Finegold, Kenneth, and Theda Skocpol. 1995. *State and Party in America's New Deal*. Madison: University of Wisconsin Press.

Finer, S. E. 1966. *Anonymous Empire*. London, UK: Pall Mall Press.

______. 1997. *The History of Government from the Earliest Times*. Oxford, UK: Oxford University Press.

Finifter, Ada. 1974. "The friendship group as a protective environment for political deviants." *American Political Science Review* 68:607–25.

Finnemore, Martha, and Kathryn Sikkink. 1998. "International norm dynamics and political change." *International Organization* 52(4):897–917.

Fiorina, Morris. 1981. *Retrospective Voting in American National Elections*. New Haven, CT: Yale University Press.

______. 1990. "Comment: The problems with PPT." *Journal of Law, Economics, and Organization* 6:255–61.

Firebaugh, Glenn, and Kevin Chen. 1995. "Vote turnout of Nineteenth Amendment women: The enduring effect of disenfranchisement." *American Journal of Sociology* 100:972–96.

Fireman, Bruce, and William Gamson. 1979. "Utilitarian logic in the resource mobilization perspective." Pp. 8–44 in John D. McCarthy and Mayer Zald (ed.), *The Dyanamics of Social Movements*. Cambridge, MA: Winthrop.

Fischer, Claude, et al. 1996. *Inequality by Design*. Princeton, NJ: Princeton University Press.

Fischer, Roger, and William Ury 1981. *Getting to Yes*. Harmondsworth, UK: Penguin.

Fishkin, James. 1991. *Democracy and Deliberation*. New Haven, CT: Yale University Press.

Fishkin, James, and Peter Laslett. 2003. *Debating Deliberative Democracy*. London: Blackwell.

Fishman, Robert. 1990. *Working Class Organization and the Return to Democracy in Spain*. Ithaca, NY: Cornell University Press.

Fitzgerald, Keith. 1996. *The Face of the Nation: Immigration, the State and National Identity*. Stanford, CA: Stanford University Press.

Flacks, Richard. 1988. *Making History: The American Left and the American Mind*. New York: Columbia University Press.

Flanagan, Robert J. 1999. "Macroeconomic performance and collective bargaining: An international perspective." *Journal of Economic Literature* 37:1150–75.

Flavio de Almeida, Lucio, and Felix Ruiz Sanchez. 2000. "The landless workers' movement and social struggles against neoliberalism." *Latin American Perspectives* 22, 5:11–32.

Fligstein, Neil. 1990. *The Transformation of Corporate Control*. Cambridge, MA: Harvard University Press.

______. 2001. *The Architecture of Markets: An Economic Sociology of Twenty-First-Century Capitalist Societies*. Princeton, NJ: Princeton University Press.

Fligstein, Neil, and Iona Mara-Drita. 1996. "How to make a market: Reflections on the attempt to create a single market in the European Union." *American Journal of Sociology* 102:1–32.

Fligstein, Neil, and Alec Stone Sweet. 2001. "Institutionalizing the Treaty of Rome." Pp. 29–55 in Alec Sweet, Wayne Sandholtz, and Neil Fligstein (eds.), *The Institutionalization of Europe*. New York: Oxford University Press.

______. 2002. "Constructing polities and markets: An institutionalist account of European integration." *American Journal of Sociology* 107:1206–43.

Flora, Peter, and Jens Alber. 1981. "Modernization, democratization and the development of welfare states in Western Europe." Pp. 37–80 in Peter Flora and Arnold Heidenheimer (eds.), *The Development of Welfare States in Europe and America*. New Brunswick, NJ: Transaction Books.

Flora, Peter and Jens Alber (eds.). 1983. *State, Economy, and Society in Western Europe 1815–1975: A Data Handbook in Two Volumes*. Frankfurt am Main: Campus Verlag; London: Macmillan.

Flora, Peter, and Arnold J. Heidenheimer. 1981. "Modernization, democratization, and the development of welfare states in Western Europe." Pp. 37–80 in Flora and Heidenheimer (eds.), *The Development of the Welfare State in Europe and America*. New Brunswick, NJ: Transaction.

______. 1986. *Growth to Limits: the Western European Welfare State Since World War II*, Volumes 1, 2, 3, 4. New York, NY: Walter de Gruyter.

Flyvbjerg, Bent. 1998. *Rationality and Power: Democracy in Practice*. Chicago: University of Chicago Press.

Folbre, Nancy. 1994. *Who Pays for the Kids? Gender and the Structures of Constraint*. New York: Routledge.

______. 2001. *The Invisible Heart*. New York: New Press.

Foley, Michael W., and Bob Edwards, 1996. "The paradox of civil society." *Journal of Democracy* 7(3):38–52.

Foner, Eric. 1988. *Reconstruction: America's Unfinished Revolution, 1863–1877*. New York: Harper & Row.

Font, Joan, and Rosa Viros (eds.). 1995. *Electoral Abstention in Europe*. Barcelona: ICPS.

Foran, John. 1992. "A theory of third world social revolutions: Iran, Nicaragua, and El Salvador compared." *Critical Sociology* 19:3–27.

______. 1993. "Theories of revolution revisited: Toward a fourth generation." *Sociological Theory* 11: 1–20.

______. 1997a. "The future of revolutions at the *Fin-de-siècle*." *Third World Quarterly* 18:791–820.

______. 1997b. "The comparative-historical sociology of third world social revolutions: Why a few succeed, why most fail." Pp. 227–67 in John Foran (ed.), *Theorizing Revolutions*. London: Routledge.

Forbath, William. 1989. "The Changing Shape of the American Labor Movement." *Harvard Law Review*, 102:1111–256.

Fording, Richard C. 2001. "The political response to black insurgency: A critical test of competing theories of the state." *American Political Science Review* 95:115–30.

Form, William. 1985. *Divided We Stand: Working Class Stratification in America*. Urbana: University of Illinois Press.

______. 1990. "Institutional analysis: An organizational approach." Pp. 257–71 in Maureen T. Hallinan, David M. Klein, and Jennifer Glass (ed.), *Change in Societal Institutions* New York: Plenum.

Foucault, Michel. 1965/1961. *Histoire de la Folie*. Paris: Librairie Plon.

______. 1973/1963. *The Birth of the Clinic: An Archaeology of Medical Perception*. New York: Pantheon.

______. 1973/1966. *The Order of Things*. New York: Pantheon.

______. 1977/1969. *Language, Counter-Memory, Practice*. Ithaca, NY: Cornell University Press.

______. 1978/1975. *Discipline and Punish: The Birth of the Prison*. New York: Pantheon.

______. 1978/1976. *The History of Sexuality, Volume I: An Introduction*. New York: Pantheon.

______. 1979. *Discipline and Punish*. Harmondsworth, UK: Penguin.

______. 1980. "Truth and Power." Pp. 107–133 in Colin Gordon (ed.), *Power/Knowledge*. New York: Pantheon.

______. 1984. "Politics and Ethics: An Interview." Pp. 373–380 in Paul Rabinow (ed.), *The Foucault Reader*. Harmondsworth, UK: Penguin.

______. 1985. *The Archaeology of Knowledge*. London: Tavistock.

______. 1986a. *Power/Knowledge*. Brighton, UK: Harvester.

______. 1986b. "Nietzsche, genealogy, history." Pp. 32–75 in Rabinow (ed.), *The Foucault Reader*. Harmondsworth, UK: Penguin Books.

______. 1986c. "Power and the subject." Pp. 208–26 in Dreyfus and Rabinow (eds.), *Michel Foucault: Beyond Structuralism and Hermeneutics*. Brighton, UK: Harvester.

______. 1990. *Politics, Philosophy, Culture* (Lawrence Kritzman, ed.). New York: Routledge.

______. 1990. *History of Sexuality*. Harmondsworth, UK: Penguin Books.

______. 1991. "Governmentality." Pp. 87–104 in G. Burchell, C. Gordon, and P. Miller (eds.), *The Foucault Effect: Studies in Governmentality*. London: Harvester Wheatsheaf.

Fourcade-Gourinchas, Marion, and Sarah Babb. 2002. "The rebirth of the liberal creed: paths to neo-liberalism in four countries." *American Journal of Sociology* 108(3):533–79.

Fowler, Roger, et al. 1979. *Language and Control*. London: Routledge.

Fox, Elizabeth, and Silvio Waisbord. (eds.). 2002. *Latin Politics, Global Media*. Austin: University of Texas Press.

Fox, Jonathan. 1994. "The difficult transition from clientelism to citizenship. Lessons from Mexico." *World Politics* 46 (January):51–84.

Fox, Jonathan A., and L. David Brown. 1998. *The Struggle for Accountability: The World Bank, NGOs, and Grassroots Movements, Global Environmental Accord*. Cambridge, MA: MIT Press.

Francisco, Ronald. 1995. "The relationship between coercion and protest." *Journal of Conflict Resolution* 39:263–82.

Frank, David John, Ann Hironaka, and Evan Schofer. 2000. "The nation-state and the natural environment over the twentieth century." *American Sociological Review* 65(1):96–116.

Frank, Robert. 1988. *Passions Within Reason*. New York: Norton.

Franklin, Mark. 1992. *Electoral Change: Responses to Evolving Social and Attitutinal Structures in Western Countries*. Cambridge, UK: Cambridge University Press.

______. 1992. "The decline of cleavage politics." Pp. 383–405 in Mark Franklin, Thomas Mackie, and Henry Valen (eds.). *Electoral Change*. New York: Cambridge University Press.

Franklin, Mark, Thomas Mackie, and Henry Valen. 1992. "Introduction." Pp. 3–32 in Mark Franklin, Thomas Mackie, and Henry Valen (eds.), *Electoral Change*. New York: Cambridge University Press.

Franzese, Robert J. 1999. "The interaction of credibly conservative monetary policy with labor- and goods-market institutions: A review of an emerging literature." Unpublished manuscript. Department of Political Science, University of Michigan.

______. 2002. *Macroeconomic Policies of Developed Democracies*, New York: Cambridge University Press.

Fraser, Nancy. 1989. *Unruly Practices: Power, Discourse and Gender in Contemporary Social Theory*. Oxford, UK: Polity.

______. 1992. "Rethinking the public sphere: a contribution to the critique of actually existing democracy." Pp. 109–42 in Craig Calhoun (ed.), *Habermas and the Public Sphere*. Cambridge, MA: MIT Press.

______. 1997. *Justice Interruptus: Critical Reflections on the "Postsocialist" Condition*. New York and London: Routledge.

______. 2003. "Rethinking recognition: Overcoming displacement and reification in cultural politics." Pp. 21–35 in Barbara Hobson (ed.), *Recognition Struggles and Social Movements: Contested Identities, Agency and Power*. Cambridge, UK: Cambridge University Press.

Fraser, Nancy, and Linda Gordon. 1994. "A genealogy of dependency–tracing a keyword of the United States welfare-state." *Signs* 19:309–36.

Frederickson, George M. 1998. "America's diversity in comparative perspective." *Journal of American History* 85:859–75.

______. 2002. *Racism: A Short History*. Princeton, NJ: Princeton University Press.

Freeman, Gary P. 1979. *Immigrant Labor and Racial Conflict in Industrialized Societies*. Princeton, NJ: Princeton University Press.

______. 1985. "National styles and policy sectors: Explaining structured variation." *Journal of Public Policy* 5:467–96.

______. 1994. "From populate or perish to diversify or decline: Immigration and Australian national security." Pp. 9–106 in Myron Weiner (ed.), *International Migration and Security*. Boulder, CO: Westview.

______. 1995. "Modes of immigration politics in liberal democratic states." *International Migration Review* 29(4):881–902.

______. 1997. "A reply to Perlmutter." *International Migration Review* 30(1):389–93.

______. 1998. "The decline of sovereignty? Politics and immigration restriction in liberal states?" Pp. 86–108 in Christian Joppke (ed.), *Challenge to the Nation State*. Oxford, UK: Oxford University Press.

Freeman, Jo. 1979. "Resource Mobilization and Strategy." Pp. 167–89 in Mayer Zald and John D. McCarthy (ed.), *The Dynamics of Social Movements*. Cambridge, MA: Winthrop.

______. 1986. "The political culture of Democratic and Republican parties." *Political Science Quarterly* 101:327–56.

Freeman, Laurie A. 2000. *Closing the Shop: Information Cartels and Japan's Mass Media*. Princeton, NJ: Princeton University Press.

Freeman, Richard B. 2004. "What, the Vote?" Pp. 703–28 in Kathryn Neckerman (ed.), *Social Inequality*. New York: Russell Sage Foundation.

Frendreis, John, and Richard Waterman. 1985. "PAC contributions and legislative behavior: Senate voting on trucking deregulation." *Social Science Quarterly* 66:401–12.

Freud, Sigmund. 1986. *The Interpretation of Dreams*. Harmondsworth, UK: Penguin.

Frey, R. Scott, Thomas Dietz, and Linda Kalof. 1992. "Characteristics of successful American protest groups." *American Journal of Sociology* 98:368–87.

Frieden, Jeffry. 1991. "Invested interests: The politics of national economic policies in a world of global finance." *International Organization* 45:425–51.

Friedland, Roger. 2001. "Religious nationalism and the problem of collective representations." *Annual Review of Sociology* 27:125–52.

______. 2003. "Bob Alford" pp. 1–2 in *Remembering Bob Alford 1928–2003*. Ph.D. Program in Sociology. The Graduate Center, the City University of New York, September 12th.

Friedman, Milton. 1953. *Essays in Positive Economics*. Chicago: University of Chicago Press.

______. 1962. *Capitalism and Freedom*. Chicago: University of Chicago Press.

Friedmann, Harriet, and Philip McMichael. 1989. "Agriculture and the state system: The rise and decline of national agricultures, 1870 to the present." *Sociologia Ruralis* XIX, 2:93–117.

Friedmann, John, and Haripriya Rangan (eds.). 1993. *In Defense of Livelihood: Comparative Studies on Environmental Action*. West Hartford, CT: UNRISD and Kumarian.

Friedrich, Carl J. (ed.) 1953. *The Philosophy of Hegel*. Modern Library Edition. New York: Random House.

Friedrich, Carl J., and Zbigniew Brzezinski. [1956] 1965. *Totalitarian Dictatorship and Autocracy*. New York: Praeger.

Frymer, Paul. 1999. *Uneasy Alliances: Race and Party Competition in America*. Princeton, NJ: Princeton University Press.

______. 2002. "Race, representation, and elections: The politics of parties and courts." Pp. 29–55 in R. Singh (ed.), *American Politics and Society Today*. Cambridge, UK: Polity.

Fung, Archon. 2003. "Associations and democracy: between theories, hopes, and realities." *Annual Review of Sociology* 29:515–39.

Fung, Archon, and Eric Olin Wright. 2003. *Deepening Democracy: Institutional Innovations in Empowered Participatory Governance*. London: Verso.

Fung, Archon, Dara O'Rourke, Charles F. Sabel, Joshua Cohen, and Joel Rogers. 2001. *Can We Put an End to Sweatshops?, New Democracy Forum Series*. Boston: Beacon.

Furet, François. 1981/1978. *Interpreting the French Revolution*. Cambridge, UK: Cambridge University Press.

Furet, François, and Ernst Nolte. 1998. *Fascisme et communisme*. Paris: Librairie Plon. Also published in Spanish in 1999, *Fascismo y Comunismo*. México DF: Fondo de Cultura Económica.

Furetière, Antoine. 1970[1690]. *Dictionnaire universel, contenant généralement tous les mots français, tant vieux que modernes, et les termes de toutes les sciences et des arts*. Geneva: Slatkine Reprints.

Furlong, Scott R. 1997. "Interest group influence on rule making." *Administration & Society* 29: 325–47.

Gaffney, John (ed.). 1996. *Political Parties and the European Union*. New York: Routledge.

Gais, Thomas, Mark Peterson, and John Walker. 1984. "Interest groups, iron triangles, and representative institutions in American National Government." *British Journal of Political Science* 14:161–85.

Gaither, Avalaura L., and Eric C. Newburger. 2001. "The emerging American voter: An examination of the increase in the black vote in November 1998." United States Bureau of the Census: Population Division.

Gal, Susan. 2003. "Movements of feminism: The circulation of discourses about women." Pp. 93–120 in Barbara Hobson (ed.), *Recognition Struggles and Social Movements: Contested Identities, Agency and Power*. Cambridge, UK: Cambridge University Press.

Gal, Susan, and Gail Kligman. 2000. *The Politics of Gender after Socialism: A Comparative-Historical Essay*. Princeton, NJ: Princeton University Press.

Galaskiewicz, Joseph. 1985. "Interorganizational relations." *Annual Review of Sociology* 11:281–304.

Galbraith, John Kenneth. 1952. *American Capitalism*. Boston: Houghton Mifflin.

______. 1967. *The New Industrial State*. New York: New American Library.

Galenson, David W. 1981. *White Servitude in Colonial America*. New York: Cambridge University Press.

Gallin, Rita S. 1990. "Women and the export industry in Taiwan: The muting of class consciousness." Pp. 179–98 in Kathryn Ward (ed.), *Women Workers and Global Restructuring*. Ithaca, NY: Cornell University Press.

Gamble, Andrew, Marsh, David, and Tony Tant (eds.), 1999. *Marxism and Social Science*. Urbana, IL: University of Illinois Press.

Gamson, Joshua. 1995. "Must identity movements self-destruct? a queer dilemma." *Social Problems* 42:390–407.

______. 1968. *Power and Discontent*. Homewood, IL: The Dorsey Press.

Gamson, William A. 1975. *The Strategy of Social Protest*. Homewood, IL: Dorsey.

______. 1990[1975]. *The Strategy of Social Protest*, 2nd ed. Belmont, CA: Wadsworth.

______. 1992. *Talking Politics*. Cambridge, UK: Cambridge University Press.

______. 1995. "Constructing social protest." Pp. 85–106 in H. Johnston and B. Klanderman (eds.), *Social Movements, Protest and Contention, 4*. London: UCL.

Gamson, William A., and David Meyer. 1996. "Framing Political Opportunity." Pp. 265–90 in Doug McAdam, John D. McCarthy, and Mayer N. Zald (eds.), *Comparative Perspectives on Social Movements*. New York: Cambridge University Press.

Gamson, William A., and Joshua Gamson. 1998. *The Strategy of Social Protest*, 2nd ed. Belmont, CA: Wadsworth.

Gans, Herbert J. 1979. *Deciding What's News: A Study of CBS Evening News, NBC Nightly News,* Newsweek, *and* Time. New York: Random House.

______. 1985. "Are U.S. Journalists Dangerously Liberal?" *Columbia Journalism Review* November/December:29–33.

______. 1988. *Middle American Individualism*. New York: Free Press.

______. 2003. *Democracy and the news*. New York: Oxford University Press.

Ganz, Marshall. 2000. "Resources and resourcefulness: Strategic capacity in the unionization of California agriculture, 1959–1966." *American Journal of Sociology* 105(4):1003–62.

Garand, James C. 1988. "Explaining governmental growth in the U.S. States." *American Political Science Review* 82:837–49.

Garman, Christopher, Stephan Haggard, and Eliza Willis. 2001. "Fiscal decentralization: A political theory with Latin American cases." *World Politics* 53(January):205–36.

Garnham, Nicholas. 1990. *Capitalism and Communication*. London: Sage.

Garretón, Manuel Antonio. 1989–2001. "Popular mobilization and the military regime in Chile: The complexities of the invisible transition." Pp. 259–277 in Susan Eckstein (ed.), *Power and Popular Protest: Latin American Social Movements*. Berkeley: University of California Press. Updated and Expanded Edition.

Garrett, Geoffrey, and Christopher Way. 1999. "Public sector unions, corporatism, and macroeconomic performance." *Comparative Political Studies* 32:411–34.

Garrett, Geoffrey, and Barry R. Weingast. 1993. "Ideas, interests, and institutions: Constructing the

European Community's internal market." Pp. 173–206 in Judith Goldstein and Robert O. Keohane (eds.), *Ideas and Foreign Policy: Beliefs, Institutions, and Political Change*. Ithaca, NY: Cornell University Press.

Garrett, Geoffrey. 1998a. *Partisan Politics in the Global Economy*. New York: Cambridge University Press.

______. 1998b. "Global Markets and National Politics: Collision Course or Virtuous Circle?" *International Organization* 52(4):787–810.

Garrow, David J. (ed.). 1989. *We Shall Overcome: The Civil Rights Movement in the United States in the 1950's and 1960's*. Brooklyn, NY: Carlson.

______. 1978. *Protest at Selma: Martin Luther King, Jr. and the Voting Rights Act of 1965*. New Haven, CT: Yale University Press.

Garvey, Gerald. 1995. "False promises: The NPR in historical perspective." Pp. 87–106 in Donald F. Kettl and John J. Dilulio, Jr. (eds.), *Inside the Reinvention Machine: Appraising Governmental Reform*. Washington, DC: Brookings Institution.

Gatrell, Peter. 1999. *A Whole Empire Walking: Refugees in Russia During World War I*. Bloomington: Indiana University Press.

Gauthier, A. 1996. *The State and the Family*. Oxford, UK: Clarendon.

Gavanas, A., and F. Williams. 2004. "Eine neue variante des herr-knecht verhältnisses (After the breadwinner model: welfare states and gender in transition)." Pp. 308–31 in Sigrid Leitner, Ilona Ostner, and Margit Schratzenstaller (eds). *Wholfahrtsstant und Geschlechterverhältnis im Unbruch*. Wiesbaden: Verlag für Sozialwissenchaften. Press.

Geddes, Andrew. 2003. *The Politics of Migration and Immigration in Europe*. London: Sage.

Geertz, Clifford. 1973/2000. *The Interpretation of Cultures*. New York: Basic Books.

______. 1983. *Local Knowledge*. New York: Basic Books.

______. 1995. *After the Fact: Two Countries, Four Decades, One Anthropologist*. Cambridge, MA: Harvard University Press.

Gelb, Joyce. 1989. *Feminism and Politics: A Comparative Perspective*. Berkeley: University of California Press.

Gelb, Joyce, and Marian Lief Palley. 1981. *Women and Policy Change*. Princeton, NJ: Princeton University Press.

Gellner, Ernest. 1983. *Nations and Nationalism*. Oxford, UK: Blackwell.

______. 1983. *Nations and Nationalism*. Ithaca, NY: Cornell University Press.

Gentile, Emilio. 1975. *Le origini dell'ideología fascista*. Rome: Ta Terza.

Geras, Norman. 1987. "Post-Marxism?" *New Left Review* 163:40–82.

______. 1990. *Discourses of Extremity: Radical Ethics and Post-Marxist Extravagances*. London: Verso.

Gerber, Alan. 1998. "Estimating the effect of campaign spending on senate election outcomes using instrumental variables." *American Political Science Review* 92:401–11.

Gerber, Alan, and Donald P. Green. 2000. "The effects of canvassing, telephone calls, and direct mail on voter turnout: A field experiment." *American Political Science Review* 94:653–63.

Gerber, Robin. 1999. "Building to win, building to last: AFL-CIO COPE takes on the Republican Congress." Pp. 77–93 in Robert Biersack, Paul S. Herrnson, and Clyde Wilcox (eds.), *After the Revolution: PACs, Lobbies, and the Republican Congress*. Boston: Allyn and Bacon.

Gereffi, Gary, and Miguel Korzeniewicz (eds.). 1994. *Commodity Chains and Global Capitalism*. New York: Praeger.

Gerlach, Luther, and Virginia Hine. 1970. *People, Power and Change*. Indianapolis, IN: Bobbs-Merrill.

Gerlach, Michael L. 1992. *Alliance Capitalism: The Social Organization of Japanese Business*. Berkeley: University of California Press.

Gershenkron, Alxander. [1943]1989. *Bread and Democracy in Germany*. Ithaca, NY: Cornell University Press.

Gerteis, Joseph. 2002. "The possession of civic virtue: Movement narratives of race and class in the Knights of Labor." *American Journal of Sociology* 108:580–615.

Geyer, Michael, and Charles Bright. 1995. "World history in a global age." *American Historical Review* 100:1034–60.

Gibson-Graham, J. K. 2002. *The End of Capitalism (as We Knew It): A Feminist Critique of Political Economy*. London: Blackwell.

Giddens, Anthony. 1973. *The Class Structure of Advanced Societies*. New York: Harper.

______. 1976. *New Rules of Sociological Method: A Positive Critique of Interpretive Sociologies*. New York: Basic Books.

______. 1977. *Studies in Social and Political Theory*. London: Hutchinson.

______. 1979. *Central Problems in Social Theory: Action, Structure and Contradiction in Social Analysis*. London: Macmillan.

______. 1984. *The Constitution of Society: Outline of the Theory of Structuration*. Cambridge, UK: Polity Press.

______. 1985. *The Nation-State and Violence, vol. 2 of Contemporary Critique of Historical Materialism*. Berkeley, CA: University of California Press.

______. 1990. *The Consequences of Modernity*. Cambridge, UK: Cambridge University Press.

______. 2000. *The Third Way and its Critics*. Cambridge, UK: Polity Press.

______. 2002. *Power: A Reader.* Manchester, UK: Manchester University Press.

Gilbert, Martin. 1978. *Exile and Return: The Struggle for a Jewish Homeland*. Philadelphia: Lippincott.

______. 1993. *The Dent Atlas of the Arab–Israeli Conflict*. London: J. M. Dent.

Gilens, Martin. 1999. *Why Americans Hate Welfare: Race, Media, and the Politics of Antipoverty Policy*. Chicago: University of Chicago Press.

Gill, Stephen. 1992. "Economic globalization and the internationalization of authority: Limits and contradictions." *Geoforum* 23, 3:269–83.

______. 2002. *Power and Resistance in the New World Order*. London: Palgrave.

Gilligan, C. 1982. *In a Different Voice: Psychological Theory and Women's Development*. Cambridge, MA: Harvard University Press.

Gilmore, Glenda. 1996. *Gender and Jim Crow: Women and the Politics of White Supremacy in North Carolina, 1896–1920*. Chapel Hill: University of North Carolina Press.

Gimbel, Cynthia, and Alan Booth. 1996. "Who fought in Vietnam?" *Social Forces* 74:1137–57.

Gimpel, James, and James Edwards. 1999. *The Congressional Politics of Immigration Reform*. Boston: Allyn and Bacon.

Gitlin, Todd. 1980. *The Whole World Is Watching: Mass Media in the Making and Unmaking of the New Left*. Berkeley: University of California Press.

______. 1983. *Inside Prime Time*. New York: Random House.

______. 1995. *The Twilight of Common Dreams: Why America Is Wracked by Culture Wars*. New York: Henry Holt.

Giugni, Marco. 1998. "Was it worth the effort? The outcomes and consequences of social movements." *Annual Review of Sociology* 24:371–93.

______. 1999. "How social movements matter." Pp. xii–xxxiii in Marco Giugni, Doug McAdam and Charles Tilly (eds.), *How Social Movements Matter*. Minneapolis: University of Minnesota Press.

Glasberg, Davita, and Dan Skidmore. 1997. *Corporate Welfare Policy and the Welfare State*. New York: Aldine de Gruyter.

Glassman, Ronald M., and William H. Swatos, Jr. (eds.). 1986. *Charisma, History and Social Structure*. Westport, CT: Greenwood Press.

Glassner, Barry. 1999. *The Culture of Fear*. New York: Basic Books.

Glendon, Mary Ann. 1987. *Abortion and Divorce in Western Law: American Failures: European Challenges*. Cambridge, MA: Harvard University Press.

______. 1991. *Rights Talk: The Impoverishment of Political Discourse*. New York and Toronto: Free Press; Collier Macmillan; Maxwell Macmillan.

Glenn, Evelyn N. 2002. *Unequal Freedom: How Race and Gender Shaped American Citizenship and Labor*. Cambridge, MA: Harvard University Press.

Glyn, Andrew. 1995. "The assessment: Unemployment and inequality." *Oxford Review of Economic Policy* 11:1–25.

Goffman, Erving. 1959. *The Presentation of Self in Everyday Life*. New York: Doubleday.

______. 1961. *Asylums*. Garden City, NY: Doubleday.

Goidel, Robert K., Donald A. Gross, and Todd G. Shields. 1999. *Money Matters: Consequences of Campaign Finance Reform in U.S. House Elections*. New York: Rowman and Littlefield.

Gold, David A., Clarence Y. H. Lo, and Erik O. Wright. 1975a. "Recent developments in marxist theories of the capitalist state." *Monthly Review* 27(5):29–43.

______. 1975b. "Recent developments in marxist theories of the capitalist state, part 2." *Monthly Review* 27(6):36–51.

Goldberg, David Theo. 2002. *The Racial State*. Malden, MA: Blackwell.

Golden, Miriam. 1997. *Heroic Defeats: The Politics of Job Loss*. New York: Cambridge University Press.

Goldfrank, Walter. 2001. "Rational kernels in a mystical shell: A comment on Robinson." *Theory and Society* 30, 2:211–13.

Goldstein, Robert. 2001. "Political repression of the American labor movement during its formative years." Paper presented at the 2001 Annual Meeting of the American Political Science Association, San Francisco, August 29–September 2.

Goldstone, Jack A. 1980. "The weakness of organization." *American Journal of Sociology* 85:1017–42.

______. 1986. "Revolutions and superpowers." Pp. 38–48 in Jonathan R. Adelman (ed.), *Superpowers and Revolution*. New York: Praeger.

______. 1991. *Revolution and Rebellion in the Early Modern World*. Berkeley/Los Angeles: University of California Press.

______. 1998. "Social movements or revolutions?" Pp. 125–45 in Marco Giugni, Doug McAdam, and Charles Tilly (eds.), *From Contention to Democracy*. Lanham, NJ: Rowman & Littlefield.

______. 2001. "Toward a fourth generation of revolutionary theory." *Annual Review of Political Science* 4:139–87.

______. 2003. "Comparative historical analysis and knowledge accumulation in the study of revolutions." Pp. 41–90 in James Mahoney and Dietrich Rueschemeyer (eds.), *Comparative Historical*

Analysis in the Social Sciences. Cambridge, UK: Cambridge University Press.

Goldstone, Jack A., and Charles Tilly. 2001. "Threat (and opportunity): Popular action and state response in the dynamics of contentious action." Pp. 79–94 in Ronald R. Aminzade, Jack A. Goldstone, Doug McAdam, Elizabeth J. Perry, William H. Sewell, Jr., Sidney Tarrow, and Charles Tilly (eds.), *Silence and Voice in the Study of Contentious Politics*. Cambridge, UK: Cambridge University Press.

Goldthorpe, John H. 1999. "Modeling the pattern of class voting in British elections, 1964–1992." Pp. 60–82 in G. Evans (ed.), *The End of Class Politics? Class Voting in Comparative Context*. New York: Oxford University Press.

______. 2000. *On Sociology*. Oxford, UK: Oxford University Press.

______. 2001. "Class politics in advanced industrial societies." Pp. 105–20 in Terry Nichols Clark and Seymour Martin Lipset (eds.). *The Breakdown of Class Politics: A Debate on Post-Industrial Stratification*. Washington, DC: Woodrow Wilson Center Press.

Goodin, Robert E., Bruce Headey, Ruud Muffels, and Henk-Jan Dirven. 1999. *The Real Worlds of Welfare Capitalism*. Cambridge, UK: Cambridge University Press.

Goodliffe, Jay. 2001. "The effect of war chests on challenger entry in U.S. House elections." *American Journal of Political Science* 45:830–44.

Goodwin, Jeff. 1994. "Toward a new sociology of revolutions." *Theory and Society* 23:731–66.

______. 2001. *No Other Way Out: States and Revolutionary Movements, 1945–1991*. Cambridge, UK: Cambridge University Press.

______. 2003. "The renewal of socialism and the decline of revolution." Pp. 59–72 in John Foran (ed.), *The Future of Revolutions: Rethinking Radical Change in the Age of Globalization*. London/New York: Zed Books.

Goodwin, Jeff, and James M. Jasper (eds.). 1999. "Caught in a winding, snarling, vine: The structural bias of political process theory." *Sociological Forum* 14:27–54.

______. 2004. *Rethinking Social Movements: Structure, Meaning and Emotion*. Lanham, MD: Rowman and Littlefield.

Goodwin, Jeffrey, and Theda Skocpol. 1989. "Explaining revolutions in the contemporary third world." *Politics and Society* 17:489–507.

Goodwin, Jeff, James M. Jasper, and Francesca Polletta, eds. 2001. *Passionate Politics: Emotions and Social Movements*. Chicago: University of Chicago Press.

Goodwin, Robert, and Hans-Dieter Klingemann. 1997. *A New Handbook of Political Science*. New York: Oxford University Press.

Gopnik, Adam. 1996. "The first Frenchman." *New Yorker*, October 7, 1996.

Gopoian, J. David. 1984. "What makes PACs tick? an analysis of the allocation patterns of economic interest groups." *American Journal of Political Science* 28:259–81.

Gordon, A. A. 1996. *Transforming Capitalism and Patriarchy: Gender and Development in Africa*. Boulder, CO: Lynne Rienner.

Gordon, Linda (ed.). 1990. *Women, the State, and Welfare*. Madison: University of Wisconsin Press.

______. 1994. *Pitied But Not Entitled*. New York: Free Press.

Gordon, Linda, and Nancy Fraser. 1994. "Dependency demystified: Inscriptions of Power in a keyword of the welfare state." *Social Politics* 1:4–31.

Gordon, Wendy M. 2002. *Mill Girls and Strangers: Single Women's Independent Migration in England, Scotland, and the United States, 1850–1881*. Albany: State University of New York Press.

Gornick, Janet C. 1999. "Gender equality in the labour market." Pp. 210–42 in Diane Sainsbury (ed.), *Gender and Welfare State Regimes*. New York: Oxford University Press.

Gornick, Janet, Marcia K. Meyers, and Katherine E. Ross. 1977. "Supporting the employment of mothers." *Journal of European Social Policy* 7:745–70.

Gorriti, Gustavo. 1999. *The Shining Path: A History of the Millenarian War in Peru*. Chapel Hill, NC: University of North Carolina Press.

Gorski, Philip S. 1993. "The Protestant ethic revisited: Disciplinary revolution and state formation in Holland and Prussia." *American Journal of Sociology* 99:265–316.

______. 1995. "The Protestant Ethic and the spirit of bureaucracy." *American Sociological Review* 60(5):783–6.

______. 1998. "Review of Thomas Ertman, Birth of the Leviathan."*Contemporary Sociology* 27 (2): 186– 8.

______. 1999. "Calvinism, confessionalism and state-formation in early modern Europe." Pp. 147–81 in George Steinmetz (ed.), *State Culture, State Formation after the Cultural Turn*. Ithaca, NY: Cornell University Press.

______. 2003. *The Disciplinary Revolution: Calvinism, Confessionalism and the Growth of State Power in Early Modern Europe*. Chicago: Chicago University Press.

Gosnell, Harold F. 1927. *Getting Out the Vote: An Experiment in the Stimulation of Voting*. Chicago: University of Chicago Press.

______. 1968. *Machine Politics: Chicago Model*, 2nd ed. Chicago: University of Chicago Press.

Gottdiener, M., and N. Komninos. 1989. *Capitalist Development and Crisis Theory: Accumulation,*

Regulation and Spatial Restructuring. New York: St. Martins Press.

Gottschalk, Peter, and Timothy M. Smeeding. 1997. "Cross-national comparisons of earnings and income inequality." *Journal of Economic Literature* 35:633–87.

Gough, Ian. 1975 "State expenditure in advanced capitalism." *New Left Review* 92:53–92.

______. 1979. *The Political Economy of the Welfare State*. London: Macmillan.

Gould, Mark. 1987. *Revolution in the Development of Capitalism: The Coming of the English Revolution*. Berkeley: University of California Press.

Gould, Roger V. (ed.). 2004. *The Rational Choice Controversy in Sociology*. Chicago: University of Chicago Press.

______. 1995. *Insurgent Identities: Class, Community, and Protest in Paris from 1848 to the Commune*. Chicago: University of Chicago Press.

______. 2000. "Revenge as sanction and solidarity display: An analysis of vendettas in nineteenth-century Corsica." *American Sociological Review* 65(5):682–704.

Gouldner, Alvin W. 1954. *Patterns of Industrial Bureaucracy*. Glencoe, IL: Free Press.

______. 1970. *The Coming Crisis of Western Sociology*. New York: Basic Books.

Graber, Doris. 2002. *Mass Media and Politics*, 6th ed. Washington, DC: CQ Books.

Graber, Doris, Denis McQuail, and Pippa Norris (eds.). 1998. *The Politics of News: The News of Politics*. Washington, DC: CQ Press.

Graham, Lawrence S. 1992. "Redefining the Portuguese Transition to Democracy." Pp. 282–99 in John Higley and Richard Gunther (eds.), *Elites and Democratic Consolidation in Latin America and Southern Europe*. Cambridge, UK: Cambridge University Press.

Gramsci, Antonio. 1971. *Selections from the Prison Notebooks*. London: New World Paperbacks.

Gramsci, Antonio. 1971[1934]. *Selections from the Prison Notebooks*. London, UK: Lawrence and Wishart.

______. [1924]1983. "Democracy and fascism." Pp. 121–4 in Beetham Davis (ed.), *Marxists in Face of Fascism*. Manchester: Manchester University Press.

______. 1999/1971. *Selections from the Prison Notebooks of Antonio Gramsci*. (Quintin Hoare and Geoffrey Nowell-Smith, eds.). New York: International Publishers.

______. 2000. *The Antonio Gramsci Reader*. New York: New York University Press.

Granovetter, Mark. 1985. "Economic action and social structure: The problem of embeddedness." *American Journal of Sociology* 91:481–510.

Graus, Frantisek. 1970. "Slavs and Germans." Pp. 15–42 in G. Graus, K. Bosl, F. Seibt, M. Postan, and A. Gieysztor (eds.), *Eastern and Western Europe in the Middle Ages*. London: Thames & Hudson.

Gray, Virginia, and David Lowery. 1996. *The Population Ecology of Interest Representation: Lobbying Communities in the American States*. Ann Arbor, MI: University of Michigan Press.

Green, Daniel M. 1999. "Liberal moments and democracy's durability: Comparing global outbreaks of democracy – 1918, 1945, 1989." *Studies in Comparative International Development* 34:83–120.

Green, Donald P., and Jonathon Krasno. 1988. "Salvation for the spendthrift incumbent: Reestimating the effects of campaign spending in House elections." *American Journal of Political Science* 32:884–907.

Green, Donald P., and Ian Shapiro. 1994. *Pathologies of Rational Choice Theory: A Critique of Applications in Political Science*. New Haven, CT: Yale University Press.

______. 1995. *Pathologies of Rational Choice Theory: A Critique of Applications in Political Science*. New Haven, CT: Yale University Press.

Green, Donald P., Bradly Palmquist, and Eric Schickler. 2002. *Partisan Hearts and Minds: Political Parties and the Social Identities of Voters*. New Haven, CT: Yale University Press.

Green, John C. 1997. "The Christian Right and the 1996 elections: An overview." Pp. 1–14 in Mark J. Rozell and Clyde Wilcox (eds.), *God at the Grass Roots: The Christian Right in American Elections*. New York: Rowman and Littlefield.

______. 2000. "The Christian Right and the 1998 elections: An overview." Pp. 1–20 in John C. Green, Mark J. Rozell, and Clyde Wilcox (eds.), *Prayers in the Precincts: The Christian Right in the 1998 Elections*. Washington, D.C.: Georgetown University Press.

Green, John C., Mark J. Rozell, and Clyde Wilcox. 2001. "Social movements and party politics: The case of the Christian right." *Journal for the Scientific Study of Religion* 40:413–26.

Green, John C., Paul Herrnson, Lynda Powell, and Clyde Wilcox. 1998. "Individual congressional campaign contributors." Department of Political Science, University of Akron, Akron, OH. Unpublished manuscript.

Green-Pedersen, C., and M. Haverland. 2002. "The new politics and scholarship of the welfare state." *Journal of European Social Policy* 12(1):43–51.

Greenberg, Stanley B., and Theda Skocpol. 1997. *The New Majority: Toward a Popular Progressive Politics*. New Haven, CT: Yale University Press.

Greenfeld, Liah. 1992. *Nationalism: Five Roads to Modernity*. Cambridge, MA: Harvard University Press.

______. 1993. "Nationalism and democracy: The nature of the relationship and the cases of England, France, and Russia." *Research in Democracy and Society* 1:327–52.

______. 1995. "Russian nationalism as a medium of revolution: An exercise in historical sociology," *Qualitative Sociology* 18(2):189–209.

______. 1996a. "The modern religion?" *Critical Review* 10(2):169–91.

______. 1996b. "Nationalism and modernity." *Social Research* 62(1):3–40.

______. 2001. *The Spirit of Capitalism: Nationalism and Economic Growth*. Cambridge, MA: Harvard University Press.

______. 2001. "Etymology, definitions, types." In Alexander J. Moytl (ed.), *Encyclopedia of Nationalism*. New York: Academic Press.

Greenfeld Liah, and Daniel Chirot. 1994. "Nationalism and aggression." *Theory and Society* 23(1):79–130.

Greenhalgh, Susan. 2001. "Fresh winds in Bejing: Chinese feminists speak out on the one-child policy and women's lives." *Signs: Journal of Women in Culture & Society* 26(3):847–86.

Greenstein, Fred, and Nelson Polsby. 1975. *Handbook of Political Science*. Reading, MA: Addison–Wesley.

Greenwood, Justin, Jürgen R. Grote, and Karsten Ronit. 1992. *Organized Interests and the European Community*. London: Sage.

Greenwood, Justin. 1997. *Representing Interests in the European Union*. Basingstoke, UK: Macmillan.

Greif, Avner. 1998. "Self-enforcing political systems and economic growth." Pp. 23–63 in Bates et al. (eds.), *Analytic Narratives*. Princeton, NJ: Princeton University Press.

Grenzke, Janet M. 1989. "PACs and the congressional supermarket: The currency is complex." *American Journal of Political Science* 33:1–24.

Grier, Kevin, and Michael Munger. 1991. "Committee assignments, constituent preferences, and campaign contributions to House incumbents." *Economic Inquiry* 29:24–43.

Griffin, Larry, Joel Devine, and Michael Wallace. 1982. "Monopoly capital, organized labor, and military expenditures in the United States, 1949–1976." *American Journal of Sociology* 88:S113–S153.

Griffin, Larry. 1992. "Temporality, events, and explanation in historical sociology: an introduction." *Sociological Methods & Research* 20(4):403–27.

______. 1993. "Narrative, event-structure analysis, and causal interpretation in historical sociology." *American Journal of Sociology* 98:1094–1133.

Griffin, Roger. 1995. *Fascism*. New York: Oxford University Press.

Griffith, Kati L., and Leslie C. Gates. 2002. "A state's gendered response to political instability: Gendering labor policy in semiauthoritarian El Salvador (1944–1972)." *Social Politics* 9(2):248–92.

Griffiths, Paul E. 1997. *What Emotions Really Are*. Chicago: University of Chicago Press.

Grofman, Bernard, and Chandler Davidson. 1994. "The effect of municipal election structure on black representation in eight Southern states." Pp. 301–34 in C. Davidson and B. Grofman (eds.), *Quiet Revolution in the South: The Impact of the Voting Rights Act, 1965–1990*. Princeton, NJ: Princeton University Press.

Grofman, Bernard, William Koetzle, and Anthony J. McGann. 2002. "Congressional leadership 1965–96: A new look at the extremism versus centrality debate." *Legislative Studies Quarterly* 27:87–105.

Groot, Gerard-René de. 1989. *Staatsangehörigkeitsrecht im Wandel*. Köln: Carl Heymanns Verlag.

Grosby, Steven. 1999. "The chosen people of ancient Israel and the occident: Why does nationality exist and survive?" *Nations and Nationalism* 5(3):357–80.

Grosfoguel, Ramon. 1996. "From cepalismo to neoliberalism: A world systems approach to conceptual shifts in Latin America." *Review* 19:131–54.

Gross, Larry. 2001. *Up from Invisibility: Lesbians, Gay Men, and the Media in America*. New York: Columbia University Press.

Gross, Michael L. 1994. "Jewish rescue in Holland and France during the Second World War: Moral cognition and collective action." *Social Forces* 73:463–96.

Grote, Jürgen R. 1998. *The Political Ecology of Regionalism: State-Society Relations in Nine European Regions*. Doctoral dissertation. Florence, Italy: European University Institute.

Grote, Jürgen R., and Philippe C. Schmitter 1999. "The renaissance of national corporatism: Unintended side-effect of European economic and monetary union or calculated response to the absence of European social policy?" *Transfer European Review of Labour and Research* 5:34–64.

Gubrium, Jaber F., and James A. Holstein. 1997. *The New Language of Qualitative Method*. Oxford, UK: Oxford University Press.

Guevara, Che. 1985[1960]. *Guerrilla Warfare*. Lincoln: University of Nebraska Press.

Guha, Ramachandra, and Juan Martínez-Alier. 1997. *Varieties of Environmentalism. Essays North–South*. London: Earthscan.

Guild, Elspeth. 1996. "The legal framework of citizenship of the European Union." Pp. 30–55 in David Cesarini and Mary Fulbrook (eds.), *Citizenship, Nationality and Migration in Europe*. New York: Routledge.

Guinier, Lani. 1994. *The Tyranny of the Majority: Fundamental Fairness in Representative Democracy*. New York: Free Press.

Gunlicks, Arthur P. "The new German party finance law." *German Politics* 4(1):104–21.

Gunther, Richard, Giacomo Sani, and Goldie Shabad. 1986. *Spain After Franco: The Making of a Competitive Party System*. Berkeley: University of California Press.

Gunther, Richard. 1992. "Spain: the very model of the modern elite settlement." Pp. 38–80 in John Higley and Richard Gunther (eds.), *Elites and Democratic Consolidation in Latin America and Southern Europe*. Cambridge, UK: Cambridge University Press.

Gurin, Patricia, Shirley Hatchett, and James S. Jackson. 1989. *Hope and Independence: Blacks' Response to Electoral and Party Politics*. New York: Russell Sage.

Gurr, Ted Robert. 1971. *Why Men Rebel*. Princeton, NJ: Princeton University Press.

______. 1986. "Persisting patterns of repression and rebellion: Foundations for a general theory of political coercion." Pp. 149–68 in M. Karns (ed.), *Persistent Patterns and Emergent Structures in a Waning Century*. New York: Praeger.

Gusfield, Joseph R. 1981. *The Culture of Public Problems: Drinking–Driving and the Symbolic Order*. Chicago: University of Chicago Press.

______. 1986[1963]. *Symbolic Crusade: Status Politics and the American Temperance Movement*. Urbana: University of Illinois Press.

Gustafsson, Bjorn, and Mats Johansson. 1999. "In search of smoking guns: What makes income inequality vary over time in different countries?" *American Sociological Review* 64:585–605.

Haas, Ernst B. 1958. *The Uniting of Europe: Political Social and Economic Forces 1950–1957*. London: Stevens and Son.

Haas, Peter M. 1992. "Introduction: Epistemic communities and international policy coordination." *International Organization* 46:1–36.

Habermas, J. 1990. *Moral Consciousness and Communicative Action*. Cambridge, UK: Polity.

______. 1998. *Between Facts and Norms: Contributions to a Discourse Theory of Law and Democracy*. Cambridge, MA, and London: MIT Press.

Habermas, Jürgen. 1973. *Legitimation Crisis*. Boston: Beacon Press.

______. 1979. *Communication and the Evolution of Society*. Boston: Beacon.

______. 1981. "New social movements." *Telos* 49:33–7.

______. 1984. *The Theory of Communicative Action, Vol. I: Reason and the Rationalization of Society* (T. McCarthy, trans.). Boston: Beacon Press.

______. 1986. "The new obscurity: the crisis of the welfare state and the exhaustion of utopian energies." *Philosophy and Social Criticism* 11:1–18.

______. 1987a. *The Philosophical Discourse of Modernity*. Cambridge, MA: MIT Press.

______. 1987b. *The Theory of Communicative Action*. Volume II: *Lifeworld and System: A Critique of Functionalist Reason*. Boston: Beacon/Cambridge, U.K. Polity.

______. 1989. *The Structural Transformation of the Public Sphere*. Cambridge, MA: MIT Press.

______. 1990. *The Philosophical Discourse of Modernity: Twelve Lectures*. Cambridge, UK: Polity.

______. 1992. *Faktizität und Geltung: beiträge zur diskurstheorie des rechts und des demokratischen rechtsstaats*. Frankfurt am Main: Suhrkamp Verlag.

______. 1996. *Between Facts and Norms: Contributions to a Discourse Theory of Law and Democracy*. Cambridge, MA: MIT Press.

Hacker, Jacob S., and Paul Pierson. 2002. "Business power and social policy: Employers and the formation of the American welfare state." *Politics and Society* 30:277–325.

Hacking, Ian. 1999. *The Social Construction of What?* Cambridge, MA: Harvard University Press.

Haeri, Shahla. 2001. "Obedience versus autonomy: Women and fundamentalism in Iran and Pakistan." Pp. 350–8 in Frank J. Lechner and John Boli (eds.), *The Globalization Reader*. Oxford, UK: Blackwell.

Hage, Jerald, Robert Hanneman, and Edward T. Gargan. 1989. *State Responsiveness and State Activism: An Examination of the Social Forces that Explain the Rise in Social Expenditures in Britain, France, Germany and Italy 1870–1968*. London: Unwin Hyman.

Haggard, Stephan, and Robert Kaufman. 1995. *The Political Economy of Democratic Transitions*. Princeton, NJ: Princeton University Press.

Haines, Herbert. 1984. "Black radicalization and the funding of civil rights." *Social Problems* 32:31–43.

Hainsworth, Paul, 2000a. "Introduction: The extreme Right." Pp. 1–17 in Paul Hainsworth (ed.), *The Politics of the Extreme Right. From the Margins to the Mainstream*. London: Pinter.

______. (ed.). 2000b. *The Politics of the Extreme Right. From the Margins to the Mainstream*. London: Pinter.

Halfmann, Drew. 2000. "Historical institutions, opposing movements and the macro-social consequences of the antiabortion movement." Paper presented at the annual meeting of the American Sociological Association, Washington, DC.

Hall, Jerome. 1952. Theft, Law and Society. Second edition. Indianapolis: Bobbs-Merrill.

Hall, John (ed.). 1998. *The State of the Nation: Ernest Gellner and the Theory of Nationalism*. New York: Cambridge University Press.

______. 1995. "Public narratives and the apocalyptic sect: From Jonestown to Mt. Carmel." Pp. 205–35 in Stuart A. Wright (ed.), *Armageddon in Waco*. Chicago: University of Chicago Press.

______. 1995. *Civil Society: Theory, History, Comparison*. Cambridge, UK: Polity Press.

Hall, Peter A. 1986. *Governing the Economy*. Oxford: Polity Press.

______. 2003. "Aligning ontology and methodology in comparative politics." Chapter 9 in James Mahoney and Dietrich Rueschemeyer (eds.), *Comparative and Historical Analysis in the Social Sciences*. New York: Cambridge University Press.

Hall, Peter A., and Robert J. Franzese, Jr. 1998. "Mixed signals: Central bank independence, coordinated wage bargaining, and European Monetary Union." *International Organization* 52:505–35.

Hall, Peter A., and David Soskice (eds.). 2001. *Varieties of Capitalism*. New York: Oxford University Press; *Economist* 147(3):364–6.

Hall, Peter A., and Rosemary C. R. Taylor. 1996. "Political science and the three new institutionalisms." *Political Studies* 44:936–57.

Hall, Richard, and Frank Wayman. 1990. "Buying time: Moneyed interests and the mobilization of bias in congressional committees." *American Political Science Review* 84:797–820.

Hall, Stuart, and Tony Jefferson. 1976. *Resistance through Rituals: Youth Subcultures in Post-War Britain*. London: Hutchinson & Co.

Hall, Thomas D. 2002. "World systems analysis and globalization directions for the twenty first century." Pp. 81–122 in Betty A. Dobratz, Timothy Buzzell, and Lisa K. Waldner (eds.), *Theoretical Directions in Political Sociology for the 21st Century*. Greenwich, CT: JAI Press.

Hallin, Daniel C. 1986. *"The Uncensored War": The Media and Vietnam*. New York: Oxford.

______. 1994. *We Keep America on Top of the World*. London: Routledge.

Hallin, Daniel C. and Paolo Mancini. 1984. "Speaking of the president: Political structure and representational form in U.S. and Italian television news." *Theory and Society* 13:829–50.

______. 2004. *Comparing Media Systems: Three Models of Media and Politics*. Cambridge: Cambridge University Press.

Hallin, Daniel C., and Stylianos Papathanassopoulos. 2002. "Political clientelism and the media: Southern Europe and Latin America in comparative perspective." *Media, Culture, and Society* 24:175–95.

Hallin, Daniel C., Robert K. Manoff, and Judy K. Weddle. 1993. "Sourcing patterns of national security reporters." *Journalism Quarterly* 70:753–66.

Hamelink, Cees J. 1983. *Cultural Autonomy in Global Communications: Planning National Information Policy*. New York: Longman.

Hamilton, Gary G., and Nicole Woolsey Biggart. 1988. "Market, culture, and authority: A comparative analysis of management and organization in the Far East." *American Journal of Sociology* 94:S52–S94.

Hamilton, Richard F. 1972. *Class and Politics in the United States*. New York: Wiley.

______. 1995. "Some difficulties with cultural explanations of national socialism." Pp. 197–216 in Houchan Chehabi and Alfred Stepan (eds.), *Politics, Society and Democracy*. Boulder, CO: Westview.

Hamilton, Roberta. 1995. "Pro-natalism, feminism, and nationalism." Pp. 133–52 in François-Pierre Gigras (ed.), *Gender Politics in Contemporary Canada*. Toronto: Oxford University Press.

Hammar, Tomas. 1964. *Sweden for the Swedes. Immigration Policy, Aliens Control and Right of Asylum 1900–1932*. [*Sverige åt svenskarna*] Stockholm: Caslon.

______. 1985. "Dual citizenship and political integration." *International Migration Review* 19(3):438–50.

Hammond, Thomas, and Jack Knott. 1996. "Who controls the bureaucracy?: Presidential power, congressional dominance, legal constraints, and bureaucratic autonomy in a model of multi-institutional policy-making." *Journal of Law, Economics, and Organization* 12:119–66.

Handler, Joel. 1978. *Social Movements and the Legal System*. New York: Academic.

Handley, Lisa, and Bernard Grofman. 1994. "The impact of the Voting Rights Act on minority representation: Black officeholding in southern state legislatures and congressional delegations." Pp. 335–50 in C. Davidson and B. Grofman (eds.), *Quiet Revolution in the South: The Impact of the Voting Rights Act, 1965–1990*. Princeton, NJ: Princeton University Press.

Haney, Lynne. 1996. "Homeboys, babies, men in suits: The state and the reproduction of male dominance." *American Sociological Review* 61:759–78.

Hannan, Michael, and John Freeman. 1989. *Organizational Ecology*, Cambridge, MA: Harvard University Press.

Hansen, Randall. 2000. *Citizenship and Immigration in Post-War Britain: The Institutional Origins of a Multicultural Nation*. Oxford, UK: Oxford University Press.

Hansen, Randall, and Patrick Weil. 2002. *Dual Nationality, Social Rights and Federal Citizenship in the US and Europe*. New York: Berghahn.

Hantrais, Linda. 2000. "From equal pay to reconciliation of employment and family life." Pp. 1–26 in Linda Hantrais (ed.), *Gendered Policies in Europe*. New York: St. Martin's.

Hardin, Russell. 1995. *One for All: The Logic of Group Conflict*. Princeton, NJ: Princeton University Press.

Hardt, Michael, and Antonio Negri. 2000. *Empire*. Cambridge, MA and London: Harvard University Press.

Hardt, Michael. 2002. "Today's Bandung?" *New Left Review* March–April:112–18.

______. 2000. *Empire*. Cambridge, MA: Harvard University Press.

Hargreaves, Alec. 1995. *Immigration, Race and Ethnicity in Contemporary France*. London: Routledge.

Harmel, Robert, and John D. Robertson. 1985. "Formation and success of new parties: A cross-national analysis." *International Political Science Review* 6(4):501–23.

Harrington, Michael. 1962. *The Other America; Poverty in the United States*. New York: Macmillan.

Harris, Fredrick C. 1999. *Something Within: Religion in African American Political Activism*. New York: Oxford University Press.

Harris, Jamie, and John F. Zipp. 1999. "Black candidates, roll-off, and the black vote." *Urban Affairs Review* 34:489–98.

Harrison, C. E. 1988. *On Account of Sex: The Politics of Women's Issues, 1945–1968*. Berkeley: University of California Press.

Harrison, Trevor. 1995. *Of Passionate Intensity: Right-Wing Populism and the Reform Party of Canada*. Toronto: University of Toronto Press.

Hartlyn, Jonathan. 1993. "The Dominican Republic: Contemporary problems and challenges." Pp. 150–72 in Jorge I. Domínguez, Robert A. Pastor, and R. Delisle Worrell (eds.), *Democracy in the Caribbean. Political, Economic, and Social Perspectives*. Baltimore, MD: The Johns Hopkins University Press.

Hartmann, Elizabeth. 1995. *Reproductive Rights and Wrongs*. Boston: South End.

______. 1997. "Cairo consensus sparks new hopes, old worries." *Forum for Applied Research and Public Policy* 12:33–40.

Hartmann, H. 1986. "The unhappy marriage of Marxism and feminism: Towards a more progressive union." Pp. 1–14 in L. Sargent (ed.), *The Unhappy Marriage of Marxism and Feminism: A Debate on Class and Patriarchy*. Boston: South End Press.

Hartsock, Nancy. 1985. *Money, Sex, and Power: Toward a Feminist Historical Materialism*. Boston: Northeastern University Press.

Harvey, David. 1989. *The Condition of Postmodernity*. Oxford, UK: Basil Blackwell.

______. 2000. *Spaces of Hope*. Berkeley: University of California Press.

Harvey, Neil. 1998. *The Chiapas Rebellion. The Struggle for Land and Democracy*. Durham, NC: Duke University Press.

Haskell, John. 1996. *Fundamentally Flawed: Understanding and Reforming Presidential Primaries*. New York: Rowman and Littlefield.

Hastie, R. 2001. "Problems for judgment and decision-making." *Annual Review of Psychology* 52(1):653–84.

Hastings, Adrian. 1997. *The Construction of Nationhood*. Cambridge, UK: Cambridge University Press.

Hatem, Mervat F. 1994. "Privatization and the demise of state feminism in Egypt." Pp. 40–60 in Pamela Sparr (ed.), *Mortgaging Women's Lives*. London: Zed Books.

Hattam, Victoria C. 1993. *Labor Visions and State Power: The Origins of Business Unionism in the United States*. Princeton, NJ: Princeton University Press.

Haugaard, Mark. 1997. *The Constitution of Power: A Theoretical Analysis of Power, knowledge and Structure*. Manchester, UK: Manchester University Press.

Haus, Leah A. 2002. *Unions, Immigration and Internationalization: New Challenges and Changing Coalitions in the United States and France*. London: Palgrave MacMillan.

Havelkova, Hana. 2000. "Abstract citizenship? women and power in the Czech Republic." Pp. 118–38 in Barbara Hobson (ed.), *Gender and Citizenship in Transition*. London: Macmillan.

Haveman, Robert H. 1996. "Reducing poverty while increasing employment: A primer on alternative strategies and a blueprint." *OECD Economic Studies* 26:7–42.

Hawkins, Darnell F. 2001. "Commentary on Randall Kennedy's overview of the justice system." Pp. 32–51 in N. J. Smelser, W. J. Wilson, and F. Mitchell (eds.), *America Becoming: Racial Trends and Their Consequences*, vol. 2. Washington, DC: National Academy.

Hawley, Willis D. 1973. *Nonpartisan Elections and the Case for Party Politics*. New York: Wiley.

Hay, Colin. 2001. "The crisis of keynsianism and the rise of neo-liberalism in Britain: an ideational institutionalist approach." Pp. 192–218 in John L. Campbell and Ove K. Pedersen (eds.), *The Rise of Neoliberalism and Institutional Analysis*. Princeton, NJ: Princeton University Press.

______. 2002. "Common trajectories, variable paces, divergent outcomes? Models of European capitalism under conditions of complex economic interdependence." Paper presented at the Biannual *Conference of Europeanists*, Chicago, March 14–16.

Hay, Douglas. 1975a. "Poaching and the Game Laws on Cannock Chase." Pp. 189–353 in Douglas Hay et al. (eds.), *Albion's Fatal Tree: Crime and Society in Eighteenth Century England*. New York: Pantheon Books.

______. 1975b. "Property, Authority, and the Criminal Law." Pp. 17–63 in Douglas Hay et al. (eds.),

Albion's Fatal Tree: Crime and Society in Eighteenth Century England. New York: Pantheon Books.

Hayles, N. Katherine. 1990. *Chaos Bound: Orderly Disorder in Contemporary Literature and Science*. Ithaca, NY: Cornell University Press.

Haynes, S. E., and D. Jacobs. 1994. "Macroeconomics, economic stratification, and partisanship: A longitudinal analysis of contingent shifts in political identification." *American Journal of Sociology* 100:70–103.

Hazlett, Joseph M. II. 1992. *The Libertarian Party and Other Minor Political Parties in the United States*. Jefferson, NC: McFarland.

Headrick, Rita. 1978. "African soldiers in World War II." *Armed Forces and Society* 4(3):501–26.

Heath, Anthony, John Curtice, Roger Jowell, Geoff Evans, Julia Field, and Sharon Witherspoon. 1991. *Understanding Political Change*. Oxford, UK: Pergamon.

Heath, Anthony, Roger Jowell, and John Curtice. 1985. *How Britain Votes*. London: Pergamon.

______. 1987. "Trendless Fluctuation: A reply to Crewe." *Political Studies* 35:256–77.

______. 1991. *Understanding Political Change: The British Voter, 1964–1987*. London: Pergamon.

______. 2001. *The Rise of New Labour: Party Policies and Voter Choices*. New York: Oxford University Press.

Heath, Melanie, and Judith Stacey. 2002. "Transatlantic family travail." *American Journal of Sociology* 108:658–68.

Hebdige, Dick. 1979. *Subculture: The Meaning of Style*. London: Methuen.

Heberle, Rudolph. 1951. *Social Movements: An Introduction to Political Sociology*. New York: Appleton–Century–Crofts.

Hechter, Michael and Elizabeth Borland. 2001. "National Self-Determination: The Emergence of an International Norm." *Social Norms*. New York: Russell Sage:186–233.

______. 2001. "National self-determination: The emergence of an international norm." Pp. 89–110 in Michael Hechter and Karl Dieter-Opp (eds.), *Social Norms*. New York: Russell Sage Foundation.

Hechter, Michael, and Karl Dieter-Opp (eds.). 2001. *Social Norms*. New York: Russell Sage Foundation.

Hechter, Michael, and Satoshi Kanazawa. 1997. "Sociological rational choice theory." *Annual Review of Sociology* 23:191–214.

Hechter, Michael. 1975. *Internal Colonialism. The Celtic Fringe in British National Development, 1536–1966*. Berkeley: University of California Press.

______. 1987. *Principles of Group Solidarity*. Berkeley: University of California Press.

______. 1999. *Containing Nationalism*. Oxford, UK: Oxford University Press.

Heckman, S. 1996. *Feminist Approaches to Michel Foucault*. University Park: Pennsylvania State University Press.

Heckscher, Charles. 1996. *The New Unionism*, 2nd ed. Ithaca, NY: ILR Press.

Heclo, Hugh. 1974. *Modern Social Policy in Britain and Sweden from Relief to Income Maintenance*. New Haven, CT: Yale University Press.

______. 1978. "Issue networks and the executive establishment." Pp. 87–124 in Anthony King (ed.), *The New American Political System*. Washington, DC: American Enterprise Institute.

Hedström, Peter. 2005. *Dissecting the Social: On the Principles of Analytic Sociology*. New York: Cambridge University Press.

Hedström, Peter, and Richard, Swedberg, (eds.), 1998. *Social Mechanisms: An Analytical Approach to Social Theory*. Cambridge, UK: Cambridge University Press.

Hegel, Georg F. W. 1983[1820]. *Philosophie des Rechts: Die Vorlesung von 1819/20 in einer Nachschrift* (Dieter Henrich, ed.). Frankfurt Main: Suhrkamp.

Hein, Jeremy. 1993. "Refugees, immigrants, and the state." *Annual Review of Sociology* 19:43–59.

Heinemann, Eduard. 1929. *Soziale Theorie der Kapitalismus*. Frankfurt: Suhrkamp.

Heinrich, Carolyn. 2002. "Outcomes-based performance management in the public sector: implications for government acccountability and effectiveness." *Public Administration Review* 62(6):712–25.

Heinz, John P., Edward O. Laumann, Robert L. Nelson, and Robert H. Salisbury. 1993. *The Hollow Core: Private Interests in National Policymaking*. Cambridge, MA: Harvard University Press.

Heisler, Martin O., and Barbara Schmitter Heisler. 1986. "Transnational migration and the modern democratic state." *Annals* 485(5):12–22.

______. 1991. "Citizenship – old, new and changing: Inclusion, exclusion and limbo for ethnic groups and migrants in the modern democratic state." Pp. 91–128 in Jurgen Fijalkowski, Hans Merkens, and Folker Schmidt (eds.), *Dominant National Cultures and Ethnic Identities*, vol. 1. Berlin: Free University Press.

Heitlinger, Alena. 1991. "Pronatalism and women's equality policies." *European Journal of Population* 7:343–75.

______. 1993. *Women's Equality, Demography and Public Policies*. New York: St. Martin's.

Held, David. 1989. *Political Theory and the Modern State: Essays on State, Power and Democracy*. Cambridge, UK: Polity.

______. 1995. *Democracy and the Global Order: From the Modern State to Cosmopolitan Governance*. Stanford, CA: Stanford University Press.

______. 1996. *Models of Democracy (2nd Edition)*. Stanford, CA: Stanford University Press.

______. 2000. "Regulating globalization. The reinvention of politics." *International Sociology* 15 (2):394–408.

Held, David, Anthony McGrew, David Goldblatt, and Jonathan Perraton. 1999. *Global Transformations: Politics, Economics and Culture*. Stanford, CA: Stanford University Press.

Helgason, Sigurdur. 1997. "International benchmarking experiences from OECD countries." Paper presented at a conference organized by the Danish Ministry of Finance on International Benchmarking. Copenhagen, February 20–1.

Hellebust, Lyn (ed.). 1997. *Think Tank Directory: A Guide to Nonprofit Public Policy Research Organizations*. Topeka, KS: Government Research Service.

Helleiner, Eric. 1994. *States and the Reemergence of Global Finance*. Ithaca, NY: Cornell University Press.

______. 1997. "Braudellian reflections on economic globalization: The historian as pioneer." Pp. 90–104 in Stephen Gill and James H. Mittelman (eds.), *Innovation and Transformation in International Studies*. Cambridge, UK: Cambridge University Press.

Hellman, Joel, Geraint Jones, Daniel Kaufmann, and Mark Schankernan. 2000. "Measuring governance corruption and state capture. How do firms and bureaucrats shape the business environment in transition economies?" World Bank, Policy Research Working Paper 2312. Washington, DC.

Henderson, David. 1998. *The Changing Fortunes of Economic Liberalism*. London: Institute of Economic Affairs.

Heng, Geraldine, and Janadas Devan. 1992. "State fatherhood: The politics of nationalism, sexuality, and race in Singapore." Pp. 343–64 in Andrew Parker, Mary Russo, Doris Sommer, and Patricia Yaeger (eds.), *Nationalisms and Sexualities*. New York: Routledge.

Hennis, Wolfgang. 1987. "A science of man, Max Weber and the political economy of the German Historical School." Pp. 25–58 in Wolfgang Mommsen and Jürgen Osterhammel (eds.), *Max Weber and his Contemporaries*. London: Allen & Unwin.

______. 1988. *Max Weber: Essays in Reconstruction*. London: Allen & Unwin.

Herda-Rapp, Ann. 1998. "The power of informal leadership: Women leaders in the civil rights movement." *Sociological Focus* 31:341–55.

Héritier, Adrienne, and Susanne Schmidt. 2000. "After liberalization: Public interest services and employment." Pp. 554–98 in Fritz W. Scharpf and Vivien A. Schmidt (eds.), *Welfare and Work in the Open Economy. Volume II. Diverse Responses to Common Challenges*. Oxford, UK: Oxford University Press.

Herman, Edward S. 1981. *Corporate Control, Corporate Power.* New York: Cambridge University Press.

Herman, Edward S., and Noam Chomsky. 1988. *Manufacturing Consent*. New York: Pantheon.

Hermet, Guy. 1984. "Prédestination ou Stratégie." *Esprit* 90:131–41.

Hernes, Helga Marie. 1984. "Women and the welfare state: The transition from private to public dependence." Pp. 20–46 in Harriet Holter (ed.), *Patriarchy in a Welfare Society*. Oslo: Universitetsforlaget.

______. 1987. *Welfare State and Woman Power*. Oslo: Norway University Press.

Herrnson, Paul S. 1993. "Political parties and congressional elections: Out of the eighties and into the nineties." Pp. 7–19 in Michael Margolis and John Green (eds.), *Machine Politics, Sound Bites and Nostalgia*. Lanham, MD: University Press of America.

______. 2000. *Congressional Elections*, 3rd ed. Washington, DC: CQ Press.

Herron, Michael, and Jasjeet Sekhon. 2002. "Black candidates and black voters: Assessing the impact of candidate race on uncounted vote rates." Unpublished manuscript, Department of Political Science, Northwestern University.

Hess, Stephen. 1981. *The Washington, Reporters*. Washington, DC: Brookings Institution.

Hesse, Carla, and Robert Post (eds.). 1999. *Human Rights in Political Transition: Gettysburg to Bosnia*. New York: Zone Books.

Hewitt, Christopher. 1977. "The effects of political democracy and social democracy on equality in industrial societies. *American Sociological Review* 42:450–64.

______. 2002. *Understanding Terrorism in America*, London: Routledge.

Hibbs, Douglas. 1982. "The dynamics of political support for American president among occupational and partisan groups." *American Journal of Political Science* 26:313–32.

______. 1987. *The American Political Economy*. Cambridge, MA: Harvard University Press.

Hibbs, Jr., Douglas A. 1986a. *The Political Economy of the United States*. Cambridge, MA: Harvard University Press.

Hicks, Alexander. 1988. "National collective action and economic performance." *International Studies Quarterly* 32:131–153.

______. 1991. "Unions, social democracy, welfare and growth." *Research in Political Sociology.* 5:209–234.

______. 1999. *Social Democracy and Welfare Capitalism: A Century of Income Security Politics*. Ithaca, NY: Cornell University Press.

______. 2003. "Back to the future?" *Socioeconomic Review* 1:271–88.

Hicks, Alexander, and Lane Kenworthy. 1998. "Cooperation and political economic performance in affluent democratic capitalism." *American Journal of Sociology* 103:1631–72.

______. 2003. "Varieties of welfare capitalism." *Socio-Economic Review* 1:27–62.

Hicks, Alexander, and Joya Misra. 1993. "Political resources and the expansion of welfare effort." *American Journal of Sociology* 99(3):678–710.

Hicks, Alexander, and Duane H. Swank. 1984. "Governmental redistribution in rich capitalist democracies." *Policy Studies Journal* 613:265–86.

______. 1992. "Politics, institutions, and welfare spending in industrialized democracies, 1960–1982." *American Political Science Review* 86:658–74.

Hicks, Alexander, and Christopher Zorn. 2006. "Economic globalization, the macro-economy, and reversals of welfare expansion in affluent democracies, 1978–1994." *International Organization*, 60: forthcoming.

Highton, Benjamin, and Raymond Wolfinger. 2001. "The first seven years of the political life cycle." *American Journal of Political Science* 45:202–09.

Higley, John, and Gwen Moore. 1981. "Elite integration in the United States and Australia." *American Political Science Review* 75:581–97.

Hilferding, Rudolf. 1981[1910]. *Finance Capital* (Tom Bottomore, ed., Morris Watnick and Sam Gordon, trans.). London: Routledge & Kegan Paul.

Hill, Christopher. 1952. "Puritans and the Poor." *Past and Present, 2.*

Hill, Raynard E., and Bernard J. White. 1979. *Matrix Organization and Project Management.* Ann Arbor: University of Michigan Press.

Hines, Colin. 2000. *Localization. A Global Manifesto.* London: Earthscan.

Hingham, John. 1965. *Strangers in the Land: Patterns of American Nativism 1860–1925.* New York: Antheneum.

Hintze, Otto. 1902. "The formation of states and constitutional development." Pp. 157–77 in Felix Gilbert (ed.), *The Historical Essays of Otto Hintze.* New York: Oxford University Press.

______. 1906. "Military organization and the organization of the state." Pp. 178–215 in Felix Gilbert (ed.), *The Historical Essays of Otto Hintze.* New York: Oxford University Press.

______. 1910. "The commissary and significance in general administrative history: A comparative study." Pp. 267–301 in Felix Gilbert (ed.), *The Historical Essays of Otto Hintze.* New York: Oxford University Press.

______. 1913. "Machtpolitik und Regierungsverfassung." Pp. 424–56 in Otto Hintze (ed.), *Staat und Verfassung. Gesammelte Abhandlungen zur Allgemeinen Verfassungsgeschichte*, 3rd ed. Goettingen: Vandenhoeck & Ruprecht.

______. 1915. *Die Hohenzollern und ihr Werk 1415–1915.* Berlin: Paul Parey.

______. 1922. "Max Webers Religionssoziologie." Pp. 126–34 in Otto Hintze (ed.), *Soziologie und Geschichte* 3rd ed. Goettingen: Vandenhoeck & Ruprecht.

______. 1924. "Staatenbildung und Kommunalverwaltung." Pp. 216–41 in Otto Hintze (ed.), *Staat und Verfassung. Gesammelte Abhandlungen zur Allgemeinen Verfassungsgeschichte*, 3rd ed. Goettingen: Vandenhoeck & Ruprecht.

______. 1926. "Max Webers Soziologie." Pp. 135–47 in Otto Hintze (ed.), *Soziologie und Geschichte*, 3rd ed. Goettingen: Vandenhoeck & Ruprecht.

______. 1927a. "Max Weber, ein Lebensbild." Pp. 148–54 in Otto Hintze (ed.), *Soziologie und Geschichte*, 3rd ed. Goettingen: Vandenhoeck & Ruprecht.

______. 1927b. "Troeltsch and the Problem of Historicism: Critical Studies." Pp. 368–421 in Felix Gilbert (ed.), *The Historical Essays of Otto Hintze.* New York: Oxford University Press.

______. 1930. "Typologie der Standischen Verfassungen des Abendlandes." Pp. 120–39 in Otto Hintze (ed.), *Staat und Verfassung. Gesammelte Abhandlungen zur Allgemeinen Verfassungsgeschichte*, 3rd ed. Goettingen: Vandenhoeck & Ruprecht.

______. 1931. "Calvinism and raison d'etat in early seventeenth-century Brandenburg." Pp. 88–107 in Felix Gilbert (ed.), *The Historical Essays of Otto Hintze.* New York: Oxford University Press.

______. 1967. *Regierung und Verwaltung: Gesammelte Abhandlungen zur Staats-, Rechts-, und Sozialgeschichte Preussens.* Goettingen: Vandenhoeck & Ruprecht.

______. 1970. *Staat und Verfassung. Gesammelte Abhandlungen zur Allgemeinen Verfassungsgeschichte*, 3rd ed. Goettingen: Vandenhoeck & Ruprecht.

______. 1975. *The Historical Essays of Otto Hintze.* Felix Gilbert (ed.), New York: Oxford University Press.

______. 1982. *Soziologie und Geschichte*, 3rd ed. Goettingen: Vandenhoeck & Ruprecht.

Hirsch, Paul, Stuart Michaels, and Ray Friedman. 1987. " 'Dirty hands' versus 'clean models:' is sociology in danger of being seduced by economics?" *Theory and Society* 16:317–36.

Hirschman, Albert O. 1970. *Exit, Voice, and Loyalty: Responses to Decline in Firms, Organizations, and States.* Cambridge, MA: Harvard University Press.

______. 1979. "The turn to authoritarianism in Latin America and the search for its economic determinants." Pp. 61–98 in David Collier (ed.), *The New Authoritarianism in Latin America.* Princeton, NJ: Princeton University Press.

______. 1982. *Shifting Involvements.* Princeton, NJ: Princeton University Press.

Hirst, Paul Q., and Graeme Thompson. 1996. *Globalization in Question*. Cambridge, UK: Polity.

______. 1999. *Globalization in Question, 2nd Edition*. Cambridge, UK: Polity.

Hirst, Paul. 1994. *Associative Democracy: New Forms of Economic and Social Governance*. Amherst: University of Massachusetts Press.

Hix, Simon. 2002. "Parliamentary behavior with two principals: Preferences, parties, and voting in the European parliament." *American Journal of Political Science* 46:688–98.

Hix, Simon, and Christopher Lord. 1997. *Political Parties in the European Union*. London: Macmillan.

Hixson, William B., Jr. 1992. *Search for the American Right Wing*. Princeton, NJ: Princeton University Press.

Hobbes, Thomas. 1958. *The Leviathan*. Indianapolis: Bobbs-Merrill.

Hobsbawm, Eric. 1990. *Nations and Nationalism since 1780: Programme, Myth, Reality*. Cambridge, UK: Cambridge University Press.

Hobson, Barbara. 1990. "No exit no voice: Women's economic dependency and the welfare state." *Acta Sociologia* 33:235–50.

______. 1994. "Solo mothers, policy regimes and the logics of gender." Pp. 170–87 in D. Sainsbury (ed.), *Gendering Welfare States*. London: Sage.

______. 2000. *Gender and Citizenship in Transition*. New York: Routledge.

______. 2000. "Agencies, identities, institutions." *Social Politics* 7:2:238–43.

Hobson, Barbara (ed.). 2002. *Making Men into Fathers*. Cambridge, UK: Cambridge University Press.

______. 2003. *Recognition Struggles and Social Movements*. Cambridge, UK: Cambridge University Press.

Hobson, Barbara, and Marika Lindholm. 1997. "Collective identities, power resources, and the making of welfare states." *Theory and Society* Fall:1–34.

Hobson, Barbara, and Ruth Lister. 2002. "Citizenship." Pp. 23–54 in B. Hobson, J. Lewis, and B. Siim (eds.), *Contested Concepts in Gender and Social Politics*. Cheltenham: Elgar.

Hobson, Barbara, and D. Morgan. 2002. "Introduction: Making men into fathers." Pp. 1–24 in Barbara Hobson (ed.), *Making Men into Fathers: Men, Masculinities and the Social Politics of Fatherhood*. Cambridge, UK: Cambridge University Press.

Hobson, Barbara, and Mieko Takahashi. 1997. "The parent-worker model: Lone mothers in Sweden." Pp. 121–39 in Jane Lewis (ed.), *Lone Mothers in European Welfare Regimes: Shifting Policy Logics*. London: Jessica Kingsley.

Hochschild, Arlie Russell. 1983. *The Managed Heart: Commercialization of Human Feeling*. Berkeley: University of California Press.

______. 1995. "The culture of politics. Traditional, postmodern, cold-modern, and warm-modern ideals of care." *Social Politics* 2:(3):331–46.

______. 2000. "The nanny chain." *American Prospect* 11 online www. prospect.

Hochschild, Jennifer L. 1995. *Facing Up to the American Dream*. Princeton, NJ: Princeton University Press.

______. 2002. "Multiple racial identifiers in the 2000 Census, and then what?" Pp. 340–53 in J. Perlmann and M. C. Waters (eds.), *The New Race Question: How the Census Counts Multiracial Individuals*. NY: Russell Sage Foundation.

Hodgson, Dennis, and Susan Cotts Watkins. 1997. "Feminists and neo-Malthusians: Past and present alliances." *Population and Development Review* 23 (3):469–524.

Hoffer, Eric. 1951. *The True Believer*. New York: Harper and Row.

Hofferbert, Richard I., and Ian Budge. 1992. "The party mandate and the Westminster model: Election programmes and government spending in Britain, 1945–1985." *British Journal of Political Science* 22:151–82.

Hoffman, Andrew J. 1997. *From Heresy to Dogma: An Institutional History of Corporate Environmentalism*. San Francisco, CA: New Lexington Press. Reprinted by Stanford University Press, 2001.

Hofstadter, Richard. 1964. "Pseudo-conservatism revisited: A postscript" Pp. 97–104 in Daniel Bell (ed.), *The Radical Right*. Garden City, NY: Anchor.

______. 1972. *The Idea of a Party System: The Rise of Legitimate Opposition in the United States, 1780–1840*. Berkeley: University of California Press.

Holliday, Ian. 2000. "Productivist welfare capitalism: Social policy in East Asia." *Political Studies* 48:706–23.

Hollifield, James. 1992. *Immigrants, Markets and States: The Political Economy of Post War Europe*. Cambridge, MA: Harvard University Press.

______. 2000. "The politics of international migration." Pp. 137–85 in Caroline Brettell and James Hollifield (eds.), *Migration Theory: Talking Across Disciplines*. London: Routledge.

Hollingsworth, J. Rogers, and Wolfgang Streeck. 1994. "Countries and sectors: Concluding remarks on performance, convergence, and competitiveness." Pp. 270–300 in J. Rogers Hollingsworth, Philippe C. Schmitter, and Wolfgang Streeck (eds.), *Governing Capitalist Economies: Performance and Control of Economic Sectors*. Oxford, UK: Oxford University Press.

Holmes, Geoffrey. 1982. *Augustan England*. London: George Allen & Unwin.

Holsti, Ole R. 1969. *Content Analysis for the Social Sciences and Humanities*. Reading, MA: Addison-Wesley.

Holton, Robert J., and Bryan S. Turner. 1986. *Talcott Parsons on Economy and Society*. London: Routledge & Kegan Paul.

Homans, George C. 1964. "Bringing men back in." *American Sociological Review* 29:809–18.

Honig, Bonnie. 1995. "Towards an agonistic feminism: Hanna Arendt and the politics of identity." Pp. 135–166 in Bonnie Honig (ed.), *Feminist Interpretations of Hanna Arendt*. University Park: Pennsylvania State University Press.

Honneth, Axel. 1991. *Critique of Power*. Cambridge, MA: MIT Press.

______. 1996. *The Struggle for Recognition: The Moral Grammar of Social Conflicts*. Cambridge, MA: MIT Press.

Honneth, Axel, Eberhard Knödler-Bunte, and Arno Widmann. 1981. "The dialectics of rationalization: an interview with Jürgen Habermas." *Telos* 49:5–31.

Hoogvelt, Ankie. 1997. *Globalisation and the Postcolonial World: The New Political Economy of Development*. London: Macmillan.

Hooks, B. 1995. *Killing Rage: Ending Racism*. New York: H. Holt.

Hooks, Gregory. 1990. "The rise of the Pentagon and U.S. state building: The defense program as industrial policy." *American Journal of Sociology* 96:358–404.

______. 1992. "The ambiguous legacy of C. Wright Mills: A reply to G. William Domhoff." *Critical Sociology* 18:57–74.

______. 1993. "The weakness of strong theories: The U.S. state's dominance of the World War II investment process." *American Sociological Review* 58:37–53.

______. 1994. "Regional processes in the hegemonic nation: Political, economic, and military influences on the use of geographic space." *American Sociological Review* 59:746–72.

Hooks, Gregory, and Leonard E. Bloomquist. 1992. "The legacy of World War II for regional growth and decline: The cumulative effects of wartime investments on U.S. manufacturing, 1947–1972." *Social Forces* 71:303–37.

Hooks, Gregory, and William Luchansky. 1996. "Warmaking and the accommodation of leading firms." *Political Power and Social Theory* 10:3–37.

Hooks, Gregory, and Gregory McLauchlan. 1992. "The institutional foundation of warmaking: Three eras of U.S. warmaking, 1939–1989." *Theory and Society* 21:757–88.

Hopcroft, Rosemary. 1999. *Regions, Institutions, and Agrarian Change in European History*. Ann Arbor, MI: University of Michigan Press.

Horkheimer, Max, and Theodor W. Adorno. 1979/1944. *Dialectic of Enlightenment*. London: Verso.

Horowitz, Donald L. 1985. *Ethnic Groups in Conflict*. Berkeley: University of California Press.

______. 2002. "The primordialists." In Daniele Conversi (ed.), *Ethnonationalism in the Contemporary World*. New York: Routledge.

Horowitz, Gad. 1968. *Canadian Labour in Politics*. Toronto: University of Toronto Press.

Hout, Michael, Clem Brooks, and Jeff Manza. 1995. "The democratic class struggle in the United States, 1948–1992." *American Sociological Review* 60:805–28.

Houtman, Dick. 2001. "Class, culture, and conservatism: Reassessing education as a variable in political sociology," Pp. 161–95 in Terry Nichols Clark and Seymour Martin Lipset (eds.), *The Breakdown of Class Politics: A Debate on Post-Industrial Stratification*. Washington, DC: Woodrow Wilson Center Press.

Howard, Christopher. 1999. "The American welfare state, or states?" *Political Research Quarterly* 52:421–42.

Howard, David. 1989. *Defining the Political*. Basingstoke, UK: Macmillan.

______. 1998. "Discourse theory and political analysis." Pp. 268–93 in Scarbrough and Tannenbaum (eds.), *Research Strategies in the Social Sciences*. Oxford, UK: Oxford University Press.

______. 2000. *Discourse*. Buckingham, UK: Open University Press.

Howarth, David, Aletta J. Norval, and Yannis Stavrakakis. 2000. *Discourse Theory and Political Analysis*. Manchester, UK: Manchester University Press.

Howarth, David, and Jacob Torfing (eds.). 2003. *Discourse Theory and European Politics: Identity, Policy and Governance*. Basingstoke, UK: Palgrave.

Howell, Jude. 1998. "Gender, civil society, and the state in China." Pp. 166–94 in Vicky Randall and Georgina Waylen (eds.), *Gender, Politics, and the State*. New York: Routledge.

Hsiung, Ping-Chun. 1996. *Living Rooms as Factories*. Philadelphia: Temple University Press.

Huber, Evelyne. 1996. "Options for social policy in Latin America: Neoliberal versus social democratic models." Pp. 141–191 in Gøsta Esping-Andersen (ed.), *Welfare States in Transition: National Adaptations in Global Economies*. London: Sage Publications.

Huber, Evelyn, Charles Ragin, and John Stephens. 1993. "Social democracy, Christian democracy, constitutional structure, and the welfare state." *American Journal of Sociology* 99(3):711–49.

______. 1997. Comparative Welfare States Data Set, Northwestern University and University of North Carolina.

Huber, Evelyne, and John D. Stephens. 1998. "Internationalization and the social democratic model." *Comparative Political Studies* 31:353–97.

______. 2001. *Development and Crisis of the Welfare State: Parties and Policies in Global Markets*. Chicago: University of Chicago Press.

Huber, Evelyne, John Stephens, David Bradley, Stephanie Moller, and François Nielsen. 2001. "The welfare state and gender inequality." Luxembourg Income Study Working Paper No. 278.

Huberts, Leo W. 1989. "The influence of social movements on government policy." Pp. 395–441 in Bert Klandermans (ed.), *Organizing for Change*. Greenwich, CT: JAI Press.

Huckeldt, Robert, and John Sprague. 1993. "Citizens, contexts, and politics." Pp. 281–303 in *Political Science: The State of the Discipline II*. Washington, DC: American Political Science Association.

______. 1995. *Citizens, Politics and Social Communication: Information and Influence in an Election Campaign*. New York: Cambridge University Press.

Huckfeldt, Robert. 1986. *Politics in Context: Assimilation and Conflict in Urban Neighborhoods*. New York: Agathon.

Huckle, Patricia. 1988. "The womb factor: Policy on pregnancy and the employment of women." Pp. 131–45 in Ellen Boneparth and Emily Stoper (eds.), *Women, Power, and Policy, 2nd edition*. New York: Pergamon.

Huddy, Leonie, and David O. Sears. 1995. "Opposition to bilingual education: Prejudice or the defense of realistic interests?" *Social Psychology Quarterly* 58:133–43.

Hula, Kevin W. 1999. *Lobbying Together: Interest Group Coalitions in Legislative Politics*. Washington, DC: Georgetown University Press.

Hulsink, Willem. 1999. *Privatisation and Liberalisation in European Telecommunications: Comparing Britain, the Netherlands, and France*. London: Routledge.

Human Rights Watch. 1999. *Human Rights Watch Report 1999*. New York: Human Rights Watch.

Hume, David. 1987[1739]. *Essay, Moral and Political*. Boston: Liberty Fund.

Hunt, Lynn A. 1984. *Politics, Culture, and Class in the French Revolution*. Berkeley: University of California Press.

Hunt, Scott A., Robert D. Benford and David A. Snow. 1994. "Identity fields: framing processes and the social construction of movement identities," Pp. 185–206 in E. Larana, H. Johnston and J. Gusfield (eds.), *New Social Movements: From Ideology to Identity*, Philadelphia: Temple University Press.

Hunter, Floyd. 1953. *Community Power Structure*. Chapel Hill: Univeristy of North Carolina Press.

______. 1959. *Top Leadership, U.S.A.* Chapel Hill, NC: University of North Carolina Press.

Hunter, James Davison 1991. *Culture Wars: The Struggle to Define America*. New York: Basic Books.

Huntington, Samuel P. 1968. *Political Order in Changing Societies*. New Haven, CT: Yale University Press.

______. 1991. *The Third Wave: Democratization in the Late Twentieth Century*. Norman, OK: University of Oklahoma Press.

Hutchinson, Robert. 1981. *Legislative History of American Immigration Policy 1798–1965*. Philadelphia: University of Pennsylvania Press.

Huttenback, Robert. 1976. *Racism and Empire: White Settlers and Colored Immigrants in the British Self-Governing Colonies 1830–1910*. Ithaca, NY: Cornell University Press.

Huyssen, Andreas. 1986. *After the Great Divide: Modernism, Mass Culture, Postmodernism*. Bloomington, IN: Indiana University Press.

Hyman, Herbert H., and Charles R. Wright. 1979. *Education's Lasting Effect on Values*. Chicago: University of Chicago Press.

IADB. 1991. Economic and Social Progress in Latin America. 1991 Report. Washington, DC: Inter-American Development Bank.

______. 1997. "Latin America after a decade of reforms." Economic and Social Progress in Latin America. 1997 Report. Washington, DC: Inter-American Development Bank.

Ignatieff, Michael. 1994. *Blood and Belonging: A Journey into the New Nationalism*. New York: Farrar, Straus, and Girout.

Ignazi, Piero. 1997. "The extreme Right in Europe: A survey." Pp. 300–19 in P. H. Merkl and L. Weinberg (eds.), *The Revival of Right Wing Extremism in the 90s*. London: Frank Cass.

Ignazi, Piero, and Colette Ysmal. *The Organization of Political Parties in Southern Europe*. Westport, CT: Praeger.

Ikegami, Eiko. 1995. *The Taming of the Samurai: Honorific Individualism and the Making of Modern Japan*. Cambridge, MA: Harvard University Press.

Ilchman, Warren. 1984. "Administración Pública Comparativa y el 'Sentido Común Académico.'" Pp. 54–120 in Oscar Oszlak (ed.), *Teoría de la Burocracia Estatal: Enfoques Críticos*. Buenos Aires: Paidós.

Ilchman, Warren, and Todd La Porte. 1970. "Comparative public organization" (mimeo).

Ilchman, Warren, and Norman Uphoff. 1969. *The Political Economy of Change*. Berkeley: University of California Press.

Immergut, Ellen M. 1992. *Health Politics: Interests and Institutions in Western Europe*. Cambridge, UK: Cambridge University Press.

______. 1998. "The theoretical core of the new institutionalism." *Politics and Society* 26:5–34.

Inglehart, Ronald. 1977. *The Silent Revolution: Changing Values and Political Styles among Western Publics*. Princeton, NJ: Princeton University Press.

______. 1989. *Changing Culture*. Princeton, NJ: Princeton University Press.

______. 1990. *Culture Shift in Advanced Industrial Societies*. Princeton, NJ: Princeton University Press.

______. 1997. *Modernization and Post-Modernization: Cultural, Economic, and Political Change in 43 Societies*. Princeton, NJ: Princeton University Press.

Inglehart, Ronald, and Wayne E. Baker. 2000. "Modernization, cultural change, and the persistence of traditional values." *American Sociological Review* 65:19–51.

Inkeles, Alex (ed.). 1991. *On measuring democracy: its consequences and concomitants*. New Brunswick, NJ: Transaction.

______. 1983. *Exploring Individual Modernity*. New York: Columbia University Press.

International Institute for Democracy and Electoral Assistance (IDEA). 1997. *Voter Turnout from 1945 to 1997: A Global Report*. Stockholm: IDEA.

Ippolito, Dennis S., and Thomas G. Walker. 1980. *Political Parties, Interest Groups, and Public Policy*. Englewood Cliffs, NJ: Prentice Hall.

Ireland, Patrick. 1994. *The Policy Challenge of Ethnic Diversity: Immigrant Politics in France and Switzerland*. Cambridge, MA: Harvard University Press.

Irons, Jenny. 1998. "The shaping of activist recruitment and participation: A study of women in the Mississippi civil rights movement." *Gender and Society* 12:692–709.

Irvin, Cynthia L. 1999. *Militant Nationalism: Between Movement and Party in Ireland and the Basque Country*. Minneapolis: University of Minnesota Press.

Isaac, Larry W., and William R. Kelly. 1981. "Racial insurgency, the state and welfare expansion." *American Journal of Sociology* 86:1338–86.

Isaacs, Harold Robert. 1989. *Idols of the Tribe: Group Identity and Political Change*. Cambridge, MA: Harvard University Press.

Ishay, Micheline (ed.). 1997. *The Human Rights Reader: Major Political Essays, Speeches and Documents from the Bible to the Present*. New York: Routledge.

Ishiyama, John T. 1999. "The communist successor parties and party organizational development in post-communist politics." *Political Research Quarterly* 52:87–112.

Isin, Engin F. 2002. *Being Political. Geneologies of Citizenship*. Minneapolis: University of Minnesota Press.

Iversen, Torben. 1999. *Contested Economic Institutions: The Politics of Macroeconomics and Wage Bargaining in Advanced Democracies*. New York: Cambridge University Press.

______. 2001. "The dynamics of welfare state expansion." Pp. 45–79 in Paul Pierson (ed.), *The New Politics of the Welfare State*. Oxford, UK: Oxford University Press.

Iverson, Torben, and Thomas Cusack. 2000. "The causes of welfare state expansion." *World Politics* 52:313–49.

Iyengar, Shanto, and Donald, Kinder, 1987. *News That Matters*. Chicago: University of Chicago Press.

Jackman, Mary R. 1978. "General and applied tolerance: Does education increase commitment to racial integration?" *American Journal of Political Science* 22:302–24.

______. 1994. *The Velvet Glove: Paternalism and Conflict in Gender, Class, and Race Relations*. Berkeley: University of California Press.

Jackman, Robert W. 1987. "The politics of economic growth in the industrial democracies, 1974–1980: Leftist strength or North Sea oil?" *Journal of Politics* 49:242–57.

Jacob, Charles. 1966. *Policy and Bureaucracy*. Princeton, NJ: DV Nostrand.

Jacobs, David, and Ronald Helms. 2001. "Racial politics and redistribution: Isolating the contingent influence of civil rights, riots, and crime on tax progressivity." *Social Forces* 80: 91–121.

Jacobs, Jane. 1961. *The Death and Life of Great American Cities*. New York: Random House.

Jacobs, Lawrence R., and Robert Y. Shapiro. 2000. *Politicians Don't Pander.* Chicago: University of Chicago Press.

______. 2000. *Politicians Don't Pander: Political Manipulation and the Loss of Political Responsiveness*. Chicago: University of Chicago Press.

Jacobs, Ronald. 2003. "Toward a political sociology of civil society." Pp. 19–47 in Betty, Dobratz, and Liza Waldnes and Timothy Bizzell (eds.), *Reaserch in Political Socilogy*: Vol. 12. *Political Sociology for the 21st Century.* New York: JAI/Elsevier Science.

Jacobsen, John Kurt. 1995. "Much ado about ideas: The cognitive factor in economic policy." *World Politics* 47:283–310.

Jacobson, Gary. 1980. *Money in Congressional Elections*. New Haven, CT: Yale University Press.

______. 1990. "The effects of campaign spending in House elections: New evidence for old arguments." *American Journal of Political Science* 34:334–62.

Jacoby, Gerhard. 1944. *Racial State, the German Nationalities Policy in the Protectorate of Bohemia-Moravia*. New York: Institute of Jewish Affairs of the American Jewish Congress and World Jewish Congress.

Jain, Anrudh (ed.). 1998. *Do Population Policies Matter?* New York: Population Council.

James, David R. 1986. "Local state structure and the transformation of Southern agriculture." Pp. 150–78 in E. Havens, G. Hooks, P. Mooney, and M. Pfeffer (eds.), *Studies in the Transformation of United States Agriculture*. Boulder, CO: Westview.

______. 1988. "The transformation of the Southern racial state: class and race determinants of local-state structures." *American Sociological Review* 53:191–208.

______. 1989. "City limits on racial equality: The effects of city–suburb boundaries on public-school desegregation, 1968–1976." *American Sociological Review* 54:963–85.

______. 1994. "Review symposium: American apartheid: Segregation and the making of the underclass." *Law & Social Inquiry* 19:407–32.

______. 2000. "Colorblind vs. color-conscious justice." *Social Science History* 24:429–34.

James, David R., and Sara Heiliger. 2000. "Slavery and involuntary servitude." Pp. 2596–2610 in E. F. Borgatta and R. J. V. Montgomery (eds.), *Encyclopedia of Sociology*, vol. 4. New York: Macmillan Reference USA.

James, David R., and Michael Soref. 1981. "Profit constraints on managerial autonomy: Managerial theory and the unmaking of the corporation president." *American Sociological Review* 46:1–18.

James, Winston, and Clive Harris. 1993. *Inside Babylon: The Caribbean Diaspora in Britain*. London: Verso.

Jameson, Fredric. 1981. *The Political Unconscious: Narrative as a Socially Symbolic Act*. Ithaca, NY: Cornell University Press.

Jamieson, Kathleen Hall, and Paul Waldman, 2003. *The Press Effect: Politicians, Journalists and the Stories That Shape the Political World*. Oxford, UK: Oxford University Press.

Jamieson, Kathleen Hall. (ed.). 1988. *Eloquence in an Electronic Age*. New York: Oxford University Press.

______. 1996. *The Media and Politics*. Thousand Oaks, CA: Sage Periodicals. Special issue of *The Annals of the American Academcy of Political and Social Science*, 56.

Janoski, Thomas. 1990. *The Political Economy of Unemployment*. Berkeley: University of California Press.

______. 1994. *The Political Economy of Unemployment: Active Labor Market Policy in West Germany and the United States*. Berkeley: University of California Press.

______. 1998. *Citizenship and Civil Society: A Framework of Rights and Obligations in Liberal, Traditional, and Social Democratic Regimes*. New York: Cambridge University Press.

______. 2001. "Neo-pluralism and neo-functionalism in political sociology: citizen groups, openness and responsiveness in politics." Paper presented at Conference on "Theories of Political Sociology," New York University, May, 2001.

______. Forthcoming. *The Ironies of Citizenship: The Naturalization and Integration of Strangers in Advanced Industrialized Countries.*

Janoski, Thomas and Alexander Hicks (eds.). 1994. "Methodological Innovations in Comparative Political Economy: An Introduction." Pp. 1–30 in Thomas Janoski and Alexander Hicks (eds.), *The Comparative Political Economy of the Welfare State*. New York: Cambridge University Press.

Janoski, Thomas, and Brian Gran. 2002. "Political citizenship: Foundations of rights." Pp. 13–52 in Engin Isin and Brian Turner (eds.), *Handbook of Citizenship Studies*. Thousand Oaks, CA: Sage.

Janoski, Thomas, and Elizabeth Glennie. 1995a. "The integration of immigrants in advanced industrialized nations." Pp. 11–39 in Marco Martiniello (ed.), *Migration, Citizenship and National Identities in the European Union*. Aldershot, UK: Avebury.

______. 1995b. "The double irony of granting citizenship: Colonialism and indigenous decline as causes of naturalization rates." Paper presented at the ASA convention Annual Meetings in Washington, D.C., August.

Janoski, Thomas, Christa McGill, and Vanessa Tinsley. 1997. "Making institutions dynamic in cross-national research: Time-space distancing in explaining unemployment." *Comparative Social Research* 16:227–68.

Janoski, Thomas, Darina Lepadatu, and Karen Diggs. 2003. "Dynamics of barriers to naturalization." Pp. 135–170 in Atushi Kondo (ed.), *New Concepts of Citizenship*. Stockholm: CEIFO.

Janowitz, Morris. 1960. *The Professional Soldier*. London: Macmillan.

______. 1988. *Military Institutions and Coercion in the Developing Nations: An Essay in Comparative Analysis*. Chicago: University of Chicago Press.

______. 1970. *Political Conflict: Essays in Political Sociology*. Chicago: Quadrangle.

Jaquette, Jane S. 1994. *The Women's Movement in Latin America*. Boulder, CO: Westview.

Jaquette, Jane S., and Sharon L. Wolchik (eds.). 1998. *Women and Democracy*. Baltimore, MD: Johns Hopkins University Press.

Jardim, Claudia. 2003. "Interview with Joao Pedro Stedile (MST)." *Brasil de Fato* July 10–16.

Jarquín, Edmundo, and Fernando Carrillo (eds.). 1998. *Justice Delayed: Judicial Reform in Latin America*. Washington, DC: Johns Hopkins University Press/Inter-American Development Bank.

Jasper, James M. 1990. *Nuclear Politics: Energy and the State in the United States, Sweden, and France*. Princeton, NJ: Princeton University Press.

______. 1997. *The Art of Moral Protest: Culture, Biography, and Creativity in Social Movements*. Chicago: University of Chicago Press.

______. 1998. "The emotions of protest: Affective and reactive emotions in and around social movements." *Sociological Forum* 13:397–424.

______. 2000. *Restless Nation: Starting Over in America*. Chicago: University of Chicago Press.

______. 2004. "The intellectual cycles of social-movement research: From psychoanalysis to culture." Pp. 234–53 in Jeffrey Alexander, Gary T. Marx, and Christine Williams (eds.), *Self, Social Structure, and Beliefs: Explorations in Sociology*. Berkeley: University of California Press.

______. In press, a. "Modernity, threat, nostalgia: Common responses to the moment of modernization." In Craig Calhoun, Jeff Goodwin, and Emma Naughton (eds.), *The Sociology of Islamic Movements*.

______. In press, b. *Strategy, a Social Approach*.

Jasper, James M., and Jane D. Poulsen. 1993. "Fighting back: Vulnerabilities, blunders and countermobilization by the targets of three animal rights campaigns." *Sociological Forum* 8:639–57.

Jasso, Guillermina. 2001. "Rule Finding About Rule Making: Comparison Processes and the Making of Rules." In Michael Hechter and Karl-Dieter Opp. (eds.), *Social Norms*. New York: Russell Sage.

Jay, Martin. 1973. *The Dialectical Imagination*. Boston: Little, Brown.

Jaynes, Arthur. 2002. "Insurgency and policy outcomes." *Journal of Political and Military Sociology* 30:90–112.

Jenkins, J. Craig. 1983. "Resource mobilization theory and the study of social movements." *Annual Review of Sociology* 9:527–53.

______. 1985. *The Politics of Insurgency: The Farm Worker Movement of the 1960s*. New York: Columbia University Press.

Jenkins, J. Craig, and Zeynep Benderliglou. 2003. "The velvet glove revolutions: A comparative analysis of protest and democratization in Eastern Europe, 1984–1993." Unpublished Paper Dept. of Sociology, Columbus, OH: Ohio State University.

Jenkins, J. Craig, and Doug Bond. 2001. "Conflict carrying capacity, political crisis, and reconstruction: A framework for the early warning of political system vulnerability." *Journal of Conflict Resolution* 45:3–31.

Jenkins, J. Craig, and Barbara Brents. 1989. "Social protest, hegemonic competition, and social reform: a political struggle interpretation of the origins of the American welfare state." *American Sociological Review* 54:891–909.

Jenkins, J. Craig, and Augustine J. Kposowa. 1990. "Explaining military coups d'etat: Black Africa, 1957–1984." *American Sociological Review* 55:861–75.

Jenkins, J. Craig, and Teri Shumate. 1985. "Cowboy capitalists and the rise of the 'New Right': An analysis of contributors to conservative policy formation." *Social Problems* 33:130–45.

Jenkins, J. Craig, and Charles Perrow. 1977. "Insurgency of the powerless: Farm workers' movements (1946–1972)." *American Sociological Review* 42:249–68.

Jenkins, Henry, and David Thorburn (eds). 2003. *Democracy and New Media*. Cambridge, MA: MIT Press.

Jenkins, J. Craig, and Michael Wallace. 1996. "The generalized action potential of social movements." *Sociological Forum* 11:183–207.

Jenkins, J. Craig, David Jacobs, and Jon Agnone. 2003. "Political opportunities and African-American protest." *American Journal of Sociology* 109:277–303.

Jenkins, Philip. 1992. *Intimate Enemies: Moral Panics in Contemporary Great Britain*. New York: Aldine de Gruyter.

______. 1998. *Moral Panic: Changing Concepts of the Child Molester in Modern America*. New Haven, CT: Yale University Press.

Jenkins, Richard. 1992. *Pierre Bourdieu*. London: Routledge.

Jennings, Edward T. 1983. "Racial insurgency, the state and welfare expansion." *American Journal of Sociology* 88:1220–36.

Jenson, Jane. 1990. "Representations of gender: Policies to 'protect' women workers and infants in France and the United States before 1914." Pp. 152–7 in L. Gordon (ed.), *Women, the State and Welfare*. Madison, WI: University of Wisconsin Press.

Jenson, Jane, and Mariette Sineau. 1995. *Mitterrand et les Francaises: Un rendez-vous manqué*. Paris: Press de la Fondation Nationale des Sciences Politiques.

Jessop, Bob. 1977. "Recent theories of the capitalist state." *Cambridge Journal of Economics* 1(4):353–73.

______. 1990. *State Theory: Putting the Capitalist State in Its Place*. University Park: Pennsylvania State University Press.

Jewell, Malcolm E., and Sarah M. Morehouse. 2001. *Political Parties and Elections in American States*. Washington, DC: CQ Press.

Jhally, Sut, and Justin Lewis. 1992. *Enlightened Racism: The Cosby Show, Audiences, and the Myth of the American Dream*. Boulder, CO: Westview.

John, Peter. 2001. "Policy networks." Pp. 139–48 in Kate Nash and Alan Scott (ed.), *Blackwell Companion to Political Sociology*. Malden, MA: Blackwell.

Johnson, Chalmers. 1982[1966]. *Revolutionary Change*, 2nd ed. Stanford, CA: Stanford University Press.

Johnson, G. Wesley. 1971. *The Emergence of Black Politics in Senegal*. Stanford, CA: Stanford University Press.

Johnson, Hubert. 1975. *Frederick the Great and His Officials*. New Haven, CT: Yale University Press.

Johnston, Hank. 1994. "New social movements and old regional nationalisms." Pp. 267–86 in Enrique Laraza, Hank Johnston, and Joseph R. Gusfield (eds.), *New Social Movements: From Ideology to Identity*. Philadelphia: Temple University Press.

Johnston, John. 1998. *Information Multiplicity: American Fiction in the Age of Media Saturation*. Baltimore, MD: Johns Hopkins University Press.

Jones, A. 2001. "The death of Barricada: Politics and professionalism in the post–Sandinista press." *Journalism Studies* 2:243–59.

Jones, K. 1990. "Citizenship in a woman-friendly polity." *Signs* 15:781–812.

______. 1994. *The Making of Social Policy in Britain, 1830–1990*. London: Athlone.

Jones, Woodrow Jr., and K. Robert Keiser. 1987. "Issue visibility and the effects of PAC money." *Social Science Quarterly* 68:170–6.

Joppke, Christian. 1999. *Immigration and the Nation State: The United States, Germany, and Great Britain*. Oxford, UK: Oxford University Press.

Jordan, Grant. 1990. "Sub-government, policy communities and networks: Refilling the old bottles?" *Journal of Theoretical Politics* 2(3):319–38.

Jordan, Grant and Klaus Schubert. 1992. "A preliminary ordering of policy network labels." *European Journal of Political Research* 21:7–27.

Jutte, Robert. 1994. *Poverty and Deviance in Early Modern Europe*. New York: Cambridge University Press.

Kabeer, Naila. 2000. *The Power to Choose: Bangladeshi Women and Labour Market Decisions in London and Dhaka*. London: Verso.

Kahneman, Daniel, and Amos Tversky. 1979. "Prospect theory: An analysis of decision under risk." *Econometrica* 47:263–91.

Kahneman, Daniel, Paul Slovic, and Amos Tversky, eds. 1982. *Judgment under Uncertainty: Heuristics and Biases*. Cambridge, UK: Cambridge University Press.

Kaid, Lynda Lee, and Christina Holtz-Bacha (eds.). 1995. *Political Advertising in Western Democracies: Parties and Candidates on Television*. Thousand Oaks, CA: Sage.

Kaiser, Daniel H. (ed.). 1987. *The Workers' Revolution in Russia, 1917: The View from Below*. Cambridge, UK: Cambridge University Press.

Kalb, Marvin. 1998. "The rise of the new news": A case study of two root causes of the modern scandal coverage." Cambridge, MA: Joan Shorenstein Center on Press, Politics, and Public Policy, Discussion Paper D–34.

Kalberg, Stephen. 1985. "The role of ideal interests in Max Weber's comparative historical sociology." In Robert J. Antonio and Ronald M. Glassman (eds.), *A Marx–Weber Dialogue*. Lawrence, KS: University Press of Kansas.

______. 1980. "Max Weber's Types of Rationality." *American Journal of Sociology* 85:1145–79.

Kaldor, Mary. 1981. *The Baroque Arsenal*. New York: Hill and Wang.

______. 1999. "Transnational civil society." Pp. 195–213 in T. Dunne and N. Wheeler (eds.), *Human Rights in Global Politics*. New York: Cambridge University Press.

Kamerschen, David R. 1968. "The influence of ownership and control on profit rates." *American Economic Review* 58:432–47.

Kangas, Olie. 1991. *The Politics of Social Rights*. Stockholm: Swedish Institute for Social Research.

Kantorowicz, Ernst H. 1957. *The King's Two Bodies: A Study in Medieval Political Theology*. Princeton, NJ: Princeton University Press.

Kantrowitz, Stephen. 2000. *Ben Tillman and the Reconstruction of White Supremacy*. Chapel Hill: University of North Carolina Press.

Kapstein, Ethan B. 1997. "Social policy and the transition." *Social Research* 64:1423–43.

Karagiannis, Nathalie. 2004. *Avoiding Responsibility. The Politics and Discourse of European Development Policy*. London: Pluto Press.

Karatnycky, Adrian. 1998. *Freedom in the World. The Annual Survey of Political Rights and Civil Liberties, 1997–1998*. New Brunswick, NJ: Transaction.

Karides, Marina. 2001. "Self-employment for all: Race, gender, and micro-enterprise development in Port of Spain, Trinidad." Doctoral dissertation, University of Georgia.

Karl, Terry Lynn. 1986. "Petroleum and Political Pacts: the Transition to Democracy in Venezuela." Pp. 196–219 in Guillermo O'Donnell, Philippe C. Schmitter, and Laurence Whitehead (eds.), *Transitions from Authoritarian Rule: Prospects for Democracy*. Baltimore, MD: Johns Hopkins University Press.

______. 1990. "Dilemmas of democratization in Latin America." *Comparative Politics* 23(1):1–21.

______. 1995. "The hybrid regimes of Central America," *Journal of Democracy* 6:72–86.

Karlson, Nils. 2002. *The State of State: Invisible Hands in Politics and Civil Society*. New Brunswick, NJ: Transaction.

Karsh, Efraim. 2002. *The Iran–Iraq War, 1980–1988.* Oxford, UK: Osprey.

Karsh, Efraim, and Inari Rautsi. 2003. *Saddam Hussein: A Political Biography*. New York: Grove.

Kastoryano, Riva. 2002. *Negotiating Identities: States and Immigrants in France and Germany* (B. Harvshav, trans.). Princeton, NJ: Princeton University Press.

______. 2003. *Arafat's War: The Man and his Battle for Israeli Conquest*. New York: Grove.

Katouzian, Homa. 1998. "The Pahlavi Regie in Iran." Pp. 182–205 in H. E. Chehabi and Juan J. Linz (eds.), *Sultanistic regimes*. Baltimore, MD: Johns Hopkins University Press.

Katz, Elihu, and Daniel, Dayan, 1992. *Media Events: The Live Broadcasting of History*. Cambridge, MA: Harvard University Press.

Katz, Elihu, and Paul F. Lazarsfeld. 1955. *Personal Influence*. New York: Free Press.

Katz, Jack. 1987. "What makes crime 'news'?" *Media, Culture and Society* 9:47–76.

Katz, Mark N. 1997. *Revolutions and Revolutionary Waves*. New York: St. Martin's Press.

Katz, Richard S. 2001. "Are Cleavages Frozen in the English-Speaking Democracies?" Pp. 65–92 in Lauri Karvonen and Stein Kuhnle (eds.), *Party Systems and Voter Alignments Revisited*. London: Routledge.

Katz, Richard, and Peter Mair. 1995. "Changing models of party organization and party democracy: The emergence of the cartel party." *Party Politics* 1:5–28.

Katzenstein, Mary F. 1998. *Faithful and Fearless: Moving Feminism in the Church and the Military.* Princeton, NJ: Princeton University Press.

Katzenstein, Peter J. 1984. *Corporatism and Change: Austria, Switzerland, and the Politics of Industry*. Ithaca, NY: Cornell University Press.

______. 1985. *Small States in World Markets: Industrial Policy in Europe*. Ithaca, NY: Cornell University Press.

______. 1993. "Coping with Terrorism: Norms and Internal Security in Germany and Japan." Pp. 265–98 in Peter Katzenstein (ed.), *Ideas and Foreign Policy: Beliefs, Institutions and Political Change*. Ithaca, NY: Cornell University Press.

Katznelson, Ira. 1973. *Black Men, White Cities: Race, Politics and Migration in the United States, 1900–1930 and Britain, 1948–1968*. London: Oxford University Press.

______. 1982. *City Trenches: Urban Politics and the Patterning of Class in the United States*. Chicago: University of Chicago Press.

______. 1997. "Structure and configuration in comparative politics." Pp. 81–112 in Mark Irving Lichbach and Alan S. Zuckerman (eds.), *Comparative Politics: Rationality, Culture, and Structure*. New York: Cambridge University Press.

Katznelson, Ira, and Helen V. Milner. 2002. *Political Science: The State of the Discipline, Centennial Edition*. New York/Washington, DC: W. W. Norton/American Political Science Association.

Katznelson, Ira, and Aristide R. Zolberg. 1986. "Working class formation: Nineteenth century patterns in Western Europe and the United States." Princeton, NJ: Princeton University Press.

Kaufman, Jason. 2001. "Rise and fall of a nation of joiners: The knights of labor revisited." *Journal of Interdisciplinary History* 31:553–79.

Kaufman, Robert R., and Alex Segura-Ubiergo. 2001. "Globalization, domestic politics, and social spending in Latin America – A time-series cross-section analysis, 1973–1997." *World Politics* 4:553–88.

Kautsky, Karl. 1971. *The Class Struggle: (Erfurt Program)*. New York: W. W. Norton.

Kavanagh, Dennis. 1980. "Political culture in Great Britain." Pp. 124–76 in Gabriel A. Almond and Sidney Verba (eds.), *The Civic Culture Revisited*. Boston: Little, Brown.

Kay, Tamara. forthcoming. "Labor relations in a post-NAFTA era: The impact of NAFTA on transnational labor cooperation and collaboration in North America." Ph.D. Dissertation, Department of Sociology, University of California–Berkeley.

Kaysen, Carl. 1957. "The social significance of the modern corporation." *American Economic Review* 47:311–319.

Keane, John (ed.). 1987a. *Re-discovering Civil Society* London: Verso.

Keane, John. 1988a. *Democracy and Civil Society.* London: Verso.

______. (ed.). 1988b. *Civil Society and the State*. London: Verso.

______. 1991. *The Media and Democracy*. Cambridge, UK: Polity Press.

______. 1991. *Media and Democracy*. London: Verso.

______. 1998. *Civil Society: Old Images, New Visions*. Stanford, CA: Stanford University Press.

Keat, John, and Russell Urry. 1983. *Social Theory as Science*. London/New York: Routledge & Kegan Paul.

Keck, Margaret E. 1995. "Social equity and environmental politics in Brazil – lessons from the rubber tappers of Acre." *Comparative Politics* 27(4):409–24.

______. 1998. "Planafloro in Rondôia: The limits of leverage." in Pp. 181–218 J. A. Fox and L. D. Brown (eds.), *The Struggle for Accountability: The World Bank, NGOs, and Grassroots Movements*. Cambridge, MA: MIT Press.

Keck, Margaret E., and Kathryn Sikkink. 1998. *Activists beyond Borders: Advocacy Networks in International Politics*. Ithaca, NY: Cornell University Press.

______. 1999. "Transnational advocacy networks in international and regional politics." *International Social Science Journal* 159:89–101.

Keddie, Nikki R. 1998. "The new religious politics: Where, when, and why do 'fundamentalisms' appear?" *Comparative Studies in Society and History* 40(4):696–723.

______. 1999. "The new religious politics and women worldwide: A comparative study." *Journal of Women's History* 10:11–34.

Keech, William R. 1968. *The Impact of Negro Voting: The role of the Vote in the Quest for Equality*. Chicago: Rand McNally.

Keister, Lisa. 1998. "Engineering growth: Business group structure and firm performance in China's transitional economy." *American Journal of Sociology* 104:404–440.

Kelley, Jonathan, and H. S. Klein. 1980. *Revolution and the Rebirth of Inequality.* Berkeley: University of California Press.

Kellner, Douglas. 1990. *Television and the Crisis of Democracy*. Boulder, CO: Westview Press.

Kelly, William, and David Snyder. 1980. "Racial violence and socioeconomic changes among Blacks in the United States." *Social Forces* 58:739–60.

Kelsey, Jane. 1995. *Economic Fundamentalism*. London: Pluto.

Kenis, Patrick, and Volker Schneider. 1991. "Policy networks and policy analysis: Scrutinizing a new analytical toolbox." Pp. 25–62 in Bernd Marin and Renate Mayntz (eds.), *Policy Networks: Empirical Evidence and Theoretical Considerations*. Boulder, Co: Campus/Westview Press.

Kennedy, Randall. 2001. "Racial trends in the administration of criminal justice." Pp. 1–20 in N. J. Smelser, W. J. Wilson, and F. Mitchell (eds.), *America Becoming: Racial Trends and Their Consequences*, vol. 2. Washington, DC: National Academy.

Kenworthy, Lane. 1996. "Unions, wages, and the common interest." *Comparative Political Studies* 28: 491–524.

______. 1999. "Do social-welfare policies reduce poverty? A cross-national assessment." *Social Forces* 77:1119–39.

______. 2001. "Wage-setting measures: A survey and assessment." *World Politics* 54:57–98.

______. 2002. "Corporatism and unemployment in the 1980s and 1990s." *American Sociological Review* 67:367–88.

Kenworthy, Lane, and Bernhard Kittel. 2002. *Indicators of Social Dialogue: Concepts and Measurement*. Report prepared for the International Labour Organization, Geneva.

Kenworthy, Lane, and Jonas Pontusson. 2002. "Inequality and redistribution in OECD countries." Paper presented at the Annual Meetings of the Society for the Advancement of Soceioeconomics, Minneapolis, MN, June 27–30, 2002.

Keohane, Robert. 1989. *International Institutions and State Power*. Boulder, CO: Westview Press.

Keohane, Robert, and Joseph Nye. 1977. *Power and Interdependence: World Politics in Transition*. Boston: Little, Brown.

Kepel, Gilles. 1984. *Muslim Extremism in Egypt*. Berkeley: University of California Press.

Kerkvliet, Benedict J. 1977. *The Huk Rebellion: A Study of Peasant Revolt in the Philippines*. Berkeley: University of California Press.

Kernell, Samuel. 1986. *Going Public: New Strategies of Presidential Leadership*. Washington, DC: Congressional Quarterly Press.

Kerr, Clark, J. T. Dunlop, F. Harbison, and Charles A. Meyers, 1964. *Industrialism and Industrial Man: The Problems of Labor and Management in Economic Growth*. Cambridge, MA: Harvard University Press.

Kershaw, Ian, and Moshe Lewin(eds.), 1997. "Introduction: The regimes and their dictators." Pp. 1–25 in Kershaw Ian and Moshe Lewin (eds.), *Stalinism and Nazism: Dictatorships in Comparison*. Cambridge, UK: Cambridge University Press.

Kertzer, David I. 1988. *Ritual, Politics, and Power*. New Haven, CT: Yale University Press.

Keuchler, Manfred, and Russell J. Dalton. 1990. "New Social Movements and the Political Order: Inducing Change for Long-term Stability?" Pp. 277–300 in Russell J. Dalton and Manfred Kuechler (eds.), *Challenging the Political Order*. New York: Oxford University Press.

Key, V. O. 1964[1942]. *Politics, Parties, and Pressure Groups*, 5th Edition, New York: Crowell.

______. 1964[1949]. *Southern Politics in State and Nation*. Cambridge, MA: Harvard University Press.

Key, V. O., Jr., and Frank Munger. 1959. "Social determinism and electoral decision: The case of Indiana." Pp. 281–299 in Eugene Burdick and Arthur J. Brodbeck (eds.), *American Voting Behavior*. Glencoe, IL: Free Press.

Keyssar, Alexander. 2000. *The Right to Vote. The Contested History of Democracy in the United States*. New York: Basic Books.

Khagram, Sanjeev. 2004. "Dams, and development: Transnational struggles for water power." Ithaca, NY: Cornell University Press.

Khagram, Sanjeev, James V. Riker, and Kathryn Sikkink. 2002. *Restructuring World Politics: Transnational Social Movements, Networks, and Norms. Social Movements, Protest, and Contention; v. 14.* Minneapolis: University of Minnesota Press.

Khomeini, Imam. 1981. *Islam and Revolution: Writings and Declarations of Imam Khomeini* (Hamid Algar, trans.). Berkeley: Mizan.

Kiewiet, D. Roderick. 1983. *Macroeconomics and Micropolitics.* Chicago: University of Chicago Press.

Kiewiet, D. Roderick, and Matthew D. McCubbins. 1991. *The Logic of Delegation: Congressional Parties and the Appropriations Process.* Chicago: University of Chicago Press.

Kilkey, Majella, and Jonathan Bradshaw. 1999. "Lone mothers, economic well-being, and policies." Pp. 147–83 in Diane Sainsbury (ed.), *Gender and Welfare State Regimes.* Oxford, UK: Oxford University Press.

Killian, Lewis M. 1964. "Social movements." Pp. 426–455 in Robert E. Ferris (ed.), *Handbook of Sociology.* Chicago: Rand McNally.

______1968. *The Impossible Revolution? Black Power and the American Dream.* New York: Random House.

Kim, Jae-On, and Mahn-Geum Ohn. 1992. "A theory of minor party persistence: Election rules, social cleavage, and the number of political parties." *Social Forces* 70:575–99.

Kimmel, Michael S. 1990. *Revolution: A Sociological Interpretation.* Philadelphia: Temple University Press.

Kimmerling, Baruch. (ed.). 1996. *"Political sociology at the crossroads."* Special issue of *Current Sociology* 44(3):1–186.

Kinder, Donald R., and Tali Mendelberg. 2000. "Individualism reconsidered: Principles and prejudice in contemporary American opinion." Pp. 44–74 in D. O. Sears, J. Sidanius, and L. D. Bobo (eds.), *Racialized Politics: The Debate About Racism in America.* Chicago: University of Chicago Press.

Kinder, Donald R., and Lynn M. Sanders. 1996. *Divided by Color: Racial Politics and Democratic Ideals.* Chicago: University of Chicago Press.

______. 1996. *Divided by Color.* Chicago: University of Chicago Press.

Kinder, Donald R., and David O. Sears. 1981. "Prejudice and politics: Symbolic racism versus racial threats to the good life." *Journal of Personality and Social Psychology* 40:414–31.

Kinder, Donald R., and Nicholas Winter. 2001. "Exploring the racial divide: Blacks, whites, and opinion on national policy." *American Journal of Political Science* 45:439–53.

King, Anthony D. (ed.) 1997. *Culture, Globalization and the World-System: Contemporary Conditions for the Representation of Identity.* Minneapolis: University of Minnesota Press.

______. 1998. "The accidental derogation of the lay actor: A critique of Giddens' concept of structure." *Philosophy of the Social Sciences* 30:362–83.

______. 2000. "Thinking with Bourdieu against Bourdieu: A 'practical' critique of the habitus." *Sociological Theory* 18:417–33.

King, Gary, Ian Budge, Richard I. Hofferbert, Michael Laver, and M. McDonald. 1993. "Party platforms, mandates, and government spending." *American Political Science Review* 87:744–50.

King, Gary, Robert O. Keohane, and Sidney Verba. 1994. *Designing Social Inquiry: Scientific Inference in Qualitative Research.* Princeton, NJ: Princeton University Press.

King, Leslie. 2002. "Demographic trends, pronatalism, and nationalist ideologies in the late twentieth century." *Ethnic and Racial Studies* 25(3):367–89.

King, Leslie, and Ginna Husting. 2003. "Anti-abortion activism in the United States and France: Comparing opportunity environments of rescue tactics." *Mobilization* 8(3):297–312.

King, Roger. 1986. *The State in Modern Society: New Directions in Political Sociology.* Chatham, NJ: Chatham House.

Kingdon, John W. 1984. *Agendas, Alternatives, and Public Policies.* Boston: Little, Brown.

Kingston, Paul. 1985. *Chicago Divided: The Making of a Black Mayor.* DeKalb: Northern Illinois University Press.

______. 2000. *The Classless Society.* Stanford, CA: Stanford University Press.

Kirby, Andrew (ed.). 1992. *The Pentagon and the Cities.* Newbury Park, CA: Sage.

Kirchheimer, Otto. 1966. "The transformation of the western European party systems." Pp. 177–200 in Joseph LaPalombara and Joseph Weiner (eds.), *Political Parties and Political Development.* Princeton, NJ: Princeton University Press.

Kiser, Edgar. 1994. "Markets and hierarchies in early modern tax systems: A principal-agent analysis." *Politics and Society* 22(3):284–315.

______. 1996. "The revival of narrative in historical sociology: What rational choice theory can contribute." *Politics and Society* 24:249–71.

______. 1999. "Comparing varieties of agency theory in economics, political science, and sociology: An iIllustration of state policy implementation." *Sociological Theory* 17:146–70.

Kiser, Edgar, and Justin Baer. In press. "The bureaucratization of states: Toward an analytical Weberianism." In Julia Adams, Elizabeth Clemens, and Ann Orloff (eds.), *Remaking Modernity.* Durham, NC: Duke University Press.

Kiser, Edgar, and Yoram Barzel. 1991. "The origins of democracy in England." *Rationality and Society* 3(4):396–422.

Kiser, Edgar, and Joshua Kane. 2001. "Revolution and state structure: The bureaucratization of tax administration in early modern England and France." *American Journal of Sociology* 107(1):183–223.

Kiser, Edgar, and April Linton. 2000. "Determinants of the growth of the state: War and taxation in early modern France and England." *Social Forces* 80(2):411–48.

______. 2002. "The hinges of history: state-making and revolt in early modern France." *American Sociological Review* 67(6):889–910.

Kiser, Edgar, and Joachim Schneider. 1994. "Bureaucracy and efficiency: An analysis of taxation in early modern Prussia." *American Sociological Review* 59:187–204.

Kitschelt, Herbert. 1986. "Political opportunity structures and political protest: Anti-nuclear movements in four democracies." *British Journal of Sociology* 16:57–85.

______. 1988. "Left-libertarian parties: Explaining innovation in competitive party systems." *World Politics* 40:194–234.

______. 1989. *The Logics of Party Formation: Ecological Politics in Belgium and West Germany*. Ithaca, NY: Cornell University Press.

______. 1990. "New social movements and the decline of party organization." Pp. 179–208 in Russell J. Dalton and Manfred Kuechler (eds.), *Challenging the Political Order: New Social and Political Movements in Western Democracies*. New York: Oxford University Press.

______. 1994. *The Transformation of European Social Democracy*. Cambridge, UK: Cambridge University Press.

______. 1995a. "Formation of party cleavages in post-communist democracies." *Party Politics* 1:447–72.

______. 1995b. *The Radical Right in Western Europe*. Ann Arbor, MI: University of Michigan Press.

Kittay, E. F. 1998. "Dependency, equality, and welfare." *Feminist Studies* 24:32–43.

______. 1999. *Love's Labor: Essays on Women, Equality and Dependency*. New York: Routledge.

Kitschelt, Herbert, Peter Lange, Gary Marks, and John D. Stephens (eds.). 1999. *Continuity and Change in Contemporary Capitalism*. Cambridge, UK: Cambridge University Press.

Kitschelt, Herbert, Zdenka Mansfeldova, Radoslaw Markowski, and Gabor Toka. 1999. *Post-Communist Party Systems: Competition, Representation, and Inter-Party Cooperation*. Cambridge, UK: Cambridge University Press.

Kittel, Bernhard. 2000. "Trade union bargaining horizons in comparative perspective: The effects of encompassing organization, unemployment, and the monetary regime on wage pushfulness." *European Journal of Industrial Relations* 6:181–202.

Klapp, Orrin. 1969. *Collective Search for Identity*. New York: Holt, Rinehart and Winston.

Klausen, Jytte. 1998. *War and Welfare: Europe and the United States, 1945 to the Present*. New York: St. Martin's.

Klein, E. 1987. "The diffusion of consciousness in the United States and Western Europe." Pp. 23–45 in Mary Katzenstein and Carol Mueller (eds.), *The Women's Movements in the United States and Western Europe: Consciousness, Political Opportunity and Public Policy*. Philadelphia: Temple University Press.

Klein, Gary. 1998. *Sources of Power: How People Make Decisions*. Cambridge, MA: MIT Press.

Kligman, Gail. 1992. "The politics of reproduction in Ceausescu's Romania: A case study in political culture." *East European Politics and Societies* 6(3): 364–418.

Klinker, Philip. 1994. "Party culture and party behavior." Pp. 275–87 in Daniel M. Shea and John C. Green (eds.), *The State of the Parties: The Changing Role of Contemporary American Parties*. Lanham, MD: Rowman and Littlefield.

Klinkner, Philip A., and Rogers M. Smith. 1999. *The Unsteady March: The Rise and Decline of Racial Equality in America*. Chicago: University of Chicago Press.

Kluegel, James R., and Lawrence D. Bobo. 2001. "Perceived group discrimination and policy attitudes: The sources and consequences of the race and gender gaps." Pp. 163–213 in A. O'Connor, C. Tilly, and L. D. Bobo (eds.), *Urban Inequality: Evidence from Four Cities*. New York: Russell Sage Foundation.

Knack, Stephen. 1995. "Does motor voter work? evidence from state-level data." *Journal of Politics* 57:796–811.

______. 2000. "Aid dependence and the very quality of need for sustained and rapid income growth. A cross-country empirical analysis." The World Bank Development Research Group Regulation and Competition Policy. Policy Research Working Paper 2396, July. Washington, DC.

Knight, Jack. 1992. *Institutions and Social Conflict*. Cambridge, UK: Cambridge University Press.

Knight, Jack, and Itai Sened. 1995. *Explaining Social Institutions*. Ann Arbor: University of Michigan Press.

Knijn, Trudie. 2000. "Marketization and the struggling logics of (home) care in the Netherlands." Pp. 232–48 in Madonna Harrington Meyer (ed.), *Care Work*. New York: Routledge.

Knijn, Trudie, and M. Kremer. 1997. "Gender and the caring dimension of welfare states: Toward inclusive citizenship." *Social Politics* 4:328–61.

Knijn, Trudie, and Ilona Ostner. 2002. "Commodification and de-commodification." Pp. 141–69 in Barbara Hobson, Jane Lewis, and Birte Siim (eds.), *Contested Concepts in Gender and Social Politics*. Cheltenham: Elgar.

Knoke, David. 1976. *The Social Bases of Political Parties*. Baltimore: Johns Hopkins University Press.

______. 1990a. *Organizing for Collective Action: The Political Economies of Associations*. New York: Aldine de Gruyter.

______. 1990b. Political Networks: The Structural Perspective. New York: Cambridge University Press.

______. 1998. "The organizational state: Origins and prospects." *Research in Political Sociology* 8:147–63.

______. 2001. *Changing Organizations: Business Networks in the New Political Economy*. Boulder, CO: Westview.

______. 2004. "The sociopolitical construction of national policy domains." In Christian H. C. A. Henning and Christian Melbeck (eds.), *Interdisziplinäre Sozialforschung: Theorie und empirische Anwendungen*. Frankfurt, Germany: Campus Verlag.

Knoke, David, and Miguel Guilarte. 1994. "Networks in organizational structures and strategies." *Current Perspectives in Social Theory, Supplement* 1:77–115.

Knoke, David, Franz Pappi, Jeffrey Broadbent, and Yutaka Tsujinaka. 1994. *Comparing Policy Networks*. Cambridge, UK: Cambridge University Press.

Knoke, David, Franz Urban Pappi, Jeffrey Broadbent, and Yutaka Tsujinaka. 1996. *Comparing Policy Networks: Labor Politics in the U.S., Germany, and Japan*. New York: Cambridge University Press.

Knoke, David, and Christine Wright-Isak. 1982. "Individual motives and organizational incentive systems." *Research in the Sociology of Organizations* 1: 209–54.

Knorr Cetina, Karin. 1999. *Epistemic Cultures: How the Sciences Make Knowledge*. Cambridge, MA: Harvard University Press.

Koch, Jeffrey W. 1993. "Is group membership a prerequisite for group identification?" *Political Behavior* 15:49–60.

Koenigsberger, H. G. 1977. "Dominium regale or dominium politicum et regale? Monarchies and Parliaments in Early Modern Europe." Pp. 43–68 in Karl Bosl (ed.), *Der moderne Parlamentarismus und seine Grundlagen in der standischen Reprasentatation*. Berlin: Duncker & Humbolt.

Kohli, Atul (ed.). 2001. *The Success of India's Democracy*. Cambridge, UK: Cambridge University Press.

Kohli, Martin, Martin Rein, Anne Marie Guillemard, and Herbert van Gunsteren. 1991. *Time for Retirement*. Cambridge, UK: Cambridge University Press.

Kohn, Hans. 1946. *The Idea of Nationalism*. New York: MacMillan.

Kolakowski, Leszek. 1978. *Main Currents of Marxism*, vol. 3: *The Breakdown*. New York: Oxford University Press.

Kolko, Gabriel. 1994. *Century of War: Politics, Conflicts, and Society Since 1914*. New York: Hill and Wang.

Koltsova, Olessia. 2001. "News production in contemporary Russia: Practices of power." *European Journal of Communication* 16(3):315–35.

Kopecky, Petr, and Cas Mudde(eds.). 2003. *Uncivil Society? Contentious Politics in Post-Communist Europe*. London: Routledge.

Korchak, Alexander. 1994. *Contemporary Totalitarianism. A Systems Approach*. East European Monographs. New York: Columbia University Press.

Kornhauser, William. 1959. *The Politics of Mass Society*. Glencoe, IL: Free Press.

Korpi, Walter. 1972. "Some problems in the measurement of class voting." *American Journal of Sociology* 78:627–42.

______. 1978. *The Working Class in Welfare Capitalism*. London: Routledge and Kegan Paul.

______. 1982. *The Democratic Class Struggle*. Boston: Routledge & Kegan Paul.

______. 1985a. "Economic growth and the welfare system: leaky bucket or irrigation system?" *European Sociological Review* 1(2):97–118.

______. 1985b. "Power resources approach vs. action and conflict: on causal and intentional explanations in the study of power." *Sociological Theory* 3(2):31–45.

______. 1989. "Power, politics, and state autonomy in the development of social citizenship." *American Sociological Review* 54:309–28.

______. 2000. "Faces of Inequality: Gender, Class, and Patterns of Inequalities in Different Types of Welfare States." *Social Politics*. 7:2:127–91.

______. 2003. "Welfare state regress in Western Europe: politics, institutions, globalization and Europeanization." *Annual Review of Sociology* 29: 489–609.

Korpi, Walter, and Joakim Palme. 1998. "The paradox of redistribution and strategies of equality: welfare state institutions, inequality, and poverty in the Western countries." *American Sociological Review* 63:661–87.

______. 2003. "New politics and class politics in the context of austerity and globalization: welfare state regress in 18 countries; 1975–1995." *American Political Science Review* 97(3):425–58.

Korpi, Walter, and Michael Shalev. 1980. "Strikes, power and politics in the western nations, 1900–1976." *Political Power and Social Theory* 1:301–34.

Korsch, Karl. 1969[1922]. *Arbeitsrecht für Betriebsräte*. Erich Gerlach (ed.). Frankfurt am Main: Europäische Verlagsanstalt.

Kostakopoulou, Theodora. 2001. *Citizenship, Identity and Immigration in the European Union*. Manchester, UK: Manchester University Press.

Kotz, David. 1978. *Bank Control of Large Corporations in the United States*. Berkeley: University of California Press.

Kourvetaris, George. 1990. "Beyond the arms race: A search for a new paradigm for a peaceful world." *Journal of Political and Military Sociology* 19:233–52.

______. 1997. *Political Sociology: Structure and Process*. Boston: Allyn & Bacon.

Kousser, J. Morgan. 1974. *The Shaping of Southern Politics: Suffrage Restriction and the Establishment of the One-Party South, 1880–1910*. New Haven, CT: Yale University Press.

______. 1999. *Colorblind Injustice: Minority Voting Rights and the Undoing of the Second Reconstruction*. Chapel Hill: University of North Carolina Press.

______. 2000. "Response to commentaries." *Social Science History* 24:443–50.

Koven, Seth, and Sonya Michel. 1993. *Mothers of a New World: Maternalist Politics and the Origins of Welfare States*. New York: Routledge.

Kowalewski, David. 1991. "Core intervention and periphery revolution, 1821–1985." *American Journal of Sociology* 97:70–95.

Kposowa, Augustine J., and J. Craig Jenkins. 1993. "The structural sources of military coups in postcolonial Africa, 1957–1984." *American Journal of Sociology* 99:126–63.

Krasner, Stephen D. 1978. *Defending the National Interest: Raw Materials Investments and U.S. Foreign Policy*. Princeton, NJ: Princeton University Press.

Krasno, Jonathon S., and Donald Philip Green. 1988. "Pre-empting quality challengers in House elections." *Journal of Politics* 50:920–36.

Krasno, Jonathon S., Donald Philip Green, and Jonathon Cowden. 1994. "The dynamics of campaign fundraising in House elections." *Journal of Politics* 56:459–74.

Krauss, Ellis. 1998. "Changing television news in Japan." *Journal of Asian Studies* 57:663–92.

______. 2000. *Broadcasting Politics in Japan: NHK TV News*. Ithaca, NY: Cornell University Press.

Krehbiel, Keith. 1991. *Information and Legislative Organization*. Ann Arbor: University of Michigan Press.

Kreps, David M. 1990. *Game Theory and Economic Modeling*. New York: Oxford University Press.

Krieger, Joel, and David Held. 1978. "A theory of the state? A comment on Block's 'The Ruling Class Does Not Rule.'" *Socialist Review* 8(4–5):189–207.

Kryder, Daniel. 2000. *Divided Arsenal: Race and the American State During World War II*. New York: Cambridge University Press.

Krysan, Maria. 2000. "Prejudice, politics, and public opinion: Understanding the sources of racial policy attitudes." *Annual Review of Sociology* 26:135–68.

Kuhn, Raymond. 2002, "The first Blair government and political journalism." Pp. 47–68 in Erik Neveu and Raymond Kuhn (eds.), *Political Journalism: New Challenges, New Practices*. London: Routledge.

Kuhn, Thomas S. 1970. *The Structure of Scientific Revolutions*. Chicago: University of Chicago Press.

Kuklinski, James H., Robert C. Luskin, and John Bolland. 1991. "Where is the schema?" *American Political Science Review* 85:1341–56.

Kuran, Timar. 1995. "The inevitability of future revolutionary surprises." *American Journal of Sociology* 100(6):1528–51.

Kurzman, Charles. 1998. "Waves of democratization." *Studies in Comparative International Development* 33:37–59.

Kwon, Yong Yeok, and Jonas Pontusson. 2002. "Welfare spending in OECD countries revisited: Has salience of partisanship really declined?" Paper presented at the 2002 Meeting of the American Political Science Association, Boston, Massachussetts, August, 2002.

Kyle, David, and Rey Koslowski (eds.). 2001. *Global Human Smuggling: Comparative Perspectives*. Baltimore, MD: Johns Hopkins University Press.

Kymlicka, W. 1989. *Liberalism, Community and Culture*. Oxford, UK: Clarendon.

______. 1995. *Multicultural Citizenship: A Liberal Theory of Minority Rights*. Oxford, UK: Oxford University Press.

______. (ed.). 1996. *The Rights of Minority Cultures*. Oxford, UK: Oxford University Press.

______. 1999. "Liberal complacencies." Pp. 31–4 in Susan Moller Okin and Joshua Cohen (eds.), *Is Multiculturalism Bad for Women?* Princeton, NJ: Princeton University Press.

La Palombara, Joseph. 1963. *Bureaucracy and Political Development*. Princeton, NJ: Princeton University Press.

La Porta, Rafael, Florencio Lopez-de-Silanes, and Andrei Shleifer, 1999. "Corporate ownership around the world." *Journal of Finance* 54:471–517.

La Porte, Todd. 1971. "The recovery of relevance in the study of public organizations." Pp. 17–48 in Frank Marini (ed.), *Toward a New Public Administration*. The minnowbrook perspective. Scranton, PA: Chandler.

Labov, William, and David Fanshel. 1977. *Therapeutic Discourse: Psychotherapy as Conversation*. New York: Academic.

Lacan, Jacques. 1977/1966. *Ecrits: A Selection*. New York: W. W. Norton.

Lacher, Hannes. 1999. "The politics of the market: Re-reading Karl Polanyi." *Global Society* 13, 3:313–26.

Laclau, Ernesto. 1975. "The specificity of the political: the Poulantzas–Miliband debate." *Economy and Society* 5(1):87–110.

______. 1977. *Politics and Ideology in Marxist Theory*. London: Verso.

______. 1990. *New Reflections of the Revolution of Our Time*. London: Verso.

______. 1993. "Discourse." Pp. 431–7 in Gooding and Pettit (eds.), *The Blackwell Companion to Contemporary Political Philosophy*. Oxford, UK: Blackwell.

______. 1996a. "The death and resurrection of ideology." *Journal of Political Ideologies* 1:201–20.

______. 1996b. *Emancipations*. London: Verso.

______. 2000. "Identity and hegemony," "Structure, history and the political," and "Constructing universality." Pp. 44–89, 182–212, 281–308 in Butler, Laclau, and Žižek (eds.), *Contingency, Hegemony, Universality*. London: Verso.

Laclau, Ernesto, and Chantal Mouffe. 1985. *Hegemony and Socialist Strategy*. London: New Left Books.

______. 1987. "Post-Marxism without apologies." *New Left Review* 166:79–106.

______. 2001. *Hegemony and Socialist Strategy*. 2nd Edition. London: Verso.

Lacquer, Walter. 1968. *The Road to Jerusalem: The Origins of the Arab–Israeli Conflict*. New York: MacMillan.

Lacquer, Walter, and Barry Rubin (eds.). 2001. *The Arab–Israeli Reader: A Documentary History of the Middle East Conflict*. New York: Penguin Books.

Lahav, Gallya. 2004. *Immigration and Politics in the New Europe: Reinventing Borders*. NY: Cambridge University Press.

Laitin, David D. 1988. *Identity in Formation*. Ithaca, NY: Cornell University Press.

Lakatos, Imre. 1978. *The Methodology of Scientific Research Programs*. Cambridge, UK: Cambridge University Press.

Lakatos, Imre, and Alan Musgrave (eds.). 1974. *Criticism and the Growth of Knowledge*. Cambridge, UK: Cambridge University Press.

Lake, Marilyn. 1993. "A revolution in the family': The challenge and contradiction of maternal citizenship." Pp. 378–95 in Seth Koven and Sonya Michel (eds.), *Mothers of a New World: Maternalist Politics and Welfares States in Comparative Perspective*. New York: Routledge.

______. 2000. "The ambiguities for feminists of national belonging: Race and gender in the imagined Australian community." Pp. 159–76 in Ida Blom, Karen Hagemann, and Catherine Hall (eds.), *Gendered Nations: Nationalisms and Gender Order in the Long Nineteenth Century*. Oxford, UK: Berg.

Lakunina, Liana, Natalia Stepantchikova, and Tatyana Tchetvernina. 2001. "Social support for home-based care in the Russian Federation." Pp. 125–39 in Mary Daly (ed.), *Care Work*. Geneva: International Labour Office.

Lamont, Michèle. 1992. *Money, Morals, and Manners*. Chicago: University of Chicago Press.

Landau, Martin. 1969. "Redundancy, rationality, and the problem of duplication and overlap." *Public Administration Review* 29:348–356.

Landes, J. B. 1998a. *Feminism, the Public and the Private*. Oxford, UK: Oxford University Press.

______. 1998b. "The public and the private sphere: A feminist reconsideration." Pp. 135–63 in Joan B. Landes (ed.), *Feminism the Public and the Private*. Oxford, UK: Oxford University Press.

Lane, Jan-Erik. 1999. *The Public Sector. Concepts, Models and Approaches, 2nd ed.* New Delhi: Sage.

Lane, Robert E. 1962. *Political Ideology: Why the American Common Man Believes What He Does*. New York: Free Press.

______. 1978. "Autonomy, Felicity, Futility: the Effects of the Market Economy on Political Personality." *The Journal of Politics*, 40:2–24.

Langbein, Laura I. 1985. "The politics of growth." *Journal of Politics* 47:792–827.

______. 1986. "Money and access: Some empirical evidence." *The Journal of Politics* 48:1052–62.

Lange, Peter, and Geoffrey Garrett. 1985. "The politics of growth: strategic interaction and economic performance in advanced industrial societies; 1974–1980." *Journal of Politics* 47:792–827.

______. 1987. "The politics of growth reconsidered." *Journal of Politics* 49:257–74.

Langford, John W., and K. Lorne Brownsey (eds.). 1991. *Think Tanks and Governance in the Asia-Pacific Region*. Canada: Institute for Research on Public Policy.

Larner, Robert J. 1970. *Management Control and the Large Corporation*. New York: Dunellen.

Lasswell, Harold. 1941. "The garrison state." *American Journal of Sociology* 46:555–68.

______. 1950. *Politics: Who Gets What, When, How*. New York: P. Smith.

______. 1971. *A Pre-View of Policy Sciences*. New York: Elsevier.

Lasswell, Harold and Abraham Kaplan. 1950. *Power and Society*. New Haven, CT: Yale University Press.

Laumann, Edward O., and David Knoke. 1987. *The Organizational State: Social Choice in National Policy Domains*. Madison: University of Wisconsin Press.

Laurell, Asa Cristina. 2000. "Structural adjustment and the globalization of policy in Latin America." *International Society* 15:306–25.

Lawler, Edward J. 1986. "Bilateral deterrence and conflict spiral: A theoretical analysis." *Advances in Group Processes* 3:107–30.

Lawrence, Regina. 2000. *The Politics of Force: Media and the Construction of Police Brutality*. Berkeley: University of California Press.

Lawson, Kay. 1980. "Political parties and linkage." Pp. 3–24 in Kay Lawson (ed.), *Political Parties and Linkage: A Comparative Perspective*. New Haven, CT: Yale University Press.

______ (ed.). 1994. *How Political Parties Work*. Westport, CT: Praeger

______. 1999a. "How state laws undermine parties." Pp. 330–55 in A. James Reichley (ed.), *Elections American Style*. Washington, DC: Brookings Institution.

______. 1999b. "Cleavages, parties and voters." Pp. 19–34 in Kay Lawson, Andrea Rommele, and Georgi Karasimeonov (eds.), *Cleavages, Parties and Voters: Studies from Bulgaria, the Czech Republic, Hungary, Poland and Romania*. Westport, CT: Praeger.

Lawson, Kay, and Peter Merkl (eds.). 1988. *When Parties Fail: Emerging Alternative Organizations*. Princeton, NJ: Princeton University Press.

Lawson, Kay, Andrea Rommele, and Georgi Karasimeonov (eds.). 1999. *Cleavages, Parties and Voters: Studies from Bulgaria, the Czech Republic, Hungary, Poland, and Romania*. Westport, CT: Praeger.

Lawson, Steven F. 1976. *Black Ballots: Voting Rights in the South, 1944–1969*. New York: Columbia University Press.

______. 1985. *In Pursuit of Power: Southern Blacks and Electoral Politics, 1965–1982*. New York: Columbia University Press.

______. 1990. *Running for Freedom: Civil Rights and Black Politics in America since 1941*. Philadelphia: Temple University Press.

______. 1991. "Freedom then, freedom now: The historiography of the civil rights movement." *American Historical Review* 96:456–71.

Layard, Richard, Stephen Nickell, and Richard Jackman. 1991. *Unemployment: Macroeconomic Performance and the Labor Market*. Oxford, UK: Oxford University Press.

Layman, Geoffrey C. 2001. *The Great Divide: Religious and Cultural Conflict in American Party Politics*. New York: Columbia University Press.

Layman, Geoffrey C., and Thomas M. Carsey. 2002. "Party polarization and 'conflict extension' in the American electorate." *American Journal of Political Science* 46:786–802.

Layton-Henry, Zig. 1984. *The Politics of Race in Britain*. London: Allen & Unwin.

______. 1988. "The political challenge of migration for West European states." *European Journal of Political Research* 16:587–95.

______. 1992. *The Politics of Immigration: Immigration, Race and Race Relations in Post-war Britain*. Oxford, UK: Blackwell.

______. 1996. "Immigration and the Heath government." Pp. 215–34 in Stuart Ball and Anthony Seldon (eds.), *The Heath Government 1970–1974*. London: Longman.

Layton-Henry, Zig, and C. Wilpert. 1994. *Discrimination, Racism and Citizenship*. London: Anglo-German Foundation for the Study of Industrial Society.

Lazarovici, Laureen. 2002. "Elected to Serve." *America @ Work*, June:14–17.

Lazarsfeld, Paul F. 1944. "The election is over." *Public Opinion Quarterly* 8:317–30.

Lazarsfeld, Paul F., Bernard Berelson, and Hazel Gaudet. 1944. *The People's Choice*. New York: Duell, Sloane, and Pearce.

______. 1948. *The People's Choice*, 2nd Ed. New York: Columbia University Press.

Le Bot, Yvon. 1992. *Communauté, violence et modernité: luttes sociales, questions ethniques et conflits armés en Amérique Centrale et Amérique andine*. Paris: Ecole de Hautes Etudes en Sciences Sociales.

______. 1995. *La guerra en tierras mayas: comunidad, violencia y modernidad en Guatemala 1970–1992*. México DF: Fondo de Cultura Económica.

______. 1997. *El sueño zapatista. Entrevistas con el subcomandante Marcos, el Mayor Moisés y el comandante Tacho, del Ejército Zapatista de Liberación Nacional*. México DF: Plaza y Janés.

Lee, Mordecai. 2002. "Politicians and administrators: A partnership doomed to a superior–subordinate relationship." *PA Times* Archives, Special Section. American Society for Public Administration. (25), 9. September. www.unpan1.un.org/intradoc/groups/public/document/ASPA/UNPAN005261.html

Lee, Phil-Sang. 2000. "Economic crisis and chaebol reform in Korea." Discussion paper #14. APEC Study Center, Columbia University. http://www.columbia.edu/cu/business/apec/publications/PS-Lee.PDF

Lee, Sharon M. 1993. "Racial classification in the U.S. Census: 1890–1990." *Ethnic and Racial Studies* 16:75–94.

Lefebvre, Georges. 1947. *The Coming of the French Revolution*. Princeton, NJ: Princeton University Press.

Leffler, Melvyn. 1992. *A Preponderance of Power: National Security, the Truman Administration, and the Cold War*. Stanford, CA: Stanford University Press.

Legorreta Díaz, María del Carmen. 1998. *Religión, política y guerrilla en las cañadas de la Selva Lacandona*. México DF: Cal y Arena.

Lehman, Edward. 1977. *Political Society: Macrosociology of Politics*. New York: Columbia University Press.

______. 1988. "The theory of the state versus the state of theory." *American Sociological Review* 53:807–23.

Lehmbruch, Gerhard. 1974. "Consociational democracy, class conflict, and the new corporatism." International Political Science Association, ed., Round Table on Political Integration. Jerusalem.

______. 1977. "Liberal corporatism and party government." *Comparative Political Studies* 10:91–126.

______. 1979. "Liberal corporatism and party government." Pp. 147–83 in P. C. Schmitter and G. Lehmbruch (eds.), *Trends Toward Corporatism Intermediation*. Beverly Hills, CA: Sage.

______. 1984. "Concertation and the structure of corporatist networks." Pp. 60–80 in John H. Goldthorpe (ed.), *Order and Conflict in Contemporary Capitalism*. Oxford, UK: Clarendon.

______. 2001. "The institutional embedding of market economies: The German 'model' and its impact on Japan." Pp. 39–93 in Wolfgang Streeck and Kozo Yamamura (eds.), *The Origins of Nonliberal Capitalism: Germany and Japan in Comparison*. Ithaca, NY and London: Cornell University Press.

Lehmbruch, Gerhard, and Philippe C. Schmitter (eds.). 1982. *Patterns of Corporatist Policy-Making*. Beverly Hills, CA: Sage.

Leighley, Jan E. 1991. "Participation as a stimulus of political conceptualization." *Journal of Politics* 53:198–211.

______. 2001. *Strength in Numbers? The Political Mobilization of Racial and Ethnic Minorities*. Princeton, NJ: Princeton University Press.

Leighley, Jan E., and Jonathan Nagler. 1992. "Socioeconomic class bias in turnout: The voters remain the same." *American Political Science Review* 86:725–36.

Leira, A., and C. Saraceno. 2002. "Care: Actors, relationships and contexts." Pp. 55–83 in B. Hobson, J. Lewis, and B. Siim (eds.), *Recognition Struggles and Social Movements: Contested Identities, Agency and Power*. Cambridge: Cambridge University Press.

Lembo, Ron. 2000. *Thinking through Television*. Cambridge, UK: Cambridge University Press.

Lemert, Charles. *Social Things: An Introduction to the Sociological Life*. Lanham, MD: Rowman & Littlefield.

Lenin, Vladimir Il'ich. 1932/1943. *State and Revolution*. New York: International.

Lenin, Vladimir Il'ich. 1933[1916]. *Imperialism, the Highest State of Capitalism*. New York: International.

______. 1968. *Lenin on Politics and Revolution: Selected Writings* (James E. Connor, ed.). New York: Pegasus.

______. 1971. *El Estado y la revolución*. Buenos Aires: Cartago.

Lenski, Gerhard. 1966. *Power and Privilege*. New York: McGraw–Hill.

Leontidu, Lila, and Alex Afouxenidis. 2001. "Boundaries of social exclusion in Europe." Pp. 131–248 in Janet Fink, Gail Lewis, and John Clarke (eds.), *Rethinking European Welfare*. London: Open University and Sage.

Levi, Margaret. 1981. "The predatory theory of rule." *Politics and Society* 10(4):431–65.

______. 1988. *Of Rule and Revenue*. Berkeley: University of California Press.

______. 1997. *The Contingencies of Consent*. Cambridge, UK: Cambridge University Press.

Lévi-Strauss, Claude. 1969/1949. *The Elementary Structures of Kinship*, rev. ed. Boston: Beacon.

______. 1967/1958. *Structural Anthropology*. New York: Anchor Books.

Levitas, R. 1998. *The Inclusive Society?: Social Exclusion and New Labour*. Basingstoke: Macmillan.

Levitt, Peggy. 2001. *The Transnational Villagers*. Berkeley and Los Angeles: University of California Press.

Levitt, Steven. 1998. "Are PACs trying to influence politics or voters?" *Economics and Politics* 10:19–35.

Levy, Daniel C. 1995. "Latin America's think tanks: The roots of nonprofit privatization." *Studies in Comparative International Development* 30(2):3–25.

Lewin, Lief. 1988. *Self-Interest and Public Interest in Western Politics*. New York: Oxford University Press.

______. 1991. *Ideology and Strategy*. New York: Oxford University Press.

Lewis, Gail. 2000. *"Race," Gender and Social Welfare*. Cambridge, UK: Polity.

Lewis, Jane. 1992a. "Gender development of welfare regimes." *Journal of European Social Policy* 2:159–73.

______. 1992b. *Women in Britain Since 1945: Women, Family, Work and the State in the Post-War Years*. Oxford, UK: Blackwell.

______. 1994. "Gender and family and women's agency in the building of the welfare state." *Social History* 19:37–55.

Lewis, Jane, with Barbara Hobson. 1997. "Introduction." Pp. 1–20 in Jane Lewis (ed.), *Lone Mothers in European Welfare Regimes*. London: Jessica Kingsley.

Lewis, Paul G. 1996. "Introduction and Theoretical Overview." Pp. 1–19 in Paul G. Lewis (ed.), *Party Structure and Organization in East Central Europe*. Cheltenham: Edward Elgar.

Lewis-Beck, Michael A., and Peverill Squire. 1995. "The politics of institutional choice: Presidential ballot access for third parties in the United States." *British Journal of Political Science* 25:419–27.

Leys, Colin. 1996. *The Rise and Fall of Development Theory*. Bloomington: Indiana University Press.

Li, Bobai, and Andrew Walder. 2001. "Career advancement as party patronage: Sponsored mobility into the Chinese administrative elite, 1949–1996." *American Journal of Sociology* 106(5):1371–1408.

Li, T. M. 2000. "Articulating indigenous identity in Indonesia: Resource politics and the tribal slot." *Comparative Studies in Society and History* 42(1):149–79.

Liang, Zai. 1994. "Social contact, social capital, and the naturalization process: Evidence from six immigrant groups." *Social Science Research* 23:407–37.

Lichbach, Mark Irving. 1996. *The Cooperator's Dilemma*. Ann Arbor: University of Michigan Press.

Lichbach, Mark I., and Seligman, Adam. 2000. *Market and Community: The Bases of Social Order, Revolution, and Relegitimation*. University Park: Pennsylvania State University Press.

Lichbach, Mark Irving, and Alan S. Zuckerman (eds.). 1997. *Comparative Politics. Rationality, Culture, and Structure*. Cambridge, UK: Cambridge University Press.

Lichtenberg, Judith (ed.). 1990. *Democracy and the Mass Media*. Cambridge, UK: Cambridge University Press.

Lichtenstein, Nelson. 2002. *State of the Union: A Century of American Labor.* Princeton, NJ: Princeton University Press.

Lichter, S. Robert, Stanley. Rothman, and Linda S. Lichter. 1986, *The Media Elite: America's New Powerbrokers*. Bethesda, MD: Adler and Adler.

Lichterman, Paul. 1999. "Talking identity in the public sphere: Broad visions and small spaces in sexual identity politics." *Theory and Society* 28:101–41.

Lieberman, Robert C. 1998. *Shifting the Color Line: Race and the American Welfare State*. Cambridge, MA: Harvard University Press.

______. 2002. "Weak state, strong policy: Paradoxes of race policy in the United States, Great Britain, and France." *Studies in American Political Development* 16:138–61.

Lieberson, Stanley. 1971. "An empirical study of military–industrial linkages." *American Journal of Sociology* 76:562–84.

Liebert, Ulrike, and Stefanie Stifft. 2003. *Gendering Europeanisation*. Bruxelles: P.I.E.–Peter Lang. Multiple Europes Series. Number 19.

Liebes, Tamar, and Elihu Katz. 1990. *The Export of Meaning: Cross-Cultural Readings of Dallas*. New York: Oxford University Press.

Liebman, Robert C., and Robert Wuthnow (eds.). 1983. *The New Christian Right: Mobilization and Legitimation*. New York: Aldine.

Lijphart, Arend. 1968. *The Politics of Accommodation: Pluralism and Democracy in the Netherlands*. Berkeley: University of California Press.

______. 1977. *Democracy in Plural Societies: A Comparative Exploration*. New Haven, CT: Yale University Press.

______. 1984. *Democracies: Patterns of Majoritarian and Consensus Government in Twenty-One Countries*. New Haven, CT: Yale University Press.

______. 1994. *Electoral Systems and Party Systems: A Study of Twenty-Seven Democracies 1945–1990*. Oxford, UK: Oxford University Press.

______. 1997. "Unequal participation: Democracy's unresolved dilemma." *American Political Science Review* 91:1–14.

______. 1999. *Patterns of Democracy. Government Forms and Performance in Thirty-Six Countries*. New Haven, CT: Yale University Press.

Lijphart, Arend, and Markus M. L. Crepaz. 1991. "Corporatism and consensus democracy in 18 countries: Conceptual and empirical linkages." *British Journal of Political Science* 21:345–56.

Lim, Linda. 1990. "Women's work in export factories: The politics of a cause." Pp. 101–19 in Irene Tinker (ed.), *Persistent Inequalities*. New York: Oxford University Press.

Lim, Nelson. 2001. "On the back of blacks? Immigrants and the fortunes of African Americans." Pp. 186–227 in Roger Waldinger (ed.), *Strangers at the Gates: New Immigrants in Urban America*. Berkeley: University of California Press.

Lincoln, James R., Michael L. Gerlach, and Peggy Takahashi. 1992. "Keiretsu networks in the Japanese economy: A dyad analysis of intercorporate ties." *American Sociological Review* 57: 561–85.

Lindbeck, Assar. 1995. "Welfare state disincentives with endogenous habits and norms." *Scandinavian Journal of Economics* 97:477–94.

Lindblom, Charles E. 1977. *Politics and Markets. The World's Political-Economic Systems*. New York: Basic Books.

Lindblom, Charles, and Edward Woodhouse. 1993. *The Policy-Making Process*, 3rd ed. Englewood Cliffs: Prentice Hall.

Lindenberg, Siegwart. 1989. "Social production functions, deficits, and social revolutions." *Rationality and Society* 1:51–77.

Lindenfeld, Frank. 1968. *Reader in Political Sociology*. New York: Funk & Wagnells.

Ling, Peter J., and Sharon Monteith. 1999. *Gender in the civil rights movement*. New York: Garland.

Linz, Juan J. 1970a. "An authoritarian regime: The case of Spain." Pp. xxx in Erik Allard and Stein Rokkan (eds.), *Mass Politics. Studies in Political Sociology*. New York: Free Press.

______. 1970b. "From Phalange to Movimiento-organización: The Spanish single party and the Franco regime 1936–1968. Pp. 128–203 in Samuel P. Huntington and Clement H. Moore (eds.), *Authoritarian Politics in Modern Society: The Dynamics of Established One-Party Systems*. New York: Basic Books.

Linz, Juan. 1990 "The perils of presidentialism." *Journal of Democracy* 1:51–69.

Linz, Juan J., and Stepan, Alfred (eds.). 1978. *The Breakdown of Democratic Regimes*. Baltimore, London: Johns Hopkins University Press.

______. 1978. *Crisis, Breakdown and Reequilibration*. Baltimore, MD: Johns Hopkins University Press.

______. 1978a. *The Breakdown of Democratic Regimes: Crisis, Breakdown and Re-equilibration: Europe*. Baltimore, MD: Johns Hopkins University Press.

______. 1978b. *The Breakdown of Democratic Regimes: Crisis, Breakdown and Re-equilibration: Latin America*. Baltimore, MD: Johns Hopkins University Press.

______. 1990. "The perils of presidentialism." *Journal of Democracy* 1:51–69.

______. 1996. *Problems of Democratic Transition and Consolidation. Southern Europe, South America, and Post-Communist Europe*. Baltimore: Johns Hopkins University Press.

______. 2000[1975]. *Totalitarian and Authoritarian Regimes*. Boulder, CO and London: Lynne Rienner.

Lipschutz, Ronnie D., and Judith Mayer. 1996. *Global Civil Society and Global Environmental Governance: The Politics of Nature from Place to planet. SUNY Series in International Environmental Policy and Theory*. Albany: State University of New York Press.

Lipset, Seymour Martin. 1960. *Political Man: The Social Bases of Politics*. Garden City, NY: Doubleday.

______. 1962. "Introduction." Pp. 15–39 in Robert Michels, *Political Parties*. New York: Free Press.

______. 1963. *The First New Nation: The United States in Historical and Comparative Perspective*. New York: Basic Books.

______. 1968[1950]. *Agrarian Socialism: The Cooperative Commonwealth Federation in Saskatchewan. A Study in Political Sociology*, updated. Garden City, NY: Doubleday Anchor.

______. 1970. *Revolution and Counter-revolution*. Garden City, NY: Anchor.

______. 1981[1960]. *Political Man: The Social Bases of Politics*, revised edition. Baltimore, MD: Johns Hopkins University Press.

______. 1988. *Revolution and Counterrevolution: Change and Persistence in Social Structures*, revised edition. New Brunswick, NJ: Transaction.

______. 1990. *Continental Divide: The Values and Institutions of the United States and Canada*. New York: Routledge.

Lipset, Seymour Martin, Paul Lazarsfeld, Allan Barton, and Juan Linz. 1954. "The psychology of voting: An analysis of political behavior." Pp. 1124–75 in Gardiner Lindzey (ed.), *Handbook of Social Psychology*. Cambridge, MA: Addison-Wesley.

Lipset, Seymour Martin, and Gary Marks. 2000. *It Didn't Happen Here: The Failure of Socialism in America*. New York: W.W. Norton.

Lipset, Seymour Martin, and Stein Rokkan (eds.). 1967a. *Party Systems and Voter Alignments*. New York: Free Press.

______. 1967b. "Cleavage structures, party systems, and voter alignments: An introduction." Pp. 1–64 in S. M. Lipset and Stein Rokkan (eds.), *Party Systems and Voter Alignments*. New York: Free Press.

Lipset, Seymour Martin, and William Schneider. 1983. *The Confidence Gap: Business, Labor, and Government in the Public Mind*. New York: Free Press.

Lipset, Seymour Martin, Martin A. Trow, and James S. Coleman. 1956. *Union Democracy: The Internal Politics of the International Typographical Union*. New York: Anchor Books.

Lipsky, David. 1970. *Protest in City Politics*. Chicago, IL: Rand McNally.

Lipsmeyer, Christine S. 2000. "Reading between the welfare lines: Politics and policy structure in post-communist Europe." *Europe–Asia Studies* 52:1191–211.

Lipstadt, Deborah. 1986. *Beyond Belief: The American Press and the Coming of the Holocaust 1933–1945*. New York: Free Press.

Lis, Catharina and Hugo Soly. 1979. *Poverty and Capitalism in Pre-Industrial Europe*. Atlantic Highland, NJ: Humanities Press.

Lisk, Franklyn, and Yvette Stevens. 1987. "Government policy and rural women's work in Sierra Leone." Pp. 182–202 in Christine Oppong (ed.), *Sex Roles, Population and Development in West Africa*. Portsmouth, NH: Heinemann.

Lister, Ruth. 1997. *Citizenship: Feminist Perspectives*. Basingstoke: Macmillan.

______. 1998. "Citizenship and difference. Towards a differentiated universalism." *European Journal of Social Theory* 1:71–90.

Litwack, Leon. 1998. *Trouble in Mind: Black Southerners in the Age of Jim Crow*. New York: Alfred A. Knopf.

Livingston, Steven. 1997. "Beyond the 'CNN effect': The media–foreign policy dynamic." Pp. 291–318 in Pippa Norris (ed.), *Politics and the Press*. Boulder, CO: Lynne Rienner.

Livingston, Steven, and Todd, Eachus. 1995. "Humanitarian crisis and U.S. foreign policy: Somalia and the CNN effect reconsidered." *Political Communication* 12:413–29.

Llobera, Joseph. 1994. *The God of Modernity: The Development of Nationalism in Western Europe*. Oxford, UK: Berg.

Lo, Clarence Y. H. 2002. "Marxist models of the capitalist state and politics." Pp. 197–231 in Betty A. Dobratz, Timothy Buzzell, and Lisa K. Waldner (eds.), *Theoretical Directions in Political Sociology for the 21st Century*. Greenwich, CT: JAI Press.

Loeb, Paul. 1986. *Nuclear Culture: Living and Working in the World's Largest Atomic Complex*. Philadelphia: New Society.

Loescher, Gil. 1993. *Beyond Charity: International Cooperation and the Global Refugee Crisis*. New York: Oxford University Press.

Lofland, John. 1993. *Social Movement Organizations*. New York: Aldine de Gruyter.

Lohkamp-Himmighofen, Martene and Christiane Dienel. 2000. "Reconciliation policies from a comparative perspective." Pp. 49–67 in Linda Hantrais (ed.), *Gendered Policies in Europe*. New York: St. Martin's.

Lohmann, Susanne. 1995. "Information, access, and contributions: A signaling model of lobbying." *Public Choice* 85(3–4):267–84.

______. 1993. "A signaling model of informative and manipulative political action." *American Political Science Review* 87:319–33.

______. 1998. "An information rationale for the power of special interests." *American Political Science Review* 92(4):809–27.

Lora, Eduardo. 2001. Structural Reforms in Latin America: What Has Been Reformed and How to Measure It. Washington, DC: Inter-American Development Bank, Research Department, Working Paper #466 (December).

Lora, Eduardo, and Ugo Panizza. 2002. *Measuring the progress of reform*. Latin American Economic Policies. vol. 17, first quarter. Washington, DC: Inter-American Development Bank, Research Department.

Loveman, Brian. 1994. "Protected democracies and military guardianship: Political transition in Latin America, 1978–1993. *Journal of Interamerican Studies and World Affairs* 36(2):105–89.

Lowi, Theodore J. 1967. "The public philosophy: Interest-group liberalism." *American Political Science Review* 61:5–24.

______. 1964. "American business case studies, political theory and public policy." *World Politics* 16:677–715.

______. 1969. *The End of Liberalism: The Second Republic of the United States*. New York: W. W. Norton.

______. 1972. "Four systems of policy, politics, and choice". *Public Administration Review* 32:298–310.

Löwy, Michael. 1981. *The Politics of Combined and Uneven Development: The Theory of Permanent Revolution*. London: Verso.

Lubbers, Marcel, Peer Scheepers, and Jaak Billiet. 2000. "Multilevel modelling of Vlaams blok voting: Individual and contextual characteristics of the Vlaams blok vote." *Acta Politica* 35:363–98.

Lublin, David Ian. 1995. "Race, representation, and redistricting." Pp. 111–25 in P. E. Peterson (ed.), *Classifying by Race*. Princeton, NJ: Princeton University Press.

Luebbert, Gregory M. 1987. "Social foundations of political order in interwar Europe." *World Politics* 39:449–78.

______. 1991. *Liberalism, Fascism, or Social Democracy: Social Classes and the Political Origins of Regimes in Interwar Europe*. Oxford, UK: Oxford University Press.

Luhmann, Niklas. 1982. *The Differentiation of Society*. New York: Columbia University Press.

______. 1990. *Political Theory in the Welfare State*. Berlin: Walter de Gruyter.

______. 1995. *Social Systems*. Stanford, CA: Stanford University Press.

Luker, Kristin. 1984. *Abortion and Politics of Motherhood*. Berkeley, CA: University of California Press.

______. 1996. *Dubious Conceptions*. Cambridge, MA: Harvard University Press.

Lukes, Steven. 1974. Power: *A Radical View*. New York: Macmillan.

Lukes, Timothy. 2001. "Lionizing Machiavelli." *American Political Science Review* 95(3):561–75.

Luskin, Robert C., James S. Fishkin, and Roger Jowell. 2002. "Considered opinions: Deliberative polling in Britain." *British Journal of Political Science* 32:455–87.

Lyotard, Jean-François. 1984. *The Postmodern Condition*. Minneapolis: University of Minnesota Press.

Määttä, Paula. 1998. "Equal pay policies: International review of selected developed and developing countries." Working Paper, International Labour

Organization, ISBN 92-2-111451-1. http://www.ilo.org/public/english/dialogue/govlab/legrel/papers/equalpay/index.htm. Retrieved July 30, 2003.

Macdonald, Laura, and Mildred A. Schwartz. 2002. "Political parties and NGOs in the creation of new trading blocs in the Americas." *The International Journal of Political Science* 23(2):135–58.

Mace, Myles L. 1971. *Directors: Myth and Reality.* Boston: Harvard Business School Press.

Macfarlane, Alan. 1978. *The Origins of English Individualism: The Family, Property, and Social Transition.* Cambridge, UK: Cambridge University Press.

Macfarquhar, Roderick. 1960. *The Hundred Flowers.* New York: Atlantic Books.

______. 1974. *The Origins of the Cultural Revolution.* New York: Columbia University Press.

Macfarquhar, Roderick, and Seyyed Vali Resa Narr. 2001. *Islamic Leviathan. Islam and the Making of State Power.* New York: Oxford University Press.

Mackie, Thomas, and Richard Rose. 1982. *The International Almanac of Electoral History*, 2nd ed. London: Macmillan.

MacKinnon, Catherine A. 1983. "Feminism, Marxism, method and the state." *Signs: Journal of Women, Culture and Society* 8:635–8.

______. 1989. *Toward a Feminist Theory of the State.* Cambridge, MA: Harvard University Press.

Madeley, John. 2000. *Hungry for Trade.* London and New York: Zed.

Madison, James. 1973. *The Complete Madison: His Basic Writings* (ed.) Saul K. Padover. New York: Harper & Row.

Magleby, David B. (ed.). 2002. *Financing the 2000 Election.* Washington, DC: Brookings Institution.

______. 2002. "A high-stakes election." Pp. 1–21 in David B. Magleby (ed.), *Financing the 2002 Election.* Washington, D.C.: Brookings Institute.

Magleby, David B., and Candice J. Nelson. 1990. *The Money Chase: Congressional Campaign Finance Reform.* Washington, D.C.: Brookings Institute.

Maguire, Diarmuid. 1993. "Protestors, counter-protestors and the authorities." *Annals of the American Academy of Political and Social Science* 528:101–13.

Mahler, Vincent A., David K. Jesuit, and Douglas D. Roscoe. 1999. "Exploring the impact of trade and investment on income inequality: A cross-national sectoral analysis of the developed countries." *Comparative Political Studies* 32:363–95.

Mahoney, James. 1999. "Nominal, ordinal, and narrative appraisal in macrocausal analysis." *American Journal of Sociology* 104(4):1154–96.

______. 2000. "Path dependence in historical sociology." *Theory and Society* 29:507–48.

______. 2001. *The Legacies of Liberalism. Path Dependence and Political Regimes in Central America.* Baltimore: Johns Hopkins University Press.

______. 2002. "Knowledge accumulation in comparative historical research: The case of democracy and authoritarianism." In James Mahoney and Dietrich Rueschemeyer (eds.), *Comparative Historical Analysis in the Social Sciences.* Cambridge, UK: Cambridge University Press.

Mahoney, James, and Dietrich Rueschemeyer (eds.). 2003. *Comparative Historical Analysis in the Social Sciences.* New York: Cambridge University Press.

Mahoney, James, and Dietrich Rueschemeyer. 2003. "Comparative and historical analysis: Achievements and agendas." In Dietrich Rueschemeyer and James Mahoney (eds.), *Comparative and Historical Analysis in the Social Sciences.* New York: Cambridge University Press.

Mahoney, James, and Richard Snyder. 1999. "Rethinking agency and structure in the study of regime change." *Studies in Comparative International Development* 34:3–32.

Mainwaring, Scott. 1999. "The surprising resilience of elected governments."*Journal of Democracy* 10: 101–14.

Mainwaring, Scott, and Timothy R. Scully (eds.). 1995. *Building Democratic Institutions: Party Systems in Latin America.* Stanford, CA: Stanford University Press.

Mainwaring, Scott, Daniel Brinks, and Anibal Pérez-Liñán, 2000. "Classifying political regimes in Latin America, 1945–1999." Working Paper #280, September 2000, Kellogg Institute of Political Studies.

______. 2001. "Classifying political regimes in Latin America, 1945–1999." *Studies in Comparative International Development* 36:37–65.

Mainwaring, Scott, Guillermo O'Donnell, and J. Samuel Valenzuela (eds.). 1992. *Issues in Democratic Consolidation. The New South American Democracies in Comparative Perspective.* Notre Dame: University of Notre Dame Press.

Maioni, Antonia. 1998. *Parting at the Crossroads: The Emergence of Health Insurance in the United States and Canada.* Princeton, NJ: Princeton University Press.

Mair, Peter. 1994. "Party organizations: from civil society to the state." Pp. 1–22 in Richard S. Katz and Peter Mair (eds.), *How Parties Organize: Change and Adaptation in Party Organizations in Western Democracies.* Thousand Oaks, CA: Sage.

______. 1997. *Party System Change.* New York: Oxford University Press.

Mair, Peter, Seymour Martin Lipset, Michael Hout, and John H. Goldthorpe. 1999. "Critical commentary." Pp. 308–22 in Geoffrey Evans (ed.), *The*

End of Class Politics. Oxford, UK: Oxford University Press.

Maiz, Ramon. 2003. "Politics and the nation: Nationalist mobilisation of ethnic differences." *Nations and Nationalism* 9:195–212.

Makkai, Toni. 1994. "Social policy and gender in Eastern Europe." Pp. 188–205 in Diane Sainsbury (ed.), *Gendering Welfare States*. London: Sage.

Malbin, Michael J. 1980. "Of mountains and molehills: PACs, campaigns, and public policy." Pp. 152–84 in Michael J. Malbin (ed.), *Parties, Interest Groups, and Campaign Finance Laws*. Washington, D.C.: American Enterprise Institute.

Maleck-Lewy, E. 1995. "Between self-determination and state supervision: Women and the abortion law in post-unification Germany." *Social Politics* 2:62–76.

Malloy, James. (ed.). 1977. *Authoritarianism and Corporatism in Latin America*. Pittsburgh: Pittsburgh University Press.

Maltese, John Anthony, 1994. *Spin Control: The White House Office of Communications and the Management of Presidential News*. Chapel Hill: University of North Carolina Press.

Maman, Daniel. 1997. "The power lies in the structure: Economic policy forum networks in Israel." *British Journal of Sociology* 48:267–85.

Mamdani, Mahmood. 1996. *Citizen and Subject. Contemporary Africa and the Legacy of Late Colonialism*. Princeton, NJ: Princeton University Press.

Mancini, Paolo. 2001. "How to combine media commercialization and party affiliation: The Italian experience." *Political Communication* 17:319–24.

Mandel, Ernest. 1979. *Trotsky: A Study in the Dynamic of His Thought*. London: New Left Books.

Mandel, H., and M. Shalev. 2003. "Class conditioning of welfare state effects on gender inequality: A preliminary comparative analysis." In *Annual Conference of Research Committee 19*. Toronto.

Manley, John F. 1983. "Neo-Pluralism: A Class Analysis I and Pluralism II." *American Political Science Review* 77:368–83.

Mann, Michael. 1970. "The social cohesion of liberal democracy." *American Sociological Review* 35:423–40.

______. 1986. *The Sources of Social Power, vol. 1*. Cambridge, UK: Cambridge University Press.

______. 1986. "The autonomous power of the state: its origins, mechanisms, and results." Pp. 109–36 in John A. Hall (ed.), *States in History*. New York: Basil Blackwell.

______. 1988. *States, War, and Capitalism*. New York: Basil Blackwell.

______. 1993. *The Sources of Social Power, Volume II: The Rise of Classes and Nation-States, 1760–1914*. New York: Cambridge University Press.

______. 1994. *The Sources of Social Power, Vol. 2*. Cambridge, UK: Cambridge University Press.

______. 1997. "Has globalization ended the rise of the nation-state?" *Review of International Political Economy* 4(3):472–96.

______. 1997. "The contradictions of continuous revolution." Pp. 135–57 in Ian Kershaw and Moshe Lewin (eds.), *Stalinism and Nazism: Dictatorships in Comparison*. Cambridge, UK: Cambridge University Press.

______. 1999. "The dark side of democracy: the modern tradition of ethnic and political cleansing." *New Left Review* 235:18–45.

______. 2000. "Were the perpetrators of genocide "ordinary men" or "real Nazis"? results from fifteen hundred biographies." *Holocaust & Genocide Studies* 14(3):331–66.

______. 2001. "Globalization is (among other things) transnational, inter-national and american." *Science and Society* 65(4):464–9.

Mannheim, Karl. 1952/1928. "The problem of generations." Pp. 286–323 in Paul Kecskemeti (ed.), *Essays on the Sociology of Knowledge*. London: Routledge and Kegan Paul.

Mansfield, Harvey C., Jr. 1965. *Statesmanship and Party Government: A Study of Burke and Bolingbroke*. Chicago: University of Chicago Press.

Manza, Jeffrey. 2000. "Race and the underdevelopment of the American welfare state." *Theory and Society* 30:819–32.

Manza, Jeffrey, and Clem Brooks. 1997. "The religious factor in U.S. presidential elections, 1960–1992." *American Journal of Sociology* 103:38–81.

______. 1998. "The gender gap in U.S. presidential elections: When? why? implications?" *American Journal of Sociology* 103:1235–66.

______. 1999a. "Group size, turnout, and political alignments in the development of U.S. party coalitions, 1960–1992." *European Sociological Review* 15:369–90.

______. 1999b. *Social Cleavages and Political Change: Voter Alignments and U.S. Party Coalitions*. New York: Oxford University Press.

Manza, Jeffrey, and Fay Lomax Cook. 2002. "Policy responsiveness to public opinion: The state of the debate." In Jeff Manza, Fay Lomax Cook, and Benjamin I. Page (eds.), *Navigating Public Opinion: Polls, Policy, and the Future of American Democracy*. New York: Oxford University Press.

______. 2002. "A democratic polity? Three views of policy responsiveness to public opinion in the United States." *American Politics Research* 30:630–67.

Manza, Jeffrey, and Nathan Wright. 2003. "Religion and political behavior." Pp. 297–314 in Michele

Dillon (ed.), *Handbook of the Sociology of Religion*. New York: Cambridge University Press.

Manza, Jeffrey, Michael Hout, and Clem Brooks. 1995. "Class voting in capitalist democracies since World War II: Dealignment, realignment, or trendless fluctuation?" *Annual Review of Sociology* 21:137–63.

Maravall, José María, and Julián Santamaría. 1986. "Political change in Spain and the prospects for democracy." Pp. 71–108 in Guillermo O'Donnell, Philippe C. Schmitter, and Laurence Whitehead (eds.), *Transitions from Authoritarian Rule. Prospects for Democracy*. Baltimore, MD: Johns Hopkins University Press.

March, James G., and Johan P. Olsen. 1989. *Rediscovering Institutions: The Organizational Basis of Politics*. New York: Free Press.

______. 1995. *Democratic Governance*. New York: Free Press.

Marchand, M. H., and A. S. Runyan. 2000. *Gender and Global Restructuring: Sightings, Sites and Resistances*. London: Routledge.

Marchblank, Jennifer. 2000. *Women, Power and Policy*. New York: Routledge.

Marcuse, Herbert. 1967. "La lucha del liberalismo en la concepción totalitaria del Estado." Pp. 43–79 in O. Bauer, H. Marcuse, and A. Rosenberg (eds.), *Fascismo y Capitalismo*. Barcelona: Ediciones Martínez Roca, S. A. (Translated from *Faschismus und Kapitalismus*. Frankfurt am Main: Europäische Verlagsanstalt, 1967).

Marger, Martin N. 1987. *Elites and Masses*. Belmont, CA: Wadsworth.

Marin, Bernd, and Renate Mayntz (eds.). 1991. *Policy Networks: Empirical Evidence and Theoretical Considerations*. Boulder, CO: Westview Press.

Markoff, John. 1995. "Violence, emancipation and democracy: The countryside and the French Revolution." *American Historical Review* 100:360–86.

______. 1996. *Waves of Democracy: Social Movements and Political Change*. Thousand Oaks, CA: Pine Forge Press.

______. 2002. "Archival methods." Pp. 637–42 in Neil J. Smelser and Paul B. Baltes (eds.), *International Encyclopedia of the Social and Behavioral Sciences*. Oxford, UK: Elsevier.

______. 2003a. "Who will construct the global order?" In Bruce William Morrison (ed.), *Transnational Democracy in Critical and Comparative Perspective: Democracy's Range Reconsidered*. London: Ashgate.

______. 2003b. "Margins, centers, and democracy: The paradigmatic history of women's suffrage." *Signs: Journal of Women in Culture and Society* 29:85–116.

Markoff, John, and Verónica Montecinos. 1993. "The ubiquitous rise of economists." *Journal of Public Policy* 13:37–68.

Marks, Gary, and Doug McAdam. 1999. "On the relationship of political opportunities to the form of collective action: The case of the European Union." Pp. 97–111 in D. d. Porta, H. Kriesi, and D. Rucht (eds.), *Social Movements in a Globalizing World*. New York: St. Martin's Press.

Marks, Gary, Carole J. Wilson, and Leonard Ray. 2002. "National political parties and European integration." *American Journal of Political Science* 46:585–94.

Markusen, Ann, and Joel Yudken. 1992. *Dismantling the Cold War Economy*. New York: Basic Books.

Markusen, Ann, Peter Hall, Scott Campbell, and Sabina Deitrick. 1991. *The Rise of the Gunbelt: The Military Remapping of Industrial America*. New York: Oxford University Press.

Maroney, Heather Jon. 1992. "'Who has the baby?' Nationalism, pronatalism and the construction of a 'demographic crisis' in Quebec 1960–1988." *Studies in Political Economy* 39:7–36.

Marris, Robin L. 1964. *The Economic Theory of Managerial Capitalism*. London: Macmillan.

Marsh, David, and Martin Smith. 2000. "Understanding policy networks: Towards a dialectical approach." *Political Studies* 48(4):4–21.

Marsh, David, and R. A. W. Rhodes (eds.). 1992. *Policy Networks in British Government*. Oxford: Clarendon Press.

Marshall, Monty G., and Keith Jaggers. 2000. "Polity Project: Dataset Users Manual." http://www.bsos.umd.edu/cidcm/polity/

Marshall, S. E. 1994. "Confrontation and cooptation in anti-feminist organizations." In M. M. Ferree and P. Y. Martin (eds.), *Feminist Organizations: Harvest of the New Women's Movement*. Philadelphia, PA: Temple University Press.

Marshall, T. H. 1992[1950.] *Citizenship and Social Class and Other Essays*. Cambridge, UK: Cambridge University Press.

______. 1964. *Class, Citizenship and Social Development: Essays*. Garden City, NY: Doubleday.

______. 1992[1950]. "Citizenship and social class." Pp. 3–51 in T. B. Bottomore. (ed.), *Citizenship and Social Class*. London: Pluto.

Martínez, Nogueira. 1978. "Bases para la formulación de una política de desarrollo de los recursos humanos del sector público de Guatemala." New York: Programa de Naciones Unidas para el Desarrollo.

Martínez-Alier, J. 2002. *The Environmentalism of the Poor. A Study of Ecological Conflicts and Valuation*. London: Edward Elgar.

Marty, Martin E., and Appleby R. Scott. 1995. *Fundamentalisms Comprehended*. Chicago: University of Chicago Press.

Marwell, Gerald, and Pamela Oliver. 1993. *The Critical Mass in Collective Action: A Micro-Social Theory*. Cambridge, MA: Cambridge University Press.

Marx, Anthony W. 1998. *Making Race and Nation: A Comparison of South Africa, the United States, and Brazil*. Cambridge, UK: Cambridge University Press.

Marx, Karl. 1904. *A Contribution to the Critique of Political Economy* (N. I. Stone, trans.). New York: The International Library.

______. 1909. *Capital: A Critique of Political Economy* (Frederic Engles, ed., Ernest Untermann, trans.). Chicago: C. H. Kerr & Co.

______. 1954. *The Communist Manifesto*. Chicago: Henry Regnery Company.

______. 1963. *The Eighteenth Brumaire of Louis Bonaparte*. New York: International.

______. 1964. In Eric Hobsbawm (ed.), *Pre-Capitalist Economic Formations*. London: Lawrence and Wishart.

______. 1967. *Capital*, Vol. 1. Moscow: Progress.

______. 1972. "Civil wars in France." Pp. 526–76 in Robert Tucker (ed.), *The Marx-Engels Reader*. New York: W. W. Norton.

______. 1978[1843]. "On the Jewish question." Pp. 26–52 in R. C. Tucker (ed.), *The Marx-Engles Reader*. New York: W. W. Norton.

Maslow, Abraham. 1954. *Motivation and Personality*. New York: Harper.

Mason, David. 1995. *Race and Ethnicity in Modern Britain*. Oxford, UK: Oxford University Press.

Mason, T. David, and Dale A. Krane. 1989. "The political economy of death squads: Toward a theory of the impact of state-sanctioned terror." *International Studies Quarterly* 33:175–98.

Massey, Douglas S. 1990. "American apartheid: Segregation and the making of the underclass." *American Journal of Sociology* 96:329–57.

______. 2001. "Segregation and violent crime in urban America." Pp. 317–44 in E. Anderson and D. S. Massey (eds.), *Problem of the Century: Racial Stratification in the United States*, New York: Russell Sage Foundation.

Massey, Douglas S., and Nancy A. Denton. 1993. *American Apartheid: Segregation and the Making of the Underclass*. Cambridge, MA: Harvard University Press.

Massey, Douglas, Joaquin Arango, Graeme Hugo, Ali Kouaoci, Adela Pellegrino, and J. Edward Taylor. 1988. "Economic development and international migration in comparative perspective." *Population and Development Review* 14(3): 383–413.

______. 1998. *Worlds in Motion: Understanding International Migration at the End of the Millennium*. Oxford, UK: Clarendon.

Matear, Ann. 1997. "Gender and the state in rural Chile." *Bulletin of Latin American Research* 16:97–105.

Matthews, Donald R., and James Warren Prothro. 1966. *Negroes and the New Southern Politics*. New York: Harcourt Brace & World.

Maxwell, Kenneth. 1986. "Regime overthrow and the prospects for democratic transition in Portugal." Pp. 109–37 in Guillermo O'Donnell, Philippe C. Schmitter, and Laurence Whitehead (eds.), *Transitions from Authoritarian Rule: Southern Europe*. Baltimore: Johns Hopkins University Press.

May, John D. 1973. *Of the Conditions and Measures of Democracy*. Morristown, NJ: General Learning Press.

Mayer, Frederick W. 1998. *Interpreting NAFTA: The Science and Art of Political Analysis*. New York: Columbia University Press.

Mayer, Nonna. 1998. "The French National Front." Pp. 11–26 in Hans Georg Betz (ed.), *The New Politics of the Right: Neopopulist Parties and Movements in Established Democracies*. New York: St Martin's.

Mayhew, David R. 1974. *Congress: The Electoral Connection*. New Haven, CT: Yale University Press.

______. 1986. *Placing Parties in American Politics: Organization, Electoral Settings and Government Activity in the Twentieth Century*. Princeton, NJ: Princeton University Press.

______. 1991. *Divided We Govern: Party Control, Lawmaking, and Investigations 1946–1990*. New Haven, CT: Yale University Press.

Mayntz, Renate. 1979. "Public bureaucracies and policy implementation." *International Social Science Journal*, (4):633–45.

______. 1993. "Modernization and the logic of interorganizational networks." *Knowledge and Policy* 6:3–16.

Mazey, Sonia, and Jeremy Richardson (eds.). 1993. *Lobbying in the European Community*. Oxford, UK: Oxford University Press.

______. 2001a. "Institutionalizing Promiscuity: Commission-Interest Group Relations in the European Union." Pp. 71–93 in Alec Sweet, Wayne Sandholtz, and Neil Fligstein (eds.), *The Institutionalization of Europe*. New York: Oxford University Press.

______. 2001b. *Filling the Hollow Core? Interest Intermediation in the European Union*. London: Routledge.

Mazur, Amy. G. 2001. *State Feminism, Women's Movements, and Job Training: Making Democracies Work in the Global Economy*. New York: Routledge.

______. 2001. "Comparative conclusions." Pp. 293–318 in Amy G. Mazur (ed.), *State Feminism, Women's Movements, and Job Training: Making Democracies Work in the Global Economy*. New York: Routledge.

______. 2002. *Theorizing Feminist Policy*. Oxford, UK: Oxford University Press.

Mazzoleni, Gianpietro, and Winifrid, Schulz. 1999, "'Mediatization' of politics: A challenge for democracy?" *Political Communication* 16:247–61.

Mazzoleni, Gianpietro, Stewart, Julianne, and Horsfield, Bruce (eds.). 2003. *The Media and Neo-Populism*. Westport, CT: Praeger.

McAdam, Doug, 1982/1999. *Political Process and the Development of Black Insurgency, 1930–1970*. Chicago: University of Chicago Press.

______. 1988. *Freedom Summer.* New York: Oxford University Press.

______. 1996a. "Conceptual origins, current problems, future directions." Pp. 23–40 in Doug McAdam, John D. McCarthy, and Mayer N. Zald (eds.), *Comparative Perspectives on Social Movements*. New York: Cambridge University Press.

______. 1996b. "The framing function of movement tactics." Pp. 338–55 in Doug McAdam, John D. McCarthy, and Mayer N. Zald (eds.), *Comparative Perspectives on Social Movements*. New York: Cambridge University Press.

McAdam, Doug, and David A. Snow (eds.) 1997. *Social Movements.* Los Angeles, CA: Roxbury.

McAdam, Doug, and Ronelle Paulsen. 1993. "Specifying the relationship between social ties and activism." *American Journal of Sociology* 99(3):640–67.

McAdam, Doug, John D. McCarthy, and Mayer N. Zald, eds. 1996. *Comparative Perspectives on Social Movements*. Cambridge, UK: Cambridge University Press.

______. 1988. "Social movements." Pp. 695–737 in Neil Smelser (ed.), *The Handbook of Sociology*. Newbury Park, CA: Sage.

______. 1996. *Comparative Perspectives on Social Movements.* New York: Cambridge University Press.

McAdam, Doug, Sidney Tarrow, and Charles Tilly. 1996. "To map contentious politics." *Mobilization: An International Journal* 1:17–34.

______. 2001. *The Dynamics of Contention*. Cambridge, UK: Cambridge University Press.

McAdam, Douglas, and Yang Su. 2002. "The war at home: Antiwar protests and congressional voting, 1965 to 1973." *American Sociological Review* 67:696–721.

McCammon, Holly. 1994. "Disorganizing and reorganizing conflict: outcomes of the state's legal regulation of the strike since the Wagner Act." *Social Forces* 72(4):1011–49.

McCammon, Holly, Ellen M. Granberg, Karen E. Campbell, and Christine Mowery. 2001. "How movements win: Gendered opportunity structures and U.S. women's suffrage movements, 1866 to 1919." *American Sociological Review* 66:49–70.

McCargo, Duncan. 2002, "Political journalists and their sources in Thailand." Pp. 92–107 in Erik Neveu and Raymond Kuhn (eds.), *Political Journalism: New Challenges, New Practices*. London: Routledge.

McCarthy, John. 1996. "Accessing public, media, electoral and governmental agendas." Pp. 291–311 in Doug McAdam, John McCarthy and Mayer Zald (eds.), *Comparative Social Movements*. New York: Cambridge University Press.

______. 1997. "The globalization of social movement theory." Pp. 243–259 in J. G. Smith, C. Chatfield, and R. Pagnucco (eds.), *Transnational Social Movements and Global Politics: Solidarity Beyond the State*. Syracuse, NY: Syracuse University Press.

McCarthy, John D., and Mayer N. Zald. 1977. "Resource mobilization and social movements: A partial theory." *American Journal of Sociology* 82:1212–41.

______. 1973. *The Trend of Social Movements in America*. Morristown, NJ: General Learning Press.

McCarty, Nolan, and Lawrence Rothenberg. 1996. "Commitment and campaign contract." *American Journal of Political Science* 40:872–904.

McCaughey, Martha, and Michael D. Ayers. (eds.) 2003. *Cyberactivism*. London: Routledge.

McChesney, Robert W. 1997. *Corporate Media and the Threat to Democracy*. New York: Seven Stories Press.

______. 1999. *Rich Media, Poor Democracy: Communication Politics in Dubious Times*. Chicago: University of Illinois Press.

______. 2000. *Rich Media, Poor Democracy: Communication Politics in Dubious Times*. New York: New Press.

McConnell, Grant. 1966. *Private Power and American Democracy*. New York: Alfred A. Knopf.

McCormick, John P. 2001. "Machiavellian democracy: controlling elites with ferocious populism." *American Political Science Review* 95(2): 297–313.

McCubbins, Matthew. 1985. "The legislative design of regulatory structure." *American Journal of Political Science* 29:721–48.

McCubbins, Matthew, and Thomas Schwartz. 1984. "Congressional oversight overlooked: Policy patrols vs. fire alarms." *American Journal of Political Science* 28:165–79.

McCubbins, Matthew, Roger Noll, and Barry Weingast. 1987. "Administrative procedures as instruments of political control." *Journal of Law, Economics, and Organization* 3:243–77.

McDaniel, Tim. 1991. *Autocracy, Modernization, and Revolution in Russia and Iran*. Princeton, NJ: Princeton University Press.

McDonald, Michael P., and Samuel L. Popkin. 2001. "The myth of the vanishing voter." *American Political Science Review* 95:963–74.

McDonough, John E. 1997. *Interests, Ideas and Deregulation*. Ann Arbor: University of Michigan Press.

McGann, James G., and R. Kent Weaver (eds.). 2000. *Think Tanks and Civil Societies: Catalysts for Ideas and Action*. New Brunswick, NJ: Transaction Press.

McGarry, John. 2002. "'Democracy' in Northern Ireland: Experiments in self-rule from the Protestant ascendancy to the Good Friday Agreement." *Nations and Nationalism* 8:451–74.

McGlynn, C. 2001. "European Union family values: Ideologies of 'family' and 'motherhood' in European Union law." *Social Politics* 8:325–50.

McGuire, James W. 1999. "Labor union strength and human development in East Asia and Latin America." *Studies in Comparative International Development* 33(Winter):3–34.

McIntosh, M. 1978. "The State and the oppression of women." Pp. 254–289 in A. M. Wolpe and A. Kuhn (eds.), *Feminism and Materialism: Women and Modes of Production*. London: Routledge.

McKelvey, R. 1976. "Intransitivities in multidimensional voting models and some implications for agenda control." *Journal of Economic Theory* 12:472–82.

McKenzie, R. T. 1956. *British Political Parties*. London: Heineman.

McLaren, Lauren M. 2003. "Anti-immigrant prejudice in Europe: Contact, threat perception, and preferences for the exclusion of migrants." *Social Forces* 81:909–36.

McLauchlan, Gregory, and Gregory Hooks. 1995. "Last of the dinosaurs? Big weapons, big science, and the American state from Hiroshima to the end of the Cold War." *Sociological Quarterly* 36:749–76.

McLaughlin, Abraham. 2000. "After election, are promises kept?" *Christian Science Monitor* (September 15).

McLeod, Douglas M., Gerald M., Kosicki, and Jack M. McCleod. 2002. "Resurveying the boundaries of political communication effects." Pp. 215–67 in Jennings Bryant and Dolf Zillman (eds.), *Media Effects: Advances in Theory and Research*. Mahwah, NJ: Erlbaum.

McMichael, Philip. 1990. "Incorporating comparison within a world-historical perspective: An alternative comparative method." *American Sociological Review* 55, 3:385–97.

______. 2000a. "Sleepless since Seattle: What is the WTO about?" *Review of International Political Economy* 7, 3:466–74.

______. 2000b. "World-systems analysis, globalization and incorporated comparison," *Journal of World-System Research* VI, 3:668–91.

______. 2000c. *Development and Social Change: A Global Perspective*. Thousand Oaks, CA: Pine Forge.

______. 2001. "Revisiting the question of the transnational state: A comment on William Robinson's 'Social Theory and Globalization'." *Theory and Society* 30, 2:201–10.

______. 2003. "Food security and social reproduction: Issues and contradictions." Pp. 169–89 in Isabella Bakker and Stephen Gill (eds.), *Power, Production and Social Reproduction*. Hampshire: Palgrave Macmillan.

______. 2004. *Development and Social Change. A Global Perspective*, 3rd ed. Thousand Oaks, CA: Pine Forge.

McMillen, Neil R. 1971. *The Citizens' Council: Organized Resistance to the Second Reconstruction, 1954–1964*. Urbana: University of Illinois Press.

McNair, Brian. 2000. *Journalism and Democracy*. London: Routledge.

McNeely, Connie. 1995. *Constructing the Nation-State: International Organization and Prespective Action*. Westport, CT: Greenwood.

McRae, Susan. 1998. "Part-time employment in a European perspective." Pp. 100–11 in Eileen Drew, Ruth Emerek, and Evelyn Mahon (eds.), *Women, Work, and the Family in Europe*. New York: Routledge.

Mead, George Herbert. 1936. *Mind, Self and Society*. Chicago: University of Chicago Press.

Medvic, Stephen K. 2001. "The impact of party financial support on the electoral success of US House candidates." *Party Politics* 7(2):192–242.

Meertens, Roel W., and Thomas F. Pettigrew. 1997. "Is subtle prejudice really prejudice?" *Public Opinion Quarterly* 61:54–71.

Meeusen, Wim and Ludo Cuyvers. 1985. "The interaction between interlocking directorships and the economic behaviour of companies." Pp. 45–72 in Frans N. Stokman, Rolf Ziegler, and John Scott (eds.), *Networks of Corporate Power*. Cambridge, UK: Polity Press.

Meier, August, and Elliott Rudwick. 1973. *CORE: A Study in the Civil Rights Movement, 1942–1968*. New York: Oxford University Press.

Melbeck, Christian. 1998. "Comparing local policy networks." *Journal of Theoretical Politics* 10:531–52.

Mellors, Colin, and John McKean. 1984. "The politics of conscription in Western Europe." *West European Politics*7(3):25–42.

Melman, Seymour. 1970. *Pentagon Capitalism: The Political Economy of War.* New York: McGraw–Hill.

Melucci, Alberto. 1989. *Nomads of the Present: Social Movements and Individual Needs in Contemporary Society*. Philadelphia: Temple University Press.

______. 1996. *Challenging Codes: Collective Action in the Information Age*. Cambridge, UK: Cambridge University Press.

Mendelberg, Tali. 2001. *The Race Card: Campaign Strategy, Implicit Messages, and the Norm of Equality*. Princeton, NJ: Princeton University Press.

Mendez, Juan E., Guillermo O'Donnell, and Paulo Sergio Pinheiro.(eds.), 1999. *The (Un)rule of Law and the Underprivileged in Latin America.* Notre Dame: Notre Dame University Press.

Meny, Yves, and Jean-Claude Thoenig. 1992. *Las Políticas Públicas*. Barcelona: Ariel Ciencia Política.

Merelman, Richard M. 1984. *Making Something of Ourselves: on Culture and Politics in the United States*. Berkeley: University of California Press.

Merkl, P. H., and L. Weinberg (eds.). 1997. *The Revival of Right Wing Extremism in the 90s*. London: Frank Cass.

Mermin, Jonathan. 1997. "Television news and American intervention in Somalia: The myth of a media–driven foreign policy." *Political Science Quarterly* 112:385–403.

Mernissi, Fatima. 1988. "Muslim women and fundamentalism." *Middle East Report* 18 (July/August):8–11.

Merton, Robert K. 1968. *Social Theory and Social Structure*, enlarged edition. New York: Free Press.

Mesa-Lago, Carmelo. 1978. *Social Security in Latin America: Pressure Groups, Stratification, and Inequality*. Pittsburgh: University of Pittsburgh Press.

______. 1989. *Ascent to Bankruptcy: Financing Social Security in Latin America.* Pittsburgh: University of Pittsburgh Press.

______. 1994. *Changing Social Security in Latin America: Toward Alleviating the Social Costs of Economic Reform*. Boulder, CO: Lynne Rienner.

Meyer, David S. 1990. *A Winter of Discontent.* New York: Praeger.

______. 2005. "Social movements and public policy." In David S. Meyer, Valerie Jenness, and Helen Ingram (eds.), *Routing the Opposition: Social Movements, Public Policy, and Democracy in America.* Minneapolis: University of Minnesota Press.

Meyer, David S., and Nancy Whittier. 1993. "Social movement spillover." *Social Problems* 41:277–98.

Meyer, David S., and Sidney Tarrow. 1998. *The Social Movement Society.* Lanham, MD: Rowman & Littlefield.

Meyer, David S., and Suzanne Staggenborg. 1996. "Movements, counter-movements, and the structure of political opportunity." *American Journal of Sociology* 100:1628–60.

Meyer, John W. 1999. "The changing cultural content of the nation-state: A world society perspective." Pp. 125–42 in George Steinmetz (ed.), *State/Culture: State Formation after the Cultural Turn.* Ithaca, NY: Cornell University Press.

______. 2001a. "The changing cultural content of the nation-state: a world society perspective." Pp. 123–44 in George Steinmetz (ed.), *State/Culture: State-Formation after the Cultural Turn.* Ithaca, NY: Cornell University Press.

______. 2001b. "Globalization, national culture, and the future of the world polity." Wei Lun Lecture, delivered at the Chinese University of Hong Kong, November 28.

Meyer, John W., and Brian Rowan. 1977. "Institutionalized organizations: Formal structure as myth and ceremony." *American Journal of Sociology* 83:340–63.

Meyer, John W., and Ronald L. Jepperson. 2000. "The 'actors' of modern society: The cultural construction of social agency." *Sociological Theory* 18:100–20.

Meyer, John W., John Boli, George M. Thomas, and Francisco O. Ramirez 1997. "World society and the nation state." *American Journal of Sociology* 103:144–81.

Meyers, Eytan. 2000. "Theories of international immigration policy – a comparative analysis." *International Migration Review* 34(4):1245–82.

Meyers, Marcia, Janet C. Gornick, and Katherin E. Ross. 1999. "Public childcare, parental leave, and employment." Pp. 117–46 in Diane Sainsbury (ed.), *Gender and Welfare State Regimes*. Oxford, UK: Oxford University Press.

Meyrowitz, Joshua. 1985. *No Sense of Place: The Impact of Electronic Media on Social Behavior.* New York: Oxford University Press.

Michael Hechter and Karl-Dieter Opp. 2001. "What Have We Learned About the Emergence of Social Norms?" In Michael Hechter and Karl-Dieter Opp. (eds.), *Social Norms*. New York: Russell Sage.

Michael, George. 2003. *Confronting Right-Wing Extremism and Terrorism in America.* London: Routledge.

Michel, Sonya. 1999. *Children's Interests/Mothers' Rights*. New Haven, CT: Yale University Press.

Michels, Robert. 1915/1959. *Political Parties.* New York: Dover.

______. 1958. *Political Parties: A Sociological Study of the Oligarchical Tendencies of Modern Democracy*. Glencoe, IL: Free Press.

______. 1962. *Political Parties: A Sociological Study of the Oligarchical Tendencies of Modern Democracy* (Eden and Cedar Paul, trans.). New York: Collier.

______. 1989[1911/1925]. *Zur Soziologie des Parteiwesens in der modernen Demokratie. Untersuchungen über die oligarchischen Tendenzen des Gruppenlebens*. Stuttgart: Kröner.

Mickelson, Sig. 1989. *From Whistle Stop to Sound Bite*. New York: Praeger.

Mies, Maria. 1998[1986]. *Patriarchy and Accumulation on a World Scale: Women in the International Division of Labour*. New York: Zed Books.

Miles, Robert. 1982. *Racism and Migrant Labour*. London: Routledge & Kegan Paul.

Miles, Robert, and Annie Phizacklea. 1980. *Labor and Racism*. London: Routledge and Kegan Paul.

Milgram, Stanley. 1974. *Obedience to Authority*. New York: Harper and Row.

Miliband, Ralph. 1969. *The State in Capitalist Society*. New York: Basic Books.

______. 1972. "Reply to Nicos Poulantzas." Pp. 253–62 in R. Blackburn (ed.), *Ideology in Social Science*. London: Fontana. Originally published in the *New Left Review*, No. 59, January–February 1970.

______. 1973. "Poulantzas and the capitalist state." *New Left Review* 82:83–92.

______. 1977. *Marxism and Politics*. London: Oxford University Press.

______. 1990. "Gender and trade unions in historical perspective." Pp. 87–107 in Louise A. Tilly and Patricia Gurin (eds.), *Women, Politics and Change*. New York: Russell Sage Foundation.

Mill, John Stuart. 1977[1861]. "Considerations on representative government." Pp. 371–577 in *Collected Works of John Stuart Mill*. TorontoLondon: University of Toronto Press and Routledge & Kegan Paul.

Miller, Carol. 1998. "Gender advocates and multilateral development organizations: Promoting change from within." Pp. 138–71 in Carol Miller and Shahra Razavi (eds.), *Missionaries and Mandarins*. London: United Nations Research Institute for Social Development.

Miller, Carol, and Shahra Razavi (eds.). 1998. *Missionaries and Mandarins*. London: United Nations Research Institute for Social Development.

Miller, Daniel, (ed.) 1995. *Worlds Apart: Modernity through the Prism of the Local*. New York: Routledge.

Miller, James. 1979. *History and Human Existence: From Marx to Merleau-Ponty*. Berkeley, CA: University of California Press.

Miller, John. 2003. "Why economists are wrong about sweatshops and the antisweatshop movement." *Challenge* 46(1):93–122.

Miller, Mark. 1981. *Foreign Workers in Western Europe: An Emerging Political Force?* New York: Praeger.

Miller, Warren E., and J. Merrill Shanks. 1996. *The New American Voter*. Cambridge, MA: Harvard University Press.

Mills, C. Wright. 1956. *The Power Elite*. New York: Oxford University Press.

______. 1958. *The Causes of World War Three*. New York: Simon & Schuster.

______. 1959. *The Sociological Imagination*. New York: Oxford University Press.

______. 1962. *The Marxists*. New York: Dell.

______. 1963. *Power, Politics and People*. New York: Oxford University Press.

Mills, Kay. 1988. *A Place in the News*. New York: Dodd, Mead.

Milyo, Jeffrey. 1997. "The economics of political campaign finance: FECA and the puzzle of the not very greedy grandfathers." *Public Choice* 93:245–70.

Milyo, Jeffrey, David Primo, and Timothy Groseclose. 2000. "Corporate PAC campaign contributions in perspective." *Business and Politics* 2:75–88.

Milza, Pierre. 1984. *Fascisme français. Passé et Présent*. Paris: Flammarion.

______. [1985] 2001. *Les Fascismes*. Paris: Editions du Seuil.

Mink, Gwendolyn. 1986. *Old Labor and New Immigrants in American Political Development: Union, Party and State, 1875–1920*. Ithaca, NY: Cornell University Press.

______. 1995. *The Wages of Motherhood*. Ithaca, NY: Cornell University Press.

______. 1999. *Whose Welfare?* Ithaca, NY: Cornell University Press.

Minkoff, Debra C. 1995. *Organizing for Equality*. New Brunswick, NJ: Rutgers University Press.

______. 1997. "The sequencing of social movements." *American Sociological Review* 62:779–99.

______. 1998. "Bending with the wind: Strategic change and adaptation by women's and racial minority organizations." *American Journal of Sociology* 104:1666–1703.

Minow, Mortha. 1990. *Making All the Difference: Inclusion, Exclusion, and American Law*. Ithaca, NY: Cornell University Press.

Mintrom, Michael, and Sandra Vergari. 1998. "Policy networks and innovation diffusion: The case of state education reforms." *Journal of Politics* 60:126–48.

Mintz, Alex, and Randolph Stevenson. 1995. "Defense expenditure, economic growth, and the peace dividend." *Journal of Conflict Resolution* 39(2):283–305.

Mintz, Beth, and Michael Schwartz. 1985. *The Power Structure in American Business*. Chicago: University of Chicago Press.

Mintzberg, Henry. 1999. *La estructuración de las organizaciones*. Barcelona: Ariel Economía.

Mirowsky, John, and Catherine Ross. 1981. "Protest group success." *Sociological Focus* 14:177–92.

Misra, Joya. 1998a. "Mothers or workers? The value of unpaid labor." *Gender & Society* 12:376–99.

______. 1998b. "Gender, culture, and the state: Family policies in Catholic countries." July 19 Paper presented at the Annual Meetings of the International Society for the Advancement of Socio-Economics, Vienna, Austria.

______. 2000. "Gender and the world system." Pp. 105–27 in Thomas Hall (ed.), *A World Systems Reader: New Perspectives on Gender, Urbanism, Cultures, Indigenous Peoples and Ecology*. Lanham, MD: Rowman & Littlefield.

______. 2003. "Women as agents in welfare state development." *Socioeconomic Review* 1:185–245.

Misra, Joya, and Frances Akins. 1998. "Structure, agency, and diversity: Women in the welfare state." *Social Politics: International Studies in Gender, State, and Society* 5:259–89.

Mitchell, Timothy. 1991. *Colonising Egypt*. Berkeley: University of California Press.

Mizruchi, Mark S. 1982. *The American Corporate Network, 1904–1974*. Beverly Hills: Sage.

______. 1989. "Similarity of political behavior among large American corporations." *American Journal of Sociology* 95:401–24.

______. 1990. "Determinants of political opposition among large American corporations." *Social Forces* 68:1065–88.

______. 1992. *The Structure of Corporate Political Action: Interfirm Relations and Their Consequences*. Cambridge, MA: Harvard University Press.

______. 1996. "What do interlocks do? An analysis, critique, and assessment of research on interlocking directorates." *Annual Review of Sociology* 22:271–98.

Mizruchi, Mark S., and Gerald F. Davis. 2004. "The globalization of American banking, 1962–1981." Pp. 95–126 in Frank Dobbin (ed.), *The Sociology of the Economy*. New York: Russell Sage Foundation.

Mizruchi, Mark S., and Thomas Koenig. 1986. "Economic sources of corporate political consensus: an examination of interindustry relations." *American Sociological Review* 51:482–91.

Moaddel, Mansoor. 1994. "Political conflict in the world economy: A cross-national analysis of modernization and world-system theories." *American Sociological Review* 59:276–303.

______. 2002. *Jordanian Exceptionalism: A Comparative Analysis of State-Religion Relationships in Egypt, Iran, Jordan, and Syria*. New York: Palgrave.

Moe, Terry M. 1987. "Interests, institutions, and positive theory: the politicis of the NLRB." *Studies in American Political Development* 2:236–299.

______. 1980. *The Organization of Interests: Incentives and the Internal Dynamics of Political Interest Groups*. Chicago: University of Chicago Press.

______. 1985. "Control and feedback in economic regulation: The case of the NLRB." *American Political Science Review* 79:1094–1116.

______. 1990. "Political institutions: The neglected side of the story." *Journal of Law, Economics, and Organization* 6:213–53.

Moghadam, Valentine M. 1994. *Identity Politics and Women*. Boulder, CO: Westview.

______. 1997. *Women, Work, and Economic Reform in the Middle East and North Africa*. Boulder, CO: Lynne Rienner.

______. 1999. "Gender and the global economy." Pp. 128–60 in Myra Marx Ferree, Judith Lorber, and Beth B. Hess (eds.), *Revisioning Gender*. Thousand Oaks, CA: Sage.

______. 2000. "Transnational feminist networks: Collective action in an era of globalization." *International Sociology* 15:57–85.

______. 2002. "Violence, terrorism, and fundamentalism: Some feminist observations." *Global Dialogue* 4:66–76.

______. 2003a. *Modernizing Women: Gender and Social Change in the Middle East (second edition)*. Boulder, CO: Lynne Rienner.

______. 2003b. Personal E-mail Communication, September 23.

Mohan, Dia. 2004. "Reimagining Community: Scripting Power and Changing the Subject through Jana Sanskriti's Political Theatre in Rural North India." *Journal of Contemporary Ethnography* 33, 2:178–217.

Mohanty, Chandra. T. 1991. *Third World Women and the Politics of Feminism*. Bloomington: Indiana University Press.

______. 2003. *Feminism without Borders: Decolonizing Theory, Practicing Solidarity*. Durham, NC and London: Duke University Press.

Molho, Ian. 1986. "Theories of migration: A review." *Scottish Journal of Political Economy* 33(4): 396–419.

Molina, Oscar, and Martin Rhodes. 2002. "Corporatism: The past, present, and future of a concept." *Annual Review of Political Science* 5:305–31.

Moller, Stephanie, David Bradley, Evelyne Huber, François Nielsen and John D. Stephens. 2003. "Determinants of relative poverty in advanced capitalist democracies." *American Sociological Review* 68:22–52.

Molyneaux, M. 1979. "Beyond the domestic labour debate." *New Left Review* 116: 3–27.

______. 1985. "Mobilization without emancipation? women's interests, the state and revolution in Nicaragua." *Feminist Studies* 11:227–54.

Monbiot, George. 2003. *The Age of Consent. A Manifesto for a New World Order.* London: Flamingo.

Money, Jeannette. 1999. *Fences and Neighbors: The Political Geography of Immigration Control.* Ithaca, NY: Cornell University Press.

Monroe, Alan D. 1998. "Public opinion and public policy, 1980–1993." *Public Opinion Quarterly* 62:6–28.

Monroe, J. P. 2001. *The Political Party Matrix: The Persistence of Organization.* Albany: State University of New York Press.

Monsen, R. Joseph, John. S. Chiu, and David E. Cooley. 1968. "The effect of separation of ownership and control on the performance of the large firm." *Quarterly Journal of Economics* 82:435– 51.

Moore, Barrington Jr. 1962[1958]. *Political Power and Social Theory.* New York: Harper-Torchbooks.

______. 1965. *Social Origins of Dictatorship and Democracy.* Boston: Beacon.

______. 1967. *The Social Origins of Dictatorship and Democracy.* Boston: Beacon Press.

______. 1978. *Injustice: The Social Bases of Obedience and Revolt.* White Plains, NY: M. E. Sharpe.

______. 1996. *Social Origins of Dictatorship and Democracy. Lord and Peasant in the Making of the Modern World.* Boston: Beacon.

Moore, Kelly. 2002. *Democratizing Science.* Princeton, NJ: Princeton University Press.

Moore, Mark. 1998. *Gestión estratégica y creación de valor en el sector público.* Buenos Aires: Paidos.

Moore, Robert. 1975. *Racism and Black Resistance in Britain.* London: Pluto.

Morgan, Edmund S. 1975. *American Slavery, American Freedom.* New York: Norton.

Morley, J. T. 1984. *Secular Socialists: The CCF/NDP in Ontario, A Biography.* Kingston and Montreal: McGill–Queen's University Press.

Morris, Aldon D. 1984. *The Origins of the Civil Rights Movement: Black Communities Organizing for Change.* New York: Free Press.

______. 1993. "Birmingham confrontation reconsidered: An analysis of the dynamics and tactics of mobilization." *American Sociological Review* 58:621–36.

______. 1999. "A retrospective on the civil rights movement: Political and intellectual landmarks." *Annual Review of Sociology* 25:517–39.

Morriss, Peter. 1987. *Power: A Philosophical Analysis.* New York: St. Martins.

Morrow, Duncan. 2000. "Jörg Haider and the new FPÖ: Beyond the democratic pale." Pp. 33–63 in Paul Hainsworth (ed.), *The Politics of the Extreme Right. From the Margins to the Mainstream.* London: Pinter.

Mortensen, F., and E. N. Svendsen. 1980. "Creativity and control: The journalist betwixt his readers and editors." *Media, Culture and Society* 2:169–77.

Morton, Desmond. 1986. *The New Democrats, 1961–1986.* Toronto: Copp Clark Pitman.

Mosca, Gaetano. 1939. *The Ruling Class.* New York: McGraw–Hill.

Moskos, Charles. 1988. *Soldiers and Sociology.* Washington, D.C.: Government Printing Office.

Moss, Philip I., and Chris Tilly. 2001. *Stories Employers Tell: Race, Skill, and Hiring in America.* New York: Russell Sage Foundation.

Mouffe, Chantal. 1979. "Hegemony and ideology in Gramsci." Pp. 168–205 in Mouffe (ed.), *Gramsci and Marxist Theory.* London: Routledge and Kegan Paul.

______. 1981. "Hegemony and the integral state in Gramsci: Towards a new concept of politics." Pp. 167–87 in Bridges and Brunt (eds.), *Silver Linings: Some Strategies for the Eighties.* London: Lawrence and Wishart.

______. 1988. "Hegemony and new social movements: Towards a new concept of democracy." Pp. 89–101 in Nelson and Grossberg (eds.), *Marxism and the Interpretation of Culture.* Basingstoke, UK: Macmillan.

______. 1989. "Radical democracy: Modern or postmodern?" Pp. 31–45 in Ross (ed.), *Universal Abandon?* Edinburgh: Edinburgh University Press.

Mouffe, C. 1992a. "Feminism, citizenship and radical democratic politics." Pp. 369–84 in Joan Wallach Scott and Judith Butler (eds.), *Feminists Theorize the Political.* New York: Routledge.

______ (ed.). 1992b. *Dimensions of Radical Democracy.* London: Verso.

______. 1993a. *The Return of the Political.* London: Verso.

______. 1993b. "Citizenship." Pp. 138–9 in Joel Krieger et al. (eds.), *The Oxford Companion to Politics of the World.* New York: Oxford University Press.

______. 1996. "Deconstruction, Pragmatism and the Politics of Democracy." Pp. 1–11 in Chantal Mouffe (ed.), *Deconstruction and Pragmatism.* New York: Routledge.

______ (ed.). 1996. *Deconstruction and Pragmatism.* New York: Routledge.

Mouzelis, Nicos P. 1988. "Marxism or post-Marxism." *New Left Review* 167:107–25.

Mudde, Cas. 2000a. "Extreme Right parties in Eastern Europe." *Patterns of Prejudice* 34(1):5–27.

______. 2000b. *The Ideology of the Extreme Right.* Manchester: Manchester University Press.

______. 2001. "In the name of the peasantry, the proletariat, and the people: Populism in Eastern Europe." *East European Politics and Societies* 15(1): 35–53.

______. 2002. "Extreme Movements." Pp. 135–48 in Paul Heywood, Erik Jones, and Martin Rhodes (eds.), *Developments in West European Politics.* 2nd ed. Houndsmills: Macmillan.

Mueller, Adam. 1922[1809]. *Die Elemente der Staatskunst* J. Baxa (ed.), Jena.

Mueller, Carol. 1994. "Conflict networks and the origin of women's liberation." Pp. 234–266 in H. Johnston, J. R. Gusfield, and E. Laràna (eds.), *New Social Movements: From Ideology to Identity.* Philadelphia: Temple University Press.

Muetzelfeldt, Michael, and Gary Smith. 2002. "Civil society and global governance: The possibilities for global citizenship." *Citizenship Studies* 6, 1 (March):55–76.

Mukerji, Chandra. 1997. *Territorial Ambitions and the Gardens of Versailles.* Cambridge, UK: Cambridge University Press.

Muller, Katharina. 2002. "Privatising old-age security: Latin America and Eastern Europe compared." Research Report. Frankfurt: Institute for Transformation Studies (March).

Müller, Wolfgang C. 1994. "The development of Austrian party organizations in the post-war period." Pp. 51–79 in Richard S. Katz and Peter Mair (eds.), *How Parties Organize: Change and Adaptation in Party Organizations in Western Democracies.* Thousand Oaks, CA: Sage.

Münch, Richard. 2001. *Nation and Citizenship in the Global Age.* Basingstoke, UK: Palgrave.

Mundigo, Axel I. 2000. "Re-conceptualizing the role of men in the post-Cairo era." *Culture, Health and Society* 2(3):323–37.

Murillo, Maria Victoria. 2001. *Labor Unions, Partisan Coalitions, and Market Reforms in Latin America.* New York: Cambridge University Press.

Murphy, Raymond. 1988. *Social Closure: The Theory of Monopolization and Exclusion.* Oxford, UK: Clarendon Press.

Murschetz, Paul. 1998. "State support for the daily press in Europe: A critical appraisal." *European Journal of Communication* 13:291–313.

Mutch, Robert E. 2001. "Three centuries of campaign finance law." Pp. 1–24 in Gerald C. Lubenow (ed.), *A User's Guide to Campaign Finance Reform.* New York: Rowman & Littlefield.

Mutz, Diana C. 2002. "The consequences of cross-cutting networks for political participation." *American Journal of Political Science* 46:838–55.

Mutz, Diane, and Paul Martin. 2001. "Facilitating communication across lines of political difference." *American Political Science Review* 95(1):97–114.

Myles, John, and Jill Quadagno. 2002. "Political theories of the welfare state." *Social Service Review* (March):34–57.

Myles, John, and Paul Pierson. 1997. "Friedman's revenge." *Politics and Society* 25:442–72.

______. 2000. "The political economy of pension reform." Pp. 305–33 in Paul Pierson (ed.), *The New Politics of the Welfare State.* Oxford: Oxford University Press.

Myles, John. 1989[1979]. *Old Age in the Welfare State: The Political Economy of Public Pensions*, second ed. Boston: Little, Brown.

Nagel, Joane. 1982. "The political mobilization of Native Americans." *Social Science Journal* 19:37–46.

______. 1986. "The political construction of ethnicity." Pp. 93–112 in S. Olzak and J. Nagel (eds.), *Competitive Ethnic Relations.* Orlando, FL: Academic.

______. 1995. "American Indian ethnic renewal: Politics and the resurgence of identity." *American Sociological Review* 60:947–65.

______. 1997. *American Indian Ethnic Renewal: Red Power and the Resurgence of Identity and Culture.* New York: Oxford University Press.

Naples, Nancy A., and Manisha Desai (eds.). 2002. *Women's Activism and Globalization: Linking Local Struggles and Transnational Politics.* New York: Routledge.

Narayan, Deepa. 2000. *Voices of the Poor: Crying out for Change.* New York: Oxford University Press.

Nash, Kate. 2000a. *Contemporary Political Sociology: Globalization, Politics, and Power.* Oxford, UK: Blackwell.

______. 2000b. *Readings in Contemporary Political Sociology.* Oxford, UK: Blackwell.

Nayar, Jayan. 2000. "Doing law differently." *New Internationalist* 330:20–1.

Naylor, Phillip. 2000. *France and Algeria.* Gainesville: University of Florida Press.

Nelson, Candice J., David A. Dulio, and Stephen K. Medvic (eds.). 2002. *Shades of Gray: Perspectives on Campaign Ethics.* Washington, DC: Brookings Institution.

Nelson, Joan. M. 1987. "Political participation." Pp. 103–59 in Myron Weiner and Samuel P.

Huntington (eds.), *Understanding Political Development*. BostonToronto: Little, Brown.

Nettl, J. P. 1968. "The state as a conceptual variable." *World Politics*, 20, July: 559–92.

Neumann, Sigmund (ed.). 1956. *Modern Political Parties.* Chicago: University of Chicago Press.

Neustadtl, Alan. 1990. "Interest-group PACsmanship: An analysis of campaign contributions, issue visibility, and legislative impact." *Social Forces* 69:549–64.

Neustadtl, Alan, and Dan Clawson. 1988. "Corporate political groupings: PAC contributions to the 1980 congressional elections." *American Sociological Review* 51:781–96.

Neustadtl, Alan, Denise Scott, and Dan Clawson. 1991. "Class struggle in campaign finance? Political action committee contributions in the 1984 election." *Sociological Forum* 6:219–38.

Newman, Bruce I. 1994. *Marketing of the President: Political Marketing as a Campaign Strategy*. Thousand Oaks, CA: Sage.

Nicholson, Linda, ed. 1990. *Feminism/Postmodernism*. New York: Routledge.

Nie, Norman H., Sidney Verba, and John R. Petrocik. 1981. *The Changing American Voter*, 2nd ed. Cambridge, MA: Harvard University Press.

Niemi, Richard, and Henry Weisberg. 2001. *Controversies in Voting Behavior*, 4th ed. Washington, D.C.: Congressional Quarterly.

Nieuwbeerta, Paul. 1996. "The democratic class struggle in postwar societies: Class voting in twenty countries, 1945–1990." *Acta Sociologica* 39:345–83.

______. 2001. "The democratic struggle in postwar societies: Traditional class voting in twenty countries, 1945–1990." Pp. 121–35 in Terry Nichols Clark and Seymour Martin Lipset (eds.), *The Breakdown of Class Politics: A Debate on Post-Industrial Stratification*. Washington, DC: Woodrow Wilson Center Press.

Nieuwbeerta, Paul, Clem Brooks, and Jeffrey Manza. 2004. 'Social Cleavages and Voter Alignments in Comparative Perspective.' *Social Science Research* 33: forthcoming.

Nieuwbeerta, Paul, and Nan Dirk De Graaf. 1999. "Traditional class voting in twenty postwar societies." Pp. 23–56 in Geoffrey Evans (ed.), *The End of Class Politics*? Oxford, UK: Oxford University Press.

Nimmo, Dan, and James E. Combs. 1980. *Subliminal Politics: Myths and Mythmakers in America*. Englewood Cliffs, NJ: Prentice Hall.

______. 1983. *Mediated Political Realities*. New York: Longman.

Nisbet, Robert. 1966. *The Sociological Tradition*. New York: Basic Books.

Niskanen, William. 1971. *Bureaucracy and Representative Government*. Chicago: Aldine-Atherton.

Nixon, Richard. 1968. "Richard Nixon for President 1968 Campaign Brochures. The Nixon Stand on 'Progress with Order.'"

Nobles, Melissa. 2000. *Shades of Citizenship: Race and the Census in Modern Politics*. Stanford, CA: Stanford University Press.

Noiriel, Gerard. 1996. *The French Melting Pot: Immigration, Citizenship, and National Identity*. Minneapolis: University of Minnesota Press.

Norberg-Hodge, Helena, Peter Goering, and John Page. 2001. *From the Ground Up. Rethinking Industrial Agriculture*. London: Zed.

Nordlinger, Eric. 1981. *On the Autonomy of the Democratic State*. Cambridge, UK: Harvard University Press.

Norris, Pippa (ed.). 1997. *Passages to Power: Legislative Recruitment in Advanced Democracies*. Cambridge, UK: Cambridge University Press.

Norris, Pippa, John, Curtice, David, Sanders, Margaret, Scammell, and Holli A. Semetko. 1999. *On Message: Communicating the Campaign*. London: Sage.

North, Douglass. 1981. *Structure and Change in Economic History*. New York: W. W. Norton.

______. 1990. *Institutions, Institutional Change and Economic Performance*. Cambridge, UK: Cambridge University Press.

North, Douglass, and Barry Weingast. 1989. "Constitutions and commitment: The evolution of institutions governing public choice in seventeenth century England." *Journal of Economic History* 99(4): 803–32.

North, Douglass, and Robert Paul Thomas. 1973. *The Rise of the Western World*. Cambridge, UK: Cambridge University Press.

Norval, Aletta J. 1996. *Deconstructing Apartheid*. London: Verso.

Oberschall, Anthony. 1973. *Social Conflict and Social Movements.* Englewood Cliffs, NJ: Prentice-Hall.

______. 1993. *Social Movements: Ideologies, Interests, and Identities*. New Brunswick, NJ: Transaction.

______. 1996. "Opportunities and framing in the East European revolts of 1989." Pp. 93–121 in Doug McAdam, John McCarthy and Mayer Zald (eds.), *Comparative Social Movements.* New York: Cambridge University Press.

Oberschall, Anthony, and Eric M. Leifer. 1986. "Efficiency and social institutions: Uses and misuses of economic reasoning in sociology." *Annual Review of Sociology* 12:233–53.

O'Brien, Kevin. 1990. *Reform without Liberalization*. Cambridge, UK: Cambridge University Press.

O'Brien, Richard. 1992. *Global Financial Integration: The End of Geography*. London: Pinter Publishers.

O'Brien, Robert. 2000. *Contesting Global Governance: Multilateral Economic Institutions and Global Social Movements. Cambridge Studies in International Relations; 71*. Cambridge, UK; New York: Cambridge University Press.

O'Connor, James. 1973. *The Fiscal Crisis of the State*. New York: St. Martin's Press.

O'Connor, Julia. 1996. "From women in the welfare state to gendering welfare state regimes." *Current Sociology*, 44(2):67–95.

O'Connor, Julia S., Ann Shola Orloff, and Sheila Shaver. 1999. *States, Markets, Families: Gender, Liberalism and Social Policy in Australia, Canada, Great Britain and the United States*. Cambridge, UK: Cambridge University Press.

O'Donnell, Guillermo. 1973. *Modernization and Bureaucratic Authoritarianism: Studies in South American Politics*. Berkeley: University of California Press.

______. 1979. "Tensions in the bureaucratic–authoritarian state and the question of democracy." Pp. 285–318 in David Collier (ed.), *The New Authoritarianism in Latin America*. Princeton, NJ: Princeton University Press.

______. 1993. "On the state, democratization and some conceptual problems: A Latin American view with glances at some postcommunist countries." *World Development* 21(8):1355–69.

______. 1994. "Delegative democracy?" *Journal of Democracy* 5:55–69.

O'Donnell, Guillermo, and Schmitter, Philippe C. 1986. "Tentative conclusions about uncertain democracies." In Guillermo O'Donnell, Philippe C. Schmitter, and Laurence Whitehead (eds.), *Transitions from Authoritarian Rule: Prospects for Democracy*. Baltimore, MD: Johns Hopkins University Press.

O'Donnell, Guillermo, Philippe Schmitter, and Laurence Whitehead (eds.). 1986. *Transitions from Authoritarian Rule*. Baltimore, MD: Johns Hopkins University Press.

O'Dwyer, Conor. 2002. "Civilizing the state bureaucracy: The unfulfilled promise of public administration reform in Poland, Slovakia, and the Czech Republic (1990–2000)." Working Paper, Institute of Slavic, East European, and Eurasian Studies. Berkeley: University of California.

OECD (Organization for Economic Cooperation and Development). 1995. *Historical Statistics 1960–1993*. Paris: Organization for Economic Cooperation and Development.

______. 1997. "Economic performance and the structure of collective bargaining." Pp. 63–93 in *OECD Employment Outlook*. Paris: OECD.

OECD-SOPEMI. 1983–2002. *Trends in International Migration*. Paris: OECD.

OECD/HRDC. 1997. *Literacy Skills for the Knowledge Society: Further Results from the International Adult Literacy Survey*. Paris: Organization for Economic Co-operation and Development, Human Resources Development Canada.

Oestreich, Gerhard. 1970. "Die Niederlande und Brandenburg-Preussen." *Nachbarn* 7:1–28.

______. 1981. "Calvinismus, Neustoizismus und Preussentum." Pp. 1268–93 in Otto Buesch and Wolfgang Neugebauer (eds.), *Moderne Preussische Geschichte 1648–1947*. Berlin: De Gruyter.

Offe, Claus. 1972a. *Strukturprobleme des kapitalistischen Staates*. Frankfurt: Suhrkamp.

______. 1972b. "Advanced capitalism and the welfare state." *Politics and Society* 2(4):479–88.

______. 1972c. "Political authority and class structures – an analysis of late capitalist societies." *International Journal of Sociology* II(1):73–108.

______. 1974. "Structural problems of the capitalist state, class rule and the political system: On the selectiveness of political institutions." Pp. 31–57 in Klaus Von Beyme (ed.), *German Political Studies*, Vol. 1. London: Sage.

______. 1975a. "Introduction to part III." Pp. 245–59 in Leon N. Lindberg, Robert R. Alford, Colin Goud and Claus Offe, (eds.), *Stress and Contradiction in Modern Capitalism*. Lexington, MA: Lexington Books.

______. 1975b. "The theory of the capitalist state and the problem of policy formation." In L. Lindberg, R. Alford, C. Crouch, and C. Offe (eds.), *Stress and Contradiction in Modern Capitalism*. Lexington, MA: D. C. Heath and Company.

______. 1976. "Crises of crisis management: elements of a political crisis theory." *International Journal of Politics* VI(3):29–67.

______. 1984a. *Contradictions of the Welfare State*. London: Hutchinson.

______. 1984b. "Korporatismus als System nichtstaatlicher Makrosteuerung? Notizen über seine Voraussetzungen und demokratischen Gehalte." *Geschichte und Gesellschaft* 10:234–56.

Offe, Claus, and Volker Ronge. 1975. "Theses on the theory of the state." *New German Critique* 6:137–47.

Offe, Claus, and Helmut Wiesenthal. 1980. "Two logics of collective action: Theoretical notes on social class and organizational forms." *Political Power and Social Theory* 1:167–15.

Offen, K. 1988. "Defining feminism – a comparative historical approach." *Signs* 14:119–57.

Ogburn, William F., and Lolagene Coombs. 1940. "The economic factor in the Roosevelt elections." *American Political Science Review* 34:719–27.

Ogburn, William F., and Delvin Peterson. 1916. "Political thought of social classes." *Political Science Quarterly* 31:300–17.

Ogliastri, Enrique, and Carlos Davila. 1987. "The articulation of power and business structures: A study of Colombia." Pp. 233–63 in Mark S. Mizruchi and Michael Schwartz (eds.), *Intercorporate Relations: The Structural Analysis of Business.* New York: Cambridge University Press.

Ohlander, Ann-Sofie. 1991. "The invisible child? The struggle for a social democratic family policy in Sweden, 1900–1960s." Pp. 60–72 in Gisela Bock and Pat Thane (eds.), *Maternity and Gender Policies*, New York: Routledge.

Ohmae, Kenichi. 1995. *The End of the Nation State: The Rise of Regional Economies.* New York: Free Press.

Okin, Susan Moller. 1989. *Justice, Gender, and the Family.* New York: Basic Books.

Okin, Susan Moller, Joshua Cohen, et al. 1999. *Is Multiculturalism Bad for Women?* Princeton, NJ: Princeton University Press.

Oliver, Pamela E. 1980. "Rewards and punishments as selective incentives for collective action: Theoretical investigations." *American Journal of Sociology* 85:1356–75.

______. 1984. "'If you don't do it, nobody else will': Active and token contributors to local collective action." *American Sociological Review* 49:601–10.

Oliver, Pamela E., and Gerald Marwell. 1988. "The paradox of group size in collective action—a theory of the critical mass." *American Sociological Review* 53(1):1–8.

Oliver, Pamela E., and Hank Johnston. 2000. "What a good idea! Ideologies and frames in social movement research." *Mobilization* 5:37–54.

Olson, Mancur. 1965. *The Logic of Collective Action: Public Goods and the Theory of Groups.* Cambridge, MA: Harvard University Press.

______. 1971. *The Logic of Collective Action: Public Goods and the Theory of Groups.* Cambridge, MA: Harvard University Press.

______. 1982. *The Rise and Decline of Nations.* New Haven, CT: Yale University Press.

Olzak, Susan. 1989. "Labor unrest, immigration, and ethnic conflict in urban America." *American Journal of Sociology* 94(6):1303–33.

______. 1992. *The Dynamics of Ethnic Competition and Conflict.* Stanford, CA: Stanford University Press.

Omi, Michael and Howard Winant. 1994. *Racial Formation in the United States: From the 1960s to the 1980s*, 2nd ed. New York: Routledge & Kegan Paul.

______. 1994. *Racial Formation in the United States*, rev. ed. New York: Routledge.

Ong, Aihwa. 1987. *Spirits of Resistance and Capitalist Discipline: Factory Women in Malaysia.* Albany: State University of New York Press.

______. 1999. *Flexible Citizenship: The Cultural Logics of Transnationality.* Durham, NC: Duke University Press.

Opp, Karl-Dieter. 2001. "Social networks and the emergence of protest norms." Pp. 234–73 in Michael Hechter and Karl Dieter-Opp (eds.), *Social Norms.* New York: Russell Sage Foundation.

Opp, Karl-Dieter, P. Voss, and C. Gern. 1995. *Origins of a Spontaneous Revolution.* Ann Arbor: University of Michigan Press.

Oppenheimer, Valerie, and Anne Jensen. 1995. *Gender and Family Change in Industrialized Countries.* Oxford, UK: Clarendon.

Orfield, Gary. 1978. *Must We Bus?: Segregated Schools and National Policy.* Washington, DC: Brookings Institution.

Orfield, Gary, and Susan E. Eaton. 1996. *Dismantling Desegregation: The Quiet Reversal of Brown v. Board of Education.* New York: New Press.

Orfield, Gary, Mark D. Bachmeier, David R. James, and Tamela Eitle. 1997. "Deepening segregation in American public schools: A special report from the Harvard Project on School Desegregation." *Equity & Excellence in Education* 30:5–24.

Orlanda Pinnasi, Maria, Fatima Cabral, and Mirian Claudia Lourencao. 2000. "An interview with Joao Pedro Stedile." *Latin American Perspectives* 27, 5:46–62.

Orloff, Ann Shola. 1993. "Gender and the social rights of citizenship – the comparative analysis of gender relations and welfare states." *American Sociological Review* 58:303–28.

______. 1993. *The Politics of Pensions: A Comparative Analysis of Britain, Canada, and the United States, 1880–1940.* Madison: University of Wisconsin Press.

______. 1996. "Gender in the welfare state." *Annual Review of Sociology* 22:51–78.

Orloff, Ann Shola, and Theda Skocpol 1986. "Explaining the origins of welfare states: Britain and the United States, 1880s–1920s." Pp. 229–254 in Siegwart Lindenberg, James S. Coleman, and Stefan Nowak (eds.), *Approaches to Social Theory.* New York: Russell Sage Foundation.

______. 1984. "Why not equal protection? Explaining the politics of public social welfare in Britain and the United States, 1880s–1920s." *American Sociological Review* 49:726–50.

Orum, Anthony. 1988. "Political sociology." Pp. 393–443 in Neil Smelser (ed.), *The Handbook of Sociology*. Newbury Park, CA: Sage.

______. 1996. "Political Sociology in the United States." In Baruch Kimmerling (ed.) *Political Sociology at the Crossroads. Current sociology*. 44(3).

______. 2001[1977, 1983, 1989]. *Introduction to Political Sociology*, 4th ed. Upper Saddle River, NJ: Prentice Hall.

Osborne, Thomas, and Nikolas Rose. 1999. "Do the social sciences create phenomena? The example of public opinion research." *British Journal of Sociology* 50:367–96.

Ost, David. 2000. "Illusory corporatism in Eastern Europe: Neoliberal tripartism and postcommunist class identities." *Politics & Society* 28:503–30.

Ostner, Ilona. 1997. "Lone mothers in Germany before and after unification." Pp. 21–49 in Jane Lewis (ed.), *Lone Mothers in European Welfare Regimes*. London: Jessica Kingsley.

Ostrogorski, Mosei. 1970. *Democracy and the Organization of Political Parties*. (Frederick Clarke, trans.). New York: Haskell House Publishers. (Original published as *Démocratie et l'organisation des partis politiques*, Paris, Calmann-Lévy, 1903.)

Ostrom, Elinor. 1990. *Governing the Commons: The Evolution of Institutions for Collective Action*. Cambridge, UK: Cambridge University Press.

Oszlak, Oscar. 1972. "Diagnóstico de la Administración Pública Uruguaya." New York: United Nations.

______. 1973. "Indicators of bureaucratic performance in Third World countries: Uses and limitations." *Philippine Journal of Public Administration*, Manila, July, 334–53.

______. 1976. *El INTI y el Desarrollo Tecnológico en la Industria Argentina*. Buenos Aires: Instituto Nacional de Tecnología Industrial.

______. 1977. "Notas críticas para una Teoría de la burocracia estatal." Working paper *CEDES/G.E. CLACSO*, Number 8. Buenos Aires.

______. 1982. *La formación del Estado Argentino*. Buenos Aires: Editorial Belgrano.

______. 1984. "Public policies and political regimes in Latin America." The Wilson Center, Latin American Program. Working Papers, Number 139. Washington, D.C.

______. 2001. "La Construcción de conceptos en ciencias sociales: una discusión sobre el desarrollo humano y la gobernabilidad democrática." *Magazine DHIAL*, Number 17. Barcelona: Instituto Interznacional de Gobernabilidad. www.iigov.org/dhial/?p=17_1.

Oszlak, Oscar, and Guillermo O'Donnell. 1976. "Estado y políticas públicas en América Latina: hacia una estrategia de investigación." *Documento G.E. CLACSO*. Number 4. Buenos Aires: CEDES.

Oszlak, Oscar, Jorge E. Roulet, Jorge F. Sábato and Néstor Lavergne. 1971. *Determinación de Objetivos y Asignación de Recursos en el Instituto Nacional de Tecnología Agropecuaria*. Buenos Aires: INTA.

Ottati, Victor C., and Robert S. Wyer, Jr. 1993. "Affect and political judgment." Pp. 264–95 in Shanto Iyengar and William J. McGuire (eds.), *Explorations in Political Psychology*. Durham, NC: Duke University Press.

Outhwaite, William, and Luke Martell. 1998. *The Sociology of Politics*. Cheltenham, UK: Edward Elgar.

Outshoorn, Joyce. 2004. *The Politics of Prostitution: Women's Movements, Democratic States, and the Globalisation of Sex Commerce*. Cambridge, UK: Cambridge University Press.

Overacker, Louise. 1932. *Money in Elections*. New York: Macmillan.

Overbeek, Henk. (ed.). 1993. *Restructuring Hegemony in the Global Political Economy: The Rise of Transnational Neo-liberalism in the 1980s*. London, UK: Routledge.

Ozouf, Mona. 1988/1976. *Festivals and the French Revolution*. Cambridge, MA: Harvard University Press.

Page, Benjamin. 1983. *Who Gets What from Government*. Berkeley: University of California Press.

Page, Benjamin I., and James Simmons. 2001. *What Government Can Do*. Chicago: University of Chicago Press.

Page, Benjamin I., and Robert Y. Shapiro. 1992. *The Rational Public: Fifty Years of Trends in Americans' Policy Preferences*. Chicago: University of Chicago Press.

Paige, Jeffery M. 1975. *Agrarian Revolution: Social Movements and Export Agriculture in the Underdeveloped World*. New York: Free Press.

______. 1997. *Coffee and Power: Revolution and the Rise of Democracy in Central America*. Cambridge, MA: Harvard University Press.

______. 1999. "Conjuncture, comparison, and conditional theory in macrosocial inquiry." *American Sociological Review* 105:781–800.

Pakulski, Jan, and Malcolm Waters. 1996. *The Death of Class*. London: Sage.

Paletz, David L. 1998, "The media and public policy." Pp. 218–237 in Doris Graber, Denis McQuail, and Pippa Norris (eds.), *The Politics of News/The News of Politics*. Washington, DC: CQ Press.

Palme, Joakim. 1990. *Pensions in Welfare Capitalism*. Stockholm: Swedish Institute for Social Research.

Palmer, Bryan D. 1988. *A Communist Life: Jack Scott and the Canadian Workers Movement, 1927–1985*.

St. John's, NFLD: Committee on Canadian Labour History.

______. 1990. *Descent into Discourse: The Reification of Language and the Writing of Social History*. Philadelphia: Temple University Press.

Palmer, Donald, and Brad M. Barber. 2001. "Challengers, elites, and owning families: A social class theory of corporate acquisitions in the 1960s." *Administrative Science Quarterly* 46:87–120.

Palmer, John. 1973. "The profit-performance effects of the separation of ownership from control in large United States corporations." *Bell Journal of Economics and Management Science* 4:293–303.

Pammett, Jon H., and Joan De Bardeleben. 2000. "Citizen orientations and political parties in Russia." *Party Politics* 6(3):373–84.

Pampel, Fred C., and John B. Williamson. 1985. "Age structure, politics and cross-national patterns of public pension expenditures." *American Sociological Review* 50:782–98.

______. 1989. *Age, Class, Politics and the Welfare State*. New York: Cambridge University Press.

Panebianco, Angelo. 1988. *Political Parties: Organization and Power*. Cambridge, UK: Cambridge University Press.

Panitch, Leo. 1998. "'The state in a changing world': Social-democratizing global capitalism?" *Monthly Review* 50(5):11–22.

Papathanassopoulos, Stylianos. 2001. "Media commercialization and journalism in Greece." *European Journal of Communication* 16:505–21.

Pappi, Franz Urban, and Christian H. C. A. Henning. 1998. "Policy networks: More than a metaphor?" *Journal of Theoretical Politics* 10:553–75.

Pareto, Vilfredo. 1963. *The Treatise on General Sociology*. New York: Dover.

Park, Robert Ezra. 1922. *The Immigrant Press and Its Control*. New York: Harper & Row.

______. 1928. "Human migration and the marginal man." *American Journal of Sociology* 33:881–93.

______. 1934. "Collective behavior." In *Encyclopedia of the Social Sciences*. New York: Macmillan.

Parkin, Frank. 1979. *Marxism and Class Theory*. New York: Columbia University Press.

______. 1982. *Max Weber*. Chinchester: Ellis Harwood.

Parsa, Misagh. 2000. *States, Ideologies, and Social Revolutions: A Comparative Analysis of Iran, Nicaragua, and the Philippines*. Cambridge, UK: Cambridge University Press.

Parsons, Talcott. 1935. "The Place of Ultimate Values in Sociological Theory." *International Journal of Ethics*, XLV, January: 282–316.

______. 1949. *The Structure of Social Action*. Glencoe, IL: The Free Press.

______. 1960. *Structure and Process in Modern Societies*. Glencoe, IL: The Free Press.

______. 1963. "On the concept of political power." *Proceedings of the American Philosophical Society* 107:232–62.

______. 1967. *Sociological Theory and Modern Society*. New York: The Free Press.

______. 1969. *Politics and Social Structure*. New York: The Free Press.

Pascall, G. 1986. *Social Policy: A Feminist Analysis*. London: Routledge.

______. 1988. *The Sexual Contract*. Stanford, CA: Stanford University Press.

______. 1989. *The Disorder of Women: Democracy, Feminism and Political Theory*. Cambridge, UK: Polity.

Patel, Rajeev. 2002. *Solidarity in a Time of Fascism: Feminism, Global Capital and Resistance from Zimbabwe*. Unpublished Ph.D. dissertation, Department of Sociology, Cornell University.

Patillo-McCoy, Mary. 1998. "Black church culture as a community strategy of action." *American Sociological Review* 63:767–84.

Patterson, Thomas E. 1993. *Out of Order*. New York: Alfred A. Knopf.

______. 1998. "Political roles of the journalist." Pp. 17–32 in Doris Graber, Denis McQuail, and Pippa Norris (eds.), *The Politics of News/The News of Politics*. Washington, DC: CQ Press.

Paul, Kathleen. 1996. *Whitewashing Britain: Race and Citizenship in the Postwar Era*. Ithaca, NY: Cornell University Press.

Pavalko, Eliza K., and Glen H. Elder Jr. 1990. "World War II and divorce: A life-course perspective." *American Journal of Sociology* 95:1213–34.

Pavarala, Vinod. 1996. *Interpreting Corruption: Elite Perspectives in India*. Thousand Oaks, CA: Sage.

Paxton, Pamela. 2000. "Women's suffrage in the measurement of democracy: Problems of operationalization." *Studies in Comparative International Development* 35:92–111.

Paxton, Robert. 1998. "The five stages of fascism." *Journal of Modern History*, March:1–23.

Payne, Leigh A. 2000. *Uncivil Movements. The Armed Right Wing and Democracy in Latin America*. Baltimore, MD: Johns Hopkins University Press.

Payne, Stanley G. 1980. Fascism, *Comparison and Definition*. Madison: University of Wisconsin Press.

______. 1995. *A History of Fascism* 1914–1945. Madison: University of Wisconsin Press.

Pearce, Frank. 1973. "How to be immoral and ill, pathetic and dangerous, all at the same time: Mass media and the homosexual." Pp. 284–301 in S. Cohen and J. Young (eds.), *The Manufacture of News: A Reader*. Beverly Hills: Sage.

Pearce, Jenny. 1986. *Promised Land: Peasant Rebellion in Chalatenango, El Salvador*. London: Zed Books.

Pearson, R. 2000. "All change? men, women and reproductive work in global economy." *European Journal of Development Research* 12:219–37.

Pêcheux, Michel. 1982. *Language, Semantics and Ideology*. London: Macmillan.

Pedazur, Ami, and Leonard Weinberg. 2003. *Political Parties and Terrorist Groups*. London: Routledge.

Pedersen, Mogens N. 1979. "The dynamics of European party systems: Changing patterns of electoral volatility." *European Journal of Political Research* 7:1–26.

Pedersen, Susan. 1989. "The failure of feminism in the making of the British welfare state." *Radical History Review* 43:86–110.

______. 1993. *Family, Dependence, and the Origins of the Welfare State*. New York: Cambridge University Press.

Pempel, T. J., and Keichi Tsunekawa. 1979. "Corporatism without labor? The Japanese anomaly." Pp. 231–70 in Philpge C. Schmitter and Gerhard Lehmbruch (eds.), *Trends toward Corporatist Intermediation*. London: Sage.

Pepper, Stephen C. 1972. *World Hypotheses: A Study in Evidence*. Berkeley: University of California Press.

Pérez-Liñan, Aníbal. 2003. "Presidential crisis and democratic accountability in Latin America (1990–1999)." In Susan Eckstein and Timothy Wickham-Crowley (eds.), *Whose Justice? What Justice?* Berkeley: University of California Press.

Pèrez-Stable, Marifeli. 1999. *The Cuban Revolution: Origins, Course, and Legacy*, second ed. New York: Oxford University Press.

Peri, Yoram. 1997. "The Rabin myth and the press: Reconstruction of the Israeli collective identity." *European Journal of Communication* 12:435–58.

Perkin, Harold. 1969. *The Origins of Modern English Society 1780–1880*. London: Routledge and Kegan Paul.

Perlmann, Joel, and Mary C. Waters. 2002. "The new race question: How the Census counts multiracial individuals." NY: Russell Sage Foundation.

Perlmutter, Ted. 1995. "Bringing parties back in: Comments on modes of immigration politics in liberal democratic societies." *International Migration Review* 30(1):375–88.

Perloff, Richard M. 1998. *Political Communication: Politics, Press and Public in America*. Mahwah, NJ: Erlbaum.

Perman, Michael. 1984. *The Road to Redemption: Southern Politics, 1869–1879*. Chapel Hill: University of North Carolina Press.

______. 2001. *Struggle for Mastery: Disfranchisement in the South, 1888–1908*. Chapel Hill: University of North Carolina Press.

Perrow, Charles. 1986. *Complex Organizations: A Critical Essay*. 3rd ed. New York: Random House.

______. 2002. *Organizing America: Wealth, Power, and the Origins of Corporate Capitalism*. Princeton, NJ: Princeton University Press.

Persinos, John F. 1994. "Has the Christian Right taken over the Republican Party?" *Campaigns and Elections* 15:21–4.

Peters, Guy. 1999. *La Política de la Burocracia*. México DF: Fondo de Cultura Económica. 1st ed. in Spanish, 4th ed. in English.

Petersen, William. 1978. "International migration." *Annual Review of Sociology* 4:533–75.

Peterson, Paul E. 1981. *City Limits*. Chicago: University of Chicago Press.

Peterson, V. Spike, and Anne Sisson Runyan. 1993. *Global Gender Issues*. Boulder, CO: Westview.

Petras, James F., and Maurice Zeitlin. 1967. *Latin America, Reform or Revolution?* Greenwich, CT: Fawcett.

Petras, James F., and Morris H. Morley. 1990. *U.S. Hegemony Under Siege: Class, Politics, and Development in Latin America*. London: Verso.

Petry, Francois. 1999. "The opinion–policy relationship in Canada." *Journal of Politics* 61:540–50.

Pettigrew, Thomas F., and Roel W. Meertens. 2001. "In defense of the subtle prejudice concept: A retort." *European Journal of Social Psychology* 31:299–309.

Pfaff, Steven, and Guobin Yang. 2001. "Double-edged rituals and the symbolic resources of collective action: Political commemorations and the mobilization of protest in 1989." *Theory and Society* 30:539–89.

Pfaff, William. 1993. *The Wrath of Nations: Civilization and the Furies of Nationalism*. New York: Simon and Schuster.

Pfeffer, Jeffrey. 1982. *Organizations and Organization Theory*. Boston: Pitman.

Pfeffer, Jeffrey, and Gerald Salancik. 1978. *The External Control of Organization: A Resource Dependence Perspective*. New York: Harper & Row.

Phillips, A. 1991. *Engendering Democracy*. Cambridge, UK: Polity, in association with Blackwell.

______. 1992. "Universal pretensions in political thought." Pp. 10–20 in A. Phillips and M. Barrett (eds.), *Destabilizing Theory: Contemporary Feminist Debates*. Cambridge, UK: Polity.

______. 1995. *The Politics of Presence*. Oxford, UK: Oxford University Press.

Phillips, Ulrich B. 1928. "The central theme of Southern history." *American Historical Review* 34: 30–43.

Phizacklea, Annie. 1980. *Labour and Racism*. London: Routledge & Kegan Paul.

Piazza, James. 2001. "De-linking labor: Labor unions and social democratic parties under globalization." *Party Politics* 7:413–35.

Picard, Robert G. 1998, "Media concentration, economics, and regulation." Pp. 193–217 in Doris Graber, Denis McQuail, and Pippa Norris (eds.), *The Politics of News/The News of Politics*. Washington, DC: CQ Press.

Pierson, Paul. 1993. "When effect becomes cause: Policy feedback and political change." *World Politics* 45:595–628.

______. 1994. *Dismantling the Welfare State: Reagan, Thatcher and the Politics of Retrenchment*. Cambridge, UK: Cambridge University Press.

______. 2000. "Increasing returns, path dependence, and the study of politics." *American Political Science Review* 94(2):251–67.

______. 2001a. "Coping with permanent austerity: welfare state restructuring in affluent democracies." Pp. 410–56 in Paul Pierson (ed.), *The New Politics of the Welfare State*. Oxford, UK: Oxford University Press.

______. 2001b. "Post-industrial pressures on mature welfare states." Pp. 80–104 in Paul Pierson (ed.), *The New Politics of the Welfare State*. New York: Oxford.

Pinto, António Costa. 1995. *Salazar's Dictatorship and European Fascism Problems of Interpretation*. Boulder, CO: Social Science Monographs.

Piven, Frances Fox, and Richard A. Cloward. 1977. *Poor People's Movements: Why They Succeed, How They Fail*. New York: Vintage/New York: Pantheon.

______. 1971. *Regulating the Poor*. New York: Vintage.

______. 1988. *Why Americans Don't Vote*. New York: Pantheon.

______. 1997. *The Breaking of the American Social Compact*. New York: The New Press.

______. 2000. *Why Americans Still Don't Vote*. New York: New Press.

Pizzorno, Alessandro. 1978. "Political exchange and collective identity in industrial conflict." Pp. 277–98 in Colin Crouch and Alessandro Pizzorno (eds.), *The Resurgence of Class Conflict in Western Europe since 1968*, vol. 2. London: Macmillan.

Plantenga, Janneke, and Johan Hansen. 1999. "Assessing the equal opportunities in the European Union." *International Labour Review* 138(4):351–79.

Plantenga, Janneke, and Kea Tijdens. 1995. "Segregation in the European Union: Developments in the 1980s." Pp. 15–30 in Anneke van Doorne-Huiskes, Jacques van Hoof, and Ellie Roelofs (eds.), *Women and the European Labor Markets*. London: Paul Chapman.

Plasser, Fritz, and Ulram, Peter A. 2003. "Striking a responsive chord: Mass media and right-wing populism in Austria." In Gianpietro Mazzoleni, Julianne Stewart, and Bruce Horsfield (eds.), *The Media and Neo-Populism*. Westport, CT: Praeger.

Platt, Gerald M., and Michael R. Fraser. 1998. "Race and gender discourse strategies: Creating solidarity and framing the civil rights movement." *Social Problems* 45:160–79.

Plotke, David. 2002. "The success and anger of the modern American Right." Pp. xxx in Daniel Bell (ed.), *The Radical Right*. 3rd ed. New Brunswick, NJ: Transaction.

Plummer, Brenda Gayl. 1996. *Rising Wind: Black Americans and U.S. Foreign Affairs, 1935–1960*. Chapel Hill: University of North Carolina Press.

Plutzer, Eric, and John F. Zipp. 1996. "Identity politics, partisanship, and voting for women candidates." *Public Opinion Quarterly* 60:30–57.

Pluvier, Jan. 1974. *South-East Asia from Colonialism to Independence*. Kuala Lumpur: Oxford University Press.

Pochet, Philippe, and Gustav Fajertag. 2000. "A new era for social pacts in Europe." Pp. 9–40 in G. Fajertag and P. Pochet (eds.), *Social Pacts in Europe – New Dynamics*. Brussels: OSE-ETUI.

Poggi, Gianfranco. 1978. *The Development of the Modern State: A Sociological Introduction*. Palo Alto, CA: Stanford University Press.

______. 1990. *The State: Its Nature, Development and Prospects*. Stanford, CA: Stanford University Press.

______. 2001. *Forms of Power*. Malden, MA: Polity Press.

Polanyi, Karl. 2001[1944]. *The Great Transformation: The Political and Economic Origins of Our Time*. Boston: Beacon.

______. 1957. *The Great Transformation. The Political and Economic Origins of Our Times*. Boston: Beacon.

______. 1971. "Our obsolete market mentality" (1947). Pp. 59–77 in George Dalton (ed.), *Primitive, Archaic and Modern Economies. Essays of Karl Polanyi*. Boston: Beacon.

Polletta, Francesca. 1998. "'It was like a fever . . .': Narrative and identity in social protest." *Social Problems* 45:137–59.

Polletta, Francesca, and James M. Jasper. 2001. "Collective identity and social movements." *Annual Review of Sociology* 27:283–305.

Polsby, Nelson W. 1960. "How to study community power: the pluralist alternative." *Journal of Politics* 22:474–84.

______. 1980. *Community Power and Political Theory: A Further Look and Problems of Evidence and Inference*, 2nd ed. New Haven, CT: Yale University Press.

"Polyarchy Dataset, The. Tatu Vanhanen's Index of Democracy." 2000. http://www.sv.ntnu.no/iss/data/vanhanen/ University of Helsinki, Finland.

Pomper, Gerald M. 1978. "The impact of *The American Voter* on political science." *Political Science Quarterly* 91:617–28.

Poole, Keith, and Howard Rosenthal. 1997. *Congress: A Political Economic History of Roll Call Voting*. Oxford, UK: Oxford University Press.

Pope, James Gray. 1997. "Labor's Constitution of Freedom." *Yale Law Journal* 106:941–1031.

Popkin, Samuel L. 1991. *The Reasoning Voter: Communication and Persuasion in Presidential Campaigns*. Chicago: University of Chicago Press.

Popper, Karl. 1959. *The Logic of Scientific Discovery*. London: Hutchinton.

Porter, John. 1965. *The Vertical Mosaic*. Toronto, Canada: University of Toronto Press.

Portes, Alejandro. 1997. "Immigration theory for a new century: Some problems and opportunities." *International Migration Review* 31(4):799–825.

______. 2000. "The hidden abode: Sociology as the analysis of the unexpected." *American Sociological Review* 65:1–18.

Portugese, Jacqueline. 1998. *Fertility Policy in Israel: The Politics of Religion, Gender, and Nation*. Westport, CT: Praeger.

Poster, Mark. 1990. *The Mode of Information*. Chicago: University of Chicago Press.

Potter, Jonathan, and Margaret Wetherell. 1987. *Discourse and Social Psychology*. London: Sage.

Potter, Trevor. 1997. "Issue advocacy and express advocacy." Pp. 227–39 in Anthony Corrado, Thomas E. Mann, Daniel Ortiz, Trevor Potter, and Frank Sorauf (eds.), *Campaign Finance Reform: A Sourcebook*. Washington, D.C.: Brookings Institute.

Poulantzas, Nicos. 1967. "Marxist political theory in Great Britain." *New Left Review* 43:57–74.

______. 1972. "The problem of the capitalist state." Pp. 238–53 in R. Blackburn (ed.), *Ideology in Social Science*. London: Fontana.

______. 1973a. *Political Power and Social Classes* (Timothy O'Hagan, trans.). London: NLB.

______. 1973b. "On social classes." *New Left Review* 78:27–54.

______. 1976. "The capitalist state: a reply to Miliband and Laclau." *New Left Review* 95:63–83.

______. 1978a. *State, Power Socialism* (Timothy O'Hagan, trans.). London: NLB.

______. 1978b. *Classes in Contemporary Capitalism*. London, UK: Verso.

Powell, G. Bingham. 2000. *Elections as Instruments of Democracy: Majoritarian and Proportional Views*. New Haven, CT: Yale University Press.

Powell, Walter W. 1990. "Neither market nor hierarchy: Network forms of organizations." Pp. 295–336 in Barry M. Staw and Larry L. Cummings (eds.), *Research in Organizational Behavior*, Vol. 12. Greenwich, CT: JAI Press.

Powell, Walter W., and Paul J. DiMaggio (eds.). 1991. *The New Institutionalism in Organizational Analysis*. Chicago: University of Chicago Press.

Power, Margaret. 2000. "Class and gender in the anti-Allende women's movement: Chile 1970–1973." *Social Politics* 7(3):289–308.

Prechel, Harland. 1990. "Steel and the state: industry politics and business policy formation, 1940–1989." *American Sociological Review* 55:634–47.

______. 1991. "Conflict and historical variation in steel capital-state relations: the emergence of state structures and a more prominent, less autonomous state." *American Sociological Review* 56:693–98.

______. 2000. *Big Business and the State: Historical Transitions and Corporate Transformation, 1880s–1990s*. Albany, NY: State University of New York Press.

______. 2003. "Historical contingency theory, policy paradigm shifts, and corporate malfeasance at the turn of the 21st century." Pp. 311–40 in Betty Dobratz, Lisa Waldner, and Timothy Buzzell (eds.), *Research in Political Sociology Vol. 12: Political Sociology for the 21st Century*. Amsterdam: JAI.

Presser, Harriet. 1997. "Demography, feminism, and the science-policy nexus." *Population and Development Review* 23(2):295–331.

Presthus, Robert. 1962. *The Organizational Society. An Analysis and a Theory*. New York: Vintage.

______. 1964. *Men at the Top: A Study of Community Power*. New York: Oxford University Press.

Preston, Paul. 1990. *The Politics of Revenge. Fascism and the Military in 20th Centuary Spain*. London: Unwin Hyman.

Prewitt, Kenneth. 2002. "Race in the 2000 Census: A turning point." Pp. 354–61 in J. Perlmann and M. C. Waters (eds.), *The New Race Question: How the Census Counts Multiracial Individuals*. NY: Russell Sage Foundation.

Prewitt, Kenneth, and Norman H. Nie. 1971. "Election studies of the survey research center." *British Journal of Political Science* 1:479–502.

Prillaman, William C. 2000. *The Judiciary and Democratic Decay in Latin America: Declining Confidence in the Rule of Law*. Westport, CT: Praeger.

Provan, Keith, and H. Brinton Milward. 2001. "Do networks really work? A framework for evaluating public-sector organizational networks." *Public Administration Review* 61(4):414–23.

Przeworski, Adam, 1985a. "Marxism and rational choice." *Politics & Society* 14(4):379–409.

______. 1985b. *Capitalism and Social Democracy*. Cambridge, UK: Cambridge University Press.

______. 1986. "Some problems in the study of transitions to democracy." Pp. 47–63 in G. O'Donnell, P. C. Schmitter, and L. Whitehead (eds.), *Transitions from Authoritarian Rule: Comparative Perspectives*. Baltimore: Johns Hopkins University Press.

______. 1991. *Democracy and the Market: Political and Economic Reforms in Eastern Europe and Latin America*. Cambridge, UK: Cambridge University Press.

______. 1997. "Democratization Revisited." *Items* 51(1):6–11.

______. 2004. "Politics and Administration." Pp. 195–215 in Bresser Pereira, et al., *Politica y Gestión Publica*. Buenos Aires: Fondo de Cultura Económica.

Przeworski, Adam, and Henry Teune. 1970. *The Logic of Comparative Social Inquiry*. New York: Wiley-Interscience.

Przeworski, Adam, and John Sprague, 1988. *Paper Stones: A History of Electoral Socialism*. Chicago: University of Chicago Press.

Przeworski, Adam, and Michael Wallerstein. 1982. "The structure of class conflict in democratic capitalist societies." *American Political Science Review* 76:215–238.

______. 1988. "Structural dependence of the state on capital." *American Political Science Review* 82:11–31.

Przeworski, Adam, Michael E. Alvarez, José Antonio Cheibub, and Fernando Limongi. 2000. *Democracy and Development: Political Institutions and Material Well-Being in the World, 1950–1990*. Cambridge, UK: Cambridge University Press.

Pulver, Simone. 2003. Power in the Public Sphere: Oil companies and environmental groups in the UN climate change negotiations: Book manuscript. Watson Institute for International Studies, Brown University.

Putnam, Hilary. 1983. *Realism and Reason*. New York: Cambridge University Press.

Putnam, Robert D. 1993. *Making Democracy Work: Civic Traditions in Modern Italy*. Princeton, NJ: Princeton University Press.

______. 1993. "Diplomacy and domestic politics: the logic of two level games." In Peter Evans, Harold Jacobson, and Robert Putnam (eds.), *Doubled-Edged Diplomacy*. Berkeley: University of California Press.

______. 1995. "Bowling alone: America's declining social capital." *Journal of Democracy* 6:65–78.

______. 2000. *Bowling Alone: The Collapse and Revival of American Community*. New York: Simon and Schuster.

Pyle, Jean. 1997. "Women, the family, and economic restructuring: The Singapore model?" *Review of Social Economy* LV(2):215–53.

Quadagno, Jill S. 1984. "Welfare capitalism and the Social Security Act of 1935." *American Sociological Review* 49:632–47.

______. 1985. "Two models of welfare state development: Reply to Skocpol and Amenta." *American Sociological Review* 50:575–8.

______. 1988. *The Transformation of Old Age Security: Class and Politics in the American Welfare State*. Chicago: University of Chicago Press.

______. 1994[1996, paperback]. *The Color of Welfare: How Racism Undermined the War on Poverty*. New York: Oxford University Press.

Quadagno, Jill, and S. J. Knapp. 1992. "Have historical sociologists forsaken theory – thoughts on the history–theory relationship." *Sociological Methods and Research* 20(4):481–507.

Quattrone, George A., and Amos Tversky. 1988. "Contrasting rational and psychological analysis of political choice." *American Political Science Review* 82:719–36.

Quine, Willard van Orman. 1971. *From a Logical Point of View*. Cambridge, MA: Harvard University Press.

Quinn, Dennis, and Carla Inclan. 1997. "The origins of financial openness: A 21 country study of its determinants, 1950–1988." *American Journal of Political Science* 41:771–813.

Quinney, Richard. 1973. *The Social Reality of Crime*. Boston: Little Brown.

Quintilian. 2001. *Quintilian: The Orator's Education*. Cambridge, MA: Harvard University Press, Loeb Classical Library.

Quirk, Paul J., and Joseph Hinchliffe. 1998. "The rising hegemony of mass opinion." *Journal of Policy History* 10:19–50.

Raab, Charles D. 1992. "Taking networks seriously: Education policy in Britain." *European Journal of Political Research* 21:60–90.

Raab, Jörg. 2002. "Where do policy networks come from?" *Journal of Public Administration Research and Theory* 12:581–622.

Raadschelders, Jos, and Mark Rutgers. 1996. "The evolution of civil service systems." Pp. 67–100 in H. Bekke, J. Perry, and T. Toonen (eds.), *Civil Service Systems*. Bloomington: Indiana University Press.

Rabin, Matt. 1998. "Psychology and economics." *Journal of Economic Literature* 36:11–46.

Radcliff, Benjamin, and Patricia Davis. 2000. "Labor organization and electoral participation in industrial democracies." *American Journal of Political Science* 44:132–41.

Radice, Hugo. 1998. "Responses to globalization: A critique of progressive nationalism." *New Political Economy* 5(1):5–19.

Ragin, Charles. 1987. *The Comparative Method*. Berkeley: University of California Press.

______. 1994. "A Quantitative Comparative Analysis of Pension Systems." Pp. 320–45 in Thomas Janoski and Alexander Hicks (eds.), *The Comparative Political Economy of the Welfare State*. New York: Cambridge University Press.

______. 2000. *Fuzzy Set Social Science*. Chicago: University of Chicago Press.

Raiffa, Howard. 2003. *Negotiation Analysis*. Cambridge, MA: Belknap Press/Harvard University Press.

Rama, Martín. 1997. "Efficient public sector downsizing." *Policy Research Working Paper 1840*. Washington, DC: World Bank.

Ramirez, Manuel Becerra. 2000. "Nationality in Mexico." Pp. 312–41 in T. Alexander Aleinkoff and Douglas Klusmeyer (eds.), *From Immigrants to Citizens*. Washington, D.C.: Carnegie Endowment for International Peace.

Randall, Vicky. 1998. "Gender and power: Women engage the state." Pp. 185–205 in Vicky Randall and Georgina Waylen (eds.), *Gender, Politics, and the State*. New York: Routledge.

Ranney, David. 2003. *Global Decisions/Local Collisions: Urban Life in the New World Order*. Philadelphia, PA: Temple University Press.

Rasler, Karen. 1996. "Concessions, repression and political protest in the Iranian revolution." *American Sociological Review* 61:132–52.

Rasler, Karen, and William Thompson. 1988. "Defense burdens, capital formation, and economic growth." *Journal of Conflict Resolution* 32:61–86.

Ratcliff, Richard E. 1980. "Banks and corporate lending: An analysis of the impact of the internal structure of the capitalist class on the lending behavior of banks." *American Sociological Review* 45:553–70.

Ratcliff, Richard E., Mary Elizabeth Gallagher, and Kathryn Strother Ratcliff. 1979. "The civic involvement of bankers: An analysis of the influence of economic power and social prominence in the command of civic policy positions." *Social Problems* 26:298–313.

Razavi, Shahra. 1998. "Becoming multilingual: The challenges of feminist policy advocacy." Pp. 20–41 in Carol Miller and Shahra Razavi (eds.), *Missionaries and Mandarins*. London: United Nations Research Institute for Social Development.

Redding, Kent. 2003. *Making Race, Making Power: North Carolina's Road to Disfranchisement*. Urbana: University of Illinois Press.

Redding, Kent, and David R. James. 2001. "Estimating levels and modeling determinants of black and white voter turnout in the South, 1880 to 1912." *Historical Methods* 34:141–58.

Redding, Kent, and Jocelyn S. Viterna. 1999. "Political demands, political opportunities: Explaining the differential success of left-libertarian parties." *Social Forces* 78:491–510.

Reed, Adolph, Jr. 2000. *Class Notes: Posing as Politics and Other Thoughts on the American Scene*. New York: New Press.

______. 2002. "Unraveling the relation of race and class in American politics." *Political Power and Social Theory* 15:265–74.

Reed, Adolph, Jr., and Julian Bond. 1991. "Equality: Why we can't wait." *The Nation* 253:733–8.

Reeves, Keith. 1997. *Voting Hopes or Fears?* New York: Oxford University Press.

Regini, Marino. 2000. "Between deregulation and social pacts: The responses of European economies to globalization." *Politics and Society* 28:5–33.

Regnerus, M., D. Sikkink, and C. Smith. 1999. "Voting with the Christian Right: Contextual and individual patterns of electoral influence." *Social Forces* 77:375–401.

Reinarman, Craig. 1987. *American States of Mind: Political Beliefs and Behavior among Private and Public Workers*. New Haven, CT: Yale University Press.

Reiter, Dan, and Allan Stam. 2002. *Democracies at War*. Princeton, NJ: Princeton University Press.

Reiter, Howard L. 1979. "Why is turnout down?" *Public Opinion Quarterly* 43:297–311.

______. 1993. *Parties and Elections in Corporate America*. New York: Longman.

Rémond, René. 1982. *Les Droites en France*. Paris: Aubier.

Renan, Ernest. 1994. *Qu'est-ce qu'une nation*. Leiden: Academic Press.

Renfro-Sargent, Matthew, and Thomas Janoski. 2001. "Citizen deliberation in the political process: Sociological theories of town meetings, citizen boards and deliberative polls." Paper presented at the 2002 American Sociological Association Meetings in Chicago.

Rex, John. 1979. "Black militancy and class conflict." Pp. 72–92 in Robert Miles and Annie Phizacklea (eds.), *Racism and Political Action in Britain*. London: Routledge & Kegan Paul.

Rex, John, and Robert Moore. 1967. *Race, Community and Conflict*. Oxford, UK: Oxford University Press.

Rham, Gérard de. 1990. "Naturalisation: The politics of citizenship acquisition." Pp. 158–85 in Zig Layton-Henry (ed.), *The Political Rights of Migrant Workers in Western Europe*. Newbury Park, CA: Sage.

Rhoades, Gary. 1990. "Political competition and differentiation in higher education." Pp. 187–221 in Jeffrey C. Alexander and Paul Colomy (eds.), *Differentiation Theory and Social Change*. New York: Columbia University Press.

Rhodes, R. A. W. 1985. "Power dependence, policy communities and inter-governmental networks." *Public Administration Bulletin* 49:4–29.

______. 1990. "Policy networks: A British perspective." *Journal of Theoretical Politics* 2(3):293–317.

______. 1996. "The new governance: Governing without government." *Political Studies* 44:652–67.

Ricci, David. 1993. *The Transformation of American Politics: The New Washington and the Rise of Think Tanks.* New Haven, CT: Yale University Press.

Rice, Stuart A. 1969 [1928]. *Quantitative Methods in Politics.* New York: Russell and Russell.

Richardson, Jeremy J. 2000. "Government, interests groups and policy change." *Political Studies* 48:1006–25.

Richardson, Jeremy J., and A. Grant Jordan. 1979. *Governing Under Pressure.* Oxford, UK: Martin Robertson.

Richardson, Jeremy. 2001. "Policy-making in the EU: Interests, ideas and garbage cans of primeval soup." Pp. 3–26 in Jeremy Richardson (ed.), *European Union: Power and Policy-Making, 2nd Edition.* London: Routledge.

Ricoeur, Paul. 1984. *Time and Narrative.* Vol. I. Chicago: University of Chicago Press.

Rieder, Jonathan. 1985. *Canarsie: The Jews and Italians of Brooklyn against Liberalism.* Cambridge, MA: Harvard University Press.

Riesman, David. 1953. *The Lonely Crowd.* Garden City, NY: Anchor.

Riggs, Fred W. 1950. *Pressures on Congress: A Study of the Repeal of Chinese Exclusion.* New York: King's Crown.

______. 1964. *The Theory of Prismatic Society.* Boston: Houghton Mifflin.

______. 1971. *Frontiers of Development Administration.* Durham, NC: Duke University Press.

Riker, William H. 1962. *The Theory of Political Coalitions.* New Haven, CT: Yale University Press.

______. 1984. "The heresthetics of constitution-making." *American Political Science Review* 78:1–16.

Riker, William H., and Peter C. Ordeshook. 1973. *An Introduction to Positive Political Theory.* Englewood Cliffs, NJ: Prentice Hall.

Rimlinger, Gaston V. 1971. *Welfare Policy and Industrialization in America, Germany and Russia.* New York: Wiley.

Ringdal, K., and K. Hines. 1999. "Changes in class voting in Norway, 1957–1989." Pp. 182–202 in Geoffrey Evans (ed.), *The End of Class Politics? Class Voting in Comparative Context.* New York: Oxford University Press.

Riordon, William L. 1963. *Plunkitt of Tammany Hall.* New York: E. P. Dutton.

Ripley, Randall and Grace Franklin. 1982. *Bureaucracy and Policy Implementation.* Chicago: Dorsey.

Risse-Kappen, Thomas. 2000. "The power of norms versus the norms of power: Transnational civil society and human rights." Pp. 177–209 in A. Florini and N. K. K. Senta (eds.). *The Third Force: The Rise of Transnational Civil Society.* Tokyo: Japan Center for International Exchange; Washington, D.C.: Carnegie Endowment for International Peace.

Risse-Kappen, Thomas, Steve C. Ropp, and Kathryn Sikkink. 1999. *The Power of Human Rights: International Norms and Domestic Change. Cambridge. Studies in International Relations; 66.* New York: Cambridge University Press.

Rist, Gilbert. 1997. *The History of Development. From Western Origins to Global Faith.* London: Zed.

Ritchey, P. Neal. 1976. "Explanations of migration." *Annual Review of Sociology* 2:363–404.

Ritchie, Mark. 1993. *Breaking the Deadlock. The United States and Agricultural Policy in the Uruguay Round.* Minneapolis: Institute for Agriculture and Trade Policy.

Robbin, Alice. 2000. "Administrative policy as symbol system: Political conflict and the social construction of identity." *Administration & Society* 32:398–431.

Roberts, G. 2001. *Leaving Readers Behind: The Age of Corporate Newspapering.* Fayetteville, AK: University of Arkansas Press.

Roberts, Nancy. 2002. "Keeping public officials accountable through dialogue: Resolving the accountability paradox." *Public Administration Review* 62(6):658–69.

Robin, Ron. 2001. *The Making of the Cold War Enemy: Culture and Politics in the Military–Industrial Complex.* Princeton, NJ: Princeton University Press.

Robinson, William. 1996. *Promoting Polyarchy: Globalization, US Intervention, and Hegemony.* Cambridge, UK: Cambridge University Press.

Robnett, Belinda. 1997. *How Long? How Long? African American Women in the Struggle for Civil Rights.* New York: Oxford University Press.

Roche, Jeff. 1998. *Restructured Resistance: The Sibley Commission and the Politics of Desegregation in Georgia.* Athens: University of Georgia Press.

Rochon, Thomas R. 1998. *Culture Moves.* Princeton, NJ: Princeton University Press.

Rockwell, R., and N. Janus. 2001. "Stifling dissent: The fallout from a Mexican media invasion of Central America." *Journalism Studies* 2:497–512.

Rodriguez, Clara E. 2000. *Changing Race: Latinos, the Census, and the History of Ethnicity in the United States.* New York: New York University Press.

Rodrik, Dani. 1997. *Has Globalization Gone Too Far?* Washington, D.C.: Institute for International Economics.

______. 1998. "Why do more open economies have bigger governments?" *Journal of Political Economy* 106:997–1032.

Roe, Mark J. 1994. *Strong Managers, Weak Owners.* Princeton, NJ: Princeton University Press.

Roebroek, Joop, and Theo Berben. 1987. "Netherlands." Pp. 751–810 in P. Flora (ed.), *Growth to Limits*, Vol. 4. New York: Walter de Gruyter.

Roemer, John (ed.). 1986. *Analytical Marxism.* Cambridge, UK: Cambridge University Press.

Rogers, Mary F. 1974. "Instrumental and infra-resources: the bases of power." *American Journal of Sociology* 79:1418–33.

Rokeach, Milton. 1968. "The role of values in public opinion research." *Public Opinion Quarterly* 32:547–59.

Rokkan, Stein. 1966. "Norway: Numerical democracy and corporate pluralism." Pp. 70–115 in Robert A. Dahl (ed.), *Political Oppositions in Western Europe.* New Haven, CT: Yale University Press.

______. 1973. "Cities, states and nations: A dimensional model for the study of contrasts in development." Pp. 73–97 in S. N. Eisenstadt and Stein Rokkan (eds.), *Building States and Nations.* Beverly Hills: Sage.

______. 1975. "Dimensions of state formation and nation-building: A possible paradigm for research on variations in Europe." Pp. 562–600 in Charles Tilly (ed.), *The Formation of National States in Western Europe.* Princeton, NJ: Princeton University Press.

______. 1981. "Territories, nations, parties: Toward a geoeconomic-geopolitical model for the explanation of variations within Western Europe." Pp. 70–95 in Richard Merritt and Bruce Russett (eds.), *From National Development to Global Community.* London: George Allen & Unwin.

______. 1999. *State Formation, Nation-Building and Mass Politics in Europe: The Theory of Stein Rokkan* (Peter Flora, ed.). Oxford, UK: Oxford University Press.

Romer, Thomas, and James Snyder. 1994. "An empirical investigation of the dynamics of PAC contributions." *American Journal of Political Science* 38:745–69.

Rommele, Andrea. 1999. "Cleavage structures and party systems in East and Central Europe." Pp. 3–17 in Kay Lawson, Andrea Rommele, and Georgi Karasimeonov (eds.), *Cleavages, Parties and Voters: Studies from Bulgaria, the Czech Republic, Hungary, Poland and Romania.* Westport, CT: Praeger.

Romzeck, Barbara, and Melvin Dubnick. 1987. "Accountability in the public sector: Lessons from the Challenger tragedy." *Public Administration Review*, 47(3):227–38.

Ronit, Karsten, and Volker Schneider. 1999. "Global governance through private organizations." *Governance* 12(3):243–66.

Rønning, H., and T. Kupe. 2000. "The dual legacy of democracy and authoritarianism: The media and the state in Zimbabwe." Pp. 157–77 in J. Curran and M. Park (eds.), *De-Westernizing Media Studies.* London: Routledge.

Root, Hilton. 1994. *Fountains of Privilege.* Berkeley: University of California Press.

Rorty, Richard. 1989. *Contingency, Irony, and Solidarity.* Cambridge, UK: Cambridge University Press.

Roscigno, Vincent J. 1992. "Conservative and critical approaches to the power structure debate: An assessment and critique of empirical findings." *Journal of Political and Military Sociology* 20:63–81.

Rose, Arnold M. 1967. *The Power Structure.* New York: Oxford University Press.

Rose, Melody. 2001. "Losing control: The intraparty consequences of divided government." *Presidential Studies Quarterly* 31: 679–98.

Rose, Richard. 1980. *Do Parties Make a Difference?* Chatham, NJ: Chatham House Press.

Rose, Richard, and Doh Chull Shin. 2001. "Democratization backwards: The problem of third-wave democracies." *British Journal of Political Science* 31: 331–54.

Rose, Richard, William Mishler, and Christian Haerpfer. 1998. *Democracy and its alternatives: Understanding Post-Communist Societies.* Baltimore, MD: The Johns Hopkins University Press.

Rose, Tricia. 1994. *Black Noise: Rap Music and Black Culture in Contemporary America.* Hanover, NH: University Press of New England.

Rosenau, Pauline Marie. 1992. *Post-Modernism and the Social Sciences.* Princeton, NJ: Princeton University Press.

Rosenberg, Justin. 2000. *The Follies of Globalisation Theory.* London: Verso.

______. 2001. *The Empire of Civil Society.* 2nd ed. London: Verso.

Rosenfeld, Susan. 2001. *A Revolution in Language: The Problem of Signs in Late Eighteenth-Century France.* Stanford, CA: Stanford University Press.

Rosenstone, Steven J., and John M. Hansen. 1993. *Mobilization, Participation, and Democracy in America.* New York: MacMillan.

Rosenstone, Steven J., Roy L. Behr, and Edward H. Lazarus. 1996. *Third Parties in America*, 2nd ed. rev. and enlarged. Princeton, NJ: Princeton University Press.

Rosenthal, H. 1990. "The setter model." Pp. 61–87 in J. M. Enelow and M. J. Hinich (eds.), *Advances in the Spatial Theory of Voting*. New York: Cambridge University Press.

Rosenthal, Jean-Laurent. 1998. "The political economy of absolutism reconsidered." Pp. 64–108 in Robert Bates, Avner Greif, Margaret Levi, Jean-Laurent Rosenthal, and Barry Weingast (eds.), *Analytic Narratives*. Princeton, NJ: Princeton University Press.

Rostow, W. W. 1967[1961]. "Guerrilla warfare in underdeveloped areas." Pp. 108–16 in Marcus G. Raskin and Bernard B. Fall (eds.), *The Viet-Nam Reader*, revised ed. New York: Random House.

Roth, Guenther. 1963. *The Social Democrats in Imperial Germany: A Study in Working-Class Isolation and National Intergration*. Totowa, NJ: Bedminster Press.

Rothenberg, Larry. 1992. *Linking Citizens to Government: Interest Group Politics in Common Cause*. Cambridge, UK: Cambridge University Press.

Rouhana, Nadim N., and Daniel Bar-Tal. 1998. "Psychological dynamics of intractable ethnonational conflicts: the Israeli–Palestinian case." *American Psychologist* 53:761–70.

Rouquié, Alain. 1984. *O Estado Militar na América Latina*. São Paulo: Alpha-Omega. Also published in English in 1987, *The Military and the State in Latin America*. Berkeley: University of California Press.

Rourke, Francis. 1984. *Bureaucracy, Politics and Public Policy*, 3rd ed. Boston: Little, Brown.

Rousseau, Jean Jacques. 1762. *Emilius and Sophia: Or, a New System of Education*, vol. 2. London: T. Becket and P. A. Hondt.

Rousseau, Jean-Jacques. 1964. *Du Contrat Social. Ecrits Politiques*, vol. 3. Paris: Gallimard.

Rowthorn, Robert. 1992. "Corporatism and labour market performance." Pp. 82–131 in Jukka Pekkarinen, Matti Pohjola, and Bob Rowthorn (eds.), *Social Corporatism*. Oxford, UK: Oxford University Press.

______. 1995. "Capital formation and unemployment." *Oxford Review of Economic Policy* 11:29–39.

Rozell, Mark J., and Clyde Wilcox. 1999. *Interest Groups in American Campaigns*. Washington, DC: CQ Press.

Rubio-Marín, Ruth. 2000. *Immigration as a Democratic Challenge: Citizenship and Inclusion in Germany and the United States*. Cambridge, UK: Cambridge University Press.

Ruddick, Sara. 1984. "Maternal thinking." Pp. xxx in Joyce Trebilcot (ed.), *Mothering: Essays in Feminist Theory*. Totowa, NJ: Rowman & Allanheld.

______. 1984. "Maternal thinking." *Feminist Studies.* 6:2:342–67.

Rude, George. 1964. *The Crowd in History*. New York: Wiley.

Rueda, David, and Jonas Pontusson. 2000. "Wage inequality and varieties of capitalism." *World Politics* 52:350–83.

Rueschemeyer, Dietrich, and Peter B. Evans. 1985. "The state and economic transformation: Toward an analysis of the conditions underlying effective intervention." Pp. 44–77 in P. Evans, D. Rueschemeyer, and T. Skocpol (eds.), *Bringing the State Back In*. Cambridge, UK: Cambridge University Press.

Rueschemeyer, Dietrich, Evelyne Huber Stephens, and John D. Stephens. 1992. *Capitalist Development and Democracy*. Chicago: University of Chicago Press.

Ruffner, Michael. 2002. "Governing for results." Paper presented at *Congreso Internacional del CLAD sobre la Reforma del Estado y de la Administración Pública*. Lisboa, October 8–11.

Ruggie, John G. 1982. "International regimes, transactions, and change: Embedded liberalism in the postwar economic order." *International Organization* 36(2):195–231.

______. 1983. "International regimes, transactions and change. Embedded liberalism in the post-war economic order." In Stephen D. Krasner (ed.), *International Regimes*. Ithaca, NY: Cornell University Press.

______. 1994. "At home abroad, abroad at home.' International liberalization and domestic stabilization in the new world economy." *Millennium: Journal of International Studies* 24(3):507–26.

______. 1996. "Globalization and the embedded liberalism compromise: end of an era?" Working paper 97/1, Max Planck Institut für Gesellschaftsforschung, Cologne.

Ruggie, Mary. 1996. *Realignments in the Welfare State. Health Policy in the United States, Britain, and Canada*. New York: Columbia University Press.

Ruiz, Javier Astudillo. 2001. "Without unions, but socialist: The Spanish Socialist party and its divorce from its union confederation (1982–96)." *Politics and Society* 29:273–96.

Rule, James B. 1997. *Theory and Progress in Social Science*. Cambridge, UK: Cambridge University Press.

Rule, Wilma, and Joseph F. Zimmerman (eds.). 1992. *United States Electoral Systems: Their Impact on Women and Minorities*. Westport, CT: Praeger.

Rupp, Leila J. 1997. *Worlds of Women: The Making of an International Women's Movement*. Princeton, NJ: Princeton University Press.

Russell, Bertrand. 1938. *Power: A New Social Analysis.* London: George Allen and Unwin.

Ryan, M., C. Swanson, and R. Buchholz. 1987. *Corporate Strategy, Public Policy and the Fortune 500: How America's Major Corporations Influence Government.* Oxford, UK: Blackwell.

Saatci, Mustafa. 2002. "Nation-states and ethnic boundaries: Modern Turkish identity and Turkish–Kurdish conflict." *Nations and Nationalism* 8:549–64.

Sabato, Larry J. 1984. *PAC Power: Inside the World of Political Action Committees.* New York: Norton.

______. (ed.). 1989. *Campaigns and Elections.* Glenview, IL: Scott, Foresman.

______. 2000. *Feeding Frenzy: Attack Journalism and American Politics.* Baltimore, MD: Lanahan.

Sachs, Jeffrey. 1998. "The IMF and the Asian flu." *The American Prospect* March–April:16–21.

Sachs, Wolfgang. 1992. "One world." Pp. 3–21 in Wolfgang Sachs (ed.), *Global Ecology.* London: Zed.

Sacks, K. 1974. "Engels revisited." Pp. 207–222 in M. Rosaldo and L. Lamphere (eds.), *Woman, Culture and Society.* Stanford, CA: Stanford University Press.

Sadik, Nafis. 1997. "Cairo conference goals begin to gain momentum." *Forum for Applied Research and Public Policy* 12:16–19.

Safa, Helen I. 1993. "The new women workers: Does money equal power?" *NACLA Report on the Americas,* 27(1):24–29.

Saguy, Abigail C. 1999. "Puritanism and promiscuity? Sexual attitudes in France and the United States." *Comparative Social Research* 18:227–47.

______. 2000. "Sexual harrassment in France and the United States: Activists and public figures defend their definitions." Pp. 56–93 in M. Lamont and L. Thévenot (eds.), *Rethinking Comparative Cultural Sociology.* New York: Cambridge University Press.

Said, Edward W. 1978. *Orientalism.* New York: Pantheon.

Sainsbury, Diane. 1994. *Gender and Welfare State Regimes.* New York: Oxford University Press.

______. 1996. *Gender, Equality, and Welfare States.* Cambridge, UK: Cambridge University Press.

______. 1999. *Gendering Welfare States.* London: Sage.

______. 1999. "Gender, policy regimes, and politics." Pp. 245–75 in Diane Sainsbury (ed.), *Gender and Welfare State Regimes.* Oxford, UK: Oxford University Press.

Saliba, Therese, Carolyn Allen, and Judith A. Howard (eds.), 2002. *Gender, Politics, and Islam.* Chicago: University of Chicago Press.

Salisbury, Robert H. 1969. "An exchange theory of interest groups." *Midwest Journal of Political Science* 13:1–32.

______. 1979. "Why no corporatism in America?" In P. C. Schmitter and G. Lehmbruch (eds.), *Trends Toward Corporatist Intermediation.* Beverly Hills, CA: Sage.

Samaha, Joseph. 2002. "L'Islam est-il soluble dans la démocratie?" *Courrier International* 628 (November) 14–22.

Sampson, Robert J., and John H. Laub. 1996. "Socioeconomic achievement in the life course of disadvantaged men: Military service as a turning point, circa 1940–1965." *American Sociological Review* 61:347–67.

Samuels, David. 2001. "Does money matter? Credible commitments and campaign finance in new democracies: Theory and evidence from Brazil." *Comparative Politics* 34(1):23–42.

Santoro, Wayne. 2002. "The civil rights movement's struggle for equal employment rights: A 'dramatic events-conventional politics' model." *Social Forces* 81:177–206.

Saraceno, Chiara. 1997. "Family change, family policy and the reconstruction of welfare." Paper presented at OECD Conference "Beyond 2000," Paris, July 12–13.

Sartori, Giovanni. 1969. "From the sociology of politics to political sociology." Pp. 65–100 in Seymour Martin Lipset (ed.), *Politics and the Social Sciences.* Oxford, UK: Oxford University Press.

______. 1976. *Parties and Party Systems: A Framework for Analysis.* Cambridge, UK: Cambridge University Press.

Sassen, Saskia. 1996. *Losing Control? Sovereignty in an Age of Globalization.* New York: Columbia University Press.

______. 1998. *Globalization and Its Discontents: Essays on the New Mobility of People and Money.* New York: New Press.

Sawer, Marian. 1993. "Reclaiming social liberalism: The women's movement and the state." *Journal of Australian Studies*:1–21.

______. 1998. "Femocrats and ecorats: Women's policy machinery in Australia, Canada, and New Zealand." Pp. 112–37 in Carol Miller and Shahra Razavi (eds.), *Missionaries and Mandarins: Feminist Engagement with Development Institutions.* London: Intermediate Technology Publications with United Nations Research Institute for Social Development.

Sawyers, Tracy M., and David S. Meyer. 1999. "Missed opportunities: Social movement abeyance and public policy." *Social Problems* 46:187–206.

Saxenian, Anna Lee. 2002. "Brain circulation: How high-skill immigration makes everyone better off." *Brookings Review* 20(1):28–32.

Sayer, Andrew. 1984. *Method in Social Science: A Realist Approach.* London: Hutchinton.

Sayer, Derek. 1987. *The Violence of Abstraction*. London: Routledge.

Scannell, Paddy. 1989. "Public service broadcasting and modern public life." *Media, Culture and Society* 11:135–66.

Scarrow, Susan E. 2000. "Parties without members? Party organization in a changing electoral environment." Pp. 79–101 in Russell J. Dalton and Martin P. Wattenberg (eds.), *Parties Without Partisans: Political Change in Advanced Industrial Democracies*. New York: Oxford University Press.

Scarrow, Susan E., Paul Webb, and David M. Farrell. 2000. "From social integration to electoral contestation: The changing distribution of power within political parties." Pp. 129–53 in Russell J. Dalton and Martin P. Wattenberg (eds.), *Parties Without Partisans: Political Change in Advanced Industrial Democracies*. New York: Oxford University Press.

Schaffner, Brian F., Matthew Streb, and Gerald Wright. 2001. "Teams without uniforms: The nonpartisan ballot in state and local elections." *Political Research Quarterly* 54:7–30.

Schain, Martin. 1988. "Immigration and changes in the French party system." *European Journal of Political Research* 16:597–621.

______. 1990. "Immigration and politics." Pp. 253–68 in Peter Hall, Jack Hayward and Howard Machin (eds.), *Developments in French Politics*. New York: St. Martin's.

Scharpf, Fritz W. 1991[1987]. *Crisis and Choice in European Social Democracy*. Ithaca, NY: Cornell University Press.

______. 1992. "Die Handlungsfähigkeit des Staates am Ende des zwanzigsten jahrhunderts." *Politische Vierteljahresschrift* 32:621–34.

______. 2000a. "The viability of advanced welfare states in the interrnational economy: Vulnerabilities and options." *European Review* 8:399–425.

______. 2000b. "Economic changes, vulnerabilities, and institutional capabilities." Pp. 21–124 in Fritz W. Scharpf and Vivien A. Schmidt (eds.), *Welfare and Work in the Open Economy. Volume 1: From Vulnerability to Competitiveness*. New York: Oxford University Press.

Scharpf, Fritz W., and Vivien A. Schmidt (eds.). 2000. *Welfare and Work in the Open Economy. Volume II. Diverse Responses to Common Challenges*. Oxford, UK: Oxford University Press.

______. 2000. "Conclusions." Pp. 310–36 in Fritz W. Scharpf and Vivien A. Schmidt (eds.), *Welfare and Work in the Open Economy. Volume 1: From Vulnerability to Competitiveness*. New York: Oxford University Press.

Schattschneider, E. E. 1942. *Party Government*. New York: Rinehart.

______. 1960. *The Semisovereign People: A Realist's View of Democracy in America*. New York: Holt, Reinhart, & Winston.

Schedler, Andreas. 2001. "Measuring democratic consolidation." *Studies in Comparative International Development* 36:66–92.

Scheepers, Peer, Merove Gijsberts, and Marcel Coenders. 2002. "Ethnic exclusionism in European countries: Public opposition to civil rights for legal migrants as a response to perceived ethnic threat." *European Sociological Review* 18:17–34.

Schelling, Thomas. 1978. *Micromotives and Macrobehavior*. New York: Norton.

Schermerhorn, R. A. 1978. *Comparative Ethnic Relations: A Framework for Theory and Research*. Chicago: University of Chicago Press.

Schill, Michael H. 1994. "Race, the underclass, and public policy." *Law & Social Inquiry* 19:433–56.

Schiller, Herbert I. 1992. *Mass Communications and American Empire*, 2nd ed. Boulder, CO: Westview.

Schippers, Joop. 1995. "Pay differences between men and women in the European Labor Market." Pp. 31–52 in Anneke van Doorne-Huiskes, Jacques van Hoof, and Ellie Roelofs (eds.), *Women and the European Labor Markets*. London: Paul Chapman.

Schlesinger, Arthur, Jr. 1962. "The humanist looks at empirical social research." *American Sociological Review* 27:768–71.

Schlesinger, Joseph, 1968. "Party units." *International Encyclopedia of the Social Sciences*. New York: Macmillan.

______. 1984. "On the theory of party organization." *Journal of Politics* 46:369–400.

Schlesinger, Philip. 1990. "Rethinking the sociology of journalism: Source strategies and the limits of media–centrism." Pp. 61–83 in M. Ferguson (ed.), *Public Communication*. London: Sage.

Schlesinger, Philip, and Hoard, Tumber. 1994. *Reporting Crime: The Media Politics of Criminal Justice*. Oxford, UK: Clarendon Press.

Schlozman, Kay Lehman, and John T. Tierney. 1986. *Organized Interests and American Democracy*. New York: Harper & Row.

Schluchter, Wolfgang. 1981. *The Rise of Western Rationalism: Max Weber's Developmental History*. Berkeley: University of California Press.

Schmidt, Manfred. 1982. "Does corporatism matter? Economic crisis, politics, and rates of unemployment in capitalist democracies in the 1970s." Pp. 237–58 in Gerhard Lehmbruch and Philippe C. Schmitter (eds.), *Patterns of Corporatist Policy-Making*. London: Sage.

Schmitt, Carl. 1976/1932. *The Concept of the Political.* New Brunswick, NJ: Rutgers University Press.

______. 1985/1923. *The Crisis of Parliamentary Democracy*. Cambridge, MA: MIT Press.

Schmitter Heisler, Barbara. 1981. "Trade unions and immigration politics in West Germany and Switzerland." *Politics and Society* 10:317–34.

______. 1985. "Sending countries and the politics of emigration and destination." *International Migration Review* 6(3):469–84.

______. 2000. "The sociology of immigration." Pp. 77–96 in Caroline Brettell and James Hollifield (eds.), *Migration Theory: Talking Across the Disciplines*. New York: Routledge.

Schmitter, Philippe C. 1974. "Still the century of corporatism?" *The Review of Politics* 36:85–131.

______. 1981. "Interest intermediation and regime governability in contemporary Western Europe and North America." Pp. 285–327 in Suzanne D. Berger (ed.), *Organizing Interests in Western Europe*. Cambridge, UK: Cambridge University Press.

______. 1989. "Corporatism is dead! Long live corporatism!" *Government and Opposition* 24:54–73.

______. 1996. "Imagining the future of the Euro-polity with the help of new concepts." Pp. 121–50 in Gary Marks, Fritz W. Scharpf, Philippe C. Schmitter, and Wolfgang Streeck (eds.), *Governance in the European Union*. Thousand Oaks, CA: Sage.

Schmitter, Philippe C., and Gerhard Lehmbruch (eds.). 1979. *Trends Toward Corporatist Intermediation*. Beverly Hills, CA: Sage.

Schmitter, Philippe C., and Wolfgang Streeck. 1999 [1982]. "The organization of business interests: Studying the associative action of business in advanced industrial societies." Discussion Paper 99/1. Max Planck Institute for the Study of Societies, Cologne, Germany. Available at: www.mpi-fg-koeln.mpg.de.

Schmitter, Philippe C., with Terry Lynn Karl. 1994. "The conceptual travels of transitologists and consolidoligists: How far to the East should they attempt to go?" *Slavic Review* 53:173–85.

______. 1991. "Cinco reflexiones sobre la cuarta onda de democratización." Pp. 101–40 in Carlos Barbas Solano, J. L. Barros Horcasitas, and Javier Hurtado (eds.), *Transiciones hacia*.

Schneider, Volker. 1992. "The structure of policy networks: A comparison of the 'chemical control' and 'telecommunications' policy domains in Germany." *European Journal of Political Research* 21:91–130.

Scholte, Jan Aart. 2000. *Globalization. A Critical Introduction*. New York: St. Martin's.

Schotter, A. 1981. *The Economic Theory of Social Institutions*. New York: Cambridge University Press.

Schram, Martin. 1995. *Speaking Freely*. Washington, D.C.: Center for Responsive Politics.

Schram, Sanford. 2000. *After Welfare: The Culture of Postindustrial Social Policy.* New York: New York University Press.

Schroedel, Jean Reith. 1986. "Campaign contributions and legislative outcomes." *Western Political Quarterly* 39:371–89.

Schuck, Peter. 1998. *Citizens, Strangers and In-Betweens.* Boulder, CO: Westview.

______. 2000. "Law and the study of migration." Pp. 187–204 in Caroline Brettell and James Hollifield (eds.), *Migration Theory*. New York: Routledge.

Schudson, Michael. 1978. *Discovering the News: A Social History of American Newspapers*. New York: Basic Books.

______. 1982. "The politics of narrative form: The emergence of news conventions in print and television." *Daedalus* 111:97–113.

______. 1994. "Question authority: A history of the news interview in American journalism, 1860s–1930s." *Media, Culture & Society* 16:565–87.

______. 1995. *The Power of News*. Cambridge, MA: Harvard University Press.

______. 1998. *The Good Citizen*. New York: Free Press.

______. 1999. "Social origins of press cynicism in portraying politics." *American Behavioral Scientist* 42:998–1008.

______. 2000. "The sociology of news production revisited (again)." Pp. 175–200 in J. Curran and M. Gurevitch, (eds.), *Mass Media and Society*, 3rd ed. London: Arnold.

______. 2003. *The Sociology of News*. New York: W. W. Norton.

Schulz, M. S. 1998. "Collective action across borders: Opportunity structures, network capacities, and communicative praxis in the age of advanced globalization." *Sociological Perspectives* 41:587–616.

Schumacher, Bruno. 1958. *Geschichte Ost- und Westpreßens*. Würzburg: Holzner Verlag.

Schumaker, Paul. 1975. "The scope of political conflict and the effectiveness of constraints in contemporary urban protest." *Sociological Quarterly* 19:168–84.

______. 1978. "The scope of political conflict and the effectiveness of constrains in contemporary urban protest." *Sociological Quarterly* 19:168–84.

Schuman, Howard. 1995. "Velvet glove: Paternalism and conflict in gender, class, and race relations [book review]." *Public Opinion Quarterly* 59:144–7.

______. 2000. "The perils of correlation, the lure of labels, and the beauty of negative results."

Pp. 302–23 in D. O. Sears, J. Sidanius, and L. Bobo (eds.), *Racialized Politics: The Debate About Racism in America.* Chicago: University of Chicago Press.

Schuman, Howard, and Cheryl Rieger. 1992. "Historical analogies, generational effects, and attitudes towards war." *American Sociological Review* 57:315–26.

Schuman, Howard, and Stanley Presser. 1981. *Questions and Answers in Attitude Surveys.* New York: Academic Press.

Schuman, Howard, Charlotte Steeh, Lawrence Bobo, and Maria Krysan. 1997. *Racial Attitudes in America: Trends and Interpretations,* revised ed. Cambridge, MA: Harvard University Press.

Schumpeter, Joseph. 1942. *Capitalism, Socialism, and Democracy.* New York: Harper & Row.

Schumpeter, Joseph. 1950. *Capitalism, Socialism & Democracy,* 3rd ed. New York: Harper.

Schwartz, Barry. 1996. "Memory as a cultural system: Abraham Lincoln in World War II." *American Sociological Review* 61:908–27.

Schwartz, Herman. 1994a. "Public choice theory and public choices: Bureaucrats and state reorganization in Australia, Denmark, New Zealand and Sweden in the 1980s." *Administration and Society* 26:48–77.

______. 1994b. "Small states in big trouble: The politics of state organization in Australia, Denmark, New Zealand, and Sweden." *World Politics* 46:527–55.

______. 1998. "Social democracy going down or down under: Institutions, internationalized capital, and indebted states." *Comparative Politics* 30:253–72.

Schwartz, Michael. 1976. *Radical Protest and Social Structure.* New York: Academic Press.

Schwartz, Michael, and Shuva Paul. 1992. "Resource mobilization versus the mobilization of people." Pp. 205–23 in Aldon Morris and Carole Mueller (eds.), *Frontiers of Social Movement Theory.* New Haven, CT: Yale University Press.

Schwartz, Mildred A. 1990. *The Party Network: The Robust Organization of Illinois Republicans.* Madison: University of Wisconsin Press.

______. 1990a. *A Sociological Perspective on Politics.* Englewood Cliffs, NJ: Prentice Hall.

______. 1991. "Political protest in the western borderlands: Can farmers be socialists?" Pp. 28–53 in Robert Lecker (ed.), *Borderlands: Essays in Canadian–American Relations.* Toronto: ECW.

______. 1994a. "Party organization as a network of relations: The Republican party of Illinois." Pp. 75–101 in Kay Lawson (ed.), *How Political Parties Work.* Westport, CO: Praeger.

______. 1994b. "North American social democracy in the 1990s: The NDP in Ontario." *Canadian-American Public Policy* 17:1–46.

______. 2000. "Continuity strategies among political challengers: The case of Social Credit." *The American Review of Canadian Studies.* 30:455–77.

______. 2002. "Factions and the continuity of political protest movements." Pp. 157–70 in David Meyer, Nancy Whittier, and Belinda Robnett (eds.), *Social Movements: Identity, Culture and the State.* New York: Oxford University Press.

Sciolino, Elaine. 2002. "European Union turns down Turkey's bid for membership." *New York Times,* December 13:A16.

Sciulli, David. 1990. "Differentiation and collegial formations: implications of societal constitutionalism." Pp. 367–405 in Jeffrey C. Alexander and Paul Colomy (eds.), *Differentiation Theory and Social Change.* New York: Columbia University Press.

Scott, James C. 1976. *The Moral Economy of the Peasant: Rebellion and Subsistence in Southeast Asia.* New Haven, CT: Yale University Press.

______. 1985. *Weapons of the Weak: The Everyday Forms of Peasant Resistance.* New Haven, CT: Yale University Press.

______. 1990. *Domination and the Arts of Resistance: Hidden Transcripts.* New Haven, CT: Yale University Press.

______. 1998. *Seeing Like a State.* New Haven, CT: Yale University Press.

Scott, Joan Wallach. 1988. *Gender and the Politics of History.* New York: Columbia University Press.

Scott, John (ed.). 1990. *The Sociology of Elites.* Aldershot, UK: Edward Elgar.

Scott, John Finley. 1963. "The changing foundations of the Parsonian action scheme." *American Sociological Review,* October, 28:716-35.

Scott, John. 1979. *Corporations, Classes, and Capitalism.* New York: St. Martin's Press.

______. 1987. "Intercorporate structures in Western Europe: A comparative historical analysis. Pp. 208–32 in Mark S. Mizruchi and Michael Schwartz (eds.), *Intercorporate Relations: The Structural Analysis of Business.* New York: Cambridge University Press.

______. 1996. *Stratification and Power.* London: Polity Press.

Scott, W. Richard. 1995. "Introduction: Institutional theory and organizations." Pp. xi–xxiii in W. Richard Scott and Soren Christensen (eds.), *The Institutional Construction of Organizations: International and Longitudinal Studies.* Thousand Oaks, CA: Sage.

______. 1998. *Organizations: Rational, Natural, and Open Systems*, 4th ed. Upper Saddle River, NJ: Prentice Hall.

Sears, David O. 1988. "Symbolic racism." Pp. 53–84 in P. A. Katz and D. A. Taylor (ed.), *Eliminating Racism: Means and Controversies*. New York: Plenum.

Sears, David O., Collete Van Laar, Mary Carrillo, and Rick Kosterman. 1997. "Is it really racism? The origins of white Americans' opposition to race-targeted policies." *Public Opinion Quarterly* 61:16–53.

Sears, David O., Jack Citrin, Sharmaine V. Cheleden, and Colette Van Laar. 1999. "Cultural diversity and multicultural politics: Is ethnic balkanization psychologically inevitable?" Pp. 35–79 in D. A. Prentice and D. T. Miller (eds.), *Cultural Divides: Understanding and Overcoming Group Conflict*. New York: Russell Sage Foundation.

Sears, David O., Jim Sidanius, and Lawrence Bobo (eds.). 2000. *Racialized Politics: The Debate About Racism in America*. Chicago: University of Chicago Press.

Sears, David O., John J. Hetts, James Sidanius, and Lawrence D. Bobo. 2000. "Race in American politics: Framing the debates." Pp. 1–43 in D. O. Sears, J. Sidanius, and L. D. Bobo (eds.), *Racialized Politics: The Debate About Racism in America*. Chicago: University of Chicago Press.

Sears, David O., Leonie Huddy, and Robert Jarvis. 2003. *Oxford Handbook of Political Psychology*. New York: Oxford University Press.

Seccombe, W. 1974. "The housewife and her labour under capitalism." *New Left Review* 83:3–24.

Segal, David R. 1994. "National security and democracy in the United States." *Armed Forces & Society* 20(3):375–93.

Seidman, Gay W. 1994. *Manufacturing Militance: Workers' Movements in Brazil and South Africa, 1970–1985*. Berkeley/Los Angeles: University of California Press.

Seidman, Steven. 1983. *Liberalism and the Origins of European Social Theory*. Berkeley: University of California Press.

Seils, Eric, and Philip Manow. 2000. "Adjusting badly: The German welfare state, structural change, and the open economy." Pp. 264–307 in Fritz W. Scharpf and Vivien A. Schmidt (eds.), *Welfare and Work in the Open Economy. Volume II. Diverse Responses to Common Challenges*. Oxford, UK: Oxford University Press.

Selbin, Eric. 1993. *Modern Latin American Revolutions*. Boulder, CO: Westview Press.

Selle, P., and L. Karvonen. 1995. *Women in Nordic Politics*. Aldershot: Dartmouth.

Selnow, Gary W. 1994. *High Tech Campaigns: Computer Technology in Political Communication*. Westport, CT: Praeger.

Selznick, Philip. 1949. *TVA and the Grass Roots: A Study of Politics and Organization*. Berkeley: University of California Press.

Sen, Gita, and Caren Grown. 1987. *Development, Crises, and Alternative Visions*. New York: New Feminist Library.

Sevenhuijsen, S. 1998. *Citizenship and the Ethics of Care: Feminist Considerations on Justice, Morality and Politics*. London: Routledge.

Sewell, William H. Jr., 1980. *Work and Revolution in France*. New York: Cambridge University Press.

______. 1985. "Ideologies and social revolutions: Reflections on the French case." *Journal of Modern History* 57:57–85.

______. 1992. "A theory of structure: Duality, agency and transformation." *American Journal of Sociology* 98(1):1–29.

______. 1994. *A Rhetoric of Bourgeois Revolution*. Durham, NC: Duke University Press.

______. 1996. "Historical events as transformations of structures: Inventing revolution at the Bastille." *Theory and Society* 25:841–81.

Shafritz, Jay, and E. W. Russell. 1996. *Introducing Public Administration*. New York: Addison Wesky Longman.

Shaiken, H. 1994. "Advanced manufacturing and Mexico – a new international division-of-labor". *Latin American Research Review* 29(2):39–71.

Shain, Yossi, and Juan J. Linz. 1995. *Between States. Interim Governments and Democratic Transitions*. Cambridge, UK: Cambridge University Press.

Shalev, Michael. 1983. "The social democratic model and beyond: Two generations of comparative research on the welfare state." *Comparative Social Research* 5:315–51.

______. 1992. *Labor and the Political Economy in Israel*. Oxford, UK: Oxford University Press.

Shamir, Michael. 1984. "Are Western party systems 'frozen'? A comparative analysis." *Comparative Political Studies* 12:35–79.

Shanks, Cheryl. 2001. *Immigration and the Politics of American Sovereignty, 1890–1990*. Ann Arbor: University of Michigan Press.

Shapiro, Michael J. 1992. *Reading the Postmodern Polity: Political Theory as Textual Practice*. Minneapolis: University of Minnesota Press.

Shapiro, Robert Y., and John T. Young. 1989. "Public opinion and the welfare state: The United States in comparative perspective." *Political Science Quarterly* 104:59–89.

Sharp, Rhonda, and Ray Broomhill. 1988. *Shortchanged: Women and Economic Policies*. Boston: Allen and Unwin.

Shaver, S. 1993/1994. "Bodyrights, social rights and the liberal welfare state." *Critical Social Policy* 39:66–93.

______. 2002. "Gender, welfare regimes and agency." *Social Politics* 9:2:203–11.

Shavit, Y., and H. P. Blossfeld. 1993. *Persistent Inequalities*. Boulder, CO: Westview.

Shavit, Yossi, Claude S. Fischer, and Yael Koresh. 1994. "Kin and nonkin under collective threat: Israeli networks during the Gulf War." *Social Forces* 72:1197–215.

Shaw, Martin (ed.). 1984. *War, State and Society*. London: Macmillan.

______. 1999. "Global voices: Civil society and the media in global crises." Pp. 214–32 in T. Dunne and N. Wheeler (eds.), *Human Rights in Global Politics*. New York: Cambridge University Press.

Sheehan, Robert J. 1967. "Proprietors in the world of big business." *Fortune* (June 15):178–83,242.

Shefter, Martin. 1978. "Party, bureaucracy and political change in the United States." Pp. 211–65 in Louis Maisel and Joseph Cooper (eds.), *Political Parties: Development and Decoy.* Beverly Hills, CA: Sage.

Shepsle, Ken, and Barry Weingast. 1987. "The institutional foundations of committee power." *American Political Science Review* 81:85–194.

Sherman, Arnold K., and Aliza Kolker. 1987. *The Social Bases of Politics* Belmont, CA: Wadsworth.

Sherman, Howard J. 1995. *Reinventing Marxism.* Baltimore, MD: Johns Hopkins Press.

Shields, Todd G., and Robert Goidel. 1997. "Participation rates, socioeconomic class biases, and congressional elections: A crossvalidation." *American Journal of Political Science* 41:683–91.

Shiffman, Jeremy, Marina Skrabalo, and Jelena Subotic. 2002. "Reproductive rights and the state in Serbia and Croatia." *Social Science and Medicine* 54:625–42.

Shils, Edward A. 1954. "Authoritarianism: Right and Left." Pp. 24–49 in Richard Christie and Marie Jahoda (ed.), *Studies in the Scope and Method of The Authoritarian Personality*. Glencoe, IL: Free Press.

______. 1960. *Political Development in the New States.* The Hague: Mouton.

______. 1975. *Center and Periphery: Essays in Macrosociology*. Chicago: University of Chicago Press.

Shiva, Vandana. 1997. *Biopiracy. The Plunder of Nature and Knowledge.* Boston: South End.

Siaroff, Alan. 1999. "Corporatism in 24 industrial democracies: Meaning and measurement." *European Journal of Political Research* 36:175–205.

Siebert, Horst. 1997. "Labor market rigidities: At the root of unemployment in Europe." *Journal of Economic Perspectives* 11(3):37–54.

Sifry, Micah L. 2002. *Spoiling for a Fight: Third-Party Politics in America.* New York: Routledge.

Sigal, Leon V. 1973. *Reporters and Officials.* Lexington, MA: Lexington Books.

______. 1986. "Sources make the news." In R. K. Manoff and M. Schudson. (eds.), *Reading the News.* New York: Pantheon.

Sigmund, Paul E. 1978. *The Overthrow of Allende and the Politics of Chile, 1964–1976.* Pittsburgh: University of Pittsburgh Press.

Siim, B. 2000. *Gender and Citizenship: Politics and Agency in France, Britain and Denmark.* Cambridge, UK: Cambridge University Press.

Sikkink, Kathryn. 2002. "Restructuring world politics: The limits and asymmetries of soft power." Pp. 301–17 in S. Khagram, J. V. Riker, and K. Sikkink (eds.), *Restructuring World Politics: Transnational Social Movements, Networks, and Norms.* Minneapolis: University of Minnesota Press.

Sikkink, Kathryn, and Jackie G. Smith. 2002. "Infrastructures for change: transnational organizations, 1953–1993. Pp. 24–44 in S. Khagram, J. V. Riker, and K. Sikkink (eds.), *Restructuring World Politics: Transnational Social Movements, Networks, and Norms.* Minneapolis: University of Minnesota Press.

Silberman, Jonathon, and Garey C. Durden. 1976. "Determining legislative preferences on the minimum wage: An economic approach." *Journal of Political Economy* 84:317–29.

Silverstein, Helen. 1996. *Unleashing Rights: Law, Meaning and the Animal Rights Movement.* Ann Arbor: University of Michigan Press.

Simmel, George. 1950. In Kurt H. Wolff (ed.), *The Sociology of George Simmel.* Glencoe, IL: The Free Press.

______. 1955. *Conflict: the Web of Group Affiliations.* New York: Free Press.

Simmons, Beth. 1999. "The internationalization of capital." Pp. 36–69 in Herbert Kitschelt, Peter Lange, Gary Marks, and John D. Stephens (eds.), *Continuity and Change in Contemporary Capitalism.* New York: Cambridge University Press.

Simmons, Beth, Geoffrey Garrett, and Frank Dobbin. 2003. "The international diffusion of democracy and markets." Paper presented at Conference on The International Diffusion of Democracy and Markets, Weatherhead Center for International Affairs, Harvard University, Cambridge, MA, October 3–4.

Simon, Gerhard. 1987. *Nationalism and Policy Toward Nations within the Soviet Union.* Boulder, CO: Westview.

Simon, Herbert. 1958. *Administrative Behavior.* New York: Macmillan.

Simon, J., and L. Lynch. 1999. "A comparative assessment of public opinion toward immigration and immigration policies." *International Migration Review* 30(2):455–67.

Simon, Rita, and Susan Alexander. 1993. *The Ambivalent Welcome: Print Media, Public Opinion and Immigration*. Westport, CT: Praeger.

Sinclair, John M., and Malcolm Coulthard. 1975. *Towards an Analysis of Discourse*. Oxford, UK: Oxford University Press.

Singer, Daniel. 2002. *Prelude to Revolution: France in May 1968*, 2nd ed. Cambridge, MA: South End Press.

Singh, Jitendra V., David J. Tucker, and Agnes G. Meinhard. 1991. "Institutional change and ecological dynamics." Pp. 390–422 in Walter W. Powell and Paul J. DiMaggio (eds.), *The New Institutionalism in Organizational Analysis*. Chicago: University of Chicago Press.

Skidmore, Thomas E. 1989. *The Politics of Military Rule in Brazil, 1964–1985*. New York: Oxford University Press.

Sklair, Leslie. 1993. *Assembling for Development*. San Diego: University of California Center for U.S.-Mexican Studies.

______. 2001. *The Transnational Capitalist Class*. Oxford, UK: Blackwell.

Sklar, R. 1987. "Postimperialism: A class analysis of multinational corporate expansion." In D. Becker, J. Frieden, S. Schatz, and R. Sklar (eds.), *Postimperialism*. Boulder, CO: Lynne Reinner.

Skocpol, Theda. 1973. "A critical review of Barrington Moore's *Social Origins of Dictatorship and Democracy*." Pp. 25–54 in Theda Skocpol, *Social Revolutions in the Modern World*. Cambridge, UK: Cambridge University Press.

______. 1977. "Wallerstein's world capitalist system: A theoretical and historical critique." Pp. 55–71 in Theda Skocpol (ed.), *Social Revolutions in the Modern World*. Cambridge, UK: Cambridge University Press.

______. 1979. *States and Social Revolutions: A Comparative Analysis of France, Russia, and China*. Cambridge, UK: Cambridge University Press.

______. 1980. "Political response to capitalist crisis: neo-marxist theories of the state and the case of the New Deal." *Politics and Society* 10(2):155–201.

______. 1984. *Vision and Methods in Historical Sociology*. New York: Cambridge University Press.

______. 1985. "Bringing the state back in: Strategies of analysis in current research." Pp. 3–37 in Peter Evans, Dietrich Rueschemeyer, and Theda Skocpol (eds.), *Bringing the State Back In*. Cambridge, UK: Cambridge University Press.

______. 1986/87. "A brief reply." *Politics and Society* 15:331–2.

______. 1992. *Protecting Soldiers and Mothers: Political Origins of Social Policy in the United States*. Cambridge, MA: Belknap Press of Harvard University Press.

______. 1994. *Social Revolutions in the Modern World*. Cambridge, UK: Cambridge University Press.

______. 1996. *Boomerang: Clinton's Health Security Effort and the Turn Against Government in U. S. Politics*. New York: W. W. Norton.

______. 2000. "Theory tackles history." *Social Science History* 24(4):669–76.

Skocpol, Theda, and Ann Shola Orloff. 1986. "Explaining the origins of welfare states." Pp. 229–64 in Siegwart Lindenberg, James Coleman, and Stefan Nowak (eds.), *Approaches to Social Theory*. New York: Russell Sage Foundations.

Skocpol, Theda, and Edwin Amenta. 1985. "Did capitalists shape social security?" *American Sociological Review* 50(4):572–5.

Skocpol, Theda, and John L. Campbell. 1994. *American Society and Politics*. New York: McGraw–Hill.

Skocpol, Theda, and Margaret Somers. 1980. "The uses of comparative history in macrosocial inquiry." *Comparative Studies of Society and History* 22:174–97.

Skocpol, Theda, Marshall Ganz, and Ziad Munson. 2000. "A nation of organizers: The institutional origins of civic voluntarism in the United States." *American Political Science Review* 94(3):527–46.

Skogerbo, Eli. 1997. "The press subsidy system in Norway." *European Journal of Communication* 12:99–118.

Skowronek, Stephen. 1982. *Building a New American State: The Expansion of National Administrative Capacities*, 1877–1920. Cambridge, UK: Cambridge University Press.

______. 1999. *The Politics Presidents Make: Leadership from John Adams to George Bush*. Cambridge, MA: Belknap Press of Harvard University.

Skrentny, John David. 1996. *The Ironies of Affirmative Action: Politics, Culture, and Justice in America*. Chicago: University of Chicago Press.

______. 1998. "The effect of the Cold War on African-American civil rights: America and the world audience, 1945–1968." *Theory and Society* 27:237–85.

______. 2001. *Color Lines: Affirmative Action, Immigration, and Civil Rights Options for America*. Chicago: University of Chicago Press.

______. 2002. *The Minority Rights Revolution*. Cambridge, MA: Harvard University Press.

Sleeper, Jim. 1997. *Liberal racism*. New York: Viking.

Smelser, Neil J. 1959. *Social Change in the Industrial Revolution: An Application of Theory to the Lancashire Cotton Industry 1770–1840*. London: Routledge & Kegan Paul.

______. 1962. *The Theory of Collective Behavior.* Glencoe, IL: Free Press.

______. 1968. "Social and psychological dimensions of collective behavior." Pp. 92–121 in Smelser (ed.), *Essays in Sociological Explanation*. Englewood Cliffs, NJ: Prentice-Hall.

______. (ed.). 1988. *Handbook of Sociology*. Beverly Hills, CA: Sage.

______. 1990. "The contest between family and schooling in nineteenth-century britain." Pp. 165–86 in Jeffrey C. Alexander and Paul Colomy (eds.). *Differentiation Theory and Social Change.* New York: Columbia University Press.

Smith, Abbot Emerson. 1947. *Colonists in Bondage.* Chapel Hill: University of North Carolina Press.

Smith, Adam. 1776/1976. *The Wealth of Nations.* Chicago: University of Chicago Press.

Smith, Adam. 1982. *Lectures on Jurisprudence.* R. L. Meek (ed.). London: Oxford Clarendon Press.

Smith, Anna Marie. 1994. *New Right Discourse on Race and Sexuality*. Cambridge, UK: Cambridge University Press.

Smith, Anthony D. 1983. *Theories of Nationalism.* London: Duckworth.

______. 1987. *The Ethnic Origins of Nations.* New York: Basil Blackwell.

______. 1991. *National Identity*. London: Penguin.

______. 1995. *Nations and Nationalism in a Global Era.* Maiden, MA: Blackwell.

Smith, David Horton. 2000. *Grassroots Associations.* Thousand Oaks, CA: Sage.

Smith, Jackie G., and Hank Johnston. 2002. *Globalization and Resistance: Transnational Dimensions of Social Movements.* Lanham, MD: Rowman & Littlefield.

Smith, Mark A. 2000. *American Business and Political Power: Public Opinion, Elections, and Democracy.* Chicago: University of Chicago Press.

Smith, Martin J. 1990. "Pluralism, reformed pluralism, and neopluralism: The role of policy groups in policymaking." *Political Studies* 38:302–22.

______. 1993. *Pressure, Power and Policy.* New York: Harvester Wheatsheaf.

Smith, Michael R. 1992. *Power, Norms, and Inflation.* New York: Aldine de Gruyter.

Smith, R. P. 1980. "Military expenditures and investment in OECD countries, 1954–1973." *Journal of Comparative Economics* 4:19–32.

Smith, Rogers. 1997. *Civic Ideals: Conflicting Visions of Citizenship in U.S. History*. New Haven, CT: Yale University Press.

Smith, Steven B. 1984. *Reading Althusser: An Essay on Structural Marxism*. Ithaca, NY: Cornell University Press.

Smith, Tom W. 1990. "Liberal and conservative trends in the United States since World War II." *Public Opinion Quarterly* 54:479–507.

Smooha, Sammy. 2002a. "Types of democracy and modes of conflict management in ethnically divided societies." *Nations and Nationalism* 8:423–31.

______. 2002b. "The model of ethnic democracy: Israel as a Jewish and democratic state." *Nations and Nationalism* 8:475–503.

Sniderman, Paul M., and Edward G. Carmines. 1997. *Reaching Beyond Race.* Cambridge, MA: Harvard University Press.

Sniderman, Paul M., and Thomas Piazza. 1993. *The Scar of Race.* Cambridge, MA: Belknap.

Sniderman, Paul M., Edward G. Carmines, Geoffrey C. Layman, and Michael Carter. 1996. "Beyond race: Social justice as a race neutral ideal." *American Journal of Political Science* 40:33–55.

Sniderman, Paul M., Gretchen C. Crosby, and William G. Howell. 2000. "The politics of race." Pp. 236–79 in D. O. Sears, J. Sidanius, and L. D. Bobo (eds.), *Racialized Politics: The Debate About Racism in America.* Chicago: University of Chicago Press.

Sniderman, Paul, Henry Brody, and Philip Tetlock. 1991. *Reasoning and Choice: Explorations in Political Psychology*. New York: Cambridge University Press.

Snipp, C. Matthew. 2003. "Racial measurement in the American census: Past practices and implications for the future." *Annual Review of Sociology* 29:563–88.

Snow, David A., and Robert D. Benford. 1992. "Master frames and cycles of protest." Pp. 133–55 in A. D. Morris and C. M. Mueller (eds.), *Frontiers in Social Movement Theory*. New Haven, CT: Yale University Press.

______. 1988. "Ideology, frame resonance, and participant mobilization." Pp. 197–217 in Bert Klandermans, Hanspeter Kriesi, and Sidney Tarrow (eds.), *From Structure to Action*. Greenwich, CT: JAI Press.

______. 2000. "Clarifying the relationship between framing and ideology." *Mobilization* 5:55–60.

Snow, David A., Daniel M. Cress, Liam Downey, and Andrew W. Jones. 1998. "Disrupting the 'quotidian': Reconceptualizing the relation between breakdown and the emergence of collective action." *Mobilization* 3:1–22.

Snow, David A., E. Burke Rochford, Jr., Steven K. Worden, and Robert D. Benford. 1986.

"Frame alignment processes, micromobilization, and movement participation." *American Sociological Review* 51(4): 464–81.

Snyder, James M. 1992. "Long-term investing in politicians; or, give early, give often." *Journal of Law and Economics* 35:15–43.

Snyder, Richard. 1992. "Explaining transitions from neopatrimonial dictatorships." *Comparative Politics* 24:379–99.

______. 1998. "Paths out of sultanistic regimes: Combining structural and voluntarist perspectives." Pp. 49–81 in Houchang E. Chehabi and Juan J. Linz (eds.), *Sultanistic Regimes*. Baltimore: Johns Hopkins University Press.

Soboul, Albert. 1974. *The French Revolution, 1789–1799*. London: New Left Books.

Social Security Administration (SSA). 1999. *Social Security Programs Throughout the World, 1999*. http://www.ssa.gov/policy/docs/progdesc/ssptw/1999/index.html.

______. 2002. *Social Security Programs Throughout the World: Europe, 2002*. http://www.ssa.gov/policy/docs/progdesc/ssptw/2002/europe/index.html.

______. 2003. *Social Security Programs Throughout the World: Asia and the Pacific, 2002*. http://www.ssa.gov/policy/docs/progdesc/ssptw/2002/asia/index.html.

Sohrabi, Nader. 1995. "Historicizing revolutions: Constitutional revolutions in the Ottoman Empire, Iran, and Russia, 1905–1908." *American Journal of Sociology* 100:1383–447.

______. 2002. "Global waves, local actors: what the young Turks knew about other revolutions and why it mattered." *Comparative Studies in Society and History* 44(1):45–79.

Solomos, John. 1993. *Race and Racism in Britain*, 2nd ed. New York: St. Martin's.

______. 1995. "The politics of citizenship in nationality in a european perspective." Pp. 40–52 in Martin Martiniello (ed.), *Migration, Citizesnhip and Ethno-National Identities in the European Union*. Brookfield, VT: Ashgate.

Solomos, John, and Les Back. 1995. *Race, Politics and Social Change*. London: Routledge.

Sombart, Werner. 1976[1906]. *Why Is There No Socialism in the United States*? (P. M. Hocking and C. T. Husbands, trans.). White Plains, NY: International Arts and Sciences Press. (Originally published as *Warum gibt es in den Vereinigten Staaten keinen Sozialismus*? Tübingen: J. C. B. Mohr (P. Siebech) 1906.)

Somers, Margaret R. 1995. "What's political or cultural about political culture and the public sphere?" *Sociological Theory* 13:113–44.

______. 1998. "We're no angels: Realism, rational choice, and relationality in social science." *American Journal of Sociology* 104(3):722–84.

Sorauf, Frank J. 1988. *Money in American Elections*. Glenview, IL: Scott, Foresman.

______. 1992. *Inside Campaign Finance: Myths and Realities*. New Haven, CT: Yale University Press.

Soref, Michael. 1976. "Social class and a division of labor within the corporate elite: A note on class, interlocking, and executive committee membership of directors of U.S. industrial firms." *Sociological Quarterly* 17:360–8.

Sorj, Bila. 2001. "Child care as public policy in Brazil." Pp. 105–24 in Mary Daly (ed.), *Care Work*. Geneva: International Labour Office.

Soroka, Stuart N., and Christopher Wlezien. 2002. "Opinion–policy dynamics: Public preferences and public expenditure in the United Kingdom." Paper presented at the Elections, Public Opinion and Parties Annual Conference, Salford, England.

Soskice, David. 1990. "Wage determination: The changing role of institutions in advanced industrialized countries." *Oxford Review of Economic Policy* 6(4):36–61.

______. 1999. "Divergent production regimes: Coordinated and uncoordinated market economies in the 1980s and 1990s." Pp. 101–34 in Herbert Kitschelt, Peter Lange, Gary Marks, and John D. Stephens (eds.), *Continuity and Change in Contemporary Capitalism*. New York: Cambridge University Press.

Soysal, Yasemin. 1994. *Limits of Citizenship: Migrants and Postnational Membership in Europe*. Chicago: University of Chicago Press.

Spain, Daphne, and Suzanne Bianchi. 1996. *Balancing Act: Motherhood, Marriage, and Employment Among American Women*. New York: Russell Sage Foundation.

Sparks, Colin, and A. Reading. 1998. *Communism, Capitalism, and the Mass Media*. London: Sage.

Sparks, Colin, and John. Tulloch. 2000. *Tabloid Tales: Global Debates Over Media Standards*. Lanham, MD: Rowman & Littlefield.

Sparr, Pamela. 1994. "Feminist critiques of structural adjustment." Pp. 13–39 in Pamela Sparr (ed.), *Mortgaging Women's Lives*. London: Zed Books.

Spengler, Joseph. 1979. *France Faces Depopulation, 1936–1976*. Durham, NC: Duke University Press.

Sperling, Valerie, Myra Marx Ferree, and Barbara Risman. 2001. "Constructing global feminism: Transnational advocacy networks and Russian women's activism." *Signs* 26(4):1155–86.

Spiro, Peter. 2002. "Explaining the end of plenary power." *Georgetown Immigration Law Journal* 16:339–63.

Spivak, Gayatri. 1996. "'Woman' as theater: United Nation's Conference on Women, Beijing, 1995." *Radical Philosophy* 75:2–4.

Springhall John. 1998. *Youth, Popular Culture and Moral Panics: Penny Gaffs to Gangsta-Rap, 1830–1996.* New York: St. Martin's.

Spruyt, Hendrik. 1994. *The Sovereign State and Its Competitors.* Princeton, NJ: Princeton University Press.

______. 2002. "The origins, development, and possible decline of the modern state." *Annual Review of Political Science* 5:127–50.

Sreberny, Annabelle. 2000. "Television, gender and democratization in the Middle East." Pp. 63–78 in J. Curran and M. Park (eds.), *De-Westernizing Media Studies.* London: Routledge.

Stack, Carol. 1974. *All Our Kin: Strategies for Survival in a Black Community.* New York: Harper and Row.

Staggenborg, Suzanne. 1998. *Gender, Family and Social Movements.* Thousand Oaks, CA: Pine Forge Press.

Stahl, Charles. 1989. "Overview: Economic perspectives." Pp. 361–80 in Reginald Appleyard (ed.), *The Impact of International Migration on Developing Countries.* Paris: OECD.

Stallings, Barbara, and Wilson Peres. 2000. *Growth, Employment, and Equity: The Impact of the Economic Reforms in Latin America and the Caribbean.* Washington, DC: Brookings Institution Press/United Nations Economic Commission for Latin America and the Caribbean.

Stampp, Kenneth. 1965. *The Era of Reconstruction, 1865–1877.* New York: Vintage.

Stanley, Harold, and Richard Niemi. 1993. "Partisanship and group support over time." Pp. 350–67 in Richard Niemi (ed.), *Controversies in Voting Behavior.* Washington, D.C.: Congressional Quarterly.

Starr, Amory. 2000. *Naming the Enemy. Anti-Corporate Movements Confront Globalization.* London: Zed.

Starr, Paul. 1992. "Social categories and claims in the liberal state." *Social Research* 59:263–95.

Staudt, Kathleen A. 1997. *Women, International Development, and Politics: The Bureaucratic Mire.* Updated and expanded ed., *Women in the Political Economy.* Philadelphia: Temple University Press.

______. 1998. *Policy, Politics, and Gender: Women Gaining Ground.* West Hartford, CT: Kumarian.

Stearns, Peter N. (ed.). 2001. *The Encyclopedia of World History, Ancient, Medieval, and Modern, Chronologically Arranged.* Boston: Houghton Mifflin.

Stedile, João Pedro. 2002. "Landless battalions." *New Left Review* 15 (May/June):77–104.

Stedman-Jones, Garth. 1983. *Languages of Class: Studies in English Working Class History, 1832–1902.* New York: Cambridge University Press.

Steedley, H. R., and J. Foley. 1979. "The success of protest groups." *Social Science Research* 8:1–15.

Steeh, Charlotte, and Maria Krysan. 1996. "Affirmative action and the public, 1970–1995." *Public Opinion Quarterly* 60:128–58.

Stefancic, Jean, and Richard Delgado. 1996. *No Mercy: How Conservative Think Tanks and Foundations Changed America's Social Agenda.* Philadelphia: Temple University Press.

Stein, Arlene. 1997. *Sex and Sensibility: Stories of a Lesbian Generation.* Berkeley: University of California Press.

Steinberg, Marc W. 1999. "The talk and back talk of collective action: A dialogic analysis of repertoires of discourse among nineteenth-century English cotton spinners." *American Journal of Sociology* 105:736–80.

Steinberg, Stephen. 2003. "No mere atavism: Race as a world system." *Contemporary Sociology* 32:415–17.

Steinmetz, George. 1993. *Regulating the Social: The Welfare State and Local Politics in Imperial Germany.* Princeton, NJ: Princeton University Press.

______. 1998. "Critical realism and historical sociology." *Comparative Studies in Society and History* 40(1):170–86.

______ (ed.). 1999. *State/Culture: State Formation after the Cultural Turn.* Ithaca, NY: Cornell University Press.

______. 1999. "Introduction: Culture and the State." In George Steinmetz (ed.), *State/Culture: State-Formation after the Cultural Turn.* Ithaca, NY: Cornell University Press.

______. 2003. " 'The devil's handwriting': precolonial discourse, ethnographic acuity, and cross-identification in German colonialism." *Comparative Studies in Society and History* 45(1):41–95.

______. (ed.). (Forthcoming). *Politics of Method in the Human Sciences: Positivism and Its Epistemological Others.* Durham, NC: Duke University Press.

Steinmo, Sven. 1993. *Taxation and Democracy: Swedish, British and American Approaches to Financing the Modern State.* New Haven, CT: Yale University Press.

Steinmo, Sven, Kathleen Thelen, and Frank Longstreth. 1992. *Structuring Politics.* New York: Cambridge University Press.

Stepan, Alfred. 1986. "Paths toward Redemocratization: Theoretical and Comparative Considerations." Pp. 64–84 in Guillermo O'Donnell, Philippe C. Schmitter, and Laurence Whitehead (eds.), *Transitions from Authoritarian Rule. Prospects for Democracy.* Baltimore: Johns Hopkins University Press.

Stephens, Evelyne Huber, and John D. Stephens. 1986. *Democratic Socialism in Jamaica: The Political

Movement and Social Transformation in Dependent Capitalism. London: Macmillan, and Princeton, NJ: Princeton University Press.

Stephens, John D. 1979. *The Transition from Capitalism to Socialism*. London: Macmillan.

______. 1979. "Class formation and class consciousness." *British Journal of Sociology* 30:389–414.

______. 1980. *The Transition from Capitalism to Socialism*. Atlantic Highlands, NJ: Humanities Press.

______. 1989. "Democratic transition and breakdown in Western Europe, 1870–1939: A test of the Moore thesis." *American Journal of Sociology* 94:1019–77.

______. 1991. "Explaining crossnational differences in union organization: Why are small countries more organized than large ones?" *American Political Science Review* 85:941–9.

______. 1996. "The Scandinavian welfare states." Pp. 32–65 in Gosta Esping-Andersen (ed.), *Welfare States in Transition*. London: Sage.

Stephens, John D., Evelyne Huber, and Leonard Ray. 1999. "The welfare state in hard times." Pp. 164–93 in Herbert Kitschelt, Peter Lange, Gary Marks, and John D. Stephens (eds.), *Continuity and Change in Contemporary Capitalism*. New York: Cambridge University Press.

Stephens, John, Dietrich Rueschemeyer, and Evelyn Huber Stephens. 1992. *Capitalist Development and Democracy*. New York: Cambridge University Press.

Stern, Phillip M. 1992. *Still the Best Congress Money Can Buy*. Washington, D.C.: Regnery Gateway.

Stetson, D. M. 2001. *Abortion Politics, Women's Movements, and the Democratic State: A Comparative Study of State Feminism*. Oxford, UK: Oxford University Press.

Stetson, D. M., and A. G. Mazur. 2000. "Women's movements and the state: Job-training policy in France and the US." *Political Research Quarterly* 53:597–623.

Stetson, Dorothy McBride, and Amy G. Mazur. 1995. *Comparative State Feminism*. Thousand Oaks, CA: Sage.

Stewart, Angus. 2001. *Theories of Power and Domination*. Thousand Oaks, CA: Sage.

Stienstra, D. 1994. *Women's Movements and International Organizations*. Basingstoke: Macmillan.

Stiglitz, Joseph E. 2002. *Globalization and Its Discontents*. New York and London: Norton.

Stimson, James A. 1999. *Public Opinion in America: Moods, Cycles, and Swings*, 2nd ed. Boulder, CO: Westview.

Stimson, James A., Michael MacKuen, and Robert S. Erikson. 1995. "Dynamic Representation." *American Political Science Review*, 89:543–65.

Stinchcombe, Arthur L. 1985 "The functionalist theory of social insurance." *Politics and Society* 4(4):411–30.

______. 1964. "Social structure and organizations." Pp. 142–193 in James March (ed.), *Handbook of Organizations*. Chicago: Rand McNally.

______. 1974. *Creating Efficient Industrial Administrations*. New York: Academic.

______. 1968. *Constructing Social Theories*. New York: Harcourt, Brace, and World.

______. 1997. "On the virtues of the old institutionalism." *Annual Review of Sociology* 23:1–18.

______. 1999a. "Ending revolutions and building new governments." *Annual Review of Political Science* 2:49–73.

______. 1999b. *Information and Organizations*. Berkeley: University of California Press.

Stoecker, Helmuth. 1985. "The position of Africans in the German colonies." Pp. 119–30 in Arthur Knoll and Lewis Gann (eds.), *Germans in the Tropics*. New York: Greenwood.

______. 1986. "The First World War." Pp. 270–96 in Helmuth Stoecker (ed.), *German Imperialism in Africa*. London: C. Hurst.

Stokman, Frans N., and Jaco Berveling. 1998. "Dynamic modeling of policy networks in Amsterdam." *Journal of Theoretical Politics* 10:577–601.

Stokman, Frans N., Rolf Ziegler, and John Scott (eds.). 1985. *Networks of Corporate Power: A Comparative Analysis of Ten Countries*. Cambridge, UK: Polity Press.

Stolle, D., and J. Lewis. 2002. "Social capital – an emerging concept." Pp. 195–231 in B. Hobson, J. Lewis, and B. Siim (eds.), *Contested Concepts in Gender and Social Politics*. Cheltenham: Elgar.

Stone, Clarence N. 1989. *Regime Politics: Governing Atlanta, 1946–1988*. Lawrence, KS: University Press of Kansas.

Stone, Diane, and Mark Garnett. 1998. "Think tanks, policy advice and governance." Pp. 1–20 in D. Stone, A. Denham, and M. Garnett (eds.), *Think Tanks Across Nations: A Comparative Approach*. Manchester, UK: Manchester University Press.

Stone, Diane. 2000. "Think tank transnationalisation and non-profit analysis, advice and advocacy." *Global Society* 14:153–72.

Stouffer, Samuel A., Edward A. Suchman, Leland C. DeVinney, Shirley A. Star, and Robin M. Williams, Jr. 1949. *The American Soldier*. Princeton, NJ: Princeton University Press.

Strange, Susan. 1996. *The Retreat of the State*. Cambridge, UK: Cambridge University Press.

Stratmann, Thomas. 1992. "Are campaign contributions rational? Untangling strategies of political action committees." *Journal of Political Economy* 100:647–64.

______. 1998. "The market for congressional votes: Is the timing of contributions everything?" *Journal of Law and Economics* 41:85–114.

Strauss, Anselm. 1958. *Mirrors and Masks.* New York: Free Press.

Streeck, Wolfgang. 1984. "Neo-corporatist industrial relations and the economic crisis in West Germany." Pp. 291–314 in John H. Goldthorpe (ed.), *Order and Conflict in Contemporary Capitalism.* Oxford, UK: Clarendon.

______. 1992. *Social Institutions and Economic Performance.* London: Sage.

______. 1997a. "German capitalism: Does it exist? Can it survive?" *New Political Economy* 2:237–56.

______. 1997b. "German capitalism: Does it exist? Can it survive?" Pp. 33–54 in Colin Crouch and Wolfgang Streeck (eds.). *The Political Economy of Modern Capitalism.* London: Sage.

______. 2001. "Introduction: Explorations into the origins of nonliberal capitalism in Germany and Japan." Pp. 1–38 in Wolfgang Streeck and Kozo Yamamura (eds.), *The Origins of Nonliberal Capitalism: Germany and Japan in Comparison.* Ithaca, NY: Cornell University Press.

Streeck, Wolfgang, Volker Schneider, Jelle Visser, and Jürgen R. Grote (eds.). 2003. *Governing Interests: Business Associations in the National, European and Global Political Economy.* Oxford, UK: Oxford University Press.

Streeck, Wolfgang, and Philippe C. Schmitter (eds.). 1985. *Private Interest Government: Beyond Market and State.* London: Sage.

______. 1991. "From national corporatism to transnational pluralism: Organized interests in the single European market." *Politics and Society* 19:133–64.

Stryker, Robyn. 1989. "Limits on technocratization of the law." *American Sociological Review* 54:341–358.

Stryker, Robin, and Scott Eliason. 2002. "Gender, class, and the welfare state: Left–center–right political preferences in France, Belgium, Germany, Italy, Denmark, and Britain, 1977–1994." Paper presented at the Gender Studies Program, Robert Schuman Center, European University Institute, Florence, Italy, February 13.

Stryuck, Raymond J. 1999. *Reconstructive Critics: Think Tanks in Post-Soviet Bloc Democracies.* Washington, DC: Urban Institute Press.

Stuempfle, Stephen. 1995. *The Steelband Movement: The Forging of a National Art in Trinidad and Tobago.* Philadelphia: University of Pennsylvania Press.

Stumpp, Karl. 1973. *The Emigration from Germany to Russia in the Years 1763 to 1862.* Lincoln, NE: American Historical Society of Germans from Russia.

Su, Tie-ting, Alan Neustadtl, and Dan Clawson. 1995. "Business and the conservative shift: Corporate PAC contributions, 1976–1986." *Social Science Quarterly* 76:20–40.

Subirats, Joan. 1994. *Análisis de políticas públicas y eficacia de la administración.* Madrid: MAP.

Sun, Ying. 2002. "Guli Haiwaixuezi Guiguo Chuangye Harbin Geiyu 10 Wan Chuangyefei" [Harbin gives out 100,000 RMB to attract overseas students]. *Harbin Daily*, June 27. http://edu.sina.com.cn/a/2022-06-27/26951.html

Suret-Canale, Jean. 1971. *French Colonialism in Tropical Africa, 1900–1945.* London: C. Hurst.

Sutherland, Edwin H. 1943. "Crime and the conflict process." Pp. 99–111 in Karl Schuessler (ed.), *Edwin H. Sutherland, On Analyzing Crime.* Chicago: University of Chicago Press.

Suzumura, Kotaro. 1989. *Rational Choice, Collective Decisions, and Social Welfare.* New York: Cambridge University Press.

Swain, Carol M. 1993. *Black Faces, Black Interests: The Representation of African Americans in Congress.* Cambridge, MA: Harvard University Press.

______. 2001. "Affirmative action: Legislative history, judicial interpretations, public consensus." Pp. 318–47 in N. J. Smelser, W. J. Wilson, and F. Mitchell (eds.), *America Becoming: Racial Trends and Their Consequences*, vol. 1. Washington, DC: National Academy.

Swank, Duane. 1988. "The political economy of governmental domestic expenditures in affluent democracies, 1960–1980." *American Journal of Political Science* 32:1121–50.

______. 1992. "Politics and the structural dependence of the state in democratic capitalist nations." *American Political Science Review* 86:38–54.

______. 2001. "Political institutions and welfare state restructuring." Pp. 197–237 in Paul Pierson (ed.), *The New Politics of the Welfare State.* Oxford, UK: Oxford University Press.

______. 2002a. *Diminished Democracy? Globalization, Political Institutions, and the Welfare State in Advanced Market Economies.* New York: Cambridge University Press.

______. 2002b. *Global Capital, Political Institutions, and Policy Change in Developed Welfare States.* New York: Cambridge University Press.

______. 2003. "Tax policy in an era of internationalization: An assessment of a conditional diffusion model of the spread of neoliberalism." Paper presented at Conference on The International Diffusion of Democracy and Markets, Weatherhead

Center for International Affairs, Harvard University, Cambridge, MA, October 3–4.

Swank, Duane, and Cathie Jo Martin. 2001. "Employers and the welfare state: The political economic organization of firms and social policy in contemporary capitalist democracies." *Comparative Political Studies* 34:889–923.

Swank, Duane, and Hans-Georg Betz. 2003. "Globalization, the welfare state, and right-wing populism in Western Europe." *Socio-Economic Review* 1:215–45.

Swank, Duane, and Sveum Steinmo. 2002. "The new political economy of taxation in advanced capitalist democracies." *American Journal of Political Science* 46(3):642–55.

Swann, Dennis. 1988. *The Retreat of the State: Deregulation and Privatization in the UK and US.* Ann Arbor: University of Michigan Press.

Swanson, David, and Paolo. Mancini. 1996. *Politics, Media and Modern Democracy*. Westport, CT: Praeger.

Swanson, Guy E. 1956. "Agitation through the press: A study of the personalities of publicists." *Public Opinion Quarterly* 20:441–56.

______. 1957. "Agitation in face-to-face contacts: A study of the personalities of agitators." *Public Opinion Quarterly* 21:288–94.

Swarns, Rachel L., and Onishi, Norimitsu. 2002. "Africa creeps along path to democracy," *New York Times*, June 2.

Swedberg, Richard. 2003. "The changing picture of Max Weber's sociology." *Annual Review of Sociology* 29:283–306.

Sweezy, Paul M. 1968[1956]. "Power elite or ruling class?" Pp. 115–32 in G. William Domhoff and Hoyt B. Ballard (eds.), *C. Wright Mills and The Power Elite.* Boston: Beacon Press.

Swenson, Peter. 1997. "Arranged alliance: Business interests in the New Deal." *Politics and Society* 25 (1):66–116.

______. 2001. *Talk of Love: How Culture Matters.* Chicago: University of Chicago Press.

______. 2002. *Capitalists Against Markets: The Making of Labor Markets and Welfare States in the United States and Sweden.* New York: Oxford University Press.

Swidler, Ann. 1986. "Culture in action: Symbols and strategies." *American Sociological Review* 51:273–86.

Szalai, J. 1991. "Some aspects of the changing situation of women in Hungary." *Signs* 17:151–70.

Tabb, William. 2000. "After Seattle: Understanding the politics of globalization." *Monthly Review* 51, 10:1–18.

Taira, Koji, and Teiichi Wada. 1987. "Business–government relations in modern Japan: A Todai–Yakkai–Zaikai complex?" Pp. 264–97 in Mark S. Mizruchi and Michael Schwartz (eds.), *Intercorporate Relations: The Structural Analysis of Business.* New York: Cambridge University Press.

Tarrow, Sidney G. 1994. *Power in Movement: Social Movements, Collective Action and Politics.* New York: Oxford University Press.

______. 1995a. "The Europeanisation of conflict: Reflections from a social movement perspective." *West European Politics* 18:223–251.

______. 1995b. "Linking politics and collective action." Paper presented at the annual meeting of the American Sociological Association, Washington, DC, August.

______. 1996. "States and opportunities." Pp. 41–61 in Doug McAdam, John D. McCarthy, and Mayer Zald (eds.), *Comparative Perspectives on Social Movements.* New York: Cambridge University Press.

______. 1998. *Power in Movement Social Movements and Contentious Politics*, 2nd ed. *Cambridge Studies in Comparative Politics.* New York: Cambridge University Press.

______. 2001. "Transnational politics: Contention and institutions in international politics." *Annual Review of Political Science* 4:1–20.

______. 2002. "From lumping to splitting: Inside 'globalization' and 'resistance'. " Pp. 222–49 in Jackie Smith and Hank Johnston (eds.), *Globalization and Resistance.* Lanham, MD: Rowman and Littlefield.

______. 2003. "Confessions of a recovering structuralist." *Mobilization* 8:134–41.

Tatalovich, Raymond. 1995. *Nativism Reborn: The Official English Language Movement and the American States.* Lexington: University Press of Kentucky.

Tate, Katherine. 1993. *From Protest to Politics.* Cambridge, MA: Harvard University Press.

Tawney, R. H. 1931. *Equality.* London: Allen and Unwin.

Taylor, C. 1994. "The politics of recognition." Pp. 25–74 in C. Taylor, A Gutmann, A. Appiah, and J. Habermas (eds.), *Multiculturalism: Examining the Politics of Recognition.* Princeton, NJ: Princeton University Press.

Taylor, Charles. 1989. *Sources of the Self: The Making of the Modern Identity.* Cambridge, MA: Harvard University Press.

Taylor, Verta, and Nancy Whittier. 1995. "Analytical approaches to social movement culture." Pp. 163–87 in Hank Johnston and Bert Klandermans (eds.), *Social Movements and Culture.* Minneapolis: University of Minnesota Press.

Taylor, Verta. 1989. "Social movement continuity: The women's movement in abeyance." *American Sociological Review* 54:461–75.

Teichman, Judith A. 2001. *The Politics of Freeing Markets in Latin America.* Chapel Hill: University of North Carolina Press.

Teixeira, Ruy. 1992. *The Disappearing American Voter*. Washington, D.C.: Brookings Institute.

Teles, Steven M. 1998. "Why is there no affirmative action in Britain?" *American Behavioral Scientist* 41:1004–26.

Tettey, W. J. 2001. "The media and democratization in Africa: Contributions, constraints and concerns of the private press." *Media, Culture and Society* 23:5–31.

Thaler, Richard H. 1991. *Quasi-Rational Economics*. New York: Russell Sage.

______. 1992. *The Winner's Curse: Paradoxes and Anomalies of Economic Life*. New York: Free Press.

Thatcher, Mark. 1998. "The development of policy network analysis. From modest origins to overarching frameworks" *Journal of Theoretical Politics* 10(4):389–446.

Thayer, Millie. 2000. "Traveling feminisms: From embodied women to gendered citizenship. Pp. 203–33 in M. Burawoy, J. A. Blum, S. George, Z. Gille, T. Gowan, L. Haney, M. Klawiter, S. H. Lopez, S. Riain, and M. Thayer (eds.), *Global Ethnography: Forces, Connections, and Imaginations in a Postmodern World*. Berkeley: University of California Press.

______. 2001. "Transnational feminism: Reading Joan Scott in the Brazilian sertão." *Ethnography* 2 (2):243–71.

______. 2002. "Feminists and funding: Plays of power in the social movement market." Unpublished.

Thelen, Kathleen. 1999. "Historical institutionalism in comparative politics." *Annual Review of Political Science* 2:369–404.

______. 2001. "Varieties of labor politics in the developed democracies." Pp. 71–103 in Peter Hall and David Soskice (eds.), *Varieties of Capitalism*. Oxford, UK: Oxford University Press.

Thelen, Katheen, and Sven Steinmo. 1992. "Historical institutionalism in comparative politics." Introduction in Sven Steinmo, Kathleen Thelen, and Frank Longstreth (eds.), *Structuring Politics: Historical Institutionalism in Comparative Analysis*. New York: Cambridge University Press.

Therborn, Göran. 1976. *Science, Class and Society: On the Formation of Sociology and Historical Materialism*. London: NLB.

______. 1977. "The rule of capital & the rise of democracy." *New Left Review* 103:3–41.

______. 1978. *What Does the Ruling Class Do When It Rules? State Apparatuses and State Power Under Feudalism, Capitalism and Socialism*. London: New Left Books.

______. 1983. "When, how, and why does a welfare state become a welfare state?" Paper presented at the ECPR Workshops, Freiburg (March).

______. 1987. "Does corporatism really matter? The economic crisis and issues of political theory." *Journal of Public Policy* 7:259–84.

Thernstrom, Abigail M. 1987. *Whose Votes Count?: Affirmative Action and Minority Voting Rights*. Cambridge, MA: Harvard University Press.

Thernstrom, Stephan, and Abigail M. Thernstrom. 1997. *America in Black and White: One Nation, Indivisible*. New York: Simon & Schuster.

Thomas, Clive A., and Ronald J. Hrebenar. 1995. "The interest group political party connection: Fundamentals of the relationship." Paper presented to the annual meeting of the American Political Science Association, Chicago, September.

Thomas, Clive S. (ed.). 1993. *First World Interest Groups*. Westport, CT: Greenwood Press.

Thomas, George, and John Meyer. 1984. "The expansion of the state." *Annual Review of Sociology* 10:461–82.

Thompson, E. P. 1963. *The Making of the English Working Class*. New York: Vintage.

______. 1971. "The Moral Economy of the English Crowd in the Eighteenth Century." *Past and Present*, 50.

______. 1975. *Whigs and Hunters: The Origin of the Black Act*. New York: Pantheon Books.

______. 1978. *Poverty of Theory and Other Essays*. New York: Monthly Review Press.

______. 1982. "Notes on exterminism, the last stage of civilisation." Pp. 41–79 in E. P. Thompson (ed.), *Beyond the Cold War: A New Approach to the Arms Race and Nuclear Annihilation*. New York:Merlin.

______. 1993. "Time, work-discipline and industrial capitalism." Pp. 352–403 in E. P. Thompson (ed.), *Customs in Common*. New York: New Press.

Thompson, James D. 1967. *Organizations in Action*. New York: McGraw–Hill.

Thompson, John B. 1995. *The Media and Modernity: A Social Theory of the Media*. Cambridge, UK: Polity.

______. 2000. *Political Scandal: Power and Visibility in the Media Age*. Cambridge, UK: Polity.

Thränhardt, Dietrich. 2000. "Conflict, consensus, and policy outcomes." Pp. 162–86 in Ruud Koopmans and Paul Statham (eds.), *Challenging Immigration and Ethnic Relations Politics*. Oxford, UK: Oxford University Press.

Thurber, James A., and Candice J. Nelson (eds.). 1995. *Campaigns and Elections American Style*. Boulder, CO: Westview

Tianjin City. 1998. "Guli Tianjin Jishu Chanye Yuanxu Huayuan Ruanjianyuan Jianli Ruanjian Qiye de Zhanxing Banfa" [The implementing measures to encourage setting up software companies in the Tianjin Advance and New Technology area at Huayuan Software Park]. http://www.ctitj.com/zcfg/disp.asp?recno=93.

Tichenor, Daniel. 2002. *Dividing Lines: The Politics of Immigration Control in America*. Princeton, NJ: Princeton University Press.

Tickner, J. A. 2001. *Gendering World Politics: Issues and Approaches in the Post-Cold War Era*. New York: Columbia University Press.

Tigar, Michael with the assistance of Madeleine R. Levy. 1977. *Law and the Rise of Capitalism*. New York: Monthly Review Press.

Tilly, Charles. 1969. "Collective Violence in European Perspective." In Hugh Davis Graham and Ted Robert Gurr (eds.), *The History of Violence in America*. New York: Praeger.

______ (ed.). 1975. *The Formation of National States in Western Europe*. Princeton, NJ: Princeton University Press.

______. 1975. "Reflections on the history of European state-making." Pp. 3–83 in Charles Tilly (ed.), *The Formation of National States in Western Europe*. Cambridge, MA: Harvard University Press.

______. 1978. *From Mobilization to Revolution*. Reading, MA: Addison-Wesley.

______. 1981a. "Stein Rokkan's conceptual map of Europe." Working Papers of the Center for Research on Social Organizations, University of Michigan, No. 229.

______. 1981b. "Sinews of War." Pp. 108–26 in Per Torsvik (ed.), *Mobilization, Center-Periphery Structures and Nation-Building, A Volume in Commemoration of Stein Rokkan*. Bergen, Norway: Universitetsforlaget.

______. 1982. "Britain Creates the Social Movement." Pp. 21–52 in James E. Cronin and Jonathan Schneer (eds.). *Social Conflict and the Political Order in Modern Britain*. New Brunswick, NJ: Rutgers University Press.

______. 1984. "Social Movements and National Politics." In Charles Bright and Susan Harding (eds.), *Statemaking and Social Movements.* Ann Arbor, MI: University of Michigan Press.

______. 1984a. *Big Structures, Large Processes, Huge Comparisons*. New York: Russell Sage Foundation.

______. 1984b. "The state as a protection racket." Pp. 169–91 in Peter Evans, Dietrich Rueschemeyer, and Theda Skocpol (eds.), *Bringing the State Back In*. New York: Cambridge University Press.

______. 1985. "War making and state making as organized crime." Pp. 169–91 in Peter Evans, Dietrich Rueschemeyer, and Theda Skocpol (eds.), *Bringing the State Back In*. Cambridge, UK: Cambridge University Press.

______. 1986. "Structural Change and Contention in Great Britain, 1758–1834." Center for Studies of Social Change, New School of Social Research Working Paper no. 36.

______. 1986. *The Contentious French*. Cambridge, MA: Harvard University Press.

______. 1990. *Coercion, Capital and European States AD 990–1990*. Oxford, UK: Basil Blackwell.

______. 1991. "Prisoners of the state." New York: Center for Studies of Social Change Working Papers, #129.

______. 1993. *European Revolutions, 1492–1992*. Oxford, UK: Blackwell.

______. 1995. "To explain political processes." *American Journal of Sociology* 100:1594–610.

______. 1995. "Globalization threatens labor's rights." *International Labor and Working Class History* 47:1–23.

______. 1997. "Democracy is a lake." Pp. 193–215 in Charles Tilly (ed.), *Roads from Past to Future*. Lanham, MD: Rowman Littlefield.

______. 1998. *Durable Inequality*. Berkeley: University of California Press.

______. 1999. "From interactions to outcomes in social movements." Pp. 253–70 in Marco Giugni, Doug McAdam, and Charles Tilly (eds.), *How Social Movements Matter*. Minneapolis: University of Minnesota Press.

______. 2001. "Mechanisms in political processes." *Annual Review of Political Science* 4:21–41.

______. 2003. *The Politics of Collective Violence*. Cambridge, UK: Cambridge University Press.

Tilly, Chris, Philip Moss, Joleen Kirschenman, and Ivy Kennelly. 2001. "Space as signal: How employers perceive neighborhoods in four metropolitan labor markets." Pp. 304–38 in A. O'Connor, C. Tilly, and L. D. Bobo (eds.), *Urban Inequality: Evidence from Four Cities*. New York: Russell Sage Foundation.

Tinbergen, Jan. 1952. *On the Theory of Economic Policy*. Amsterdam: North Holland.

Tingsten, Herbert. 1963 [1937]. *Political Behavior: Studies in Election Statistics*. Totowa, NJ: Bedminster.

Tirman, J. (ed.). 1984. *The Militarization of High Technology*. Cambridge, MA: Ballinger.

Titmuss, Richard. 1958. *Essays on the Welfare State*. London: Allen and Unwin.

______. 1974. *Social Policy*. London: Allen & Unwin.

Tokman, Victor. 2002. "Jobs and solidarity: Challenges for labor market policy in Latin America." Pp. 159–94 in Evelyne Huber (ed.), *Models of Capitalism: Lessons for Latin America*. University Park: Pennsylvania State University Press.

Tomlinson, John. 1991. *Cultural Imperialism: A Critical Introduction*. London: Pinter.

______. 1999. *Globalization and Culture*. Chicago: University of Chicago Press.

Topf, Richard. 1995. "Electoral participation." Pp. 27–51 in Hans-Dieter Klingemann and Dieter Fuchs (eds.), *Citizens and the State*. New York: Oxford University Press.

Torfing, Jacob. 1998. *Politics, Regulation and the Modern Welfare State*. Basingstoke, UK: Macmillan.

______. 1999. *New Theories of Discourse: Laclau, Mouffe and Žižek*. Oxford, UK: Blackwell.

Tossutti, Livianna A. 2002. "How transnational factors influence the success of ethnic, religious and regional parties in 21 states." *Party Politics* 8:51–74.

Tourain, Alain. 1971. *The Post-Industrial Society*. New York: Random House.

Tranparency International. 2001. "2001 Corruption Perceptions Index," http://www.tranparency.org/cpi/2001/ pi2001.html

______. 2003. "2002 Corruption Perceptions Index," in "Global Corruption Report 2003," http://www.globalcorruptionreport.org/download.shtml

Traxler, Franz, and Bernhard Kittel. 2000. "The bargaining system and performance: A comparison of 18 OECD countries." *Comparative Political Studies* 33:1154–90.

Traxler, Franz, Sabine Blaschke, and Bernhard Kittel. 2001. *National Labour Relations in Internationalized Markets*. Oxford, UK: Oxford University Press.

Trelease, Allen W. 1971. *White Terror: The Ku Klux Klan Conspiracy and Southern Reconstruction*. New York: Harper & Row.

Trent, Judith S., and Robert V. Friedenberg. 2000. *Political Campaign Communication: Principles and Practices*, 4th ed. Westport, CT: Praeger.

Trice, Harrison M., and Janice M. Beyer. 1993. *The Cultures of Work Organizations*. Englewood Cliffs, NJ: Prentice Hall.

Trigilia, Carlo. 1990. "Work and politics in Third Italy's industrial districts." Pp. 160–84 in F. Pyke, G. Becattini, and W. Sengenberger (eds.), *Industrial Districts and Inter-Firm Cooperation in Italy*. Geneva: International Institute for Labor Studies.

Trimberger, Ellen Kay. 1978. *Revolution From Above: Military Bureaucrats and Development in Japan, Turkey, Egypt, and Peru*. New Brunswick, NJ: Transaction Books.

Tronto, J. 1993. *Moral Boundaries: A Political Argument for an Ethic of Care*. New York: Routledge.

Trotsky, Leon. 1961[1932]. *The History of the Russian Revolution*. New York: Monad Press.

Truman, David B. 1951. *The Governmental Process: Political Interests and Public Opinion*. Westport, CT: Greenwood Press.

______. 1993[1951]. *The Governmental Process: Political Interests and Public Opinion*, 2nd ed. Berkeley, CA: Institute of Governmental Studies.

Tsebelis, George. 1990. *Nested Games: Rational Choice in Comparative Politics*. Berkeley: University of California Press.

______. 1999. "Veto players and law production in parliamentary democracies." *American Political Science Review* 93(3):591–608.

Tu, Weiming. 1996. "Beyond the Enlightenment mentality: A Confucian perspective on ethics, migration, and global stewardship." *International Migration Review* 30(1):58–75.

Tuch, Steven A., and Michael Hughes. 1996. "Whites' racial policy attitudes." *Social Science Quarterly* 77:723–45.

Tuchman, Gaye. 1972. "Objectivity as strategic ritual: An examination of newsmen's notions of objectivity." *American Journal of Sociology* 77: 660–79.

______. 1978. *Making News: A Study in the Construction of Reality*. New York: Free Press.

Tully, James. 1995. *Strange Multiplicity*. Cambridge, UK: Cambridge University Press.

Turk, Austin. 1966. "Conflict and Criminality." *American Sociological Review*. 31:338–351.

______. 1982. *Political Criminality*. Beverly Hills, CA: Sage.

Turkey. 1987. *The Constitution of the Republic of Turkey*. http://www.hri.org.docs/turkey/.

Turner, Bryan. 1981. *For Weber*. London: Routledge & Kegan Paul.

______. 1986a. *Citizenship and Capitalism. The Debate Over Reformism*. London: Allen & Unwin.

______. 1986b. "Personhood & Citizenship." *Theory, Culture and Society* 3(1):1–16.

______. 1988. *Status*. Minneapolis: University of Minnesota Press.

______. 1990. "Outline of a theory of citizenship." *Sociology* 24:189–217.

______. 1992. *Max Weber: From History to Modernity*. London: Routlege.

______. (ed.). 1993. *Citizenship and Social Theory*. London: Sage.

______. 1993a. "Contemporary problems in the theory of citizenship." Pp. 1–18 in Bryan Turner (ed.), *Citizenship and Social Theory*. Newbury Park, CA: Sage.

______. 1997. "Citizenship studies: A general theory." *Citizenship Studies* 1:5–18.

______. 2000. "Cosmopolitan virtue: Loyalty and the city." Pp. 129–47 in Engin F. Isin (ed.), *Democracy, Citizenship and the Global City*. London and New York: Routledge.

Turner, Jonathan, and C. Power. 1981. "Theory and political sociology." Pp. 139–201 in Samuel Long (ed.). *Handbook of Political Behavior*. New York: Plenum.

Turner, Ralph, and Lewis Killian. 1987[1957, 1972]. *Collective Behavior*, 1st, 2nd, and 3rd eds. Englewood Cliffs, NJ: Prentice Hall.

Turner, Stephen P. 1994. *The Social Theory of Practices: Tradition, Tacit Knowledge and Presuppositions*. Chicago: University of Chicago Press.

______. 2002. *Brains/Practices/Relativism: Social Theory after Cognitive Science*. Chicago: University of Chicago Press.

Turner, Victor. 1967. *The Forest of Symbols: Aspects of Ndembu Ritual*. Ithaca, NY: Cornell University Press.

______. 1974. *Dramas, Fields, and Metaphors: Symbolic Action in Human Society*. Ithaca, NY: Cornell University Press.

TWIG/This Week in Germany. "Controversial immigration law passed." 6/24/2002.

Tyler, Tom R., and Heather Smith. 1998. "Social justice and social movements." Pp. xxx in Daniel T. Gilbert, Susan T. Fiske, and Gardner Lindzey (eds.), *Handbook of Social Psychology*, 4th ed. New York: Oxford University Press.

U.S. Bureau of the Census. 2000. *Statistical Abstract of the United States*. Washington, DC: U.S. Bureau of the Census.

______ 2002. *Statistical Abstract of the United States*. Washington, DC: U.S. Bureau of the Census.

Uggen, Christopher, and Jeff Manza. 2002. "Democratic contraction? the political consequences of felon disenfranchisement in the United States." *American Sociological Review* 67:777– 803.

United Nations Development Report, 1999. *Human Development Report*. Oxford, UK: Oxford University Press.

UNIFEM. 2003. *Progress of the World's Women 2002: Volume 2*. New York: United Nations Development Fund for Women. http://www.unifem.org.

United Nations. 1994. "The 20-year programme of action." *UN Chronicle* 31:66–8.

United Nations, Population Division, Department of Economic and Social Affairs. 2003. *Fertility, Contraception and Population Policies*. New York: United Nations.

Urry, John. 2000. "Global flows and global citizenship." Pp. 62–78 in Engin F. Isin (ed.), *Democracy, Citizenship and the Global City*. London and New York: Routledge.

Useem, Michael. 1979. "The social organization of the American business elite and the participation of corporate directors in the governance of American institutions." *American Sociological Review* 44:553–572.

______. 1982. "Classwide rationality in the politics of managers and directors of large corporations in the United States and Great Britain." *Administrative Science Quarterly* 27:199–226.

______. 1984. *The Inner Circle: Large Corporations and the Rise of Political Activities in the U.S. and U.K.* New York: Oxford University Press.

______. 1996. *Investor Capitalism*. New York: Basic Books.

Useem, Michael, and Jerome Karabel. 1986. "Pathways to top corporate management." *American Sociological Review* 51:184–200.

Usui, Chikako. 1991. "The origins and development of modern welfare policies." *Research in Political Sociology* 6:39–70.

Valelly, Richard M. 1995a. "National parties and racial disfranchisement." Pp. 188–216 in P. E. Peterson (ed.), *Classifying by Race, Princeton Studies in American Politics*. Princeton, NJ: Princeton University Press.

______. 1995b. "The vanishing voters." Pp. 194–201 in Theda Skocpol and John Campbell (eds.), *American Politics and Society*. New York: McGraw–Hill.

______. 2004. *The Two Reconstructions: The Struggle for Plack Enfranchisement*. Chicago: University of Chicago Press.

Valiente, Celia. 2001. "A closed sub-system and distant feminist demands block women-friendly outcomes in Spain." Pp. 111–30 in Amy G. Mazur (ed.), *State Feminism, Women's Movements, and Job Training: Making Democracies Work in the Global Economy*. New York: Routledge.

Van Arnheim, J., M. Corina, and Geurt J. Schotsman. 1982. "Do parties affect the distribution of income? The case of advanced capitalist democracies." In Francis Castles (ed.), *The Impact of Parties*. Beverly Hills, CA: Sage.

van Creveld, Martin. 1989. *Technology and War: From 2000 BC to the Present*. New York: Free Press.

van den Berg, Axel. 2003. *The Immanent Utopia: From Marxism on the State to the State of Marxism*. Brunswick, NJ: Transaction.

van den Berghe, Pierre L. 1967. *Race and Racism: A Comparative Perspective*. New York: Wiley.

______. 1987. *The Ethnic Phenomenon*. New York: Praeger.

______. 2002. "Multicultural democracy: Can it work?" *Nations and Nationalism* 8:433–49.

van der Eijk, Cees, et al. 1992. "Cleavages, conflict resolution and democracy." Pp. 406–431 in Mark Franklin, Thomas Mackie, and Henry Valen (eds.), *Electoral Change*. New York: Cambridge University Press.

Van Doorne-Huiskes, Anneke. 1995. "The comparable worth strategy." Pp. 203–16 in Anneke van Doorne-Huiskes, Jacques van Hoof, and Ellie

Roelofs (eds.), *Women and the European Labor Markets*. London: Paul Chapman.

Van Doorne-Huiskes, Anneke, Laura den Dulk, and Joop Schippers. 1999. "Work-family arrangements in the context of welfare states." Pp. 1–20 in Laura den Dulk, Anneke Van Doorne-Huiskes, and Joop Schippers (eds.), *Work-Family Arrangements in Europe*. Amsterdam: Netherlands School for Social and Economic Policy Research.

Van Dyke, Nella. 2003. "Protest cycles and party politics." Pp. 226–45 in Jack Goldstone (ed.), *Parties, Politics and Movements*. New York: Cambridge University Press.

van Kersbergen, Kees. 1996. *Social Capitalism: A Study of Christian Democracy and the Welfare State*. London: Routledge.

van Steenbergen, Bart (ed.). 1994. *The Condition of Citizenship*. Thousand Oaks, CA: Sage.

Van Vleuten, Tineke. 1995. "Legal instruments at the EU level." Pp. 143–62 in Anneke van Doorne-Huiskes, Jacques van Hoof, and Ellie Roelofs (eds.), *Women and the European Labor Markets*. London: Paul Chapman.

Van Waarden, Frans. 1992. "Dimensions and types of policy networks." *European Journal of Political Research* 21:29–52.

Van Young, Eric. 2001. *The Other Rebellion: Popular Violence, Ideology, and the Struggle for Mexican Independence, 1810–1821*. Palo Alto, CA: Stanford University Press.

Vanhanen, Tatu. 1997. *Prospects of Democracy. A Study of 172 Countries*. London: Routledge.

Verba, Sidney. 1980. "On revisiting the civic culture: A personal postscript." Pp. 394–410 in Gabriel A. Almond and Sidney Verba (eds.), *The Civic Culture Revisited*. Boston: Little, Brown.

Verba, Sidney, Kay Lehman Schlozman, and Henry E. Brady. 1995. *Voice and Equality*. Cambridge, MA: Harvard University Press.

Verba, Sidney, Norman H. Nie, and Jae-On Kim. 1978[1987]. *Participation and Political Equality*. Chicago: University of Chicago Press.

Verba, Sidney, Norman H. Nie, and John R. Petrocik. 1979. *The Changing American Voter*, enlarged ed. Cambridge, MA: Harvard University Press.

Verdery, Katherine. 1996. *What Was Socialism, and What Comes Next*? Princeton, NJ: Princeton University Press.

Vilas, Carlos M. 1995. *Between Earthquakes and Volcanoes: Market, State, and the Revolutions in Central America* (Ted Kuster, trans.). New York: Monthly Review Press.

Virgil, Maurilio. 1990. "The ethnic organization as an instrument of political change: MALDEF, a case study." *Journal of Ethnic Studies* 18(1):15– 31.

Visser, Jelle, and Anton Hemerijck. 1997. *"A Dutch Miracle": Job Growth, Welfare Reform, and Corporatism in the Netherlands*. Amsterdam: Amsterdam University Press.

Visser, Jelle, and Bernhard Ebbinghaus. 1992. "Making the most of diversity." In J. Greenwood, J. R. Grote, and K. Ronit (eds.), *Organized Interests and the European Community*. London: Sage.

Vogel, David. 1989. *Fluctuating Fortunes: The Political Power of Business in America*. New York: Basic Books.

______. 1996. *Kindred Strangers: The Uneasy Relationship Between Politics and Business in America*. Princeton, NJ: Princeton University Press.

Vogel, Lise. 1983. *Marxism and the Oppression of Women: Toward a Unitary Theory*. London: Pluto.

Vogel, Ursula. 1994. "Marriage and the boundaries of citizenship." Pp. 76–89 in B. V. Steenbergen (ed.), *The Condition of Citizenship*. London: Sage.

Vold, George B. 1958. *Theoretical Criminology*. New York: Oxford University Press.

von Beyme, Klaus. 1982. *Parties in Western Democracies*. Munich: Piper Verlag.

Von Eschen, Penny. 1997. *Race Against Empire: Black Americans and Anticolonialism*. Ithaca, NY: Cornell University Press.

Voss, Kim. 1993. *The Making of American Exceptionalism: The Knights of Labor and Class Formation in the Nineteenth Century*. Ithaca, NY: Cornell University Press.

______. 1996. "The collapse of a social movement: The interplay of mobilizing structures, framing, and political opportunities in the Knights of Labor." Pp. 227–60 in Doug McAdam, John D. McCarthy, and Mayer N. Zald (eds.), *Comparative Perspectives on Social Movements*. New York: Cambridge University Press.

Voss, Kim, and R. Sherman. 2000. "Breaking the iron law of oligarchy: Union revitalization in the American labor movement." *American Journal of Sociology* 106(2):303–49.

Vuola, Elina. 2002. "Remaking universals?—transnational feminism(s) challenging fundamentalist ecumenism." *Theory Culture & Society* 19(1–2): 175–195.

Wacquant, Loïc. 2002. "Scrutinizing the street: Poverty, morality, and the pitfalls of urban ethnography." *American Journal of Sociology* 107:1468–1532.

Wade, Robert. 2001. "The US role in the malaise at the World Bank: Get up, Gulliver!" Paper presented at the meetings of the American Political Science Association, San Francisco, August.

Wagner-Pacific, Robin Erica. 1986. *The Moro Morality Play: Terrorism as Social Drama*. Chicago: University of Chicago Press.

Wagner-Pacifici, Robin, and Barry Schwartz. 1991. "The Vietnam Veterans Memorial: Commemorating a difficult past." *American Journal of Sociology* 97:376–420.

Waisbord, Silvio. 1995. "Leviathan dreams: State and broadcasting in South America." *Communication Review* 1:201–26.

______. 1994. "Knocking on newsroom doors: The press and political scandals in Argentina." *Political Communication* 11:19–33.

______. 1997. "The narrative of exposes in South American journalism." *Gazette* 59:189–203.

______. 2000. *Watchdog Journalism in Latin America*. New York: Columbia University Press.

Walby, Sylvia. 1990. *Theorizing Patriarchy*. Oxford, UK: Basil Blackwell.

______. 1994. "Is citizenship gendered? *Sociology*. 28:(2): 379–95.

______. 1997. *Gender Transformations*. London: Routledge.

Wald, Kenneth, Dennis E. Owen, and Samuel S. Hill, Jr. 1990. "Political cohesion in churches." *Journal of Politics* 52:197–215.

Walder, Andrew, Bobai Li, and Donald Treiman. 2000. "Politics and life chances in a state socialist regime: Dual career paths into the urban Chinese elite, 1949–1996." *American Sociological Review* 65(2):191–209.

Waldinger, Roger. 2001. "Strangers at the gates." Pp. 1–29 in Roger Waldinger (ed.), *Strangers at the Gates: New Immigrants in Urban America*. Berkeley: University of California Press.

Waldner, Lisa, Timothy Buzzell, and Dobratz, Betty. 2002. "Introduction." Pp. xiii–xvi in *Theoretical Directions for Political Sociology for the 21st Century*, Vol. 11. New York/Amsterdam: JAI/Elsevier Science.

Waldrauch, Harald, and Christoph Hofinger. 1997. "An index to measure the legal obstacles to the integration of migrants." *New Community* 23(2):271–85.

Walker, Jack L. 1966. "A critique of the elitist theory of democracy." *American Political Science Review* 60:285–95.

Walker, Mack. 1964. *Germany and the Emigration, 1816–1885*. Cambridge, MA: Harvard University Press.

______. 1971. *German Home Towns*. Ithaca, NY: Cornell University Press.

Walker, Samuel, Cassia Spohn, and Miriam DeLone. 2004. *The Color of Justice: Race, Ethnicity, and Crime in America*. Belmont, CA: Wadsworth.

Waller, Willard. 1951. *The Family: A Dynamic Interpretation*. New York: Dryden.

Wallerstein, Immanuel M. 1974. *The Modern World System I: Capitalist Agriculture and the Origins of the European World System in the Sixteenth Century*. New York: Academic Press.

______. 1980. *The Modern World System II*. San Diego, CA: Academic Press.

______. 1989. *The Modern World System III*. San Diego, CA: Academic Press.

______. 1995. *After Liberalism*. New York: Vintage.

______. 1997. "The National and the universal: Can there be such a thing as world culture?" Pp. xxx in Anthony D. King (ed.), *Culture, Globalization and the World-System*. Minneapolis: University of Minnesota Press.

______. 2000. *The Essential Wallerstein*. New York: New Press.

______. 2002. "New revolts against the system." *New Left Review* 18:29–40.

Wallerstein, Michael. 1987. "Unemployment, collective bargaining, and the demand for protection." *American Journal of Political Science* 31:729–52.

______. 1989. "Union organization in advanced industrial democracies." *American Political Science Review* 83:481–501.

______. 1991. "Industrial concentration, country size, and union membership: Response to Stephens." *American Political Science Review* 85:949–53.

______. 1999. "Wage-setting institutions and pay inequality in advanced industrial societies." *American Journal of Political Science* 43:649–80.

Walton, John. 1976. "Structures of power in Latin American cities: Toward a summary and interpretation." Pp. 136–78 in Alejandro Portes and John Walton (eds.), *Urban Latin America: The Political Condition from Above and Below*. Austin: University of Texas Press.

______. 1984. *Reluctant Rebels: Comparative Studies of Revolutions and Underdevelopment*. New York: Columbia University Press.

Walton, John, and David Seddon. 1994. *Free Markets and Food Riots: The Politics of Global Adjustment*. Oxford: Blackwell.

Walzer, Michael. 1997. *On Toleration*. New Haven, CT: Yale University Press.

Wapner, P. 1995. "Politics beyond the state–environmental activism and world civic politics." *World Politics* 47 (3):311–40.

Ward, Brian. 1998. *Just My Soul Responding: Rhythm and Blues, Black Consciousness, and Race Relations*. Berkeley: University of California Press.

Ward, Kathryn. 1990. "Introduction and overview." Pp. 1–22 in Kathryn Ward (ed.), *Women Workers and Global Restructuring*. Ithaca, NY: Cornell University Press.

______. 1993. "Reconceptualizing world-system theory to include women." Pp. 43–68 in Paula

England (ed.), *Theory on Gender/Feminism on Theory*. New York: Aldine de Gruyter.

Ward, Kathryn, and Jean Larson Pyle. 1995. "Gender, industrialization, corporations, and development." Pp. 37–63 in Christine E. Bose and Edna Acosta-Belén (eds.), *Women in the Latin American Development Process*. Philadelphia: Temple University Press.

Ware, Alan. 1987a. *Citizens, Parties and the State: A Reappraisal*. Cambridge, UK: Polity Press.

______. (ed.). 1987b. *Political Parties: Electoral Change and Structural Response*. New York: Basil Blackwell.

______. 1988. *The Breakdown of Democratic Party Organization, 1940–1980*. New York: Oxford University Press.

______. 1996. *Political Parties and Party Systems*. Oxford, UK: Oxford University Press.

Washburn, Philo C. 1982. *Political Sociology: Approaches, Concepts, Hypotheses*. Englewood Cliffs, NJ: Prentice Hall.

Watkins, Kevin. 1996. "Free trade and farm fallacies: From the Uruguay Round to the World Food Summit." *The Ecologist* 26, 6:244–55.

Wattenberg, Martin P. 1996. *The Decline of American Political Parties, 1952–1994*. Cambridge, MA: Harvard University Press.

______. 2000. "The Decline of Party Mobilization." Pp. 64–76 in Russell J. Dalton and Martin P. Wattenberg (ed.), *Parties Without Partisans: Political Change in Advanced Industrial Democracies*. New York: Oxford University Press.

Watts, Duncan J. 1999. *Small Worlds: The Dynamics of Networks Between Order and Randomness*. Princeton, NJ: Princeton University Press.

Watts, Julie R. 2002. *Immigration Policy and the Challenge of Globalization: Unions and Employers in Unlikely Alliance*. Ithaca: Cornell University Press.

Wawro, Gregory. 2000. *Legislative Entrepreneurship in the U.S. House of Representatives*. Ann Arbor: University of Michigan Press.

______. 2001. "A panel probit analysis of campaign contributions and roll-call votes." *American Journal of Political Science* 45:563–79.

Waylen, Georgina. 1997. "Women's movements, the state, and democratization in Chile: The establishment of SERNAM." Pp. 90–103 in Anne Marie Goetz (ed.), *Getting Institutions Right for Women in Development*. New York: Zed Books.

Wayne, Stephen J. 2001. *The Road to the White House, 2000: The Politics of Presidential Elections*. New York: Palgrave.

Wazir, Rekha. 2001. "Early childhood development and care in India: Some policy issues." Pp. 91–104 in Mary Daly (ed.), *Care Work*. Geneva: International Labour Office.

Weakliem, David L. 1991. "The two lefts? Occupation and party choice in France, Italy, and the Netherlands." *American Journal of Sociology* 66:1327–61.

______. 1997. "Race versus class? Racial composition and class voting, 1936–1992." *Social Forces* 75:939–56.

______. 2002. "The effects of education on political opinions." *International Journal of Public Opinion Research* 14:141–57.

Weakliem, David L., and Anthony Heath. 1994. "Rational choice and class voting." *Rationality and Society* 6:243–70.

______. 1999. "The secret life of class voting: Britain, France, and the United States since the 1930s." Pp. 98–133 in Geoff Evans (ed.), *The End of Class Politics? Class Voting in Comparative Context*. New York: Oxford University Press.

Weaver, David, and G. Cleveland. Wilhoit. 1996. *The American Journalist in the 1990s*. Mahwah, NJ: Erlbaum.

Weaver, Paul. 1975. "Newspaper news and television news." In D. Cater and R. Adler (eds.), *Television as a Social Force*. New York: Praeger.

Weaver, R. Kent, and James G. McGann. 2000. "Think tanks and civil societies in a time of change." Pp. 1–35 in J. G. McGann and R. K. Weaver (eds.), *Think Tanks and Civil Societies*. New Brunswick, NJ: Transaction.

Webb, Paul D. 1992. *Trade Unions and the British Electorate*. Aldershot: Dartmouth.

______. 1994. "Party Organizational Change in Britain: The Iron Law of Centralization." Pp. 108–33 in Richard S. Katz and Peter Mair (ed.), *How Parties Organize: Change and Adaptation in Party Organizations in Western Democracies*. Thousand Oaks, CA: Sage.

Webber, Michael J. 2000. *New Deal Fat Cats: Business, Labor, and Campaign Finance in the 1936 Presidential Election*. New York: Fordham University Press.

Webber, Michael J., and G. William Domhoff. 1996. "Myth and reality in business support for Democrats and Republicans in the 1936 presidential election." *American Political Science Review* 90:824–33.

Weber, Douglas. 2002. *Sex, Money and Politics: The Gender Gap in Campaign Contributions*. Center for Responsive Politics: <www.opensecrets.org/pubs/gender/index.asp>.

Weber, Eugen J. 1976. *Peasants into Frenchmen: the modernization of rural France, 1870–1914*. Stanford, CA: Stanford University Press.

Weber, Max. 1930. *The Protestant Ethic and the Spirit of Capitalism* (Talcott Parsons, trans.). London: G. Allen & Unwin.

______. 1946. *From Max Weber: Essays in Sociology* (Hans H. Gerth and C. Wright Mills, eds. and trans.). New York: Oxford University Press.

______. 1946. "Politics as a vocation." Pp. 77–128 in H. H. Gerth and C. Wright Mills (eds.), *From Max Weber*. New York: Oxford University Press.

______. 1964[1922]. *The Sociology of Religion* (Ephraim Fischoff, trans.). Boston: Beacon Press.

______. 1964. *Wirtschaft und Gesellschaft*. Studienausgabe (Johannes Winckelmann, ed.). Koeln and Berlin: Kiepenheuer & Witsch.

______. 1968[1920]. *Economy and Society*. Three volumes, edited by Gunther Roth and Claus Wittich. New York: Bedminister Press.

______ 1968[1922]. *Economy and Society*. Berkeley: University of California Press.

______. 1978a[1920]. *Economy and Society*, Vol. 1 (Guenther Roth and Klaus Wittich, ed.). Berkeley: University of California Press.

______. 1978b[1920]. *Economy and Society* Vol. 2. (Guenther Roth and Claus Wittich, eds.). Berkeley: University of California Press.

______. 2002 [1918]. "Parlament und Regierung im neugeordneten Deutschland." Pp. 395–435 in Dirk Kaesler (ed.), *Schriften 1894–1922*. Stuttgart: Kröner.

Weedon, Chris. 1987. *Feminist Practice and Poststructuralist Theory*. Oxford, UK: Basil Blackwell.

______. 1998. *Feminist Theory and the Politics of Difference*. Oxford, UK: Blackwell.

Weiher, Gregory. 1991. *The Fractured Metropolis: Political Fragmentation and Metropolitan Segregation*. Albany: State University of New York Press.

Weil, Patrick. 2001. "Access to citizenship: A comparison of twenty-five nationality laws." Pp. 17–35 in T. Alexander Aleinikoff and Douglas Klusmeyer (eds.), *Citizenship Today*. Washington, D.C.: Carnegie Endowment.

______. 2002. *Qu'est-ce qu'um Française? Histoire de la nationalité française de la Révolution à nos jours*. Paris: Bernard Grasset.

Weilhouwer, Peter W., and Brad Lockerbie. 1994. "Party contacting and political participation, 1952–1990." *American Journal of Political Science* 38:211–29.

Weiner, Martin J. 1981. *English Culture and the Decline of the Industrial Spirit 1850–1980*. Cambridge, UK: Cambridge University Press.

Weiner, Myron. 1987. "Empirical democratic theory." Pp. 3–34 in Myron Weiner and Ergun Özbudun (eds.), *Competitive Elections in Developing Countries*. Durham, NC: Duke University Press.

Weingast, Barry R. 1984. "The congressional-bureaucratic system: A principle-agent perspective." *Public Choice* 44:147–92.

______. 1996. "Political institutions: Rational choice perspectives." Pp. 167–90 in Robert E. Goodin and Hans-Dieter Klingemann (eds.), *A New Handbook of Political Sociology*. New York: Oxford University Press.

Weingast, Barry, and M. Moran. 1983. "Bureaucratic discretion or congressional control?: Regulatory policy making by the Federal Trade Commission." *Journal of Political Economy* 91:765–800.

Weir, Margaret. (ed.). 1998. *The Social Divide: Political Parties and the Future of Activist Government*. Washington, D.C.: Brookings Institute.

Weir, Margaret, and Theda Skocpol. 1985. "State structures and the possibility for 'Keynesian' responses to Great Depression in Sweden, Britain and the United States." In P. B. Evans, D. Rueschemeyer, and T. Skocpol. *Bringing the State Back In*. Cambridge, UK: Cambridge University Press.

Weir, Margaret, Ann Shola Orloff, and Theda Skocpol. 1988. "Understanding American social politics." Pp. 3–27 in Margaret Weir, Ann Shola Orloff, and Theda Skocpol (eds.), *The Politics of Social Policy in the United States*. Princeton, NJ: Princeton University Press.

Weiss, Carol H. 1992. *Organizations for Policy Analysis: Helping Government Think*. Newbury Park: Sage.

Weiss, Linda. 1997. "Globalization and the myth of the powerless state." *New Left Review* 225:3–27.

Wekkin, Gardy D., Donald E. Whistler, Michael A. Kelley, and Michael A. Maggiotto. 1993. *Building Democracy in One-Party Systems: Theoretical Problems and Cross-Nation Experiences*. Westport, CT: Praeger.

Welch, Claude. 2001a. "Amnesty International and Human Rights Watch: A comparison." Pp. 85–118 in Claude Welch (ed.), *NGOs and Human Rights: Promise and Performance*. Philadelphia: University of Pennsylvania Press.

______. 2001b. "Introduction." Pp. 1–22 in Claude Welch (ed.), *NGOs and Human Rights: Promise and Performance*. Philadelphia: University of Pennsylvania Press.

Welch, Susan. 1975. "The impact of urban riots on urban expenditures." *American Journal of Political Science* 29:741–60.

Welch, William F. 1982. "Campaign contributions and legislative voting: Milk money and dairy price supports." *Western Political Quarterly* 35:478–95.

Wells, Amy Stuart, and Robert L. Crain. 1997. *Stepping Over the Color Line: African-American Students in White Suburban Schools*. New Haven, CT: Yale University Press.

Wennemo, Irene. 1992. "The development of family policy." *Acta Sociologica* 35:201–17.

West, Darrell M. 2000. *Checkbook Democracy: How Money Corrupts Political Campaigns*. Boston: Boston University Press.

Western, Bruce. 1991. "A comparative study of corporatist development." *American Sociological Review* 56:283–94.

______. 1997. *Between Class and Market: Postwar Unionization in the Capitalist Democracies*. Princeton, NJ: Princeton University Press.

______. 2001. "Institutions, investment, and the rise in unemployment." Pp. 71–93 in John L. Campbell and Ove K. Pedersen (eds.), *The Rise of Neoliberalism and Institutional Analysis*. Princeton, NJ: Princeton University Press.

Westerstahl, Jurgen, and Folke Johansson. 1986. "News ideologies as moulders of domestic news." *European Journal of Communication* 1:133–49.

Weyland, Kurt. 1998. "Swallowing the bitter pill: Sources of popular support for neoliberal reform in Latin America." *Comparative Political Studies* 31 (October):539–68.

______. 2002. *The Politics of Market Reform in Fragile Democracies: Argentina, Brazil, Peru, and Venezuela*. Princeton, NJ: Princeton University Press.

Wheeler, Mark. 1997. *Politics and the Mass Media*. Oxford, UK: Blackwell.

Whitby, Kenny J. 1997. *The Color of Representation: Congressional Behavior and Black Interests*. Ann Arbor: University of Michigan Press.

Whitby, Kenny J., and George A. Krause. 2001. "Race, issue heterogeneity and public policy: The Republican revolution in the 104th US Congress and the representation of African-American policy interests." *British Journal of Political Science* 31:555–72.

White, Harrison C. 2002. *Markets from Networks: Socioeconomic Models of Production*. Princeton, NJ: Princeton University Press.

Whitehead, Laurence. 1986. "International aspects of democratization". Pp. 3–46 in Guillermo O'Donnell, Philippe C. Schmitter, and Laurence Whitehead (eds.), *Transitions from Authoritarian Rule: Prospects for Democracy*. Baltimore: Johns Hopkins University Press.

Whitehorn, Alan. 1992. *Canadian Socialism: Essays on the CCF-NDP*. Toronto: Oxford University Press.

Whiteley, Paul. 1986. "Predicting the Labour vote in 1983: Social background versus subjective evaluation." *Political Studies* 34:82–98.

Whitt, J. Allen. 1979a. "Toward a class-dialectical model of power: an empirical assessment of three competing models of political power." *American Sociological Review* 44(1):81–99.

______. 1979b. "Can capitalists organize themselves?" *The Insurgent Sociologist* 9(2–3):51–9.

______. 1982. *Urban Elites and Mass Transportation: The Dialectics of Power*. Princeton, NJ: Princeton University Press.

Whittier, Nancy. 1995. *Feminist Generations: The Persistence of the Radical Women's Movement*. Philadelphia: Temple University Press.

______. 2001. "Emotional strategies: The collective reconstruction and display of oppositional emotions in the movement against child sexual abuse." Pp. 233–50 in Jeff Goodwin, James M. Jasper, and Francesca Polletta (eds.), *Passionate Politics: Emotions and Social Movements*. Chicago: University of Chicago Press.

Wiarda, Howard J. 1997. *Corporatism and Comparative Politics: The Other Great. "Ism."* Armonk, NY: M. E. Sharp.

Wickham, Carrie Rosefsky. 2002. *Mobilizing Islam: Religion, Activism, and Political Change in Egypt*. New York: Columbia University Press.

Wickham-Crowley, Timothy P. 1992. *Guerrillas and Revolution in Latin America: A Comparative Study of Insurgents and Regimes since 1956*. Princeton, NJ: Princeton University Press.

Wicksell, Knut. 1954. *Value, Capital, and Rent* (S. H. Frowein, trans.). New York: Rinehart.

Wiener, Jonathan. 1978. *Social Origins of the New South: Alabama, 1860–1885*. Baton Rouge: Louisiana State University Press.

Wiktorowicz, Quintan. 2001. *The Management of Islamic Activism: Salafis, the Muslim Brotherhood, and State Power in Jordan*. Albany: State University of New York Press.

Wilcox, Clyde. 1994. "Premillennialists at the millennium: Some reflections on the Christian Right." *Sociology of Religion* 55:243–62.

Wilensky, Harold. 1975. *The Welfare State and Equality*. Berkeley: The University of California Press.

______. 1990. "Common problems, divergent policies: An 18-nation study of family policy." *Foreign Affairs Report* 31:1–3.

______. 2002. *Rich Democracies: Political Economy, Public Policy, and Performance*. Berkeley: University of California Press.

Wilensky, Harold L., and Charles Nathan Lebeaux. 1964. *Industrial Society and Social Welfare; The Impact of Industrialization on the Supply and Organization of Social Welfare Services in the United States*. New York: Russell Sage Foundation.

Wilks, Stephen, and Maurice Wright (eds.). 1987. *Government-Industry Relations: West Europe, U.S. and Japan*. Oxford, UK: Clarendon Press.

Williams, Fiona. 1995. "Race ethnicity, gender, and class in welfare states – a framework for comparative-analysis." *Social Politics* 2:127–59.

______. 2003. "Contesting 'race' and gender in the European Union: A multi-layered recognition struggle for voice and visibility." Pp. 121–44 in B. Hobson (ed.), *Recognition Struggles and Social Movements: Contested Identities, Agency and Power.* Cambridge, UK: Cambridge University Press.

Williams, Kim M. 2003. "Parties, movements, and constituencies in categorizing race." Pp. 197–225 in J. A. Goldstone (ed.), *States, Parties, and Social Movements.* Cambridge, UK: Cambridge University Press.

Williams, Raymond. 1973. *The Country and the City.* New York: Oxford University Press.

______. 1977. *Marxism and Literature.* Oxford, UK: Oxford University Press.

Williams, Richard E. 1990. *Hierarchical Structures and Social Value: The Creation of Black and Irish Identities in the United States.* Cambridge, UK: Cambridge University Press.

Williamson, Joel. 1984. *The Crucible of Race: Black–White Relations in the American South Since Emancipation.* New York: Oxford University Press.

Williamson, John (ed.). 1990. *Latin American Adjustment: How Much Has Happened?* Washington, DC: Institute for International Economics.

Williamson, John B., and Fred C. Pampel. 1993. *Old-Age Security in Comparative Perspective.* New York: Oxford University Press.

______. 1990. "What Washington means by policy reform." In John Williamson (ed.), *Latin American Adjustment: How Much Has Happened?* Washington, DC: Institute for International Economics. www.iie.com/publications/papers/willianson0102_2.html.

Williamson, Oliver. 1975. *Markets and Hierarchies.* New York: Free Press.

______. 1981. "The economics of organization: The transaction cost approach." *American Journal of Sociology* 87:548–77.

Williamson, Peter J. 1985. *Varieties of Corporatism.* Cambridge, UK: Cambridge University Press.

______. 1989. *Corporatism in Perspective.* Newbury Park, CA: Sage.

Willis, Eliza, Christopher Garman, and Stephan Haggard. 1999. "The politics of decentralization in Latin America." *Latin American Research Review* 34, no. 1:7–56.

Willis, Paul. 1977. *Learning to Labour.* New York: Columbia University Press.

Wilson, Elizabeth. 1977. *Women and the Welfare State.* London: Tavistock.

Wilson, Graham K. 1977. *Special Interests and Policy Making.* Chichester: Wiley.

______. 1982. "Why Is There No Corporativism in the United States?" Pp. 219–36 in G. Lehmbruch and P. C. Schmitter (eds.), *Patterns of Corporatist Policy Marking.* Beverly Hills, CA: Sage.

Wilson, James Q. 1973. *Political Organizations.* New York: Basic Books.

______. 1980. "The politics of regulation." Pp. 357–94 in James Wilson (ed.), *The Politics of Regulation.* New York: Basic Books.

______. 1989. *Bureaucracy: What Government Agencies Do and Why They Do It.* New York: Basic Books.

______. 1999. "The rise of the bureaucratic state." Pp. 38–57 in Frederick Lane (ed.), *Current Issues in Public Administration.* 6th ed. Boston: Bedford/St. Martin's.

Wilson, John. 1973. *Introduction to Social Movements.* New York: Basic.

Wilson, William J. 1978. *The Declining Significance of Race: Blacks and Changing American Institutions.* Chicago: University of Chicago Press.

______. 1987. *The Truly Disadvantaged: The Inner City, the Underclass, and Public Policy.* Chicago: University of Chicago Press.

______. 1996. *When Work Disappears: The World of the New Urban Poor.* New York: Knopf.

______. 1999. *The Bridge Over the Racial Divide: Rising Inequality and Coalition Politics.* Berkeley: University of California Press.

Winant, Howard. 1994. *Racial Conditions: Politics, Theory, Comparisons.* Minneapolis: University of Minnesota Press.

______. 2001. *The World Is a Ghetto: Race and Democracy since World War II.* New York: Basic Books.

Winders, Bill. 1999. "The roller coaster of class conflict: Class segments, mass mobilization, and voter turnout in the U.S., 1840–1996." *Social Forces* 77:833–60.

Windolf, Paul. 2002. *Corporate Networks in Europe and the United States.* New York: Oxford University Press.

Winger, Richard. 1995. "How ballot access laws affect the U.S. party system." *American Review of Politics* 16:321–50.

Witte, Jan Martin, Wolfgang H. Reinicke, and Thorsten Benner. 2000. *Beyond Multilateralism: Global Public Policy Networks.* Internationale Politik und Gesellschaft 2/2000.

Witte, Rob. 1996. *Racist Violence and the State.* London: Longman.

Wittgenstein, Ludwig. 1958. *Philosophical Investigations.* Oxford, UK: Basil Blackwell.

Wlezien, Christopher. 1995. "The public as thermostat: Dynamics of preferences for spending." *American Journal of Political Science* 39:981–1000.

Wolf, Eric R. 1969. *Peasant Wars of the Twentieth Century.* New York: Harper and Row.

Wolfe, Alan. 1977. *The Limits of Legitimacy.* New York: The Free Press.

Wolfinger, Raymond E., and Jonathan Hoffman. 2001. "Registering and voting with motor voter." Political Science and Politics 35:85–92.

Wolfinger, Raymond E., and Steven J. Rosenstone. 1980. *Who votes?* New Haven, CT: Yale University Press

Wolin, Richard. 1992. *The Terms of Cultural Criticism: the Frankfurt School, Existentialism, Poststructuralism.* New York: Columbia University Press.

Wolinetz, Steven B. 1979. "The transformation of western European party systems revisited." *West European Politics* 2:4–28.

______. (ed.). 1988. *Parties and Party Systems in Liberal Democracies.* London/New York: Routledge.

Wood, Elisabeth Jean. 2000. *Forging Democracy from Below: Insurgent Transitions in South Africa and El Salvador.* Cambridge, UK: Cambridge University Press.

Wood, Gordon S. 1992. *The Radicalism of the American Revolution.* New York: Random House.

Woodiwiss, Anthony. 1990. *Social Theory after Postmodernism.* London: Pluto.

Woodman, Harold D. 1987. "Economic reconstruction and the rise of the New South, 1865–1900." Pp. 254–307 in John B. Boles and Evelyn Thomos Nola (eds.), *Interpreting Southern History: Historiographical Essays in Honor of Sanford W. Higginbotham.* Baton Rouge: Louisiana State University.

World Social Forum. 2001. "Porto Alegre call for mobilization." Postscript, pp. 122–5 in Francois Houtart and Francous Polet (eds.), *The Other Davos.* London and New York: Zed.

Wright, Augas, and Wendy Wolford. 2003. *To Inherit the Earth.* San Francisco: Food First.

Wright, Erik Olin. 1985. *Classes.* New York: Verso.

______. 1997. *Class Counts: Comparative Studies in Class Analysis.* New York: Cambridge University Press.

______. 2002. "The shadow of exploitation in Weber's class analysis." *American Sociological Review* 67:832–53.

Wright, Gerald C., and Brian F. Schaffner. 2002. "The influence of party: Evidence from the state legislatures." *American Political Science Review* 96:367–79.

Wright, John. 1985. "PACs, contributions and roll calls: An organizational perspective." *American Political Science Review* 75:400–14.

______. 1989. "PAC contributions, lobbying and representation." *Journal of Politics* 51:713–29.

______. 1990. "Contributions, lobbying, and committee voting in the U.S. House of Representatives." *American Political Science Review* 84:417–38.

Wrong, Dennis. 1979. *Power: Its Forms, Bases, and Uses.* Chicago: University of Chicago Press.

______. 1999. *The Oversocialized Conception of Man.* New Brunswick, NJ: Transaction Books.

Wuthnow, Robert. 1987. *Meaning and Moral Order: Explorations in Cultural Analysis.* Berkeley: University of California Press.

______. 1988. *The Restructuring of American Religion: Society and Faith since World War II.* Princeton, NJ: Princeton University Press.

______. 1989. *Communities of Discourse: Ideology and Social Structure in the Reformation, the Enlightenment and European Socialism.* Cambridge, MA: Harvard University Press.

______. 1993. *The Future of Christianity.* New York: Oxford University Press.

Wuthnow, Robert, and John H. Evans. 2002. *Quiet Hand of God: Faith Based Activism and the Public Role of Mainline Protestantism.* Berkeley: University of California Press.

Yamamoto, Tadashi (ed.). 1995. *Emerging Civil Society in the Asia-Pacific Community.* Singapore and Tokyo: Institute of Southeast Asian Studies/Japan Center for International Exchange.

Yarwood, Dean, and D. Nimmo. 1997. "Bureaucratic roles and participation: Variation on two themes." Pp. 63–80 in George Frederickson and Charles Wise (eds.), *Public Administration and Public Policy.* Lexington, MA: Lexington Books.

Yashar, Deborah J. 1997. *Demanding Democracy. Reform and Reaction in Costa Rica and Guatemala, 1870s–1950s.* Stanford, CA: Stanford University Press.

Yeatmann, A. 1997. "Feminism and power." Pp. 144–57 in Mary L. Shanley and Uma Narayan (eds.), *Reconstructing Political Theory: Feminist Perspectives.* Cambridge, UK: Polity.

Yishai, Yael. 1994. "Interest parties: The thin line between groups and parties in the Israeli electoral process." Pp. 197–225 in Kay Lawson (ed.), *How Political Parties Work: Perspectives from Within.* Westport, CT: Praeger.

York, Jodi. 2002. "Forests for whom? Ethnic politics of conservation in Northern Thailand 1996–2001." *Berkeley Journal of Sociology: A Critical Review* 46:132–54.

Young, I. M. 1990. *Justice and the Politics of Difference.* Princeton, NJ: Princeton University Press.

______. 1995. "Gender as seriality: Thinking about women as a collective." Pp. 99–124 in Y. Arat, J. Brenner, and B. Laslett (eds.), *Rethinking the Political: Gender, Resistance, and the State.* Chicago: University of Chicago Press.

______. 2000. *Inclusion and Democracy*. Oxford, UK: Oxford University Press.

Young, Iris Marion. 1990. *Justice and the Politics of Difference*. Princeton, NJ: Princeton University Press.

Young, Marilyn B. 1991. *The Vietnam Wars, 1945–1990*. New York: Herper Collins.

Young, Walter D. 1969. *The Anatomy of a Party: The National CCF*. Toronto: University of Toronto Press.

Yuval-Davis, Nira. 1989. "National reproduction and 'the demographic race' in Israel." Pp. 92–109 in Nira Yuval-Davis and Floya Anthias (eds.), *Woman–Nation–State*. London: Macmillan.

______. 1997. *Gender and Nation*. London: Sage.

______. 2000. "Citizenship, territoriality and the gendered construction of difference." Pp. 171–88 in Engin F. Isin (ed.), *Democracy, Citizenship and the Global City*. London and New York: Routledge.

Yuval-Davis, N., and P. Werbner. 1999. *Women, Citizenship and Difference*. London: Zed.

Zakaria, Fareed. 1997. "The rise of illiberal democracy." *Foreign Affairs* 76(6):22–43.

Zald, Mayer. 2000. "Ideologically structured action: An enlarged agenda for social movement research." *Mobilization* 5:1–16.

Zaller, John R. 1992. *The Nature and Origins of Mass Opinion*. Cambridge, UK: Cambridge University Press.

______. 1994. "Elite leadership of mass opinion: New evidence from the Gulf War." Pp. 186–209 in W. L. Bennett, and D. L. Paletz (eds.), *Taken by Storm: The Media, Public Opinion, and U.S. Foreign Policy in the Gulf War*. Chicago: University of Chicago Press.

______. 1999 "Monica Lewinsky's contribution to political science." *Political Science and Politics* 31:82–89.

______. (forthcoming). *A Theory of Media Politics*. Chicago: University of Chicago Press.

Zaretsky, Eli. 1976. *Capitalism, the Family, and Personal Life*. New York: Harper Colophon Books.

Zeigler, Harmon. 1988. *Pluralism, Corporatism, and Confucianism: Political Association and Conflict Regulation in the United States, Europe, and Taiwan*. Philadelphia: Temple University Press.

Zeitlin, Maurice; 1970. *American Society, Inc.: Studies of the Social Structure and Political Economy of the United States*. Chicago: Markham.

______. 1974. "Corporate ownership and control: The large corporation and the capitalist class." *American Journal of Sociology* 79:1073–119.

______. 1999. "Veto players and law production in parliamentary democracies." *American Political Science Review* 93(3):591–608.

Zeitlin, Maurice, and Richard E. Ratcliff. 1988. *Landlords and Capitalists: The Dominant Class of Chile*. Princeton, NJ: Princeton University Press.

Zeitlin, Maurice, W. Lawrence Neuman, and Richard Ratcliff. 1976. "Class segments: Agrarian property and political leadership in the capitalist class of Chile." *American Sociological Review* 41:1006–1029.

Zelizer, Julian. 2004. *On Capital Hill: The Struggle to Reform Congress and its Consequences, 1948–2000*. Cambridge, UK: Cambridge University Press.

Zhao, Yuzhei. 1998. *Media, Market, and Democracy in China: Between the Party Line and the Bottom Line*. Urbana: University of Illinois Press.

Zimmermann, Ekkart. 1983. *Political Violence, Crises, and Revolutions: Theories and Research*. Cambridge, MA: Schenkman.

Zinn, Howard. 1964. *SNCC: The New Abolitionists*. Boston: Beacon.

Zipp, John F. 1986. "Social class and social liberalism." *Sociological Forum* 1:301–29.

Žižek, Slavjo. 1989. *The Sublime Object of Ideology*. London: Verso.

______. 1990. "Beyond discourse analysis." Pp. 249–60 in Ernesto Laclau (ed.), *New Reflections on the Revolution of Our Time*. London: Verso.

______. 1999. *The Ticklish Subject*. London: Verso.

______. 2000a. "Class struggle or postmodernism? Yes please!" Pp. 90–135 in Judith Butler, Ernesto Laclau, and Slavoj Žižek (eds.), *Contingency, Hegemony, Universality*. London: Verso.

______. 2000b. "Da Capo Sensa Fine" Pp. 213–62, in Judith Butler, Ernesto Laclau, and Slavoj Žižek (eds.), *Contingency, Hegemony, Universality*. London: Verso.

______. 2000c. "Holding the Place." Pp. 308–29 in Judith Butler, Ernesto Laclau, and Slavoj Žižek (eds.), *Contingency, Hegemony, Universality*. London: Verso.

Zolberg, Aristide R. 1978. "International migration policies in a changing world system." Pp. 241–86 in W. H. McNeill and R. Adams (eds.), *Human Migration, Patterns and Policies*. Bloomington: Indiana University Press.

______. 1981. "International migrations in political perspective." Pp. 3–27 in Mary Kritz, Charles Keely, and Sivano Tomasi (eds.), *Global Trends in Migration*. New York: Center for Migration Studies.

Zolberg, Aristide, Astri Suhrke, and Sergio Aguayo. 1989. *Escape from Violence: Conflict and the Refugee Crisis in the Developing World*. New York: Oxford University Press.

Zonabend, Françoise. 1993. *The Nuclear Peninsula*. Cambridge, UK: Cambridge University Press.

Name Index

Subject Index